UNITED STATES HISTORY

**Globe Fearon
Foundations Series**

**Program Consultant
Peter J. Myers**
Palo Alto College
San Antonio, Texas

GLOBE FEARON EDUCATIONAL PUBLISHER
Upper Saddle River, New Jersey
www.globefearon.com

Globe Fearon gratefully acknowledges the contributions of the following consultants and reviewers.

PROGRAM CONSULTANT

Peter J. Myers
Assistant Professor of History
Palo Alto College
San Antonio, TX

CONTENT CONSULTANTS

William Brescia
Director of Development
Harmony School
Bloomington, IN
American Indian educational consultant

Gordon Chang, Ph.D.
Associate Professor
Department of History
Stanford University
Stanford, CA
Asian American studies

Frank De Varona, Ed.S.
Visiting Associate Professor
College of Education
Florida International University
Miami, FL
Latino studies

Robin Kilson, Ph.D.
Department of History
University of Texas at Austin
Austin, TX
Twentieth-century African American history/women's studies

Stephen Middleton, Ph.D.
Department of History
North Carolina State University
Raleigh, NC
U.S. constitutional history

CONSULTANT

Joseph J. Ellis, Ph.D.
Department of History
Mount Holyoke College
South Hadley, MA

REVIEWERS

Elaine S. Abelson, Ph.D.
Associate Professor of History
New School for Social Research
New York, NY

Nelson Acevedo
Chairman, Social Studies Department
Norman Thomas High School
New York, NY

David F. Cattran
Social Studies Department Head
Sheridan High School
Thornville, OH

Kathy C. Coley
Bearden High School
Knoxville, TN

Dennis Cross
Mentor Teacher—Social Sciences
Anaheim High School
Anaheim, CA

Robert T. Davis
Supervisor, Social Studies/
 Multicultural Studies
Newark, NJ Public Schools
Newark, NJ

Veronica Disque
Learning Disabilities Teacher
DeKalb High School
Waterloo, IN

Simone T. Dorman, Ph.D.
Philip and Sala Burton Academic
 High School
San Francisco, CA

Nannetta Durnell, Ph.D.
Associate Professor
Department of Communication
Florida Atlantic University
Boca Raton, FL

Carol Enseki-Miller
Roosevelt High School
Los Angeles, CA

William Fetsko, Ph.D.
Social Studies Coordinator
Liverpool Central Schools
Liverpool, NY

Kenneth F. Gill
Social Studies Teacher
Stephenson High School
Dekalb County, GA

Catherine Head
Mentor Teacher/
 Social Studies Chairperson
Fairfax High School
Los Angeles, CA

Rob Hines
Instructor of History
Palo Alto College
San Antonio, TX

Nadolyn Y. Hoskins
Department Head of Social Studies
Northern High School
Detroit, MI

Richard J. Hryniewicki
Social Studies Department Chairperson
Cudahy Public Schools
Cudahy, WI

Raymond B. McClain, Ph.D.
Pittsburgh Public Schools
Pittsburgh, PA

Tom Murray
Social Studies Chairman
Glenbard South High School
Glen Ellyn, IL

Dianne S. Partee
Curriculum Specialist
School District of Philadelphia
Philadelphia, PA

Joyce Prenner
Chair of Social Studies
Francis Lewis High School
New York, NY

Ninfa Anita Sepulveda
Social Studies Chairperson
Stephen F. Austin High School
Houston, TX

David Silberberg
Teacher, Social Studies Department
Satellite Academy High School
New York, NY

John Smith
Franklin High School
Los Angeles, CA

J. Kelli Sweet
Kalamazoo Public Schools
Western Michigan University
Kalamazoo, MI

Ellen Vasta
Curriculum Specialist
Elk Grove Unified School District
Elk Grove, CA

Glenn Walker
Fayette County Schools
Fayette County, GA

Brook Whitmire
Duluth High School
Duluth, GA

Dana Willens
Assistant Principal, Social Studies
Theodore Roosevelt High School
Bronx, NY

Printed in the United States of America
  3 4 5 6 7 8 9 10   02 01 00

ISBN 0-835-92258-8

GLOBE FEARON EDUCATIONAL PUBLISHER
Upper Saddle River, New Jersey
www.globefearon.com

Contents

▲ *Which Native American group lived at the site of present-day Mexico City? See page 8.*

▲ *How did this snake symbol help convince colonists to fight for independence? Find out on page 73.*

▲ What event did this parade celebrate? Find out on page 96.

▲ How did this small machine, invented in 1793, powerfully affect America's economy? See page 117.

▲ *What two-minute long speech by President Abraham Lincoln is considered one of the greatest in American history? See page 194.*

▲ *How did these little bullets change the way wars were fought? See page 205.*

▲ *What equipment did cowhands use as they worked in the American West? Find out on page 237.*

▲ *Why was this event at Promontory Point, Utah, important to U.S. history? See page 254.*

▲ *For what cause are these people protesting? Turn to page 308.*

▲ *How did this poster help convince Americans to support World War I? Find out on page 349.*

▲ *What form of music gave its name to an entire era in American history? You can find its name on page 359.*

▲ What did Americans do for entertainment before television was invented? See page 417.

Unit *7* THE UNITED STATES IN TIMES OF CRISIS, 1922–1961 421

▲ Why was this battle a turning point in World War II? See page 449.

▲ *How did launching this dog and satellite into space lead to a space race? Turn to page 495.*

▲ *What's wrong with this headline? Find out on page 508.*

▲ *How did television help this man become President? See page 549.*

▲ What historic legislation became effective just before this handshake? Turn to page 561.

Unit 9 FOREIGN AND DOMESTIC CHALLENGES, 1960–1981

Chapter 28
The Fight for Social Change, 1960–1980

Chapter 29
The Vietnam War, 1960–1973

Chapter 30
Searching for Stability, 1969–1981

▲ Cars like this did not get many miles to the gallon, but they were very popular. Why? See page 568.

▲ Why did Americans boycott grapes? Find out on page 582.

Unit *10* ENTERING A NEW CENTURY, 1980 – the future . .633

▲ These people were among those who fought for the most sweeping civil rights bill ever passed. Whom did it help? See page 647.

▲ Why did this showdown between students and armed forces in China capture the attention of the United States? See page 658.

Building Skills

Connecting History &...

Person to Person

Point of View

Connecting Past and Present

Maps

Graphs, Charts, Tables, and Timelines

Documents

"Primary Sources

These entries read as follows: **source,** topic, date, student edition page number.

What Is Social Studies?

Social Studies is more than a collection of dates, names, and facts. Although as you read this book you will learn the who, what, where, and when of United States history, you will also trace patterns, or themes, that make up Social Studies. By tracing these themes, you can learn lessons that can help us shape our country's future.

Seven major interrelated themes are woven throughout this book. As you read, pay close attention to the ways in which these themes have changed and developed throughout our country's history.

History

History is the study of people and events of the past. We study the past so that we can understand the connections between events and their consequences. These connections prepare us for the roles we can take in shaping the future of our country. As you read this book, think about:

- When—and why—did events happen?

- How is today's world affected by events that happened long ago?

- Which people helped guide important events of the past?

- What lessons can be learned from history?

Geography

Geography is the study of the land, and its climate, physical features, and resources. The geography of the United States, which varies widely, greatly affected the development of the country. As you read this book, think about:

- What are the different ways in which people adapt to their environment?

- What were the advantages and challenges of geography to early settlers?

- In what ways has the geography of the United States had an effect on its development?

Economics

Economics is the way a country produces and uses natural resources, goods, and services to meet people's needs. The early U.S. economy was based largely on agriculture. As the nation grew, business and industry became important economic factors. As you read this book, think about:

- How has the economy influenced our nation's history?

- How has technology affected the economics of the United States?

- What is the relationship between the geography and the economy of different U.S. regions?

Government

Government is a system of rules or laws by which a community of people live together. In the United States, citizens abide by the laws of the nation and elect people to provide just and fair leadership. As you read this book, think about:

- Who were the people that shaped the system of U.S. government?

- How does government struggle to balance the good of the country with the protection of individual rights?

- How has the power of government changed over the years?

Culture

Culture is the values, customs, and traditions of a people. Because the United States is home to people with origins from all over the world, it is a unique, culturally diverse nation. As you read this book, think about:

- What are the similarities and differences between the cultures of various groups in America today?

- Through what means—music, art, literature—do people express themselves?

- In what ways does the culture of the United States reflect its diverse population?

Social Issues

Social issues are the matters that are important to the public. Important to Americans throughout their history have been their political, economic, and religious freedom, as well as their civil rights. As you read this book, think about:

- Which issues have motivated people to fight for equal rights and justice?

- How do people work to improve conditions in society today?

- What role can you or your community play in helping to bring about positive change?

Citizenship

Citizenship is having the rights and duties of a member of a nation. The rights of U.S. citizens are guaranteed by the Bill of Rights and amendments to the Constitution. As you read this book, think about:

- What responsibilities do U.S. citizens have for their country and toward each other?

- How can good citizens contribute to their community?

- How did the desire for people's basic rights influence U.S. history?

"While we read history
we make history.
—George William Curtis

Unit *1*

Early America Prehistory–1783

> **"** Here in our home of Texcoco, your birthplace, things are coming to an end.... Now everywhere our Lord is destroying and reducing the land. We are coming to an end and disappearing. Why? For what reason? Perhaps we have incurred His wrath and offended Him with our sins and wrong doing. But what are we to do? **"**
>
> *An Aztec woman commenting on the destruction of Aztec civilization after the Spanish conquest, 1520s*

▲ *This painting depicts one artist's idea of North America's natural beauty before the arrival of Europeans.* **◆ Connecting Past and Present** *What does the artist want to convey about this landscape? What place in the United States would you choose to illustrate the country's natural beauty today?*

Chapter 1
Three Cultures Meet
Prehistory–1570

CHAPTER PREVIEW

Section 1 Early Americans

Shaped by different environments, Native American groups developed a wide variety of cultures.

Section 2 Europe Looks Outward

The Crusades and trade with the Middle East and Asia opened a world of new products and new ideas to Europeans.

Section 3 Africa's Trading Kingdoms

More than one thousand years ago in Africa, three powerful and sophisticated kingdoms built extensive trade networks linking West Africans with other peoples.

Section 4 Exploration and Its Consequences

As Europeans became more skilled at navigation in the late 1400s and 1500s, they expanded their explorations, encountering lands and peoples previously unknown to them.

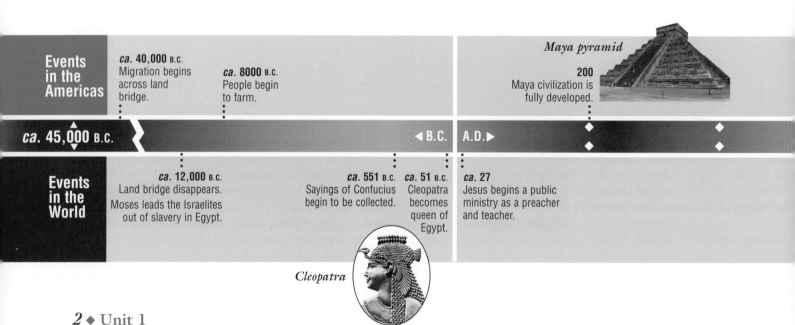

Events in the Americas

ca. **40,000** B.C.
Migration begins across land bridge.

ca. **8000** B.C.
People begin to farm.

Maya pyramid

200
Maya civilization is fully developed.

ca. **45,000** B.C.   ◄ B.C.   A.D. ►

Events in the World

ca. **12,000** B.C.
Land bridge disappears.
Moses leads the Israelites out of slavery in Egypt.

ca. **551** B.C.
Sayings of Confucius begin to be collected.

ca. **51** B.C.
Cleopatra becomes queen of Egypt.

ca. **27**
Jesus begins a public ministry as a preacher and teacher.

Cleopatra

▲ Europeans brought many changes to the lands and peoples of the Americas. ◆◆ **Connecting Past and Present** *How does the artist want you to feel about the Europeans' arrival? How do Americans influence other parts of the world today?*

Portfolio Project

A NEWS STORY

There were no newspapers from the 1400s and 1500s that presented a picture of daily life in the Americas. If we had them, we would have additional insights into the lifestyles, values, and traditions of the people. As you read this chapter, note some topics you might use to create your own news story, editorial, or editorial cartoon about some aspect of life in the 1400s or 1500s.

Christopher Columbus

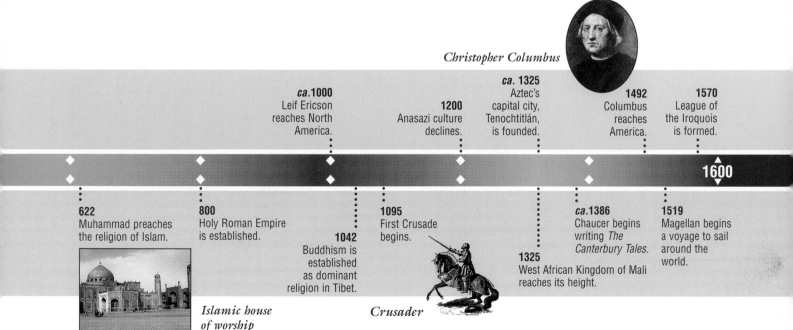

ca.1000
Leif Ericson reaches North America.

1200
Anasazi culture declines.

ca. 1325
Aztec's capital city, Tenochtitlán, is founded.

1492
Columbus reaches America.

1570
League of the Iroquois is formed.

1600

622
Muhammad preaches the religion of Islam.

800
Holy Roman Empire is established.

1042
Buddhism is established as dominant religion in Tibet.

1095
First Crusade begins.

1325
West African Kingdom of Mali reaches its height.

ca.1386
Chaucer begins writing *The Canterbury Tales.*

1519
Magellan begins a voyage to sail around the world.

Islamic house of worship

Crusader

Early Americans

PREVIEW

Objectives

- To analyze how people may have come to the Americas

- To evaluate how the environment influenced the development of Native American cultures

- To identify characteristics of Native American cultures

- To describe the major achievements of the Maya and Aztec civilizations in Central America and Mexico

Vocabulary

nomad	civilization
glacier	tribute
migrate	empire
surplus	

The history of the United States is more than a collection of dates, battles, and laws. It is the dramatic story of how many people came together and developed a nation and a way of life.

The story begins long before European explorers came upon the land that became known as the Americas. It began during prehistoric times—before people kept written records. Playing leading roles were Ice Age hunters from Asia and their descendants, the Native Americans, who established rich traditions on two continents.

◆ ACROSS A LAND BRIDGE

Not everyone agrees how people first came to the Americas. Some Native Americans believe that their people have always lived on the American continents. Many scientists, however, theorize that the first people to arrive in North America were **nomads,** groups of people constantly on the move in search of food. It is thought that these nomads journeyed by foot from Asia to North America many thousands of years ago

during the last Ice Age. The routes of their probable migrations are shown on the map below.

The Ice Ages were periods when the Earth's temperature dropped so steeply that giant sheets of ice, called **glaciers,** covered much of the Earth. With so much of Earth's water trapped in the form of ice, the water level of the oceans fell, and some of the higher areas of the ocean floor appeared. One such place may have been the Bering Strait, a 50-mile stretch of ocean that today separates Asia from North America. During the last Ice Age, a bridge of land connected the two continents. Bighorn sheep, bison, bears, and moose moved back and forth across the land bridge. Some scientists believe that the nomads **migrated,** or

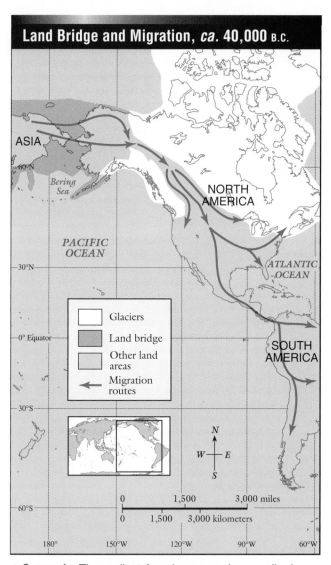

Land Bridge and Migration, *ca.* 40,000 B.C.

ASIA
60°N
Bering Sea
PACIFIC OCEAN
NORTH AMERICA
30°N
0° Equator
ATLANTIC OCEAN
SOUTH AMERICA
30°S
60°S

	Glaciers
	Land bridge
	Other land areas
←	Migration routes

N
W—E
S

0   1,500   3,000 miles
0   1,500   3,000 kilometers

180°   150°W   120°W   90°W   60°W

▲ **Geography** *The earliest Americans may have walked across this land bridge in search of food.* **Interpreting the Map** *What present-day continents does the land bridge connect?*

moved, across the land bridge from Siberia to North America to hunt these animals.

About 10,000 years ago, the Ice Age ended, and Earth began to warm. Glaciers melted and the water level of the oceans rose once again, covering the land bridge between Asia and North America. No longer could humans or animals walk from one continent to another. But by that time, hundreds of thousands of people lived in North and South America.

? **According to some scientists, how was it possible for nomads to reach North America during the Ice Age?**

◆ FLOURISHING NORTH AMERICAN CULTURES

The descendants of those early migrants are called Native Americans because they are believed to be the first to be native to, or born on, the American continents. As the climate changed, groups of these people slowly moved south and modified their way of life to suit the new environments they encountered.

From hunting animals and gathering plants, some Native Americans gradually turned to agriculture, the practice of growing crops. Some historians believe that women were most likely the first to plant because, as seed gatherers, they probably noticed that seeds began to sprout after lying in the ground.

Planting and harvesting meant that by 8000 B.C., people no longer had to be constantly on the move in search of food. Instead, they could settle in one place. Small groups began to build shelters and form permanent villages. This led to a division of labor. While some people produced food for the village, others were able to become specialized at tasks such as pottery making, weaving, teaching, and healing. Native Americans were engaged in the agricultural revolution that was taking place in Europe, Asia, and Africa at about the same time.

The land and climate where each group settled influenced the kinds of houses they built, the foods they ate, and the ways they traveled. The chart on page 6 shows how Native American groups in different regions of North America developed ways of life to adjust to their environments.

Two of the largest groups of Native Americans living in North America were located in the Eastern Woodlands and the Southwest. Their cultures are evidence of how people adapt to their surroundings to create different ways of life.

Native Americans of the Eastern Woodlands

The Eastern Woodlands included an area that stretched from the pine forests of Canada, along the Atlantic coast, and as far west as the Mississippi River. Eastern Woodlanders hunted and trapped animals, gathered wild plants for food, and fished in the rivers and streams. They were also successful farmers, often growing a **surplus** of food, or more than they needed. Surplus food was traded with neighboring groups for other goods. With food so plentiful, populations grew. One Huron town that was uncovered in the Great Lakes region had a population of about 5,000 people. It was larger than the average European town of the 1500s.

The Eastern Woodlands was inhabited by two major groups. The largest group was the Algonquin (al-gän′-kwin), which included at least 50 distinct cultures. They lived in small bands, hunting and gathering as well as farming. Several of these peoples, including the Ojibwas (also known as the Chippewas), would become the first fur traders.

The most powerful people of the Eastern Woodlands were the Iroquois. They lived in the area of present-day New York State. They were expert farmers, growing as many as 15 varieties of maize (or corn) and more than 60 different kinds of beans. Like some of the Algonquins, the Iroquois lived in permanent villages. They built long, rectangular-shaped houses from wooden poles made from saplings and tree bark. These longhouses were sometimes about

Major Native American Cultures in North America Through 1500

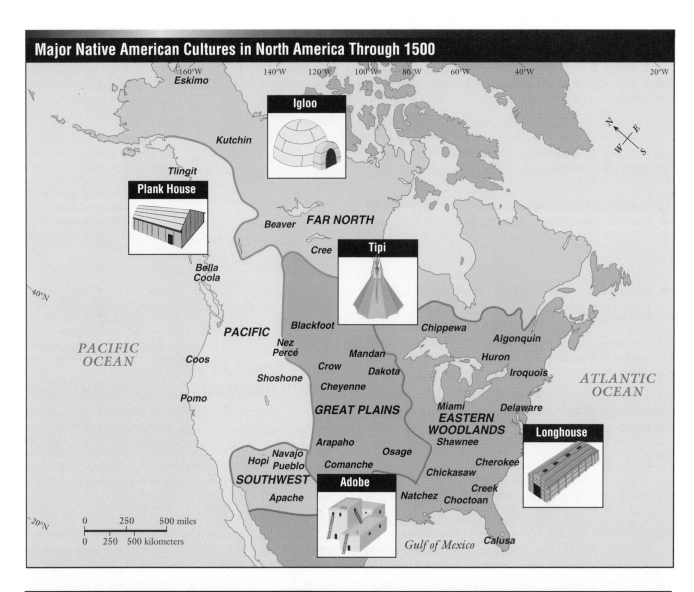

REGION	WAY OF LIFE	HOUSES	DIET
Far North	Nomadic; hunting and fishing	Wooden houses covered with bark, called plank houses; farther north, houses built of ice bricks, called igloos	Moose, caribou, plants, berries, nuts
Pacific	Lived in villages; hunting and fishing	Large houses, called plank houses, made of wood	Fish, seal, whale, bear, elk
Great Plains	Part nomadic; lived in villages when not hunting	Tipis made of buffalo skin	Buffalo
Eastern Woodlands	Lived in villages; hunting, fishing, and farming	Longhouses or dome-shaped houses covered with bark	Deer, corn, beans, squash, nuts, berries
Southwest	Some nomadic, some lived in villages; hunting and gathering, some farming	Houses often made of stone and sun-dried clay bricks, called adobe	Antelope, rabbit, corn, cactus fruit

▲ **Geography** *Native American ways of life were influenced by the regions in which they lived.* **Interpreting the Map and Chart** *How did the climates in the Far North and the Southwest affect the style of houses built by the Native Americans in those regions?*

150 feet long and 20 feet wide. A hallway, with a central fireplace and rooms on either side, ran the length of the building. Each room was home to one family.

A woman and her relatives presided over each longhouse. In addition to owning the house and its belongings, the women were in charge of planting and harvesting crops. Women were powerful in the village as well. They selected the chiefs and determined the fate of captured enemy warriors.

Over time, the Iroquois became the largest and most powerful of all the Native American groups that lived in the east. Their power came from an alliance of five groups—the Mohawk, Seneca, Onondaga, Oneida, and Cayuga—founded to control warfare among themselves. According to legend, a religious leader, calling for an end to the violence, inspired the Mohawk chief Hiawatha to organize the union. The founders of the League of the Iroquois made this promise:

> We bind ourselves together by taking hold of each other's hands.... Our strength shall be in union, our way the way of reason, righteousness, and peace.... Be of strong mind, O chiefs. Carry no anger and hold no grudges.

The League of the Iroquois operated as a representative government. A council of 50 members, who were chosen by women, spoke for the group and made decisions for the League. Each nation had one vote. The council could take action only if all nations agreed.

Native Americans of the Southwest

In contrast to the Eastern Woodlands region, the Southwest region, which was made up of parts of present-day Arizona and New Mexico, was dry and barren. Native Americans of the Southwest had to learn to irrigate the land. Using only stone and wooden tools, they dug ditches that carried water to farmland from nearby streams. Their fields produced corn, beans, and squash.

The Anasazi (an-uh-sah´-zee) were one of the most highly developed cultures of the Southwest. In addition to producing baskets and pottery, the Anasazi were talented architects. They built stacked, multistoried houses, or cliff dwellings, out of sun-dried

bricks, called *adobe*. Their homes were similar to modern-day apartment houses. In fact, their unique style of architecture gave some of the descendants of the Anasazi a new name. When the Spaniards arrived, they called some of these people *pueblo* (pwĕb´lō), the Spanish word for *village*. The Pueblos had adapted the Anasazi style of architecture as protection against warlike neighbors, building their homes into the faces of cliffs. Toeholds cut into the rock allowed them to climb up and down from the top of the cliff.

? What environmental factors caused the Eastern Woodlands and the Southwest peoples to develop different ways of life?

▲ The Anasazi lived in this village, in an area that is now part of Arizona, from around A.D. 800 to 1100. The village is 5 stories high and 70 feet wide. These prehistoric cliff dwellings have been preserved as a national monument.

◆ CIVILIZATIONS OF CENTRAL AMERICA AND MEXICO

Central America and the southern and central portions of Mexico were home to some of the largest and most powerful of the early Native American cultures. Historians have estimated that the region supported a population of 25 million people who established complex **civilizations,** the society and culture of a particular people.

The Maya

The Maya civilization emerged in the rain forests of present-day southern Mexico, Honduras, Belize, and Guatemala, where the Maya planted fields of corn, cocoa, cotton, tomatoes, beans, and squash. They built elaborate irrigation systems. As the food supply increased, the culture blossomed. Trade centers sprang up, and large cities, such as Tikal, were built.

The Maya developed a group of city-states that competed in battle and in building grand public works, such as enormous stone pyramids. Fascinated with time and mathematics, the Maya created a 365-day calendar and a number system.

The Aztec Empire

The Aztecs had a powerful army whose goal was to conquer others, gaining new lands and demanding **tribute,** or forced payment from conquered peoples. With these riches the Aztecs built an enormous **empire,** vast lands and many people controlled by one ruler. The Aztec Empire lasted for nearly 200 years.

The capital city of the Aztec civilization was Tenochtitlán (ta-noch-tēt-län´). Built in the middle of a lake, it had floating gardens, markets, and drawbridges. Mexico City, founded over the ruins of Tenochtitlán, is one of the largest populated cities of the world today. When a Spanish explorer saw Tenochtitlán in the early 1500s, he wrote:

When we saw all those . . . great towns and temples and buildings rising from the water, all made of stone [it] seemed like an enchanted vision.

The Aztecs ruled millions of people from the Gulf of Mexico to the Pacific Ocean. The emperor had absolute power and was treated almost like a god.

This is a statue of Quetzalcoatl (ket´-zəl-kō-ah´-təl), an Aztec god. ▶

The demands for tribute caused revolts among the people conquered by the Aztecs. Powerful Aztec armies, however, put down the uprisings. As one Aztec poet asked, "Who could conquer Tenochtitlán? Who could shake the foundation of heaven?"

What features of the Maya civilization are in use in our civilization today?

Section 1 Review

Check Understanding

1. **Define** (a) nomad (b) glacier (c) migrate (d) surplus (e) civilization (f) tribute (g) empire

2. **Explain** scientists' theory about how people reached North America.

3. **Describe** how the development of agriculture made it possible for civilization to progress in ancient times.

4. **Identify** two characteristics of the Maya civilization and two of the Aztec civilization.

Critical Thinking

◈ **Connecting Past and Present** How was the Iroquois government similar to the U.S. government today?

Write About Culture

Create a chart showing the similarities and differences of the cultures of two Native American cultures.

BUILDING *SKILLS*

Reading a Timeline: Events in Early History

A **timeline** is a tool used to organize information in chronological order or time order. One kind of timeline, a horizontal timeline, shows information that is read from left to right.

Here's How

Follow these steps to read and study a timeline:

1. Look at the beginning and end of the timeline. Identify the period of time covered.
2. Note the length of time between events. These intervals may be one year, five years, or some other span of time. A break in the timeline shows where a period of time has been left out.
3. Determine relationships between events on the timeline. Look for cause-and-effect developments and changes over time.

Here's Why

A timeline is a visual tool that can help you put key events into chronological order and determine historical relationships.

Practice the Skill

Study the timeline on this page and practice reading it by answering the following questions.

1. How many years exist between each interval from 5000 B.C. to 1000 B.C.?
2. About how many years after the Maya abandoned Tikal did the Anasazi stop building their homes?
3. What events show progress in the development of early civilizations?

Apply the Skill

Each day for seven days, record at least two news events that you find in your local newspaper and the date on which they occurred. Then create a timeline for those events. Compare your events with those recorded by your classmates. What similarities and differences do you notice?

Events in Early History

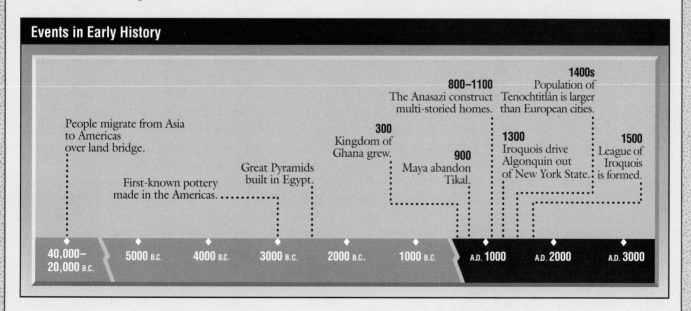

People migrate from Asia to Americas over land bridge.

First-known pottery made in the Americas.

Great Pyramids built in Egypt.

300 Kingdom of Ghana grew.

900 Maya abandon Tikal.

800–1100 The Anasazi construct multi-storied homes.

1400s Population of Tenochtitlán is larger than European cities.

1300 Iroquois drive Algonquin out of New York State.

1500 League of Iroquois is formed.

40,000–20,000 B.C. | 5000 B.C. | 4000 B.C. | 3000 B.C. | 2000 B.C. | 1000 B.C. | A.D. 1000 | A.D. 2000 | A.D. 3000

Section 2

Europe Looks Outward

PREVIEW

Objectives

- To describe how the Crusades helped change Europe and its people

- To explain how and why trade with the East became important in Europe

- To analyze how countries and their rulers grew more powerful as a result of trade

Vocabulary

colony	monopoly
Crusades	monarch
commerce	

In A.D. 1000, Europe was less advanced in certain ways than the major civilizations of the Americas. In Europe, small, decentralized states were led by weak rulers. Wealth and resources were limited, and education was restricted to church officials and the nobility. Most people lived in small villages and devoted their time to raising what they needed to eat or defending their lands against invaders. They had little reason or desire to look beyond life in their own villages. Trade and exploration were limited, and Europe remained insulated from the rest of the world.

◆ HORIZONS WIDEN

The Vikings, farmers and traders from Scandinavia, were the first Europeans to visit the Americas. Scandinavia is the area of present-day Norway, Sweden, and Denmark. Between 700 and 1000, the Scandinavian population steadily increased as their food supply decreased. Facing starvation, some Vikings ventured into areas in western Europe. Others explored and raided lands along the rivers of eastern Europe and Russia.

Some time around 1000, a Viking leader named Leif Ericson landed on the eastern coast of North America in what is today Newfoundland. Here, the Vikings founded a **colony,** a settlement made up of people who retain ties to their homeland.

The Crusades

The Vikings were not the only travelers, however. Beginning in 1095, religious wars known as the **Crusades** caused nobles and peasants all over Europe to flock to what is often called the Middle East today.

The Crusades, which lasted for almost 200 years, were an attempt by Christians to recapture the Holy Land, or the area of the Middle East around Palestine, from the Muslims. Muslims are followers of a religion called Islam that began in Arabia. The Muslims created an enormous empire extending from India in the east through the Holy Land and across North Africa to the Atlantic Ocean. About the same time the Vikings were exploring, the Muslim ruler of Palestine began to persecute Christians. It became impossible for Europeans to visit the Holy Land. Christians considered the region holy to their faith because Jesus had lived there. The Muslims, too, regarded the land as sacred because their prophet Muhammad had lived in Palestine.

The Crusades did not regain the Holy Land for Christians. Two hundred years later, it was still controlled by Muslims and would remain so until the twentieth century. But Europe had changed in important ways. More people had traveled to distant lands. They saw another world and heard new ideas. In the markets they tasted rice, oranges, and dates. They noticed how ginger, pepper, cloves, and other spices both improved the taste of food and helped preserve it. Their new clothes of silk and cotton were much more comfortable than their usual wool clothing. They sat on colorful rugs and ate from beautiful china dishes. When the Crusaders brought these treasures home, everyone was impressed with the new luxurious goods.

Trade with the East

For the small number of Europeans back home who could read, *The Travels of Marco Polo* aroused tremendous curiosity. Written in 1298, it described the wonders an Italian merchant, Marco Polo, claimed to have seen during his 20-year trip to Asia. For the next three centuries, Marco Polo's Asia remained the focus of European dreams of wealth and adventure.

Spices, silks, rugs, and jewels came to the Holy Land by trade routes from India and China, and from the Indies, islands off the coast of Southeast Asia. They came either by ship across the Indian Ocean or by camel caravan on the 4,000-mile overland Silk Road. To recover the costs of these long journeys, Middle Eastern merchants charged high prices for their merchandise.

▲ *This painting from a manuscript of Marco Polo's book shows that goods from Asia were unfamiliar to Europeans. The elephant was probably drawn by someone who had never seen one before.*

Having transported Crusaders across the Mediterranean Sea to the Holy Land, Italian sea captains realized that their ships could also carry luxury goods from the Middle East to Europe. Soon, Italian traders became masters of **commerce,** the large-scale buying and selling of goods that goes on between cities or countries. Some traders flourished and gained a **monopoly,** or exclusive control, of trade. Europeans who wanted Asian goods had to deal with these traders. To recover the high costs of obtaining the goods, Italian merchants charged a great deal of money for them. The goods became so expensive that only very wealthy Europeans could afford them. Other European nations sought to break Middle Eastern and Italian control by finding their own trade routes to Asia.

 In what way did the Crusades stimulate interest in Asia?

◆ STRONG NATIONS EMERGE

During the Middle Ages, much of Europe was broken into small kingdoms under the control of nobles, who often fought with one another. With the growth of trade, however, strong **monarchs,** or

rulers, were needed to build roads, protect trade routes against robbers, and keep the peace. Merchants and bankers willingly loaned money to rulers, who used the funds to build large armies and unite their kingdoms. By the late 1400s, powerful monarchs in England, France, Spain, and Portugal were looking for ways to increase their wealth.

By the middle of the fifteenth century, European cultures were much different from what they had been. Agricultural production had increased, cities had expanded, and the crafting of handmade articles for sale had begun. Commerce became more organized, and, along with the opening of new trade routes, economic growth soon followed. A spirit of curiosity and adventure ignited the Age of Exploration.

Why were new trade routes so important to European countries and their rulers?

Section 2 Review

Check Understanding

1. **Define** (a) colony (b) Crusades (c) commerce (d) monopoly (e) monarch

2. **Identify** ways in which the Crusades benefited the people of Europe.

3. **Explain** why goods from Asia were so expensive in Europe.

4. **List** several ways that trade led to the strengthening of European rulers and their nations.

Critical Thinking

Analyzing Cause and Effect How and why did Italian merchants come to dominate European trade with Asia?

Write About Economics

◆ **Connecting Past and Present** Make a list of treasures brought home by Crusaders. Write a paragraph about why you think items like these are considered treasures today.

Section 3

Africa's Trading Kingdoms

PREVIEW

Objectives

- To examine how Africa's trading kingdoms grew and prospered

- To describe features of West African culture

- To identify traditions that people of West Africa shared

Vocabulary

pilgrimage
kinship
griot

In the 1400s, Europe was entering the Age of Exploration. By then, several powerful states had arisen in Africa. Kush, a state in East Africa, dates back to Ancient Egypt. The prosperity of the Kushites grew from its wealth in iron ore, which it traded for goods from India and Arabia. Axum, another East African state, grew rich and powerful from trading its gold and ivory. Other African states arose in the savannahs and the forests of West Africa.

◆ WEST AFRICAN KINGDOMS

Between A.D. 300 and 1500, three kingdoms rose and fell in West Africa. Their world began to change in the 1400s when Europeans landed on the West African coast.

Ghana

The earliest of the West African kingdoms, Ghana, developed from a simple trading post. Because of its location on the southern edge of the Sahara, it was a stopping point for camel caravans that came to trade salt and copper for gold from central African mines. Salt was, quite literally, worth its weight in gold because it prevented meat from spoiling in the heat. North Africans and desert traders also purchased slaves here to work in the desert salt mines. Ghana prospered until Muslims from the north took over the kingdom in the eleventh century.

Mali

The Muslim empire of Mali replaced Ghana as the primary trading kingdom in West Africa. Mansa Musa, who ruled the area from 1307 to 1332, made Mali famous when he went on a **pilgrimage,** or religious journey, to Mecca, the holiest city in the Muslim world. Although details of his caravan—which included 80 camels, each carrying a 300-pound bag of gold dust—seem almost fictional, he did attract much attention. Mansa Musa's trip was widely reported, and stories of Mali's wealth spread far beyond the Muslim world. In a Spanish map of West Africa, seen on page 13, Musa is shown sitting on a throne and holding a huge gold nugget. Accompanying the map was this note:

> **The gold which is found in [Mansa Musa's] country is so abundant that he is the richest and noblest lord in all the region.**

The strength of Mali weakened after Mansa Musa died in 1332.

Songhai

Like Ghana and Mali, Songhai grew rich from trade. As it prospered, it expanded. In 1468, Songhai armies conquered Mali and its capital, making Songhai the most powerful and the largest kingdom in West Africa. Songhai's cavalry, or troops trained to fight on horseback, became important in controlling the flow of trade.

Songhai's traders obtained gold and ivory from central Africa and kola nuts from the forests. Kola nuts were used to flavor a beverage that was the original version of the colas people drink today. Traveling in caravans with as many as 12,000 camels, they crossed the Sahara to trade with the North Africans. On the return trip, they brought salt, weapons, cloth, horses, books, and paper. The books were for Tombouctou (or Timbuktu), which became the center of Islamic learning and the home of 3 universities and 180 other schools. By the mid-1500s, education rivaled trade as the city's major activity. Scholars came from northern Africa and the Middle East to study law, history, and religion.

At a time when European countries were just beginning to develop, African kingdoms like Songhai were already stable and organized. As Ramusio, secretary to the rulers of Venice, said in 1563,

" Let them go and do business with the King of Timbuktu and Mali and there is no doubt that they will be well-received there with their ships and their goods and treated well, and granted the favours that they ask. "

To control Songhai, which extended over part of western Africa, as shown on the map on page 14, its ruler, Askia Muhammad, hired paid officials to administer laws, keep the peace, and collect taxes. Under Askia's direction, they also ran a banking system.

Songhai's great wealth attracted other nations. In 1591, the kingdom fell to an invading army from Morocco, in North Africa.

What made West Africa an important center of trade?

◆ WEST AFRICAN CULTURE

While the people of West Africa differed in many of their customs and beliefs, they did hold many things in common. Family and **kinship** were the basis of West African society. Kinship is a relationship based on common ancestors. Families tended to be large, including immediate family members as well as kin through marriage.

Kinship had a place in West African religion as well. West Africans believed that the spirits of their ancestors had power to influence their lives. They worshiped these ancestors along with other gods, praying for protection from evil and help in solving life's daily problems.

Knowledge of past generations was extremely important to West Africans. The achievements of ancestors were kept alive by **griots** (grē´-ōz), or storytellers. Griots told stories of the past that had been handed down through generations from parents to children. Griots were the major link people had with their past.

Away from the trading centers, most people were farmers who worked on the same land their ancestors had cleared. This land belonged to communities, not to individual farmers. Decisions about production, storage, and distribution were made by clan leaders and village chiefs. Local courts settled disputes.

◀ This Spanish map, created in 1375, includes a drawing of Mansa Musa. It gives clues about Musa's power, his wealth, and the extent of his rule.

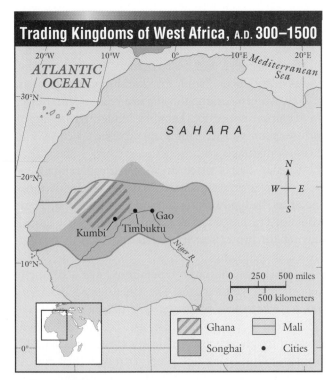

ATLANTIC OCEAN

SAHARA

Kumbi • Timbuktu • Gao

Niger R.

Mediterranean Sea

N
W — E
S

0   250   500 miles

0   500 kilometers

▨ Ghana   Mali

▨ Songhai   • Cities

▲ **Geography** *Each of the early kingdoms of West Africa reached the height of its power in different time periods. On this map, Mali encompasses most of Ghana and Songhai.* **Interpreting the Map** *Which kingdoms had access to the Atlantic Ocean?*

Both men and women shared many of the same jobs, such as clearing fields for planting and harvesting crops. Both also produced housewares, tools, and weapons from iron and bronze.

Because farming had been going on for thousands of years, farming methods were exceptionally sophisticated. Farmers grew grains and rice on the grassy plains and fruits and vegetables in the tropical forests near the equator. In some areas, poor, thin soil demanded "shifting cultivation," which meant that after several years of farming on a plot of land, farmers would need to move on and allow that plot to recover.

The fact that the people of West Africa were so accustomed to farming was significant when European slave traders arrived. The nomadic peoples of other parts of Africa were not accustomed to working the land, but West Africans were experienced and able farmers.

A form of slavery was a part of the social system of West Africa. People who had been cut off from their kinship relationships, such as prisoners of war and criminals, were the most likely to be enslaved. However, orphans, people with disabilities, and others

were also commonly robbed of their freedom. Enslaved people were adopted into new kinship networks and were protected by the same laws as everyone else. Slaves could own or inherit property, including their own slaves. Their enslavement was not necessarily permanent, and it did not automatically pass to their children.

Like the native peoples of the Americas, the West Africans were diverse peoples with highly developed civilizations. They, too, had little contact with Europeans. All these worlds would soon change with the arrival of European explorers.

 What were some important traditions in early West African culture?

Section 3 Review

Check Understanding

1. **Define** (a) pilgrimage (b) kinship (c) griot

2. **Explain** how the government of Songhai was run.

3. **Identify** Mansa Musa and the importance of his journey to Mecca.

4. **Describe** how slavery operated in West Africa.

5. **Discuss** the ways in which family ties were important to the people of West Africa.

Critical Thinking

◆**Connecting Past and Present** Compare the way in which early West Africans learned about their ancestors with ways Americans learn about their ancestors today.

Write About Geography

Study the map of trading kingdoms in West Africa on this page. Write a paragraph that explains how the location of the region might have affected the development of the three trading kingdoms.

Section 4

Exploration and Its Consequences

PREVIEW

Objectives

- To evaluate Portugal's role in the age of discovery

- To explain how Native American cultures in the Caribbean changed as a result of European influence

- To examine why Africans were captured and taken to the Americas

Vocabulary

navigator	plantation
compass	conquistador
astrolabe	encomienda system

In the 1400s, Europe began an age of discovery that would lead explorers to Africa, Asia, and the Americas in hopes of finding gold and a direct sea route to Asia. The country of Portugal was responsible for promoting the advancement of navigation techniques. With these techniques, European explorers began to search for new trade routes.

◆ PORTUGUESE EXPLORATION

The prince of Portugal, known as Prince Henry the Navigator, had long dreamed of making his country the world's leading sea power. He realized that Portugal needed better ships and more able **navigators** to accomplish the task. Navigators are people who plan and direct the course of a ship. In 1419, he established a school for sailors, where he brought astronomers, geographers, and mathematicians to share their learning. Students were taught to use tools such as the **compass** and **astrolabe.** The compass is an instrument that shows direction, while the astrolabe shows distance north of the equator. Students also learned math and geography, the study of Earth's physical features and climate.

By the time the prince died in 1460, Portuguese ships had sailed south along the African coast as far as Sierra Leone. In 1498 the explorer Vasco da Gama rounded Africa, sailed all the way to India, and then returned to Portugal. With this discovery, Portugal commanded the all-important water route to Asia. The accomplishments of Vasco da Gama and other explorers are shown in the chart on page 17.

One of Portugal's major goals during the fifteenth century was to take advantage of the wealth of West Africa. The area, dotted with Portuguese trading stations, became known as the Gold Coast. But gold was not the only contribution to the economy. Soon ships were returning home with wrought iron, ivory, tortoise shell, textiles, and slaves as well as gold.

Household slaves were not new in parts of Europe. Prisoners of war were sold to wealthy families, who put them to work as servants. Some Europeans, however, were disturbed about enslaving fellow Christians. They were less troubled about enslaving Africans and Muslims, who differed from them in culture and appearance.

Most captured Africans were sold to Portuguese sugar cane **plantations,** or large farms for growing one major crop, located on the island of Madeira, off the coast of northern Africa. Portuguese planters worked their slaves to death because the costs of replacing them were small in comparison to the profits from growing sugar cane. Trading for slaves to

▲ By aligning the crosspiece of the astrolabe with the horizon, and aligning the rotating pointer with the North Star, navigators on ships could tell how many degrees north of the equator they were.

Chapter 1 ◆ *15*

supply a large, cheap labor force laid the foundation for a new kind of slavery that would eventually find its way to the Americas.

? How did Prince Henry the Navigator contribute to the age of exploration?

◆ FIRST CONTACTS IN THE AMERICAS

The voyage of an Italian ship captain, Christopher Columbus, began centuries of interaction and change around the world. It also marked the beginning of conflict among Native Americans, Europeans, and Africans. During the first years explorers spent in the Americas, new societies were formed, but old ones were destroyed.

The Voyages of Christopher Columbus

In the 1480s, Christopher Columbus proposed to the king of Portugal that Portuguese ships could reach Asia by sailing west across the Atlantic Ocean. He believed that sailing westward would provide a shorter route to Asia. Columbus's plan was rejected by the king's science advisors, who said that the ocean was too vast to cross.

Columbus was not discouraged. He took his plan to King Ferdinand and Queen Isabella of Spain. It took Columbus six years to convince them to finance his quest. In August 1492, Columbus sailed from Spain with three small ships—the *Niña, Pinta,* and *Santa María.* Two months later he landed on an island and claimed it for Spain.

Columbus assumed that this island was located off the coast of India. Thus, he called the people who came to meet him "Indians." He had actually landed on one of the islands of the Bahamas, just off the coast of North America in the Caribbean Sea. The people he met were Native Americans who called themselves Taíno (tä-ē-nō). The Taíno had a complex social structure and a distinctive art.

Over the next several weeks, Columbus explored other islands in the Bahamas and Cuba. He then sailed to Hispaniola, or "Little Spain" (known today as Haiti and the Dominican Republic), where he built a fort. He left 40 of his crew members behind to hunt for gold.

On his return to Spain, Columbus was hailed as a hero. The monarchs gave him the title "Admiral of the Ocean Sea" and quickly organized a second trip. This time, Columbus left with 17 ships and about

▲ *Columbus is portrayed next to a map showing an idea of how much of the world was still left to explore.*

1,500 people. Their goal was to make Hispaniola a thriving Spanish colony.

Columbus arrived back in Hispaniola to make a grim discovery. All 40 crew members left behind had been killed by the Taíno, who were outraged at the Spaniards' cruel treatment. In retaliation, Columbus destroyed Taíno villages, demanding gold tribute and enslaving the people.

Columbus made two more trips to the Americas. He died in Spain in 1506, still convinced that he had opened the way to Asia. One of his important contributions was the discovery of the clockwise circulation of the Atlantic winds and currents that would carry other European explorers back and forth to the Americas.

Amerigo Vespucci

Columbus died believing he had reached Asia. After Columbus, European explorers continued their quests to find new passages to Asia, as shown in the chart on page 17. In 1501, Amerigo Vespucci (ve-spoō-chē) explored South America's coast for Portugal. He described the lands as *Mundus Novus,* a "new world." When geographers finally named these continents in the sixteenth century, they called them America after Vespucci.

Spain Conquers the Caribbean

After Columbus reached the West Indies—the islands in the Caribbean Sea—the Spaniards continued to explore and settle several of the islands. By 1511, they had conquered Puerto Rico, Jamaica, and Cuba. Long before the English arrived in the Americas, the Spaniards had built a huge and wealthy empire there.

The Spaniards came to the Americas for different reasons. Spanish priests came hoping to convert Native Americans to Christianity. **Conquistadors,** the Spanish term for *conquerors*, came for fame and gold.

Some Spaniards even came to farm. They divided the land into large plantations and planted sugar cane. The Spanish conquerors enslaved Native American people such as the Taíno and put them to work growing and harvesting the cane. Columbus and his successors established a practice known as the **encomienda system,** in which Native Americans were forced to work for Spanish lords. Faced with continual labor shortages, soldiers raided the Bahamas and soon had severely depopulated them.

Not all Europeans supported the cruel treatment of Native Americans. One of the most vocal was Bartolomé de Las Casas, a Spanish priest who himself had taken part in the conquest of the island of Cuba. Several years later he denounced the conquest, saying that the Christian mission in the Americas was to convert its inhabitants to Christianity, not to destroy them. In his *Destruction of the Indies*, Las Casas noted that when he arrived on Hispaniola in 1508,

> "There were 60,000 people living on this island, including the Indians; so that from 1494 to 1508, over three million people had perished from war, slavery, and the mines. Who in future generations will believe this? I myself writing it as a knowledgeable eyewitness can hardly believe it."

But war and enslavement were not the only causes of death to the Native Americans of the Caribbean. With the arrival of the Spaniards came new diseases, such as yellow fever, smallpox, measles, and tuberculosis.

History *Many explorers brought fame and riches to Spain and Portugal between 1488 and 1522.* **Interpreting the Chart** *Which explorers were looking for a route to Asia? Which were looking for gold?* ▼

Early Portuguese and Spanish Explorations, 1488–1522

Explorer	Country Represented	Year	Goal	Accomplishment
Bartholomeu Dias	Portugal	1488	To find southern tip of Africa	Sailed around southern tip of Africa (Cape of Good Hope) into Indian Ocean
Christopher Columbus	Spain	1492–1504 (4 voyages)	To find western route to Asia	Explored West Indies, Caribbean Islands, and Central and South America
Vasco da Gama	Portugal	1497–1498	To sail around Africa to eastern Asia	Reached India
Amerigo Vespucci	Portugal	1499–1502 (2 voyages)	To explore the Americas	Explored coast of South America and identified it as a continent
Juan Ponce de León	Spain	1513, 1521	To find gold and the Fountain of Youth	Explored Florida and Puerto Rico
Vasco Núñez de Balboa	Spain	1513	To find gold	Crossed Isthmus of Panama and saw Pacific Ocean
Ferdinand Magellan	Spain	1519–1522	To find western route to Asia	Sailed across Atlantic, around South America, and across Pacific Ocean; survivors of voyage were first to sail around the world

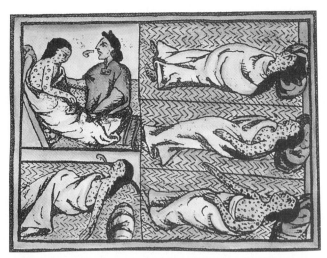

▲ *Diseases brought by Europeans devastated Native Americans, who had had no previous exposure to them. Victims of smallpox are pictured here.*

Repeated outbreaks of these diseases took a heavy toll on Native Americans, and tens of thousands of them died.

The Trade in Humans

Many Native Americans died working for the Spaniards. Soon, there were not enough people left to work in the gold mines and on the plantations. In 1517, Spain brought about 4,000 Africans to the Caribbean islands and forced them to work there. By the middle of the 1500s, the Spaniards were shipping about 2,000 enslaved Africans each year just to Hispaniola.

Slave raiders from Europe tore hundreds of thousands of people away from their homes in West Africa and shipped them to the islands in the Caribbean. To escape the horrible conditions of enslavement, some Africans chose to jump overboard and drown. One West African who survived the trip later wrote of the ordeal on the ship:

"The men who fastened irons on the mothers took the children out of their hands and threw them over the side of the ship into the water. Two of the women leaped overboard after the children. They were carried down by the weight of their irons before they could be rescued."

Many others died on the slave ships before they arrived in the Caribbean. They died from diseases that spread rapidly within the confines of the slave ships. Others perished from tainted food or abusive treatment.

 Why did the Spaniards force West Africans into enslavement?

Section 4 Review

Check Understanding

1. **Define** (a) navigator (b) compass (c) astrolabe (d) plantation (e) conquistador (f) encomienda system

2. **Identify** Prince Henry's role in promoting exploration by Europeans.

3. **Describe** the skills that students learned in the school for navigators.

4. **Explain** the negative effects that Portuguese explorers had on West Africa.

5. **Identify** the reason for Christopher Columbus's failure to reach India. What long-range effects did this "error" have?

6. **Explain** how European explorers affected Native American cultures in the Caribbean.

Critical Thinking

◆ **Connecting Past and Present** One of Columbus's companions wrote of the Native Americans: "Amongst them, the land belongs to everybody, just as does the sun or the water." Would most people today agree with the Native Americans' point of view? Explain.

Write About History

Write a brief essay explaining why you think Bartolomé de Las Casas was concerned that people might not believe his statement about the deaths of Native Americans in the Caribbean.

CONNECTING HISTORY
&Geography

THE COLUMBIAN EXCHANGE

When Christopher Columbus arrived in the Americas, different cultures came into contact for the first time. In addition to language and customs, Europeans, Native Americans, and West Africans exchanged crops, animals, and ideas. Because this cultural mingling began with Columbus, the transfer is called the Columbian Exchange.

Native Americans taught Europeans to eat maize and potatoes and to smoke tobacco. With the addition of nutritious beans, squash, tomatoes, and peppers to European diets, the population of Europe nearly doubled by the 1700s. At the same time, livestock, wheat, sugar cane, bananas, and citrus fruits from Europe, Africa, and Asia changed the meals of Native Americans. During the 1500s the first pigs, sheep, horses, and cattle were brought to the Americas. These animals provided new sources of protein, as well as materials for many products.

Not all aspects of the Columbian Exchange were positive, however. Native Americans, never before exposed to the diseases carried by Europeans, fell victim to smallpox, measles, and tuberculosis. These diseases killed 80 percent of the Native American population.

The Columbian Exchange is a striking illustration of cultural interaction—long before modern communication and transportation were available. Forever changed were the ways people ate, dressed, fought, and lived. Within 100 years of the arrival of the first Europeans, a new environment had developed in the Americas.

Making the Geographic Connection

1. What was the Columbian Exchange?
2. How did the Columbian Exchange cause the populations of different continents to change?
3. What was a negative aspect of the Columbian Exchange?

Connecting Past and Present

What kinds of cultural and economic exchanges occur today between nations? What are the effects of this interaction?

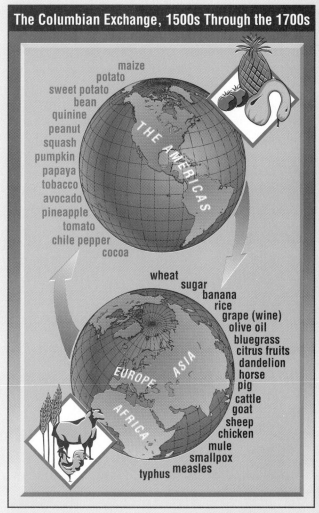

The Columbian Exchange, 1500s Through the 1700s

maize
potato
sweet potato
bean
quinine
peanut
squash
pumpkin
papaya
tobacco
avocado
pineapple
tomato
chile pepper
cocoa

THE AMERICAS

wheat
sugar
banana
rice
grape (wine)
olive oil
bluegrass
citrus fruits
dandelion
horse
pig
cattle
goat
sheep
chicken
mule
smallpox
measles
typhus

EUROPE
ASIA
AFRICA

▲ **Economics** *Traders in the Columbian Exchange introduced foods, animals, and diseases to the people of the Americas.* **Interpreting the Map** *Which goods originally brought from Europe, Asia, and Africa are most common in your life today?*

Chapter 1
Review

CHAPTER SUMMARY

Section 1

Many scientists believe that the first Americans migrated to North America many thousands of years ago during the Ice Age. The first Americans, the ancestors of present-day Native Americans, migrated throughout the Americas. In different regions, they created cultures that adapted to and changed their environments.

Section 2

Europeans knew little of the outside world until the Crusades. The Crusades changed Europe, though they did not regain the Holy Land from the Muslims. Exposed to Asian goods for the first time, Europeans quickly developed a taste for them. To avoid paying the high prices charged by the merchants from Italy, other countries began to search for trade routes to the East.

Section 3

Highly developed civilizations had already been prospering in West Africa while European nations were growing. Ghana, Mali, and Songhai developed as a result of active trading. Even though cultures varied from place to place within West Africa, all groups shared certain fundamental beliefs.

Section 4

With the help of Prince Henry of Portugal, who sponsored a school for navigators, explorers set off from Europe to find new trade routes to Asia. Christopher Columbus, looking for a route to India, landed on an island in the Caribbean. Other explorers followed, with negative effects on Native Americans. In the early 1500s, West Africans were enslaved and brought to the Americas to work.

Connecting ◆◆ Past and Present

What might your life be without the rice, oranges, spices, cotton, jewels, and rugs that Europeans encountered on the Crusades?

Using Vocabulary

From the list below, select the term that best completes each sentence.

griot	monopoly
civilization	nomad
migrate	Crusades
plantation	compass
surplus	commerce

1. A _____ is exclusive control of a product.

2. A person who moves from place to place is called a _____ .

3. The _____ were a series of wars fought between Muslims and Christians over the part of the Middle East known as the Holy Land.

4. A large farm producing one major crop is called a _____ .

5. A _____ is an instrument for showing direction.

6. A _____ is a West African storyteller.

7. A _____ is the society and culture of a particular people.

8. When people have produced a _____ they have more food than they need.

9. _____ is the large-scale buying and selling of goods done by cities and countries.

10. One factor that caused people to _____ was the need for food.

Check Understanding

1. **Explain** how the Ice Age may have contributed to the migration of people to the Americas.

2. **Analyze** why women may have been the first farmers.

3. **Identify** some of the cultural differences between the Native Americans of the Eastern Woodlands and the Native Americans of the Southwest.

4. **Summarize** some of the beliefs that Native American groups had in common.

5. **Discuss** some of the accomplishments of the Aztec and the Maya civilizations.

6. **Describe** some of the outstanding features of Mali's capital, Timbuktu.

7. **Explain** how Columbus's journey resulted in his landing on a Caribbean island.

8. **Discuss** the role of enslaved Africans in the Caribbean economy under Spanish rule.

Critical Thinking

1. **Analyzing Cause and Effect** Why would more advanced cultures tend to develop in agricultural societies rather than among hunters and gatherers?

2. **Drawing Conclusions** How did disease affect the conquest of the Caribbean in the 1500s?

3. **Evaluating** How did the Italian monopoly on trade with Asia both help and hurt Europeans?

4. **Drawing Conclusions** Why did Christopher Columbus have trouble finding support for his plan to find a water route to Asia?

◆ **Connecting Past and Present** Why are the trade links that were vital to the civilizations of Central America, Africa, and Europe still vital today?

Writing to Persuade

Write a brochure to encourage engineers, sailors, scientists, and mathematicians to study at Prince Henry's school for navigators. Explain what skills they will learn, and be sure to include the benefits they might expect from their studies.

Putting Skills to Work

READING A TIMELINE

In the Building Skills lesson on page 9, you learned how to read events chronologically. You also learned how a timeline can help you analyze historical relationships. Use the vertical timeline on this page to answer these questions. (In a vertical timeline, you read the events from the bottom to the top.)

1. What years are covered by the timeline?

2. What was the length of time of Marco Polo's visit to China?

3. Which event on the timeline most likely benefited the explorers in the 1400s and 1500s?

4. About how many years before Columbus crossed the Atlantic did Marco Polo visit China?

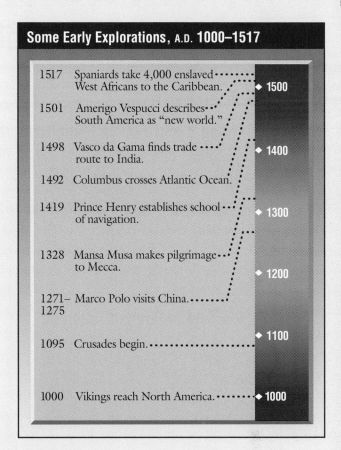

Some Early Explorations, A.D. 1000–1517

1517	Spaniards take 4,000 enslaved West Africans to the Caribbean.	1500
1501	Amerigo Vespucci describes South America as "new world."	
1498	Vasco da Gama finds trade route to India.	1400
1492	Columbus crosses Atlantic Ocean.	
1419	Prince Henry establishes school of navigation.	1300
1328	Mansa Musa makes pilgrimage to Mecca.	1200
1271– 1275	Marco Polo visits China.	
1095	Crusades begin.	1100
1000	Vikings reach North America.	1000

Portfolio Project

A NEWS STORY

Choose a place, event, or person from this chapter that you think is newsworthy. Then decide if you will write a news story, write an editorial, or draw an editorial cartoon. Remember that a news story presents information that answers the questions *who, what, when, where, why,* and *how.* An editorial and an editorial cartoon present a point of view about a topic or person. Include details that convey the most important information you want the reader to know about your topic. You and your classmates may want to create a newspaper, using your news stories, editorials, and editorial cartoons. Consider including advertisements. File your completed work in your portfolio.

Chapter 2
Europeans Settle New Colonies 1519–1760

CHAPTER PREVIEW

Section 1 Spain and France Establish Colonies

Spain and France had different economic goals in settling the Americas and, as a result, established different kinds of colonies.

Section 2 Settling Virginia and New England

England's colonies in Virginia and New England began to thrive in the mid-1600s, making rules and advocating rights that would lead to important principles of government for Americans.

Section 3 Thirteen English Colonies

By 1750 each of the 13 English colonies located along the Atlantic coast of North America had developed its own distinct economy and society.

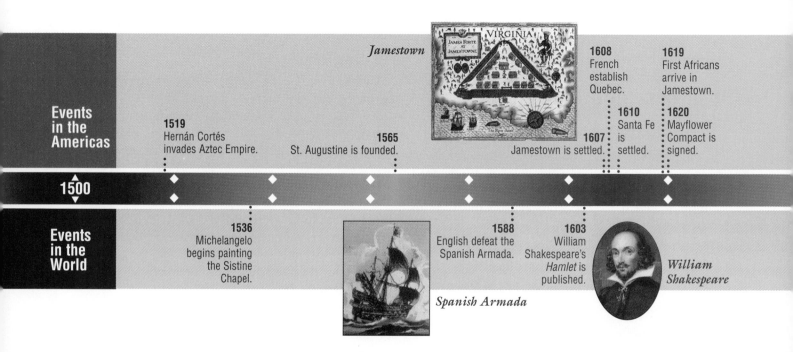

Events in the Americas

Jamestown

1519 Hernán Cortés invades Aztec Empire.

1565 St. Augustine is founded.

1607 Jamestown is settled.

1608 French establish Quebec.

1610 Santa Fe is settled.

1619 First Africans arrive in Jamestown.

1620 Mayflower Compact is signed.

1500

Events in the World

1536 Michelangelo begins painting the Sistine Chapel.

1588 English defeat the Spanish Armada.

1603 William Shakespeare's *Hamlet* is published.

Spanish Armada

William Shakespeare

Portfolio *Project*

AN ADVERTISEMENT FOR SETTLERS

As the colonization of North America began in the 1600s, people left Europe for a variety of reasons. As you read about the American colonies, look for information that you could use to promote the benefits of leaving England to settle in the colonies. At the end of this chapter, you will write an advertisement to encourage people in England to come to the colonies.

▲ *William Penn made a treaty with the Native Americans for the land that became Pennsylvania.* ◈ **Connecting Past and Present** *How does the artist convey a mood of cooperation? How do nations today interact peacefully?*

Anne Hutchinson

1637
Anne Hutchinson is put on trial.

1664
English take over New Netherland.

1682
La Salle claims Mississippi River region for France.

Oglethorpe, of Georgia

1733
Georgia, last of the 13 colonies, is settled.

1760

1639
Foreigners are expelled from Japan.

1689
English Bill of Rights passes Parliament.

1711
Bubonic plague kills more than 500,000 people in Austria and Germany.

1750
The Industrial Revolution has begun in Great Britain.

Japanese shogun

Section 1

Spain and France Establish Colonies

PREVIEW

Objectives

- To explain how Spanish conquistadors overtook the powerful Aztec Empire

- To identify reasons for expansion into what is today the U.S. South and Southwest

- To analyze the impact of the Spanish conquest on Native American cultures

- To identify reasons for French settlements in the Americas

Vocabulary

famine	hacienda
mission	vaquero
mestizo	Californio
presidio	aristocrat

In 1519, a small Spanish army appeared on the east coast of Mexico near the present-day city of Veracruz. Led by a conquistador named Hernán Cortés, 500 Spaniards prepared to march on the Aztec capital of Tenochtitlán. Their goal was to claim the rich and powerful Aztec Empire.

◆ THE FALL OF THE AZTECS

As the Spaniards prepared to march, Cortés met a Native American woman named Malíntzin, who came to be called Doña Marina by the Spaniards. Cortés learned that Malíntzin hated the Aztecs because they had sold her into slavery as a child. She was happy to help Cortés, offering to serve as an interpreter for the Spaniards during meetings with the Aztecs. Malíntzin told Cortés that many Native Americans, opposed to the Aztecs because of their cruel rule, would be eager to make alliances with the Spaniards. She also reported that some Aztecs believed that a fair-skinned god called Quetzalcoatl would one day appear from the east to rule the Aztecs. Cortés was able to use that belief to his advantage.

At the gates of Tenochtitlán, the Aztec emperor Moctezuma greeted Cortés with the high honors due a god. The Spaniards were presented with dazzling gifts. Cortés accepted Moctezuma's invitation to enter the city but then made the emperor a prisoner. To stop the fighting that broke out, Cortés persuaded the emperor to announce that Cortés was now ruler of the Aztecs. Some Aztecs responded angrily and hurled stones at the emperor. Moctezuma was gravely wounded and died a few days later.

The Aztecs and Spaniards battled for control of Tenochtitlán for more than one year. In the end, the Spaniards, though far outnumbered, proved too powerful. Aztec bows, arrows, and spears could not compete with the swords, guns, and cannons of the Spanish forces. And Native Americans on foot were no match for Spaniards on horseback. Many Aztecs succumbed to the diseases brought by the European adventurers. Cortés was also helped by many people who, like Malíntzin, resented living under Aztec rule. He forged Spanish-Indian alliances that became models for later European colonization in the Americas.

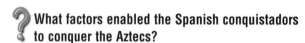

What factors enabled the Spanish conquistadors to conquer the Aztecs?

◆ A SPANISH EMPIRE

By the year 1600, Spain had conquered lands that stretched from present-day New Mexico and Florida almost to the southern tip of South America. To organize and control this huge empire, the Spaniards divided it into two parts. In the north, New Spain consisted of present-day Mexico, Central America, and the Caribbean islands. In the south, Spanish claims stretched over a large part of the continent of South America. Brazil was controlled by Portugal.

Finding it difficult to keep enough supplies coming from Europe to feed all of its soldiers, Spain seized control of central Mexico's valuable farm and ranch lands. Throughout New Spain, large estates soon appeared as the Spanish crown rewarded conquistadors with grants of land. The land grants gave the new owners the right to force Native Americans to work on their lands. Traveling through New Spain, church leader Bartolomé de Las Casas protested the mistreatment he observed. He wrote,

> "The Indians were totally deprived of their freedom . . . Even beasts enjoy more freedom when they are allowed to graze in the field."

Because of Las Casas's protest, by 1550 landowners had to pay wages to Native American farm workers. However, the wage was so low that Native Americans had to borrow from the landowners to survive. Since Spanish law stated that workers could not leave an estate until all debts were paid, workers were sometimes trapped for life.

Native Americans were also forced to work in mines. In 1546, a Spanish miner found a vein of silver northwest of present-day Mexico City. Within a few years, there were about 5,000 silver mines producing ore for shipment to Spain. Many Native Americans working in the mines died from disease and mistreatment. Seeking new workers, the Spaniards began to import Africans as slave laborers. In the following years, the African slave trade grew in the Spanish colonies and elsewhere in the Americas.

Why were Native Americans often trapped working on Spanish estates and in Spanish mines?

This painting from an Aztec manuscript shows Cortés with his interpreter, Malíntzin (Doña Marina), at right. Cortés and his Spanish army entered Tenochtitlán in 1519. ▼

◆ EXPLORING FLORIDA AND THE BORDERLANDS

As New Spain grew, the Spaniards looked north from Mexico, into the region they called "the borderlands." The borderlands stretched across the present-day United States from Florida to California. There, the Spaniards hoped to find and conquer other rich empires.

The first conquistador to set foot within the present boundaries of the United States was Juan Ponce de León. He had traveled with Columbus on the voyage of 1493 and soon afterward conquered the island of Puerto Rico. Ponce de León left Puerto Rico in 1513 in search of a mythical fountain that would restore youth to anyone who bathed in its waters. On Easter morning, de León landed on a peninsula he named *Pascua Florida*, or "Flowering Easter." Today, this land is called Florida.

Spanish Missions

Because Spain was preoccupied with other conquests, it was not until 1565 that the Spaniards built a permanent settlement in Florida. This settlement, which they named St. Augustine, is the oldest European-built city in the United States. In its early days, the residents of St. Augustine faced **famine**, long periods in which there was not enough food. However, the settlement survived and, in time, grew. From St. Augustine, Roman Catholic priests built **missions** along the coast of the Atlantic Ocean. A mission is a group of people sent by a church to carry on religious work. Some Native Americans resisted the activities of the missionaries, but by 1655 there were several dozen missions in Florida and Georgia.

The Journeys of De Soto and Coronado

In 1539, the explorer Hernán De Soto arrived in Florida in search of golden treasure. For the next few years, he explored the southwestern part of the present-day United States. Aided by Native American allies, he was the first European to reach the Mississippi River. As was the case with almost all European explorers, De Soto died without finding gold.

Around the same time, explorer Francisco Vásquez de Coronado heard stories about seven cities with streets of gold. Leading an expedition into the southwestern borderlands in 1540, he found only Native American villages with dusty roads. Coronado's journey, as well as de León's and De Soto's, is shown on the map on page 26.

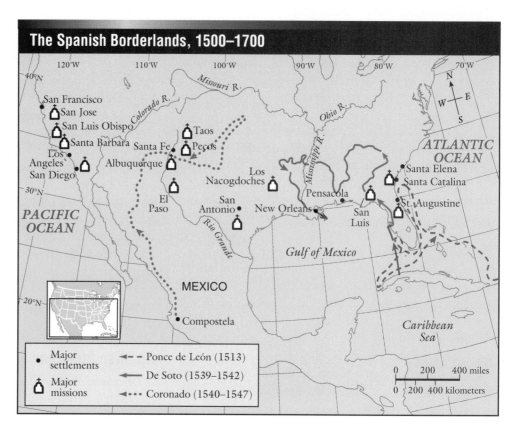

The Spanish Borderlands, 1500–1700

Major settlements •
Major missions ⛪
- - - Ponce de León (1513)
→ De Soto (1539–1542)
····◄ Coronado (1540–1547)

Geography *From 1500 to 1700 the southern United States, located at the edge of Spain's territory, was called the Spanish borderlands. Explorers journeyed through these lands for wealth and fame.* **Interpreting the Map** *Name the missions along the Rio Grande.* ▶

Because the borderlands did not produce great riches, the government of New Spain showed little interest in the area. In time, however, Spain came to fear that other European nations might try to move into the borderlands.

 **What did the Spaniards hope to find in the borderlands?**

◆ SETTLING THE BORDERLANDS

The farming communities of the Native Americans did not offer the wealth the Spaniards were looking for. By the 1580s, however, Franciscan missionaries from Spain had arrived in the area. In the missions that they built, priests taught Native Americans the Roman Catholic religion, the Spanish language, and how to grow the crops that the Spaniards introduced. In addition to missions, villages were established by some Spaniards in the borderlands. One of the first permanent villages to be settled was Santa Fe, located in present-day New Mexico.

New Mexico

The Spanish settlement at Santa Fe was established by 1610 along a branch of the Rio Grande.

Though Santa Fe was peaceful on the surface, Pueblo resentment was growing over the strict rule of Spanish landowners.

In 1675, the Spaniards in Santa Fe stopped Pueblos from practicing their traditional religion. Many Pueblo priests were arrested, whipped, or hanged. One religious leader, named Popé, vowed to drive out the hated Spaniards. In 1680, the Pueblos, under Popé, drove the Spaniards from Santa Fe and burned the town.

Popé ordered the destruction of everything Spanish, but the Pueblos refused to obey him. The colonists had introduced horses and sheep, fruit trees and grains, and new tools and crafts—all of which the Pueblos found useful.

For 12 years the Pueblos controlled the northern borderland. However, over time other groups of Native Americans began fighting among themselves. When the Spaniards attempted to retake the settlement, the Native Americans were too divided to resist. In 1693, Spanish soldiers retook Santa Fe and restored their rule over the northern borderlands.

Both sides had learned a lesson. Over the next generation, the settlers and the Native Americans reached an understanding. The Pueblos observed Catholicism in the missionary chapels, and the missionaries allowed the Pueblos to practice their traditional religion in their own homes.

Texas

During the late 1600s, Spain made few attempts to settle the land today known as Texas. Then, in 1718, a group of Spanish priests and soldiers built a mission in central Texas. In its first years, the mission barely survived. It was not until 1731, when about 200 Spanish families arrived, that the mission began to thrive. This mission grew into the Texas colony's capitol in 1773. Eventually, it became the city of San Antonio.

Outside San Antonio, growth was slow. In the 1740s, Spain had only a few missions and forts in its Texas colony. By 1800, only about 3,000 colonists lived there. Despite the small population, Native American and Spanish cultures endured. The **mestizo** population grew. A mestizo is a person of mixed Spanish and Native American ancestry. Mestizo culture incorporated elements of both Spanish and Native American cultures.

In addition to cultural growth in the Texas colony, an important new industry—ranching—was developing. Spanish travelers in the mid-1600s had left cattle and horses on the Texas plains. By the early 1700s, large numbers of wild cattle and horses roamed the grasslands. Large ranches owned by Spanish families soon spread over the Texas plain. Many of these ranches later grew into cities, such as Laredo.

During the 1700s, hundreds of Spaniards passed under the stone archways of the Conception Mission, located in present-day San Antonio, Texas. ▼

California

Throughout the 1600s and 1700s, Spain had shown little interest in California. Spain's attitude changed when it realized that the area could be lost to the British or the Russians. It was not until the 1760s that Spanish priests built a series of missions and **presidios,** or forts, along the Pacific coast to protect their claims. The first presidios were built in the present-day cities of San Diego and San Francisco. In addition to presidios, the Spaniards built 21 missions along the coast of California.

The California settlements did not become firmly established until Spanish and mestizo settlers began moving north from New Spain. A wealthy few laid out huge **haciendas** (hä-sē-ěn´-das), or estates, for cattle ranching. Other new settlers worked as **vaqueros** (vä-ker´-ōs) on the haciendas. *Vaqueros* is the Spanish word for "cowhands." Soon, many of these settlers began to think of themselves as **Californios,** citizens of California. The Spaniards were delighted. In addition to becoming a symbol of Spanish authority and a center for missionary activity, California was becoming an important center of trade.

Why did Spain establish settlements in New Mexico, Texas, and California?

◆ THE FRENCH, ENGLISH, AND DUTCH IN NORTH AMERICA

Spain was not the only country to lay claim to lands in North America. In 1608, the French explorer Samuel de Champlain sailed up the St. Lawrence River and founded Quebec, the first French settlement in North America. Here the French established a profitable fishing and fur trading network. Soon they expanded their territory into eastern Canada.

Samuel de Champlain made 20 more exploratory trips throughout the region, gaining the title Father of New France. Champlain went on to become the governor of France's first colony in the Americas.

Meanwhile the French were also exploring elsewhere in North America. In 1673, Louis Joliet, a Canadian fur trader, and Jacques Marquette, a Jesuit missionary, began a canoe journey up the Mississippi River. During this journey, Marquette and Joliet charted hundreds of miles of the Mississippi River.

In 1682, Robert de La Salle further explored the Mississippi, leading an expedition down the river to its mouth on the Gulf of Mexico. La Salle named the area Louisiana for the French king, Louis XIV. By 1700, French explorers had also sailed through the Great Lakes and up the Missouri River to the Rocky Mountains. In addition to what is now Canada, France claimed the entire Mississippi Valley.

Settling New France

The colonies established by France in North America formed a long string of outposts, extending from Canada to the Gulf of Mexico. One of these settlements, New Orleans—at the mouth of the Mississippi River—soon became a busy trading center.

While New Orleans and Quebec were thriving trading centers, the rest of New France grew slowly. Most of the French who had come to the colony were fur trappers and traders. Continually on the move searching for animals to trap, fur trappers and traders seldom settled in any one place for long. Their temporary settlements would not lay the foundation for a lasting empire in North America.

In an effort to attract permanent settlers, the French king granted land in New France to **aristocrats,** people of the ruling class. The aristocrats were supposed to find people willing to emigrate to New France and then rent their land from the aristocrats. The aristocrats were expected to pay for the settlers' passage to the colony. But this system failed. Settlers wished to own the land, but the aristocrats would agree only to rent it out. Therefore, most of New France remained unsettled. By the early 1700s, only about 10,000 settlers lived in New France. Of those, one third established farms along the St. Lawrence and Mississippi rivers, while the rest were fur trappers.

Cabot and Hudson

Lands explored by the French were also claimed by England and the Dutch East India Company of Holland, or the Netherlands. John Cabot, an Italian navigator, set out from England in 1497, hoping to find a northwest passage to Asia. Cabot crossed the Atlantic Ocean, landed on the northeastern coast of North America, and claimed the region for England.

In 1609, the Dutch East India Company hired an English explorer, Henry Hudson, to find a route to China. Hudson sailed west across the Atlantic until he reached North America. During his search for a northwest passage to China, Hudson found the river in present-day New York State that now bears his name. He followed it inland to what is now Albany and claimed the area for the Dutch.

In 1610, Hudson made another journey to North America, this time sailing for an English company. He explored the northeastern coast of Canada, reaching what is today called the Hudson Bay.

Due to the explorations of John Cabot and Henry Hudson, England claimed land in North America that overlapped some of the French claims. Many battles would be fought for control of these disputed territories.

 Why did the French have difficulty establishing colonies in North America?

Section 1 Review

Check Understanding

1. **Define** (a) famine (b) mission (c) mestizo (d) presidio (e) hacienda (f) vaquero (g) Californio (h) aristocrat

2. **Identify** the factors that contributed to the fall of the Aztec Empire.

3. **Explain** the reasons for Spanish interest in North America.

4. **Discuss** the importance of Popé's rebellion in the Spanish borderlands.

5. **Explain** the role missions played in the settlement of California and Texas.

6. **Compare** the differences between Spanish and French settlements in the Americas.

Critical Thinking

Connecting Past and Present What riches were the Spaniards seeking in the borderlands? What riches have been found there in recent times?

Write About Geography

Write about a trip from France to a settlement in New France in the early 1700s. Name and describe the settlements and bodies of water you encounter in New France.

BUILDING SKILLS

Sequencing Information: Spain and the Borderlands

Sequencing information involves putting facts and ideas in a logical order so that they can be understood. In history, chronological order, or time order, usually works best.

Here's How

Follow these steps to sequence information:

1. Determine the first and last events in a sequence. Check for specific dates that tell you when events occurred.

2. Look for clues that imply when an event happened. Words such as *soon, before, after, later, then, while, first,* and *last* can tell you that one event happened before, after, or at the same time as another event.

3. Make a chart like the one on this page to help you sequence events.

4. Identify relationships between events. Determine if or how one event leads directly to another.

Here's Why

Sequencing events helps you understand how historical events are related. By putting a series of events into chronological order, you can understand how they unfold and how patterns emerge.

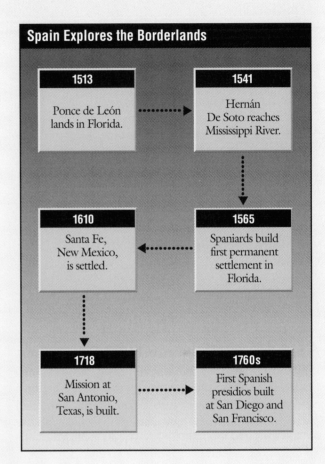

Spain Explores the Borderlands

1513 — Ponce de León lands in Florida.

1541 — Hernán De Soto reaches Mississippi River.

1565 — Spaniards build first permanent settlement in Florida.

1610 — Santa Fe, New Mexico, is settled.

1718 — Mission at San Antonio, Texas, is built.

1760s — First Spanish presidios built at San Diego and San Francisco.

Practice the Skill

Use the following events to make a chain-of-events chart. Then write a paragraph about Spanish settlements in the borderlands.

1740s	Spanish had a few missions in Texas.
1600–1700	Spain shows no interest in California.
By 1850	21 missions had been established in California.
1760s	Spanish priests built missions and forts in California.
1731	200 Spanish families arrived in Texas.

Apply the Skill

Scan a news magazine and select an article that describes one event. Read the article and write five or six of the most important facts on five or six slips of paper. Make sure to use dates, wherever appropriate, or key words. Give the slips to a classmate and ask him or her to arrange them in sequence. Check to see how the person did.

Section 2

Settling Virginia and New England

PREVIEW

Objectives

- To describe how English settlers established a permanent colony in Virginia

- To explain how religious change in England led to the founding of the Plymouth and Massachusetts Bay settlements

- To describe events in Virginia and Massachusetts that led to political freedoms in the colonies

Vocabulary

joint-stock company	Separatist
charter	Pilgrim
cash crop	Puritan
indentured servant	tax

As Spain's empire in the Americas grew powerful, England looked on with envy. The English also wished to increase their wealth by colonizing lands in North America. To pay for expeditions, England organized **joint-stock companies** in which people invested money, sharing both the risks and the profits of colonization.

In 1606, King James I of England gave a group of English merchants of the London Company a **charter,** a written document from the government. This charter granted the joint-stock company the right to establish a colony in North America. In May of the next year, three ships landed in present-day Virginia. In honor of King James I, the colonists named their new settlement Jamestown.

◆ THE ENGLISH SETTLE VIRGINIA

From the beginning, Jamestown had problems. The land was swampy and unhealthful. In addition, few settlers had the skills, such as carpentry or farming, that were needed to build houses, clear forests, and plant

crops to live in the new land. As the colonists searched for gold—as instructed by the London merchants who had granted them the land—their supplies and strength diminished.

With winter approaching, the colonists realized that they were quickly running out of food. But it was too late to plant the crops that were necessary to survive. Nearly two thirds of the settlers died within the first eight months of the settlement. The others barely survived the cold, illness, and famine.

Only Captain John Smith's leadership saved the Jamestown settlement. Smith, a soldier and adventurer, took charge, visiting Native American villages and forming relationships with the inhabitants. With the help of Powhatan and his daughter Pocohantas, Smith obtained enough food to keep the remaining colonists alive until spring. Then he forced the men to cut trees, plant crops, and fish. He warned the colonists, "He that will not work, will not eat."

Jamestown's problems were not over. Hard times returned when Smith was burned in an explosion, requiring his return to England. New colonists arrived without bringing fresh food. During the winter of 1609, bitter cold and food shortages killed some 60 of the nearly 500 settlers. It was a winter that came to be known as "the starving time."

A New Cash Crop

The future of Jamestown and Virginia remained uncertain until settlers began to grow tobacco. Using methods learned from the Native Americans, colonist John Rolfe first raised this crop in 1612. By 1619, tobacco was the colony's biggest **cash crop.** A cash crop is a plant, such as rice or tobacco, that is grown for sale rather than for use by a farmer. Tobacco became known as "green gold" because it was often used in place of money to trade for other goods.

Growing tobacco not only fueled the colony's economy but also led to Virginia's physical expansion. A plot of land could only support tobacco crops for about three years. After that, the soil lost the nutrients necessary for growing crops. Settlers then had to clear more land. As a result, the Virginia colony expanded rapidly toward the west and south. Tobacco would remain the backbone of the colony's economy for more than 200 years.

The Growth of Jamestown

Over the years, more Europeans wished to come to Virginia. Many who could not afford to pay for the passage signed contracts with Virginia's tobacco

Study Hint

Before reading a section of text, preview the pictures, graphs, charts, and maps in the section. As you preview, read the captions of each visual. Scanning the visual elements of a section will help you anticipate key topics in your reading. Try this before you read the next sections of this chapter.

started on their own. Most servants, however, headed west in hope of starting a farm of their own.

In 1619 the first Africans arrived in Jamestown on a Dutch trading ship. The captain of the ship had traded the Africans for much-needed food. Some Africans were treated as indentured servants and were put to work in the tobacco fields. After serving their terms, some Africans acquired land and became planters themselves. For a short time, a few Africans owned property, testified in court, and voted in the colony's elections.

As Virginia grew, however, the colonists faced a severe labor shortage. By 1650, Africans in large numbers were forcibly taken from their homes on the West African coast and enslaved in Virginia.

The growth of the Virginia colony led to the need for better management. To meet this need, the Virginia Company created a government in 1619 to deal directly with local issues. This government granted all free males the right to elect burgesses, or representatives to a lawmaking body, known in Virginia as the House of Burgesses. The House of Burgesses helped the governor make laws and run the colony. It was the first elected lawmaking body in colonial America.

How did tobacco influence the development of the Virginia colony?

planters. The planters, who were always in need of more workers to plant and harvest tobacco, paid the fare. In return the newcomers worked for the planter until the debt was paid. These **indentured servants** became an important part of the Virginia labor force. At the end of their term, servants were eligible for clothing, tools, a gun, and perhaps a plot of land to help them get

◄ Situated at the mouth of two rivers, the land at Jamestown, Virginia, was once swampy and unproductive. The economy of the region improved when settlers learned to grow tobacco.

Cramped beneath the deck of their ship, 41 of the Pilgrims signed the Mayflower Compact, a document that proclaimed their right to create and enforce their own laws. ▶

◆ ENGLISH SETTLEMENTS IN NEW ENGLAND

The 1500s and 1600s were a time of great religious unrest in England. In the early 1500s, religious leaders broke away from the Roman Catholic Church and established their own church, the Church of England. Religious disagreements continued. Some English people believed that the new Church of England was still too similar to the Roman Catholic Church. Some of these people were called **Separatists** because they wished to detach themselves from the Church of England.

In 1608, about 100 Separatists fled to Holland, the only country in Europe at that time where people were not punished for their religious beliefs. The Separatists, however, wished for a more permanent home. They soon won permission from the London Company to settle within its territory in North America. On September 16, 1620, the ship *Mayflower* sailed from Plymouth, England. On board were almost 50 Separatists who called themselves **Pilgrims,** or religious travelers to a new land. They were joined by a smaller number of other passengers.

The *Mayflower* missed its target site in Virginia by many hundreds of miles. After sailing along the coast of North America for several weeks, the Pilgrims—as all the passengers aboard the *Mayflower* would come to be called—chose a site for their new settlement farther up the Atlantic coast, in the region now called New England. The Pilgrims named their settlement Plymouth. Before leaving the ship, they signed an agreement known as the Mayflower Compact. In this document, the settlers first acknowledged the authority of King James of England. They then agreed to elect officers, make fair laws, and obey them. Some historians see the Mayflower Compact as the first document to state that American colonists had the right to make their own laws and govern themselves.

The Pilgrims at Plymouth

Plymouth Colony was very different from Jamestown. While only men and boys made up the first settlers in Jamestown, whole families settled Plymouth. Jamestown settlers were often wealthy gentlemen who were unaccustomed to physical labor. The Pilgrims, on the other hand, expected that hard physical labor would be required to make their new settlement successful.

Like Jamestown, the first year at Plymouth required back-breaking work, such as cutting trees for shelter and clearing fields for growing food. Before the end of December, 6 Pilgrims had died of disease. Each month brought another 10 or 12 deaths. William Bradford, who served as governor of the colony for 30 years, wrote,

> **Having thus passed the vast ocean . . . [we] had now no friends to welcome [us], no houses to provide protection. . . . It was winter and they that know the winters of that country know them to be sharp and violent, and subject to cruel and fierce storms. . . . Yet all [difficulties] might be borne or overcome through the help of God.**

By spring, nearly half the colonists had died. As had happened at Jamestown, only the help of local Native Americans allowed the Pilgrims to survive. During the following spring and summer, Native Americans taught the Pilgrims how to use fish to fertilize the soil, how to grow corn, and how to trap beavers.

As the colony grew, its economy developed. Plymouth's economic strength rested on trading English goods with Native Americans in exchange for otter and beaver skins. The Pilgrims shipped these goods back to England, where they sold for high prices. By 1640, prosperity had attracted enough newcomers so that Plymouth Colony contained eight towns and 2,500 people.

The Puritans

In 1628, a group of English people called **Puritans** visited Plymouth. Puritans wanted to purify, or simplify, the traditions of the Church of England. After visiting Plymouth, the Puritans wished to establish their own permanent settlement. They obtained a charter from King Charles and organized the Massachusetts Bay Company, which allowed them to settle the Massachusetts Bay Colony.

During 1630, English ships took more than 1,000 Puritans to the new colony. The Puritans carried with them all their household goods, farm tools, and livestock. Before long, they moved to a town they named Salem.

From the beginning, the colony did well. Puritan settlers worked hard, often cooperatively, clearing fields in which they planted wheat, barley, and corn. Between 1630 and 1640, more than 10,000 Puritans arrived. Within a few years, groups of Puritans had left Salem and began building other settlements nearby. Boston, on the banks of the Charles River, soon became the colony's leading town. Other groups besides the Puritans were allowed to live in the colony, but they were required to follow Puritan ways and to contribute to the colony's Puritan-controlled church.

The Puritans placed a high value on education, believing that a person needed to be educated in order to study the Bible. In 1636, they established Harvard College. In 1647, the Puritans passed one of the most important laws in American history. Towns with more than 50 families were required to set up schools that were paid for by **taxes,** or monies paid to a government in return for services. Towns with 100 families had to set up more advanced schools to prepare students for a college education. That was the beginning of the public school system in the United States.

 What was the major reason for early English settlement in New England?

Section 2 Review

Check Understanding

1. **Define** (a) joint-stock company (b) charter (c) cash crop (d) indentured servant (e) Separatist (f) Pilgrim (g) Puritan (h) tax

2. **Identify** the importance of the Virginia House of Burgesses.

3. **Discuss** the reason that slavery grew in Virginia in the late 1600s.

4. **Explain** the significance of the Mayflower Compact.

Critical Thinking

Connecting Past and Present For what reasons do people wish to settle in the United States today?

Write About Geography

Write a paragraph to compare the effects of the geographic locations of Plymouth and Jamestown on their inhabitants. Identify which colony had the harsher climate.

Thirteen English Colonies

PREVIEW

Objectives

- To explain how religious differences led to the founding of new colonies in New England

- To identify how the Middle colonies were founded

- To explain why the economy of the Southern colonies was built on farming

- To identify ways in which the 13 English colonies differed

Vocabulary

dissenter	civil rights
patroon	royal colony

There were many reasons why people came to the American colonies, as shown on the chart on page 38. Some made the dangerous voyage in hopes of getting rich. Others came to be free to practice their religions. Many came because they wanted a fresh start in a land with few restrictions. However, once these newcomers arrived in the American colonies, they needed to learn about, adapt to, and modify their environments. Different ways of life began to emerge in the colonies based on differing geographies and natural resources.

◆ THE NEW ENGLAND COLONIES

Both in climate and geography, New England was much different from the Chesapeake region where Virginia was located. Because farming was difficult in the northern colonies, the region was less favored for investment and settlement. However, New England became a haven for religious **dissenters**, or people who refused to conform to authority. This gave the northern colonies a distinctive character.

Massachusetts

Although the Massachusetts Bay Colony prospered, religious differences among the Puritans soon caused difficulties. Popular ministers challenged other local leaders. One such minister was Roger Williams, who believed strongly that the colonists should pay Native Americans for the land they were taking. He also preached that everyone had the right to worship as he or she wished. Another outspoken colonist was Anne Hutchinson, who disputed the teachings and authority of the Puritan-controlled church. Both Anne Hutchinson and Roger Williams were banished from Massachusetts.

Rhode Island

In 1635, when called before a court in Boston, Roger Williams boldly told the judges that they had no power over him or his congregation. The court found him guilty of spreading "new and dangerous opinions." It ordered him to be arrested and sent back to England. Friends, however, warned Williams. He fled south to the area around Narragansett Bay, where he bought land from the Narragansett people and founded the settlement he called Providence.

In 1644, the English government gave Williams's colony a charter, which brought together several settlements into the colony of Rhode Island. Under the charter, all people in Rhode Island enjoyed the right to worship as they pleased.

Rhode Island was the first American colony to promote religious freedom. This freedom attracted many people who had been persecuted for their religious beliefs. Rhode Island welcomed Jews as well as Christians. In 1658, groups of Jewish people settled in Newport and built one of the earliest synagogues in North America. Rhode Island also attracted many Quakers, a religious group opposed to warfare and any kind of force.

Connecticut and New Hampshire

The pressure for land in a growing Massachusetts led many colonists to look elsewhere for farmland. Thomas Hooker, a Puritan minister, led his followers westward in 1636. In the fertile valley of the Connecticut River, they set up a number of settlements. In 1639 the leaders from some of these towns drew up a plan of union. Their plan, called the Fundamental Orders of Connecticut, was the basis for documents that would establish rights and responsibilities in the United States.

Anne Hutchinson

Anne Hutchinson and her husband came to Boston from England in 1634. Soon, their home was a gathering place for people to discuss church sermons and religious ideas. Anne Hutchinson told people who attended these meetings that church attendance and prayer were less important than leading a holy life. Her words challenged the beliefs of Puritan ministers, who were furious when they heard that Hutchinson was voicing her views. They felt that Hutchinson's opinions were filled with religious errors and that she had no right to explain God's law.

▲ Anne Hutchinson
(about 1591–1643)

Opposing the authority of church law was the same as speaking against the state. In November 1637, Anne Hutchinson was put on trial. Defending herself to a jury of ministers, she challenged their right to tell her how to practice religion. At first they could not prove that she had broken any Puritan laws. However, when Anne Hutchinson told the court that God spoke directly to her, the ministers knew that they had found a way to pronounce her "dangerous." Because the Puritans believed that God spoke only through ministers or through the Bible, she could be conceived of as "a dangerous instrument of the devil." As a result, Anne Hutchinson and her family were banished from the Massachusetts Bay Colony in 1637.

Looking Back: Why do you suppose that a statue of Anne Hutchinson stands beside the entrance to the Massachusetts State House? How might people react to her beliefs today?

The Fundamental Orders created a government much like that of the Massachusetts Bay Colony. There were two important differences, however. First, the Fundamental Orders gave the vote to all men who were property owners, including men who were not church members. Second, the Fundamental Orders limited the governor's power. In this way the Fundamental Orders expanded the idea of representative government in the English colonies.

Other colonists moved from Massachusetts Bay north into the area that is today New Hampshire, Maine, and Vermont. New Hampshire, though settled in 1623, became a separate colony in 1679. Maine and Vermont were parts of other colonies when the American Revolution began in 1775.

? How did problems within the Massachusetts Bay Colony lead to the founding of other English colonies in New England?

◆ THE MIDDLE COLONIES

Located south of the New England colonies on the Atlantic seaboard were a group of colonies that became known as the Middle colonies, as shown on the map on page 37. The Middle colonies attracted large numbers of people from different nations on the European mainland.

New York

Economic factors played a major role in the development of the area now known as New York. In 1609, Henry Hudson sailed about 100 miles up the river that now bears his name. He reported to his employers, the Dutch, that the river valley was teeming with beaver. Beaver skins were very valuable because beaver-skin hats were fashionable in Europe. For this reason, Holland claimed the area around the Hudson River. In 1626, the Dutch started a village on an island at the mouth of the river, naming the settlement New Amsterdam.

The land on both sides of the Hudson River had been founded and named New Netherland in 1624. Most people came to the colony to trade furs. To encourage more permanent farming settlements, the Dutch government gave landowners, called **patroons,** huge grants of land along the Hudson River. Each patroon had to bring 50 settlers to the colony within four years.

People from France, Africa, and Sweden all found a home in the Dutch colony of New Netherland.

However, the colony did not remain in Dutch hands for long. In 1664, the English seized the colony and renamed it New York. New Amsterdam became New York City.

New Jersey

When the English took over New Netherland in 1664, they divided the territory into two pieces. Back in England, the Duke of York, King Charles's brother, granted to two of his friends a large piece of the land that stretched south from the Hudson River to the Delaware River. One of these friends came from the English island of Jersey, which is why the colony took the name New Jersey.

Because New Jersey had rich soil and an abundance of other natural resources, settlers had been attracted to the colony since 1624. The new settlers were not only English and Dutch who had moved from the colony of New York but also newcomers from Finland, Ireland, Germany, and Sweden. In addition, many colonists from the New England colonies moved to New Jersey in hopes of finding better farmland. By 1650, the colony had built a network of roadways connecting all its boundaries. Because of this network, New Jersey was given one of its earliest nicknames—the Crossroads colony.

Pennsylvania

The Quakers were a religious group with a loyal following in England. Although the Quakers believed in equality, kindness to others, and religious freedom, English leaders considered them dangerous and unmanageable. Because Quakers were against wars and killing, they refused to serve in the king's army. Imprisoned and beaten in England, the Quakers looked to North America for a safe home.

A young Quaker lawyer named William Penn pleaded with King Charles II to grant the Quakers land for such a home. At first, Charles resisted, but he changed his mind at the death of Penn's father, Admiral Penn, to whom Charles owed a large amount of money. The king suggested to William Penn that instead of repaying the money, he would satisfy the debt by giving the son a large grant of land on the eastern coast of North America.

Penn journeyed to his new land and named it Pennsylvania, meaning "Penn's woods." Because he did not believe in taking land that did not belong to him, Penn paid Native Americans already living there, the Delaware people, for the land. He spoke of his colony as a "holy experiment" because it would be a place where people of all nationalities and religions could live in peace.

Pennsylvania grew rapidly, in part because Penn sent agents to the European mainland to promote his colony. Soon, thousands of eager immigrants came to Pennsylvania to farm. Germans settled mainly along the Delaware River. Other farmers came from Ireland, Scotland, Holland, and France. By 1700, Pennsylvania was the richest of the 13 colonies. It was also a place where people of all faiths enjoyed religious freedom.

Delaware

Just as the Dutch were settling along the Hudson River, a small band of Swedes settled on the Delaware River. At the place where today's city of Wilmington is located, the Swedes built a settlement they called Fort Christina. In time they established other settlements as well.

Unfortunately, the tiny colony became the victim of Europe's quarrels. The Dutch sent an army that wiped out the colony. Soon after, the English took over New Netherland and with it Fort Christina. For a while, the region was part of Pennsylvania, but in 1704, representatives from the area started making their own laws. However, they did not break away to form the colony of Delaware until the time of the American Revolution.

 How did the reasons for settling New York differ from those for settling Pennsylvania?

◆ THE SOUTHERN COLONIES

Like the New England and Middle colonies, the Southern colonies developed a distinctive way of life and an economy suited to the region. Within some Southern colonies, culture and industry varied. For example, large farms with slave labor were widespread along the coastal plain regions of Virginia and Georgia but were uncommon in the mountainous western regions of those colonies.

Maryland

An English noble named George Calvert, Lord Baltimore, founded the colony of Maryland. In 1625, Lord Baltimore had become a Roman Catholic. At that time, Roman Catholics in England had no **civil rights,** or political, economic, and social rights. Lord Baltimore wanted to start a colony where Roman

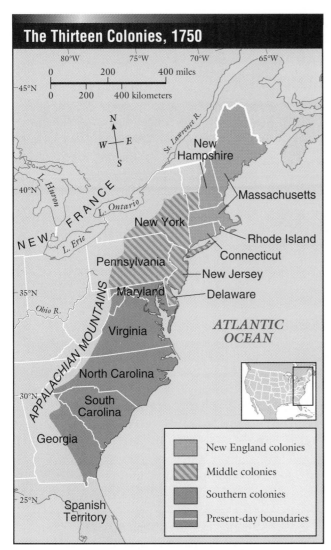

The Thirteen Colonies, 1750

Legend:
- New England colonies
- Middle colonies
- Southern colonies
- Present-day boundaries

▲ **Geography** *The 13 colonies may be divided into three geographic regions. The regions differed in climate, land, and natural resources.* **Interpreting the Map** *Name the states that made up the New England and the Middle colonies.*

Catholics could worship in peace. In 1632 the king of England granted him land along Chesapeake Bay, in North America, for his colony. Although Baltimore died before a colony could be established, his son Cecilius inherited his father's grant and started the settlement of St. Mary's in 1634. It became part of the Maryland colony.

Because Maryland's land was so rich, the colony attracted many newcomers. Many of these newcomers were Protestants or Christians who did not belong to the Roman Catholic Church. So many Protestants came to live in Maryland that before the colony was ten years old, Roman Catholics made up less than one fourth of the population. To protect the Roman Catholics, the colony passed a Toleration Act in 1649. This act granted religious freedom to Christian settlers, Protestant and Roman Catholic alike.

The Toleration Act was the first law protecting religious freedom in the colonies. By leaving out non-Christians, the Maryland colony was less tolerant toward non-Christians than were the colonies of Rhode Island or Pennsylvania. However, Maryland set down on paper ideas that would become important later as people throughout the colonies struggled with the principles of freedom.

Virginia

The colony of Virginia, which began with the Jamestown settlement in 1607, continued to attract settlers not only from England but also from the New England and Middle colonies. At first the economy of Virginia was based on simple farming. Colonists raised the food they needed to keep their own families alive. But in Virginia, tobacco proved to be so profitable that eventually settlers came to rely on slave labor to raise this important cash crop. Many landowners began to purchase items their families needed from other farmers or from overseas traders. They began to pursue additional activities—developing trade relations with other colonies and with England, and formulating a government.

While tobacco ensured that the Virginia colony would be one of the richest on the Atlantic coast, King James I of England was already speaking against it. He remarked that smoking tobacco was

> **a custom loathsome to the eye, hateful to the nose, harmful to the brain, and dangerous to the lungs.**

While King James loathed tobacco, he disliked something about the Virginia colony even more—the House of Burgesses. In 1624, King James took back the charter he had granted to the Virginia Company. Virginia was then made a **royal colony,** that is, a colony directly under the king's control. King James planned to do away with the House of Burgesses, but he died in 1625 before he could put his plan into action. His successor, Charles I, permitted the House of Burgesses to meet. Virginia remained a royal colony for the next 150 years.

NEW ENGLAND COLONIES

NEW ENGLAND COLONIES

COLONY	DATE OF SETTLEMENT	FOUNDER OR EARLY LEADER	REASONS FOR SETTLEMENT
Plymouth	1620	William Bradford	Religious freedom
Massachusetts Bay[1]	1630	John Winthrop	Religious freedom
New Hampshire	1623	John Wheelwright	Trade, religious freedom
Rhode Island	1635–1636	Roger Williams	Religious freedom
Connecticut	1636	Thomas Hooker	Establish a separate Puritan settlement; religious and political freedom

MIDDLE COLONIES

MIDDLE COLONIES

COLONY	DATE OF SETTLEMENT	FOUNDER OR EARLY LEADER	REASONS FOR SETTLEMENT
New York[2]	1624	Peter Minuit James, Duke of York	Trade and land
New Jersey[3]	1624	Dutch and Swedish settlers; George Berkeley and William Carteret	Trade and land
Pennsylvania	1637	William Penn	Establish a Quaker colony; land, religious and political freedom
Delaware	1638[4]	William Penn	Self-government from Pennsylvania colony

SOUTHERN COLONIES

SOUTHERN COLONIES

COLONY	DATE OF SETTLEMENT	FOUNDER OR EARLY LEADER	REASONS FOR SETTLEMENT
Virginia (Jamestown settlement)	1607	London Company, John Smith	Trade and land
Maryland	1632	George and Cecilius Calvert	Establish a Roman Catholic settlement
South Carolina	1663[5]	Sir Anthony Ashley	Trade and land; religious freedom
North Carolina	1663	John Cooper	Trade and land; religious freedom
Georgia	1733	James Oglethorpe	Home for debtors

1. Plymouth and the Massachusetts Bay Colonies combined into one colony, 1691.   2. Called New Netherland until 1664.
3. English proprietors from 1664–1702.   4. Created own laws in 1704.   5. Separate colony established in 1712.

▲ **Citizenship** *The colonies were founded for different reasons. The different reasons give each region a distinctive character even today.* **Interpreting the Chart** *What was the most common reason that settlers left their homelands? What was the second reason?*

The Carolinas

Many colonies were first settled by people who came directly from Europe. In Carolina, however, colonists spread slowly into the northern part of Carolina from Virginia and some of the Middle colonies. These colonists were mostly poor farmers, independent people who distrusted the wealthy landowners who were settling the southern coastal region of the Carolina colony at the same time.

Many of the landowners who settled in the southern coastal region of Carolina were English colonists from the West Indies. When they came to Carolina, they brought their slaves with them. Thus, Carolina was the first English colony in North America to have enslaved Africans brought into the colony from the very start. By 1710, Africans were the largest single group populating the Carolina colony.

Most enslaved Africans worked on plantations. Rice and indigo, a plant that produces a blue dye, were the main crops. Tobacco was also grown along the coastal plain. These crops were shipped to the West Indies, to other colonies on the mainland, and to England.

In time, the tensions between the wealthy farmers of southern Carolina and the poorer farmers of northern Carolina became so great that the northerners insisted that Carolina be divided. In 1729, the Carolina colony was divided into North and South Carolina.

Georgia

Georgia, the last English colony to be settled, was founded by James Oglethorpe. In England, Oglethorpe was involved in a study of prisons and prisoners who had not been able to pay their debts. At the time, people were often imprisoned if they were unable to repay even small debts. Oglethorpe decided to do something to assist English debtors. With some friends, he proposed to King George II that he start a colony for debtors in North America. Oglethorpe believed that:

> **In America, there are enough fertile lands to feed all the poor of England.**

The king did not care much about debtors, but he was concerned about the Spaniards in Florida. There were no English colonies in the area between the Carolinas and Spanish Florida. An English settlement in that in-between area would provide protection for the colonies around it.

In 1733, colonists started a settlement at Savannah. At first, the colony grew slowly because Oglethorpe told settlers where to settle and what crops to plant. He forbade slavery. This limited the amount of crops planters could grow, since they did not have enough laborers to harvest large cash crops. It was only after Oglethorpe lifted these restrictions that white Georgia colonists began to prosper.

By the 1750s slavery was well established in Georgia. Between 1750 and 1760, the number of enslaved Africans in Georgia grew from 1,000 to 4,000. In total, there were about 10,000 people living in the Georgia colony.

 How did settling the Carolinas differ from settling the other Southern colonies?

Section 3 Review

Check Understanding

1. **Define** (a) dissenter (b) patroon (c) civil rights (d) royal colony

2. **Discuss** how the government formed by the Fundamental Orders of Connecticut differed from the government of Massachusetts.

3. **Describe** why the Middle colonies attracted more people than the New England colonies.

4. **Explain** why there were different styles of living among the Southern colonies.

Critical Thinking

Connecting Past and Present Which of the reasons for settling the original colonies might still be important for newcomers today?

Write About Economics

Write an essay that explains the ways in which the growing and selling of tobacco affected the economies of the Southern colonies.

Chapter 2
Review

CHAPTER SUMMARY

Section 1

When the Spanish conquistadors arrived in Mexico, Central America, and South America, they found great civilizations. Spanish rule altered the life and customs of the native peoples in the lands they claimed for their own. Mexico, when conquered by Spain, became part of New Spain. The French, who were mainly interested in furs, established forts in Canada and along the Mississippi River. The lives of the Native Americans were disrupted less by the French than they were by the Spanish.

Section 2

In the early 1600s, the English established their first North American colony at Jamestown, Virginia. Settlers experienced hard times until they established tobacco as a cash crop. In Virginia, the colonists set up the House of Burgesses, the first representative government in North America. The first Africans arrived in Jamestown in 1619 as indentured servants. Puritans and Pilgrims, who opposed the Church of England, founded colonies in New England based on their religious beliefs.

Section 3

Religious freedom was a key factor in establishing many of the American colonies, such as Massachusetts, Rhode Island, Connecticut, and Pennsylvania. By the 1750s, there were 13 English colonies on the Atlantic coast. These colonies may be broadly divided into three geographic regions: the New England colonies, the Middle colonies, and the Southern colonies. The regions differed from one another in geography, economy, population, and religious practices.

Connecting ◆▶ Past and Present

What positive characteristics of the Pilgrims and the Puritans continue to inspire Americans today?

Using Vocabulary

From the list below, select the term that best completes each sentence.

cash crop	hacienda
mestizo	Pilgrim
charter	famine
indentured servant	patroon

1. King James I of England gave a group of English merchants a _____ , allowing them the right to set up a colony.
2. A large cattle ranch owned by wealthy Spaniards in California was called a _____ .
3. One of the main crops in Virginia was tobacco, which became an important _____ for landowners.
4. The Dutch government gave a person called a _____ huge grants of land along the Hudson River.
5. A person who agreed to work for a certain number of years in exchange for passage to America was called an _____ .
6. A person with both Native American and Spanish ancestry is a _____ .
7. A _____ was a religious traveler to a new land.
8. Despite the threat of _____ , the settlers of St. Augustine survived.

Check Understanding

1. **Describe** the reasons why a small band of conquistadors was able to conquer the powerful Aztec Empire.
2. **Discuss** what happened to Native Americans under Spanish rule.
3. **Explain** the elements of the new culture that grew up in New Spain.
4. **Explain** how the English settlers overcame many difficulties to establish a permanent colony at Jamestown.
5. **Discuss** why the Separatists and the Puritans came to North America.

6. **Explain** how Spanish missionaries and Native Americans worked out a compromise in New Mexico.

7. **Identify** two important ways that the 13 colonies differed from one another.

8. **Discuss** the reasons why William Penn established a colony that had freedom of religion.

Critical Thinking

1. **Understanding Cause and Effect** What are two causes and two effects of the fall of the Aztecs?

2. **Evaluating** How did the House of Burgesses and the Mayflower Compact contribute to the idea of self-government in the colonies?

3. **Expressing a Point of View** Did the founders of the Massachusetts Bay Colony benefit from the experiences of the Plymouth Colony and the Jamestown settlement? Explain.

4. **Compare and Contrast** What were some of the similarities and differences between colonies set up by Spain and colonies set up by England?

◆ **Connecting Past and Present** The Puritans believed that church and state should be one and the same. What is the relationship between church and state in the United States today?

Writing to Persuade

Suppose the settlers at Jamestown in 1607 were so overcome by hardship that they began to think about returning to their homeland in England. As one of the leaders of the settlement, you must try to persuade the colonists to work together to build a successful settlement. **Write** a persuasive speech to the colonists, explaining the reasons why they should remain at Jamestown. Include some suggestions about how they might improve the conditions at Jamestown.

Putting Skills to Work

SEQUENCING INFORMATION

In the Building Skills lesson on page 29, you learned that *sequence* means "order." One way to sequence information is to put it into chronological order, or time order. Rewrite the following paragraph in time sequence. Include several words that give clues about when events happened.

France claimed land in North America from numerous explorations. Robert de La Salle further explored the Mississippi River in 1682 and named the area Louisiana in honor of the French king, Louis XIV. Samuel de Champlain made 20 expeditions throughout eastern Canada. He gained the title Father of New France. Champlain started the first French colony along the St. Lawrence River at Quebec in 1608. Jacques Marquette and Louis Joliet explored the Mississippi River in 1673, charting hundreds of miles. Samuel de Champlain became the governor of France's first colony in North America.

Interpreting the Timeline

Use the timeline on pages 22–23 to answer these questions.

1. How many years after St. Augustine was settled did the English defeat the Spanish Armada?

2. What two events on the timeline show French influence in North America?

3. What European countries were establishing settlements in the Americas?

Portfolio Project

AN ADVERTISEMENT FOR SETTLERS

Choose one of the colonies you read about in this chapter. Write an advertisement directed to people in England to encourage them to move to a colony in the 1600s. You can highlight what they can expect to find in this new land, such as its geography, climate, and natural resources. List any important items settlers should bring with them to the colony. File your advertisement in your portfolio.

Chapter 3
Colonial Societies Take Shape 1630–1760

CHAPTER PREVIEW

Section 1 The Economies of the Colonies
As American settlements grew and prospered, different economies and ways of life developed in the New England, Middle, and Southern colonies.

Section 2 Africans in the Colonies
Although slavery was legal in all the colonies, the number of enslaved people and the work they performed differed throughout the northern and southern colonies.

Section 3 New Ideas Take Hold
Separated from England by a wide ocean, American colonists developed new ideas and traditions, sometimes challenging old beliefs.

U.S. Events					
	1636 Harvard College is founded.	**1650** A collection of poetry by Anne Bradstreet is published.	*Nathaniel Bacon*	**1676** Bacon's Rebellion takes place.	

1620

World Events					
	1635 Sale of tobacco in France only on doctor's prescription.	**1653** Taj Mahal is completed in India.	**1660** Charles II is crowned king of England.		**1685** Louis XIV begins persecution of French Protestants.

Taj Mahal

Louis XIV, king of France

Portfolio Project

THE INTERACTION OF ECONOMY AND GEOGRAPHY

Three distinct ways of life emerged in the New England, Middle, and Southern colonies. This was due, in part, to differences in location, geography, climate, natural resources, and the people who lived in these three regions. At the end of the chapter, you will choose one of these regions and prepare an oral or written presentation describing the region's economy. As you read, note details about agriculture and industry and how both were influenced by geography.

▲ *This Quaker Meeting House was used for town meetings, religious services, and other public functions.* ◆ **Connecting Past and Present** *How does the artist show the building's central role in the community? Where are community meetings usually held today?*

Printing press

Olaudah Equiano

1735
Zenger trial is about freedom of the press.

1739
Stono slave rebellion put down.

1750
Great economic growth occurs in Southern colonies.

1756
Equiano sold into slavery.

1732
Benjamin Franklin first publishes *Poor Richard's Almanac.*

1760

1707
Act of Union unites England and Scotland to form Great Britain.

1726
Jonathan Swift's *Gulliver's Travels* is published.

1740
Freedoms of press and of worship are introduced in Prussia.

1754
First woman doctor graduates from a German university.

English coat of arms

Section 1

The Economies of the Colonies

PREVIEW

Objectives

- To evaluate how geography influenced the economies and ways of life in the New England, Middle, and Southern colonies

- To analyze how and why England controlled colonial trade

- To analyze the growth of slavery in the colonies

- To discuss city life and the role of women in the 13 colonies

Vocabulary

subsistence	export
common	mercantile system
frontier	import
backcountry	duty

As England's colonies in North America expanded between 1650 and 1750, three distinct regions formed—New England, the Middle Atlantic, and the South. Colonists in each region faced different challenges due to variations in climate, location, and natural resources. As a result of these challenges, diverse economies developed in the regions.

◆ THE NEW ENGLAND COLONIES

The New England colonies prospered despite the conditions that made it difficult to grow crops. With climate and soil largely unsuited for farming, many people of the New England colonies turned to shipbuilding, fishing, and trading as their major occupations and sources of income.

Using Natural Resources

The colonial settlers who hoped to make a success of farming in New England found the work difficult. In general, the region's rocky and infertile soil was not ideal farmland. Winters were long and cold, with howling winds and violent storms. Furthermore, dense forests had to be cleared before land could be farmed. Some settlers managed to earn a living as farmers. However, most lived at a **subsistence** level, producing just enough food to feed their families.

The forests and the sea offered other opportunities for making a living. Many New Englanders worked in the lumber industry, cutting down trees, building sawmills, and shipping timber to other colonies. Wood from New England's forests was used to build ships, houses, and furniture.

The lumber industry fueled New England's shipbuilding industry. With lumber both plentiful and cheap, building ships in the colonies cost half as much as it did in England. Port cities, such as Boston, Portsmouth, and Newport, became major shipbuilding centers as the industry rapidly expanded. By 1700, the city of Boston alone had 12 shipyards.

The shipbuilding industry was related to other successful industries—fishing and whaling. New England's jagged coastline, with its numerous inlets and bays, provided excellent harbors from which fishing and whaling ships set sail. Large fishing boats drew huge catches of cod, halibut, and other fish from New England's coastal waters.

New England Communities

Because shipping and fishing were important economic activities, most New England colonists lived and worked in cities or small towns located near harbors. In these towns, people worked in a number of trades, such as carpentry, blacksmithing, or shopkeeping.

Boston, the largest city in Massachusetts, developed into one of the most prosperous ports in the colonies. Each year, hundreds of ships loaded with animal hides, fish, and timber left Boston for England. In turn, English merchants shipped food, clothing, and other supplies to Boston. Trade became the key to prosperity in the New England colonies, making some merchants and shipowners wealthy.

Many colonists lived in villages. They built their church, meeting house, and school around a **common,** a piece of land shared by all inhabitants of a place. The colonists' houses lined the common, and the fields they farmed lay outside the village. By the 1700s small communities like this appeared throughout New England.

 How did the land and resources affect the economy of New England?

◀ As settlers expanded into the wooded areas of the New England colonies, they were able to supply inexpensive lumber to shipbuilders.

◆ THE MIDDLE COLONIES

In New England most people were of English background. In contrast, the Middle colonies had a much more diverse population. Many colonists who lived in the Middle colonies came from northern Ireland, the Netherlands, Sweden, Finland, and Germany—as well as from England.

People from Many Lands

Pennsylvania became one of the fastest growing of the 13 colonies. William Penn's policy of religious tolerance attracted people from many nations. For example, Germans came to escape religious wars that devastated their homeland. In the Pennsylvania countryside, some Germans purchased rich farmland and grew crops. Other Germans moved to Philadelphia, whose name meant "city of brotherly love," to work in various trades, such as weaving and shoemaking.

During the 1700s thousands of people migrated to the Middle colonies from northern Ireland. These immigrants, known as Scots-Irish, had moved to Ireland from Scotland. Once in America, the Scots-Irish usually moved to the **frontier,** a region that marks the point of farthest settlement in a territory. There, they cleared land and made a living by hunting and farming.

New York also attracted people of many nationalities. By the late 1600s, New York's population included English, Scots-Irish, Germans, Poles, Dutch, French, Danes, Portuguese, Italians, and Africans. The Dutch owned large estates along the Hudson River, and by the mid-1700s, they controlled many large banking and trading companies.

Farming in the Middle Colonies

The Middle colonies contained some of the most fertile farmland in eastern North America. Most of the land in the Middle colonies was far richer and much less rocky than the land in New England. The climate of the region was also milder, allowing for a longer growing season.

The majority of people in the Middle colonies made their living by farming. Their farms tended to be much larger than those in New England. Therefore, some landowners needed to hire workers to help with the planting, harvesting, and other tasks. Although enslaved Africans worked on a few large farms, most farmhands were hired workers who labored alongside the families that owned the land.

How did farming in the Middle colonies differ from farming in New England?

◆ THE SOUTHERN COLONIES

There were two ways of life in the Southern colonies: the life in the coastal region and the life in the **backcountry,** or the remote, less developed part of a region. A major difference between the regions was slavery. Although slavery was widespread on the large plantations on the coast, few enslaved people worked on smaller farms in the backcountry.

Southern Plantations and Backcountry Farming

Many of the first European settlers to arrive in the South established plantations on the coast and raised tobacco, rice, and indigo—a plant used to make a blue dye. In the beginning, plantation owners hired workers to farm the fields along with enslaved Africans, who were brought from West Africa to the colonies by slave traders. Later, as pressure increased to produce enormous quantities of these cash crops, field work was done almost entirely by enslaved Africans. Less than a century after the first Africans came as indentured servants to Virginia, most had lost their rights. By the 1700s, most Africans in the Southern colonies were enslaved.

With the rich farmland along the coast already claimed, European settlers who arrived during the late 1600s settled in the hilly country to the west. There in the backcountry, they carved small farms from the forested valleys and foothills of the Appalachian Mountains.

Backcountry farmers in the South tilled small plots, growing such garden crops as beans and peas. Because their farms were small, backcountry farmers did not need slaves to plant and harvest their crops. With the South's long growing season, they produced all the food they needed for themselves and their families. In addition, these farmers traded surplus at local markets.

Bacon's Rebellion

As backcountry farmers pushed farther west, they came into conflict with Native Americans already living on the land. These conflicts led to violent confrontations on the frontier. When farmers in Virginia asked their governor to intervene, he refused. The farmers accused the governor of avoiding action because he profited from his own fur trade with the Native Americans. In 1676 one farmer, Nathaniel Bacon, organized raids on Native Americans to drive them farther west and to take their land.

Bacon then turned his attention to the government. He and his followers objected to unfair taxes and laws favoring wealthy coastal planters. In an incident later called Bacon's Rebellion, Bacon led his forces to Jamestown, Virginia's capital, and burned the town. When Bacon died suddenly of disease, the rebellion fell apart. Virginia's governor caught the remaining leaders, tried them, and hanged them. However, conflict between frontier settlers and Native Americans continued. The resentment of backcountry farmers toward coastal plantation owners over taxes remained an issue after Nathaniel Bacon's rebellion.

 How did life on the coast differ from life in the backcountry of the Southern colonies?

Angry at the unfair treatment of backcountry farmers, Nathaniel Bacon protested against the government by burning down houses in Jamestown. ▼

◆ COLONIAL TRADE

By the mid-1700s almost all of the British colonies depended on overseas trade. In New England, lumber, fish, and whale oil had their main markets in England. The Middle colonies **exported,** or sent abroad, many farm products, including garden vegetables and fruits such as apples, pears, and cranberries. The Southern colonies shipped tobacco, rice, and indigo to markets in England.

The Mercantile System

Colonial merchants wanted to sell their products wherever they could get the most money for them. However, England's purpose in creating colonies in North America was not to make the colonies rich, but to make England rich.

The economy of England, like the economy of many European countries at the time, was based on the **mercantile system.** The mercantile system was based on the theory that a nation grew in strength by building up its gold supply and expanding its trade. To build up its gold supply, a nation needed to sell more goods to other countries than it purchased from them. A favorable balance of trade was needed. A nation gains a favorable balance of trade when it exports more products than it **imports,** or buys from other nations.

The colonies were an essential part of England's mercantile system. The colonies provided England with raw materials, such as timber, furs, and cotton. These raw materials were used by English manufacturers to produce finished products, which were then sold worldwide. People in the colonies were not allowed to make their own finished products. They were forced to buy their manufactured goods from England.

The Navigation Acts

To strictly regulate trade in the colonies, England passed several laws. Under this series of laws, called the Navigation Acts, only English ships or ships made in the English colonies could be used to transport goods between England and the colonies. Ships carrying goods to the colonies from other European countries were required to stop first in England so that England could collect **duties,** or taxes, on the goods. Another law listed items from the colonies that could be shipped only to England. These specific items, known as enumerated articles, included important products—tobacco, indigo, cotton, furs, and sugar cane—that England needed but did not produce. Some of the

Study Hint

Each time you begin a reading assignment, preview the content. You can do this by making a list of the section titles and headings. Leave space after each heading so that you can fill in main ideas and details as you read. Try this previewing technique as you read the next section.

laws enacted by the Navigation Acts helped the colonial economy. For example, the order to use only English- or colonial-made ships encouraged the colonies to develop their own shipbuilding industry. By the 1770s, colonial shipyards were building one third of all merchant ships sailing under the British flag.

Still, colonists disliked the Navigation Acts because they believed the acts favored English merchants. In addition, the colonists had to pay more for European goods because the English placed taxes on goods that the colonies imported.

 What actions did England take to control trade in the colonies?

◆ COLONIAL LIFE

Early settlers in the 13 colonies were influenced by English traditions. However, during the late 1600s and early 1700s, settlers developed their own practices. The new colonial culture tended to flourish in the growing cities.

Cities as Centers of Culture

Because the colonial economy depended on shipping and trade, port cities developed rapidly. Philadelphia, the leading city of the colonies, was the first to be laid out in a grid pattern, with streets crossing at right angles. It had a fire department, the first public library, and the only public hospital in the English colonies.

▲ These colonial women perform the tasks for making cloth. One combs the wool, a second spins it into thread, and a third weaves it into cloth. Such tasks were part of women's responsibilities in colonial America.

In colonial cities, such as Philadelphia, educated people produced fresh ideas. Benjamin Franklin, Philadelphia's most prominent citizen, was a printer, publisher, scientist, inventor, and politician. Franklin served as deputy postmaster of Philadelphia, and he started a college that later became the University of Pennsylvania. He drew up plans to improve the paving and lighting of city streets. Franklin also wrote numerous books, including his autobiography and *Poor Richard's Almanac*, which included proverbs praising hard work and honesty. One saying still quoted today is "Never leave that till tomorrow which you can do today."

Women in the Colonies

Women played a key role in the economic life of the colonies, working as shopkeepers, printers, inn managers, and even as shipbuilders. They were responsible for all household jobs, and they assisted their husbands in planting crops and managing family businesses. Frequently, colonial women would take over the family business when a husband or father died.

Yet colonial women had few rights. In all the colonies, decision-making power rested in the hands of white male property owners. At home, most women were legally under the control of men. For example, when a woman married, she was required to turn over control of her property to her husband.

A married woman could not run a business without her husband's permission. Women could not vote or serve on juries.

Despite these restrictions, some women took on more than their traditional duties. On the frontier, where life was more difficult, women had to know how to hunt as well as how to spin wool and weave cloth. One colonist left this description of a frontier woman in 1710:

" **She is very civil . . . yet she will carry a gun in the woods and kill deer, turkeys, shoot down wild cattle, catch and tie hogs, knock down cattle, and perform the most manful exercises as well as most men in those parts.** "

? Why was achieving success in business difficult for a woman during colonial times?

Section 1 Review

Check Understanding

1. **Define** (a) subsistence (b) common (c) frontier (d) backcountry (e) export (f) mercantile system (g) import (h) duty

2. **Discuss** why farming was, in general, more difficult in the New England colonies than in the Middle and Southern colonies.

3. **Explain** why the colonists opposed the Navigation Acts.

Critical Thinking

Analyzing How did the economies of the New England, Middle, and Southern colonies differ?

Write About Citizenship

◈ **Connecting Past and Present** Write a brief paragraph describing how Benjamin Franklin's contributions to Philadelphia live on today.

BUILDING *SKILLS*

Reading a Map: Economy of the New England Colonies

Reading a map helps you learn about a particular place. Some maps show the locations of physical features such as mountains and lakes. Others show information about population, economics, or natural resources.

Here's How

Follow these steps to read and study a map:

1. Look at the title, which gives the subject.
2. Look at the map key. The key tells what the colors and symbols on the map represent.
3. Check the compass rose, which shows direction—north, south, east, and west.
4. Note the map scale, which shows how distances on the map relate to real distances.
5. Locate places and other details on the map.

Here's Why

Maps help people understand the world around them. Although it is sometimes possible to present the information on a map in another form, such as a paragraph or chart, a map is usually the most effective way to show the locations, physical features, and special characteristics of places.

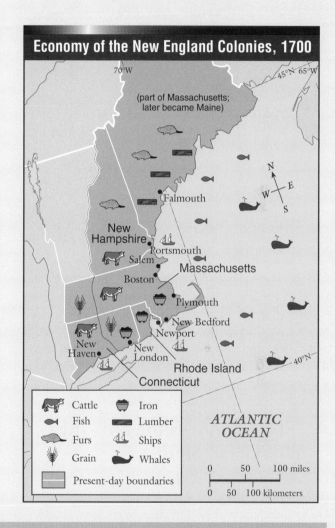

Economy of the New England Colonies, 1700

Practice the Skill

Study the map and answer the questions.

1. Which colonies are shown on this map?
2. What do the symbols on the map show?
3. From which Connecticut seaport might iron have been exported?
4. What conclusions can you draw about geography and economic activity in Maine?

Apply the Skill

Choose a map shown in a section of the textbook you have not read. Use the *Here's How* steps to analyze the map. Then write a brief explanation of how studying the map helped you to understand the area.

Section 2

Africans in the Colonies

PREVIEW

Objectives

- To explain the link between the triangular trade and the slave trade
- To describe the Middle Passage
- To compare the lives of Africans in the South and in the North

Vocabulary

Middle Passage
sanitation
restriction

Colonial prosperity depended to a large extent on trade. A great deal of trade was conducted with Great Britain, of which England was now a part, where colonial merchants sent raw materials such as iron, lumber, and cotton. In Great Britain, these materials were transformed into finished products and then sold to markets in the colonies and elsewhere.

◆ TRIANGULAR TRADE AND THE MIDDLE PASSAGE

Some trade was called triangular trade because three separate voyages were involved in the trading. During the colonial period there were several different triangular trade routes connecting the American colonies to Europe and Africa.

One triangular trade route connected North America to Africa and the West Indies. This route, shown on the map on the right, involved trading goods for enslaved Africans.

In the first leg of this triangle, ships carried rum, iron goods, and cloth from the New England colonies to the coast of West Africa. At West African ports, New England sea captains exchanged these goods for Africans who had been captured by slave hunters and then sold to European or American sea

captains. To prevent their escape, the captives were forced to wear iron collars and were linked together by chains.

In the second leg of the trade route, the colonial ships took the enslaved Africans to the West Indies. This part of the voyage was called the **Middle Passage.** In the West Indies, the sea captains traded some of the Africans for molasses and sugar. They then sailed on to the colonies. There, the molasses was sold to makers of rum. The remaining Africans were auctioned to the highest colonial bidders. Considered property of their owners, they were then transported to plantations as slaves.

The living conditions on the ships during the Middle Passage were unimaginably horrid. As many bodies as could fit were packed aboard. Africans were housed in an area a little over five feet high between the main deck and the cargo hold. There were no mattresses, sheets, pillows, or blankets. Captives lay between decks, gasping for air. Their muscles cramped, and iron chains cut into their legs and wrists. Bodies were packed tightly together. There was not enough room to stand.

At the brink of death, many captured people were forced to stay alive. Sailors often pried open the Africans' mouths and forced food down their throats. There was no **sanitation,** or disposal of waste, on

Economics *One triangular trade route moved goods, supplies, and people between Africa, the West Indies, and the colonies.* **Interpreting the Map** *What goods were brought to Africa from North America?* ▼

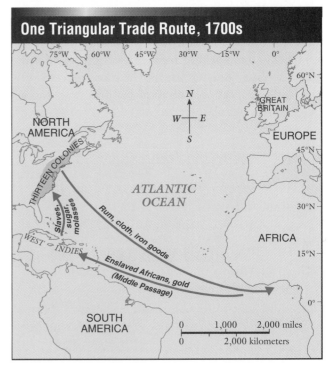

One Triangular Trade Route, 1700s

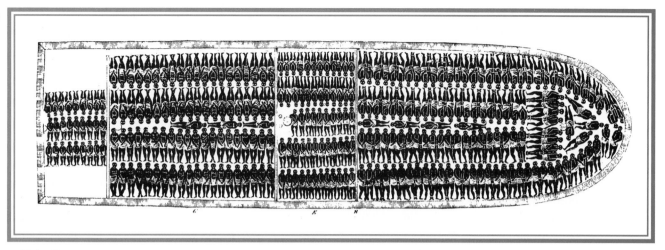

▲ *This diagram shows how enslaved Africans, forced into tightly confined areas on slave ships, were transported across the Atlantic Ocean.*

board. Contagious diseases such as smallpox swept through the ships. Many died from sickness, filthy conditions, and spoiled food. Sharks trailed the ships and fed on the bodies that were thrown overboard. There were some revolts against the inhumane conditions, but they were seldom successful.

Records show that about 10 percent of all Africans shipped to North America in the 1700s did not survive the Middle Passage. On some tragic voyages, the number of deaths was even higher. This heavy loss of life did not discourage the slave traders, who made enormous profits.

 In what ways did slavery become a key part of colonial trade?

◆ **SLAVERY GROWS IN THE SOUTH**

The number of enslaved people increased as the English colonies grew. Faced with the need for a large supply of labor, southern landowners looked to Africans to provide it. By 1700, plantation owners depended on enslaved Africans to clear land, tend livestock, plant and harvest crops, and care for their homes and children. In Virginia and North Carolina, enslaved Africans grew tobacco. In South Carolina, they worked on rice and indigo plantations.

Some Africans had a great deal of experience growing rice in their homeland, so when they were brought to the Americas, they improved rice-growing techniques. Their skills and labor helped to make rice growing highly profitable in the Southern colonies.

Enslaved people typically worked from dawn to dusk. Those who worked in the fields on large plantations usually toiled in gangs. Overseers, or men who were hired by plantation owners to "oversee" the work of the enslaved people, sometimes beat them in an effort to get them to work harder or faster. Household slaves generally received better treatment.

Because they were considered valuable property, enslaved Africans usually received enough food to keep them healthy. Their meals consisted mostly of rice, corn, beans, and molasses. However, since slave owners used Africans to increase their profits, they generally spent as little as possible on them. For example, slave quarters were typically shacks with a few pieces of furniture, some straw to sleep on, and perhaps an iron pot.

Enslaved people lived at the mercy of their owners. They had no rights and were treated not as people but as possessions. If an owner chose to sell a child and keep the child's mother, there was no way for a slave to prevent it. Enslaved people lived in constant fear of being torn from their families.

As the number of enslaved Africans increased in the colonies, so did **restrictions,** or limitations, on their behavior. In order to have complete control over slaves, colonies adopted laws called slave codes. These slave codes barred enslaved Africans from gathering in groups and from striking back if they were attacked by their owners. Enslaved Africans were forbidden to learn to read or write. They were not allowed to go to court to testify against white people.

 In what ways did slave codes control enslaved Africans?

◆ AFRICANS IN THE NORTH

Although slavery was legal in all 13 colonies, there were far fewer slaves in the North. The smaller farms of the New England and Middle colonies required less labor than the large southern plantations. Since the cold climate prevented northern farms from being worked during the winter, it was not profitable to feed and clothe enslaved Africans all year round. Therefore, slavery never became the basis for the economy in the North as it did in the South.

About 500,000 Africans lived in the Southern colonies by the late 1700s, compared to about 50,000 in the New England and Middle colonies combined. In the colony of Virginia, 5 percent of the population was African in 1671 but rose to 24 percent by 1715. In 1756, that figure climbed to more than 40 percent. Not one colony in the New England or Middle Atlantic region came close to this population figure for Africans in the 1700s.

Although slavery did not play a dominant role in the New England and Middle colonies, northern merchants were involved in building, sailing, and financing the ships that brought Africans across the Atlantic Ocean on the Middle Passage. These merchants sold thousands of Africans to plantation owners in the West Indies and in the Southern colonies.

Africans in the North worked on farms as field-hands or servants, in the forests as lumberjacks, and on the seacoast as sailors, dockworkers, and fishers. Others worked in the cities of Boston, New York, and Philadelphia in lumber mills, gristmills, paper mills, and iron works. Still others worked as servants in the homes of wealthy people.

Free Africans

Not all Africans in colonial times were enslaved. Some had gained freedom by escaping from their owners. Others were descendants of people who had come as indentured servants. A few had been able to buy freedom from their owners.

More free Africans lived in the New England colonies than in any of the other colonies. Free Africans could own land in New England. Although these free Africans were better off than enslaved Africans, their lives were still filled with restrictions. Most of the colonies passed laws limiting their activities. Free Africans could work for wages, but colonial society usually kept them in menial positions, working as servants. Laws in most colonies denied them the right to vote.

A few African children attended schools with white children, but most were not able to get a formal education. Most other public facilities were arranged to separate Africans from white people. Free Africans in the South could not assemble for any purpose. Africans were seated in different areas of churches and were buried in separate graveyards. In a graveyard in Concord, Massachusetts, a gravestone tells a great deal about the plight of free Africans:

*Economics Between 1690 and 1750, the economy of the Southern colonies depended on the labor of enslaved Africans. **Interpreting the Chart** Compare the number of Africans in the Southern colonies in 1750 to the number of Africans in the rest of the colonies combined. ▼*

Africans in the Colonies, 1690–1750

Year	New England Colonies	Middle Colonies	Southern Colonies
1690	905	2,472	13,307
1700	1,680	3,361	22,476
1710	2,585	6,218	36,063
1720	3,956	10,825	54,058
1730	6,118	11,683	73,220
1740	8,541	16,452	125,031
1750	10,982	20,736	204,702

" Here lies the body of John Jack,
a native of Africa who died March 1773,
aged about 60 years.
Tho born in the land of slavery
He was born free:
Tho he lived in a land of liberty
He lived a slave.
Till by his honest,
tho stolen labors,
He acquired . . . his freedom.
Tho not long before Death the great Tyrant
Gave him his final emancipation [freedom]
And put him on a footing with kings. "

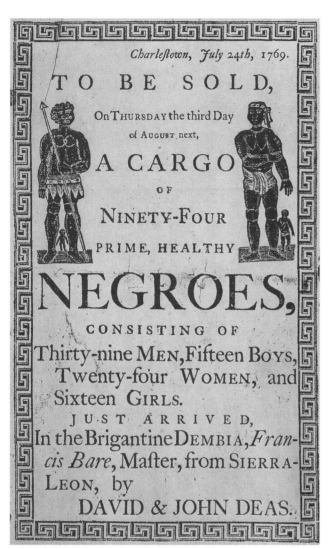

Charleſtown, July 24th, 1769.

TO BE SOLD,

On THURSDAY the third Day of AUGUST next,

A CARGO

OF

NINETY-FOUR

PRIME, HEALTHY

NEGROES,

CONSISTING OF

Thirty-nine MEN, Fifteen BOYS, Twenty-four WOMEN, and Sixteen GIRLS.

JUST ARRIVED,

In the Brigantine DEMBIA, *Francis Bare*, Maſter, from SIERRA-LEON, by

DAVID & JOHN DEAS.

▲ The sale of Africans was advertised by traders. This advertisement lists the details of the sale. Africans were considered the property of their buyers.

Slave Resistance

Enslaved Africans did not accept their conditions willingly. Resistance was common. Some slaves broke their owners' tools and worked slowly on purpose. Some set fire to farm buildings and destroyed other property. Some enslaved Africans were allowed to leave their plantations to visit elsewhere. Running away was rarely successful since there were few places to hide.

On occasion, enslaved Africans plotted revolts against their owners. In New York several revolts took place in the 1700s. For instance, in 1712 a group of enslaved Africans burned down a house and fought with the white colonists who tried to put out the fire. In the battle that followed, nine colonists died and six were injured. Soldiers tracked down the enslaved

Africans, who were tried and executed. Other slave revolts in the North were also brutally put down.

In South Carolina, the Stono Uprising of 1739 started with about 20 enslaved Africans gathering along the Stono River. At a supply store, they killed two guards and stole guns and gunpowder. The slaves then headed south, hoping to reach freedom in Spanish Florida. Other slaves joined them, and their number grew to about 80. Eventually, a colonial force from South Carolina caught up with them and crushed the revolt. The Stono Uprising prompted slaveholders to take more and more elaborate precautions to protect themselves.

 How did the lives of Africans in the North and the South differ?

Section 2 Review

Check Understanding

1. **Define** (a) Middle Passage (b) sanitation (c) restriction

2. **Identify** one triangular trade route.

3. **Explain** why slavery grew faster in the Southern colonies than in the New England and Middle colonies.

4. **Discuss** some of the restrictions that free Africans faced.

5. **Describe** the ways in which enslaved Africans resisted slavery.

Critical Thinking

Connecting Past and Present Many slave codes forbade the education of enslaved Africans. How do laws today protect a young person's right to an education?

Write About Culture

Study the quote on page 52. In your own words, explain the meaning of the inscription on the gravestone.

POINT *of* VIEW

THE EVILS OF SLAVERY

Olaudah Equiano was born in Benin, Africa, around 1745. When Equiano was 11, his world was shattered. Stolen from his home and enslaved to a series of African masters, Equiano was ultimately put aboard a British slave ship bound for the Americas.

Equiano was a rare example of an enslaved person who eventually was able to buy his freedom. As a freed man, Equiano moved to Great Britain. Until the end of his life, Equiano spoke out against the evils of slavery. In the following passages from his book, *The Interesting Narrative of the Life of Olaudah Equiano*, published in 1789, Equiano describes the shock of his capture, the hardship of the Middle Passage, and the mistreatment suffered by slaves.

One day, when all our people were gone out to their works as usual, and only I and my dear sister were left to mind the house, two men and a woman got over our walls, and in a moment seized us both; and, without giving us time to cry out, or make resistance, they stopped our mouths, and ran off with us into the nearest wood. Here they tied our hands, and continued to carry us as far as they could, till night came on....

• • • •

I now saw myself deprived of all chance of returning to my native country.... Soon, to my grief, two of the white men offered me eatables and on my refusing to eat, one of them held me fast by the hands and laid me across the windlass [a machine used to pull sails up and down] and tied my feet while the other flogged me severely....

• • • •

It was very common in several of the islands, particularly in St. Kitt's, for the slaves to be branded with the initial letters of their master's name, and a load of heavy iron hooks hung about their necks. Indeed on the most trifling occasions they were loaded with chains, and often instruments of torture were added.... I have seen a Negro beaten till some of his bones were broken for even letting a pot boil over.

Examining Point of View

1. Describe Equiano's capture by the two men and the woman.

2. What kinds of treatment does Equiano both endure and observe?

3. How would you describe Equiano's response to his experiences?

4. What can you tell about Equiano from his writings?

What's Your Point of View?

All civilized people agree about the brutality and injustice of slavery. Nothing emphasizes this position more than an account from the point of view of a person who lived through it.

Write an essay in which you consider how slavery—a calamity for enslaved people—is also severely damaging to an entire society.

New Ideas Take Hold

PREVIEW

Objectives

• To discuss how religious tolerance developed in the 13 colonies

• To trace the effect of the Great Awakening on education, politics, and religion

• To explain how the political rights and freedoms of the colonists expanded

Vocabulary

Enlightenment	militia
assembly	libel

With each passing year, life in the American colonies resembled life in Great Britain less and less. The colonists developed their own new ideas and new traditions. Separated by an ocean from their homeland, they came to view themselves as different from their British counterparts.

◆ CHANGES IN COLONIAL SOCIETY

The desire to freely practice the religion of their choice had provided the incentive for many settlers to come to the colonies. Yet, by the early 1700s, religion had become less important to many settlers. In 1720, only about 25 percent of New Englanders belonged to a church. The figure was even lower in other colonies. As the colonies became more prosperous, younger people developed a greater interest in trade than in religion. This alarmed many ministers, especially in the New England colonies.

Ministers tried to revive religion through emotional and dramatic sermons beginning around the 1730s. Many succeeded in awakening a religious sense in their listeners. For that reason, this period of religious enthusiasm came to be known as the Great Awakening. The Great Awakening helped promote religious tolerance as preachers emphasized religion as a sincere set of beliefs rather than an attachment to a particular church.

The Great Awakening

Jonathan Edwards, one of the leaders of the Great Awakening, called on people to examine their lives. His most famous sermon, entitled "Sinners in the Hands of an Angry God," became known throughout the colonies. In it, Edwards compared a listener to a spider hung over a fire. He thundered,

> **Oh sinner! Consider the fearful danger you are in. It is a great furnace of wrath, a wide and bottomless pit, full of the fire of wrath. You hang by a slender thread.**

The Great Awakening encouraged religious freedom. As a result, many new religious groups sprang up during this period. One of the first truly national movements in the American colonies, the Great Awakening affected the way people viewed themselves, their political rights, and their governments. Ordinary people began to realize that if they could figure out how to worship God on their own, then they could also figure out how to govern themselves. More colonists came to oppose government support of any one religious group.

Colonists were also becoming interested in the ideas of the **Enlightenment,** the European belief that

George Whitefield, pictured here, was a popular preacher during the Great Awakening. Crowds gathered to hear his enthusiastic sermons. ▼

the spread of new ideas and reason would improve society. People believed that through the power of the human mind, they could improve themselves and the world around them. Many took part in the search for new inventions and practical knowledge.

Education and Religion

The Great Awakening and the Enlightenment further resulted in a new emphasis on education. Education and religion had been closely linked during early colonial times. Now, colleges and universities were established for the purpose of training ministers. Harvard, the first college founded in the colonies in 1636, began as a college for Puritan ministers. In 1693, James Blair, a minister in the Church of England, founded the College of William and Mary in Virginia. It was the first college in the Southern colonies. Religious groups that began during the Great Awakening wanted colleges to train their ministers as well. Institutions such as Princeton, Brown, Rutgers, and Dartmouth were founded as a result of the movement. In time all these schools became places where lawyers, doctors, teachers, and others were educated.

How did the Great Awakening influence politics and education as well as religion?

◆ ESTABLISHING POLITICAL RIGHTS

Even as the colonists grew apart from England, most considered themselves loyal subjects of the king. As such, the colonists believed they deserved the same rights as any English person. These rights had been written in a document known as the Magna Carta (1215), Latin for "Great Charter." The Magna Carta stated that even the king was not above the law. For example, before raising taxes, he had to have the consent of a representative body.

Rights for Citizens

In England only wealthy landowners had the right to vote. In general, the colonists followed the same tradition: white men who owned property could vote. Voters elected people to represent them in an **assembly,** or lawmaking body.

In each colony, the assembly established a trained **militia**—an army of citizens who served in times of emergency. The militias often acted to protect the rights of the wealthy, such as responding to a call to crush a slave revolt.

In addition to their elected assemblies, 8 of the 13 American colonies were ruled by royal governors. Royal governors were not elected, but rather were appointed by the King of England. The job of a royal governor

Many colleges were founded to train religious leaders. One of them, the College of William and Mary, in Virginia, is pictured here. ▶

▲ *When John Peter Zenger printed his opinions about corrupt New York City leaders, soldiers were ordered to burn his newspaper.*

the paper and ordered it closed. Cosby then accused Zenger of **libel,** or making a false statement in writing to injure a person's reputation. Zenger was thrown in jail and brought to trial in 1735. Zenger's trial raised the issue of freedom of the press—whether the press should be free to criticize the acts of public officials. Zenger's lawyer, Andrew Hamilton, asked, "Shall the press be silenced that evil governors may have their way?" He defended the rights of Americans to have

> **the liberty—both of exposing and opposing arbitrary power . . . by speaking and writing truth.**

The jury found Zenger not guilty after just ten minutes of deliberation. This decision paved the way for freedom of the press in the American colonies.

? How did English history and traditions affect political freedoms enjoyed by the colonists?

was to ensure that the colonists obeyed British laws in addition to those proposed by the assembly. When the views of the assembly and the royal governor clashed, the governor had the power to dissolve the assembly.

In matters of justice, juries—made up of people from a community—made decisions about guilt or innocence. White men and women accused of crimes in the colonies were tried before such juries. Trial by jury helped promote new ways of thinking. Decisions about guilt or innocence were made not by a judge, but by people from the community.

The Zenger Case

One of the most important means of colonial communication was the weekly newspaper. Early in the eighteenth century, the press functioned as a mouthpiece for the government. In fact, editors who criticized public officials could land in jail.

In 1733, some prominent New Yorkers started a newspaper called *The New York Weekly Journal.* They hired John Peter Zenger, a German immigrant, as a journalist. Together they opposed the corrupt government of New York Governor William Cosby. Zenger published a number of articles criticizing the governor's dishonesty and greed. The governor felt threatened by

Section 3 Review

Check Understanding

1. **Define** (a) Enlightenment (b) assembly (c) militia (d) libel

2. **Discuss** the impact the Great Awakening had on the development of religious freedom in the colonies.

3. **Describe** how early colonial government worked.

4. **Explain** the purpose of early colleges.

Critical Thinking

Making Connections Why would the spirit of the Enlightenment be welcomed in the colonies?

Write About Government

◆ **Connecting Past and Present** Write a brief essay about the influence of the Zenger decision on the freedom of the U.S. press today.

Chapter 3
Review

CHAPTER SUMMARY

Section 1

By the 1700s three distinct regions had developed in the English colonies—the New England, the Middle, and the Southern colonies. Each region developed an economy influenced by its geography and the people who settled there. Trade helped the colonies to flourish, although the English controlled and limited that trade.

Section 2

Enslavement of Africans played an important role in the colonial economy. The slave trade bolstered the economies of both the New England and the Southern colonies. The Middle Passage brought Africans to the Americas under harsh conditions. Once in the colonies, most Africans faced a life of enslavement. Even free Africans were restricted in their rights.

Section 3

The Great Awakening encouraged religious freedom throughout the 13 colonies. Colonists tended to think of themselves as having the freedoms and political rights of English citizens. Over time, however, the colonists developed values distinct from those of most British citizens. The value of education, the right to religious freedom, and the right to freedom of the press were especially important to the colonists.

Connecting ◆◆ Past and Present

What rights and freedoms enjoyed by Americans today had their beginnings in colonial times?

Using Vocabulary

For each word, write the letter of the correct definition in the blank on a separate sheet of paper.

____ 1. frontier   ____ 5. import

____ 2. duty   ____ 6. export

____ 3. common   ____ 7. subsistence

____ 4. militia   ____ 8. libel

a. a type of organized army that can be called on in an emergency

b. bring foreign-made products or goods into a country

c. a land shared by all the inhabitants of a place

d. a false statement in writing that injures a person's reputation

e. a region that marks the point of farthest settlement in a territory

f. a tax paid on goods brought into a country

g. send products abroad for sale

h. the minimum level of food and clothing necessary to live

Check Understanding

1. **Describe** two major ways in which New Englanders made their living.

2. **Discuss** how the population of the Middle colonies differed from that of New England.

3. **Compare** the lives of southern backcountry farmers with coastal plantation owners.

4. **Explain** what the Navigation Acts were and how they affected the colonies.

5. **Describe** the three legs of one triangular trade route.

6. **Summarize** the treatment of enslaved Africans during the Middle Passage.

7. **Identify** some of the limitations on the rights of free Africans.

8. **Examine** the way in which religious tolerance was affected by the Great Awakening.

9. **Summarize** one influence of the Magna Carta on colonial thought.

10. **Identify** John Peter Zenger and describe the importance of his trial.

Critical Thinking

1. **Understanding Economics** How do the Navigation Acts show the difference between how England viewed the role of its colonies and how the colonial settlers viewed their role?

2. **Comparing** In what ways were Southern plantations different from Middle Atlantic and New England farms?

3. **Understanding Cause and Effect** What were the causes and effects of the Great Awakening?

4. **Evaluating** Why was resistance by enslaved Africans largely unsuccessful?

◆ **Connecting Past and Present** Is the relationship between geography and economics as strong in your community today as it was in seventeenth-century New England? Explain.

Interpreting the Timeline

Use the timeline on pages 42–43 to answer these questions.

1. What event on the timeline shows evidence of the conflict between backcountry farmers and plantation owners in the Southern colonies?

2. In what year was Zenger brought to trial?

3. How might Louis XIV's action have affected immigration to the American colonies?

Putting Skills to Work

READING A MAP

In the Building Skills lesson on page 49, you learned about some features of a map. Review the map on this page, then answer the following questions:

1. What is the purpose of this map?

2. What kinds of information does the map convey?

3. What areas on the map indicate the most population density?

4. What conclusions can you draw about colonial settlement from the map?

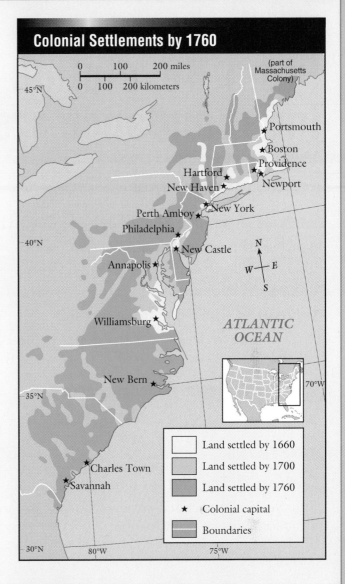

Colonial Settlements by 1760

- Land settled by 1660
- Land settled by 1700
- Land settled by 1760
- ★ Colonial capital
- Boundaries

Writing to Persuade

As a young English resident in the 1700s, you have decided to move to America. **Write** a letter to the king, asking permission to settle in a particular colony. Explain the reasons for your choice.

Portfolio Project

THE INTERACTION OF ECONOMY AND GEOGRAPHY

Choose one of the three regions you have read about in Section 1. Research and prepare a presentation about how its economic growth related to its geography from the 1600s to the 1700s. Include population statistics, economic data, and maps. File it in your portfolio.

Chapter 4
From Revolution to Independence 1754–1783

CHAPTER PREVIEW

Section 1 French Settlement and Conflict

French settlement in North America prospered with an expanding fur trade. This trade threatened British claims, leading to conflict between Britain and France.

Section 2 The Road to Revolution

British efforts to make the colonists pay the costs of the French and Indian War sparked a spirit of rebellion in the colonies.

Section 3 Declaring Independence

The Declaration of Independence set forth ideals of freedom and liberty that became the foundation upon which the United States was built.

Section 4 The War for Independence

Eight years of war ended in victory for the American colonists and in the founding of a new nation.

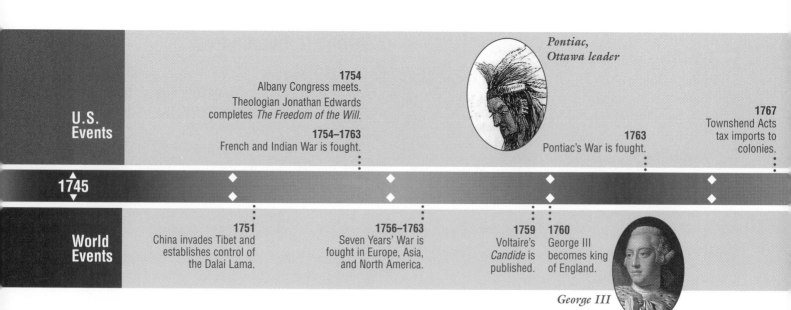

Pontiac, Ottawa leader

U.S. Events

1754
Albany Congress meets.
Theologian Jonathan Edwards completes *The Freedom of the Will.*

1754–1763
French and Indian War is fought.

1763
Pontiac's War is fought.

1767
Townshend Acts tax imports to colonies.

1745

World Events

1751
China invades Tibet and establishes control of the Dalai Lama.

1756–1763
Seven Years' War is fought in Europe, Asia, and North America.

1759
Voltaire's *Candide* is published.

1760
George III becomes king of England.

George III

Portfolio Project

MAPPING THE REVOLUTION

In 1763 few colonists could imagine that within 20 years they would belong to an independent nation of united states. Yet, in the years after 1763, one event after another widened the gap of trust between the colonists and the British. As you read this chapter, watch for significant events in the march toward independence. At the end of the chapter, you will create a map that shows how the events you selected led the 13 colonies to independence.

▲ *In 1775, George Washington was named commander of the Continental Army, which fought against the British in the Revolutionary War.* ◆◆ **Connecting Past and Present** *How does the artist convey Washington's power? How are military leaders portrayed today?*

A minuteman

Mary Ludwig Hays, also called Molly Pitcher

1776
Declaration of Independence is signed.

1775
American Revolution starts at Lexington and Concord.

1773
Boston Tea Party takes place.

1778
Molly Pitcher helps win Battle of Monmouth, NJ.

1783
Treaty of Paris ends the American Revolution.

1789
✪ George Washington elected.

1790

1770
James Cook discovers Botany Bay, in Australia.

1774
British establish control in India.

1780
Tupac Armaru, descendant of Incas, leads revolt against Spain.

Incan statue

1785
Russians settle in Aleutian Islands.

1787
Sierra Leone is founded by Great Britain for freed slaves.

Section 1

French Settlement and Conflict

PREVIEW

Objectives

- To identify characteristics of French settlement in the Americas

- To explain why Britain and France clashed in the French and Indian War

- To explain how the British managed to win the French and Indian War

Vocabulary

coureur de bois   muster
representative   cede

The French came to North America in small numbers. Their patterns of settlement were influenced by geography, economics, and their relations with the Native Americans they encountered.

◆ THE FRENCH FUR TRADE

What the French sought in the Americas was not gold and silver, but fish and furs. Quebec, their first permanent settlement, was located near the villages of the Huron people. French missionaries had established a friendship with the Hurons, thereby becoming enemies of the Hurons' enemy, the Iroquois. The alliance with the Hurons proved to be a mistake because the Iroquois, in turn, attempted to block French expansion to the south and west.

Meanwhile the French continued to focus on trade, sending their fur traders, called **coureurs de bois** in French, deep into the heart of North America. They followed water routes through the Great Lakes, the Ohio River Valley, and down the Mississippi River. Each spring, the coureurs de bois paddled their canoes filled with animal skins to their trading center in Quebec. The French hoped to develop this vast territory while confining British settlements to a narrow band of land along the Atlantic coast.

The fur trade quickly became the backbone of France's colony in the Americas. While almost everyone in New France had something to do with the fur trade, the coureurs de bois played the key role. They built strong alliances with many Native Americans that would prove beneficial to France in its struggle to control British expansion in North America.

The fur trade brought great profits to France, but it did not increase the population of New France. As late as 1750, approximately 55,000 colonists lived in all of New France. By contrast, more than one million people lived in the British colonies. The strength of New France lay in its trade system.

 What role did the coureurs de bois play in the growth of New France?

◆ THE FRENCH AND INDIAN WAR

In the early 1700s, people in the British colonies were not concerned about the scattered forts and trading posts of the French. By the middle of the 1700s, however, the situation had changed. Not only were Great Britain and France rivals in Europe, but British fur traders from New York, Pennsylvania, and Virginia were also crossing the Appalachian Mountains into land the French coureurs de bois considered their own. Both nations claimed the Ohio River Valley, and each was determined to drive out

Europeans traded firearms, tools, and trinkets for furs from the Hurons. Below, a Dutch trader inspects a pelt that he might be willing to trade for the goods he has placed on a blanket. ▼

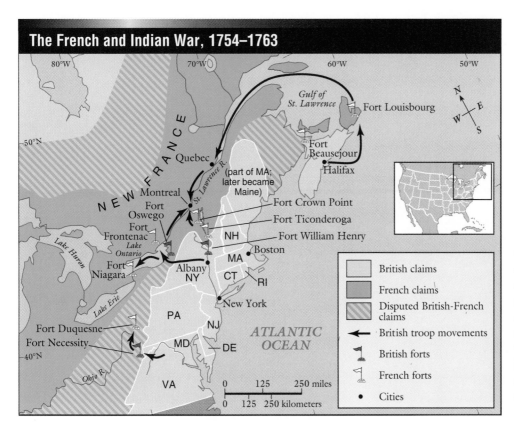

The French and Indian War, 1754–1763

British claims
French claims
Disputed British-French claims
British troop movements
British forts
French forts
Cities

◀ **Geography** *The French and Indian War was fought between the British and the French with their Indian allies. The colonists, as British subjects, named the war after their enemies.* **Interpreting the Map** *Explain how British troops traveled from Halifax to Quebec.*

the other. The stern orders that the French government sent to its officials in New France were evidence of their determination:

“ **Drive from the Ohio River any European foreigners, and do it in a way that will make them lose all taste for trying to return.** ”

The Albany Plan of Union

To some in the American colonies, the French threat looked like the beginning of war. In 1754, the British government organized the Albany Congress. **Representatives,** or people selected to act for others, from seven colonies met in Albany, New York, to discuss the threat of French expansion into British territories. At this first intercolonial gathering, Benjamin Franklin presented the delegates with a plan for a close alliance of colonies. In his Albany Plan of Union, Benjamin Franklin proposed that all the colonies form a council that would be headed by a president appointed by the British king. The council would have the power to raise taxes in the 13 colonies and lead military operations if war broke out.

Both the colonies and the British government rejected the plan. The colonies opposed it because they wanted to control their own taxes and military forces. The British government did not want a colonial council interfering with its powers. However, the Albany Plan of Union was the first step toward uniting the 13 colonies in a common cause.

Native Americans Take Sides

There was a second reason for the Albany Congress. The delegates also wanted to persuade the Iroquois to help them against the French. The Iroquois were cautious about taking sides, however. As Hendrick, a Mohawk chief, pointed out,

“ **the British and French are quarreling about lands which belong to us. And such a quarrel as this may end in our destruction.** ”

Ultimately, the Iroquois—who had never forgiven the French for joining with the Huron—allied with the British. This close alliance was an important defense on the northern frontier during the wars that followed.

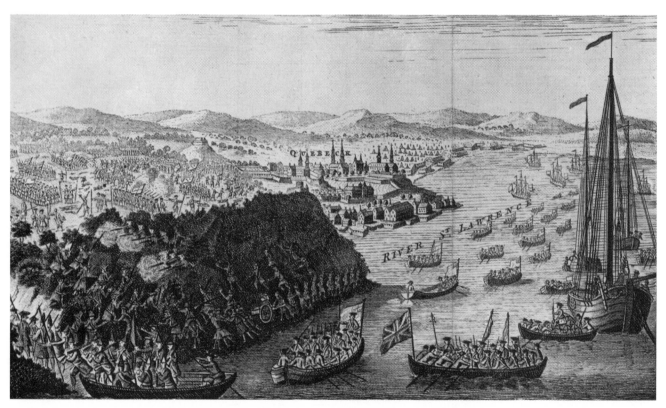

▲ *This illustration depicts British ships in the St. Lawrence River. British soldiers wait to climb the cliffs to the fort protecting the city of Quebec. The capture of Quebec by the British greatly weakened French control of the region.*

In general, Native Americans sided with the French, who did not endanger their way of life as drastically as did the British. French fur traders did not destroy Native American hunting grounds or build many permanent settlements. British settlers, on the other hand, cleared forests, killed forest animals, and planted crops.

The Ohio River Valley, claimed by the Iroquois and the Hurons, had become a refuge for Native Americans who had fled the Northeast—the Delaware and the Shawnee. These groups were anxious to preserve the Appalachians as a barrier to westward expansion. As much as possible, they took advantage of playing the British and the French against each other so that the existing colonial deadlock was maintained.

The War Begins

By 1753 the French began building several forts between Montreal and the Ohio River in preparation for war with the British. These forts are shown on the map on page 63. Later that year, Governor Dinwiddie of Virginia sent a 21-year-old officer, George Washington, to warn the French that the Ohio River Valley belonged to the British and that the French were invading their territory. Washington reported that the French were determined to stay in the Ohio River Valley and could not be moved except by force.

Britain and France did not declare war until 1756, but fighting began in 1754. In that year, Washington was sent to defend a British fort near the Ohio River. Before Washington and his men reached the fort, they learned that the French had seized it and renamed it Fort Duquesne (dōō-kān´). Washington's army was no match for the combined French and Native American force. Washington was forced to surrender, but the French soldiers allowed him and his soldiers to return home.

In 1755, the British sent an army under General Edward Braddock to defeat the French. Braddock knew nothing about fighting in America. As the British marched through the forest wearing bright red coats, they made perfect targets. When a combined French and Native American force attacked, Braddock and over 900 of his soldiers were killed or wounded.

The British Seize Quebec

After almost three years of fighting, the course of war began to turn in favor of the British. The new head of the British government, William Pitt, realizing the value to Great Britain of its North American colonies, poured men and money into destroying France's colonies. Older military commanders were dismissed, and younger, more aggressive officers, such as General James Wolfe, were installed. In 1758, Wolfe helped lead a force that captured the fort at Louisbourg, Canada, the most important French fortress in the Americas. The British then captured Fort Duquesne and renamed it Fort Pitt. From that fort, the present-day city of Pittsburgh received its name. The British next turned their attention to launching attacks on Canada.

Quebec was important to New France. Without it, the French would not be able to supply their forts farther up the St. Lawrence River. On top of a hill, the fort was well defended. However, in 1759, an army of British soldiers and American colonists under General Wolfe made a daring attack on Quebec. During the night, the British army scaled the cliffs around the city. The French commander failed to **muster,** or call together, reinforcements. In the morning, 4,000 British troops were outside the city.

The capture of Quebec was the most important British victory of the French and Indian War. Fighting went on for another year, with the British easily capturing Montreal and other French settlements in Canada. Fearing a British victory, Spain entered the war on the side of France in 1762. Spanish aid was too little and too late. In 1763 the governments of Great Britain and France signed the peace treaty that formally ended the war.

To take revenge against the French-speaking colonists of Acadia, who inhabited what today are the provinces of Nova Scotia and New Brunswick, the British forcibly removed 10,000 of them. These people had lived peacefully under British rule for over 40 years, but their refusal to swear an oath of allegiance to the British crown was used as a reason for their expulsion. The British sold their farms at bargain prices to immigrants from New England. The Acadians were dispersed throughout the Atlantic seacoast—approximately 3,000 of them settled in Louisiana. Known as Cajuns, they reassembled their distinctive community, which survives today as a strong, separate culture.

The power of France in North America had come to an end. The country lost all of its American territory except Guadeloupe, St. Pierre, Miquelon, and Martinique. It **ceded,** or surrendered possession of, its claims east of the Mississippi River to Great Britain. New Orleans was an exception. The city was given to Spain. In addition to New Orleans, Spain got the vast territory west of the Mississippi River. Spain, as an ally of France, was forced to give Florida to Great Britain.

American colonists celebrated Great Britain's victory with as much enthusiasm as the people in England. However, despite the apparent unity of the colonists and the British government, the French and Indian War did change their relationship. The colonists expected that, despite the Navigation Acts that controlled trade, the British would not interfere in other ways. However, faced with enormous war debts, the British could not afford to ignore the colonies any longer.

 How did alliances with Native Americans affect the outcome of the French and Indian War?

Section 1 Review

Check Understanding

1. **Define** (a) coureur de bois (b) representative (c) muster (d) cede

2. **Identify** one difference in the ways the French and British settled their North American colonies.

3. **Explain** the causes of the French and Indian War.

Critical Thinking

Analyzing Why did the Native Americans tend to side with the French?

Write About Government

◆ **Connecting Past and Present** Write an essay explaining in what ways the U.S. government today resembles the Albany Plan of Union.

BUILDING SKILLS

Classifying Information: Fighting the French and Indian War

Classifying information is the process of putting things that go together in categories. Classification makes things easier to locate and also easier to examine, understand, and use. Anything can be classified, as long as there are features by which to group the information. A chart is a handy tool to use for classifying.

Here's How

Follow these steps to classify historical information:

1. Review the information you wish to classify and decide on your purpose for classifying the facts and details. For example, you may want to study for a test, create an outline for a paper, or illustrate a comparison or contrast.

2. Decide on the best categories to use to classify your information. Historians often group ideas, people, objects, and events from the same time or the same region of the world.

3. Find the key characteristics of each piece of information and locate the category where it belongs. Record your information in a chart like the one on this page.

4. Use the information in your chart to draw conclusions.

Here's Why

Suppose you were asked to write an essay about the people who played important roles in the French and Indian War. Classifying information can help you to understand the relationships between people and events. By searching for appropriate and logical features by which to group facts, you can see patterns among them.

Practice the Skill

Copy the chart below on a sheet of paper. Reread Section 1 of this chapter, adding other names to the first column and filling in the second and third columns. Then use your classifications to write an essay about the role each person played in the French and Indian War.

Colonial Leader	Contribution	Date
Benjamin Franklin	Proposed Albany Plan	1754
George Washington		
Edward Braddock		
James Wolfe		

Apply the Skill

As you read the remaining sections of this chapter, think of ways you can classify information. For example, after reading Section 4 on pages 75–79, decide on two categories for classifying the information, such as Advantages of the British, Advantages of the Patriots; or African American Contributions, Native American Contributions. Make a chart and classify the information. Use your chart as a study tool.

Section 2

The Road to Revolution

PREVIEW

Objective

- To identify the reasons why Great Britain tried to block colonial expansion across the Appalachian Mountains

- To explain why British taxes stirred colonial anger

- To explain the importance of the First Continental Congress

Vocabulary

denounce
boycott
propaganda

massacre
minuteman

For many years, French fur traders had sent back glowing reports of the land beyond the Appalachian Mountains. With the French and Indian War finally over, settlers began to move there. They were eager to build homes on the lands newly won from the French. Native Americans watched with anger and sadness as the settlers set to work building houses and fences and driving away the game that the Native Americans had depended on for food. These Native Americans saw their way of life disappearing, just as it had vanished for groups east of the mountains.

◆ PONTIAC'S WAR AND COLONIAL EXPANSION

By 1763, Native Americans found a leader, Pontiac, of the Ottawa nation. As he called together Shawnee, Delaware, Chippewa, and Ottawa leaders, Pontiac stated,

> It is important for us, my brothers, that we exterminate [destroy] from our land this nation which only seeks to kill us.... Whom fear we? It is time.

In the spring of 1763, Native Americans began an attack on British settlements along the frontier, capturing 10 of 14 posts. Pontiac's War, as it was called, did not last long. British and colonial forces struck back and regained much of what they had lost. By December 1763, Pontiac had fled to the west and the fighting was over.

Pontiac's War was a warning to the British to expect constant conflict on the western boundaries of their settlements. To defend the frontier, forts had to be built and supplied, and soldiers had to be paid to defend them. Because of these expenses, the British were eager to take steps to keep the peace. The first step they took was to sign an agreement called the Proclamation of 1763, which closed lands west of the Appalachian Mountains to further colonial settlement.

Unhappy with the Proclamation, the colonists simply ignored it. Thousands of farmers, land buyers, and traders continued to move across the mountains. It was clear that the British government was unable to enforce its orders. American scorn for the British rules was reflected in this verse of a popular poem written by Benjamin Franklin.

> We have an old Mother that peevish [bad tempered] has grown. She snubs us like children that scarce walk alone. She forgets we've grown up and have sense of our own.

 Why did the British issue the Proclamation of 1763?

◆ TAXES AND RESISTANCE

Although the British had won the French and Indian War, they had also gone deeply into debt to pay for it. The British government had borrowed large amounts of money to pay British and colonial soldiers and Native American allies, and to ship supplies across the ocean. The British were determined to make the American colonists, who had benefited from the war, help repay those debts. Furthermore, the costs had not ended with the war. Great Britain would continue to require soldiers on the frontier to keep the settlers and Native Americans apart. Great Britain intended to force the colonists to share those costs, too.

The Sugar Act

With those expenses in mind, the British Parliament passed the Sugar Act in 1764. This law increased the duties, or import taxes, on non-British products and allowed the British to seize any ship that evaded the law.

The Sugar Act was the first of many laws taxing the colonists. After each law went into effect, the colonists reacted with anger at being forced to pay taxes that Great Britain had placed on them without their consent. Some colonists began to consider an action that had been unthinkable a few years earlier—breaking away from Great Britain.

The Stamp Act

No act outraged the colonists more than the Stamp Act of 1765. The act taxed all printed items—such as marriage licenses, newspapers, diplomas—and more than 50 other items. All items named in the law had to carry a stamp showing that the tax had been paid.

The colonists most affected by the Stamp Act were lawyers, newspaper editors, teachers, and merchants who used printed items. Many of them were influential people in a position to sway public opinion. They argued that it was not fair for the British Parliament to impose taxes on the colonies because the colonists did not elect representatives to Parliament. According to James Otis,

> **Taxation without representation is tyranny.**

On the day the Stamp Act went into effect, colonists in Boston showed their opposition by flying

▲ *Novelties such as this ceramic teapot were produced to protect the Stamp Act.*

flags at half mast. In October 1765, the Boston lawyer Samuel Adams organized a meeting of colonists to protest the taxes. Delegates from nine colonies met in New York. This meeting, the Stamp Act Congress, was the first time that any of the colonies had united to protest British actions. They **denounced,** or sharply condemned, the Stamp Act as an attack on colonial liberties.

Tax Protests

As small protests and riots spread, some angry colonists organized to fight the taxes. The best-known group, the Sons of Liberty, organized demonstrations and burned piles of stamps in town squares. Some officials were tarred and feathered, a practice that involved pouring hot tar over a person and covering the individual with bird feathers. The punishment was intended to be both painful and humiliating.

In the face of widespread opposition, Parliament cancelled the Stamp Act in 1766. The colonists rejoiced, but few of them noticed that the cancellation of the Stamp Act did nothing to address Parliament's right to tax the colonies.

In 1767, Parliament passed a new set of taxes and rules called the Townshend Acts, which put duties on several products imported from Britain, including paint, glass, paper, and tea. Once again, protests swept the colonies. But more effective than all the protests was the **boycott** of British business. A boycott is an economic protest in which people refuse to buy certain goods. The boycott of products such as cloth and paper was effective because the British government lost out on the money that would have come from the taxes on the goods. However, it was also a sacrifice for the colonists because they were accustomed to having British products.

The Boston Massacre

Protest against the Townshend Acts kept Boston in turmoil and forced Great Britain to send two regiments of soldiers to quiet the protests. On March 5, 1770, a mob gathered outside a British government office in the city. Some protesters began shouting insults at the British soldiers guarding the building. The scene grew uglier as snowballs mixed with stones and ice began to fly at the soldiers. Suddenly the British troops fired on the mob. When the smoke cleared, five colonists lay dead or dying. One was Crispus Attucks, an escaped slave who worked as a sailor. The five colonists are remembered as the first Americans to die in the struggle

▲ *This painting depicts the protest in which an African American sailor, Crispus Attucks, and four other protesters were killed by British soldiers. Attucks and the four others are considered the first casualties of the Revolutionary War.*

for freedom from British rule. The deaths of the colonists were tragic, but the incident had some value to the colonists' cause. Samuel Adams, a cousin of John Adams and a leader of the Sons of Liberty, saw the **propaganda** value of the incident. Propaganda is the promotion of certain ideas to improve or damage a cause. Adams made sure all colonists heard what had happened in Boston.

Several paintings showed the British soldiers firing on colonists, depicting the incident as a **massacre,** the merciless killing of many people. Again, the British were forced to cancel the taxes, although the tax on tea remained.

Even though calm was restored for several years, the possibility of conflict with the British made many of the colonists doubtful about the future. They worried that at any time, Parliament might again threaten colonial liberties.

To keep colonists informed of British actions, Samuel Adams set up a Committee of Correspondence. Members of this committee wrote letters and pamphlets reporting events in Massachusetts. The idea worked well, and soon all but two colonies had their own committees. The committees played an important role in uniting the colonists against Britain.

The Boston Tea Party

In 1773 the British Parliament issued the Tea Act. According to mercantile rules, the colonists were supposed to buy tea only from British companies. One such company was the British East India Company, a private company with substantial amounts of tea that it wanted to sell in the American market. However, Dutch tea, which was illegally smuggled into the colonies, was far cheaper.

The Tea Act removed certain taxes on British tea and permitted Americans to buy tea directly from the British East India Company and not from middlemen such as American tea merchants. Buyers would have to pay only one tax, and it was small. However, by making it cheaper and easier to buy British tea, the law cut into the business of American tea merchants.

The Tea Act had given the British East India Company a monopoly on the tea trade. Merchants warned that other products might suffer the same fate. While the tea tax was meant to calm colonial outrage, it instead became another source of anger and mistrust. Again, the colonists responded with a boycott. One colonial newspaper warned,

Do not suffer yourself to sip the accursed, dutied STUFF. For if you do, the devil will immediately enter into you, and you will instantly become a traitor to your country.

In November 1773 three ships loaded with tea from India arrived in Boston Harbor. On the evening of December 16, a band of colonists boarded the ships. Dressed as Native Americans to conceal their identities, they worked quickly, tossing chests of tea overboard. Soon more than 300 chests of valuable tea had been emptied into Boston Harbor. The Boston Tea Party was a powerful and effective display that was meant to show Britain that the colonists could act decisively.

The British government was convinced that something had to be done about the rebellious colony of Massachusetts. When King George III heard about the colonists' actions, he angrily exclaimed, "The die is now cast. The colonies must either submit or triumph."

Retaliation in the form of punishment came swiftly to the people of Boston. The British decided to make an example of them by closing the port to all shipping until Boston had paid for the wasted tea. This punishment threatened the very life of Boston, for the city's economy was based on trade conducted through this important port.

Great Britain also suspended local self-government and sent in more troops to enforce the punishment. Furthermore, British commanders could force citizens to house troops in their homes. The colonists, outraged by British retaliation, called these laws the Intolerable Acts because they were so harsh.

? Why did colonists react with anger to the Sugar Act and other tax acts?

◆ THE COLONIES UNITE

The Committees of Correspondence quickly spread news of the Intolerable Acts. At the urging of the Virginia burgesses, colonial leaders called a meeting in Philadelphia in September 1774 to discuss the British outrages.

The First Continental Congress

Delegates called their meeting the First Continental Congress. Every colony except Georgia sent representatives to the Continental Congress. Georgia agreed to accept all decisions made by the Congress.

The colonists viewed the Boston Tea Party as a bold protest against tyrannical British laws. The British called the participants in the Party thieves and rebels. ▶

The mood of the delegates was angry as they came to the First Continental Congress. After much debate, they issued a statement charging that Parliament did not have the right to tax the colonies. The Congress urged each colony to set up militia units to prepare for war with Great Britain. As the delegates departed, they agreed to meet again the following May if demands were not met.

Lexington and Concord

In Massachusetts, colonists had been preparing for war for some time. Special groups within the militia were arming themselves and drilling on village greens. They called themselves **minutemen** because they believed that they could be ready for action at a minute's notice. In towns near Boston, they collected weapons and gunpowder.

Meanwhile, Britain built up its forces. More British soldiers landed at Boston, bringing the total number of troops there to 7,000. On the night of April 18, 1775, British General Thomas Gage ordered 700 of his men to march from Boston to the town of Concord, where colonists were keeping a store of military supplies. It was Gage's intent to seize the supplies so that these storehouses would be empty. The British troops left Boston quietly, hoping not to be noticed.

Observant colonists saw the British movements. Three messengers, one of whom was named Paul Revere, rode through the night to alert the minutemen. During the night, Captain John Parker assembled 70 minutemen on the village green in nearby Lexington. He told them:

> **Stand your ground. Don't fire unless fired upon, but if they mean to have a war, let it begin here.**

In the early morning of April 19, the first British troops reached Lexington on their way to Concord. Six companies of troops wearing red coats advanced toward the minutemen. The British general commanded the minutemen to return to their homes. When they turned to leave without dropping their weapons, a shot rang out. After a brief skirmish, eight colonists were dead.

The British then marched on to Concord, six miles away, where they destroyed all the colonists' supplies that they found. At a Concord bridge outside of town, the colonists and the British became involved in a second skirmish, and the British were forced to retreat.

Word of the battles spread quickly. Farmers left their fields and picked up their muskets. As the British retreated toward Boston, from behind stone walls and trees on both sides of the road, the farmers kept up a steady fire on the retreating troops. By the time the British reached Boston, they had lost nearly 300 men. The colonists had delivered a strong message: there was nothing that would stop them from fighting for their rights.

 What was the outcome of the First Continental Congress?

Section 2 Review

Check Understanding

1. **Define** (a) denounce (b) boycott (c) propaganda (d) massacre (e) minuteman

2. **Explain** how the British discouraged further colonial settlement.

3. **Describe** methods the colonists employed to protest British taxes.

4. **Explain** what the First Continental Congress accomplished.

5. **Analyze** the role of the Committees of Correspondence prior to the start of the American Revolution.

Critical Thinking

Connecting Past and Present Compare "taxation without representation" to today's system of taxation in the United States.

Write About History

Review the painting shown on page 69 showing the Boston Massacre. Write a paragraph explaining what you have learned about weapons and battle conditions from your study of the painting.

Declaring Independence

PREVIEW

Objectives

- To analyze the arguments for and against independence for the American colonies

- To explain why the Declaration of Independence is a powerful political statement

- To analyze the differences between the ideals expressed in the Declaration and the reality of colonial society in the late 1700s

Vocabulary

declaration	Patriot
preamble	Loyalist
ideal	

Although the British soldiers still held Boston, colonial militias were close to the city. Their position on hills across the Charles River was ideal for storming into the city or firing on ships in Boston Harbor. In an attempt to prevent an advance on Boston, British troops attacked one of the hills on June 17. In the Battle of Bunker Hill, the colonists turned back two British attacks and retreated only when they ran out of gunpowder. One British officer remarked after the battle, "A few such victories will ruin our army."

◆ DEBATING INDEPENDENCE

Delegates from 12 of the 13 colonies came together in Philadelphia for the Second Continental Congress on May 10, 1775. The delegates included many leaders who had strong views about dealing with Britain.

On one side were the cousins John and Samuel Adams, of Massachusetts, and Richard Henry Lee and Patrick Henry, of Virginia—men who favored a complete break with Britain. On the other side were delegates such as John Dickinson of Pennsylvania who hoped for a continued relationship with Britain. Most

of the delegates, including Thomas Jefferson of Virginia and Benjamin Franklin of Pennsylvania, held views somewhere in the middle. Even the delegates in the middle, however, realized that bold action was necessary. Since fighting had begun, the first need seemed to be the colonies' defense. One of the Congress's first acts was to create an army out of the different colonial militia. Congress appointed George Washington as commander of the newly formed Continental Army.

In January 1776 a pamphlet was published that argued forcefully for colonial independence. The pamphlet, called *Common Sense*, had been written by an Englishman named Thomas Paine, who had arrived in the colonies only 13 months before. Paine argued that the colonists should follow "common sense" and break with the government led by King George III. Nothing but misery had come from kings, Paine said. It was up to the American colonies to lead the way in overthrowing monarchs. In one passage of the pamphlet, Paine wrote these memorable words:

> " The cause of America is in great measure the cause of all mankind. "

▲ The title page of this famous pamphlet was well-known to the thousands who were influenced by it. Thomas Paine was the author.

All the members of the Continental Congress read *Common Sense,* and most were convinced by its arguments. It sold 500,000 copies in less than six months, a huge number considering that there were only two and a half million people in the colonies. *Common Sense* gave the fighting in Massachusetts a new meaning. To many Americans the battle was not just a struggle to defend their rights as British subjects. The American cause was a revolution on behalf of liberty.

On June 7, 1776, Richard Henry Lee of Virginia proposed that the colonies declare their independence. Congress voted to put off a decision until July 1. In the meantime it appointed a committee to write a statement declaring why independence was justified. That statement was mostly the work of Thomas Jefferson.

On July 2, 1776, the committee presented the **declaration,** or formal statement, to Congress, and on July 4, Congress approved it. At the signing, John Hancock, the president of the Congress, wrote his name "large enough for King George to read without his spectacles." He urged the other delegates to approve the declaration, saying "There must be no pulling in different ways." "Yes," replied Benjamin Franklin of Pennsylvania. He added,

> We must all hang together, or assuredly, we shall all hang separately.

In what ways did Paine's *Common Sense* influence colonists to declare independence?

◆ THE DECLARATION OF INDEPENDENCE

The Declaration of Independence is one of the world's most important political documents. At different times in history, this document has inspired citizens to achieve equal rights, equal opportunities, and equal voice in government. The text of the Declaration of Independence appears on pages 688–691.

Few people today realize the courage it took to sign the Declaration of Independence. In voting for independence, the delegates were committing treason against their king and an empire that dominated much of the world.

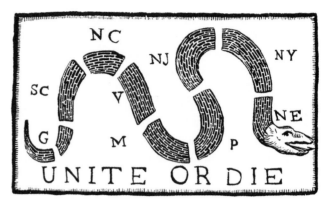

▲ *Drawn by Benjamin Franklin, this snake is divided into pieces representing the colonies. The "NE" section represents the New England colonies.*

Provisions of the Declaration

The first part of the Declaration of Independence, called the **preamble,** states basic principles of democracy, such as respect for the individual. In the past, the colonists had emphasized the rights they had as British citizens. Now they spoke of natural rights that all human beings have. Among these rights are "life, liberty, and the pursuit of happiness." According to the Declaration, people form governments to protect these rights. The people, not a king, are the basic source of government power.

The next part of the Declaration lists the grievances that led the Americans to break away from Britain. It states that King George III taxed the colonists without their consent, destroyed self-government, tried to stop the colonists from moving west, and stationed British troops in the colonies during peacetime. Because of the king's actions, the colonies declared their independence.

The last part of the Declaration announces that the colonies had become the United States of America. All political ties with Britain were cut. As a free and independent nation, the United States could make alliances and trade with other countries.

Matching Reality to Ideals

The ideas set forth in the Declaration of Independence set a high goal for the colonies. One of the hardest goals to reach was the statement in the preamble that reads "all men are created equal." In the 1700s this statement was an **ideal,** a perfect model, not a reality. In 1776, "all men" really meant "white men who could vote." This left out women, African Americans, Native Americans, and other groups.

Half a million enslaved men, women, and children in the colonies were evidence of how far the nation had to travel to achieve the goal of equality. Many of the men who signed the Declaration, including Thomas Jefferson, owned slaves. Jefferson, who believed that slavery would slowly disappear in the United States, never freed his own slaves.

Other southern signers intended to make sure that the Declaration of Independence had no impact on the institution of slavery. Slavery was legal in all 13 colonies in 1776, and slavery formed the basis of the southern economy. Yet many Americans of the late 1700s were troubled by slavery. Benjamin Franklin, for example, urged all colonists to free their slaves.

The debate over slavery nearly derailed the Declaration of Independence. In his first draft, Jefferson had attacked the slave trade. Southern delegates refused to sign the document, forcing the Congress to drop this clause and create a new draft.

Abigail Adams, the wife of the Massachusetts delegate John Adams, wanted something about the status of women written into the document. She sent her husband this message:

> Remember the ladies and be more generous and favorable to them than your ancestors [were]. Do not put such unlimited power in the hands of husbands. Remember all men would be tyrants if they could.

Despite Mrs. Adams's urging, however, the Declaration of Independence states only that "all men are created equal."

Still, the powerful words of the Declaration provided a foundation for a society built on equal rights. They encouraged Americans to work for democratic principles, such as free speech, freedom of the press, the rights of citizens to participate in government, and the rights of individuals.

Debating Loyalties

Colonists were divided about whether to support the new nation or remain loyal to Britain. On one side were **Patriots,** people who favored independence. On the other side were **Loyalists,** people who remained faithful to the British king.

It was an issue that even divided some colonial families. Benjamin Franklin, for example, was a Patriot, but his son, the royal governor of New Jersey, supported the king. John Adams estimated that one third of the Americans were Patriots, one third were Loyalists, and one third took no side.

Being a Loyalist in the colonies was not easy. Committees of Patriots drove many Loyalists from their communities. Others returned to Great Britain or fled to Canada. Perhaps as many as 80,000 people left the United States during the war rather than give up their allegiance to the British crown. This made it easier for the Patriots. Once independence was finally won, they were able to start immediately on the challenge of building a nation.

 Why do you think the Declaration of Independence has inspired other nations?

Section 3 Review

Check Understanding

1. **Define** (a) declaration (b) preamble (c) ideal (d) Patriot (e) Loyalist

2. **Discuss** Thomas Paine's influence on the colonists in their struggle for independence from Great Britain.

3. **Explain** the major ideas of the preamble of the Declaration of Independence.

4. **Identify** the rights, according to the Declaration of Independence, that government is obligated to protect.

Critical Thinking

Connecting Past and Present Today, what does "all men are created equal" mean to you?

Write About Citizenship

You have read about many events that led to the writing of the Declaration of Independence. Which event would have convinced you to support independence? Write an essay that describes your views.

Section 4

The War for Independence

PREVIEW

Objectives

- To analyze the strengths and weaknesses of the Patriot and British sides

- To describe the role of the Battle of Saratoga as a turning point in the war

- To explain the importance of African Americans, Hispanics, Native Americans, and women to the American victory

Vocabulary

mercenary	peninsula
Hessian	neutral

Americans who supported independence had good reason to celebrate the Declaration of Independence. The first year of the war had gone well. The Continental Army had chased the British out of Boston. Few people thought the rebellion would last long, but they were wrong. The Revolution would go on for almost eight years, making it the longest war in America's history—until the Vietnam conflict nearly 200 years later.

◆ THE OPPOSING SIDES

The Americans faced financial problems and a larger, better-equipped British army. However, the American army was fighting on its own ground with strong leadership. Both sides had advantages and disadvantages that were played out on the battlefields.

The British Forces

Britain had many advantages when the war began. The British army was tough, well-trained, and well-armed; therefore British officers were confident that they could stamp out the rebellion in a short time. Furthermore, the British navy ruled the seas, making it possible to supply their forces with ease and move their troops anywhere along the coast. Britain also had more support from Native Americans than the Patriots had. As in the French and Indian War, many Native Americans sided against the settlers who threatened their lands and ways of life.

On the other hand, the British had difficulty getting reinforcements. Army pay was so low and living conditions were so bad that few Englishmen volunteered. Accordingly, the British were forced to hire soldiers to help fight the war. These soldiers were called **mercenaries.** In 1776 the British hired 30,000 German mercenaries to fight in the colonies. Since many of the Germans were from the state of Hesse, all the mercenaries came to be known as **Hessians.**

The Patriot Forces

Although Britain's strength was impressive, the Patriots did have some advantages in the fighting. Most of all, they were fighting for their freedom and defending their own homes and families, while the British had no such cause and were fighting far from home. In time, many Hessians began to hate the war. When they saw how much free land there was in the colonies, some deserted to the Patriot side.

Familiarity with the land was another American advantage. The colonists knew the trails and coastlines, the good lookouts, and the best places to hide. The size of the American colonies was yet another advantage. Individual families of colonists living on scattered farms over a vast area could survive even if Britain controlled all the cities.

Finally, the Patriots had excellent leaders, including the top commander, George Washington. Washington was so devoted to his duty that he returned home to Mount Vernon, in Virginia, only once during the war and then only for a few hours. During some of the darkest days of war, it was the soldiers' respect for Washington that kept them fighting. Many soldiers stayed with the army even after their times of duty were over because of Washington's leadership.

 What was one great advantage and one great disadvantage to Great Britain in the war?

◆ FIGHTING THE WAR

A month after the signing of the Declaration of Independence, the war started to turn against the Patriots. The British attacked first at Brooklyn Heights,

Chapter 4 ◆ *75*

now a part of New York City, and easily drove off the Americans. Two weeks later, Britain's General William Howe captured New York City. With this defeat, the American army had to retreat across the East River.

By December of 1776, the Patriots were discouraged. Some soldiers deserted the army. Washington knew that an American victory was badly needed. To this end, he devised a plan that had his army cross into New Jersey to battle Hessian mercenaries. On Christmas night, Washington ordered his men to row silently across the icy Delaware River. Their target was the Hessian garrison at Trenton, New Jersey. The

Hessians had spent the evening celebrating, and the Americans hoped to catch them by surprise. The plan worked perfectly. At dawn, the Hessians stumbled out of bed to the sound of gunfire. With only five casualties, the Americans easily took Trenton. Ten days later, Washington captured nearby Princeton, New Jersey. These battles gave the Americans encouragement to continue the fighting.

 How did Washington's Christmas night plan defeat the Hessians at Trenton?

◆ **TURNING POINT OF THE WAR**

The British, spurred by their defeats at Trenton and Princeton, came up with a plan. Their plan was to have three armies meet at Albany—one was to come north from New York City, one would march from the west, and the third was to come south from Canada. If the plan worked, the New England colonies would be split from the Southern colonies. The British would then march south, seize the Southern colonies, and end the rebellion.

However, instead of moving north towards Albany, the British army in New York went south. It sailed to the head of Chesapeake Bay and disembarked. The British army overcame the Americans at Brandywine. Despite this victory, the British plan to split the colonies had failed.

Meanwhile, British general John Burgoyne (bur-goin´) led his army from Canada toward Albany. At Saratoga they faced a force of American volunteers and were defeated. After several weeks of minor fighting, the forces met again near Saratoga in October 1777. The Americans once more defeated the British. Burgoyne's army, badly outnumbered, was forced to surrender to the Americans. The map on this page shows some battles of the war.

The battle at Saratoga proved to be the turning point of the war because it sent an important message. It demonstrated to the French that the Americans could win the war. After Saratoga, France began making open war on Great Britain, and French soldiers and ships began to support the Patriots actively. In February 1778, France became the first nation to sign a treaty with the United States. In the treaty, Louis XVI recognized the new nation and agreed to supply it with military assistance.

 Why was Saratoga an important American victory?

Turning Point of the Revolution, 1776–1777

0   50   100 miles
0   50   100 kilometers

75°W   Quebec   70°W

Montreal

CANADA
(Great Britain)

45°N

St. Lawrence R.

Fort Ticonderoga

Lake Ontario

Saratoga

Oriskany

New York

Albany

Bennington

Vermont
(claimed
by NY)

(part of MA;
later became
Maine)

New
Hampshire

N
W   E
S

Boston

Massachusetts

Susquehanna R.

Delaware R.

Hudson R.

Connecticut

Rhode
Island

Brooklyn
Heights

Morristown

Pennsylvania   Trenton

Valley Forge

Princeton

New York

Philadelphia

40°N

New
Jersey

Brandywine

ATLANTIC OCEAN

Potomac R.   Maryland

Delaware

Shenandoah R.

Virginia

James R.

Yorktown

Chesapeake Bay

← American forces
✸ American victories
← British fleet and land forces
✸ British victories
• Cities

▲ **Geography** In 1776 and 1777, American and British troops fought many battles over a large land area. **Interpreting the Map** How did British forces travel between New York City and Brandywine?

◄ While the British held Philadelphia in the winter of 1777–1778, Washington and his soldiers camped outside the city at Valley Forge.

◆ VICTORY FOR THE AMERICANS

French aid came too late to help Washington and his army. Despite the victory at Saratoga, the next few months proved difficult. The British still held Philadelphia, and their army spent the winter of 1777–1778 in comfort in the city. Meanwhile, Washington's poorly clothed and poorly fed troops spent the winter at Valley Forge, outside Philadelphia. Washington's troops shivered, sickened, and died from lack of clothing and medicine. Hundreds of soldiers died during that terrible winter, and over 2,000 deserted.

War in the South

Later in 1778 the British shifted the war to the South. Here the British believed that Loyalists in large numbers were ready to join them. South Carolina and Georgia now felt the fury of the British attack. British forces captured Savannah, Georgia, in 1778 and Charleston, South Carolina, less than two years later. They burned houses and barns, killed cattle, destroyed crops, and drove the survivors into prison camps.

Yet slowly the Patriots made headway. The British might control the cities, but the Americans remained strong in rural areas. In October 1780 a force of volunteers from Tennessee, Kentucky, and North Carolina defeated a Loyalist army in western Carolina. A series of colonial victories followed. The British general commander Lord Cornwallis took his force to Yorktown, Virginia, located on a narrow **peninsula.** A peninsula is a narrow finger of land surrounded on three sides by water. At Yorktown, Cornwallis waited for British ships to bring him new supplies. But French ships got there first and blocked the British navy from resupplying Cornwallis. The British were trapped.

Final Victory

With support from soldiers sent by France, a force of American troops pounded British defenses. On October 14 a combined force of Americans and French captured two British posts. The allies were now able to fire directly into the British camp at Yorktown. On October 19, 1781, a British officer stepped out from British lines waving the white cloth of surrender. Although the war was not officially over until 1783, the British defeat at Yorktown meant that the Americans' fight for independence had been won.

The Treaty of Paris was signed on September 3, 1783. Under the treaty, Great Britain agreed to recognize the colonies as an independent nation. The United States gained all the lands between the Appalachian Mountains and the Mississippi River from the Great Lakes south to Florida.

How did France contribute to the Patriots' final victory?

◆ CONTRIBUTIONS TO VICTORY

African Americans, Hispanics, Native Americans, and women took part in the American Revolution from the beginning. Their help took many forms, all vital to the successful outcome for the United States.

Women in the Revolution

In 1774, while the all-male First Continental Congress was debating in Philadelphia, Patriot women formed the Daughters of Liberty. They refused to buy British goods and made family clothes from rough homespun, or hand-woven cloth.

When the fighting started in 1775, many women took their husbands' places on farms or at trades.

Women made arms and ammunition, provided food and clothing, and raised money to equip troops. Nearly 20,000 women marched with troops, serving as doctors, nurses, cooks, guides, and spies. Some women even took part in battle. Mary Ludwig Hays, better known as Molly Pitcher, took her place at her husband's cannon, helping to win the Battle of Monmouth, New Jersey, in 1778.

Though women played important roles in the activities of the Revolution, they found at the end of the struggle that their rights had not changed at all. In fact, though laws were written for the new nation, many years would pass before laws were enacted that gave women their full rights.

The Role of Native Americans

At first, most Native Americans tried to avoid the war by staying **neutral,** or not taking either side in the dispute. Many agreed with Little Abraham, a chief of the Mohawk, who called the fighting "a family affair" and who preferred "to sit still and see you fight it out." However, they could not remain neutral. A good deal of the fighting took place near Native American lands on the frontier. Furthermore, as settlers continued to push west of the Appalachians during the Revolution, they clashed with Native Americans over the control of lands.

Nancy Hart, like many other women, displayed courage during the war. This picture shows her confronting British soldiers who had taken over her home. ▶

Native American groups, while no longer neutral, were not united in their loyalties. The League of the Iroquois officially declared its neutrality, but the strongest of the six nations decided to support the British. The Algonquin nations of New England tended to support the Patriots. In the South, however, the Cherokee supported the British. In the West, where settlers had been taking Native American land since 1763, many Native American groups joined the British.

Hispanics and the Revolution

The American Revolution was greatly helped by Hispanic participation in the colonists' struggle for independence. Spain made vast financial contributions to help the Patriots purchase military supplies. The governor of Cuba gave funds to support Washington's Yorktown campaign.

On the battlefield, Spanish troops fought and defeated the British at St. Louis and in Michigan. One of the most effective soldiers in the war was Colonel Bernardo de Gálvez, who led a force that drove the British from along the Mississippi Valley and the Gulf of Mexico. The city of Galveston, in Texas, is named in honor of this courageous leader.

African Americans and the War

More than half a million African Americans lived in the colonies when the Revolution began. At first, the Continental Army prevented African Americans from enlisting. However, when the British offered slaves their freedom in return for fighting with them, Washington decided to accept free African Americans. About 5,000 African Americans served in the Continental Army. About 2,000 others served in the Patriot navy. African Americans fought in every major battle of the war, and their presence as drummers, spies, guides, and soldiers sometimes made the crucial difference between victory and defeat.

Despite their efforts during the Revolution, most African Americans were still enslaved. In the North, slavery was declining by the 1770s. Several states—including Vermont, New Hampshire, Massachusetts, and Pennsylvania—moved to outlaw slavery.

Elsewhere, the debate about slavery continued. With the words of the Declaration of Independence ringing in Americans' ears, it became harder for some to tolerate slavery in a nation that had been founded on equality and individual rights. As James Otis wrote,

> The colonists are by the law of nature free born, as indeed all men are, white or black.

In what ways did African Americans, Hispanics, Native Americans, and women contribute to the war?

Section 4 Review

Check Understanding

1. **Define** (a) mercenary (b) Hessian (c) peninsula (d) neutral

2. **Identify** some of the advantages the Patriots had at the outbreak of the American Revolution.

3. **Describe** the contributions women made to the war effort.

Critical Thinking

Connecting Past and Present How might your life today be different if the British had won the Revolution?

Write About Geography

Study the map of the American Revolution on page 76. Write a news article about the war during 1776–1777, using information from the map.

Chapter 4
Review

CHAPTER SUMMARY

Section 1

In the 1600s and 1700s, the French and British competed for control of the fur trade in North America. This rivalry resulted in a war that began in 1754, though it was not officially declared until 1756. In 1763, the British won the French and Indian War, giving them control of much of Canada and the land east of the Mississippi.

Section 2

To support the continuing defense of the western frontier against conflict with Native Americans, Britain imposed a number of taxes on the colonies. American colonists were furious and staged protests against the taxes and British rule. Colonists began to talk seriously of breaking away from Britain. When the colonial militia and British soldiers fought near Boston, the American Revolution began.

Section 3

The Declaration of Independence was issued on July 4, 1776. This important political document states that "all men are created equal," lists what led the Americans to break away from Britain, and officially announces that the United States is a new nation.

Section 4

Not all colonists supported the American Revolution. Many were Patriots, but some colonists remained loyal to the British crown. The war between the colonists and the British was a long one, ending in victory for the Americans. The British signed the Treaty of Paris in 1783, recognizing American independence. Although African Americans, Hispanics, Native Americans, and women played roles during the American Revolution, these groups did not yet gain their full rights.

Connecting ◆◆ Past and Present

How do current methods of protest compare with protests during colonial times?

Using Vocabulary

From the list below, select the term that best completes each sentence.

representative	muster
peninsula	preamble
denounce	Loyalist
boycott	neutral

1. When generals _____ their troops, they call them together.
2. A _____ is a person selected to act on behalf of others.
3. General Cornwallis took his army to Yorktown, located on a narrow finger of land called a _____ .
4. An American colonist who chose to side with the British during the Revolution was called a _____ .
5. The _____ , which is the first part of the Declaration of Independence, states basic principles of democracy.
6. An economic protest in which citizens refuse to buy certain goods is called a _____ .
7. The Stamp Act Congress voted to _____ the Stamp Act as an attack on colonial liberties.
8. To refrain from choosing sides over an issue is to remain _____ .

Check Understanding

1. **Explain** why the population of Britain's American colonies far outnumbered the population of New France.
2. **Describe** the reasons for the outbreak of the French and Indian War.
3. **Explain** why the British issued the Proclamation of 1763.
4. **Discuss** colonial arguments for and against independence from Britain.
5. **Identify** the reason France sided with the Patriots during the American Revolution.

6. **Identify** the major ways in which the views of Patriots clashed with those of Loyalists.

7. **Explain** why the colonists and the British did not support the Albany Plan of Union.

8. **Explain** why the Battle of Saratoga was a turning point in the war.

9. **Discuss** the important points of the Treaty of Paris of 1783.

10. **Describe** the ways in which African Americans contributed to the war effort.

Critical Thinking

1. **Understanding Cause and Effect** What was the cause of the Boston Tea Party? What were some of its effects?

2. **Drawing Conclusions** Why do you think *Common Sense* had an impact on the American Revolution?

3. **Making Inferences** Why would some Americans be disturbed by the words "all men are created equal" in the Declaration of Independence?

4. **Synthesizing Information** Discuss the reasons why Native American nations had divided loyalties during the French and Indian War and during the American Revolution.

◆ **Connecting Past and Present** Explain why the Declaration of Independence is considered one of the most important political documents in the world.

Interpreting the Timeline

Use the timeline on pages 60–61 to answer these questions.

1. How many years was the American Revolution fought?

2. In which year was the Declaration of Independence signed?

3. Though Great Britain was losing control in the American colonies, where was it expanding its empire?

Putting Skills to Work

CLASSIFYING INFORMATION

In the Building Skills lesson on page 66, you learned that classifying information helps you to recall, locate, examine, understand, and use facts. Copy the chart below. In the column labeled Event, write at least five events that led to the American Revolution. In the Year column, write the year each event occurred. In the Importance column, explain briefly the significance of the event. Use the information in the chart to write an essay about the causes of the American Revolution.

The Road to Revolution		
Event	**Year**	**Importance**

Writing to Persuade

Write a dialogue between a British citizen and an American citizen. The dialogue should include their points of view about such issues as colonial taxes, laws, and regulations imposed by Britain. In your dialogue, have each person justify his or her position.

 *Portfolio Project*

MAPPING THE REVOLUTION

Draw or trace a map that shows the 13 colonies. Label the places where battles and other important events took place. Then draw a line from each mark on the map to the margin of your paper. Write a two-sentence description of the event, where it happened, and its main significance. Display your map for the class and then file it in your portfolio.

Connecting Past and Present

THE FUR TRADE

People have long valued wearing fur not only for its beauty and warmth but also for the high status it seems to offer. Historically, fur has had important economic and political connections. During the 1600s the desire for fur stimulated much of the early exploration in North America. Today, portions of the economy of some nations are threatened because wildlife protection and animal rights groups are protesting the raising and trapping of animals for fur.

Then During the sixteenth, seventeenth, and eighteenth centuries in Europe, people wore clothing made of fur. Even then, furs were costly because of the expense of importing the skins and then sewing them together into garments. When it became clear that North America was rich in fur-bearing animals, Europeans competed to control the lands and the animals that lived there. The scramble for beaver and other animal pelts, or skins, led the French and English to trade and trap throughout New England, the Great Lakes region, and the Ohio River Valley—and then range north and west in search of more fur. Furs were so valuable that they helped spark the French and Indian War. The fur trade prospered until the mid-1800s, when fur-bearing animals became scarce.

Now Today, the treatment of animals is more controversial than it was in the 1600s and 1700s. People for the Ethical Treatment of Animals (PETA), Coalition to Abolish the Fur Trade (CAFT), and other animal protection groups stage demonstrations in protest of the inhumane treatment of animals, particularly those used to make fur coats. Their efforts have led to the development of fur ranches, where animals are bred scientifically, and to padded traps that do not inflict pain or injury. These more humane methods have not silenced the protesters, however. PETA and CAFT members, who number over 400,000 worldwide, have used violent tactics to disrupt the fur business and influence people not to wear fur. During the 1980s and 1990s, considerable numbers of fur stores in the United States closed due to lack of business. With fake fur becoming more popular, it is clear that the efforts of these protesters influenced many people's notions of what is fashionable.

▲ Anti-fur protesters rally in New York City on a day they called "Fur Free Friday."

You Decide

1. What would the French fur traders in the 1600s and 1700s have thought about PETA and CAFT?

2. Should wearing fur be a political and economic issue or a matter of individual choice? Explain your point of view and give some examples.

Growth of a New Nation 1780–1860

> **"** ...few of us are natives of the country, we are all adventurers, coming from a distance to seek a fortune or make a name; we had very little to bring with us...migration was a necessity of life. **"**
>
> *Edward Bates, 1849, speaking about what it felt like to be an immigrant to the United States*

▲ *The engraving above shows immigrants arriving in New York City in the 1850s. The news of opportunities in the United States brought people from all over the world.* ◈ **Connecting Past and Present** *What conclusions about immigration can you draw from the busy port scene above? What are some of the reasons people emigrate to the United States today?*

Chapter 5
Americans Build a New Government 1780–1815

CHAPTER PREVIEW

Section 1 The Articles of Confederation

With independence won, the leaders of the United States set themselves to the task of forming a new government.

Section 2 Creating a Constitution

When the weaknesses of the Articles of Confederation became apparent, the nation's leaders created a new constitution for a strong federal government.

Section 3 Approving the Constitution

Supporters of the U.S. Constitution worked hard to get the document approved. Later, the Bill of Rights was added to the Constitution.

Section 4 The New Government Begins

George Washington, John Adams, and Thomas Jefferson provided strong leadership in the new nation. The Louisiana Purchase greatly enlarged the country's territory.

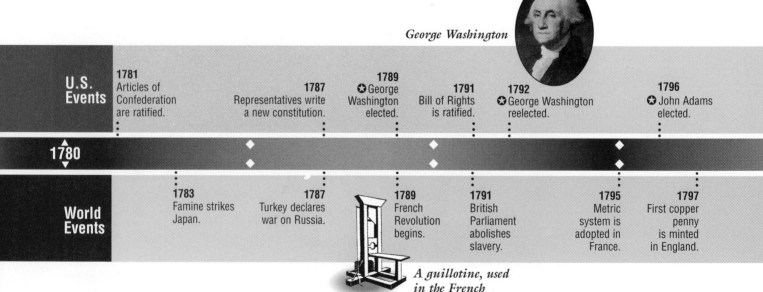

George Washington

U.S. Events

1781 Articles of Confederation are ratified.

1787 Representatives write a new constitution.

1789 ✪ George Washington elected.

1791 Bill of Rights is ratified.

1792 ✪ George Washington reelected.

1796 ✪ John Adams elected.

1780

World Events

1783 Famine strikes Japan.

1787 Turkey declares war on Russia.

1789 French Revolution begins.

1791 British Parliament abolishes slavery.

1795 Metric system is adopted in France.

1797 First copper penny is minted in England.

A guillotine, used in the French Revolution

Portfolio Project

FROM BILL TO LAW

The way in which laws are made is one of the most important elements in the U.S. Constitution. Passing a law is one way the government can go about solving its problems. In this chapter, you will learn how a bill becomes a law. At the end of the chapter, you will write a proposal for a bill and create a flow chart to show the process your bill would follow to become a law.

▲ On September 17, 1787, George Washington looked on as delegates from the 13 colonies signed the Constitution of the United States. **◆◆ Connecting Past and Present** *How does the painting reflect the magnitude of the event? What recent national event would you choose to commemorate with a work of art?*

Lewis and Clark with their guide, Sacajawea

1800
✪ Thomas Jefferson elected.

1803
Louisiana Territory is purchased.

1804
✪ Thomas Jefferson reelected.
Lewis and Clark begin journey.

1808
✪ James Madison elected.

1812
✪ James Madison reelected.
United States declares war on Great Britain.

1815

1804
Napoleon crowns himself emperor of France.
Ludwig van Beethoven composes Symphony No. 3.

Ludwig van Beethoven

1810
Mexicans fight for independence.

1813
Jane Austen's novel *Pride and Prejudice* is published.

Father Hidalgo, Mexican priest and revolutionary leader

The Articles of Confederation

PREVIEW

Objectives

- To explain the purpose of the Articles of Confederation

- To examine how settlers were encouraged to move to the Northwest Territory

- To examine the weaknesses of the Articles of Confederation

Vocabulary

constitution   survey

confederation   treasury

ratify

When the American Revolution ended, the 13 colonies had won independence from Great Britain. Now, these states faced the task of forming a government that would create a single nation. Many Americans understood that this was a great challenge. One of them was Dr. Benjamin Rush, a well-known American physician and patriot, who said,

> The American war is over, but this is far from being the case with the American revolution. . . . nothing but the first act of a great drama is closed.

◆ THE FIRST GOVERNMENT

Once Americans declared their independence from Britain in 1776, they had to begin governing themselves. The first step was to write a **constitution,** a document that states the principles according to which a nation is governed.

Because many Americans felt more loyal to their state than to the nation, establishing a national government would be a difficult task. However, some

Americans were ready to declare loyalty to the new nation. They agreed with Patrick Henry who said, "I am not a Virginian, sir, but an American." Also, having united in the war against the British, Americans had come together for a common goal. In June 1776, the Continental Congress began work on a plan for a national government.

The Continental Congress decided to create a **confederation** of states. A confederation is a union of independent states or nations that decide to work together. In November 1777, the Continental Congress made public their plan of government. Their constitution was called the Articles of Confederation.

Based on their experience with the British king and Parliament, most Americans were distrustful of a strong central government. Therefore, the Articles left more power in the hands of the state governments than in the hands of the national government. In Congress, each state had one vote, regardless of the size of its population. Most laws needed the support of at least nine states to be passed. Approval of major changes to the Articles of Confederation required agreement by all 13 states.

To be official, the Articles of Confederation had to be **ratified,** or approved, by all 13 states. Maryland refused to ratify unless states gave up lands they claimed west of the Appalachian Mountains. Maryland worried that larger states would become too powerful if they were allowed to keep all their western territories. The dispute dragged on for more than two years. Finally, the states claiming western lands agreed to Maryland's demand, and the Articles of Confederation officially took effect on March 1, 1781.

? **Why did the Americans create the Articles of Confederation?**

◆ THE NORTHWEST TERRITORY

The problem facing the national government was how to organize and govern the western lands given up by the states. To solve the problem, Congress passed two laws.

The Land Ordinance of 1785 set up a method of selling the land, as shown on the map and chart on page 87. It provided for a **survey** of the region. A survey is an examination and measurement of a region to determine its boundaries. Each region would be divided into townships consisting of 36 sections. Congress planned to sell sections to settlers for $640 each. A section would be one square mile in area, which settlers could sell to individuals in smaller units. One section in every township was set aside to support public schools.

The second law, the Northwest Ordinance (1787), was a plan to govern the lands. It provided that the Northwest be divided into territories. When the population of a territory reached 60,000, it could apply for statehood. New states were required to meet two conditions: government representatives must be elected by the people, and slavery was prohibited. Eventually, the Northwest Territory was divided into five states: Ohio, Indiana, Illinois, Michigan, and Wisconsin.

 What was the purpose of the Northwest Ordinance?

◆ WEAKNESSES OF THE ARTICLES

The Northwest Ordinance was a success, but the weaknesses of the Articles of Confederation soon would become obvious. Under the Articles, the Congress had limited powers. Congress could declare war but could not enforce treaties with other countries. It could not regulate trade between states, or even between states and foreign countries. Congress could issue money, but it did not have the power to collect taxes. In addition, the government had no president to carry out laws passed by Congress. Other difficulties would arise because no national court system was set up.

The Problem of Debt

Without the power to collect taxes, the national government had no **treasury,** or reserve of money. With no reserves of money, the first major problem for Congress to tackle was the country's debt. During the Revolution, the United States borrowed money from individuals and from foreign countries. Congress, without the power to tax, could not force the states to contribute money to pay the debt. To get money, Congress had to ask each state for it.

The national debt was increasing. Money was owed to many people, and they were growing impatient. The soldiers who had served in the Continental Army had not been paid. Farmers demanded money for the food they had provided throughout the Revolution. The situation caused veterans and farmers to talk of rebellion.

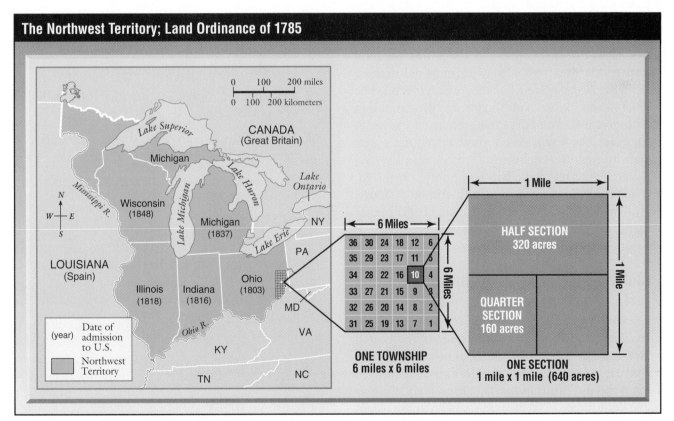

▲ **Economics** *Settlers could purchase one section and divide it into smaller units.*
Interpreting the Map and Chart *What was the western boundary of the territory?*

Study Hint

As you read, write down questions that occur to you. While reading Chapter 5, compose questions about content that you do not understand. When you complete the chapter, answer the questions or ask questions in class to get the answers. Keep these questions and answers as a guide to help you study.

Shays' Rebellion

One of the worst rebellions faced by the new United States government was staged by farmers in western Massachusetts in 1786. The Massachusetts legislators, determined to pay off the state's large debts, raised taxes. Not able to pay the taxes, farmers grew worried about losing their land. They demanded lower taxes on their farms and lower fees for local courts and lawyers. When Massachusetts did nothing to help the farmers, a rebellion broke out. It was led by Daniel Shays, who had fought in the American Revolution at Bunker Hill, Lexington, and Saratoga. A poor man, Shays was deeply troubled by the state's actions to pay off its debts.

Because Shays' Rebellion was poorly organized, the state militia stopped it quickly. Although Shays' Rebellion failed, it added to the growing belief among Americans that something had to be done to strengthen the central government.

Problems with Foreign Countries

The weak U.S. government also ran into difficulties with other countries. Powerful foreign nations, such as Great Britain and Spain, took advantage of the United States. Though still buying American raw materials and manufactured goods, the British forbade American farmers and merchants from selling many types of goods in the West Indies. Even more serious, the British would not evacuate forts and trading posts in the Northwest Territory, saying that the posts would be held until the states paid debts owed to British citizens. Britain's refusal to leave violated the 1783 peace treaty, but there was little the United States could do about it.

The United States also had problems with Spain. Spain would not allow Americans to use the port of New Orleans, in Louisiana, to export their goods. Spain also refused to allow Americans to trade with its Latin American colonies. Even though Congress was authorized to deal with foreign countries, it had trouble gaining respect abroad for the United States.

With each passing year, it was becoming clearer that the Articles of Confederation were not working. The government could not solve the country's economic, political, and foreign policy problems. By 1787, the time had come to bring the country's leaders together to strengthen the government.

 What were two weaknesses of the Articles of Confederation?

Section 1 Review

Check Understanding

1. **Define** (a) constitution (b) confederation (c) ratify (d) survey (e) treasury

2. **Describe** the Americans' need for the Articles of Confederation.

3. **Explain** why Congress was unable to pay its debts under the Articles of Confederation.

4. **Analyze** why farmers in western Massachusetts revolted in 1786.

Critical Thinking

Connecting Past and Present Patrick Henry stated, "I am not a Virginian, sir, but an American." Do you think of yourself primarily as a citizen of your state, or as a citizen of the United States? Why?

Write About Government

Write a paragraph about the plan to establish statehood in the Northwest Territory.

BUILDING SKILLS

Using Graphic Organizers: The Articles of Confederation

Graphic organizers are useful tools to organize information in a variety of ways. A graphic organizer is a kind of chart that shows how ideas relate to one another. Types of graphic organizers include flow charts, spider diagrams, word webs, cause and effect charts, and charts of main idea and details.

Here's How

Follow these steps to develop one type of graphic organizer, a main idea and detail chart:

1. Identify a topic or main idea. Use it for the heading or title.
2. Create a chart with the main idea in the large box; then list supporting details in the smaller boxes.
3. Use the information on the chart to summarize ideas or draw conclusions about the material you have read.

Here's Why

Graphic organizers show the connections between ideas. They help you visualize related ideas, follow steps in a process, or compare and contrast two or more ideas. A graphic organizer provides an effective way to take notes while you read, and it is a good source of information while you study for a test.

Practice the Skill

Study the main idea and detail chart on this page. Practice reading it by answering the questions that follow:

1. What is the main idea of the chart?
2. What are the supporting details?
3. Copy the chart on a piece of paper. Add two more details about weaknesses of the Articles of Confederation.

Apply the Skill

As you read Section 2, use what you have learned about the Articles of Confederation and the new Constitution to create a chart of comparison and contrast. Use the following heads as main ideas: Characteristics of the Articles of Confederation, Characteristics of the New Constitutional Government. Under each head, list details that describe characteristics of each government. Then write a brief paragraph summarizing the characteristics and comparing strengths and weaknesses of each government.

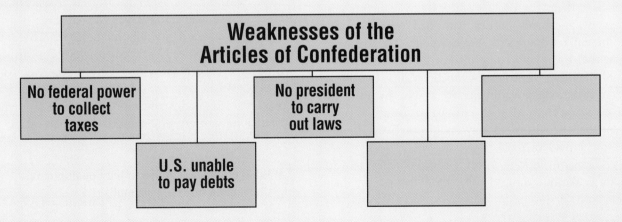

Weaknesses of the Articles of Confederation

- No federal power to collect taxes
- U.S. unable to pay debts
- No president to carry out laws

Creating a Constitution

PREVIEW

Objectives

• To determine why delegates met in Philadelphia in 1787

• To discuss the role of compromise at the Constitutional Convention

• To describe the principal ideas of the U.S. Constitution

Vocabulary

compromise
bicameral
electoral college
federalism
tariff

separation of powers
unconstitutional
checks and balances
veto

In May 1787, representatives from 12 states gathered in Philadelphia for a Constitutional Convention. Only Rhode Island did not attend. Some leaders in that state feared that a strong central government would take away power the state had gained. The Convention's goal was to solve the problems caused by the Articles of Confederation. In the end, the representatives drafted an entirely new constitution.

◆ THE CONSTITUTIONAL CONVENTION

The delegates who came to Philadelphia were leaders in their states. Many were wealthy young men in their twenties and thirties who had served in the Continental Congress or in the Army. They realized that the time had come to revise the Articles of Confederation. Most delegates believed that creating a stronger national government would solve many of the nation's problems. Most also wished to create a government that would prevent any one group from gaining too much power.

The Convention's most respected delegate was George Washington, of Virginia. One of the first things the Convention did was to elect Washington

president of the convention. James Madison also belonged to the Virginia delegation. At age 36, Madison's knowledge of both history and politics enabled him to have a great influence on the meeting. Madison took detailed notes at the Convention. These notes later became important pieces of information to historians. After the Convention, Madison remarked,

> **I chose a seat in front of the presiding member, with the other members on my right and left hand. In this favorable position for hearing all that passed, I noted . . . what was read from the chair or spoken by the members; . . . I was not absent a single day, nor more than a casual fraction of an hour in any day; so that I could not have lost a single speech, unless a very short one.**

Another delegate with an outstanding reputation was Alexander Hamilton, of New York. Hamilton had worked closely with Washington during the Revolution. Only 30 years old, Hamilton was one of the most forceful supporters of a strong national government. The oldest delegate at the Convention was Benjamin Franklin of Pennsylvania, who was 81. The delegates respected him for his common sense and wisdom.

Before beginning its work, the Constitutional Convention set a number of rules. The first was that each state would have one vote. The Convention also adopted a rule of secrecy to allow delegates to speak freely. This was important because they did not want the press or local people to influence their talks. They wanted to be free to speak their minds openly. The rule of secrecy was carefully kept. To make sure that outsiders could not listen in, the large windows of Philadelphia's State House were nailed shut.

Secrecy made it possible for delegates to control the debate. As James Madison said, "No Constitution would ever have been adopted by the convention if the debates had been public." Shutting the windows, however, made their work more difficult. Summers in Philadelphia are hot and humid. The men inside the State House worked in uncomfortable heat.

 What did the delegates to the Constitutional Convention hope to accomplish?

▲ Philadelphia had become one of the largest cities in the United States by the time the Constitutional Convention met there in 1787.

◆ COMPROMISES SHAPE THE CONSTITUTION

Although most delegates believed in a strong national government, they disagreed about how that government should be organized. It would take a great deal of **compromise** to write the Constitution. A compromise is a settlement of differences in which both sides give up something they want.

The Great Compromise

One of the most serious issues the delegates faced was the question of representation. Under the Articles of Confederation, all states had one vote in Congress. This meant that Rhode Island, with its small population, had power equal to that of Virginia, with its large population.

To make representation more directly linked to population, James Madison and Edmund Randolph, both of Virginia, proposed the Virginia, or "large states," Plan. The plan called for a national government divided into three branches, or parts: the legislative, executive, and judicial branches. The legislative branch would be responsible for passing laws. The executive branch would enforce, or carry out, the laws. The judicial branch would evaluate laws to make sure they were fair.

The Virginia Plan recommended a **bicameral** Congress. That meant it would have two legislative houses with large states having more votes in both houses. Thus, the Virginia Plan would shift power from the smaller to the larger states.

The smaller states objected strongly to the Virginia Plan. They backed the New Jersey, or small states, Plan. According to the New Jersey Plan, Congress would consist of only one house, with each state having one vote. It also called for a three-branch government.

The delegates finally reached a compromise. There would be a bicameral Congress, with an upper and a lower house. In the upper house—the Senate—there always would be two senators and two votes for each state. In the lower house—the House of Representatives—representation and number of votes would be based on population. The delegates finally approved this plan, later called the Great Compromise.

The Three-Fifths Compromise

After the debate on representation was settled, the delegates argued over another sensitive issue. In figuring out the population of a state, how were enslaved people to be counted? Northerners pointed out that Southerners considered enslaved people to be property, not human beings. Therefore, Northerners argued, enslaved people should not be counted in determining representation in Congress. Southerners said that slaves should be counted. If enslaved African Americans were counted, the South would have more representatives in Congress and therefore more power.

The Convention seemed headed for failure. Finally, the delegates to the Convention reached another compromise. They agreed to count three fifths of the slave population in any state when determining representation in Congress. To determine the population of a state, five enslaved people would be counted as three people.

With the question of representation resolved, the issue of slavery caused yet another debate. Many northern delegates wanted the slave trade to be stopped completely. The southern states opposed such a ban, claiming that it would ruin their economy. Again, Convention delegates reached a compromise. The slave trade would continue for 20 years. After that period, Congress could regulate the trade if it wished.

Signing the Constitution

The delegates to the Constitutional Convention worked long hours through the hot summer making more compromises and finalizing details. On September 17, 1787, the delegates met to hear a final reading of the Constitution. Not all delegates were happy with the results. There were rumors that some would not sign.

After the reading, Benjamin Franklin asked for the delegates' attention. He was too weak to deliver his speech, so James Wilson read it. Franklin wrote that he doubted whether:

> any other convention . . . may be able to make a better constitution. . . .
> It . . . astonishes me . . . to find this system approaching so near perfection as it does. . . . Thus I consent to this Constitution because I expect no better, and because I am not sure it is not the best.

Franklin's plea did not convince all the delegates. However, most delegates signed the Constitution. As he watched, Franklin looked toward Washington's chair. A rising sun was painted on its back. Franklin said that during the Convention he had often looked at the sun on the chair "without being able to tell whether it was rising or setting." Now, he added, "I have the happiness to know that it is a rising and not a setting sun."

 What differences of opinion led to the Three-Fifths Compromise?

◆ IDEAS THAT FORM OUR GOVERNMENT

The United States of America was the first nation to write a constitution that set out its principles of government. However, many of the basic ideas about government and the rights of the people expressed in the Constitution were drawn from other sources.

The ideas of John Locke, a seventeenth-century Englishman, influenced a number of members of the Constitutional Convention. Locke argued that people set up governments to protect their rights, and they can remove governments that fail in that duty. Voltaire, a French philosopher, contributed the ideals of personal liberties and certain rights that were due to everyone.

Some historians believe that the delegates to the Constitutional Convention were influenced by the way in which the Iroquois organized their government. The Iroquois had formed a union called the League of the Iroquois that included five Iroquois nations. The League was formed of delegates from each nation. Each nation had one vote, but each also retained the right to govern itself at the local level. In the same way, the delegates to the Constitutional Convention decided to create a system of government with two levels—a national level and a state level.

Government of and by the People

The most important principle in the Constitution of the United States is clearly stated in its introduction, or Preamble. The Preamble begins, "We the people of the United States." This statement says that the government gets its power from the people, even though many of the people were not allowed to participate in its early development. The Preamble also states the purpose of the Constitution: to establish a united country that will provide justice, security, and liberty for the American people.

The Constitution established a powerful national government that stood apart from state governments. Congress was elected directly by the people. The President, a strong executive who served the nation as a whole, was not elected directly by the people. The founders set up an **electoral college** to select the President and Vice President. Each state had a number of votes in the electoral college equal to its total number of representatives in Congress. When people vote, they are actually voting for electors who are pledged to a particular team of candidates. This system is still in effect today.

A Framework for Government

The Constitution set up a government according to the principles of **federalism.** In a federal system of government, power is divided between national government and state governments.

Under the Constitution, the national, or federal, government has many powers. One of the most important is the power to collect taxes. The United States could now raise money to pay its expenses without depending on state legislatures. The federal government could also place **tariffs** on imported goods. A tariff is a system of duties placed on imports or exports.

The Constitution also gave the federal government the power to make treaties with foreign countries and to maintain an army and a navy. The government could also regulate interstate trade. Other powers include Congress's ability to make laws to carry out the government's duties. The Constitution gave Congress the right to make all laws that shall be "necessary and proper" to carry out the powers of the federal government. Called the Elastic Clause, this clause allows Congress to stretch its power to pass laws it finds necessary.

The Constitution is the highest law of the land. Though it grants the states a number of powers, it is more powerful than the laws of any one state. Even the members of state legislatures are required to take an oath to support the U.S. Constitution. At the same time, there are limits on what the federal government can do. The Constitution grants the states a number of powers. The chart on this page shows how power is shared between the national and state governments.

Three Branches of Government

The Constitution divided the federal government into three branches, each with separate duties and powers. These branches are the legislative, executive, and judicial. The system of dividing the powers of government among different branches is called **separation of powers.**

Congress, the legislative branch of the federal government, is divided into two houses: the Senate and House of Representatives. The major function of Congress is to make the laws for the country. It also has the power to declare war and to remove a President from office. The President is the head of the executive branch of the federal government. The executive branch carries out the laws passed by Congress. The President is commander-in-chief of the armed forces. With the approval of the Senate, the President has the power to appoint federal judges and to make treaties with foreign powers.

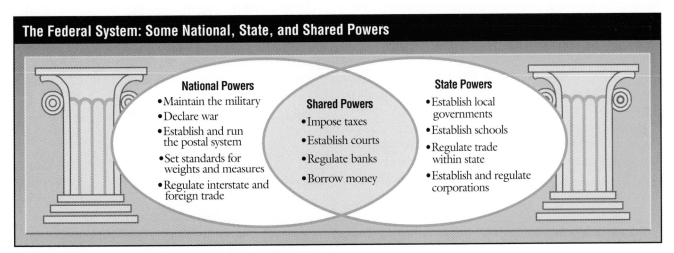

The Federal System: Some National, State, and Shared Powers

National Powers
- Maintain the military
- Declare war
- Establish and run the postal system
- Set standards for weights and measures
- Regulate interstate and foreign trade

Shared Powers
- Impose taxes
- Establish courts
- Regulate banks
- Borrow money

State Powers
- Establish local governments
- Establish schools
- Regulate trade within state
- Establish and regulate corporations

▲ **Government** *The Constitution divided the responsibility for running the country between the state and the national governments.* **Interpreting the Chart** *Which powers do state governments and the national government share?*

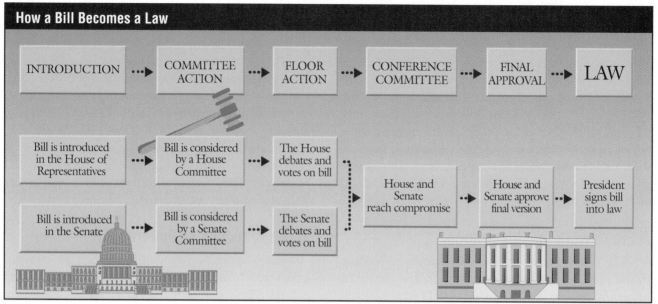

How a Bill Becomes a Law

INTRODUCTION ···► COMMITTEE ACTION ···► FLOOR ACTION ···► CONFERENCE COMMITTEE ···► FINAL APPROVAL ···► LAW

Bill is introduced in the House of Representatives ···► Bill is considered by a House Committee ···► The House debates and votes on bill

Bill is introduced in the Senate ···► Bill is considered by a Senate Committee ···► The Senate debates and votes on bill

House and Senate reach compromise ···► House and Senate approve final version ···► President signs bill into law

▲ **Government** *This chart shows the process by which a bill becomes a law in the United States.* **Interpreting the Chart** *Which branches of the federal government are involved in passing a law?*

The judicial branch has the power to interpret federal laws. The most important federal court is the U.S. Supreme Court, which has the final word on what federal laws mean. The Supreme Court decides if a law is **unconstitutional,** or violates the Constitution.

Checks and Balances

The delegates of Philadelphia wanted to create a strong central government, but they were also concerned about the possible misuse of power. They tried to prevent misuse by creating a system of **checks and balances.** This system makes sure that each branch of government has powers that limit and control those of the other branches. For example, the President is commander-in-chief of the armed forces, but only Congress can declare war. The President can **veto,** or reject, a law passed by Congress, but Congress can override the veto with a two-thirds majority. The President can make a treaty with a foreign nation, but the Senate must approve it. Congress can pass a law and the President can sign it, but the Supreme Court can rule the law unconstitutional. These are a few examples of how the powers of each branch of the government are checked, or restrained, by the others.

What are two ways that the Constitution protects the American people?

Section 2 Review

Check Understanding

1. **Define** (a) compromise (b) bicameral (c) electoral college (d) federalism (e) tariff (f) separation of powers (g) unconstitutional (h) checks and balances (i) veto

2. **Describe** the provisions of the "Great Compromise."

3. **Name** two powers of the executive branch.

Critical Thinking

Comparing and Contrasting What were the similarities and differences between the Constitution and the Articles of Confederation?

Write About Government

◆ **Connecting Past and Present** At the Constitutional Convention, the delegates adopted a rule of secrecy. Explain in writing how this differs from today's coverage of congressional meetings.

Section 3

Approving the Constitution

PREVIEW

Objectives

- To compare the points of view of the Federalists and Antifederalists

- To explain how the Constitution was ratified

- To indicate how the Bill of Rights expanded Americans' freedoms

Vocabulary

Federalist

Antifederalist

bill of rights

amend

On September 28, 1787, the Constitutional Convention met to carry out its last important task. It voted to send the new Constitution to the states for approval. Before the Constitution could go into effect, 9 of the 13 states had to ratify it.

◆ DEBATING THE CONSTITUTION

Delegates to the Constitutional Convention included those who supported a strong central government and those who did not. Those who favored the Constitution and a strong central government were called **Federalists.** Led by bankers, landowners, and other business people, they wanted a strong central government to protect their interests. Among them were George Washington, James Madison, and John Adams.

The opponents of the new Constitution, called **Antifederalists,** were mainly small farmers and shopkeepers. To them, liberty was more important than property. They included Patrick Henry, Governor George Clinton of New York, and Governor John Hancock of Massachusetts.

The Federalists

Many Federalist leaders had worked together at the Convention. Their goal was to win acceptance of the Constitution.

The best-known arguments for the Constitution were made in *The Federalist Papers,* a series of 85 essays written by James Madison, Alexander Hamilton, and John Jay. They appeared in a New York newspaper between October 1787 and April 1788. The most famous of these essays is *Federalist No. 10* by James Madison. In it he argued that the Constitution would protect the rights of all citizens. He said that the Constitution contained safeguards that would not allow any group to gain too much power. He also pointed out that the Constitution left the states with important powers.

Alexander Hamilton made another argument to support the Constitution and a strong central government. He said that a government had to be strong enough to protect its people against foreign powers. Hamilton warned,

> No government could give us . . . happiness at home, which did not possess [enough] . . . strength to make us respectable abroad.

The Antifederalists

The Antifederalists feared that the Constitution gave too much power to the national government. Many believed that the federal government would become like the British monarchy.

One Antifederalist said the Constitution had been written

> by a few tyrants, whose views are to lord it over the rest of their fellow citizens.

Patrick Henry, a respected lawmaker and speaker from Virginia, said that the Constitution was a threat to liberty. He said that people at the state and local level knew best what their needs were. It made no sense to give so much power to "the chosen few who go to Congress."

Another Virginian, Richard Henry Lee, wrote an attack on the Constitution called *Letters from a Federal Farmer.* He said that the changes made in the Constitution went too far. The Constitution had left the states without any direct role in the national government. Lee also complained that the Constitution did not guarantee the basic liberties and rights that the people had fought so hard to obtain.

❓ **What was the main difference between the Federalists and the Antifederalists?**

◆ RATIFYING THE CONSTITUTION

The Federalists got off to a fast start in their campaign to ratify the Constitution. In December, Delaware became the first state to ratify, followed by Pennsylvania and New Jersey. In January 1788, Georgia and Connecticut did the same.

Opposition in Massachusetts

Massachusetts was an important state with a large population. It had played a leading role in the Revolution. The Constitution had well-known supporters from Massachusetts, such as Paul Revere. However, Massachusetts was the first state in which the Constitution ran into serious opposition. A number of prominent people, including patriot Samuel Adams and Governor John Hancock, were against ratification.

With such opposition, the vote at the Massachusetts convention was going to be close. The Federalists

gained an important supporter when Hancock switched sides. Hancock suggested that a **bill of rights** be added to the Constitution. A bill of rights would be a list of basic freedoms for all people. With such guarantees of their freedom, Hancock believed that Americans would never be provoked to rebel again. Hancock's suggestion was attached to the motion for ratification. Other Antifederalists then agreed to support ratification. The motion was approved in February by a slim margin.

Ratification

By the end of May, Maryland and South Carolina had also ratified the Constitution. That brought the total number of states to eight, one short of the necessary number. The prospects for ratification did not look good in North Carolina or Rhode Island. Virginia and New York also had not ratified. Since they were two of the largest states, the Federalists desperately needed these states to vote in favor of the Constitution.

While the debate in Virginia dragged on, New Hampshire voted to ratify on June 21, 1788. Officially, the Constitution was now in force. Still, ratification by Virginia and New York was critical to the future of the new nation.

Patriotic Americans celebrated the ratification of the Constitution with banners and parades. This float was part of the New York City celebration. ▶

THE BILL OF RIGHTS

Amendment 1
Guarantees freedom of religion, speech, and the press, and the right to assemble.

Amendment 2
Guarantees the right to bear arms.

Amendment 3
Sets conditions for housing of soldiers.

Amendment 4
Prohibits searches and seizures without warrants.

Amendment 5
Guarantees due process of law.

Amendment 6
Guarantees the right to a jury trial in criminal cases.

Amendment 7
Guarantees the right to a jury trial in civil cases.

Amendment 8
Prohibits excessive fines and cruel and unusual punishment.

Amendment 9
Gives rights not mentioned in the Constitution to the people.

Amendment 10
Reserves powers not delegated to the national government for the states.

You may read the Constitution on pages 692–711

▲ **Citizenship** *The Bill of Rights was ratified in 1791.*
Interpreting the Chart *Which amendment guarantees the right to disagree with the government?*

On June 25, despite the opposition of Patrick Henry, Virginia ratified the Constitution. Like Massachusetts and several other states, Virginia called for a bill of rights. When the news from Virginia reached New York, it too fell into line. The struggle to ratify the Constitution had been hard fought and the victory narrow, but the Federalists had realized their goal.

North Carolina ratified the Constitution in November. Rhode Island did so in May 1790. The country had already held its first national election, electing Washington as President, in January 1789.

The Bill of Rights

When the Antifederalists strongly complained that the Constitution failed to protect individual liberties such as freedom of speech and freedom of religion, the Federalists presented a plan. Their plan was a way to **amend**, or change, the Constitution.

The Constitution is often called "a living document" because it allows for amendments, or additions and changes. When the Constitution was ratified, one of the first tasks of Congress was to create the Bill of Rights, the first ten amendments to the Constitution. By 1791 the states had ratified the Bill of Rights.

The first eight amendments protect individual rights such as speech, religion, assembly, and trial by jury. They also describe procedures that courts must follow when trying people for crimes. The Fifth Amendment to the Constitution says that no person "shall . . . be deprived of life, liberty, or property, without due process of law." Brief summaries of the first ten amendments to the Constitution are listed in the chart on this page.

? What are three rights guaranteed by the Bill of Rights?

Section 3 Review

Check Understanding

1. **Define** (a) Federalist (b) Antifederalist (c) bill of rights (d) amend

2. **Describe** a major concern of the Antifederalists.

3. **Identify** the number of states needed to ratify the Constitution for it to go into effect.

4. **Explain** the purpose of the Bill of Rights.

Critical Thinking

◆ **Connecting Past and Present** The Bill of Rights was written to protect individual rights. If you were adding a new amendment to the Bill of Rights, what would it be? Explain your choice.

Write About Government

Write a letter to persuade a friend to support ratification of the Constitution in 1788.

Section 4

The New Government Begins

PREVIEW

Objectives

- To describe the early accomplishments of the young nation
- To compare the Federalists and the Democratic-Republicans
- To analyze the causes and effects of the War of 1812

Vocabulary

inauguration	judicial review
Cabinet	impressment
bond	embargo
precedent	nationalism
nullify	

The new government of the United States faced many challenges. Important issues were national unity and independence. Ahead were the tasks of building a strong political system and a sound economy.

◆ THE FIRST PRESIDENT AND HIS GOVERNMENT

George Washington's **inauguration** as the first President of the United States under the Constitution took place on April 30, 1789, in New York City. An inauguration is a formal ceremony to officially induct a President into office. In President Washington's inaugural address, he spoke of the importance of representative government.

Building the New Government

Congress and the President began setting up a new government immediately. Congress passed laws establishing three executive departments under the President: the Departments of State, of War, and of the Treasury. Congress also set up the offices of

Attorney General and Postmaster General. The heads of these five departments were called the **Cabinet.**

The Judiciary Law set up the federal judiciary system with three levels. At the top was the Supreme Court made up of six justices, one of them the Chief Justice.

Building a Strong Economy

When George Washington took office, the country was 50 million dollars in debt. Most of the debt was due to the Revolutionary War. The U.S. government, however, had almost no money.

Washington appointed Alexander Hamilton to be Secretary of the Treasury. Hamilton wanted the government to honor its debts. He said the United States should issue **bonds** for the money it owed and pay them off over time. A bond is a certificate of debt that a government issues to raise money. The bonds are sold with the promise of paying back the buyer with interest.

The southern states argued against Hamilton's plan. Most southern states had already paid their war debts. They did not want to be responsible for the debts of the rest of the country.

Congress debated Hamilton's plan furiously. James Madison led the opposition. Supporters of Hamilton and Madison argued with each other. There was even talk that the union might break up. However, in June 1790, Hamilton, Madison, and Jefferson worked out a compromise. Hamilton's bond plan would be adopted. In return, the nation's new capital would be in the South. It would be located along the Potomac River between Virginia and Maryland. At first called Federal City, it was renamed in Washington's honor after his death.

Debate Over the National Bank

Hamilton next suggested establishing a national bank. In 1791, Congress set up the Bank of the United States to hold taxes the government collected and to issue paper money. Hamilton believed that the Bank of the United States would help the nation's economy grow.

However, a number of people, including Thomas Jefferson, were opposed to the bank. Jefferson believed that the bank gave too much power to the federal government and to the wealthy investors who would control the bank. Besides, Jefferson asked, where in the Constitution was Congress permitted to establish a bank? Jefferson said that any powers not specifically given to the federal government belonged to the states.

◄ *The liquor tax angered farmers in Pennsylvania, who protested by tarring and feathering the tax collectors.*

Hamilton believed in the establishment of the bank. He explained that the Elastic Clause gave Congress the power to make all laws that were "necessary and proper" to carry out its duties. Hamilton was convinced that the bank helped the government carry out its economic functions.

Hamilton also wanted to put a tariff on foreign goods brought into the United States. He felt that taxes would make foreign goods more expensive, encouraging people to buy American goods instead. Taxes on imports, Hamilton maintained, would help American industry. Arguments about tariffs arose between the North and the South. Although tariffs would help northern manufacturers, southern farmers resented paying more for foreign goods.

The Whiskey Rebellion

Congress passed a bill in 1791 that taxed all liquor made and sold in the nation. This tax led to one of the young nation's most serious crises: the Whiskey Rebellion. The Whiskey Rebellion began in western Pennsylvania, where farmers raised corn, sometimes turning it into whiskey. Whiskey was easy to ship and was very profitable.

Faced with a tax, farmers started to rebel. In the spring of 1794, angry farmers began attacking tax collectors. About 7,000 farmers marched to the city of Pittsburgh, Pennsylvania, to protest the whiskey tax. President Washington decided to take forceful action. He ordered more than 13,000 militia to the region.

When the farmers heard that soldiers were coming, the rebellion ended immediately. President Washington had succeeded in showing that the new government would not tolerate rebellion.

George Washington set many such **precedents,** or examples, in his two terms as President. One of the most important was his decision to serve only two terms in office.

In Washington's farewell speech, he urged the nation to stay unified. He also warned of the dangers of getting involved in foreign affairs. He said,

> 'Tis our true policy to steer clear of permanent alliances with any portion of the foreign world.

What were two ways in which President Washington demonstrated strong leadership?

◆ THE FIRST POLITICAL PARTIES

Political parties developed in the United States during the 1790s. The first political parties were the Federalists and the Democratic-Republicans. The supporters of Hamilton formed the Federalist party. Supporters of Jefferson and Madison organized the Democratic-Republican party.

John Adams

Each party had its own Presidential candidate in the election of 1796. John Adams ran as a Federalist, and Thomas Jefferson ran as a Democratic-Republican. According to the Constitution, the candidate with the most electoral votes would become President. The person who came in second would be Vice President. In the 1796 election, Adams won the most votes. Jefferson, in second place, became Vice President.

During the 1790s, France was going through its own revolutionary period. As the revolution gained strength, many Federalists in Congress worried that the violence would spread to the United States. This fear led Congress to pass the Alien and Sedition Acts of 1798. These laws restricted immigration and allowed the President to expel any alien, or foreign person, regarded as dangerous. The acts also limited freedom of speech so that it became a crime to express or publish opinions against the government.

Federalists used the Alien and Sedition Acts to attack their political rivals. They closed Democratic-Republican newspapers and arrested people who supported Democratic-Republicans.

Jefferson called on the states to act against the Alien and Sedition Acts. Jefferson believed that the states had the right to **nullify,** or cancel, federal laws. Kentucky and Virginia followed Jefferson's advice. The Kentucky and Virginia resolutions stated that if states decide that a law is unconstitutional, they can nullify it within their borders.

The tension of the Adams presidency led to a bitter election in 1800. Adams was the Federalist candidate for President. Thomas Jefferson and Aaron Burr ran as Democratic-Republican candidates. When the electoral college voted, Jefferson and Burr, in the same party, each had 73 votes. It was unclear which man would be President.

It was up to the House of Representatives to decide the outcome of the election. The House voted 35 times, and each time Jefferson and Burr tied. Finally, Jefferson won by a small margin, and Burr became Vice President. As a result of this election, Congress passed the Twelfth Amendment to the Constitution. This amendment required electors to vote separately for President and Vice President. In 1804, this amendment was ratified.

? What were the main differences between Federalists and Democratic-Republicans?

◆ JEFFERSON GUIDES THE NATION

Thomas Jefferson believed strongly in doing away with many formal ceremonies and events that were customary under previous Presidents. For example, he greeted guests by shaking hands, not by having guests bow. Under Jefferson, many events at the executive mansion were opened to the public. Jefferson, determined to set the country on a more democratic course, still did not extend these rights to enslaved African Americans or to women.

Jefferson had Congress repeal many Federalist taxes. He cut government expenses by cutting the size of the army and the navy. Some parts of the Alien and Sedition Acts were dropped. Other parts were changed.

Powers of the U.S. Supreme Court

One of the most important developments during Jefferson's presidency involved the U.S. Supreme Court. In 1803 a case called *Marbury* v. *Madison* was presented to the Court. William Marbury had been appointed a federal judge at the very end of John Adams's presidency. James Madison, Secretary of State under Jefferson, refused to give Marbury the official papers that would allow Marbury to become a judge. Marbury decided to sue Madison.

According to the Judiciary Act of 1789, the Supreme Court was required to decide cases brought against federal officials. However, Chief Justice John Marshall ruled that the Judiciary Act was unconstitutional. He said that the Constitution denied the Supreme Court the right to decide cases involving federal officials. Furthermore, since the Constitution was the highest law in the land, Congress could not pass a law that violated it. After much debate, the Supreme Court decided not to hear *Marbury* v. *Madison*.

The Court's ruling meant that Marbury could not become a judge. But the main importance of the ruling was that for the first time the Supreme Court claimed the power to declare a law unconstitutional. This concept is called **judicial review.** It has become a part of the U.S. court system.

The Louisiana Purchase

In 1801, President Jefferson believed that the United States had a special opportunity at hand. That year, France signed a treaty with Spain that turned the Louisiana Territory over to France. The treaty gave France control over the port of New Orleans. Wanting Americans to have access to the port, Jefferson sent ambassadors to France to try to buy New Orleans. To the ambassadors' surprise, France offered to sell all of the Louisiana Territory, a huge region stretching from the Mississippi River to the Rocky Mountains. The map on this page shows the vast area of the Louisiana Purchase. The purchase would open a rich new territory to farmers and fur traders.

When the ambassadors offered $15 million for the territory, the French agreed. President Jefferson, eager to buy Louisiana, was not certain that the Constitution gave him the authority to purchase territory. After a great deal of thought, Jefferson reasoned that he could purchase the territory by using the President's power to make treaties with foreign nations. Approaching the Louisiana Purchase as a

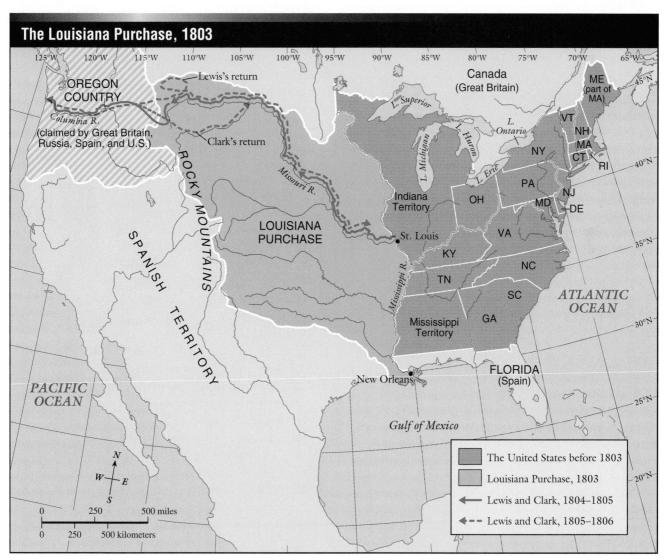

The Louisiana Purchase, 1803

	The United States before 1803
	Louisiana Purchase, 1803
←	Lewis and Clark, 1804–1805
◄--	Lewis and Clark, 1805–1806

▲ **Geography** *The land in the Louisiana Purchase almost doubled the size of the United States.* **Interpreting the Map** *Which of the present-day states were carved from the Louisiana Purchase? Use the atlas in the back of the book for help.*

treaty with France, he presented it to the Senate. The Senate approved the treaty, and in 1803, the United States took control of the territory.

People in the United States considered the Louisiana Territory ripe for settlement and exploration. Few thought of consulting the thousands of Native Americans who lived on these lands. In 1804, Jefferson sent Meriwether Lewis and William Clark to explore the new territory. Their guides were a Native American woman, Sacajawea, and her husband. Their trip, which took them beyond the Louisiana Territory to the Pacific Ocean, lasted two years.

 How did the *Marbury* v. *Madison* case expand the powers of the U.S. Supreme Court?

◆ THE WAR OF 1812

Thomas Jefferson was reelected President in 1804. At that time, relations with Great Britain were becoming strained. Britain, at war with France, tried to cut off U.S. trade with France by seizing American ships. Americans were especially angry when the British navy stopped U.S. ships and impressed their sailors into the British navy. **Impressment** is the act of seizing someone and forcing that person into service. In 1807, Jefferson tried to solve the problem by placing an **embargo,** or ban, on U.S. trade with foreign countries.

After a second term, Jefferson refused to run again. In the election of 1808, James Madison was chosen President. During Madison's term, tensions with Great Britain grew.

President Madison wished to avoid a conflict with Great Britian, but a number of representatives in Congress were pressing for war. Those in favor, called War Hawks, saw several advantages to a war with Great Britain. They sought to gain Canada in a war against Great Britain, and they wanted to push the Spanish—allies of Great Britain—out of Florida.

War Hawks were also concerned that Britain was aiding Native Americans against U.S. settlers in the Northwest. A Shawnee chief named Tecumseh managed to unite many Native American groups in the territory. Tecumseh's goal was to drive the settlers out of the Northwest Territory. He knew that if the white settlers did not stop moving onto Native American land, war would surely come. Tecumseh warned the whites,

Person ◆ *to* ◆ *Person*

Lewis and Clark

The Lewis and Clark Expedition (1804–1806) was the result of President Thomas Jefferson's interest in learning about the lands acquired in the Louisiana Purchase. Jefferson hoped to establish political boundaries in Louisiana and gather information to develop the area economically. Jefferson hired Meriwether Lewis, his secretary and a man familiar with the frontier, to lead the exploration. Lewis chose his friend William Clark to join him. Twenty-six men signed on with them.

▲ Meriwether Lewis (1774–1809)

The explorers set off from St. Louis, traveling up the Missouri River in boats. They followed the river through what is today North and South Dakota and carried canoes around the Great Falls of the Missouri. After a difficult crossing of the Rocky Mountains, they traveled by river to the Pacific Ocean. By the time the expedition returned more than two years

▲ William Clark (1770–1838)

later, the group had traveled 6,000 miles.

Lewis and Clark brought back valuable information about the West. They created maps of the region and kept detailed journals of their expedition. They worked to establish relationships with the Native Americans they encountered. Most importantly, their expedition opened the way for settlement of the West. For the first time, people would be able to cross the continent from one side to the other.

Looking Back: What are some reasons people might have had for joining Lewis and Clark's expedition?

▲ Tecumseh studied the Bible, Shakespeare, and European history. He worked to unite all Native Americans against white settlers.

"You are continually driving the red people [from their land,] when at last you will drive them into the [ocean] where they can't either stand or work. Brother. You ought to know what you are doing with the Indians. . . . It is a very bad thing and we do not like it."

However, Americans were determined to build their permanent settlements. In 1811, General William Henry Harrison defeated the Shawnee at the Battle of Tippecanoe, in what is now the state of Indiana. Some of the Shawnee carried British guns. The Americans accused the British of backing the Shawnee.

Madison finally gave in to the War Hawks. In June 1812, he asked Congress to declare war on Great Britain. After a great deal of debate, war was declared in 1812.

The British won most of the early battles of the war. In 1813, they captured Washington, D.C., and burned the Capitol Building and the President's mansion. In 1814, they tried to capture Baltimore. They failed because they could not take Fort McHenry, a fort that protected Baltimore.

The all-night battle for Fort McHenry was watched by a young lawyer named Francis Scott Key. The next morning Key saw that Americans still held the fort. Inspired, he wrote a poem called "The Star Spangled Banner." His poem, later set to music, became the United States' national anthem.

Both sides were weary of war. British and American representatives held peace talks in Ghent, Belgium, that ended the fighting. Under the provisions of the treaty, neither the British nor the United States gained any territory. However, the United States had shown that it could stand up to the world's strongest power and defend itself. Even more important, the war produced a rise of **nationalism** among many Americans. Nationalism is pride in one's country. Feelings of nationalism led to an even greater urge to expand U.S. boundaries. Nationalism and expansionism would be important themes in the years to come.

? How did tension with the British lead to the War of 1812?

Section 4 Review

Check Understanding

1. **Define** (a) inauguration (b) Cabinet (c) bond (d) precedent (e) nullify (f) judicial review (g) impressment (h) embargo (i) nationalism

2. **Differentiate** between the Federalist and Democratic-Republican positions regarding the Alien and Sedition Acts.

3. **Explain** the significance of the Louisiana Purchase.

4. **Identify** causes and effects of the War of 1812.

Critical Thinking

Connecting Past and Present In what ways are the goals of space explorations similar to and different from the goals of Lewis and Clark's expedition?

Write About Economics

Write a brief essay describing how the young American government tried to strengthen the U.S. economy.

Chapter 5
Review

CHAPTER SUMMARY

Section 1
The Continental Congress wrote the Articles of Confederation in 1777. This plan created a weak national government. After several years, it became obvious that the nation needed a new, stronger foundation.

Section 2
Compromise led to the creation of the Constitution in 1787. The Constitution called for a government with three branches and a bicameral Congress. It created a government based on federalism, which divided power between state and national government.

Section 3
During the ratification process, Federalists and Antifederalists debated the merits of the Constitution. The Constitution was ratified in 1788. A Bill of Rights was ratified in 1791.

Section 4
The nation's first President under the Constitution was George Washington, who set the United States on a strong course. Governmental departments were formed, and important economic issues were addressed. During Thomas Jefferson's presidency, the country was greatly enlarged with the purchase of the Louisiana Territory. After James Madison became President, the United States went to war with Britain. The U.S. victory led to a heightened pride of country in most Americans.

Connecting ◆ Past and Present

How does the Constitution of the United States protect you in your daily life?

Using Vocabulary

For each word, write the letter of the correct definition on a separate sheet of paper.

1. ratify
2. unconstitutional
3. confederation
4. veto
5. compromise
6. amend
7. embargo
8. federalism
9. impressment
10. precedent

a. to reject
b. a loose union of individual states or nations
c. a form of government that divides power between national and state government
d. a settlement of differences in which both sides give up something they want
e. to change
f. an example
g. to approve
h. in violation of the Constitution
i. a government order banning foreign trade
j. an act of seizing someone and forcing the person into service

Check Understanding

1. **Describe** the major strengths and weaknesses of the Articles of Confederation.
2. **Explain** why some people opposed ratification of the Constitution.
3. **Explain** the purpose of the Northwest Ordinance.
4. **Identify** the reasons why delegates gathered for the Constitutional Convention in 1787.
5. **Explain** the Great Compromise and the Three-Fifths Compromise.
6. **Describe** the three branches of government under the U.S. Constitution.
7. **Summarize** the reasons for tension between the United States and Great Britain in the early 1800s.

8. **Explain** the differences between the Federalists and the Antifederalists.

9. **Explain** why the states wanted a bill of rights added to the Constitution.

10. **Summarize** the provisions of the Alien and Sedition Acts.

Critical Thinking

1. **Evaluating** How did the federal government become stronger under the Constitution?

2. **Comparing** What were the main differences between the Virginia Plan and the New Jersey Plan, and how were they resolved?

3. **Understanding Economics** Why were Northerners generally more supportive of Alexander Hamilton's ideas about the economy than were Southerners?

4. **Analyzing** Why did Thomas Jefferson call on the states to act against the Alien and Sedition Acts? What did Jefferson's actions tell about his beliefs in states' rights versus the power of the national government?

◆ **Connecting Past and Present** The Bill of Rights was written to protect the rights of people. Which three rights are most important to you today?

Writing to Compare

The Americans who framed the Constitution and participated in government during the early days of the United States had many different ideas. **Write** an essay comparing one of the following: (a) the ideas of the Federalists and the Antifederalists during the ratification of the Constitution; (b) the beliefs of the Federalist party and the Republican party in the late 1700s and early 1800s.

Putting Skills to Work

USING GRAPHIC ORGANIZERS

In the Building Skills lesson on page 89, you learned about the value of using graphic organizers. Now you will create one of your own. Entitle it "The Three Branches of Government." In each of three large boxes, write the name of a branch of the federal government. In smaller boxes extending from the larger ones, list the functions of each branch.

Interpreting the Timeline

Use the timeline on pages 84–85 to answer these questions.

1. How soon after the Articles of Confederation were ratified did a convention meet to write a new plan for the government?

2. What world event occurred the same year George Washington was elected President?

3. What events in the world might have been influenced by the American Revolution?

Portfolio Project

FROM BILL TO LAW

Read your local newspaper or speak to people in your community to find out about issues that need to be addressed. Choose one issue and write a proposal for a bill to address this issue. For example, you may see a need in your community to establish a program to help the homeless.

Then create a flow chart to show how you could introduce your bill to Congress and see it through the process. Find out the names of your representatives in Congress—in the Senate and in the House of Representatives. Include their names in your flow chart. File your flow chart in your portfolio.

Chapter 6
Taking Different Economic Paths 1789–1860

CHAPTER PREVIEW

Section 1 Industrialization in the North

The Industrial Revolution, which brought new ways of working and living to the United States, increased the number of women in the workforce, introduced a market economy, and reinforced the idea of free enterprise.

Section 2 Cotton Is King in the South

With technological advances and the use of slave labor, the plantations of the South prospered. In a number of instances, enslaved African Americans rose in revolt.

Section 3 Policies of Monroe and Jackson

A new democratic spirit seized the land with the administration of Andrew Jackson, though the treatment of Native Americans did not uphold democratic principles.

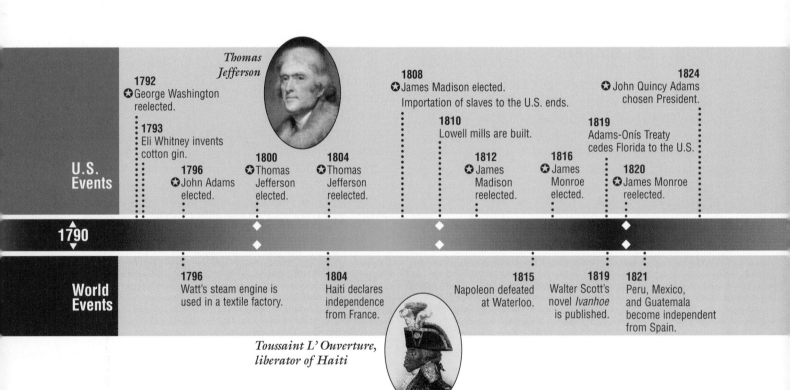

U.S. Events

Thomas Jefferson

1792 ✪George Washington reelected.

1793 Eli Whitney invents cotton gin.

1796 ✪John Adams elected.

1800 ✪Thomas Jefferson elected.

1804 ✪Thomas Jefferson reelected.

1808 ✪James Madison elected. Importation of slaves to the U.S. ends.

1810 Lowell mills are built.

1812 ✪James Madison reelected.

1816 ✪James Monroe elected.

1819 Adams-Onís Treaty cedes Florida to the U.S.

1820 ✪James Monroe reelected.

1824 ✪John Quincy Adams chosen President.

1790

World Events

1796 Watt's steam engine is used in a textile factory.

1804 Haiti declares independence from France.

Toussaint L' Ouverture, liberator of Haiti

1815 Napoleon defeated at Waterloo.

1819 Walter Scott's novel *Ivanhoe* is published.

1821 Peru, Mexico, and Guatemala become independent from Spain.

Portfolio Project

THE SPIRIT OF MUSIC

Enslaved Africans often turned to activities that reminded them of their homelands. Singing was one way to keep their cultures and spirits alive. Their songs were often accompanied by West African instruments, such as three-stringed banjos and drums. As you read this chapter, think of the kinds of songs people might have created during this time period. At the end of the chapter, you will present a report about African American music and culture in the 1800s.

▲ This illustration depicts the Erie Canal in the nineteenth century. Canals throughout the Northeast improved transportation and trade. ◈ **Connecting Past and Present** *How do the animals help the canal boat move? How does the improved transportation of today help increase trade?*

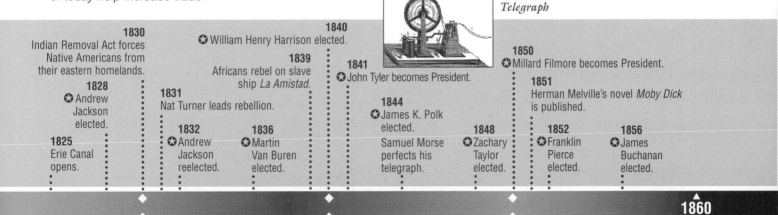

Telegraph

1830
Indian Removal Act forces Native Americans from their eastern homelands.

1828
✪ Andrew Jackson elected.

1825
Erie Canal opens.

1831
Nat Turner leads rebellion.

1832
✪ Andrew Jackson reelected.

1836
✪ Martin Van Buren elected.

1840
✪ William Henry Harrison elected.

1839
Africans rebel on slave ship *La Amistad.*

1841
✪ John Tyler becomes President.

1844
✪ James K. Polk elected.

Samuel Morse perfects his telegraph.

1850
✪ Millard Filmore becomes President.

1851
Herman Melville's novel *Moby Dick* is published.

1848
✪ Zachary Taylor elected.

1852
✪ Franklin Pierce elected.

1856
✪ James Buchanan elected.

1860

1825
Bolivia proclaims independence from Spain.

Simón Bolívar, liberator of South America

1834
Slavery is abolished in British empire.

1845
Famine breaks out in Ireland.

1847
Charlotte Brontë's novel *Jane Eyre* is published.

1859
Work begins on Suez Canal.

Section 1

Industrialization in the North

PREVIEW

Objectives

- To analyze the factors that led to the Industrial Revolution

- To describe how the factory system changed working conditions

- To explain the impact of improved transportation and communication

Vocabulary

artisan	mass production
factory system	turnpike
textile	canal
capitalist	

In 1800 the United States was an agricultural, or farming, society. Yet by 1840, nearly 10 percent of workers were employed in factories. The ideas and inventions of the Industrial Revolution changed the very nature of work and had an impact on people around the world.

◆ THE INDUSTRIAL REVOLUTION

Before the Industrial Revolution, most goods were produced by hand with simple tools. **Artisans,** or craftsworkers, worked at home or in small shops. During the Industrial Revolution, inventors began building machines that were able to do much of the work. At first, water power ran the machines. Then more efficient sources of energy were found: first steam and then electricity, oil, and gas.

The Factory System

The first inventions of the Industrial Revolution were machines for making cotton thread and cloth. The spinning jenny, for example, which was invented in England, increased the speed at which a worker could spin thread from raw cotton.

The new machines were too big to use in a home or a small shop. Owners began to adopt the **factory system,** which brought workers and machines together in one place to produce goods. In factories, everyone had to work a certain number of hours each day. Workers were paid daily or weekly wages. The factory system made it possible to produce more goods each day than individual workers at home ever could.

The Industrial Revolution in the United States

The British worked hard to keep the new technology secret. They made it a crime to take the plans for the new machines out of the country and even prevented factory workers from leaving Britain. However, American investors offered money to skilled workers who would come to the United States. A young British mechanic named Samuel Slater heard that the Americans were offering rich rewards. Slater had worked in British cotton mills and had even helped make some of the new machines. Slater memorized the plans of his machines, and in 1789 he managed to get past British officials and sail to the United States.

Slater went to work for Moses Brown, a Rhode Island investor, and began designing machines to make **textiles,** or cloth. Brown's new cotton-spinning mill in Pawtucket, Rhode Island, became the first successful factory in the United States.

New England soon became the first major U.S. manufacturing center. The region's fast-running rivers supplied the water power to turn the water wheels that ran the machines. New England also had **capitalists** to invest in new factories. A capitalist is a person with money to invest in business to make a profit. From New England, the Industrial Revolution spread throughout the Northeast. New York City became an industrial center as well as a center for trade.

The Steam Engine

One of the most important machines developed during the Industrial Revolution was the steam engine. The steam engine freed industry from depending on the power of rushing water, which limited the location of factories to the banks of streams or rivers. The steam engine used coal to heat water to produce steam for its source of power. Now, factories could be built anywhere.

James Watt, in Great Britain, developed the first efficient steam engine in the late 1760s. By 1785, he had built a steam engine that could be used in textile

◄ Textile factories such as this one in Lowell, Massachusetts, employed many women who were eager to leave farms and earn their own wages.

factories. Moses Brown's cotton mills switched from water power to steam power in 1828. By the middle of the 1800s, steam engines were powering factories, ships, and railroads throughout western Europe and the United States.

 **How did New England become a manufacturing center?**

◆ FACTORIES IN THE NORTH

The vast change sweeping the United States made an impression on foreigners who visited. A French visitor named Alexis de Tocqueville noted the changes.

... no people in the world had made such rapid progress in trade and manufactures as the Americans.

The War of 1812 spurred the growth of American industry. By blockading American ports, Britain cut the United States off from foreign manufacturers. American industry began to grow to meet the demand for goods.

After the war's end, the government gave a further boost to American industry with the Tariff Act of 1816. By taxing imports, the Tariff Act made foreign goods more expensive and American goods more attractive.

The Lowell Factory System

As in Britain, the textile factories in the United States pioneered important industrial advances. A Boston merchant, Francis Cabot Lowell, came up with the idea that all the operations needed to make a product could be carried out in one factory. This saved time and increased profits.

Lowell joined a group of capitalists in establishing a huge textile factory in Waltham, Massachusetts, outside Boston. Workers labored around the clock spinning and weaving thread to make cloth. When Lowell died, the group built a larger factory along the Merrimack River. With it, they built an entire town, named Lowell, to support the factory.

At first, most workers in the Lowell factory were unmarried young women—usually the daughters of nearby farmers. Young women were eager to work in the Lowell cotton mills, where they were paid more money than they could earn from farm labor. To assure parents of their daughters' safety, the Lowell group provided dormitories that were supervised by older women. The company also provided education, religious instruction, and entertainment.

Working conditions, quite good at first, soon declined. Beginning in the 1830s, wages went down and the working day grew longer. The workers' day began at 5 A.M. and did not end until 7:30 P.M. Many factories employed young children.

In 1845, a weaver named Sarah Bagley and 11 other mill workers in Lowell founded the Female Labor Reform Association. Though the group worked to fight against wage cuts and increased work loads, they never could persuade lawmakers to limit these practices.

Conditions in the Lowell textile industry mirrored changing conditions in American industries. A main reason for the worsening conditions in the factories was increased competition. As the factory system grew, the products of new factories competed with established factories. Competition meant lower prices, which forced factory owners to cut their operating costs. A second reason for the worsening of factory conditions was the arrival of waves of immigrants in the United States. Recognizing that immigrants would accept lower pay, the owners hired them and fired higher-paid workers.

Mass Production

The United States swiftly became a world leader in manufacturing. A German visitor to the United States during the 1820s, noticed that,

Everything new is quickly introduced here. There is no clinging to old ways.

One new technique was the use of interchangeable parts—parts that were identical and that could be used in place of each other to assemble a product. A young Connecticut inventor named Eli Whitney realized that if the parts of a musket or gun were made by machine, individual parts could be identical. Then the parts could be used in any musket the factory made. Until then, if a part broke, a new one had to be made for the particular gun. Whitney's method made it cheaper and easier to manufacture and repair muskets. The use of interchangeable parts spread slowly to other industries. Factories began to produce clocks, knives, locks, and other items with interchangeable parts. Interchangeable parts led to **mass production.**

Mass production is the making of many items in a short period of time. As the system spread to other industries, it came to be known as the "American system of manufacturing."

How did the Industrial Revolution change the way goods were produced?

◆ MOVEMENT WESTWARD

During the first half of the 1800s, large numbers of Americans were heading for the western frontier. In those days, the West was the land between the Appalachians and the Mississippi River. Americans from every state along the Atlantic seaboard crossed the Appalachian Mountains and fanned out in all directions toward the Mississippi River. Between 1810 and 1816, Ohio's white population almost doubled and Indiana's almost tripled. On the other hand, most of the original 13 states lost population during that same period. Although some of the westward bound pioneers were immigrants, most were Americans moving to another part of the country.

As the territories filled with people, they became eligible to apply for statehood. Between 1812 and 1819, five states—Louisiana, Mississippi, Illinois, Indiana, and Alabama—joined the union.

Cheap land was particularly appealing to many pioneers. They were excited by tales of rich, fertile soil in the western regions. Land was becoming more expensive in the East, and opportunities seemed to be lessening.

Better Transportation

In the early days in the United States, getting from one place to another had been very difficult. Roads were terrible—where they even existed. Often they were little more than trails that were too narrow for even a single wagon. While rivers and coastal waterways moved traffic more efficiently, they often did not lead where people wanted to go. After 1800, improved transportation helped people move westward. Later, new means of transportation also helped them get their goods to market in the East.

Most of the earliest roads were built by private companies that charged tolls. These new **turnpikes** were named after the pikes, or spiked poles, that were used at toll roads. The pikes were turned aside to let travelers pass after they had paid their tolls. Turnpikes soon connected a number of eastern cities with the important rivers of the West.

State governments began to take an active role in road building. Transportation costs were lowered, but moving goods along the roads was still too costly for most farmers and manufacturers.

In 1807, Robert Fulton successfully adapted the steam engine to a boat, the *Clermont*. Within a few years, steamboats were in use on the Mississippi River, and within 30 years, hundreds of steamboats were in service on major rivers and lakes. Steamboats could move upstream as easily as downstream.

While steamboats revolutionized water travel, people still needed to find ways to overcome waterfalls and rapids that were obstacles to steamboat travel. They also needed to find a way to connect individual rivers to form continuous water routes. The solution to these problems was to build **canals,** or channels dug out of the ground and filled with water. Barges, or flat-bottomed vessels that traveled the canals, were towed by mules walking along dirt paths that paralleled the canal. A mule could pull a load 50 times heavier on water than it could over a road.

During the early 1800s, canal-building proceeded at a frenzied pace in the United States. One of the largest and most impressive of the canals was the Erie Canal, which opened in New York State in 1825 after eight years of construction. More than 360 miles long, the canal enabled traffic to move from Lake Erie to the Hudson River and down to New York City. By 1840, about 3,300 miles of canals had been built.

The Erie Canal reduced the cost of moving a ton of freight from Buffalo to New York City by more than 90 percent. It made New York City the center for goods being shipped from the Atlantic coast to the West. It was such a success that communities all over the East competed with each other to build the longest, cheapest canal route to the West. The era of canal building came to an end when a new invention—the railroad—came into use.

The first major railroad line, the Baltimore and Ohio, was chartered in 1828. The first railroad trains were simply steam-powered engines placed on top of a wagon moving along a set of tracks. These early railroads were dangerous and unreliable. Tracks fell apart, and the boilers that powered the steam engines often blew up. However, as travel expanded, safety improved. Robert Stevens designed a new type of rail, which made derailment more unlikely. By the 1850s, railroads were as safe as steamboats—and much quicker. The map on page 112 shows railroads, canals, and roads that were in use by 1840.

By 1860, more than 30,000 miles of railroad tracks covered the country. Trains on these tracks could travel

◄ The steamboat *Clermont,* developed by Robert Fulton, was larger and more powerful than other boats in the early 1800s. For the first time, it was easy to move goods upriver.

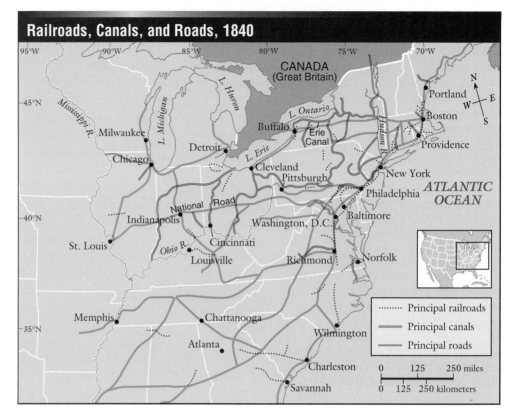

Railroads, Canals, and Roads, 1840

CANADA
(Great Britain)

ATLANTIC
OCEAN

Portland
Boston
Providence
Buffalo
Erie Canal
New York
Philadelphia
Baltimore
Washington, D.C.
Cleveland
Pittsburgh
Detroit
Milwaukee
Chicago
National Road
Indianapolis
St. Louis
Cincinnati
Louisville
Richmond
Norfolk
Memphis
Chattanooga
Atlanta
Wilmington
Charleston
Savannah

L. Superior
L. Michigan
L. Huron
L. Erie
L. Ontario
Mississippi R.
Ohio R.
Hudson R.

.... Principal railroads
———— Principal canals
———— Principal roads

0   125   250 miles
0   125   250 kilometers

Geography *The roads, canals, and railroads that crisscrossed the eastern United States made trade faster, easier, and cheaper.* **Interpreting the Map** *What routes could be taken to transport goods from New York to Baltimore?* ▶

at the then amazing speed of 20 to 30 miles per hour. Faster transportation over the lines of tracks helped connect distant regions of the United States.

The growth of transportation led to a legal question concerning the regulation, or control, of trade between the states. In 1824 the Supreme Court decided in the case of *Gibbons* v. *Ogden* that the federal government, which had the right to control interstate commerce, or trade between the states, could not control trade within a single state.

Inventions in Communications

While strides in transportation were made during the 1800s, technological advances improved communication. In 1844, the introduction of the telegraph by Samuel F. B. Morse helped tie the nation together. The telegraph made it possible for Americans to communicate with one another from different areas of the country. By 1860 there were 50,000 miles of telegraph wire crisscrossing the nation. In 1861, the first telegraph line reached San Francisco on the Pacific coast.

 How did new methods of communication and transportation affect the growth of the nation?

Section 1 Review

Check Understanding

1. **Define** (a) artisan (b) factory system (c) textile (d) capitalist (e) mass production (f) turnpike (g) canal

2. **Describe** how the Industrial Revolution changed the way people worked.

3. **Analyze** some of the reasons people moved west in the early 1800s.

Critical Thinking

◆ **Connecting Past and Present** Do you think the quotation on page 110 is an accurate description of the United States today? Explain.

Write About Social Issues

Write a diary entry from the point of view of a young woman working in the Lowell mills.

BUILDING *SKILLS*

Distinguishing Fact from Opinion: Women Workers

Telling the difference between **fact** and **opinion** is important when you read history. A fact is something that can be proven or observed. For example, the statement "John Adams was elected President in 1796" is a fact. An opinion is a judgment that reflects a person's own ideas and attitudes. Opinions may be true or false, and people may have different opinions about the same topic. People often use facts to support their opinions. In general, opinions supported by many facts, or opinions held by experts in a particular field, stand a better chance of being accurate.

Here's How

Follow these steps to distinguish fact from opinion:

1. Decide which statements are facts. When you read something, think about which parts of it can be proven or observed.

2. Decide which statements are opinions. *I think* or *I believe* may signal an opinion statement, but many opinions are not identified that obviously.

3. Identify the purpose. What does the writer want you to believe or do with the information?

4. Evaluate the way in which a writer or speaker mixes facts and opinions. Are opinions supported by a number of verifiable facts?

Here's Why

Distinguishing between fact and opinion helps you determine the truth about what happened in the past. By identifying and evaluating various opinions, you can interpret the meaning of historical events with greater accuracy.

Practice the Skill

The passage below is part of a description of a textile mill in Waltham, Massachusetts. It was written in 1834 by Harriet Martineau, an English traveler. After you have read the passage, answer the questions that follow.

The girls earn two, and sometimes three, dollars a week, besides their board. The little children earn one dollar a week.... Some of the girls have [paid off] mortgages from their fathers' farms.... Many are rapidly accumulating an independence.... The girls work about 70 hours per week, on the average. The time of work varies with the length of the days.... All look like well-dressed young ladies.... [It was] a pleasure to make the acquaintance with the [working women] of the United States.

1. Which statements of the excerpt seem to be fact?

2. Which statements seem to be opinion?

3. Do you think Harriet Martineau had a favorable or unfavorable opinion of the girls she describes?

Apply the Skill

Choose one of the opinions below. Then, as you read the chapter, write three facts to support the statement.

1. Andrew Jackson was a skilled President.

2. The Industrial Revolution was good for workers.

3. Life on a plantation was difficult.

Section 2

Cotton Is King in the South

PREVIEW

Objectives

- To describe how cotton became a profitable crop in the South

- To describe the conditions of enslaved African Americans on cotton plantations

- To explain how enslaved people protested against their situation

Vocabulary

cotton gin
spiritual

In the early 1790s, the southern part of the United States was in financial trouble. Since American independence, southern exports of tobacco, rice, and indigo to European markets had dropped. The sale of wheat and corn did not earn much money. The South needed a new cash crop.

◆ THE ECONOMY OF THE SOUTH CHANGES

Cotton would be the answer to the South's economic problems. The booming textile mills of England had created a huge demand for cotton. However, producing pure cotton fiber was difficult and costly because it involved removing seeds by hand.

A new invention made cotton the chief cash crop of the South. In 1793, Eli Whitney, who had invented interchangeable gun parts, designed a machine called the cotton engine. The cotton engine could remove the seeds much faster than had been done before. People shortened the name of the new machine to **cotton gin.**

Suddenly, cotton could be grown profitably throughout the region. Even a small farmer could afford a cotton gin. The owners of large plantations built large cotton gins powered by horses or mules. Costs could be further contained by using enslaved people to pick

cotton. Southern cotton shipped to English mills became the nation's largest export. As the cotton economy grew, so did the number of enslaved people.

? How did industrialization affect the economy of the South?

◆ CONDITIONS OF SLAVERY

When the United States gained its independence, about 500,000 African Americans were held in slavery. Less than a century later, in 1860, there were nearly four million enslaved people in the South. One of every three persons living in the South was an enslaved African American.

About three out of four white families in the South owned no slaves. Even though these families were in the majority, however, most of them supported the institution of slavery. Since enslaved people played a critical role in raising and harvesting crops, slavery had grown to be an essential part of the farming economy in the South.

Some enslaved people worked as skilled servants in plantation houses. Women learned to sew, weave, and spin. Some became cooks, maids, and child-care workers. Men became blacksmiths, shoemakers, jewelers, carpenters, and painters. Occasionally, a plantation owner hired out enslaved people to work in factories, in flour and sugar mills, or in iron works.

This painting depicts the poverty and hardship of slave living quarters that were typical on southern plantations. ▼

Some were hired out to build roads, canals, or railroads. Many worked on the docks, lifting and carrying heavy loads on and off ships.

Most enslaved people, however, worked long hard days in the fields. Normally working from dawn to dusk, they might be forced to work even longer at planting or harvest time. They were closely watched by a driver, often another enslaved person. One enslaved person in Louisiana described a typical day in the fields:

> The hands are required to be in the cotton field as soon as it is light in the morning, and, with the exception of fifteen minutes, they are not permitted to be a moment idle until it is too dark to see.

Plantation owners introduced Christianity to enslaved people. Many accepted the religious teachings and adapted them to their lives. Some of them identified with the ancient Israelites, who were enslaved in Egypt but eventually freed. In the African American **spiritual** "Go Down, Moses," Moses tells the Egyptian pharaoh to "Let my people go." A spiritual is an expressive religious song. In spirituals, the enslaved people of the Americas sang of their misfortunes and unhappiness—and of freedom in the future.

Enslaved people created a rich cultural and social life, blending elements of their West African traditions with the customs and styles of the white culture in which they lived. Yet an important fact of American slavery remained. Enslaved people were considered property, and their lives could be completely regulated by their owner.

❓ What was life like for enslaved African Americans on cotton plantations?

◆ REVOLTS AGAINST SLAVERY

Enslaved Africans found a variety of ways to show their discontent. Some struck back in ways that would not be seen as openly rebellious. They might make a tool unusable or agree among themselves to work more slowly. In indirect ways, they protested against their unjust and enforced situation. Some slaves tried to run away, which was extremely risky. Runaway slaves who were captured faced severe punishment,

▲ Eli Whitney's invention, the cotton gin, made it easier to process cotton. However, as the cotton industry grew, so did the exploitation of slaves.

sometimes even death. Most slaves did not attempt to leave their plantations.

Discipline was strict. If enslaved people showed signs of disobedience or independence, they might be flogged or whipped. A greatly feared punishment was to be sold at auction. There was always the threat that children would be separated from their parents, and husbands from their wives.

Gabriel Prosser and Denmark Vesey

Some groups of enslaved people made several attempts to revolt. With perhaps 1,000 other enslaved people, Gabriel Prosser tried and failed to capture Richmond, Virginia, in 1800. He was executed with many of his followers. Several hundred enslaved people marched on New Orleans in 1811, but they were also defeated. In 1822, Denmark Vesey, a free African American living in Charleston, South Carolina, planned a rebellion. Vesey's plans were discovered and he was hanged with 34 of his followers.

Nat Turner's Revolt

In 1831, Nat Turner led the largest rebellion of enslaved people in U.S. history. Believing that he was urged by God to lead an uprising against slavery, Turner and five other enslaved people attacked Virginia farmers. Other enslaved people joined Turner. It was two days before the revolt was stopped. When Turner was captured, he admitted what he had done. When asked why he pleaded "not guilty," he answered, "Because I don't feel guilty." About 60 whites were killed during the revolt, and more than 100 enslaved people lost their lives. Turner was hanged for his part in the revolt.

In the South, most white people reacted to the uprisings by creating stricter rules for enslaved people. Legislatures strengthened slave codes. Most critics of slavery either left the South or remained silent. However, antislavery feeling was growing in the North.

The Amistad Mutiny

After 1808 it was illegal to bring enslaved Africans into the United States. In Cuba, however, slave trade was still legal.

In May 1839, a man named Sengbeh Pieh was captured in Sierra Leone, West Africa, and taken to Cuba. There, Pieh was purchased, renamed Joseph Cinqué, and forced on board the ship *La Amistad* with 53 other enslaved Africans.

Three days into their voyage to another Cuban port, Cinqué and several other captives stormed the deck, killing most of the crew. They spared the lives of two Spaniards who had the navigational skills to sail them back to Africa. However, the sailors tricked the Africans and guided the ship northward, ending up off the coast of New York City. There, the Africans were spotted by a U.S. Navy vessel, arrested, and taken to jail.

Led by Lewis Tappan, a New York businessman, a group of abolitionists decided to publicize the incident to expose the brutalities of slavery and the slave trade. Tappan wrote detailed newspaper accounts about the incident and found Africans who could translate for the captives, most of whom spoke their native language and not English. He also hired an attorney to defend the Africans against charges of murder and piracy.

The judge in the case ruled that the Africans had been kidnapped, and he ordered their return to Africa. The government filed an appeal, and after a series of trials the case was sent to the U.S. Supreme Court. Abolitionists hired former President John Quincy Adams to defend the Africans. Adams challenged the Court to free the Africans on the basis of rights granted in the Declaration of Independence.

The Court handed down a decision that freed the African mutineers. For the first and only time in history, Africans seized by slave dealers and brought to the United States won their freedom in American courts. In January 1842, almost three years after their capture by slave traders, Joseph Cinqué and the 35 remaining captives returned to Sierra Leone.

 In what ways did enslaved people try to rebel?

Section 2 Review

Check Understanding

1. **Define** (a) cotton gin (b) spiritual

2. **Identify** the effect of the cotton gin on the economy of the South.

3. **Describe** the typical working conditions of an enslaved person.

4. **Identify** Gabriel Prosser, Nat Turner, and Joseph Cinqué.

Critical Thinking

Drawing Conclusions Although most Southerners owned no slaves, many defended slavery. Why do you think this was so?

Write About Culture

Connecting Past and Present Enslaved people expressed their thoughts and feelings in spirituals. These spirituals continue to have meaning for people today. Write an essay explaining what qualities make some music of lasting value to people living in different times.

CONNECTING HISTORY & The Economy

THE COTTON ECONOMY

In the late 1700s, the development of power-driven machinery for spinning thread and weaving cloth led to the opening of textile factories. These mills, many of them in New England, ordered ever larger amounts of raw cotton fiber from southern farmers.

The invention of the cotton gin brought about an efficient and inexpensive way to process cotton. Before the cotton gin, a man or woman could separate by hand only a few pounds of fiber a day. With the cotton gin, it was possible for one person to separate more than 50 pounds a day.

More and more southern farmers and plantation owners began to raise cotton. On many farms, enslaved people were used to fill the increased demand for labor. Large 500-pound bales of raw fiber were shipped to factories in New England. The cultivation of cotton made possible the rapid growth of the northern cotton cloth industry. After being woven on looms, the cloth was sent to clothing manufacturers to be made into dresses, shirts, and suits for markets around the world.

In 1791 southern production of cotton fiber was 4,000 bales. By 1830, it was 732,000 bales. By 1860, production was more than four million bales, two thirds of the world's total production of cotton. Cotton farmers grew prosperous as textile manufacturers paid higher and higher prices.

The demand for cotton increased, and the cotton-growing area widened. Farmers and plantation owners moved west and cleared the rich soil. And as the profits of the cotton economy grew, so did the institution of slavery.

Making the Economic Connection

1. What was the relationship between the economy of the South and the economy of New England?

2. How did the cotton gin affect the economy of the South?

3. Why did the practice of slavery increase after the invention of the cotton gin?

◆ Connecting Past and Present

During the past 100 years, a number of inventions have changed the world. Choose the invention you believe has made the greatest impact during this century. Write an essay defending your point of view.

▲ *The cotton gin had sets of wire teeth on a cylinder turned by a hand crank. The teeth pulled the raw cotton fiber through a fine grid, leaving the seeds behind.*

Section 3

Policies of Monroe and Jackson

PREVIEW

Objectives

- To describe the relationship between the United States and Latin America in the early 1800s

- To discuss how democracy was extended in the 1820s

- To explain the effects of Jackson's Native American policy

Vocabulary

annex
spoils system
kitchen cabinet

During the first half of the 1800s, colonies in Latin America fought for independence from Spain and Portugal. American public opinion was strongly in favor of independence for the colonies, mainly because it wished to free the Western Hemisphere of European influence and power.

◆ THE UNITED STATES AND LATIN AMERICA

In the years following 1800, Europe was involved in a series of wars, known as the Napoleonic wars. Most of these wars were fought in Spain, France, Austria, Germany, Italy, and Russia. Major battles fought in Spain had sapped Spain's strength. As a result of the wars, its hold on its colonies in the Western Hemisphere was weakened.

The United States Takes Florida

In 1813 the United States took over the western tip of Spain's Florida colony, territory that is located in Alabama and Louisiana today. The United States claimed the area was part of the Louisiana Purchase. Spain protested but was too weak to do much else.

Not wanting a European colony on its southeastern flank, the United States continued to eye the rest of Florida. In 1818, General Andrew Jackson crossed the Florida border, seized two Spanish forts, and raised the American flag.

Spain protested this action, but again its power was limited. Spain was having great problems with its colonies in South America. In 1819, Spain and the United States signed the Adams-Onís Treaty. For five million dollars, Spain allowed the United States to **annex** Florida, or take possession of it. The two countries also agreed on a border between the Louisiana Territory and Spain's possessions farther west.

The Monroe Doctrine

War and revolution soon cost Spain most of its other territories in the Western Hemisphere. By 1822 most of Spain's colonies from Mexico to the southern tip of South America had won their independence. Spain held only Cuba and Puerto Rico. Portugal lost its huge colony Brazil, which won independence in 1822.

The United States supported the newly independent countries, but enthusiasm was soon replaced by concern. The United States feared that France might attempt to take over Cuba, a colony still held by Spain. Russia, which owned Alaska, was rumored to be planning an expansion along the Pacific coast. There was also fear that Spain would try to recover its colonies. The United States wanted to ensure that European nations would not threaten Latin America's new freedom. To its surprise, it found it had an ally in Great Britain, which saw profits in trade with the newly independent Latin American countries.

In December 1823, President James Monroe, knowing he had British backing, issued what later became known as the Monroe Doctrine. In a speech to Congress, he warned European powers against establishing new colonies in North and South America. The United States would consider any attempt to do so "dangerous to our peace and safety." Furthermore, Monroe stated that if European powers intervened in affairs of a country in the Western Hemisphere, the United States would consider it an act against the United States itself. Monroe also promised that the United States would not interfere in European affairs.

 **How did the United States respond to fears of European interference in Latin America?**

◆ THE AGE OF JACKSON

In the presidential election of 1824, one of the four leading candidates was John Quincy Adams, the son of John Adams. Another was Andrew Jackson, a self-made man from a poor background. Born in the Carolina backcountry, he had educated himself and had become a wealthy lawyer and a supporter of democratic causes. Jackson was especially popular because of a successful military career.

In the election of 1824, Jackson won the most popular votes and electoral votes, but he did not have the majority of the electoral votes needed for election. According to the Constitution, the election then was to be decided by the House of Representatives.

The House chose John Quincy Adams for President. Adams was backed by Henry Clay, a congressman from Kentucky, who was then appointed Secretary of State. Jackson's supporters called the deal between Adams and Clay a "corrupt bargain."

The Election of 1828

In 1828, Jackson once again opposed Adams. Adams, a National-Republican, was considered by some to be remote from ordinary people. He was easily defeated by Jackson. Formerly known as the Democratic-Republicans, the members of Jackson's party now called themselves simply the Democrats.

For the first time in its history, the United States had a President born west of the Appalachian Mountains. Before Jackson, all Presidents were men of wealthy backgrounds. Andrew Jackson had been born into poverty and had risen through his own efforts. He presented himself as being in touch with the "common man."

King Andrew

Jackson was a complicated man. Viewed by many as a man of the people, he was seen by some as tough, a man who expected to get his way.

Jackson had a terrible temper and a ruthless streak. By the time he reached the White House, he had already been involved in two duels and countless street brawls. In Florida, in 1819, he had dealt harshly with Native Americans and rudely with the Spaniards. Jackson's supporters admired him as a leader, but his opponents hated him as a tyrant. When he became President, they sarcastically called him "King Andrew." Jackson intended to be a strong President by expanding the powers of the presidency.

Jacksonian Democracy

Though Jackson believed in the power of the presidency, he also believed in the common sense of ordinary people. One of his goals as President was to get as many people as possible involved in government.

Jackson gave government positions to many of his supporters. The jobs became available after Jackson removed people—usually political opponents—from office. These government jobs became known as the "spoils of office." The practice of a victorious political party filling government jobs with party supporters was called the **spoils system.**

Jackson felt it was good democratic practice to rotate the jobs among as many people as possible. After a certain period of time, most officeholders were replaced. Jackson believed that holding out the possibility of government jobs to loyal party supporters was a good way to attract people to politics.

Considered unfair by some, the spoils system was defended by Jackson. He believed that government was improved when ordinary citizens—not only those with special qualifications—were allowed to participate.

Distrusting the old established privileged class, Jackson relied instead on a small group of friends and supporters. They met with Jackson informally at the White House. The President's enemies called the group his **"kitchen cabinet."**

Despite Jackson's restricted notion of democracy—only white men were qualified to vote—his beliefs led to some important reforms. For example, under his administration the nominating process to choose candidates for federal office became more democratic. Until that time, candidates for federal office had been selected by legislators gathered in closed meetings. Voters had little voice in the nominating process.

The system was different on the local level. Groups of voters chose delegates to attend county conventions to nominate candidates for county offices. During Jackson's administration, this practice gradually spread to state and national politics. By 1832, the present practice of choosing the party's candidates for President and Vice President in nominating conventions had been established.

Nullification

A challenge that arose during Jackson's administration was the issue of nullification, or the idea that states could declare federal laws unconstitutional and without legal force. Senator John Calhoun, of South Carolina, first raised the idea of nullification in 1828. Angry over a new tariff law that put a high tax on imported products in order to encourage manufacturing within the United States, he claimed that the states had the right to nullify any congressional act that violated their rights.

Government *"King Andrew" Jackson was ridiculed by the press for his tyrannical temper.* **Interpreting the Cartoon** *Why do you think the artist portrayed President Jackson stepping on the Constitution?* ▼

A senator from Massachusetts, Daniel Webster, disagreed. In a speech to Congress in 1830, Webster argued that the people, not the states, had created the Constitution and the national government. Therefore the states had no right to interpret the Constitution as they wanted. Webster said,

> **It is the people's Constitution, the people's government, made for the people, by the people, and answerable to the people.**

In 1832, Congress lowered the tariff slightly. That did not satisfy Vice President Calhoun or most of the South Carolina legislators. They declared the tariffs of 1828 and 1832 null in South Carolina. Jackson asked Congress to pass a Force Bill, giving him the right to use his power to enforce the law. Calhoun resigned as Vice President and returned to Washington as a senator from South Carolina.

Finally, Henry Clay helped arrange a compromise. Congress passed the Force Bill as well as a lower tariff. South Carolina accepted this compromise and revoked its nullification of the earlier tariffs.

The problem of nullification and states' rights would soon become tied to a much more difficult issue than tariffs. Antislavery feeling was building in the North. The South was determined to defend its right to keep slavery. A much greater contest between federal powers and states' rights lay ahead.

 In what ways did democracy advance under President Jackson?

◆ JACKSON AND NATIVE AMERICANS

Andrew Jackson saw Native Americans as an obstacle to American expansion westward. When Jackson became President, about 125,000 Native Americans lived east of the Mississippi River. About 60,000 lived in the South, including the Cherokee, Creek, Choctaw, Chickasaw, and Seminole nations. Known as the Five Tribes, these Native Americans inhabited 33 million acres of land. Jackson's goal was to make this land available for settlers.

Settlers had an intense desire for this land. In 1830, Congress passed the Indian Removal Act, with Jackson's support. The terms of the bill applied to all Native Americans east of the Mississippi, though it

In 1838, Native Americans were uprooted from their homes in the east and forced to travel west. Though many resisted, 15,000 Native Americans were forced to set out on a journey of hardship and death. ▶

was meant primarily for the Five Tribes. They were to exchange their lands in the East for new lands that lay west of the Mississippi River.

Native Americans resisted the forced move in a number of ways. The Cherokee went to court to defend their lands. Though the Supreme Court supported their claims, Jackson went ahead with the removal. In 1838, more than 15,000 Cherokee were made to leave their homes in Georgia and relocate in Oklahoma Territory. Many died during the long walk, called the Trail of Tears. For the survivors, the ordeal ended only when they arrived in the dry and foreign land that would be their new home. Many Seminoles resisted by going to war. The war lasted from 1835 to 1842. The defeated Seminoles were pushed to move west, although some remained in Florida. Their descendants still live there today.

During the 1830s the federal government continued to move most of the Native Americans off eastern lands. Thousands headed west to unfamiliar territory with little food or means of shelter. By 1840, the forced removal of 60,000 Native Americans had been carried out.

 What was Andrew Jackson's policy toward Native Americans?

Section 3 Review

Check Understanding

1. **Define** (a) annex (b) spoils system (c) kitchen cabinet

2. **Identify** the Monroe Doctrine and explain its purpose.

3. **Evaluate** the effect of the Indian Removal Act on Native Americans.

Critical Thinking

◆ **Connecting Past and Present** Which viewpoint regarding states' rights—that of John C. Calhoun or Daniel Webster—do you think should prevail today? Explain.

Write About Government

In a letter to Daniel Webster, explain what you think of the ideas expressed in his 1830 speech.

Chapter 6
Review

CHAPTER SUMMARY

Section 1

The early 1800s brought the Industrial Revolution to the United States, changing production techniques and working conditions. One development was the growth of mills and factories in the North. At the same time, improved roads and canals made travel between the regions easier. Using these new transportation routes, Americans began heading west in record numbers to find better and cheaper land.

Section 2

The invention of the cotton gin made cotton easier to prepare for sale, turning it into the South's most important crop. The growth of cotton as the main cash crop of the South led to rising numbers of enslaved people. While many Africans endured terrible conditions, some resisted slavery in direct and indirect ways.

Section 3

By 1820, Spain's colonies in the Americas were gone. Fearing a return of European control, President Monroe warned European countries against any attempt to create new colonies in the Americas. President Andrew Jackson advanced some democratic measures, but he dealt harshly with Native Americans, relocating many from their original homes in the Southeast to lands in the West.

Connecting ◆◆ Past and Present

The inventions of the 1800s transformed people's working conditions. How has modern technology changed today's workplace?

Using Vocabulary

From the list below, select the term that best completes each sentence.

capitalist	mass production
artisan	turnpike
annex	spiritual
spoils system	kitchen cabinet
canal	factory system

1. A road built by a private company that charged a toll was called a _____ .
2. A wealthy merchant who played a major role in investing in new factories was a _____ .
3. Jackson's method of giving jobs to his supporters was called the _____ .
4. A craftsperson who works at home or in a small shop is called an _____ .
5. An expressive religious song is called a _____ .
6. The Industrial Revolution made it possible for the _____ of goods.
7. The group of Jackson's friends who met informally was called his _____ .
8. A channel dug into the ground and filled with water is a _____ .
9. For $5 million, Spain agreed to let the United States _____ Florida.
10. The _____ brought workers and machines together in one place.

Check Understanding

1. **Explain** how the Industrial Revolution spurred the growth of factories in the North.
2. **Describe** the impact that improved means of transportation and communication had on the United States.
3. **Compare** the conditions of workers before the Industrial Revolution and after it began.
4. **Explain** why slavery persisted in the South even though most Southerners owned no slaves.

5. **Identify** two instances of revolt against slavery.

6. **Describe** the outcome of the *Amistad* mutiny.

7. **Explain** how independence for Latin American countries affected American foreign policy.

8. **Analyze** the impact of Jackson's presidency on Native Americans.

9. **Explain** how the tariff issue turned into a nullification controversy in 1832.

10. **Discuss** how democracy expanded in the United States during President Jackson's administration.

Critical Thinking

1. **Analyzing** Why was the United States so quick to adopt the new manufacturing methods of the Industrial Revolution?

2. **Understanding Causes and Effects** What were the effects of the invention of the steam engine?

3. **Comparing** Compare the economic systems of the North and the South in the early 1800s.

4. **Evaluating** Was Andrew Jackson an effective President? Use examples of his actions to justify your answer.

◆ **Connecting Past and Present** In your opinion, what event mentioned in this chapter had the greatest long-term impact on the United States? Defend your answer with reasons.

Writing to Describe

A French writer, Alexis de Tocqueville became famous for his observations of Americans in 1831. Imagine that, like De Tocqueville, you are visiting somewhere in the United States in the early 1800s. The place could be a cotton plantation, a cotton mill in Lowell, a settler's new home in the West, or another place mentioned in this chapter. **Write** a paragraph describing the scene you see and explaining what you think it shows about the changes occurring at that time in America.

Putting Skills to Work

DISTINGUISHING FACT FROM OPINION

In the Building Skills lesson on page 113, you learned how to distinguish fact from opinion. Read the statements below and decide which are fact and which are opinion. Be prepared to explain the reasons for your choices.

1. British citizens who came to the United States and built factories were traitors to Great Britain.

2. The Lowell factory workers were mostly young, unmarried women.

3. Andrew Jackson's "spoils" policy rewarded his political supporters.

4. Jackson's policy toward Native Americans was the only way for the United States to expand westward.

5. Between 1812 and 1819, four states joined the Union.

Interpreting the Timeline

Use the timeline on pages 106–107 to answer these questions.

1. What was the outcome of the 1812 presidential election?

2. What happened in Ireland one year after Samuel Morse successfully tested his telegraph?

3. What advances were made in the textile industry during this time period?

 *Portfolio Project*

THE SPIRIT OF MUSIC

Enslaved people often communicated their feelings in songs called spirituals. These songs almost always expressed a deep desire for freedom. Use library resources to find out about the role music played in the lives of enslaved African Americans. You might investigate the kinds of instruments they played or choose one song and analyze the meaning of the words. Present your findings to the class in an oral report. File the written version in your portfolio.

Chapter 7
Expansion of the United States 1820–1850

CHAPTER PREVIEW

Section 1 Native Americans in the West

Native Americans in the West developed ways of life suited to the different environments of the Plains, the Southwest, and California.

Section 2 Tensions in the West

As the United States expanded westward, Spanish and Mexican control of colonies in the West and Southwest weakened.

Section 3 An Expanding Nation

An agreement with Great Britain and a war with Mexico resulted in great territorial gains for the United States.

Section 4 Californians and a New State

The discovery of gold in California led to rapid population growth as people from all over the world flocked to the region.

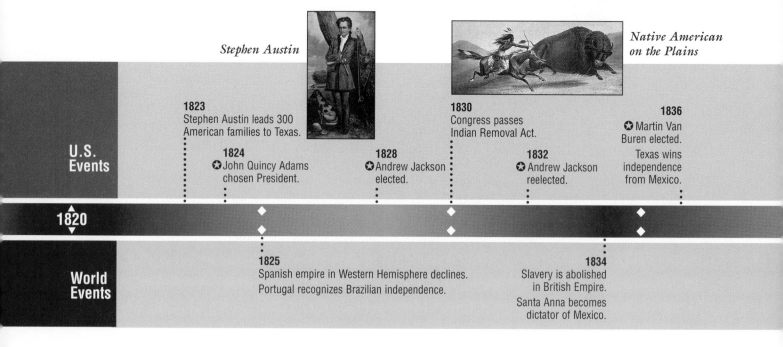

Stephen Austin

Native American on the Plains

U.S. Events

1823
Stephen Austin leads 300 American families to Texas.

1824
✪ John Quincy Adams chosen President.

1828
✪ Andrew Jackson elected.

1830
Congress passes Indian Removal Act.

1832
✪ Andrew Jackson reelected.

1836
✪ Martin Van Buren elected.
Texas wins independence from Mexico.

1820

World Events

1825
Spanish empire in Western Hemisphere declines.
Portugal recognizes Brazilian independence.

1834
Slavery is abolished in British Empire.
Santa Anna becomes dictator of Mexico.

▲ *Native Americans on horseback hunted the buffalo, which they relied on for food, clothing, and shelter. Until the Spaniards brought horses to the Americas in the 1500s, Native Americans had hunted on foot.*

Horses on the Plains

Hunting buffalo was central to the way of life on the Plains. Groups that hunted buffalo used every part of the animal. They ate buffalo meat, wore buffalo skins, and shaped tools from animal bones. They even built shelters, called **tipis,** from buffalo hide. Buffalo skins that had been pounded, stretched, and dried were used like paper to record important events.

Spanish conquistadors had brought horses and cattle to the Americas in the 1500s. Spaniards who lived in what is now the American Southwest employed local Native Americans, some of whom they called Pueblos, to tend their horses.

Horses, and knowledge about riding them, spread from group to group. Once, Native Americans had hunted buffalo on foot. With horses, hunters could kill as many buffalo in a day as they once had killed in a week. Horses and the buffalo hunt became a central part of life for many groups. It turned some from semi-sedentary people into nomadic hunters.

By the time white settlers arrived from the East, Native Americans had become skilled horse riders. No group rode horses better than the Comanche people.

One visitor said a Comanche on a horse seemed to be "half horse, half man . . . so [skillfully] managed that it appears but one animal, fleet and furious."

Native Americans from the East

The Indian Removal Act of 1830 forced the Five Tribes, who lived in the East, to move west. Their new home was in a region called Indian Territory, an enormous area that today includes much of Oklahoma. Fearing that the newcomers would take their lands, Plains groups sometimes attacked them.

The Five Tribes tried to rebuild their lives in a foreign and hostile land. They never regained their former prosperity, although the Cherokee adopted many of the customs of white settlers. The Five Tribes built schools and churches where both boys and girls studied. The Five Tribes also had a printing press, which they used to publish a newspaper and print books.

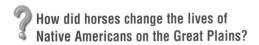 **How did horses change the lives of Native Americans on the Great Plains?**

▲ Navajo pottery often depicts animals from the southwestern environment.

◆ NATIVE AMERICANS IN THE SOUTHWEST

The Native Americans in the Southwest lived in a land of extreme temperatures. They had to grow or find food in a place with little rainfall.

One group that farmed successfully under these difficult conditions were the Hopi, whose name means "Peaceful Ones." They lived in northern Arizona and were descended from people who had lived in the region for at least 2,000 years.

The Hopi people were farmers who grew corn, squash, tobacco, and beans. These crops were easy to grow in the hot climate of the Southwest. The Hopi dug irrigation ditches to water their fields. Although these were a peaceful people, the Hopi were forced to do battle when the Apache and the Navajo raided them for food.

The Apache and Navajo were closely related. At first, both were hunter-gatherers. Unlike the Hopi, the Apache and Navajo were relative newcomers, arriving in the region in the 1400s. The Navajo gradually settled in villages and began to farm as well as hunt. After the Spaniards arrived, the Navajo learned how to raise sheep and horses. They increased their sheep herds and became skilled wool weavers. The Apache remained nomads who hunted and raided their neighbors. In the late 1600s, the Apaches first used horses and became skilled riders.

Many groups of Native Americans also lived in California. By the late 1700s, Spain had set up many missions in California. Native Americans were forced to live and work on mission lands. By the mid-1800s, about 30,000 of California's 300,000 Native Americans lived on mission lands.

Most of the California peoples were hunters and gatherers. In this region of abundant natural resources, wild plants, fish, and game were readily available. The groups that farmed lived along the Colorado River in the southern California deserts. One of these groups was the Mojave (ma´-häve-ē), a prosperous people who fished the Colorado River and grew corn, beans, pumpkins, and melons. Many of the Mojave died from diseases European settlers brought to the United States.

 How did Native Americans in the Southwest and in California live?

Section 1 Review

Check Understanding

1. **Define** (a) drought (b) semi-sedentary (c) tipi

2. **Explain** how horses changed buffalo hunting for the Native Americans of the Plains.

3. **Describe** how the buffalo was used by Native Americans living in the Great Plains.

4. **Tell** how the Native Americans of the Great Plains sometimes responded to the arrival of the Five Tribes.

5. **Describe** how the climate of the Southwest affected the lives of the people who lived there.

Critical Thinking

◆ **Connecting Past and Present** Spain's introduction of the horse changed the Native American way of life. What contributions from other countries have changed your way of life?

Write About Culture

Write a brief letter to the Plains people that George Catlin might have sent after visiting them.

BUILDING SKILLS

Reading a Graph: Population Changes in California

Graphs are drawings that present numerical information. A line graph may show change over time—it is a useful tool for revealing trends. A trend is the general direction taken by something that has changed or is changing. The graph on this page is a line graph. Other types of graphs include pictographs, pie graphs, and bar graphs.

Here's How

Follow these steps to read a line graph:

1. Read the title of the graph to determine the subject of the graph.

2. Identify the horizontal axis. The horizontal axis is the line running across the bottom of the graph. It shows one variable, or item that changes. What variable does the horizontal axis on the graph on this page show?

3. Identify the vertical axis. The vertical axis is the line running up and down the left side of the graph. The vertical axis shows another variable. What variable does the vertical axis on the graph on this page show?

4. Analyze the graph to identify trends. Does the line on the graph run in a particular direction? Are there increases, decreases, or sudden shifts in direction?

5. Draw conclusions from the graph. Study the information on the graph. What trends or patterns appear?

Here's Why

Graphs are good ways to present numerical information about historical topics. A graph presents information visually. A graph can help people compare numbers, identify increases and decreases, spot trends, and see the relation of parts to a whole. Graphs, like other visuals, help people understand information more easily than if the information were written.

Practice the Skill

Study the graph and answer the six questions that follow.

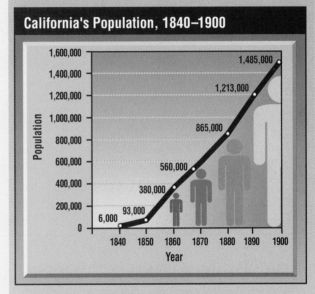

California's Population, 1840–1900

1. What time period does the graph represent?

2. How many people are represented by each point on the vertical axis? How much time is represented by each point on the horizontal axis?

3. How many people lived in California in 1840?

4. How many lived there in 1860?

5. About how much did the population increase between 1840 and 1890?

6. In a sentence, describe the trend shown in this graph.

Apply the Skill

Find another line graph in this textbook and write a brief description of the graph's content. Explain the trends shown and how you determined the trends.

Tensions in the West

PREVIEW

Objectives

- To examine how Spanish power declined in North America

- To describe how Mexico's control weakened in California, New Mexico, and Texas

- To explain how Texas won independence from Mexico

Vocabulary

rancho
Tejano

Beginning in the early 1500s, Spain built a huge empire in North America. As the United States expanded westward, American and Spanish settlers came into conflict. After winning its independence from Spain, Mexico faced pressures from American settlers moving westward into Texas.

◆ THE SPANISH IN NORTH AMERICA

At its peak in the last part of the 1700s, the Spanish empire stretched from the southern tip of South America to Canada. It included all the states of the present-day southern and southwestern United States and the western states from the Mississippi River to the Rocky Mountains.

Spain's Grip Weakens

When Spain began building its American empire, it was the most powerful nation in Europe. However, during the 1600s and 1700s, Spain's influence declined, and Great Britain and France became the most powerful European nations. These countries also began building large empires in the Americas.

Spain feared it might lose much of its North American empire to Britain. Hoping to reduce British control in North America, Spain provided important help to the 13 colonies during the American

Revolution. However, the American victory hurt Spain. The ideas of the American Revolution—liberty and freedom—soon spread to the people in the Spanish empire. The struggle against Spanish control occurred in both North and South America.

By 1825, Spain had lost most of its territory in the Americas. Mexico had become independent in 1821. In South America, one of the heroes in the wars for independence was Simón Bolívar, whose leadership was so effective that he became known as "the Liberator." Under Bolívar, the Spaniards were driven from the northern part of South America. Other leaders helped eject the Spaniards from today's Chile, Argentina, Ecuador, and Peru.

Some of the newly independent countries began to face problems governing their own far-flung territories. Mexico's control over its three provinces to the north— California, New Mexico, and Texas—was weak. The provinces, lightly settled with Mexicans, were hundreds of miles away from Mexico's main population centers. To their east was the United States.

California

In the 1820s, the Spanish presence in California mainly consisted of 21 missions, four presidios, or forts, and a few small cities along the coast. The missions were agricultural settlements where Native Americans were forced to provide most of the labor.

When Mexico gained independence, it decided that the economic growth of the missions was too slow. The government took the land from the missions and gave it to private individuals. Most of the new landowners were government officials or other wealthy people who knew political leaders. These people set up huge cattle farms, called **ranchos.**

The owners of the ranchos, called Californios, were wealthy people who lived well. However, the Native Americans, who did most of the work, were poor. Their lives on the ranchos were even harder than they had been on the missions.

Native Americans often raided Mexican settlements in California. When the Californios asked for protection from the Mexican government, they found that their government offered little help. Mexico maintained no courts, no police force, and no schools in its California lands. With no regular postal service, communication between California and Mexico City was rare.

In the 1820s, Californios began trading with the United States, selling leather and other products

▲ *Missions such as this one were built and maintained by Mexicans in the area that is now the southwestern United States. Many missions, beginning as religious and economic centers, became the foundations for flourishing cities.*

to supply New England's shoe industry. They used their earnings to buy American manufactured goods. This growing trade and cooperation led some Californios to begin thinking about joining the United States.

New Mexico

Mexico's control over New Mexico was also weak. Hundreds of miles of dry plains and high mountains lay between New Mexico and Central Mexico. In addition, the Native Americans of the region resisted Mexican rule and fought to maintain their traditional way of life. The Apache and other groups that lived in New Mexico wanted to keep their own customs.

Like the Californios, the New Mexicans traded with the United States. Most traders used the Santa Fe Trail, which connected Santa Fe with Independence, Missouri. By the mid-1820s, traders carried a great variety of goods in both directions along that route. The commerce helped strengthen the relationship between New Mexico and the United States. Some traders who traveled the difficult route also settled along it. Their presence tied the area more strongly to the United States.

Texas

Mexico's control was in greatest danger in Texas. In the 1820s, only about 2,500 Mexican Texans, called **Tejanos,** lived in Texas.

The Mexicans, eager to attract Americans to Texas, hoped they would help develop the area. The Mexicans also hoped American settlers might help take control of the Texas plains from Native Americans. In 1823 the Mexican government reached an agreement with Stephen A. Austin, an American. Austin would bring 300 American families to Texas. Each family would receive about 4,000 acres of land for farming and raising cattle. In return the Americans would become both Mexican citizens and Roman Catholics. They would obey the laws of Mexico.

Americans continued to migrate to Texas, and by 1830, there were about 16,000 settlers in the region. Many of them brought their enslaved Africans to work their farms and ranches. Meanwhile, the Tejano population was hardly growing.

Mexico began to worry about the strong American presence in Texas. The Americans had established their own schools and resisted learning Spanish.

Most Americans in Texas were Protestants and refused to become Catholics, as Mexican law required. Most of their trade was with the United States. To try to regain control over Texas, Mexico decided to force the Americans to obey Mexican laws, including a law outlawing slavery. The Americans resented the Mexican troops who came into Texas to enforce the laws.

 Why did Spain's and Mexico's power in North America decline?

◆ TEXAS INDEPENDENCE

By the 1830s, the situation in Texas was unstable and tense. The Americans living there were increasingly angry with the Mexican government. American settlers and a number of Tejanos hoped to become a self-governing state within Mexico. However, the Mexican government refused to grant this right.

In 1830 the Mexican government tightened its control over Texas. It outlawed further American immigration and the importation of more slaves into Texas. It also placed heavy taxes on goods coming from the United States and sent more troops to enforce Mexican laws in Texas.

In 1833, General Antonio López de Santa Anna became president of Mexico. Soon he ended constitutional government, making himself sole ruler of the country. Santa Anna refused to allow Texas to become a separate state within Mexico.

The Texans began to hear rumors about a possible attack by Santa Anna. In 1835, armed Texans attacked Mexican soldiers in Gonzales. Two months later, Texans took control of San Antonio. Then in early 1836, 59 Texans gathered for an important meeting in the small town of Washington-on-the-Brazos. On March 2, 1836, Texas declared its independence and set up the Republic of Texas. American-born Sam Houston became president, and Lorenzo de Zavala, a Tejano, became vice president.

Leading an army of several thousand men into Texas, Santa Anna moved quickly to end the rebellion. The first major battle took place in San Antonio, where about 190 Texans held a mission called the Alamo. Among the Alamo's defenders were Davy Crockett, Jim Bowie, and William B. Travis. They are remembered today as frontier heroes.

The battle for the Alamo took 12 days. When it was over, on March 6, 1836, all its adult defenders were dead. Among them were several Tejanos who had joined the fight for Texan independence. All

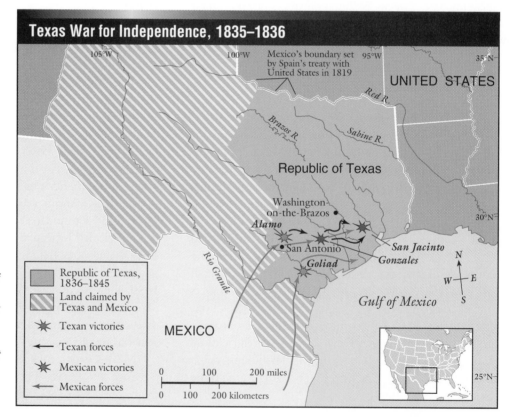

Geography *All the battles of the Texas War for Independence were fought on land that became the Republic of Texas in 1836.* **Interpreting the Map** *In what direction did Mexican forces have to travel to fight at Goliad?* ▶

Texas War for Independence, 1835–1836

Mexico's boundary set by Spain's treaty with United States in 1819

UNITED STATES

Red R.

Brazos R.

Sabine R.

Republic of Texas

Washington-on-the-Brazos

Alamo

San Antonio

Goliad

San Jacinto

Gonzales

Rio Grande

Gulf of Mexico

MEXICO

Republic of Texas, 1836–1845

Land claimed by Texas and Mexico

Texan victories

Texan forces

Mexican victories

Mexican forces

0   100   200 miles

0   100   200 kilometers

▲ As a teenager, Sam Houston served as a negotiator between the Cherokee and the U.S. government regarding land claims and agreements. This statue is in the Texas city of Houston, named after him.

across Texas the battle cry rang out, "Remember the Alamo."

As a young boy, Enrique Esparza lived through the battle of the Alamo. His father and mother made the decision to stay and fight. Later in his life, Esparza remembered,

" Bowie asked my father if he wished to go. . . . My father replied: 'No. I will stay and die fighting.' My mother then said: 'I will stay by your side and with our children die too. . . .' So we stayed. And so my father died as he said, fighting. He struck down one of his foes as he fell in the heap of slain. "

Shortly after the Alamo fell, 300 Texans surrendered to Santa Anna at the town of Goliad. Santa Anna had every one of them killed.

Sam Houston led the remaining Texan forces. He vowed to avenge the Alamo and Goliad. An experienced soldier, Houston retreated to gain time to build up and train his army. Volunteers from the United States joined him, and soon he had a force of 800 experienced fighters.

In April 1836, Sam Houston and his forces surprised Santa Anna and his army by attacking the Mexican camp near the San Jacinto (jə-sin´-tō) River. Within 18 minutes, the Texans had killed 630 Mexican soldiers and captured 730 others. The Texans quickly defeated the Mexican army and succeeded in capturing General Santa Anna. The map on page 132 shows the locations of the major battles of Texas's war for independence.

Sam Houston forced Santa Anna to sign a treaty granting Texas independence. Though the Mexican congress refused to honor the treaty, Mexico did not have the strength to continue the war. Texas was independent, whether Mexico recognized it or not.

What is the importance of the Alamo to the history of Texas?

Section 2 Review

Check Understanding

1. **Define** (a) rancho (b) Tejano

2. **Explain** why Spain's power in North America declined.

3. **Describe** how Mexico tried to maintain control over its land in North America.

4. **Relate** how the Texans and Tejanos won independence from Mexico.

Critical Thinking

Analyzing Why do you think Mexico tried to stop American immigration into Texas?

Write About Geography

Connecting Past and Present Compare the map showing the Republic of Texas on page 132 with a map of the United States in the atlas in the back of the book. Write a paragraph about how the boundaries of the Republic of Texas compare with the boundaries of Texas today.

Section 3

An Expanding Nation

PREVIEW

Objectives

- To explain how the mountain men helped the United States expand westward

- To describe the routes and conditions of the trails to the West

- To identify the causes and effects of the war with Mexico

Vocabulary

mountain man	communal
wagon train	Manifest Destiny

During the 1840s the United States expanded as far west as the Pacific coast. In the Northwest, the United States and Great Britain agreed to divide Oregon. Further expansion into the Southwest resulted from war.

◆ THE MOUNTAIN MEN

Meriwether Lewis and William Clark were the first Americans to blaze a trail across the vast interior of the United States to the West. Their expedition gave the United States a great deal of information about a rich and beautiful territory. Their journey also helped establish a United States claim to the Oregon Territory.

The first Americans to follow Lewis and Clark westward were the **mountain men.** They were fur trappers and traders who went west to make money. Later, many of them used their knowledge to become scouts for settlers and other travelers.

Mountain men lived difficult lives in a rough environment. They had to cope with floods, blizzards, and bitter cold. Mountain men learned from Native Americans how to survive by living off the land.

The mountain men were a varied group. They included men from every nationality and social class. One, John Colter, had been a member of Lewis and Clark's expedition. Another, James P. Beckwourth, was an African American who had been born a slave.

The mountain men hunted and explored in the mountains of the West. In their journeys, the mountain men helped open the main routes between the Great Plains and the Pacific Ocean.

How did the mountain men help people move West?

◆ TRAILS TO THE FAR WEST

Americans moving west took a number of different routes, as shown on the map on page 135. The weather could be unbearable, and the mountains and rivers were difficult to cross. Traders and pioneers faced many dangers.

The Santa Fe Trail

Trade along the Santa Fe Trail began in 1821, the year Mexico became independent. The Santa Fe Trail was a dangerous route. Travelers had to cross the desert and find their way over mountain passes. Pawnee, Apache, and Comanche warriors sometimes attacked. Diseases such as cholera and dysentery were common.

To protect themselves from attack, the traders rode in **wagon trains,** as many as 100 wagons traveling together. At night, they parked their wagons in a square with their wheels linked to each other. This kept their valuable animals inside and provided protection against attack.

Settlers moving west in covered wagons began their long journey early in the spring to avoid the danger of deadly winter storms. ▼

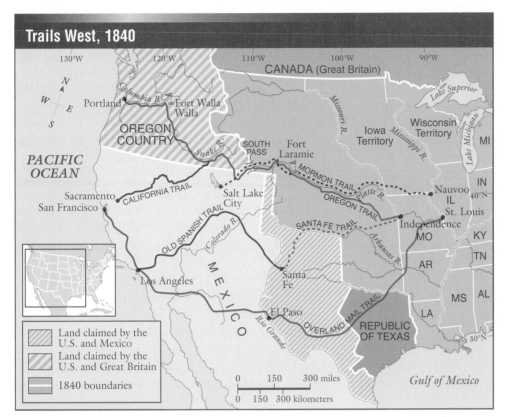

Trails West, 1840

130°W · 120°W · 110°W · 100°W · 90°W

CANADA (Great Britain)

Columbia R.

Portland · Fort Walla Walla

OREGON COUNTRY

PACIFIC OCEAN

Snake R.

SOUTH PASS · Fort Laramie

Missouri R.

Iowa Territory

Wisconsin Territory

Mississippi R.

Lake Superior

Lake Michigan

MI

IN

MORMON TRAIL

Platte R.

Nauvoo

IL

40°N

Sacramento · San Francisco

CALIFORNIA TRAIL

Salt Lake City

OLD SPANISH TRAIL

OREGON TRAIL

St. Louis

Independence

MO

KY

Colorado R.

SANTA FE TRAIL

Arkansas R.

TN

AR

MEXICO

Los Angeles

Santa Fe

El Paso

Rio Grande

OVERLAND MAIL TRAIL

REPUBLIC OF TEXAS

MS · AL

LA

30°N

Gulf of Mexico

Land claimed by the U.S. and Mexico

Land claimed by the U.S. and Great Britain

1840 boundaries

0 · 150 · 300 miles

0 · 150 · 300 kilometers

◄ **Geography** *Most trails heading west began in St. Louis or Independence, Missouri. Supplies such as wagons and horses could be purchased in these cities for the long trip.* **Interpreting the Map** *Which trail would you take if you were traveling from Independence to Fort Walla Walla?*

Each year the amount of goods transported along the trail increased. By the 1830s a trail ran from Independence, Missouri, through Santa Fe and all the way to the Pacific coast. By the 1850s, a regular stage coach line ran from Independence to Santa Fe.

The Oregon Trail

The Oregon Trail was the main route westward for American settlers from the East. Like the Santa Fe Trail, it began in Independence, Missouri. The Oregon Trail ran northwest for 2,000 miles to western Oregon and the Columbia River. Pioneers bound for California left the Oregon Trail in the Rocky Mountains and continued west on the California Trail. The Oregon Trail was the most direct route to the Pacific coast. It took the South Pass through the Rocky Mountains.

The Oregon Trail, considered easier than many other trails, presented some difficult challenges. South Pass, thought to be narrow, was actually 20 miles wide, surrounded by high walls of rock. The trail required pioneer families to travel without rest for about six months to avoid winter in the mountains. They had to get their wagons across fast-running rivers and face the storms, the bitter heat of the Great Plains, and the biting cold of the Rocky Mountains.

One traveler, Samuel Hancock, wrote of the dangers of the journey.

> We lost two of our men, Ayres and Stringer. Ayres got into trouble with his mules in crossing the stream. Stringer... went to his relief, and both were drowned in sight of their women folks. The bodies were never recovered.

The Mormons Head West

In 1846 members of the Church of Jesus Christ of Latter Day Saints began one of the largest migrations westward by a single group. The Mormons, as members of this religious group were called, were organized in 1830 in Palmyra, New York, by a man named Joseph Smith. The Mormons accepted the Bible as the word of God but added a book they called The Book of Mormon. They believed in **communal** land ownership, or land shared by members of the community. They also believed in polygyny, the practice of having more than one wife at a time. The Mormons were persecuted for their religious beliefs and were continually moving to new locations. Their last home east of the Mississippi was in Illinois, where a mob murdered Smith in 1844. Brigham Young became the new leader of the Mormon church. In 1846, he led several thousand Mormons westward along the Oregon Trail.

After crossing South Pass, Young headed southwest into Utah and came to the Great Salt Lake. There in the summer of 1847, the Mormons began building their new home. By the time Young died in 1877, more than 100,000 Mormons lived in Utah. They had settled in Salt Lake City and in 200 other communities in Utah.

 What difficulties were encountered on the trails to the far West?

◆ MANIFEST DESTINY

In the 1840s many Americans, proud of their country, wanted to expand it. They believed in **Manifest Destiny**—the belief that the U.S. had the right to extend its boundaries to the Pacific Ocean.

After Texas won its independence from Mexico, many Americans hoped it would join the United States. Most Texans agreed. They feared Mexico, which did not recognize Texan independence. However, Jackson and a majority in Congress refused to add Texas as a state. Slavery was the main issue. At the time there were 13 slave states and 13 free states in the nation. Slavery was legal in Texas. If Texas joined the United States, the balance would be upset. The President and the Congress feared also that annexing Texas would lead to war with Mexico.

The annexation of Texas was delayed for almost ten years. In the presidential campaign of 1844, James Polk proposed annexing both Texas and the Oregon Territory. Oregon, which did not practice slavery, would balance the impact of admitting Texas. Polk was elected in part because of his position on expansion. In 1845, Congress finally voted for annexation of Texas, although by only a small margin.

American settlers had started arriving in the Oregon Territory in the 1830s and 1840s. As stories filtered eastward about the good land and abundant resources available in Oregon, "Oregon fever" took

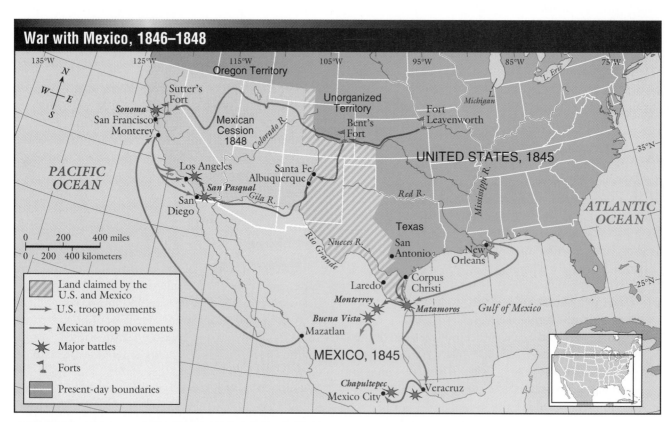

War with Mexico, 1846–1848

Land claimed by the U.S. and Mexico
→ U.S. troop movements
→ Mexican troop movements
✳ Major battles
⚑ Forts
Present-day boundaries

▲ **Geography** *The three battle fronts in the war with Mexico were (1) northern Mexico, (2) Central Mexico, and (3) the coast of California.* **Interpreting the Map** *Based on the map, what role did the Pacific Ocean and the Gulf of Mexico play in the war?*

136 ◆ Unit 2

hold and more settlers came. By the mid-1840s, there were about 6,000 Americans in Oregon. Some Americans were ready to go to war with Britain to control the Oregon Territory. Despite his expansionist beliefs, President James Polk did not want a war. In 1846, he agreed to a compromise. Oregon was divided at latitude 49°N. Britain got the lands north of the line, and the United States got the lands south of the line. Eventually, the U.S. states of Oregon, Washington, and Idaho, and parts of Wyoming and Montana were carved from the territory.

 How did the United States expand in the 1840s?

◆ WAR WITH MEXICO

The annexation of Texas angered Mexico. Mexico's leaders believed their soldiers could defeat the small U.S. Army. In 1845, President Polk offered to give Mexico $5 million for New Mexico and $25 million for California. Outraged, the Mexicans turned down the offer.

President Polk was determined to acquire California and New Mexico. When Mexico refused to sell its territory, Polk decided to fight.

Polk already had sent an army under General Zachary Taylor to Texas. At first, the army camped along the Nueces (nōō-ā´-sās) River, which Mexico claimed was the southern border of Texas. Polk then ordered General Taylor to move south to the Rio Grande, which Texas claimed as its border. Mexico's president ordered his troops across the Rio Grande. In a small battle, several Americans were killed.

On May 13, 1846, Congress declared war on Mexico. The United States attacked Mexico from three directions. One group of U.S. soldiers overran New Mexico in two months. Naval and land forces attacked California. They were helped when American settlers revolted and set up a "Republic of California," replacing the Mexican flag with their own flag. By January 1847, California was in U.S. hands.

Despite these defeats, Mexico did not surrender. To end the war, President Polk sent an army to capture Mexico City. After several battles, the Americans took Mexico City. Still, Mexico fought on for another month before surrendering. The map on page 136 shows the major battles of the war.

The United States and Mexico signed a peace treaty on February 2, 1848. With a stroke of the pen, Mexico lost about half of its territory. The United States agreed to pay Mexico $15 million for the newly acquired territory. It also agreed to pay about $3 million in claims owed to American citizens by the Mexican government. The Treaty of Guadalupe Hidalgo recognized the United States' annexation of Texas and turned over to the United States the territories that now form the states of Arizona, California, Nevada, New Mexico, and Utah, and half of Colorado. Mexico accepted the Rio Grande as its border with Texas. The U.S. government promised to fully protect the rights of Mexicans living in U.S. territory. However, these agreements were soon violated. Many Mexicans lost their property when the area where they lived became part of the United States.

 What were the causes of the war with Mexico?

Section 3 Review

Check Understanding

1. **Define** (a) mountain man (b) wagon train (c) communal (d) Manifest Destiny

2. **Explain** how the mountain men's way of life differed from that of many other Americans of their time.

3. **Explain** how the United States expanded in the 1840s.

4. **Describe** the causes and effects of the war with Mexico.

Critical Thinking

◆ **Connecting Past and Present** Compare the relationship between the United States and Mexico in the 1800s with their relationship today.

Write About History

As an advisor to President Polk, let him know in writing why you do or do not support his position on war with Mexico.

Californians and a New State

PREVIEW

Objectives

- To explain how the discovery of gold affected the growth of California

- To describe how California became a state

Vocabulary

forty-niner
boom town
water rights

In January 1848 a California landowner named John Sutter instructed his carpenters to build a sawmill on the American River. Sutter's land was in the fertile Sacramento Valley, about 75 miles northeast of San Francisco. The settlement he built there for his workers was called Sutter's Fort. On January 24, James Marshall, one of the carpenters, was inspecting a ditch near the construction site. He later recorded his observations:

> My eye was caught by something shining in the bottom of the ditch. . . . I reached my hand down and picked it up; it made my heart thump, for I was certain it was gold. The piece was about half the size and shape of the pea. Then I saw another.

Sutter tried to keep his discovery a secret. However, in March, the *Californian*, a San Francisco newspaper, announced Marshall's find. Almost immediately, gold fever swept California and quickly spread. The California gold rush was on.

◆ THE CALIFORNIA GOLD RUSH

The gold rush changed California. In 1848 the state had fewer than 20,000 people. By the end of 1849, almost 90,000 gold seekers had arrived.

Getting to California

The gold seekers who rushed to California in 1849, known as **forty-niners,** came by boat and by land from the United States and all over the world. No matter how they came, the journey was difficult and dangerous. Some came from the east by sea, taking a ship to the Isthmus of Panama. There they crossed overland through the jungle and then sailed north to California. Others made the stormy and dangerous voyage around South America. Many of the ships used on that route were not seaworthy, and some sank with all aboard. The ocean voyage could take as long as six months.

The overland route on the Oregon Trail and through the Rockies was not much easier or safer than the sea route. Many of the gold seekers who began the California Trail did not reach its end. They died in storms or drowned crossing flooded rivers. In 1849 alone, about 5,000 died of cholera between South Pass and Sutter's Fort.

Life in the Gold Fields

Life was hard in the gold fields. Prospectors in mining camps lived in tents and spent months digging and panning for gold with picks, shovels, and wash pans. It was backbreaking work. Miners had to pay outrageous prices for the goods they needed. Flour cost as much as $800 a barrel, and eggs were $4 a dozen. A toothpick cost 50 cents, and a newspaper from the East was $5.

The main escapes from the hard work were drinking and gambling. Professional gamblers often cheated miners out of their earnings. Miners could also not easily find safety. Fights and murder were common as law and order broke down. Often men took the law into their own hands, which only made the violence worse. Many of the victims of this violence were Californios and Mexicans. They were often forced out of the mines and beaten.

As mining camps grew, they became **boom towns,** or towns that seemed to spring up overnight. Many boom towns often died as quickly as they began. When gold ran out, they were often abandoned as miners pressed on to search for new deposits of gold.

Only a small number of miners actually struck it rich. Of the tens of thousands of people searching for gold in 1850, most barely covered their expenses. Those who prospered most during the gold rush were not miners at all. They were merchants and traders who sold the miners equipment and other goods. Some miners gave up and went home. Many others gave up mining but stayed in California. They took different kinds of jobs in the mining region or in the growing cities. Their efforts helped build a prosperous community in a region that had much to offer. These new Californians firmly established the United States on the Pacific coast.

Opportunity and Prejudice in the Gold Fields

Most of those who came to California during the gold rush were men. In 1850 fewer than 2 percent of the people in the gold mining areas were women.

Most women who went to the gold fields had come overland to California with their husbands. Those who came to California alone usually stayed and worked in the large cities. Single women who did make it to the mining region found opportunities to make money cooking or washing clothes.

African Americans also found opportunity in the gold fields. Among the forty-niners were hundreds of free African Americans. Some enslaved African Americans came with their owners. However, white miners objected to slaves working in the gold fields. They refused to compete with slave labor. In 1849 a group of Texans tried to put their enslaved people to work panning for gold. In response, the white miners got together and ordered them to leave. But by 1852 there were 2,000 African Americans in California, many working in the area's mines.

Immigrants from China also found opportunity in the gold fields. The gold rush drew 20,000 Chinese immigrants to California within three years. After the gold rush ended, many stayed in California and worked in a wide variety of jobs and businesses.

Chinese immigrants faced widespread discrimination in the gold fields, as did other foreign immigrants. In 1850 the California legislature passed a Foreign Miners' Tax requiring miners who were not citizens to pay a high fee to dig for gold. The law, written to restrict Chinese miners, also counted Californios as foreigners, even though they were U.S. citizens. Californios, Mexicans, and other Hispanics were expelled from the mines. If they resisted, violence was often used against them.

How did the gold rush affect the population of California?

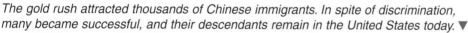

The gold rush attracted thousands of Chinese immigrants. In spite of discrimination, many became successful, and their descendants remain in the United States today. ▼

▲ With the influx of thousands of miners, boom towns sprang up overnight. Poorly built shacks were separated by roads that often were nothing more than dirt ruts.

◆ STATEHOOD FOR CALIFORNIA

The gold rush brought people to California from all over the world, giving California a broad and varied cultural heritage. People came from China, Hawaii, Australia, many European countries, and a number of Latin American countries.

By 1849, California's population was large enough for it to apply for statehood. The people elected delegates to a convention to write a constitution. The convention delegates unanimously agreed to ban slavery in California.

Eight of the forty-eight delegates to the convention were Californios. One of their goals was to protect their rights, particularly the right to vote.

After the convention, Californios played an important role in California's early state government. In several areas, California law followed Spanish and Mexican practices. One example was **water rights,** which determined who had the right to use water that flowed from one person's land to another. This was a key issue in dry regions, such as southern California. A law that gave women more property rights also was based on Spanish tradition.

When California applied for statehood, the debate over slavery became more heated than ever before.

Southerners were angry because California had banned slavery. In Washington, D.C., a senator from Georgia warned northern congressmen:

> **If . . . you seek to drive us supporters of slavery from the territories of California and New Mexico, I am for disunion.**

Finally, in 1850 opposing forces in Congress reached a compromise. There were four parts to the compromise: (1) territories that were obtained from Mexico could decide the issue of slavery for themselves; (2) slave trade was banned in Washington, D.C.; (3) stricter laws required state governments to help return runaway slaves; and (4) California was admitted as a free state.

 How was slavery an issue in the debate over California's statehood?

Section 4 Review

Check Understanding

1. **Define** (a) forty-niner (b) boom town (c) water rights

2. **Explain** how the gold rush provided opportunities for many people.

3. **Describe** how the issue of slavery in California was resolved.

Critical Thinking

◆ **Connecting Past and Present** Where are population shifts taking place in the United States today? Explain why they occur.

Write About Economics

Look back at the graph on page 129. Explain in writing why California's population increased dramatically between 1848 and 1900.

POINT of VIEW

THE CALIFORNIA GOLD RUSH

When the San Francisco newspaper the *Californian* announced James Marshall's discovery of gold, it set off a case of gold fever. The fever was so contagious that before the year was out, 10,000 men were staking out their claims. In 1849, about 90,000 people made their way to California, beginning one of the largest mass migrations in history.

The diaries of the travelers to California tell stories of hunger, thirst, and hardship willingly undertaken. All forty-niners believed that riches awaited them at the end.

Here are several entries from the diary of Ansel McCall, who traveled to California from New York.

How times change and men change with them! I look in vain among the ragged, grave and bronzed codgers, dragging themselves wearily along, for those dashing, sprightly…young fellows, full of song and laughter, whom I saw in the valley of the Blue, on the banks of the Platte, two months ago.

• • • •

While our animals were resting, we selected an overturned wagon wheel, built a fire in the tarred hub, and boiled thereon a pot of coffee, and then squatted around it on the ground, like merry knights of the round table, and partook of our midnight meal of coffee and hard tack, the only refreshment we had taken for twelve hours.

• • • •

Others had arrived here before us. Their baleful camp fires gleamed here and there, and in their pale and misty light, tall gaunt figures, with long disheveled locks, long beards, and tattered garments, perfectly white from the fine impenetrable dust which covered them, flitted about in moody silence.

• • • •

The ground was covered with bleached and whitened bones of horses and cattle, the wrecks of other years, and the dried and decaying carcasses of innumerable animals of this, broken carts and wagons, and all imaginable debris.

From the diaries of Ansel McCall, 1849

Examining Point of View

1. In the first entry, McCall describes the men around him. How have they changed in the last two months?

2. What clues do you have about the outcome of earlier journeys along the trail?

3. Judging from these passages, what were some of the hardships the travelers faced?

4. What can you tell about Ansel McCall from reading his diary entries?

What's Your Point of View?

The 10,000 people who made their way to the gold fields were motivated by the promise of riches. What else might motivate people to make a dangerous trip?

Write a brief story describing the motivations for, as well as the fears and expectations of, relocating to an unfamiliar place.

Chapter 7
Review

CHAPTER SUMMARY

Section 1

Native Americans on the Great Plains, in the Southwest, and in California developed different ways of life. Some became semi-sedentary, while others were nomadic. The horse changed the way many Native Americans of the Plains lived. The relocation of the Five Tribes to the West caused some apprehension among the Native Americans of the Plains.

Section 2

After Mexico won its independence, its control of the borderlands was weakened. As more U.S. settlers moved west, tension between the United States and Mexico increased. Led by U.S. settlers, Texas declared its independence from Mexico in 1836. In the war that followed, Texas defeated Mexico.

Section 3

In the 1840s many Americans believed in the idea of Manifest Destiny. Mountain men blazed trails west, and thousands of settlers soon followed. The United States annexed Texas in 1845. In 1846 the Oregon Territory was divided between the United States and Britain. The United States and Mexico went to war over territorial disputes. As a result of winning the war with Mexico, the United States gained a huge amount of territory.

Section 4

Once gold was discovered in California in 1848, people arrived by the thousands to seek their fortunes. Many people who went to California stayed and built lives there. As settlements grew, Californios and Native Americans lost a great deal of their land. In 1850, California became a state.

Connecting ◆◆ Past and Present

The lives of Native Americans were radically changed when settlers arrived. How would you feel if newcomers to your community forced you to change your way of life?

Using Vocabulary

From the list below, select the term that best completes each sentence.

drought	mountain man
semi-sedentary	Manifest Destiny
Tejano	tipi
wagon train	boom town

1. Many times, people who made their way west traveled as a group in a _____ for safety.

2. When a mining camp grew extremely fast, it became a _____ .

3. A shelter made from buffalo hides by some Native Americans was called a _____ .

4. _____ was the belief that the United States had a right to expand as far as the Pacific coast.

5. The Native Americans who hunted buffalo on the Plains but then returned to their villages are referred to as _____ .

6. A Mexican settler in Texas was called a _____ .

7. A _____ was a fur trapper and trader who went west to make money.

8. The lack of rain for a long period of time is called a _____ .

Check Understanding

1. **Describe** some of the main characteristics of the cultures of the Plains peoples.

2. **Discuss** how Native Americans of the Southwest and of California developed distinct ways of life.

3. **Explain** how the arrival of the Five Tribes affected the Plains peoples.

4. **Examine** why Spain's and Mexico's control over the borderlands became weak.

5. **Describe** how Californios built a culture based on raising cattle.

6. **Describe** the outcome of the battle for the Alamo.

7. **Identify** the influence of Lewis and Clark on Western settlement.

8. **Describe** the hardships that settlers faced as they traveled the trails west.

9. **Identify** at least one cause and one effect of the war with Mexico.

10. **Explain** the basic idea of Manifest Destiny.

Critical Thinking

1. **Analyzing** Why was the United States able to acquire so much territory in such a short span of time?

2. **Evaluating** What were the conditions endured by most settlers going west?

3. **Comparing** What were some similarities and differences between the lives of the mountain men and the lives of the people in the gold fields?

4. **Drawing Conclusions** What were some of the outcomes of the gold rush?

◆ **Connecting Past and Present** Does any kind of frontier still exist today? Explain.

Writing to Persuade

Imagine that you are a forty-niner. **Write** a letter to your relatives or friends persuading them to come to California. In your letter, describe both the positive and negative aspects of life in California during the gold rush.

Interpreting the Timeline

Use the timeline on pages 124–125 to answer these questions.

1. When was slavery outlawed in the British Empire?

2. How many years after gold was discovered in California did California become a state?

3. What is the relationship between the events of 1823 and 1836, shown on the timeline?

Putting Skills to Work

READING A GRAPH

Study the graph below and answer the questions that follow.

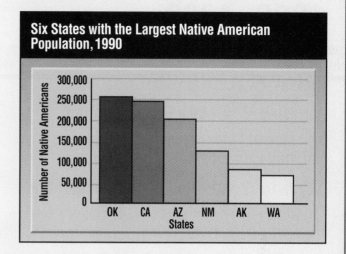

Six States with the Largest Native American Population, 1990

1. Which three states have the largest Native American population?

2. Approximately how many Native Americans live in the state of Washington?

3. About how many more Native Americans live in Arizona than in Alaska?

Portfolio Project

CULTURAL CHANGE

Choose a group of people affected by U.S. westward expansion. You might consider the Californios, the Tejanos, or a Native American group. Use library resources to collect information about how westward expansion affected the people you chose. Then create a bulletin board display of maps, pictures, and articles that help you tell their story.

Chapter 8
Immigration and Reform
1820–1860

CHAPTER PREVIEW

Section 1 A More Diverse Nation
The United States changed as its cities rapidly expanded and immigrants arrived in great numbers.

Section 2 A Period of Experimentation
Caught up in the excitement of religious reform, Americans went through a period of religious awakening and social experimentation.

Section 3 An Age of Reform
Turning their attention toward problems at home, Americans spoke out against slavery, as well as against alcohol, and worked to improve education and the care of the mentally disabled.

Section 4 The Women's Rights Movement
Having played key roles in earlier reform movements, a number of American women devoted their lives to achieving equal rights for all women.

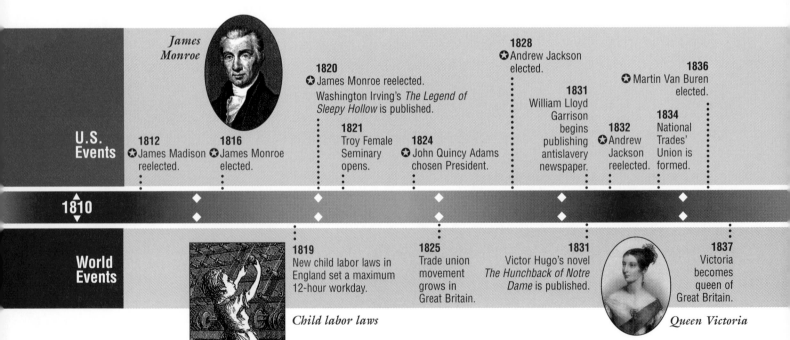

U.S. Events

James Monroe

1812 ✪ James Madison reelected.

1816 ✪ James Monroe elected.

1820 ✪ James Monroe reelected. Washington Irving's *The Legend of Sleepy Hollow* is published.

1821 Troy Female Seminary opens.

1824 ✪ John Quincy Adams chosen President.

1828 ✪ Andrew Jackson elected.

1831 William Lloyd Garrison begins publishing antislavery newspaper.

1832 ✪ Andrew Jackson reelected.

1834 National Trades' Union is formed.

1836 ✪ Martin Van Buren elected.

1810

World Events

1819 New child labor laws in England set a maximum 12-hour workday.

Child labor laws

1825 Trade union movement grows in Great Britain.

1831 Victor Hugo's novel *The Hunchback of Notre Dame* is published.

1837 Victoria becomes queen of Great Britain.

Queen Victoria

Portfolio Project

AMERICAN CITIES, THEN AND NOW

Throughout the history of the United States, cities and towns have changed dramatically. Yet most communities, whatever their size, show some evidence of their early days. As you read how immigration and reform changed the nation, keep in mind how the events in the chapter might have affected your community. At the end of this chapter, you will complete an assignment about a community as it was in its early days and as it is today.

▲ Immigrants from around the world arrived in the United States seeking new opportunities. ◆◇ **Connecting Past and Present** *How might these newcomers have felt? How would you feel if you were moving to a new country?*

Seneca Falls convention

1841
✪ John Tyler becomes President.

1840
✪ William Henry Harrison elected.

1844
✪ James K. Polk elected.

1847
Frederick Douglass founds the antislavery newspaper, *North Star.*

1848
✪ Zachary Taylor elected. Seneca Falls convention is held.

1850
✪ Millard Fillmore becomes President. Know-Nothing Party is formed.

1852
✪ Franklin Pierce elected.

1856
✪ James Buchanan elected.

1860
✪ Abraham Lincoln elected.
Women's property rights are protected by a New York State law.

1864
✪ Lincoln reelected.

1865

1848
Revolutions sweep Europe, fueled by the problems of the Industrial Revolution.

1859
Darwin's theory of evolution arouses bitter controversy.

1860
Giuseppe Garibaldi forms a volunteer army to unify Italy.

A More Diverse Nation

PREVIEW

Objectives

• To explain why people flocked to American cities after the 1820s

• To analyze the reasons for the formation of unions

• To identify the causes for a wave of immigration from western Europe

Vocabulary

labor union	thresher
rural	tenement
urban	strike
mechanical reaper	nativism

Americans not only moved westward between 1820 and 1860, but they also moved into the growing cities of the United States. Though people found new opportunities there, they faced new problems, too. Often they had to live and work in overcrowded conditions. Factory workers in the cities worked long hours. To improve their lives, workers tried to band together to form the first American **labor unions**. A labor union is a group of workers who organize to protect their rights and improve working conditions.

◆ CITIES GROW AND FARMS CHANGE

In the early 1800s, the United States was almost completely a **rural** nation, where most Americans lived on farms in the country. Only 6 percent of the five million Americans lived in towns with a population of 2,500 or more. There were just six cities with populations of more than 10,000 people. Only Philadelphia and New York each had more than 50,000 people.

In the 1820s, American cities began to expand. Anne Royall, a self-educated woman who traveled widely, portrayed the excitement and energy of New York City in 1826. Touring the waterfront, she wrote,

"The warehouses, docks, shipyards [contain] a flood of human beings. Here the sound of axes, saws, and hammers from a thousand hands; there the ringing of the blacksmith's anvil . . . the whole city surrounded by masts; the Hudson, East rivers, and the bay covered with vessels. In short, imagine upwards of a hundred thousand people, all engaged in business. Add to these more than a thousand strangers which swarm in the streets. Such is New York."

By 1850, the United States was being transformed into an **urban** nation, or a place with many cities. In 1850 more than 60 cities each had more than 10,000 people. Seven had populations of more than 100,000 people. New York City, the largest city, had more than 500,000 people. Beyond the Appalachians, new cities, such as Chicago and St. Louis, were growing quickly.

Changes on the Farm

Between 1820 and 1850, a number of inventions changed the way Americans farmed. One invention was Cyrus McCormick's **mechanical reaper,** a machine for harvesting grain. Before the mechanical reaper, farmers had to cut and gather wheat using hand tools. With McCormick's reaper, farmers could harvest as much in a day as they could in two weeks using a hand-held cutting implement, the sickle.

Other inventions also helped farmers work faster and produce more. A mechanical hay mower made it possible for one farmer to do the work of eight farmers working by hand. The mechanical **thresher** speeded the work of separating the valuable kernels of the wheat plant from the husks. John Deere's new steel plows helped farmers turn over the soil of the Great Plains. Farmers no longer produced food just for themselves and their families, as they had in 1800. There was now a surplus of crops to sell.

New methods of transportation also changed farming. By 1850, American farmers were sending their products by train to customers in distant markets. They also were buying machines, tools, nails, and other products from factories in the cities.

As machines took over jobs once done by hand, there was a surplus of labor on the farms. People who were no longer needed to work on farms were forced to go to the cities to find work.

Life and Work in the Cities

There were many jobs in the cities for people leaving the farms. Businesses and industries needed salespeople, clerks, laborers, skilled craftworkers, and factory workers.

However, the rapid growth of cities created many problems. Services did not keep up with the population growth. Sewer systems were inadequate. Human waste and garbage often polluted drinking water. The huge numbers of animals living in the cities made conditions even more unhealthful. Overcrowding in poorer neighborhoods bred disease. Smallpox, diphtheria, and yellow fever spread quickly.

Slums such as New York's Five Points neighborhood appeared during the 1820s. Immigrants from Ireland and Germany, native-born laborers, free African Americans, and working people without job skills crowded into these neighborhoods. They lived in **tenements,** apartment buildings that often did not meet high standards for sanitation and safety. Sometimes a dozen or more people lived in a single room. Fire was a constant danger to tenement dwellers.

As difficult as city life was, many cities were places of technological change, as well as examples of social and political reform. Boston introduced gas street lights in 1817. New York started a public transportation system in 1832. Several cities set up police forces for public safety. New York started its police force in 1844. Boston and Philadelphia followed.

? Why did American cities experience rapid growth in the first half of the 1800s?

◆ LABOR BEGINS TO ORGANIZE

During the first half of the 1800s, many American factory workers endured poor working conditions and low wages. So, too, did laborers who dug canals or built railways.

Artisans, who were skilled workers in crafts, enjoyed much better conditions. Shoemakers, carpenters, tailors, cabinet makers, printers, and house builders were the first American workers to form labor unions. The first artisans to organize were shoemakers in Philadelphia in the 1790s. Craftworkers in other trades and in other cities quickly did the same. Membership in each new union was limited to skilled workers in a particular craft.

The rapid growth of cities often created overcrowding in poorer neighborhoods. Many immigrants were forced to live in cramped and dirty neighborhoods, such as the one pictured here. ▼

▲ In 1860 in Massachusetts, 800 women shoemakers went on strike to demand better working conditions.

The first unions tried to get their members and employers to agree to certain wages or conditions. Some workers went on **strike,** or work stoppage to protest an act or condition, when employers refused. The early labor unions did not survive for long after courts began ruling that these strikes, which interfered with trade, were illegal. Until the mid-1800s, the effectiveness of unions increased during times of economic prosperity and decreased during economic downturns. When jobs were scarce, workers did not make demands. During bad times, employers found people willing to work even under undesirable conditions. For example, after an economic downturn in 1819, almost every existing union closed.

Unions Revive

When better economic times returned in the mid-1820s, artisans from many trades organized again. As before, they protested against competition from unskilled workers. The artisans were especially upset over the new competition from factories. Often, women and children worked in these factories for low wages and under poor conditions. The goods they produced could be sold more cheaply .han goods made by skilled craftworkers.

By the mid-1830s, there were more than 200 active labor unions with more than 300,000 members. More than 160 strikes took place between 1833 and 1837. Yet most of these strikes were unsuccessful. Employers hired nonunion workers at lower wages to take the place of the strikers.

The National Trades' Union

The labor union movement slowly grew in spite of the unions' inability to change working conditions. In 1834, delegates from a number of craft unions in New York, Boston, Philadelphia, and other cities met in New York to form the National Trades' Union. During 1835 and 1836, shoemakers and carpenters formed national unions.

However, in 1837 hard economic times returned. Workers were willing to accept almost any wage in order to survive. Neither the National Trades' Union nor the national craft unions survived the difficult years that followed.

When prosperity returned in the 1840s, workers once again began to organize unions. They won a small victory with an 1842 court decision in Massachusetts. The Massachusetts Supreme Court ruled that unions had a legal right to exist. The court said it was not "criminal for men to agree together to exercise their. . . rights . . . to serve their own interests."

Unskilled workers had less success in organizing. Young women in factories frequently were paid $3 for working six 12-hour days per week. Strikes were unusual because the women knew that immigrants were cheap replacements. Immigrants, eager to get work, would often take very low-paying jobs. Women's unions formed, but they did not last. In 1834, factory owners in Lowell, Massachusetts, cut women's wages by 15 percent. One thousand women went out on strike, but the owners threatened to hire other workers, and the strike collapsed.

What conditions led workers to form labor unions?

Study Hint

To understand the main idea of a section, look at the heads and the subheads that follow. For example, in the following section, Immigration from Europe is the main idea. Find three subheads that tell more about the main idea.

◆ IMMIGRATION FROM EUROPE

Between independence, in 1776, and the early 1820s, only about 300,000 immigrants came to the United States. From 1830 to 1840, more than half a million immigrants arrived in the United States. Forty-four percent came from Ireland, 15 percent came from Great Britain, and the rest came from other European countries. A million and a half immigrants came between 1840 and 1850. Forty-nine percent of them were from Ireland.

To reach the United States, the immigrants endured terrible hardships. They were packed into crowded, poorly managed, and poorly ventilated vessels. Hunger and disease were common. Many did not survive the voyage or were hospitalized when they arrived.

Immigration from Ireland

Large numbers of Irish immigrants came to the United States after disease wiped out the entire potato crop in 1845. Potatoes were the staple diet in Ireland, and the next several years brought terrible famine and widespread starvation. More than one million people died.

Though most of the new Irish immigrants had been farmers, few had the money to buy land in the United States. Instead, most settled in the cities of the Northeast, where low-paying jobs were available. By the 1850s the Irish made up half the population of New York and Boston. They also found homes in other growing cities, such as Albany, Baltimore, St. Louis, Cincinnati, and New Orleans.

Because they had few job skills, most Irish immigrant men took jobs as laborers or factory workers. They helped build railroads, worked on the docks, and did other hard manual work. Irish women often worked as servants in private homes or in factories. The growing industrialization of the United States was creating many jobs for these and other immigrants.

German Immigration

Unlike the Irish, many Germans immigrated to the United States because of political conditions in their homeland. In 1848 a revolution swept Germany. The goal of the revolutionaries was to establish democracy, but the revolution failed. Many supporters of democracy were forced to flee. Between 1848 and 1860, one million Germans came to the United States.

▲ The challenges immigrants faced in adapting to a new land were often expressed in songs. Pictured above is the cover of one such song.

Many of the German immigrants found little difficulty in settling in the United States. Most had some money, and many were skilled in crafts or farming. Some immigrants moved to farms in the Midwest. Others settled in midwestern cities and towns and opened businesses. Soon there were large communities of German immigrants in St. Louis, Chicago, Milwaukee, and Cincinnati.

A German immigrant who arrived in Chicago in the 1850s described life in his new home:

"The houses in which we lived in those days in Chicago were modest one- or two-story frame dwellings. . . . Business houses were at no great distance from the homes and the men were generally to be found with their families after business hours. The women occupied themselves with needlework, household duties, and reading. The children were reared to honor and obey their parents."

A small minority of the immigrants from Germany were Jewish. German Jews began immigrating to the

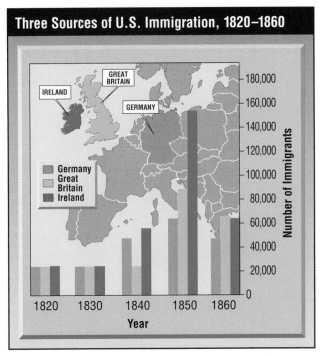

Three Sources of U.S. Immigration, 1820–1860

GREAT BRITAIN

IRELAND

GERMANY

Number of Immigrants

- Germany
- Great Britain
- Ireland

180,000
160,000
140,000
120,000
100,000
80,000
60,000
40,000
20,000
0

1820 1830 1840 1850 1860

Year

▲ **Citizenship** *Throughout the 1800s, many immigrants came to the U.S. from Great Britain, Ireland, and Germany.* **Interpreting the Graph** *About how many more Irish immigrants arrived in 1850 than in 1840?*

United States in the 1820s. By the time of the Civil War, there were about 150 communities with large Jewish populations across the United States. The graph above provides information on immigration from Great Britain, Ireland, and Germany between 1820 and 1860.

Reaction to Immigration

The arrival of many foreign-born people caused problems among native-born Americans. Many distrusted the customs, dress, and language of the immigrants. Also, native-born workers complained that immigrants were willing to work for low wages. Competition for jobs tended to drive wages down. Furthermore, when native-born workers went out on strike, owners often hired immigrants to replace them.

In the 1840s a wave of resentment against immigration swept the United States. This reaction against foreign-born people is called **nativism** because it came from native-born Americans. By the 1850s, hostility to immigrants was so strong that the nativists formed a new political party, the American Party. Members promised to say nothing about their involvement. When asked about their party, they were told to say, "I know nothing." As a result, the party became known as the Know-Nothings. The Know-Nothings were

anti-Catholic and anti-immigrant. They claimed that Catholics who won government posts would be under the control of the Pope in Italy. They also feared that the immigrants would threaten their jobs.

The party's message was popular, and the party did well in elections during the mid-1850s. Some of its members were elected to Congress. However, the Know-Nothing movement faded in the late 1850s, when members became divided over the issue of slavery. Yet nativism did not disappear with the end of the Know-Nothings. Over the years it continued to rise and fall. In periods of high immigration, nativist feelings tended to rise again, only to recede when the gates were closed to immigrants.

 What led to a rise in immigration from Ireland in the mid-1800s?

Section 1 Review

Check Understanding

1. **Define** (a) labor union (b) rural (c) urban (d) mechanical reaper (e) thresher (f) tenement (g) strike (h) nativism

2. **Explain** how labor-saving machinery on farms caused people to flock to American cities after the 1820s.

3. **Explain** why unskilled workers were less successful than skilled workers at union organizing in the early 1800s.

4. **Describe** how revolution and famine led to a wave of immigration to the United States after the 1820s.

Critical Thinking

◈**Connecting Past and Present** How do you think farm life today differs from farm life in the early 1800s?

Write About Economics

Create an advertisement for mechanical threshers and reapers, telling how these machines will benefit farmers.

BUILDING SKILLS

Recognizing Causes and Effects: Immigration

Recognizing causes and effects will help you understand why an event happened and what occurred as a result of the event. Causes are conditions that lead to an event; effects are the outcome of the event.

Since history is a series of events, the effect of one event may be the cause of another. For example, the desire for new trade routes was a cause of early explorations. These explorations caused other events to occur. Among the effects of these explorations were encounters that took place between different cultures. These encounters, in turn, led to great changes for many people.

Here's How

Follow these steps to recognize the relationship between causes and effects:

1. Study the conditions that led to the event. These are the causes.

2. Study what happened as a result of the causes. These are the effects.

3. Look for the connections between one event and another.

4. Look for key words. *Since, due to,* and *because* often indicate causes. *So, therefore,* and *as a result* often indicate effects.

Here's Why

If you recognize causes and effects, you will see that a connection may exist between what came before an event and what came afterward. You will understand that there are reasons that things happen—and there are consequences.

Practice the Skill

The chart below lists some causes and effects of immigration between 1820 and 1860. Answer the questions, using information from the chart.

CAUSES AND EFFECTS
OF IMMIGRATION TO THE U.S. FROM IRELAND AND GERMANY

- Famine in Ireland
- Revolution and civil war in Germany

- Immigration from Ireland and Germany to the United States, 1820–1860

- Millions of people arrive in the cities.
- The United States becomes more diverse and multicultural.
- Immigrants become a source of labor for factory owners.
- Anti-immigrant groups are formed.

1. What was one cause of immigration to the United States?

2. What was one effect of the immigration?

3. Choose one effect. Viewing it as a cause, create a new diagram showing several effects.

Apply the Skill

Choose one event that you have already studied in history, such as the American Revolution or the gold rush, and create a cause-and-effect chart. Then, use your chart to write an essay, explaining the cause of the event and what consequences it had.

Section 2

A Period of Experimentation

PREVIEW

Objectives

- To explain the importance of religious reform groups in the early 1800s

- To describe what motivated African Americans to form their own churches

- To explain the goal of the utopian communities that sprang up in the early 1800s

Vocabulary

utopia   socialism

revival   self-sufficient

During the early years of the 1800s, new attitudes among Americans led to new religious feelings and the desire to reform their forms of worship. African Americans formed their own congregations to meet their religious needs. Hoping to add meaning to their lives, some people tried to shut themselves off from the outside world and establish a **utopia,** a perfect society on Earth.

◆ A RELIGIOUS AWAKENING

During the last years of the 1700s, it seemed to many Americans that religion was losing its influence on American life. Many Americans had moved away from their communities, either to the frontier or to the cities. In their new communities, they were not as influenced by traditional religious leaders.

Many preachers began to call for a religious **revival,** or reawakening, in the United States. This revival began with Protestant preachers who traveled from one small community to another, urging people to change their ways and follow the teachings of the Bible. The traveling preachers often spoke at huge outdoor gatherings called revival meetings. Some of these meetings went on for several days or even a week, attracting entire families from miles around.

Perhaps the most famous revival meeting was held in 1801 in the small town of Cane Ridge, Kentucky. The meeting lasted for one week and was attended by about 25,000 people, about 10 percent of Kentucky's entire population. A young man who was there described what he saw,

The noise was like the roar of Niagara. . . . I counted seven ministers all preaching at once, some on stumps, some on wagons. . . . Some people were singing, others praying, some crying for mercy . . . while others were shouting. "

The message of the revival preachers was that life on Earth was not just a preparation for heaven. People had a duty to improve the society in which they lived. Good Christians might try to help poor people improve their lives, or work to stop the widespread drinking of alcohol. They might work for world peace, or try to end slavery in their own country. The revival movement led to many of the reform movements that began to form in the early 1800s.

? What were the concerns of religious groups in the early 1800s?

◆ AFRICAN AMERICAN CHURCHES

For many years, African American worshippers at Philadelphia's St. George's Methodist Episcopal Church were allowed to sit where they wanted. That changed suddenly one Sunday in 1787. White church officials, who had grown uneasy about the large number of African Americans who were regularly attending the church, decided to take action. When African American worshippers arrived, they were told to sit upstairs.

Two of the worshippers, Richard Allen and Absalom Jones, were leaders of Philadelphia's free African American community. Allen and

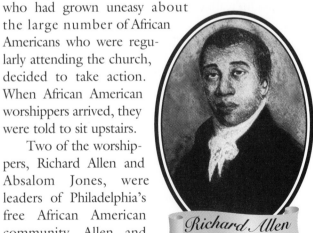

Richard Allen

◀ One of the first African American churches in the United States was Mother Bethel African Methodist Episcopal Church in Philadelphia. It was founded in 1794 to ensure that African Americans would not be treated unfairly during worship services.

Jones refused to be treated as second-class members of their church. In 1794, Allen founded a new church for African Americans called the Mother Bethel African Methodist Episcopal Church. Jones founded an African American church called St. Thomas's Free African Church. Other African Americans in the North also formed their own churches. The new African American churches at first were part of Protestant denominations, such as the Methodists, that were controlled by white ministers. African American ministers eventually decided they wanted more control over their churches. In 1816, African American Methodist ministers organized their own denomination, the African Methodist Episcopal (AME) church.

African Americans in the South could not follow the example of Northerners. After 1830, white Southerners increasingly feared that more enslaved people might rebel as Nat Turner had. Southern states therefore made African American churches operate under tight controls.

Whether in the North or in the South, African American churches grew out of a tradition of self help in the community. The church took a leading role in dealing with community problems and helping people in need. For example, African American ministers were important in the struggle to end slavery.

They held meetings, wrote letters to public officials, and provided hiding places for enslaved people escaping from the South. African American churches also fought slavery by organizing boycotts of products made by slave labor. They encouraged people to buy products made only by free workers.

 Why did African Americans establish their own churches?

◆ UTOPIAN COMMUNITIES

In the first half of the 1800s, Americans saw the rise of a number of movements whose goal was to build a utopia. In a utopian society, cooperation—not competition—would be the foundation. There would be no rich or poor, and all people would be treated fairly. Members of a utopian society would share equally in what they produced.

Between 1800 and 1850, about 100 utopian communities sprang up in the United States. Some had only a few dozen people. Others had more than a thousand. Some were organized around religions, while others were not. However, all were based in some way on **socialism.** Socialism is an economic and political system in which society as a whole—rather

▲ *The quality and simplicity of these chairs are characteristics of Shaker furniture.*

the people who worked in his factories. He also insisted that children of workers receive an education.

In New Harmony, Owen tried to change living conditions that had deteriorated because of industrial growth. He believed that through true cooperation, a community could be **self-sufficient,** able to provide for itself without the aid of others. Every person would work at some trade or occupation and, in return, gain credit for food and other goods at the public stores.

New Harmony was not harmonious, however. Members argued constantly among themselves about goals and actions. Furthermore, the community lacked skilled labor and never truly became self-sufficient. New Harmony dissolved after about two years.

What did utopian societies hope to accomplish?

than private individuals—owns property, operates businesses, and provides for its members.

Most of these societies failed quickly. Members soon began quarreling over trivial matters. Only a few of the societies lasted for more than a few years. Two well known but short-lived experiments were the Oneida Community, in New York State, and Brook Farm, near Boston, Massachusetts.

The Shakers

The Shakers were one of the first utopian movements in the United States. By 1800, there were a dozen Shaker communities in the United States, and by the 1820s, there were 18. The Shakers believed in equality of the sexes and complete separation from what they saw as the disorder of American life. Shakers did not marry or have children. Their communities survived by converting others to their way of life. The Shaker movement reached its peak before 1860 and then steadily declined. Today few Shakers are left, but the furniture they made remains highly valued for its simple style and fine craftsmanship. It is often copied by craftworkers today.

New Harmony

The first important non-religious community in the United States was founded in 1825 in New Harmony, Indiana. Robert Owen, its founder, had made a fortune as a cotton manufacturer in Britain. However, what made him well known and respected was his concern for providing decent housing and working conditions for

Section 2 Review

Check Understanding

1. **Define** (a) utopia (b) revival (c) socialism (d) self-sufficient

2. **Explain** the message of the revival preachers in the early 1800s.

3. **Describe** the reasons for the founding of the African Methodist Episcopal Church.

4. **Identify** a utopian community and tell what it attempted to do.

Critical Thinking

◆ **Connecting Past and Present** In the 1800s, many religious organizations reached out to their local communities. Many religious organizations continued to function in a similar way. How do religious organizations today reach out to improve local communities?

Write About Culture

Your local newspaper has sent you to cover a revival meeting like the one described in this section. Write a brief news story with a headline, describing what happened at the meeting.

An Age of Reform

PREVIEW

Objectives

- To explain the growth of the abolitionist movement
- To identify social issues that concerned reformers in the 1800s

Vocabulary

abolition
militant
temperance

The urge to reform American society swept the northern and western states in the first half of the 1800s. Reformers worked for change for different reasons. Some believed that they were fulfilling the teachings of their religion. Others believed that they were furthering the promise of the Declaration of Independence, which said that "all men are created equal." Others believed that science could solve all human problems.

Whatever their reasons, the reformers believed that people did bad things only because conditions were bad. If conditions improved, they thought, people would behave much better.

◆ THE ANTISLAVERY MOVEMENT

Perhaps the most controversial of all reforms was **abolition,** or the act of doing away with slavery. A few small abolitionist groups had existed in the United States as far back as the late 1700s. A Protestant group, the Religious Society of Friends, commonly called the Quakers, was the most important of the early groups fighting slavery. They insisted that a person could not be both a slave owner and a Christian. In 1758 the Philadelphia Quakers Meeting prohibited their members from owning slaves.

The American Colonization Society

In 1816, people opposed to slavery formed the American Colonization Society. The Society hoped to convince southern planters to free enslaved African Americans, who would then settle in Africa.

The idea was a result of widespread racial prejudice against African Americans in the United States. This prejudice was strong in the North as well as in the South. Supporters of the "back to Africa" plan hoped that more Americans would support abolition if the freed African Americans were allowed to leave the United States.

In 1822 a small group of free African Americans set up a settlement on the coast of West Africa. That settlement later became the African nation of Liberia, "The Land of the Free." However, because there was a lack of funding and because few free African Americans wanted to go to Africa, the colonization plan never took hold.

William Lloyd Garrison

During the early 1800s, the antislavery movement grew stronger and more **militant,** or aggressive, with the help of William Lloyd Garrison. Garrison was a strong-willed man who expressed his ideas through his newspaper, the *Liberator*. In 1831, on the first page of his first issue, he wrote,

> I will be as harsh as truth, and as uncompromising as justice. On this subject [slavery] I do not wish to think, or speak, or write, with moderation. . . . I am in earnest. . . . I will not excuse— I will not retreat a single inch— AND I WILL BE HEARD.

In 1833, Garrison helped found the American Anti-Slavery Society. Over the next few years, hundreds of abolitionist groups organized in northern cities and towns.

The abolitionists worked hard to spread their message throughout the North. Theodore Weld's book *American Slavery As It Is* used reports from southern newspapers to show the cruelty of slavery.

Still, progress was slow. Most Northerners disliked slavery and opposed it in new western territories. At the same time, however, they practiced widespread discrimination against the free African Americans in the North. Many white Northerners saw slavery as a remote problem, of little concern to the North. They viewed Garrison as a troublemaker. Sometimes mobs broke up abolitionist meetings.

▲ *William Lloyd Garrison (1805–1879) published his abolitionist opinions in the* Liberator.

Abolitionism was also slowed by disputes within the movement. While abolitionist leaders had the same goal—ending slavery—they often engaged in disputes over strategy and personal differences. Some abolitionists wanted to advance their cause by persuasion. Others urged that people should have nothing to do with a government that allowed slavery. Still others focused on preventing the spread of slavery to new territories, rather than abolishing it entirely.

Frederick Douglass and Abolition

In the 1840s, free African Americans began to play a larger role in the movement. The most powerful voices came from formerly enslaved people, especially a young man named Frederick Douglass.

Douglass was born into slavery in Maryland about 1817. It was against the law at the time to teach enslaved people to read and write. Even so, with the help of the plantation owner's wife, Douglass taught himself to read and write when he was eight years old. At the age of 21, Douglass escaped to Massachusetts. He began to speak at antislavery meetings. Douglass's fame as a speaker grew. He spoke out against slavery in London and in the West Indies. In one speech, he described seeing escaped slaves captured and returned to the South:

" In the deep stillness of midnight, I have been often aroused by the dead, heavy footsteps, and the piteous [pitiful] cries of the chained gangs that passed our door. I see the bleeding footsteps; I hear the doleful [sad] wail of chained humanity. My soul sickens at the sight! "

How did the abolitionists spread their message?

◆ REFORMING SOCIETY

During the 1830s and 1840s, hundreds of reform movements sprang up. Reformers began urging changes in public education, the care of the mentally disabled, and the consumption of alcohol.

Public Education

During the early 1800s, there were few free public schools. Children from wealthy families were educated in private schools or by tutors. Poor children generally received no education outside the home.

By the 1830s support was growing for free public education financed by government tax dollars. People

▲ *Frederick Douglass (1817–1895) was a forceful, well-known African American antislavery activist.*

◄ Boys and girls of all ages commonly took their lessons in the same room in the 1800s. Older children helped younger ones with their work.

increasingly agreed that to participate in a democracy effectively, voters should be educated. Most reformers believed that education was necessary to make sure that voters were intelligently informed. They also viewed education as the way to prevent the spread of crime and social disorder. With the rise in immigration, support for public education grew because it prepared immigrant children for life in the United States.

Horace Mann was the leader in the struggle to establish good public schools for all children. He saw education as "the great equalizer" and essential for democracy to work. Mann once wrote in a report,

" If we do not prepare children to become good citizens—if we do not develop their capacities, if we do not enrich their minds with knowledge, imbue [fill] their hearts with the love of truth and duty, then our republic must go down to destruction, as others have gone before it. "

Mann's efforts brought results. Massachusetts set up a state board of education in 1837, with Horace Mann in charge. Under his leadership, Massachusetts lengthened the school year and began to spend money to train teachers and improve teaching methods. Mann also fought the practice of beating students to maintain discipline.

Women helped spread the new public education. By 1850 they dominated primary school teaching. Teaching school had come to be regarded as an acceptable occupation for women between their own school years and the time of their marriage.

In 1852, Massachusetts became the first state to require all children to attend public school. Some other states followed in support of free public education. However, little was done at first to set up public high schools. In 1860, there were only 300 in the entire country, one third of them in Massachusetts.

Improving Conditions for Mental Patients

In 1841, when Dorothea Dix visited a prison in East Cambridge, Massachusetts, she was shocked to find mentally disabled patients confined under terrible conditions. She decided at that moment to dedicate herself to the improvement of facilities and treatment for mental patients. Dix then investigated other places in Massachusetts that housed mental patients. She wrote a highly critical report to the

▲ *Women were some of the most vocal anti-alcohol protesters. Their organizations were called temperance societies.*

The Temperance Movement

In the 1820s, the use of alcoholic beverages in America began to cause concern. A connection was made between alcoholism and poor health, crime, and other social problems. Some reformers warned that problems related to drinking threatened democracy, which depended on active and involved citizens. Some focused on convincing people to change their habits. Others wanted to get rid of alcohol completely by getting states to outlaw all alcoholic beverages.

The **temperance** movement, supporting limited drinking or total rejection of alcoholic beverages, began as a result of these concerns. In 1826, religious leaders and other reformers organized the American Temperance Society. Soon there were hundreds of anti-alcohol groups throughout the country.

 What were some goals of reformers in the mid-1800s?

state legislature. Dix found mental patients were kept in "cages, closets, cellars, stalls, pens!" [and were] "chained, naked, beaten with rods, and lashed into obedience." Her description of the horrors she witnessed had the effect she wanted. As a result of her efforts, Massachusetts passed a law establishing asylums. These were hospitals where mentally disabled people would be treated as patients, not criminals. Dorothea Dix took her campaign to the rest of the country. Because of her tireless efforts, public pressure forced most states to improve their treatment of the mentally disabled.

Advances in Medicine

Improvements in other areas of health care also were taking place. People began to benefit from various advances in the field of medicine. Patients who required surgery, for instance, were helped greatly by the use of anesthetics. Anesthetics are chemicals that deaden feeling, making it possible for surgeons to perform operations without causing pain to patients. In 1846 a Boston dentist began using ether when removing teeth. Doctors and dentists throughout the country were soon using ether to deaden pain during surgery.

In the 1860s it was discovered that diseases were caused by germs. People began to use antiseptics to kill germs. By making sure that hospitals and sick rooms were kept clean, health workers helped prevent the spread of diseases.

Section 3 Review

Check Understanding

1. **Define** (a) abolition (b) militant (c) temperance

2. **Identify** William Lloyd Garrison and Frederick Douglass.

3. **Explain** Dorothea Dix's influence on the treatment of the mentally disabled.

4. **Describe** the concerns that led to the temperance movement.

Critical Thinking

Evaluating Information How did Horace Mann believe free public education would benefit American society?

Write About Social Issues

Connecting Past and Present The reformers of the mid-1800s were dedicated to improving society. Write an essay discussing an important problem that people are working to solve today.

The Women's Rights Movement

PREVIEW

Objectives

- To describe the status of women in the 1800s

- To analyze the impact of the Seneca Falls convention

- To enumerate the gains women made in the 1800s

Vocabulary

suffrage
resolution

Toward the mid-1800s, women reformers turned their attention for the first time to the conditions of women workers in the mills. In 1845 the Female Labor Reform Association joined forces with male workers to fight for a 10-hour workday. The failure of this movement convinced many women that without equal political rights, they would not achieve equal economic rights.

◆ THE STRUGGLE FOR RIGHTS BEGINS

At the beginning of the 1800s, American women had few of the rights that were enjoyed by men. A woman was not allowed to vote or hold public office. Any property a woman owned was turned over to her husband when she married. When a man died, his widow lost control of that property completely. There were few divorces, but if a couple did divorce, the husband had custody of the children. As late as 1850, in most states it was legal for a husband to beat his wife. A woman could not bring a lawsuit in court or make a legal contract. In short, the law in many ways treated women as if they were children.

In colonial times, families produced much of what they needed at home. This gave women an important economic role. However, after 1800, factories gradually took over much of that work. Many women, especially middle-class women, were then limited to housekeeping and child-care duties.

Women and the Reform Movements

Even when they tried to make life better for others, women did not receive equal treatment. For example, the reform movements of the early 1800s did not allow women to participate on the same level as men. Therefore, American men were shocked when Sarah Grimké stood before the Massachusetts legislature. She came to present a petition demanding an end to slavery. She also asked that women be given the right to be heard on any subject:

> These petitions relate to the great and solemn subject of slavery. . . . Because it is a political subject, it has often been . . . said that women had nothing to do with it. . . . Are we bereft of citizenship? Have women no country?

As women began to play a major role in the antislavery movement, they started to take a look at their own unjust position in society. By 1840 the American Anti-Slavery Society had decided to allow women to participate fully in its work. In its delegation to the World Anti-Slavery Convention in London, England, several women were included. However, the convention's organizers in London refused to admit them. The American women had to sit in a balcony and watch the convention.

Outstanding Women's Rights Leaders

Two of the women delegates excluded from the London antislavery convention were Elizabeth Cady Stanton and Lucretia Mott. After sharing their views with one another, they realized that an organized movement was needed to advance women's rights.

Another significant leader was Lucy Stone, who gave her first lecture on behalf of the women's rights movement in the mid-1840s. Stone once refused to pay property taxes because "women suffer taxation, and yet have no representation."

Susan B. Anthony became the best known American champion for women's rights. As a young teacher, she bitterly resented earning less money than men earned for doing the same work. Anthony, who eventually became the movement's organizer, began working for the temperance, antislavery, and women's rights movements in the late 1840s.

Sojourner Truth, an enslaved person for half her life, also became a leading speaker for abolition and women's rights. She was one of only a few African American women to attend meetings on the issue of **suffrage.** Suffrage is the right to vote.

 How did women's rights differ from men's rights in the early 1800s?

◆ THE SENECA FALLS CONVENTION

In July 1848, Lucretia Mott and Elizabeth Cady Stanton, who lived in nearby Seneca Falls, met in Waterloo, New York, to discuss the problems they faced in American society. The women decided to involve others as well. On July 14, 1848, an announcement in *The Seneca County Courier* reported that a convention would be held on July 19th and 20th in Seneca Falls "to discuss the social, civil, and religious rights of women."

A major achievement of the convention was a Declaration of Sentiments, which was modeled on the Declaration of Independence. The Declaration of Sentiments, which is excerpted on page 714, said that "We hold these truths to be self-evident; that all men and women are created equal." The declaration then listed 16 injustices women suffered, including being shut out from educational opportunities and good jobs. Another inequality was that every woman had to "submit to laws, in the formation of which she has no voice." The Declaration demanded full equality for women in every area of life.

The Declaration of Sentiments was followed by 12 **resolutions,** or formal expressions of intention. All but one was passed unanimously. That resolution called for woman suffrage. In 1848, when many women were interested in other reform issues, suffrage was a radical idea. At that time the main concerns were to be able to control property, have educational opportunities, and change divorce laws. Yet women such as Stanton were convinced that women's opportunities would remain limited until they had the vote. The vote on suffrage passed by only a narrow margin.

The convention was significant because it was the first time an organized group of women came together in large numbers to address the issues that concerned them. The next women's rights convention took place in Rochester, New York. Others were held nearly every year during the 1850s. The meetings took place in large cities and in small towns. The meetings continued

The Seneca Falls convention was attended by about 200 women and 40 men. Energetic speakers brought attention to injustices against women. ▶

▲ *Women activists Elizabeth Cady Stanton (left) and Susan B. Anthony (right), two of the most well-known suffragists, secured the first laws in New York guaranteeing women control of property and wages.*

despite the widespread scorn that women suffragists faced from the male-dominated press.

Women worked especially hard at the state level to get laws passed that would give them more rights. In 1860, the efforts of Susan B. Anthony and Elizabeth Cady Stanton led to a New York State law protecting women's property rights. It allowed married women to own property and collect their own wages. It also allowed them to sue in court and enter into contracts. Women in several other states won passage of similar laws.

 What was the importance of the Seneca Falls convention?

◆ EQUALITY IN EDUCATION

Women made gains in a number of fields during the first half of the 1800s, but the area in which the most progress was made was education. An outstanding leader in that effort was Emma Willard.

In 1819, Willard sent a letter to the governor of New York, requesting state money to open a school for girls. Willard intended to teach subjects such as science

and mathematics, which girls rarely had a chance to learn. The New York legislature refused to supply the money. However, the city of Troy, New York, did. In 1821, Emma Willard opened the Troy Female Seminary. Ninety students enrolled the first year. By 1831 the seminary had more than 300 students. Willard developed the courses, the teaching methods, and even wrote some of the textbooks herself. Many of her students became teachers who spread Willard's methods throughout the country. The school's courses included mathematics, history, geography, and several sciences. In 1895, 25 years after Emma Willard's death, the school was renamed in her honor.

Mary Mason Lyon also wanted to improve standards in women's education. Lyon managed to raise $27,000, and in 1837, Mt. Holyoke Female Seminary opened in Massachusetts. Today, Mt. Holyoke is a highly respected college for women.

 In what ways did women's education improve in the 1800s?

Section 4 Review

Check Understanding

1. **Define** (a) suffrage (b) resolution

2. **Summarize** the curbs to women's rights that existed in the 1800s.

3. **Describe** the results of the Seneca Falls convention.

4. **Explain** the advances that women made during the first part of the 1800s.

Critical Thinking

◆**Connecting Past and Present** What trends led to the growth of the women's rights movement during the 1840s? What areas of equality are women in the United States still fighting for today?

Write About Citizenship

Write a flyer persuading people to attend the Seneca Falls convention.

Chapter 8
Review

CHAPTER SUMMARY

Section 1

American cities grew rapidly in the early 1800s, fueled by an increase in immigration and a movement of people from rural areas to cities. To protect their jobs against unskilled laborers, skilled workers organized unions. Immigrants from Europe, especially Ireland and Germany, swelled the United States' population. The surge in immigration led to a rise in nativism.

Section 2

At the beginning of the 1800s, new religious groups emerged that focused on the need to improve American life. Huge crowds attended revival meetings. To combat discrimination, African Americans formed their own churches. Efforts to improve society led to a number of utopian experiments.

Section 3

The urge to improve society in the 1800s gave rise to a number of reform movements. The antislavery movement grew, with free African Americans playing a large role. Reformers supported a variety of other causes, including public education, better conditions for mental patients, and temperance.

Section 4

In the first half of the 1800s, women began to organize for their rights, such as the right to own and manage property. Interest in women's rights led to the Seneca Falls convention, which proposed a Declaration of Sentiments. Although women had made some advances by 1860, they still had not gained the right to vote.

Connecting ◆ Past and Present

Which reform movement of the 1800s do you think could be effective today? What do you think it should work to accomplish?

Using Vocabulary

From the list below, select the term that best completes each sentence.

abolition	suffrage
labor union	tenement
nativism	thresher
utopia	revival
temperance	urban

1. The _____ movement believed in restricting the consumption of alcohol.

2. A _____ is an apartment building that may have unsafe conditions.

3. The negative reaction to immigrants was called _____.

4. As the cities grew, the United States was transformed into an _____ nation.

5. Farmers used a _____ to separate the kernels from the husks of wheat plants.

6. A religious _____ drew many people to sing and pray at meetings.

7. The right to vote is called _____.

8. Some reformers believed they could create a _____ and live in a perfect society.

9. The act of doing away with slavery is called _____.

10. A _____ is a group of workers who organize to protect their rights and working conditions.

Check Understanding

1. **Explain** how labor-saving machinery on farms caused people to migrate to American cities after the 1820s.

2. **Explain** why workers in trades organized unions in the 1800s.

3. **Describe** what led to a wave of immigration from western Europe after the 1820s.

4. **Describe** the effects of the religious revival of the early 1800s on reform movements in the United States.

5. **Explain** why African Americans began their own churches in the 1800s.

6. **Identify** the reasons for the rise of utopian communities in the first half of the 1800s.

7. **Discuss** the wide variety of policies supported by reformers.

8. **Explain** William Lloyd Garrison's and Frederick Douglass's roles in the antislavery movement.

9. **Describe** the many restrictions women faced in the early 1800s.

10. **Analyze** what happened at the women's rights convention in Seneca Falls in 1848.

Critical Thinking

1. **Drawing Conclusions** What led to the revival meetings of the 1800s?

2. **Analyzing** What impact did African Americans have on the abolitionist movement in the 1800s?

3. **Contrasting** What was the difference between the utopian communities of the 1800s and other reform movements of that time?

4. **Drawing Conclusions** Why did women reformers of the early 1800s have trouble winning the vote?

◆ **Connecting Past and Present** Reformers in the 1800s held meetings, made speeches, and distributed pamphlets to spread their ideas. What would be the most effective methods of working for reform today? Explain.

Interpreting the Timeline

Use the timeline on pages 144–145 to answer these questions.

1. William Lloyd Garrison's antislavery newspaper was first printed in what year?

2. In what year did the Troy Female Seminary open?

3. What events on the timeline show the effects of the Industrial Revolution on working people?

WESTON HIGH SCHOOL
115 School Road
Weston, CT 06883

Putting Skills to Work

RECOGNIZING CAUSES AND EFFECTS

On page 151, you learned about the relationship between cause and effect. Review the Building Skills lesson and then look at the list below. Decide which items on the list are causes and which are effects of the women's rights movement during the mid-1800s. Then, in your notebook create a cause-and-effect chart similar to the one on page 151.

- Seneca Falls convention takes place.
- Troy Female Seminary and other schools for women are opened.
- Declaration of Sentiments is issued.
- Women cannot vote, hold public office, or sue in court.
- New York passes a law that gives women some property rights.
- Husbands control wives' property.
- Women cannot enter professional careers.

Writing to Persuade

The 1800s in the United States was a time of passionate belief in reform. From women's rights to abolition to temperance to better conditions for mental patients, reformers worked fiercely for causes. **Write** a persuasive letter to the editor of a local paper about one of the reform movements described in this chapter. Explain why the newspaper should support that reform.

Portfolio Project

AMERICAN CITIES, THEN AND NOW

Choose a city or town in the United States. It can be your own community or any other you choose. Use library resources to compare what your community was like 100 years ago with what it is today. Make a chart that shows similarities between then and now. Consider using categories such as population, biggest businesses, tallest buildings, recreation, schools, and transportation. You may want to write a report to accompany your chart, explaining what has changed and what has stayed the same. File your work in your portfolio.

ATTITUDES TOWARD MENTAL HEALTH

Throughout the years, people with mental disabilities have been viewed by some with a mixture of fear and anxiety. Because many people did not understand the reasons for mental disturbances, the sufferers were often rejected, neglected, or abused. Mentally disabled people had to struggle to get the help and understanding they needed.

Then When Dorothea Dix first became interested in the mentally disabled in the 1840s, she saw scenes that appalled her. People with mental problems were jailed with criminals, forced to live under unsanitary conditions, chained, and even beaten. These conditions prompted Dix in her crusade to create special hospitals for the mentally disabled. Through her untiring efforts, Dorothea Dix helped to change the horrible conditions under which many of these people lived. In doing so, she also helped change public opinion toward people with mental disabilities.

Now The modern mental health movement continually searches for ways to improve the necessary care and treatment of mental problems. Various medications and therapies have improved or restored the lives of people who formerly were seriously disabled. Educational efforts have increased the public's understanding and tolerance. The Americans with Disabilities Act, passed by Congress in 1990, insures that people with mental disabilities no longer can be discriminated against or isolated in the community or the workplace.

You Decide

1. How might Dorothea Dix have reacted to the passage of the Americans with Disabilities Act?
2. How does society benefit from modern attitudes toward mental disabilities?

▲ A rotating chair was used to treat mental disorders during the late 1700s. People believed the device relieved mental illness by increasing the blood supply to the brain.

A Nation Divided 1820–1877

" A house divided against itself cannot stand. I believe this government cannot endure, permanently half slave and half free. "

Abraham Lincoln,
1858

▲ *Bitter disagreements between the North and the South over the issue of slavery escalated into a war that tore the country apart.* ◈ **Connecting Past and Present** *What can you learn from this image about the way battles were fought during the Civil War? How does this battle compare to the way battles are fought today?*

Chapter 9
Slavery Divides the Nation 1820–1861

CHAPTER PREVIEW

Section 1 Slavery and Westward Expansion

As the United States expanded west and territories sought admission to the Union, the issue of slavery created tension between the North and the South.

Section 2 Differences Between North and South Widen

Although the widening gap between the North and the South made compromise more difficult, Congress passed the Kansas-Nebraska Act, which allowed settlers in those territories to decide the issue of slavery for themselves.

Section 3 The Final Break

Differences between the North and the South continued to grow. Abraham Lincoln's election to the presidency pushed a number of southern states to withdraw from the Union.

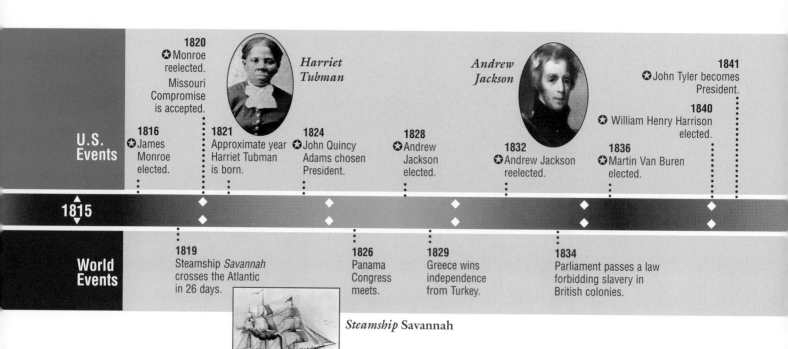

U.S. Events

1816 ✪ James Monroe elected.

1820 ✪ Monroe reelected. Missouri Compromise is accepted.

Harriet Tubman

1821 Approximate year Harriet Tubman is born.

1824 ✪ John Quincy Adams chosen President.

1828 ✪ Andrew Jackson elected.

Andrew Jackson

1832 ✪ Andrew Jackson reelected.

1836 ✪ Martin Van Buren elected.

1840 ✪ William Henry Harrison elected.

1841 ✪ John Tyler becomes President.

1815

World Events

1819 Steamship *Savannah* crosses the Atlantic in 26 days.

1826 Panama Congress meets.

1829 Greece wins independence from Turkey.

1834 Parliament passes a law forbidding slavery in British colonies.

Steamship Savannah

Portfolio Project

ART AND HISTORY

Art that portrays historical events offers a point of view about those events. Artists use a number of devices to emphasize particular aspects of the people and events they show in their work. As you read this chapter, be aware of how artists illustrate the era. At the end of the chapter, you will analyze several pieces of art to determine what they reveal about history.

▲ *The Underground Railroad was a secret network of routes that helped enslaved African Americans escape from the South.*

◆ **Connecting Past and Present** *How are people in this painting helping one another? What organizations help people in need today?*

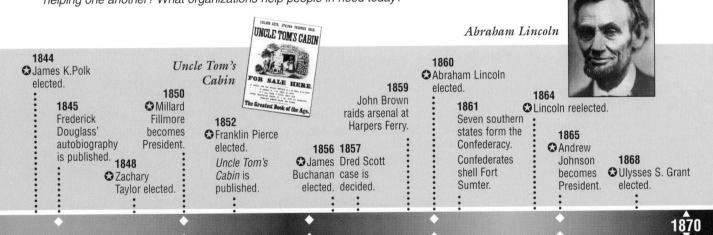

Abraham Lincoln

1844
✪James K.Polk elected.

1845
Frederick Douglass' autobiography is published.

1848
✪Zachary Taylor elected.

1850
✪Millard Fillmore becomes President.

Uncle Tom's Cabin

UNCLE TOM'S CABIN

FOR SALE HERE.

The Greatest Book of the Age.

1852
✪Franklin Pierce elected.
Uncle Tom's Cabin is published.

1856
✪James Buchanan elected.

1857
Dred Scott case is decided.

1859
John Brown raids arsenal at Harpers Ferry.

1860
✪Abraham Lincoln elected.

1861
Seven southern states form the Confederacy. Confederates shell Fort Sumter.

1864
✪Lincoln reelected.

1865
✪Andrew Johnson becomes President.

1868
✪Ulysses S. Grant elected.

1870

1847
Republic of Liberia is established by former African American slaves.

1854
Japan is reopened to the West.

1855
Florence Nightingale reforms military hospitals.

Florence Nightingale

1862
Victor Hugo's novel *Les Misérables* is published.

1866
Austro-Prussian War ends.

Section 1

Slavery and Westward Expansion

PREVIEW

Objectives

- To analyze how the issue of slavery affected the admission of new states to the Union in the mid-1800s

- To identify the key ideas behind the various compromises reached by Congress

- To explain why the Fugitive Slave Law increased antislavery feelings in the North and drove the nation closer to breaking apart

Vocabulary

free state	popular sovereignty
slave state	Free-Soiler
sectionalism	fugitive
proviso	

On May 19, 1856, Massachusetts Senator Charles Sumner gave a speech in the U.S. Senate. He attacked slavery and harshly criticized several proslavery senators, including Andrew Butler of South Carolina.

Several days later, Congressman Preston Brooks of South Carolina walked into the Senate. Brooks, who was Butler's nephew, hit Sumner on the head with a cane. Several senators pulled Brooks away, but not before he had beaten Sumner unconscious. The issue of slavery aroused strong feelings and sometimes even violent behavior. It was tearing the nation apart.

◆ THE MISSOURI COMPROMISE

The different views of slavery in the North and the South had been a continuing source of conflict as the United States added new territory or admitted new states. If these territories or states allowed slavery, then the South would grow in power. If they banned slavery, then the power would shift to the North. Not only slavery, but the future of the Union—the federal union of all the states—was at stake.

By 1819, there were 11 **free states,** or states that banned slavery, and 11 **slave states,** or states that permitted slavery, in the Union. When Missouri, which was part of the Louisiana Territory, asked to join the Union as a slave state, a sharp debate took place in Congress. Admitting Missouri as a slave state would mean that there would be 12 slave states and 11 free states, upsetting the balance of equal representation in the Senate. Naturally, Northerners opposed Missouri's admission as a slave state.

Congress argued over Missouri's statehood until 1820. Finally, Senator Henry Clay of Kentucky suggested a compromise that both sides accepted. The agreement, called the Missouri Compromise, allowed Missouri to enter the Union as a slave state and Maine to be admitted as a free state, thus preserving the balance between free and slave states in the Senate.

The Missouri Compromise also divided the remaining territory acquired through the Louisiana Purchase into slave and free regions. The dividing line was Missouri's southern border, which is at a latitude of 36°30'N, as the map on the next page shows. Except for Missouri itself, Congress banned slavery north of that line. Therefore, slavery would not be permitted in most of the remaining territory.

Many people hoped that the slavery question was settled. However, the Missouri Compromise proved to be only a temporary solution.

How did the Missouri Compromise deal with the issue of slavery in the Louisiana Territory?

◆ THE DEBATE OVER SLAVERY

Because the Missouri Compromise maintained the balance between the number of free states and slave states, the North and the South had the same number of senators. However, the population of the North was growing faster than that of the South. Because representation in the House of Representatives is based on population, the North's strength in Congress was growing.

Southerners began looking for a way to protect their power. Southern leaders, such as Senator John C. Calhoun of South Carolina, feared that with the North's majority, it would pass laws limiting slavery.

Texas Becomes a State

The Missouri Compromise applied only to the territories included in the Louisiana Purchase. When

Sam Houston, the president of Texas, asked the United States to annex Texas in 1836, the issue of slave or free status in new states arose again. Southerners wanted to admit Texas as a slave state, while Northerners protested against increasing the number of slave states in the Union. The debate continued until 1845, when Texas entered the Union as a slave state.

Hardened Positions

As the slavery debate continued, positions on both sides hardened. Feelings of **sectionalism,** or loyalty to a region rather than to the whole country, grew. When Northerners called for an end to slavery, southern leaders accused them of trying to destroy tradition.

Senator John C. Calhoun of South Carolina insisted that slaves were property. According to him, the Constitution protected property, and people had the right to take their property, including slaves, where they wanted. Therefore, Calhoun said, slavery should be allowed in all the territories.

Congressman David Wilmot of Pennsylvania expressed what many Northerners believed—slavery should be banned in all newly acquired territory.

In 1846, during the war with Mexico, he had proposed a ban on slavery in all territory the United States might win from Mexico. The House of Representatives passed Wilmot's proposal, called the Wilmot Proviso, but the Senate rejected it. A **proviso** is a part of a document that makes restrictions.

Senator Stephen Douglas of Illinois and others held a compromise position. They proposed **popular sovereignty**—a practice that allows the people to decide their own policies, such as whether to allow slavery. This compromise shifted decision making on this issue from national politicians to territorial legislators who often thought in terms of their own self-interests. When the war with Mexico ended in 1848, Congress still had to decide whether the territory won in that war would permit slavery. A decision would not be reached until the Compromise of 1850.

The Free-Soilers

The Democrats and the Whigs were the two major parities in the 1848 presidental election. The Whig party had been formally organized in 1834 by opponents of Andrew Jackson. Both the Democrats

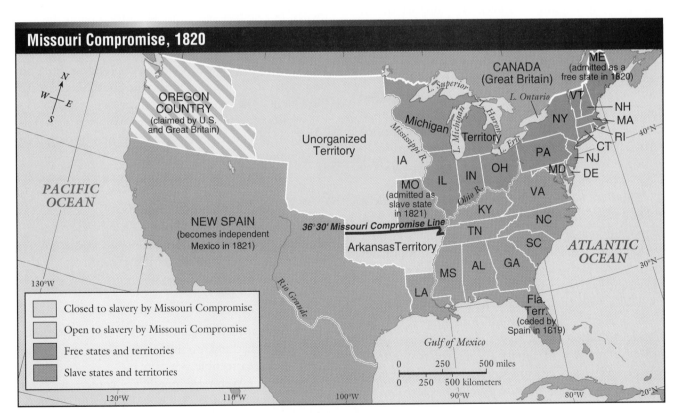

Missouri Compromise, 1820

Closed to slavery by Missouri Compromise
Open to slavery by Missouri Compromise
Free states and territories
Slave states and territories

▲ **Geography** *This map shows how the Missouri Compromise affected the balance of free and slave states and territories.* **Interpreting the Map** *In the territories, was more land opened or closed to slavery as a result of the Missouri Compromise?*

Posters similar to this one offered large rewards for the capture and return of fugitive slaves.

and the Whigs wanted to keep the support of the South, so both parties refused to take a strong stand on slavery as they prepared for the election.

The refusal of the parties to take a firm position angered antislavery people in both parties, some of whom organized the Free-Soil party. Supporters called themselves **Free-Soilers,** or people who opposed slavery and popular sovereignty. The newly formed party called for excluding slavery from all the territories. Its slogan was "Free Soil, Free Speech, Free Labor, Free Men." Most Free-Soilers were Northerners.

The Free-Soiler candidate who ran for President in 1848 was former President Martin Van Buren. The Democrats selected Lewis Cass of Michigan as their presidential candidate. He was a supporter of popular sovereignty. The Whigs chose Zachary Taylor, a slave owner and hero of the war with Mexico.

Taylor won the election but died in the summer of 1850. His Vice President, Millard Fillmore, became President. Although the Free-Soil party did not carry a single state, it won almost 10 percent of the total vote as well as 13 seats in Congress. The nation continued to be divided over the issue of slavery.

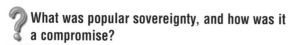 **What was popular sovereignty, and how was it a compromise?**

◆ THE COMPROMISE OF 1850

When California applied to join the Union in 1849, there were 15 free states and 15 slave states. If California was admitted as a free state, the balance would be uneven again. The question of California's statehood again opened the issue of whether slavery should be allowed in the territory won from Mexico.

During this period, there were other issues dividing the North and South. Northerners wanted the slave trade abolished in Washington, D.C. They believed that it was a disgrace to have auctions and slave pens in the nation's capital. On the other hand, Southerners wanted Northerners to catch runaway slaves. They called for a law that would force the return of **fugitive,** or runaway, slaves.

For months it looked as if no solution would be found to solve these problems. Members of Congress were badly divided over the issue. Many representatives from the North were determined to stop the expansion of slavery, while some southern leaders spoke of leaving the Union.

In 1850, Senator Henry Clay again stepped forward, as he had in 1820, to propose a compromise to save the Union. Clay was a Southerner and a slave owner, but he believed above all in the Union.

Senator John C. Calhoun was against compromise. As a strong believer that states should determine whether to allow slavery, Calhoun opposed any limit on slavery in the territories. He said the South should leave the Union if the North did not meet its demands.

Massachusetts Senator Daniel Webster answered Calhoun. In one of his greatest speeches, he defended the Union:

> **I wish to speak today not as a Massachusetts man, nor as a Northern man, but as an American. . . . I speak for the preservation of the Union. Hear me for my cause.**

Webster argued that both sides must compromise. He warned that any attempt to break up the Union would lead to a terrible war.

Even after Webster's speech, no compromise was reached until Senator Stephen Douglas of Illinois brought the two sides together. His efforts produced several new laws that together made up the Compromise of 1850. Under this compromise,

California joined the Union as a free state. Congress divided the rest of the territory won from Mexico into the territories of New Mexico and Utah. The settlers in those territories would decide according to the principles of popular sovereignty whether to permit slavery. Another provision in the Compromise of 1850 banned the slave trade in Washington, D.C. The compromise also included a strong new law concerning runaways—the Fugitive Slave Law.

 What were the provisions of the Compromise of 1850?

◆ THE FUGITIVE SLAVE LAW

It was not long before the Compromise of 1850 caused problems. One was the bitter opposition by Northerners to the Fugitive Slave Law, who viewed it as drastic and cruel. The law denied runaway slaves trial by jury and most other rights. Worse, the law required Northerners to cooperate in capturing runaways by hunting them down and turning them in. This made Northerners feel as if they were a part of the slave system. They did not want to be associated with slave catchers, who often used attack dogs to hunt down runaways. Anyone who did not cooperate with the law could be fined or imprisoned. Federal commissioners and marshals were charged with enforcing the law.

Opposition to the Law

Calhoun had hoped that the Fugitive Slave Law would force Northerners to acknowledge the rights of slave owners. Instead, each time the law was enforced, it convinced more Northerners that slavery was evil.

A number of Northerners risked punishment by disobeying the Fugitive Slave Law. Several states enacted "personal liberty laws," which prevented state authorities from helping to return runaways.

In several cases, crowds tried unsuccessfully to rescue runaway slaves from jail. In 1854, a group of abolitionists in Boston tried to free Anthony Burns, a runaway slave from Virginia. They broke down the courthouse door but were turned away by marshals. Burns was escorted back to Viriginia by armed guards.

The Fugitive Slave Law was enforced vigorously in the courts. Out of 191 cases tried in northern federal courts, 157 people were judged to be runaway slaves and returned to the South. Northern marshals did their jobs, even when they disagreed with the law. Southerners paid more attention to the few dramatic and widely reported instances of slave rescues than to the ways in which Northerners complied with the law.

The Election of 1852

The election of 1852 showed that the nation continued to be divided over slavery. Southern Democrats supported the Compromise of 1850. The Whigs were unable to agree among themselves. Most Whigs from the North were antislavery, while those from the South were proslavery. The Whigs' candidate lost the election, and the Whigs ceased to exist as a national political party. The Democratic candidate, Franklin Pierce of New Hampshire, won the presidency.

 In what ways was the Fugitive Slave Law unacceptable to most Northerners?

Section 1 Review

Check Understanding

1. **Define** (a) free state (b) slave state (c) sectionalism (d) proviso (e) popular sovereignty (f) Free-Soiler (g) fugitive

2. **Explain** why adding a territory or state created tension between the North and the South.

3. **Describe** the purpose of the Missouri Compromise.

4. **Identify** the major provisions of the Compromise of 1850.

5. **Explain** how the Fugitive Slave Law heightened sectional conflict.

Critical Thinking

◈ **Connecting Past and Present** What types of sectionalism exist in this country today?

Write About Citizenship

Write an editorial from a northern newspaper that attacks the law requiring Northerners to cooperate in capturing runaway slaves.

BUILDING *SKILLS*

Interpreting Fine Art: A Famous Abolitionist

Interpreting fine art involves understanding and explaining the kinds of information that drawings, paintings, and sculpture communicate. Fine art can provide details about people or events of the past. Visual images, such as historical paintings, can give the viewer insight into an artist's version of a historical event. Drawings, paintings, and sculpture can also provide a vivid record of daily life during a historical period.

Here's How

Follow these steps to interpret a piece of fine art:

1. Identify the subject. Describe the action, the scenery, and the people.

2. Was the artist present at the event, or is he or she reacting to secondhand reports?

3. What mood, or atmosphere, has the artist created? How does the artist use composition (the placement of people and objects) to draw your eye to what is important?

4. What was the artist's purpose in creating the painting? Does the picture reveal a political, social, or personal bias? How can you tell?

5. What conclusions can you draw from the painting? In what way does it support or contradict your ideas about the event, person, or place? What attitudes and ideas does the painting reveal?

Here's Why

The ability to analyze fine art is useful in identifying points of view. By analyzing and interpreting fine art, you can better understand the attitudes and ideas of and about a historical period.

Practice the Skill

John Brown was an abolitionist who tried to start a slave uprising in 1859. He was found guilty of treason and murder and sentenced to death. Brown became a hero to the antislavery movement.

This painting by a northern artist shows Brown kissing an African American child as Brown is led to his hanging. The artist based his painting on a newspaper account. At the actual event, Brown did not kiss a child. Interpret the painting by answering the questions from *Here's How.*

Apply the Skill

After you read about John Brown's raid on page 178, look again at this painting. Now that you know more about Brown, review your answers to the questions. Then write a brief essay about the kind of information a historical painting can provide.

Section 2

Differences Between North and South Widen

PREVIEW

Objectives

- To compare ways of life in the North and the South

- To explain how antislavery sentiment in the North became stronger during the mid-1800s

- To describe the role of the Underground Railroad as an escape route for enslaved people

Vocabulary

literacy rate
Underground Railroad
repeal

During the 1850s, conflict between the North and the South continued to grow. The differences between the two regions were not just political, however. They were economic and social as well.

◆ A WIDENING GAP

One major difference between the North and the South was in the growth of cities. During the 1850s, cities in the North grew much faster than cities in the South. As northern cities grew, so did industry. Most of the country's factories were located in the North, and over 90 percent of industrial workers lived close by.

The South concentrated on farming. Cotton, the region's most important cash crop, doubled in the 1850s and thus increased the value of the enslaved African Americans who worked in the fields.

Education in the North and the South also differed. The **literacy rate,** or the proportion of people who could read, varied widely between these regions. In 1850, about 20 percent of southern white adults could not read. In contrast, in New England less than one half of one percent could not read. Fewer children attended school in the South than in the North, and the school year in the South was shorter.

The Underground Railroad

Abolitionists in the North tried to find ways to help enslaved African Americans escape from the South, even if it caused conflict with southern slave owners. An example was the **Underground Railroad,** a network of escape routes African Americans followed to freedom. Both whites and African Americans set up this network to help slaves flee to the North.

The Underground Railroad included "tracks," "stations," and "conductors." Its tracks were hundreds of routes along back roads and rivers. These routes began in the South and ran north to Canada or south to Cuba, the Bahamas, or Mexico. The "stations" were houses, churches, or caves, where runaways could hide, rest, and get food. The "conductors" were people who guided the slaves during their journeys. The major routes of the Underground Railroad are shown on the map below.

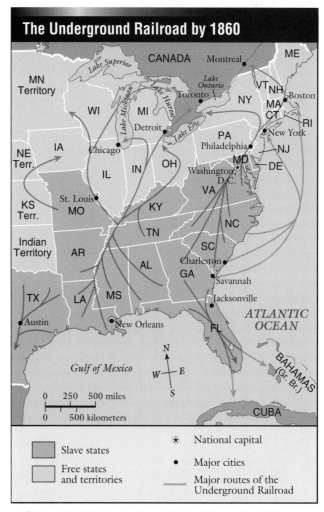

▲ Geography *This map shows the major routes of the Underground Railroad.* **Interpreting the Map** *Identify three routes used to escape from Georgia.*

One of the railroad's conductors was John Mason, a former slave who had escaped from Kentucky. Mason returned to the South and in less than two years helped 265 slaves escape. Finally authorities captured Mason by using bloodhounds to track him down as he was leading a group of runaways north. Mason was sold back into slavery, but he escaped again. He returned to work on the Underground Railroad and led more than 1,000 slaves to freedom.

Harriet Tubman was another conductor of the Underground Railroad. After escaping slavery by traveling the railroad herself in 1849, she, too, risked her freedom by helping others escape. Slave owners offered $40,000 for Tubman's capture.

Swaying Public Opinion

The Fugitive Slave Law was not the only reason Northerners turned against slavery. Writers influenced public opinion by telling about the cruelty of slavery, angering slave owners.

One influential book was *Twelve Years a Slave*, by Solomon Northup. Northup was a freed African American who lived in the North. While he was visiting Washington, D.C., slave traders kidnapped him and took him to New Orleans, where a planter bought him. Northup worked as a slave for the next 12 years. He finally regained his freedom with the help of a family friend.

Based on Northup's experiences, *Twelve Years a Slave* describes the feelings of an enslaved African American. This passage describes his fear related to weighing a basket of cotton:

> . . . no matter how much he longs for sleep and rest—a slave never approaches the gin-house with his basket of cotton but with fear. If it falls short in weight, he knows that he must suffer.

No event, book, or person did more to turn Northerners against slavery than *Uncle Tom's Cabin*. Its author, Harriet Beecher Stowe, saw the cruelty of slavery when she visited Kentucky. She also saw runaway slaves arrested where she lived in Cincinnati, Ohio. Her novel tells the story of an enslaved African American named Uncle Tom who is known for his kindness. His master is a brutal planter named Simon Legree, who eventually beats Tom to death for trying to prevent the whipping

Person ◆ to ◆ Person

Harriet Tubman

Often compared to Florence Nightingale or Joan of Arc, Harriet Tubman faced danger and death to relieve human suffering. The most famous leader of the Underground Railroad, she was also a Civil War scout, nurse, and spy.

In 1849, Harriet Tubman escaped from a plantation on Maryland's eastern shore. Once free, she was determined to help other enslaved African Americans escape. Between 1850 and 1860, she made 19 trips as a "conductor" on the Underground Railroad and helped more than 300 slaves escape to Canada.

Harriet Tubman's trips were very successful because she was a master at planning. She provided for all possibilities, including forged passes and even sedatives for crying babies. One of her more famous trips involved a passenger who panicked. Tubman feared that if he turned back, he would be captured and tortured until he told all he knew about the Railroad. The unwilling passenger changed his mind when Tubman pointed a gun at his head, telling him that dead folks "tell no tales."

Harriet Tubman's efforts strengthened the abolitionist movement. She chose to help because she wanted to heal the wounds slavery had left on her people.

▲ Harriet Tubman
(about 1821–1913)

Looking Back: Why do you think Harriet Tubman took the risk of helping others after she herself had escaped to freedom? Would you have done the same? Why or why not?

of a female slave. Stowe made Legree a Northerner who lived in the South in order to show how slavery could corrupt even those born outside the system.

When *Uncle Tom's Cabin* appeared in 1852, it was a bestseller—and another source of conflict. In just over a year, it sold 300,000 copies. Southerners claimed that Stowe's novel did not give a fair or accurate picture of the lives of enslaved African Americans. They claimed that *Uncle Tom's Cabin* was filled with insults and lies. However, the book presented northern readers with a vivid picture of slavery and life in the South. Many readers began to ask how one person could own another. *Uncle Tom's Cabin* showed that slavery was not just a political conflict. It was a human problem.

How did literature have the power to change public opinion about slavery?

◆ THE KANSAS-NEBRASKA ACT

Senator Stephen Douglas of Illinois raised the slavery issue in Congress once again in 1854, when he introduced a bill to set up a territorial government in Nebraska. Douglas wanted to see a railroad built from Illinois through the Nebraska Territory to the Pacific coast, which would increase settlement in the West and also help business in Chicago. However, before a railroad could be built, the Nebraska Territory had to be settled and organized.

Douglas considered it his responsibilty to promote the settlement of the West, since he was the chairman of the Senate Committee on Territories and the Democratic party's leading spokesperson for western interests. According to him,

> There is a power in the nation greater than either the North or the South. That power is the country known as the Great West. . . . There, sir, is the hope of this nation.

Douglas suggested dividing the area into two territories: the Nebraska Territory and the Kansas Territory. According to the Missouri Compromise, slavery was already outlawed in those territories because they were north of latitude 36°30'N. Douglas needed the support of Southerners to get his bill passed.

To gain the support of the South, Douglas called for the issue of slavery in Kansas and Nebraska to be decided by popular sovereignty. This meant **repealing,** or canceling, the Missouri Compromise. Southerners supported Douglas because they hoped Kansas would vote for slavery. Nebraska, they knew, was located too far north to have a climate suitable for the plantation system. Northerners, however, were furious and believed that Douglas had betrayed them by reopening territory that was protected from slavery by the Missouri Compromise. After a struggle, Douglas got the Kansas-Nebraska Act through Congress, and President Franklin Pierce signed it into law.

Why did Senator Stephen Douglas want to promote the organization and settlement of the Nebraska Territory?

Section 2 Review

Check Understanding

1. **Define** (a) literacy rate (b) Underground Railroad (c) repeal

2. **Explain** how the growth of cities affected the economy of the North.

3. **Identify** the reasons why the value of enslaved African Americans increased during the 1850s.

4. **Explain** how the Underground Railroad was organized.

Critical Thinking

Understanding Points of View Explain how a Southerner and a Northerner might have responded to the descriptions of slavery in *Twelve Years a Slave* and in *Uncle Tom's Cabin.*

Write About Social Issues

Connecting Past and Present Several books in the 1800s influenced the public's view of slavery. Write about current books or movies that have swayed public opinion on a social issue.

The Final Break

PREVIEW

Objectives

- To describe the violence that took place in Kansas from 1855 to 1856

- To explain the Supreme Court's decision in the Dred Scott case

- To identify the effects of Abraham Lincoln's victory in the election of 1860

Vocabulary

border ruffian	extremist
arsenal	secede
insurrection	

The Kansas-Nebraska Act repealed the Missouri Compromise and reopened the question of where slavery could expand. In the years after the act was passed, Kansas became the center of a violent struggle between proslavery and antislavery forces. Because politicians in Washington could not agree on whether Kansas should be a free or a slave state, they left the question to the white settlers of the territory, who tried to solve it by killing each other. This struggle earned the region the name Bleeding Kansas.

◆ KANSAS BECOMES A BATTLEGROUND

The struggle over Kansas began in 1854, when supporters and opponents of slavery rushed to send settlers to Kansas. Each side wanted a majority in the territory before the vote concerning slavery took place.

By 1855 there were about 9,000 settlers in Kansas—enough to hold an election to establish a territorial government. Just before the election date, thousands of armed proslavery men from Missouri poured into Kansas. These **border ruffians,** as antislavery people called them, were not settlers and were not able to vote legally in the election. They crossed into Kansas to terrorize free-soil settlers. A witness described what happened in one town:

> "On the morning of the election before the polls were opened, some 300 to 400 Missourians and others were collected in the yard . . . where the election would be held, armed with bowie-knives, revolvers, and clubs. They said they came to vote and whip the yankees [Northerners], and would vote without being sworn. Some said they came to fight."

Although the proslavery forces won the election, the voting was dishonest. Only about 1,500 men were registered to vote in all of Kansas, but more than 6,000 votes were cast—a clear indication that cheating was taking place.

The new proslavery legislature immediately passed proslavery laws. One law called for the death penalty for anyone caught helping a runaway slave.

In the fall of 1855, antislavery people set up their own government with a constitution that banned slavery. There were now two governments in Kansas, one proslavery and one antislavery.

Bleeding Kansas

By the fall of 1855, a civil war raged in Kansas. On May 21, 1856, about 800 border ruffians from Missouri attacked the town of Lawrence, the capital of the antislavery Kansas government. The attackers

Study Hint

A good way to study for a test is to turn headings into questions. Main idea questions often begin with how, why, and what. Detail questions often begin with when, where, which, and who. Write a main idea question and a detail question for the headings on this page, "Kansas Becomes a Battleground" and "Bleeding Kansas," and then answer them.

looted some houses, destroyed two printing presses, and wrecked the Free State Hotel.

Three days after the attack on Lawrence, Kansas, an antislavery group led by the abolitionist John Brown murdered five proslavery men and boys. Proslavery forces struck back with raids and killings of their own. By the end of the year, Kansas had truly earned the nickname Bleeding Kansas. More than 200 people from both sides were dead.

The Election of 1856

While the violence in Kansas increased, antislavery people organized a new political party that was opposed to the spread of slavery into the western territories. This new organization, the Republican party, began in Michigan in 1854. It attracted northern Whigs, northern Democrats, Free-Soilers, and other opponents of slavery. It included older established leaders, such as Charles Sumner of Massachusetts, and younger faces such as Abraham Lincoln of Illinois.

The presidential election of 1856 was split along regional lines. All the southern states except Maryland voted for James Buchanan, the Democratic candidate. The Republican candidate, John C. Fremont, won the majority of the northern states. Millard Fillmore, the candidate of both the Whig and American parties, carried only Maryland. The national growth policies of the Whig party and the anti-immigrant policies of the American party could no longer attract voters, who were now more concerned with taking sides over the issue of slavery.

Buchanan won the election with less than 50 percent of the popular vote. The vote, split clearly along regional lines, showed that feelings about slavery ran high and that the Union was in danger.

Why was Kansas at the center of the struggle between proslavery and antislavery forces?

◆ THE DRED SCOTT CASE

Another sign that slavery was dividing the nation was the Dred Scott case. Dred Scott was a slave in Missouri who sued for his freedom in 1846. His suit was based on the fact that between 1834 and 1838, his owner had taken him and his wife to live in the free state of Illinois and the free territory of Wisconsin. Scott argued that by living in free areas, their status as slaves ended, even though the owner later took them back to Missouri.

▲ Dred Scott, shown with his wife Harriet, sued for freedom in 1846. The Supreme Court decision against Scott in 1857 led to protest in the North. This poster announces a meeting to discuss the decision.

In 1850 a Missouri court ruled that Scott was a free man. However, in 1852 the Missouri Supreme Court overruled that decision. It said that Scott and his wife were still slaves. The case went to the U.S. Supreme Court, which ruled on it in early 1857.

The U.S. Supreme Court, headed by Chief Justice Roger Taney, used the case to decide the status of slavery in U.S. territories. The Court's decision, which denied Dred Scott his freedom, was based on the following conclusions. First, the Court ruled that Scott had no right to sue in a federal court because as an African American, Scott was not a U.S. citizen nor could he ever become one. Second, according to the Court, slaves were considered property, and the Fifth Amendment of the Constitution protects a citizen's right to own property. As a result, a citizen has a right to take his or her property, including slaves, anywhere. Finally, the Missouri Compromise was declared to be unconstitutional because the Constitution did not give Congress the power to prohibit slavery in a territory. After a territory became a state, it could ban slavery. The Court's decision meant that all territories were once again open to slavery.

President James Buchanan and southern leaders welcomed the Dred Scott decision. They saw it as a confirmation of the institution of slavery. However, the decision's extreme proslavery point of view caused an uproar in the North.

? On what basis did Dred Scott sue to obtain his freedom?

◆ THE LINCOLN-DOUGLAS DEBATES

In the congressional elections of 1858, Illinois Democrat Stephen Douglas was running for reelection to the Senate. His Republican opponent was Abraham Lincoln, a lawyer who had served one term as a member of the Illinois House of Representatives. Lincoln took a strong stand against the expansion of slavery in the territories. Lincoln began his campaign with one of his most famous defenses of the Union:

> **A house divided against itself cannot stand. I believe this government cannot endure, permanently half slave and half free. I do not expect the Union to be dissolved—I do not expect the house to fall—but I do expect it to cease to be divided.**

Lincoln challenged Douglas to a series of public debates from August into October. The debates gave voters a chance to compare the candidates' views on the status of slavery in the territories. During the debates, Lincoln spoke forcefully against permitting slavery in the territories, "If slavery is not wrong, nothing is wrong."

Douglas supported popular sovereignty as a means of determining the future of slavery in the U.S. territories. Douglas defeated Lincoln in the Senate race. However, Lincoln became a major contender for the Republican party's presidential nomination in 1860.

? What positions on slavery did Lincoln and Douglas express during the debates?

◆ JOHN BROWN'S RAID

The Lincoln and Douglas debates were not the only place the issue of slavery was being confronted. John Brown, a leader in the effort to make Kansas a free state, took matters into his own hands. A dedicated abolitionist, Brown decided that it was his destiny to end slavery.

Brown led 18 of his followers on an attack in October 1859. They took several hostages and seized control of an **arsenal** at Harpers Ferry, Virginia, that was loaded with weapons and ammunition. Brown planned to use the arms to start an uprising. He believed, as did many northern abolitonists, that discontent among enslaved African Americans was so great that a general uprising needed only a spark to begin. Brown never found out whether he was right. Federal troops led by Colonel Robert E. Lee surrounded the arsenal, killed several of Brown's forces, and captured Brown, who was tried for treason and hanged.

Brown's raid symbolized Southerners' deepest fear: the fear of slave **insurrection,** or rebellion against established authority. Plantation owners fortified their homes while leaders prepared for more slave rebellions. Southerners believed that northern abolitionists supported slave uprisings, a suspicion that was confirmed when documents found at Harpers Ferry revealed that Brown had the financial support of half a dozen wealthy Northerners. The Richmond, Virginia, *Enquirer* reported, "The Harpers Ferry invasion has advanced the cause of disunion more than any other event that has happened since the formation of [the] government."

Many northern leaders condemned Brown's actions, including Abraham Lincoln. However, abolitionists such as Ralph Waldo Emerson and Louisa May Alcott called him a hero. As the election of 1860 approached, the differences dividing North from South were growing wider.

? What effect did John Brown's raid have on Southerners?

◆ THE ELECTION OF 1860

The election of 1860 reflected the country's opposing views of slavery. Southern Democrats wanted protection of slavery in the territories. Northern Democrats wanted popular sovereignty. When the Democratic party tried to nominate a candidate, the membership split. Stephen Douglas was nominated by the northern Democrats. John C. Breckinridge of Kentucky was nominated by the southern Democrats.

The Republicans nominated Abraham Lincoln. Lincoln firmly supported the idea that slavery could not be allowed to expand but promised to leave slavery alone where it already existed. The Republican party attracted western voters when it promised public land at a low cost. The Republicans also called for tariff protection for American manufactured goods, which appealed to northern voters. Entering the election, the party had a program and a candidate with broad appeal.

Lincoln won the election with a clear majority of the electoral vote but not a majority of the popular vote. He also won the election without the South, confirming many Southerners' fear that the South was becoming powerless. **Extremists,** who drastically deviated from the political opinions held by most people, believed that both the President and the Congress were against their interests, especially slavery. They argued that the Constitution was only a compact, or agreement, among the states. If the North was not going to keep its part of the compact and respect the rights of Southerners, then the South should **secede,** or withdraw, from the Union. After all, the Declaration of Independence said that "it is the right of the people to alter or abolish" a government that denies the rights of its citizens. Southerners believed that the Northerners had broken the compact by preventing the return of fugitive slaves. Using arguments like this, extremists persuaded other Southerners to secede.

The Nation Breaks Apart

In December 1860, South Carolina became the first state to secede. By February 1861, Georgia, Florida, Mississippi, Louisiana, Alabama, and Texas had also left the Union. In none of these states was the vote for secession unanimous, as it had been in South Carolina. Throughout the South, secession occurred because Southerners felt they had no other choice.

In February, delegates from the seven seceding states met in Montgomery, Alabama, and created the Confederate States of America, or the Confederacy. They wrote a constitution similar to the Constitution of the United States, with a few important exceptions. It strongly supported the right of the states to decide on the slavery issue. The convention chose Jefferson Davis as president of the new Confederate States of America.

Fort Sumter: The War Begins

When Lincoln took office in March 1861, the Confederacy had already begun to seize forts, post offices, and other federal buildings. Lincoln, who believed it was unconstitutional for the southern states to leave the Union, did not want to allow the Confederates to take over government property. However, if he sent troops to hold the forts, he might start a war.

Fort Sumter became the center of the conflict. The Confederacy wanted to gain control of the fort because it guarded the Charleston, South Carolina, harbor. Fort Sumter was running low on supplies, so President Lincoln decided to send unarmed merchant ships to resupply the fort. If the Confederates attacked the fort, then the Confederacy—and not the federal government—would be responsible for starting the war.

After the Union commander of the fort refused a Confederate demand to surrender before the supply ships arrived, Confederate guns opened fire on Fort Sumter on the morning of April 12, 1861. Thirty-three hours later, the Union commander surrendered. The Civil War had begun.

 What events caused the South to fire the first shot of the war?

Section 3 Review

Check Understanding

1. **Define** (a) border ruffian (b) arsenal (c) insurrection (d) extremist (e) secede

2. **Explain** why Kansas became a site of violence between proslavery and antislavery forces.

3. **List** the key parts of the U.S. Supreme Court decision in the Dred Scott case.

4. **Analyze** how John Brown's raid affected Southerners' desire to leave the Union.

5. **Explain** why southern secession occurred.

Critical Thinking

Connecting Past and Present How did the Dred Scott decision add to the tension between the North and the South? What present-day court decisions have caused conflict?

Write About Government

Write the headline and the first paragraph of an editorial in a southern newspaper about the election of Lincoln as President.

Review

CHAPTER SUMMARY

Section 1
The issue of slavery sharply divided the North and South as the United States added new territory or admitted new states during the 1800s. Congress struggled to find compromises on the issue, but tensions between the two regions only increased. Part of one compromise, the Fugitive Slave Law, severely punished runaway slaves and those who aided them. The law served only to turn many more Northerners against slavery.

Section 2
In the 1850s the issue of slavery continued to pit North against South. Accounts of the horrors of slavery greatly stirred northern emotions. During this time, the Underground Railroad helped countless enslaved African Americans escape from the South. In 1854 the Kansas-Nebraska Act was passed, which repealed the Missouri Compromise. Slavery would now be decided according to popular sovereignty in Kansas and Nebraska.

Section 3
In 1854, Kansas became the focus of the slavery struggle when widespread violence broke out over the issue of whether Kansas would be a free or a slave state. Tensions escalated still further in 1857, when the U.S. Supreme Court ruled in the Dred Scott decision that slaves were property and thus slavery could not be prohibited in the territories. After Abraham Lincoln, a Republican, was elected President in 1860, southern states began seceding from the Union. In 1861 the Civil War began with the South's first shot on Fort Sumter in South Carolina.

Connecting ◆ Past and Present

Do you think states should have the right to secede from the United States today? Under what circumstances? Explain the reasons for your point of view.

Using Vocabulary

For each term below, write a sentence that shows its meaning.

1. free state
2. sectionalism
3. slave state
4. Free-Soiler
5. popular sovereignty
6. Underground Railroad
7. secede
8. border ruffian
9. arsenal
10. insurrection

Check Understanding

1. **Explain** the Missouri Compromise.
2. **Contrast** the beliefs of Daniel Webster and John C. Calhoun toward slavery.
3. **Summarize** the provisions of the Compromise of 1850.
4. **Describe** how the North changed economically and socially in the 1850s.
5. **Explain** how the Underground Railroad was organized.
6. **Explain** why Kansas had two governments in 1855.
7. **Discuss** why John Brown and his activities concerned the South.
8. **Explain** why the U.S. Supreme Court's decision in the Dred Scott case angered people who opposed slavery.
9. **Describe** how the election of 1860 revealed the conflict between the North and the South.
10. **Explain** the importance of Fort Sumter in the Civil War.

Critical Thinking

1. **Understanding Causes and Effects** What were the effects of the Fugitive Slave Law on Northerners and Southerners?

2. **Making Inferences** How might the growing economic differences between the North and the South have helped lead to the Civil War?

3. **Comparing Ideas** In what ways were the provisions of the Missouri Compromise, the Compromise of 1850, and the Kansas-Nebraska Act similar and different?

4. **Analyzing** Why was the surrender of Fort Sumter important?

◆ **Connecting Past and Present** In the 1850s, Harriet Beecher Stowe wrote a novel to influence public opinion. If you wanted to reach people and change their opinions today, how would you do it? Explain.

Interpreting the Timeline

Use the timeline on pages 166–167 to answer these questions.

1. Who was President when Japan was reopened to the West?

2. How many years separated the Missouri Compromise and the shelling of Fort Sumter?

3. Which events led to increased tensions over the issue of slavery?

Writing to Create

John Brown's raid on Harpers Ferry was a forceful attempt to end slavery. **Write** a short, dramatic scene based on the event. Use dialogue that the people involved might have used. Write a script, select classmates to play particular roles, rehearse your scene, and perform it for the class.

Putting Skills to Work

INTERPRETING FINE ART

Look carefully at the painting *The Bombardment of Fort Sumter* on this page. Then answer these questions.

1. What is the subject of the painting? How would you describe the actions, the scenery, and the people?

2. What mood or atmosphere has the artist created?

3. How does the artist use composition (the placement of people and objects) to draw your eye to what is important?

4. What conclusions can you draw from the painting? In what ways does the painting support or contadict your ideas about the event?

▲ *The Confederate attack on Fort Sumter in 1861 pushed the troubled nation into war.*

Portfolio Project

ART AND HISTORY

Look through the drawings and paintings in this unit. You can also use library resources to find a book with art from the pre-Civil War era. Note how the artists draw attention to their subjects through the use of light and dark spaces. Also notice how subjects are positioned. Choose two paintings or drawings and explain how the artist uses light and position to emphasize details. Present a report to your class, explaining how the paintings reveal information about this period in history. Show the paintings to your classmates, and lead a discussion about them.

Chapter 10
The Civil War
1861–1865

CHAPTER PREVIEW

Section 1 Preparing for War
As the North and the South prepared for war, both gathered troops and accumulated resources.

Section 2 A Country at War
The Battle of Bull Run began a war that would be fought for four years.

Section 3 The War and American Life
Although most soldiers were white men, many African Americans, Hispanics, and women made significant contributions to the war effort.

Section 4 The War Ends
While the Union army's victory ensured the restoration of the nation, President Lincoln's death cast a shadow over the Union.

Gettysburg Address

U.S. Events

1861
Eleven states form the Confederate States of America.
War begins between the North and the South.
South wins the First Battle of Bull Run.
North develops the Anaconda Plan.

1862
Battle of Antietam is fought.
Ironclad battleships clash.

1863
Lincoln delivers Gettysburg Address.
Emancipation Proclamation takes effect.
Grant wins control of Mississippi River valley.
Violent draft riots occur in North.

1860

World Events

1861
Russian serfs are emancipated.
New Zealand gold rush begins.

1862
International Red Cross is proposed.

1863
French offer to make Maximilian of Austria emperor of Mexico.

Maximilian of Austria

Portfolio Project

A CIVIL WAR TIMELINE

A complex historical event that spans a number of years, such as the Civil War, usually includes many smaller events—battles, changes in leadership, and treaties. A timeline is a useful tool for organizing these events in a visual format. At the end of this chapter, you will create a timeline for events of the Civil War and draw conclusions about it.

▲ *These soldiers gathered on a ridge at Cumberland Landing, Virginia, before attacking Confederate forces.* ◆ **Connecting Past and Present** *What do you think these soldiers thought about as they rested before battle? How do armies prepare for battle today?*

Robert E. Lee surrenders in Appomattox, Virginia

1864
✪ Lincoln reelected.
Grant takes command of all Union forces.
Sherman begins "march to the sea."

1865
Civil War ends at Appomattox Court House.
Lincoln is assassinated.
✪ Andrew Johnson becomes President.
Walt Whitman's elegy to Lincoln is published.

1867

1864
Louis Pasteur develops pasteurization.

1866
Great Britain unites West African colonies.
Fyodor Dostoyevsky's novel *Crime and Punishment* is published.

Louis Pasteur memorial stamp

Preparing for War

PREVIEW

Objectives

• To identify the states that stayed in the Union and those that seceded

• To describe the advantages of the North and of the South at the start of the Civil War

• To explain how the Union planned to win the war

Vocabulary

border state
martial law

Until 1861 the central issue dividing the North and the South was the expansion of slavery. Once the South seceded from the Union, Jefferson Davis, president of the Confederate States of America, was faced with the task of building and maintaining the unity of the Confederacy.

President Lincoln's main goal was the preservation of the Union—more important even than finding a solution to the issue of slavery. Lincoln made his objective clear when he wrote, in 1862,

❝ I would save the Union. I would save it the shortest way under the Constitution. . . . My paramount [main] object in this struggle is to save the Union, and is not either to save or destroy slavery. If I could save the Union without freeing any slave I would do it, and if I could save it by freeing all the slaves I would do it; and if I could save it by freeing some and leaving others alone I would also do that. . . . I have here stated my purpose according to my view of official duty; and I intend no modification [change] of my oft-expressed personal wish that all men everywhere could be free. ❞

◆ THE NATION DIVIDES

Although seven states had seceded from the Union by February 1861, eight other slave states had not decided if they would join the Confederacy or remain in the Union. Their indecision related to Lincoln's promise not to interfere with slavery in the states where it already existed.

The Confederate bombardment of Fort Sumter, in the harbor of Charleston, South Carolina, determined the final choice by the eight undecided slave states. A few days after the Confederacy fired the first shots on Fort Sumter, Lincoln declared that a rebellion against the U.S. government was taking place. On April 15, the President called for 75,000 volunteers to put down the rebellion. This call for volunteers led four of the undecided states—Virginia, North Carolina, Tennessee, and Arkansas—to secede from the Union.

In Virginia, the choice to join the Confederacy had serious consequences, leading to the formation of a new state. Small farmers in the northwestern part of Virginia had never supported slavery, and they opposed secession. When Virginia seceded, the northwestern part of the state broke away. Its citizens banned slavery and entered the Union in 1863 as the state of West Virginia.

The election of Abraham Lincoln in 1860 convinced many southern states that their rights would no longer be protected. ▼

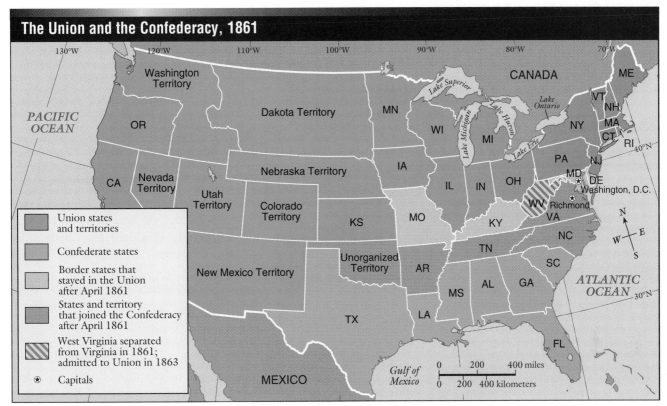

The Union and the Confederacy, 1861

Union states and territories

Confederate states

Border states that stayed in the Union after April 1861

States and territory that joined the Confederacy after April 1861

West Virginia separated from Virginia in 1861; admitted to Union in 1863

★ Capitals

▲ **Geography** *At the start of the Civil War, some states, called border states, had divided loyalties between the Union and the Confederacy.* **Interpreting the Map** *How many border states stayed in the Union? Name the states that were part of the Confederacy.*

The four remaining slave states—Missouri, Kentucky, Delaware, and Maryland—became known as the **border states,** or states located between the North and the South. Though all the border states officially stayed in the Union, citizens within these states were often fiercely divided in their loyalties. It was not uncommon for some citizens in these states to join the Confederate army, while others joined the Union army.

In the state of Maryland, the division of loyalties was particularly obvious. This created a tense situation that concerned President Lincoln. He knew that Maryland, which bordered the nation's capital of Washington, D.C., was in a strategic geographic location. This location made Maryland crucial to the Union cause. If the Confederate army reached Washington, D.C., by way of a nearby state such as Maryland, the Union center of power would be at risk. In one incident, a pro-Confederate group attacked Union soldiers in Baltimore, Maryland, on April 19, 1861. Fearing that the state might turn to the Confederacy, President Lincoln sent federal troops to the city. He declared statewide **martial law,** or the temporary rule by the army instead of by elected officials.

Maryland was not the only border state that concerned the Union. In fact, the Union regarded all the border states as critical to its success in the war. That these four border states chose to stay in the Union was a severe blow to the Confederacy. They could have added much needed military manpower and manufacturing capacity to the Confederacy. Because of this, Lincoln was careful not to do or say anything that would upset the balance in these states, thus forcing them to leave the Union and join the Confederacy. Since slavery was legal in the border states during the war, Lincoln stated that his main purpose in leading the Union into war against the Confederacy was not to abolish slavery but to restore the Union.

The map above shows the states and territories that remained in the Union in 1861. The map also shows the eleven states and one territory that made up the Confederacy. The new capital of the Confederacy was Richmond, Virginia.

 Why were the border states important to both the North and the South?

◆ PREPARATION FOR WAR

The North and the South each had certain advantages as they prepared for war. The strengths and weaknesses of each side, shown on the chart on page 187, greatly influenced the outcome of the war.

Strengths of the North

One of the North's greatest advantages was the size of its population. More than 21 million people lived in the North, while only about 9 million people lived in the South. Of those, about 3.5 million Southerners were enslaved African Americans.

The North had many more people to produce food, guns, and ships. Because of its larger population, more people were available to serve in its army and navy. For example, northern soldiers greatly outnumbered Confederate soldiers even though less than half the North's white males of fighting age went off to war. In contrast, about 90 percent of the South's white males of fighting age enlisted, or signed up, to serve in the war. This left few people to run the factories and farms vital to the production of military goods and other supplies needed to fight the war.

The North had an even greater advantage in its industry and railroads. In 1860 it had many more factories than the South. This gave Northerners the ability to produce more artillery, uniforms, and locomotives. The Union could easily replace equipment as it wore out. The South had to depend on getting many of these goods from countries in Europe. In its transportation networks, the North also had the advantage, with more than twice as many miles of railroad track as the South. Railroads helped the North disperse goods and soldiers in a more timely manner and with greater efficiency than with other methods of transportation. The North was able to feed, clothe, arm, and transport all its soldiers.

The North also had a decisive leader—Abraham Lincoln. As President, Lincoln understood the North's military problems and was able to rally Northerners to the cause of war. He also had the courage and political skill to take on the task. As he explained, the struggle to save the Union was deeply connected to the ideals of freedom and democracy.

By 1861 more than 70 percent of all factories were located in the North. The factories produced better rifles and better cannons, such as the one pictured below, which would be used to the North's advantage in the Civil War. ▼

Northern and Southern Economic Strengths, 1861

	Northern and Border States	Southern States
Railroad track	22 thousand miles	9 thousand miles
Number of factories	110 thousand	21 thousand
Number of workers	1.2 million	111 thousand
Value of products	$1.6 billion	$155 million
Agriculture totals in bushels—corn, wheat, oats	728 million bushels	331 million bushels
Agriculture totals in pounds—rice and tobacco	279 million pounds	386 million pounds
Agriculture totals in bales—cotton	4 thousand bales	5 million bales

▲ **Economics** *The northern and southern states had different economic strengths.* **Interpreting the Chart** *In which areas did the South have an economic advantage? Overall, which side was economically stronger?*

Strengths of the South

Despite the North's advantages, the South had strengths of its own. Many of the country's best military leaders in 1860 were from the South, including the Confederacy's commander, General Robert E. Lee of Virginia. Generally, Southerners were better-trained and more experienced at handling weaponry and horses than soldiers who enlisted in the North.

Furthermore, the goal of the Confederacy was to be recognized as an independent country. The forces of the South did not need to conquer territory in the North to achieve their independence. Southern forces had to fight a defensive war mainly on their own soil. Confederates had strong motivation to

fight hard, since they were defending their land, their homes, and their way of life.

Since the main goal of the North was to preserve the Union, it had to invade and conquer the South. To do so, the Union army needed enough supplies for its journey into Confederate territory, as well as enough supplies to sustain its soldiers once the fighting began. Long supply lines that allowed goods and people to be moved both by rail and by horse were necessary because of the long distances. Traveling these distances slowed Union troop movements, giving the South the advantage in moving both people and weaponry more quickly from battle to battle.

The South hoped that its cotton industry would help it gain support. Since southern cotton was vital to Great Britain's booming textile factories, the South hoped to receive British support in its struggle with the North.

 **What was one advantage of the North and one advantage of the South as the Civil War began?**

◆ EARLY BATTLES AND STRATEGIES

When Abraham Lincoln called for volunteers in April 1861, he expected the war to be over by winter. Therefore, Lincoln asked Union volunteers to enlist for only 90 days. Lincoln believed that if the Confederate capital could be captured, the rest of the South would fall. The slogan "On to Richmond" became the cry to win the war.

The Battle of Bull Run

The first major battle of the Civil War proved Lincoln wrong. The Battle of Bull Run, named for a creek in the area, took place on July 21, 1861. The battlefield was about 20 miles southwest of Washington, D.C. Some members of Congress and a number of other civilians came to watch the battle. The spectators expected to enjoy a picnic as they watched the battle they thought would quickly end the rebellion.

As the battle began, both the inexperienced Union and Confederate troops fought well and held their ground. Then, as Confederate reinforcements arrived and pushed forward, the Union lines broke. Instead of marching "On to Richmond," confused and disorganized Union soldiers dropped their guns. As they turned back, they ran into their congressmen and other civilians who were watching the battle. It was a chaotic scene as soldiers and panicky civilians

▲ *The Confederate victory at the Battle of Bull Run ended the hope in the North for a brief war.*

fled back to Washington. The Union's defeat at the Battle of Bull Run proved that there would be no easy victory in the Civil War.

The Anaconda Plan

The North realized the need for a well-planned strategy to defeat the South. Union leaders devised a three-part plan, called the Anaconda Plan, after a snake that coils around its victims and crushes them to death. The plan contained several key strategies. First, the Union would blockade southern ports to cut off the Confederacy's export of cotton and import of military supplies from Europe. At the same time, land and naval forces would seize the Mississippi valley and split the Confederacy in two. Finally, Union armies in the East would attack the Confederacy with the intention of capturing its capital, Richmond, Virginia.

It was a good plan, but one that would take years to carry out. Abraham Lincoln and his advisors understood that the war ahead would present a long and difficult challenge.

 How did the North's strategy change after the Battle of Bull Run?

Section 1 Review

Check Understanding

1. **Define** (a) border state (b) martial law

2. **List** the advantages of each side at the start of the Civil War.

3. **Describe** the plan the Union devised to defeat the South.

Critical Thinking

Connecting Past and Present What social and political issues create divided opinions among Americans today?

Write About Economics

Based on economic factors, was the North or the South better equipped to fight a long war? Write an essay, defending your position with reasons and examples.

BUILDING SKILLS

Drawing Conclusions: Saving the Union

Drawing conclusions is the process of making reasoned judgments based on information you have learned. Historians draw conclusions based on evidence from primary and secondary sources. These sources include diaries, newspapers, journals, letters, fine art, political cartoons, maps, charts, and graphs.

Here's How

Follow these steps to draw conclusions:

1. Study the primary or secondary source carefully.
2. Consider the information you are learning in light of what you already know about the subject.
3. Look for details that support what you know. Consider details that contradict what you already know.
4. If possible, compare the new information with other reliable sources. Look for similarities and differences between the different sources.
5. Make a summary statement as a conclusion about a group of details.
6. Test your conclusions and revise them to fit additional facts you learn. The more supporting information you have, the more likely you are to draw accurate conclusions.

Here's Why

Putting together new information with what you already know and comparing information in several reliable sources are important in studying history. Drawing conclusions allows you to go beyond what you have learned to form new insights.

Practice the Skill

The Crittenden Resolution, which was passed by the House of Representatives on July 25, 1861, clarified the Union's reasons for waging war against the Confederacy. After reading the passage, answer the questions below.

This war is not waged upon our part in any spirit of oppression, nor for any purpose of conquest or subjugation [to bring under control], nor purpose of overthrowing or interfering with the rights or established institutions of those [seceding] States, but to defend and maintain the supremacy of the Constitution and to preserve the Union, with all the dignity, equality, and rights of the . . . States unimpaired [undamaged].

1. What conclusions can you draw about the Union's reasons for waging war against the Confederacy?
2. What evidence from the passage supports your conclusion?
3. What conclusions can be drawn about the Union's policy toward slavery?
4. What evidence from the passage supports your conclusion?

Apply the Skill

Choose one of the photographs or maps in this chapter. Draw several conclusions by combining what you already know about the Civil War with the new information provided in the photo or map. As you continue to read the chapter, test your conclusions and revise them if necessary.

Section 2

A Country at War

PREVIEW

Objectives

- To explain the significance of the early battles of the Civil War

- To describe Robert E. Lee's strategy to win the war for the South

- To explain how the Union won control of the Mississippi River valley

- To discuss why Gettysburg was a turning point in the Civil War

Vocabulary

war of attrition	stalemate
casualty	ironclad warship

The Confederacy probably would have had its best chance of succeeding if it had worn down the Union by a **war of attrition.** In this kind of war, the weaker army inflicts continuous losses of soldiers and supplies that gradually add up to an unbearable burden for the other side. Fighting such a war, however, meant avoiding direct battle, a policy the South did not want to follow.

◆ THE FIRST WAR YEARS

After Bull Run, Lincoln appointed General George B. McClellan to lead the Union army. Though a good organizer, McClellan was less aggressive than Lincoln had hoped.

Once he built his army, General McClellan showed a reluctance to take it into battle. At one point, President Lincoln became impatient with McClellan's inaction and remarked, "If McClellan is not using the army, I should like to borrow it." Even when McClellan was in the field, however, he was not a good military commander.

Lincoln finally convinced McClellan to take action in March 1862. McClellan moved his Union army of 135,000 soldiers by boat to a peninsula south of Richmond. From there, he planned to attack the Confederate capital.

As usual, McClellan moved slowly, which gave the Confederate army time to organize its troops. On May 31 and June 1, the armies fought the Battle of Seven Pines. Among those wounded was the Confederate commander, General Joseph E. Johnston.

General Robert E. Lee replaced Johnston as commander. Lee believed the South had to win the war quickly to prevent the North from gathering its greater resources and putting pressure on the South. The only way to win the war quickly was to take chances. If he hit the northern armies hard and often, Lee hoped he might win a decisive victory and end the war.

From June 25 through July 1, 1862, Lee repeatedly struck at McClellan in a series of battles known as the Seven Days Battles. The **casualties,** or those killed and injured, on both sides were huge, reaching 30,000. McClellan retreated and took his army back to Washington. Lee claimed victory because he had successfully defended Richmond. Frustrated that McClellan failed to take the Confederate capital, Lincoln temporarily relieved him from command.

Antietam

The next major battle in the East occurred in September 1862. In keeping with his strategy, Lee

President Lincoln and General McClellan are shown at Antietam, Maryland, in October 1862. When McClellan failed to meet Lincoln's military expectations, he was replaced by General Ambrose Burnside.▼

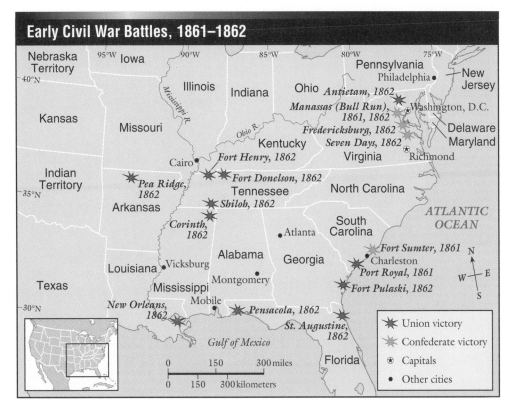

Early Civil War Battles, 1861–1862

◄ **Geography** *Many early battles of the Civil War centered around the capital cities and along the southeastern coast.* **Interpreting the Map** *Which battles threatened the capitals of the Union and the Confederacy?*

decided to advance his army into Maryland. However, McClellan, with a reorganized army, had an enormous stroke of luck. A Union soldier found Lee's battle plans wrapped around three cigars and turned the battle plans over to McClellan. Still, McClellan moved slowly. He finally attacked Lee on September 17, at Antietam Creek, in Maryland.

The Battle of Antietam started at dawn. Union forces attacking through a cornfield ran into Confederate rifle and cannon fire. Both sides suffered huge losses in what turned out to be the bloodiest day of the war. There were more than 23,000 casualties. That was nearly double the total killed in the War of 1812 and the war with Mexico combined.

A newspaper reporter on the scene described the battlefield after the fighting ended:

"The field and its ghastly harvest which the Reaper [death] had gathered in those fatal hours remained finally with us. Four times it had been lost and won. The dead are strewn so thickly that as you ride over it you cannot guide your horse's steps too carefully. Pale and bloody faces are everywhere upturned."

On the night of September 18, Lee retreated with his battered army to Virginia. To Lincoln's dismay, McClellan did not pursue Lee. Because of Lee's retreat, the Union called Antietam a victory—but Lincoln looked for a replacement for McClellan.

Lee continued to carry out bold moves in the East, but he still was not able to defeat the Union armies. By 1863 the fighting in the East had reached a **stalemate,** or deadlock.

Warfare at Sea

As part of the Anaconda Plan, the North's blockade against the South proved to be effective in stopping military supplies and other products, such as sugar, salt, and coffee, from entering southern ports. Shortages of food in the South reached critical levels. By 1863, Southerners in several cities staged bread riots, in which starving civilians took to the streets to demand food from the Confederate government.

The blockade also kept the South from shipping cotton to Great Britain. The South hoped that Great Britain would break the blockade to get the cotton it needed. However, this would have meant war with the North, and Great Britain did not want a war. In 1861 the British had enough cotton on hand to last for more than a year. In addition, Great Britain needed

The Civil War ushered in a new era for naval warships. No longer driven by wind and sail, the new warships were steam driven and covered with protective iron. On the right is the South's Virginia, *originally named the* Merrimac *by the North, fighting against the North's* Monitor, *on the left.* ▶

northern grain as much as it needed southern cotton. British factories also prospered by selling the North manufactured goods for its war effort. Therefore, Great Britain was unwilling to enter the war to help the South and, as much as possible, tried to maintain a neutral position in its dealings with the states.

Southerners tried to break the blockade by running small, quick boats, called blockade runners, through the line. Then the South tried a new strategy—building and using **ironclad warships.**

The South's first ironclad warship, covered with iron plates four inches thick, was originally named the *Merrimac.* The vessel was a Union ship that had sunk, was recovered by the Confederates, and was renamed the *Virginia.* On March 8, 1862, this strange-looking ship steamed into Norfolk Bay in Virginia and attacked northern ships. Despite its unusual appearance, the *Virginia* destroyed two Union ships. Union cannon fire simply bounced off its iron-plated sides. On March 9, the *Virginia* returned to continue attacking the Union navy. However, this time it faced the Union's ironclad ship, the *Monitor.* The two ironclad ships fought for several hours but did little damage to one another.

Although the inventor of the ironclad ships had a hard time convincing authorities that the ship could float, let alone fight, ironclads ushered in a new age in naval warfare. The Union and the Confederacy built more ironclad ships. Since the South lacked shipyards, skilled workers, metal, and other essential resources, it could not build enough ironclads or keep them in working order. The North, however, had plenty of shipyards, workers, and materials. The Union built 200 new warships during the war, including more than 70 ironclads. New ironclads helped it to maintain control of the sea and the inland waters of the Confederacy.

Control of the Mississippi River Valley

In the West—the region that included Tennessee, Arkansas, Mississippi, and Louisiana—the North experienced success in battles during 1861 and 1862. The location of these battles can be seen on the map on page 191. In February 1862, Union forces under General Ulysses S. Grant attacked and captured Fort Henry and Fort Donelson, two Confederate forts in Tennessee. The North then moved ahead with its plan to divide the South by taking control of the Mississippi River valley. Although General Grant's army suffered high losses in April at the Battle of Shiloh, which was fought near the Tennessee River, in the end the Confederate soldiers retreated.

While Union forces under Grant attacked the Confederacy near the Mississippi River in the North, a Union naval force under Admiral David Farragut forced the surrender of New Orleans in the South. New Orleans was the South's largest and wealthiest city, and its loss badly hurt the Confederacy.

The Union victory at New Orleans and the Confederacy's retreat at Shiloh gave control of the northern and southern ends of the Mississippi River to the Union. The South could no longer use the Mississippi as a supply line. To gain complete control of the river, the Union still had to capture the Confederate stronghold in Vicksburg, Mississippi. Grant tried and failed to capture it in early 1863. Then Grant tried to capture Jackson, Mississippi, and attack Vicksburg from the rear. After a six-week siege, Vicksburg surrendered on July 4, 1863. The Union now controlled the Mississippi River and had split the South in half. Texas, Arkansas, and most of Louisiana were now cut off from the other Confederate states.

 How did the Union win control of the Mississippi River?

◆ GETTYSBURG

Despite Confederate victories in Fredericksburg, Virginia, in December 1862 and at Chancellorsville, Virginia, in May 1863, General Lee knew it would take more to win the war. He decided to stop defending Virginia. His goal was to win a large battle and force the North to make peace.

The Turning Point

As Lee moved north into Pennsylvania, Lincoln put George G. Meade in command of the main Union army in the East. On July 1, 1863, the two armies clashed in the small town of Gettysburg, Pennsylvania.

The Battle of Gettysburg lasted for three days. More than 50,000 men on both sides were killed or wounded. It was the deadliest battle of the entire Civil War.

The decisive point in the battle came on July 3, when Lee ordered troops under General George Pickett of Virginia to attack the center of the Union lines. It was one of the few military mistakes Lee ever made.

About 15,000 Confederate soldiers took part in the attack known as Pickett's Charge. They had to cross

▲ *The Confederate army suffered a major defeat at the Battle of Gettysburg, shown above. Afterward, General Lee apologized to his troops, declaring, "It's all my fault."*

▲ *In 1863, President Lincoln delivered a two-minute speech in Gettysburg. The Gettysburg Address, not considered successful at the time, is one of the most famous speeches in United States history.*

more than a mile of open field to reach the Union lines. Northern soldiers waited for them behind stone walls on an area of high ground called Cemetery Ridge. The Confederate troops charged into rifle and cannon fire. A witness remembered how the noise was "strange and terrible, a sound that came from thousands of human throats . . . like a vast mournful human roar." More than 6,500 southern soldiers fell dead or wounded. The rest retreated to their lines.

Although General Lee was not forced to flee Gettysburg, but instead chose to retreat, the battle was a disastrous defeat for the South. His army was badly weakened. Never again would the Confederate army have the strength to attack the North.

The Gettysburg Address

In November 1863, a ceremony was held to dedicate a cemetery for soldiers who had died in the Battle of Gettysburg. President Lincoln was invited to attend the ceremony. In little more than two minutes, he delivered what is now known as the Gettysburg Address, regarded as one of the greatest speeches in American history. In just a few sentences, Abraham Lincoln summed up the ideals upon which the United States is based. Lincoln stressed that the Civil War was a struggle to preserve those ideals.

Lincoln began the address by reminding his audience that the United States was "conceived in Liberty, and dedicated to the proposition that all men are created equal." The Civil War, he said, was "testing whether that nation or any nation so conceived and so dedicated, can long endure." The soldiers who fought and died at Gettysburg did so to make sure the United States would last. The President ended by saying that it was the duty of those gathered at Gettysburg to complete the soldiers' unfinished work. That "great task" was to make sure that the United States had

 . . . a new birth of freedom, and that government of the people, by the people, and for the people, shall not perish from the earth. ""

Why is the Battle of Gettysburg called a turning point in the Civil War?

Section 2 Review

Check Understanding

1. **Define** (a) war of attrition (b) casualty (c) stalemate (d) ironclad warship

2. **Discuss** General McClellan's strengths and weaknesses as a military commander.

3. **Outline** General Lee's plan for southern victory.

4. **Analyze** why control of the Mississippi River was important to the Union.

5. **Explain** why Lee did not invade the North after the Battle of Gettysburg.

Critical Thinking

Connecting Past and Present What was the significance of the Gettysburg Address? How are its ideas relevant today?

Write About History

You are a newspaper reporter who witnessed General George Pickett's charge at Gettysburg. Write a news report in which you describe the charge and explain its importance.

Section 3

The War and American Life

PREVIEW

Objectives

- To discuss opposition to the Civil War

- To explain how the Union and Confederate armies drafted soldiers

- To describe the contributions of African Americans, Hispanics, and women to the Civil War

Vocabulary

due process	conscription
censorship	emancipation
bounty	reconnaissance

In spite of early hopes for a quick war that avoided excessive damage to either side, the toll of the Civil War was devastating. While the numbers of dead and injured increased on the battlefield, social and economic problems plagued both sides at home.

◆ OPPOSITION TO THE WAR

Northerners who opposed the Civil War did so for a variety of reasons. Some were not opposed to slavery and believed the South should be allowed to secede. Others believed that the cost of keeping the South in the Union was not worth the loss of life and property. Most of the opponents of the war came from the Democratic party.

The Democratic party divided into two wings—War Democrats and Peace Democrats. Supporters of the war were known as War Democrats. They often differed with Lincoln about how to achieve victory, but they supported the struggle to save the Union.

The Peace Democrats strongly opposed the war. These Northerners who wanted peace with the South were called Copperheads by Republicans and other critics. A copperhead is a poisonous snake that is able to hide easily due to its natural camouflage and is said

to strike without warning. The Copperheads opposed the war in a variety of ways. Some gave speeches and wrote articles, others violated the law by trying to persuade Union soldiers to desert or by smuggling guns to the South.

Opponents of the war posed a dilemma for President Lincoln. The North was in theory a free and democratic society where people had the right to say what they wanted. However, the President did not want the Copperheads to stir up feelings against the war and weaken the war effort.

Lincoln pushed the powers of the presidency under the Constitution as far as possible, expanding presidential powers in wartime and setting a precedent for future wartime Presidents. During the war he had more than 13,000 opponents of the war arrested. They were held in prison without being tried. This violated the Fifth Amendment, which says that no citizen can be deprived of liberty without **due process,** or the required procedures of the law. In addition the government shut down more than 300 newspapers for various periods of time. This silencing of free speech, called **censorship,** violated the First Amendment of the Constitution. Lincoln justified this unconstitutionality by claiming that the people he arrested and the newspapers he shut down were breaking military law, which does not have the same guarantees of freedom as civilian law.

 How did President Lincoln exceed constitutional powers during the Civil War?

History *The woman holding the shield with* Union *written on it is threatened by serpents representing Peace Democrats.* **Interpreting the Cartoon** *Why are the serpents attacking the woman?* ▼

◆ RAISING THE ARMIES

When the war began, the North and the South relied on volunteers to build their armies. The North gave the enlisting soldiers money, called a **bounty,** to encourage them to sign up. The bounty system, however, proved to be expensive and led to abuses. Men would enlist and collect their bounty, then desert the army, go to another place, and enlist again to collect another bounty.

Eventually neither the North nor the South could fill their ranks with volunteers, so they both passed **conscription** laws, drafting people to serve in the armed forces. The South passed a conscription law in 1862 and the North in 1863. The South's law permitted few people to be exempt from the draft, but it did allow planters with more than 20 slaves to avoid serving in the army. The high productivity of their plantations was considered necessary for the war. This angered poor southern farmers who had no slaves to do their work when they went off to war. They complained that the rich were not carrying their share of the burden.

The North's conscription law allowed men to stay out of the army if they could afford $300 or find a substitute to serve in their place. Of course, only the wealthy could pay to get substitutes. Many people complained that the Civil War was "a rich man's war and a poor man's fight."

Draft Riots

In the North, opposition to the draft sometimes led to violence. Many people did not want to risk losing their lives to win freedom for African Americans. There were riots in Ohio, Illinois, Wisconsin, and Pennsylvania. The worst draft riot occurred in mid-1863 in New York City. There was great anger among workers at being drafted. Tempers rose when white workers heard rumors that African Americans would take their places at work once they were in the army.

The riot in New York lasted several days. The rioters attacked both African Americans and abolitionists. As many as 100 people were killed, and casualties reached 1,000. Damage to property from looting and fires was as high as 1.5 million dollars. It took 20,000 federal soldiers to restore order.

Billy Yank and *Johnny Reb*

During the Civil War, people used the term *Yankee* to apply to all Northerners and *Rebel* for all

As the war continued, draft laws were passed in the North and the South to increase the number of men serving in the armies. Names were drawn by lottery from draft wheels, such as the one shown here. ▶

Southerners. They called the men who fought in the two armies *Billy Yank* and *Johnny Reb*. These soldiers came from every walk of life. They were farmers, skilled craftworkers, laborers, office workers, and professionals. Most Union and Confederate soldiers were under the age of 21. However, as the death toll climbed higher each year, the age limits were expanded. The South eventually drafted boys who were as young as 17 and men as old as 50.

Many of the soldiers who fought in the Civil War were immigrants from Europe. About one fourth of the men in the Union army and one tenth of those in the Confederate army were born outside the United States. In the last years of the war, many immigrants became soldiers as soon as they arrived.

Few of the soldiers had any military experience. Although most knew how to use a gun, battle strategy was a mystery to them. The armies of both sides were little better than armed mobs. Most regiments were made up of men from one town or region. Since the soldiers chose their own officers, popularity rather than ability determined leadership. Desertion was common: one out of every seven Union soldiers and one out of every nine Confederate soldiers deserted.

Life in camp was difficult. Poor sanitation made army camps breeding grounds for disease. As the war dragged on, Confederate soldiers often lacked adequate food, clothing, and shelter. Fighting took up only part of the time. Between battles, soldiers cared for their equipment, played cards and baseball, wrote letters, and sang.

Why did some people oppose the draft during the Civil War?

◆ THE EMANCIPATION PROCLAMATION

By the summer of 1862, Lincoln was ready to announce the **emancipation,** or freeing, of the slaves in the Confederacy. Lincoln's decision was not an indication that he was bending to pressure from abolitionists. Instead, he reasoned that the Confederacy needed the labor of enslaved African Americans to continue fighting the war. If the Union promised them their freedom, many slaves might refuse to work or might leave their owners. This would seriously weaken the South and help end the war.

Lincoln also thought that emancipation would rally support for the war in the North. Discouraged by the number of casualties, many Northerners were questioning the need for war. The President believed the abolition of slavery would provide a larger moral reason for the war and gain the Northerners' support.

President Lincoln issued the Emancipation Proclamation on September 22, 1862. A proclamation is a public announcement. You can read Lincoln's words in the historical document appendix on pages 712 and 713. The Emancipation Proclamation did not free any slaves immediately. Instead, the proclamation called on the South to end the war and rejoin the Union by the end of the year. It said that enslaved people in the areas in open rebellion against the Union on January 1, 1863, would be "forever free." That included slaves in North Carolina, South Carolina, Georgia, Florida, Alabama, Mississippi, Arkansas, Texas, and the parts of Virginia and Louisiana that were not under Union control. It did not apply to areas under Union control, including the slaveholding border states. In those states more than 400,000 African Americans still remained enslaved. The proclamation was a promise that enslaved people living under Confederate rule would be free when the Union won the war. Lincoln's purpose in issuing the proclamation was to meet the abolitionist demand for a war against slavery while not losing the support of those who favored slavery, especially in the border states.

The North now had an important new war aim. The goal of ending slavery in the South succeeded in rallying support for the Union. Public opinion in Europe swung strongly to the Union side, ending any chance that Great Britain or France might support the Confederacy.

? What were Lincoln's motives in issuing the Emancipation Proclamation?

▲ *Although the Emancipation Proclamation did not immediately free any African Americans, it did provide a moral purpose to help rally support for the war.*

◆ AFRICAN AMERICANS IN THE CIVIL WAR

When the war began, many free African Americans in the North wanted to serve in the army, but the government turned them down. President Lincoln feared that if African Americans were permitted to join the Union army, the border states would defect to the Confederacy.

Abolitionists urged the President to recruit African American troops. Frederick Douglass pointed out that the government was hurting the war effort by not using all its available men. Douglass also wanted African Americans to fight for the North for another reason:

> Let the black man get upon his person the brass letters U.S. Let him get an eagle on his button and a musket on his shoulder and bullets in his pocket, and there is no power on earth which can deny that he has earned the right to citizenship in the United States.

African Americans in the Union Army

President Lincoln reversed his decision to allow African American soldiers to serve in the Union army at about the same time he issued the Emancipation Proclamation. Ultimately, nearly 185,000 African Americans served in the Union army, including about 100,000 formerly enslaved people. Nearly 40,000 African Americans lost their lives in battle. Approximately 29,000 African Americans served in the Union navy. More than 100,000 additional African Americans served the North as valuable laborers and spies. Twenty African American soldiers and sailors received the Congressional Medal of Honor for bravery.

Even after they were allowed to enlist, African Americans faced discrimination. In the North, many whites believed that African Americans were inferior both in intelligence and in courage. Thus, African American soldiers had to prove themselves in battle, particularly to their commanding officers. They served in all-African American units, usually commanded by white officers. Often, African Americans received weapons and horses that were inferior to those issued to white troops. Furthermore, medical

These men served in the Fourth United States Colored Infantry. African American soldiers made up 10 percent of the Union forces. ▼

care in African American units was not as good as that found in white units.

Initially, African American soldiers were paid less than white troops, ten dollars a month rather than thirteen. This changed in June 1864, when Congress equalized the pay of black and white soldiers and authorized back pay for those who had not received their fair share.

The excellent performance of African American soldiers helped bring about a change in the policy that excluded them from becoming officers. By the end of the war, more than 75 African Americans had become officers in the Union army. One was William Harvey Carney, a sergeant who became famous for his refusal to allow the American flag to touch the ground during battle.

African American soldiers in the Union army and their officers faced special dangers. The Confederacy passed a law that said any captured white officer from an African American unit would be punished severely or even put to death. The Confederacy also warned that captured African American soldiers might be executed or sold into slavery. In a famous incident at Fort Pillow in Tennessee, soldiers of Confederate General Nathan B. Forrest gunned down hundreds of African American and white Union soldiers who had fought side by side and were trying to surrender.

Regiments of Distinction

The best-known African American regiment was the 54th Massachusetts Volunteers. Its enlisted soldiers were free African Americans, such as Robert Fitzgerald from Pennsylvania and Frederick Douglass' two sons, and its officers were white abolitionists. Colonel Robert Shaw, who came from a well-known abolitionist family, was its commander.

The unit earned fame in July 1863, when it attacked Fort Wagner in Charleston Harbor, South Carolina. The regiment attacked across an open beach, and despite heavy fire and huge losses, it reached the walls of the fort. When no other Union units came to its aid, the regiment had to retreat. Almost half of its men were killed or wounded, including Colonel Shaw.

Another African American unit was the First South Carolina Volunteers. Most of its soldiers were escaped slaves. The unit helped win control of South Carolina for the Union.

 How did African Americans contribute to the Union's war effort?

▲ Approximately 400 women disguised themselves as men in order to fight in the Civil War. Francis Clalin, shown in these photographs, served with the Missouri cavalry.

◆ WOMEN DURING THE WAR

During the Civil War, women from both the North and the South helped the war effort in countless ways. While some took on the jobs of their fathers, husbands, or brothers, others found new occupations they had not been allowed to hold before.

At Home

Women played a number of different roles at home. When able-bodied men left for the army, southern women had to take their places, managing plantations and operating farms. Women took jobs making uniforms and weapons. They worked in government offices and did many other jobs that in the past had been done by men.

Women in the North took jobs as secretaries and clerks in government offices, such as the Treasury Department in Washington, D.C. The number of women working in private businesses, in offices, and factories also increased. Their entry into the workforce in both the North and the South had effects that lasted long after the war.

On the Battlefield

Hundreds of women became battlefield nurses. Dorothea Dix, well known for her work helping the mentally disabled, volunteered to serve as a nurse. The Secretary of War appointed her to take charge of all Union nurses. Clara Barton and abolitionist activist Sojourner Truth also served as nurses for the Union. Clara Barton believed that the war created employment opportunities that normally would have taken another 50 years for women to obtain.

Women played other important medical roles as well. Dr. Elizabeth Blackwell trained nurses for work in Union hospitals. Sally Louisa Tompkins founded small clinics and hospitals in the South. She was commissioned as a captain in the Confederate army so that her facilities could qualify as military hospitals.

A few women served as spies. Belle Boyd went behind Union lines to get information for the Confederacy. Pauline Cushman spied for the North, pretending to be an actress while behind enemy lines in the South. Elizabeth Bowser and Harriet Tubman supplied information to the Union from behind enemy lines.

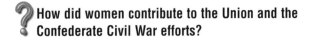 How did women contribute to the Union and the Confederate Civil War efforts?

◆ HISPANICS IN THE CIVIL WAR

Approximately 10,000 Hispanics fought for the North and the South during the Civil War. In addition to Hispanic regiments led by Hispanic officers, such as the all-Californio Union regiment led by Salvador Vallejo, many Hispanics fought side by side in army or volunteer units with soldiers who were not of Latin descent.

David Glasgow Farragut was one of the most famous Hispanic heroes of the war. Commander of the Union ships charged with blockading Confederate ports, he captured New Orleans in 1862. Two years later, in attempting to launch an assault on the heavily protected harbor in Mobile, Alabama, he voiced his famous cry, "Damn the torpedoes! Full speed ahead!" Farragut avoided the torpedoes, entered the harbor, and captured the town. In 1866, he became the first four-star admiral in the nation.

Other Hispanics did equally daring tasks during the war. Manuel Chaves, known as *El Leoncito* ("the Little Lion"), led 490 New Mexicans in a spectacular attack on a Confederate spy train. Cuban-born Lieutenant Colonel Federico Fernández Cavada did airborne **reconnaissance,** or exploratory surveys, from hot-air balloons for the Union. Cuban-born Loreta Janeta Velaquez was both a soldier and a spy for the Confederacy. Disguised as a man, she fought at Bull Run in 1861. Even after being discovered and discharged, she enlisted as a man and fought at Shiloh in 1862. Later working as a spy, she described her adventures in the book *The Woman in Battle.*

 What were some of the major contributions made by Hispanics during the Civil War?

Section 3 Review

Check Understanding

1. **Define** (a) due process (b) censorship (c) bounty (d) conscription (e) emancipation (f) reconnaissance

2. **Describe** the reasons for opposition to the Civil War.

3. **Explain** the strategies the Union and Confederacy used to build their armies.

4. **Discuss** the kinds of discrimination African Americans faced in the Civil War.

5. **Describe** the contributions women and Hispanics made to the Civil War.

Critical Thinking

◆ **Connecting Past and Present** What are some reasons people oppose war today? How might a President create support for a war?

Write About Citizenship

You are an abolitionist in the North during the Civil War. Explain what the events at Fort Pillow and Fort Wagner mean to the struggle for African American freedom.

Section 4

The War Ends

PREVIEW

Objectives

• To analyze General Grant's strategy for defeating the Confederacy

• To explain the concept of total war

• To analyze the impact technological advances had on fighting the Civil War

• To describe the costs of the Civil War in terms of human life and property loss

Vocabulary

total war
assassinate

Union General Ulysses S. Grant commanded troops in the Mississippi River valley. Grant's success in the western campaign earned him status as a hero and helped to bring about the end of a long, destructive, and costly war.

◆ ULYSSES S. GRANT

A West Point graduate, Grant had fought in the war with Mexico, then left the army in 1854. When the Civil War broke out, the North needed officers. Grant took advantage of the opportunity, and shortly after rejoining the army, he became a general.

Unlike some other Union generals, Grant had an iron will and the ability to stay calm under fire. He also had an excellent military mind and could develop strategies for large modern armies. His victories in the West under difficult conditions caught President Lincoln's attention, and Grant received more important assignments.

After Grant's victory at Vicksburg, he became the North's greatest military hero. Lincoln then appointed him commander of Union forces in the West. Grant's next target was Chattanooga, Tennessee, an important railway center and the gateway to the center of the Confederacy.

The attack took a month, but in November, Chattanooga finally fell. Once again, Grant had demonstrated his ability to manage a large and difficult campaign. In March 1864, Lincoln appointed Grant commander of all Union forces. Grant now moved his army east to attack Robert E. Lee.

General Grant decided that to win the war, he would need to engage in **total war**—destroying food, equipment, and resources that would be of use to civilians as well as armies. Civilians would thus suffer as much as the soldiers.

 Why did Lincoln choose Grant to lead the Union forces?

◆ TOTAL WAR

Grant launched two main attacks in the spring of 1864. He went after Lee's army and at the same time began driving southeast from Chattanooga toward Atlanta. His philosophy of war was simple: get the enemy. As Grant put it: "Get at him as soon as you can. Strike at him as hard as you can, and keep moving on."

Grant Fights Lee's Army

Grant followed his no-nonsense war strategy in his pursuit of Lee. Before Grant took command, the Union armies had advanced 35 miles toward Richmond in 3 years. Under Grant's leadership, the Union advanced 75 miles in 45 days. The Union paid a high price in human life, since the army fought terrible battles at almost every turn. By June, half of Grant's army of 120,000 men were casualties.

Nevertheless Grant continued to push Lee toward Virginia. In June, Lee reached Petersburg, a town south of Richmond. By then, Lee had lost one third of his army and had only 40,000 troops left. Lee continued to hold off Grant, but that was all he could do. His battered army made no more advances.

Sherman's March to the Atlantic Ocean

While Grant fought Lee's army, Union General William Tecumseh Sherman pushed southeast toward Atlanta, Georgia, the heart of the Confederacy. It was a vital railroad, manufacturing, and trade center. Sherman took control of Atlanta in September 1864, as shown on the map on the next page.

After taking Atlanta, Sherman began his "march to the sea" through Georgia to the Atlantic Ocean.

It was this campaign, more than any other, that brought total war to the South. Sherman began his campaign by expelling the people of Atlanta from their homes and burning a large part of the city. As Sherman's army marched southeast to Savannah, it cut a path 60 miles wide in which it destroyed everything. Union forces tore up railroad tracks, blew up bridges, burned barns, destroyed crops, and killed livestock. Sherman explained the reason behind total war:

" We cannot change the hearts of those people of the South, but we can make war so terrible . . . make them so sick of war that generations would pass away before they would again appeal to it. "

The Union army reached the sea and the city of Savannah in December. Southern forces retreated from the city, and Sherman took it without a fight. In February 1865 he turned north and moved through South Carolina and North Carolina. Then Sherman's army headed for Richmond, Virginia.

As General Sherman marched through Georgia, Union General Philip Sheridan marched through Virginia's Shenandoah Valley. Like Sherman, Sheridan waged total war, carrying out Grant's order to leave nothing in the valley that Lee could use to carry on the war. During the campaign, Sheridan's troops burned 2,000 barns filled with grain. They left nothing behind for Lee's hungry troops.

Why did General Grant use the strategy of total war to defeat the Confederacy?

◆ **SURRENDER AT APPOMATTOX**

By early 1865 the Confederacy was beaten. Many troops deserted, hoping to get home to protect their families. In late March and early April, Union forces struck at what was left of Lee's army. Meanwhile, on April 3, Union troops entered a burning Richmond. Lee retreated until Grant surrounded his forces at Appomattox Courthouse in central Virginia. There, Lee decided he must surrender. On April 9 the two generals met and quickly agreed to terms. Grant's terms were generous. Lee's 28,000 troops would surrender and give up their weapons. Officers could keep their pistols and swords, their baggage, and their horses. Enlisted men who had horses or mules could take them home "for the spring plowing." Grant also

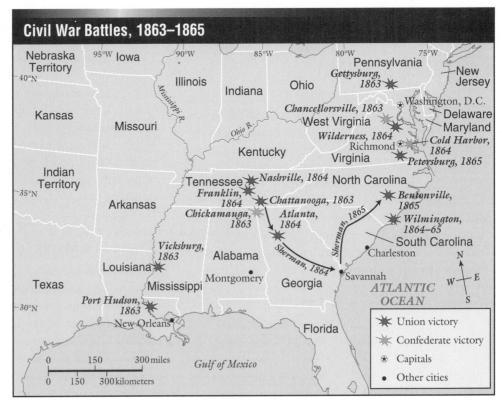

Geography *The Union won many battles between 1863 and 1865.* **Interpreting the Map** *Compare the number of Union victories with that of Confederate victories. Which army had more victories? Trace the route of Union forces from Chattanooga to Bentonville. Who was the victor at Bentonville?* ▶

ordered that Lee's hungry soldiers be fed. When Union troops started firing their guns in celebration, he stopped them. Grant told his men,

> **The long war is over. The rebels are our countrymen again.**

The next day, Lee left for Richmond. The rest of the Confederate commanders quickly surrendered. On April 14, 1865, Major Robert Anderson returned to Fort Sumter. Anderson had surrendered the fort four years earlier. "I thank God that I have lived to see this day," Anderson said. Then he raised the same frayed and shell-torn flag he had lowered four years earlier.

What were the terms of the surrender at Appomattox?

◆ LOSSES AND CHANGES

The Civil War was finally over. Abraham Lincoln had played the leading role in saving the Union. His next task was to overcome the bitterness between North and South and bring the nation together. In his second inaugural address in 1865, he explained,

> **With malice [anger] toward none, and with charity for all . . . let us strive to finish the work we are in, to bind up the nation's wounds, . . . to do all which may achieve and cherish a just and lasting peace among ourselves and with all nations.**

By reelecting Lincoln, voters showed their approval not only of his war policy but of his goal to end slavery. In February 1865, Congress supported this goal by passing the Thirteenth Amendment to the U.S. Constitution, which abolished slavery. Before the amendment could be made into law, however, it had to be ratified by the states.

The Murder at Ford's Theater

Lincoln did not get the chance to witness the ratification of the Thirteenth Amendment or to heal the Union. On Friday, April 14, he and his wife attended a play at Ford's Theater in Washington, D.C. There he was **assassinated,** or murdered, by John Wilkes Booth.

Born in Maryland, Booth was a talented actor who sympathized with the South. His hatred for the Union was focused on its central figure, Abraham Lincoln. On the evening of April 14, Booth entered Ford's theater, crept into the President's box, and shot Lincoln in the back of the head.

When Lincoln died the next day, grief swept the nation. On almost every home in the North, a strip of black cloth appeared as a sign of mourning. The train carrying Lincoln's body back to Illinois for burial passed through New York City, Chicago, and many other cities. Millions of Americans came to pay their last respects as the train passed through their communities. On May 4, 1865, Abraham Lincoln was buried in Springfield, Illinois.

Study Hint

While a heading states a main idea, the paragraphs that follow explain or give examples related to the heading. Each paragraph in the next section explains a consequence of the Civil War. As you read, take notes on the five consequences.

The Consequences of the War

The Civil War was by far the most costly war in American history. First and foremost, it claimed the lives of more than 618,000 men. That is more than the total dead of all of the other wars in U.S. history combined, from the Revolution to the middle of the Vietnam War. Another 275,000 Union and 190,000 Confederate troops were wounded.

The financial cost of the war was staggering. Government loans and tax revenues spent on the war totaled nearly $3 billion for the Union government. The Confederacy spent more than $2 billion. Twenty years after the war ended, the United States was still devoting more than 60 percent of the federal budget for interest on the war debt and veterans' benefits. However, government spending amounted to only a fraction of the $20 billion or so of the total cost of the war. Much of the rest represented the physical destruction of the South.

The Civil War left large parts of the South in ruins. Property losses were never officially counted, but certainly added up to billions of dollars. Much of the best agricultural land had been destroyed, and planting again would not be possible for years. Many towns and cities—including Richmond, Virginia; Atlanta, Georgia; and Columbia, South Carolina— were nothing but rubble. It would take the South's economy a generation to overcome the severe blows dealt by the war.

Furthermore, the war left wounds of bitterness that took generations to heal. Conquered, and in their view robbed of their slave property, white people in the South were forced to redefine their world. They were no longer allowed to view themselves as masters of anyone else. The possibility of political power and social equality for African Americans was not easy for most white Southerners to accept.

Finally, the Civil War dramatically changed the United States. Americans no longer saw the nation as a group of separate states that had made a compact to work together. Instead, they saw it as a single nation led by a strong central government. From time to time since the end of the Civil War, some states have insisted on their sovereignty, or right to determine their own laws. However, no state has ever seriously threatened to secede from the Union since the Civil War.

A New Kind of War

The American Civil War was the first major war to take place after the Industrial Revolution, making it the world's first modern war. It was the first war in which the railroad and telegraph played a major role. These inventions speeded the movement of men and supplies and the flow of information. New forms of technology made weapons more deadly. For the first time, armies used long-range rifles; iron-plated, steam-powered gunboats; and hot-air balloons to fight battles.

The Civil War armies were much larger than armies in earlier American wars. In the War of 1812 and in the war with Mexico, no more than 15,000 soldiers fought in a single battle. In the Civil War, some battles involved more than 100,000 soldiers.

The Effect of War on Government

The federal government itself changed as a result of the Civil War. Abraham Lincoln extended the powers of the President in wartime as no other President before

him had. For example, he expanded the army when he thought it was necessary, though the Constitution of the United States grants that power only to Congress. Lincoln also took away the civil rights of thousands of citizens who were imprisoned because of their opposition to the war. These actions formed a powerful precedent for later Presidents to follow in wartime.

Lincoln, along with Congress, also created another kind of civil rights precedent during the war years. The idea that the protection of Americans' civil rights was the job of the federal government, especially if the states failed to protect these rights, took hold during the Civil War. This idea was to grow stronger over the next century, resulting in strong federal civil rights laws in the 1950s and 1960s.

 How did the Civil War affect the expansion of presidential powers?

Section 4 Review

Check Understanding

1. **Define** (a) total war (b) assassinate

2. **Explain** what made Ulysses S. Grant's strategy for winning the war effective.

3. **Describe** how technological advances affected the Civil War.

4. **Analyze** the effect of Lincoln's assassination.

5. **Summarize** the consequences of the Civil War in terms of both human life and property.

Critical Thinking

Connecting Past and Present General Grant engaged in total war to defeat the South. What strategies do armies use against each other today to win battles?

Write About Economics

In an essay, explain why it took so many years for the South to recover from the Civil War.

CONNECTING HISTORY & Technology

THE TECHNOLOGY OF WARFARE

By the time the Civil War was over, 2 percent of the American population had died in battle. These deaths were a horrifying tribute to the effectiveness of new weapons technology.

In addition to better warships and cannons, perhaps the most important technological change during the Civil War was a new kind of bullet. Old-fashioned muskets with their smooth bores, or interiors, and their lead ball ammunition did not have much fire power. Gunfire hardly reached more than 100 yards. The new minié ball, however, made rifles more accurate and deadly. For the first time in a war, bullets killed many more men than did bayonets.

The minié ball, which was invented by Captain Claude Minié of France, was simply an inch-long slug of metal. The new bullet was shot from a special rifle that had grooves worked into its bore. The minié ball spun around the grooves and out of the rifle at a very fast speed. This allowed the bullet to travel much farther, up to 1,500 yards, and with more accuracy. An enemy standing one half mile away could become a casualty when shot with the minié ball.

Using the new kind of bullet had several important effects. Armed with the minié ball, Civil War soldiers were much safer defending themselves against attack than they were initiating an assault. Frontal charges were no longer effective because they resulted only in heavy casualties. This meant that the cavalry lost its importance. Men on horseback were now used to scout and screen the enemy's movements rather than to lead assaults. Fighting also became much more impersonal. In the past, soldiers had seen their opponents as recognizable human beings because they had to get close enough to shoot or stab them. Now the enemy was simply a cloud of smoke and a storm of bullets. The advanced technology and the new military strategies it promoted ushered in a new and deadly age of warfare.

Making the Technological Connection

1. How did the minié ball get its name?
2. Why did the minié ball require a special rifle?
3. How were the minié ball and its rifle improvements over the old-fashioned musket?
4. How did technological advances affect battlefield tactics?

Connecting Past and Present

What technological advances help to defend the United States today? How have these inventions changed the nature of war?

The minié ball was invented in 1848. This new type of bullet improved a shooter's speed and accuracy. ▼

Chapter 10
Review

CHAPTER SUMMARY

Section 1

As the Civil War began, the North's strengths included its large population and its numerous factories. The South had skilled military leaders and a population with training and experience with horses and weapons. Since the South was defending its own territory, it was motivated to fight hard to protect its land and its way of life.

Section 2

At first the South won a number of battles, but many of them resulted in huge losses of life on both sides. Then, General Ulysses S. Grant, of the North, began winning battles in the western part of the Confederacy. The Battle of Gettysburg was a turning point in the Civil War. The South was fatally weakened and from then on was unable to attack the North.

Section 3

Not everyone in the North or the South supported the war. To rally support in the North, Lincoln issued the Emancipation Proclamation. In addition, the North began allowing African Americans to serve in the military. African Americans, Hispanics, and women made numerous contributions to the war effort.

Section 4

General Grant's philosophy of war was costly but effective: keep hitting the enemy. As a result, the Union suffered many deaths but won the war. As part of the effort, General Sherman marched to the Atlantic Ocean through Georgia, burning everything in his path. By 1865 the Confederacy was beaten. Five days after the South surrendered, President Lincoln was assassinated.

Connecting ◆ Past and Present

What values, ideas, or rights do you think people in the United States would be willing to fight for in order to protect them?

Using Vocabulary

From the list below, select the term that best completes each sentence.

martial law	border states
stalemate	due process
assassinate	bounty
conscription	emancipate

1. John Wilkes Booth planned to _____ Abraham Lincoln.

2. Lincoln declared _____ in Baltimore so the army would rule instead of elected officials.

3. In 1862, President Lincoln issued the announcement that would _____ slaves in the Confederate-controlled South.

4. The North offered men a _____ if they signed up to be soldiers.

5. Neither side defeated the other early in the Civil War, which led to a _____ .

6. When not enough volunteers offered to fight, both sides in the Civil War began _____ to obtain soldiers.

7. Lincoln violated the Fifth Amendment by denying _____ to 13,000 opponents of the war who were arrested.

8. The _____ stayed with the Union, though many of their citizens wanted to join the Confederacy.

Check Understanding

1. **Describe** how technology changed warfare during the Civil War.

2. **Identify** states in the Union, states in the Confederacy, and those classified as border states.

3. **Describe** the South's plans to win the war.

4. **Summarize** the events of the Battle of Gettysburg.

5. **List** the provisions of the Emancipation Proclamation.

6. **Summarize** the arguments of the Copperheads.

7. **Describe** the contributions of Hispanics to the Civil War.

8. **Describe** the contributions of African Americans to the Civil War.

9. **Describe** the contributions of women to the Civil War.

10. **Explain** how General Sherman waged total war against the South.

Critical Thinking

1. **Comparing** What were the relative strengths and weaknesses of the North and the South at the start of the Civil War?

2. **Analyzing** What reasons did Abraham Lincoln have for issuing the Emancipation Proclamation?

3. **Drawing Conclusions** During the war how did methods for building armies change on both sides, and why did they change?

4. **Identifying Assumptions** At the beginning of the war, what did Lincoln and the people in Washington, D.C., assume about the length of the war?

Connecting Past and Present Why do you think differences within the United States have never again resulted in a civil war?

Interpreting the Timeline

Use the timeline on pages 182–183 to answer these questions.

1. How many years separate the First Battle of Bull Run from the end of the Civil War?

2. Did the Emancipation Proclamation take effect during Lincoln's first or second term?

3. Which 1864 event most contributed to ending the war in 1865? Explain your choice.

Writing to Describe

Put yourself in the place of a freed African American during the Civil War. **Write** a diary entry describing the provisions of the Emancipation Proclamation and how you believe it will affect the lives of succeeding generations of your family.

Putting Skills to Work

DRAWING CONCLUSIONS

In the Building Skills lesson on page 189, you learned that drawing conclusions helps you to develop new insights by going beyond what you read. Read the following excerpt from a Union soldier's diary that describes conditions at Andersonville Prison in Georgia. Use what you know about drawing conclusions to answer the questions that follow.

July 6 [1864]

Boiling hot, camp reeking with filth and no sanitary privileges; men dying off over 140 per day. Stockade enlarged, taking in eight or ten more acres, giving us more room, and stumps to dig up for wood to cook with. Mike Hoare is in good health; not so Jimmy Devers. Jimmy has now been a prisoner over a year and, poor boy, will probably die soon. Have more mementos than I can carry, from those who have died, to be given to their friends at home. At least a dozen have given me letters, pictures, etc., to take North. Hope I shan't have to turn them over to someone else.

1. What details does the writer provide about his life at the prison?

2. What conclusions can you draw about conditions at Andersonville Prison?

3. What conclusions can you draw about the writer's state of mind from his words and sentence structure?

Portfolio Project

A CIVIL WAR TIMELINE

The Civil War was a long and complex event in American history. To help you study the war and all its significant battles and important events, create a timeline of the war based on events described in this chapter. Begin by making a list of all the key events. Then decide how you will organize the timeline. Use your timeline to help you draw conclusions about the causes and effects of the Civil War.

Chapter 11
The Reconstruction Era
1865–1877

CHAPTER PREVIEW

Section 1 Reuniting a Divided Nation

Post-Civil War Reconstruction proved to be a difficult task, with the President and Congress fighting for control of the process.

Section 2 Congress Takes Charge of Reconstruction

Radical Republicans seized control of the Reconstruction process and began impeachment proceedings against President Andrew Johnson in an attempt to eliminate opposition to their program of Reconstruction.

Section 3 African Americans Build New Lives

As African Americans built new lives in the South, they gained a voice in politics that was limited or lost with the end of Reconstruction.

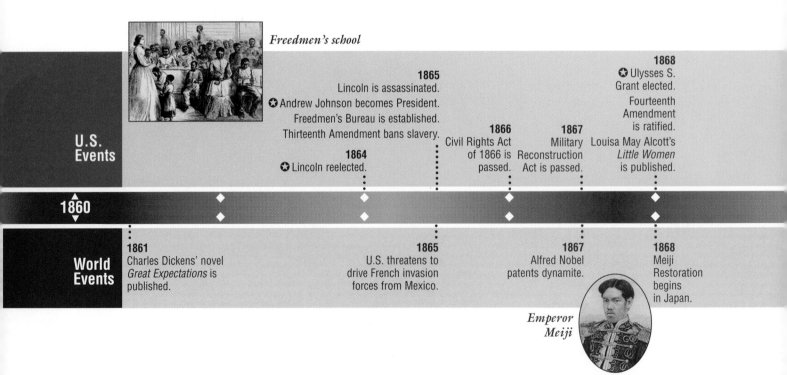

Freedmen's school

U.S. Events

1864
✪ Lincoln reelected.

1865
Lincoln is assassinated.
✪ Andrew Johnson becomes President.
Freedmen's Bureau is established.
Thirteenth Amendment bans slavery.

1866
Civil Rights Act of 1866 is passed.

1867
Military Reconstruction Act is passed.

1868
✪ Ulysses S. Grant elected.
Fourteenth Amendment is ratified.
Louisa May Alcott's *Little Women* is published.

1860

World Events

1861
Charles Dickens' novel *Great Expectations* is published.

1865
U.S. threatens to drive French invasion forces from Mexico.

1867
Alfred Nobel patents dynamite.

1868
Meiji Restoration begins in Japan.

Emperor Meiji

Portfolio Project

POLITICAL CARTOONS

Political cartoons are visual messages that express a point of view about an issue, person, or event. In the post-Civil War era, there were many points of view about how Republicans affected Reconstruction policies. At the end of the chapter, you will draw a political cartoon that reflects a point of view about events during Reconstruction.

▲ *These ruins in Richmond, Virginia, show the destruction in the South shortly after the end of the Civil War.* ◆◆ **Connecting Past and Present** *How would this destruction make it difficult for the South to recover? What agencies provide assistance to communities in need today?*

Hiram Revels

Rutherford B. Hayes

1870
Fifteenth Amendment is ratified.
Hiram Revels becomes first African American senator.

1872
✪ Grant reelected.

1876
✪ Rutherford B. Hayes chosen President.
Mark Twain's novel *Tom Sawyer* is published.

1877
Reconstruction ends.

1878

1871
Germany is unified under Prussian leadership.

Pierre Auguste Renoir's **The Dancer**

1874
The first exhibition of Impressionist paintings is held.

1877
Queen Victoria is proclaimed empress of India.

Reuniting a Divided Nation

PREVIEW

Objectives

- To compare the differences between President Lincoln's Reconstruction plan and the plan proposed by Radical Republicans

- To explain President Andrew Johnson's Reconstruction plan

- To describe the importance and impact of the Thirteenth Amendment

Vocabulary

Reconstruction	radical
amnesty	black codes
moderate	

The period after the Civil War from 1865 to 1877 is called the **Reconstruction** era. It was a time when the national government tried various plans to reunite the former Confederate states with the Union. During Reconstruction, the government also attempted to redefine the rights and status of African Americans, rebuild the devastated South, and heal the wounds of a divided nation.

◆ RECONSTRUCTING THE UNION

Before the end of the Civil War, President Lincoln had formulated a plan for reuniting the nation. A main goal of his plan was to win back the South's loyalty. Lincoln announced his program for bringing the South back into the Union in December 1863. It became known as the Ten Percent Plan.

According to the plan, most former Confederates, excluding high-ranking civil and military officers, could receive **amnesty,** or a pardon from their war actions (including joining the Confederacy), by taking an oath of loyalty to the Union. Those taking the oath had to pledge to support the U.S. Constitution and obey laws passed by Congress. They also had to accept the end

of slavery. Once 10 percent of a Confederate state's voters who had voted in the 1860 election swore loyalty to the Union, they could elect a new state government. Only after the new state government endorsed the Thirteenth Amendment, which abolished slavery, could the state reenter the Union. The Union would return any property, with the exception of former slaves, to voters who took the oath.

The Radical Republicans

Although Lincoln was a Republican, not all Republicans in Congress supported his plan. **Moderates,** or those who were opposed to extreme measures, supported Lincoln's plan. However, the plan did not go far enough to satisfy others. They wanted to take **radical,** or drastic, steps to change southern society and help the former slaves acquire civil rights. They also wanted to punish the white South severely for its secession. For these reasons, they were known as the Radical Republicans. The two leading Radical Republicans in Congress in 1864 were Representative Thaddeus Stevens of Pennsylvania and Senator Charles Sumner of Massachusetts.

The Radical Republicans had their own plan, called the Wade-Davis Bill, to bring the South back into the Union. The Wade-Davis Bill required that over 50 percent of all voters take an ironclad, or unbreakable, oath pledging to support the federal Constitution. Only then could a southern state form a new government. The ironclad oath was much stronger than the oath in

Study Hint

Not all facts in a paragraph or section have the same importance. When you read, look for important details that help explain, or clarify, the main idea. Ask yourself questions to identify who, what, where, when, why, and how in order to understand the main idea or topic.

Lincoln's plan. People had to swear that they had never voluntarily supported the Confederacy. Congress passed the Wade-Davis Bill in mid-1864. President Lincoln vetoed it and went ahead with his own plan. During late 1864 and early 1865, Virginia, Louisiana, Arkansas, and Tennessee met the terms of Lincoln's plan. The President restored these states to the Union.

But trouble was still brewing over Lincoln's plan. Even some moderate Republicans thought the President's plan was too lenient, and they joined forces with the Radicals. To show their rejection of Lincoln's plan, Congress refused to admit the congressmen and senators elected from the four southern states back into the national government. By early 1865, President Lincoln and Congress had reached a stalemate.

President Johnson's Plan

Lincoln's Vice President, Andrew Johnson, believed deeply in the rights of the common man. When Johnson entered politics in Tennessee as a Democrat, he had defended poor farmers against plantation owners. Johnson had served as a state legislator and governor in Tennessee before winning election to the U.S. Senate.

Johnson supported the Union when the war broke out. He was the only Southerner to remain in Congress after secession. To promote national unity, the Republicans chose him to run for Vice President with Lincoln in 1864. After Lincoln was assassinated on April 14, 1865, Andrew Johnson assumed the presidency.

Based on Johnson's beliefs about wealthy plantation owners and his support for the Union, the Radicals thought that as President, Johnson would be firm with the South. They hoped Johnson would ban former Confederate leaders from holding positions of power in the South. They also hoped Johnson would require former Confederate states to ratify the Thirteenth Amendment, banning slavery, and would require states to help freed African Americans rebuild their lives.

However, Johnson surprised the Radicals by adopting a plan for Reconstruction that was similar to Lincoln's. He did not ban slavery. Instead, Johnson pardoned most Confederates, restoring both their political and property rights. By doing so, Johnson allowed many of the same people who had run the South before 1861 to take charge once again.

The Thirteenth Amendment

One of the strongest messages Congress had issued just prior to Johnson's becoming President was the passage of the Thirteenth Amendment in

▲ President Andrew Johnson was a southern Democrat from Tennessee. One of his first acts as President was to continue Lincoln's plan of Reconstruction.

January 1865, abolishing slavery. Republicans felt strongly about the need for such an amendment as early as 1863. In that year slavery still legally existed in Tennessee and in the four border states that had joined the Union—Maryland, Missouri, Kentucky, and Delaware. This situation existed because the Emancipation Proclamation applied only to areas in rebellion against the United States. When the Proclamation took effect on January 1, 1863, these four Union border states, as well as the state of Tennessee, still supported slavery but were not in rebellion. These states were now under Union control.

The Thirteenth Amendment was ratified by most of the southern and northern states and became law in December 1865. With ratification, slavery was now officially illegal in the United States.

The Congressional Plan for Reconstruction

When Andrew Johnson took office, Congress was not in session. He therefore could carry out his Reconstruction policies with little interference until the end of 1865. When Congress, led by Radical Republicans, returned to Washington in December, it immediately challenged Johnson's polices.

Congress refused to seat the representatives and senators elected by the southern states under

Johnson's plan. It then formed a Joint Committee on Reconstruction to oversee policy in the South. The Radicals wanted to break the power of southern planters, prevent the Democratic party from recovering its strength in the South, and ensure African Americans a position in society.

In early 1866, moderates joined with the Radicals to pass the Civil Rights Act of 1866. The act granted citizenship to all people born in the United States except Native Americans. The act said that all citizens should have the same protection of the law "as is enjoyed by white persons."

Johnson vetoed the Civil Rights Act because he did not believe in the principles of the act. Congress, however, overrode Johnson's veto. The struggle for control of Reconstruction had begun.

How did the beliefs of President Johnson differ from the views of the Radical Republicans regarding Reconstruction?

◆ SOUTHERN STATES AND THE BLACK CODES

President Johnson's original Reconstruction plan allowed southern states to form new governments with few controls and conditions. This infuriated Radicals and angered moderate Northerners, who demanded that former Confederate leaders not be allowed to run these new governments. The President therefore added new conditions. One of the conditions included requiring the new governments to ratify the Thirteenth Amendment.

Johnson's changes did not satisfy the Radicals, however. They became more upset when, in 1865, the southern states elected dozens of former Confederate officials to serve in Congress. Even worse, the southern states passed laws called **black codes.** The black codes were a series of laws that aimed to limit the freedom African Americans had gained with the passage of the Thirteenth Amendment and the Civil Rights Act.

The black codes made it difficult for African Americans to enter many occupations, such as politics and banking. The codes banned them from carrying arms or from serving on juries. In addition the black codes allowed authorities to arrest and impose a monetary fine on African Americans who did not work. If a person could not pay the fine, the authorities could rent the person out as a laborer to landowners. No

southern state allowed African Americans the right to vote. In many ways, African Americans lived under conditions that were not much different from those they had endured under slavery.

Radical Republicans in Congress were angered by the black codes and sent President Johnson a report condemning southern practices. The report said,

There is yet among the Southern people a desire to preserve slavery in its original form as much and as long as possible.

When Johnson ignored the report, members of Congress vowed to take Reconstruction into their own hands.

In what ways were the black codes a setback for African Americans?

Section 1 Review

Check Understanding

1. **Define** (a) Reconstruction (b) amnesty (c) moderate (d) radical (e) black codes

2. **Identify** the differences between President Lincoln's Reconstruction plan and the Radical Republican plan.

3. **Discuss** the ways in which the Thirteenth Amendment and the black codes contradicted one another.

Critical Thinking

Hypothesizing How might the period of Reconstruction have been frustrating for African Americans who were no longer enslaved?

Write About Government

◆**Connecting Past and Present** Write a paragraph discussing what issues today cause conflict between the President and Congress.

BUILDING *SKILLS*

Interpreting Political Cartoons: The Reconstruction Era

Political cartoons are drawings that express a point of view on a political issue or current event. Artists of political cartoons generally use humor, exaggeration, and satire, or sarcastic wit, to get their point across. Their goal is generally to influence public opinion about important issues. Some political cartoonists present a positive point of view, but most are critical of a policy, situation, or person.

Here's How

Follow these steps to interpret a political cartoon:

1. Identify the symbols and caricatures in the political cartoon. A symbol stands for something. For example, "Uncle Sam" is a symbol often used to represent the United States. A caricature is a picture that deliberately exaggerates a person's features to make that character immediately recognizable or to produce a comic effect.

2. Analyze what the symbols mean and whether they show the subject in a positive or negative light.

3. Read any titles or labels. Decide how they add to the cartoon's message.

4. Identify the cartoonist's point of view about the subject.

5. Draw conclusions about the event or person by combining the artist's perspective with what you already know about the event, issues, or person.

Here's Why

Knowing how to interpret political cartoons can help you understand how some people thought and felt about certain issues during a particular time period in the past. Interpreting political cartoons can also help you understand different viewpoints expressed in today's political cartoons.

Practice the Skill

The cartoon below portrays President Lincoln trying to repair the Union. Study the cartoon and answer the questions that follow.

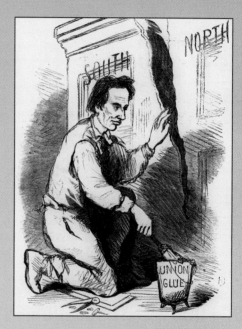

1. What symbols does the cartoon contain, and what do they represent?

2. How is President Lincoln portrayed?

3. What was the artist's purpose in creating this cartoon?

Apply the Skill

Find a political cartoon in the newspaper. Bring it to class and interpret it, using the steps you have learned in *Here's How*. With your classmates, draw conclusions about the way the artist wants you to interpret the event or issue.

Objectives

- To explain the ideas behind the Fourteenth and Fifteenth Amendments

- To describe the Radical Republican plan to readmit the southern states into the Union

- To discuss the impeachment proceedings against Andrew Johnson

- To identify the reasons why Reconstruction came to an end

Vocabulary

disenfranchise   carpetbagger
pardon   scalawag
impeachment

President Johnson and Congress disagreed about how to respond to the southern resistance to Reconstruction. For the next two years, they fought to control what happened in the South.

◆ THE FOURTEENTH AMENDMENT

In mid-1866, Congress took steps to protect the laws it had passed. Republicans were especially concerned that the U.S. Supreme Court would vote down the Civil Rights Act by ruling it unconstitutional. To prevent this, Congress proposed the Fourteenth Amendment to the Constitution.

The Fourteenth Amendment defined who qualified as an American citizen. Except for Native Americans, every person born in the United States and subject to its laws was a citizen. This overturned the ruling in the U.S. Supreme Court's Dred Scott decision, which said that African Americans were not citizens. The amendment also said that no state could interfere with the rights granted to citizens by the Constitution, such as "life, liberty, or property, without due process of law" or equal protection of the law.

The Fourteenth Amendment also dealt with voting rights. It gave each southern state a choice: either give all adult males the right to vote, or limit the right to vote and face reduced representation in the House of Representatives. Congress believed this choice would encourage southern states to give African American males the right to vote.

In addition, the Fourteenth Amendment banned many former Confederate officeholders from being elected to any state or federal office. Only Congress could remove this ban.

How did the Fourteenth Amendment define who was a U.S. citizen?

◆ RADICAL RECONSTRUCTION

Congress passed the Fourteenth Amendment in June 1866 and sent it to the states for ratification. It told the southern states that in order to be readmitted to the Union, they had to ratify the amendment. President Johnson, who was promoting his own plan for readmission, urged the states to refuse. Of the 11 former Confederate states, only Tennessee ratified the amendment.

Johnson and the other ten states hoped the issue would be resolved in the congressional elections of 1866. They hoped the Republicans, and especially the Radicals, would be replaced. Then Johnson and his supporters could continue with their Reconstruction plan.

During the election campaign of 1866, Johnson vehemently spoke out against the Republicans and the Fourteenth Amendment. He urged the public to elect people who supported him in Congress. His angry speeches alienated many voters and ultimately swung support to the Republicans. As a result, the Republicans won a huge victory, and they ended up with the votes needed to pass laws over Johnson's veto. Radical Republicans wasted no time in pursuing their goals, and so began the era of Radical Reconstruction.

To ensure that its Reconstruction measures were carried out, Congress passed the Military Reconstruction Act on March 2, 1867. Wanting to control what it called the "rebel states," Congress put the ten southern states that had rejected the Fourteenth Amendment under military rule. This act gave Congress the power to declare the new state governments in the South illegal. Federal troops were sent into those states to maintain law and order and to prepare the way for new state governments. The law divided the South into five military regions and placed an army general as military governor in charge of each district.

The military governors began Reconstruction with voter registration campaigns. The campaigns registered African American males to vote for the first time. Voters in each state then elected delegates to conventions, which wrote new state constitutions to guarantee suffrage, or voting rights, to African American males. The governors also **disenfranchised,** or denied the voting rights of, Confederate leaders and other whites who had supported the Confederacy. During 1868, voters in seven states were required to ratify their constitutions and the Fourteenth Amendment before being recognized. These states were then readmitted to the Union. Many whites boycotted the elections. In 1870, the remaining southern states rejoined the Union.

> How did Congress begin its plan of Radical Reconstruction to reorganize and readmit the southern states to the Union?

◆ IMPEACHMENT PROCEEDINGS

President Andrew Johnson did what he could to oppose Radical Reconstruction. He appointed military governors who disagreed with the Radical Republicans.

Johnson also **pardoned,** or released from punishment, former Confederates and then helped them regain their property.

The Radicals wanted to remove Johnson from office, but according to the Constitution, this could be done only if the President had committed "treason, bribery, or high crimes and misdemeanors." Removing a President involves a two-part process. First, the House of Representatives must vote by majority to accuse the President of a very serious crime. Then the Senate puts the President on trial. It must vote by a two-thirds majority to convict. Only if the Senate convicts the President can he be removed from office. This process is called **impeachment.**

In 1867, Congress passed the Tenure of Office Act, designed to limit Johnson's power. The act stated that the President needed the Senate's approval in order to remove a Cabinet member whom the President had appointed. In February 1868, Johnson dismissed Secretary of War Edwin Stanton without the Senate's approval. The Radicals claimed that in doing so Johnson had violated the 1867 law. Johnson denied the charge. The stage was set for a showdown between Johnson and the Radical Republicans who controlled Congress.

The House of Representatives voted to impeach President Johnson in February 1868. The articles of impeachment focused on violations of the Tenure of

◀ Republicans voted to impeach President Johnson because they disagreed with his Reconstruction policies. Admission tickets were available for the public to attend the trial. On the first day, the galleries were full.

Office Act. It ignored the Republicans' real reasons for wanting the President removed: Johnson's political views and his opposition to Congress's Reconstruction acts. A long and bitter trial to decide whether to convict Johnson lasted for almost two months. Johnson's lawyer showed convincingly that the President had not broken the law.

When the Senate voted, the outcome was 35 votes for and 19 against impeachment. The Radicals were one vote short of the two-thirds majority they needed to convict Johnson and remove him from office. Johnson's narrow escape established the precedent that only criminal actions by a President—not political disagreement—warrant removal from office. President Johnson finished out his term, but by mid-1868, he had lost most of his influence.

? Why did President Johnson's opponents seek to impeach him?

◆ REPUBLICANS CONTROL SOUTHERN GOVERNMENTS

The Republican governments of the Radical Reconstruction era were formed by an alliance of three groups: African Americans, Northerners who moved to the South and entered politics, and Southerners who broke their ties with the white majority to side with the Republicans.

African Americans provided many of the votes to support Reconstruction governments. However, Northerners who moved to the South after the Civil War actually controlled many of the new governments. Many Northerners came to the South with only a few possessions in a small cloth bag made of carpet fabric, called a carpetbag. White Southerners called these Northerners **carpetbaggers.**

Southern whites accused carpetbaggers of being corrupt politicians who used their government positions to get rich. This was true of some, but most were people of principle who tried to rebuild the South.

Many Northerners who went South after the war packed their belongings in carpetbags, such as this one. ▶

▲ The character of the carpetbagger became a part of American popular culture. Pictured here is the sheet music cover for a song that was written about the carpetbagger around 1869.

Southern whites who sided with the Republicans were called **scalawags** by many white people. The word *scalawag,* used to describe a small, scruffy horse, was a term that had been used in the South to insult people. Most southern whites considered scalawags traitors. In fact, many scalawags were business people who supported Republican economic policies. Others were farmers who had always disliked slavery.

State Governments Make Changes

The Republican governments made many improvements in the southern states. They established public school systems and built hospitals. They rebuilt and improved roads, railroads, bridges, and public buildings destroyed during the Civil War.

These governments also made changes that expanded democracy in the South. For example, supporters of Reconstruction reorganized legislative districts to no longer favor large planters at the expense of small farmers. They eliminated property qualifications for voting and holding office, enabling many poor whites to vote for the first time. More offices were filled through elections, rather than through appointments. Women benefited from laws that increased their rights regarding property and divorce. Poor people benefited when new tax laws shifted more of the tax burden to the wealthy. .

Reconstruction legislatures repealed the black codes. They passed civil rights laws that banned discrimination in public places and on public transportation. Overall, they gave African Americans the same political and civil rights as white people.

The Fifteenth Amendment

In 1869, Radical Republicans made another effort to guarantee that African Americans would keep their right to vote. They convinced Congress to propose the Fifteenth Amendment to the Constitution.

The Fifteenth Amendment stated that the right to vote could not be denied because of "race, color, or previous condition of servitude." After considerable debate the states ratified the Fifteenth Amendment in February 1870.

Although the amendment's intent was to guarantee male African Americans the right to vote, the language of the Fifteenth Amendment was vague, or unclear. After Reconstruction, southern governments found ways to get around the Fifteenth Amendment to keep African Americans from voting. For example, some states denied the vote to people who were illiterate, or could not read or write. This excluded many African Americans, who had not been able to go to school.

Despite efforts by southern governments to find ways of depriving African Americans of the right to vote, the passage of the Fifteenth Amendment made a strong statement, on paper at least, of the federal government's intent to support African American equality.

African Americans' Involvement in Government

African Americans in the South became politically active during Reconstruction. In addition to voting, they took part in all the conventions that wrote new state constitutions. Thousands joined the Union League, an organization that promoted Republican candidates and helped African Americans exercise their new civil rights.

Many African Americans were elected to office during Reconstruction. Hiram Revels and Blanche Bruce were the first African Americans to serve in the United States Senate. Sixteen African Americans served in the U.S. House of Representatives in 1869. Others held high state offices or became sheriffs and mayors in the South's new local elections. One African American, P.B.S. Pinchback, served as governor of Louisiana.

 What changes did Reconstruction governments bring to the South?

◀ *The Fourteenth and Fifteenth Amendments made it possible for African Americans to participate in politics. Seated here are Hiram R. Revels (left), the first U.S. African American senator, and newly elected members of the U.S. House of Representatives.*

◆ THE END OF RECONSTRUCTION

By the mid-1870s, many Northerners lost interest in reconstructing the South. They believed the government had done enough to help African Americans rebuild their lives—first by ending slavery and then by passing the Civil Rights Act of 1866. As a result, many Northerners sympathized with southern resistance to Reconstruction. Economic hard times in 1873 also drew support away from Reconstruction as people worried about their own economic survival.

Military leader Ulysses S. Grant, elected President in 1868, also reflected these concerns. As a Republican, Grant had initially supported Reconstruction when elected, but by 1872 he no longer wanted to keep federal soldiers in the South. Grant also was occupied by corruption scandals in his administration.

The Election of 1876

Corruption in Grant's administration and economic hard times hurt the Republicans and strengthened the Democrats. The presidential election of 1876 between Republican Rutherford B. Hayes and Democrat Samuel J. Tilden was very close. Although Tilden won more popular votes, he was one electoral vote short of winning the election. To make the situation more complicated, Hayes questioned who had won 20 of the electoral votes that Tilden claimed to have won. Hayes believed he had won the presidency based on his victories in Florida, Louisiana, Oregon, and South Carolina, states still under Republican and federal control. However, another set of election returns sent by the Democrats showed Tilden as the victor in those states. In a vote of 8 to 7, Congress decided to form a commission to investigate the disputed electoral votes. In each disputed state, the commission awarded the vote to Hayes, thus making him President.

The election results and their aftermath threw the country into a political crisis. Tilden reportedly called Hayes "RutherFRAUD" for stealing the election. In the end, however, the two sides worked out a compromise. Hayes became President, and in return removed federal troops from the remaining southern states. This action effectively returned power to southern politicians, who began to take control of their state governments. With this, Reconstruction came to an end early in 1877.

The Results of Reconstruction

Reconstruction succeeded in the limited political sense of reuniting a nation torn apart by the Civil War. It laid the foundation for many changes. The states had ratified two historic constitutional amendments, granting African American males full rights of citizenship and the right to vote, at least in theory. The federal government was not yet fully committed to protecting these rights, but the Reconstruction era at least pointed to how that goal might be achieved.

Reconstruction also marked the beginning of a major increase in the responsibilities of the federal government. The passage of the Thirteenth, Fourteenth, and Fifteenth Amendments and the Civil Rights Act of 1866 took power from the states and concentrated it at the national level. Although the states retained the responsibility for regulating civil rights, they did so under the watchful eye of the federal government.

 How did the election of 1876 lead to the end of Reconstruction?

Section 2 Review

Check Understanding

1. **Define** (a) disenfranchise (b) pardon (c) impeachment (d) carpetbagger (e) scalawag

2. **Describe** the impeachment proceedings against Andrew Johnson.

3. **Describe** the role African Americans played in government in the South.

4. **Explain** why Reconstruction came to an end.

Critical Thinking

Examining Causes and Effects Why did attitudes toward Reconstruction change in the 1870s?

Write About Citizenship

◆ **Connecting Past and Present** Explain in writing how democracy has been advanced by the passage of the Fourteenth and Fifteenth Amendments.

POINT *of* VIEW

RECONSTRUCTION

During Reconstruction, the Radical Republicans wanted to make dramatic changes in southern society. Many of the Radical Republicans were abolitionists. One of their main concerns was improving life for the newly freed African Americans. When the Civil War ended, they insisted that Congress play an active role in ensuring that African Americans would receive the same civil liberties and freedoms as white Southerners.

The following selections illustrate how the goals of Reconstruction were not always achieved. The first selection, which represents the goals of Radical Reconstruction, is by Senator Henry Wilson of Massachusetts. The second selection is from a letter written by Charles Harris, an African American who fought in the Union army. In his letter, Harris describes his frustration at the ways in which equality for African Americans living in the South has not been achieved.

"[Congress] must see to it that the man made free by the Constitution is a freeman indeed; that he can go where he pleases, work when and for whom he pleases . . . go into the schools and educate himself and his children; that the rights and guarantees of the common law are his, and that he walks the earth proud and erect in the conscious dignity of a free man."

Henry Wilson, Senator of Massachusetts

"We obey laws; others make them. We support state educational institutions, whose doors are virtually closed against us. We support . . . hospitals, and our sick, deaf, . . . or blind are met at the doors by . . . unjust discriminations. . . . From these and many other oppressions . . . our people long to be free."

Charles Harris, 1877

Examining Point of View

1. According to Henry Wilson, what were the objectives of Reconstruction?

2. What do you think Henry Wilson meant when he said that African Americans should walk "the earth proud and erect in the conscious dignity of a free man"?

3. Summarize the problems Charles Harris described.

4. How do you think Henry Wilson would react to Charles Harris's description of the ways in which Reconstruction affected African Americans' lives?

What's Your Point of View?

While Reconstruction did not achieve everything the Radical Republicans wanted to accomplish, it did create significant changes in African Americans' lives and in southern society.

Write an essay discussing the successes and failures of Reconstruction. As you continue reading this chapter, consider how the new information you are learning might change your original ideas and perspective on Reconstruction.

African Americans Build New Lives

PREVIEW

Objectives

- To explain the function of the Freedmen's Bureau

- To describe how the end of Reconstruction affected African Americans in the South

- To examine the ways in which southern whites tried to prevent African Americans from exercising their rights

Vocabulary

Freedmen's Bureau	poll tax
sharecropping	segregation
credit	Jim Crow laws
lynch	

For four million enslaved African Americans, freedom arrived in various ways in different parts of the South. Individuals as well as communities were affected by emancipation and the changes brought about by Reconstruction. African Americans struggled to establish economic, political, and cultural independence. At the same time, many southern white people sought to restrict the boundaries of that independence.

◆ THE FREEDMEN'S BUREAU

In March 1865, Abraham Lincoln had signed a bill creating the **Freedmen's Bureau,** a temporary agency that was intended to help newly emancipated African Americans, or "freedmen," adjust to freedom. Operating as part of the War Department and directed by military officers, the Bureau helped African Americans and poor white people acquire food, shelter, employment, medical care, legal aid, and schooling.

Among the Bureau's tasks was to arrange labor contracts between freedmen and landowners to make sure that landowners agreed to pay freedmen a fair wage. To further increase the likelihood of justice for

African Americans, the Bureau set up its own courts, as well as assigning agents to civil courts. By far the most successful task performed by the Freedmen's Bureau was setting up schools, which became the basis of the first free public school system in the South. With the help of northern charitable organizations, such as the American Missionary Association, by 1870 the Bureau had enrolled about one quarter of a million African Americans in 4,300 schools. It staffed these Bureau schools with volunteer teachers from the North.

The establishment of schools offered African Americans the chance to improve their lives through education. Reading and writing were necessary skills in defending civil rights, in negotiating new job contracts, and in keeping informed about important community and national events.

Adults and children attended schools run by the Freedmen's Bureau. Since students were required to pay tuition, sometimes as much as 10 percent of a family's income, both parents needed to work. Adults often attended school at night after a long day's work.

Although most schools established by the Bureau were elementary schools, it also set up institutions for teaching industrial skills and for training teachers. In addition it established the first colleges for African Americans, including Howard University in Washington, D.C., Hampton Institute in Virginia, and Fisk University in Tennessee.

The Freedmen's Bureau lasted until 1872. During its existence the Bureau accomplished what it had set out to do—help formerly enslaved people rebuild their lives. The Bureau was, without a doubt, one of the most important and effective tools of Reconstruction.

Why was the Freedmen's Bureau created?

◆ NEW LIVES FOR AFRICAN AMERICANS

Emancipation greatly expanded the choices available to African Americans. It helped them build confidence in their ability to cause change without having to rely on white people. Freedom also meant greater uncertainty and risk, but the vast majority of African Americans were ready and willing to take their chances.

Testing New Freedoms

The first impulse of many emancipated slaves was to test their freedom. By walking off a plantation and coming and going without fear of punishment,

▲ *Unable to attend school when they were enslaved, freed African Americans were enthusiastic about the Freedmen's schools.*

African Americans could enjoy the taste of freedom. When urged to stay on with the South Carolina family where she had worked for years as a cook, one woman replied firmly,

> No, Miss, I must go. If I stay here I'll never know I am free.

Although many African Americans actually returned to the plantations they had left, others moved away to seek jobs in nearby towns and cities. Between 1865 and 1870, the African American population of the South's ten largest cities doubled, while the white population increased only by 10 percent.

Juneteenth and Family Reunions

Some African Americans working on remote plantations in Texas did not find out about emancipation until June 19, 1865. Once they found out about their freedom, they expressed their joy in celebration. African Americans in Texas and around the United States continue today to observe "Juneteenth" as a family and community celebration with parades, picnics, and bands.

Juneteenth is considered the first holiday celebration for African Americans as a completely free people.

For many African Americans, emancipation meant the opportunity to reunite with long-lost family members. To track down relatives, freed people traveled to far-off plantations, put ads in newspapers, sought help from the Freedmen's Bureau, and questioned anyone who might have information about loved ones who had been sold to different owners.

Once separated families could live together, thousands of African American couples demanded to be legally married. They regarded this as an important symbol of their freedom and equality. Agents of the Freedmen's Bureau often conducted group ceremonies for 20 to 30 couples who had brought their children and grandchildren to celebrate the occasion.

Land and Labor

During Reconstruction some Radical Republicans wanted to take abandoned property from southern landowners and distribute it to African Americans. The idea was for each family to get "forty acres and a mule." President Johnson did not support this idea, however, and ordered that tens of thousands of freed people be evicted from the land.

Most African Americans could not afford to buy or rent land. Meanwhile, white landowners needed laborers to work their plantations. The system that developed to meet these needs was called **sharecropping.** Under this system, African Americans and many poor southern whites worked small plots of land owned by white landowners. Because the sharecroppers had no money, the landowners gave them the supplies and land they needed on **credit,** a form of borrowing. Sharecroppers used part of their crop to pay for use of the land and farming supplies.

Sharecropping had advantages and disadvantages. For landowners the system provided a stable work force. For sharecroppers the system allowed families to set their own hours and tasks and offered freedom from white supervision and control. However, since many African Americans owned little equipment, they continually borrowed against future earnings to afford farming tools and supplies. As a result many fell into a cycle of poverty and debt. A sharecropper named Solomon Lewis described the problem in this way:

> I was in debt and the man I rented land from said every year I must rent again to pay the other year, so I rent and rent and each year I get deeper and deeper in debt.

African American Churches

The creation of African American churches proved to be one of the most lasting and important changes to occur after the Civil War. Tired of being treated as second-class members of white churches, where they were forced to sit in the back during services and excluded from Sunday schools, African Americans pooled their resources to buy land and build their own churches.

As the first social institution fully controlled by African Americans, the churches became the centers not only of religious practice but also of community life. During the Reconstruction years, schools, political groups, lodges, clubs, and trade associations grew up around the church. In nearly every community, ministers, respected for their speaking and organizational skills, were among the most influential leaders.

 **In what ways did the lives of African Americans change during Reconstruction?**

▲ The Ku Klux Klan began as a Confederate veterans organization in 1866. The Klan openly threatened and terrorized African Americans.

◆ WHITE RESISTANCE

Many white Southerners were reluctant to acknowledge that slavery had ended. They had enjoyed their positions of authority, expecting obedience and loyalty from African Americans. White Southerners resented northern interference and feared they would lose control if African Americans became property owners. They were also concerned about the new political role that freed slaves had begun to play during the time of Reconstruction.

Secret Societies

To keep African Americans from exercising their new rights, a number of white Southerners formed secret organizations, such as the Ku Klux Klan, or KKK. The Ku Klux Klan, founded in 1866, terrorized African Americans by intimidation, beating, and **lynching,** or hanging. The Klan primarily targeted African American landowners, business people, and political leaders. Teachers of African American children were also targets of Klan violence. Some freed men were known to have been murdered by the Klan just because they could read or write. In addition, Klansmen burned African American houses and churches.

When President Grant was first elected, he tried to avoid conflict with the Ku Klux Klan. By 1871, however, it became impossible for him and others in the federal government to ignore the terror that was sweeping the South. Joseph Rainey, an African American congressman from South Carolina who had received death threats from the Klan spoke about the fear and violence that the Klan invoked:

"Why myself and colleagues shall leave these Halls and turn our footsteps toward our Southern home we know not but that the assassin may await our coming. Be it as it may, we have resolved to be loyal and firm, and if we perish, we perish!"

Responding to the general outcries of the public, Grant asked Congress to pass a tough law against the Ku Klux Klan. Congress approved an Anti-Klan Bill, which allowed the federal government to send marshals to the South to establish order. These marshals arrested many hundreds of Klansmen and generally curtailed Klan activity. When Reconstruction ended in 1877, however, Klan violence resumed and, in fact, increased.

Discriminatory Laws

When Democrats returned to power in the South, they used every possible method to keep their political power. Thousands of African Americans were deprived of the right to vote. To accomplish that, state authorities used property requirements and **poll taxes,** or sums of money paid before people were allowed to vote. Although, in theory, these requirements applied to both African American and white voters, the "grandfather clause" assured that the requirements would apply only to African Americans. This clause stated that any man whose father or grandfather had the right to vote as of January 1, 1867, was automatically entitled to vote. Since few African Americans could meet that requirement, the African American vote was reduced to a fraction of its former size.

Southern governments replaced laws that had guaranteed equal rights with laws that discriminated against African Americans. New laws imposed **segregation,** or the separation of races, on all aspects of southern life—schools, restaurants, railroad cars, and other public facilities. These **Jim Crow laws** were named after an African American character in a song—

a character who never made any trouble. Later, the name came to stand for the policy of segregation.

The U.S. Supreme Court also helped deprive African Americans of their rights. In 1873 the Court ruled to limit the rights protected by the Fourteenth Amendment, declaring that state governments would no longer be required to guarantee due process of law to their citizens. In 1876 the Court ruled in the case of *United States* v. *Reese* that the Fifteenth Amendment did not guarantee every male citizen the right to vote. This decision essentially made property requirements and poll taxes constitutional. With these decisions, the Supreme Court gave its permission for the enforcement of a full range of discriminatory laws in the South.

 In what ways were African Americans deprived of their rights at the end of Reconstruction?

Section 3 Review

Check Understanding

1. **Define** (a) Freedmen's Bureau (b) sharecropping (c) credit (d) lynch (e) poll tax (f) segregation (g) Jim Crow laws

2. **Describe** how African Americans in the South made use of their freedom.

3. **Discuss** how the Freedmen's Bureau was an effective tool of Reconstruction.

4. **Describe** the ways white Southerners tried to prevent African Americans from exercising their new rights and political power.

Critical Thinking

Analyzing Information How did emancipation and Reconstruction affect the structure of African American family life?

Write About Citizenship

◆ **Connecting Past and Present** Secret societies, such as the Ku Klux Klan, threatened communities in the 1800s. Write suggestions to protect your community against such threats today.

Chapter 11
Review

CHAPTER SUMMARY

Section 1

After the Civil War, President Lincoln's plan for Reconstruction focused on reuniting the Union, while the Radical Republicans wanted to change southern society dramatically. In 1865, the Thirteenth Amendment freed slaves everywhere, but black codes restricted the freedom of former slaves. After Lincoln's death, the Radical Republicans and President Johnson continued the struggle over Reconstruction.

Section 2

In 1866, Congress proposed the Fourteenth Amendment, which protected citizenship for those born in the United States, including African Americans. Radical Republicans won control of Congress and challenged Johnson, even going so far as to begin impeachment proceedings, though he was not convicted. In 1870, the Fifteenth Amendment passed with the aim of ensuring that African American men could vote.

Section 3

Freedom changed life for African Americans in the South. They now had the freedom to move to towns and cities, marry, and search for family members. However, under the system of sharecropping, many African Americans remained tied to the land. For a time, African Americans voted, held office, and enjoyed many civil rights. Some whites objected to these new freedoms and used violence and discriminatory laws to frighten and limit the rights of the new citizens. As Reconstruction ended in 1877, the U.S. Supreme Court made rulings that supported segregation in the South.

Connecting ◆◆ Past and Present

During Reconstruction, the United States attempted to achieve equality, but the goal remained elusive. In what ways does the nation still struggle today to fulfill its promise of justice and equality for all?

Using Vocabulary

For each term below, write a sentence that shows its meaning.

1. amnesty
2. radical
3. black codes
4. disenfranchise
5. impeachment
6. carpetbagger
7. Freedmen's Bureau
8. sharecropping
9. Jim Crow laws
10. segregation
11. poll tax
12. scalawag

Check Understanding

1. **Describe** the impact of the black codes on African Americans' rights.
2. **Identify** the Thirteenth Amendment and tell why it is important.
3. **Describe** the work of the Freedmen's Bureau.
4. **Explain** the provisions of the Fourteenth and Fifteenth Amendments.
5. **Describe** the Radical Republican plan to readmit the southern states.
6. **Summarize** the reasons why the Radical Republicans brought impeachment proceedings against President Johnson.
7. **Describe** the reasons why Northerners lost interest in reconstructing the South.
8. **Discuss** how freedom affected the lives of African Americans in the South.
9. **Discuss** African American involvement in politics during Reconstruction.
10. **Describe** how white resistance affected African Americans in the South.

Critical Thinking

1. **Comparing Ideas** In what ways were the Reconstruction plans of Lincoln, the Radical Republicans, and Congress similar?

2. **Analyzing** Why could President Johnson's impeachment and subsequent trial be called "politically motivated"?

3. **Synthesizing Information** What were the greatest problems and opportunities African Americans faced at the end of the Civil War?

4. **Drawing Conclusions** Why do you think the KKK grew so strong during Reconstruction?

◆ **Connecting Past and Present** What provisions would you have added to the Fifteenth Amendment to make it stronger in 1876? Have these provisions been addressed today in subsequent legislation?

Writing to Explain a Point of View

The era after the Civil War was a time of intense battling over the future of the South and the African Americans who lived there. **Write** an essay in which you explain how Reconstruction affected the lives of African Americans. Consider the efforts of the Radical Republicans, the laws and Constitutional amendments that were passed during this period, and the ways in which southern whites reacted to Reconstruction policies.

Interpreting the Timeline

Use the timeline on pages 208–209 to answer these questions.

1. How soon after the passage of the Civil Rights Act was the Fourteenth Amendment ratified?

2. Which happened first, ratification of the Fifteenth Amendment or the unification of Germany?

3. In what way are the two events of 1870 related?

Putting Skills to Work

INTERPRETING POLITICAL CARTOONS

In the Building Skills lesson on page 213, you learned how to interpret political cartoons. The cartoon below depicts the white supremacy groups that threatened African Americans during Reconstruction. As the words "Worse Than Slavery" indicate, many whites used lynchings and other acts of violence to make life for African Americans worse than it had been during slavery. Study the cartoon below and answer the questions.

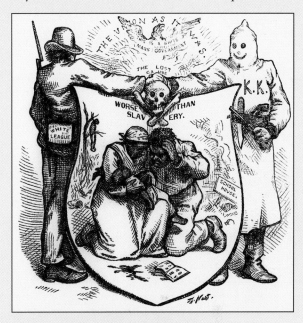

1. Why are the figures shaking hands?

2. How is the threat of violence portrayed? What symbols are used?

3. What do you think the artist's point of view was regarding conditions in the South?

Portfolio Project

POLITICAL CARTOONS

Choose a point of view about the impeachment of President Johnson or the impact of the carpetbaggers and Republican governments in the South, and create a political cartoon that expresses that point of view. Consider the symbols you will use. Keep in mind that your ideas are more important than your drawing ability. Exchange cartoons with a classmate and write an interpretation of each other's cartoons. Then file your cartoon in your portfolio.

Connecting Past and Present

EDUCATION: AGENCIES AND PEOPLE WHO MAKE A DIFFERENCE

Reading and writing are necessary tools that enable people to achieve their goals, such as obtaining good jobs and being responsible citizens. Providing these skills to people who have limited access to educational resources is a task that has long occupied the efforts of American society. Whether funded publicly or privately, many programs work toward providing all citizens with the opportunity to have an excellent education.

▲ *Teach For America recruits recent college graduates who commit to teach students in school districts where there are not enough qualified instructors.*

Then When the Civil War ended, the United States government helped newly emancipated African Americans prepare for jobs and the responsibilities of voting through the Freedmen's Bureau. By 1870, schools set up by the Bureau were attended by more than 250,000 African Americans. Between 1860 and 1870, illiteracy dropped from 90 percent to less than 80 percent among the adult African American population.

Northern charitable organizations provided money, textbooks, and teachers, who were mostly women from abolitionist families in Massachusetts, New York, and Ohio. These volunteers taught both children and adults to read, write, and keep business accounts. In a combined effort, the federal government and volunteers had given African Americans some of the tools they needed to construct new lives.

Now The combined efforts of the federal government and charitable organizations continue to help ensure that children receive an excellent education. For example, Teach For America recruits recent college graduates who commit to teach for two years in urban and rural public schools which do not have enough educational resources. About 1,000 members a year reach more than 100,000 students. As one teacher explained, "This is not something we merely choose to do. I believe it is our responsibility."

You Decide

1. Why was the creation of the Freedmen's schools of lasting importance to African Americans in the South?

2. Volunteerism is being encouraged and rewarded today in many businesses and required of many high school students. Why do you think volunteerism is being encouraged?

Unit

New Challenges and Achievements 1860–1920

> **❝** Now, four centuries from the discovery of America, at the end of a hundred years of life under the Constitution, the frontier has gone and with its going has closed the first period of American history. **❞**
>
> *Frederick Jackson Turner, 1893, in an address to the American Historical Association*

▲ This sketch of Atlanta in the nineteenth century shows a growing city. **◆ Connecting Past and Present** *How did the railroad impact life in Atlanta? How have twentieth century innovations in transportation affected city life?*

Chapter 12
Americans Move West
1860–1900

CHAPTER PREVIEW

Section 1 Conflict on the Great Plains

The end of the Civil War sent a large number of settlers onto the Great Plains. This movement westward set the stage for conflict between Native Americans and the U.S. government.

Section 2 Ranchers and Miners

The growth of two industries—ranching and mining—provided new opportunities and challenges and attracted more people to the West.

Section 3 Settling the Great Plains

Despite the harsh environment, farmers overcame many difficulties in cultivating the Great Plains. Increasing economic problems brought farmers together in protest.

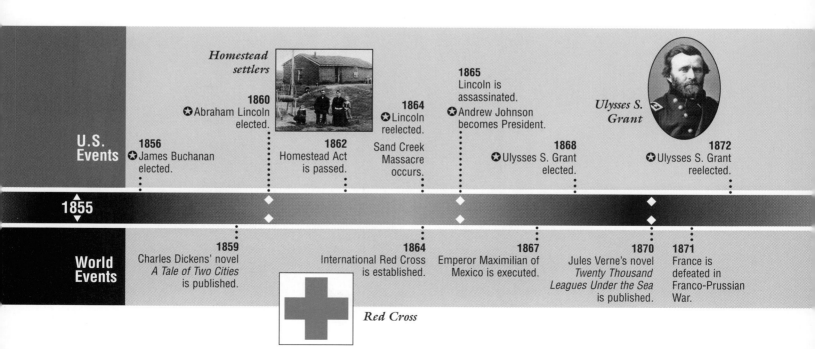

Homestead settlers

Ulysses S. Grant

U.S. Events

1856 ✪ James Buchanan elected.

1860 ✪ Abraham Lincoln elected.

1862 Homestead Act is passed.

1864 ✪ Lincoln reelected.

Sand Creek Massacre occurs.

1865 Lincoln is assassinated.
✪ Andrew Johnson becomes President.

1868 ✪ Ulysses S. Grant elected.

1872 ✪ Ulysses S. Grant reelected.

1855

World Events

1859 Charles Dickens' novel *A Tale of Two Cities* is published.

1864 International Red Cross is established.

Red Cross

1867 Emperor Maximilian of Mexico is executed.

1870 Jules Verne's novel *Twenty Thousand Leagues Under the Sea* is published.

1871 France is defeated in Franco-Prussian War.

▲ *A family heading west to Custer County, Nebraska, in 1866 stands next to its loaded wagon.* ◈ **Connecting Past and Present** *What kinds of difficulties might this family experience on their journey? What challenges might a family today encounter when moving to an unfamiliar place?*

Portfolio Project

A MUSEUM DISPLAY

During the last half of the nineteenth century, information about conflicts on the Great Plains was recorded in photographs and newspapers. Observers traveled west to witness firsthand the impact of western settlement. As you read this chapter, watch for the kinds of subjects observers might have chosen to document the era. At the end of this chapter, you will create an exhibit that captures the period in words and pictures.

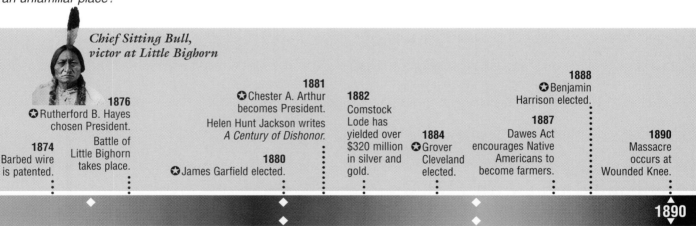

Chief Sitting Bull, victor at Little Bighorn

1874
Barbed wire is patented.

1876
✪ Rutherford B. Hayes chosen President.
Battle of Little Bighorn takes place.

1881
✪ Chester A. Arthur becomes President.
Helen Hunt Jackson writes *A Century of Dishonor.*

1880
✪ James Garfield elected.

1882
Comstock Lode has yielded over $320 million in silver and gold.

1884
✪ Grover Cleveland elected.

1888
✪ Benjamin Harrison elected.

1887
Dawes Act encourages Native Americans to become farmers.

1890
Massacre occurs at Wounded Knee.

1890

1875
London Medical School for Women is founded.

1876
Korea becomes independent.

1878
Electric street lights are introduced in London.

1885
Trancontinental railroad is completed in Canada.

Trancontinental railroad

Section 1

Conflict on the Great Plains

PREVIEW

Objectives

- To summarize how the slaughter of the buffalo ended a way of life for Native Americans on the Great Plains

- To show how Native Americans resisted the U.S. government

- To discuss the attempt to force Native Americans to adapt to white society

Vocabulary

transcontinental	reenlistment
reservation	Ghost Dance
buffalo soldier	assimilate

Beginning in the 1840s, wagon trains rumbled at a steady pace over trails leading west to the Pacific coast. As they traveled west of the Mississippi River, early settlers came upon the Great Plains region. With little rain and few trees, the region seemed an endless wasteland. Some observers called it the "Great American Desert."

In the late 1800s, Americans tried to settle the Great American Desert. They built railroads, towns, and farms. In so doing, they changed the landscape of the Great Plains and ended the traditional way of life for Native Americans who lived there.

◆ DISRUPTION ON THE PLAINS

Destruction followed in the tracks of the wagon trains. Diseases carried by settlers spread rapidly to some Native American groups. Settlers burned whatever timber they found, and their livestock trampled and ate the grass, destroying the environment. Wherever the wagons traveled, hunters shot antelope and other animals for food. The movement of settlers also disrupted the migration patterns of the buffalo. Native Americans living on the Plains relied on the buffalo for food, clothing, and shelter. They ate buffalo meat; they used hides to make blankets and robes, skins to make clothing and shoes, and bones to make tools.

In the late 1800s, Native Americans watched with alarm as railroad crews laid iron track across the grasslands. President Lincoln had approved plans to build the **transcontinental** railroad in 1862. This railroad would span the continent, connecting cities of the Midwest with new settlements on the west coast. The Civil War interrupted the project, but once the war ended, work continued until the project was completed in 1869.

The railroads played a large part in reducing the number of buffalo. To feed hungry crews, railroad companies hired hunters to shoot the buffalo. One such sharpshooter, William F. Cody, killed nearly 4,300 buffalo in just eight months, earning him the nickname "Buffalo Bill."

 How did wagon trains and railroads affect Native American life on the Great Plains?

◆ YEARS OF STRUGGLE

Before the Civil War, the United States had reserved nearly all the land on the Great Plains for Native Americans. In the late 1860s, however, the government reversed its policies as settlers who were eager to farm land on the Great Plains began to claim it for themselves. In response, the U.S. government set aside tracts of land, called **reservations,** for Native Americans. The government promised that Native Americans would hold these lands, in the words of one treaty, for "as long as waters run and the grass shall grow."

Broken Promises

The promise held for only a few years. As settlers continued to move onto Native American lands, as shown on the map on page 232, some Native Americans resisted. They did not want to give up lands where they had lived, hunted, and buried their dead. Others signed treaties that sold their lands. Often the treaties were negotiated in English, which was not their language. Many Native Americans did not realize that by signing a treaty they would no longer be allowed to continue using the land. Their traditions had taught them that the land belonged to everyone.

In 1859, Native Americans from the Cheyenne and Arapaho nations fought with gold miners who had moved onto their land. Cheyenne Chief Black Kettle asked for peace and moved about 700 of his followers to a camp at Sand Creek, Colorado. On the morning of November 29, 1864, a U.S. Army colonel, John M. Chivington, led his soldiers in an attack on the camp. Black Kettle tried to stop the assault, first by raising a U.S. flag as a sign of peace and then by raising a white flag to signal surrender. Neither worked. The soldiers killed most of the men, women, and children in the camp.

The Sand Creek Massacre set off a wave of protests. While the U.S. government condemned the attack, it still insisted that Native Americans on the southern Plains give up their lands for smaller reservations. In a treaty signed in 1867, most major Native American groups on the southern Plains agreed to move, but only on the condition that they could continue to hunt buffalo. However, since the buffalo population had begun to be greatly reduced by hunters, this promise had little meaning.

The Black Hills

On the northern Plains, the Lakota and Dakota Sioux resisted the construction of a trail that ran through the Black Hills of the Dakota Territory, an area sacred to the Sioux.

The Lakota and Dakota battled U.S. troops for two years. Then, in 1868, the two sides negotiated a treaty. Under this treaty, the government agreed to close the trail and to abandon all forts in the area. In exchange, most Native Americans on the northern Plains agreed to move onto a reservation north of the Black Hills region of what is now South Dakota.

In 1874 the government sent Colonel George Armstrong Custer into the Black Hills to find a spot to build a fort. Upon his return, Custer told reporters that the Black Hills had "gold among the roots of grass." The story set off a stampede of gold prospectors into the area. This violated the 1868 treaty, which had promised to keep white settlers away from reservation land.

 **How did the U.S. government break its promises to Native Americans?**

◆ FIGHTING BACK

Conflicts between government troops and Native Americans over land rights on the Great Plains continued. Treaty violations and mistreatment on reservations led some Native Americans to fight back.

▲ *The battle of Little Bighorn, led by Chief Sitting Bull and others, was a brief victory for Native Americans. Most were soon forced onto reservations.*

Showdown in Dakota

The U.S. government had hoped that the influx of gold prospectors would force the Sioux to sell the Black Hills. The Sioux reacted to this with scorn. "One does not sell the land upon which the people walk," a respected Sioux chief named Crazy Horse responded.

President Ulysses S. Grant reacted to Native American defiance with a warning, "White people outnumber the Indians by at least 200 to one." He told them to make the region safe for white prospectors or face federal troops.

Many Native Americans chose to fight back. In March 1876, Grant sent General George Crook to attack a Sioux camp. When Cheyenne Chief Sitting Bull heard the news, he exclaimed, "These soldiers have come shooting; they want war. All right, we'll give it to them."

Little Bighorn

In June 1876 Sioux and Cheyenne warriors under Crazy Horse's leadership attacked Crook's soldiers near Rosebud Creek in Montana. The two evenly matched sides fought for more than six hours. By sunset, however, the Native Americans had the upper hand and Crook's army retreated.

Crazy Horse and his supporters withdrew to Sitting Bull's main camp, located along the Little Bighorn River in Montana. The camp grew to approximately 5,000 warriors. Unaware of Crook's defeat, Custer led about 225 troops toward the camp.

Custer ignored his scouts' warnings of a large Native American force nearby. As his troops neared the camp, they saw a cloud of dust. "The Sioux must be running away," yelled one soldier. When Native Americans burst through the dust cloud, Custer's soldiers faced an assault by Sioux and Cheyenne warriors.

Native Americans killed Custer and all his soldiers, except one scout who escaped to tell the story. Newspapers in the East labeled the battle a "massacre."

Native Americans paid a high price for their victory at Little Bighorn. The government sent troops to find Crazy Horse. He was captured and then murdered by a government soldier. Sitting Bull fled to Canada. In 1881 he led his homesick followers back to the United States and onto a reservation.

Conflicts in the Far West

In 1877 the government sent troops to open up the Walla Walla valley in present-day Oregon for white settlement. The Nez Percé, who lived in the valley, had 30 days to move to a reservation.

Rather than submit to reservation life, Chief Joseph of the Nez Percé decided to flee to Canada. For over three months, he led some 800 people through the mountains on a journey that covered more than 1,000 miles. By October 1877 they were exhausted and could go no farther. Less than 40 miles from the Canadian border, they were forced to surrender. Chief Joseph said,

> I am tired of fighting. Our chiefs are killed. . . . It is cold and we have no blankets. The little children are freezing to death. . . . My heart is sick and sad. From where the sun now stands, I will fight no more forever.

The government sent the captured Nez Percé to Indian Territory in Oklahoma. There, many died from the heat and malaria. Later, Chief Joseph and the remaining Nez Percé returned to the reservation that had been established for them in present-day Idaho.

? How did Native Americans resist being forced onto reservations?

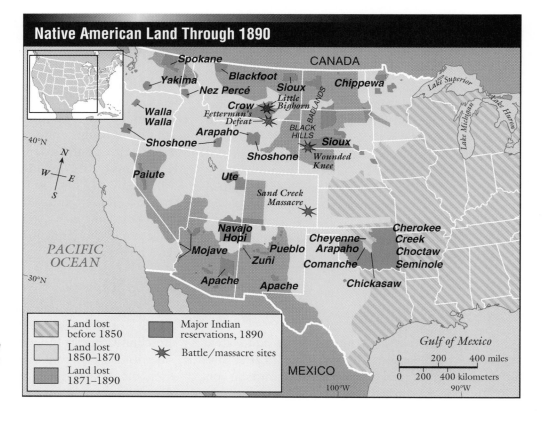

Geography As settlers pushed west toward the Pacific Ocean, they took over the lands on which Native Americans lived. By 1890 many Native Americans were forced to live on reservations. **Interpreting the Map** When did Native Americans lose most of their lands as shown on the map? ▶

Native American Land Through 1890

CANADA

Spokane
Yakima
Blackfoot
Nez Percé
Sioux
Chippewa
Crow
Little Bighorn
Walla Walla
Fetterman's Defeat
BADLANDS
BLACK HILLS
Arapaho
Sioux
Shoshone
Shoshone
Wounded Knee
Paiute
Ute
Sand Creek Massacre
Navajo
Hopi
Mojave
Zuñi
Pueblo
Cheyenne–Arapaho
Comanche
Cherokee
Creek
Choctaw
Seminole
Chickasaw
Apache
Apache

PACIFIC OCEAN

40°N
30°N

Lake Superior
Lake Michigan
Lake Huron

Gulf of Mexico

MEXICO

100°W   90°W

Land lost before 1850
Land lost 1850–1870
Land lost 1871–1890
Major Indian reservations, 1890
✳ Battle/massacre sites

0   200   400 miles
0   200   400 kilometers

◄ *Buffalo soldiers were sent to guard Native American reservations on the Great Plains.*

◆ BUFFALO SOLDIERS

By 1881 most Native Americans in the United States lived on reservations. Guarding many of the reservations were African American army units stationed on the frontier—the Ninth and Tenth Cavalries and the Twenty-fourth and Twenty-fifth Infantries. Because their dark, curly hair resembled buffalo hair, these soldiers were called **buffalo soldiers** by Native Americans.

The government formed the African American units at the end of the Civil War to keep the peace on the frontier. African Americans saw the units as a chance to build careers denied to them elsewhere. Of all the units assigned to the Plains, the buffalo soldiers had the lowest rates of desertion and the highest rates of **reenlistment,** or signing up again for service in the army. The buffalo soldiers fought in nearly all the major battles on the Plains and received 18 Congressional Medals of Honor for bravery during their service.

 Why did many African Americans volunteer to serve in army units stationed on the frontier?

◆ WOUNDED KNEE

In the late 1880s, Wovoka, a Paiute (pī-yo͞ot) spiritual leader, spread a vision of hope to Plains Native Americans. Wovoka taught his followers, including the Sioux, a ritual dance that he claimed would restore their lands and their traditional ways of life, as well as unite them with their ancestors. A religious movement formed around this dance, which became known as the **Ghost Dance.** Federal officials, fearing that the dance might actually be a war dance, ordered a crackdown on the Sioux and attempted to arrest Sioux Chief Sitting Bull. In the confusion of arrest, Sitting Bull and several others were killed. Many Sioux, fearing for their lives, fled the reservation for the South Dakota Badlands. On December 28, 1890, U.S. soldiers in the Seventh Cavalry caught up with them and ordered the 120 men and 230 women and children to camp along the nearby Wounded Knee Creek.

The following morning, soldiers began collecting guns from the Native Americans. According to one version of the story, a rifle went off when one of the men resisted. The gunshot set off a round of fire from the soldiers. "We tried to run," recalled Louise Weasel Bear, "but they shot us like buffalo."

When the smoke cleared, nearly all the Native Americans lay dead. Black Elk, a Sioux spiritual leader who arrived at Wounded Knee soon after the massacre, described the feelings of many Native Americans:

 I can see [now] that something else died there in the bloody mud. . . . A people's dream died there.

 Why did federal officials feel threatened by the Ghost Dancers?

◆ CALL FOR REFORM

Reformers tried to bring the plight of Native Americans to public attention. In Helen Hunt Jackson's 1881 book *A Century of Dishonor,* she documented the many broken promises made to Native Americans. Her message gave a boost to the growing movement for reform of federal policies toward Native Americans.

The protests of reformers prompted the government to act, but not in a way most Native Americans welcomed. Well-meaning groups, such as the Women's National Indian Association (WNIA) and the Indians Rights Association (IRA), called for programs to help Native Americans **assimilate,** or be absorbed, into the main culture of the nation.

To force Native Americans to adapt to white society, Native American children were sent to boarding schools far away from their homes. Teachers cut the children's long hair and took away their traditional clothes. In describing his education at Pennsylvania's Carlisle Indian School, a Hopi youth named Sun Elk recalled,

Many Native American children were sent to schools where they were forced to give up their customs. Left: These boys from the Sioux nation were sent to the Carlisle Indian School, Pennsylvania, in the late 1800s. Right: The same boys are pictured three years later. ▶

"They taught us that being an Indian was bad. They said that we must get civilized. I remember that word too. It means 'be like a white man.'"

Congress attempted to end the reservation policy through passage of the Dawes Act in 1887. The Dawes Act encouraged Native Americans to live more like white settlers and farm separate plots of land distributed to individual families. But many Native Americans had little experience in agriculture. Although the government provided them with seeds, Native Americans received no instructions on how to plant. Once-proud men, who had regarded farming as women's work, were now forced to plant and harvest in order to survive. Many Native Americans had little interest in farming and eventually sold their large tracts of fertile land to white settlers for low prices.

With each passing year, Native Americans lost more of their land. Between 1887 and 1934, Native American land holdings shrank from 138 million acres to 55 million acres. In 1900 the government counted 200,000 Native Americans living in the United States, most of them on reservations. "We are prisoners of war," lamented Black Elk. "Our power is gone, and we are dying as a people."

❓ **What was the goal of government programs for Native Americans in the late 1800s?**

Section 1 Review

Check Understanding

1. **Define** (a) transcontinental (b) reservation (c) buffalo soldier (d) reenlistment (e) Ghost Dance (f) assimilate

2. **Explain** how the destruction of the buffalo affected Native American life.

3. **Discuss** how the federal government changed its policies toward Native Americans.

4. **Explain** how Native Americans resisted the U.S. government.

Critical Thinking

◈ **Connecting Past and Present** How do we protect animals such as the buffalo today?

Write About Social Issues

Review the primary source quotation on this page that describes a Native American who was forced to adapt to white society. Write a letter to the editor of a newspaper in which you support or criticize the United States' policy of assimilation.

CONNECTING HISTORY
& Fine Arts

PORTRAYING NATIVE AMERICANS

The way in which paintings and illustrations of the 1700s and 1800s portrayed Native Americans depended to a large extent on the point of view of the artist. Early artists who painted scenes of Native Americans rarely visited them or knew much, if anything, about their ways of life. In the 1700s, European artists showed Native Americans as noble people whose culture and dress were similar to Europeans'. Many later artists emphasized the alarm some white people felt about Native Americans. As the illustration on the bottom left shows, these artists often portrayed Native Americans as fearsome warriors. Their art was intended to terrify white Americans.

In the 1830s a number of artists traveled west to portray the way Native Americans actually lived. For example, Karl Bodmer, a Swiss artist, traveled up the Missouri River in 1833. Bodmer had a keen eye for detail. His painting, shown on the right, depicts a proud and strong Native American. Artists such as Bodmer began to paint Native Americans in more realistic ways.

These images show two different ideas about Native Americans. ▶

Making the Artistic Connection

1. Why did European artists of the 1700s portray Native Americans as if they were Europeans?

2. What was the point of view of many later artists toward Native Americans?

3. What distinguished the art of Karl Bodmer from that of many other artists?

4. How do you think Native Americans today feel about the different style and content in the art examples below?

◆▷ Connecting Past and Present

How does the way artists portray people of different cultures influence the ideas other people have about them?

BUILDING SKILLS

Making Predictions: Native Americans in the West

Predicting means making a logical guess about something that might happen. You can predict consequences, or the results of actions, by analyzing information and suggesting possible outcomes. When you watch a movie or read a book, you might try to guess how it will end, based on what you already know. In this way, you are predicting consequences or outcomes.

Here's How

Follow these steps to predict consequences:

1. Review the information you have gathered from books or other sources.

2. Think about what you already know about a subject. Compare how the new situation is similar to what you already know.

3. What kind of trends can you spot? What patterns can you detect among the facts you have gathered?

4. Predict possible consequences, based on facts you have gathered. Your predictions may not always be accurate, but they should be logical. You should be able to explain the reasons you made the predictions you did.

5. Analyze the possibilities. Are some consequences more likely to occur than others?

6. Verify your predictions or make new predictions.

Here's Why

Predicting consequences helps you understand how the past affects the future. By studying what has happened already, you can try to predict what might happen next.

Practice the Skill

Copy the organizer below on a sheet of paper. Use it to chart the problems encountered by Native Americans when settlers moved west. In each small circle, write one consequence of westward expansion on Native American life. Once you have analyzed this information, make a prediction about the future of Native Americans after 1900. Write an essay explaining how you came to your conclusion.

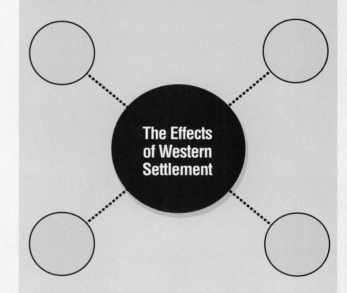

The Effects of Western Settlement

Apply the Skill

Work with two or three classmates to identify an issue, such as pollution or crime, in your school or community. Analyze what you know about this issue, noting trends and patterns that emerge from the facts. Finally, make predictions based on the information you have gathered. Present your predictions and reasons to the class.

Section 2

Ranchers and Miners

PREVIEW

Objectives

- To explain how a huge cattle industry developed on the Great Plains
- To identify the reasons why the cattle boom began and ended
- To evaluate the reasons for the rise and fall of the mining boom

Vocabulary

bonanza
railhead
vigilante committee

The American West attracted new industries by providing opportunities for ranchers and miners. These ranchers and miners produced two great **bonanzas,** or sources of sudden wealth. One bonanza was built on beef, the other on silver and gold.

◆ THE CATTLE BOOM

The vast open range of the Great Plains provided a natural grazing area for cattle. Herds of cattle had been introduced by the Spaniards onto the open range in the sixteenth century. By the early 1800s, herds of cattle roamed southern Texas. These herds bred with cattle brought into the region by U.S. settlers. The result was the Texas longhorn—a cow with a horn spread of up to seven feet. Ranchers began to turn the Great Plains into a cattle region.

Before the Civil War, the demand for longhorns remained small. A few adventurous ranchers tried to attract interest in the breed. In 1854, for example, a pair of ranchers drove their cattle to Muncie, Indiana, and shipped them to New York City. The cattle caused quite a stir as they broke loose from their pens and stampeded down a New York City street.

The Civil War delayed other cattle drives while Texas ranchers marched off to fight. When the ranchers returned home to Texas, they found the grasslands teeming with five to six million longhorns.

Other factors helped spur the cattle boom. The original value of the Texas longhorn was based on its hide, which was processed in tanneries in the Northeast. Soon, however, the growth of industrial cities and the flood of immigrants into the United States created a new demand for beef, which the cattle boom helped meet. There were also other new markets right on the Great Plains. The railroad companies bought cattle to feed their crews. The federal government had to buy cattle for Native Americans on reservations since it had cut off their food supply by reducing the number of buffalo.

Longhorns suddenly became very valuable. A steer that cost $4 in Texas could be sold for $40 in big cities, such as Chicago, New York, and Philadelphia. Such huge profits spurred the growth of a new cattle industry on the Great Plains.

The Life of the Cowhands

The cattle industry's workers were the cowhands who rode the open range. Cowhands have been portrayed to generations of Americans as adventurous heroes. Their daily lives, however, were not spent riding the open range shooting at villains.

The cowhands' way of life evolved from that of the vaqueros—Mexican cowhands who worked the ranches of California and the Southwest. About one out of every six cowhands in the 1870s was Mexican. The cowhands used many of the tools and clothes developed by the vaqueros, and the English words for them were adopted from Spanish. The lariat that cowhands used to rope a steer came from the Spanish words *la reata*. The heavy leather chaps worn to protect their legs from thorns came from *chaparreras*.

Texas cowhands used some of the same equipment as Mexican vaqueros. Like the vaqueros, Texas cowhands wore high-heeled boots with spurs, pictured here. ▼

Buckaroo, the cowhands' nickname for themselves, probably came from *vaquero*.

The dangerous work of a cowhand attracted a wide mix of people. Formerly enslaved African Americans who learned to herd cattle on the ranches of Texas made up about 15 percent of all cowhands. They rode alongside former Confederate soldiers seeking to escape the war-torn South. Joining them were former Union soldiers who found farm life boring after the war. A small number of Native Americans joined them, seeking a chance to ride the Plains once again.

Most cowhands were young—with an average age of 24. They lasted only about seven years in a job that exposed them to choking dust, blistering sun, and sleet-driven, freezing nights. They worked for about $25 a month, less than $1 a day, and whatever food the chuck wagon served.

The Roundups and Long Drives

For much of the year, the cowhands rode back and forth along the boundary of the ranch, keeping cattle from wandering off or being stolen. However, the spring and fall roundups set the rhythm of cowhands' lives. In the spring they rode the range and chased all the cattle they could find into corrals. Then they sorted out cattle marked with the brand of their owner's ranch and newborn calves that still needed to be branded. In the fall, the cowhands gathered the herds that were ready for market and set out on the long drive—the movement of thousands of cattle to railroad centers.

One long drive lasted for two to three months. Cowhands spent 18 hours a day in the saddle, with no days off. They slept on the ground and bathed in the rivers. Cowhands drove cattle to the nearest **railhead,** or end of the track, for shipment to markets in the East.

In 1866 the railhead closest to most Texas ranches was in Sedalia, Missouri, which made each long drive a dangerous trip over the Great Plains. Sometimes, farmers blocked the way to stop cattle from trampling their crops and spreading disease. Many cattle were lost or stolen, or they died along the way. The journey to Sedalia also exposed cowhands to the unpredictable weather of the Plains. Heavy rainstorms often turned the cattle trails to mud. Lightning from those storms was a constant danger.

In 1867 a cattle dealer from Springfield, Illinois, named Joseph McCoy shortened the journey and reduced the dangers. McCoy traveled to several new railheads in Kansas to find the best site for a "cow town," a place where cattle trails and railheads might come together. McCoy settled upon Abilene, where he built huge stockyards to hold the cattle. A widespread advertising campaign by McCoy brought 35,000 cattle into Abilene the first year. Business more than doubled to 75,000 by the end of the second year. In 1871 about 600,000 cattle left Kansas on rails bound for Chicago.

The profits were enormous. Wealthy investors traveled from as far away as Great Britain to establish cattle ranches on the Plains. Cow towns sprang up along the railheads, and ranching spread from Texas to as far north as present-day Montana.

The End of the Cattle Boom

The cattle boom ended almost as quickly as it had begun. The huge profits from the sale of beef led

Nat Love, an African American cowhand, was an expert with the lariat. He won several roping contests in a rodeo in Deadwood, South Dakota. ▼

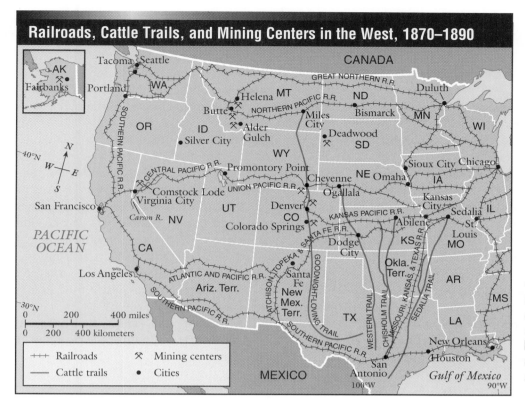

Railroads, Cattle Trails, and Mining Centers in the West, 1870–1890

◀ **Geography** *Railroads connected many mining centers with other cities in the West and Midwest.* **Interpreting the Map** *Which cattle trails connected to the Kansas Pacific Railroad?*

ranchers to raise even more cattle. However, the supply of beef began to far exceed the demand, which led to a sharp drop in prices.

Meanwhile the grazing herds ate parts of the grassland bare. In addition, drought struck in 1885, drying up streams and water holes. The hot sun turned the overgrazed land into desert. Blizzards hit the Great Plains in the winters of 1886 and 1887, bringing death to millions of cattle and nearly 300 cowhands who were looking after the herds. One cowhand wrote, "They are lost, all lost together, out here on the pitiless Plains."

The end of the cattle boom also resulted from the use of barbed wire, which increased after 1874. Farmers could now fence their land and keep out grazing cattle. With barbed wire there was no longer an open range where ranchers could graze their herds. Cowhands became ranch hands, harvesting the hay, feeding it to the cattle, and fixing fences and equipment. About all that remained were the rodeos in which the cowhands performed—a memory of when cowhands and ranchers symbolized the boom years of the American West.

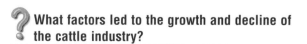 **What factors led to the growth and decline of the cattle industry?**

◆ WESTERN MINING

In 1859 a prospector named George Jackson found nuggets of gold in a frozen stream at Clear Creek, Colorado. Later he recalled,

> **That night I went to bed and dreamed of riches. I had struck it rich! There were millions in it.**

George Jackson never became a millionaire, but news of his gold strike inspired dreams of wealth similar to those created by the California gold discovery of 1849. A widespread belief began to circulate that huge deposits of gold lay hidden in the mountains of the West.

In the next decade, Colorado became the biggest gold producer in the United States, a position that had previously been held by California. For the next 30 years, thousands of miners swarmed into the western mountain ranges looking for wealth. Although a handful of these prospectors actually struck it rich, most did not. Much of the wealth from mining went to large companies.

Boom Towns

In 1859, the same year Jackson discovered the gold nuggets, a Canadian-born former fur trapper named Henry Comstock stumbled across a rich vein of silver along Nevada's Carson River. The strike turned out to be one of the richest in history, yielding nearly $320 million in silver before 1882. It became known as the Comstock Lode. A lode is a rich vein of ore lying in the cracks of rocks.

Wherever people struck gold or silver, thousands of miners rushed to the region to stake their claims. News of a big discovery created boom towns, turning mining camps into towns in just days. For example, within months of a gold strike near Alder Gulch, Montana, 10,000 miners swarmed into the area. Cities such as Denver, Colorado, and Helena, Montana, originated as mining camps, as shown on the map on page 239.

Not everybody who rushed into the boom towns worked at mining. Some made their fortunes by setting up businesses. People brought mule teams carrying tools, food, and clothing to sell to the miners. A formerly enslaved woman named Clara Brown, for example, went to Colorado to earn money by cooking and washing clothes. From the tips she was paid by prospectors, Brown invested her money in mining stocks. She eventually earned enough money to bring her entire family out of the South and into Colorado. Often, women ran boarding houses, restaurants, laundries, and small hotels.

Mining towns had no organized law or law officials at first. The flood of people into these towns often led to lawlessness. Gamblers, thieves, and outlaws lurked about the mining towns. Citizens responded to the lawlessness by forming **vigilante committees,** or groups of people who make and enforce their own laws. Vigilante committees hunted down suspected criminals and handed out punishment. People who were suspected of committing crimes were often sentenced to death by hanging without benefit of a trial.

One of the last big gold strikes took place in 1898 near Fairbanks, Alaska. By this time many other boom towns had dwindled in size. Gold and silver had run out in much of the continental United States, and miners drifted into other jobs.

▲ *"Gold fever" lured thousands of people west to make their fortunes. Many prospectors, such as the ones above, panned for gold nuggets in streams, while others used pickaxes and shovels to search for gold veins in rocks and earth.*

The End of the Mining Boom

One reason for the end of the mining boom was the way that miners had to extract ore from the ground. Gold or silver that lay on the surface could be mined by simply separating the nuggets from the stones and dirt. However, the bulk of the ore existed in underground veins of rock. Mining these veins meant digging tunnels, breaking up the ore, and hauling it out of the mine shafts.

Mining was difficult work. A famous American author, Mark Twain, tried his hand at it. Twain was a reporter for a newspaper in Virginia City, near the Comstock Lode. After digging an eight-foot shaft in a mine near Virginia City and getting hit with rocks from his own shovel, he gave up. Twain wrote,

> I never said a word, but climbed out [of the shaft] and walked home. I inwardly resolved that I would starve before I would make a target of myself with a long-handled shovel.

Miners faced dangerous, unhealthful conditions. They worked for days in dark shafts far underground where temperatures could soar to more than 100°F. Pressure in the underground rock became so intense that it sometimes caused deadly explosions. The miners breathed dangerous fumes, developed fatal diseases of the lung, and were often killed when dynamite misfired. Cave-ins and flooding claimed many lives. In the 1870s one miner in every 30 was disabled, and one in every 80 was killed.

Only the large mining companies, with their money and power, could afford the heavy equipment needed for underground mining and the new systems for breaking down the ore. Machines as large as houses pounded large chunks of ore into pellet-sized pieces. Hundreds of these machines were used to reduce the huge mountains of ore. In time, many miners who had left home to seek their fortunes wound up working for large mining companies.

Why was mining more successful for large companies than for individuals?

Section 2 Review

Check Understanding

1. **Define** (a) bonanza (b) railhead (c) vigilante committee

2. **Discuss** how the Great Plains provided opportunities for the growth of the cattle industry.

3. **Describe** what life was like for the cowhands who herded on the open range.

4. **Identify** the factors that helped bring the cattle boom to an end.

5. **Explain** why boom towns declined.

Critical Thinking

Connecting Past and Present Where do boom towns exist in the country today? How do they compare with boom towns of earlier times?

Write About History

Review the descriptions of life for cowhands and miners. Write a diary entry in which you describe a day in the life of a cowhand or a miner.

Section 3

Settling the Great Plains

PREVIEW

Objectives

- To summarize the opportunities that attracted people to the Great Plains

- To describe the difficulties faced by settlers on the Great Plains

- To explain how farmers organized alliances to protest economic conditions

- To trace the rise of the Populist party

Vocabulary

homesteader	cooperative
right-of-way	Populist
Exoduster	platform
squatter	

As John East of Missouri rolled his covered wagon onto the Kansas prairie, he looked over his shoulder and shouted: "Farewell to America!" To most Americans in the mid-1800s, the West seemed like a foreign land. Although Native Americans had lived in the West for thousands of years, and Spanish settlers had lived there for nearly 200 years, pioneers saw the Great Plains as a largely unsettled area.

The "wild west," as the land was called, gave birth to many legends that are still told today. The era began and ended with the pioneers who used their plows to turn millions of acres of grassland into farms.

◆ FARMING ON THE FRONTIER

The frontier, as most Americans in the 1800s thought of it, generally took the form of an imaginary line that ran from north to south and marked off the limit of western settlement. Since colonial times, settlers had pushed that line steadily westward. By the end of the Civil War, the frontier lay just east of the Mississippi River. Three major pockets of

settlement lay beyond the Mississippi. About 440,000 people lived along the Pacific coast in what are today the states of California, Oregon, and Washington. Approximately 100,000 people lived in the New Mexico area and another 40,000 lived in the basin of the Great Salt Lake. When the Civil War ended, hundreds of thousands more settlers were ready to stream onto the 400 million acres of the Great Plains.

Environment of the Plains

When people thought of the Great Plains, they thought first of its size. The Plains stretched from Canada to the Texas Panhandle, from the Missouri River to the Rocky Mountains. Settlers who crossed the Great Plains remembered it as an ocean of grass that swept as far as the eye could see. One traveler, who crossed the Great Plains in a slow-moving train, wrote,

> **It was a world almost without feature. An empty sky, and empty earth. On either hand, the green plain ran till it touched the skirts of heaven.**

At first the white settlers failed to see the tremendous wealth locked up in the prairies. The area was one of the largest grazing lands in the world. The wide-bladed "buffalo grass" supported huge herds of antelope, bison, and cattle. Anchoring the buffalo grass was a tough sod cover, a thick mat of roots and earth. Beneath the sod lay up to six feet of fertile topsoil. Deeper in the earth ran underground streams.

The Homestead Act

The government encouraged farm settlement on the Great Plains with the passage of the Homestead Act of 1862. This act offered free land grants of 160 acres to anyone who would live on the land and farm it for five years. Those who received land, the **homesteaders,** had to be 21 years of age or older, pay a $10 registration fee, build a shelter within six months, and improve and cultivate the land.

When the Civil War ended, people took advantage of the Homestead Act to start new lives. Many Union and Confederate soldiers tried to put the war behind them by packing up their families and moving onto the Great Plains.

The 160-acre limit under the Homestead Act proved too little for those who claimed lands on drier parts of the Plains. To help homesteaders, the government passed the Timber Culture Act of 1873. This act gave homesteaders an additional 160 acres if they planted 40 acres with trees. For areas with little rainfall, the government passed the Desert Act of 1877, giving settlers 640 acres at $.25 an acre if they agreed to irrigate part of the land within three years.

These laws triggered one of the largest migrations in United States history. More than 400,000 families acquired land under the Homestead Act alone.

News of the Homestead Act reached all the way across the Atlantic. Urged on by land promoters, waves of immigrants from England, Ireland, Germany, Sweden, Denmark, Norway, Russia, and other European countries migrated to the United States and onto the Great Plains.

Expansion of the Railroads

The railroads benefited greatly from the Transcontinental Railroad Act of 1862. This act gave railroad builders huge **rights-of-way** on which to lay track. A right-of-way is a strip of land on which a railroad, highway, or power line is built. For building the transcontinental railroad, both the Union Pacific and Central Pacific railways received 10 square acres of public land for every mile of track they laid in a state and 20 square acres for every mile they laid in a territory. By 1872 the United States Congress had awarded railroad companies more than 170 million acres of land worth one-half billion dollars. Not surprisingly, members of Congress received large contributions from the railroad companies in return.

The railroad companies sold these lands to raise cash. When railroads sold to farmers who worked the land and needed to transport their goods to cities, the railroads profited even more. The railroads thus became some of the biggest promoters of westward settlement and the largest corporate monopoly. They hired agents to advertise the sale of land both in the United States and in Europe. These advertisements helped bring some 2.2 million European immigrants onto the Great Plains.

Women on the Plains

The 1870 census counted 384,898 men and 172,145 women in the western states and territories. The ratio of men to women varied from place to place, with California having the largest number of women of any area. The number of women on the Great Plains steadily increased with the passage of

◄ *Life was hard for settlers on the prairie. This woman pushes a wheelbarrow full of buffalo chips, which she will use for fuel.*

▲ By 1900 nearly half a million farmers had settled on the Great Plains as a result of the Homestead Act. Because building materials were scarce on the Plains, many families dug up sod in strips and cut it into bricks to build their houses.

the Homestead Act, which applied to all heads of households, including women.

Women's rights leaders found the West a place where women could take leadership roles. Said one suffrage leader, "It takes brains, not brawn, to make farms pay. We need more women farmers!" Many territories, eager to claim enough people for statehood, attracted women onto the Plains by promising them the vote. By 1910, more than 10 percent of all heads of households in the West were women.

On the Plains, "women's work" came to mean anything that had to be done—trapping animals, herding cattle, or seeding rows of corn. Women plowed the land, harvested the crops, and raised the children. Some women found they could earn $1 a day just by showing new arrivals how to break land or use a pair of oxen to pull a plow. Women also made clothing, quilts, soap, and candles by hand. They cooked, washed the clothes, and treated the sick. Women on the Plains lived much as women had in colonial times. "Every imagination," said one woman, "was fired up with dreams and visions of new homes and fortunes to be made in the Fertile West."

Exodusters from the South

Opportunities on the Great Plains held special appeal for African Americans, particularly those from the South who were formerly enslaved. After the Civil War, African Americans faced abuse from those who resented their newly won freedom. To help African Americans escape from racial prejudice, a one-time conductor on the Underground Railroad, named Benjamin "Pap" Singleton, began a colony for African Americans on the Plains.

Singleton set up his first settlements in Kansas. By mid-1879 "Kansas fever" gripped much of the South as thousands of African Americans boarded trains and riverboats and headed west. African American settlers compared their journey to the Exodus—the biblical story of the Hebrews who left slavery in Egypt for freedom in Israel. Those who took part in the movement became known as **Exodusters.** By the time the movement ended in the 1880s, some 80,000 Exodusters had moved onto the Great Plains.

The large-scale arrival of African Americans in Kansas stirred up fears among some white homesteaders. Open hostility against African Americans forced many to move on to the Oklahoma Territory, where they set up more than 30 towns between 1890 and 1910. In these towns and elsewhere on the Plains, they joined thousands of other settlers who sought to make a living in spite of the harsh environment.

 What opportunities lured large numbers of people to settle the Great Plains?

◆ LIFE ON THE PLAINS

For many, the dream of owning a homestead soon turned into a nightmare as they fought to survive. Exaggerated advertisements from railroads and lies from land promoters promised cheap land and fertile soil. However, the advertisements neglected to mention the forces of nature. In some places the harsh environment drove nearly half of all newcomers off the Great Plains.

Surviving the Climate

Settlers began their life on the Great Plains by building shelters and planting crops. Both required wrestling with the tough prairie sod. The iron plows used in the East made little headway, so settlers turned to new and more expensive sharp-edged steel plows.

With so few trees on the Great Plains to supply lumber, settlers learned to use blocks of sod to build houses. Although the sod houses cost little and withstood the fierce prairie winds, they leaked dirt in dry weather and mud in wet weather.

One of the greatest challenges on the Great Plains was the weather. The temperature might soar past 110°F in summer and dip to −40°F in winter. Nature provided other hardships: sky-blackening tornadoes, hail storms with fist-sized balls of ice, flash floods, and lightning bolts that set the grasslands ablaze.

When weather favored the homesteaders, it also favored insects. In the 1870s and 1880s, clouds of locusts—giant grasshoppers—descended on the Great Plains, eating everything in sight. "Hoppers left behind nothing but the mortgage," moaned one farmer.

Hard times on the Plains discouraged many farmers. Some packed up and went back east. Others headed for the milder climate in the far west. Those who hung onto the land were fiercely proud in their determination. As time passed, those who could afford new inventions, from improved windmills to mechanical grain-binders for harvesting crops, found

their lives got easier. Survivors looked back upon their experiences with a kind of awe. As Colorado homesteader Lena Ely Stoddard explained,

 I guess, homesteading like we did— seeing all the beauty of it—just gets to you. You just have to love it. "

Oklahoma Land Rushes

The last major movement onto the Great Plains took place in the late 1880s when settlers cast their eyes to one more expanse of land—the Indian Territory. Responding to pressures by **squatters,** people who settle land without having a legal claim, Congress opened up nearly two million acres of land not yet assigned to Native Americans. These lands were in what is now the state of Oklahoma.

At noon on April 22, 1889, about 50,000 people lined up at the Oklahoma border. The land was to be given away on a first come, first served basis. At the sound of a starter's gun, people rushed in to stake a claim. Those who slipped past government patrols and staked an early claim became known as sooners. Because of the sooners, the entire parcel of land was divided up in a matter of hours. New towns sprang up even faster than they had in mining country. Oklahoma City, for example, grew from a population of zero to 10,000 in just a few hours.

 What challenges did homesteaders face on the Great Plains?

◆ FARMERS UNITE

Farming the Great Plains proved more difficult than most homesteaders ever imagined. Along with natural disasters, they faced harsh economic realities. New farm machinery had increased crop production. There were now more farm goods than buyers needed, causing prices to drop. Farmers were forced to use credit to finance homesteads or farm equipment. Credit is a loan that is scheduled to be paid back with regular payments. Without adequate income, they did not have the money to make their payments. Many farmers faced economic ruin. "We can see nothing but starvation in the future if relief does not come," said one farmer in 1874.

Rise of the Grange

Faced with these problems, farmers turned to an organization called the Grange. Oliver Kelley, a clerk in the Department of Agriculture, organized the Grange in 1867 to help relieve the loneliness of farm life on the Great Plains. The original purpose of the Grange was to provide a place for farmers and their families to gather together for social and educational purposes. Farmers used the organization to discuss their common problems and how to deal with them.

By 1875 the Grange had nearly 20,000 local branches and close to one million members. As the economic conditions of farmers became more serious, the Grange moved from social matters into political action. The Grange focused much of its energy and attention on battles with the railroads, to force them to lower freight rates for shipping goods to market. The Grange also set up **cooperatives,** organizations that were jointly owned by those who used their services, so farmers could save money by buying goods in large quantities. The cooperatives were set up primarily to allow farmers to market their own goods.

By the late 1870s, membership had slipped in the Grange. Some farmers lost interest in the organization when an economic depression caused many cooperatives to fail. Others left when better crop prices returned in the late 1870s. From membership in the Grange, farmers had learned that they could organize themselves to improve their lives.

Two powerful regional Farmers' Alliances moved in to replace the Grange—one on the Great Plains and one in the South. Together their combined membership totaled nearly four million people. In addition, African Americans in 16 states formed the Colored Farmers' National Alliance, which had more than one million members. The Farmers' Alliances sponsored rallies and educational meetings and supported political issues that were important to farmers, such as federal regulation of the railroads.

This 1873 poster illustrates a farmer surrounded by scenes of ideal farm life. These scenes were not realistic for most farmers. ▶

Drought and falling prices of crops pushed the Alliances into the political arena. Many farmers believed that neither of the political parties—the Republican party nor the Democratic party—had farmers' interests as a priority. By 1890, the Alliances had helped elect a number of officeholders sympathetic to farmers. During campaigns that year, members of the Kansas Alliance ran candidates on a third-party ticket called the People's, or **Populist,** party. The name "populist" came from *populus*, the Latin word for "people."

Rise of the Populists

The election results of 1890 stimulated the Alliances throughout the United States. Members of the Alliances called a Populist party convention on July 4, 1892, to draw up a statement of political beliefs and policies, or **platform.**

The platform proposed a list of reforms. It called for federal regulation of the railroads and demanded an income tax that taxed higher incomes more than lower incomes. The platform also proposed a loan program so that farmers could repay their debts. It included a number of political reforms, such as the direct election of senators and use of the secret ballot. Finally, to win the support of laborers, the platform supported an eight-hour workday.

The Populist party chose General James Weaver of Iowa, a Civil War veteran, to run for President in 1892. The Republican candidate, President Benjamin Harrison, was running for reelection against the Democratic candidate, former President Grover Cleveland. Although Cleveland was elected, the Populist candidate received more than one million votes.

An economic depression in 1893, causing a further drop in the price of crops, brought the Populists new support. Sensing victory in the presidential election of 1896, the Populists launched an all-out campaign. The Democrats tried to counter the Populists by nominating William Jennings Bryan, a pro-farmer representative from Nebraska.

At the 1896 Democratic convention, Bryan electrified the audience with his strong message challenging Americans to rally in support of American farms and farmers. Bryan's pro-farmer message rang out so clearly that the Populists nominated him as their candidate, too. Bryan now tried to carry his message across the country, traveling more than 18,000 miles and delivering more than 600 speeches. His Republican rival, William McKinley, relied on his party's superior financial resources. Republicans

pumped an estimated $3.5 to $7 million into the campaign. For the most part, McKinley talked to reporters from the back porch of his Ohio home. McKinley knew that bankers and business people supported him. They were afraid that Bryan would ruin the economy.

Bryan won the entire West and South but failed to carry a single industrial state. These heavily populated states handed victory to McKinley. The Populist party itself all but disappeared after 1908, but many of its ideas lived on in reforms the country would make.

 What reforms did the farmers' organizations introduce?

Section 3 Review

Check Understanding

1. **Define** (a) homesteader (b) right-of-way (c) Exoduster (d) squatter (e) cooperative (f) Populist (g) platform

2. **Explain** how the Homestead Act of 1862 promoted settlement of the Great Plains.

3. **Describe** the new opportunities women found in the West.

4. **Explain** the economic problems farmers faced on the Great Plains.

5. **Discuss** the goals of the Populist party.

Critical Thinking

Connecting Past and Present What organizations today serve the same functions as the Grange?

Write About Geography

You have read about the opportunities and challenges in the West in the mid-1800s and later. Create a one-page newspaper advertisement that encourages settlers to move to the Great Plains.

Chapter 12
Review

CHAPTER SUMMARY

Section 1

After the Civil War, white settlers headed to the Great Plains in record numbers. Native Americans were pushed onto ever smaller pieces of land and saw the slaughter of the buffalo they depended on for survival. Native Americans lost access to their lands and their traditions and often fought back against government troops. Reformers tried to force Native Americans to adapt to white society.

Section 2

The cattle and mining booms attracted ranchers and miners to the West. Cowhands rode the Plains, bringing cattle for shipment to eastern markets. The discovery of precious metals brought many others west, with hopes of striking it rich. Boom towns developed, but eventually only huge companies had the money to finance mining precious ores from deep underground.

Section 3

The Homestead Act attracted many to farm on the Great Plains, but new settlers faced a number of hardships. Difficult weather conditions drove some back home. Those who remained encountered new economic problems. Farmers joined together to gain power through organizations such as the Grange and the Farmers' Alliances. The Populist party represented the interests of many farmers.

Connecting ◆◆ Past and Present

Many movies, television shows, and books today portray life in the American West as exciting and heroic. How does that image compare with what you have learned?

Using Vocabulary

From the list below, select the term that best completes each sentence.

transcontinental	assimilate
homesteader	squatter
right-of-way	cooperative
bonanza	vigilante committee
Exoduster	Populist

1. Some people in western boom towns reacted to the lawlessness by forming a _____ to act as police.

2. Some farmers joined a _____ to save money on purchases, as well as to market their own goods.

3. The _____ railroad, which went from coast to coast, was completed after the Civil War.

4. After Native Americans were sent to reservations, several groups tried to force them to _____ into white culture.

5. A _____ took a grant of free land on the Plains in exchange for farming the land.

6. An African American who moved to Kansas from the South was called an _____.

7. The federal government gave railroads a generous _____ on which to lay track.

8. One who settled land without a legal claim was called a _____.

9. The riches of western mines were a _____ for those who found gold.

10. The _____ party was also called the "People's party."

Check Understanding

1. **Compare** the views of white settlers and Native Americans over land ownership and settlement of the Great Plains.

2. **Explain** how the Populist party represented the interests of farmers.

3. **Evaluate** the impact of attempts to force Native Americans to adapt to white society.

4. **Summarize** the obstacles farmers overcame in settling the Great Plains.

5. **Analyze** how the Homestead Act helped settle the Great Plains.

6. **Describe** the reasons why the Populist party grew in popularity.

7. **Explain** the pattern of conflict between the U.S. government and Native Americans.

8. **Describe** several factors that led to the growth of cattle ranching.

9. **Explain** the effect of the Dawes Act on Native Americans.

10. **Describe** the growth of boom towns.

Critical Thinking

1. **Analyzing** Why did the U.S. government break its promises to Native Americans?

2. **Making Inferences** Why do you think the religious movement called the Ghost Dance became so popular among Native Americans?

3. **Evaluating Information** Near the turn of the century, Native American Black Elk wrote, "We are prisoners of war." Do you agree with this statement or not? Give your reasons.

4. **Drawing Inferences** Why do you think settlers put up with the hardships of life on the Great Plains?

◆ **Connecting Past and Present** Why do you think the stories of miners and cowhands live on in legends today?

Writing to Express an Opinion

In recent times, Native Americans have taken the U.S. government to court, asking for the return of lands that were theirs by right. Often these lands are now the sites of homes and businesses. Should the Native American claims be respected? What should be done about the homes and businesses? Suppose you are the judge in such a case. **Write** an essay to express your opinion about whether to honor the Native American claims.

Putting Skills to Work

MAKING PREDICTIONS

Read this 1892 excerpt from the Populist party's platform. Use what you have learned about predicting consequences on page 236 to answer the questions.

> *The land, including all the natural sources of wealth, is the heritage of the people, and should not be monopolized [used exclusively] for speculative [economic risk-taking] purposes, and alien [foreign] ownership of land should be prohibited. All land now held by railroads and other corporations in excess of their actual needs, and all lands now owned by aliens should be reclaimed by the government and held for actual settlers only.*

1. How do the Populists feel about foreign ownership of western lands?

2. What would you predict the Populists would say about Native American lands? Explain.

Interpreting the Timeline

Use the timeline on pages 228–229 to answer these questions.

1. In what year was the Homestead Act passed?

2. How many years passed between the defeat of Custer's forces at Little Bighorn and the massacre at Wounded Knee?

3. Which events on the timeline reflect conflict between Native Americans and the U.S. government?

Portfolio Project

A MUSEUM DISPLAY

A museum is preparing an exhibit showing the impact of westward expansion on the Great Plains. Contribute to the exhibit by creating a display that shows some aspect of settlement of the West. Use quotations, pictures, and data from several sources. When your project is completed, discuss what your display shows about the time period.

Chapter 13
The Nation Industrializes 1860–1900

CHAPTER PREVIEW

Section 1 A Revolution in Technology

A revolution in technology and a growing transportation network spread people, products, and information across the nation.

Section 2 The Rise of Big Business

The United States became a major industrial power with the rise of big business in control of major industries.

Section 3 The Industrial Work Force

Dangerous working conditions, long hours, and low pay led to a renewed interest in the labor union movement.

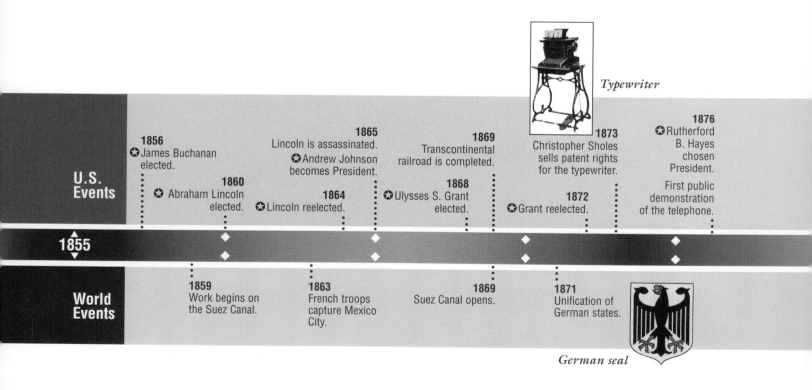

Typewriter

U.S. Events

1856
✪ James Buchanan elected.

1860
✪ Abraham Lincoln elected.

1865
Lincoln is assassinated.
✪ Andrew Johnson becomes President.

1864
✪ Lincoln reelected.

1869
Transcontinental railroad is completed.

1868
✪ Ulysses S. Grant elected.

1873
Christopher Sholes sells patent rights for the typewriter.

1872
✪ Grant reelected.

1876
✪ Rutherford B. Hayes chosen President.

First public demonstration of the telephone.

▲
1855
▼

World Events

1859
Work begins on the Suez Canal.

1863
French troops capture Mexico City.

1869
Suez Canal opens.

1871
Unification of German states.

German seal

▲ *These women are working in a corset factory in the 1800s.*
◆◆ **Connecting Past and Present** *How would you describe the working conditions in this factory? How does this compare to working conditions in factories today?*

Portfolio Project

SCRIPT WRITING

Many people became famous during the time when industries expanded, big business dominated the economy, and workers began to organize. One way to bring the people and events of this period to life is through dramatization. As you read about this era, look for people and events to include in a script. At the end of the chapter, you will use facts to dramatize how one person or event changed technology, business, or labor.

Women Knights of Labor

Pullman Strike

1881
✪ Chester A. Arthur becomes President.

Knights of Labor extend membership to women.

1880
✪ James Garfield elected.

1882
Edison opens the first electric lighting power station.

1884
✪ Grover Cleveland elected.

1886
American Federation of Labor is founded.

1887
Congress passes the Interstate Commerce Act.

1888
✪ Benjamin Harrison elected.

1890
Sherman Antitrust Act outlaws trusts.

1892
✪ Grover Cleveland elected again.

1894
Railroad workers go on nationwide strike.

1895
Stephen Crane's novel *The Red Badge of Courage* is published.

1896
✪ William McKinley elected.

1900

1879
London's first telephone exchange is established.

1883
Robert Louis Stevenson's novel *Treasure Island* is published.

1884
Berlin Conference carves out European colonies in Africa.

1887
Queen Victoria of England celebrates her Golden Jubilee.

1891
Java man bones are discovered.

1896
First modern Olympics are held in Athens.

Olympic symbol

Section 1

A Revolution in Technology

PREVIEW

Objectives

- To summarize the advances in technology that contributed to growth in the U.S. economy after the Civil War

- To explain how an expanding transportation network helped to unite the nation

- To describe advances in communication that speeded the flow of information

Vocabulary

patent	branch line
kerosene	railroad time
Bessemer process	Pullman car

Between 1860 and 1900, the United States changed from a rural nation into the world's leading industrial power. During these years, the nation's manufacturing output grew from $1.8 billion a year to more than $13 billion. This increase of economic growth led industrialist Andrew Carnegie to boast,

" While the old Nations of earth creep on at a snail's pace, the [United States] thunders past with the rush of an express. "

New ideas about ways in which people lived, worked, and traveled, as well as technological advances, spurred industrial expansion. In the 70-year period following the Civil War, the U.S. government granted 1.5 million **patents** for new inventions. A patent grants an inventor the sole right to make, use, and sell an invention for a set period of time. Business leaders began to invest heavily in these inventions, and new products—electric light bulbs, sleeping cars on railroad trains, typewriters, and hundreds of other devices—changed the way people lived.

◆ THE OIL AND STEEL INDUSTRIES

In the early 1840s, Samuel Kier began collecting oil from places where it oozed up from underground pools. He urged people in Pennsylvania to buy **kerosene**—an oil-based liquid produced from crude oil, saying,

" Hurry, before this wonderful product is depleted from Nature's laboratory! "

In 1854 the Pennsylvania Rock Oil Company was set up to refine, or purify, oil into kerosene. Before Kier started refining oil, no one quite knew what to do with the dark, gooey substance. By turning it into kerosene, Kier offered a cheap substitute for whale oil, used for lighting lamps. As the demand for kerosene increased, people sought out new sources. In 1859, Edwin L. Drake, a retired railroad conductor, drilled the first oil well. News of his "gusher" in Titusville, Pennsylvania, sent people rushing to the region. A new industry was born.

The oil industry brought new problems, such as pollution and dangerous working conditions, but it also created vast new economic opportunities. Products made from oil would soon power the machines of the new industrial age and eventually provide new means of transportation. This would lead to the creation of new jobs for the American people.

While Samuel Kier refined oil into kerosene, two other inventors discovered a way to make steel quickly and cheaply. Until the middle of the nineteenth century, it took several weeks to turn just 50 pounds of iron into steel. In the 1850s, an American ironmaker, named William Kelly, and a British manufacturer, named Henry Bessemer, each developed a way to make steel by passing air through iron and coal in a furnace. Working independently of one another, Kelly and Bessemer blasted air at molten, or melted, iron. By doing this, they could remove impurities and turn the iron into high quality steel.

The **Bessemer process,** as the technique came to be known, reshaped the steel industry. Using this process, manufacturers could make steel at a far lower cost than in the past. In the 1860s, before widespread use of the Bessemer process, U.S. manufacturers produced fewer than 2,000 tons of steel a year. In the late 1800s, manufacturers produced more than seven million tons. By 1880 more than 90 percent of the steel in the United States was produced using the new method.

▲ *The Bessemer process was the beginning of modern steelmaking. This wood engraving shows the huge furnaces used to change molten iron into steel.*

Steel became the building material of the industrial age, used to make longer bridges, taller buildings, and an extensive network of railroads. It proved to be stronger, easier to work with, and far more resistant to rust than iron.

How did oil and steel contribute to the growth of the economy after the Civil War?

◆ A NETWORK OF RAILROADS

The biggest consumer of steel in the late 1800s was the railroad industry, as steel rails replaced iron rails. At the start of the Civil War, railroads were a relatively new form of transportation in the U.S. There were only about 35,000 miles of railroad track in the United States, most of them in the Northeast. By 1900 more than 193,000 miles of railroad track crisscrossed the nation. The United States had more miles of track than all the countries of Europe put together.

The Transcontinental Railroad

One of the main arteries of trade was the transcontinental railroad, built by crews working for the Union Pacific and Central Pacific railroads. Americans viewed construction of the transcontinental railway as a race between two competing teams. The government encouraged the construction by offering loans that came to about $65 million, and by promising land for each mile of track laid by the crews. A railroad company received 10 square miles of land for each mile of track laid in a state, and 20 square miles of land for each mile of track in a territory. The government later increased the land to 20 square miles in states.

Starting in Omaha, Nebraska, crews of the Union Pacific Railroad, made up of large numbers of Irish immigrants and Civil War veterans, worked their way westward. This railroad would link up with one being built by the Central Pacific Railroad, whose crew worked eastward from its starting point in Sacramento, California. Among the laborers who worked on this project were about 15,000 Chinese immigrants.

The dangerous job of blasting tunnels through the rocks, ice, and snow of the Sierra Nevada range fell to the Chinese laborers. Working with only pickaxes and shovels, they won the admiration of the Central Pacific owners. Chinese workers set the one-day record for track laid—an astounding ten miles. They lifted 1,000 tons of steel to lay the ten miles of track in 12 hours. When other workers demanded that the Central Pacific stop hiring the Chinese workers, owner Charles Crocker responded, "If you can't get along with them, we have only one alternative. We'll let you go and hire nobody but them."

On May 10, 1869, after seven years of labor, the two railroad lines met at Promontory Point, near the northern tip of the Great Salt Lake, in what is now the state of Utah. In a ceremony to mark the historic occasion, the presidents of the Union Pacific and the Central Pacific drove a golden spike into the final railroad tie, followed by a steel spike. A telegraph operator flashed news to a waiting nation that the Atlantic and Pacific oceans were linked by rail: "Dot. Dot. Dot. . . . Done." All over the country, Americans celebrated the event.

Many people did not believe it was possible to build a railroad across the continent. Two railroad companies took on the challenge. Here, the completion of the transcontinental railroad is celebrated at Promontory Point. ▶

Uniting the Country

By 1885 four more railroads crossed the continent while numerous other companies built smaller lines connecting major cities. These **branch lines** reached out to smaller cities in the nation like strands in a spider's web.

Railroads changed the way Americans thought about space and time. Instead of talking about travel in terms of miles, people referred to the time it took to travel from one place to another. However, the way Americans measured time was a major obstacle to efficient travel. There was no standard accepted time. Most towns kept their own time, creating great confusion. The time kept in one town might vary by several minutes from the time kept in another town. For example, there were 27 different local times in Illinois, making it almost impossible for the railroads to establish accurate schedules.

To help make time standard, a professor named C.F. Dowd proposed that Earth be divided into 24 time zones. Four of these zones—Eastern, Central, Mountain, and Pacific—would cut through the United States. Railroads supported the plan with great enthusiasm.

On November 18, 1883, railroad crews and people in towns along railroad lines all over the United States reset their watches and clocks. In 1884 an international conference adopted the rest of Dowd's plan, putting the world on **railroad time.**

A standard time system was just one way in which railroads helped unite the country. People and goods now flowed in all directions. Trains carried raw materials to faraway factories. They took finished products to markets all over the United States. Railroads shipped crops from farmers in the West to markets in the East. They also transported people farther and faster than ever before.

Improving Service on the Railroads

Passengers aboard the first transcontinental railroads endured risk-filled trips. Locomotives sometimes broke down or blew up from overheating, and brakes often failed on steep grades. Wooden trestles buckled under the weight of 50-ton locomotives. Railroad cars broke free of one another and ran off the tracks.

Inventors took steps to improve safety. Elijah McCoy, the son of formerly enslaved persons, invented a device that automatically lubricated, or greased, the moving parts on a train. Another African American scientist, Granville Woods, invented a telegraph that allowed trains to communicate with each other to prevent head-on collisions. George Westinghouse developed improved air brakes, allowing trains to stop in a fraction of the distance it had previously taken.

A number of other innovations made rail travel safer. Railroad companies built two sets of tracks so that traffic could move in two directions. The companies also installed signal lights to warn people of the approach of a rushing train.

In the 1870s, George Mortimer Pullman developed a parlor car for people who could afford a first-class ticket. The so-called **Pullman cars** provided passengers with reclining seats and sleeping spaces. The cars came with plush carpets, wooden panels, and gourmet meals. "The prairie schooner has passed away," announced one newspaper, "and is replaced by the railway coach with all its modern comforts."

 How did the expansion of railroads help to unite the nation?

◆ THE POWER TO COMMUNICATE

While railroads quickened the pace of travel in the United States, a revolution in communications quickened the flow of information. Messages once carried by riders on horseback began to travel over wires in a matter of seconds.

The Telegraph

The introduction of the telegraph by Samuel F.B. Morse in 1844 marked the start of a communications revolution. Morse invented a code of long and short electrical impulses to represent letters of the alphabet. Using what became known as the Morse Code, he tapped out messages in dots and dashes.

Telegraph wires soon spread across the nation. By 1853, about 23,000 miles of telegraph wire stretched across the country. In 1868, telegraph companies combined to form the Western Union Telegraph Company. By 1900, Western Union owned 933,000 miles of wire and sent more than 63 million messages each year.

The telegraph had a far-reaching impact on American companies. It allowed business managers to keep track of shipments and to stay informed of prices across the nation. Western Union also set up a financial service so that people could wire money to each other.

The Telephone

In 1876, visitors at the Centennial Exhibition in Philadelphia stood in long lines to witness the "talking telegraph." This new invention was the telephone, developed by Alexander Graham Bell, a teacher whose work with hearing impaired people had led him to study the science of sound. Through this study, he learned to transmit speech electronically.

On March 10, 1876, Bell sent an electronic message to his assistant, Thomas A. Watson. In the world's first telephone call, he said, "Mr. Watson, come here. I want you."

Two years after Bell uttered those words, President Rutherford B. Hayes installed a telephone in the White House. By 1895 there were over 325,000 telephones in the United States. By 1915 there were ten million.

The Typewriter

New inventions led to the growth of business and industry. The expansion created a huge volume of paperwork. More than 50 inventors had tried to produce a typing machine to speed up writing. However, inventor Christopher A. Sholes was the first to produce a machine that could actually write faster than clerks could.

In 1868, Sholes patented his invention. In 1873 he sold the patent to E. Remington & Sons. By 1886, Remington was producing about 1,500 typewriters a month. A business journal wrote of the typewriter:

▲ *The first typewriter was manufactured in 1873.*

> "Today its monotonous click can be heard in almost every well-regulated business establishment in the country. A great revolution is taking place, and the typewriter is at the bottom of it."

The typewriter provided new employment opportunities for women. Typing jobs paid no better than factory work. However, women, who had few opportunities to receive high wages, found the office environment an attractive alternative to factories.

 What impact did inventions have on businesses in the United States?

◆ INVENTIONS CHANGE LIVES

The same year that Bell invented the telephone, Thomas Alva Edison set up the nation's first industrial research laboratory in Menlo Park, New Jersey. Edison called his lab an idea factory. Working with a team of scientists, the self-educated Edison promised to produce "a minor invention every ten days and a big one every six months." By the time of Edison's death in 1931, the "Wizard of Menlo Park" had patented over 1,000 inventions. Many of the inventions made basic changes in the ways Americans lived. For example, Edison used his knowledge of sound to produce a "sound writer," or phonograph, in 1877. He then turned his efforts to producing a long-burning light bulb that could be used indoors.

With the light bulb perfected, Edison built the first central power plant for producing and carrying electricity into homes and offices. In 1882 he opened Edison Illuminating Company in New York City. His power plant furnished lighting for 85 buildings.

Electricity sparked the rise of a new industry. Backed by investment bankers, power-generating stations went up around the nation. By 1892 electric companies, such as General Electric, sold electricity and equipment worth more than $22 million.

Although electricity was not used nationwide until the 1940s, it started to make changes in American cities immediately. By 1890 more than 50 cities had electric streetcars. Steel frames and electrically-powered elevators were brought together by engineers to build taller buildings and, later, skyscrapers. Electric lights allowed people to stay on city streets after nightfall with some degree of safety.

Inventions set the stage for the United States to become an industrial nation. Some inventions improved transportation and communication, while others led to the creation of entire new industries, such as food processing, packaging, and preservation. Jar makers, such as John L. Mason, developed bottles that kept out air. Gail Borden invented the process for condensing and then canning milk. Henry J. Heinz canned and bottled vegetables, fruits, and a sauce known as ketchup. Meat processing, or the preparation of meat for consumer use, and meat packing also benefited from improvements in machinery and in the rail transportation that carried these perishable products to markets.

 How did the invention of the electric light bulb change the way people lived in cities?

BUILDING SKILLS

Interpreting Primary Sources: Thomas A. Edison

Primary sources are firsthand accounts of events in history. Letters, diaries, speeches, autobiographies, newspaper articles, and other documents are examples of primary sources. Paintings, drawings, and photographs can also be primary sources. Even physical objects, such as utensils and clothing, can provide direct evidence about an event or a person. All of these provide factual information, but they do something else important. They also reveal the feelings, attitudes, and motives of the author. Because they reflect the point of view of the author, you need to analyze how reliable the source is.

Here's How

Follow these steps to interpret a primary source:

1. Identify the document or source. Determine who wrote it, when it was written, where it was written, and what it is about.

2. Analyze the author's point of view. Decide how the author feels about the issue or event. Watch for words and phrases that signal a one-sided point of view.

3. Draw conclusions about the event or issue. You can discover information about conditions in the period in which the document was written.

Here's Why

Historians use primary sources to view history through the eyes of those who were involved in an event. By analyzing and interpreting primary sources, you can gain insight into the attitudes of people in a particular historical period. The insights you gain will help you make your own judgments about the events and issues of that period.

Practice the Skill

Below is a newspaper account from *The New York Herald* of January 17, 1879, of a visit to Thomas Edison's workshop at Menlo Park. Read the excerpt and answer the questions.

The ordinary rules of industry seem to be reversed at Menlo Park. Edison and his numerous assistants turn night into day and day into night. At six o'clock in the evening, the machinists and electricians assemble in the laboratory. Edison is already present, attired in a suit of blue flannel, with hair uncombed and straggling over his eyes, his whole air that of a man with a purpose and indifferent to everything save that purpose. By a quarter past six, the quiet laboratory has become transformed into a hive of industry. . . .

Edison, himself, flits about first to one bench, then to another, examining here, instructing there. At one place drawing out a new fancied design, at another earnestly watching the progress of some experiment.

1. What is the reporter's point of view toward Edison? What words or details helped you to draw these conclusions?

2. What did you learn about the way in which Thomas Edison worked?

3. How do you think Edison's assistants responded to him?

Apply the Skill

As you read the primary source quotation about the working conditions of children in factories on page 264, use the three steps on this page to form your own judgments about those conditions.

Section 2

The Rise of Big Business

PREVIEW

Objectives

- To explain the growth of corporations in the late 1800s

- To show how big business tried to eliminate competition

- To describe the beginnings of government regulations on business in the late 1800s

Vocabulary

corporation	horizontal integration
stock	trust
rebate	capitalism
vertical integration	Social Darwinism
philanthropist	

Expansion of the nation's transportation and communication systems made it possible for industrial leaders to conduct business on a large scale. As these leaders bought small companies and merged them into huge national operations, giant business enterprises emerged.

The business leaders who ran these operations had great wealth and power. Their critics called them "robber barons," charging them with building their fortunes from the sweat of workers. Admirers saw the new business leaders as "captains of industry," praising them for expanding U.S. markets and increasing production of goods. Many Americans regarded the business leaders simply as a necessary evil. Said one economist in 1889, "There is no other way in which the work of production and distribution can be done."

◆ BUSINESS EXPANSION

Until the late 1800s, most businesses were run by single owners or partnerships, with few employees. However, new business leaders brought about basic changes in how industry was run.

At the start of the 1900s, for example, the Singer Sewing Machine Company operated eight factories nationwide. Singer employed more than 90,000 workers who made and sold 1.25 million sewing machines each year. Even bigger enterprises emerged in the railroad, meat packing, steel, sugar, and oil businesses. These operations required new methods of organization.

Corporations and Investment Bankers

The business expansion of the late 1800s required large amounts of capital, or money that is invested in factories, machines, or other businesses. To get the capital, industrialists now formed **corporations.** Corporations are businesses authorized by law to act as one person, though they are often made up of many investors. A corporation often sells **stock,** or shares of ownership in the business, in order to raise capital. The people who buy these stocks, the stockholders, gain the right to share in the profits. They also elect a board of directors that runs a company.

To acquire the huge sums of money they needed, corporations relied on investment bankers. These bankers arranged the sale of stocks and negotiated loans. J.P. Morgan, the most powerful investment banker of the late 1800s, believed the most efficient way to earn a profit was through the merger of businesses. This avoided what Morgan called the "wasteful" practice of competition.

In the 1890s, Morgan and other bankers helped finance the growth of the railroad business. In the

Study Hint

When you read an unfamiliar word, look for context clues about its meaning. Context clues are nearby words and phrases that help make the meaning clearer. For example, if you do not know the meaning of robber barons in column 1, the phrases critics and sweat of workers can help you learn that robber barons is a negative term.

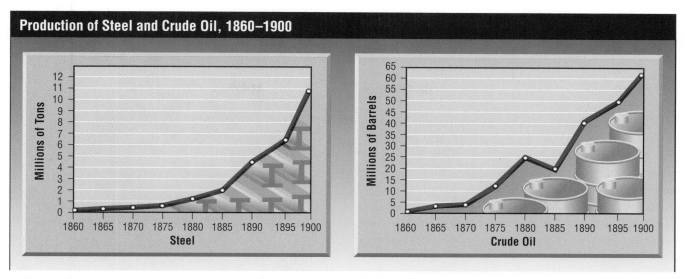

Production of Steel and Crude Oil, 1860–1900

▲ **Economics** *These graphs show the dramatic rise of steel and oil production from 1860 to 1900.* **Interpreting the Graphs** *Which five-year period shows the greatest increase for (a) steel production? (b) oil production?*

process, they bought control of the industry. They increased profits by cutting wages and by granting **rebates,** or partial refunds or discounts, to large companies that promised them large amounts of business. Smaller railroads could not compete with such practices, and many were forced to sell out to investment bankers.

By 1900, seven giant railroad systems controlled nearly two thirds of the nation's track. All these railroads were under the control of J.P. Morgan or other banking firms. This pattern was repeated in other large American industries.

Carnegie and Steel

Andrew Carnegie, the son of a poor Scottish weaver, learned how to succeed in business at an early age. After arriving in the United States in 1848 at age 13, Carnegie quickly worked his way up the economic ladder, rising from cotton mill worker to telegraph operator to private secretary for Thomas A. Scott, a superintendent of the Pennsylvania Railroad.

One evening while Scott was out, Carnegie used his telegraph skills to unsnarl a tangle of freight and passenger trains. Scott rewarded him by giving him a stock tip in a promising new company. To raise the money to buy the stock, Carnegie convinced his mother to mortgage the family home. The tip paid off, and Carnegie was on his way to building a fortune.

Through wise investments and knowing the right people, young Carnegie became a millionaire. In 1873 he used the money to enter the steel business, a

growing industry, as shown in the graph above. Carnegie kept his steel mills running around the clock and took every opportunity to cut prices and still earn a profit. This drove most of his competitors out of business. Between 1890 and 1900, the annual profits from Carnegie's mills increased from $5.4 million to $40 million.

Carnegie cut costs by owning or controlling most of the operations needed to make steel. He invested in iron mines in Michigan and Wisconsin, tens of thousands of acres of coal fields, a shipping fleet on the Great Lakes, and several railroad lines. Controlling the raw materials, transportation systems, and all stages of the manufacturing process—called **vertical integration**—gave Carnegie total power over the quality and cost of the product. By 1900 he ran the world's largest steel-making enterprise.

J.P. Morgan watched Carnegie's success and decided he could build an even larger steel empire. In 1901 Morgan asked Carnegie to name a price for his company. Carnegie scribbled a figure of almost a half billion dollars on a piece of paper. Morgan glanced at it and said, "I accept this price." Merging this company with others, Morgan created the United States Steel Corporation. It was a $1.4 billion firm with 200 companies and 168,000 employees.

Carnegie, now retired from business, spent the rest of his life as a **philanthropist,** giving away his fortune. He donated money to museums, libraries, and other public works. "The man who dies rich," wrote Carnegie, "dies disgraced."

Rockefeller and Oil

About the same time that Carnegie entered the steel business, a young Cleveland merchant named John D. Rockefeller began to take control of the new oil industry. Like J.P. Morgan, Rockefeller considered competition wasteful.

In the early 1860s, Rockefeller visited the oil fields of Pennsylvania. He saw that someone who could buy and combine the claims of several oil drillers might make a fortune. This merger of competing businesses, or individual claims in the same business, was known as **horizontal integration.** In 1863, at the age of 24, Rockefeller bought his first oil refinery. By 1878 his company, Standard Oil, controlled over 90 percent of the oil business in the United States.

Rockefeller used the same cost-cutting methods as Carnegie to build his empire. He paid careful attention to the smallest details. After counting the number of drops of an alloy used to seal each kerosene can, he ordered workers to cut the number of drops from 40 to 39. On a larger scale, he bought everything his company needed: timberlands to make wooden barrels, refineries to process the oil, warehouses to store it, and tankers to ship it around the world. Rather than passing the savings on to employees or customers, Rockefeller kept huge profits for himself.

To manage this complex operation, Standard Oil developed a new business organization called the **trust.** The trust was a legal agreement under which stockholders of different companies in one industry turn over their stock to one group of directors, called trustees. The trustees then run the companies as one giant corporation. Rockefeller had created a monopoly, control by a business over an entire industry. By 1900 the oil industry had grown phenomenally, as shown in the graph on page 259.

When Rockefeller retired, he had a personal fortune of $1 billion. Standard Oil continued to amass wealth. Later it would become the target, along with other trusts, of reformers who felt the trusts endangered the American system of free enterprise.

How did industrialists in the 1800s change the way some businesses were run?

◆ THE ANTITRUST MOVEMENT

Traditionally, many Americans had wanted the government to stay out of business affairs, a policy known as *laissez-faire*, the French expression meaning

▲ **Economics** *This cartoon compares several big companies to the tentacles of an octopus.* **Interpreting the Cartoon** *What does the cartoonist say about the attitude of the big companies toward the public?*

"leave alone." Many wealthy Americans believed that government should not interfere with **capitalism,** the system in which privately owned businesses, farms, and factories compete with one another for profits.

Some business people tried to justify capitalism through the findings of science. In 1859, Charles Darwin, an English scientist, presented his theory of biological evolution. Darwin believed that all life had evolved through a process he called natural selection, in which only the strongest or fittest survive. Some business people applied this scientific theory to the relationship between government and business. Their theory of **Social Darwinism** argued that if government would stay out of the affairs of business, the strong would survive and the weak would fail. The success of the fittest would benefit all society. Based on this hands-off approach, the government neither taxed the profits of big business nor regulated the treatment of the workers.

Regulating the Railroads

Although large operations were often able to make goods more efficiently and less expensively than small companies, many people became concerned about the growth of big business. The power of the trusts led many to believe that big business needed closer governmental supervision.

Farmers were among the first to demand government action. While they had to pay high rates to railroads to ship their crops to market, big business often paid lower prices, or rates. Farmers believed that the rebates given to big business by railroads were unfair. John D. Rockefeller, for instance, was able to ship his oil for less money by forcing railroads into secret deals to give him rebates on shipping costs. Farmers also protested that the lack of competition among railroads kept freight rates high.

In 1887, Congress reacted to these demands for federal regulation of the railroads by passing the Interstate Commerce Act. This law stated that railroads traveling through more than one state must set rates that are "reasonable and just." It also made rebates illegal and required railroads to make their rates public.

To enforce these terms, the act created the Interstate Commerce Commission (ICC). Although the ICC received a flood of complaints about unfair rate practices, it lacked the power to enforce its decisions. To change an unfair rate, the ICC had to file suit against the railroad charged with a rate violation and take it to court. Winning such cases, said one ICC official, "was like cutting a path through a jungle." The courts usually ruled in favor of the railroads. Out of 16 cases brought to trial between 1887 and 1905, the ICC won only one.

The Sherman Antitrust Act

The Interstate Commerce Act was passed to make sure that the railroads did not cheat the public. Its purpose was not to break up or control the size of corporations and trusts. Several states tried to prohibit trusts, but most trusts did business in more than one state. Since state efforts had little effect, reformers began to demand that the federal government take action.

In 1890, Congress sought to protect free competition with passage of the Sherman Antitrust Act. This act outlawed "every . . . form of trust or otherwise" that promoted the "restraint [limitation] of trade." According to the act, any attempt to interfere with free trade among the states by forming a trust was illegal.

The law, however, had some big loopholes. Its vague wording failed to define either *trust* or *restraint of trade*. Between 1890 and 1900, the government prosecuted only 18 cases under the act, and it lost most of them. Furthermore, most trusts escaped prosecution entirely. They simply dissolved when charged and re-formed into different corporations. Eventually, the government stopped trying to enforce the Sherman Antitrust Act against trusts. Instead, ironically, the law was often used to prevent labor unions from using strikes, boycotts, and other tactics that were said to interfere with interstate trade.

By 1900, giant business firms controlled nearly two fifths of all the capital invested in American manufacturing. The failure of the government to enforce the Sherman Antitrust Act led to an antitrust movement among reformers.

 How did the government begin to take action against big business?

Section 2 Review

Check Understanding

1. **Define** (a) corporation (b) stock (c) rebate (d) vertical integration (e) philanthropist (f) horizontal integration (g) trust (h) capitalism (i) Social Darwinism

2. **Identify** the conditions that encouraged the growth of corporations in the late 1800s.

3. **Explain** how industrialists such as Andrew Carnegie and John D. Rockefeller drove out competition.

4. **Explain** why the Interstate Commerce Act was passed in 1887.

Critical Thinking

Hypothesizing Why do you suppose Andrew Carnegie spent the later years of his life giving away his fortune?

Write About Economics

Connecting Past and Present Many people still have both positive and negative feelings about big business today. Divide a sheet of paper into two columns. List positive qualities in one column and negative qualities in the other.

POINT *of* VIEW

STANDARD OIL COMPANY

In 1903, a journalist named Ida Tarbell published a series of articles in *McClure's Magazine* that caused a storm of controversy. Tarbell told a story of widespread corruption at the world's largest oil company, Standard Oil. She created this story from documents that traced some of the practices of the company.

Following are two passages. In the first, Ida Tarbell describes how the South Improvement Company, the small company that grew into Standard Oil, fixed railroad rates so that the company paid less than its competitors. In the second, John D. Rockefeller defends his methods for expanding his business and eliminating the competition.

Ida Tarbell

The oil men found that the contracts which the new company had made with the railroads [increased] the rates of freight from the Oil Regions over 100 percent— an advance which [took away] their margin of profit on their business. But it was not the railroad that got the greater part of this advance; it was the South Improvement Company.... cheap oil? Mr. Rockefeller's fundamental reason for forming his first combination was to keep <u>up</u> the price of oil. It has been forced down by the inventions and discoveries of his competitors. He has never lowered it a point if it could be avoided, and in times of public stress he had taken advantage of the very misery of the poor to demand higher prices.

John D. Rockefeller

I have often wondered if the criticism which centered upon us did not come from the fact that we were among the first, if not the first, to work out the problems of direct selling to the user on a broad scale. This was done in a fair spirit and with due consideration of everyone's rights. We did not ruthlessly go after the trade of our competitors and attempt to ruin it by cutting prices or instituting a spy system.... It was never our purpose to interfere with a dealer who adequately cultivated his field of operations, but when we saw a new opportunity or a new place for extending the sale by further and effective facilities, we made it our business to provide them.

Examining Point of View

1. What do you think Ida Tarbell was trying to accomplish with her series of articles on the Standard Oil Company?

2. Why do you think John Rockefeller wrote the passage reprinted here?

3. Whose writing is more persuasive to you? Explain your answer.

What's Your Point of View?

In a monopoly, one company controls the supply of a product or service many people want or need. As the 1900s progressed, Congress passed laws intended to stop monopolies in industry.

Write an essay explaining whether you feel that monopolies are still a danger today, and whether laws to stop them should still be in place.

Section 3

The Industrial Work Force

PREVIEW

Objectives

- To discuss how the growth of industry changed the way people worked

- To summarize the reasons for the rise of labor unions

- To explain the results of strikes in several industries

Vocabulary

company town	blacklist
scrip	anarchist
lockout	closed shop
scab	yellow-dog contract

Industry could not have grown in this country without a huge labor force. By 1880 nearly five million men, women, and children worked in manufacturing, construction, and transportation. The conditions under which they worked became a major source of controversy in the years that followed.

◆ LIFE IN THE WORKPLACE

"A mere machine" is how one factory worker described himself. The arrival of machines in the workplace made great changes in the way people worked, largely destroying the old crafts, such as glassmaking and iron molding. As small workshops gave way to factories, the work was broken down into separate steps. Each step was performed by a different worker who always did the same task. Now most workers in manufacturing labored at tasks they performed over and over. Their work was set to rigid schedules. One woman worker in a pickle factory wrote,

> I have stood ten hours. I have fitted 1,300 corks; I have hauled and loaded 4,000 jars of pickles. My pay is seventy cents.

Poor Working Conditions

Before the machine age, most workers were producers—people who made products they sold themselves. They received rates of pay based on the quality of their work and the willingness of a customer to meet a price.

By the late nineteenth century, workers found jobs in growing factories, where they routinely put in 12-hour shifts. In most factories a whistle signaled the start and end of a worker's day. As one shift left the factory, another came into it.

Working conditions in factories were often unsafe. Accidents resulted from many factors. The rapid pace of production and the use of dangerous machines caused many accidents. Poor lighting, polluted air, and worker fatigue were also responsible. Steel mills claimed the largest number of lives. Steel workers faced the dangers of molten metal and fast-moving overhead cranes. The noise of machines in the new factories was deafening.

A steel worker faced with these conditions for the first time said, "I stood numb, afraid to move, until a man came to me and led me out of the mill." The steel worker, however, came back. Because he needed the work, he forced himself to endure unpleasant and unsafe conditions.

In some places, particularly in the coal mining industry, workers were forced to live in company-owned housing and shop for goods in company-owned stores. Communities like this were called **company towns.** They were set up and run by a company for its employees. However, company towns were established to increase company profits, not to benefit workers. Employees returned most of their wages to the company in rent and store purchases. Their low wages were partially paid in **scrip,** certificates for use in the company store, which were useless anywhere else.

Workers in company towns easily fell into debt to the company. These debts further bound them to their employers. The company towns also made strikes or other protests difficult. If workers tried to organize for higher wages or better working conditions, they risked being fired from their jobs and evicted from their homes.

New Sources of Labor

Heavy industry required an army of unskilled workers. Many employers hired laborers and shopped for raw materials in the same way. One railroad official explained,

> **If I wanted boiler iron, I would go out on the market and buy it where I could get it cheapest, and if I wanted to employ men, I would do the same.**

Often the best "buys" were not men at all, but women and children who were paid far cheaper wages than the men. Between 1880 and 1900, the number of working women grew from 2.6 million to 8.6 million. By 1910 the number of child workers between the ages of 10 and 15 swelled to nearly two million.

The work that women did in the late 1800s varied widely. In large part it depended upon a woman's education and social class. When the typewriter and telephone came into wide use, middle-class women with high school educations moved into clerical jobs once held by men. They also took jobs in the growing numbers of department stores.

Many working women contributed to the incomes of their families. With men earning low wages, families found it difficult to get by on one income. Since men dominated jobs in heavy industries, such as mining and steel, women took jobs in the textile, food processing, and garment industries. Here they endured the same long hours and poor working conditions as men, but often at far lower wages.

Children received even lower pay. The use of machines had reduced the physical effort of many jobs. Employers gave these jobs to children for a fraction of the rate paid to adults. There were few protections for the children. Some states had child labor laws that set minimum ages and maximum working hours for children. However, these laws did not apply to industries that did business in more than one state. Most states did not rigorously enforce the laws. Mary Harris Jones, an early union organizer, described the working conditions endured by children in some mills:

> **Little girls and boys, barefooted, walked up and down between endless rows of spindles. They reached their little hands into the machinery to repair snapped threads. They crawled under the machinery to oil it. . . . Tiny babies of six years old with faces of sixty did an eight hour shift for ten cents a day.**

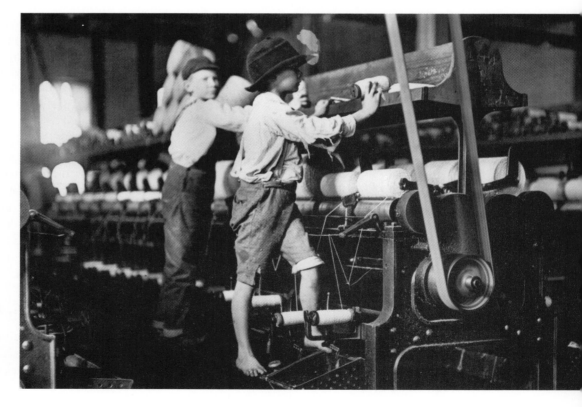

In 1910 almost two million children worked long hours in factories, mines, and fields. Six- and seven-year-olds often started work in factories at two o'clock in the morning. ▶

Even with the addition of women and children to the work force, booming industries needed more workers. They found willing laborers in the hundreds of thousands of immigrants arriving in the United States. To survive, these newcomers took the hardest and most physically demanding jobs because they saw the work as a short-term sacrifice for a long-term gain. They believed that someday things would get easier, perhaps not for themselves, but for their children.

African American men had long held some of the most labor intensive jobs. As immigration increased, fierce competition for work as laborers also increased. Competition for the same jobs led to growing hostility toward African Americans from native-born and immigrant white laborers. African American women were shut out of industrial work almost entirely. They were forced to take jobs as domestics, working as cooks and maids, earning half the wages of white women. Most lived in deep poverty.

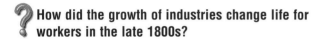 **How did the growth of industries change life for workers in the late 1800s?**

◆ LABORERS FORM UNIONS

Working long hours for low wages led some workers in the late 1800s to turn to labor unions for help. As industrial development raced ahead, the number of laborers increased dramatically. In the years following the Civil War, labor leaders talked of creating a national labor movement. To realize this goal, they would have to overcome resistance from employers. Companies imposed **lockouts** in which armies of private guards kept striking workers from entering the factories. Then they hired **scabs** to take their place. The word *scab* is a negative term for a person hired to replace a striking worker.

To prevent union organizers from working elsewhere, employers put their names on **blacklists** and sent the lists to other companies. Despite these efforts, employers could not stop workers from organizing to better their lives.

In 1869, nine Philadelphia garment cutters met in secret to form the Noble Order of the Knights of Labor. Their goal was to organize both skilled and unskilled workers into a single union. In 1881, the Knights extended membership to women over the age of 16. By 1886, membership in the Knights peaked at 700,000. Its numbers included some 50,000 white women and 60,000 African Americans.

▲ *Approximately 60,000 African Americans belonged to the Knights of Labor. Here, a delegate to a Knights' convention introduces Terence Powderly (center), the leader of the Knights.*

The Knights of Labor

The Knights of Labor fell apart after a violent incident in Chicago. In May 1886, union members went out on strike against the McCormick Harvester factory. When fights broke out at the factory, several workers who clashed with the police were killed. A group of Chicago radicals known as **anarchists,** or those who want to do away with all forms of government, organized a rally at Chicago's Haymarket Square. When police tried to break up the rally, somebody threw a bomb. After an exchange of gunfire between police and some of the protesters, about 100 people, including 70 police, lay injured. Seven of the police died.

To this day no one knows for sure who threw the bomb. However, a jury convicted eight anarchists on charges of conspiracy to commit murder. Four died by hanging, and one committed suicide. Because of a lack of clear-cut evidence, the governor of Illinois pardoned the remaining three anarchists.

Most American workers were not interested in violence and rejected the union. In addition to the basic issues of higher wages, fewer working hours, and safer working conditions, the Knights were also involved in political issues not directly related to working conditions. Furthermore, financial trouble depleted the union's resources. A series of failed strikes led to a sharp decline in Knight membership, and the union soon disappeared as a national force.

The American Federation of Labor

Two weeks after the Haymarket bombing, trade union leaders formed a new union, the American Federation of Labor (AFL). Its membership included 25 labor groups composed of about 150,000 members. The American Federation of Labor, unlike the Knights of Labor, sought to organize only skilled workers.

The AFL elected Samuel Gompers as its first president. Gompers, born in London, had learned the cigarmaker's trade before coming to the United States in 1863. He joined the Cigarmakers' Union in 1864 and became its president in 1877. Except for one year in the 1890s, Gompers remained the president of the AFL from 1886 until his death in 1924.

The AFL advocated a **closed shop,** or a business that hired only union members. It was responsible for the abolition of **yellow-dog contracts,** or contracts that required newly hired employees to promise never to join a labor union. The AFL focused on wages and hours—what workers called the "bread-and-butter" issues. It generally opposed the membership of women and Asians and did not actively recruit African Americans. However, some women and African Americans got into the AFL through membership in craft unions. The Ladies Federal Labor Union

Elizabeth Rodgers, holding her baby, was among the first women to join the Knights of Labor. ▼

Number 2703 received an AFL charter. Its outspoken leader, Elizabeth Morgan, wrote to Gompers,

> ❝ My education is but poor, but I will do the best I can, as I like many other children had to work when [I was] but 11 years old. I went to work in a mill and worked from 10 to 16 hours a day. For that reason I cannot read or write very well. ❞

Morgan was the only woman delegate at the 1894 AFL convention. Her forceful arguments convinced the convention to pass resolutions supporting school attendance laws for children and an eight-hour workday for women and children in manufacturing plants.

Under Gompers the AFL grew to more than one million members by 1901. The organization then began a series of boycotts and strikes to force employers to negotiate with union leaders.

❓ How did labor unions attempt to meet the needs of employees in the late 1800s?

◆ UNIONS ON STRIKE

Employers resisted unions, and the struggle between employers and workers grew. The late 1800s was a time marked by industrial strikes and violence.

The Homestead Strike

In 1892, Andrew Carnegie's steel company in Homestead, Pennsylvania, announced a wage cut. The union retaliated with a strike. The company tried to crush it by bringing in private armed guards to battle the strikers. When the strikers fired on the guards, people on both sides were killed. Eventually the strike was broken and the union acknowledged defeat. The company rehired only a few strikers, and Carnegie Steel remained nonunionized until the 1930s.

The Pullman Strike

The Pullman Strike was the last big strike of the 1800s. The strike was against the company run by George Pullman, the inventor and manufacturer of the Pullman sleeping cars. Pullman considered himself a friend of labor.

Workers felt otherwise. In 1894, an economic depression led Pullman to cut wages, while keeping

▲ In July 1894, armed federal troops were called in to break up the Pullman Strike. It took more than 14,000 police, state militia, and federal troops to end this violent strike.

rents and prices high in the company town he had set up for his workers. When workers decided to strike in protest, Pullman laid them off and shut down the company in a lockout.

News of the lockout caught the attention of Eugene Debs, founder of the American Railroad Union. Debs encouraged some 120,000 railroad workers throughout the nation to join in a sympathy strike with the Pullman workers. The walkout had crippling effects on the railroad industry.

To break the strike, the railroad appealed to the federal government for help. Using the reasoning that trains carried mail across state lines, President Grover Cleveland charged that the strike violated the restraint of trade clause in the Sherman Antitrust Act. He ordered all union members back on the job, sending in troops to back up the order.

When Debs refused to obey the order, federal troops arrested him, setting off a rash of violence. Strikers burned more than 700 railroad cars. By the time troops crushed the strike, seven people had died and dozens lay wounded.

The strike caused a major setback in the union movement. For nearly 30 years after the strike, the federal government followed the example set by President Cleveland and settled labor disputes in favor of factory owners. Not until the 1930s did government decisions begin to swing in the direction of the workers.

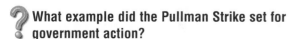 **What example did the Pullman Strike set for government action?**

Section 3 Review

Check Understanding

1. **Define** (a) company town (b) scrip (c) lockout (d) scab (e) blacklist (f) anarchist (g) closed shop (h) yellow-dog contract

2. **Explain** why manufacturers hired women and children whenever possible.

3. **Explain** the purpose and goals of labor unions.

4. **Discuss** the methods employers used to break unions.

Critical Thinking

Forming Generalizations How powerful were labor unions at the end of the 1800s?

Write About Economics

◆**Connecting Past and Present** Review the primary source quotations in this section that deal with the hardships factory workers faced in the late 1800s. Write an essay that compares how workers were treated with the ways workers are treated today.

Chapter 13
Review

CHAPTER SUMMARY

Section 1
A revolution in technology triggered a surge in U.S. economic growth after the Civil War. Expanding transportation and communication networks across the country led to the increased movement of people, products, and information as the nation entered a new industrial age.

Section 2
By the turn of the century, technology changed the United States from a nation of small businesses to a nation of large industry. Corporations provided a way to finance industrial growth. Many corporations tried to eliminate competition by controlling all aspects of an industry, and the government began to take actions to regulate big business.

Section 3
The growth of industry changed the way people worked. Workers faced harsh conditions in large factories with low pay. The reaction to these conditions led to the rise of a national labor movement, the formation of the American Federation of Labor, and industrial strikes.

Connecting ◆◆ Past and Present

How have technological changes made during your lifetime affected the way people work?

Using Vocabulary

Select the letter of the phrase that best completes each sentence.

1. The **Bessemer process** is (a) a technique for canning food; (b) an assembly line; (c) a cheap way to make large amounts of steel.

2. If you have a **patent,** you have (a) the sole right to your invention for a set period of time; (b) a plant for milling steel; (c) a ready work force that has no right to form a union.

3. **Rebates** are (a) partial refunds or discounts; (b) poorly paid immigrants or child workers; (c) the same as a monopoly.

4. A **corporation** is (a) a financing scheme; (b) the right to work; (c) a business that can raise money by selling stock.

5. **Stock** in a company is (a) sold to raise money for business operations; (b) available only to members of a trust; (c) a way to keep workers from having control of a company.

6. A **scab** is (a) a labor leader's word for a boss; (b) a union worker; (c) a negative label for a person hired to replace a striker.

7. **Anarchists** (a) are the same as labor leaders; (b) believe in labor unions; (c) oppose all government.

Check Understanding

1. **Summarize** the advances in technology that helped the U.S. economy grow after 1865.

2. **Describe** how the growth of railroads helped unite the country.

3. **List** three inventors and inventions that added to the communications and transportation revolution of the late 1800s.

4. **Describe** how some business owners raised money needed to expand their businesses in the late 1800s.

5. **Identify** the advantages of a corporation in financing the business expansion of the late 1800s.

6. **Identify** the differences between vertical integration and horizontal integration.

7. **Describe** changing conditions in factories after the machine age began.

8. **Explain** the causes of renewed interest in labor unions in the late 1800s.

9. **Summarize** why early actions to limit the power of big business failed.

10. **Discuss** why the struggle between workers and employers sometimes resulted in strikes.

Critical Thinking

1. **Analyzing** How did the revolution in technology help create a transportation network after the Civil War?

2. **Understanding Cause and Effect** What impact do you think railroads had on the development of communities that were not along the rights-of-way?

3. **Making Inferences** Why do you suppose the leaders of the AFL were not enthusiastic about recruiting women?

4. **Predicting Outcomes** What would be the impact of large numbers of immigrant factory workers joining the American Federation of Labor?

◆ **Connecting Past and Present** Should government today be concerned with the way corporations conduct their business? Explain.

Writing to Explain Cause and Effect

The late 1800s in the United States saw a series of dramatic changes in the way the country's businesses operated. **Write** an essay that explains what caused these changes and what resulted from them.

Interpreting the Timeline

Use the timeline on pages 250–251 to answer these questions.

1. In what year did the Queen of England mark her 50-year anniversary (Golden Jubilee)?

2. In what year did a union extend its membership to women?

3. What events on the timeline are related to either the completion of the transcontinental railroad in 1869 or the first public demonstration of the telephone?

Putting Skills to Work

INTERPRETING PRIMARY SOURCES

The primary source below is an account of working conditions in the 1800s by Leonora Barry, a member of the Knights of Labor. Read the excerpt and answer the questions that follow.

> **1877**—*Went to Auburn, NY, Feb. 20. I found the working-women of this city in a deplorable [awful] state, there being none of them organized. There were long hours, poor wages and the usual results consequent upon such a condition. Not among male employers alone in this city, but a woman in whose heart we would expect to find a little pity and compassion for the suffering of her own sex. . . . I found one who . . . owns and conducts an establishment in which is manufactured women's and children's wear. Upon accepting a position in her factory, an employee is compelled to purchase a sewing machine . . . and the thread for doing the work . . . [After paying a weekly sum for these items] the unfortunate victim has $2.50 wherewith to board, clothe and care for herself generally; and it is only experts who can make even this.*

1. What is Barry's attitude toward the woman who owns the clothing manufacturing firm?

2. Based on what you know about labor in the late 1800s, do you think this report is accurate? Explain.

 *Portfolio Project*

SCRIPT WRITING

Working with several classmates, create a script about one of the following subjects: a revolution in technology, a monopoly hurting a small company, or workers organizing for their rights. Use library resources and information in the chapter to write the script. Focus on making people and events memorable by including an interesting conflict and realistic dialogue. Ask several classmates to play parts, and perform a dramatic reading for the class.

Chapter 14
Cities and Immigration
1870–1920

CHAPTER PREVIEW

Section 1 Immigrants from Eastern and Southern Europe

Beginning in the mid-1800s, a flood of new immigrants from eastern and southern Europe arrived in the United States, many of them passing through Ellis Island, in New York Harbor.

Section 2 Immigrants from Asia and Latin America

As immigrants from Europe began their journey, others from Asia and Latin America made their way to the west coast of the United States.

Section 3 The Growth of Cities

Immigration and industrialization encouraged the economic expansion of American cities, which led to growth in industry and technology.

Section 4 Life in American Cities

Rapid urban growth resulted in housing problems and unfair labor practices for immigrants, stirring reformers to take action on their behalf.

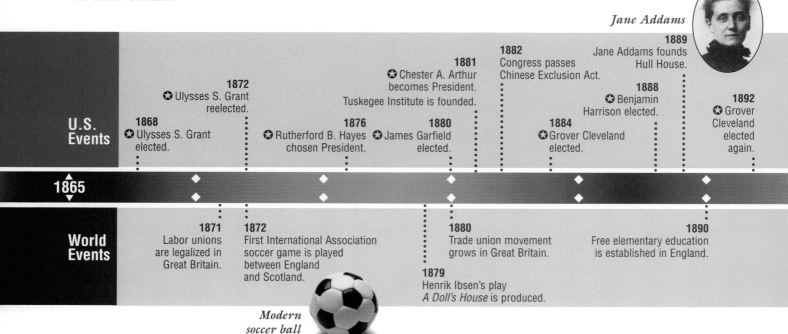

Jane Addams

U.S. Events

1868 ✪ Ulysses S. Grant elected.

1872 ✪ Ulysses S. Grant reelected.

1876 ✪ Rutherford B. Hayes chosen President.

1880 ✪ James Garfield elected.

1881 ✪ Chester A. Arthur becomes President. Tuskegee Institute is founded.

1882 Congress passes Chinese Exclusion Act.

1884 ✪ Grover Cleveland elected.

1888 ✪ Benjamin Harrison elected.

1889 Jane Addams founds Hull House.

1892 ✪ Grover Cleveland elected again.

1865

World Events

1871 Labor unions are legalized in Great Britain.

1872 First International Association soccer game is played between England and Scotland.

1879 Henrik Ibsen's play *A Doll's House* is produced.

1880 Trade union movement grows in Great Britain.

1890 Free elementary education is established in England.

Modern soccer ball

Portfolio Project

A LETTER HOME

An immigrant's first experiences in a new land often form impressions that last a lifetime. Imagine the journey and the anticipation, confusion, and excitement of seeing your new home for the first time. In letters to relatives in the homeland, nineteenth-century immigrants wrote of the experiences that overwhelmed them upon reaching the new land. As you read about this age of immigration, watch for the kinds of experiences these immigrants faced. At the end of the chapter, you will write a letter home describing what it meant to settle in the United States at the beginning of the twentieth century.

▲ *The Statue of Liberty welcomed many immigrants to the United States.* ◆ **Connecting Past and Present** *What do you think these immigrants were thinking when they saw the statue? Why do thousands of people visit the Statue of Liberty today?*

Triangle Shirtwaist factory fire

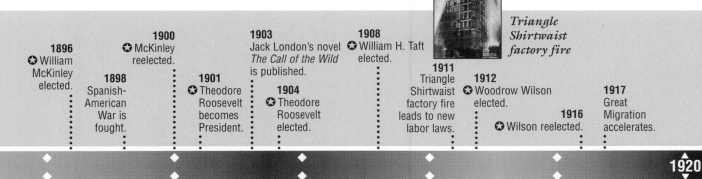

1896
✪ William McKinley elected.

1898
Spanish-American War is fought.

1900
✪ McKinley reelected.

1901
✪ Theodore Roosevelt becomes President.

1903
Jack London's novel *The Call of the Wild* is published.

1904
✪ Theodore Roosevelt elected.

1908
✪ William H. Taft elected.

1911
Triangle Shirtwaist factory fire leads to new labor laws.

1912
✪ Woodrow Wilson elected.

1916
✪ Wilson reelected.

1917
Great Migration accelerates.

1920

1896
Klondike gold rush begins in Canada.

1898
Cuba becomes independent.

1903
Madame Curie receives Nobel Prize for physics.

1910
Revolution continues in Mexico.

1911
Manchu dynasty overthrown in China.

Madame Curie

Gold rush tools

Immigrants from Eastern and Southern Europe

PREVIEW

Objectives

- To describe the reasons for European immigration at the end of the 1800s

- To discuss the problems that immigrants faced, particularly in cities

- To explain the steps taken by immigrants to ease the difficulties of adjusting to American life

Vocabulary

scapegoat
pogrom
steerage

The story of the United States is the story of immigrants: why they came to this country and how they have shaped its history through the centuries. Time and again, leaders have reminded Americans of their immigrant past. "We are, one and all, immigrants or sons and daughters of immigrants," said President Dwight D. Eisenhower in the 1950s.

The newcomers who arrived in the United States in the late 1800s and early 1900s came mostly from countries in southern and eastern Europe—countries such as Italy, Greece, Russia, Czechoslovakia, Poland, and Hungary. Americans called the wave of people arriving at this time the "new immigrants" because they came from different places than had earlier immigrants. Most of the "old immigrants," who had arrived in the 1700s and early 1800s, had come from countries in western and northern Europe, such as England, Scotland, Ireland, and Germany.

◆ THE NEW IMMIGRANTS

Throughout the 1700s and early 1800s, hopes of a better life drew millions of immigrants across the Atlantic, as shown on the map on page 273. Immigration from northern and western Europe

peaked in the 1840s and 1850s. These immigrants helped settle areas of the American frontier, energize the growing number of cities, and begin building the transportation networks that would link the nation.

By 1885 the country was begining to welcome growing numbers of immigrants from countries in southern and eastern Europe. While immigrants continued to come from northern and western Europe, by the early 1900s they were outnumbered by these "new immigrants," as shown on the pie charts below. For almost 30 years, Italians, Slavs, Greeks, Russians, Armenians, and others immigrated to the United States in large numbers. By 1920 the foreign-born population of the United States totaled more than 14 million people, out of a total U.S. population of 106 million.

The new immigrants included people of many different religious traditions. They introduced their religious faiths, including Roman Catholicism, Eastern Orthodoxy, and Judaism to parts of the United States. The levels of education of the new immigrants varied, from schoolmasters to those who were unable to read and write. Their religion, customs, and language made them seem strange to many Americans.

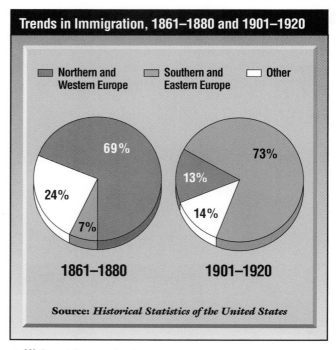

Trends in Immigration, 1861–1880 and 1901–1920

- Northern and Western Europe
- Southern and Eastern Europe
- Other

1861–1880: 69%, 24%, 7%

1901–1920: 73%, 13%, 14%

Source: *Historical Statistics of the United States*

▲ **History** *These pie charts show trends in immigration from 1861 to 1880 and from 1901 to 1920.* **Interpreting the Charts** *According to the charts, how did immigration from northern and western Europe change?*

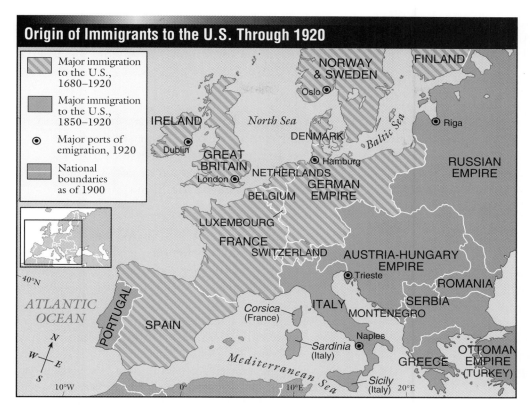

Origin of Immigrants to the U.S. Through 1920

Major immigration to the U.S., 1680–1920

Major immigration to the U.S., 1850–1920

Major ports of emigration, 1920

National boundaries as of 1900

◀ **Geography** *This map shows patterns of European immigration from 1680 to 1920.* **Interpreting the Map** *During which years did many people immigrate to the United States from Italy?*

Leaving European Homelands

As with earlier immigrants, including the American colonists of the seventeenth century, people left their European homelands for a variety of reasons. Many of the new immigrants left because of overpopulation and lack of economic opportunity. Personal freedom and abundant land attracted many to America.

Others left their homelands because of religious persecution. This was especially true of Jews who had lived in Russia and eastern Europe. In Russia, the government used Jews as **scapegoats**—people unfairly blamed for a bad situation or a problem. Scapegoating sometimes occurs when a country experiences economic and political unrest. Jews became the object of prejudice, with Russian law forcing them to live in separate towns in a region called the *Pale of Settlement.* Here, Jews often became targets for **pogroms,** or organized attacks on unarmed people. The threat of violence and death led nearly one third of all Jews in Russia and eastern Europe to leave the region. Most looked to one place for freedom—the United States.

Going to America

Advertisements by U.S. railroad and steamship companies beginning in the mid-1800s, encouraged people to come to the United States. These advertisements told of cheap land on the prairies and numerous jobs in growing U.S. industries. To encourage passengers, steamship lines lowered their prices. Those willing to travel in **steerage,** a large open area beneath the ship's deck, could purchase a ticket for $15—about one month's wage for some passengers. Thousands took advantage of these offers.

Immigrants who packed into steerage spent the entire two- or three-week journey tossed about in an overcrowded, unsanitary area. In recalling the trip, one woman wrote,

> The ship heaved and turned. People threw up, dishes fell, women screamed . . . but I didn't care what happened. I was going to America!

Immigrants entered the United States through several ports. However, about seven out of every ten arrivals from Europe sailed into New York Harbor. Those who arrived after 1892 first landed at Ellis Island, near Liberty Island, the location of the Statue of Liberty. They could see the statue, erected in 1886, as a symbol of hope and refuge.

Nearly two thirds of all nineteenth-century immigrants were males between the ages of 15 and 39.

A large percentage of them could not read and write in their native languages. Among those who reported occupations, almost one half listed a skilled trade, while the remainder were farmers. Because many immigrants had little money for further transportation, they often settled near the ports of entry, in cities such as New York City, New York, or Newark, New Jersey. A large number, however, traveled inland to live at railroad and industrial centers, such as Cleveland, Detroit, Milwaukee, or Chicago.

Of those immigrants who came to the United States seeking free land and rich soil, most never realized this dream. By the late 1800s, the era of frontier settlement was drawing to a close. The farmland promised by many railroad and steamship lines had already been carved up into large farms and ranches. Would-be farmers found that they did not have the money to buy land, and instead settled in midwestern cities to pursue other work.

What contributed to the rise in immigration from southern and eastern Europe in the late 1800s?

◆ A NEW LIFE

The wave of new arrivals had an enormous impact on the cities where they settled, causing the population to soar. For example, in 1890, New York City had twice as many Irish residents as Dublin, Ireland; as many Germans as Hamburg, Germany; half as many Italians as Naples, Italy; and two-and-a-half times as many Jews as Warsaw, Poland. That same year, four out of five children in the New York City area had either been born in another country or were the children of immigrants.

Because cities were populated by immigrants from so many different backgrounds, neighborhoods reflecting each group's culture and origin emerged. People who shared the same customs, language, and religion felt they belonged to the same community. Although these neighborhoods, sometimes called ghettos, often had overcrowded tenements, they helped immigrants adjust to the United States.

Adjusting to a New Land

During the first difficult months of adjustment to life in the United States, many immigrants struggled to learn the English language. Peddlers, landlords, and employment agencies charged them inflated prices for their goods. Other immigrants were targets of insults hurled by native-born Americans. Such practices caused one immigrant to write these words of caution to a friend back home:

> " When you land in America, you will find many who will offer their services, but beware of them because there are so many rascals who make it their business to cheat the immigrants. "

Difficult living conditions also created stress for immigrants. Many immigrants lived in almost windowless apartments called railroad flats, so named because the rooms connected in a straight line, like the cars of a railroad train. Many of the flats lacked plumbing and heating. Some immigrant families lived in tenement houses with poor sanitation and little space for each family member.

The jobs offered to most immigrants, in factories, warehouses, and ship and train yards, required few skills but a great deal of physical labor. It was often the new immigrants who paved streets, dug sewers and subways, and built bridges in eastern cities. For the first time in their lives, many of the immigrants worked according to the clock instead of the rising and setting of the sun, as was the custom throughout rural Europe.

Study Hint

A word's denotation, or dictionary definition, is often different from its connotation, or suggested meaning. For example, many people think the word peddler is a negative term for a kind of salesperson. However, the dictionary meaning is "one who offers merchandise for sale along the street or from door to door." Always check a dictionary to find the denotation of a word.

◄ *These immigrants waited in line on Ellis Island for a ferry to take them to New York City. From there, many boarded trains to other cities.*

Living in Immigrant Communities

The motto of many immigrants to the United States was "cooperate and survive." In some ethnic neighborhoods, immigrants pooled their money to form self-help associations. The New York Hebrew Free Loan Society, for example, founded in 1892, gave loans of $10 to $200 to Jewish immigrants who wanted to set up small businesses in New York City. In Bridgeport, Connecticut, Italian immigrant Pasquale Cruci helped found a medical and life insurance fund for fellow Italian immigrants in the area. "I felt that the Italian people of this city should have some security from death and accidents," explained Cruci.

Gradually through their children's schools and then through newspapers, marketplaces, and work environments, immigrants were introduced to American ways of doing things, and also to the English language. Learning English helped newcomers blend into American culture, making it easier for them to find jobs, raise their families, and socialize with other Americans. In time, immigrants learned to cook American foods, sew American fashions, and sing American tunes. At the same time they also contributed their native foods, fashions, and songs to the culture of the United States.

How did living together in neighborhoods help immigrants to adjust to American life?

Section 1 Review

Check Understanding

1. **Define** (a) scapegoat (b) pogrom (c) steerage

2. **Identify** the conditions that led large numbers of Jews to leave Russia and eastern Europe.

3. **Discuss** some of the problems new immigrants faced in adjusting to life in America.

4. **Explain** the appeal of immigrant neighborhoods to newcomers to the United States.

Critical Thinking

Connecting Past and Present How are the problems faced by today's immigrants similar to and different from those faced by previous immigrants?

Write About Culture

Write an essay in which you describe why many immigrants were willing to sacrifice the comfort and security they had known in their homelands for the chance to come to the United States.

BUILDING *SKILLS*

Making Valid Generalizations: The Age of Immigration

Making generalizations means that you extend meaning beyond the specific facts and ideas you read about. Generalizing allows you to connect information you have learned in a broader, less specific way. You add up facts and details and draw some general ideas from that particular information. A generalization is valid, or sound, when it is broad enough to apply to a number of different examples of a group or topic. A sound generalization is also logical and based on facts. For example, based on what you have read in this chapter, you may generalize that many nineteenth-century immigrants suffered great hardships.

Here's How

Follow these steps to make a valid generalization:

1. Focus on a topic and compile a list of relevant facts about the topic.

2. Study the facts and find a single feature that is true of all examples of the topic. If there is no relationship among the facts, then you should not try to make a generalization.

3. Make a general statement based on the facts. Accurate generalizations often have one of the following clue words: *many, most, often, usually, some, few,* and *sometimes.* Faulty generalizations may include the words *all, none, always, never,* or *every.*

Here's Why

Without generalizations, history would not have much meaning. Isolated facts are not memorable or even important until they can be unified to show relationships and patterns. This skill can help you clarify your understanding of material you have read.

Practice the Skill

Try making a valid generalization about why immigrants came to the United States during the mid- to late 1800s. First, copy the diagram below into your notebook to help you organize your facts. Then use the steps in *Here's How* to write a valid generalization based on the facts.

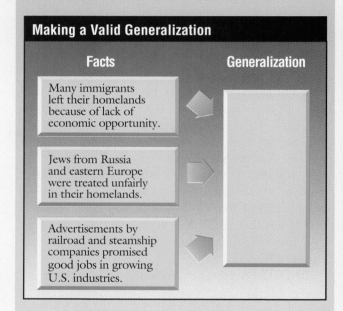

Making a Valid Generalization

Facts / **Generalization**

Many immigrants left their homelands because of lack of economic opportunity.

Jews from Russia and eastern Europe were treated unfairly in their homelands.

Advertisements by railroad and steamship companies promised good jobs in growing U.S. industries.

Apply the Skill

Turn the following statements into valid generalizations by revising the statements and supplying facts.

1. The presence of neighborhoods of immigrants triggered uncontrollable panic among the native-born population in every American city.

2. All Americans feared the growing number of immigrants who practiced religions different from their own.

Immigrants from Asia and Latin America

PREVIEW

Objectives

- To describe the reasons why large numbers of Asian immigrants came to the United States

- To evaluate the reasons for a rise of anti-immigrant feeling against Asians

- To explain why people from Mexico, Puerto Rico, and Cuba emigrated to the United States

Vocabulary

migrant
ethnic
detention center

As immigrants from Europe, Asia, the Caribbean, and Mexico poured into the United States, some Americans feared that the new arrivals would not be able to assimilate into American society. Others resented the newcomers because they competed for jobs. Some opponents of immigration demanded that the government eliminate immigration into the United States or at least lessen the number of people allowed to enter. Beginning in the 1880s, the government essentially excluded Chinese immigrants and severely limited the number of European and Japanese immigrants.

◆ FROM ASIA TO AMERICA

When the United States acquired California from Mexico in 1848, it welcomed Asian immigrants, especially those from China. Some policy makers saw Chinese immigrants as a key to the region's future. "No people in all of the East are so well adapted for clearing wild lands and raising every species of agricultural product as the Chinese," wrote one government official.

In China, labor recruiters, or people paid to bring laborers to America, painted a glowing picture of the United States. One brochure circulated in Chinese ports declared,

> Americans are very rich people. They want the [Chinese] to come.... You will have great pay, large houses and food and clothing of the finest description.... It is a nice country.... Money is plentiful in America.

Immigrants from China

News of the 1848 California gold rush reinforced the excitement generated by labor recruiters in China. Until 1860 about two thirds of the Chinese population in the United States labored in the gold mines. The majority of these workers had paid their own fares to the United States. They planned to work for a short while, then return to China with the money they earned.

Many Chinese eventually settled in western cities. When mining began to decline in the 1860s, some helped build the first transcontinental railroad. When it was completed in 1869, thousands of these workers moved to San Francisco to find work. By 1870 the city had a Chinese population of more than 12,000, making it the center of Chinese culture in the United States. Wherever Chinese people settled in large numbers, they built neighborhoods known as Chinatowns.

As with other immigrant groups, Chinese laborers, largely men, were an important part of the work force. By the 1870s they made up nearly 75 percent of San Francisco's woolen-mill workers and almost 90 percent of the city's cigarmakers. Others took agricultural jobs in the San Joaquin and Sacramento river deltas. Draining swamps and building irrigation ditches, they were among the laborers who turned the area into one of the most productive farming regions in the nation.

Immigrants from Japan

The Japanese immigration boom began in the 1880s when the Japanese government allowed laborers to travel to Hawaii, then an independent nation. There, workers on American-owned sugar plantations could earn six times more than they could in Japan.

When the United States acquired Hawaii in 1898, some Japanese **migrants,** or workers who travel from job to job, headed to the mainland. Between 1885 and 1924, about 300,000 Japanese immigrants came directly to the continental United States. Many settled in California, where they took jobs in agriculture, in railroad construction, or in canneries, which are factories that produce canned

Other Asian Groups

The first Korean immigrants came to Hawaii and then to the California coast of the United States between 1903 and 1905. Small in number, Koreans generally were absorbed into other Asian communities. Initially, they worked at the same kinds of low-paying jobs as Chinese and Japanese immigrants.

Filipino immigrants began coming to the United States as early as 1899. Because the Philippines were under American rule after that year, Filipinos were able to bypass the usual immigration procedures. Escaping from the poverty of their homeland, many Filipinos migrated throughout the West, following the crops. Others worked in canneries in Washington and Alaska.

? Why did large numbers of Chinese and Japanese immigrants come to the United States?

◆ OPPOSITION TO IMMIGRATION

The hostility directed toward Japanese immigrants by some Americans reflected a widespread opposition to immigration in general. This opposition had been growing steadily since the mid-1800s. Many native-born Americans liked to think of the United States as a huge "melting pot" where different immigrant cultures would blend together and into American society. However, the reality was that many of the newcomers chose to maintain their own cultural identity.

The strong presence of **ethnic** neighborhoods, or those based on a common racial, national, religious, or cultural tradition, triggered anti-immigrant feelings among many native-born Americans. These prejudices grew as competition for jobs increased. The result was renewed nativism, which put the interests of native-born Americans above those of immigrants.

The Rise of Nativism

Nativism was not a new reaction. It had gained force at the height of the German and Irish immigrations of the 1840s and 1850s. It now reemerged as a reaction against the immigrants arriving at the close of the 1800s. Some Protestants, for example, feared the growing number of Catholics and Jews arriving from southern and eastern Europe. These religions were unfamiliar, and anxiety of the unknown produced fear. While many supported the admission of immigrants

▲ By 1870, more than 100,000 Chinese had emigrated to the United States. Many were men who hoped to return eventually to their families in China.

goods. Their goal was to earn enough money to fulfill their dreams of buying farmland.

By 1920 the value of Japanese American farm products was more than $67 million—about 10 percent of the value of all California crops. Japanese American farmers grew nearly 70 percent of California's strawberries. The success of Japanese immigrants was due in part to the completion of the transcontinental railroad in 1869. Farming became more profitable in California when fruits and vegetables could be shipped to markets in the East all year long.

The success of Japanese immigrants triggered jealousy among some native-born Americans. Newspapers used the term "Yellow Peril" to describe the Japanese. This racial insult implied that somehow Japanese immigrants threatened the United States.

from the European nations that had built the 13 colonies, they opposed admission of immigrants from other parts of the world, including Asia.

On the east coast, nativists focused their efforts on curbing immigration from southern and eastern Europe. The Immigration Restriction League, formed in 1894, demanded that immigrants from those regions pass a literacy test, a test of ability to read English, before entering the United States. In 1896, Congress passed such a law, but President Grover Cleveland vetoed it.

Anti-Asian Policies

On the west coast, prejudice fell heaviest on Asian immigrants, particularly those from China. In addition to speaking a different language and practicing unfamiliar customs, Chinese men made little effort to assimilate to American styles. They wore their hair in long pigtails, called *queues,* and wore clothes from their home country—wide-brimmed hats and quilted jackets.

A depression from 1873 to 1878 increased anti-Chinese sentiment as native-born workers grew concerned that they would lose their jobs to Chinese workers. Violent anti-Chinese riots erupted throughout California. Meanwhile, some American labor leaders called for a ban on Chinese immigration. In 1882 the U.S. government passed the Chinese Exclusion Act. The act denied citizenship to those born in China and banned immigration of Chinese laborers for ten years. It was renewed through 1902, when it was made "permanent" until it was repealed in 1943.

The Chinese Exclusion Act did not prevent entry to those who had previously lived in the United States or who had family already living in the country. In 1910 the government built a **detention center** on Angel Island in San Francisco Bay. Here immigrants could be held temporarily until their claims of prior residence or relationship to U.S. citizens could be examined.

With most Chinese excluded from entering the country, Japanese immigrants stepped in to take jobs once filled by Chinese laborers. However, they too soon fell victim to anti-Asian attitudes. In 1906, efforts were made to exclude Japanese children from public schools in San Francisco.

Soon after, the United States negotiated a so-called "Gentlemen's Agreement" with Japan. Under this agreement only the parents, wives, and children of Japanese people already living in the United States were permitted entry. In exchange, the U.S. government convinced officials in San Francisco to drop efforts to exclude Asian children from the city's free public schools.

 What actions did nativists take to curb immigration to the United States?

◆ IMMIGRATION FROM LATIN AMERICA

As the United States limited Asian immigration, increasing numbers of people from Latin America began to emigrate to the United States. The greatest number of newcomers were from Mexico, which had won its independence from Spain in 1821. Other Latin American immigrants came from the islands of Puerto Rico and Cuba, which gained independence from Spain in 1898.

Anti-immigration restrictions passed by Congress in the late 1800s and early 1900s applied mainly to Asians and not to Latin Americans. As a result, the United States experienced the start of a huge influx of largely Spanish-speaking, Roman Catholic immigrants. Their arrival signaled the start of a movement of people that would continue throughout the 1900s.

Mexican Immigrants

Like other immigrants, Mexicans saw the United States as a land of opportunity. They lived close enough to its borders to hear positive reports from friends and relatives who already lived there. Many states—such as Texas, California, Nevada, Arizona, and New Mexico—had large Spanish-speaking populations that had been there for generations before the United States acquired the area in the 1840s.

In 1902, Congress passed the Newlands National Reclamation Act to fund the irrigation of southwestern lands. This act turned millions of acres of desert into fertile farmland and created new jobs. In 1902 alone, about 3 percent of the population of Mexico entered the United States through El Paso, Texas.

In 1910, revolution broke out in Mexico. War and economic disorder forced many Mexicans to flee. The United States offered them opportunities for jobs in mining, railroad construction, and especially farming. In orchards and fields throughout the Southwest, Mexican workers picked artichokes, grapefruits, and melons. Between 1910 and 1919, during the years of the Mexican Revolution, approximately 185,000 Mexicans entered the United States.

These children belonged to the Cuban Club in Ybor City, Florida. The town was built by Vincente Ybor, who employed many Cubans in his cigar factory. ▶

Immigrants from Cuba and Puerto Rico

By 1860, Cuba was one of Spain's last colonies in the Americas. Efforts by Cubans to throw off Spanish rule resulted in fighting between Cuba and Spain, beginning in the 1860s.

In 1898 the United States entered into the conflict to help free Cuba of Spanish rule in the Spanish-American War. After Spain lost the war, Cuba gained its independence. During the late 1800s, many Cubans emigrated to the United States to escape the fighting and discontent in their homeland. They settled in cigarmaking centers in New York City and near Tampa, Florida.

Like Cuba, the island of Puerto Rico was one of Spain's last colonies in the Americas. As a result of the U.S. victory in the Spanish-American War, the United States gained possession of Puerto Rico in 1898. Soon after, Puerto Ricans began moving to the United States to look for job opportunities. After 1917, however, Puerto Ricans were not immigrants. In 1917, Congress passed the Jones Act, which granted all Puerto Ricans U.S. citizenship. Puerto Ricans could move freely to and from the U.S. mainland. Many took advantage of this and moved to New York City, which still has one of the mainland's largest Puerto Rican populations.

Why did people from Latin America emigrate to the United States in the late 1800s and early 1900s?

Section 2 Review

Check Understanding

1. **Define** (a) migrant (b) ethnic (c) detention center

2. **Explain** why nativists tried to restrict immigration from southern and eastern Europe.

3. **Identify** the steps Congress took to exclude Chinese immigrants from the United States.

4. **Discuss** why Mexican immigrants came to the United States in growing numbers after 1910.

5. **Identify** reasons why Cubans and Puerto Ricans came to the United States in the 1800s.

Critical Thinking

Analyzing Why did newcomers to the United States tend to move into ethnic neighborhoods?

Write About Social Issues

◆ **Connecting Past and Present** Write an essay explaining what factors today could help overcome racial or religious prejudice from the past.

280 ◆ Unit 4

Section 3

The Growth of Cities

PREVIEW

Objectives

• To analyze the reasons why U.S. cities grew dramatically in the years following the Civil War

• To explain how cities became cultural and entertainment centers

• To describe actions taken by African Americans to organize to gain their rights

Vocabulary

entrepreneur	discrimination
suburb	Great Migration
circulation	de facto
vaudeville	

Between 1870 and 1920, the number of Americans living in cities swelled from 10 million to 54 million. By 1900, New York City's 3.4 million people equaled the nation's entire urban population in 1850. No wonder one observer exclaimed, "We live in an age of great cities!"

◆ THE LURE OF CITIES

Like giant magnets, cities drew people from all over the United States and abroad. Cities became the new frontier—places that held out opportunities to build a new life. Cities represented jobs, adventure, and a chance to glimpse the marvels of a new technological age.

The new city dwellers came from many places. While immigration brought millions of newcomers into urban areas, so did migration within the United States. In the late 1800s, thousands of people left farms and small towns for the jobs and higher wages found in cities. So great was the migration that some farming communities in New England disappeared altogether.

There were a number of reasons for the rapid migration from farms to cities. First, large farm machinery eliminated farm jobs by doing work that previously had been done by hand. Second, low crop prices and high debts made it difficult for small farmers to compete with the huge farms of the Great Plains. Third, birth rates in rural areas were high, while death rates dropped because of improved medical care. There was no work for the extra rural population, so much of it moved into the cities.

Buildings That Scraped the Sky

Cities grew so rapidly that some neighborhoods became overcrowded fire traps, with wooden houses packed tightly together. In October 1871, Chicago, with a population of nearly 300,000 people, went up in flames. The raging blaze destroyed more than 61,000 buildings and left nearly 100,000 people homeless.

Out of that disaster emerged a miracle in city planning. The destruction gave architects a chance to rebuild Chicago's business district. They chose to

The first metal-frame skyscraper was the Home Insurance Company in Chicago. Built in the mid-1880s, its stories were supported by iron girders. ▼

THE CHICAGO BUILDING OF THE HOME INSURANCE CO. OF NEW YORK

experiment with a new building style known as the skyscraper—a building of many stories supported by steel frames. The skyscraper grew out of the ideas of Louis L. Sullivan, an architect who moved to Chicago in hopes of rebuilding the city. Sullivan imagined that modern cities could grow upward as well as outward.

Three innovations made the skyscraper possible: internal steel frames, fireproofing, and electric elevators. In the past, tall buildings had been entirely supported by their walls. Now engineers used steel beams to build a central skeleton. The beams supported the entire weight of the building, including the walls. To fireproof the structure, clay tiles were placed between the exterior and interior walls. Finally, to make the structure practical, electric elevators were installed.

Before the Civil War, no building stood more than five stories high. Sullivan erected a building in Chicago that stood 22 stories high. **Entrepreneurs,** or business people who take risks in hope of earning a profit, took advantage of the opportunities offered by tall buildings. Now they needed to invest in only a small piece of land to build a huge vertical building. Skylines once dominated by church spires became studded with office buildings and apartments.

Streetcars and Suspension Bridges

While skyscrapers made it possible for cities to expand upward, other innovations made it possible for them to grow outward. In the 1800s, horses pulled streetcars over iron rails in the streets. Then, in the 1880s, an electric streetcar moved out of Thomas Edison's idea factory at Menlo Park, New Jersey, and onto American streets.

Frank J. Sprague, who worked for Edison, designed an electric motorcar that drew its power from an overhead wire. In 1888, Sprague won permission to install a 17-mile line in Richmond, Virginia. Ten years later, 40,000 electric streetcars were in use in cities all over the United States.

Before the streetcar, most cities were confined to a two- or three-mile square area—the distance a person might reasonably walk to work. Electric streetcars allowed people to commute, or travel to work from communities at the edges of cities, called **suburbs.** In 1860, for example, Chicago occupied only about 17 square miles. By 1890 the city and its outlying suburbs covered more than 178 square miles. By this time nearly 70,000 people commuted into Chicago each day from suburbs. In New York City, more than 100,000 commuters made their way into the city daily.

When the Brooklyn Bridge was completed in 1883, it was the largest suspension bridge in the world. It cost $15 million to build. ▶

Technology also made it possible for cities to span rivers. In one of the great architectural feats of the late 1800s, John A. Roebling and his son Washington Roebling built the Brooklyn Bridge. It was a 16-year effort that cost the father's life and the son's health. When the bridge opened in 1883, it crossed 1,595 feet of New York's East River and connected New York City to Brooklyn. The towers from which the bridge was suspended rose higher than any structure made by humans except the great pyramids of Egypt. Soon, suspension bridges reached across other bodies of water in cities such as Newark, New Jersey, and San Francisco, California, allowing cities to expand even more.

 What technological developments contributed to the expansion of cities?

◆ URBAN CULTURE

The attraction of the city was more than jobs. Cities also provided great possibilities for entertainment, education, and culture.

A Golden Age for Reading

People received news about local, national, and international events from newspapers. A big lure for buying a newspaper was its advertisements. People wanted to see all the new products and find out about the latest prices. In 1879, Philadelphia's Wanamaker's department store placed the first full-page newspaper advertisement. In 1900, advertisers spent more than $95 million on newspaper ads. By 1919 the total climbed to $500 million.

Advertisers placed their ads in the newspapers that had the largest **circulation,** or number of readers. Joseph Pulitzer, a Hungarian immigrant, discovered a way to increase sales of his newspaper. Pulitzer, the publisher of the New York *World*, included human-interest stories as well as news. He also was the first to bring a sports section, a women's page, and comics into newspapers.

Readers liked what they read. In just one year, the *World's* circulation climbed from 20,000 to 100,000. By the 1890s, it reached more than one million. Soon another entrepreneur named William Randolph Hearst bought the New York *Journal* and started competing with Pulitzer.

Increased leisure time gave people an opportunity to read more books. Seeking an escape from the sometimes harsh realities of the cities, readers turned to

▲ *Some city people spent their leisure time on rides at amusement parks, such as this one at Coney Island in Brooklyn, New York.*

romance and adventure. Zane Grey's novels about the American West and Edgar Rice Burroughs' *Tarzan* tales attracted many people. Mark Twain's *Huckleberry Finn* appealed to those who enjoyed humor, while more serious readers liked the novels of William Dean Howells, which explore the greed of American businesses and the plight of industrial workers to meet that need.

A natural outgrowth of more reading was the need for libraries. Industrialist Andrew Carnegie donated $60 million to meet that need. By 1900 there were about 9,000 public libraries in the United States.

Mass Entertainment

The growth of newspaper readership was one result of leisure time, which increased in the late 1800s due to improved transportation and labor-saving devices, such as the washing machine and gas cooking range. Americans spent this extra time in a variety of ways. People poured into amusement parks, such as Coney Island in Brooklyn, New York; attended circuses; and frequented theaters to watch live entertainment, such as **vaudeville.** Vaudeville was a variety show that featured singing, dancing, and comedy skits.

The most popular entertainment of all was sports. In the 1890s a bicycling craze swept the nation. To take part in the craze, women replaced their dresses with shorter split skirts that would not get caught in the bicycle chains. Suffragist leader Susan B. Anthony declared, "I think [cycling] has done more to emancipate women than anything in the world."

The bicycle changed American society in numerous ways. Not only did it add a new dimension to women's wardrobes, but it also provided a new sense of independence and mobility for young people.

Spectator sports were equally popular, especially boxing and baseball. Of the two, baseball had the wider appeal. By 1903 the United States had two professional leagues—the National League and the American League—and they competed in the first World Series. Baseball had become what historians called a "national pastime." It also grew into a big business. By the late 1800s, most large cities had a team of their own.

Public Education

The cities also offered opportunities for Americans who wanted to advance their education. In a time when few nations offered public education, the United States was expanding its system of public schools and colleges.

By the early 1900s, the United States had made strides toward educating all its youth. Between the late 1870s and 1900, the number of public high schools in the nation rose from 160 to 514. During these same years, 31 states passed laws that required children between the ages of 8 and 14 to receive 12 to 16 weeks of education per year. By 1900 almost 75 percent of children between those ages attended public schools.

Although few Americans attended universities, the opportunity for higher education began to grow. Between 1880 and 1900, nearly 150 colleges and universities opened. Almost 70 colleges developed as a result of the Morrill Land Grant Act of 1862. This act gave large grants of land to states to establish colleges to teach "agriculture and the mechanical arts." Famous land-grant colleges founded as a result of the act include Cornell University and the state university systems of Wisconsin, California, Minnesota, and Illinois.

These new and expanded educational opportunities rarely benefited African Americans. Most universities refused to accept their applications. Segregation also kept African American children in run-down schools or out of school entirely. In 1890, nearly two thirds of all African Americans could not read and write. Conditions like these caused African American leaders to organize against **discrimination**, or the unjust treatment of one individual by another based on prejudice.

What cultural and educational attractions did cities hold for people?

◆ AFRICAN AMERICANS UNITE

Since the end of Reconstruction, African Americans had faced particular difficulties in the South. Southern states had imposed Jim Crow laws that restricted voting and imposed segregation. African Americans protesting these laws faced the threat of being insulted, beaten, run off their land, or even lynched by organized groups of whites, such as the Ku Klux Klan.

Violence, poverty, racism, and a lack of jobs and educational opportunities caused about 200,000 African Americans to leave the South and head to the North between 1890 and 1900. This was the beginning of what has been called the **Great Migration.** After 1917, when the United States entered World War I, the movement of African Americans north accelerated. By 1920, more than 1.4 million African Americans lived in northern cities.

Prejudice in the North

In the North, African Americans found discrimination of a different sort than in the South. It was **de facto** discrimination, or discrimination *in practice* instead of *by law.* Some employers refused to hire African Americans or offered them the least desirable jobs at low pay. Rental agents would not show them apartments or houses in white neighborhoods.

As African American migration increased, racial tensions in the North also rose. Riots erupted in several places. The worst riot, in Chicago in 1919, involved 10,000 people. It took state police nearly three days to end the fighting.

Organizing for Rights

Faced with continuing racial hostility, African Americans took action against discrimination. In 1905 a group of African American leaders came together at a meeting in Niagara Falls, Canada. The site had once been an important station on the Underground Railroad. Under the leadership of W.E.B. Du Bois (dōō-bois′), a historian, editor, and sociologist, members of the so-called "Niagara Movement" met annually to plan ways to resist racism. They demanded full civil rights and an end to racial discrimination. "We do not hesitate to complain, and to complain loudly and insistently," they warned in a statement.

In 1909 a lynch mob terrorized African Americans in Springfield, Illinois. A small group of white reformers, shocked at the violation of African American rights, offered their support. Together with Du Bois,

◄ These students are studying history at Tuskegee Institute in Alabama. Founded by Booker T. Washington, Tuskegee became a major college for African Americans.

Ida B. Wells, and other African American leaders, they formed the National Association for the Advancement of Colored People (NAACP). Its objective was to secure "equal rights and opportunities for all." The NAACP soon became the most active and effective fighter for the rights of African Americans. Another group, the Black Colleges Urban League, was established in 1910 to provide opportunities for African Americans to gain jobs and adequate housing.

Advances in Education

Despite discrimination, African Americans made advances in U.S. society. Barred from most white universities, African Americans established their own colleges and universities, including Hampton Institute in 1868, and Spelman College and Tuskegee Institute in 1881. Many future leaders of the civil rights movement received their training at these institutions.

Teachers at these colleges had overcome great odds to build their careers. George Washington Carver, a noted chemist and inventor, taught agricultural science at Tuskegee Institute in Alabama. Carter Woodson taught history at Howard University in Washington, D.C., and wrote books establishing African American studies as a discipline. Such pioneering teachers and scholars began to arm African American students with the knowledge to bring about change.

What actions did African Americans take to oppose racial discrimination?

Section 3 Review

Check Understanding

1. **Define** (a) entrepreneur (b) suburb (c) circulation (d) vaudeville (e) discrimination (f) Great Migration (g) de facto

2. **Discuss** why many people moved from rural areas to the cities in the late 1800s.

3. **Analyze** how discrimination was different in the North and the South.

4 **Discuss** some of the accomplishments of W.E.B. Du Bois.

Critical Thinking

Analyzing How was the economy of the United States spurred by the rise of cities from 1890 to 1900?

Write About Social Issues

◆**Connecting Past and Present** What attracted people to cities in the past? What attracts people to cities today? Explain the most significant attractions in a brief paragraph.

Life in American Cities

PREVIEW

Objectives

- To explain how rapid city growth in the late 1800s created problems

- To discuss the need for improved labor conditions in U.S. factories

- To describe how a reform movement developed to help poor people improve their lives

Vocabulary

sweatshop   social gospel movement

task force   settlement house

Although cities offered many new opportunities, they had many problems as well. The rapid urban growth of the late 1800s did not allow for city planning. Factories spewed smoke and pollution into the air of urban neighborhoods. People packed into whatever housing they could afford. Crime and disease were common. In 1898 a visitor from Britain described what he saw when he arrived in the industrial city of Pittsburgh, Pennsylvania:

> A cloud of smoke hangs over it by day. The glow of scores of furnaces light the river banks by night. . . . All nations are jumbled up here, the poor living in . . . wooden shanties thrown up or dumped down with very little reference to roads.

Wealthy people could avoid the filth and poverty of the cities by living in exclusive districts or by moving to the new suburbs. The widening gap between rich and poor increasingly concerned a group of reformers, or people who seek to bring about social change. Many of these reformers were well-to-do women who set out to improve the harsh conditions endured by impoverished people in the large cities of the nation.

◆ PROBLEMS OF CITY LIFE

Urban reformers faced serious challenges. They struggled to provide adequate housing for the workers who made up the bulk of city dwellers. They also tried to find ways to raise health and safety standards and to deal with rising crime rates.

Every industrial city at the turn of the century had its run-down neighborhoods, which were home to workers and immigrants who were too poor to live elsewhere. Run-down apartment buildings meant to hold several families held hundreds—turning neighborhoods into slums. One reformer reported,

> I shudder at the filthy and rotten tenements, the dingy courts and tumbled-down sheds, the foul stables and dilapidated outhouses, the broken sewer-pipes, the piles of garbage fairly alive with diseased odors, and the children . . . seeming literally to pave every scrap of yard.

Such conditions were breeding grounds for disease. Epidemics of typhoid fever, smallpox, and diphtheria swept through slums. Cities proved especially harsh for children. Childhood diseases, such as whooping cough, measles, and scarlet fever, took a frightening toll. In one immigrant neighborhood in Chicago in 1900, more than 20 percent of all infants died in their first year of life. Diseases were spread, in part, by the lack of indoor plumbing in many slum areas. Children set off fire hydrants to wash themselves, played in polluted puddles, and drank impure water.

Sweatshop Labor

Equally dangerous to the health of workers were the **sweatshops,** factories where workers labored under unhealthy conditions for long hours and little pay. Workers often found themselves crammed together in poorly lit buildings with inadequate fresh air.

The clothing industries of the Northeast had the largest number of sweatshops. Here women and children—often immigrants—worked from 60 to 80 hours per week. On March 25, 1911, a disaster occurred that made it impossible for the public to ignore the dangerous conditions in sweatshops. A fire swept through the Triangle Shirtwaist factory in New York City. Oil-soaked machines, bolts of cloth, and the lint-filled air fed the fire until it turned into a blazing inferno. When the women tried to escape, they found that the company had locked most of the doors to prevent theft and to keep out union organizers.

The toll of this fire was horrendous. The one unlocked door was blocked by fire. The company had no sprinkler system, and the old fire escape soon collapsed. Some women threw themselves out of windows rather than die in the blaze. Headlines the next day summarized the horror: "Street Strewn With Bodies! Piles of Dead Inside!"

Public outrage forced New York State to set up a **task force,** a group of experts organized to solve a specific problem, to investigate sweatshops. The findings of the task force resulted in the passage of strict fire codes, a 54-hour maximum work week, and a ban on child labor under the age of 14.

Rise in Crime

The overcrowding and poverty in cities encouraged an increase in crime. Pickpockets and thieves stole wallets and purses. Street gangs sometimes beat up or robbed people. In some cities, murder rates nearly tripled in a year.

To curb crime, cities set up or expanded their police departments. However, the police made little headway against gambling, drunkenness, and disorderly conduct. Worse yet, the police sometimes accepted bribes to look the other way. Scandalized by the corruption, city governments worked to make law enforcement more professional. In New York City, for example, reformers took the hiring of police out of the hands of politicians and placed it in the hands of an elected commission. The commission made the police subject to regular reviews.

? What challenges faced reformers who wanted to improve life in the cities?

◆ IMPROVING CITY LIFE

By the 1890s a group of men and women began to expose the conditions faced by people trapped in the slums. They also tried to bring about change by helping poor people learn the skills needed to break the cycle of poverty.

Jacob Riis, an immigrant from Denmark, had experienced poverty firsthand. Arriving in the United States in 1870 at age 21, Riis wandered the streets trying to find work. Sometimes he went without food for days. At one point, robbers stole what little Riis owned, and he considered throwing himself into New York's East River. Instead, he continued to search for a job. Eventually, he was hired by a New York newspaper.

As a reporter, Riis described the lives of the poorest New Yorkers. Visits to the tenements filled Riis with anger. He called them "hotbeds of the epidemics that carry death to rich and poor alike." He especially detested the impact miserable housing had on children.

The Social Gospel Movement

Like many others at the time, Riis believed missions sponsored by Christian churches would best help the poor by offering them housing and the

▲ During the Triangle Shirtwaist factory fire, 146 of the company's 500 employees died. The fire led to laws improving working conditions.

skills needed to find jobs. Reformers who adopted this approach urged fellow Christians to help the poor just as Jesus had. This movement, called the **social gospel movement,** introduced youth to habits and skills based on Christian teachings to help them escape the conditions in which they lived.

The YMCA and YWCA

One organization that worked to provide the disadvantaged with skills needed for everyday living was the Young Men's Christian Association, or YMCA. This organization began in England but was brought to the United States in the 1850s. The YMCA provided shelters for many of the young farm boys who arrived in the cities in the late 1800s. The Young Women's Christian Association (YWCA), founded in England in 1855, provided a similar service for girls. By 1900 more than 1,500 YMCAs and YWCAs offered temporary lodgings and supervision to young people as they tried to begin new lives in unfamiliar cities.

The Settlement Houses

Inspired by the social gospel movement, a group of young reformers decided to adopt a more direct approach to change. Led by a reformer named Jane Addams, they insisted that relief workers live in poor neighborhoods where they could work directly with poor people to reduce the hardships of daily life.

In 1889, Addams, together with her friend Ellen Gates Starr, opened Chicago's first **settlement house,** which was named Hull House, to provide community services for the poor. Jane Addams believed that Hull House had two main goals. The first was to help the many immigrants in the city. The second goal was to provide a place where educated young people, especially women, could do useful and productive work.

From its start, Hull House was successful. Immigrants from 18 different countries visited the house. Addams offered them classes in English and in American history, but she also encouraged them to preserve their heritage through ethnic festivals and art.

Addams' example inspired the spread of the settlement house movement. In 1890, Janie Porter Barrett founded the first settlement house for African Americans in Hampton, Virginia. In 1893, Lillian D. Wald opened New York's Henry Street Settlement House. In 1900, Los Angeles's Bronson House opened to help Mexican Americans. By this time, several hundred settlement houses had opened in cities around the United States.

Person to Person

Jane Addams

As a young girl living in Illinois, Jane Addams was troubled by the gap that existed between the wealthy and the poor. She vowed to help change the lives of poor and disadvantaged people one day.

In 1889, Addams bought a large, old house in a poor area of Chicago. She turned it into a neighborhood center for the immigrants who lived around her. Within a few months she had set up a nursery, and classes for those who wanted to become citizens. Within a few years, Hull House had become the center of a complex of 13 buildings that offered everything from theater classes to hot meals.

▲ Jane Addams (1860–1935)

Through her work at Hull House, Addams became deeply involved with women's issues. She became a passionate worker for woman suffrage and also took up the cause of the factory workers who lived around her. When Addams discovered that many children often worked 14 hours a day in a neighborhood candy factory, she became a tireless campaigner against child labor.

"Human beings are becoming more humane," she said on her 70th birthday. "But there are always new causes to work for, new conflicts to be resolved and settled, another foot of progress to be made." Today the work of Hull House continues as dedicated reformers keep Jane Addams' dream alive.

Looking Back: Why do you suppose Jane Addams devoted her life to helping others?

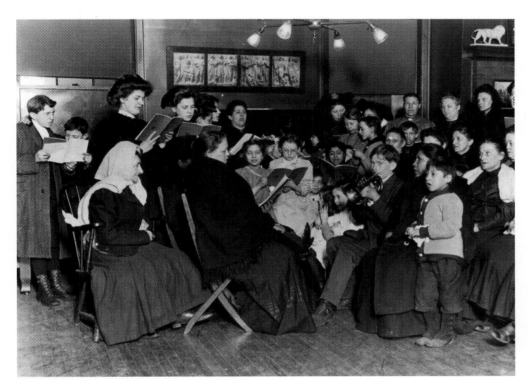

◄ *In addition to providing hot meals and teaching English, Jane Addams held singing classes for children and their parents.*

Over time, settlement houses helped to relieve some of the difficulties of city life. They provided daycare centers, gymnasiums, music schools, social clubs, adult education classes, and other services that had not been available to poor people.

In addition, reformers also influenced city governments. By providing a model for social change, settlement houses encouraged local governments to expand their social services, especially to the poor. In the process, a new profession was created—social work.

 How did reformers try to improve the lives of poor city dwellers?

Section 4 Review

Check Understanding

1. **Define** (a) sweatshop (b) task force (c) social gospel movement (d) settlement house

2. **Identify** the conditions in slums that created health problems for the people who lived there.

3. **Explain** how the results of the fire at the Triangle Shirtwaist factory led to reform of labor practices.

4. **Discuss** how the social gospel movement worked to initiate change in poor people's lives.

Critical Thinking

Connecting Past and Present How are the problems of cities today similar to the problems of cities in the late 1800s? In what ways are the problems different?

Write About Social Issues

Write a newspaper article detailing your suggestions for lowering the health risks found in a city's crowded areas.

Chapter 14
Review

CHAPTER SUMMARY

Section 1
At the end of the 1800s, large numbers of immigrants from southern and eastern Europe entered the United States. They came for a variety of reasons, but mostly to take advantage of new opportunities and to escape discrimination in their homelands. Once here, many moved to cities where people of similar backgrounds had already established neighborhoods.

Section 2
Asians came to California in the late 1800s until prejudice led to sharp limits on their entry into the United States. Latin Americans came to the United States in increasing numbers. Many Mexicans came north to escape the upheavals of the Mexican Revolution, while Cubans and Puerto Ricans came as a result of the Spanish-American War.

Section 3
Between 1870 and 1920, American cities grew rapidly due to an influx of immigrants and the opportunities that city life afforded. Skyscrapers stretched the urban landscape, and an urban culture developed. African Americans moved north in the Great Migration. Seeking civil rights and opportunity, they were subjected to a different form of discrimination.

Section 4
The dramatic growth of cities led to overcrowding, disease, and tragedies such as the Triangle Shirtwaist factory fire, which produced some reforms of the sweatshop system. Many reformers tried to improve conditions by opening settlement houses to care for the needs of poor people.

Connecting ◆◆ Past and Present

America has sometimes been labeled "the land of opportunity." What opportunities exist for immigrants coming to the United States today?

Using Vocabulary

Select the letter of the phrase that best completes each sentence.

1. A person caught in a **pogrom** would be (a) in fear of his or her life; (b) injured in an assembly line accident; (c) accused of breaking immigration laws; (d) forced to leave the United States.

2. A **scapegoat** is (a) a concerned reformer; (b) the kind of animal that could live in the city; (c) someone unfairly blamed for a problem; (d) a new kind of office building.

3. An **entrepreneur** is (a) an employee of a large company; (b) a business person who takes a risk in hope of making money; (c) a union organizer; (d) a task force.

4. Those who face **de facto** discrimination face discrimination (a) in theory; (b) in law; (c) in practice; (d) only in the workplace.

5. A **sweatshop** was a place where people worked (a) for long hours under harsh conditions; (b) in rural settings; (c) turning out products for tropical countries; (d) under conditions set by unions.

6. A **settlement house** is a (a) union; (b) community center that provides services to the poor; (c) club for members of one immigrant group; (d) group of poor, young immigrant women.

Check Understanding

1. **Explain** the difference between the old immigrants and the new immigrants of the late 1800s and early 1900s.

2. **List** two reasons why Europeans emigrated to the United States in the late 1800s.

3. **Describe** the lives immigrants led in their urban, ethnic communities.

4. **Explain** the reasons Asians emigrated to the United States in the late 1800s.

5. **Describe** the reason for the rise of anti-Asian feeling in the United States in the 1800s.

6. **Explain** why people from Mexico, Puerto Rico, and Cuba came to the United States in the late 1800s.

7. **Explain** why many people found cities attractive places to live in the late 1800s.

8. **Identify** the organizations founded by African Americans in the early 1900s to fight for equality.

9. **List** four problems that rapid urban growth caused in the late 1800s.

10. **Analyze** the contributions of Jane Addams and W.E.B. Du Bois.

Critical Thinking

1. **Drawing Conclusions** Would Asians have emigrated to the United States had they known of the prejudice they would encounter in this country? Explain your answer.

2. **Hypothesizing** Which age groups do you think came to the cities from rural areas? Why?

3. **Drawing Conclusions** What conditions led to the Triangle Shirtwaist factory fire?

4. **Making Inferences** How did the immigrants of the late 1800s change American society?

◆ **Connecting Past and Present** How do turn-of-the-century cities compare with cities today?

Interpreting the Timeline

Use the timeline on pages 270–271 to answer these questions.

1. In what year did a reformer open a settlement house?

2. What major event of 1882 affected immigration to the United States?

3. What world event(s) may have had an impact on United States immigration in the early 1900s?

Writing to Describe

Imagine you are a reformer helping residents of slums in the late 1800s. In one particular family you visit, the youngest child has contracted a disease due to poor sanitary conditions. **Write** a report for the health department in which you describe the conditions you see. Include the causes of the problems and your suggestions for solving them.

Putting Skills to Work

MAKING VALID GENERALIZATIONS

In the Building Skills lesson on page 276, you learned how to form generalizations based on a series of facts. Read the three facts below. Then from the four listed generalizations, choose the generalization that best explains a general trend supported by the three facts. Explain your answer.

Facts

a. Many native-born Americans left farms in search of jobs in industries in the 1800s.

b. African Americans left the South for northern cities in record numbers in the early 1900s.

c. Asian immigrants came to U.S. cities seeking opportunities at the end of the 1800s.

Generalizations

1. Anti-immigrant feelings grew on the Pacific coast of the United States.

2. U.S. cities grew rapidly in the late 1800s as many people sought new opportunities.

3. New transportation and communications methods helped suburbs grow up outside the major cities.

4. In the 1800s, organized groups, such as the Ku Klux Klan, spurred racial prejudice in the South, often resulting in violence.

Portfolio Project

A LETTER HOME

In 1890 you landed in the United States and went to live with a cousin in a large city. Write a letter home to your younger brothers and sisters telling them of your impressions of the United States. Share the feelings you had as you explored the city. Describe the new sights and sounds you found, and use specific details to bring your experiences to life for your readers.

PUBLIC HEALTH

Dim, undrained courts oozing with pollution; the dark, narrow stairways, decayed with age, reeking with filth, overrun with vermin; the rotten floors; ceilings begrimed, and often too low to permit you to stand upright.

Horrified writers of the late 1800s described the conditions under which some people lived in New York City. It has been more than 100 years since that description was written. Many people believe conditions for poor people in cities have not improved.

Then The United States paid little attention to public health until 1866, when a cholera epidemic struck the nation for the eighteenth consecutive year. Up until that time, some streets were littered with human and animal filth. The air reeked with the smell of garbage, which had been allowed to pile up, layer upon layer, on city streets. Epidemics of such diseases as diphtheria, tuberculosis, dysentery, and typhoid fever spread through overcrowded tenements. The American Public Health Association, which was founded in 1872, took the first steps to change these unhealthful conditions.

Now Much has changed in American cities since 1872. Preventive measures, such as the Clean Water Act, hygiene education, and sewage treatment, have been introduced. They have generally solved the problem of contaminated drinking water. Epidemics of diseases such as cholera and typhoid fever are now rare, as they and other diseases have been brought under control by vaccination programs. Playgrounds have been built to promote health and exercise in crowded city neighborhoods, and "fresh-air funds" have given generations of children vacations in the country. Although conditions are far from perfect, people continue to use modern science and technology to combat public health issues.

Over the years the emphasis on public health has shifted from the impersonal approach of environmental controls to the more personal approach of preventive treatment. Visiting nurses' associations give free medical and nursing care, and mobile hospital units offering tests and screenings are fixtures in many cities.

You Decide

From your perspective, what aspect of public health should be addressed next? Consider such problems as communicable diseases, infant mortality, drug abuse, and violence. Give reasons and examples to support your point of view.

▲ This photograph from 1895 shows a New York City street littered with trash.

Entering the Modern Age 1870–1920

**" It is a fearful thing
to lead this great
people into war....
But the right is
more precious
than peace, and
we shall fight for
the things we have
always carried
nearest our
hearts—for
democracy,...for
the rights and
liberties of small
nations. "**

*Woodrow Wilson,
in a message to
Congress
asking for a
declaration of war
on Germany,
April 2, 1917*

▲ *U.S. soldiers in World War I climb out of a sandbag-lined trench, ready to charge into
battle.* ◆ **Connecting Past and Present** *What battle equipment are these soldiers using?
What battle equipment do soldiers use today?*

Chapter 15
Efforts to Reform Society 1870–1920

CHAPTER REVIEW

Section 1 The Gilded Age
During the Gilded Age, business leaders amassed unequaled wealth, and government corruption was widespread.

Section 2 The Progressive Movement
Wishing to reform business and government, many people joined the progressive movement in the early 1900s.

Section 3 Social Reform Continues
The Progressives were an active force throughout the early 1900s, passing laws that reformed railroad practices, trade between states, and labor conditions.

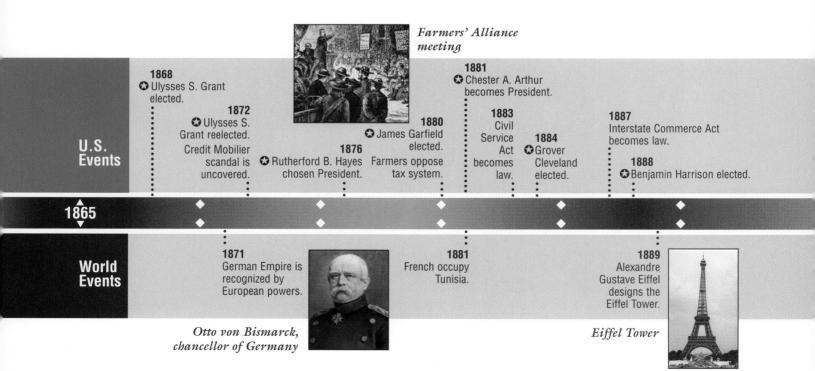

Farmers' Alliance meeting

U.S. Events

1868
❂ Ulysses S. Grant elected.

1872
❂ Ulysses S. Grant reelected.
Credit Mobilier scandal is uncovered.

1876
❂ Rutherford B. Hayes chosen President.

1880
❂ James Garfield elected.
Farmers oppose tax system.

1881
❂ Chester A. Arthur becomes President.

1883
Civil Service Act becomes law.

1884
❂ Grover Cleveland elected.

1887
Interstate Commerce Act becomes law.

1888
❂ Benjamin Harrison elected.

1865

World Events

1871
German Empire is recognized by European powers.

1881
French occupy Tunisia.

1889
Alexandre Gustave Eiffel designs the Eiffel Tower.

Otto von Bismarck, chancellor of Germany

Eiffel Tower

Portfolio Project

A BIOGRAPHICAL REPORT

Studying the lives of prominent Americans does more than teach us about them. It gives us a window into the mood of the era in which they lived. As you read about the progressive era, look for people whose lives might give you an insight into what the time was really like. At the end of this chapter, you will write a biography about one of the people you have studied.

▲ *The end of the Civil War to about 1900 was a period of great wealth and luxury for some Americans, including these women. At times the wealth led to corruption, which made many Americans try to reform the excesses of the age.* ◆ **Connecting Past and Present** *What items indicate the women's wealth? What items indicate great prosperity today?*

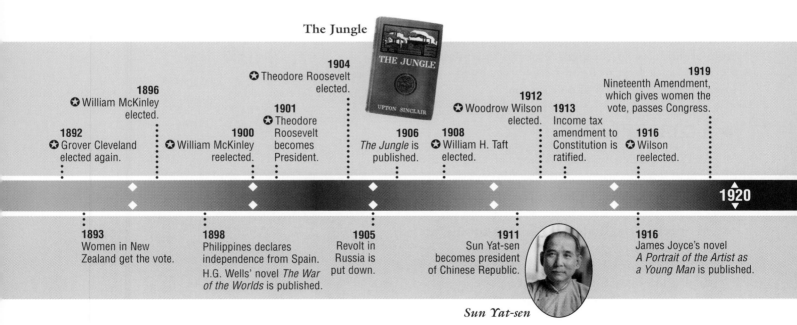

The Jungle

THE JUNGLE

UPTON SINCLAIR

1892
✪ Grover Cleveland elected again.

1896
✪ William McKinley elected.

1900
✪ William McKinley reelected.

1901
✪ Theodore Roosevelt becomes President.

1904
✪ Theodore Roosevelt elected.

1906
The Jungle is published.

1908
✪ William H. Taft elected.

1912
✪ Woodrow Wilson elected.

1913
Income tax amendment to Constitution is ratified.

1916
✪ Wilson reelected.

1919
Nineteenth Amendment, which gives women the vote, passes Congress.

1920

1893
Women in New Zealand get the vote.

1898
Philippines declares independence from Spain. H.G. Wells' novel *The War of the Worlds* is published.

1905
Revolt in Russia is put down.

1911
Sun Yat-sen becomes president of Chinese Republic.

1916
James Joyce's novel *A Portrait of the Artist as a Young Man* is published.

Sun Yat-sen

The Gilded Age

PREVIEW

Objectives

- To explain how corruption in government during the Gilded Age sparked an era of reform

- To describe the steps reform-minded Presidents took to improve government

Vocabulary

Gilded Age	kickback
censure	merit system

In the years after the Civil War, the United States became a strong industrial nation. During this period, factories, steel mills, and railroads grew rapidly. Millions of people immigrated to the United States, attracted by the promise of a better life.

Yet there was a dark side to this growth. Some leaders of industry built fortunes of astonishing size and lived extravagant lifestyles. They used their wealth to try to influence government officials. Seeing the corruption and extravagance around them, writers Mark Twain and Charles Warner called the period the **Gilded Age.** Gilding is a process of applying a thin layer of gold over a cheaper metal. To these writers, the lavish lives lived by a few people concealed widespread poverty, greed, and corruption.

◆ A CORRUPT AGE

In 1892 a delegate at the Cincinnati convention of the new Populist party wrote this stinging description of politics in the United States:

> We meet in the midst of a nation brought to the verge of moral, political, and material ruin. Corruption dominates the ballot-box, the Legislatures, the Congress. . . . Public opinion is silenced . . . and the land concentrated in the hands of the capitalists.

The capitalist hands that the delegate mentioned belonged to the wealthy few who ran the nation's growing industries. These leaders of business and industry had amassed enormous power. Although their enterprising ways helped lead the nation to great prosperity, their ruthless business tactics were not appreciated by many people.

Cornelius Vanderbilt was a captain of industry who mixed vision, hard work, courage, ruthlessness, and corruption. Vanderbilt started out poor, working on the crew of a ferry that took people across New York Harbor from Staten Island to Manhattan. In his teens, he purchased his first boat. By the time he was in his fifties, he owned the largest steamboat fleet in the United States. During the gold rush days, he made a fortune transporting gold seekers to California.

He then made a bold move. Vanderbilt saw that the future of transportation in the United States lay in railroads, not ships. During the Civil War, he sold his ships to the government at a big profit and used the money to invest in railroads. Vanderbilt then bought a number of small railroads and merged them to form the New York Central and Hudson River Railroad. By the early 1870s, Vanderbilt controlled railroad shipping lines between the Midwest and the east coast.

As Vanderbilt became richer, he also became more daring and corrupt. He destroyed competitors who tried to challenge him. When he was taken to court, he bribed judges to rule in his favor. When told that

Study Hint

Words can have different shades of meaning when used in different contexts. For example, the word gilded means "covered with gold." Used in the context of the Gilded Age, though, it refers to the way in which a thin layer of luxury covered corruption. As you read, look for familiar words that may have another meaning.

he was violating the law, Vanderbilt replied: "Law! What do I care about the law! Hain't I got the power?" Robber barons often displayed the belief that they were above normal legal restraints.

Corruption in the Federal Government

Corruption could be found at all levels of government. Perhaps the biggest scandal of the time involved a construction company known as Credit Mobilier, which had been hired by the Union Pacific Railroad to lay railroad tracks. The managers of the railroad paid Credit Mobilier more than double what the job actually cost.

Later it turned out that the owners of Credit Mobilier were also the managers of the railroad. They had pocketed the extra money and enriched themselves at the expense of unsuspecting Union Pacific shareholders. When it seemed that Congress might investigate the company, Credit Mobilier managers bribed members of Congress. In the end, a few members of Congress were **censured,** or officially reprimanded, and some resigned in disgrace.

Corruption in City and State Government

Corruption was common not just in the federal government but also in state and city governments. Immigration and industrialization had created explosive growth in the nation's cities, causing people in the developing cities to depend more heavily on city government services. This dependence created a vast opportunity for corrupt government officials to enrich themselves by controlling the services the city provided.

For example, each city was made up of neighborhoods, or wards. Each ward had a local leader, called a boss. Bosses were responsible for getting voters to support their party's candidates for local offices. Bosses increased the likelihood of this happening by doing favors for voters—finding them jobs in government or giving them gifts. In return, bosses often received **kickbacks,** or illegal payments, from those who had received the favors or services.

One of the most corrupt figures of the time was William Marcy "Boss" Tweed. Tweed, a senator in the New York State legislature, cheated New York City of at least $30 million by adding unneeded charges to city contracts. He pocketed some of the profit himself and shared the rest with his supporters, including city employees like police and workers in the mayor's office. Many New Yorkers were not aware of the extent of the corruption until Thomas Nast created and published a

▲ **Government** *In this political cartoon, the policeman is overshadowed by Boss Tweed.* **Interpreting the Cartoon** *How does the cartoon illustrate the relationship between Boss Tweed and the law?*

series of political cartoons exposing Tweed and his associates. In the days when many people could not read well, Nast's cartoons hit hard. As Tweed said,

> **I don't care a straw for your newspaper articles. My people don't know how to read. But they can't help seeing them . . . pictures.**

The cartoons were one factor that led to an investigation of Tweed's activities. Tweed was arrested, convicted, and jailed. He escaped, was re-arrested, and was sent back to jail, where he remained until his death.

Why were the late 1800s called the Gilded Age?

◆ FIRST TRIES AT REFORM

Excesses in business and government led to a reaction against corruption. One of the first targets was the spoils system, which had been first used by Andrew Jackson. It allowed newly elected Presidents to give government jobs to friends and supporters, not necessarily to the people who were most qualified.

President Rutherford B. Hayes tried to reform the spoils system. When Hayes took office in 1877, he announced that no officeholder would be dismissed from a government job for political reasons. However, Republican leaders opposed his efforts, and Hayes was unable to win support for his reform ideas.

In 1880 the Republicans chose another presidential candidate, James Garfield of Ohio. Once elected, Garfield spent his first months in office being pestered by eager job seekers. Hoping to get away from this pressure, he scheduled a vacation in New England. As he was leaving for his vacation, he was shot and killed in Washington, D.C., by a man angered because he had been denied a government job.

Chester A. Arthur, Garfield's Vice President, became the new President. Reformers were dismayed, since Arthur himself had been involved in corrupt deals with a New York boss. However, as President, Arthur worked hard to reform the spoils system. In 1883, Congress passed the Pendleton Civil Service Act. This law established a **merit system,** in which jobs are granted on the basis of ability. Under the law, candidates for some government jobs now had to show they were suitable by passing a civil service examination. The number of jobs covered was small, but the civil service act was an important start.

The Reformers and the Presidents

In 1884, angered by Arthur's reforms and by trouble in the economy, the Republicans did not renominate Arthur. Instead they chose James G. Blaine of Maine. A group of Republican reformers, fearing that Blaine would not carry out reform, split from the party.

The reformers threw their support behind the Democratic candidate, Grover Cleveland, who, as governor of New York, had built a strong record fighting government corruption. Cleveland and the Democrats captured the presidency for the first time in 28 years.

Democratic party members expected Cleveland to appoint large numbers of loyal Democrats to offices. Cleveland had different ideas. He did appoint many Democrats to public office, but not as many as wanted

jobs. Instead he urged the expansion of the merit system. He extended it to cover about 27,000 employees, almost twice as many as when he took office.

Cleveland tried to steer a middle course between eager office seekers and reformers. In the end, he pleased neither side. As a result he lost the election of 1888 to Republican Benjamin Harrison.

Harrison's one term in office was marked mainly by the attempts of wealthy business interests to pass legislation that benefited themselves. Harrison was voted out of office in 1892, losing to Democrat Grover Cleveland. Cleveland thus became the only President to serve two terms that were not consecutive.

Farmers, Big Business, and the Federal Government

While reform stalled on the federal level, it pushed ahead on the state level. During the late 1800s, many states sought ways to regulate big business in the public interest. By 1900 almost every state had laws regulating the railroads. These laws attempted to reduce unfair pricing practices. For example, some railroads charged small farmers higher rates for transporting crops than they charged big businesses. During the 1870s angry farmers convinced many state legislatures to outlaw this practice. Railroad companies challenged the state laws in court, claiming that states had no authority to regulate their business

▲ Grover Cleveland, who had a reputation for fighting government corruption, became the first Democratic President in 28 years.

◄ *Farmers held meetings to express their dissatisfaction with the tax system. One of the signs in this illustration reads, "Let us organize and educate for knowledge is power."*

practices. In the case of *Munn v. Illinois* (1877), the U.S. Supreme Court said that states had the right to regulate businesses in the public interest. The Court ruled that any private property that affected the public interest "must submit to be controlled by the public for the common good."

The impact of the state laws, however, was undercut by the Supreme Court's 1886 ruling in the case of *Wabash, St Louis and Pacific Railroad Company v. Illinois.* In this case, the Court said that only the federal government, not the states, had the power to regulate interstate commerce. Public anger at this decision led Congress to pass the Interstate Commerce Act of 1887. The act required railroads that passed through more than one state to set reasonable rates. The act also set up a five-member Interstate Commerce Commission to investigate complaints.

Farmers also resented the federal tax system, which was based on the amount of land a person owned. They felt that this system aided wealthy businesses at the farmers' expense. Farmers proposed a system that would tax wealth, not land. The federal government eventually adopted that system.

How did the federal government try to reform politics and industry during the Gilded Age?

Section 1 Review

Check Understanding

1. **Define** (a) Gilded Age (b) censure (c) kickback (d) merit system

2. **Explain** how the corruption of political bosses and captains of industry led to reform.

3. **Describe** the Credit Mobilier scandal.

Critical Thinking

Evaluating How did two Supreme Court rulings in the late 1800s affect U.S. businesses?

Write About Government

◆**Connecting Past and Present** Today many people seeking government jobs are required to pass civil service examinations. In an essay, explain how the present system differs from the spoils system.

BUILDING SKILLS

Using Secondary Sources: The Progressives

Secondary sources are historical materials that are written after events have occurred by people who did not participate in those events. Secondary sources are usually based on primary sources. Encyclopedia articles, biographies, history books, and some magazine articles are examples of secondary sources.

Here's How

Follow these steps to use secondary sources:

1. Determine who wrote the piece, and when and why it was written.
2. Consider what motivated the author to write about the event. Does the author have biases?
3. Compare the secondary source to other sources. Are there references to primary sources in the text or in the acknowledgments or footnotes?
4. Evaluate the source. Decide if it gives an accurate account of the events, based on other sources you have used.

Here's Why

Secondary sources may offer broad explanations of people, events, and issues. Compared with primary sources, secondary sources may give a more unbiased view, since their authors can be less emotional about people and events. But secondary sources may be less accurate, since sometimes a long time has passed since the event occurred. Secondary sources are useful when you need background and basic facts about a topic.

Practice the Skill

The commentary below was written by Gary B. Nash, Professor of History at the University of California, Los Angeles, and Julie Roy Jeffrey, Professor of History at Goucher College. After you have read the excerpt, answer the questions below.

The progressive era was a time when many Americans set out to promote reforms because they saw poverty, despair, and disorder in the country . . . Progressivism was largely a middle-class movement that sought to help the poor, the immigrants, and the working class. Yet the poor were rarely consulted about policy, and many groups . . . were almost entirely left out of reform plans. Progressives . . . talked of the need for more democracy, but they often succeeded in promoting a government run by experts. In the end, their regulatory laws tended to aid business and to strengthen corporate capitalism, while social justice and equal opportunity remained difficult to achieve.

From: The American People: Creating a Nation and a Society, *by Gary Nash and Julie Roy Jeffrey, HarperCollins, 1994, p.742*

1. How can you tell that this commentary is a secondary source?
2. What is the point of view of Nash and Jeffrey toward the Progressives?
3. Which statements in the sources might be facts? Which might be opinions?

Apply the Skill

As you read pages 301–308, find an article about the Progressives in an encyclopedia or other book. Write a paragraph comparing and contrasting the viewpoint of that secondary source to the one above.

Section 2

The Progressive Movement

PREVIEW

Objectives

- To list the major goals of the Progressives

- To describe reforms that went into effect in local and state governments

- To identify the progressive ideas that were promoted by Theodore Roosevelt

Vocabulary

muckraker   direct primary
city manager   recall

As the United States entered the twentieth century, it faced a number of problems. Some people argued that these problems were caused by capitalism. They believed that only an entirely new system could solve these problems. Most reformers, however, believed that the best way to solve the nation's ills was to reform the capitalist system. Those who tried to reform the system were known as Progressives. As the name suggests, the Progressives believed in progress. They believed that no matter how difficult problems were, they could be solved.

◆ MAKING GOVERNMENT MORE RESPONSIVE

The progressive movement grew out of concern about the vast economic and social gap between rich and poor Americans. Progressives believed that if reforms did not take place, disorder and revolution would tear the country apart. The major goals of the Progressives were to end political corruption and to create a government that was responsive to all citizens.

Reforming Local Government

Americans came to understand the goals of the Progressives thanks to a group of journalists. These writers investigated and exposed corrupt practices in government, unions, corporations, and other businesses. Critics of these writers called them **muckrakers,** charging they did nothing but rake up filth and muck, but the writers accepted the label with pride. Their articles made Americans aware of problems that had long been covered up. For example, one muckraker, Ida Tarbell, wrote about corruption in the oil industry.

The writer Lincoln Steffens exposed urban corruption. In a series of articles, he described how political bosses filled offices with loyal followers and took large bribes from businesses. Steffens wrote that in St. Louis, "nothing was passed free of charge." For example, a shopkeeper who wanted a new sign had to bribe a city official to get a permit.

To limit the power of the political bosses, Progressives worked to change the form of city government. Perhaps the most important change was the introduction of the **city manager** system in some cities. A city manager is a professional manager—not an elected politician—who is hired to run a city government.

Another important reform dealt with public utilities such as water, gas, and electricity. City governments generally supplied water, but gas and electric companies were privately owned. Progressives feared that privately owned utilities could charge whatever they wanted for gas and electricity. Some city governments began to run these services themselves, and others began regulating the private companies. Either way, the Progressives believed, utilities would be provided at a price that everyone could afford.

The journalist Ida Tarbell, shown here in her office, exposed corruption in the oil industry. ▼

Reforming State Governments

Some of the most important progressive reforms were begun at the state government level. One reform was the **direct primary,** an election in which the members of a political party choose the party's candidates for office. No longer would party bosses alone choose the candidates. Another reform was the **recall.** A recall allows voters to remove an elected official from office. Another important progressive reform was the direct election of U.S. senators. Under the Constitution, state legislatures named senators to office. In 1913 the Seventeenth Amendment allowed voters to elect senators directly.

? What reforms gave citizens more control of local and state governments?

◆ THEODORE ROOSEVELT AND THE SQUARE DEAL

The role of the federal government in progressive reform increased when Theodore Roosevelt became President in 1901. Roosevelt was a dynamic man with a variety of interests. He wrote 20 books on history, travel, sports, and politics. He was a cowhand, a hero of the Spanish-American War, and a recreational boxer. Elected Vice President on the McKinley ticket in 1900, Roosevelt became President when McKinley was assassinated in 1901.

Roosevelt believed that a President should lead. He had a chance to put his beliefs into practice when coal miners went on strike in 1902. Though the miners had received no wage increases in 20 years, mine owners refused to negotiate with the miners' union.

Roosevelt threatened to seize the mines and force the owners to deal with the miners. That threat forced the owners to the bargaining table. The miners went back to work and eventually won most of their demands. Later, Roosevelt said that he had given the miners a "square deal."

Theodore Roosevelt was the first President to take both labor and management issues into consideration during a strike. He established a new principle: the federal government was responsible for solving conflicts that threatened the welfare of the American people.

The Trustbuster

Roosevelt believed that only the federal government had the power to control the giant trusts. He believed big corporations played an important role in making the United States powerful, but he was determined to bust what he called "bad" trusts. These were corporations that forced competitors out of business or charged customers too much.

Roosevelt's most famous target was the Northern Securities Company, which controlled railroads in the Pacific Northwest region. At the urging of the President, the government sued Northern Securities for restricting trade. In 1904 the government won a stunning victory when the U.S. Supreme Court ruled against Northern Securities and ordered the company to be broken up. Other suits quickly followed. Roosevelt won every one of them—and the American public loved it.

The Jungle and the Square Deal

Restating his promise of a square deal for all Americans, Roosevelt easily won the election of 1904. He introduced a wide range of bills as part of the square deal program. Congress passed laws to clear slums, to make factories safer, and to prohibit rebates in the railroad industry. The Food and Drug Administration (FDA) was created to help keep food pure.

▲ Upton Sinclair's novel The Jungle *revealed to thousands of people the unsanitary conditions in the meat-packing industry. Its publication helped support the policies of Roosevelt's square deal program.*

▲ Theodore Roosevelt (left) was concerned with protecting America's natural beauty. He is shown with naturalist John Muir at Glacier Point in Yosemite Valley, California.

The square deal received a major boost from a novel published in 1906. In *The Jungle*, Upton Sinclair described the unsanitary and unsafe conditions in the meat-packing and processing industries. Descriptions like this aroused widespread disgust and anger:

" There would be meat that had tumbled out on the floor, in the dirt and sawdust, where the workers had tramped and spit uncounted billions of consumption germs. There would be meat stored in great piles in rooms; and the water from leaky roofs would drip over it, and thousands of rats would race about on it. . . . These rats were nuisances, and the packers would put poisoned bread out for them, they would die, and then rats, bread, and meat would go [out] together. "

Sinclair's book raised people's anger so much that Congress reacted quickly. The Meat Inspection Act of 1906 gave federal officials the right to inspect all meat shipped in interstate commerce. Inspectors were to ensure that the meat came from healthy animals and that it was packed and processed under sanitary conditions.

Conserving American Treasures

Roosevelt was especially interested in protecting the country's natural beauty. Throughout his presidency,

Roosevelt championed conservation efforts. The National Conservation Commission was established to conserve, or preserve, the nation's natural resources. During his administration more than 150 million acres were set aside as preserved or public lands—three times the area of federal lands when he took office. Muir Woods, Crater Lake, and the Petrified Forest were among the areas that became national parks or national monuments during his presidency. Roosevelt once said,

" . . . the conservation of our natural resources and their proper use [is] the fundamental problem which underlies almost every other problem of our national life. "

? Under Roosevelt's leadership, what reforms were introduced in the early 1900s?

Section 2 Review

Check Understanding

1. **Define** (a) muckraker (b) city manager (c) direct primary (d) recall

2. **Identify** the main goals of the progressive movement.

3. **Describe** how the muckrakers promoted the reform movement.

4. **Analyze** Theodore Roosevelt's attitude toward big corporations.

Critical Thinking

Understanding Point of View Using the passage from *The Jungle*, compare and contrast possible attitudes toward the book from consumers and from owners of meat-packing plants.

Write About Citizenship

◆ **Connecting Past and Present** In a pamphlet, suggest ways to carry out Theodore Roosevelt's ideas about conserving natural resources today.

Section 3

Social Reform Continues

PREVIEW

Objectives

- To recognize the achievements as well as the shortcomings of President Taft

- To summarize the progressive reforms enacted by President Wilson

- To explain the impact of the Federal Reserve Board and the Federal Trade Commission on the U.S. economy

- To explain how women gained the vote in 1920

Vocabulary

graduated income tax
interest rate
price-fixing

When Theodore Roosevelt decided not to run for President in 1908, he recommended that his Secretary of War, William Howard Taft, be nominated as the Republican candidate. Roosevelt had great faith in Taft's abilities. The Republican party agreed with him and nominated Taft on the first ballot.

The Democrats chose William Jennings Bryan to run against Taft. Both Taft and Bryan ran on progressive platforms. However, Taft won the election, in part because of Roosevelt's support.

◆ TAFT TAKES A MIDDLE ROAD

Taft had been an effective secretary of war, but when he was President, things did not go well for him. An intelligent and well-meaning person, he lacked the forcefulness that had marked Roosevelt's presidency. Cautious and thoughtful, Taft missed many opportunities to persuade Congress to follow his advice.

Problems over Tariffs

One missed opportunity concerned tariffs, or taxes, on imported goods. The Republicans, believing that high tariffs meant high prices for consumers, had pledged to lower tariffs.

Immediately after taking office, Taft called a special session of Congress to lower tariffs. There was much opposition among domestic manufacturers to doing so. Therefore, Congress accepted part, but not all, of Taft's approach to tariffs. The Payne-Aldrich Tariff Act of 1909 lowered tariffs on some imported items but raised them on others. Although Taft felt the act protected the interests of business, not consumers, he signed it into law. In doing so, he lost the support of the Progressives he needed to push through other legislation.

Taft and the Environment

Taft ran into more trouble over the issue of conservation. The trouble began when Taft's secretary of the interior, Richard Ballinger, sold some wilderness lands in Alaska, Wyoming, and Montana to private investors. Although Ballinger had done nothing illegal by selling these lands, his political enemies accused him of misconduct. Ballinger was eventually cleared of any wrongdoing, but Taft was criticized widely for not preventing the sale. Newspapers and magazines printed unflattering stories about the land sales. They damaged Taft's reputation and branded him an enemy of conservation. The truth was that Taft created more national park and forest land than Roosevelt had. However, the facts emerged too late to help Taft.

This 1908 campaign poster pictures Republican party candidates William Howard Taft for President (left) and James S. Sherman for Vice President (right). ▼

◀ Woodrow Wilson was president of Princeton University and governor of New Jersey before being elected President of the United States. He is shown here throwing the first pitch on opening day of the 1916 major league baseball season.

Reforms Made Under Taft

Although Taft missed a number of opportunities to make certain changes, he did manage to sign several important progressive reforms. For example, during Taft's administration the attorney general filed twice as many antitrust suits as had been filed during Roosevelt's presidency.

Taft initiated other reforms as well. He proposed the Sixteenth Amendment, which gave Congress the power to collect income tax. The amendment was ratified in 1913, the year after Taft left office. Taft also nominated six justices to the Supreme Court and signed legislation that regulated railroads.

 **What reforms went into effect under President Taft?**

◆ THE ELECTION OF 1912

The presidential election of 1912 was one of the most unusual elections in American history. Theodore Roosevelt, disappointed with Taft's performance and wanting to reenter politics, decided to run for the Republican nomination. Taft also decided to seek renomination from the Republicans. In doing so, he acknowledged that the odds were against him:

❝ I am afraid I am in for a hard fight, but I am going to stay in anyhow. . . . I believe I represent a safer and saner view of our government and its Constitution than Theodore Roosevelt. ❞

The once friendly relations between Taft and Roosevelt became bitter. In the end, Taft's supporters managed to nominate him as the Republican candidate for President. An enraged Theodore Roosevelt decided to run for President on his own ticket. He formed a new Progressive party, which became known as the Bull Moose party.

The Democratic convention nominated Woodrow Wilson as their candidate. A progressive politician, Wilson had been elected governor of New Jersey in 1910. As governor, he had passed laws that punished corrupt politicians, increased state aid for schools, and called for strict inspection of food. Before becoming governor, he was a law professor and a president of Princeton University.

Both Wilson and Roosevelt were labeled progressive candidates. Despite some of Taft's accomplishments, his image was that of a conservative. In the weeks before the election, Wilson and Roosevelt campaigned vigorously, while Taft stayed in Washington.

On election night, it was clear that the Democrats would win. The popular vote showed that the Republican split had given Wilson 42 percent of the popular vote. Roosevelt won 27.5 percent and Taft 23 percent. In the electoral vote, however, Wilson claimed a landslide victory. He won 435 votes to Roosevelt's 88 and Taft's 8.

The election of 1912 showed that progressive reform was the major issue of the day. Together the two candidates labeled Progressives, Wilson and Roosevelt, had received the most popular votes.

 Why was the presidential election of 1912 an unusual election?

◆ WILSON AS PRESIDENT

The election over, Wilson took office and began to put into practice a program he called the New Freedom. His first action was to call a special joint session of Congress. He then proceeded to address the joint session directly, something that had not been done since John Adams had been President.

Wilson would address Congress again and again. It was an action that demonstrated his belief in the power of the presidency. Wilson believed his role was to lead Congress, and he insisted on party loyalty. In that way he managed to guide a great many important laws through Congress.

Wilson and Economic Reform

Under pressure from Wilson, Congress passed the Underwood-Simmons Tariff Act in 1913. The act decreased tariffs to their lowest rate since the Civil War. In addition the Underwood-Simmons Act provided for a **graduated income tax,** which had been made possible by the passage of the Sixteenth Amendment. A graduated income tax assesses money owed to the government based on income. The tax meant that those with higher incomes would pay higher taxes—a principle that is still followed today.

Wilson then set out to reform the banking system. He suggested the establishment of the Federal Reserve Board. This was to be a group of financial experts, appointed by the President, who would manage the nation's financial policy. The Board would manage 12 large banks, called Federal Reserve Banks, across the country. These banks would in turn supervise local banks. The Board would also set the nation's **interest rate,** or the rate that Federal Reserve Banks

charge other banks for borrowing money. Wealthy bankers, who saw this Federal Reserve System as a scheme to take away their power, opposed Wilson's idea. But Wilson was determined to get his bill passed. On December 23, 1913, Congress passed the Federal Reserve Act. The act created institutions and rules still in use today.

In 1914, Wilson convinced Congress to pass an act establishing the Federal Trade Commission (FTC). The commission's function was to identify companies that were engaging in unfair competition. The commission could bring these companies to court if they failed to change the way they conducted business.

The Clayton Antitrust Act of 1914 outlawed a number of business tactics that gave large companies

Reforms of the Federal Government, 1903–1920

1903	Dept. of Commerce and Labor established
1903	Elkins Act placed controls on unfair corporate practices
1904	Northern Securities Company ruling broke up railroad trust
1905	Swift and Company beef trust broken up
1906	Pure Food and Drug Act
1906	Meat Inspection Act
1908	White House Conservation Conference
1911	Standard Oil trust broken up
1913	16th Amendment to the Constitution ratified; authorized income tax
1913	17th Amendment provided for direct election of U.S. senators
1919	18th Amendment prohibited manufacture and sale of alcoholic beverages
1920	19th Amendment ratified; guaranteed woman suffrage

▲ **Government** *Between 1903 and 1920 the federal government approved reforms that affected many areas of American society.* **Interpreting the Chart** *Which reforms addressed food safety?*

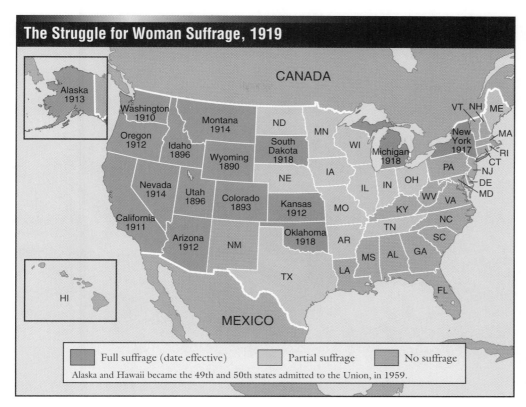

The Struggle for Woman Suffrage, 1919

CANADA

Alaska 1913

Washington 1910

Oregon 1912

Idaho 1896

Montana 1914

Wyoming 1890

ND

South Dakota 1918

MN

WI

Michigan 1918

VT NH ME

New York 1917

MA

RI

CT

NJ

DE

MD

Nevada 1914

Utah 1896

Colorado 1893

NE

IA

IL

IN

OH

PA

California 1911

Kansas 1912

MO

KY

WV VA

Arizona 1912

NM

Oklahoma 1918

AR

TN

NC

SC

MS AL GA

TX

LA

FL

HI

MEXICO

◀ **Geography** *By 1919, women were given full suffrage in many states.* **Interpreting the Map** *Which was the first state to give full suffrage to women? Which states gave only partial suffrage?*

| ■ Full suffrage (date effective) | ■ Partial suffrage | ■ No suffrage |

Alaska and Hawaii became the 49th and 50th states admitted to the Union, in 1959.

power over small ones. The act ended **price-fixing,** the practice of several companies raising or lowering their prices in order to drive competitors out of business. The act also declared that companies could not refuse to sell to a dealer who sold a competitor's product. The Clayton Antitrust Act protected unions and legalized strikes, boycotts, and picket lines.

Wilson and Limited Social Reform

President Wilson's record on business and banking reform was impressive. However, his record on social reform—changes that might improve conditions for individuals or minority groups—was poor.

While he was campaigning, Wilson asked for support from African Americans. In return, Wilson promised to fight for civil rights and to appoint a commission to study race relations. Once in office, however, Wilson told African American leaders that the time was not right for such a commission.

Wilson became the first President since the Civil War to follow a policy of official segregation in the federal government. African Americans were forced to use separate offices, shops, restrooms, and restaurants. If an employee objected to using segregated facilities, he or she was fired. African Americans were angered by Wilson's actions.

Wilson did little for civil rights or for woman suffrage, though he did support the passage of some social legislation—especially as his reelection campaign of 1916 approached. For example, he signed legislation that established an eight-hour workday for railroad workers. Wilson also supported legislation dealing with child labor, compensation for injured workers, and educational aid for farmers.

 **In what ways did Wilson encourage fair business practices?**

◆ THE SUFFRAGE MOVEMENT

Even though President Wilson did not support the suffrage movement, women were not easily stopped. Among the women who led the suffrage movement during the early 1900s was Carrie Chapman Catt. Catt headed the National American Woman Suffrage Association (NAWSA). Catt and her followers decided that the best strategy for winning the vote for women was to win suffrage in the individual states. They believed that when a number of states succeeded in allowing women to vote, it would be easier to pass a constitutional amendment giving all women the vote.

Although women were sometimes jailed for their attempts to gain suffrage, they continued to organize demonstrations. These women are attending a suffrage meeting held around 1920. ▶

Another woman suffrage organization, the National Woman's Party, was headed by Alice Paul. This group called for quick action by the government to pass an amendment giving women the vote. Paul's group organized a parade through Washington, D.C., to celebrate Wilson's inauguration. After Wilson was in office, Paul and her supporters picketed in front of the White House for 18 months. Some picketers were put in jail, where they went on hunger strikes and were force fed. The arrests and hunger strikes attracted the attention of the nation.

In the meantime, Catt's state-by-state strategy of gaining the vote was working. By 1919, women had gained full suffrage in 15 states plus Alaska. Another 14 states allowed partial suffrage. Partial suffrage meant that women could vote in local or state elections, but not in national elections. There were still 19 states plus Hawaii that would not allow women to vote at all. The map on page 307 shows how the states stood on the suffrage issue.

Women and their male supporters kept up the struggle until they convinced Congress to pass the Nineteenth Amendment in 1919. After the states completed ratification in 1920, women had finally gained the right to vote.

 What was Carrie Chapman Catt's strategy to gain the vote for women?

Section 3 Review

Check Understanding

1. **Define** (a) graduated income tax (b) interest rate (c) price-fixing

2. **List** President William Howard Taft's major accomplishments.

3. **Contrast** Wilson's record on business reform with his record on social reform.

4. **Describe** how the National Woman's Party helped pass the Nineteenth Amendment.

Critical Thinking

Connecting Past and Present Today, what political goals for women remain to be achieved?

Write About Economics

Make an outline for an article about economic reforms during President Wilson's administration.

POINT *of* VIEW

SHOULD WOMEN HAVE THE VOTE?

Today it seems odd even to discuss whether women should be allowed to vote. Before the passage of the Nineteenth Amendment, however, the subject was hotly debated. Not even all women agreed that they should have the vote.

Following are two examples of arguments for and against woman suffrage. The first is from the January 1909 issue of *The Remonstrance*, a magazine published by a Massachusetts anti-suffrage organization of women. The second excerpt is from a congressional hearing about a constitutional amendment to give women the vote. The hearing was held February 18, 1902, and Mrs. Mariana Chapman spoke.

The Remonstrance

The average man, by the very nature of his ordinary employments, is familiar with the practical question of local government, questions of the care of the streets, lighting, policing, sewer construction, and the like. He is familiar also with the character, capacity, and records of men who are candidates for office. The average woman, on the other hand, is already overburdened with duties which she cannot escape and from which no one proposes to relieve her. If she is given the suffrage, it is an added duty. Is it reasonable to suppose that, called upon to perform a duty which lies outside of the ordinary employments of her life, she would do it more wisely than the average man?

Mrs. Mariana W. Chapman

Boys will vote at twenty-one, but their mothers are minors forever in the eyes of the law. They are legislated for and governed and, to some extent, protected. . . . We ask for something more precious—the jewel of justice. We ask for it because we are individual human beings who average well with men in intelligence, in virtue, and in sobriety. We ask for it as taxpayers, because we help to maintain the expense of this great Capitol and other buildings, and to pay the salaries of those who serve them. We desire it for our own protection just as men desire it for theirs.

Examining Point of View

1. *The Remonstrance* states that "[t]he average woman . . . is already overburdened with duties which she cannot escape and from which no one proposes to relieve her." Contrast the attitude toward women expressed here with the prevailing attitude today.

2. Summarize the argument for suffrage that Mariana Chapman makes.

3. Based on what you read above, what can you tell about the authors of these passages?

What's Your Point of View?

Many young people today have considerable responsibilities. Some have jobs, others help take care of younger children. There are those who believe that young people with such responsibilities should be given the right to vote.

Write a speech you would make if you were to testify either for or against giving the right to vote to citizens over the age of 15.

Chapter 15
Review

CHAPTER SUMMARY

Section 1
After the Civil War, corruption in business and government became more widespread, as officeholders gave jobs to their friends and did favors for business. Although some U.S. Presidents tried to end the corruption, reformers had some success on the state and federal level.

Section 2
Progressives worked to make government more responsive to all citizens. Muckraking writers brought abuses in government and business to light. President Theodore Roosevelt, a trustbuster and conservationist, helped advance the reformers' cause.

Section 3
William Howard Taft, although not a forceful President, added federal park and forest lands, filed many antitrust suits, and initiated other reforms. His successor, Woodrow Wilson, implemented a graduated income tax and set up federal agencies to regulate banking and stop unfair business competition. However, Wilson had little interest in social reform. Even without firm support from Wilson, though, the Nineteenth Amendment, giving women the right to vote, was passed by Congress in 1919.

Connecting ◆ Past and Present

What issues do you think would be of interest to a muckraker today?

Using Vocabulary

Select the letter of the phrase that best completes each sentence.

1. If you have been given a **kickback,** you (a) have landed in jail; (b) have been elected to national office; (c) have been given an illegal payment in return for services.

2. Under the **merit system** (a) politicians have control of government jobs; (b) government jobs are granted on the basis of ability; (c) people who want jobs must know someone in government.

3. A **recall** (a) allowed voters to remove officials from office; (b) gave legislation a needed boost; (c) made sure that prices were regulated.

4. **Muckrakers** were (a) foreign-born workers; (b) writers paid by businesses to write positive articles; (c) writers who exposed corrupt practices.

5. A **direct primary** is an election (a) in which politicians choose the candidates; (b) without political parties; (c) in which the members of a political party choose the party's candidates.

6. A **city manager** is a (a) professional hired to run the city government; (b) politician who was elected to run a city; (c) candidate for mayor.

7. A **graduated income tax** (a) favors the rich; (b) makes the wealthy pay a higher rate than the poor; (c) abolishes the income tax.

8. If you have been **censured,** you have been (a) complimented; (b) applauded; (c) officially reprimanded.

9. Corporations that practiced **price-fixing** (a) raised prices to collect larger profits; (b) kept prices at a constant level; (c) raised or lowered prices to drive competitors out of business.

10. The **Gilded Age** referred to a time when the luxury of a few concealed (a) widespread poverty; (b) large gold deposits; (c) overseas riches.

Check Understanding

1. **Explain** why many people thought government was corrupt during the Gilded Age.

2. **Describe** how U.S. Presidents tried to institute reforms in government in the 1880s.

3. **Discuss** local and state reforms of the political process that took effect near the turn of the century.

4. **Explain** the goals of the Progressives.

5. **Identify** the progressive ideas of President Theodore Roosevelt.

6. **Explain** what made the election of 1912 different from many others.

7. **Describe** Wilson's economic programs.

8. **List** the business and banking reforms for which Wilson was able to gain passage.

9. **Summarize** how women won the right to vote.

10. **Explain** the role played by muckrakers in the reform movement.

Critical Thinking

1. **Drawing Conclusions** Why do you think the corruption of the Gilded Age occurred?

2. **Analyzing** Why do you suppose the Civil Service Act was not passed earlier in the century?

3. **Understanding Causes and Effects** What were the effects of the novel *The Jungle* on public policy?

4. **Comparing** Compare how the personalities of Roosevelt and Taft affected their presidencies.

◆ **Connecting Past and Present** Do you think Theodore Roosevelt would be a popular President today? Explain your answer.

Interpreting the Timeline

Use the timeline on pages 294–295 to answer these questions.

1. In what years was Grover Cleveland elected President? Why was this unusual?

2. What happened in China the year before Woodrow Wilson was elected President?

3. In what year was a law passed that changed the way many federal government jobs were filled?

Putting Skills to Work

USING SECONDARY SOURCES

In the Building Skills lesson on page 300, you learned how to use secondary sources. Read the following excerpt and answer the questions that follow.

> *Perhaps initially he was disappointed when Taft, as Roosevelt's personal choice for the presidency, failed to campaign with the kind of enthusiasm that Roosevelt expected in a candidate. Perhaps the former President realized that retiring at age 51 was a big mistake, that he was too young and vigorous to bow out of the political scene at such an early age. Taft, in turn, was upset with Roosevelt's constant contact with the insurgents [rebels] in the Republican Party.*

From: William H. Taft,
by Lucille Falk, 1990

1. What reasons does Falk give for Roosevelt's decision to run for the presidency in 1912?

2. What new information has this excerpt given you about the election of 1912?

3. What factors forced Teddy Roosevelt to change his mind about his friend William Taft and to decide to run for the presidency himself?

Writing to Express a Point of View

Imagine you are a reformer in New York City. **Write** an explanation of your position on Boss Tweed's political actions. What should be done about Boss Tweed?

Portfolio Project

A BIOGRAPHICAL REPORT

Choose one of the reformers you have read about in this chapter. Use secondary sources from your school or local library to learn more about this person. Then create a two-page biography. In what area—business, government, politics, or society—did this person choose to work? What interested the person in this field? What changes were brought about as a result of this person's work?

Chapter 16
The United States as a World Power 1890–1916

CHAPTER PREVIEW

Section 1 The United States and Overseas Expansion

In the 1890s the United States began an aggressive colonial policy in Asia and Latin America.

Section 2 The Big Stick in Latin America

Citing a moral responsibility, the United States exercised control over events in Latin America and created a legacy of distrust.

Section 3 The Origins of Global War

A tangle of jealousies and alliances forced European powers to enter a war that no European leader wanted.

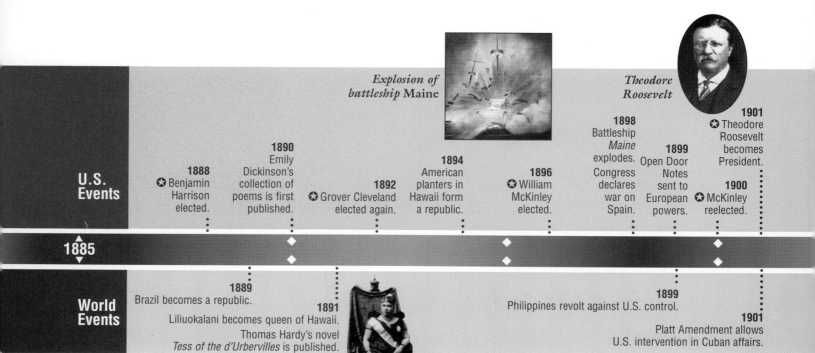

Explosion of battleship Maine

Theodore Roosevelt

U.S. Events

1888
✪ Benjamin Harrison elected.

1890
Emily Dickinson's collection of poems is first published.

1892
✪ Grover Cleveland elected again.

1894
American planters in Hawaii form a republic.

1896
✪ William McKinley elected.

1898
Battleship *Maine* explodes. Congress declares war on Spain.

1899
Open Door Notes sent to European powers.

1901
✪ Theodore Roosevelt becomes President.

1900
✪ McKinley reelected.

1885

World Events

1889
Brazil becomes a republic.

1891
Liliuokalani becomes queen of Hawaii.
Thomas Hardy's novel *Tess of the d'Urbervilles* is published.

1899
Philippines revolt against U.S. control.

1901
Platt Amendment allows U.S. intervention in Cuban affairs.

Queen Liliuokalani of Hawaii

Portfolio Project

NEWSPAPER ARTICLES

Newspapers were important sources of local, national, and international news in the late 1800s. Although many journalists were committed to presenting facts fairly and objectively, others adopted a more sensational style. Sometimes this meant manipulating the truth to arouse interest or reaction. As you read this chapter, pay close attention to emotional or controversial issues. At the end of the chapter, you will try two different approaches to journalism.

▲ *During the 1880s and 1890s, the United States increased its military strength by building more ships. Part of the Great White Fleet is shown here.* ◆◆ **Connecting Past and Present** *How did a strong U.S. Navy change the world's view of the United States? Is it important for the United States to be a strong naval power today?*

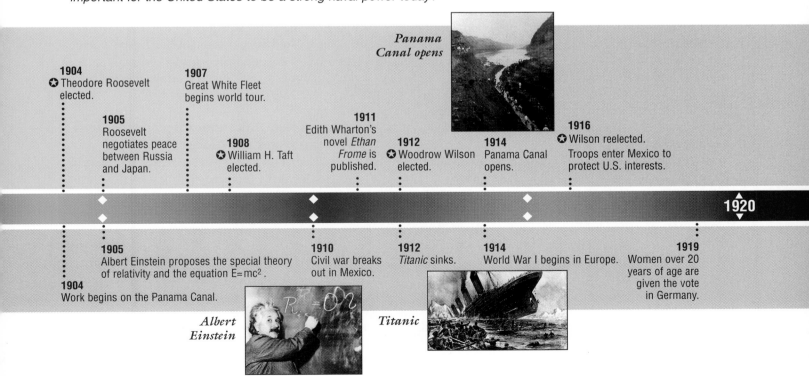

Panama Canal opens

1904
✪ Theodore Roosevelt elected.

1905
Roosevelt negotiates peace between Russia and Japan.

1907
Great White Fleet begins world tour.

1908
✪ William H. Taft elected.

1911
Edith Wharton's novel *Ethan Frome* is published.

1912
✪ Woodrow Wilson elected.

1914
Panama Canal opens.

1916
✪ Wilson reelected. Troops enter Mexico to protect U.S. interests.

1920

1904
Work begins on the Panama Canal.

1905
Albert Einstein proposes the special theory of relativity and the equation E=mc².

1910
Civil war breaks out in Mexico.

1912
Titanic sinks.

1914
World War I begins in Europe.

1919
Women over 20 years of age are given the vote in Germany.

Albert Einstein

Titanic

Section 1

The United States and Overseas Expansion

PREVIEW

Objectives

- To explain why the United States began to acquire territory overseas

- To describe how overseas expansion led the United States into conflicts in Latin America

- To analyze differences between U.S. goals in East Asia and the goals of other world powers

Vocabulary

imperialism	jingoism
isolationism	yellow journalism
protectorate	sphere of influence

After the 1500s many European countries built huge empires in Asia, Africa, and the Americas. During this time, parts of what is today the United States belonged to the empires of Great Britain, the Netherlands, Spain, France, Mexico, and Russia.

The Industrial Revolution in Europe only increased the need for and pace of empire building. It created a need for raw materials for factories. It also produced a need for new markets for Europe's manufactured goods. Out of these needs grew the age of **imperialism,** the policy of one nation gaining control of other territories and using them to build a foreign empire.

At the beginning of this age, the United States did not join Europe's powers in building overseas empires. For one thing, Americans were busy expanding their own country's boundary to the Pacific. Many Americans also disliked the idea of imperialism because it conflicted with the ideals of the Declaration of Independence and its support of the right of people to govern themselves. In addition, many Americans strongly believed that the United States should not get involved in Europe's problems. They supported **isolationism,** or staying out of the political affairs of other countries. George Washington had established this policy during his administration. For the most part, Presidents who succeeded Washington shared this view.

◆ FIRST STEPS IN OVERSEAS EXPANSION

By the 1880s, however, American opinion had begun to change. Farms and factories in the United States were producing more food and manufactured goods than could be used at home. United States trade with other countries was, as a result, rapidly increasing. Foreign trade grew from $450 million in 1870 to more than $1 billion in the mid-1890s. Many Americans agreed with James G. Blaine, secretary of state under President Benjamin Harrison, who said,

> We have developed a volume of manufactures which, in many departments, overruns the demands of the whole market. . . . Our great demand is for expansion of trade.

More than economic factors were behind the urge to expand. Extending the idea of Manifest Destiny, some American leaders believed that a prosperous power such as the United States had a responsibility and a right to impose its way on the people it colonized and on the nations with which it traded. They believed the United States had an obligation to change the lives of people around the world. Senator Albert J. Beveridge of Indiana explained this obligation:

> American law, American order, American civilization, and the American flag will plant themselves on shores hither to bloody and benighted [suffering], but by the agencies of God henceforth to be made beautiful and bright.

In the late 1800s, the United States began to expand beyond its Pacific boundary. The first move was the purchase of Alaska from Russia in 1867. Secretary of State William Seward, a firm believer in expansion, negotiated the purchase for the United States.

The United States paid $7.2 million for Alaska. It was a huge sum at the time, and when Americans received the news, they thought they had been cheated. Many Americans believed Alaska was an icy wasteland, calling the purchase "Seward's Folly" and "Seward's Icebox." Few Americans saw any reason to buy a huge expanse of land where they believed nobody would want to live.

Seward, on the other hand, was happy with the price. He thought Alaska, at about two cents per acre, was a great value. But Seward did not live long enough to see the true worth of his purchase. He died in 1872, and in 1898 vast gold deposits were discovered in the Alaska Territory. What had been called Seward's Folly turned out to be one of the wisest investments the United States ever made.

 Why was the United States interested in overseas expansion by the mid- and late 1800s?

◆ EXPANDING IN THE PACIFIC

Alaska was just a first step. Bigger markets and greater resources lay in East Asia, especially in the countries of China and Japan.

Americans had been trading with China since the mid-1700s. However, until 1842 the Chinese had opened only one port, Canton, to foreign trade. The Chinese had little desire to trade with the West. They thought the West had nothing worth trading for. In 1842, however, the British scored a resounding victory over China in the Opium War. As the price of peace, Britain forced China to open more ports to foreign trade. Now western nations were free to increase their trade with China.

Japan was just as distrustful of Westerners as China had been. For many hundreds of years, Japan, like China, had kept itself isolated from the outside world.

All that began to change on July 8, 1853. On that day, Tokyo residents saw a fleet of steam-powered warships flying the American flag enter their harbor. Commodore Matthew Perry had been sent by President Millard Fillmore to persuade Japan's emperor to open the country to foreign trade. Perry made a second trip in 1854 and, by a mixture of threats and gifts, persuaded the Japanese to open their country to the rest of the world.

In just a few years, Japan's outlook on dealing with other nations changed markedly. A new emperor came to power in 1868 and rejected Japan's policy of

▲ A Japanese artist painted this picture of Commodore Matthew Perry. Perry helped to open trade between Japan and the United States.

isolationism. Over the next few years, the Japanese studied the Industrial Revolution in Britain and the United States and built new factories based on these models. They studied the British navy and began to build one of their own. Within a few decades, the Japanese had transformed their country into a modern industrialized nation and a world power.

As U.S. trade increased with countries in East Asia, the United States realized it needed to control harbors in the Pacific, where ships could refuel. The United States was especially attracted to the Hawaiian Islands, an independent country ruled as a monarchy. Pearl Harbor, on Oahu (ō-ä´-hoo) Island, was the best sheltered port between San Francisco and China.

In the 1800s the Hawaiian Islands became an important stopping point for American whalers and commercial ships. American businesses began buying Hawaiian land to harvest an important natural resource, sugar. They established huge sugar cane plantations. Over the years wealthy American planters gained a good deal of power over Hawaii's government.

This changed after Liliuokalani (li-lē´-ōō-ō-ká-lä-nē) became queen of the Hawaiian Islands. Liliuokalani was a proud woman who resented the influence Americans wielded. Shortly after ascending to the throne, she

▲ *Queen Liliuokalani ruled the Hawaiian Islands from 1891 to 1893. She appealed to her country to keep "Hawaii for Hawaiians."*

began a program to reduce American influence. Alarmed by this program, the American planters began plotting to overthrow her. In 1894 the planters executed their plot and established a republic, putting themselves in charge. American diplomat John Stevens then declared that Hawaii was an American **protectorate,** an independent country that is actually controlled by a more powerful country. It was then proposed that the United States annex the protectorate.

In the United States there was a mixed reaction to these events. American expansionists were thrilled. Before Congress could approve the annexation, Grover Cleveland became President. Like many Americans, Cleveland was generally against imperialism and, in particular, U.S. acquisition of overseas territories. Believing that the United States had no right to take control of an independent country, he withdrew the annexation treaty from Congress. However, Cleveland's successor, William McKinley, did not have the same qualms. In 1898, during the Spanish-American War, the United States annexed the Hawaiian Islands.

? Why did many Americans oppose imperialist policies during the 1800s?

◆ THE SPANISH-AMERICAN WAR

Spain's American empire shrank dramatically during the 1800s. By 1890, Spain controlled only Cuba and Puerto Rico. Although Spain was no longer a world power, it still clung stubbornly to its two Caribbean islands. Spain was especially determined not to give up Cuba, which the Spaniards called "the ever-faithful island."

Many Cubans, however, had no desire to be Spain's faithful colony. They wanted independence. Fighting in Cuba began in the 1860s and continued off and on into the 1890s.

The Road to War

Although the U.S. government was not formally involved in the conflict, Americans were very sympathetic to the Cubans, as Cuba was only 90 miles from Florida. Many Americans volunteered to fight with the Cubans against Spain. Some Americans were killed in battle, and the Spaniards executed others who were captured. The harsh measures taken by the Spanish government stopped the revolution, but only temporarily. Rebellion also broke out in Puerto Rico, but like the Cuban uprising, it was put down. Puerto Rican leaders then tried to negotiate with Spain for more freedom.

A tax imposed by the U.S. government caused revolution in Cuba to flare anew. In 1895 the U.S. Congress put a high tariff on Cuban sugar. As a result, Cuban sugar prices rose and demand dropped. Cuban sugar plantations laid off thousands of cane cutters, and discontent increased. Beginning in 1895, rebels waged war against forces from Spain.

Spain was determined to put down the rebellion once and for all. General Valeriano Weyler, the commander of the Spanish forces, set up what he called reconcentration camps. Weyler's aim was to prevent the rebels in the countryside from receiving food and supplies from their supporters. He forcibly herded thousands of Cuban peasants into the camps, where they lived with little food or proper sanitation.

Weyler's methods earned him the nickname "the Butcher" in the United States. Many Americans, horrified at the conditions in the reconcentration camps, demanded that the U.S. government intervene to stop Weyler. Others called for action—but for a different reason. Expansionists saw the fighting as an opportunity to spread American influence in the Caribbean. The expansionists stirred up aggressive patriotism, called **jingoism,** to win support for the war.

The jingoists might not have succeeded had it not been for the actions of some American newspapers. Seeing the events in Cuba as a way to increase circulation, they printed sensational stories about the war. Distorted news stories like these came to be called **yellow journalism.** For example, an article in the New York *World* included these words:

> Blood on the roadsides, blood in the fields, blood on the doorsteps, blood, blood, blood! The old, the young, the weak, the crippled—all butchered without mercy.

"Remember the *Maine*!"

President William McKinley wanted to avoid war, but the fighting in Cuba concerned him. If rebellion continued, U.S. business interests might be harmed, and U.S. citizens living there might be in danger. In January 1898, McKinley sent the battleship *Maine* to Havana to stand by in case Americans had to be evacuated. On February 15, the *Maine* exploded in Havana harbor, killing about 260 of the crew.

The explosion aboard the *Maine* caused an uproar in the United States. Although an investigation many years later concluded that the explosion was probably internal and accidental, most Americans were convinced at the time that Spain had been responsible. A newspaper headline became the battle cry for war: "Remember the *Maine*!" With feelings running high, the U.S. Congress demanded that Spain get out of Cuba. When Spain failed to reply, the U.S. government declared war on April 25, 1898.

War in the Pacific

As the United States prepared for war, some Americans realized the conflict would be a good opportunity to increase American influence in the Pacific. Spain had controlled the Philippine Islands for about 300 years. Because of U.S. interest in trade with China and Japan, the Philippines would be a valuable prize for the United States. The port of Manila was an ideal location to maintain and control trade with East Asia.

Shortly after the *Maine* had exploded—but before war was declared—Theodore Roosevelt, who was Assistant Secretary of the Navy at the time, had sent a secret message to Commodore George Dewey in Hong Kong harbor. Roosevelt ordered Dewey's U.S. fleet to head toward Manila Bay if war were declared. On April 25, the day the United States declared war, Roosevelt ordered Dewey to attack the

◄ *This painting depicts the explosion of the battleship* Maine *in Havana, which killed about 260 of the crew. Many Americans believed that Spain was responsible for the disaster.*

Spanish fleet at Manila Bay. On April 30, the U.S. fleet sailed into Manila Bay, where it attacked and destroyed the Spanish fleet the next morning.

With the Spanish fleet destroyed, gaining control of the Philippine Islands was relatively simple. Dewey armed a Filipino leader named Emilio Aguinaldo (ä-gē-näl´-dō), who had long fought Spanish rule. A combined Filipino and American force quickly routed Spanish forces and left the victors in control of almost all the islands. This sudden victory took Americans by surprise. Almost overnight, Dewey became a national hero, and the Navy promoted him to admiral.

War in the Caribbean

Shortly after the American victory in Manila Bay, Theodore Roosevelt resigned his position in the Navy Department. Wanting to test himself in war, he decided to join the U.S. Army as an officer. There he helped organize the First Volunteer Cavalry.

This special unit consisted of cowhands from the West and miners, college athletes, and young men from throughout the country who were looking for adventure. Because of their riding skills, they soon became known as the Rough Riders. After a brief period of training in San Antonio, Texas, the unit shipped out to Cuba. They landed on Cuba's south coast and marched inland toward the city of Santiago.

Outside Santiago, American troops met Spanish troops at San Juan Hill. The Rough Riders charged recklessly up the hill on foot, meeting stiff resistance. Several other units took part in the charge, including the Ninth and Tenth Cavalry regiments, made up of African American soldiers. Many Latino soldiers also fought in a number of American units. Particularly helpful was the role played by Cuban soldiers who fought side by side with the Americans.

Roosevelt, who was on horseback, made an easy target for Spanish soldiers. Nevertheless, he escaped injury and galloped from one end of the battlefield to the other, rallying his men. The fight ended with the Americans in control of the hill.

San Juan Hill was the turning point of the Spanish-American War. Soon after, the U.S. Navy defeated the Spanish fleet at Santiago, Cuba. With Cuba under control, the U.S. Army invaded Puerto Rico, meeting little resistance. The fighting ended in less than four months. The map below shows some major battles.

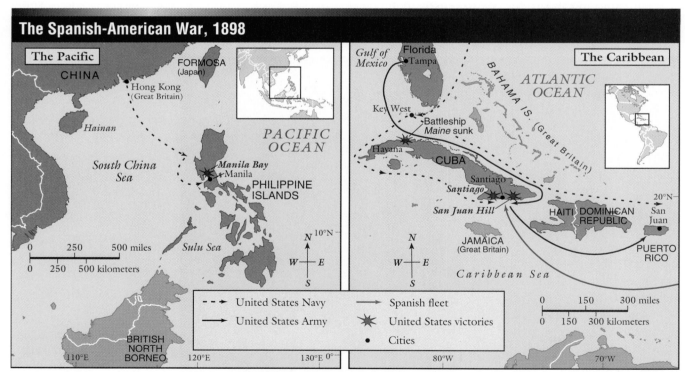

The Spanish-American War, 1898

The Pacific

CHINA
FORMOSA (Japan)
Hong Kong (Great Britain)
Hainan
PACIFIC OCEAN
South China Sea
Manila Bay
Manila
PHILIPPINE ISLANDS
Sulu Sea
BRITISH NORTH BORNEO

0 250 500 miles
0 250 500 kilometers

The Caribbean

Gulf of Mexico
Florida
Tampa
BAHAMA IS. (Great Britain)
ATLANTIC OCEAN
Key West
Battleship Maine sunk
Havana
CUBA
Santiago
Santiago
San Juan Hill
HAITI
DOMINICAN REPUBLIC
San Juan
JAMAICA (Great Britain)
PUERTO RICO
Caribbean Sea
20°N

0 150 300 miles
0 150 300 kilometers

- - -▶ United States Navy
——▶ United States Army
——▶ Spanish fleet
✴ United States victories
• Cities

▲ **Geography** *The map on the left shows the route of Admiral Dewey's fleet to the Philippine Islands. The map on the right shows the victory sites of the American forces in the Caribbean.* **Interpreting the Map** *Where in the Philippines and in the Caribbean were American forces victorious?*

▲ *Theodore Roosevelt and the Rough Riders posed for this photograph after the victory on San Juan Hill in 1898.*

In December 1898, Spain and the United States signed a peace treaty. As part of the treaty, Cuba became a U.S. protectorate. The United States took direct possession of Puerto Rico, the Philippines, and the Pacific island of Guam. In a few short years, the United States had gone from an isolationist nation to a world power with an empire that sprawled from the Caribbean Sea to the Pacific Ocean.

How were American expansionists able to spread their beliefs to other people?

◆ POLICIES IN ASIA

Over the years, Asia continued to be of interest to Americans. With new acquisitions in the Pacific, Americans began to think that they should play a larger political and economic role there.

Relations with Japan

In the first years of the twentieth century, Japan and Russia clashed over the Chinese province of Manchuria. Japan, which had been building up its military strength, sought to control Manchuria. However, Russia was already exploiting the mineral resources there. To settle their disputes, Japan and Russia signed a series of agreements, which Russia proceeded to break. In February 1904, Japan attacked Russian ships anchored in Port Arthur in northern China. Several days later, Japan declared war on Russia.

Japan won great victories over Russia both on land and at sea. Yet although Japan was clearly in control, the war dragged on. By 1905 both sides wanted it to end. Japan had used up much of its resources in the struggle. Russia's defeats had angered its people and brought the nation close to revolution.

In 1905 the Japanese secretly asked President Theodore Roosevelt to help negotiate the peace. Roosevelt gathered diplomats from both sides for a peace conference at Portsmouth, New Hampshire, in August 1905. At the conference, Russia and Japan negotiated a peace. For his efforts, Roosevelt was awarded the Nobel Peace Prize.

The peace treaty left Japan greatly strengthened and caused the United States to reevaluate its policies toward Asia. While most Americans had initially favored the Japanese against the Russians, they now were concerned about Japan's growing power.

To impress upon the Japanese the strength of the U.S. Navy, Roosevelt ordered the American fleet to go on a world-wide cruise. The so-called Great White Fleet, 16 gleaming battleships, set out in December 1907. Before setting off for Asia, the ships sailed around South America and up the Pacific coast to California. At every port, people received them eagerly.

The Open Door Policy in China

Although China had once had an advanced civilization, war and internal conflict had greatly weakened the country by the 1800s. Because of China's hostility to the outside world, the country remained untouched by the Industrial Revolution.

China was weak and ripe for exploitation by powerful nations. Japan and a number of European countries established **spheres of influence** in China. A sphere of influence is a territorial area over which one nation has political and economic influence. Little by little, spheres of influence were being carved up in China.

The United States and Britain had no spheres of influence in mainland China. Both governments wanted to trade with all of China and feared they would be barred from trading in other countries' spheres of influence. The United States and China proposed what they called an Open Door Policy in which all countries would have equal opportunity to trade in China.

After defeating the Boxers in 1900, American troops marched through the Temple of Agriculture grounds in Beijing. ▶

In 1899 and 1900, U.S. Secretary of State John Hay sent letters, called the Open Door Notes, to the nations involved in China. Hay asked these powers to allow all countries to trade within each of the spheres of influence. The nations soon agreed, and the Open Door Policy was in effect.

The Boxer Rebellion

Many Chinese people resented foreign influence. Some joined societies whose purpose was to loosen the grip foreigners had on their country. One such group, I Ho Ch'uan (the Society for Harmonious Fists), was called the Boxers by the British. In 1900, members of the Boxers rose in revolt against foreign holdings. This revolt became known as the Boxer Rebellion.

The Boxers surrounded Beijing. Some 900 Western diplomats and their families were trapped in their embassies for about seven weeks. Troops from Britain, France, Germany, Russia, Japan, and the United States rescued them and crushed the rebellion. The Chinese government was forced to pay the foreign powers millions of dollars in damages.

 Why did the United States support an Open Door Policy in China?

Section 1 Review

Check Understanding

1. **Define** (a) imperialism (b) isolationism (c) protectorate (d) jingoism (e) yellow journalism (f) sphere of influence

2. **Describe** how most Americans reacted to the purchase of Alaska from Russia.

3. **Explain** why the United States wanted to gain control of Hawaii and the Philippines.

Critical Thinking

Analyzing Was the United States justified in its policy of overseas expansion? Explain.

Write About Economics

Connecting Past and Present In a brief paragraph, explain Hawaii's importance to the U.S. economy today.

BUILDING
SKILLS

Evaluating Evidence: "Remember the *Maine!*"

Evaluating evidence is the process of judging the reliability of primary source material. Although eye-witness testimonies and diary entries can be effective sources of information, they can also be biased or incomplete. You need to know whether you can believe what you read.

Here's How

Follow these steps to evaluate historical evidence:

1. Distinguish between fact and opinion as you study the evidence. Look for unsupported general statements and emotion-packed words.

2. Determine how a writer's background or experience might have affected his or her interpretation of the event.

3. Examine and judge carefully the writer's reasoning. How convincing do you find the facts or arguments the writer supplies?

Here's Why

It is important to evaluate evidence to find out the truth about events and judge how reliable the evidence is. In addition, you can determine various points of view about an event by studying the available evidence.

Practice the Skill

The two sources below provide information about the explosion that destroyed the *Maine*. Study the sources and evaluate the evidence about this event using the following questions.

1. What facts does Captain Sigsbee present in his message?

2. What do you think was the effect of Captain Sigsbee's message? What do you think was the effect of the headlines in the *World*?

3. Which piece of evidence about the sinking of the *Maine* is more reliable? Explain why you think so.

Apply the Skill

Based on what you read in this chapter and the evidence below, do you think the United States would have gone to war with Spain if the newspapers had not printed sensational articles about the *Maine*? Write an explanation of your response, citing evidence from both sources to support your point of view.

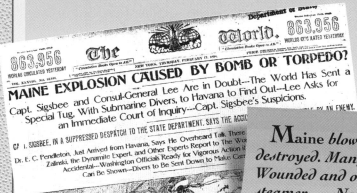

863,956
WORLDS CIRCULATED YESTERDAY

The World. 863,956
WORLDS CIRCULATED YESTERDAY

Department of Buoy?

Circulation Books Open to All.

NEW YORK, THURSDAY, FEBRUARY 17, 1898

MAINE EXPLOSION CAUSED BY BOMB OR TORPEDO?

Capt. Sigsbee and Consul-General Lee Are in Doubt---The World Has Sent a Special Tug, With Submarine Divers, to Havana to Find Out---Lee Asks for an Immediate Court of Inquiry---Capt. Sigsbee's Suspicions.

... BY AN ENEMY.

CAPT. SIGSBEE, IN A SUPPRESSED DESPATCH TO THE STATE DEPARTMENT, SAYS THE ACCID...

Dr. E. C. Pendleton, Just Arrived from Havana, Says He Overheard Talk There ...
Zalinski, the Dynamite Expert, and Other Experts Report to The Wor...
Accidental---Washington Officials Ready for Vigorous Action i...
Can Be Shown---Divers to Be Sent Down to Make Car...

M*aine blown up in Havana Harbor at nine-forty tonight and destroyed. Many wounded and doubtless more killed and drowned. Wounded and others on board Spanish man-of-war and Ward Line steamer. . . . No one has clothing other than that upon him. Public opinion should be suspended until further report. All Spanish officers, including representatives of General Blanco, now with me to express sympathy.*

Message from Captain Sigsbee to the Secretary of the Navy, February 15, 1898

The Big Stick in Latin America

PREVIEW

Objectives

- To describe how the United States tried to win a position of dominance in the Western Hemisphere
- To identify the steps that led to the building of the Panama Canal
- To explain how tension grew between the United States and Mexico

Vocabulary

autonomy   isthmus

guerrilla   dollar diplomacy

Victory in the Spanish-American War ensured that the United States would be regarded as a world power, but it also presented the country with a serious dilemma. After all, the United States was founded on freedom. Many Americans wondered how the United States could now "own" other countries.

◆ AN AMERICAN EMPIRE

By the end of the Spanish-American War, the United States controlled many islands in the Caribbean Sea. Puerto Rico was a U.S. colony, and Cuba was a U.S. protectorate. Although many Cubans and Puerto Ricans felt great enthusiasm for the United States at first, these feelings did not last. The United States soon found itself labeled an invader, not a liberator.

Cuba and Puerto Rico

Cuba's economy had been devastated by the war, and the United States decided to maintain troops on the island until the economy was running more smoothly. The United States primarily wanted to protect its large investments in the Cuban sugar industry.

In 1901, U.S. control of Cuba was given a legal basis. As a price of getting American troops out, Cuba agreed to put a clause in its new constitution that granted the United States a number of rights. This clause, known as the Platt Amendment, gave the United States the right to intervene in Cuban affairs to preserve order. It also gave the United States the right to maintain naval bases in Cuba. Today, the United States still controls Guantanamo Bay Naval Base there.

In 1900 the United States granted Puerto Rico limited **autonomy,** or independence. Puerto Ricans were allowed to elect representatives to one of Puerto Rico's two legislative houses. The United States appointed representatives to the other house, as well as the governor of the island. Additionally, a representative from Puerto Rico sat in the U.S. Congress but could not vote.

Puerto Ricans wanted greater self-government, however. Luis Muñoz Rivera, Puerto Rico's congressional representative from 1910 to 1916, was among those who worked toward this goal. Their efforts resulted in the Jones Act of 1917. It made the island a territory of the United States and gave Puerto Ricans the choice of becoming U.S. citizens. Puerto Ricans were allowed to elect representatives to both houses of their legislature. However, the governor of Puerto Rico continued to be appointed by the President of the United States.

The Philippines

The United States also chose to maintain control over the Philippine Islands. As the Spanish-American War drew to an end, American anti-imperialists argued for granting independence to the Philippines. The expansionists in government urged the United States to maintain control over the Philippines. After some hesitation, President McKinley decided to keep the Philippines as a possession.

Many Filipinos felt betrayed by this U.S. action. They had believed that American control would be short-lived and that Filipinos would regain control of their country. As a result of these feelings of betrayal, Filipinos under Aguinaldo fought for independence. For three years, beginning in 1899, Aguinaldo led a **guerrilla** campaign against the U.S. Army. Guerrillas are fighters, not part of a regular army, who make surprise raids on their enemy. The Filipino fighters hid in jungles and hills. It took more than 60,000 U.S. troops to put down the rebellion.

 **Why did the United States decide not to grant the Philippines and Puerto Rico their independence?**

Luis Muñoz Rivera

In Puerto Rico, July 17 is an important day. It is the birthday of Luis Muñoz Rivera, the journalist and politician who dedicated his life to the cause of Puerto Rican independence.

As a young man, Muñoz Rivera fought for Puerto Rican independence from Spain.

▲ Luis Muñoz Rivera (1880–1916)

When Spain gave Puerto Rico permission to set up a cabinet, he became its premier. Through his newspaper, *La Democracia*, which he founded in 1889, Muñoz Rivera continued to push for full independence for his homeland. When Spain granted Puerto Rico full self-government in 1897, he was elected to lead the new administration. Eight days after he took office, United States forces took over the island.

Under control of the American government, a representative from Puerto Rico was allowed to take a seat in the U.S. Congress but could not vote. In 1910, Muñoz Rivera went to Washington, D.C., as his people's representative. An outspoken critic of the U.S. policy towards his country, Muñoz Rivera called it "unworthy of the United States which imposed it and of the Puerto Ricans who have to endure it."

For six years, Muñoz Rivera worked tirelessly to change the policy. Sadly, he died in 1916—a year before U.S. Congress passed the Jones Act, which provided greater self-government for Puerto Rico.

Looking Back: How are the ideals of Muñoz Rivera similar to the ideals of some early Americans?

◆ RELATIONS WITH PANAMA

In 1900, Democrat William Jennings Bryan ran for President on an anti-imperialist platform. Bryan lost to William McKinley. When McKinley was assassinated in September 1901, his Vice President, Theodore Roosevelt, became President. Roosevelt continued to support U.S. expansion. One of his concerns was to deal with a problem that had cropped up in the first days of the Spanish-American War.

When war first broke out, the battleship *Oregon* was in San Francisco. To get to the fighting in Cuba, it had to sail around the southern tip of South America. The *Oregon* arrived at the war scene almost too late to take part in the fighting.

This experience renewed interest in finding a site in Central America for a canal that would link the Atlantic and the Pacific oceans. One possible route was through Nicaragua. Another was across the **isthmus,** or narrow land strip, of Panama. The French had tried to build such a canal. They began digging in Panama in 1881 but gave up after eight years. Widespread disease, including yellow fever and malaria, as well as lack of money and proper tools, forced an end to the project.

Panama and the Big Stick

In 1901 a U.S. commission recommended digging a canal through Panama, then a province of Colombia. Roosevelt offered Colombia $10 million for the right to build the canal. The Colombians wanted more money, so negotiations broke down.

In November 1903 a quick series of events changed the situation. The Panamanians revolted against Colombia and declared independence. The United States had a warship in the area, and Roosevelt sent U.S. marines to Panama to prevent Colombian troops from attacking. The United States quickly recognized Panama's new government, and within two weeks, Panama and the United States signed a treaty. In it, Panama agreed to give the United States a zone ten miles wide across the country in return for a one-time payment of $10 million and $250,000 per year in rent.

Theodore Roosevelt's actions sparked a storm of outrage in both Latin America and the United States. His willingness to use U.S. power to create a new country that would obey the United States angered some people and marked the beginning of a new era in U.S. foreign policy. It also expressed Roosevelt's faith in direct action. As he said,

> **❝I have always been fond of the West African proverb 'speak softly and carry a big stick, you will go far.'❞**

Building the Panama Canal

Before the massive job of canal building could go ahead, something had to be done about the health conditions in Panama. In 1904, Colonel William C. Gorgas took charge of improving sanitary conditions in the Canal Zone. Gorgas drew on the work of Cuban doctor Carlos Juan Finlay and American doctor Walter Reed, who had identified mosquitoes as a source of yellow fever.

Gorgas supervised the draining of swamps and the clearing of land that was infested by mosquitoes. By 1906 he had wiped out yellow fever in Panama. He had also reduced the rate of malaria and eliminated the rats that carried plague. Without these achievements, many thousands of workers would have died of disease. Thanks to the efforts of William Gorgas, the disease rate among canal workers was lower than it was in the contiguous United States.

Digging the Panama Canal was one of the biggest building projects in history. Workers labored for seven years, cutting a channel through the mountains and damming rivers. The workers were brought in from several countries. Few of them had had any construction experience, but they received the necessary training and surpassed all expectations. The canal was completed six months ahead of schedule and $23 million under budget.

In 1914 the first ship passed through the Panama Canal. With control of a vital link between the Atlantic and Pacific oceans, the United States was a first-rate world power.

 **Why was the Panama Canal important to the United States?**

◆ THE ROOSEVELT COROLLARY

By 1901 the United States was the undisputed power in the Western Hemisphere, ready to intervene wherever its interests were challenged. Roosevelt tried to put intervention in acceptable terms. The United States, he said, had a "most regrettable but necessary international duty which must be performed for the sake of the welfare of humanity."

It was not long before Roosevelt saw the need to exercise this duty. In 1902, Venezuela and Britain became involved in a dispute over a loan that Venezuela had received from Britain. The Venezuelan government refused to repay the loan. Britain, Italy, and Germany then blockaded several Venezuelan ports, preventing all ships from sailing in or out.

Although the Europeans chose to withdraw from Venezuela after forcibly collecting the money owed them, the crisis put the United States in a difficult position. If the United States had allowed foreign powers to attack a Latin American country, the Monroe Doctrine would have proved useless. On the other hand, if the United States had discouraged forcible collection of debts, that might have promoted financial dishonesty.

Roosevelt solved this dilemma by adding the Roosevelt Corollary to the Monroe Doctrine. A corollary is an addition to a document. The Roosevelt Corollary stated the United States alone had the right to interfere in the domestic affairs of Latin American nations if they were unstable or, in the case of Venezuela, unable to meet financial obligations.

In 1905, the Roosevelt Corollary was first tested when the United States took on the foreign debt of the Dominican Republic. Roosevelt did not want to annex the nation, but he fully believed it was the United States' obligation to intervene in the affairs of the country. Roosevelt defended U.S. intervention in the Dominican Republic, stating,

> **❝I want to do nothing but what a policeman has to do in Santo Domingo. As for annexing the island, I have about as much desire to annex as a gorged boa constrictor might have to swallow a porcupine wrong-end-to.❞**

During the next 30 years, the United States used the Roosevelt Corollary to excuse intervention in Latin American countries on several occasions. Each time the United States intervened, the people of Latin America reacted with anger. To Latin Americans the United States was "the colossus of the North" that would use its power without respect for the rights of Latin Americans.

 **How did the Roosevelt Corollary affect relations with Latin America?**

◆ DOLLAR DIPLOMACY AND MORAL DIPLOMACY

In 1909, William Howard Taft became President. Taft had long worked with Roosevelt and supported most of his policies. He continued to support these policies, but he used his own style to implement them as President.

Taft believed foreign trade was the key to American prosperity. He thought the United States should use its economic power to attain its foreign policy goals. This use of economic power came to be called **dollar diplomacy.** Taft hoped that by investing large amounts of money in Latin American countries, friendship as well as profits would be the result.

Taft's dollar diplomacy was a skilled way of gaining power in Latin America. With their investments, U.S. business people were able to gain control of industries and land throughout Latin America. With this power, U.S. investors were able to influence Latin American governments. Furthermore, if trouble arose, the U.S. government was more likely to intervene in order to protect U.S. investments.

Such actions created even more resentment of U.S. economic imperialism in Latin America. Many in Latin America could see little difference between the dollar diplomacy of Taft and the "big-stick" diplomacy of Roosevelt.

Woodrow Wilson, who became President in 1913, had different views from those of Taft and Roosevelt. Wilson believed that the United States had "a mission to do good" in the world. He spoke against imperialism, big-stick diplomacy, and dollar diplomacy. He hoped to show Latin Americans that U.S. policy was based on cooperation, not power. Wilson hoped to encourage political reform in Latin America, which would lead to stability. He called his policy "moral diplomacy."

Although Wilson expressed views that were different from Roosevelt's and Taft's, he continued to exercise U.S. power once he took office. In fact, he sent the U.S. military into the Caribbean and Latin America more often than Taft and Roosevelt combined. For example, the United States intervened in Haiti in 1915 and in the Dominican Republic in 1916. Political unrest and corruption in those countries threatened U.S. business interests there. Wilson felt it was necessary to show the people of those countries "how to elect good men." He sent the American marines and navy to supervise Haitian and

◀ **Government** *This political cartoon shows President Roosevelt pulling a string of ships through the Caribbean Sea while carrying a big stick on his shoulder.* **Interpreting the Cartoon** *How is Roosevelt's leadership portrayed?*

Dominican elections and take over the countries' police duties. In the Dominican Republic, American citizens were even named to positions of power in the nation's government.

? How was Woodrow Wilson's moral diplomacy similar to big-stick diplomacy?

◆ CONFLICT IN MEXICO

Wilson's actions led to serious problems with Mexico, where a revolution had broken out. Wilson believed the United States had to act to give Mexico a democratic government. This set the stage for a serious confrontation between Mexico and the United States.

In the early 1800s in Mexico, millions of peasants farmed small plots of land leased from a small group of wealthy landowners. Later in the century, under the dictatorship of Porfirio Díaz (dē´-äs), Mexico began to industrialize. Mexicans built factories, oil wells, mines, and railroads. The profits that poured into the country enriched a few people but left the majority of Mexicans as poor as ever. The huge gap between the poor and the rich led to widespread unrest. In 1910, civil war broke out. Emiliano Zapata, one of the leaders of the rebel forces, dedicated himself to land reform for the peasants of Mexico.

Wilson and Mexico

In 1911, Díaz's government was overthrown and he left the country. Díaz was succeeded by Francisco Madero, who proved to be a weak president. In 1913 a general named Victoriano Huerta seized power and had Madero assassinated. Huerta favored the wealthy landowners in Mexico. U.S. business people encouraged Wilson to recognize Huerta as the country's new leader. Wilson refused to deal with what he called a "government of butchers." In an interview with a writer, Wilson exclaimed,

" I challenge you to cite me an instance in all history of the world where liberty was handed down from above! Liberty is always attained by the forces working below, underneath, by the great movement of the people. "

Wilson put American support behind Venustiano Carranza (kär-rän´-sä), who challenged Huerta's power and promised to distribute land to the poor.

In 1914, Mexican authorities arrested some American sailors who were visiting the Mexican port of Tampico. When the United States protested the sailors' arrest, Mexico promptly released the sailors and apologized for the actions of the arresting authorities. The commander of the U.S. soldiers was not satisfied. He demanded a 21-gun salute to the American flag. The Mexican officials agreed to do this, but only if the U.S. sailors in return saluted the Mexican flag.

Wilson was infuriated with Mexico. He ordered U.S. forces to seize the major port city of Veracruz.

▲ As a leader of the Mexican Revolution, Emiliano Zapata strongly opposed the governments of Porfirio Díaz, Francisco Madero, Victoriano Huerta, and Venustiano Carranza.

▲ Francisco "Pancho" Villa tried to control Mexico after the fall of Porfirio Díaz.

capture Villa. Pershing spent 11 months trying to hunt down Villa in northern Mexico, but he never caught up with him. In the meantime, U.S. troops remained on Mexican soil. The presence of U.S. troops angered Mexicans so much that the two nations came close to war. Finally, when it became clear that Villa would not be captured, Wilson ordered Pershing home. The episode was over, but tension between the two countries would last for many years. However, the continuous fighting and civil war within Mexico brought another change to the United States. Between 1910 and 1920, thousands of Mexicans fled the violence, crossing the border and settling in cities, towns, and rural areas in the southwestern part of the United States.

 What led to growing tension between Mexico and the United States?

His real goal was to prevent a shipment of arms from Germany from reaching Huerta. Even Wilson's ally, Carranza, said the United States had no business seizing Mexican territory. When he became president of Mexico later that year, Carranza pressed the United States to remove its troops, and Wilson did so.

Pancho Villa

It soon became clear that Carranza had no intention of keeping his earlier promise to give land to the poor. One of Carranza's army generals, Francisco "Pancho" Villa (vē´-yä), revolted against his rule. He led rebel forces in the northern part of Mexico, much as Zapata was continuing to do in the south. Villa hoped that the United States would support him. Wilson considered doing so, believing Villa to be a committed reformer, but he ended up continuing to support Carranza instead. Villa, angered, threatened the United States. In January 1916, Villa's forces stopped a train in northern Mexico and killed 16 U.S. citizens. Two months later, Villa's men crossed the border and attacked Columbus, New Mexico. They killed some residents, burned the town, and then escaped back across the border. Villa, whom Wilson had once viewed as a supporter of and fighter for democracy, was now considered a dangerous bandit.

Americans were shocked by Villa's attack. President Wilson responded to it by sending 6,000 troops under General John J. Pershing to Mexico to

Section 2 Review

Check Understanding

1. **Define** (a) autonomy (b) guerrilla (c) isthmus (d) dollar diplomacy

2. **Explain** how the Roosevelt Corollary was an extension of the Monroe Doctrine.

3. **State** why it was important for the United States to build a canal between the Atlantic and the Pacific oceans.

4. **Discuss** what led to Pershing's invasion of Mexico in 1916.

Critical Thinking

Comparing and Contrasting In what ways were big-stick diplomacy, dollar diplomacy, and moral diplomacy similar? How were they different?

Write About Government

◆**Connecting Past and Present** Write an essay analyzing political relations between Mexico and the United States today.

CONNECTING HISTORY & Geography

THE PANAMA CANAL

No project tested early twentieth-century technology against the forces of geography more than the building of the Panama Canal. The builders of the Panama Canal were challenged by the health hazards and the geographical features of the area.

Several attempts had been made and abandoned to dig the passage—and no wonder! Building the canal involved cutting trenches through mountains, battling disease, and finding workers willing to put their lives on the line for a 40-mile-long hole in the ground.

Work on the canal went on for ten years. The builders had to come up with many new ideas. One very effective idea was the design for a series of locks. The locks are like giant elevators. Water is pumped into them to raise a ship and pumped out of them to lower it. The locks allow ships to be carried over the high land of Panama.

The canal cost more than half a billion dollars to build, but its worth was beyond measure. Since its completion in 1914, the canal has provided faster, less expensive passage between the Atlantic and Pacific oceans. During World War II the canal was heavily guarded against the possibility of enemy attack.

As trains, trucks, and especially airplanes increasingly came into use, the role of the Panama Canal lessened. It is still a critical shipping lane, however. Japan, for example, sends about two million tons of cars through the canal each year.

Making the Geographic Connection

1. Why was building the Panama Canal such a long-held dream of American leaders?

2. Why do you think the Panama Canal was a military target during World War II?

3. Review the map on this page. In what direction must one travel to go from the Pacific Ocean to the Caribbean Sea through the Panama Canal?

4. Is the Panama Canal as important today as it was when it was built in 1914? Explain your answer.

Connecting Past and Present

Use the maps in the atlas that begins on page 680. Identify another place where building a canal would provide economic benefits to a region. Make a drawing of your canal route. Then write a brief summary explaining the benefits.

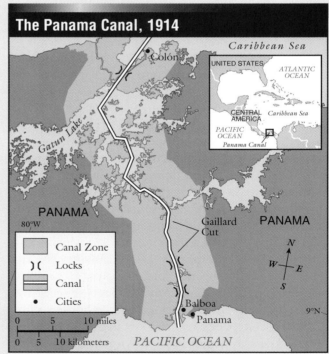

▲ **Geography** *This map shows the number of locks that ships must pass through to navigate the Panama Canal.* **Interpreting the Map** *How many locks must a ship pass through between Balboa and Gaillard Cut?*

Section 3

The Origins of Global War

PREVIEW

Objectives

- To explain how nationalism and imperialism created tension among the nations of Europe

- To analyze why the system of alliances led to war in 1914

Vocabulary

arms race	terrorist
ally	mobilize
heir	

During the late 1800s and early 1900s, many nations had taken steps toward international cooperation. Peace movements had grown in strength. Antiwar societies worked hard to convince people that war was wasteful and not a solution to problems. War was seen by many as too costly—even for the winners.

◆ ARMS RACE IN EUROPE

People from different parts of the world were being brought together in different ways. Technology made it possible for people to travel and communicate with one another. Businesses bought and sold in worldwide markets. International humanitarian organizations, such as the Red Cross, helped people in times of crisis. Leaders from Europe and the United States held conferences to encourage cooperation among their nations. Presidents Roosevelt, Taft, and Wilson all took active parts in international discussions to promote peace.

Despite all these international relationships, tensions arose in Europe in the early 1900s as European powers competed with one another to extend their control in Asia, Africa, and the Pacific. Great Britain and France had huge colonial empires, while Germany's and Italy's overseas holdings were not nearly so vast. France and Germany disagreed about who owned Alsace-Lorraine, a part of France that had been seized by Germany.

As a result of these tensions, the major European powers started to increase their military power. Germany began the process by building a powerful, modern navy. Since Germany already had the most powerful army in Europe, its rivals became concerned. Most alarmed was Britain, which, for more than 100 years, had possessed the largest navy in the world. Concerned with Germany's military buildup, Britain began to enlarge its own army and navy. Soon, Britain and Germany were joined by other European powers. Before long a dangerous **arms race,** or competition to build weapons, was underway in Europe.

European tensions increased additionally because of the forces of nationalism sweeping central and eastern Europe. By 1900 both Austria-Hungary and the Ottoman Empire were on the verge of collapse. Austria-Hungary included Austria, Hungary, what are now the Czech and Slovak republics, Slovenia, and Balkan lands such as Bosnia and Croatia. The Ottoman Empire consisted of Turkey and surrounding areas. Both empires included people from many different nationalities, all of whom wanted their independence. Nationalism grew as the two huge empires, which had ruled central and eastern Europe for many centuries, began to disintegrate.

As these empires weakened, the powers in Europe jockeyed for **allies.** An ally is a nation or person that is associated with another for a common cause or purpose. Germany, Italy, and Austria-Hungary formed one major alliance, called the Triple Alliance, in 1882.

Study Hint

A synonym is a word that has the same or similar meaning to another word. For example, in the first paragraph of this column, the words _increase_ and _enlarge_ are synonyms. Writers often use synonyms to avoid repetition. Look for other examples of synonyms as you read.

France, in 1894, signed an agreement with Russia. Each nation promised to come to the aid of the other if it were attacked. In 1907, Britain joined France and Russia to form the Triple Entente, which was an agreement among the three nations that they were allies.

The leaders of these countries believed their alliances resulted in a balance of power. They thought that by securing as many allies as possible, each alliance would become stronger. They felt that neither alliance would take advantage of the other. The theory was that respect for each other's strength would discourage either side from using aggressive tactics.

The balance, however, was not solid. National leaders were not satisfied with the empires they controlled. They wanted more territory for themselves. Also, since each member of an alliance promised to help the other when needed, an attack on one country would draw other countries into the conflict until the major European powers were involved. A European conflict could become a world war. The map below shows how Europe was divided into alliances at the outset of World War I.

By 1914, Europe was like a powder keg ready to explode. The spark was set off by a shooting in the city of Sarajevo (sä´-rä-yä-vō), capital of the Austro-Hungarian province of Bosnia.

? What factors contributed to the rise of tensions in Europe?

◆ THE WORLD GOES TO WAR

For decades, Austria-Hungary, Russia, and the Ottoman Empire fought for the control of the Balkans, a peninsula that included Albania, Bulgaria, Greece, Romania, Bosnia, Serbia, Montenegro, and other lands. Russia was interested in the Balkans because it wanted to gain control of the outlet from the Black Sea into the Mediterranean Sea.

Germany was interested in building a railroad through the Balkans to the Middle and Far East. Britain worried about this plan. It also was concerned that any trouble in the area would affect the Suez Canal, which was Britain's main route to its colonies in Asia.

▲ **Geography** *This map shows the different alliances among countries at the outset of World War I.* **Interpreting the Map** *Which countries make up the Allies? Which countries from the Central Powers border the Russian empire?*

▲ As Archduke Franz Ferdinand and his wife Sophie rode through Bosnia, Gavrilo Princip stepped forward and fatally shot them.

In June 1914, Archduke Franz Ferdinand visited Bosnia, a province within his empire of Austria-Hungary. Franz Ferdinand was the **heir** to the throne, or the person next in line to inherit it. As the archduke rode through Sarajevo, a 19-year-old Bosnian, Gavrilo Princip (gäv´-rē-lau prēnt´-sēp), shot and killed him and his wife. Princip wanted Bosnia to unite with its independent neighbor, Serbia. Princip was a member of a Serbian **terrorist** group. A terrorist is a person who is willing to use violence to promote a cause. Though there was no direct evidence that Princip was connected to the Serbian government, Austria-Hungary blamed Serbia for the murder. Austria-Hungary decided to teach the Serbs a lesson, regardless of the consequences. Austria-Hungary declared war on Serbia on July 28, 1914.

The alliance system went into effect. Serbia's ally Russia believed it had to defend Serbia or else it would be seen as a second-rate power. The Russians **mobilized** their troops, or called them to duty. Austria-Hungary's ally Germany warned the Russians to cancel the mobilization. When the Russians refused to back down, the Germans declared war on them on August 1. Then on August 3, Germany declared war on Russia's closest ally, France. On the way to France,

the German army invaded Belgium, a neutral country. Britain then declared war on Germany. Europe had now slipped into a war that nobody had wanted.

Within weeks, much of the world was divided into warring sides. The Ottoman Empire joined Germany and Austria-Hungary in a new alliance called the Central Powers. Japan joined with Britain, France, and Russia in another new alliance known as the Allies. In 1915, Italy joined the conflict on the side of the Allies. Even in the far-flung colonies controlled by these powers, people prepared to help the war effort. The spark set off by the murder of the archduke had set the stage for a worldwide war.

 How did the European alliances contribute to the causes of World War I?

Section 3 Review

Check Understanding

1. **Define** (a) arms race (b) ally (c) heir (d) terrorist (e) mobilize

2. **Analyze** the factors that led to increased tensions in Europe.

3. **Name** the European countries that made up the Triple Alliance and the Triple Entente.

4. **Evaluate** the benefits and the disadvantages of the alliance system.

Critical Thinking

Hypothesizing What might have happened in 1914 if the system of alliances had not existed?

Write About History

Connecting Past and Present Write a letter to the editor supporting or criticizing a current U.S. alliance.

Chapter 16
Review

CHAPTER SUMMARY

Section 1

Although some Americans had been wary of empire building, this attitude began to change in the 1880s as the United States industrialized and its international trade increased. In the 1890s the United States annexed Hawaii and took control of Cuba, Puerto Rico, and the Philippines after winning the Spanish-American War. After the war, Cuba won limited independence. The Philippines, Guam, and Puerto Rico became U.S. possessions. Meanwhile, with its Open Door Policy, the United States tried to keep trade open in all parts of China.

Section 2

U.S. control over Puerto Rico and the Philippines was a continuing sore point. In the Philippines it led to armed conflict. Relations with Latin America soured as a result of numerous U.S. interventions in the affairs of Latin American countries. Soon after Panama won independence, it signed a treaty granting the United States permission to build a canal between the Atlantic and the Pacific oceans. With the completion of the Panama Canal in 1914, the United States became a major power. U.S. intervention in Mexico during the Mexican Revolution continued a legacy of distrust between the two countries.

Section 3

A vigorous imperialist policy by some European powers in the early 1900s increased tensions and led to an arms race. A system of alliances set the stage for war by ensuring that European nations would come to the aid of an attacked ally. When the heir to the throne of Austria-Hungary was assassinated in Sarejevo in 1914, war began.

Connecting ◆ Past and Present

What countries are allies of the United States today? What factors promote these alliances?

Using Vocabulary

From the list below, select the term that best completes each sentence.

guerrilla	imperialism
ally	mobilize
jingoism	autonomy
isthmus	terrorist
heir	isolationism

1. In 1914, Archduke Franz Ferdinand was the _____ to the throne of Austria-Hungary.
2. The aggressive patriotism called _____ helped create public sentiment for involvement in the war against Spain.
3. To prepare for war, a country will _____ its troops.
4. _____ is the policy of extending power and influence around the world.
5. Americans who believed in _____ thought that the country should stay out of the affairs of other countries.
6. _____ fighters hide in jungles and hills and make surprise attacks.
7. In the early 1900s, Americans wanted to build a canal across the _____ of Panama.
8. The _____ was arrested for his violent activities.
9. In World War I, Britain, France, and Japan considered Russia an _____ .
10. When a country is independent, it has _____ .

Check Understanding

1. **Summarize** why the United States changed its policy of isolationism in the late 1800s.
2. **Describe** how the United States' interest in expansion led the country into war with Spain.
3. **Explain** the Open Door Policy toward China.
4. **List** the steps the United States took to prepare for building the Panama Canal.

5. **Describe** how Latin American views toward Americans changed after the Spanish-American War.

6. **Explain** why relations were tense between the United States and Mexico during the Mexican Revolution.

7. **Explain** the reasons for the Open Door Notes.

8. **Describe** how moral diplomacy was different from dollar diplomacy.

9. **Summarize** the factors that led to World War I.

10. **Review** the events that led to the Boxer Rebellion of 1900.

Critical Thinking

1. **Synthesizing Information** Describe three events that contributed to the United States becoming a world power in the early 1900s.

2. **Understanding Causes and Effects** What long-term effects did increased trade with East Asia have on U.S. foreign policy?

3. **Contrasting** How did the status of Cuba differ from that of Puerto Rico and the Philippines after the Spanish-American War?

4. **Analyzing** How did nationalism and imperialism create unrest in Europe?

◆ **Connecting Past and Present** Have U.S. responsibilities as a world power changed since the days of Theodore Roosevelt? Why or why not?

Interpreting the Timeline

Use the timeline on pages 312–313 to answer these questions.

1. Which U.S. event happened the same year that the Philippines revolted against U.S. control?

2. Who was President when the United States and Spain went to war?

3. When did the United States first declare war against a foreign country?

Putting Skills to Work

EVALUATING EVIDENCE

In the Building Skills lesson on page 321, you learned that evaluating evidence is the process of judging the reliability of material. Look at the cartoon on page 325. Study it and answer the following questions.

1. Do you think the cartoonist is exaggerating the truth?

2. What do you think the cartoonist is trying to make people think?

3. Is the cartoon a reliable source that shows all the facts of the situation?

Writing to Persuade

Choose a side for a debate on whether the United States should or should not be involved in world affairs today. **Write** your position, using supporting points from the chapter. Find classmates who took the opposite position and compare your papers.

 *Portfolio Project*

NEWSPAPER ARTICLES

Pick an event that happened in your community recently. Then write two newspaper stories about the event. The first story should be a straightforward description of the event, answering the traditional newspaper questions:

Who? What? When? Where? Why? How?

The second newspaper article should be in the style of yellow journalism, with exaggerations and eye-catching devices. If you use a computer, you may want to experiment with different fonts. For each article, be sure to write headlines that reflect the style in which you are writing. See which style your classmates prefer.

Chapter 17
World War I and Its Aftermath 1914–1920

CHAPTER PREVIEW

Section 1   The United States Is Drawn into War

As European nations entered World War I, the United States tried to stay neutral. However, a series of incidents drew the United States into the conflict.

Section 2   Fighting the War

Russian withdrawal and the collapse of the eastern front made the presence of U.S. fighting forces an immediate necessity.

Section 3   The Home Front Effort

A shortage of labor on the home front led to unusual opportunities for women and minorities and a concerted effort by the government to build public support for the war.

Section 4   The War to End All Wars

Woodrow Wilson's dreams of a just peace were dashed by the determination of European Allies to punish Germany.

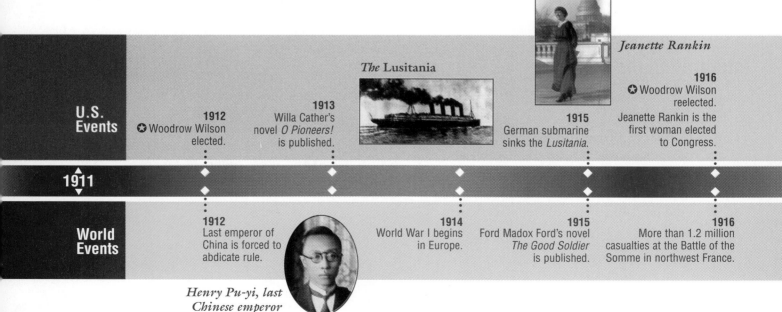

The Lusitania

Jeanette Rankin

U.S. Events

1912
✪ Woodrow Wilson elected.

1913
Willa Cather's novel *O Pioneers!* is published.

1915
German submarine sinks the *Lusitania*.

1916
✪ Woodrow Wilson reelected. Jeanette Rankin is the first woman elected to Congress.

1911

World Events

1912
Last emperor of China is forced to abdicate rule.

Henry Pu-yi, last Chinese emperor

1914
World War I begins in Europe.

1915
Ford Madox Ford's novel *The Good Soldier* is published.

1916
More than 1.2 million casualties at the Battle of the Somme in northwest France.

Portfolio Project

A PERSONAL VIEW OF THE WAR

In a short time, the United States went from being neutral to participating in the war in Europe. You will read how and why the United States changed its position on the war. You will also read about the effects of war on the soldiers who fought the battles. Pay close attention to what they experienced and what they did. At the end of this chapter, you will take a soldier's point of view and write several journal entries that capture what the war was like.

▲ A German bomb attack on November 27, 1914, destroyed these buildings in the city of Ypres, Belgium. ◈◈ **Connecting Past and Present** *How do you think the lives of the people in the photograph were affected? What are some ways people today deal with the sudden and unexpected destruction of their property?*

U.S. enters World War I

1917
Zimmermann telegram causes anger.

U.S. enters World War I.

1918
Wilson makes Fourteen Points speech.

1919
Wilson arrives in Paris to begin Peace Conference.

1920
✪ Warren G. Harding elected.
Senate rejects Treaty of Versailles.

1922

1917
Russian Revolution takes place.

Communist symbol

1918
World War I ends.

1919
Treaty of Versailles is signed. Mussolini begins to organize Fascist movement.

Benito Mussolini, Italian Fascist leader

1921
Allies set German reparations at $33 billion.

The United States Is Drawn into War

PREVIEW

Objectives

- To describe conditions of battle during the first years of World War I

- To explain how the United States tried to remain neutral in the early years of World War I

- To summarize German actions during the first years of the war

- To analyze why the United States went to war in 1917

Vocabulary

civilian
diplomatic relations
tsar

After World War I broke out in Europe in 1914, the United States government tried to remain neutral. Gradually, however, tensions with Germany increased, and in 1917 the United States entered the war, on the Allied side, against Germany.

◆ THE FIRST YEARS OF THE WAR

As war spread throughout Europe and parts of Asia, country after country was drawn in. The Ottoman Empire and Bulgaria joined the Central Powers. Italy, Serbia, Japan, and Greece were among the countries siding with the Allies. By the time the United States joined the fighting in 1917, the war involved most of the world's powers.

The Stalemate in Europe

At first, both the Allies and the Central Powers expected a quick victory. Because France had built strong fortifications along the German border, Germany decided not to attack France directly. Rather, Germany chose to send its army through Belgium and attack France from the north. With the French army surrounded, the Germans expected an easy capture of Paris and a quick end to the war. France, on the other hand, expected to advance deeply into Germany after an attack across the border. Meanwhile, France's ally Russia would attack Germany from the east, trapping the Germans between two huge forces.

The war did not go as planned for either side. The German army crossed Belgium and invaded France in a lightning attack, but the Germans could not capture Paris. The French attack across the German border failed. The Russians took a horrible beating from Austria-Hungary and Germany. Demoralized, many Russian troops fought reluctantly, and others began to desert.

Trench Warfare

The war then entered a new phase. The German and French armies dug in to defend themselves and hold their positions, digging trenches six to eight feet deep and about five feet wide. Soon a network of trenches extended for 400 miles across Belgium and northern France. If placed end to end, the trenches of both armies would have extended for 25,000 miles—enough to circle the globe at the Equator.

Each side launched huge attacks against the enemy trenches. Some of the battles lasted for months and cost hundreds of thousands of lives—they were the bloodiest battles the world had ever seen. In just one battle, the first Battle of the Somme River, from July to November 1916, more than 1.2 million soldiers were killed or wounded. Yet neither side could break through the other side's defenses.

New Technologies

One reason the battles were so horrible was that both sides had powerful new weapons. Most deadly was the machine gun, which could fire 600 bullets per minute. Because it was too heavy to be carried easily in battle, the machine gun was used primarily by soldiers in the trenches as a defensive weapon. As soldiers charged toward enemy trenches, they were often cut down by a hail of machine gun fire.

Modern technology created other weapons that were first used in World War I. Both sides used poison gas. At the urging of Winston Churchill, the naval commander, the British developed the tank, called the "iron monster." Both sides sent tanks into battle.

Modern technology also made the seas more dangerous. The Germans first used the submarine, turning it into a deadly weapon against enemy warships, merchant ships carrying supplies, and even passenger ships with thousands of **civilians** aboard. A civilian is a person who is not in the military.

Meanwhile, for the first time in history, the skies became a battleground. Airplanes flew above the battlefields to get information on opposing armies. Fighter planes shot each other from the sky. Bombers killed both soldiers at the front and civilians far behind the lines. In the beginning, both sides fought the air war with dirigibles, or zeppelins. The Germans used the huge airships to destroy ammunition factories and train depots in France and in Great Britain. When the zeppelins became easy targets for anti-aircraft guns, they were no longer used.

Even when they were not actively involved in fighting, soldiers were dying. The trenches where they

Red Cross volunteers attend to injured soldiers in a trench during World War I. ▼

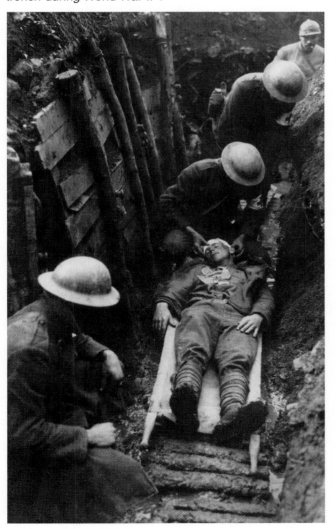

lived for months at a time were wet, muddy, and infested with rats and insects. Soldiers stood close together for long periods of time in holes filled with water. All kinds of diseases spread quickly, killing soldiers just as bullets and bombs did.

 Why was World War I more deadly than earlier wars?

◆ AMERICAN NEUTRALITY

Once the fighting began, President Wilson's main goal was to keep the United States out of the war. Wilson therefore announced a policy of neutrality—the United States would not take sides in the conflict. Wilson believed that a neutral United States might help bring the two sides together and end the war.

Divided Opinion

On August 19, 1914, President Wilson told the American people that they should be "neutral in fact as well as in name." That was not easy because from the start, most Americans favored the Allied nations. The United States had strong ties of language and culture to Great Britain. Americans also knew that France had helped the colonies win their independence from Great Britain during the American Revolution.

Furthermore, Americans had a preference for democracy. Britain had a monarch, but the monarch was a figurehead, a head of state with little power. Britain, like France, was a democratic country with an elected parliament. Germany was not. Although Germany had a parliament, its emperor held most of the power.

On the other hand, there was significant American support for the Central Powers. More than ten million Americans traced their roots to the countries that comprised the Central Powers. An additional five million more were Irish immigrants or their descendants who opposed Great Britain because it refused to grant independence to Ireland. Many American Jews who had fled Russian persecution also favored Germany against Russia.

Both the Allies and the Central Powers used propaganda to try to sway American opinion to their side. The British and French accused the Germans of murdering hundreds of thousands of women and children. The Germans said a British blockade of German ports was causing widespread starvation.

However, the propaganda from both sides was so exaggerated that it probably did not cause many Americans to change their minds.

Economic Ties with the Allies

One factor that did influence U.S. public opinion was the growing economic ties with the Allies. Since it was neutral, the United States considered itself free to trade with both sides. However, the British navy had set up a blockade of German ports, making it almost impossible for Germany to trade with the United States. As a result of the blockade, American trade with Germany and the other Central Powers dropped to almost zero.

Since Britain controlled the seas, the Allies were free to trade with the United States. They were soon buying millions of dollars of supplies from American businesses—everything from food to manufactured goods, including military supplies. This lively trade provided a welcome boost to the United States economy, which had been in a slump for more than a year.

When Britain and France ran out of money to buy American goods in 1915, Wilson agreed that American companies and banks could lend money to the warring European nations. But only Britain and France could take advantage of this trade deal, since German ships could not get past the British blockade to reach U.S. shores. Trade with Britain and France soared, as did American loans to those two countries. By 1917, those loans totaled more than three billion dollars.

 **Why was American opinion divided regarding the war in Europe?**

◆ GERMANY'S ACTIONS SPARK OUTRAGE

Germany, hurt by the British blockade of its ports, was determined to prevent American supplies from reaching Britain. In this way, it hoped to destroy Britain's ability to continue the war. To wage this battle, the Germans used a deadly new weapon—the submarine.

Under international law, a country at war could stop and search a neutral ship that was suspected of carrying war materials. Unlawfully, however, submarines could sneak up under water and sink ships on sight.

In February 1915, Germany announced that all the waters around Britain were part of a war zone and that any enemy ship entering the zone would be sunk. The Germans said they would not deliberately target ships of neutral countries, but warned that they could not prevent accidental attacks. President Wilson expressed alarm at this policy. He informed the Germans that the United States would hold Germany responsible "for property endangered or lives lost" as a result of a submarine attack. On May 1, the German government took out advertisements in American newspapers, warning Americans against becoming involved with Allied shipping.

Americans ignored the warning. Then on May 7, 1915, a German submarine sank the British passenger liner *Lusitania*. Of the 1,198 people who drowned, 128 were Americans. Even though it was later revealed that the *Lusitania* was carrying Allied war supplies, the sinking inflamed American passions against Germany.

Tension continued to grow between Germany and the United States. In April 1916, President Wilson warned Germany to stop sinking nonmilitary ships without warning. If the Germans refused, he said, the United States would break off **diplomatic relations,** or official ties, with Germany. The Germans agreed, but they attached their own conditions, which President Wilson would not accept.

Drifting Toward War

During 1916, President Wilson worried more and more about drifting into war with Germany. The United States was not adequately prepared to fight a war. The U.S. Army was tiny compared to the massive armies battling in Europe. The U.S. Navy was small and somewhat out of date. By the middle of 1916, the President convinced the Congress to more than double the size of the army. Congress also authorized a project to build the largest navy in the world.

Wilson understood that most Americans still did not want war. Indeed, he ran for reelection in 1916 on the slogan, "He kept us out of war." After the election, Wilson once again tried to take on the role of peacemaker. He repeatedly tried to bring the two sides together to negotiate an end to the war. The President called for "peace without victory" and "peace between equals." Wilson's peace effort failed because each side still believed it could win the war. Meanwhile, a new crisis pulled the United States closer to joining the conflict.

The New York Times.

EXTRA 5:30 A. M.

VOL. LXIV.,..NO. 20,928. · · · · · · · · · · · NEW YORK, SATURDAY, MAY 8, 1915.—TWENTY-FOUR PAGES. · · · · · · · · · · ONE CENT

LUSITANIA SUNK BY A SUBMARINE, PROBABLY 1,260 DEAD;
TWICE TORPEDOED OFF IRISH COAST; SINKS IN 15 MINUTES;
CAPT. TURNER SAVED, FROHMAN AND VANDERBILT MISSING;
WASHINGTON BELIEVES THAT A GRAVE CRISIS IS AT HAND

◄ *This newspaper headline recounts the sinking of the British ship, the* Lusitania. *"Remember the* Lusitania!*" became a slogan when the United States entered the war in 1917.*

The Zimmermann Telegram

On January 31, 1917, Germany announced it would start sinking all ships that neared Britain, whether they were Allied or neutral. In one three-week period, German submarines sank 134 noncombat vessels. The Germans had grown desperate because of the failure of a giant land offensive they had launched. German generals concluded that the only way to win the war was to cut off all supplies going to Britain by sea. The Germans expected all-out submarine warfare to force a British surrender within a few months.

When Germany announced it would sink all ships approaching Britain, Wilson broke off diplomatic relations with Germany. Matters went from bad to worse. Late in February, the British handed the Americans a secret telegram they had intercepted. It was from Germany's foreign minister Arthur Zimmermann to its ambassador in Mexico. The Zimmermann telegram instructed the German ambassador to arrange an alliance between Mexico and Germany. If war broke out between Germany and the United States, the ambassador was to offer a deal to Mexico. Germany would help Mexico regain Texas, New Mexico, and Arizona in return for Mexico's joining the war on the German side.

American newspapers published the telegram. Americans became outraged at Germany, although some later thought the telegram might have been forged by Great Britain to draw the United States into war. Some Americans unfairly questioned the loyalty of German Americans and Mexican Americans. Anti-German feeling swept the nation. In early March, the President ordered that all U.S. merchant ships be armed.

Why did American opinion begin to turn against Germany?

◆ AMERICA ENTERS THE WAR

In March 1917, full-fledged revolution broke out in Russia, gravely weakening the Allied cause. As part of their propaganda effort to win American support, the Allies had claimed they were fighting for democracy. But Russia, ruled by a powerful emperor known as a **tsar,** was more a dictatorship than Germany. Revolutionaries in Russia overthrew the tsar in 1917 and called for democratic freedoms.

Events in Russia pleased Wilson. By seeming to place themselves on the side of liberty, the Russian revolutionaries made it easier for Americans to back the Allied cause.

Meanwhile the military situation for the Allies continued to deteriorate. Deciding he could wait no longer,

▲ *Jeanette Rankin was the first woman elected to Congress, in 1916. She is standing at right in this photograph.*

on April 2, President Wilson asked Congress to declare war on Germany. His address to Congress stressed that the United States had to enter the war. Wilson said that Germany was a threat to the United States and to world peace and freedom. Wilson promised the American people that the United States had no territorial aims in joining the war. In his words,

> The world must be made safe for democracy. Its peace must be planted upon the tested foundations of political liberty. We have no selfish ends to serve. We desire no conquest, no domination.

Wilson's voice was quiet and serious as he concluded his speech:

> It is a fearful thing . . . to lead this great, peaceful people into war, into the most terrible and disastrous of all wars. . . .

Most members of both the Senate and the House of Representatives shared Wilson's fear about the United States entering an overseas war. But even more so, they shared with Wilson a feeling of outrage against Germany's aggressive actions in Europe. Both the Senate and the House passed resolutions supporting Wilson's call to war against Germany. The Senate voted 82 to 6 to go to war, while the House voted 375 to 50 in support of the United States entering the war. The first woman elected to Congress, Jeanette Rankin of Montana, was one of the 50 representatives who voted against the House resolution. She did so, saying, "I want to stand by my country. But I cannot vote for war." On April 6, 1917, Wilson signed the Congressional declaration of war. After nearly three years of trying to make peace, he found himself reluctantly leading the United States into World War I.

 Why did the United States enter the war in 1917?

Section 1 Review

Check Understanding

1. **Define** (a) civilian (b) diplomatic relations (c) tsar

2. **Explain** the various views in the United States about the country's entry into war.

3. **Describe** three events that prompted the United States to enter the war.

Critical Thinking

Analyzing Was Wilson's call for "peace without victory" a good idea? Why or why not?

Write About History

◆**Connecting Past and Present** Write a brief essay comparing tactics used in World War I with those of more recent wars.

BUILDING SKILLS

Identifying Point of View: Wilson and World War I

Identifying point of view is analyzing information to determine a writer's or speaker's opinion about a particular issue, event, or person. Many of the primary and secondary sources you read will have a point of view about something or someone in history. Sometimes writers or speakers will present opposite points of view about the same topic, event, or person.

Here's How

Follow these steps to identify point of view:

1. Identify the source of information. Find out who the speaker or writer is. Is the author an authority on the subject?
2. Analyze what the speaker or writer is saying about the issue, event, or person. Decide whether main ideas are supported with relevant facts and opinions.
3. Discover why the speaker or writer weighs evidence in a particular way. People may have different ideas about what is most important based on differences in their backgrounds, experiences, or basic beliefs.
4. Draw conclusions about the speaker's or writer's point of view. Try to analyze why he or she holds a particular opinion. Weigh the accuracy and reliability of the point of view.

Here's Why

Historians research, identify, and evaluate materials written from many points of view. Studying a variety of points of view about events, issues, and people in history helps historians come closer to understanding the past.

Practice the Skill

In the excerpt below, Woodrow Wilson is speaking to Frank I. Cobb, an editor and writer. Shortly afterward, Wilson would ask Congress for a declaration of war against Germany. Read the quote and answer the questions that follow.

> [If you] lead this people into war, ... they'll forget there ever was such a thing as tolerance. To fight you must be brutal and ruthless, and the spirit of ruthless brutality will enter into the very fiber of our national life, infecting Congress, the courts, the policeman on the beat, the man in the street. ... Conformity would be the only virtue ... and every man who refused to conform would have to pay the penalty.

1. What does Wilson say about the effect of war on U.S. citizens?
2. Based on this quote, what would you say is Wilson's point of view about war?

Apply the Skill

Based on what you have read in this chapter and on the quote above, identify Wilson's point of view about U.S. involvement in World War I. What was his point of view before 1917? How did his point of view change in 1917? Explain.

Fighting the War

PREVIEW

Objectives

- To describe how the United States built up its armed forces for World War I

- To explain how politics in Russia affected the Allies

- To evaluate the role of the United States in bringing about an Allied victory

Vocabulary

draft	Communist
convoy system	abdicate
depth charge	

Many Americans came to support President Wilson's decision to go to war. They, too, believed that the United States was entering the war to make the world "safe for democracy." Wilson's idealism helped Americans overcome their desire to stay out of European affairs and also built enthusiasm for the war effort.

◆ GETTING READY FOR WAR

Before the United States could fight in Europe, it had to build a larger army. Some people, such as former President Theodore Roosevelt, favored an all-volunteer army. Wilson argued that the only democratic and efficient way for the United States to raise a large army was through a military **draft,** a process for selecting people for military service. The draft would apply equally to all men of fighting age, regardless of their wealth or social position.

In May 1917, Congress passed a draft law, requiring all men from age 21 to 30 to register for military service. The law was amended in August to include all men between 18 and 45 years of age. Within 18 months, 2.8 million men had been drafted. Also, more than one million men and women had joined voluntarily.

Americans from all ethnic groups entered the army. About one out of five drafted men was an immigrant. Their military training often included learning English and American history in addition to combat skills. Because of a severe lack of weapons, some soldiers trained using broomsticks for guns.

Segregated Units

The draft law made no mention of race, and African Americans registered to serve in the armed forces in large numbers. African Americans were assigned to segregated units that were commanded by white officers, as they had been during the Civil War. Almost 400,000 African Americans served in World War I.

Most African Americans were assigned low-level jobs, such as loading and unloading ships, moving supplies, or working as laborers for fighting units in Europe. When African Americans protested the kinds of jobs they were given, the army "loaned" about 100,000 of them to the French army. The French put them on the front lines, where they served with special distinction. A number of African Americans won the French Legion of Honor for bravery in battle.

Training the Army

President Wilson gave the job of training the American army to Major General John J. Pershing,

African American soldiers in the 369th Infantry Regiment fought bravely for 191 days under enemy fire. They were awarded a French medal, the Croix de Guerre. ▼

the officer who had been assigned to capture Pancho Villa. General Pershing was much admired as a tough enforcer of military discipline and an able leader of the soldiers under his command.

Pershing believed the object of war was the total destruction of the enemy's military power. Despite heavy pressure, General Pershing refused to send American troops into battle until they had completed their training. Pershing proved to be a good choice for a very difficult job.

"Over There"

To many Americans, entering the war was a great adventure. "Over There," a song by George M. Cohan, swept the country. "Over There" meant Europe. As the words of the song promised,

> Spread the word, send the word,
> Over there,
> That the Yanks are coming
> The Yanks are coming,
> The Yanks are coming,
> Over there.
>
> We'll be over, we're coming over,
> And we won't come back till it's over,
> Over there.

Getting the Yanks "over there" proved a major problem. By early 1917, more than 100 German submarines prowled the Atlantic, sinking Allied ships faster than the United States and the Allies could build them. One out of every four British ships that left port did not return.

To provide troop and supply ships with safe passage across the ocean, the United States adopted the **convoy system.** With this system, warships accompanied groups of supply and troop transports across the Atlantic. The warships carried new weapons to defend against submarines, including **depth charges,** special bombs designed to explode underwater. The convoy system proved very effective, and by the end of 1917, the United States could send troops and supplies abroad with confidence that they would arrive safely.

? How did the United States prepare to fight in World War I?

▲ George M. Cohan wrote many plays and musicals during the early 1900s. His song "Over There" stirred American patriotism during World War I.

◆ NEW LEADERS IN RUSSIA

When war began in 1914, Russians were loosely united behind their ruler, the tsar. Russian troops played a crucial role for the Allies in the early days of the war. However, as the war continued, conditions deteriorated both in Russia and on the battlefield. In the revolution of March 1917, the tsar was overthrown and a new government was established.

Russia's new leaders believed that Russia should help the Allies defeat Germany. However, these new leaders were unable to gain a strong hold on the country. In November 1917 another revolution occurred. This time, **Communists,** led by Vladimir Lenin, seized power. A Communist believes that the government, not individuals, should own all property and businesses in a nation. The Communists took over banks and industries in Russia.

Once in power, Lenin acted to take Russia out of the war. Lenin considered both sides evil and did not care who won. Even more important, he realized that

▲ *Russian citizens, dissatisfied with their government, demonstrated in Moscow in 1917.*

if Russia left the war, the Communists could stabilize their new government.

In March 1918 the Communists sat down to sign a peace with Germany, called the Treaty of Brest-Litovsk. The treaty was a tremendous blow to the Allies. The Germans could now move troops from the Russian, or eastern, front to support their troops on the western front in France and Belgium. There they could use their full strength against the weary armies of Britain and France.

Suddenly the role of the United States was crucial. The Allies desperately needed the Americans to arrive before the German army overran the Allied forces. The timing of their arrival would decide who would win World War I.

How did Russia's signing a peace treaty with Germany affect the Allies?

◆ THE ALLIES PUSH AHEAD

The first American troops arrived in France in June 1917. To the French people, exhausted by three years of war, these young men brought new hope.

About 14,000 American soldiers paraded through the streets of Paris, stopping at the tomb of Lafayette, who had been an aide to George Washington. There an American colonel declared, "Lafayette, we are here." The colonel's words suggested that Americans had come to repay their debt to the French for having helped win the American Revolution.

These first soldiers were the nucleus of what became a force of more than one million American soldiers. It would be more than one year before General Pershing decided the Americans were trained well enough to take a major part in the conflict. However, he sent some units forward to reinforce the French and British. These forces came to the front just in time to face the full force of a huge German offensive.

The German attack was launched in desperation. By early 1918, German leaders realized that their strategy of submarine warfare was failing. Steady streams of American troops and supplies were pouring into France. Hoping to defeat the Allies before the Americans were fully established, the Germans launched a massive land attack in March 1918. The Germans broke through the Allied lines, but they could not destroy the Allies.

The Germans made a final effort to capture Paris. By May they had pushed to within 40 miles of the French capital. But American troops moved quickly to fill the holes in the British and French lines. Fresh U.S. troops helped stop the German attack.

Now the Allies took the offensive. In June 1918, American troops were ordered to the Marne River to push back the German army. The Allies stopped the

Study Hint

When you are reading history assignments, look for words and phrases that show how ideas are related. <u>Both</u>, <u>in the same way</u>, <u>also</u>, <u>the same as</u>, and <u>similarly</u> all show comparison. <u>Although</u>, <u>but</u>, <u>different</u>, <u>however</u>, <u>nevertheless</u>, <u>on the other hand</u>, <u>while</u>, and <u>yet</u> all show contrast.

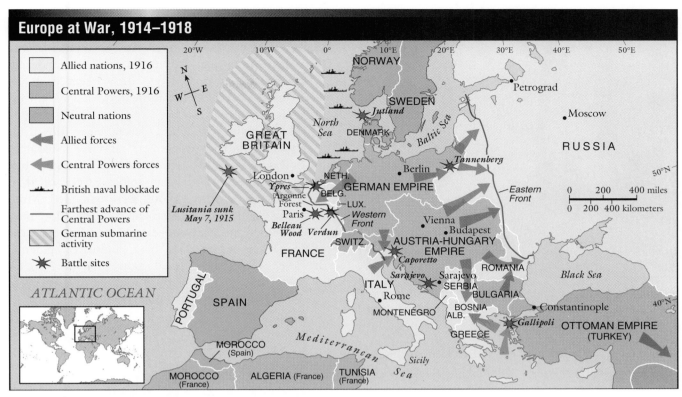

Europe at War, 1914–1918

Allied nations, 1916
Central Powers, 1916
Neutral nations
Allied forces
Central Powers forces
British naval blockade
Farthest advance of Central Powers
German submarine activity
Battle sites

▲ **Geography** *This map shows Europe at war from 1914 to 1918.* **Interpreting the Map** *Which nations were most affected by German submarine activity?*

German advance at the Marne and then began their own offensive. Now, American troops saw action up and down the line.

During the summer of 1918, U.S. Marine units were part of the force that won victories in fierce battles at Belleau (be-lō´) Wood, in France, shown on the map above. For 24 hours a day for two weeks, U.S. Marines fought their way through the forest, which was heavily defended by German machine guns. One American private noted in his journal,

> Men sought shelter behind half-finished mounds of earth and hugged the ground. Whole trees crashed down as heavy shells shook and jarred the earth.

Another soldier wrote,

> I saw blood-stained bodies everywhere, some missing an arm or a leg. My knees felt weak and I wanted to sit down.

The Allies finally took Belleau Wood—but at a cost of almost 10,000 American casualties. Said the American private, "All of us were older by a dozen years than we had been a dozen days before."

In July the Germans launched another offensive, calling upon every unit and gun that could be spared in a final effort. Night after night, the Germans fired explosives, shrapnel, and poison gas shells into the Allied lines. The Allied lines bulged, but held.

The Argonne Forest

The final Allied offensive began in late September. The plan was for the Americans to advance through the Argonne Forest in France, the most difficult part of the western front. Filled with swamps and ravines, it had also been well defended by the Germans with minefields, concrete machine gun nests, elaborate trenches, barbed wire, and heavy artillery.

Before dawn on September 26, 1918, the Americans waited quietly in their trenches to begin the attack. It rained softly. One soldier remembered that it seemed to him "as though the heavens were weeping over the sacrifice of so many lives that was so soon to be made." At dawn the American attack began.

▲ *American soldiers fought for 47 days in the Argonne Forest. It was the largest battle in American history and helped bring an end to World War I.*

A heavy fog descended on the forest. Lost in the fog, American soldiers stumbled into German lines or fell into shell holes. The German guns tore holes in the attacking force. One American soldier recalled:

> **I found myself adrift in a blind world of whiteness and noise, groping over something like the surface of the moon, half filled with rusty tangles of wire.**

The fighting in the Argonne went on for 47 days and nights. At times, soldiers fought hand to hand. More than 1.2 million Americans took part, making it the largest battle in American history. The Americans suffered 120,000 casualties, 10 percent of their force. However, they broke through the German lines and assured victory for the Allies. It was the last major battle of the war.

The battle that was fought in the Argonne Forest produced many heroes. One was Douglas MacArthur, an officer whom General Pershing called the best leader of soldiers in the American army. MacArthur later became one of the most effective American commanders during World War II.

The German Retreat

By October, the German army was in full retreat along the entire line of battle. They had suffered more than one million casualties. In early November, the German war effort totally collapsed. The army was shattered. Germany's allies—Austria-Hungary, the Ottoman Empire, and Bulgaria—had surrendered. When rebellions broke out in various parts of Germany, Kaiser Wilhelm **abdicated,** or gave up his office, and fled the country.

The French, British, and Germans had fought for four years. Although the Americans were in combat for only seven months, their losses were considerable. More than 49,000 American soldiers were killed in battle and more than 230,000 were wounded. More lives were claimed by disease than by bullets. More than 63,000 Americans died of disease while in France. Most of them were struck down by an influenza epidemic that swept through the Allied camps.

 What role did American troops play during World War I?

Section 2 Review

Check Understanding

1. **Define** (a) draft (b) convoy system (c) depth charge (d) Communist (e) abdicate

2. **State** President Wilson's goal for the United States as it entered World War I.

3. **Evaluate** the ways in which the United States prepared for war.

4. **Describe** the importance of the U.S. contribution to the Allied victory in World War I.

Critical Thinking

Connecting Past and Present Under what conditions might the government reinstate the draft today?

Write About History

Write a paragraph about what a young U.S. soldier might have felt about fighting in France during World War I.

Section 3

The Home Front Effort

PREVIEW

Objectives

- To describe how the U.S. government mobilized the economy for war

- To explain how World War I provided, for a time, new opportunities for women, Mexican Americans, and African Americans

- To analyze the efforts to build support for the war

Vocabulary

barrio
civil liberty
pacifist

No army can fight a modern war without a huge quantity of supplies. Troops need clothing, food, arms, and ammunition that only skilled workers in up-to-date factories can produce. Thus the mobilization of workers on the home front was vital to winning the war.

◆ GEARING UP THE ECONOMY

In order to mobilize the United States' industrial resources, Wilson set up the War Industries Board (WIB), headed by Bernard M. Baruch. The WIB had wide authority to regulate industries that produced war materials. It told industries what goods to produce, set production schedules, and fixed prices. The government also regulated food resources. President Wilson created the Food Administration, headed by a young business leader named Herbert Hoover. The Food Administration set out to increase food production and decrease home consumption. As head of the Food Administration, Hoover introduced a wide range of innovative programs. He encouraged Americans to plant "victory gardens" at home so that more of the food grown on farms could go to the military and to people in Europe.

The war turned out to be very expensive. New taxes provided about one third of the cost. The government placed most of the new tax burden on the wealthy, raising taxes on inheritances, high personal incomes, and corporate profits. To cover the remainder of the war costs, the government borrowed money. It did this by selling Victory and Liberty bonds to the public. Thousands of volunteers, including politicians, artists, and movie stars, helped sell these bonds. The government raised $20.5 billion through their sale.

What did the government do to mobilize the country for war?

◆ CHANGES IN THE LABOR FORCE

In order to fight World War I, the army pulled almost five million men away from their jobs, which created a huge labor shortage. As a result, workers in many industries were able to hold out for higher wages and better working conditions. The demand for laborers also created new opportunities for many people, including women, African Americans, and Mexican Americans.

New Opportunities for Women

World War I brought an important change to the role of American women. For the first time, the government admitted women into the armed forces in noncombat roles. More than 11,000 women served in the navy and several hundred served in the marines. Many others joined the Red Cross and the American Women's Hospital Service, serving overseas as nurses, doctors, and ambulance drivers.

At home, more than one million women worked in war industries, replacing the men who had entered the armed services. Women worked in factories, drove trucks, and took railroad jobs. Government contracts with war industries helped women by requiring equal pay for people holding the same jobs.

Most women working in war industries were young and single. They already were in the work force, but switched jobs when the men went off to war. After Germany's surrender, returning soldiers reclaimed their jobs, and the number of women in the work force returned to prewar levels.

The war brought a more permanent change for women in another area. The contributions of women to the war effort increased support for woman suffrage. In 1918, President Wilson reversed his earlier opposition and announced that it was important to give women the vote.

▲ During the war, women filled many jobs previously held by men. This woman is using a blowtorch in a Detroit factory.

Mexican Immigration Increases

Mexican Americans also benefited during World War I. To make up for the shortage of laborers in agriculture, the government encouraged immigration from Mexico. Between 1917 and 1920, at least 100,000 Mexicans came to the United States. Many left their country of birth to escape the fighting and upheavals caused by the Mexican Revolution.

Most of the new arrivals settled in Texas, California, New Mexico, and Arizona. Many took jobs as migrant workers, traveling from farm to farm, picking crops as they ripened. Others worked as miners or railroad workers. Still others settled in the cities of the Southwest. There many moved to Latino neighborhoods called **barrios**. In the barrios, the newly arrived Mexicans lived among relatives and friends.

For Mexican Americans whose families had lived in the United States for a generation or more, the war meant new opportunities. It provided a first chance to get skilled factory jobs that paid good wages. Mexican American women found jobs in garment factories, fish canneries, and food processing plants.

Meanwhile, thousands of Mexican Americans left the Southwest for better jobs elsewhere. They moved to cities such as Chicago, St. Louis, and Omaha to work in meat-packing houses, railroad yards, and factories.

African Americans

Like other Americans, most African Americans at home supported the war. They agreed with NAACP founder W.E.B. Du Bois, who argued, "If this is our country, then this is our war."

The war provided opportunities for African Americans to improve their living conditions. Accelerating the wave of migration that had begun earlier, 400,000 African Americans left the South for cities in the North during World War I. During the war years, the African American population of Chicago doubled, while that of Cleveland increased by four times. Detroit's African American population increased by six times.

Because of the labor shortage, many factories, mines, and other businesses in the North were eager to hire African Americans for the first time. Before the war, industries such as packing houses and steel mills had very few African American workers. By 1918 about 20 percent of Chicago packing house workers were African Americans.

Along with new opportunities, African Americans encountered the old discrimination. Most African Americans still worked in some of the lowest-paying jobs and lived in segregated neighborhoods. Although African American organizations, such as the NAACP and the Urban League, tried to help African Americans find decent housing, the task proved difficult. War or no war, residential segregation remained strong in the North.

 **How did the labor force change during World War I?**

◆ WAR PROPAGANDA

To rally public support for the war, President Wilson created the Committee on Public Information (CPI). Soon, thousands of people in the arts and in

FOR VICTORY, BUY MORE BONDS
FOURTH LIBERTY LOAN

◄ Posters such as this one urged Americans to support the war effort by purchasing Liberty bonds.

the advertising and film industries were involved. The massive propaganda compaign included 75,000 "Four-Minute Men," who gave four-minute speeches to drum up enthusiasm for the war effort. The CPI also sponsored rallies, issued reading materials, and ran other activities supporting the war and criticizing the German government.

The CPI hired artists to produce posters encouraging men to enlist in the armed services. The posters also urged Americans to buy Liberty bonds. The most famous poster the CPI produced showed a stern Uncle Sam pointing at the viewer. The caption read, "I want you for the U.S. Army."

The U.S. government sometimes acted to silence critics of the war. In 1917 the Espionage Act established heavy fines and long prison sentences for interfering with recruitment for the army. The 1918 Sedition Act made it a crime to criticize the United States government. The act led to violations of people's **civil liberties,** including the rights of free speech, thought, and action. More than 1,500 people were arrested for violating this act. Forty-one of these people received prison sentences, ranging from 10 to 20 years. Hundreds of **pacifists,** people opposed to any war, were put on trial for saying that war violated Christian teachings. In many ways, tolerance suffered in the United States during World War I.

How was propaganda used to affect public opinion during the war?

Section 3 Review

Check Understanding

1. **Define** (a) barrio (b) civil liberty (c) pacifist

2. **Recall** how the War Industry Board organized the nation's industrial resources for war.

3. **Explain** how women, African Americans, and Mexican Americans gained new opportunities during World War I.

4. **Describe** the ways in which the United States government acted to silence critics of World War I.

Critical Thinking

Connecting Past and Present Should the U.S. government have the right to silence critics during wartime? Why or why not?

Write About Citizenship

As a member of the Committee on Public Information, write a brief speech in which you encourage citizens in the United States to support the war effort.

The War to End All Wars

PREVIEW

Objectives

- To describe the results of World War I
- To review Woodrow Wilson's outline for peace
- To explain the Senate's response to the Treaty of Versailles

Vocabulary

armistice
republic

self-determination
reparation

When World War I finally ended in November 1918, Americans looked to Woodrow Wilson to lead them to a just and lasting peace. Peacemaking, however, was more difficult than Wilson had expected. In the end, he and millions of other people were deeply disappointed by the settlement that finally resulted.

◆ THE WAR ENDS

The Allied offensive during the summer and fall of 1918 finally brought an end to the fighting. In October the German government sent a telegram to Wilson. It said,

> To avoid further bloodshed, the German government requests the President to arrange the immediate conclusion of an **armistice** [a cease-fire] on land, by sea, and in the air.

Germany's allies—Bulgaria, the Ottoman Empire, and Austria-Hungary—had signed an armistice and had already stopped fighting. On November 9, Kaiser Wilhelm was forced to resign, and Germany became a **republic.** A republic is a political unit, such as a nation, with a government in which citizens rule through their elected representatives. Two days later, at 11 A.M. on November 11—the eleventh hour of the eleventh day of the eleventh month—Germany surrendered, hours after signing an armistice agreement at Rethondes, France. Soldiers from both sides immediately left their trenches to greet each other and celebrate the end of the war. A British journalist described what many people felt when the huge guns finally fell silent along the western front:

> Last night for the first time since August in the first year of the war, there was no light of gunfire in the sky, no sudden stabs of flame through the darkness, no spreading glow above black trees where for four years . . . human beings were smashed to death. The Fires of Hell had been put out.

For millions, the fires were put out much too late. More than nine million soldiers had died in battle or from disease. At least 20 million more soldiers had been wounded. Many of them had lost limbs or had been blinded.

American troops were decisive in tipping the balance against Germany. By the end of 1918, more than two million American troops were in Europe. More than 115,000 Americans died in the war, either in battle or from disease. For the survivors, it was time to come home from "over there."

The armistice that ended the fighting in World War I was signed in this railway car in Rethondes, France.▼

◀ Allied leaders (left to right) Vittorio Orlando, Premier of Italy; David Lloyd George, Prime Minister of England; Georges Clemenceau, Premier of France; and Woodrow Wilson, President of the United States met in France to sign the Treaty of Versailles.

Several million civilians also died during the war and its aftermath. When the fighting ended, disease and starvation swept across a weakened Europe. In one year, six million more people died. A worldwide flu epidemic, though not a result of the war, killed one-half million people in the United States by 1919.

What conditions did Europe face after the war?

◆ MAKING PEACE

Speaking to Congress in January 1917, a few months before the United States entered World War I, President Wilson had outlined a plan to end the war. At the time, Wilson called on both sides in the war to accept "peace without victory." In January 1918, Wilson once again spoke to Congress about making peace. This time he had a detailed plan for how it should be done.

The Fourteen Points

Wilson's plan came to be known as the Fourteen Points. His plan was intended to prevent the world from becoming involved in another war.

The Fourteen Points covered a wide range of issues. Wilson argued that nations should end secret treaties and agreements and that they should agree to the principles of freedom of the seas, free trade, arms reduction, and fair settlement of colonial claims.

In another point, Wilson put forth the principle of **self-determination.** Self-determination is the right of a nation to decide its own political status. Wilson hoped to protect Europe's small and weak countries and nationalities.

Wilson's fourteenth point called for setting up an international organization to preserve the peace. It would provide a place for countries to meet and settle their disputes peacefully. It would also bring countries together to punish any nation that broke the peace.

For Wilson, this fourteenth point was the most important. During the peace negotiations that followed, he was willing to concede on some issues. But an international peace organization, a League of Nations, was at the heart of his plan, and on this he would not compromise.

Wilson Goes to Paris

The armistice that had been signed with Germany said nothing about the shape of the peace in Europe that would follow. Representatives from 30 nations gathered in Paris in January 1919 to discuss many issues. The main decisions were made by the Big Four—Woodrow Wilson of the United States, David Lloyd George of

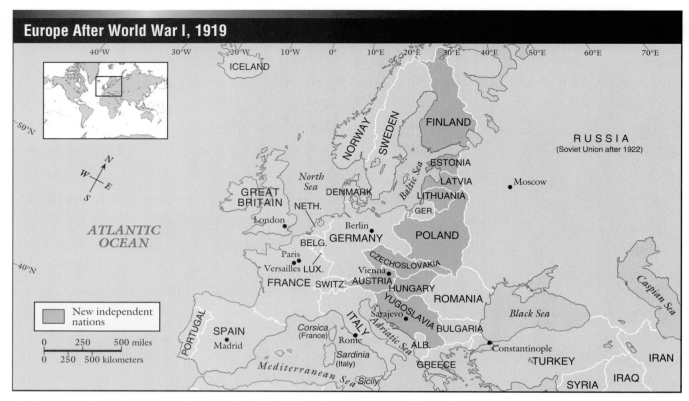

Europe After World War I, 1919

▲ **Geography** *This map shows Europe after World War I.* **Interpreting the Map** *Compare this map with the map on page 345. What new nations were created after the war?*

Great Britain, Georges Clemenceau (klā-män-sō´) of France, and Vittorio Orlando of Italy.

The European leaders did not share the idealism of President Wilson, who had brought his Fourteen Points to Paris. During the war, they had signed secret treaties for dividing up the territories of the Central Powers. Also, while Wilson called for "peace without victory," European leaders were determined to punish Germany for its role in the war.

The French leader, Clemenceau, was the force behind many of the Allied demands. It was his goal to humiliate Germany in peace as Germany had humiliated France in battle.

At one point, Wilson almost walked out of the conference. He realized, however, that leaving would be an admission of failure. What also prevented him from walking out was his fear that communism would spread from Russia into central Europe if a peace treaty did not restore stability.

In the end the European leaders forced Wilson to compromise on many issues. At the same time, the American President held firm on certain principles that became part of the final settlement.

The Treaty of Versailles

The Paris Peace Conference produced five treaties. The most important was the Treaty of Versailles (vər-sī), signed on June 28, 1919. The Treaty of Versailles treated Germany very harshly. Germany lost all its overseas colonies. Alsace-Lorraine was returned to France. In the east, Germany lost territory to the newly independent nation of Poland. Some of Germany's territory in the west was placed under foreign control for 15 years. Border changes were made to Italy, Romania, Belgium, and Greece. The map above shows how Europe changed as a result of the war.

Harshest of all, the Treaty of Versailles blamed Germany for the war and all losses in the war. A clause of the treaty, called the "war guilt" clause, justified the demand that Germany pay huge **reparations,** or damages, to the Allies. In 1921 the Allies set the amount of reparations at $33 billion, which was far more than Germany could possibly pay.

The punishing nature of the Versailles Treaty would come back to haunt the Allies. The war guilt clause and the demand for reparations created great bitterness in Germany. In time, extremist groups there would exploit that bitterness to win support. They attacked the Treaty of Versailles, the Allies that had forced it on Germany, and the democratic German government that had signed the treaty.

The Treaty of Versailles certainly did not provide Wilson with his "peace without victory." Still, it did offer him some successes, including the creation of several new eastern European nations based on the principle of self-determination. The new countries included Czechoslovakia, Estonia, Latvia, Lithuania, and Yugoslavia. Most importantly to Wilson, however, the treaty provided for an international peace organization—a League of Nations. Compare the map on page 352 to the map on page 345 to see some of the changes to Europe brought about by the war.

 What were Wilson's hopes for the future after World War I?

◆ THE SENATE AND THE TREATY

When Wilson returned to the United States, he had to persuade the U.S. Senate to approve the Treaty of Versailles—and with it, American participation in the League of Nations.

Most Americans supported the treaty and the league. A strong minority, however, opposed both. With the war over, isolationists wanted the United States to end its involvement in European affairs. Some people thought the treaty was too soft on the defeated powers. German Americans felt that the treaty dealt too harshly with Germany.

Some people believed that the League of Nations had serious weaknesses. They thought the League lacked the authority to solve economic problems that might lead to another war. The issue of reducing armaments was another serious problem they thought the League could do nothing about.

In the Senate, opposition to the treaty was led by Senator Henry Cabot Lodge of Massachusetts. Lodge wanted major changes that would reduce the United States' ties to the League. He was afraid that a strong commitment would involve the United States in future European wars. If he could not get the changes he wanted, he would let the treaty die.

Had Wilson been willing to compromise, he might have saved the treaty and the League. But Wilson would not compromise. Instead of working out a deal with Lodge, the President decided to bypass the Senate and appeal directly to the American people.

In September 1919, Wilson set out on a nationwide speaking tour. Wilson was already worn out and weak when he returned from Paris, and the tour only further exhausted him. On September 25, in Colorado, he suffered a stroke and collapsed.

Wilson never fully recovered from his illness. Although he returned to Washington, he could not work more than a few hours each day. Still, he refused to compromise with Lodge, who took full advantage of the situation to strengthen opposition to the treaty.

In November the Senate rejected the Treaty of Versailles and with it U.S. participation in the League of Nations. Wilson's dream was shattered. He served out his term as President a sick and broken man.

 Why did Wilson fail to gain support in the Senate for a world peace organization?

Section 4 Review

Check Understanding

1. **Define** (a) armistice (b) republic (c) self-determination (d) reparation

2. **Describe** the human costs of World War I.

3. **Identify** two of Wilson's Fourteen Points.

4. **Interpret** the war guilt clause in the Treaty of Versailles.

5. **Explain** why some Americans opposed the League of Nations.

Critical Thinking

◆◆**Connecting Past and Present** What new nations that were formed at the end of World War I still exist today?

Write About Government

Write a letter to your senators telling them why they should or should not reject the Treaty of Versailles.

Chapter 17
Review

CHAPTER SUMMARY

Section 1

At the outset of World War I, most Americans wanted to stay neutral, although many sympathized with the Allies. However, following a series of incidents involving Germany, the United States entered the conflict, which President Wilson called a war to make "the world safe for democracy."

Section 2

Millions of men were drafted and industry was regulated to increase wartime production. The situation looked grave when the Russians withdrew from the war. By the fall of 1917, enough Americans had arrived for the Allies to begin a massive offensive against the Germans. By October of 1918, Germany's forces were crumbling.

Section 3

At home, industries geared up to produce the materials needed for war. With so many white men away at war, women and minorities found opportunities for good jobs. To increase American support for the war, Wilson set up a propaganda committee. Those who refused to support the war faced hostility from other citizens and a loss of civil liberties.

Section 4

Wilson's Fourteen Points was a plan intended to make a fair peace. Though the Treaty of Versailles treated Germany harshly, Wilson agreed to it because it contained a provision for the establishment of the League of Nations. However, Wilson was unable to persuade the U.S. Senate to ratify the treaty.

Connecting ◆ Past and Present

In what way is today's United Nations like the League of Nations? How are their goals alike?

Using Vocabulary

From the list below, select the term that best completes each sentence.

self-determination	civil liberty
barrio	armistice
convoy system	reparation
Communist	civilian
pacifist	draft

1. The _____ is the process by which people are selected for military service.
2. They used the _____ to provide troops and supply ships with safe passage across the ocean.
3. A _____ believes that the government, not individuals, should own property and businesses.
4. Under _____, a country decides on its own government.
5. A person who is opposed to all war or violence is a _____.
6. To prevent a person from speaking her mind is a violation of a _____.
7. After the _____ was arranged, the fighting stopped.
8. The defeated countries had to pay a huge _____ to the victors.
9. A _____ is where a Mexican immigrant might have chosen to settle.
10. A person who is not a member of the armed forces is called a _____.

Check Understanding

1. **Explain** why World War I was different from wars that came before it.
2. **Explain** why the United States did not immediately take sides during the war.
3. **Summarize** the events that led the United States into war.
4. **Describe** the way the United States found soldiers to fight in World War I.
5. **Explain** why Wilson set up the War Industries Board.

6. **Summarize** the events that led to the crumbling of the German armies at the end of the war.

7. **Describe** how the war changed the working lives of women and minorities.

8. **Describe** the goal of Wilson's Fourteen Points.

9. **Explain** why the Senate did not ratify the Treaty of Versailles.

10. **Identify** the Big Four.

Critical Thinking

1. **Analyzing** Why do you think Americans were angered by the Zimmermann telegram?

2. **Hypothesizing** How do you think the Treaty of Brest-Litovsk affected later relations between the Allies and Russia?

3. **Evaluating** Why did the Allied leaders reject many of Wilson's Fourteen Points?

4. **Predicting** What impact do you think the Treaty of Versailles might have on future events in Europe?

◆ **Connecting Past and Present** Are there situations today that could justify the use of propaganda? Explain.

Writing to Persuade

You are President Wilson. You have agreed to the Treaty of Versailles. **Write** a note to a friend in the Senate explaining why you think it is important to ratify the treaty. Explain how you think the treaty will help prevent future wars.

Interpreting the Timeline

Use the timeline on pages 334–335 to answer these questions.

1. In what year did the United States enter World War I?

2. When was the *Lusitania* torpedoed?

3. In what year did an action of the Senate go against the League of Nations?

Putting Skills to Work

IDENTIFYING POINT OF VIEW

In the Building Skills lesson on page 341, you learned that identifying point of view is analyzing information to determine a writer's opinion. The excerpt below is from a *New York Times* editorial published on the day after Germany declared war on Russia in 1914. Read the excerpt and then answer the questions that follow.

> *With Germany's declaration of war against Russia, the bloodiest war ever fought on earth and the least justified of all wars since man emerged from barbarism has apparently begun . . .*
>
> *The threat of war on this unprecedented [unequaled] scale, its very nearness, the overwhelming feature that it may not be averted [avoided] are proofs of the backwardness of Europe. By permitting themselves to be brought so near to war they prove that their civilization is half a sham.*

From: The New York Times, *August 2, 1914*

1. What is the writer's point of view about the war in Europe?

2. What seems to be the writer's point of view about Europeans?

3. What facts support the writer's point of view?

4. How might the writer's point of view change by 1917? Explain.

 *Portfolio Project*

A PERSONAL VIEW OF THE WAR

The fighting in World War I was like the fighting in no previous war. Trench warfare and the introduction of new technology changed fighting techniques and created horrifying new experiences for soldiers. Imagine that you were a U.S. soldier in World War I. Write three journal entries describing your feelings about war before you reached Europe, your experiences as a soldier, and your thoughts about war after peace was won.

PROPAGANDA AND CENSORSHIP

To convince people that war is necessary, governments have used many forms of propaganda and censorship. The methods change, but the intentions remain the same—to persuade people that a certain point of view is right and to control the information people receive.

▲ Posters tried to convince Americans to join the war effort during World War I.

Then In 1916, Woodrow Wilson campaigned on a platform of keeping the United States out of war. Yet by 1917, Wilson believed that war was necessary. In order to convince Americans to support the war, he created the Committee on Public Information (CPI).

The committee had the power to censor newspaper articles that were critical of the war effort. The CPI wrote thousands of press releases, enlisted artists to create posters, and convinced the new motion picture industry to promote the war.

Now In 1990, when war broke out in the Persian Gulf, Americans were divided about using military force. As in World War I, the fighting had begun far from American borders—in this case, with an attack by Iraq on the tiny country of Kuwait. At first, some Americans did not think the attack justified American intervention. However, Kuwait was a major producer of the world's oil.

Once it made the decision to use force, the U.S. government worked hard to gain public support. Emphasis was placed on the need to protect Kuwait's sovereignty. Also, the U.S. government kept a tight rein on news coverage of the war effort. News broadcasts were reviewed by military censors. In many cases, the positive news stories about the war effort swayed public opinion.

You Decide

1. Why is it important during wartime for the government to secure favorable public opinion?

2. Was the use of censorship during the Persian Gulf War justified? Why or why not?

Unit 6

Times of Trial 1919–1941

> **❝** I am a mother of seven children, and utterly heart-broken in that they are hungry, have only 65¢ in money. The father is in L.A. trying to find something to do. Oh, President, my heart is breaking. Oh, what a burden and how helpless I am, how proud I am of my children, and how dark a future under this condition. **❞**
>
> *Mrs. H.L. in a letter to President Roosevelt, February 1, 1934*

▲ *The members of this family have been forced to leave their home in Oklahoma, taking their possessions with them.* ◆ **Connecting Past and Present** *What clues in this photograph indicate the hopelessness of the Great Depression? How might a photographer show the way homeless people live today?*

Chapter 18
The Roaring Twenties
1919–1929

CHAPTER PREVIEW

Section 1 A Time of Prosperity

During the 1920s, Republicans in the White House encouraged the growth of business and initiated a decade of consumer spending.

Section 2 The Jazz Age

New leisure pastimes and pursuits developed, changing the country's culture during the 1920s. Although some people applauded progress, others feared economic and social change.

Section 3 A Search for Social Justice

Not everyone enjoyed the prosperity of the 1920s. War veterans, immigrants, and African Americans faced the pressures of unemployment, inflation, and discrimination.

First radio broadcast

Sacco and Vanzetti

U.S. Events	**1920** ✪ Warren Harding elected. Radio station KDKA in Pittsburgh goes on the air. Nationwide arrests of so-called anarchists, Communists, and labor union organizers occur. Harlem Renaissance begins.	**1921** Sacco and Vanzetti are convicted. Teapot Dome scandal begins. Congress passes the Emergency Quota Act.	**1922** F. Scott Fitzgerald's novel *The Great Gatsby* is published.		**1923** ✪ Calvin Coolidge becomes President.

1918

World Events	**1920** World population is estimated at 1.8 billion.		**1922** Kemal Atatürk proclaims the Republic of Turkey.		**1923** Adolf Hitler leads unsuccessful attempt to take over the German government.

Atatürk, first president of Turkey

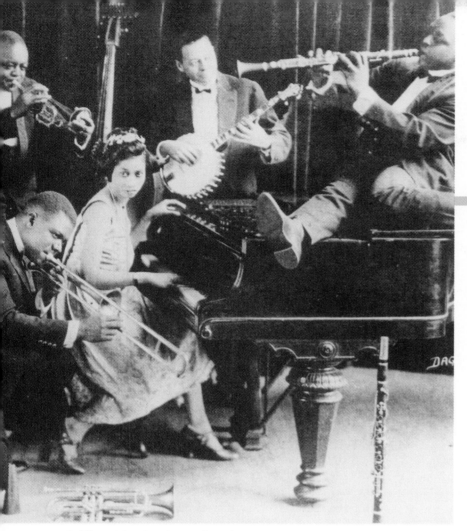

Portfolio Project

A MOVIE SCENE

People from all groups in American society, including veterans returning from World War I, women, and African Americans, experienced great cultural and social changes during the 1920s. As you read the chapter, note the changes that people experienced in this decade. At the end of the chapter, you will write a movie scene that illustrates how Americans from different groups were affected by the changes.

▲ *The 1920s is often called the Jazz Age. Newly popular jazz music captured the era's carefree atmosphere.* ◆ **Connecting Past and Present** *What emotions do you think these musicians wanted to convey? What kind of music reflects today's world?*

Babe Ruth

1924
✪ Calvin Coolidge elected.
Nellie Tayloe Ross elected governor of Wyoming.
National Origins Act cuts immigration from southern and eastern Europe.

Gertrude Ederle

1925
John Scopes arrested for teaching the theory of evolution.

1926
Gertrude Ederle swims the English Channel.

1927
Babe Ruth hits 60 home runs in the baseball season.
Lindbergh flies from New York to Paris.

1928
✪ Herbert Hoover elected.

1929

1924
Women achieve the vote in India.
E.M. Forster's novel *A Passage to India* is published.

1926
Hirohito becomes emperor of Japan.

Hirohito

1928
Sir Alexander Fleming discovers penicillin.

Sir Alexander Fleming

Section 1

A Time of Prosperity

PREVIEW

Objectives

• To describe how two Republican Presidents supported business development

• To analyze the causes and effects of the economic boom of the 1920s

• To discuss how the automobile affected American life in the 1920s

Vocabulary

assembly line
installment plan
mass media

The presidential election of 1920 signaled a dramatic change for the nation. Woodrow Wilson, the outgoing Democratic President, was deeply committed to an active role in world affairs. The newly elected President, Warren Harding, was a Republican who had little interest in foreign affairs. Harding's presidency ushered in more than a decade of Republican power and cleared the way for big business to continue its growth.

◆ REPUBLICANS IN COMMAND

Warren Harding did not have much experience in government. During the presidential campaign, he promised to return the country to "normalcy." By this he meant a return to life as it had been before World War I. Harding thought the United States should not be involved in world affairs. He was opposed to government regulation of business and to workers' demands that interfered with employers' needs. If business were left alone, Harding argued, its profits would increase and allow everyone to live better.

Corruption in the White House

Unfortunately, Harding's plans for government and business were marred by a big error. He appointed old friends from Ohio, where he had been a senator, to Cabinet positions and other high offices. Known as the

"Ohio Gang," they engaged in all kinds of questionable practices. One of Harding's appointees in the attorney general's office took bribes in return for government favors. The head of the Veterans Bureau stole millions of dollars meant for the construction of hospitals.

The biggest scandal of Harding's administration, however, was known as the Teapot Dome scandal. In 1921, Harding's secretary of the interior, Albert B. Fall, accepted more than $300,000 in bribes from private oil companies in return for selling them reserves of oil that had been set aside for the U.S. Navy. These reserves were located in Elk Hills, California, and Teapot Dome, Wyoming. Fall became the first Cabinet officer in history to be sent to prison.

President Harding died of a cerebral hemorrhage in August 1923, just as rumors of corruption in his administration were beginning to surface. The task of restoring the nation's faith in government fell to his Vice President, Calvin Coolidge.

Support for Business

Like Harding, Coolidge believed that the federal government should interfere as little as possible in the affairs of the nation. He believed that the nation's prosperity depended on big business. "The business of America," said Coolidge, "is business." Under President Coolidge, new tax laws that benefited industry were passed. He ended regulations that limited a corporation's size and the amount of money it could earn.

Government *In this cartoon, Washington officials try to outrun the Teapot Dome scandal.* **Interpreting the Cartoon** *Why is the scandal portrayed as a tank? What is the significance of the highway sign?* ▼

Coolidge's program seemed to work. The expansion of big business created more goods and more jobs. Wages rose, and the workday was shortened. Though Coolidge had not called for these particular changes, his popularity soared. He easily won the Republican nomination in 1924 and went on to resoundingly defeat the Democratic candidate, John W. Davis, in the 1924 election. He won almost every state outside the solidly Democratic South.

 How did Harding and Coolidge support big business?

◆ A BOOMING ECONOMY

By the end of the 1920s, the booming economy had changed the lives of Americans in countless ways. Factories produced a steady stream of consumer products, including refrigerators, washing machines, toasters, and automobiles. However, these factories were not only producing new goods but were also finding faster ways to make them. Necessities and luxuries were becoming more available and more affordable.

The Automobile Industry

The automobile helped spur the economic boom of the 1920s. About 7 million passenger cars were in use at the end of World War I. By 1929, however, about 24 million Americans, or one in every five persons, owned a car.

Behind this tremendous growth in auto ownership was a man named Henry Ford. Back in 1908, Ford had designed an automobile he called the Model T, a sturdy vehicle with a noisy engine that often backfired. In 1909 he began producing the car on an **assembly line.** The assembly line allowed workers to put together a product from parts that passed by on a conveyor belt in the exact order in which they were needed. In 1913 it took the average worker 13 hours to produce one automobile. By 1925, cars were rolling off the assembly line every ten seconds. Because Ford could now turn out 9,000 cars a day, he was able to lower the price. In 1908 a car had cost about $850. By 1924 a person could buy an automobile for just $290—about three months' wages for the best-paid factory workers.

The explosion in car production and sales spurred the growth of other businesses. Companies rushed to fill the auto industry's need for steel, rubber, glass, and oil. Several million Americans found jobs building, selling, servicing, parking, and driving the new cars.

▲ *Workers assemble Ford automobiles on an early production line. This new method of assembly increased production and lowered car prices.*

The nation constructed thousands of miles of new roads, making it possible for people to move away from their jobs. This led to a construction boom of new homes in suburban areas. Small roadside businesses—such as motels and diners—and billboard advertisements sprang up as motorists took to the roads.

No single development could match the automobile for changing how Americans worked, lived, and played. More than just a convenient way to get from one place to another, the car became a symbol of the American dream. It influenced where people lived, worked, and shopped, how they vacationed, and how they interacted. A car traveler described his stay at a roadside camp in North Carolina this way:

> **And for the first time in history, the common, ordinary 'fo'kes' of the North and South are meeting one another on a really large scale, mostly by means of the National chariot—the Ford car.**

In some cases the automobile caused people to go into debt for the first time. Eager to own a car, a person could put a deposit down, drive the new car away,

TWELVE YEARS OF SUCCESSFUL SERVICE

APEX
ELECTRIC
WASHING
MACHINE

▲ With the dramatic growth of consumer products in the 1920s, advertising became a large industry. This advertisement for electric washing machines appeared in magazines.

and pay on the **installment plan.** This plan allowed a person to make a small initial payment toward the total price of the car. A fixed amount—plus interest— would then be paid on a schedule until the full amount was covered.

Growing Confidence and Spending

Caught up in a spirit of optimism, more and more Americans invested in the stock market. The value of stocks skyrocketed. By 1929 the value of all stocks was $87 billion, compared to $27 million four years earlier.

Cars were not the only items that people were buying on the installment plan. A new phonograph or kitchen appliance could be purchased on the installment plan by paying as little as $5 down and $5 a month. During the 1920s, Americans became caught up in a boom of spending. Chain supermarkets spread across the country. The nation's first fast-food restaurants and the nation's first shopping center opened.

Advertising helped stimulate and change buying habits. Previously, advertisements in newspapers and magazines had offered basic information about products. Now, however, advertisers began focusing on the needs, wants, and anxieties of consumers rather than on the qualities of the product. If a product could be advertised

as contributing to the buyer's physical or emotional well-being, it was sure to be a hit. For example, a product that for years had been marketed as an antiseptic now took on a whole new dimension when it was advertised as a cure for halitosis, a scientific-sounding term for bad breath. Advertising reached a higher level of respectability and economic power in American life during the 1920s. **Mass media** was a term first used in 1923 to refer to modes of communication that reached large numbers of people. Advertisers now had billboards and radio commercials, in addition to the more traditional newspaper and magazine ads, to convince people that they needed the new products. Total advertising volume in all media jumped from $1.4 billion in 1919 to $3 billion in 1929.

 How did the popularity of the automobile affect other industries?

Section 1 Review

Check Understanding

1. **Define** (a) assembly line (b) installment plan (c) mass media

2. **Explain** Warren Harding's practices as President and how they contributed to the Teapot Dome scandal.

3. **Identify** the role advertising played in the economic boom of the 1920s.

4. **Describe** how the spending boom of the 1920s affected American life.

Critical Thinking

Connecting Past and Present How have the techniques used by advertising changed since the 1920s? In what ways are they the same?

Write About Government

From President Harding's office, write an apology to be broadcast to the American people for the actions of the Ohio gang.

BUILDING SKILLS

Comparing and Contrasting: The Impact of the Automobile

Comparing and contrasting is a skill that involves identifying the similarities and differences between two or more people, places, ideas, issues, or events. To compare is to decide what is alike between two or more things. To contrast is to identify what is different.

Here's How

Follow these steps to compare and contrast people, events, or issues:

1. Identify the characteristics of the people, events, or issues you want to compare and contrast. For example, in the activity on this page, you will compare and contrast the automobile's impact on society and industry today with its impact during the 1920s.

2. List the ways in which the people, events, or issues are similar. Words that indicate likenesses include s*imilarly, also, in addition, in the same way*, and *likewise*.

3. List the ways in which the people, events, or issues are different. Words that indicate differences include *but, although, however, nevertheless, on the other hand, in contrast, yet*, and *conversely*.

4. Draw conclusions based on your lists. Describe the similarities and the differences.

Here's Why

The ability to make accurate comparisons or contrasts between people, places, issues, and events will help you understand and organize historical information. Suppose, for example, that you were asked to compare and contrast the automobile's impact on society and industry today with its impact during the 1920s. A Venn diagram like the one on this page can help you to determine how the automobile's impact was similar and how it was different during the two time periods.

Practice the Skill

Copy the Venn diagram into your notebook. In the left circle, list the unique ways the automobile impacted society and industry during the 1920s. In the right circle, list the unique ways the automobile impacts the United States today. Where the two circles intersect, list similar ways that the automobile impacted society and industry during the 1920s and today. Then write an essay that describes the similarities and differences.

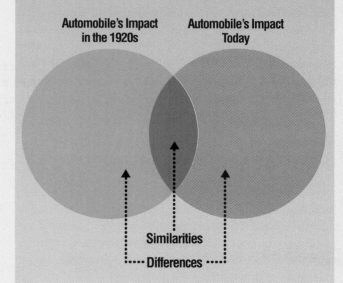

Automobile's Impact in the 1920s   **Automobile's Impact Today**

Similarities
Differences

Apply the Skill

Use information from Section 2 as well as facts that you know to create a Venn diagram showing the similarities and differences between women's roles in the 1920s and today. Then write a brief essay in which you compare and contrast those roles.

The Jazz Age

PREVIEW

Objectives

- To determine how culture changed during the 1920s
- To describe the changing role of women
- To examine conflicting values of the time period

Vocabulary

Jazz Age	prohibition
Harlem Renaissance	speakeasy
tabloid	bootlegger
expatriate	

During the 1920s a new spirit of energy swept the country, which was captured in the bouncy rhythms and melodies of the newly popular jazz music. Radio and movies created a national popular culture, while changes in society gave women more freedom in their employment.

◆ THE ROARING TWENTIES

New and improved technology brought the images and sounds of a new age to millions throughout the country. The phrase "Roaring Twenties" is an effective description for the roar of the cars, crowds, and the explosion of image- and sound-making machinery that came to dominate so much of American life. Radio, movies, music, journalism, literature, and art enabled people to explore new attitudes, habits, and experiences.

An American Sound

Music called jazz kept pace with the swiftly changing times. Created by African Americans in the South in the early 1900s, jazz drew on the rhythms and melodies of African folk songs and the harmonies of European songs. Jazz also had roots in ragtime and the blues, which African Americans had adapted from their work songs and spirituals. Musicians such as "Jelly Roll" Morton, Louis Armstrong, and Duke Ellington composed original jazz music and improvised on popular and original melodies, playing the songs in new and exciting ways.

Jazz first emerged in New Orleans, and then moved up the Mississippi River. It arrived in the North during the years of the Great Migration. New York City's Harlem and certain Chicago neighborhoods became the jazz centers of the country. By the 1920s, the popularity of jazz had spread from African Americans to white audiences. In the big cities, it was transformed from small jazz bands to large 15-piece orchestras that played in ballrooms and clubs. Nearly every American had heard jazz or danced to it. It was so popular that the decade became known as the **Jazz Age.** Leopold Stokowski, a symphony conductor, said that jazz had

> come to stay because it is an expression of the times, of the breathless, energetic, superactive times in which we are living.

▲ Bessie Smith was one of the leading jazz and blues artists of the 1920s. Her powerful singing earned her the title Empress of the Blues.

The Harlem Renaissance

During the 1920s, a New York City neighborhood called Harlem became the center for African American writers, painters, and musicians who gathered to develop and celebrate their distinctive culture. One reason writers and artists flocked to Harlem was its location. New York City was the nation's center of publishing, theater, and commerce. The artistic outpouring from African Americans during that period became known as the **Harlem Renaissance.** A renaissance is a cultural rebirth.

Writer James Weldon Johnson said in 1927 that "nothing can go farther to destroy race prejudice than the recognition of the Negro as a creator and contributor to American civilization." To help achieve that goal, *Crisis* and *Opportunity,* magazines of the National Association for the Advancement of Colored People (NAACP) and the National Urban League, offered cash prizes for outstanding work.

The atmosphere of excitement and new ideas encouraged many new talents. Countee Cullen and Claude McKay wrote poems about African American pride, and Zora Neale Hurston collected and published African American folklore. Langston Hughes was one of the first poets to use the rhythms from jazz and blues to write about city life.

Painters and sculptors also contributed to the Harlem Renaissance. Aaron Douglas and Hale Woodruff, among others, drew inspiration for their work from African art and African American history.

Radio and Print Media

The popularity of radio quickly spread. The first licensed radio station, KDKA in Pittsburgh, Pennsylvania, went on the air in 1920. By 1921 there were 27 more stations. By 1922 over 500 stations were broadcasting music, news, sports, religious services, and political speeches. By 1929 about 40 percent of American homes had radios, and soon much of the country was sharing the same music, commercials, and jokes. Radio brought entertainment and advertising to a huge market and helped spur the growth of the economy.

With more time on their hands and with more education than previous generations, Americans in the 1920s increased their reading habits. Scores of new magazines were started between 1922 and 1925, including *Reader's Digest, Time,* and *The New Yorker.* More people were reading newspapers as well, especially the **tabloids.** Tabloids, usually smaller in size, focused on sensational events.

▲ *Many of America's greatest writers flourished during the 1920s. This 1922 magazine featured a story by F. Scott Fitzgerald, author of* The Great Gatsby.

The 1920s was a time of unusual creativity in American literature. T.S. Eliot, e.e. cummings, Ezra Pound, Edna St. Vincent Millay, and Archibald MacLeish were important poets of the period. Playwrights such as Eugene O'Neill and Maxwell Anderson enriched the American theater. Novelists like John Dos Passos and Sinclair Lewis exposed the negative aspects of American culture, while F. Scott Fitzgerald wrote about the limits of success in a materialistic world. Writers like Gertrude Stein and Ernest Hemingway moved to Paris and became **expatriates,** people who leave their homeland to live in another country. Stein coined the phrase "the lost generation" to describe people who shared her sense of isolation from American culture and society.

The Popularity of Movies

Like the fresh sounds of jazz, movies provided an escape from hard work and the problems of everyday life. Many millions of Americans went to the movies at least once a week. On Saturdays, children with five cents for admission could spend the entire afternoon at the "picture show." Films were "silent;" actors mimed characters' emotions, and audiences followed the story by reading title cards that appeared on the screen.

When Charles Lindbergh, shown here with the Spirit of St. Louis, returned to New York after his historic flight, he was hailed as the Lone Eagle and given the largest ticker-tape parade held up to that time. ▶

Audiences packed the theaters to see the romantic movies of Clara Bow, Mary Pickford, and Rudolph Valentino and the comedies of Charlie Chaplin, Harold Lloyd, and Buster Keaton. Westerns and historical dramas were also popular. In 1927, Hollywood caused a sensation when it released its first major talking picture, or "talkie," *The Jazz Singer*.

Out of the love of films grew a fascination with movie stars. For many fans there was only a vague line separating the on-screen and off-screen adventures of the actors and actresses. Studio publicity, fan magazines, and gossip columns reinforced the idea that the people in films were experts in how to dress, wear their hair, and speak.

Sports Celebrities and National Heroes

Both radio and movies encouraged the growth of a national popular culture as millions of Americans now listened to the same shows and watched the same stars. Improved communications also brought news of people, places, and events into the homes of average Americans. The time was right for making famous people into heroes.

Each sport had its special stars, symbols of what could be accomplished through initiative, hard work,

and endurance. Perhaps the greatest American sports hero of the 1920s was baseball player George Herman "Babe" Ruth. However, fans also flocked to cheer for auto racer Barney Oldfield, football greats Knute Rockne and Harold "Red" Grange, and boxer Jack Dempsey.

During the 1920s, women began to distinguish themselves in the sports world. Among them, Gertrude Ederle stood out as the first woman to swim the English Channel. Tennis player Helen Wills set records on the courts.

By far the greatest hero of the decade was a pilot, Charles Lindbergh. On May 20, 1927, Lindbergh climbed aboard a single-engine plane, the *Spirit of St. Louis,* in New York. Thirty-three and a half hours later, he landed in Paris. Lindbergh was the first person to fly solo, nonstop across the Atlantic Ocean. "Lucky Lindy," as he came to be called, was an overnight sensation. When he returned to the United States, New Yorkers welcomed him with a hero's parade.

Lindbergh's flight marked a turning point for modern aviation. Two months later, planes began flying passengers and mail nonstop between San Francisco and Chicago. Lindbergh and his plane became a worldwide symbol of American imagination, determination, and technological superiority.

New Independence for Women

Increased independence marked the changing world of women in the 1920s. The young middle-class woman of the 1920s rejected the manners and dress of her mother and grandmother. The 1920s woman threw away her tight corset and shortened her skirt to her kneecaps. She cut her hair and put on makeup, once worn only on the stage. When she and her date danced to jazz music, her ankle-length boots flapped in the air, earning her the nickname "flapper."

In reality only a small percentage of women were true flappers. Still, they created an image for others to imitate and a symbol of the new social freedom of women. Although most were not ready to give up their roles as wife and mother, women slowly began to question their place in society.

The changing roles of women in the 1920s reflected deep changes in society. During World War I, a million women filled the jobs of men who had gone off to war. When the war ended, most of these women had to give up their jobs to the returning veterans. Still, by 1920 about 8.5 million women worked outside the home, a half million more than in 1910.

Women held different kinds of jobs than they had before the war, as shown on the pie charts on this page. In general, fewer white women worked as servants or domestic workers. More became office clerks, typists, and bookkeepers. A few entered professions requiring advanced study and became lawyers and professors.

Women enjoyed greater economic and intellectual independence than ever before. Freed from many household chores by labor-saving appliances, middle-class women found themselves with leisure time and looked for ways to fill it. Women began to think about going to college and having careers. By 1929, about 90 percent of the high-school girls in the Midwest said they intended to work after graduation.

After the Nineteenth Amendment gave women the right to vote, they became more active and visible in politics. At the 1920 Republican and Democratic conventions, women served as delegates for the first time. That year, the first two women governors were elected—Nellie Tayloe Ross of Wyoming and Miriam A. Ferguson of Texas.

Yet women soon learned that winning the vote was not the key to gaining equal rights in other areas. For example, although more women were employed during the 1920s, employers assumed that they would work only until they were married. Thus, women did not get the same training or pay as men did. Even though the numbers of women doctors and lawyers grew, many hospitals and law firms refused to hire them. Some women, led by New York nurse Margaret Sanger, worked to legalize the distribution of birth control information in order to expand women's economic and social options.

 In what ways did American culture change in the 1920s?

◆ CONFLICTING ATTITUDES

Although traditional attitudes and behaviors were questioned and out-of-date standards came under attack, not everyone was comfortable with the changes. Some Americans were concerned about what they viewed as the nation's moral decay. They feared that rapid social and economic changes would destroy a valuable way of life.

Prohibition

Some progressive reformers in the early 1900s who fought for government and child labor reform also believed that **prohibition,** the ban on making and

Economics *The types of jobs held by women changed between 1910 and 1930.* **Interpreting the Pie Charts** *Which occupation group had the largest increase in women's employment? Which had the largest decrease?* ▼

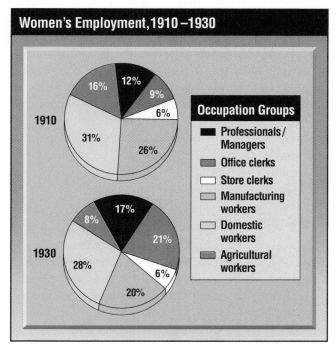

Women's Employment, 1910–1930

1910: 12%, 9%, 6%, 26%, 31%, 16%

1930: 17%, 21%, 6%, 20%, 28%, 8%

Occupation Groups
- Professionals/Managers
- Office clerks
- Store clerks
- Manufacturing workers
- Domestic workers
- Agricultural workers

▲ At the Scopes trial, Clarence Darrow, pictured above, argued against three-time presidential candidate William Jennings Bryan, who attacked Darwin's theory of evolution.

selling alcohol, would reduce poverty and wipe out crime. Although the passage of the Eighteenth Amendment in 1919 made it illegal to manufacture, sell, or transport alcohol, the reformers' victory was more symbolic than real, since prohibition was almost impossible to enforce. Designed to improve the habits and conduct of the American people, prohibition actually had the opposite effect. **Speakeasies,** or illegal saloons or bars, flourished. So did **bootleggers,** people who made alcohol themselves or smuggled it from Canada or Mexico. Gangsters like Al Capone in Chicago made enormous profits from illegal alcohol, and the fight for control of selling illegal alcohol led to a sharp increase in violence. By the time the Twenty-first Amendment was ratified in 1933, repealing prohibition, organized crime had become a feature of American life.

The Scopes Trial

Another division between modern ideas and traditional beliefs took place in Dayton, Tennessee. In 1925 a biology teacher named John Scopes was arrested for teaching the theory of evolution. The theory, proposed by Charles Darwin in 1859, suggested that all animals had developed from simpler forms of life. Although Darwin's theory received support from scientists, some religious groups viewed it as a contradiction to the Bible and a threat to basic Christian beliefs. The Tennessee legislature had made it a crime to teach the theory in state-supported schools.

The resulting trial drew international attention to the controversy. Scopes' defense team was led by Clarence Darrow, the most famous trial lawyer in the country. The prosecution was led by William Jennings Bryan. The jury took less than ten minutes to find John Scopes guilty of the crime of teaching evolution and fine him $100. Later, both the verdict and the fine were thrown out on a technicality. The struggle over the teaching of evolution continued. Laws in other states that prohibited the teaching of evolution were not repealed, but the laws were rarely enforced.

? What events reflected Americans' concerns over the rapid social changes of the 1920s?

Section 2 Review

Check Understanding

1. **Define** (a) Jazz Age (b) Harlem Renaissance (c) tabloid (d) expatriate (e) prohibition (f) speakeasy (g) bootlegger

2. **List** the ways culture changed in the 1920s.

3. **Identify** three people who contributed to the Harlem Renaissance.

4. **Explain** why the Scopes trial was an example of the clash between modern ideas and traditional beliefs.

Critical Thinking

Interpreting How did the flapper symbolize the ways that women's role in society was changing?

Write About Culture

◈ **Connecting Past and Present** Movie stars and sports figures were among the people considered heroes in the 1920s. Write a brief essay about people who are viewed as heroes today.

POINT *of* VIEW

WOMEN IN THE WORKPLACE

At the turn of the century, less than one in five women workers held professional positions. When women began to flood the workplace during the 1920s, however, many headed for offices and stores, not factories.

The typewriter, dictation machine, and switchboard made all the difference. Offices and department stores offered women alternatives to factory work or domestic service. By 1930, more than 736,000 women were shop clerks, cashiers, telephone operators, or secretaries.

These white-collar jobs involved less manual labor than factory work, and the environment was cleaner and more pleasant. The pay equaled or exceeded what women could earn in factories.

In the following passage, a woman discusses the opportunities that resulted from her taking a job outside the home. The interview comes from a community study published by sociologists Robert and Helen Lynd.

▲ Telephone switchboard operators, 1929

I began to work during the war, when everyone else did. We had to meet payments on our house and everything else was getting so high. The mister objected at first, but now he [does not] mind. I'd rather keep on working so my boys can play football and basketball and have spending money their father can't give them. No, I don't lose out with my neighbors because I work. Some of them have jobs and those who don't envy us who do. I have felt better since I worked than ever before in my life.... We have an electric washing machine, electric iron, and vacuum sweeper. I don't even have to ask my husband anymore because I buy these things with my own money....

From *Middletown: A Study in American Culture*, 1929

Examining Point of View

1. What reasons did the woman give for going out to work?

2. How are the reasons this woman gives for going to work similar to or different from the reasons women work today?

3. What reasons does the woman give for feeling better since she started working?

4. How might a woman's family and neighbors react to her working today?

What's Your Point of View?

More women work outside the home today than ever before. Some women are single parents with full responsibility for supporting their families. In other situations, both husband and wife work to make ends meet or to provide for luxury items. Some women are the chief breadwinners because their husbands prefer to stay at home and raise the children.

Write an essay about the role of working women today. Include your views about the advantages and disadvantages for the working woman and the family.

A Search for Social Justice

PREVIEW

Objectives

- To describe the economic conditions faced by returning veterans

- To analyze the reasons for the Red Scare and for limits to immigration after World War I

- To explain the causes of the Great Migration

- To discuss the rise of black nationalism

Vocabulary

inflation
Red Scare
deport

quota
black nationalism

For many veterans returning from World War I, the mood of victory soon vanished. Their reward for fighting was a quick discharge and a railroad ticket home. No one seemed interested in what these veterans were going to do now.

◆ AN UNEVEN ECONOMY

The World War I veterans who were hit hardest upon returning to the United States were those who were poor. They had no savings, and they could not depend on their families to support them while they were looking for work. Many African American and Hispanic veterans discovered that their brave efforts during the war were not enough to overcome prejudice. Jobs and schools that had been reserved for white citizens were still closed to African Americans.

Unemployment

The returning soldiers flooded the job market, but they found that there was not enough work for all of them. During the war, billion-dollar industries had been developed to produce materials for the armed forces. Now, the demand for war goods was gone.

Manufacturers needed fewer workers. By 1921 almost five million people were out of work, including women who had been employed in war industries.

Soaring Prices

Meanwhile, Americans who had stayed home during the war were eager to spend the money they had earned working in the nation's war industries. During the war, cars, new homes, and other goods had been in short supply. In the first years of peacetime, a buying craze hit the nation. Those who had money spent it on new cars, houses, clothes, and appliances. The demand for goods was so high that manufacturers could not keep up with it. As goods became scarce, prices soared. Within a year the price of milk rose by 50 percent. Eggs jumped from 32 cents to 62 cents a dozen. Even those who had jobs did not earn enough to afford the new high prices.

This **inflation,** or rise in the price of goods and services, was just one factor that made life harder for the nation's poor. They also had to compete with returning veterans for jobs—even for low-paying jobs.

Striking Workers

Labor unrest became increasingly common. From 1916 through 1920, the United States experienced between 3,350 and 4,450 strikes a year. Most were caused by disputes over wages, hours, and union recognition.

After World War I, relations between factory workers and owners continued to be tense. Workers demanded higher pay because they felt that their wages had not kept up with the price increases that had occurred during the war. The workers went on strike when the employers refused to meet their demands.

The large number of returning veterans also led to strained relations between workers and employers. Owners were now faced with a large pool of workers who were competing for jobs. Owners thus felt they could lower wages. The unions, however, struck back. Workers in the telegraph and telephone industries won higher pay, but unions in other industries were less successful.

Strikers faced hostility from veterans, who noted that the strikers had been earning money at home during the war while soldiers risked their lives overseas. Unlike soldiers, none of the strikers had been killed or wounded. Furthermore, unlike many of the veterans, the strikers had jobs.

 What economic conditions did returning veterans face after World War I?

◆ FEAR OF FOREIGNERS

As the United States tried to deal with unemployment and labor strikes, old feelings of nativism and hostility toward foreigners were revived. These feelings produced fear of ideas and people considered "un-American" and resulted in new policies limiting immigration to the United States.

The Red Scare

Many Americans distrusted strikers because people associated their actions with communism, a political movement that had led to the overthrow of the Russian government in 1917. Communism called for government ownership of all goods and property and for turning over political power to farmers and workers. Proclaiming an end to all differences between social and economic classes, Communists started the Russian Revolution with massive strikes. Thus, many Americans worried that the workers' strikes of 1919 were the start of a Communist revolution in the United States.

Widespread worries about a Communist takeover fueled what became known as the **Red Scare.** Under pressure from Congress, Attorney General A. Mitchell Palmer decided to take action against the "Reds," as Communists were sometimes called. Beginning in the fall of 1919, Palmer's agents made mass arrests of suspected Communists. One of the largest roundups came in January 1920, when raids were carried out in 33 cities. About 5,000 people were arrested, some of whom were beaten and forced to sign confessions. Most of these were foreign-born individuals who were innocent of any crime. More than 500 people were **deported,** or sent out of the country, without ever being formally charged with or convicted of any crime.

Palmer predicted that Communists would attempt to overthrow the government on May 1, 1920, which was May Day, the international workers' holiday. The day passed, however, without any Communist attacks. As a result, people began to lose faith in Palmer and for a while, the Red Scare faded away. However, applying the label "un-American" or "Communist" to a proposed reform program was enough to ensure its cancellation. Consequently, plans for state-supported housing, health and unemployment insurance, and a social security system received little or no support. A fear of communism would continue to disturb the United States repeatedly until the general collapse of the Communist system in the 1980s.

▲ **History** *During the 1920s, many Americans worried about a Communist takeover.* **Interpreting the Cartoon** *How did the artist convey the American people's fear of communism?*

Limits to Immigration

Some Americans believed that immigrants were taking jobs away from native-born Americans because the immigrants were willing to work for low wages. Fears about immigrants led the United States to change its immigration policy. In 1921, Congress passed the Emergency Quota Act. It set up a **quota,** or proportional share or allotment, for the number of people from each country that could enter the United States. Each year, immigrants from a nation were limited to 3 percent of the number of that nationality who were already living in the United States in 1910. The act also restricted the total number of immigrants to 357,000 each year. Until then, there had been few restrictions on immigration based on country of origin.

Despite the new policy, anti-immigrant sentiment continued to grow. In 1924 the National Origins Act further limited immigration. This law especially cut immigration from southern and eastern Europe while favoring immigrants from Britain, Scandinavia, and Germany. It also added the Japanese to the list of Asians who could not immigrate into the United States. In 1927, Congressman Albert Johnson from

California expressed the attitude of many Americans toward immigration:

> The United States is our land. We intend to maintain it so. The day of unalloyed [pure] welcome to all peoples, the day of indiscriminate acceptance [admitting everyone] of all races, has definitely ended.

The new immigration policies were a dramatic change from the past. The gates to the United States were now closed or, at best, open only a crack.

Sacco and Vanzetti

The intensity of anti-immigrant feelings reached its height in the trial of Nicola Sacco and Bartolomeo Vanzetti. In April 1920 robbers stole a shoe factory payroll in South Braintree, Massachusetts. A paymaster and a guard were killed. Two Italian immigrants were accused of the crime. A shoemaker and a fish peddler, Sacco and Vanzetti were carrying guns when they were arrested, and Sacco's gun was the same model used in the crime. Both were convicted and sentenced to death.

Many Americans protested that the trial was unfair. The two men admitted to being anarchists, opposed

Many Americans believed that the Sacco and Vanzetti trial was affected by hostility toward immigrants and fear of the men's political beliefs. Bartolomeo Vanzetti, left, is handcuffed to Nicola Sacco. ▼

Study Hint

Many words have more than one definition. When you come across these words, use the context—the sentence or paragraph that surrounds the word—to figure out which definition applies. For example, the word <u>races</u> has several definitions. In the quote on the left, use the sentence to figure out the meaning.

to organized government. Many people believed the prosecutor paid more attention to their heritage and political ideas than to evidence regarding their involvement in the crime. Even the judge was openly prejudiced, having commented to a friend that he was "bound to convict these men because they were 'Reds.'" When the Massachusetts Supreme Court refused to retry the case, Sacco and Vanzetti were executed in 1927. Vanzetti protested his innocence up to the moment of his death. A writer who visited him two days before his execution reported him as saying,

> This is our career and our triumph. Never in our full life could we hope to do such work for tolerance, for justice, for man's understanding of man as we now do by accident.

What contributed to the growth of anti-immigrant feelings after World War I?

◆ THE GREAT MIGRATION

Beginning about 1910, African Americans started migrating from the rural South to the cities of the North, as shown on the map on page 373. They moved northward in search of better lives and opportunities for themselves and their families. They settled in cities such as Chicago, Detroit, New York, and Philadelphia. By 1930, about two million African Americans had migrated to the North.

Reasons for Leaving

African Americans left their homes in the South for many reasons. One reason was the system of labor called sharecropping, established after the Civil War. Many freed African Americans and poor white families could not afford to buy farmland, so landowners provided them with a portion of land, and with seed, tools, and a mule. The farmers, or sharecroppers, paid for the use of the land and supplies with a share of their crops at harvest time. This system left the sharecroppers in debt since they were never able to fully pay back the landowners. Many sharecroppers hoped that the North would provide better economic opportunities.

Another reason for leaving the South was that natural disasters, such as floods and droughts, had destroyed many planting fields. Swarms of boll weevils had destroyed more than 85 percent of the cotton fields by 1922. Many African Americans could no longer make a living working on the land, and there were few jobs for them in southern cities.

Jim Crow laws in the South separated African Americans from whites by establishing a segregated way of life. African Americans were forced to use separate hospitals, restaurants, drinking fountains, restrooms, and telephone booths. They had to ride in the back of buses and sit in train cars labeled "colored." Fear for their personal safety and the desire to make a better life were important reasons for leaving the South.

While harsh conditions pushed African Americans out of the South, the lure of wartime jobs and more money pulled them north. When the United States entered World War I, U.S. factories began to produce wartime goods and the number of jobs in the North grew. When white men joined the armed forces, they created a labor shortage at home. The labor problem worsened as immigration slowed during wartime, partly because ocean travel was unsafe. Jobs now opened for African Americans, with salaries that were often much higher than those in the South.

Life in the North

Factory jobs in the North provided more money than jobs in the South, but life in the North was far from ideal. As in the South, African Americans discovered that even during wartime, many desirable jobs were closed to them. After the war, African

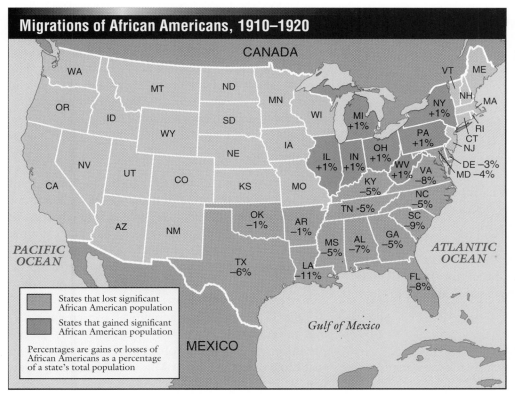

Migrations of African Americans, 1910–1920

States that lost significant African American population

States that gained significant African American population

Percentages are gains or losses of African Americans as a percentage of a state's total population

◀ **Geography** *More jobs and opportunities for a better education were among the reasons many African Americans migrated north between 1910 and 1920.*
Interpreting the Map
Which four states lost the largest percentage of African Americans during this time?

One of the Ku Klux Klan's most common symbols was a burning cross, as pictured in this initiation ceremony. ▶

American men had to compete with veterans for factory jobs. African American women had to settle for jobs as maids or cooks for well-to-do whites.

Living conditions in northern cities could also be difficult. Neighborhoods were strictly segregated. African American ghettos developed in New York City, Chicago, Philadelphia, and Washington, D.C., often in the overcrowded and unhealthy parts of these cities. Buildings fell into disrepair, and crime was widespread.

Riots Erupt

African Americans were often paid less than whites for factory jobs, and some white workers feared that employers would prefer to hire African Americans. Many white people also feared that African Americans would take over primarily white areas. Although the cost of living had more than doubled from prewar levels, and wages lagged far behind, this issue was often forgotten as resentment against African Americans sparked many bloody riots.

In 1919, 26 riots exploded across the United States, many during the summer, which became known as the "Red Summer." Riots occurred in Charleston, South Carolina; Atlanta, Georgia; and Longview, Texas. In Chicago, a riot lasted for three days and required 6,000 members of the National Guard to restore order. By the end of the riot, 36 people were dead and more than 5,000 were injured.

The Ku Klux Klan

With growing prejudice against African Americans and with nativism increasing, the Ku Klux Klan, which had died out with the end of Reconstruction, reemerged and flourished. The aim of the "new" Klan was to preserve the United States for native-born white Protestants. The Klan attacked not only African Americans but also immigrants, Catholics, and Jews.

Klan membership increased sharply in the 1920s, spreading from the South to the Midwest and the West. By 1924, four to five million Americans belonged to the Klan, more than one third of them in large cities.

To achieve its goals, the Klan turned to politics. Klan-supported candidates won elections as governors of Oklahoma and Oregon. However, after the corrupt and illegal actions of many of its leaders were exposed, the Klan began to lose members and influence. The success of immigration restriction and the general economic prosperity also contributed to the organization's rapid decline by the late 1920s.

Black Nationalism

Angered by the racially motivated violence of the Klan and other extremist groups, African Americans fought back by concentrating on their own sense of identity and racial pride. This new spirit was seen in the development of African American churches, hospitals, social clubs, businesses, and newspapers in the North. These institutions reduced dependence on white employers and organizations.

Black nationalism, a political movement seeking to establish a separate homeland for African Americans, was a reflection of the spirit of self-help that came out of the Great Migration. Marcus Garvey, who had been born in the Caribbean and migrated to

New York City, urged African Americans to reclaim their roots by returning to Africa. Through the weekly newspaper he published, the *Negro World*, Garvey set forth his ideas:

> The Negro must be united in one grand racial hierarchy [power structure]. Our union must know no clime [climate], boundary, or nationality. Like the Great Church of Rome, Negroes the world over must practice one faith, that of confidence in themselves, with One God! One Aim! One Destiny!

To promote self-reliance and other values of black nationalism, Garvey formed the Universal Negro Improvement Association (UNIA). At his urging, more than two million UNIA members invested in the Black Star steamship company. When Garvey oversold stock and was jailed on fraud charges in 1925, the UNIA faltered. Although he never set up a community in Africa, Garvey's teachings encouraged a new self-awareness among African Americans.

? How did life change for African Americans after World War I?

◆ THE ELECTION OF 1928

After completing Harding's term, Calvin Coolidge easily won the 1924 election. However, Coolidge announced that he would not run in 1928. In his place, the Republicans nominated Herbert Hoover, who had held Cabinet posts in the Harding and Coolidge administrations. His Democratic opponent was Alfred E. Smith, the governor of New York. Smith was of German and Irish ancestry and the first Roman Catholic to run for the presidency. He seemed to stand for everything small-town America was afraid of—the big city, immigrants, and Catholicism. Racial and religious prejudice helped Hoover win a landslide victory. However, for the first time in ten years, Republicans failed to win the 12 largest cities. Smith had consolidated the European ethnic vote for the Democratic party. The 1928 election revealed the important role ethnic, cultural, and economic differences played in American politics.

? What was the significance of the 1928 election?

▲ Hoover's role as Food Administrator during World War I earned him praise for preventing starvation in Europe; it also helped make him a popular presidential candidate in 1928.

Section 3 Review

Check Understanding

1. **Define** (a) inflation (b) Red Scare (c) deport (d) quota (e) black nationalism

2. **Describe** the origins of the Red Scare.

3. **Explain** why the United States limited immigration after World War I.

4. **Discuss** why many African Americans left the rural South during the Great Migration.

5. **List** two reasons for the rise of black nationalism.

Critical Thinking

◈**Connecting Past and Present** Do you believe there should be a quota system for immigrants today? Why or why not?

Write About Economics

What economic problems did the United States face after World War I, and how did these problems lead to social tensions? Write a brief report to help the candidates running for President in the election of 1928.

Chapter 18
Review

CHAPTER SUMMARY

Section 1

After a scandalous administration under Warren Harding, Vice President Calvin Coolidge, a supporter of business, took charge and won the confidence of the American people. Fueled by the manufacture of the automobile, the 1920s became a decade of business growth and consumer spending.

Section 2

Cultural life in the United States changed dramatically in the 1920s. The public's desire for entertainment and information stimulated the development of literature, music, movies, and radio. Women pursued their independence, and new heroes emerged. Not everyone was pleased by the changes in society, however. Prohibition and the controversy over the Scopes trial showed that many people wanted to maintain their traditional beliefs.

Section 3

Some people did not benefit from the prosperity of the 1920s. Returning war veterans found that jobs were scarce and unemployment was high. Inflation and unemployment resulted in widespread labor unrest and concern about immigrants competing for jobs. During this period, a fear of communism, inspired in part by the Russian Revolution, caused a panic known as the Red Scare. During the 1920s, thousands of African Americans headed north in the Great Migration to escape prejudice and get jobs. While discrimination was less apparent in the North, African Americans still found employment opportunities limited there. Fears about African Americans led to the rebirth of the Ku Klux Klan, which in turn spurred the birth of black nationalism.

Connecting ◆◆ Past and Present

The 1920s is often referred to as the Roaring Twenties or the Jazz Age. What phrase would you use to describe the present time period? Give reasons for your choice.

Using Vocabulary

For each term listed below, write a sentence that shows its meaning.

1. inflation
2. installment plan
3. deport
4. mass media
5. prohibition
6. speakeasy
7. Harlem Renaissance
8. assembly line
9. quota
10. expatriate

Check Understanding

1. **Summarize** the circumstances that led to the Red Scare after World War I.
2. **Explain** what caused about two million African Americans to leave the South between 1910 and 1930.
3. **Describe** the factors that led to black nationalism and the role played by Marcus Garvey in the movement.
4. **Identify** some of the cultural changes experienced by Americans during the 1920s.
5. **Describe** how women's lives changed during the 1920s.
6. **Explain** why the Eighteenth Amendment was passed in 1919 and what it was expected to accomplish.
7. **Explain** how artists during the Harlem Renaissance hoped to affect people's views of African Americans.
8. **Analyze** the reasons for the economic boom of the 1920s.
9. **Discuss** the factors that led to corruption during President Harding's administration.
10. **Explain** the positive and negative conditions African Americans faced living in the North.

Critical Thinking

1. **Drawing Conclusions** Which groups of people shared in the good economic times of the 1920s? Which groups did not? Explain.

2. **Understanding Causes and Effects** What were the results of the backlash against immigrants after World War I?

3. **Drawing Conclusions** How did advertising stimulate the economy?

4. **Analyzing** What factors contributed to making the 1920s a time of flourishing industry and a consumer's paradise?

◆ **Connecting Past and Present** Could another Red Scare occur today? Why or why not?

Interpreting the Timeline

Use the timeline on pages 358–359 to answer these questions.

1. Which event in the United States relates to communism?

2. What events indicate changing attitudes toward immigration in the United States?

3. What event threatened Harding's presidency?

Writing to Express a Point of View

The United States Constitution and the First Amendment were designed to protect the expression of most ideas, even those that are unpopular or controversial. Choose an incident from this chapter, such as the Red Scare, the Sacco and Vanzetti case, or the Scopes trial. **Write** an essay discussing whether free speech was limited or violated. In your essay, be sure to include an explanation of why free speech was an issue and how the time period contributed to the situation.

Putting Skills to Work

COMPARING AND CONTRASTING

In the Building Skills lesson on page 363, you learned to compare and contrast historical issues, events, ideas, or people. Choose one of the following paired subjects or things. Use this textbook as well as library resources to find out as much information as you can about them. Create a Venn diagram like the one below as you take notes about the pair of your choice. Then write an essay showing how the pair is similar or different.

1. War veterans and strikers in the 1920s
2. Herbert Hoover and Alfred Smith
3. Charles Lindbergh and Gertrude Ederle
4. Consumers in the 1920s and consumers today

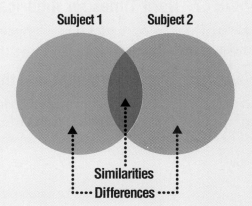

Subject 1   Subject 2

Similarities
Differences

Portfolio Project

A MOVIE SCENE

Create your own scene for a 1920s movie (silent or talkie) by choosing three of the following characters: an African American sharecropper, a flapper, a World War I veteran, a recent European immigrant, or a jazz musician. Write a script in which the characters meet by chance at a railroad station and explain how life has changed for them during the 1920s. To make a good story, create a conflict and a resolution as well as believable dialogue. You might consider revealing the characters' backgrounds, their goals, and their personal beliefs.

Chapter 19
The Great Depression
1929–1934

CHAPTER PREVIEW

Section 1   The Nation's Troubled Economy

The Great Depression created a crisis of confidence in the American economic system that affected manufacturing, industry, trade, agriculture, and consumers.

Section 2   Hard Times for Americans

The Great Depression had a major impact on the life and morale of almost every American.

Section 3   The Government and the Great Depression

President Hoover's attempts to restore confidence in the American economy failed as the nation fell deeper into economic despair.

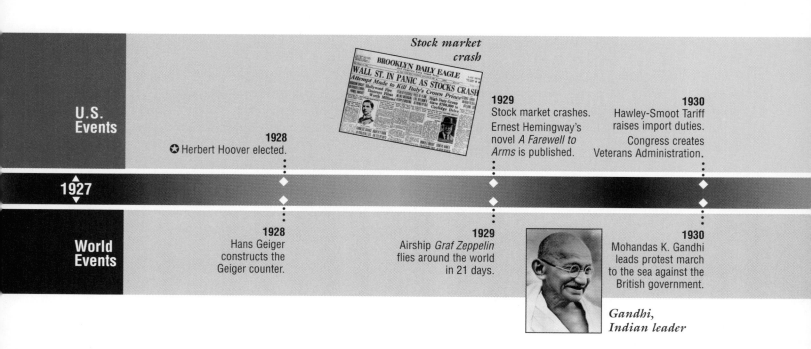

Stock market crash

BROOKLYN DAILY EAGLE
WALL ST. IN PANIC AS STOCKS CRASH

U.S. Events

1928
⭐ Herbert Hoover elected.

1929
Stock market crashes.
Ernest Hemingway's novel *A Farewell to Arms* is published.

1930
Hawley-Smoot Tariff raises import duties.
Congress creates Veterans Administration.

1927

World Events

1928
Hans Geiger constructs the Geiger counter.

1929
Airship *Graf Zeppelin* flies around the world in 21 days.

1930
Mohandas K. Gandhi leads protest march to the sea against the British government.

Gandhi, Indian leader

LOCAL HISTORY

After the prosperity of the 1920s, the hardship and suffering that accompanied the Great Depression came as a shock to Americans. The Great Depression affected every state and community in the United States. As you read the chapter, watch for ways Americans at all levels of society were affected. At the end of the chapter, you will be asked to research the impact the Great Depression had on your community.

▲ *Droughts devastated the western Great Plains during the 1930s. The lack of rain turned the soil to dust.* ◆ **Connecting Past and Present** *How does the photograph illustrate the dust storm's devastating effects on farming? What natural disasters make news today?*

Empire State Building

1932
⭐ Franklin Roosevelt elected.

Amelia Earhart is first woman to fly solo over the Atlantic.

Jobless veterans march on Washington, D.C.

Supreme Court overturns Scottsboro convictions.

Amelia Earhart

1931
Empire State Building is completed.

1933
12.6 million workers are jobless.

1934

1931
Emperor Haile Selassie gives Ethiopia its first written constitution.

British Commonwealth is established.

1933
Stalin begins great purge of the Communist party in U.S.S.R.

Haile Selassie

The Nation's Troubled Economy

PREVIEW

Objectives

- To examine the causes of the Great Depression

- To describe the effects of the Great Depression on Americans at all levels of society

- To analyze why people lost confidence in the U.S. government and economic system

Vocabulary

default   Hooverville
foreclose   Bonus Army

Though few realized it, an economic tragedy was unfolding beneath the glitter of the Jazz Age. On the surface it appeared that Americans lived a carefree and luxurious life. In reality most people had barely enough money to make ends meet, sometimes having to borrow money just to buy the bare necessities. Even the wealthy had to borrow money occasionally to maintain their style of living. In hopes of finding quick wealth, more Americans than ever risked their money by investing in the stock market. Meanwhile, important industries and agriculture were in trouble. By late 1929 the entire economic structure of the country had collapsed, plunging unprepared Americans into a state of despair.

◆ CAUSES OF THE GREAT DEPRESSION

Society magazines of the 1920s portrayed Americans as living lives of luxury and leisure. Glossy photographs presented scenes of the rich at play. Wearing silks and satins, twirling ropes of pearls, driving glamorous new cars, the wealthy seemed to have few cares in the world.

In fact, these images of a prosperous, carefree United States were deceptive, masking serious economic problems. The people who appeared in society magazines as the wealthiest Americans belonged to the 5 percent of the population that controlled almost one third of the nation's wealth. The rest of the nation, made up of hard-working people in jobs ranging from mining to secretarial work, were far from wealthy. Indeed, most of them scraped by on an annual income of $2,500 or less.

Big Business and Fading Industries

During the 1920s the government greatly favored big business, offering many corporations large tax breaks. The national government also followed a "hands-off" policy on regulating, or putting controls on, corporations. Officials argued that it was not the government's role to regulate corporate growth or finances. As a result, many corporations grew into economic giants.

By the end of the 1920s, about 200 corporations controlled half the nation's corporate wealth. General Motors, Ford Motor Company, and Chrysler Motor Company produced 90 percent of the nation's cars and trucks. Giant food market chains, such as the Atlantic and Pacific (A&P) grocery, with more than 10,000 stores across the country, put many small stores out of business.

While many industries boomed, others, such as textiles and coal mining, had been in a state of decline for years. Like farmers and factory workers, workers in these industries had little firsthand experience of prosperity.

A Wide Variety of Incomes

The executives who headed the powerful corporations were wealthy men who earned huge salaries. They had more than enough money to enjoy the flood of new consumer products pouring into the marketplace, from the latest automobiles to time-saving lawn mowers.

Meanwhile, assembly-line workers toiled long hours for small paychecks, making it difficult for families to get by. While labor unions fought for and received higher wages, the increases did not keep pace with increases in profits. This meant that the bulk of benefits from increased sales went to the business owners. Eager to share in the nation's prosperity, many workers bought goods on the installment plan.

Crisis in Agriculture

While Americans from all walks of life faced economic hardship of one sort or another during the 1920s, farmers had a particularly difficult time.

During World War I, demand for crops such as corn and wheat had boosted agricultural output in the United States. After the war, demand for crops declined and crop prices fell, often by 50 percent or more. Farmers suddenly had much less income on which to live but just as many costs. Also, American farm products faced stiffer competition from European agriculture, reviving after the war years.

To make matters worse, many farmers had secured bank loans to purchase expensive farm equipment that promised to make farm work easier and more productive. These farmers now found that they needed to borrow more money to pay loans that were secured during the war. As farmers grew deeper in debt, they began to **default,** or fail to pay their loans, causing many local banks to fail.

The Stock Market Crashes

In hopes of striking it rich, many Americans skimped, saved, and borrowed money to buy stocks and bonds on the stock market. Investors took increasing risks, often buying stocks on margin, which meant that they paid a small percentage of the stock's price as a down payment and borrowed the rest from the seller of the stock. *The Saturday Evening Post* printed a poem that captured the fever:

" Oh, hush thee, my babe, granny's bought some more shares,
Daddy's gone out to play with the bulls and the bears,
Mother's buying on tips and she simply can't lose,
And baby shall have some expensive new shoes. "

As investors lost confidence that stock prices would continue to rise, people began selling stock and its value began to fall in early September 1929. Many brokers now asked investors for the remaining money they were owed on stock that had been bought on margin. Those who could not pay were forced to sell their stock, which led to a further price decline. On October 24, stock values plunged dramatically, creating panic among investors. On October 29, "Black Tuesday," the stock market crashed due to frantic attempts to sell as much stock as possible before prices became even lower. For many stocks, there were no buyers at any price. Americans not only lost their stocks, but they also plunged into debt from loans they could not repay.

The stock market crash undermined the confidence of the business community. Manufacturers began laying

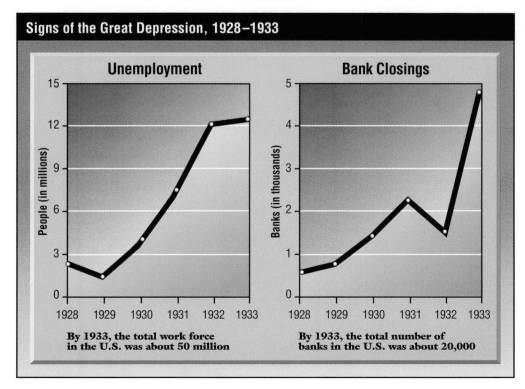

Signs of the Great Depression, 1928–1933

Unemployment

People (in millions)

By 1933, the total work force in the U.S. was about 50 million

Bank Closings

Banks (in thousands)

By 1933, the total number of banks in the U.S. was about 20,000

◄ **Economics** *The stock market crash dramatically increased unemployment and bank closings.* **Interpreting the Graphs** *Approximately how many people became unemployed between 1929 and 1932? Between which years did unemployment increase the most? Which year had the most bank closings?*

off workers, which caused further declines in consumer spending and more production cutbacks. Many banks began to fail as depositors withdrew their funds, which were not protected by insurance.

What economic problems caused the Great Depression?

◆ RESULTS OF THE GREAT DEPRESSION

By the summer of 1932, the American economy had almost totally collapsed. Factories had slashed production, and construction had almost ceased. In one year alone—1929—new investment dropped from $10 billion to $1 billion. Tens of thousands of businesses went bankrupt. Most troubling of all, however, was that millions of Americans were out of work.

Farm families were especially hard hit by the onset of the Great Depression. As more and more farmers were forced to default on their loans, banks were forced to **foreclose,** or seize their property. During a single day in 1932, banks took back 25 percent of the farmland in the state of Mississippi because farmers could not make the payments on their loans.

International Effects

Many European countries were struggling to recover from the debt they faced as a result of World War I. The Great Depression made this situation worse since it was now difficult for Americans to import foreign goods, which would have helped the European economy. Banking, manufacturing, and trade had become international. When the world's leading economy fell, the global economic system also began to crumble.

Jobless and Hopeless

Massive unemployment across America, as shown on the graph on page 381, became the most obvious sign of the deepening depression. In 1930 the Department of Labor estimated that 4.2 million workers, or roughly 9 percent of the labor force, were out of work. These figures nearly doubled in 1931, and by 1933, 12.6 million workers—over one quarter of the labor force—were without jobs.

Unable to find work, people created jobs for themselves. In New York City, for example, a group of unemployed men went to work each day before dawn. Pushing small handcarts through the dark city streets, they picked up automobile parts, old clothes, paper, rubber—anything that looked salable. Later in the

During the Great Depression, over one quarter of American workers were jobless. Unemployed people turned to soup kitchens or waited in bread lines, such as the one shown here, to receive food distributed by charities. ▶

morning, they took their pickings to a junk dealer, who gave them a few coins to buy food or other things they needed.

Many Americans lost their homes as well as their jobs during the Great Depression. Desperate for shelter, they erected shacks of scrap wood, old tin, or other materials that they could scavenge. As more and more shacks sprang up, they formed shabby little villages. The residents, who blamed their troubles on the policies of President Hoover, called these shanty-towns **Hoovervilles.** A visitor to a Hooverville expressed shock at what he saw:

> Here were all these people living in rusted-out car bodies. I mean that was their home. There were people living in shacks made of orange crates. One family with a whole lot of kids [was] living in a piano box. This wasn't just a little section. It was maybe ten miles wide and ten miles long. People living in whatever they could junk together.

In every large city, charities run by churches and other organizations set up handout lines, where free loaves of bread and other foods were handed out to the jobless. Sometimes, the lines for a handout wrapped around entire city blocks. The mood in these lines, called bread lines, was solemn and hopeless. In addition, soup kitchens were established as places where the unemployed received free meals. All kinds of people, from all levels of society, frequented the soup kitchens and bread lines.

Entire families devoted themselves to the grim task of survival. Fathers, desperate to earn a few cents to feed their families, sold apples on the street. Hungry children picked through garbage pails and scavenged in garbage dumps, looking for scraps to eat. For many Americans, begging became a way of life. In fact, begging became so widespread that a song about begging, "Brother, Can You Spare a Dime?" became a popular tune.

Economic Crisis

As the months wore on, it became clear that things were not getting better. People began to lose confidence in the American economic system and in the U.S. government. During the 1920s, business executives and government leaders had been quick to claim credit for

▲ Some Americans who lost their jobs and homes during the Great Depression were forced to live in flimsy shacks, often built among trash heaps. These shantytowns were called Hoovervilles.

the widespread prosperity. Now, they had no solution for the worst economic crisis in the nation's history.

The government also seemed helpless. As the numbers of jobless and homeless mounted, Americans appealed to President Hoover for government aid. Hoover resisted, however, believing strongly in the individual's ability to rise above the Great Depression. Government "charity," he said, would only weaken the American people and discourage them from finding solutions of their own.

The Threat of Revolution

The nation's farmers were in a rebellious mood. In some areas they banded together to prevent sheriffs from taking back the land of farmers who could not pay their mortgage loans. After the price of milk plunged in Wisconsin, dairy farmers dumped thousands of gallons of milk on the ground rather than try to sell the milk or give it away. Desperate farmers in Iowa organized the Farmers' Holiday Association, aimed at raising prices by refusing to sell produce.

In the cities there was also unrest. During the 1920s the federal government had favored big business while ignoring workers' needs. Now, millions of workers were unemployed. With little to lose, they sought radical change.

Many workers, especially those who were young and unemployed, joined the Socialist and Communist parties. These political parties challenged the traditional

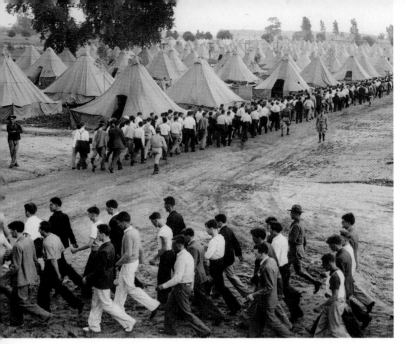

▲ Frustrated that jobs continued to be scarce, about 20,000 World War I veterans marched on Washington, D.C., in 1932, to demand their monetary bonus.

democratic and economic principles of mainstream American government. Both parties argued that the federal government should take over the nation's industries. They also urged that the wealth of the United States should be equally distributed among all Americans. The Communists believed that these goals could be accomplished only through violent revolution. On March 7, 1932, about 3,000 Detroit auto workers and unemployed people, led by Communist organizers, marched to the Ford factory. When the demonstrators refused orders to turn back, police controlled by Ford fired tear gas and bullets, killing 4 and seriously wounding more than 60 others.

The Bonus Army

After World War I, Congress had voted to give veterans a monetary bonus to be paid in 1945, but the veterans did not want to wait. About 20,000 jobless veterans of World War I, called the **Bonus Army,** marched on Washington, D.C., in the summer of 1932. They demanded payment immediately.

Congress rejected the veterans' appeal. Most veterans returned home, but between 8,000 and 10,000 men refused to leave. They vowed to stay in the tents and shacks they had set up along the Potomac River until 1945, if necessary.

President Hoover stood firm. The leaders of the Bonus Army, he said, were criminals and revolutionaries. Although the bonus marchers were generally peaceful,

a few violent incidents prompted Hoover to call in the army, led by General Douglas MacArthur, to clear them out. MacArthur exaggerated the menace of the peaceful demonstrators, insisting they were driven by "the essence of revolution." Troops equipped with bayonets and tear gas rode into the veterans' camp and burned it to the ground. The sight of soldiers chasing away war veterans shocked Americans. The incident cost Hoover what little popular support he still had. To most Americans, the treatment of the Bonus Army signaled that a change in government leadership was needed.

> **During the Great Depression, why did many Americans lose confidence in the government's ability to run the country?**

Section 1 Review

Check Understanding

1. **Define** (a) default (b) foreclose (c) Hooverville (d) Bonus Army

2. **List** some causes of the Great Depression.

3. **Describe** the economic problems of farmers in the 1920s.

4. **Discuss** why Americans lost faith in their leaders during the early years of the Great Depression.

5. **Describe** how Hoover's response to the Bonus Army affected public opinion.

Critical Thinking

Comparing and Contrasting How was the situation of farmers similar to that of factory workers during the Great Depression? How was it different?

Write About History

◈ **Connecting Past and Present** The Bonus Army marched on Washington, D.C., to protest economic conditions. Write about a recent march on Washington. Who joined the march, what was its purpose, and what was the response to it?

BUILDING *SKILLS*

Writing an Essay: The Causes of the Great Depression

Writing an essay is the process of making a generalization about something, developing the idea fully, supporting it, and drawing conclusions about it. Whether you are doing a classroom assignment or taking a standardized test, the process for writing an essay is generally the same. By synthesizing your ideas in writing, you have the chance to show what you know about a person, event, or issue.

Here's How

Follow these steps to write an essay:

1. If you have a specific question to answer, make sure you understand what is expected of you. Look for words such as *analyze, compare, describe,* and *discuss,* and use them as clues to determine how you should treat the subject.

2. If you have to choose a topic, select one that interests you. Consider what specific aspect of the topic you want to discuss and what you plan to communicate about it.

3. Think about your purpose in writing about the topic. Do you want to make recommendations, tell a story, or change someone's opinion?

4. Consider your audience as you select your topic and purpose. What do they already know about the topic? What do you want them to learn?

5. Collect your information and list all the facts and details you want to include in your essay.

6. If necessary, research your topic to find expert opinions and statistics that will support your point of view.

7. Write a thesis statement that summarizes your topic and your particular focus on it.

8. Create an outline to help you organize the information you will present.

9. Draft your essay by putting together the main points you want to make about the topic with facts, examples, and other kinds of details that develop and support it. Follow your outline, remembering that your introduction and conclusion are particularly important.

10. Revise your essay by rereading your work for meaning, for organization, and for style, including sentence structure and word choice.

11. Make a final copy of your essay that reflects your best work in both content and form.

Here's Why

Writing an essay organizes your ideas and helps you express your thoughts efficiently and accurately. It is an important skill that you will need in the future at school and at work.

Practice the Skill

Choose one of the questions on page 384 and analyze with a classmate the steps you would take to answer it. Begin by summarizing the expectations of the question as well as your purpose.

Apply the Skill

Use the steps in *Here's How* to answer the following essay question: How did public attitudes, business, and government contribute to causing the Great Depression?

Section 2

Hard Times for Americans

PREVIEW

Objectives

- To describe how the Great Depression affected American family life
- To evaluate the hardships endured by farmers and minorities during the Great Depression

Vocabulary

refugee
tenant farmer

The Great Depression affected Americans in different ways. Some wealthy investors lost their fortunes, but for most of the very rich, who represented only a small percentage of the total population, life did not change much. The average American, on the other hand, felt the Great Depression deeply. Unemployment created enormous hardship and suffering. Under the economic strain, Americans lost confidence in themselves. "No matter that others suffered the same fate, an inner voice whispered, 'I'm a failure,'" one man wrote.

Still, as is usual when hard times hit, those hurt most by the depression were those who had the least to start with: farmers, immigrants, the poor, and unskilled workers. With no resources to fall back on, these Americans quickly reached the depths of despair.

◆ CHANGES IN FAMILY LIFE

The Great Depression challenged the American family. In some cases, the struggle for survival brought family members closer together. More often, however, unemployment, homelessness, and hunger disrupted traditional family patterns and threatened to weaken the ties of family life.

Unemployment and homelessness took their toll on traditional family structures. Parental authority suffered when young adults took low-paying, unskilled jobs while fathers remained unemployed. Many unemployed husbands and fathers, humiliated at not being able to support their families, abandoned their wives and children. By 1940, more than 1.5 million men had left their homes.

Most families stayed together, however. They "made do" by renting rooms to boarders and washing other people's clothes for a fee. They found inexpensive ways to spend their time. Recreational activities included quilting bees, square dances, and stamp collecting. People's reading habits increased. Although the sale of newspapers and magazines decreased, public libraries were busy.

Along with their parents, children saw their lives change in many ways. Millions of children had to work to help their families survive. Children as young as seven years old sold newspapers, delivered groceries, mowed lawns, and took on any task that would earn a few cents.

For many children the Great Depression ended their formal education. Many families could not afford the luxury of having a child in school. Children were needed either to earn wages themselves or to help at home while parents searched for work.

Some 900,000 teenagers left home to search for work during the Great Depression. They traveled the country, riding from town to town in railroad boxcars, sleeping in makeshift camps away from the watchful eyes of the police. Riding the rails was dangerous. One railroad alone reported 433 people killed and 838 injured between 1929 and 1933.

 **How did the Great Depression change traditional family patterns?**

◆ THE DUST BOWL

Among the people hardest hit by the Great Depression were the farmers of the western Great Plains. Many of them had resettled in the region some 30 years before World War I, raising cattle and growing wheat and other crops despite the dry land. With difficulty they managed and in time even prospered.

Then, in the 1930s, just as the Great Depression was tightening its grip on the nation, a series of droughts struck the Plains region. Much of the Great Plains turned into a Dust Bowl.

Faced with total ruin, tens of thousands of Plains farmers abandoned their dusty fields and headed west as **refugees,** people who flee a difficult economic, social, or political situation in search of better living conditions. Packing up their belongings and piling them into whatever vehicle they could find, Oklahoma farmers, called "Okies," and Arkansas farmers, called "Arkies," set out for California in search of work.

When they arrived, the Dust Bowl refugees found that their troubles were not over. Californians had their own unemployment problems, and they were not eager to share the few available jobs with migrants from another state. Signs were posted to make sure the migrants knew they were not welcome. One sign said, "No Jobs in California. If you are looking for work—Keep Out."

Desperate to survive, whole families of newcomers worked for vegetable and fruit growers, picking whatever crop was ripe at the time. The money they received—as little as $1.00 to $1.50 a day—was barely enough to keep them alive. At night they crammed into tents with little to eat and only the ground to sleep on. When the job was finished, the growers chased them off the land.

? Why did Great Plains farmers abandon their land to head for California in the 1930s?

◆ AFRICAN AMERICANS IN THE GREAT DEPRESSION

The Harlem Renaissance poet Langston Hughes commented about the effect of the Great Depression on the nation's African Americans:

> **The Depression brought everyone down a peg or two. And the Negroes had but a few pegs to fall.**

As Hughes implied, African Americans had long been at the bottom of the economic ladder. With the onset of the Great Depression, things got even worse.

Life in Northern Cities

Beginning with the Great Migration after the Civil War and continuing through the early 1900s, a growing number of African Americans in the South had steadily moved to northern cities. In the North, they generally found better jobs and somewhat fairer treatment. But because of the economic decline caused by the Great Depression, most African Americans in the North quickly lost many of the advances they had worked so hard to achieve.

When times became difficult, African American workers were the first to be fired. Some bosses demanded bribes from African Americans to let them keep their jobs. Other bosses expected more work for less pay. As the Great Depression deepened, whites, desperate for work, began to take jobs that they had once scorned. Low-level jobs, usually given to African Americans, were not as unappealing as they had seemed in better times. By 1932 about 50 percent of the African American community was out of work compared to 39 percent unemployment for whites.

Due to the high percentage of unemployment, African Americans protested the firings. "Don't Buy Where You Can't Work" campaigns spread to Chicago, New York, and 23 other cities. These campaigns met with some success for African Americans, but they did not adequately solve the deep problems created by the depression.

Life in the Rural South

Despite the Great Migration, the majority of African Americans still lived in the South during the Great Depression. Most were either sharecroppers or **tenant farmers,** farmers who paid for the right to work someone else's land. While sharecroppers used part of their crop to pay for use of the land and farming supplies, tenant farmers paid money to rent the land. Whole families worked hard to survive, growing cotton as well as a few crops to feed themselves and their animals.

Plunging cotton prices in the 1930s created even greater hardship for these farmers. Most lived in shacks that had no plumbing or heating systems.

> ### Study Hint
> As you read, look for words and phrases that indicate ideas and events that have a cause-and-effect relationship. Words such as because, since, due to, and so can help you connect cause and effect.

Their diet consisted of little more than pork leftovers, cornmeal, and even weeds. Most survived on $150 to $250 a year, but often much of that money went to the landowner.

As the depression dragged on, the government began to pay landowners not to plant crops because it was thought that with fewer crops on the market, prices would rise. Most landowners decided that the unplanted land should be the land used by the tenant farmers. In response to this decision, some African American tenant farmers formed the Southern Tenant Farmers Union. Landlords hired thugs to break up the meetings, and many tenant farmers were thrown off the land where they had worked and lived for many years.

The early 1930s saw a revival of racial violence in the South, and African Americans were faced with growing discrimination. Documented lynchings increased from 8 in 1932 to 28 in 1933. Some white Americans declared openly that African Americans had no right to a job if whites were out of work. African Americans were denied civil rights, such as access to education and voting.

For African Americans in the South, there was little justice. For example, in March 1931, nine young African American men—eight of them teenagers—were accused of attacking two white women on a train near Scottsboro, Alabama. Although there was no evidence of the attack, an all-white jury convicted all nine of the so-called Scottsboro Boys. Eight were sentenced to die. The Scottsboro Boys became a nationwide symbol of injustice. In 1932 the Supreme Court overturned the conviction. All of the Scottsboro Boys eventually gained their freedom, though the last was not released until 1950.

How were African Americans affected by the Great Depression?

◆ MEXICANS AND MEXICAN AMERICANS

During the Great Depression, many Americans looked for scapegoats, or people to blame. Mexicans and Mexican Americans, as well as other groups, often became targets for prejudice and mistrust. Public resentment focused on migrant laborers, who traveled from place to place in search of work. Since the Civil War, Mexicans had been crossing into Texas to harvest cotton. After World War I they also traveled to California to harvest crops there.

Jobs were so scarce that these African Americans drove from Memphis, Tennessee, to rural Arkansas just to work for a day in the cotton fields. ▶

▲ *During the Great Depression, many people, such as this Mexican family, traveled the country searching for work.*

During prosperous times, American growers had encouraged Mexican workers to emigrate to the United States. Over the years, many of them had settled in California. Then the Great Depression struck, and farm jobs became scarce. Many migrants worked fewer days and for lower wages than in previous years. Increasingly, women and children were forced to work in the fields when work was available. Other farm laborers began to complain that Mexican farm workers were taking jobs from them by accepting lower pay.

Many Mexican immigrants settled in cities. Communities flourished in midwestern cities—such as Chicago, Illinois; Detroit, Michigan; and Gary, Indiana—as well as in cities in Texas and California. Many of the immigrants alternated between agricultural and factory work, depending on what jobs were available. Racism and segregation confined them to poor areas where disease and infant mortality rates were much higher than average.

Mexican Americans, who were citizens of the United States, faced many of the same resentments as did Mexican workers. Despite having families that had been in the United States for several generations, they were regarded as illegal aliens, foreigners who had no right to live and work in this country. Only a relatively small number of Mexican Americans owned land, but many of them lost their property because they were unable to pay taxes. Mexican Americans who had jobs in meat-packing plants, in steel factories, and on railroads found themselves working only a few days a week.

As the economic problems of the Great Depression increased, resentment against Mexican Americans grew. Mexican Americans who had jobs were accused of taking work away from "real" Americans.

? What prejudice did Mexicans and Mexican Americans face during the Great Depression?

Section 2 Review

Check Understanding

1. **Define** (a) refugee (b) tenant farmer

2. **Describe** two ways that the Great Depression disrupted family life.

3. **Describe** what happened to Dust Bowl farmers when they migrated to California.

4. **Explain** how the problems facing African Americans living in the North during the Great Depression were similar to or different from the problems facing African Americans living in the South.

5. **Discuss** the problems faced by Mexicans and Mexican Americans during the Great Depression.

Critical Thinking

Inferring Why did hard times in the United States tend to increase prejudice and discrimination?

Write About Economics

◆ **Connecting Past and Present** Economic conditions in the 1930s caused many people to relocate. Write a short essay in which you explain why people today might relocate.

CONNECTING HISTORY

& The Environment

THE DUST BOWL

During World War I, farmers plowed the grasslands of the Great Plains and planted crops to help feed starving people in Europe. After the war ended in 1918, there was less demand for wheat and corn. Consequently, prices dropped and many farmers turned to other ways of making a living.

Little rain fell on the western Great Plains during the early 1930s. The fields were exposed to the sun, and the soil had no protection as the hardy grass had been removed by the farmers. The combination of the drought and high temperatures cracked the dry earth. When the winds came in the mid-1930s, the grasslands, which would have held the earth in place, were gone, and the earth simply blew away, creating massive dust storms. From 1933 until 1939, dust storms turned this area, which became known as the Dust Bowl, into a wasteland. Winds were so strong that they blew a "curtain" of dust all the way to the east coast.

President Franklin Roosevelt began sending millions of federal dollars to the Dust Bowl states in 1933. The money was used to feed starving cattle and to plow ridges into the land to keep it from blowing away. Ten million acres of farmland were replanted with forests. Lines of trees called windbreaks were set out to protect planted fields from the winds. The government funded programs to teach farmers which crops to grow and how to plant them. Unfortunately, the programs and the money were too late to help most farmers save their land.

Making the Environmental Connection

1. What was the Dust Bowl?
2. What farming practices and acts of nature helped create the Dust Bowl?
3. What assistance did Roosevelt provide to Dust Bowl farmers?

Connecting Past and Present

Write a brief essay on the impact of a recent natural disaster. Examine the causes of the disaster, and the ways in which citizens and the government tried to repair the damage and provide aid to people in need.

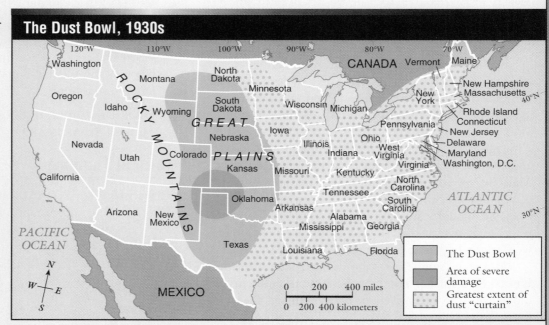

The Dust Bowl, 1930s

Legend:
- The Dust Bowl
- Area of severe damage
- Greatest extent of dust "curtain"

▲ **Geography** *This map shows the areas affected by the Dust Bowl.* **Interpreting the Map** *What states were in the Dust Bowl? What states sustained the greatest damage? What area of the United States was not affected by the Dust Bowl?*

The Government and the Great Depression

PREVIEW

Objectives

- To analyze President Hoover's approach to ending the Great Depression

- To explain why Hoover's actions were inadequate to reverse the decline in the nation's economy

- To summarize the issues and results of the election of 1932

Vocabulary

public works
relief

By 1932, most Americans blamed President Hoover for not doing enough to end the Great Depression. Many bitterly recalled the assurances of his inaugural speech, when he promised Americans that the future was bright. Hoover had said,

> **Ours is a land rich in resources . . . blessed with comfort and opportunity. . . . I have no fear for the future of our country.**

During the next three years, Hoover made many such statements, but optimistic words could not cure the nation's ills. Hoover did not see that new solutions were needed to overcome the Great Depression. His failure to do so greatly damaged his political career, and it stalled economic recovery for the country.

◆ FIGHTING THE GREAT DEPRESSION

For the millions of Americans who had voted for Hoover for President in 1928, his inability to find solutions to the Great Depression came as a surprise.

After all, Herbert Hoover's expertise in business had made him a millionaire before the age of 40. After World War I, he had headed a committee that shipped tons of food to starving Belgians. The committee had also distributed food, clothing, and medical supplies to refugees in eastern Europe. Americans wondered why President Hoover was unable to relieve the misery of people in his own country.

The Tariff Disaster

In 1930, Hoover did something that most experts condemned as a reckless blow to an already weakened economy. The President signed the Hawley-Smoot Tariff Act, which was meant to protect American goods by placing high tariffs on imports. However, as spending in the United States continued to fall, the bill did little to help U.S. manufacturers. To make matters worse, European nations responded to the act by raising their own tariffs, which then made it harder for American businesses to sell their products overseas.

Hoover's action decreased international trade when it needed to be increased. Soon, trade between the United States and Europe was at a standstill. The decline in U.S. imports and exports can be seen in the chart below. Unable to sell their goods, European nations did not have the money to repay the millions of dollars in war debts that they owed to the United States. Finally, the slowing of trade caused a deepening of the economic depression in Europe.

The United States Economy, 1920–1933

In Billions of Dollars	1920	1929	1933
National debt	24.3	17.0	22.5
General imports	2.5	4.4	1.5
General exports of U.S. merchandise	4.4	5.2	1.6
Federal government receipts of goods sold	6.7	4.0	2.0
Federal government expenditures	6.4	3.3	4.6

▲ **Economics** *This chart shows changes in the U.S. economy from 1920 to 1933.* **Interpreting the Chart** *Which figures reflect the effects of the Hawley-Smoot Tariff Act of 1930?*

▲ **History** *President Hoover is telling a dog, "You stop following me, d'hear!"* **Interpreting the Cartoon** *Why does Hoover want to distance himself from the dog?*

Too Little, Too Late

President Hoover did make some efforts to restore economic stability after the stock market crash in 1929. He met with the leaders of big business and urged them not to cut wages. But as profits slipped lower and lower, corporate leaders turned their back on Hoover's pleas. Some began mass firings and later cut wages. Hoover also cut taxes and lowered interest rates, trying to encourage Americans to spend more and thus stimulate the economy. He stepped up **public works** programs to create jobs. Public works are construction projects financed with public funds. Under Hoover's leadership, the government hired workers to build roads, dams, and other large projects. He also made it easier for farmers to get loans.

In general, however, Hoover resisted calls from Congress and local communities for a greater federal role in **relief** efforts, to provide direct money payments for the unemployed. The President's Emergency Committee for Unemployment, established in 1930, and its successor, the President's Organization for Unemployment Relief, created in 1931, did little more than encourage local groups to raise money to help the unemployed. However, these groups lacked resources and staff to deal with the worsening situation.

In 1932, Hoover set up the Reconstruction Finance Corporation (RFC), which gave government credit to banks so that they could extend loans. The purpose of the agency was to halt bank failures and business closings. The RFC reflected Hoover's theory that prosperity at the top would help the economy as a whole. To many people, however, it seemed that the government was helping bankers while ordinary people went hungry.

Three months later, bank failures had dropped from 70 a week to one every two weeks. In the long run, however, the RFC was not as effective as Hoover had hoped. Banks that received loans used the funds to strengthen their own finances. The RFC did almost nothing to finance public works.

Nothing that Hoover did worked. Eventually, he took some further steps, approving loans to businesses and allowing federal money to be spent on relief. By then, however, it was too late.

Evaluating Hoover's Actions

President Hoover underestimated the severity of the Great Depression. He believed that the economy was basically sound and that Americans would solve their own problems. He rejected the idea that the federal government should step in to halt the decline. The government, Hoover declared, had no more power to stop the depression than it had to halt a hurricane. Both had to run their course without outside interference, he said.

Though President Hoover made some efforts to combat the Great Depression, his actions had little effect. In part, his failure stemmed from his inflexible faith that individual Americans—and not the government—could pull the country out of the Great Depression. Again and again, he refused to provide direct government aid to homeless and jobless individuals on the grounds that help would weaken their self-respect.

Hoover's lack of success can also be traced to a belief that businesses, workers, and consumers would voluntarily act for the good of the nation. But as the crisis grew ever worse, Americans wanted the government to act. Resentment against the President mounted. All over the nation, people expressed their anger with signs that read, "In Hoover we trusted—now we are busted."

 Why were President Hoover's steps to end the Great Depression unsuccessful?

◆ THE ELECTION OF 1932

President Hoover's failure to end the Great Depression raised Democratic hopes for the election of 1932. For their candidate, the Democrats chose

The New York Times. 5 A.M. EDITION

ROOSEVELT WINNER IN LANDSLIDE!
DEMOCRATS CONTROL WET CONGRESS;
LEHMAN GOVERNOR, O'BRIEN MAYOR

▲ Hoover's inability to bring relief to Americans during the Great Depression provided Franklin Roosevelt with an easy victory in the 1932 election.

Franklin Delano Roosevelt, the governor of New York. Roosevelt was a cheerful, outgoing man. The Republicans, sensing defeat, nominated Hoover with little enthusiasm. With the Great Depression growing worse each day, they realized that practically any Democrat nominated could probably defeat Hoover.

Roosevelt's campaign speeches emphasized the need for bold experiment. He called for strong welfare and reform programs. He promised aid for farmers and government regulation of businesses and the stock market. Above all, he promised that the government would act. Roosevelt had a strong belief that "the national government has a positive duty to see that no citizen shall starve."

Meanwhile, Hoover's campaign strategy was to paint Roosevelt as a dangerous radical, a person who holds or follows extreme ideas. Perhaps he was even a Communist out to destroy the nation's free-enterprise system. He attacked Roosevelt's promises of government action by warning of the terrible consequences that would result if the federal government became too strong. His fears are summed up in the following words:

> You cannot extend the mastery of government over the daily lives of people without somewhere making it master of the people's souls and thoughts.

As many expected, Roosevelt won by a landslide, taking 57 percent of the popular vote compared to 39 percent for Hoover. Hoover carried only six states. At Roosevelt's inauguration, he spoke about government responsibility and efforts to end the Great Depression,

> Our greatest primary task is to put people to work. This is no unsolvable problem if we face it wisely and courageously. . . . It can be accomplished by direct recruiting by the government itself, treating the task as we would treat the emergency of a war. . . .

 What solutions did Roosevelt offer to halt the economic decline of the nation?

Section 3 Review

Check Understanding

1. **Define** (a) public works (b) relief

2. **Explain** why President Hoover opposed direct government action as a means to end the Great Depression.

3. **List** two measures taken by Hoover to halt the nation's economic decline, and describe their effect.

4. **List** the main issues of the 1932 election and describe the results of the election.

Critical Thinking

Making Inferences Why do you think Hoover could solve the problems of starvation in Europe after World War I but could not find a solution to end the Great Depression?

Write About Citizenship

◆ **Connecting Past and Present** Which President—Hoover or Roosevelt—would be a successful leader today? Explain your answer in writing.

Chapter 19
Review

CHAPTER SUMMARY

Section 1
The Great Depression exposed the United States' underlying economic problems. After World War I, the nation had overspent and gone deeply into debt. The prosperity of the 1920s had failed to spread to farmers and minority groups. The Great Depression put millions of people out of work, and confidence in government was shaken.

Section 2
The Great Depression affected everyone. Farmers and minorities were especially hard hit. Economic instability caused widespread social disruptions. The Great Plains was hit by a drought, forcing many families to move to California to find work. Millions lost jobs as farms and factories closed down.

Section 3
Americans were bitter over President Hoover's inability to stem the economic crisis. Hoover held to his beliefs that the Great Depression would cure itself and that direct aid was not the answer. Franklin Roosevelt, opposing Hoover for President in 1932, campaigned on the need for bold solutions. The nation elected him in a landslide.

Connecting ◆◆ Past and Present

What lessons from the Great Depression can we use today to help us deal with economic and social problems?

Using Vocabulary

Select the letter of the phrase that best completes each sentence.

1. When banks were forced to **foreclose** on farmers, they (a) put up temporary towns for them; (b) seized their land; (c) lent them huge sums of money.

2. A member of the **Bonus Army** was (a) a World War I veteran promised a cash payment in 1945; (b) a skilled trade worker out of work; (c) a farmer who marched on Washington.

3. A **tenant farmer** (a) owned his land; (b) paid to work someone else's land; (c) was a farmer who moved to California to find work.

4. Hoover increased **public works** programs to provide (a) jobs on projects for the unemployed; (b) charitable assistance for the hungry; (c) protection for the medical bills of the elderly.

5. **Relief** was (a) a way for poor people to help themselves; (b) charity from the wealthy; (c) direct money payments for the unemployed.

6. A **Hooverville** was (a) a shantytown; (b) a place for the wealthy to stay during the Great Depression; (c) housing for government workers.

Check Understanding

1. **Explain** the economic problems that caused the Great Depression.

2. **Describe** why the Great Depression hit farmers and minorities especially hard.

3. **Discuss** why some people lost confidence in the American economic system.

4. **Analyze** how the Great Depression affected American family life.

5. **Describe** the effects of the Dust Bowl on American farmers.

6. **Explain** how economic conditions during the 1930s affected the experiences of African Americans in the North and the South.

7. **Discuss** the problems of Mexicans and Mexican Americans during the Great Depression.

8. **Explain** Hoover's position on ending the Great Depression.

9. **Describe** the effects of the Hawley-Smoot Tariff Act on the Great Depression.

10. **Summarize** Hoover's and Roosevelt's positions on how to end the Great Depression.

Critical Thinking

1. **Analyzing Ideas** Why was the Reconstruction Finance Corporation less effective than it should have been?

2. **Making Hypotheses** What kind of positive impact do you think the Great Depression might have had on some American families?

3. **Comparing** Compare the experiences of African Americans and Mexican Americans during the Great Depression.

4. **Predicting Outcomes** What effect might the Great Depression have had on the later lives of people who grew up during that time?

◆ **Connecting Past and Present** How would Herbert Hoover's attitude toward government be received by American citizens today?

Interpreting the Timeline

Use the timeline on pages 378–379 to answer these questions.

1. Which event on the U.S. timeline had an impact on international trade?

2. Which events in the United States and the world are related to air travel?

3. Which events show the poor state of the American economy?

Writing to Persuade

Suppose you were Hoover's speechwriter in 1932. **Write** a speech that persuades voters that he should be reelected President. Provide details about Hoover's background and his program for ending the Great Depression that might attract people to vote for him.

Putting Skills to Work

WRITING AN ESSAY

In the Building Skills lesson on page 385, you learned writing an essay involves synthesizing information in order to draw conclusions about a particular topic, and then supporting those conclusions with facts and examples. Choose an essay topic from those listed below, and then answer the questions that follow.

Essay Topics

- Explain the causes that led to the stock market crash of 1929.

- Discuss the ways in which President Hoover's efforts to end the Great Depression failed.

- Describe the impact of the Great Depression on family life.

1. What is your purpose in writing an essay about this topic?

2. What thesis statement would summarize your topic and your particular focus?

3. How would an outline help structure your essay?

4. What facts would support the main points you want to make about the topic?

 *Portfolio Project*

LOCAL HISTORY

Work with several classmates to prepare a presentation that tells how your community was affected by the Great Depression. How did people help one another? What relief organizations helped people? What were unemployment figures like? Who played important leadership roles? Try to find photographs of your community during this era. If possible, interview people who lived in your community in the 1920s and 1930s. Present your findings to the class.

Chapter 20
The New Deal Renews Hope 1933–1941

CHAPTER PREVIEW

Section 1 The New Deal Begins

In three months of activity, Franklin Roosevelt won passage of a wave of laws that aggressively fought the Great Depression.

Section 2 The Second New Deal

Faced with a lagging recovery from the Great Depression, critics on the political left and right promised easy solutions.

Section 3 Life Under the New Deal

Although the New Deal improved many people's lives, it did not significantly reduce social and political inequalities.

Section 4 The New Deal and the Arts

Popular entertainment reflected the need of Americans to escape from the problems of the Great Depression.

CCC worker plants trees

Mary McLeod Bethune

U.S. Events

1933
Civilian Conservation Corps (CCC) established.
Frances Perkins becomes secretary of labor.
Roosevelt begins broadcasting his "fireside chats."

1935
Mary McLeod Bethune establishes National Council of Negro Women.
Social Security Act is passed.

1936
★ Franklin Roosevelt reelected.

1932

World Events

1933
Adolf Hitler becomes chancellor of Germany.

1934
Women gain the vote in Turkey.
Dylan Thomas' first collection of poetry is published.

1935
Italy invades Ethiopia.

1936
Olympic Games are held in Germany.
Spanish Civil War begins.

Adolf Hitler

Portfolio Project

ART AS HISTORY

During the period of the New Deal, artists, writers, sculptors, and photographers used political and economic conditions as the subject of their works more than at any other time in history. As you learn about the New Deal, watch for events and subjects that might have been used as an inspiration. At the end of this chapter, you will complete an assignment about art and the New Deal.

▲ President Roosevelt, at left on train, renewed the economy and people's spirits through government programs called the New Deal. ◆◇ **Connecting Past and Present** *What is the crowd's reaction to Roosevelt's arrival? How do politicians create support for their policies today?*

Franklin Roosevelt

Gone with the Wind

GONE WITH THE WIND
CLARK GABLE

1937
Roosevelt presents "court-packing" plan.

Zora Neale Hurston's novel *Their Eyes Were Watching God* is published.

1938
Congress passes the Fair Labor Standards Act.

1939
Gone with the Wind and *The Wizard of Oz* open.

Supreme Court rules sit-down strikes illegal.

John Steinbeck's novel *The Grapes of Wrath* is published.

1940
✪ Roosevelt reelected for a third term.

Richard Wright's novel *Native Son* is published.

1941

1937
Japan invades China.

1938
"Kristallnacht," Night of Broken Glass, results in anti-Jewish violence in Germany.

1939
World War II begins in Europe.

Los Angeles Times

GERMAN ARMY INVADES POLAND

British Mobilize Army and Fleet

World War II begins

The New Deal Begins

PREVIEW

Objectives

- To describe how Franklin Delano Roosevelt's first actions brought some relief and recovery to the American people

- To identify the actions Roosevelt took to restore a sense of confidence in the nation

- To explain the importance of programs such as the Tennessee Valley Authority and the Civilian Conservation Corps

Vocabulary

New Deal	bank holiday
Three R's	Hundred Days
Brain Trust	hydroelectric power
fireside chat	

Eleven years before Americans elected him President, Franklin Delano Roosevelt became paralyzed after contracting polio. Although medicine has almost wiped out polio today, in 1921 it was probably the most dreaded disease in the United States. Many people thought that Roosevelt's career in public service was over. However, Roosevelt chose not to allow his disability to force him into early retirement.

◆ FROM HYDE PARK TO WASHINGTON

Franklin Delano Roosevelt, known by his initials, FDR, was born in Hyde Park, New York. His parents made sure he had all the advantages wealth could buy. They also taught him that being wealthy carried a responsibility for helping people not as fortunate as he was. Roosevelt entered politics because he believed in public service. Before he was elected President, he served as assistant secretary of the navy and was elected governor of New York in 1928 and 1930.

Roosevelt took an active role in fighting the Great Depression when he was governor. He created the first state agencies to aid the poor, an unemployment commission, and a relief administration. As economic hardship worsened during the Great Depression era, this innovative statewide relief program attracted attention and praise. People all over the United States took notice. Here was a leader who actually led.

In 1932 the Democrats nominated Franklin Delano Roosevelt to run as their candidate for President. In accepting the nomination, Roosevelt said,

> "I pledge you, I pledge myself, to a new deal for the American people."

The words *new deal* became a rallying cry for the suffering country. Winning 42 out of 48 states, FDR defeated President Herbert Hoover in one of the most overwhelming victories in the history of U.S. presidential elections. Now he faced the task of making good on his promises for the **New Deal.** These economic and social programs, adopted in response to the Great Depression, were desperately needed by millions of Americans.

? What did Roosevelt mean when he pledged a new deal for the American public?

◆ ROOSEVELT TAKES CHARGE

On March 4, 1933, Franklin Delano Roosevelt was inaugurated. Inauguration Day was gray and bleak. In many ways the weather in Washington, D.C., was similar to the mood of the country. "A sense of depression has settled over the capital so that it can be felt," a newspaper reported.

President-elect Roosevelt rode to the inauguration with President Hoover. FDR was smiling and waving to the crowd, while Hoover slumped in his seat, his eyes lowered. The contrast between the two men could not have been clearer.

As Roosevelt stepped to the front of the platform to give his inaugural speech, people throughout the country sat around their radios listening. The new President knew that the times called for dramatic action. Roosevelt told his audience that the moment had come to speak the truth. He said that the nation was in a kind of war, and it needed strong leadership. Then he spoke words that sent a charge of excitement through the American public:

> Let me assert my firm belief that the only thing we have to fear is fear itself—nameless, unreasoning, unjustified terror.

Franklin Roosevelt's bold words helped reassure the American people. Almost half a million letters of support for him poured into the White House in the following week. People expected the new President to take a more active role in responding to their needs.

Ideas for Fighting the Depression

Franklin Delano Roosevelt believed in bold action. Yet he had no plan when he became President. He had only goals. They were called the **Three R's:** relief, recovery, and reform. Roosevelt promised to (1) provide quick relief for the unemployed; (2) bring economic recovery; and (3) reform practices so that a depression would never happen again.

Roosevelt began his term with few specific ideas of what to do. Rather, he brought an open mind to the presidency. He was willing to experiment with programs until he found something that worked. He was willing to use the power of the federal government to make changes. He said,

> It is common sense to take a method and try it. If it fails, admit it and try another. But above all, try something!

The Brain Trust

To plan the New Deal, Roosevelt assembled an able group of advisors. The American press quickly named the group the **Brain Trust** because many of its members were college professors, lawyers, and economists. This informal group of intellectuals helped Roosevelt formulate new policies.

Roosevelt wanted the Brain Trust to give him bold ideas. Its members had to be intelligent and imaginative. Frances Perkins, one of Roosevelt's first choices for the Brain Trust, fit this description. Perkins had worked for Jane Addams at Hull House in Chicago. Then she worked for child labor reform in New York State. Roosevelt had heard that Perkins had a plan to help the elderly and unemployed. FDR

▲ As secretary of labor, Frances Perkins made extraordinary efforts to learn about the plight of workers. Here she wades through mud to greet workers in a national defense plant in California.

appointed Perkins secretary of labor, a job she held until 1945. She became the first woman to hold a Cabinet position. Perkins would be a key figure in shaping many New Deal laws.

The Fireside Chats

To explain his actions and present his policies to the American people, Roosevelt often spoke to the nation over the radio from the comfort of a chair near a White House fireplace. His many Sunday evening radio addresses came to be known as **fireside chats.** In his first fireside chat, on March 12, 1933, Roosevelt explained the goals of the New Deal in simple, straightforward terms.

The fireside chats, which Roosevelt continued throughout his administration, did much to increase the President's popularity. In calm but confident tones, he reassured people that their problems would be solved. Moreover, he led the American people to believe that they could participate in the problem-solving process. Millions of Americans felt that the President was speaking directly to them and that they were somehow personally connected to him. Frances Perkins later described the fireside chats this way:

"I often was at the White House when he broadcast, and I realized . . . how clearly his mind was focused on the people listening on the other end. As he talked, his head would nod and his hands would move in simple, natural, comfortable gestures. His face would smile and light up as though he were actually sitting on the front porch or in the parlor with them. People felt this and it bound them to him in affection."

FDR was the first American President to use radio effectively. Today, it is a rare political figure who can achieve success without mastering the use of both radio and television.

❓ What were Roosevelt's main goals for ending the Great Depression?

◆ THE BANK CRISIS

When Roosevelt took office, many had lost confidence in the banking system. Thousands of banks had failed. People who had deposited money in these banks lost their savings. Panic quickly spread, as other people rushed to the banks to take out their savings.

Americans gathered around their radios to listen to President Roosevelt deliver his weekly radio address. ▼

Millions of Americans hid their life savings in mattresses or buried their money in their backyards.

Two days after his inauguration, FDR took action to stop the panic. On March 6, 1933, he closed all the nation's banks by declaring a four-day **bank holiday.** Banks were to refrain from conducting business other than accepting deposits and making emergency loans for food and animal feed. Then Roosevelt presented Congress with a plan to deal with the bank crisis. The plan created a board that examined the finances of all banks. The board would allow only healthy banks to reopen. In a few days, more money went into banks than came out. Soon, more than 12,000 banks were back in business.

In the next few months, Congress passed other laws to strengthen the United States banking system. Specific rules were designed to prevent bankers from speculating in unsound investments. A government board called the Federal Deposit Insurance Corporation, or FDIC, was set up to insure all bank deposits up to $5,000. This meant that even if a bank failed, depositors were guaranteed to get back any amount up to $5,000.

❓ How did FDR restore confidence in the U.S. banking system?

◆ THE HUNDRED DAYS

After the banking crisis passed, FDR continued to fight the Great Depression actively. During the first three months of his administration, Roosevelt won passage of 15 major laws. They established government agencies to fight every aspect of the Great Depression. Not all of these laws worked well, but they showed the American people that Roosevelt was serious about giving them a New Deal. This period of activity from March 9 to June 16 is known as the **Hundred Days.** Bills passed during this time dealt with the most pressing issues in the nation.

Farmers had been badly hurt by the Great Depression. The basic problem was that American farmers were producing too many crops. Demand had dropped during the Great Depression. Thus, it was hard for farmers to sell their crops. This caused prices to fall. In the New Deal solution, farmers would be paid for setting land aside and not planting it.

Early in his presidency, Roosevelt also attempted to restore confidence in the stock market, which had crashed in part because Americans had made many

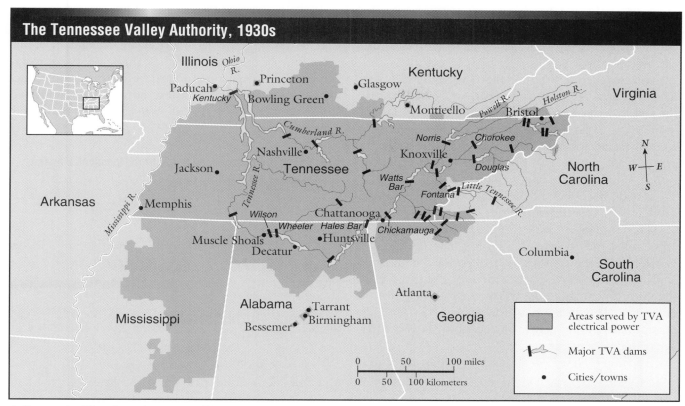

The Tennessee Valley Authority, 1930s

Illinois • Ohio R. • Princeton • Glasgow • Kentucky • Virginia • Paducah • Bowling Green • Monticello • Bristol • Holston R. • Kentucky • Cumberland R. • Powell R. • Norris • Cherokee • Nashville • Knoxville • Douglas • Tennessee • North Carolina • Jackson • Watts Bar • Little Tennessee R. • Arkansas • Mississippi R. • Memphis • Fontana • Wilson • Chattanooga • Wheeler • Hales Bar • Chickamauga • Muscle Shoals • Huntsville • Columbia • Decatur • South Carolina • Atlanta • Alabama • Tarrant • Bessemer • Birmingham • Georgia • Mississippi

Tennessee R.

Areas served by TVA electrical power

Major TVA dams

Cities/towns

0 50 100 miles
0 50 100 kilometers

▲ **Geography** *The rivers in eastern Tennessee were harnessed by dams to provide electricity.* **Interpreting the Map** *Which states benefited from the electric power generated by TVA dams? Which communities benefited?*

unwise investments. New laws required that people selling stocks provide honest information about investments. A government board was created to regulate the stock market.

Roosevelt created a number of other agencies as well. Each one came to be known by its acronym, the first letter of each word in its name. For some people, the many acronyms blurred into an "alphabet soup" of agencies. However, these new organizations, such as the EBRA, CCC, and NRA, signaled that the government was finally taking strong action to fight the Great Depression. These agencies and other New Deal acts are described in the chart on page 408.

Conserving the Land

Roosevelt had long had an interest in land conservation, or preservation. During the Hundred Days, the New Deal used the power of government to conserve land and precious resources.

One of the boldest and most successful of all the New Deal experiments was the Tennessee Valley Authority, or TVA. This agency was given control

over the valley of the Tennessee River and its tributaries. The waters of the Tennessee River run through parts of seven southeastern states—Virginia, North Carolina, Tennessee, Georgia, Alabama, Mississippi, and Kentucky, as shown on the map above. Frequent flooding by the river washed away precious topsoil in the valley. By the 1930s, most of the land was not fit to be farmed. The valley became one of the poorest parts of the United States.

People's activity in the valley made conditions worse. In the 1800s, the hills around the river had been rich in forests. However, by the 1930s, people had stripped the hills for lumber. Trees act as anchors for the soil. Without the trees, each rain washed more topsoil into the river. Soon, the hillsides were bare.

Since the beginning of the 1900s, engineers had wondered if the power of the river could be harnessed to make the valley a better place to live. Shortly after his election, Roosevelt asked Congress to create the Tennessee Valley Authority. The TVA began a program of dam building in the valley. The dams would preserve topsoil by controlling floods. They would also provide inexpensive **hydroelectric power,** or electricity produced by water power. This electricity would be sold at very cheap rates so that the people of the valley could, for the first time, afford electricity in their homes.

In the next few years, the TVA built 38 new dams, planted trees on hillsides, and helped restore the soil. It helped build hospitals and schools. It sent out doctors to rid the valley of malaria. New industries were attracted to the area because the available water power could be used to produce electricity inexpensively. Employment opportunities multiplied. The TVA made the valley of the Tennessee River a more productive and prosperous place.

The TVA also sparked a heated debate. Critics argued that the government did not have the right to interfere in the economy of the region. Supporters applauded the TVA. They said that it showed how the government could use its resources to help private enterprise. The question of how great a part the U.S. government should play in the economy is as controversial today as it was in 1933.

Another New Deal agency that reflected Roosevelt's interest in conserving the environment was the Civilian Conservation Corps, or CCC. The CCC established outdoor projects for unemployed men between 18 and 25 years old. Road construction, reforestation, flood control, and national park improvements were some of the major projects that were performed in work camps across the country. CCC workers received room and board and 30 dollars each month. By the time the program was phased out in 1941 and 1942, it had put more than 2,500,000 men to work planting trees, building irrigation projects and roads, and fighting forest fires.

Help for Businesses and Farmers

One of the most important measures taken to help businesses recover from the Great Depression was the creation of the National Recovery Administration (NRA). In each industry, the NRA set codes of conduct for the nation's businesses. Companies were allowed to fix prices with other companies in order to reduce competition. In return, they had to limit working hours and pay minimum wages. They also had to allow their workers to join unions. Businesses that promised to follow these practices were allowed to display the blue eagle, symbol of the NRA, and to print it on their products. Soon, huge factories and small shops all over the United States displayed the eagle. Americans were encouraged to buy only from NRA businesses.

Farmers' problems were addressed through the Agricultural Adjustment Administration, or AAA. The goal was to raise farm prices by cutting back the amount of crops produced. To do this, the government made payments to farmers for their crop reduction, giving income to those farmers who agreed to the plan. As the supply of farm products decreased, prices increased.

 How did Americans benefit from Roosevelt's actions during the Hundred Days?

Section 1 Review

Check Understanding

1. **Define** (a) New Deal (b) Three R's (c) Brain Trust (d) fireside chat (e) bank holiday (f) Hundred Days (g) hydroelectric power

2. **Explain** how President Roosevelt used radio to increase support for his programs.

3. **Summarize** Roosevelt's plan for fighting the Great Depression.

4. **Identify** Frances Perkins and explain why she was important to the New Deal.

5. **Discuss** why the work done by the TVA was controversial.

6. **Explain** how the creation of the National Recovery Administration helped businesses.

Critical Thinking

Connecting Past and Present How did New Deal legislation transform the country? What current laws have had an important impact on the country?

Write About History

Suppose you were out of work during the Great Depression. Write an essay explaining how President Roosevelt's accomplishments during the Hundred Days make you feel.

BUILDING SKILLS

Synthesizing Information: The New Deal and FDR

Synthesizing is the process of combining information and ideas from several sources to gain a new understanding of a subject or an event. The writing in this history book is a synthesis. The book pulls together data from different places to tell a chronological story of the United States.

Synthesizing is similar to solving a mystery. The more pieces of "evidence" you have, the more accurate your conclusions are likely to be.

Here's How

Follow these steps to synthesize information:

1. Select information that applies to the topic you are interested in.
2. Organize your information so that you can examine it closely.
3. Analyze the information and build connections.
4. Reinforce or modify your connections as you gather more information.

Here's Why

Synthesizing comes in handy on essay tests and in reports. In both cases, you draw together the material you have learned in order to make some point about it.

Suppose you were asked to answer this question: Which group felt the greatest impact from New Deal programs? Begin by selecting facts and examples that help you answer that question. For example, you might collect specific facts throughout this chapter about the ways in which women, African Americans, Native Americans, farmers, and union workers were affected. A sunburst diagram like the one on this page can help you organize this information.

The next step is to make connections between facts and details. For example, you might conclude that African Americans and Native Americans made some strides in terms of jobs and living conditions but did not overcome basic discrimination.

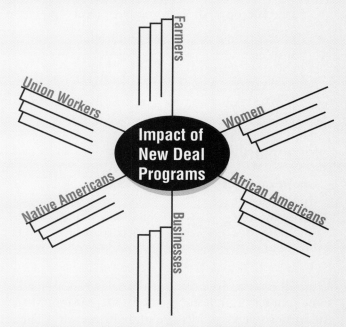

Practice the Skill

Copy the sunburst diagram on a sheet of paper. Fill in facts and details on the radiating lines relating to the impact of New Deal programs on farmers and businesses. As you continue reading the chapter, fill in facts and details for the other groups on the sunburst. After you have analyzed the information and built connections, write an essay synthesizing your data to answer the question, "Which group felt the greatest impact from New Deal programs?"

Apply the Skill

After you finish reading this chapter, synthesize the information you have learned about the Great Depression and the New Deal to explain why the following were popular during this time period: the movie *King Kong;* the board game Monopoly; and cartoon superheroes, such as Tarzan and Superman.

Section 2

The Second New Deal

PREVIEW

Objectives

- To explain opposition to the New Deal
- To describe the role played by Eleanor Roosevelt
- To explain the importance of the Social Security Act
- To identify the impact of the New Deal

Vocabulary

political right	anti-Semitic
political left	collective bargaining
conservative	sit-down strike
liberal	deficit spending

During its first two years, the New Deal made some progress in fighting the Great Depression. Most Americans were solidly behind Roosevelt. They agreed with the popular humorist Will Rogers, who said,

> The whole country is with him [Roosevelt]. Even if what he does is wrong, they are with him. Just so he does something. If he burned down the Capitol, we would cheer and say, 'Well, at least we got a fire started anyhow.'

After two years of the New Deal, the nation still faced widespread unemployment. Nine million Americans were jobless in 1935. Full recovery seemed a long way off. Faced with this situation, Roosevelt sent a flood of bills to Congress in 1935, expanding relief programs, aiding farmers and workers, and providing economic reforms. These bills became part of what historians call the Second New Deal.

◆ CRITICS ATTACK THE NEW DEAL

Because the economy was slow to recover, critics of Roosevelt became more vocal. Roosevelt faced criticism from both the **political right,** which said he was doing too much, and the **political left,** which said he was not doing enough. Some of the critics had originally supported Roosevelt.

Opposition to New Deal Programs

Conservative critics on the political right—those who wanted to preserve the current system or power structure—were convinced that strong regulation by government threatened American industry. They charged that New Deal programs were paralyzing businesses with high taxes. They also argued that many new laws were destroying individual freedoms. Conservatives said that government had no right to tell owners how to run their businesses. The critics also felt Roosevelt was spending too much money on direct relief to the unemployed.

To fight New Deal programs and policies, some conservatives formed the American Liberty League. The League warned that Roosevelt was leading the nation toward dictatorship and that his advisors were either impractical dreamers or Communists. Although the League spent a lot of money fighting Roosevelt, it had few supporters. During the Great Depression, most Americans wanted the kind of action that the conservatives opposed. More powerful opposition to the New Deal came from the political left.

Many people on the political left saw the Great Depression as the end of the free-enterprise system. They believed that New Deal reforms were like putting a small bandage on a huge open wound. The only cure, they said, was to create an entirely new system of government and economy in the United States. These **liberals** sought governmental change as a means of helping the common people.

Limitations of the New Deal

One of FDR's most powerful critics found a large following with the American people. Father Charles Coughlin was a vocal critic of FDR. Like FDR, he had mastered the use of the radio. At first, Coughlin supported the New Deal. By 1935, however, he had turned against Roosevelt because Roosevelt refused to accept his ideas. Coughlin now called the New Deal "the raw deal." He charged that the Great Depression was caused by a group of mostly Jewish bankers. By the end of the 1930s, Coughlin had grown increasingly racist and **anti-Semitic,** or prejudiced against Jewish people. Roman Catholic church officials forced him to stop his broadcasts.

Huey Long, a former governor and senator from Louisiana, appealed to struggling farmers and workers. He was an expert performer whose folksy speeches delighted audiences. Long, unlike many other southern Democrats, never used racial attacks as the basis of his power. Instead, he worked to improve education, medical care, and public services. His message was powerful. In the motto "Share Our Wealth," Long promised every American family an income of $5,000 a year—enough to buy a home, an automobile, and a radio. To pay for this program, Long would take away all income over $5 million a year earned by individuals. He would also put heavy taxes on large companies. Long was especially critical of the railroad and oil industries. He promised to tax them heavily and use the funds to build roads, schools, and hospitals. Long claimed,

> **I'm for the poor man—all poor men. Black and white, they all have to have a chance. 'Every man a king,' that's my slogan.**

Many ordinary Americans loved the "Kingfish," as Long was called. Like Roosevelt and Coughlin, Long had mastered the effective use of the radio. However, unlike Roosevelt, Long did not have a deep faith in democracy. He ruled Louisiana almost like a dictator and made many enemies. In 1935 a political enemy murdered Long, putting an end to his plans to become President of the United States.

? What did President Roosevelt's critics say about the New Deal?

◆ ELEANOR ROOSEVELT: AN ACTIVE REFORMER

In launching the Second New Deal, Roosevelt's closest advisor was his wife, Eleanor. Because FDR's paralysis limited his movement, he depended on Eleanor to meet with the American people face-to-face.

Eleanor Roosevelt was a woman of boundless energy. She traveled constantly on fact-finding trips. In 1933 she traveled more than 40,000 miles in support of the President. Her travels took her to coal mines, farms, prisons, factories, orphanages, schools, and hospitals. She was on the road so often that one newspaper poked gentle fun at her with this headline: "Mrs. Roosevelt Spends the Night at the White House."

Former First Ladies had played quiet roles in support of their husbands. Eleanor Roosevelt broke with the past. She became an active reformer. She was not afraid to speak out boldly in support of unpopular causes. At a time when there was little popular support for racial equality, Eleanor Roosevelt frequently attacked injustice. She spoke up for neglected people

Eleanor Roosevelt, on the left, became a champion of social justice. Here she is presenting the opera singer Marian Anderson with an award from the NAACP. ▼

in her own press conferences, newspaper columns, and radio talks.

Eleanor Roosevelt defied Jim Crow laws by refusing to sit in "whites only" sections. She frequently invited African American leaders to the White House. Perhaps her best known act demonstrating her outrage at prejudice occurred in 1939. During that year the African American opera singer Marian Anderson was barred from singing in a hall owned by the organization Daughters of the American Revolution, or DAR. Appalled by the DAR's decision, Eleanor Roosevelt resigned from the organization. Then she arranged for Anderson to give the concert in front of the Lincoln Memorial in Washington, D.C., where more than 75,000 people gathered to hear the singer.

 **How did Eleanor Roosevelt differ from previous First Ladies?**

◆ SOCIAL SECURITY

Before the 1930s, families had taken responsibility for the care of their oldest members. Most people whose families could not care for them worked until they died. Others went to poorhouses, institutions that provided food, clothing, and shelter paid for by public funds. During the Great Depression, however, local resources were so strained that most needy people could not be cared for. Many elderly people had lost their life savings, either through the stock market crash or through bank failures. Some were homeless, while others had to beg for food.

Providing care for the nation's elderly and the unemployed was a top priority for advisors such as Frances Perkins. Perkins supported social security, a program of insurance covering the elderly and the unemployed. With the help of Senator Robert Wagner of New York, she guided the law through Congress.

The 1935 Social Security Act became one of the most important acts of this century. The act provided monthly pensions to people over the age of 65. Pensions, or payments made on the basis of age and the number of years a person had worked, were funded by a small tax on workers and employers. There were two other important parts to the Social Security Act: (1) it provided public funds to care for people with disabilities and dependent children, and (2) it provided unemployment insurance for workers. Workers who lost their jobs would get some income for a number of weeks while they looked for new jobs.

The Social Security Act had many flaws. Benefits were quite low at first. The act did not cover many groups of workers. For example, it did not cover the self-employed. It also did not cover domestic workers and farm employees. Thus, 60 percent of African American working women, those who cleaned houses for a living, were not covered by social security.

Still, the Social Security Act was an historic step forward. Millions of Americans would not live in fear of poverty as they got older. It also provided a safety net for many Americans with financial problems. For the first time, the federal government was taking responsibility for aiding elderly, unemployed, and disabled people and dependent children.

Today the Social Security program is so large that it faces criticism. Some people argue that the United States cannot afford such an enormous expense. By 2020, the number of senior citizens may be so large that the number of wage earners contributing to social security may not be able to support them. Those who want to preserve social security are planning how to fund the system into the twenty-first century.

 **Why was the Social Security Act important, particularly during the 1930s?**

◆ PACKING THE SUPREME COURT

When parts of the New Deal faced criticism, the most effective challenge did not come from the Liberty League, Huey Long, or even Congress. Roosevelt had responded to his critics by saying that the Great Depression was a national emergency just like a war. He argued that under these circumstances, the government had to increase its powers. The Supreme Court disagreed with this view. In 1935 it struck down the National Recovery Act. The Court ruled that the federal government had no power to regulate commerce that took place within a state. It found that this expansion of federal power was unconstitutional. Later, the Court struck down other New Deal programs, ruling against laws to limit crop production and laws to provide pensions for railroad workers.

FDR was stunned by these actions. He thought that the Court was being too old-fashioned in its interpretation of the Constitution. Secretly, Roosevelt made up his mind to try to influence the Court after the presidential election of 1936.

Roosevelt was elected by a landslide to his second term in 1936, defeating the Republican candidate, Governor Alfred Landon of Kansas. He carried 46 of the 48 states, with only Maine and Vermont going to Landon. His margin of victory was 11 million votes, the largest margin in U.S. history up to that time. To Roosevelt the election showed that Americans favored his programs and would support his ideas.

With this in mind, FDR opened his second term with a startling announcement. He said that the country needed more and younger justices on the Supreme Court. Six of the nine justices had reached the age of 70. Roosevelt proposed that the President should have the power to increase the size of the Court from nine to fifteen members.

For once, FDR was unable to persuade the public to accept his idea. To his surprise, Americans reacted with a storm of protest. The public saw that Roosevelt's real goal was a Supreme Court that would favor his New Deal laws. They saw his move as a threat to the separation of powers so carefully set up in the Constitution. People called it "packing" the Court. Even his fellow Democrats did not support him. It was his first real defeat as President.

However, the Court began making more favorable rulings on New Deal policies. Also, Congress passed a law allowing justices to retire at age 70 with full pay. Over the next few years, older justices started retiring. By the time his presidency ended in 1945, President Roosevelt had appointed a majority of the Supreme Court's members.

? Why did FDR want to increase the number of justices on the Supreme Court to fifteen?

◆ LABOR WINS NEW PROTECTIONS

Roosevelt believed that the success of the New Deal depended on improving conditions for workers. This, he felt, would improve the entire economy. To protect workers' rights, Congress passed the National Labor Relations Act in 1935. This law banned certain unfair practices, such as firing workers if they joined a union. It guaranteed the right of **collective bargaining,** which meant that employers had to negotiate with unions about hours, wages, and other working conditions. It also set up the National Labor Relations Board to look into workers' complaints.

Craft Unions Versus Industrial Unions

During the 1920s and 1930s, labor unions had grown smaller as workers lost their jobs. Many workers believed that the major labor group, the American Federation of Labor (AFL), did not do a good job representing them. The AFL represented workers in skilled crafts, such as plumbing and carpentry.

ALL I SAID WAS "GIMME SIX MORE JUSTICES!"

◀ **Government** *This 1937 political cartoon shows the reaction of Democrats in Congress, symbolized by the donkey, to Roosevelt's plan to "pack" the Supreme Court.* **Interpreting the Cartoon** *How does the cartoonist portray Roosevelt? What does that tell you about the reaction Roosevelt expected to his plan?*

New Deal Legislation

ACT OR AGENCY	PURPOSE

Relief of Human Suffering

EBRA	Emergency Banking Relief Act (1933)	To regulate bank transactions
FERA	Federal Emergency Relief Act (1933)	To help states provide aid for the unemployed
CWA	Civil Works Administration (1933)	To provide emergency jobs
PWA	Public Works Administration (1933)	To create jobs in public works that would increase worker buying power and stimulate the economy
CCC	Civilian Conservation Corps (1933)	To provide jobs for young single males on conservation projects
WPA	Works Progress Administration (1935)	To create as many jobs as possible as quickly as possible in every field, from construction to art
NYA	National Youth Administration (1935)	To provide job training for unemployed youths and part-time jobs for students in need

Recovery of the American Economy

NRA	National Recovery Administration (1933)	To provide codes of fair competition and to give labor the right of collective bargaining
HOLC	Home Owners Loan Corporation (1933)	To give loans at low interest to home owners who could not make mortgage payments
FCA	Farm Credit Administration (1933)♦	To refinance farm mortgages at low rates for long terms
AAA	Agricultural Adjustment Administration (1933)	To aid farmers and to regulate crop production
TVA	Tennessee Valley Authority (1933)♦	To increase productivity and prosperity in the Tennessee Valley
FHA	Federal Housing Administration (1934)♦	To insure loans for the building and repair of houses

Reform Programs

FDIC	Federal Deposit Insurance Corporation (1933)♦	To protect bank deposits up to $5,000
SEC	Securities and Exchange Commission (1934)♦	To supervise stock exchanges and eliminate dishonest practices
	Social Security Act (1935)♦	To provide funds for retirement, unemployment insurance, and aid for children, the elderly, and the disabled
	National Labor Relations Act♦ (Wagner-Connery Act of 1935)	To define unfair labor practices and to settle differences between employers and employees
	Fair Labor Standards Act (1938)♦	To set up a national minimum hourly wage and a maximum workweek and to prohibit children under 16 from working in factories

♦Act or agency still in effect

▲ **Government** *This chart shows important acts and agencies established during the New Deal years.* **Interpreting the Chart** *How did the acts and agencies achieve Roosevelt's goal of providing the Three R's?*

However, the AFL left out the millions who worked on factory assembly lines and in other jobs that did not then call for special skills.

Since the founding of the AFL, the United States had become a huge industrial power. Giant industries, such as the steel and auto industries, had developed. Yet unskilled workers in those industries did not have a union to represent them.

Many labor leaders believed that a single union should represent workers in massive industries, such as the steel and automobile industries. That single union should represent workers whether they were skilled or unskilled. In other words, all workers in the auto industry should belong to an auto workers' union.

The campaign for industrial unions was led by one of the most distinctive leaders in American history, John L. Lewis. Lewis began working in the coal mines when he was 12, and he soon became a leader of the United Mine Workers. By 1920 he was its president. Lewis began quarreling with the leaders of the AFL when they showed resistance to supporting industrial unions. In 1935, Lewis and other industrial leaders formed the Congress of Industrial Organizations (CIO). In 1938 the CIO broke away from the AFL and began to pursue its union-organizing campaign.

The CIO had remarkable success. Hundreds of thousands of workers in steel, auto, garment, and other industries now joined unions. Unions gained more economic and political power than ever before. In contrast to many AFL branches, the CIO welcomed women, African Americans, and immigrants into the ranks of organized labor. These groups made up a large part of the unskilled work force. The CIO was responsible for much of the growth in organized labor during the remaining years of the Great Depression.

Sit-down Strikes

Auto workers faced strong opposition by employers when they tried to organize. Employers tried to stop workers from joining unions. To prevent employers from hiring other workers during a strike, the workers used a new tactic, the **sit-down strike.** Instead of walking off the job, workers simply sat down at their machines and refused to move. They ate meals by their machines and slept by their machines. All work in the factory ground to a halt.

A sit-down strike at the General Motors automobile plant in Flint, Michigan, lasted about a month and a half. During that time, workers stayed in the plant.

▲ *These strikers in the Ford Motor plant are sitting on the car seats that they were paid to install. Strikes like this one were a powerful weapon for the CIO.*

They organized their own orchestra and chorus, played games and sports, and held classes. As the strike spread to General Motors factories in other locations, weekly production of automobiles fell from 15,000 to just 151. The American public generally supported the workers, and General Motors finally agreed to negotiate a new contract. Sit-down strikes were soon used by strikers in other industries. However, in 1939 the Supreme Court ruled that sit-down strikes were illegal.

The Fair Labor Standards Act

For the millions of workers who did not belong to unions, working conditions were harsh. Hours were long and pay was low. In 1937, Roosevelt proposed a bill to improve wages and working conditions for all workers. In 1938, Congress passed the Fair Labor Standards Act. It was the last important New Deal social reform approved by Congress. It set minimum wages at 40 cents an hour initially and maximum hours of work at 40 hours per week in industries whose products crossed state lines. It also banned child labor under age 16 in industries that did business in more than one state.

How did the New Deal affect business and industry?

◆ IMPACT OF THE NEW DEAL

By 1940, FDR had dominated the Democratic party for eight years. As the presidential election approached, Americans wondered whether Roosevelt would run again. No American President had ever served more than two terms. However, war in Europe had broken out in 1939. Roosevelt used the crisis in Europe as his reason to run for office again. The Republicans nominated Wendell Willkie, who had trouble finding an issue on which to challenge Roosevelt. FDR easily won reelection, though not by as great a margin as in 1936.

Expanding the Federal Government

The expansion of the federal government into almost all aspects of people's lives was one of the major legacies of the New Deal. For the first time in history, the government assumed responsibility for the economic welfare of individuals as well as for the health of the nation's economy. During the New Deal era, the power of Congress weakened and the power of the President increased, due in part to FDR's strong personality.

The government paid for the cost of the many New Deal programs by borrowing money. In the past, both individuals and the government had tended to economize during hard times. During the 1930s the government put thousands of people to work. To do this, the government spent more than it collected in taxes. This policy, called **deficit spending,** was another controversial aspect of the New Deal.

The End of the New Deal

The New Deal did not end the Great Depression. In 1940 there were still more than seven million American people without jobs. The real end of the Great Depression came when the United States mobilized its economy to produce goods for nations fighting in World War II. Yet the New Deal did make major inroads on a troubled time, affecting the lives of those who suffered through this period.

Of all the accomplishments of the New Deal, perhaps the most important was bringing hope. Government jobs kept millions of workers off relief, while government acts and agencies helped people hold onto their farms and houses, stay in business, and bargain with their employers for better working conditions. Other government agencies insured savings accounts, regulated the stock market, and built schools, bridges, and public parks.

Another important accomplishment was that FDR proved that democracy could reform itself. With the New Deal, the government made major changes that reshaped the economy and society. Yet it did this in a peaceful and democratic way. In the end, the government and the presidency emerged stronger than ever.

To some, FDR's administration brought about a more humane and responsible government. To others, New Deal programs created government interference and regulation. Few people deny that the New Deal had a major impact on government, the economy, and society. The debate about how deeply government should be involved in people's lives continues today.

 What was the impact of the New Deal on the Great Depression?

Section 2 Review

Check Understanding

1. **Define** (a) political right (b) political left (c) conservative (d) liberal (e) anti-Semitic (f) collective bargaining (g) sit-down strike (h) deficit spending

2. **Explain** why certain groups were against the New Deal.

3. **Discuss** how Eleanor Roosevelt supported the President.

4. **Explain** what made the Social Security Act important to people in the United States.

5. **Describe** how the Fair Labor Standards Act helped workers.

Critical Thinking

Drawing Conclusions Why were sit-down strikes such a powerful tool for unions?

Write About Government

◆**Connecting Past and Present** Use the political cartoon on page 407 as a model. Create a cartoon showing reaction to a recent government proposal or new legislation.

Section 3

Life Under the New Deal

PREVIEW

Objectives

- To describe how New Deal policies both helped and hurt women, African Americans, Native Americans, and Mexican Americans

- To analyze how changing attitudes caused a change in voting behavior among African Americans

Vocabulary

Black Cabinet
repatriation

In many different ways, the Great Depression and the New Deal deeply affected American family life. Fewer people married, and the marriage rate fell from 10.14 new marriages per thousand people in 1929 to 7.8 per thousand in 1932. Families facing hard times put off having children because babies were expensive. Thus, the U.S. birthrate dropped by about 30 percent during the 1930s. The pressure of hard times caused some families to split up—fathers and even children as young as 13 left home to hunt for work.

Conditions did not immediately improve under the New Deal. Some jobless people were forced to move in with working relatives. To bring in income, families rented out rooms to boarders. Many women took in laundry and sewing to help support their families. Life was often uncomfortable and uncertain.

◆ THE NEW DEAL AND WOMEN

Women had made major economic gains during the 1920s. Many of these gains were lost during the 1930s. Large numbers of women were forced out of their jobs during the Great Depression. If jobs were available, they usually went to men. Many companies and even the federal government refused to hire a woman if her husband had a job. Although some New Deal agencies had special divisions for women, they often discriminated against them by paying them lower wages than men. On most projects, male workers received $5 a day while female workers earned only $3.

For the most part, however, New Deal laws helped women who worked outside the home. Some women's salaries rose, and working conditions improved. Women workers also benefited from the founding of the CIO, where they often became active strikers fighting for better pay.

New Deal laws did nothing to protect certain kinds of workers. African American women suffered massive unemployment in the South and elsewhere. Many of these women worked as housekeepers or cooks but were laid off when white families cut back during hard times.

In one area the New Deal broke significant new ground. During Roosevelt's first two terms, women gained political influence in the federal government. In addition to Frances Perkins, a number of other women served in important roles. Molly Dewson took control of women's affairs for the Democratic party. Florence Allen became a judge on the U.S. Court of Appeals. She was the first woman to serve

Although it was often difficult for women to find jobs during the 1930s, some women found work in nontraditional jobs, such as making airplanes. ▼

at this court level. Mary McLeod Bethune, an African American educator, became a director at the National Youth Administration. Roosevelt also appointed the first woman ambassador and a woman as director of the U.S. Mint.

? How did the New Deal policies both help and hurt women?

◆ AFRICAN AMERICANS AND THE NEW DEAL

The Great Depression was an especially difficult time for African Americans. Most were poor before the 1930s and already faced widespread prejudice in both the North and the South. The Great Depression made these conditions worse. By 1933, almost 40 percent of African American workers were unemployed. Although the New Deal helped many African Americans survive the Great Depression, it did little to eliminate unfair hiring practices and discriminatory job conditions.

Fighting Injustice

During the Great Depression, there was a marked increase in the number of lynchings. Mobs of whites hanged more than 60 African Americans between 1930 and 1934 due to prejudice. These mobs were not punished, because lynching was not a federal offense in the United States. Although Roosevelt denounced the violence, he did not take firm action to fight it. When Walter White, a leader of the NAACP, urged action on an anti-lynching bill, Roosevelt explained his difficult choice in this way:

> If I come out for the anti-lynching bill, they [Southern senators] will block every bill I ask Congress to pass to keep America from collapsing.

The rise in violence against African Americans motivated them to renew their struggles for justice. They formed a number of organizations to work for civil rights. In 1942, African Americans in Chicago formed the Congress of Racial Equality, or CORE. The founders of CORE vowed to fight racial prejudice by carrying out nonviolent actions. Groups such as the NAACP picketed to bring the violence against them to public notice. With each lynching,

Mary McLeod Bethune

Mary McLeod Bethune was the fifteenth of seventeen children born to former slaves in Mayesville, South Carolina. As a young girl, she worked in rice and cotton fields. Her parents were determined to provide her with an education. To attend school, Bethune walked ten miles a day. At the end of each day, she taught her family whatever she had learned. Later, she won scholarships and became a teacher.

▲ Mary McLeod Bethune (1875–1955)

With only $1.50, borrowed materials, and volunteer help, Bethune opened the Daytona Normal and Industrial School in Florida for African American women. At first, students sat on boxes and wrote with charred splinters dipped in berry juice. Bethune taught cooking, cleaning, and sewing, in addition to reading, writing, and arithmetic. Later, the school merged with Cookman Institute to become Bethune-Cookman College, which still exists today.

Bethune was appointed by President Franklin Roosevelt to be an advisor to the National Youth Administration. Later, she was director of the Office of Minority Affairs, the highest position in the U.S. government attained by an African American woman up to that time. FDR said of Mary McLeod Bethune: "I believe in her because she has her feet on the ground; not only on the ground but deep down in the plowed soil."

Looking Back: What traits and experiences of Bethune's early years made her a good choice to advise Roosevelt on education and youth issues?

the NAACP unfurled a flag outside its headquarters that held a simple but frighteningly factual sentence: "A Human Was Lynched Today."

New Deal Programs

Some New Deal programs benefited African Americans by providing new jobs. But the New Deal did less for African Americans than it did for whites. Many New Deal agencies refused to hire African Americans. Those that did segregated the races.

From the beginning, African Americans pressed for changes in these practices. They welcomed the appointment of African Americans to important government positions. They supported the way the Roosevelts did not tolerate segregation in the White House.

Many African Americans responded by supporting FDR. Horace Clayton, an African American professor, recalled the mood as he was growing up:

> President Roosevelt and his wife brought new hope. People could endure the miserable present if they believed there was something being done to make the future better.

This positive attitude created a major shift in the country's voting patterns. Until 1933 most African Americans favored the Republican party, which had been the party of Abraham Lincoln and abolition. In 1932 most African Americans had voted for Herbert Hoover, a Republican candidate. By 1936, however, a large majority of African Americans was solidly in the Democratic camp.

The Black Cabinet

During his early days in office, Roosevelt called together a group of African Americans to advise him. This group became known as the **Black Cabinet.** The educator Mary McLeod Bethune was a member of the Black Cabinet as was Robert C. Weaver, a young lawyer. When the Department of Housing and Urban Development was set up about 30 years later, Weaver became its first secretary. Another member was Ralph Bunche. In 1950 he won a Nobel Peace Prize for his peacekeeping work in the Middle East.

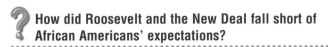 **How did Roosevelt and the New Deal fall short of African Americans' expectations?**

◆ NATIVE AMERICANS AND THE NEW DEAL

In 1933, President Roosevelt appointed John Collier to be commissioner of the Bureau of Indian Affairs. Collier was different from many of the earlier commissioners who knew or cared little about Native American life. Collier had studied Native American cultures and had seen firsthand the poor living conditions in Native American communities.

Before becoming commissioner, Collier worked to bring these conditions to the attention of all Americans. He reported how Native American cultures had been wounded by efforts to end tribal government. As commissioner, Collier convinced Congress to extend many New Deal job benefits to Native Americans.

With a strong boost from Collier, Congress created the Indian Emergency Conservation Program. This program employed about 12,000 Native Americans to work on projects that had been recommended by tribal groups. Many of these projects controlled soil erosion and provided irrigation to dry lands.

The Indian Reorganization Act

The Dawes Act of 1887 had tried to force Native Americans to abandon their traditions and customs and to adopt the practices of white society. The act ended tribal government and allowed the sale of tribal lands to individuals. These practices violated many deeply held Native American traditions. Many Native American groups had a strong sense of tribal partnership. Private ownership of land was not part of their experience or tradition.

The situation was even more complicated. Many Native Americans could not afford to farm the land they lived on, and were forced to sell it. By 1934, almost 90 million acres of once tribal lands were no longer under the control of Native Americans.

The Indian Reorganization Act of 1934 ended government efforts to take over and sell Native American tribal land. The act recognized tribal constitutions and supported the right to set up tribal courts and elect tribal governments. It promoted the preservation of Native American customs and religions and gave recognition to tribal life. Finally, it gave credit to Native American groups to buy back their land. Between 1933 and 1938, about 2.5 million acres of land were added or restored to the reservations. The government also encouraged tribal councils to develop their own businesses and corporations.

▲ *New Deal agencies, such as the Federal Art Project, sponsored the creation of public art. The artist Lucile Lloyd, lower left, is finishing a mural that depicts the variety of people who played a role in California's history. The mural was created for the California statehouse in Los Angeles.*

Native Americans who wanted to return to traditional tribal life supported the act. Those who had become more "Americanized," however, argued that the act would segregate them from the mainstream. Members of the Five Tribes in Oklahoma were opposed to the Indian Reorganization Act on these grounds. Members of the Seneca group in New York State opposed the law on other grounds. They said that the act would make it harder for Native Americans to improve themselves economically.

Government Loans

Many Native Americans made good use of the government loans that were now available. In the hills of eastern Oklahoma, Cherokees used the loans to begin raising strawberries. One Cherokee community, for example, started with one horse, no farm equipment, and no money. The people in the community borrowed $2,800 from the government to buy a team of horses. Then they planted 20 acres of strawberries.

The community soon paid off all of its debts and started earning a profit. The experiment in strawberry growing was so successful that many white neighbors of the Cherokees also became strawberry growers.

In other areas, Native Americans faced difficult times. On the northern Great Plains, the Sioux cattle ranchers could not compete with corporations that were buying up land and grazing huge herds. The corporations took valuable land away from the Sioux's cattle. One observer of the Sioux's efforts noted,

> Their [the Sioux's] loss of the cattle herds was the greatest disaster that had befallen the Pine Ridge Indians since the vanishing of the buffalo.

 How did the Indian Reorganization Act break with past government policy?

◆ MEXICAN AMERICANS AND THE NEW DEAL

The 1930s saw the first serious effort to improve conditions for Mexican American workers. During the 1930s, Mexican Americans formed organizations to help them gain their rights.

Mexican Americans Fight to Win Rights

When the Great Depression began, many Mexican Americans worked as migrant workers. Most had not lived long enough in any one state to qualify for government benefits. The terrible conditions of migrant workers continued long after the Great Depression. Citizens of Mexico living in the United States did not fare much better. Since they were not U.S. citizens, they were not eligible for many New Deal benefits.

Unemployment among Mexican Americans in the 1930s was high, as farm production fell and the number of jobs diminished. As jobs became scarcer, prejudice grew. People from the Dust Bowl region arrived in California and Arizona desperate for work. They competed for jobs with Mexicans and Mexican Americans. Mexican workers had been welcomed as a source of cheap labor in the past, but now many people complained that these migrant workers took jobs away from American citizens. Competition among workers drove wages down to eight or nine cents an hour. Although some agencies hired thousands of Mexican Americans for construction and cultural programs in the Southwest, they received little government help overall.

As a result of this widespread prejudice, thousands of Mexican families were uprooted from their homes. As many as 500,000 people were sent back to Mexico. This **repatriation** program was supposed to be voluntary. But many of the children sent back with their families had been born in the United States. That made them U.S. citizens, but the government did not respect their rights. Forced from the United States, they crossed the border back into Mexico with bitter feelings.

The Strawberry Strike

One New Deal protection that did not apply to migrant workers was the right to organize into unions. When migrant workers began to organize, they often met with resistance from farm owners. In May 1933, Mexican strawberry pickers in El Monte, California, went on strike. Their demand was to be paid 25 cents an hour. When strikers showed up to picket, police arrested them, and they were charged with disturbing the peace. Still, the strike continued. As strawberries rotted in the fields, the owners finally offered 20 cents an hour. The pickers accepted. Although this was not as much as they had demanded, at least the owners had given them the protection of a contract. It would be at least 30 years until migrant workers were able to win the right to organize their own union.

 How did the repatriation program affect Mexican families living in the United States?

Section 3 Review

Check Understanding

1. **Define** (a) Black Cabinet (b) repatriation

2. **Discuss** how the New Deal affected women in the United States.

3. **Explain** why the 1930s was a particularly difficult time for Native Americans, African Americans, and Mexican Americans.

4. **List** the accomplishments of the Indian Emergency Conservation Program.

5. **Explain** why a majority of African Americans began to vote for Democratic candidates by 1936.

6. **Discuss** why Roosevelt chose not to support the anti-lynching bill.

Critical Thinking

Evaluating Information How was the period during the New Deal a difficult time for African Americans and Mexican Americans?

Write About Citizenship

◆**Connecting Past and Present** Review the primary source quotations on pages 412 and 413. How would Roosevelt's civil rights policies be viewed today? Write an essay expressing your point of view.

The New Deal and the Arts

PREVIEW

Objectives

- To explain the role of popular entertainment during the New Deal era

- To discuss the ways in which government was involved in supporting the arts

Vocabulary

soap opera
sponsor
oral history

When times are hard, some people seek to escape their troubles through light-hearted entertainment. Others focus angrily on their problems. The writers and artists of the Great Depression took both approaches.

◆ POPULAR ENTERTAINMENT

Popular entertainment provided an escape from the troubles of the real world. Movies especially helped people flee their problems for at least a few hours. The film industry boomed during the years of the New Deal. More than 100 million Americans went to the movies each week during the New Deal years. For 25 cents, people could see two full-length movies in one sitting. Theaters began to develop special nights, when they would give away prizes such as dishes or board games. Often the dishes were made of glass, now known as depression glass.

The Wizard of Oz and *Gone with the Wind,* among the first movies in color, drew huge audiences. Comedies—with stars such as Laurel and Hardy, the Marx Brothers, and W.C. Fields—made people laugh and forget their troubles. Action films gave audiences the chance to escape to another place and time. Musicals—often starring the great dance team of Fred Astaire and Ginger Rogers—made many viewers feel like dancing themselves.

Radio also thrived in the 1930s. It became the major form of entertainment for most Americans. By 1939 almost 85 percent of American families owned a radio. Millions of people tuned in to hear comedy shows with stars such as Jack Benny and George Burns offering comic relief.

Because so many people were out of work, there was a large daytime audience for radio. New daytime dramas called **soap operas** entertained these listeners. Soap operas got their name because they had highly dramatic plots, like operas, and they were often **sponsored,** or paid for, by soap companies. Men, women, and children followed soap opera characters as they suffered through their daily crises. Radio programs were designed to help people escape reality.

Women in the Arts

In the 1930s women enjoyed a greater place in the arts than ever before in American history. Women were the most popular movie stars. Greta Garbo, Katharine Hepburn, and Carole Lombard dominated movie marquees. Pearl Buck and Margaret Mitchell were among the most popular authors. Mitchell's novel *Gone with the Wind,* an epic story of the Civil War, sold more than 13 million copies.

Athletes as Heroes

Sports events, like films, comic books, and lavish musicals, were another avenue of escape during the dark days of the Great Depression. Athletes became national heroes. They include Mildred "Babe" Didrikson, who excelled in basketball, baseball, and track; and the baseball player Lou Gehrig. Their larger-than-life accomplishments entertained millions.

Sports during the New Deal era also reflected larger political and social issues, especially during the 1936 Olympics, held in Berlin, Germany. There, African Americans Dave Albritton, Cornelius Johnson, and Jesse Owens won medals. Their impressive performances helped expose the fallacy of Nazi leader Adolf Hitler's belief that African Americans were inferior. This was further emphasized when African American boxer Joe Louis knocked out German Max Schmeling in the first round of their rematch. People made heroes of athletes to reinforce their political beliefs.

 Why was entertainment so important to people during the New Deal era?

◀ *The popularity of the radio during the 1930s brought Americans together. The entire country could hear news from around the world and enjoy comedy and drama broadcasts.*

of Okies, the characters in the novel experienced terrible living conditions and extreme poverty in California.

Richard Wright's novel *Native Son* shocked Americans when it was published in 1940. *Native Son* was a bitter attack on prejudice in the United States. Wright, an African American, was able to tell firsthand of the injustice and racism that he had experienced throughout his life. The book describes how a young African American man accidentally commits murder and ultimately is sentenced to death. The novel condemns society's racial injustice that provokes the young man into crime. Never before had Americans read such harsh honesty about racism. *Native Son* became the first best-selling book by an African American in the United States.

 How did the government help support artists in the 1930s?

◆ ART REFLECTING THE TIMES

Never before had the government become so involved in supporting the arts. Many new government groups were created to sponsor projects. Perhaps the best known of these projects came from the Works Progress Administration, or WPA. American artists working for the WPA decorated federal buildings throughout the country. The Federal Writers' Project sponsored many guidebooks. Hundreds of American writers recorded **oral histories,** the stories of immigrants, Native Americans, and former slaves. The government also created the Federal Theater Project, or FTP. The FTP employed scores of actors to put on plays in 28 states. This allowed people in rural areas to see a play for the first time.

Artists and photographers created pictures of rural life during the Great Depression. The photographer Dorothea Lange went to the Midwest to show how people were struggling to survive. Lange's photographs are still some of the most powerful reminders of the hopelessness and poverty that existed during the 1930s.

Many American artists and writers of the 1930s used the Great Depression as the theme of their works. Books and paintings focused on poverty and suffering. Perhaps one of the most powerful books of the period was John Steinbeck's *The Grapes of Wrath.* It told the story of a family from Oklahoma who left the Dust Bowl for California. Like thousands

Section 4 Review

Check Understanding

1. **Define** (a) soap opera (b) sponsor (c) oral history

2. **Explain** the reasons for interest in soap operas, movies, and sports in the 1930s.

3. **Describe** how the U.S. government became deeply involved in sponsoring the arts during the New Deal.

Critical Thinking

Connecting Past and Present How does entertainment today still reflect people's concerns and also help them forget those concerns?

Write About Culture

Suppose you were a teenager in the 1930s. Write a letter to a friend explaining what you do to have fun.

Chapter 20
Review

CHAPTER SUMMARY

Section 1

Upon becoming President in 1933, Franklin Delano Roosevelt plunged into action. He took steps to restore Americans' confidence in their banking system. During the first three months of FDR's presidency, the government passed legislation to fight every aspect of the Great Depression.

Section 2

The Social Security Act was one of the most important acts in U.S. history. Despite the intense activity of the New Deal, progress was slow in ending the Great Depression. This encouraged people on both the political right and left to criticize Roosevelt's government. Eleanor Roosevelt played an influential role in supporting the President and his New Deal. Roosevelt's attempt to "pack" the Supreme Court led to his greatest defeat as President.

Section 3

Although the New Deal employed many women in high office, it did not do much to improve the status of the average woman in the United States. The New Deal worked to improve the welfare of African Americans, Native Americans, and Mexican Americans, but it did not give a high priority to fighting prejudice.

Section 4

Popular entertainment of the 1930s reflected the desire of many Americans to escape the difficulties of the Great Depression. Some important artists, however, dealt with themes of poverty and prejudice in their writing. New Deal agencies sponsored many photographers, artists, and writers as a way of preserving the national heritage and of putting people to work.

Connecting ◆ Past and Present

How are you and your family still affected by policies and acts begun with the New Deal?

Using Vocabulary

From the list below, select the term that best completes each sentence.

Black Cabinet	fireside chat
hydroelectric power	sit-down strike
New Deal	political left
repatriation	Brain Trust
oral history	conservative

1. A writer hired by the Federal Writers' Project interviewed a former slave and recorded her _____.
2. Those who believed the New Deal did not go far enough were part of the _____.
3. Roosevelt used the radio effectively to address the American public during a _____.
4. A person who opposes strong government regulation of businesses is called a _____.
5. Roosevelt's group of African American advisors was referred to as the _____.
6. Mexican families were forced from the U.S. under the _____ program of the 1930s.
7. The _____ was an effective way for workers to prevent their employers from hiring other workers during a strike.
8. The TVA built dams that provided _____, an inexpensive form of electricity.
9. Roosevelt introduced new economic and social programs, called the _____, to fight the Great Depression.
10. Roosevelt assembled a group of advisors, called the _____, to plan the New Deal.

Check Understanding

1. **Describe** two important laws passed during the Hundred Days of Roosevelt's presidency.
2. **Identify** the importance of the fireside chats.
3. **Summarize** criticisms that the political left and the political right made against the New Deal.
4. **Explain** why the Social Security Act of 1935 was important.
5. **Explain** how Eleanor Roosevelt supported racial equality.

6. **Discuss** the role women played in the New Deal.

7. **Describe** how life improved for Mexican Americans and Native Americans during Roosevelt's presidency.

8. **Explain** the change in voting patterns among African Americans in 1936.

9. **Identify** a person who made an impact on society during the 1930s. Explain this person's impact.

10. **Discuss** why escapist entertainment was popular during the 1930s.

Critical Thinking

1. **Synthesizing** What did critics of Roosevelt from the political right and the political left have in common?

2. **Drawing Conclusions** What were Roosevelt's greatest strengths as a leader?

3. **Evaluating** Do you think that Roosevelt was right to try to pack the Supreme Court? Explain your answer.

4. **Sharing Your Point of View** Would Huey Long have made a good or bad President? Explain your point of view.

◆ **Connecting Past and Present** Roosevelt used the fireside chats to present his ideas to the American people. How do U.S. Presidents today get their ideas before the public?

Writing to Persuade

Suppose the United States were suffering from a bad economy today. Some people compare the situation to the Great Depression of the 1930s, but others say the problems will correct themselves. As an expert on the economy, you believe that the government should designate a specific time period, similar to Roosevelt's Hundred Days, to deal with pressing issues. **Write** a persuasive essay explaining why the country should have this time of focused activity to improve conditions. Include some ideas for new laws that will help to improve current economic conditions. Give the special time period a name.

Putting Skills to Work

SYNTHESIZING INFORMATION

On page 403 you learned that synthesizing requires combining various bits of information to create a complete picture. Read the following paragraphs and synthesize the information by creating a sunburst diagram with the center labeled Effects of the Dust Bowl. Decide what categories should radiate from the sunburst and then fill in facts and details from the paragraphs below. Then write an essay on the effects of the Dust Bowl.

More than 60 percent of the Dust Bowl population packed up and moved during the 1930s. Farmers and their families set out by the thousands along the western roads, looking for work. But these were the Great Depression years, and there was little work to find. Western states did not want the Dust Bowlers, whom they called "Okies." They had their own homeless and jobless.

Many of the Dust Bowlers ended up in California. There they traveled from farm to farm picking fruit and vegetables. Pay was extremely low. But few argued about pay or working conditions. For every person who would not work, there were often ten to take his or her place.

Interpreting the Timeline

Use the timeline on pages 396–397 to answer these questions.

1. What world event occurred the year before Roosevelt was elected President for a third term?

2. In what year was a law enacted to provide care for senior citizens and the unemployed?

3. Which world events are related to World War II?

Portfolio Project

ART AS HISTORY

Choose an artist, photographer, or writer from the 1930s. Select one or two of the person's works that best represent an aspect of the Great Depression or the New Deal. Write a short essay that explains the connections between the time period and the artist's work.

Connecting Past and Present

DISABILITIES IN THE PUBLIC EYE

On a spring day in 1997, President Bill Clinton dedicated a memorial in Washington, D.C., to President Franklin Delano Roosevelt. As soon as it opened, the memorial became the center of a major controversy. Roosevelt's family had made the decision that a statue in the memorial should show him seated in a regular chair. The family wanted Roosevelt to be remembered for his leadership, not for his disability. People with disabilities argued that the statue did not honestly show the man, who was paralyzed from polio for the last 24 years of his life.

Then During his lifetime, FDR made great efforts to hide the results of his polio to assure that his disability did not become an issue with the voters. The disease had severely damaged the muscles of his legs. Yet, of the 250,000 photographs of him in the Roosevelt library, only two show him in a wheelchair.

At the time, many Americans knew that Roosevelt had a physical disability. They were familiar with pictures of FDR supported by one of his sons or an aide. But few people realized that the President was paralyzed from the waist down.

Newspapers in those days did not pry into the details of a President's life. Photographers respected Franklin Roosevelt's wishes not to be photographed in his wheelchair. Reporters and even his political opponents downplayed FDR's disability and rarely made it an issue.

Now Today, many people take pride in having overcome physical or mental challenges. The achievements of participants in the Special Olympics, in which people with disabilities compete in athletic events, are celebrated throughout the country.

Many people with disabilities believe that if FDR were alive today, he would want the world to know about the disability he had overcome. President Clinton, along with 16 of FDR's grandchildren, agreed with them. In April 1997, he asked Congress to fund another statue of FDR—this time, in his wheelchair.

▲ FDR's wheelchair

◀ This is one of the few photographs that show FDR with heavy leg braces.

You Decide

1. Should a President be able to keep information about his health secret from the public? Why or why not?
2. Should a monument honor the wishes of the person honored or the wishes of the public?

The United States in Times of Crisis 1922–1961

> In the future, we look forward to a world founded upon four essential human freedoms. The first is freedom of speech and expression.... The second is freedom of every person to worship God in his own way. The third is freedom from want....The fourth is freedom from fear, which means a worldwide reduction of armaments... everywhere in the world.
>
> *Franklin Delano Roosevelt, Four Freedoms speech to Congress, 1941*

▲ *Early in the morning of June 6, 1944, the Allies launched the greatest invasion force in history—the invasion of Normandy.* ◆ **Connecting Past and Present** *From the photograph, what are the obvious dangers of the mission? How is the invasion depicted here different from possible invasions today?*

Chapter 21
Events Lead to War
1922–1941

CHAPTER PREVIEW

Section 1 **The Rise of Dictatorships in Europe**

Tough economic conditions in Europe led to the rise of dictatorships that threatened world peace.

Section 2 **Aggression in East Asia**

The Japanese waged war in East Asia in an effort to acquire land and resources.

Section 3 **From Isolationism to War**

Firmly in the grip of isolationism at the beginning of the 1930s, the United States gradually was drawn into a second world war.

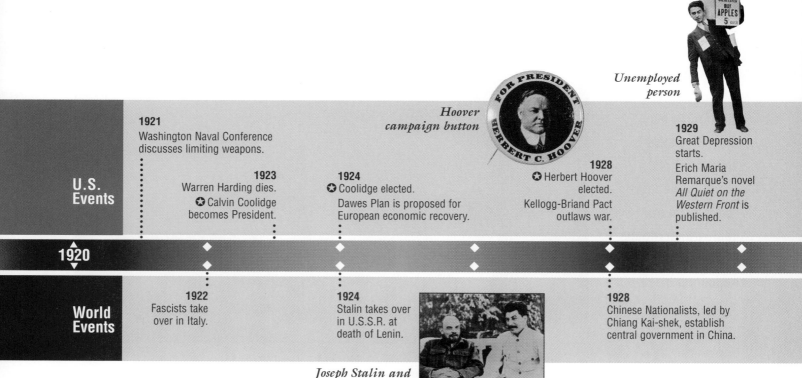

Hoover campaign button

Unemployed person

U.S. Events

1921
Washington Naval Conference discusses limiting weapons.

1923
Warren Harding dies.
✪ Calvin Coolidge becomes President.

1924
✪ Coolidge elected.
Dawes Plan is proposed for European economic recovery.

1928
✪ Herbert Hoover elected.
Kellogg-Briand Pact outlaws war.

1929
Great Depression starts.
Erich Maria Remarque's novel *All Quiet on the Western Front* is published.

1920

World Events

1922
Fascists take over in Italy.

1924
Stalin takes over in U.S.S.R. at death of Lenin.

1928
Chinese Nationalists, led by Chiang Kai-shek, establish central government in China.

Joseph Stalin and Vladimir Lenin

Portfolio Project

U.S. ENTRY INTO WORLD WAR II

Americans debated about U.S. relations with the rest of the world. On one side were interventionists, who wanted the United States to stem the threat to democracy. On the other side were isolationists, who believed in George Washington's warning to avoid "entangling alliances." As you read this chapter, take note of details that relate to this controversy. At the end of the chapter, you will use your notes to debate whether or not the United States should have entered the war.

▲ Hitler (standing in car) demonstrated his power and authority, drawing huge crowds. ◆ **Connecting Past and Present** *What tactics shown here might have added to his image of power? What methods do world leaders today use to demonstrate their authority?*

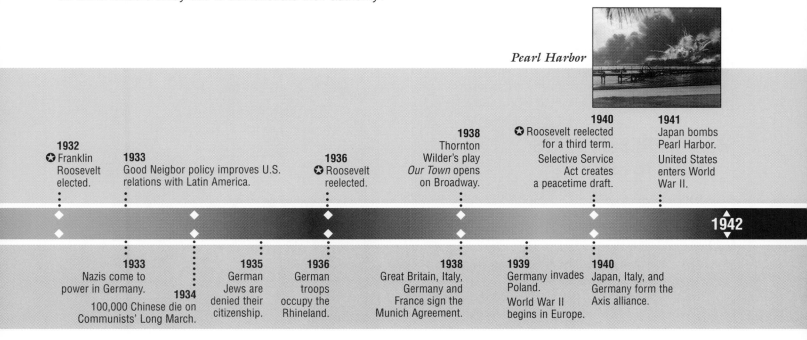

Pearl Harbor

1932
✪ Franklin Roosevelt elected.

1933
Good Neighbor policy improves U.S. relations with Latin America.

1936
✪ Roosevelt reelected.

1938
Thornton Wilder's play *Our Town* opens on Broadway.

1940
✪ Roosevelt reelected for a third term.
Selective Service Act creates a peacetime draft.

1941
Japan bombs Pearl Harbor.
United States enters World War II.

1942

1933
Nazis come to power in Germany.

1934
100,000 Chinese die on Communists' Long March.

1935
German Jews are denied their citizenship.

1936
German troops occupy the Rhineland.

1938
Great Britain, Italy, Germany and France sign the Munich Agreement.

1939
Germany invades Poland.
World War II begins in Europe.

1940
Japan, Italy, and Germany form the Axis alliance.

Section 1

The Rise of Dictatorships in Europe

PREVIEW

Objectives

- To describe the economic effects of the Great Depression on Europe during the 1930s

- To explain how dictators rose to power in Italy and Germany

- To discuss how Hitler's policies led to World War II

Vocabulary

dictator	concentration camp
Fascist	appeasement
totalitarian state	blitzkrieg
Nazi	

While the United States was enjoying a period of prosperity during the 1920s, European nations were trying to recover from World War I. An economic crisis caused by the war led some European nations to turn to **dictators,** rulers with absolute power, to solve their problems. During the 1930s, dictators gained power as other European countries failed to challenge them. In 1939, when these countries finally took a stand, Europe was engulfed in a second world war.

◆ A DEPRESSION HITS EUROPE HARD

World War I had left the nations of Europe shattered, with huge debts to pay. During the war, the United States had lent the Allies $11 billion, which had to be repaid. Furthermore, according to the Treaty of Versailles, drawn up after the war, Germany owed the Allies $33 billion in reparations.

A political dispute in 1923 deepened the economic crisis. When Germany missed a war debt payment to France, France sent troops into the Ruhr (roor) Valley and took over the steel mills and coal mines. In protest, the German government urged workers in the Ruhr

Valley to go on strike and promised to pay their wages. Its treasury almost empty, the German government began to print more paper money.

Having so much paper currency in circulation caused German inflation to spin wildly out of control. Prices rose so fast that the currency lost much of its value. By 1923, German money was worth so little, it took wheelbarrows full of paper bills to buy food.

Germany's problems soon became Europe's problems. Without the reparations payments, the Allies had trouble paying their debts to the United States. In 1924, President Coolidge appointed American banker Charles Dawes to see what could be done about the problems in Europe. Dawes worked

In the 1920s, it was cheaper for Germans to burn marks—German money—than to buy wood for kindling. This woman is using several million German marks to fuel her stove. ▼

out an agreement between Britain, France, Germany, and the United States. Under the Dawes Plan, American banks lent money to Germany. This helped the German economy, making it easier for Germany to pay its debt to the Allies and, in turn, for the Allies to pay the United States.

Although the European economy improved somewhat between 1924 and 1929, the Great Depression in the United States, which began in 1929, spread to the rest of world. American banks began demanding repayment of their European loans. Americans stopped importing foreign goods, such as clothes, machines, and wines. All over Europe, businesses and banks failed. As the European depression deepened, President Hoover suspended European debt payments for a year. Europe's economic crisis was so deep, however, that this strategy failed to improve its economy. Just as in the United States, millions of people lost their jobs and homes. All over Europe, shantytowns—areas consisting mostly of shacks—signaled economic despair. As Europeans became more desperate, some nations lost confidence in democracy and became attracted to extreme political ideas.

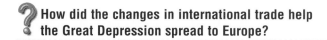
How did the changes in international trade help the Great Depression spread to Europe?

▲ *Italian Fascist leader Benito Mussolini (1883–1945) attracted crowds of supporters with his promises of peace and prosperity in their homeland.*

◆ THE RISE OF EUROPEAN DICTATORS

When the Great Depression hit Europe, people were more interested in improving their economic situation than in the kind of government that would provide the help they needed. In countries with long traditions of self-government, such as Great Britain and France, democracy survived. In others, such as Italy and Germany, people lost faith in democratic governments. This set up the opportunity for the rise of dictators in some countries in Europe.

Communism in the Soviet Union

With the end of the Russian Revolution in 1917, Russia underwent a long period of civil war. By 1921, the Communists were in charge of the entire country. As a symbol of the sweeping changes they were making, Communist leaders changed the name of the country to the Union of Soviet Socialist Republics, or Soviet Union for short. Under Vladimir I. Lenin, the Communists suppressed all opposition. They began a

campaign to wipe out private property that had been given to Russians after the Revolution.

After Lenin died in 1924, Joseph Stalin, a ruthless dictator, was determined to turn the Soviet Union into a major military and economic power. To accomplish this goal, Stalin took away political, religious, and property rights. He attempted to spread communism throughout the world by giving money to fund Communist groups in other countries.

Fascism in Italy

Partly out of fear of communism, some Italians turned to another political extreme in the early 1920s. Like other Europeans, the people of Italy faced hard times, strikes, and riots after World War I. Conditions were ripe for a strong leader to take control. Such a leader was Benito Mussolini, the founder and leader of the Italian Fascist party. A **Fascist** is a believer in fascism, a political system in which a dictator rules a state and is the supreme source of law and order. The Fascists promised peace at home by bringing an end to strikes and by crushing communism. Fascists also promised to gain respect for Italy as a world power.

In 1922, the Fascists quickly reduced the authority of the Italian parliament and crushed all opposition. Mussolini seized control of the press and set up a secret

The young German Nazis in this photograph, known as "Hitler Youth," were saluted by other Nazis as they marched in Berlin in 1934. ▶

police force. People who spoke out against the Fascists were arrested, beaten, and sometimes killed. Fascist Italy became a **totalitarian state,** a place where an individual, a group, or the government has total control over citizens' lives.

Nazism in Germany

As Mussolini gained control of Italy, Adolf Hitler began his rise to power in Germany. Hitler's National Socialist party, shortened in German to **Nazi,** had gained popularity during the 1920s because of Hitler's attacks on the Treaty of Versailles. Hitler charged that the terms of the treaty had weakened the country.

Hitler's extreme racial views were attractive to many Germans. He stated that the Germans were a "master race" destined to rule the world. According to his distorted views, other people were "inferior." Others included Jewish people, people of color, Gypsies, and the Slavic peoples of eastern Europe. Hitler blamed these people for Germany's problems.

As economic conditions worsened, more and more Germans embraced extreme views. Some enrolled in the Communist party, while others turned to Nazism. The Nazis offered a simple answer to Germany's problems. They said that the problems were the fault of Jews, Communists, and the Western democracies. According to Hitler, only the destruction of these enemies would allow Germany to rise and become the world's dominant power.

As German unemployment rose to six million people in 1932, the popularity of the Nazis rose. The Nazis legally came to power early in 1933, when the German president, Paul von Hindenberg, appointed Hitler to be chancellor of Germany.

Once in power, the Nazis cast all democratic policies aside. They arrested opponents, took power from the German parliament, and outlawed other political parties and labor unions. One of Hitler's first actions was to secretly begin building up the German military in violation of the Treaty of Versailles.

Hitler also increased his campaign against the Jews. In 1935, he stripped them of their German citizenship. Jewish students could no longer attend public schools. Jews were forced to wear yellow stars on their clothes and were subjected to humiliation from other Germans. Many Jews were brutally attacked and sent to **concentration camps,** or large prison camps, along with many of Hitler's other enemies.

How did conditions in Europe after World War I contribute to the rise of dictators?

◆ GERMAN EXPANSION

Hitler had total confidence that Germany could become the world's dominant power—by force, if necessary. When an advisor urged him not to move too boldly in attacking countries that opposed him, Hitler responded,

"**They'll never act. They'll just protest. And they will always be too late.**"

Events proved Hitler correct. On March 7, 1936, Hitler sent troops to occupy the Rhineland, an area in Germany between the Rhine River and France. This action was in violation of the Treaty of Versailles, which had made the Rhineland an unarmed zone to protect France. When German troops crossed into the Rhineland in 1936, France and Britain complained, but they took no military action because they did not want to risk another war. The policy of giving in to try to avoid more trouble is known as **appeasement**. Allied leaders believed that giving in to Hitler would satisfy him.

In reality, each success made Hitler bolder. At dawn on March 12, 1938, German troops poured across the

German and Italian Expansion, 1936–1939

- Area taken by Germany
- Area taken by Italy

▲ **Geography** *Part of Europe was under German control by September 1939.* **Interpreting the Map** *Name the countries that had been taken over by Germany by this time.*

border into Austria and annexed the country, as shown on the map on this page. Next was Czechoslovakia. Here, three million ethnic Germans lived in the Sudetenland (sŭ-dāt´-n-land), an area in the northwestern part of the country. Claiming that the government of Czechoslovakia was mistreating Sudeten Germans, Hitler demanded that Czechoslovakia give the Sudetenland to Germany. The Czech government refused and called on the Western democracies for help.

The democracies again chose to appease Hitler. In September 1938, the leaders of Britain and France met with Hitler and Mussolini in Munich, Germany. Czech leaders were not invited. Hitler said that the demand for the Sudetenland would be his last one. The leaders then signed the Munich Pact giving Germany the Sudetenland. British prime minister Neville Chamberlain announced that the Munich Pact guaranteed "peace for our time."

? Why did the European democracies avoid taking bold steps to stop Hitler?

◆ WAR BREAKS OUT

Hitler's promises at Munich were empty. In 1939, he seized the rest of Czechoslovakia. At about the same time, Italy annexed Albania, further expanding its territory.

Then Hitler turned his attention to Poland. If he provoked a war in Poland, he would be inviting a two-front war—with the Soviet Union on the eastern front and with France and Britain on the western front. In August 1939, Nazi Germany made an alliance with the Soviet Union. In the Nazi-Soviet pact, the two enemies promised not to attack each other. Germany

▲ *In October 1939, after Warsaw, Poland's capital, fell to Hitler's forces, German troops marched through the city's streets.*

and the Soviet Union also secretly agreed that they would invade and conquer Poland together. Thus, Germany's problem of fighting a two-way war seemed to have been avoided.

Hitler Attacks Poland

No longer worried about a two-front war, Hitler attacked Poland on September 1, 1939. Using a new strategy called the **blitzkrieg,** or "lightning war," the Germans attacked swiftly and massively. Waves of German bombers destroyed Polish air fields, factories, and railroads.

The invasion of Poland finally convinced France and Britain to take action. On September 3, both countries declared war on Germany. However, the Allied democracies were unprepared to fight a war and could not provide Poland with much immediate help. On October 6, Poland surrendered to the Germans.

War in France

In the spring of 1940, Hitler's tanks invaded Belgium, Luxembourg, and the Netherlands. When these countries surrendered, the Germans moved across France to the sea, swung north, and trapped the Allied soldiers on the beaches of Dunkirk, a city on the English Channel. However, the people of Britain heroically set out to rescue the trapped soldiers. From May 28 to June 4, they used small boats to pull more than 300,000 soldiers from the beaches to safety in Britain.

France, however, was doomed. Mussolini entered the war by attacking France from the south. In June 1940, France surrendered.

The Battle of Britain

With France out of the war, Britain stood alone in Europe against the Nazis. During the summer and fall of 1940, the German air force bombed Britain constantly, hoping to bring the country to its knees. But the British air force managed to fight off the German planes. Frustrated by his inability to win the Battle of Britain, Hitler turned his attention elsewhere.

 How did Hitler use both force and deception to conquer Europe?

Section 1 Review

Check Understanding

1. **Define** (a) dictator (b) Fascist (c) totalitarian state (d) Nazi (e) concentration camp (f) appeasement (g) blitzkrieg

2. **Explain** how the Great Depression weakened democracy in Europe.

3. **Identify** the conditions that helped Hitler gain power in Germany.

4. **Explain** what the appeasement policy toward Hitler was to accomplish.

Critical Thinking

Connecting Past and Present Could a dictatorship ever arise today in the United States, as it did in Germany and Italy in the early 1930s? Explain your answer.

Write About History

Make a chart showing the similarities and differences between fascism and communism. Be sure to include major leaders, countries, and political and economic goals.

BUILDING SKILLS

Recognizing Propaganda: Hitler Rises to Power

Recognizing propaganda is important so that you can form your own opinions about issues. Propaganda is the promotion of certain ideas to advance, damage, or destroy a cause. The material may contain some accurate statements. However, it usually shows only one side of an issue.

There are a number of methods propagandists use to sway opinions. One method is to tell only part of the truth, leaving out important facts. A second is to link a cause with an important person or noble idea. A third method is to use symbols or images that show the other side in a negative way.

Here's How

Follow these steps to analyze propaganda:

1. Compare the propaganda with reliable sources on the same topic.
2. Decide which propaganda technique is used. How does it distort the facts?
3. Analyze how words or images are presented in order to sway opinion or appeal to people.
4. Draw conclusions about the propaganda. What is the main purpose of the propaganda? Whom is it meant to influence?

Here's Why

Many of the primary sources historians encounter contain propaganda that has been used to influence public opinion. Recognizing propaganda helps historians analyze and draw their own accurate conclusions about events.

Practice the Skill

The poster below is from Nazi Germany. Study it, and answer the questions.

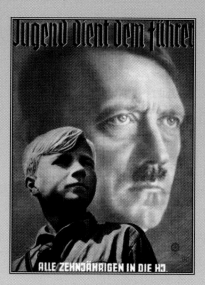

1. The poster says, "Leader, We Follow You!" What does this lead the viewer to believe about Hitler's popularity?
2. What is the purpose of this poster? What group of people is the poster meant to influence?
3. According to the image in the poster, how would you describe Hitler? Based on what you know, is this image accurate? Explain.

Apply the Skill

Find an example of propaganda in a newspaper or magazine or from a TV program. Then use the steps in *Here's How* to analyze the propaganda.

Section 2

Aggression in East Asia

PREVIEW

Objectives

- To explain how the military rose to power in Japan during the 1930s

- To describe Japan's policy of expansion in China during the 1930s

- To describe how the League of Nations and the United States responded to Japanese aggression

- To understand why Japan turned its attention from China to Southeast Asia in 1939

Vocabulary

militarism
constitutional monarchy

The rise of Hitler and Mussolini in Europe occurred around the same time that **militarism** gained a hold in Japan in the 1930s. Militarism is an aggressive policy put forth by the military or by people who follow the ideals of the military. Following a brief period of democracy during the 1920s, Japan became a military dictatorship in the early 1930s. Instead of a single dictator, as in Italy and Germany, a group of military officers gained power in Japan. The chiefs of the Imperial Army and Imperial Navy answered to the emperor. In the name of Hirohito, Japan's emperor, they set out to build an empire in East Asia.

◆ JAPAN EXPANDS ITS EMPIRE

Japan had had emperors for more than 2,500 years, but in recent centuries, they had been mostly ceremonial figures. Military leaders often held power and ruled in the emperor's name. In the late 1800s, influenced by the example of Britain, Japan became a **constitutional monarchy.** In a constitutional monarchy, democratically elected officials govern in the name of a ruler. The high point of democracy in Japan came in 1925, when the legislature passed a law granting all males over age 25 the right to vote.

Japanese Militarism

As Japan's economic troubles deepened in the 1930s, military leaders turned against democracy and began to scheme for increased military control. These leaders were extreme nationalists who were determined to use force to build a Japanese empire.

Their aim was to overcome the limits on Japanese growth that had been imposed by Japan's geography. As an island chain, Japan did not have much land or raw materials. This limited its ability to feed its growing population. Also, Japan's rapidly growing industries required even more raw materials. By the 1930s the country was facing shortages of such critical resources as oil, iron, rubber, bauxite, and tin. Bauxite is the chief source of aluminum. Japanese military leaders were determined to secure more of these natural resources—by threats or, if necessary, by war.

In 1931 the Japanese army invaded Manchuria, a province of China, against the wishes of the Japanese government. When the Japanese prime minister objected, military extremists assassinated him. In 1932 the Japanese military took full control of the government. The officers began a crash program to build up Japan's military strength. By 1938, Japanese factories were producing about 3,800 aircraft a year. By 1941 Japan had the world's third largest navy, after Britain and the United States.

Response to Japan

Japan's actions violated the laws of the League of Nations as well as several peace treaties the country had signed during the 1920s. In October 1932, the League ordered Japan to withdraw from Manchuria. Instead, Japan withdrew from the League and continued its attack on Manchuria. Within a few months, the Japanese were in total control of Manchuria.

The United States did little to actively challenge Japanese expansion. After the Japanese invasion, Secretary of State Henry Stimson announced that the United States would not recognize Japan's control of Manchuria or any other aggression. This policy became known as the Stimson Doctrine. However, the United States was not willing to use force to oppose Japan. Both Presidents Hoover and Roosevelt believed that the United States did not have the military power in the Pacific necessary to repel Japanese aggression. Indeed, the United States seemed eager to withdraw from any political role in East Asia. For example, in 1934, Congress passed the Tydings-McDuffie Act, which promised the Philippine Islands complete independence within ten years. The outbreak of World War II delayed fulfillment of that promise until July 1946.

Civil War in China

China put up little resistance to the Japanese invasion of Manchuria because for many years China had been preoccupied with a civil war. Much of China was controlled by the Nationalists, led by Chiang Kai-shek (chăng´ kī-shĕk´). The Nationalists were opposed by the Communists, led by Mao Zedong (mau´ dzŭ´-dŏong´). Fighting had begun in the late 1920s and would continue until 1949, when the Communists took control of the Chinese mainland.

At the time of the Japanese attack on Manchuria in 1931, the Chinese Nationalists had the upper hand in the civil war. After several years of struggle, the Nationalists trapped a large force of Communists. In 1934, about 100,000 men, women, and children escaped through a narrow gap in Nationalist lines and began a long trek into the Chinese interior. When they finally reached safety after more than a year, there were only 20,000 survivors. This came to be called the Long March, and it marked the beginning of a new phase in the Communist struggle. Safe from Nationalist attack,

Chiang Kai-shek was eventually driven from the Chinese mainland to the island of Taiwan, where he established a Nationalist government and continued to oppose the Communists. ▼

the Communists began to build up their strength. It was left to the Nationalists to bear the major burden of the war against Japan.

China and Japan at War

Aware that China was divided between the Nationalists and the Communists, Japan saw an opportunity to increase its conquests. In August 1936, the Japanese government announced a new policy.

❝ The fundamental national policy to be established by the Empire is to secure the position of the Empire on the East Asian continent by diplomatic policy and national debate. ❞

The claim for diplomacy and debate was false. Instead, in July 1937, the Japanese army struck deeper south into China. Japanese planes bombed China's main cities while its troops poured over the Great Wall of China and captured the cities of Beijing and Shanghai.

The Japanese attack brought about a wave of sympathy for China in the United States but little practical help. Faced with the economic problems of the Great Depression, Americans did not want to send military forces to far-off Asia. In addition, the United States had an interest in both China and Japan because the two countries bought American weapons.

Provoking the United States

After capturing Shanghai, the Japanese moved up the Yangtse River, where in December 1937, their bombers observed the American gunboat *Panay*. The *Panay* was guarding three oil tankers of the Standard Oil Company. To avoid being hit accidentally, the boat displayed two large American flags.

In spite of the flags, the Japanese bombed and machine-gunned the *Panay*. When it sank and two U.S. sailors were killed, Americans were outraged but resisted taking serious action. The U.S. government demanded and received more than $2 million from the Japanese and promises that American rights in China would be respected.

Next the Japanese stormed the Nationalist Chinese capital at Nanjing. They murdered as many as 200,000 residents of the city and destroyed farms, factories, and businesses.

In 1937, Japanese troops attacked and captured Shanghai, one of China's largest cities. This photograph shows Chinese troops behind a barricade. ▶

About 50 million Chinese fled to the western part of China. The Japanese won a considerable number of victories, but they still were not able to win the war. The outrage at Nanjing made the Chinese more determined to fight back. As the war dragged on, Japan's economy became exhausted, and the nation began to run short of important resources.

Japanese leaders began looking toward the resource-rich European colonies of Southeast Asia, which produced many raw materials. The region was especially rich in oil, which was vital to Japanese industries and armed forces. Without oil, Japan could not continue to effectively wage war.

The outbreak of war in Europe in 1939 gave the Japanese the opportunity they sought. Confident that Europe's attention was focused on the fighting there, the Japanese military made plans to take over Southeast Asia. The intention was to create an empire called the Greater East Asia Co-Prosperity Sphere. Japanese expansion would bring the island nation into direct competition with another power that had thus far stayed out of the fighting—the United States.

Why did Japanese leaders seek to expand their empire in the 1930s?

Section 2 Review

Check Understanding

1. **Define** (a) militarism (b) constitutional monarchy

2. **Identify** the factors that led to the rise of the Japanese military during the 1930s.

3. **Explain** how the League of Nations reacted to Japanese expansion in the 1930s.

Critical Thinking

Connecting Past and Present How can countries that were hostile to one another in the past improve their relationship today?

Write About Economics

Write a brief essay explaining how the desire for natural resources led to Japanese use of force in East Asia in the 1930s.

Section 3

From Isolationism to War

PREVIEW

Objectives

- To explain why the United States played a limited role in world affairs during the 1920s and early 1930s

- To describe how United States policy in Latin America changed during the 1920s and 1930s

- To describe how the United States gradually drew closer to war against the Axis powers

Vocabulary

disarmament	nationalize
cash-and-carry policy	lend-lease plan

After World War I, Americans rejected any sort of alliance that might draw the United States into another war. However, the expansion of dictatorships worried some Americans, who feared that they would not be able to remain isolated from the world's disputes.

◆ THE UNITED STATES CHOOSES NEUTRALITY

Though Americans wanted no part of Europe's alliances and rejected the League of Nations, the United States took steps to help maintain world peace in the 1920s in order to protect its economic interests. The most important step was the Washington Naval Conference that was held in 1921 and 1922. Representatives of nine nations and the United States met in Washington, D.C., to discuss **disarmament,** or the reduction of weapons. The conference produced several important treaties in which the major powers agreed to build no large battleships for the next ten years, to respect one another's territories in the Pacific, and to respect the borders of China. In addition, France and the United States put together an agreement called the Kellogg-Briand Pact, which was designed to outlaw war. Fifteen nations signed it on August 27, 1928.

These treaties could do little when a powerful nation was determined to build up its armed forces and pursue a policy of aggression. In the 1930s, the treaties—and even the League of Nations—would fail when the major powers chose not to challenge the aggressors.

Challenge to Isolationism

American support for isolationism was strengthened by charges from a committee headed by Senator Gerald P. Nye, a Republican from North Dakota. Nye's committee was formed in 1934 to investigate the weapons industry. The committee argued that American bankers and arms manufacturers had secretly tricked the United States into entering World War I. According to the committee, the bankers had wanted war to increase their profits. The Nye committee called these people "merchants of death." The committee report said,

> When Americans went into the fray [fight], they little thought they were fighting to save the skins of American bankers who had bet too boldly on the outcome of the war and had two billions of dollars of loans to the Allies in jeopardy [at risk].

This emblem urged American neutrality in the conflicts in Europe and elsewhere. ▼

Many historians did not accept these claims at the time, and many do not today. These historians have believed that the government was drawn into World War II by the threat that Germany might win and control the Atlantic shipping lanes. U.S. involvement began when German submarines sank U.S. ships.

President Franklin Roosevelt did not have isolationist views. He believed that the United States was endangered by the aggressive policies of dictators like Hitler. During Roosevelt's first term, his focus was on getting the United States out of the Great Depression. As the totalitarian states expanded, however, Roosevelt began to speak more forcefully to the American people about his concerns.

Congress, however, remained isolationist. It passed laws designed to keep the United States out of the growing European conflict. A series of neutrality acts gave the President the power to outlaw all arms shipments to countries at war. The acts also forbade Americans from making loans to nations at war and established a **cash-and-carry policy** for trading with European nations. Under this policy, nations at war could buy nonmilitary goods from the United States as long as they paid cash and carried the goods home on their own ships.

Good Neighbor in Latin America

Franklin Roosevelt came into office in 1933 pledging that the United States would be a "good neighbor" in world affairs. The Good Neighbor policy signified a major change in U.S. relations with Latin America. During the 1920s the U.S. government had continued to send marines to Central American countries to settle disputes, which angered other Latin American nations. In 1933 the United States promised to end all armed intervention in Latin America. In 1934 the United States also gave up its right to intervene in Cuba under the Platt Amendment, though the United States retained its naval base at Guantanamo Bay. Finally, the Good Neighbor policy determined how the United States reacted when, in 1938, Mexico **nationalized** the oil industry, converting the control of oil by private companies to control by the government. Instead of sending troops to protect U.S. oil interests, the government agreed to a commission to decide how much Mexico should pay U.S. companies for their losses.

What steps did Congress take to keep the United States out of the growing conflict in Europe?

◆ THE END OF NEUTRALITY

After Hitler's invasion of Poland in 1939, the United States began to move from neutrality to commitment in dealing with Europe. The fall of Poland and France convinced Roosevelt that Germany and Italy were on the verge of winning the war. Roosevelt became convinced of the need for quick action. "Even another day's delay may mean the end of civilization," he said.

To prepare the United States for the possibility of war, Roosevelt proposed the country's first peacetime draft, which Congress passed as the Selective Training and Service Act. Under this act, all men between 21 and 35 were required to sign up, or register, for the draft. Each man was given a number corresponding to his birthday. Each of the 365 numbers were drawn just before the election of 1940. Those whose numbers were drawn first had the highest probability of being drafted.

The crisis in Europe became a major issue in the presidential election of 1940. During the campaign, Roosevelt tried to quiet Americans' fears of war, saying,

> **I have said this before and I will say it again and again: Your boys are not going to be sent into any foreign wars.**

In response to the Selective Training and Service Act, many young men registered for the draft. ▼

Roosevelt continued to believe that the best way for the United States to stay out of the war was to help the British defend themselves. In December, just after the election, Roosevelt received a message from Winston Churchill saying that Britain was in financial trouble. It could no longer pay for arms and supplies as set up under the cash-and-carry policy.

Roosevelt now asked Congress to replace cash-and-carry with the **lend-lease plan.** This gave the President the power to lend or lease arms and other supplies to any country whose defense was vital to the United States. After the war, the goods that had been lent would be returned to the United States. "We must be the great arsenal of democracy," the President said. In spite of bitter resistance from isolationists, Congress passed the Lend-Lease Act in March 1941.

Getting supplies across the Atlantic to Britain exposed Americans to great dangers. The Germans attempted to cut Britain's lifeline by closing the Atlantic shipping lanes. During the first half of 1941, German submarines staged numerous attacks on British ships.

In September 1941, German submarines began attacking U.S. ships. Deeply angry, Roosevelt ordered the U.S. Navy to attack any German submarines in its path. Speaking to the nation, he said,

> When you see a rattlesnake poised to strike, you do not wait until he has struck before you crush him.

German submarines fired on two destroyers, sinking one, the *Reuben James,* on October 31, 1941. More than 100 Americans were killed. Although war had not been declared, it seemed to many Americans that they were in an undeclared war with Germany.

What actions related to the fighting in Europe did Roosevelt take in 1940 and 1941?

◆ PEARL HARBOR

The United States saw Hitler as the greatest danger to democracy. Some of his actions in the 1930s are shown in the chart above. But it was Japan that finally brought the United States into the war. The United States and Japan had not been in open conflict with each other. Roosevelt wanted to save his resources to fight against Germany. Japanese leaders

Events Leading to World War II

October 1922	Mussolini gains power in Italy.
September 1931	Japan invades Manchuria.
January 1933	Hitler becomes chancellor of Germany.
October 1935	Italy invades Ethiopia.
March 1936	Germany occupies Rhineland.
July 1937	Japanese move farther into China.
March 1938	Germany annexes Austria.
September 1938	Munich Conference held.
August 1939	Nazi-Soviet Pact signed.
September 1939	Germany invades Poland.

▲ **History** *This chart shows important events leading to World War II.* **Interpreting the Chart** *What does the chart reveal about Germany's actions in the late 1930s?*

gambled that America's preoccupation with Europe might allow Japan to conquer Asia entirely. In September 1940, Japan joined Italy and Germany in forming the Axis alliance. About the same time, Japanese soldiers moved into the French colony of Indochina, present-day Vietnam, Laos, and Cambodia. This put them in a position to easily attack the American-controlled Philippine Islands and Guam. In response, Roosevelt placed an embargo on trade with Japan, banning all oil shipments. Oil was needed by Japan to keep its military tanks, trucks, and planes working.

The oil embargo led Japan's leaders to plan for war against the United States. The Japanese decided to attack the U.S. Navy at Pearl Harbor, a U.S. naval base in Hawaii.

This photograph was taken immediately after the bombing of Pearl Harbor on December 7, 1941. ▶

On the morning of December 7, 1941, Japanese pilots climbed into more than 180 planes that were on six aircraft carriers. One by one, they took off and flew eastward toward the Hawaiian island of Oahu. Their goal was 200 miles away.

The Japanese planes soon reached Pearl Harbor and began bombing. Most of the American fleet was in a low state of alert. The Japanese sank or damaged 18 ships. About 2,400 Americans died in the attack.

On December 8, Roosevelt asked Congress to declare war on Japan.

> Yesterday, December 7, 1941—a date which will live in infamy [history of evil]— the United States was suddenly and deliberately attacked by . . . the Empire of Japan. . . .With the unbounding determination of our people—we will . . . triumph—so help us God.

The Allies had been fighting for two years. The United States would now join them in battle.

Why did Japan attack Pearl Harbor?

Section 3 Review

Check Understanding

1. **Define** (a) disarmament (b) cash-and-carry policy (c) nationalize (d) lend-lease plan

2. **Explain** how the Good Neighbor Policy affected U.S. relations with Latin America.

3. **Describe** how the United States moved from neutrality to commitment in World War II.

Critical Thinking

Evaluating If Roosevelt had taken a stronger stand against Japanese aggression earlier, how might this have affected Japanese policy?

Write About History

Connecting Past and Present Write about an event in the recent past that you would you describe as "a date which will live in infamy."

POINT *of* VIEW

ISOLATIONISTS VERSUS INTERVENTIONISTS

The decision to enter World War II was not easily made. Memories of the devastation of World War I were too fresh in American minds. The debate became heated after President Roosevelt decided to offer help to Britain through lend-lease. Below are two excerpts from the debate over this issue in 1941. The first is from a speech opposing lend-lease by Montana Representative James F. O'Connor. The second is from a radio address supporting lend-lease by Major General John F. O'Ryan, a World War I veteran.

Representative James F. O'Connor

The first World War, you will recall, was fought to "save democracy." Today the same nations are taking part in another great conflict, eyed in the same purpose, only with added fury, cruelty, barbarity, hatred, and viciousness. What is it about? The same things that caused the first World War….

Should we not appreciate that we cannot right every wrong in this man-made world? We cannot police this world. To do so would require many millions of soldiers and billions more dollars of armaments.

Major General John F. O'Ryan

This is not a European war. Hitler has not confined his ambitions to Europe. His troops and bombers are now in North Africa. An army of [spies] are hard at work in South America, in Mexico and here in our own homeland. His ships of war are at large in the North Atlantic. In the Far East he counts on the cooperation of Japan to do for him there what he cannot do himself.

In the present state of the world only resolute and forthright people who will fight and sacrifice for their freedom and rights can survive. We propose to survive.

Examining Point of View

1. What is the main point of each argument?
2. How do you think O'Connor would respond to O'Ryan's argument?
3. How would O'Ryan respond to O'Connor?
4. Which argument do you think is more persuasive? Why?

What's Your Point of View?

Americans have long held differing views about U.S. involvement in world affairs. Some believe the United States has a responsibility to make the world a better place. Others feel that the United States should not risk American lives in foreign countries.

Write an essay in which you discuss whether the United States should play a role in helping other countries resolve their problems. Support your point of view with reasons, facts, and examples.

Chapter 21
Review

CHAPTER SUMMARY

Section 1

Europe, beginning to recover from the destruction of World War I, was devastated by the Great Depression. The failure of democratic governments to deal with economic woes helped to give way to the rise of dictators. In Germany, Adolf Hitler blamed the depression on Western democracies, Jews, and Communists. Hitler seized Austria and Czechoslovakia while Europe's democracies appeased him. When Hitler attacked Poland, Britain and France finally realized that appeasement would not work and they declared war.

Section 2

In the 1930s, Japan turned to militarism. Its armed forces invaded the Chinese province of Manchuria and, later, other areas of China. Japan then focused its aggression on Southeast Asia, which was rich in resources that the Japanese economy and military needed.

Section 3

During the 1920s and 1930s, many Americans were isolationists. However, Germany's victories in the early days of World War II began to alarm the American public. Afraid that Germany would overwhelm Britain, President Roosevelt convinced Congress to help the British. In 1941 the United States took stronger steps to support the Allied war effort, but the Japanese attack on Pearl Harbor on December 7, 1941, officially brought the United States into World War II.

Connecting ◆◆ Past and Present

What can be learned from the way the United States dealt with dictatorships during the 1930s? How can the lessons be applied to dealing with undemocratic leaders today?

Using Vocabulary

From the list below, select the term that best completes each sentence.

Fascist	nationalize
totalitarian state	appeasement
blitzkrieg	militarism
cash-and-carry policy	disarmament

1. During Hitler's rule, Germany was a _____ .

2. The strategy called _____ was used by Germany in its attacks against the Allies.

3. The control of government by the armed forces is called _____ .

4. Because of talks on _____ , the major powers agreed not to build large battleships for ten years.

5. When Mexico wanted to take control of the country's oil production, it decided to _____ its oil properties.

6. The policy of _____ did not stop Hitler's demands.

7. A _____ believes in a political system in which a dictator is the supreme ruler.

8. With the _____ , nations would pay for nonmilitary goods and take the supplies home on their ships.

Check Understanding

1. **Describe** the economic effects of the Great Depression on Europe.

2. **Explain** why dictators were able to rise to power in Italy and Germany after World War I.

3. **Analyze** how Hitler's policies led to World War II.

4. **Explain** why the military assumed power in Japan in the 1930s.

5. **Describe** how Japan expanded into China in the 1930s.

6. **Explain** why the Japanese turned their attention to Southeast Asia in 1939.

7. **Draw conclusions** about why the United States was not more involved in world affairs in the 1920s and early 1930s.

8. **Identify** the Nye committee and describe its importance to American foreign policy in the 1930s.

9. **Explain** how U.S. policy toward Latin America changed during the 1920s and 1930s.

10. **Describe** why the United States found itself drawing closer to war against the Axis powers.

Critical Thinking

1. **Comparing** In what ways were Hitler and Stalin similar as leaders?

2. **Predicting Outcomes** Reread President Roosevelt's quotation on page 436. How do you think the American people reacted to what he said?

3. **Contrasting** How did Congress's attitude toward Europe's totalitarian leaders differ from the President's?

4. **Applying Information** Why did Roosevelt believe the United States was threatened by the expansionist policies of European dictators?

◆ **Connecting Past and Present** How do you think Japan's surprise attack on Pearl Harbor has affected current U.S. defense policy?

Interpreting the Timeline

Use the timeline on pages 422–423 to answer these questions.

1. How many years elapsed between the onset of the Great Depression and the Nazis' rise to power?

2. Which U.S. events during the 1920s were in response to the effects of World War I?

3. What German actions preceded America's entry into World War II?

Writing to Persuade

In the presidential campaign of 1940, Roosevelt assured Americans that "your boys are not going to be sent into any foreign wars." Now it is one year later, and Japan has attacked Pearl Harbor. **Write** a speech for Roosevelt in which he persuades Americans that going to war—with their sons as soldiers—is required for the security of the United States.

Putting Skills to Work

RECOGNIZING PROPAGANDA

In the Building Skills lesson on page 429, you learned that recognizing propaganda is important in order to form your own opinion about something. Read the statement that Adolf Hitler issued to the German army on September 1, 1939, to justify his invasion of Poland. Then answer the questions that follow.

The Polish State has refused the peaceful settlement of relations which I desired, and has appealed to arms. Germans in Poland are persecuted with bloody terror and driven from their houses. A series of violations of the frontier, intolerable to a great Power, prove that Poland is no longer willing to respect the frontier of [Germany]. . . . In order to put an end to this lunacy, I have no other choice than to meet force with force from now on. The German Army will fight the battle for the honor and the vital rights of reborn Germany with hard determination.

1. What reasons does Hitler give for the invasion of Poland?

2. What propaganda techniques does Hitler use?

3. What words does Hitler use to appeal to the Germans' emotions?

4. Why, in your opinion, did Hitler issue this statement?

Portfolio Project

U.S. ENTRY INTO WORLD WAR II

Conduct a debate about whether the United States should or should not become involved in the affairs of other nations. Begin by forming into two teams. Then create rules, such as how much time to allow for arguments and how to decide which side of the debate each team will argue. Work with your team to prepare arguments for your side in the debate. Use the chapter—as well as library resources—to find information supporting your position for isolation or for intervention. Present the debate in front of your class. Ask your classmates to vote for the side that made the more convincing argument.

Chapter 22
World War II
1941–1945

CHAPTER PREVIEW

Section 1 The War Expands

In 1941, the United States joined the Allies to fight the war in Europe, Africa, Asia, and the Pacific.

Section 2 Striking Back

In 1942, the Allies began to win victories in Africa, Europe, and the Pacific, bringing them closer to defeating the Axis powers.

Section 3 Winning the War

The war in Europe ended with an Allied victory in the spring of 1945, but the war in the Pacific continued until the summer of that year. As the Allies came closer to winning, they met to make plans for the postwar world.

World War II recruitment poster

U.S. Events

1940
★ Franklin Roosevelt reelected for a third term.
Selective Service Act of 1940 is passed.

U.S. enters World War II

1941
United States enters World War II.
Manhattan Project is begun to develop an atomic bomb.

1939

World Events

1940
Germans bomb London.
British begin night bombing of Germany.

1941
Many Latin American nations declare war on the Axis powers.

1942
Americans bomb Tokyo in surprise raid.
Battle of Midway is fought.
Germans attack Stalingrad.

Battle of Midway

Portfolio Project

PATRIOTIC MUSIC

Once the United States entered World War II, American support for the war was overwhelming. One way Americans expressed their patriotic feelings was through music. During wartime, a number of songs were written that inspired Americans to fight for democracy around the world. As you read the chapter, think of the many kinds of feelings that soldiers and civilians might have had about the war. At the end of the chapter, you will research some of the music that expressed those feelings during the World War II era.

▲ *U.S. soldiers walk through an abandoned village in France in June 1944.* ◆ **Connecting Past and Present** *How would you describe the soldier leaning against the car? Would a wartime picture today depict things differently?*

Tuskegee airman

Iwo Jima victory

1943
Squadron of African American pilots, the Tuskegee Airmen, is formed.

1944
✪ Franklin Roosevelt reelected for a fourth term.

1945
Roosevelt dies.
✪ Harry Truman becomes President.
First atomic bomb test takes place in New Mexico.
U.S. Marines take control of Iwo Jima.
World War II ends.

▲ **1946** ▼

1943
Allied victories lead to German withdrawal from North Africa.
Allied invasion of Japanese-held islands begins.

1944
Allied invasion of France begins on D-day.
Battle of the Bulge is fought.
William Somerset Maugham's novel *The Razor's Edge* is published.

1945
Germany surrenders.
U.S. drops atomic bombs on Hiroshima and Nagasaki.
Japan surrenders.

Hiroshima bombing

The War Expands

PREVIEW

Objectives

- To explain how Hitler continued his offensive in 1941, winning victories in North Africa and invading the Soviet Union

- To describe continued Japanese expansion in the Pacific in 1941 and 1942

- To identify the Allies' strategy for winning the war

Vocabulary

scorched-earth policy
siege
Big Three

After declaring war against the Axis powers, the United States began to mobilize its armed forces. Ten million men were drafted through the Selective Service Act of 1940. Approximately six million more American men and women volunteered for service. The chart on page 448 shows the branches in which they served.

◆ WAR IN AFRICA AND THE SOVIET UNION

At the time the United States mobilized its troops, the Allied position was weak. Although Germany had not defeated the British in the Battle of Britain, Germany controlled much of the European continent. The Axis powers, confident that they could deal with the British later, moved to attack North Africa and the Soviet Union.

The Battle for North Africa

Italy was the first Axis power to make a move in the battle for North Africa. In September 1940, Mussolini ordered troops in the Italian colony of Libya to move east and take Egypt and the Suez Canal from the British. This plan, if it succeeded, would give the soldiers of the Axis powers access to the oil fields of the Middle East.

The Italian army managed to get 60 miles into Egypt. Then, on December 9, the British counter-attacked and overran the Italian forces. The British pushed through northern Libya and took Tobruk, a valuable port city, in January 1941. By the end of February, the British had moved 500 miles across the desert.

Germany then stepped in to keep North Africa from falling into Allied hands. Hitler doubled the size of the newly formed Afrika Korps and sent General Erwin Rommel to lead it. Rommel's skills in desert fighting earned him the nickname Desert Fox.

By March 1941, Rommel's troops were ready for action. They defeated the British in Libya, and by June, pushed the British all the way back to Egypt. Over the next year, the Afrika Korps won battle after battle. By June 1942, Egypt seemed to be within Germany's grasp.

Hitler Invades the Soviet Union

In addition to fighting in North Africa, Hitler was getting ready to invade the Soviet Union. Although he and Stalin had promised not to attack each other in the Nazi-Soviet pact of 1939, Hitler had plans to invade the Soviet Union to win control of its rich natural resources and farmland.

On June 22, 1941, Hitler massed 3.2 million troops along the Soviet Union's western boundary. Supported by 3,000 tanks and 3,000 airplanes, the Germans hoped to conquer the country in six months—before the brutal Russian winter set in.

The British Army included soldiers from British colonies. These soldiers from India examined a Nazi flag confiscated during fighting in Libya in 1942. ▼

◀ *World War II was as brutal for many Soviet civilians as it was for soldiers. Here, Russian women move a wagon carrying the bodies of friends and relatives killed during Hitler's blitzkrieg of the Soviet Union in 1941.*

Hitler's blitzkrieg of the Soviet Union caught the Red Army, as the Soviet army was called, completely by surprise. Though the Red Army had five million soldiers, they were not well equipped or well trained. Yet, the Soviets fought hard. Forced to retreat, Soviet troops followed Stalin's orders to carry out a **scorched-earth policy.** In this plan of action, a retreating army burns or destroys crops and other valuable materials of its own country, leaving behind only "scorched earth."

In September 1941, German troops laid **siege** to the Soviet city Leningrad (called St. Petersburg today), blockading the city so that food, fuel, and other supplies could not be brought in. The Germans also bombed the city's food warehouses. Hitler planned to starve Leningrad's 2.5 million citizens into surrender.

More than 264,000 Soviets died that first winter. Nevertheless, the people of Leningrad refused to surrender. The siege lasted until January 1944, resulting in nearly two million Soviet casualties.

In October 1941, as the winter season began, Hitler began to attack Moscow, the capital of the Soviet Union. However, cold rains turned the roads into mud, slowing the German army's progress. Then temperatures dropped, and snow began to fall. German soldiers froze in their summer uniforms. Hitler, expecting a swift victory, had refused to order winter uniforms.

In early December 1941, Hitler's troops reached the outskirts of the capital. Soviet citizens, however, were determined to keep Moscow from falling into German hands. People from all over the country poured in to defend the city. The Soviet army managed to push the Germans back and kept them from taking Moscow. Hitler's generals wanted to retreat, but Hitler insisted that his soldiers "must dig into the ground where they are and hold every square yard of land!" So the Germans dug in west of Moscow and waited.

 What factors made Hitler's invasion of the Soviet Union less successful than he expected?

◆ JAPAN CONTINUES ITS WAR OF EXPANSION

After the attack on Pearl Harbor, Japan continued its war of expansion under the leadership of Prime Minister Hideki Tojo. Tojo was part of a powerful group of army officers who were eager to spread Japan's control over East Asia. By the end of December 1941, the Japanese had captured the U.S. territories of Guam and Wake Island and had landed in the Philippines. In January 1942, Japanese troops took control of the country and triumphantly entered Manila, the capital of the Philippines.

General Douglas MacArthur was in charge of defending the Philippine Islands. He pulled back his American and Filipino troops to the Bataan (ba-´tan) Peninsula and the island fort of Corregidor near Manila. His soldiers were short on ammunition, food, and medicine. Soon, they were exhausted, starving, and sick. Yet, "looking like walking dead men," they held on.

In March, Roosevelt ordered MacArthur to leave the Philippines for Australia, where he was to take command of the Allied war effort against Japan. As he was leaving, MacArthur promised the Filipinos, "I shall return."

With tremendous courage the American and Filipino soldiers on Bataan fought on, in spite of having little to eat but the animals they caught. In early April they were forced to surrender Bataan, and in May, Corregidor also fell.

The Japanese then forced 12,000 American and 63,000 Filipino prisoners on the Bataan Peninsula to march 65 miles through scorching heat with little food and water. Between 10,000 and 14,000 men died on what came to be called the Bataan Death March.

The Japanese continued their drive to control Southeast Asia. By March, the Dutch East Indies—called Indonesia today—was in Japanese hands. British Burma (called Myanmar today) fell in May. Burma is located between India and China. The Chinese received valuable Allied supplies along the passage through Burma, called the Burma Road. The Japanese expected to close the road, hoping this would finally force the Chinese to surrender. The Chinese, however, continued to hold out against the Japanese.

By June 1942 the Japanese had captured most of Southeast Asia, and 150 million people were under Japan's rule. They had also captured 500,000 European and American civilians and 150,000 prisoners of war. Japanese forces now threatened Allied forces in India, Australia, and New Zealand.

 What were some Japanese victories in the Pacific after December 1941?
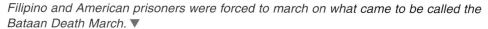

Filipino and American prisoners were forced to march on what came to be called the Bataan Death March. ▼

"THE MARINES HAVE LANDED!"

APPLY TO NEAREST RECRUITING STATION

▲ This poster, "The Marines Have Landed," was designed to recruit Americans into wartime service and to bolster support for the war in the Pacific.

◆ ALLIED STRATEGY

While the Japanese were conquering Southeast Asia and islands in the Pacific, the Allies worked out a strategy for defeating the Axis powers. Great Britain, the Soviet Union, and the United States were the strongest of the Allied powers. The leaders of these nations—Winston Churchill, Joseph Stalin, and Franklin Roosevelt—developed the war plans. These leaders came to be known as the **Big Three.**

The Big Three decided their main goal would be to defeat Germany before using all their resources against Japan. Next, the Allies had to agree on the best way to defeat the German forces. Stalin wanted Britain and the United States to invade western Europe right away, forcing Hitler to remove troops from the Soviet Union and send them west. Then, the Soviet army would have a better chance of driving the rest of the German army out of the country.

Like Stalin, General George C. Marshall, the U.S. Army chief of staff, was in favor of an invasion of western Europe. He wanted to invade France from Britain by crossing the English Channel. Marshall had put General Dwight D. Eisenhower in charge of planning. Eisenhower, who had served in World War I and in the Philippines from 1936 to 1939, believed the Allies would need until the spring of 1943 to prepare for an invasion of western Europe. General Marshall went along with Eisenhower's plans.

Churchill, however, had another plan. His idea was to strike at the weaker points of the Nazi empire—first in North Africa and then in southern Europe. He believed that this would sap Hitler's strength and would make it easier for the Allies to defeat him in western Europe later. Though believing that both plans had merit, Roosevelt agreed with Churchill in the end. The Allies decided to attack North Africa first, western Europe second, and the Pacific third. Despite this agreement, Stalin continued to insist that Britain and the United States should attack Germany from the west as soon as possible.

Why did Stalin want the Allies to invade western Europe before they fought Japan?

Section 1 Review

Check Understanding

1. **Define** (a) scorched-earth policy (b) siege (c) Big Three

2. **Describe** how the onset of winter affected Hitler's invasion of the Soviet Union.

3. **Identify** the strategy the Allies decided to use to defeat the Axis powers.

Critical Thinking

Inferring Why did Hitler break his pact with Stalin and invade the Soviet Union?

Write About History

Connecting Past and Present Write a paragraph about how today's leaders confront world problems, as the Big Three did in the 1940s.

BUILDING SKILLS

....

Analyzing Public Opinion Polls: Presidential Elections

Analyzing public opinion poll results helps you find out how people think and feel about various issues. Political parties often poll people by using surveys or questionnaires to find out how they feel about their candidates or issues. It is usually impossible to give the questionnaire to millions of people. So a poll surveys a sample—a smaller group—and uses these responses to represent what the entire group would likely have said.

Here's How

Follow these steps to analyze public opinion polls:

1. Try to find out if a large enough number of people participated in the poll. If the sample is too small, the results may not be valid.

2. Identify the type of information presented. Who would find this information important?

3. Analyze the results of the survey. What conclusions or generalizations can you make? Compare the results to other information you have about a candidate or issue.

Here's Why

Knowing how to analyze the results of a poll will help you know how people are feeling about particular national or local events and issues.

Practice the Skill

The chart below shows the results of a Gallup Poll, a frequently used public opinion poll. Study the chart and answer the questions.

1. What do the first four columns of the chart show? What does the last column show?

2. How well did the Gallup Poll predict the winner of each election? Based on these results, what conclusion would you draw about the accuracy of the results if you read a prediction for a future presidential election? Explain.

Apply the Skill

With several classmates, conduct a public opinion poll of students in your school about a political, school-related, or community issue. Create at least five questions, poll a number of students in different grades, and analyze the results. Create a chart or graph that shows the results of your poll and present your findings to the class.

Electoral and Popular Votes, 1936–1944

Year	Candidate / Political Party	Popular Votes	Predicted % Popular Vote Based on Gallup Poll	Actual % Popular Vote
1936	Franklin D. Roosevelt, Democrat	27,757,333	56%	60.8%
	Alfred M. Landon, Republican	16,684,231	44%	36%
1940	Franklin D. Roosevelt, Democrat	27,313,041	52%	54.7%
	Wendell L. Willkie, Republican	22,348,480	48%	44.8%
1944	Franklin D. Roosevelt, Democrat	25,612,610	51.5%	53.6%
	Thomas E. Dewey, Republican	22,017,617	48.5%	46%

Section 2

Striking Back

PREVIEW

Objectives

- To explain how the Allies defeated German troops in North Africa and Italy

- To describe the importance of the Battle of Stalingrad and the D-day invasion of France

- To identify the effects of the U.S. victory at Midway

Vocabulary

partisan
amphibious landing
cryptologist

As 1941 drew to a close, Hitler remarked, "Let's hope 1942 brings me as much good fortune as 1941." His wish was only partially fulfilled.

By the summer of 1942, territory under Germany's control reached from the northern boundary of Spain almost all the way to the Caspian Sea. However, this was as large as Germany's empire would get. The map on page 450 shows Allied and Axis areas of control from 1942 to 1945. By October 1942 the Allies began to win important battles that would lead eventually to victory.

◆ ALLIED VICTORIES IN NORTH AFRICA

The Allies began to carry out their strategy by first attacking the Germans in North Africa. In August 1942 the British sent Lieutenant General Bernard L. Montgomery to defeat Rommel, the Desert Fox.

On the night of October 23, 1942, Montgomery's troops attacked Rommel's forces at El Alamein, a village in Egypt. Rommel's army was outnumbered two to one, and the British Royal Air Force dominated the skies. By November 4, Rommel had lost the Battle of El Alamein and had retreated west.

On November 8, 1942, additional Allied troops invaded North Africa from Europe, beginning what was known as Operation Torch. Led by General

Dwight D. Eisenhower, more than 100,000 Allied soldiers landed in Morocco and Algeria and headed east toward Rommel. Surrounded by Allied soldiers, Rommel begged Hitler to let him withdraw. Hitler refused, calling Rommel's soldiers cowards.

Pushed from the east and the west, Rommel's army was crushed between Eisenhower's forces and Montgomery's Eighth Army. On May 12, 1943, the Germans surrendered in North Africa. The next day, Churchill received the following message:

> " All enemy resistance has ceased. We are masters of the North African shores. "

? How did the Allies defeat the Germans in North Africa?

◆ THE ALLIES INVADE ITALY

On the morning of July 10, 1943, about 180,000 Allied soldiers under General Eisenhower's command landed on the island of Sicily. British troops, led by Montgomery, and American forces, led by General

General Dwight D. Eisenhower served as Allied Supreme Commander in Europe from 1943 until the end of the war. ▶

George S. Patton, immediately began to pursue the German army stationed on the island. Montgomery and Patton had each been assigned a different route to the island. Patton was eager to reach the city of Messina before Montgomery. He believed Montgomery was hungry for glory and was willing to stop at nothing to get it. Montgomery's forces soon got bogged down, while Patton slashed his way across the island, covering twice as much ground as his rival. On August 17, after weeks of tough fighting on the rugged Sicilian landscape, Patton's soldiers dashed into Messina just minutes ahead of the British.

Hotly pursued by Patton, many Germans escaped onto mainland Italy. Many Italians who had turned against Hitler and Mussolini welcomed the Allies. By August, Sicily was in Allied hands.

By the time the Allies attacked Sicily, Mussolini's power was weakening. He had led his people into a war they had not wanted, and now Italy was being invaded. Other Fascist party leaders turned against Mussolini. On July 24 and 25, 1943, they voted to give power back to King Victor Emmanuel III. Mussolini was forced to resign and was put in jail, ending Fascist rule in Italy. Outside Italy, most Italian troops surrendered or even joined **partisan** forces fighting the Nazis. Partisans are people who strongly support a cause.

With Mussolini gone, the new Italian government surrendered to the Allies on September 8, 1943. However, the war in Italy was not yet over. Realizing that Italy's location was central to the war in Europe, Hitler had rushed to move over 400,000 German soldiers to occupy mainland Italy. Hitler also had maneuvered Mussolini's rescue and had him put in control of a new Fascist state in northern Italy.

The Allied forces began their pursuit of the Germans by slipping onto the mainland from

Americans in the Military During World War II	
Branch of Service	**Total Number of Americans**
Army	11,260,000
Navy	4,183,466
Marines	669,100
Coast Guard	241,093
Total	**16,353,659**

▲ Citizenship *This chart shows the number of Americans who served in World War II.* **Interpreting the Chart** *What percentage of the total number served in the army?*

Sicily in early September. As the Allies pushed north, they faced stiff German resistance. In an **amphibious landing**—when soldiers are brought as close as possible to shore by boat—one group of Allied forces went from Sicily to Anzio in January 1944. On June 4, 1944, the Allies entered Rome as the Germans withdrew farther north. In April 1945, Mussolini was caught and shot by fellow Italians as he tried to escape before an Allied advance. The fighting in Italy ended in May 1945 with the Allies declaring victory.

 How was the Allied invasion of Sicily aided by the attitude and actions of many Italians?

◆ THE BATTLE OF STALINGRAD

Four months before the Allies invaded Italy, the course of the German invasion of the Soviet Union began to change at the city of Stalingrad (Volgograd today). Early in the summer of 1942, German troops were still stalled at the gates of Leningrad and Moscow. Hitler turned his attention south and decided to attack Stalingrad. On August 22, 1942, the German army attacked. The Germans smashed through Soviet defenses, hoping to cut off oil shipments that passed through the city to Soviet forces in the north. Stalingrad's Communist leader called upon the city's citizens to hold their ground, saying,

" We shall never surrender the city to . . . the German invader. Let us barricade every street; transform every . . . house, into an impregnable [unconquerable] fortress. "

The Russians fiercely defended their homes, but by November 1942, the Germans controlled 90 percent of Stalingrad. The city was in ruins. On November 19, a huge Soviet army of one million men surrounded Stalingrad. The Soviets trapped the Germans inside the city, cutting off their supplies. The German commander begged Hitler to allow the army to surrender before it was destroyed. Hitler replied, "Surrender is forbidden."

The Germans held on until February 2, 1943, when they surrendered to the Soviets. Of the 230,000 German soldiers who had taken part in the attack, only 90,000 survived. The Soviets had lost 200,000 soldiers, but they had achieved their first great victory against the Germans. The Red Army went on the offensive, pushing the Germans steadily west.

 In what way was the Battle of Stalingrad a significant event in the war?

◆ **THE D-DAY INVASION**

While the Germans were being pushed back in the Soviet Union, Allied plans for the invasion of France, called Operation Overlord, were going forward. Led by General Eisenhower, troops would cross the English Channel from Great Britain and attack the Germans on the coast of Normandy, a region in northwestern France. To carry out Operation Overlord, the Allies needed a large number of landing vessels, thousands of troops, and many supplies, such as ammunition, food, medicine, and trucks. Throughout 1943 the Allies secretly built up a huge invasion force. Secrecy was vital to the success of the operation.

By May 1944 the Allied invasion force was nearly ready to attack. There were 11,000 aircraft, 600 warships, 4,000 invasion craft, 1,500 tanks, and more than 175,000 soldiers involved in an effort that would be the greatest land-and-sea attack in history. The day of the invasion, set for June 6, 1944, was code-named D-day.

General Rommel was in charge of defending Germany's position along the French coast. Rommel believed Germany's only chance to stop the Allies was where they were vulnerable. This would be on the beaches, when they were struggling to come ashore.

At dawn on D-day, the invasion of Normandy began. Once across the Channel, Allied troops fought their way ashore along a 60-mile stretch of beach. While they were landing, British and American battleships bombarded Hitler's army. Allied bombers released hundreds of tons of explosives into German positions.

◀ *More than 175,000 Allied soldiers were involved in D-day—the largest land-and-sea attack in history.*

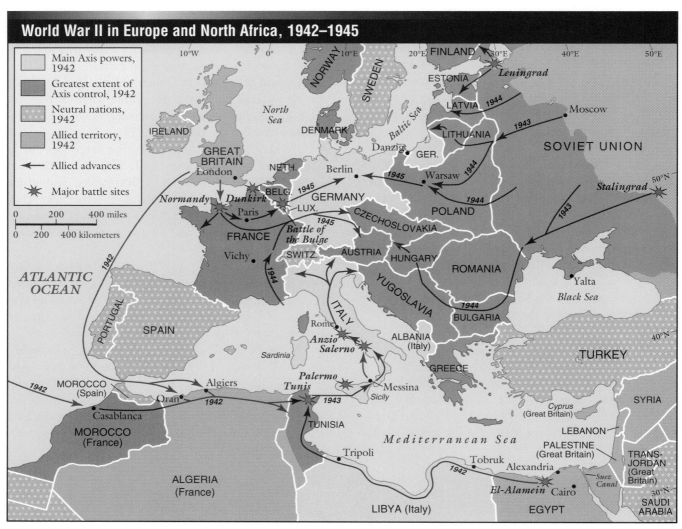

World War II in Europe and North Africa, 1942–1945

Legend:
- Main Axis powers, 1942
- Greatest extent of Axis control, 1942
- Neutral nations, 1942
- Allied territory, 1942
- ← Allied advances
- ✴ Major battle sites

▲ **Geography** *In 1942, many countries in Europe were controlled by either Axis or Allied powers.* **Interpreting the Map** *According to the map, which European countries remained neutral during World War II?*

The Americans landed on two beaches, which were code-named Omaha and Utah. Omaha was the most difficult Allied landing because the beach was surrounded on three sides by 200-foot cliffs and hills. From there, the enemy could fire down on the troops who were landing. One American soldier described what the landing was like:

> The ramp lowered and we waded ashore to the rattle of machine guns and bursting of shells. Bullets cracked over our heads and we flung ourselves on the rocky beach. . . . No one was moving forward.

Over 6,600 U.S. soldiers were killed, wounded, or lost during the first 24 hours of the invasion. Yet because of their huge numbers and their determination, U.S. troops finally moved off the beach to the land beyond.

By July, the Allies had landed an additional one million soldiers in France. After weeks of intense fighting, American tanks broke through the German line on July 25, and an army led by General Patton quickly moved inland. In mid-August, other Allied troops invaded southern France from Italy and advanced north. Meanwhile, in Paris, French resistance forces fought strenuously against the Germans. On August 25, 1944, the Allies, led by French troops, entered Paris in triumph. The Allies continued the fight to liberate the rest of France, and by the autumn of 1944, they had regained control of most of western Europe. Their next goal in Europe would be to conquer Germany.

? How were the Allies able to take France back from the Germans?

◆ THE WAR IN THE PACIFIC

As Germany faced losses in Africa and Europe, the Allied war effort in the Pacific was making steady progress. The U.S. Pacific Fleet was being rebuilt, and thousands of troops were being moved to the Pacific to take part in the next phase of the war.

Doolittle's Raid

Soon after the bombing of Pearl Harbor, U.S. colonel James Doolittle came up with a plan to bomb Tokyo in a daring raid. Although a bombing raid would be very difficult and dangerous, Colonel Doolittle's commanders approved of the idea because they hoped its success would give American troops a needed morale boost.

After several months of preparation, Doolittle led his group of 16 B-25 bombers from a U.S. aircraft carrier in the Pacific more than 600 miles east of Japan. They took off on April 18, 1942. The B-25s roared over Tokyo and, in about 30 seconds, dropped bombs that struck plane factories, railroad yards, and a naval base. On their way back, the squadron was forced to bail out over Japanese-controlled territory. Eventually, 71 of 80 crew members, including Doolittle, found their way back to base.

Doolittle's raid shocked the Japanese. No enemy had ever attacked their homeland. Until 1942 the Japanese had won many victories and had been confident of their success. Now, they began to lose that edge.

Turning Point at Midway

After recovering from the shock of the bombings, the Japanese were determined to push the United States from the Pacific. Japanese Admiral Isaroku Yamamoto decided to attack the Midway Islands, just west of the Hawaiian Islands. The Midway Islands and the Hawaiian Islands were U.S. territories.

The United States, however, managed to prevent a Japanese victory. U.S. **cryptologists,** experts in making and deciphering codes, broke the Japanese military code and found out about Yamamoto's plans.

For the Battle of Midway (June 3–6, 1942), the Japanese fleet included 150 warships and more than 270

◀ The pilots and crew in this photograph prepared fighter planes aboard the U.S.S. Enterprise prior to the Battle of Midway. Only four of the planes aboard this aircraft carrier returned after the battle.

▲ *The long struggle at Guadalcanal resulted in the United States' first successful land battle against Japan.*

fighter planes and bombers. Admiral Chester W. Nimitz, commander of the U.S. Pacific fleet, had only about half as many ships as Yamamoto did. However, Nimitz decided to use planes that took off from aircraft carriers to do most of the fighting. Nimitz, by relying more on aircraft carriers than battleships, was employing a new strategy in naval warfare.

At daybreak on June 4, Japanese bombers blasted Midway and then had to refuel. American planes suddenly swooped down and destroyed 275 airplanes and 4 aircraft carriers. Admiral Yamamoto was forced to order his crippled fleet back to Japan.

The defeat was another blow to Japan. The advantage that the Japanese had gained at Pearl Harbor had been wiped out by their losses at Midway.

On the Offensive at Guadalcanal

After the victory at Midway, the United States attacked the Japanese-held island of Guadalcanal. The United States had discovered that Japan was building an airfield there that would enable it to attack U.S. territories as far east as Samoa.

To prevent such attacks, 6,000 U.S. Marines landed on Guadalcanal at dawn on August 7, 1942. The Japanese waged a bitter struggle for the island that lasted until February 1943, when they finally abandoned Guadalcanal. They were forced to give

up their plan to fly air raids into the heart of Allied territory in the South Pacific.

Island Hopping

To achieve victory in the Pacific, the Allies had to win control of Japanese-held islands in the Pacific Ocean. It would be impossible to control all of them. Therefore, General MacArthur and Admiral Nimitz developed a strategy called "island hopping," which meant capturing some islands and bypassing others. An island, once taken, could be used as a base to attack other islands. The islands skipped over could be cut off from supplies, making them useless to the Japanese war effort. As the Allies island-hopped across the Pacific, they would move closer to Japan.

 Why was the Battle of Midway a turning point in the war?

Section 2 Review

Check Understanding

1. **Define** (a) partisan (b) amphibious landing (c) cryptologist

2. **Describe** how Montgomery and Eisenhower defeated the German army in North Africa.

3. **Explain** why German troops entered Italy after the Allied invasion in 1943.

Critical Thinking

◆**Connecting Past and Present** You have read about leaders who had to make difficult decisions during wartime. What difficult decisions do leaders of the United States have to make today?

Write About History

Shortly after the Allies invaded Italy in 1943, Fascist party leaders turned against Mussolini saying, "You believe you have the devotion of the people, but you lost it the day you tied Italy to Germany." Based on that quote, write a paragraph explaining Mussolini's downfall.

CONNECTING HISTORY
&Language

THE NAVAJO CODE TALKERS

The Japanese soldiers hunched over the radio set looked at each other in bewilderment. They were listening to the Americans transmit secret radio messages in the Pacific. However, the code was not like anything the Japanese had ever heard before.

The Japanese were listening to a special code based on the Navajo language and spoken by Navajo people. During the war, the U.S. Marines recruited a team of about 400 Navajos as "code talkers." The code these Native Americans created was never broken.

The Navajo language worked well as a code for several reasons. First, the language is complex and is extremely difficult for those who have not learned it as children. Every syllable in the language means something and must be pronounced with exactly the correct tone of voice: low, high, rising, or falling. Even small changes in the tone of voice can change the meaning of a word. For example, the words for *medicine* and *mouth* have the same pronunciation but are said in different tones. Second, there are different ways to say the same thing. For example, Navajos have several words that mean *dropped*. One word means "to drop something that is round," while another word means "to drop a stick."

During the war, the Navajos developed the special code by using words in their language to stand for military terms. For example, the code word for bombs was *a-ye-shi*, which means "eggs." The code for December was *yas-nil-tes*, or "crusted snow." The code talkers also developed an alphabet code by assigning each English letter a word in English that began with that letter. Then they translated the word into Navajo. For the letter *A*, they used the word *ant*, which in Navajo is *wol-la-chee*. Recognition for the code talkers came many years after the war ended. Their code was considered so valuable that it was not talked about until 1969.

Today code systems are based on highly complex software programs. But even computers would have had a tough time figuring out the "code talking" that the Navajos used.

Making the Language Connection

1. Why was the Navajo language so well suited to creating a secret code?

2. How did the Navajos create the code?

3. Why was finding an unbreakable code so important to the war effort?

◈ Connecting Past and Present

In 1982, the United States declared August 14 National Code Talkers Day. Imagine you are in charge of celebrating the contributions of the Navajo code talkers. Write a short speech explaining why they should be remembered today.

Navajos served as code talkers during World War II. ▼

Section 3

Winning the War

PREVIEW

Objectives

- To describe the end-of-war agreements made by the Big Three

- To analyze the Nazi murder campaign against Jews and other people in Europe

- To explain how the United States forced a Japanese surrender

- To identify the economic and social effects of World War II

Vocabulary

Holocaust	kamikaze
genocide	Manhattan Project

By the fall of 1944, the Allied powers had gained control of North Africa and had driven Germany out of France, the Soviet Union, and much of Italy. Japan was fighting for survival in the Pacific.

To force Hitler to surrender, the Allies stepped up the bombing of Germany in 1944. Aiming to cripple Germany's war industries, the Americans and British bombed roads, railroads, aircraft factories, army bases, and airfields. In more than 60 German cities, bombs killed at least 300,000 civilians, wounded 780,000, destroyed more than 3.6 million houses, and left 7.5 million people homeless.

◆ WARTIME CONFERENCES

Going ahead with the bombing of Germany's sources of supplies was a decision that Allied leaders made at their wartime conferences. At these meetings, the Allies not only worked out plans for war but also drafted programs for peace.

In Cairo, Egypt, in late November 1943, Roosevelt and Churchill met with Chinese leader Chiang Kai-shek. The leaders agreed that after the war, the Allies would return lands to China that the Japanese had taken since 1914. This would make Chiang Kai-shek stronger and tie China closer to the United States. It was hoped that the partnership of the two countries in the Far East would help make the area more stable after the war.

After Cairo, Roosevelt and Churchill traveled directly to Tehran—a city in Iran—and met with Stalin. The three leaders began to discuss what to do with Germany after the war and how to form an international organization for peace. They also talked about the future of Poland. Churchill and Roosevelt wanted a strong, democratic Poland. Stalin, however, did not say much. His armies were again on the offensive. He wanted the Soviet Union to maintain control of the region and had no intention of allowing Poland to become strong again.

The Big Three met again, this time at Yalta, in the Soviet Union, in February 1945. At the Yalta Conference, they agreed that after the war the United States, Britain, the Soviet Union, and France would divide Germany and its capital, Berlin, into four zones. Each of the four powers would occupy and administer one zone. In addition, they agreed that countries freed from Nazi rule would have democratic elections. The Allies also pledged to form a world peace organization called the United Nations.

Stalin pledged to declare war against Japan and to support the Chinese Nationalist government of Chiang Kai-shek, not the Chinese Communists. In return, the Soviets would receive certain Japanese territories and would keep Outer Mongolia, which they had already taken from China.

At Yalta, Churchill (left), Roosevelt (center), and Stalin (right) made plans for the end of the war. ▼

 Soviet troops waved their flag over the streets of Berlin to celebrate its fall to Soviet forces in May 1945.

Roosevelt agreed to Stalin's demands for territory because he believed the United States needed Soviet help to win the war against Japan. Also, he did not want the Soviets to make a separate peace with Germany. If Germany was at peace in the east, Hitler could throw all his forces against the Allies, who were closing in on Germany in the west. Roosevelt's agreement at Yalta, however, became a source of controversy in later years. Stalin took as much land as he could from the Germans in the final year of the war and did not give it up. As a result, decades would pass before eastern Europe would truly be free.

? Why did Roosevelt agree to Stalin's demands for territory at Yalta?

◆ AN END TO THE WAR IN EUROPE

While the Big Three were meeting at Yalta, the war in Europe was drawing to a close. The Americans and the British were pushing toward Germany from the west, and the Soviets were closing in from the east. Still, Hitler refused to give up.

The Battle of the Bulge

Although Germany's defeat seemed certain, Hitler believed he could still turn the war around. At a time when his armies were retreating, he decided to stage a huge counterattack in the west. It would come to be known as the Battle of the Bulge and was Hitler's last push for world power.

On December 16, 1944, the German counterattack began. Hitler's tanks pushed forward against American defenses along a 70-mile front in the Ardennes Forest in Belgium. The line "bulged," giving the Battle of the Bulge its name, but the Americans pushed the Germans back and won. With this defeat, Hitler's offensive plans were dashed. From this point on, the Germans fought a defensive war to save their homeland.

The Last Days in Berlin

After the Battle of the Bulge, the Allies crossed into Germany and moved toward Berlin. Some nine million Allied soldiers were closing in on Berlin from all directions. General Eisenhower ordered his troops to slow up their offensive. As a result, the Soviets were the first to get to Berlin. From there, they continued their advance west. The Soviet troops met up with American soldiers at the Elbe River, about 100 miles west of Berlin.

As the Soviets were attacking the German capital of Berlin, Hitler committed suicide. A week later, on May 7, 1945, Germany surrendered unconditionally. The war in Europe was over.

Perhaps the best summary of how Americans felt about the victory appeared in the simple words of a much-loved war reporter, Ernie Pyle. Pyle had followed the war from 1940, trudging through Sicily and Italy and across the beaches of France and the Pacific with American foot soldiers. His reports, published widely in the United States, told the story of the war from the soldier's point of view. As Germany neared collapse, Pyle began writing a column on the subject, in which he said:

> **And so it is over. The catastrophe on one side of the world has run its course. The day that . . . so long seemed would never come has come at last. . . . In the joyousness of high spirits it is easy for us to forget the dead. . . . Dead men by mass production—in one country after another—month after month and year after year. Dead men in winter and dead men in summer. . . .**

Pyle was killed by a sniper's bullet in the Pacific before he could finish the column. His death was one more reminder that despite the Allied victory in Europe, the world's suffering was far from over.

The Holocaust

As Allied troops stormed Europe, they began to uncover the horror of what has become known as the **Holocaust.** The Holocaust was Hitler's policy of killing Jews. Six million Jews were killed by the Nazis. Almost six million other people considered "unfit to live" were also murdered by the Nazis. They included Poles, Slavs, Gypsies, physically and mentally disabled people, and political prisoners.

In his rise to power, Hitler had loudly proclaimed his hatred of Jews. Soon, the Nazis began persecuting, or oppressing, the Jews. A wave of anti-Semitism swept Germany. Jewish businesses were shut, and Jewish homes were taken over by the Nazis. Before long, the Nazis arrived at what was called the "final solution" to

▲ These slave laborers at the concentration camp at Buchenwald, Germany, were photographed as they were about to be freed by American forces in April 1945.

the "Jewish problem." The final solution was **genocide,** or the deliberate murder of an entire people.

As soon as Hitler invaded Poland in 1939, the Nazis began killing Jews. Those who were not murdered were taken to concentration camps, mostly in Germany and Poland, where they worked as slaves. Many died from starvation or disease. Others were mercilessly beaten. Hitler also had special death camps built. These were equipped with gas chambers. The Nazis killed up to 60,000 people a day in the gas chambers and used huge crematoriums, or ovens, to burn the bodies.

After Germany's defeat, Allied soldiers arrived at the concentration camps to liberate and help the survivors. Allied governments, including that of the United States, had heard reports of the horrors of the concentration camps for several years. The reports had seemed so fantastic that most people did not believe them, although attempts were made by a number of organizations to publicize the situation.

Even the toughest soldiers were stunned by what they saw. General George S. Patton wept and grew sick when he walked through the concentration camp at Ohrdruf in mid-April. The next day he learned that the people of the nearby village claimed to know nothing of what had been going on in the concentration camp. Patton ordered them brought to the site, at gunpoint if necessary, so that they could see the conditions for themselves. Many of them were sickened by the horror. A British medical officer described the scene he found at one camp, Belsen:

> **No photograph, no description could bring home the horrors I saw. There were 56,000 people still alive in the camp. There were anywhere from 600 to 1,000 people living in accommodations which could take barely 100. The huts overflowed with inmates in every state of [starvation] and disease. . . . There were dead everywhere, some in the same bunks as the living. Lying in the compounds, in uncovered mass graves, in trenches, in the gutters, by the side of the barbed wire surrounding the camp and by the huts, were some 10,000 more.**

The Allies wanted to make sure terrible crimes such as these never happened again. In November 1945, they began a war crimes trial at Nuremberg, Germany. In the first of the Nuremberg Trials, 24 Nazi leaders were tried, and 12 were sentenced to death.

The Death of the President

Early in April 1945, shortly before Germany's surrender, President Roosevelt left for a short vacation in Warm Springs, Georgia. On April 12, he died suddenly. Newspapers, radios, and even bullhorns on American ships announced the death of the President all over the world. Roosevelt had led the nation for 12 years, through the Great Depression and World War II. Americans everywhere mourned his passing. Many stood for hours waiting to pay their respects as his funeral train carried him back to Washington, D.C. It would be the new President, Harry Truman, who would witness Germany's final surrender.

? What terrible events occurred as a result of Nazi ideas?

◆ WAR ENDS IN THE PACIFIC

After Germany surrendered, the Allies concentrated on defeating Japan. Following the victory at Guadalcanal, the United States and its allies went on the offensive.

The United States on the Offensive

By October 1944, American troops led by General MacArthur had reached the Philippines. Wading ashore Leyte Island (lāt´-ē), he reminded the world of his pledge to return. "People of the Philippines: I have returned! . . . Rally to me!" The Filipinos joined MacArthur in the fight against the Japanese. By February 1945 the Allies had retaken the Philippines.

Japan's last two island outposts fell to the Allies in the first six months of 1945. In March the U.S. Marines, with terrible losses, took tiny Iwo Jima (ē-wō jē´-mə). In June the Allies took Okinawa (ō´-kĭ-nä´-wə). The map on page 458 shows the major battles in the war in the Pacific.

At Okinawa the desperate Japanese used **kamikazes** as a special tactic, or method. Kamikazes were suicide pilots who crashed their airplanes, loaded with bombs, into enemy ships. Although the kamikazes caused a great deal of damage, they could not win the war for Japan.

Dropping the Atomic Bomb

Throughout the war, a team of Allied scientists had been working on an all-out research and design effort known as the **Manhattan Project,** aimed at building an atomic bomb. On July 16, 1945, the first atomic bomb was tested in the desert near Alamagordo, New Mexico. One scientist said, "It was the nearest thing to doomsday that one could imagine." Concerned about

In this famous photograph, United States Marines raise the American flag on February 23, 1945, at Mount Suribachi, Iwo Jima. ▼

the destructive potential of the bomb, several scientists wrote to Secretary of War Henry Stimson expressing their reservations about using it.

After Okinawa was taken in June 1945, the Japanese refused to surrender. As a result of this refusal, and after careful consideration, President Truman gave the order to drop the atomic bomb on Japan. Truman believed this action would force the Japanese to surrender and bring an end to the war more quickly. Some people believed that the power of the bomb should have been demonstrated to the Japanese on an abandoned island before it was dropped on cities. Truman later argued that the bomb would save up to one million American lives that could be lost if the Allies were forced to invade Japan.

On the morning of August 6, 1945, the United States dropped an atomic bomb on Hiroshima, a city of 250,000 residents. With a force equal to 20,000 tons of dynamite, the bomb destroyed 60 percent of the city and killed and injured about 150,000 people. Some were killed instantly, and some died later from radiation poisoning. Three days later, on August 9, the United States dropped a second bomb on Nagasaki, killing and maiming up to 70,000 people. At last, the

Japanese emperor, Hirohito, agreed to make peace. On Sunday, September 2, 1945, the Japanese officially surrendered to General MacArthur aboard the U.S.S. *Missouri* in Tokyo Bay. After great suffering and much destruction, World War II was over at last.

 What were President Truman's reasons for using the atomic bomb?

◆ **THE COSTS OF THE WAR**

The economic and social costs of World War II were great. Europe and Japan were in ruins. Cities had been bombed into rubble. Railroads, bridges, and roads had been destroyed. About 50 million people were homeless. With so many factories destroyed, millions were jobless. Schools lay in ruins. Because of the fighting, many fields had not been planted, so food was scarce.

In the months after the war's end, many died of starvation and disease. National governments could not help much because they had used up their resources to fight the war. Some governments, like those in Italy and Germany, had collapsed.

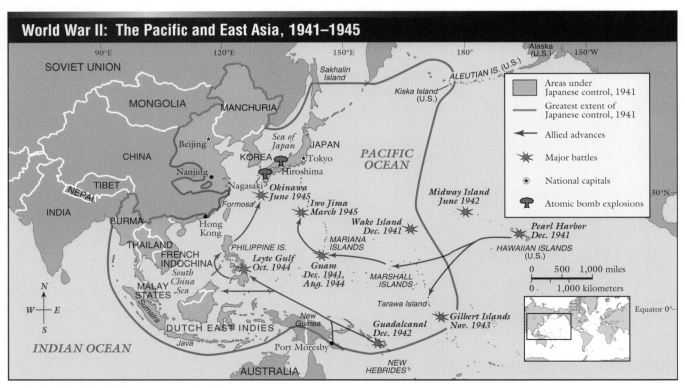

▲ **Geography** *The Allies made significant advances into areas of Japanese control between 1942 and the end of the war in 1945.* **Interpreting the Map** *About how many miles is Guam from the Marshall Islands?*

◀ Waving flags and signs, crowds of Americans gathered in Times Square, in New York City, to celebrate the surrender of German forces in 1945.

The human costs of World War II were enormous. More than 60 million people around the world had died. Although 300,000 Americans died in World War II, this was far fewer than the number of casualties in other countries. For example, there were nearly 18,000,000 Soviet military and civilian casualties.

The United States also did not experience the billions of dollars in property damage that European countries did. No battles were fought on American soil, so cities, factories, and fields remained intact.

Although the United States poured money into the Allied war effort, the country's economy came out of World War II stronger, not weaker. With factories geared up for war, the unemployment problem that had persisted during the 1930s disappeared. In fact, it was the war that had finally pulled the United States out of the Great Depression, as more and more people were needed to fill jobs.

The war also changed the position of the United States in the world. Before the war, Europe had been the center of international political power. However, as its economy suffered, Europe's power declined as well. As a result, the United States emerged as the world's strongest nation.

Why were the effects of the war less severe in the United States than in Europe?

Section 3 Review

Check Understanding

1. **Define** (a) Holocaust (b) genocide (c) kamikaze (d) Manhattan Project

2. **Explain** how the Allies planned to divide Germany after the war.

3. **Explain** why the conditions in the concentration camps were hard for people to believe.

4. **Describe** General MacArthur's strategies in the Pacific.

Critical Thinking

Evaluating How did World War II change the position of the United States in the world?

Write About History

◆**Connecting Past and Present** Write an essay about ways to prevent an event such as the Holocaust from happening again.

Chapter 22
Review

CHAPTER SUMMARY

Section 1
After the bombing of Pearl Harbor, the United States declared war on Japan and joined the Allies in the fight against the Axis. Early in the war, Hitler won victories in North Africa and staged an invasion of the Soviet Union. The Allies attacked first in North Africa, where the Axis powers were weakest, and then hit western Europe and the Pacific.

Section 2
The Allies began turning the tide of the war in 1943. By that May, Germany surrendered in North Africa. Next, the Allies invaded Italy. At the same time, the Soviet army began an offensive to drive the Germans west. On D-day, the Allies invaded the French coast and, despite huge losses, broke through German lines and liberated France. In the Pacific the Allies went on the offensive after victory at the Battle of Midway.

Section 3
In preparation for Axis surrender, Allied leaders met at Yalta in 1945 to plan how to divide Germany when the war was over. Shortly after Yalta, Roosevelt suddenly died, and Harry Truman became President. Finally, on May 7, 1945, Germany surrendered. As the Allies liberated eastern Europe and conquered Germany, they were shocked by the horrors of the Holocaust. Truman made the difficult decision to use the atomic bomb against the Japanese in the cities of Hiroshima and Nagasaki to end the war. Japan officially surrendered on September 2. The war was over, but at a high cost. The United States emerged as a powerful political and economic leader.

Connecting ◆◆ Past and Present

Many men, women, and children suffered during World War II. Do you think people today are affected any differently by war? Explain.

Using Vocabulary

From the list below, select the term that best completes each sentence.

siege	scorched-earth policy
Big Three	amphibious landing
Manhattan Project	cryptologist
genocide	kamikaze

1. The leaders of the Allied nations were known as the _____ .
2. When soldiers are brought close to shore by boat, it is called an _____ .
3. The murder of an entire people is called _____ .
4. A _____ is a blockade of a city by an army.
5. A _____ is an expert in making and deciphering codes.
6. To carry out a _____ , a country's army destroys its own crops.
7. A Japanese pilot who deliberately crashed his plane was called a _____ .
8. The building of the atomic bomb was the outcome of the _____ .

Check Understanding

1. **Explain** why Hitler was winning the war in 1941.
2. **Summarize** the strategy the Allies developed in 1941 for winning the war.
3. **Describe** how the Allies defeated Germany in North Africa.
4. **Explain** the importance of the Battle of Stalingrad.
5. **Describe** the significance of the D-day invasion of France.
6. **Explain** why the Battle of Midway was a turning point for the Allies.
7. **Summarize** the talks held at Cairo, Tehran, and Yalta.
8. **List** four problems the people of Europe faced after World War II.

9. **Explain** the major factors that led to the Allies' victory in World War II.

10. **Describe** how the war changed the position of the United States in the world.

Critical Thinking

1. **Applying Information** If you were to choose a point where the war changed in favor of the Allies, when would that point be? Explain.

2. **Comparing** How were the war strategies of Stalin and Marshall similar?

3. **Making Inferences** What might have happened had the United States not entered World War II?

4. **Evaluating Information** Some people believe that war is never justified. Was the United States justified in entering World War II? Explain your answer.

◆ **Connecting Past and Present** How have the risks associated with the use of nuclear weapons changed since World War II?

Interpreting the Timeline

Use the timeline on pages 440–441 to answer these questions.

1. During which of Roosevelt's terms of office did the Battle of Midway take place?

2. Which U.S. events in 1941 and 1945 are related?

3. According to the timeline, which cities were severely affected by the war?

Writing to Describe

Suppose you lived in London during World War II. **Write** a letter to your cousin in the United States now that the war is over, describing what you see around you and how you feel about it. Use concrete details that help your cousin understand what the war did to your country and your city.

Putting Skills to Work

ANALYZING PUBLIC OPINION POLLS

Below are the results of a public opinion poll conducted in 1942. Study the data and then answer the questions that follow.

Should all men and women over 18 who are not already in military service be required to register with the government for some kind of civilian defense or war work?

Yes	80%
No	14%
No opinion	9%

After finding out what each person can do, should the government have the power to tell each citizen what part to play in the war effort and require him or her to do it?

Yes	58%
No	33%
No opinion	9%

1. What percentage of people believed that everyone should be required to register for war work?

2. How did people feel about the government having the power to assign citizens to specific jobs during the war?

3. Based on this poll, what advice would you have given President Roosevelt about having men and women register for the service?

Portfolio Project

PATRIOTIC MUSIC

One way Americans expressed their support of the troops fighting in World War II was through patriotic songs. Work with two or three classmates to research popular songs of the World War II era. Find at least two or three examples and prepare an oral report. Explain what you think the music, the lyrics, and the mood of the songs evoke. If possible, play the original recordings for the class.

Chapter 23
Americans on the Home Front 1941–1945

CHAPTER PREVIEW

Section 1 **Mobilizing for War**

As the country prepared for war, many Americans went to work in factories producing war supplies in record numbers, helping to bring an end to the Great Depression.

Section 2 **Women in the War**

During World War II, millions of women joined the work force to help industry meet wartime demands. Thousands of women joined the armed forces.

Section 3 **The War Affects American Society**

Despite discrimination, African Americans, Latinos, Native Americans, and Japanese Americans served at home and overseas during World War II.

Women's auxiliary corps

U.S. Events	**1940** ✪ Franklin Roosevelt reelected for a third term. Carson McCuller's novel *The Heart Is a Lonely Hunter* is published.	**1941** Franklin Roosevelt orders freezing of Axis assets in the U.S. Draftee's length of service is extended to 18 months. Executive order bars discrimination in defense industries.	**1942** Congress authorizes creation of women's armed forces auxiliary units. Japanese Americans sent to internment camps. Rationing of scarce goods starts.

1939

Winston Churchill

World Events	**1940** Winston Churchill becomes British prime minister.	**1941** Churchill and Roosevelt pledge to end Nazi tyranny.	**1942** British industries produce nearly 300 tons of ships, planes, and tanks. Germans attack Stalingrad.

Portfolio Project

AN EYEWITNESS ACCOUNT

The United States endured social and economic upheaval during the war years. The changes affected nearly every American. As you read this chapter, pay close attention to the ways in which various groups of people were treated during the war years. At the end of the chapter, you will create an "eyewitness" account that narrates one person's experience on the home front.

▲ While many Americans were fighting overseas, others supported the war effort at home. ◆▶ **Connecting Past and Present** *What symbol shows these workers' support for the United States? How do people show their support for the country and the armed services today?*

Zoot suit trial

Ration coupon

1943
Zoot suit riots take place in Los Angeles.
Over 26 million tons of iron and steel is collected in scrap drives.

1944
⊙ Franklin Roosevelt reelected for a fourth term.

1945
⊙ Harry Truman becomes President.
Most rationing is ended.
Senate votes to ratify United Nations Charter.

▲1946▼

1943
Allies agree on need for unconditional surrender of Germany.
Chiang Kai-shek becomes president of Nationalist Chinese Republic.

1944
Group of German officers tries to assassinate Hitler.

1945
Churchill, Stalin, and Roosevelt meet at Yalta.
George Orwell's *Animal Farm* is published.

Chiang Kai-shek

Yalta Conference

Section 1

Mobilizing for War

PREVIEW

Objectives

- To describe the results of Roosevelt's call for mobilization

- To examine how the government controlled the economy and raised money to fight the war

- To explain how wartime industrial output ended the Great Depression

- To analyze how the government responded to labor problems in wartime

Vocabulary

rationing
wildcat strike

To defeat the powerful dictatorships in Germany, Japan, and Italy, the Allies needed a large supply of weapons. In 1940, President Franklin Roosevelt promised that the United States would become "the arsenal of democracy." Besides helping the Allies, developing and making weapons had an important impact on the American economy. As the United States began to produce goods for the war, industry revived, factories hired workers, and the nation found its way out of the Great Depression. The graph at right shows defense spending from 1940 through 1945.

◆ WINNING THE WAR IN THE FACTORIES

Roosevelt began strengthening the country as soon as he saw the war coming. In 1940, the United States was producing about 2,000 airplanes a year. Roosevelt called for an increase to 50,000 airplanes a year—a production level that most people believed was not possible. A Nazi leader scoffed at Roosevelt's plans to increase production. "Americans can't build planes," he said, "only electric iceboxes and razor blades."

By 1944, the United States was producing more than 90,000 planes a year and equally staggering quantities of other war goods. By the end of the war, the United States had produced more than 70,000 ships, 20 million guns, 40 billion bullets, 5 million tons of bombs, and about 2.4 million army trucks. This was more war equipment than had been produced by all the Axis nations combined.

When a nation mobilizes, it turns all its energy and resources to prepare to meet a challenge. In 1942, under government leadership even nonmilitary factories began making weapons and war goods. Nearly all the nation's major industries and businesses changed their products to goods that would help win the war.

 How did the United States mobilize for war?

◆ THE GOVERNMENT TAKES CONTROL OF THE ECONOMY

Guiding this production effort was a new government bureau, the War Production Board (WPB). This organization was headed by successful department store executive Donald M. Nelson.

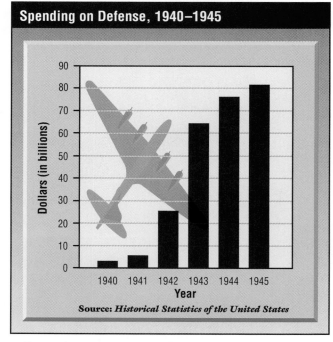

Spending on Defense, 1940–1945

Source: *Historical Statistics of the United States*

▲ Economics *This graph shows how U.S. defense spending increased dramatically between 1940 and 1945.* **Interpreting the Graph** *About how much more was spent in 1943 than in 1942?*

Through the WPB, the Office of Price Administration (OPA), and a third agency, the Office of War Mobilization (OWM), the government controlled all rents, food prices, and wages. During the war, many consumer products became scarce because factories no longer made them or because the army and navy needed them for the war effort. When products become scarce and people are willing to pay more for them, prices may increase. By freezing prices, the OPA made sure that inflation, or steady price increases, did not occur.

Another kind of U.S. government control was **rationing.** Under this system, each family could buy only a limited amount of certain foods and other vital goods. The most common system used the ration book. The OPA organized local rationing boards that gave each family in their area one of these books. In each book there were six months' worth of coupons. The coupons were labeled with the names of various rationed products. Each product was assigned a point value depending on how scarce it was. Meat, for example, had a higher point value than sugar.

The system was fairly simple. For example, when purchasing sugar, consumers had to tear the coupons labeled "sugar" out of their ration books and turn them over to the grocer. To buy meat, they would give the grocer coupons marked "meat." People could buy more sugar or meat one month and less the next, but each month their points for all rationed items could not add up to more than 48. The ration coupons did not replace money. The coupons had to be handed over along with money, or a purchase could not be made. When six months' worth of coupons for a product were used up, the consumer could purchase no more until the next ration book was issued.

Some of the other goods that were rationed were butter, coffee, cheese, canned goods, and shoes. Gasoline was usually in good supply, but it, too, was rationed. The use of cars was discouraged to preserve tires, which were made of rubber. Rubber was needed for the war effort.

Some consumer items were just not available. As material for dresses was used to make uniforms, skirts grew shorter and narrower to conserve fabric. Zippers in clothing became scarce because metal was used to manufacture guns.

Dealing with ration coupons was inconvenient, especially for store owners. They were required to stick the coupons onto cards and turn the cards over to the OPA to get more goods. In general, however, rationing did not cause severe hardship for Americans at home.

◄ During the war years, Americans used ration coupons, kept in ration books, to pay for such products as groceries and gasoline.

The system simply ensured that there was enough for everyone—especially for the soldiers on the battlefield.

Raising Money

Food and weapons are both necessary to fight a war, and they have to be paid for. Roosevelt insisted that as far as possible, the United States pay for the war as it was being fought, rather than borrow money that would have to be paid back later.

One way the government raised money was through taxes. More Americans paid taxes during World War II than ever before, although the amount varied depending on a person's or company's earnings.

Taxes, however, paid for only about 40 percent of the $321 billion cost of the war. The government borrowed the rest from banks and private investors. Citizens helped by buying U.S. war bonds. The sale of bonds provided the government with the money it needed to finance the war. After the war, the government repaid the money with interest. For example, a citizen who bought a bond for $18.75 received $25

This poster implied that the purchase of war bonds, or victory bonds, protected American women and children from Nazi aggression. ▼

KEEP THESE HANDS OFF!

BUY the New VICTORY BONDS

when the bond was turned in after a certain period of time. In spite of Roosevelt's good intentions and careful planning, the government still had to borrow huge sums of money during World War II. By the end of the war, the United States owed $250 billion, about five times its debt in 1940.

An End to the Great Depression

As the nation mobilized to produce weapons and war supplies, the economy boomed. In 1939, almost nine million American men had been unemployed. By 1944, nearly 19 million new jobs had been created. The Great Depression had finally ended.

Factory workers were not the only ones who benefited from mobilization. The government called on farmers to produce more food than ever. It was not just to feed American soldiers and citizens; it was to feed the Allied nations as well. For example, nearly 30 percent of Britain's food came from American farms. A social worker, who just a few years before had helped desperate farmers during the Great Depression, marveled at the way some of them had recovered and prospered:

> Farmers in South Dakota that I [gave] four dollars a week [during the Depression] to feed their families, when I came home [after the war], were worth a quarter of a million dollars. . . .

What were the ways in which government controlled the economy during World War II?

◆ LABOR ISSUES

In a strong economy, workers often feel bold enough to strike for better conditions. However, after Pearl Harbor was bombed, labor leaders promised that while the war lasted, they would not strike.

At first, workers kept their pledge. Hours lost due to strikes fell from 23 million in 1941 to 4 million in 1942. But by 1943, some labor leaders and workers began to resent the government's strict wage controls. Despite outraged public opinion and fierce threats from the government, workers in some industries resumed the use of strikes. In all, there were about 14,000 strikes involving about 6,770,000 workers during the war.

◄ *The shipyard workers in this photograph supported the war effort by working in defense industries on the home front.*

Most of these strikes were **wildcat strikes,** in which workers walked off the job without union approval to protest a problem.

Roosevelt reacted strongly to strikes in vital industries. When the United Mine Workers went on strike in 1943, Roosevelt ordered the government to take over the mines and forced the miners to go back to work.

Strikes caught newspapers' attention, but most Americans were too patriotic to stop working. In addition, workers' incomes actually doubled during the war. After the experience of the Great Depression, working and earning money again made the sacrifices of the war easier for most workers to tolerate.

Americans worked long hours during the war. They put in an average of six days, or 50 hours, a week. The men and women in factories were committed to turning out weapons and other war materials that would be reliable in battle. For workers with relatives at the battlefront, this need was especially strong. One story that was told and retold was about a seaman who was swept overboard at Guadalcanal but survived because of a lifebelt. He later learned it had been inspected and packed in Akron, Ohio, by his own mother!

Why did many American workers agree not to strike during World War II?

Section 1 Review

Check Understanding

1. **Define** (a) rationing (b) wildcat strike

2. **Explain** how and why America's mobilization for war was successful.

3. **Describe** how Roosevelt responded to the miners' strike.

Critical Thinking

Analyzing How did the onset of war help the United States out of the Great Depression?

Write About Economics

Connecting Past and Present If a crisis occurred today that required the government to freeze wages and ration goods, how do you think Americans would respond? Write one person's reactions in a brief monologue.

BUILDING SKILLS

....

Conducting an Interview: The Home Front

Conducting an interview is a way of acquiring information directly from someone who has experienced history firsthand. An interview offers a personal perspective on the past. The person being interviewed gives facts, as well as opinions, feelings, and impressions about the past. An interview can provide important details about life during a particular era.

Here's How

Follow these steps to conduct an interview:

1. Gather background information on the person you plan to interview and the time period during which he or she lived.

2. Set up an appointment with the person. Be sure to state clearly the purpose of the interview and the kinds of information you hope to learn so that your source is prepared. Ask permission to record the interview.

3. Formulate a list of questions you want to ask and group them into categories about events or topics. Plan the interview so that questions logically follow one another. Avoid asking questions that have *yes* or *no* replies. Allow for changes of direction or additional information that your source may provide.

4. Bring a tape recorder or video camera to record the interview. If you do not have access to equipment, ask permission to bring a classmate along to take notes so that you can concentrate on asking questions and listening to answers.

5. Conduct the interview. Allow your source to go beyond your specific questions, but keep the interview on the track you want it to follow. Ask follow-up questions to fill gaps in information or to clarify answers your source gives.

6. Analyze the interview. Review and summarize the content, identifying statements that are representative of the person's overall views.

Here's Why

Interviews can be valuable sources of information. Because they are personal recollections of an event or a period, they provide a special insight about the past.

....

Practice the Skill

Choose an older member of your family or community who was involved in the war effort, or call a local nursing home or a chapter of the Veterans of Foreign Wars (VFW) to get a source for an interview. Using this chapter as background information, prepare a list of questions that will ask your source to recall what life was like on the home front. Consider issues such as rationing, war bond campaigns, and mobilization, or concentrate on social and cultural trends, including music, movies, dress, and morale. Conduct your interview, then convert your notes into a transcript—a written record of the interview presented in a question-and-answer format.

Apply the Skill

Use your transcript as the basis for an essay, or a play script, short story, series of journal entries, or a song that reveals impressions, emotions, and insights about life during World War II.

....

Section 2

Women in the War

PREVIEW

Objectives

• To explain how the roles of American women changed during World War II

• To analyze the benefits and drawbacks to women who worked outside the home

Vocabulary

corps
foxhole

During World War II, millions of American men were hard at work on farms, in factories, and in the armed forces. But to meet the war's ever-growing need for more products and services, there were many jobs to be filled. Women began moving into the work force and the military in larger numbers than they ever had before.

The number of working women rose from 14.6 million in 1941 to about 19.4 million in 1944. More than half of all American women were employed at some point during the war. At the peak of the war effort, women made up 36 percent of the total civilian work force.

The type of women who worked during the war also changed significantly. Married women accounted for almost 75 percent of the increase. For the first time in history, married working women outnumbered single working women. More than two million women over the age of 35 held jobs, and by the end of the war, half of all women workers were over the age of 35.

◆ WOMEN GO TO WORK

Although some women had worked outside the home before World War II, many more joined the work force after the war began. A new image of the ideal woman began to be promoted. Instead of being homemakers, wartime women were urged to take jobs in the factories and fields, either working beside men or replacing those who were fighting overseas.

Before long, Americans had adopted a fictional symbol of this new woman: "Rosie the Riveter." Rosie, created by American artist Norman Rockwell, was a strong, independent woman who could do any job a man could do. She first appeared on the cover of a national magazine, balancing a heavy rivet gun in her lap. Rosie's picture, torn from the magazine, was soon found on factory and office walls, in homes, and even in soldiers' barracks overseas.

The six million women who joined the work force during the war made guns and bombs; built ships, airplanes, and tanks; and contributed in many other industries where they had never worked before. They gave a boost to the productivity that was vital to the Allied war effort.

For many of these six million women workers, however, life was not as carefree as it seemed to be for the fictional Rosie the Riveter. Those whose husbands and boyfriends were away at war often found life lonely. Women who had children had to find some way to provide care for them. To help deal with the problem, the federal government built and operated child-care centers, but these could accommodate only about 10 percent of eligible children. For the rest, mothers had to rely on makeshift arrangements. One woman's solution was typical:

▲ Posters like this encouraged the more than six million women who worked on the home front during World War II.

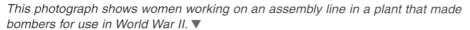

> **"My mother, my sister, and myself worked ... different shift[s] because we had little ones at home."**

Being able to juggle the care of children and still bring home a paycheck gave many women a sense of pride and independence. For some women, the experience ended as soon as the war was over. Men came back from overseas and returned to work. Most women quietly resumed their old roles as housewives. For others, however, life would never be the same. Said one woman worker,

> **"For the first time in my life I found out that I could do something with my hands besides bake a pie. I found out that I had manual dexterity and the [intelligence] to read blueprints and gauges, and to be inquisitive enough about things to develop skills other than the conventional roles that women had at that time."**

Fashions changed for many women during the war. It was no longer unusual for women to wear trousers and overalls instead of skirts. Some wartime styles, in fact, became permanent features of women's fashion.

Despite the positive effects of employment, there were also some drawbacks. Recruitment posters used stereotypes to portray working women, showing their new industrial labor as simply a variation of their domestic talents. One advertisement explained, "Instead of cutting a cake, this woman cuts the pattern of aircraft parts. Instead of baking a cake, she is cooking gears to reduce the tension."

Women continued to earn less than men doing the same jobs. Although the National War Labor Board ordered equal pay for equal work, the policy was often ignored. Women began at the bottom with the lowest-paying jobs and advanced more slowly. They earned about 65 percent of what men made at the same job.

How was Rosie the Riveter different from the traditional image of the American woman?

This photograph shows women working on an assembly line in a plant that made bombers for use in World War II. ▼

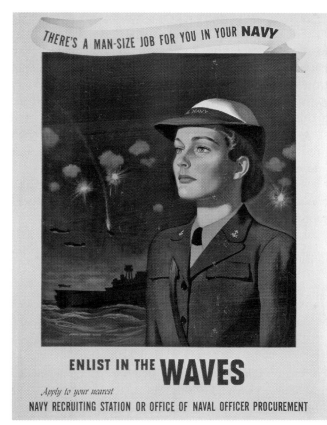

THERE'S A MAN-SIZE JOB FOR YOU IN YOUR **NAVY**

ENLIST IN THE **WAVES**

Apply to your nearest

NAVY RECRUITING STATION OR OFFICE OF NAVAL OFFICER PROCUREMENT

▲ *Recruiting posters, such as this one, encouraged women to enlist in the WAVES (Women Accepted for Volunteer Emergency Service), a division of the navy.*

◆ WOMEN IN THE ARMED FORCES

If women could work in factories, they could work in the armed services, too. In 1942, the secretary of war asked Oveta Culp Hobby, a Texas newspaper publisher, to form a **corps,** or a specialized branch of the armed forces, made up of women. The members of this Women's Auxiliary Army Corps were promptly named WAACS (later shortened to WACS). It was not long before the other branches of the military followed the army's lead. The navy had its WAVES, the Coast Guard its SPARS, and the marines its Marine Corps Women's Reserve. In all, more than 300,000 women joined the United States military.

Women soldiers were supposed to be assigned non-combat military jobs, thereby allowing more men to see action on the battlefield. Some women were translators, and others were public relations officers. Some flew supply planes and warplanes to Britain, allowing male pilots to fly in combat. Even in these supposedly safe roles, however, women soldiers often faced danger. Nurses accompanied the troops into combat, treated men

under fire, and dug and lived in their own **foxholes,** or shallow pits that provided some safety from enemy gunfire. Some women in the armed services began to question the fairness of some discriminatory practices. High-ranking female officers, for example, argued for a repeal of military policy prohibiting women from supervising male workers, even in offices.

Though women made up only about 2 percent of the 16 million members of the U.S. armed forces, they made a valuable difference. Women's contributions in the armed services, like their work in industry, demonstrated that their abilities could be applied to roles beyond the traditional ones of housewife and mother.

 What were the contributions of women in the armed forces?

Section 2 Review

Check Understanding

1. **Define** (a) corps (b) foxhole

2. **Describe** how women contributed to the productivity of the United States during World War II.

3. **List** two positive and two negative effects that working outside the home had on women during World War II.

4. **Identify** the roles women played in the armed forces during the war.

5. **Evaluate** how some women's images of themselves changed during World War II.

Critical Thinking

◆**Connecting Past and Present** In what ways are the concerns of working women today similar to those of working women in the 1940s?

Write About Citizenship

Write a paragraph for a brochure urging women to enlist in the armed forces during World War II.

The War Affects American Society

PREVIEW

Objectives

- To analyze the social upheaval that resulted when millions of Americans moved during World War II

- To discuss how African Americans forced a change in government policies on discrimination in the workplace

- To assess the means Latino servicemen used to overcome discrimination

- To describe the ordeal and the contributions of Japanese Americans during the war

Vocabulary

    executive order
    sabotage
    internment camp

During World War II, new opportunities attracted people from rural areas to the nation's industrial centers, such as Baltimore, Detroit, St. Louis, Los Angeles, and Seattle. The movement that resulted sometimes led to problems. Some rural towns lost their vitality as people moved away. Other areas, especially around large cities, became overcrowded. As often happens in uncertain times, prejudice boiled over as racial and ethnic groups that knew little about one another were thrown into close contact for the first time.

◆ SOCIAL UPHEAVAL

More than 27 million Americans relocated during World War II—the largest internal migration in the nation's history. Since many war industries were located in the West, the population surged there. During the war, the West gained about 8,000,000 people, three quarters of them from the South. In the 1940s, California's population rose by more than 50 percent.

Despite the wartime migration, in some ways Americans were more united than ever before. They formed organizations to watch for enemy planes or to patrol neighborhoods to make sure wartime restrictions were observed. They joined the Red Cross to help soldiers who were sick or wounded. In informal groups they knitted clothing for refugees or sorted scrap metal. People in many communities, when their long workdays were over, served on ration boards and draft boards without pay.

But the changes brought about by the war also created social upheaval and tensions. One government report in 1943 observed,

> **The whole pattern of our economic and social life is undergoing drastic changes, without so much as a bomb being dropped on our shores.**

For example, as thousands of defense workers crowded into cities, critical housing shortages developed. The competition for scarce housing often intensified racial tensions and even resulted in riots. In Detroit, one such riot left 25 African Americans and 9 whites dead.

What were some of the social effects of the mass movement of people during World War II?

Study Hint

Using a graphic organizer, such as a cluster diagram, is one way to recall facts. To make a cluster diagram, draw a large circle in the center of a blank page. In the circle, write a main idea or key topic. Connect a number of smaller circles around the large circle and, as you read, write down important facts that relate to the topic.

◆ AFRICAN AMERICANS DURING THE WAR

Approximately 900,000 African Americans served in the armed forces during World War II. The first recruits to sign up fought a battle even before they were shipped overseas. This battle was the fight against discrimination. The army and the navy limited many African Americans to jobs as cooks or waiters, or workers in supply units. In both branches, their units were segregated from those of white soldiers. At the start of the war, the marines refused to enlist any African Americans at all. Although changes to some of these policies occurred later in the war, such examples of discrimination made service in the armed forces a struggle for African Americans.

Despite discrimination, African Americans served with honor during the war. Dorie Miller was one of the nation's first war heroes. Miller served as a waiter on the U.S.S. *Arizona* at Pearl Harbor. When the Japanese attacked on December 7, Miller was in the galley. Hearing the enemy planes overhead, he rushed up on deck and shot down four planes with an anti-aircraft gun. For his bravery, Miller won the Navy Cross.

A number of African Americans served as fighter pilots in the Army Air Corps. The 99th Squadron was the first group trained at a government-sponsored flying school at the Tuskegee Institute in Alabama. In May 1943, they began flying combat missions in Italy and Germany. In 1944, they were merged with several other African American squadrons to form the 332nd Fighter Group, also known as the Tuskegee Airmen. The 332nd accompanied bombers on more than 1,578 missions in Europe and destroyed 400 enemy planes. They had a perfect record: no bomber escorted by the 332nd Fighter Group was ever downed by an enemy fighter.

African Americans on the Home Front

African American labor leader A. Philip Randolph saw, even before the United States entered the war, that the demand for war materials promised jobs for millions of African Americans. However, he remembered that in World War I, African Americans had been kept out of key jobs in the defense industry. Randolph determined that African Americans would not be left out again. Early in 1941, he called on President Roosevelt to take a bold stand in favor of equality. When Roosevelt did not respond, Randolph decided to act. He called on African Americans to join him in a protest march on Washington, D.C. He declared,

◀ *The 332nd Fighter Group trained at the Air Force Training Center in Tuskegee, Alabama. The inset photograph shows one of its training flights in 1943.*

> **The government will never give the Negro justice until they see masses—ten, twenty, fifty thousand Negroes on the White House lawn.**

March committees were organized, and press releases announced that 100,000 marchers were expected to converge on Washington on July 1.

Government officials feared that such a march would provide material for Hitler's anti-American propaganda campaign. President Roosevelt worried that the march might hurt him politically. If he gave in to the marchers' demands, he would lose the backing of southern Democrats in Congress, who largely opposed the marchers' cause. He was also concerned that the march might provoke racial tensions during a time the nation had to work together to mobilize. Despite the President's appeals, Randolph and his followers refused to call off the march unless the government took steps to end discriminatory hiring practices.

Finally, a few days before the march, President Roosevelt issued **Executive Order** 8802. An executive order is an order issued by the President. This one barred discrimination in defense industries and federal bureaus. The order also set up the Fair Employment Practices Committee in order to ensure that minorities did not miss out on federal jobs because of prejudice. Employers doing business with the government were ordered to support racial equality in hiring.

The executive order was a big victory for African Americans, but their struggle continued. As they moved into jobs they had never held before, white workers protested. For example, in Philadelphia white transportation workers went on strike because African American employees had been promoted to trolley car motormen for the first time.

African Americans in the Workplace

Despite continuing discrimination, there were African Americans who distinguished themselves in several professions. Ralph Bunche, a diplomat, worked for the State Department during the war. An African American doctor, Charles Drew, became director of U.S. blood banks.

The need for workers during the war years speeded the shift of African Americans from working in farming to working in manufacturing. Many left the South and moved to manufacturing centers in the Northeast, the Midwest, and the West.

Person to Person

Dr. Charles Drew

As Dr. Charles Drew was about to throw away a beaker of blood that had separated into layers, he got an idea.

The year was 1938. Doctors knew that blood could be given if needed, but after a week it was too old to be used. As he considered the different layers, Drew thought that the yellowish layer on top, the plasma, would be almost as effective as whole blood. Unlike whole blood, though, plasma could be stored for a long time.

▲ Charles Richard Drew (1904–1950)

When World War II broke out, Drew tested and proved his theory on a large scale. On the battlefield, men often died because there was not enough fresh blood stored. Drew set up blood banks and headed a "Blood for Britain" program that helped save thousands of lives. He was then named director of blood banks in the United States and Europe for the American Red Cross.

A few months after beginning his new job, Drew resigned unexpectedly. Although he never explained his reasons, many believed that he was disgusted by an order of the U.S. War Department that no white person was to be given blood from an African American. There was no medical reason for this order.

Drew continued his medical work until 1950, when his life was cut short in a car accident. Although a blood transfusion could not save the life of Dr. Charles Drew, his work continues to save the lives of countless others.

Looking Back: How would society have benefited at the time if the U.S. War Department had not issued its order about blood?

▲ *Latinos such as these Mexican Americans volunteered for military duty during World War II at a higher rate than any other ethnic group in the United States.*

Despite some whites' objections, about two million African Americans worked in defense jobs at a time when the African American population was just over 12 million. From 1940 to 1944, the number of African American skilled craftworkers and managers doubled.

As African Americans gained a foothold in the workplace, they became even more determined to acquire their full rights. During the war, African Americans in the U.S. military said they were working not for just one "V," or victory, like other Americans, but for a "Double V"—victory against the Axis and against inequality at home. An African American woman later explained what the war meant to her and other African Americans:

> Everything started opening up for us. We got a chance to go places we had never been able to go before. In ways it was too bad that so many lives were lost. But I think it was for a worthy cause, because it did make a way for us.

What advances were made toward equality for African Americans during World War II?

◆ LATINOS DURING THE WAR

Like African Americans, Latinos found new opportunities on the battlefield and in the workplace. The demands of World War II provided employment for many Latinos.

Latinos in Combat and in the Workplace

Approximately 500,000 Latinos served in the United States military during World War II. Among them were 400,000 Mexican Americans and 65,000 Puerto Ricans. About a quarter of the soldiers who endured the Bataan Death March were Latinos. All together, Latinos volunteered for military duty at a higher rate than any other group in the United States.

Latinos in the armed forces distinguished themselves for countless acts of bravery. Horacio Rivero, for example, won several medals during the war and was later promoted to four-star admiral. In all, 17 Latinos won the highest U.S. military medal, the Congressional Medal of Honor. One of these soldiers was Sergeant Cleto Rodriguez, who attacked a Japanese position and killed 82 of its defenders.

Other Latinos contributed to the war effort on the home front. In World War II, Latinos began to work in shipyards in Los Angeles for the first time. By war's end, some 17,000 worked there, helping to bring about the eventual U.S. victory. In 1942, when farmers and railroad operators in the United States found themselves desperately short of workers, the United States and Mexico teamed up to oversee a program that supplied farms and railroads with braceros, or visiting laborers, from Mexico. Some 250,000 braceros came to the United States between 1942 and 1947. They kept Americans fed and the trains running, both vital contributions to victory.

Zoot Suit Riots

Latinos also encountered discrimination as they entered workplaces previously closed to them. Tension between Latinos and whites sometimes flared into violence. The most well-known incidents became known as the zoot suit riots.

In the early 1940s, some young Latinos in Los Angeles favored a style of clothing called a "zoot suit"—a long suitcoat with wide lapels and padded shoulders, and baggy pants that narrowed at the cuffs. A broad-brimmed hat completed the outfit. The zoot suit was a badge of pride in a part of Latino culture.

The zoot suits quickly became a target for anti-Latino feeling. In 1943, white sailors on leave from ships in the port of Los Angeles clashed with young "zoot-suiters." In one major incident, a crowd of 3,000 whites beat several Latino youths.

Incidents such as these made some white Americans re-evaluate their prejudices. The federal government started the Spanish-Speaking People's Division to fight discrimination. This government office was not able to accomplish much, however. In the end, the zoot suit riots made Latinos, like African Americans, even more determined to win the respect and equality they deserved.

The American GI Forum

After helping to restore freedom in Europe, Latino servicemen returned to find little freedom at home. Instead, they met with signs reading "No Mexicans" in the windows of some restaurants and theaters. Jobs were again out of reach.

One man in particular, Dr. Hector García of Texas, stood up to this discrimination. A hero who had won a medal for courage on the battlefield, García now applied his bravery to fighting for equal rights for all veterans. In 1948, he founded the American GI Forum to help all GIs, as soldiers and former soldiers were then called, to gain their rights. *GI* stood for "government issue."

The American GI Forum has gone on to become a nationwide organization, with 500 chapters in the United States and Puerto Rico. Although most of its members are Latinos, it has members of many ethnic groups. It has promoted fair education, employment, and voting. For García's work in the American GI Forum, he was given the highest award that can be granted to an American civilian, the Medal of Freedom.

 In what ways did Latinos contribute to the war effort?

◆ JAPANESE AMERICANS

Though World War II was a time of increased opportunity for many groups, for Japanese Americans it became a period of isolation and discrimination. After the bombing of Pearl Harbor, many white Americans grew afraid that the 112,000 Japanese Americans living on the west coast might help Japan invade the United States. They ignored the fact that two thirds of these Japanese Americans were

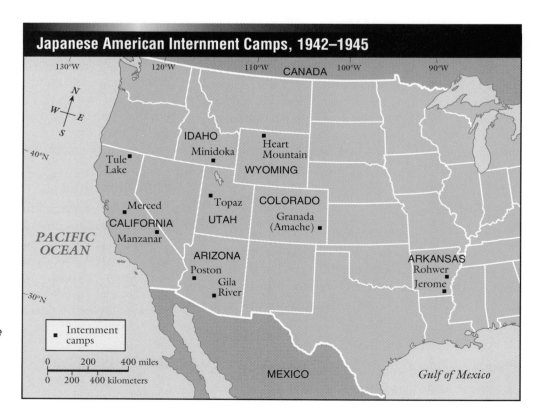

Japanese American Internment Camps, 1942–1945

Geography *Beginning in 1942, more than 100,000 Japanese Americans were sent to internment camps.* **Interpreting the Map** *Which state had the most internment camps?* ▶

▲ A Japanese American man and two young family members await relocation to an internment camp at the outbreak of World War II. They are wearing identification tags on their coats.

American citizens. Nor was there any sign that the Japanese Americans had participated in **sabotage,** or secret acts against the government.

All the same, prejudice against Japanese Americans was not uncommon. Since relatively few Japanese Americans lived in the United States, many white Americans had never met or become acquainted with them. This lack of understanding led some white Americans to believe that Japanese Americans might be spying for or aiding Japan in some way.

On the basis of this unreasonable fear, in 1942 President Roosevelt issued an order allowing the army to remove west coast Japanese Americans from their homes and ship them to **internment camps,** or prison camps. Many families lost all they owned.

The internment camps were located in barren parts of the United States far from populated areas, as shown on the map on page 476. Conditions inside the camps were rough. Housing consisted of warped boards covered with tar paper. Each family shared one room in a crowded barracks building surrounded by a barbed-wire fence. Families had almost no privacy. Food was poor, and water for personal use had to be carried from a central faucet.

For many of the interned Japanese Americans, the contrast between the life they were living and the rights they had lost was extreme. What made the contrast even more shocking was that while Japanese American families were being guarded behind barbed wire in the United States, many Japanese American

soldiers were fighting bravely on the battlefields of Europe. Some families, while still living in internment camps, received medals given for the wounding or deaths of their relatives in combat.

At last, beginning in January 1945, the government allowed Japanese Americans in the camps to leave. It was not until 1988 that the United States government decided to make reparations. The government apologized to the Japanese Americans who had been driven from their homes. It also gave every survivor of the internment camps $20,000. It was an admission from the government that it had made a serious error.

 Why were Japanese Americans imprisoned during World War II?

Section 3 Review

Check Understanding

1. **Define** (a) executive order (b) sabotage (c) internment camp

2. **Identify** one of the causes of social upheaval during World War II.

3. **Analyze** the ways in which minority groups contributed to the war effort on the home front.

4. **Explain** what African Americans meant when they said they were fighting for the Double V.

Critical Thinking

Inferring How do you think Japanese American soldiers in World War II might have felt when their families were sent to internment camps?

Write About Culture

◆ **Connecting Past and Present** During World War II, Japanese Americans were considered by many to be a threat. Write a brief story that shows how judging people unfairly today can lead to future misunderstandings.

Chapter 23
Review

CHAPTER SUMMARY

Section 1

The United States geared up for World War II, producing huge amounts of supplies and arms for the Allies. To accomplish this, the government took control of the economy. Some measures, such as wage freezes, led to workers' strikes. The overall effect of mobilization, however, was the creation of many jobs, ending the Great Depression.

Section 2

The need for workers during war brought women into the work force and the military in great numbers. When the war ended and soldiers returned to the workplace, many women resumed their traditional roles.

Section 3

The war changed the patterns of American life. People moved to urban areas. African Americans and Latinos found new jobs in the war effort but struggled against discrimination. For many Japanese Americans, the war meant the loss of businesses and homes and relocation to internment camps.

Connecting ◆▶ Past and Present

World War II drew people in many communities together as they confronted the problems that arose. How do you think the people in your community would respond to a crisis today?

Using Vocabulary

Select the letter of the phrase that best completes each sentence.

1. A person convicted of **sabotage** has (a) acted secretly against the government; (b) walked out of a job for higher wages; (c) been unfairly dismissed by an employer; (d) refused to use ration books.

2. A **corps** is a (a) military barracks; (b) military group; (c) military encampment; (d) military official.

3. An **internment camp** was a place where (a) defense workers were sent to make planes; (b) many Japanese Americans were imprisoned; (c) U.S. soldiers went to train; (d) Latino servicemen went after the war.

4. **Rationing** made sure that people (a) did not tell secrets during the war; (b) turned off the lights during air raids; (c) were not swayed by propaganda; (d) used only certain amounts of certain items.

5. An **executive order** is issued (a) by military officials; (b) by the Senate; (c) by the President; (d) by the Office of War Mobilization.

6. In a **wildcat strike,** (a) workers walk off the job without union approval; (b) employers insist that laborers work harder; (c) soldiers attack the enemy fiercely; (d) farmers raise more food for animals.

7. A **foxhole** is (a) a place to store supplies; (b) the factory where weapons were made; (c) a shallow pit that provides some safety for a soldier; (d) a defense weapon.

Check Understanding

1. **Describe** how the nation mobilized to help win World War II.

2. **Explain** how the role of government changed during the war.

3. **Explain** why the Great Depression ended during World War II.

4. **Discuss** how the relationship between government and labor changed during the war.

5. **Summarize** how war caused the roles of women to change in the United States.

6. **Discuss** the roles women played as members of the armed forces during the war.

7. **Explain** Executive Order 8802 and what it meant to African Americans.

8. **Discuss** the ways in which World War II affected employment opportunities for minority groups.

9. **Summarize** the experiences of Japanese Americans in the war years.

10. **Describe** some of the tensions brought about by the social upheavals of the 1940s.

Critical Thinking

1. **Analyzing Causes and Effects** How did mobilizing for war affect U.S. society?

2. **Defending a Position** What were the arguments for controlling businesses and labor unions during World War II? Explain whether you think these measures were justified.

3. **Making Generalizations** Were women able to overcome stereotypical treatment during World War II? Explain your answer.

4. **Drawing Conclusions** How were many women and members of minority groups able to better their lives during World War II?

◆ **Connecting Past and Present** What kind of symbol, like Rosie the Riveter, might be used to represent women workers today?

Interpreting the Timeline

Use the timeline on pages 462–463 to answer these questions.

1. When did rationing begin to take effect?

2. What U.S. event reflects Americans' fears about Japanese Americans during World War II?

3. List one event on the timeline that shows progress against discrimination. Then list one or more events that show that discrimination remained a problem during the war years.

Putting Skills to Work

CONDUCTING AN INTERVIEW

In the Building Skills lesson on page 468, you learned that interviews are a means of acquiring information from a person. Practice your interviewing techniques by questioning some of your classmates about their reactions to the treatment women and minority groups received durng World War II. Use the steps in *Here's How* to develop a questionnaire, and conduct four or five short interviews. Then draw some conclusions about your classmates' attitudes, using details from the interviews to support them.

Writing to Describe

People in the armed forces enjoy receiving mail from home. **Write** a letter from the viewpoint of a teenager in the 1940s to a soldier who is serving in World War II. Describe how your life and the lives of those around you have changed because of the war.

Portfolio Project

AN EYEWITNESS ACCOUNT

Choose one of the following people: a soldier from a minority group who has just returned from war; a woman who has gone to work in a war industry or in the armed services; an interned Japanese American; or one of the teenagers involved in the zoot suit riots. Then create an "eyewitness" account that brings that person's experiences during or after the war to life. You might present your account as a series of journal entries, a letter, or a story. Use facts from the chapter and details from your imagination to make the person's experiences believable.

Chapter 24
Cold War Grips the World 1945–1961

CHAPTER PREVIEW

Section 1 The Cold War Begins

Although the United Nations provided an opportunity for peaceful discussion of postwar issues, tensions developed between advocates of communism and advocates of democracy.

Section 2 The Cold War in Asia and the Middle East

The United States and the Soviet Union each sought allies in Asia and the Middle East. In both regions, wars broke out partly as a result of Cold War politics.

Section 3 The Cold War at Home

The tensions produced by the Cold War led to an expensive arms race and a new Red Scare led by Senator Joseph McCarthy.

Section 4 Emerging Nations and the Cold War

As colonial empires broke up, many countries won their independence. The United States and the Soviet Union competed to make alliances with these and other nations.

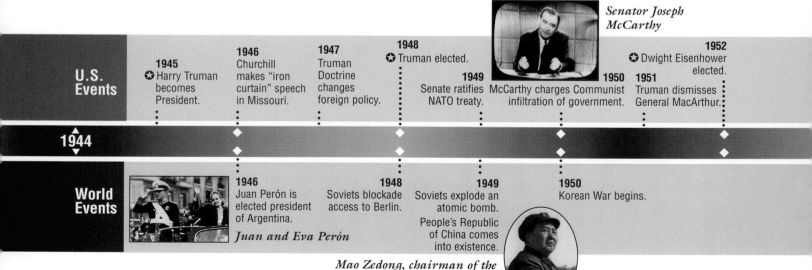

Senator Joseph McCarthy

U.S. Events

1945 ✪ Harry Truman becomes President.

1946 Churchill makes "iron curtain" speech in Missouri.

1947 Truman Doctrine changes foreign policy.

1948 ✪ Truman elected.

1949 Senate ratifies NATO treaty.

1950 McCarthy charges Communist infiltration of government.

1951 Truman dismisses General MacArthur.

1952 ✪ Dwight Eisenhower elected.

1944

World Events

Juan and Eva Perón

1946 Juan Perón is elected president of Argentina.

1948 Soviets blockade access to Berlin.

1949 Soviets explode an atomic bomb. People's Republic of China comes into existence.

1950 Korean War begins.

Mao Zedong, chairman of the People's Republic of China

Portfolio Project

A COLD WAR DOCUMENTARY

During the Cold War, tensions between the United States and the Soviet Union ran high as the two countries competed for influence and power around the globe. As you read the chapter, watch for conflicts and their turning points. At the end of the chapter, you will prepare a storyboard for a television documentary about one of the events of the Cold War.

▲ *In 1961, a wall was built to prevent Germans in East Berlin from escaping to West Berlin.* ◆❖ **Connecting Past and Present** *How did the Berlin Wall symbolize the relationship between the United States and the Soviet Union? What problems might occur when a city is controlled by two or more different countries?*

NASA *logo*

1954
Senate condemns Joseph McCarthy and recommends that he be censured.

1956
❂ Eisenhower reelected.
Eugene O'Neill's drama *Long Day's Journey into Night* opens on Broadway.

1957
Eisenhower Doctrine is announced.

1958
Congress creates NASA to coordinate space program.
National Defense Education Act puts emphasis on science and math.

1960
❂ John F. Kennedy elected.

1962

1954
Roger Bannister is first to run a mile under 4 minutes.
William Golding's novel *Lord of the Flies* is published.

Sputnik stamp

1957
West African nation Ghana gains independence.
U.S.S.R. launches *Sputnik*.

Prime Minister Kwame Nkrumah of Ghana

1961
Berlin Wall is built.

Section 1

The Cold War Begins

PREVIEW

Objectives

- To describe the founding of the United Nations and its goals

- To explain how the Soviet Union extended its influence over Eastern Europe after World War II

- To examine how U.S. aid to the war-torn countries of Europe helped stop the spread of communism

Vocabulary

satellite

iron curtain

Cold War

containment

deployment

Toward the close of World War II, President Roosevelt had begun to pursue a dream. Wanting to create a league of nations strong enough to prevent another war, Roosevelt called for a gathering of Allied leaders to plan for peace. Together, they hoped to set up a new international organization to ensure that the peace they had planned would last.

◆ THE UNITED NATIONS

Determined to avoid the mistakes made by Woodrow Wilson, President Roosevelt gained the support of Congress for this new peace organization. In April 1945, representatives from 50 nations met in San Francisco to establish the United Nations (UN). Roosevelt did not live to attend this meeting, but the new President, Harry S Truman, telephoned an address to the historic gathering.

The delegates who signed the United Nations Charter in June 1945 aimed to create an organization that would prevent wars and try to bring an end to wars that did erupt. Members pledged to work together to seek peaceful solutions to international disputes.

According to the charter, all member nations belong to the General Assembly. In this group, they debate issues and recommend action. But the General Assembly has no power to see that its recommendations are carried out.

The enforcement arm of the United Nations is the smaller Security Council. Originally, representatives of 11 nations made up the Security Council, but the number has been increased to 15. Five members—the United States, United Kingdom, Russia, China, and France—hold permanent seats on the Security Council. (The seat currently held by Russia was originally held by the Soviet Union.) The General Assembly elects the ten remaining members for two-year terms.

The Security Council has greater power than the General Assembly. For example, its members can vote to cut off trade with a nation that attacks another. Its members can also vote to send UN troops into a troubled area. However, the five permanent members have the right to veto any Security Council decision. A veto by any one permanent member can paralyze the council. In the first years of the UN, the veto was most often used by the Soviet Union to oppose the actions or beliefs of the four other permanent members. The chart on the next page shows more about the organization and some of the functions of the UN.

 What special powers does the Security Council have in the United Nations?

◆ COMMUNISM IN EUROPE

Soviet actions in Europe soon shattered the hopeful mood that had accompanied the founding of the UN. In meetings with Roosevelt and Churchill, Stalin had promised to hold free elections in Poland and the other countries of Eastern Europe. Instead, he proceeded to establish Communist governments in these nations, using Soviet troops to crush opposition. Soon after World War II, East Germany, Poland, Romania, Bulgaria, Hungary, and Czechoslovakia had all become **satellites** of the Soviet Union. A satellite is a nation that is economically or politically dependent on another nation. Yugoslavia and Albania also had Communist governments, but they followed a more independent course in foreign affairs.

The expansion of communism greatly alarmed the United States and other Western powers. It violated the principle of self-determination, which is the right of a people to freely choose their own form of government. Speaking in Fulton, Missouri, in 1946, Britain's former prime minister, Winston Churchill,

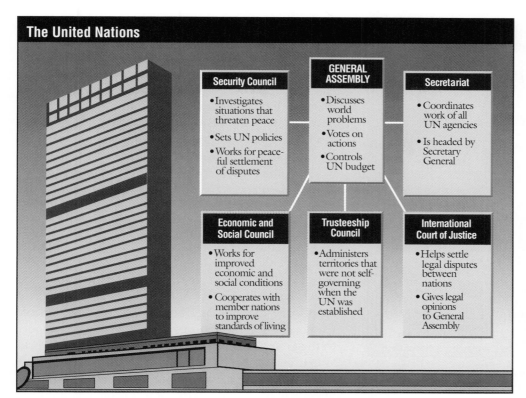

The United Nations

Security Council
- Investigates situations that threaten peace
- Sets UN policies
- Works for peaceful settlement of disputes

GENERAL ASSEMBLY
- Discusses world problems
- Votes on actions
- Controls UN budget

Secretariat
- Coordinates work of all UN agencies
- Is headed by Secretary General

Economic and Social Council
- Works for improved economic and social conditions
- Cooperates with member nations to improve standards of living

Trusteeship Council
- Administers territories that were not self-governing when the UN was established

International Court of Justice
- Helps settle legal disputes between nations
- Gives legal opinions to General Assembly

◀ **Government** *This chart shows the organizational structure of the United Nations.* **Interpreting the Chart** *If a territory needed assistance in self-government, which UN agency would most likely help?*

gave prominence to a new term as he warned of the Soviet threat:

> **From Stettin in the Baltic to Trieste in the Adriatic, an iron curtain has descended across the continent. Behind that line lie all the capitals of...Central and Eastern Europe....Warsaw, Berlin, Prague, Vienna, Budapest, Belgrade, Bucharest, and Sofia, all these famous cities and populations around them lie in what I must call the Soviet sphere.**

The **iron curtain** that Churchill spoke about was the invisible border between the Communist nations and the democratic nations of Europe. The iron curtain countries were cut off from the rest of the world. No one could easily enter them, and no one was supposed to leave. Their Soviet-style governments censored newspapers, books, and radio programs. People living behind the iron curtain had trouble getting news of the outside world. Those on the outside could not find out what was going on inside.

Within a few months after the end of World War II, the United States and the Soviet Union were involved in a new kind of war. This war was a state of tension and hostility that stopped short of actual fighting. Because of the absence of armed conflict, it became known as the **Cold War.** Only the prospect of mutual destruction prevented the disagreements between the two most powerful nations from developing into another world war. Uneasy allies in World War II, the two countries now viewed each other as enemies. Nearly all the world's other nations lined up on one side or the other.

The Berlin Blockade

The tensions of the Cold War were easily seen in Germany. At the end of World War II, the Allies had divided Germany into four zones. American, British, French, and Soviet troops were each in charge of a zone. The German capital of Berlin, which lay more than 100 miles inside the Soviet zone, was also divided among the four Allied powers. The map on page 484 shows how Germany and Berlin were divided.

The Soviets and the Western powers could not agree about the future of Germany. Having suffered during the German invasion of their country, the Soviets wanted Germany to stay weak and divided.

Germany Divided, 1945

French zone
Soviet zone
American zone
British zone

▲ **Geography** *This map shows the four zones of occupation in Germany after World War II.* **Interpreting the Map** *How was the division of Germany similar to the division of Berlin?*

The United States, Great Britain, and France, on the other hand, wanted Germany to be strong and unified so that it would serve as a barrier against the spread of communism.

In June 1948, the Western powers took a step toward reunifying Germany by announcing that they would combine the three zones they controlled. The Soviets retaliated by shutting down all rail, highway, and water routes connecting Berlin and the Western Zone of Germany. By this move they hoped to force the three Western powers out of Berlin.

Berlin had only about a month's supply of food and fuel for its two million residents. Truman knew that if he did nothing to help Berlin, the Soviets would interpret his inaction as weakness. But sending in troops would risk another world war. Truman and his advisors came up with a solution: they would send supplies to Berlin by air. Truman launched a full-scale airlift. For more than a year, Allied planes brought food and supplies to grateful Berliners.

In 1949, with the aid of the UN, the blockade was lifted. Germany—and Berlin—remained divided, however. West Berlin became part of the German Federal Republic, or West Germany. East Berlin became part of the German Democratic Republic,

or East Germany, another Soviet satellite with a Communist government.

West Germany became more and more "Americanized" as the United States guided the reconstruction of its economy. Meanwhile, the Soviets dragged industrial equipment out of impoverished East Germany for their own needs and imposed harsh discipline on the country's inhabitants. Despite promises to give greater economic control to German workers, the Soviets took no steps toward democracy in East Germany.

Civil War in Greece

The Cold War also extended to Greece. Before the Nazis left Greece in 1944, civil war had broken out between Communist rebels and supporters of the Greek king. Britain provided military and economic support to the king and his democratic government. Communists in the country of Yugoslavia gave support to the Greek Communists. However, soon after World War II ended, Britain informed the United States that it could no longer afford to help Greece. The United States had to decide whether it was willing to shoulder the burden alone.

What did Churchill mean when he said that an iron curtain had descended over Europe?

◆ AMERICAN AID TO EUROPE

On March 12, 1947, President Truman made an urgent request to Congress for $400 million to aid Greece and its neighbor Turkey. Truman said,

> **I believe that it must be the policy of the United States to support free peoples who are resisting attempted subjugation [oppression] by armed minorities or by outside pressures. . . . If we falter in our leadership, we may endanger the peace of the world—and we shall surely endanger the welfare of our own nation.**

Congress voted overwhelmingly to aid Greece and Turkey. With American help, the Greek government put down the Communist-led revolt. Turkey refused to allow Soviet warships in its waters.

Truman's pledge of help to people threatened with Communist aggression became known as the Truman Doctrine. It signaled a major shift in American foreign policy. It was part of an overall policy of **containment.** From now on, the United States would seek to contain, or halt the spread of, communism.

The Marshall Plan

Greece and Turkey were not the only countries that needed help. After World War II, all of Europe was, in Winston Churchill's words, a huge "rubble heap." Cities were bombed out. Industries were either crippled or shut down completely. Millions of Europeans endured hunger, cold, and disease. The Communists blamed these problems on the capitalist system. Many desperate Europeans believed them. Communist parties gained strength in both Italy and France.

To meet this new crisis, Truman's secretary of state, George C. Marshall, proposed a large-scale program of economic aid in June 1947. The plan called for the United States to provide economic assistance to European nations to spark an economic recovery.

The Marshall Plan, as the American plan was called, was a huge success. Between 1948 and 1951, the United States loaned or gave more than $13 billion in aid to 17 European nations. American dollars built new factories, schools, hospitals, railroads, and bridges. The Marshall Plan helped countries such as Britain, France, and West Germany recover from the war. It also helped prevent Communists from gaining influence there. Stalin denounced the Marshall Plan as an American scheme to dominate Europe and deprive Eastern European countries of desperately needed financial resources. Although the plan did not diminish Soviet control over Eastern Europe, it did help to create a sharp contrast between the East and the West and between communism and capitalism.

Marshall had invited the Soviet Union and its satellite countries to take part in the program, too, but they declined. Instead, a number of Soviet satellites formed a council of their own to provide mutual assistance. However, since they had little money, they could provide little help to each other.

The North American Treaty Organization

The Truman Doctrine and the Marshall Plan both demonstrated the United States' growing interest in world affairs. The United States was now the strongest democratic nation. In view of this new role, President Truman asked Canada and ten European

Tractors and other farm equipment were shipped to Europe under the Marshall Plan. These tractors were unloaded at the French port of Le Havre. ▼

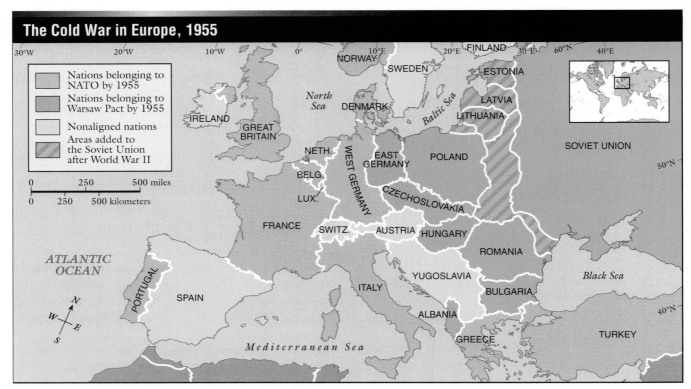

The Cold War in Europe, 1955

Nations belonging to NATO by 1955

Nations belonging to Warsaw Pact by 1955

Nonaligned nations

Areas added to the Soviet Union after World War II

0 250 500 miles
0 250 500 kilometers

NORWAY SWEDEN FINLAND
ESTONIA
North Sea DENMARK LATVIA
IRELAND GREAT BRITAIN LITHUANIA
NETH. EAST GERMANY POLAND SOVIET UNION
BELG. WEST GERMANY CZECHOSLOVAKIA
LUX.
FRANCE SWITZ. AUSTRIA HUNGARY
ATLANTIC OCEAN ROMANIA
PORTUGAL SPAIN ITALY YUGOSLAVIA Black Sea
BULGARIA
ALBANIA
Mediterranean Sea GREECE TURKEY

N W E S

▲ **Geography** *By 1955, the Cold War divided the countries of Europe into two major camps.*
Interpreting the Map *What nations belonged to the Warsaw Pact?*

nations to join the United States in a military alliance in January 1948. The North Atlantic Treaty Organization (NATO) committed all members to come to the defense of any member that was attacked. Eventually, other nations, including West Germany, joined NATO.

The United States had taken a giant step away from isolationism. The U.S. Senate had ratified the first formal military treaty with a European nation since the American Revolution. Congress had approved $1.3 billion in military aid, which involved the creation of U.S. Army bases and the **deployment** of troops, or sending out armed forces ready for battle. Critics warned that the United States could not afford to police Europe, but opinion polls revealed that there was strong support for Truman's tough line against the Soviets.

In 1955 the Soviets formed their own military alliance with their East European satellites. This alliance was called the Warsaw Pact. In addition to the Soviet Union, it included Poland, East Germany, Czechoslovakia, Hungary, Romania, Bulgaria, and Albania. As shown on the map above, Europe was again divided into two hostile camps.

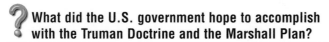 **What did the U.S. government hope to accomplish with the Truman Doctrine and the Marshall Plan?**

Section 1 Review

Check Understanding

1. **Define** (a) satellite (b) iron curtain (c) Cold War (d) containment (e) deployment

2. **Explain** the goals of the United Nations.

3. **Describe** two important ways in which the United States tried to halt the spread of communism in Europe.

Critical Thinking

Synthesizing Why was it important to the United States to help Europe recover economically?

Write About History

◆ **Connecting Past and Present** Write a brief essay that describes the ways in which the UN continues to play a role in world affairs today.

BUILDING SKILLS

Interpreting Special-Purpose Maps: Sources of Oil

Interpreting special-purpose maps can help you to understand a particular aspect of history, geography, or economics. Special-purpose maps focus on one specific topic. For example, the map could show population, railroad routes, geographic boundaries, manufacturing centers, or some other feature of an area.

Here's How

Follow these steps to interpret a special-purpose map:

1. Use basic map-reading skills. Review the steps for Reading a Map on page 49. Study the title of the map, as well as its key and labels.

2. Note any special symbols and what they represent.

3. Determine what special information the map provides and what its specific purpose is.

4. Determine whether the map supports or contradicts information you already have about the topic.

5. Draw conclusions about the information that the map presents.

Here's Why

Special-purpose maps can contribute much to your understanding of economics, geography, population, and many other topics related to your study of history. By focusing on one particular subject, they are an effective visual means of presenting important information.

Practice the Skill

Use the steps in *Here's How* to interpret the special-purpose map below. Then answer the questions that follow.

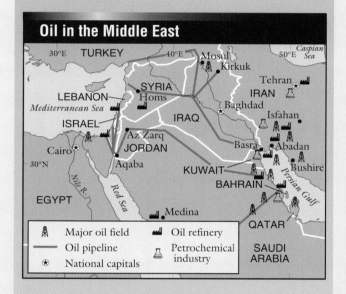

Oil in the Middle East

1. Why do you think the area around the Persian Gulf is considered to be of vital economic importance to the United States?

2. What economic activities take place in Tehran, in Iran?

3. A major oil field is located in what region of Iraq?

Apply the Skill

Look in your local newspaper for a weather map. Make a list of all the information about weather conditions that it contains.

The Cold War in Asia and the Middle East

PREVIEW

Objectives

- To describe the relationship of the United States and Japan after the war
- To explain how the Communists came to power in China
- To explain how tensions led to war in Korea
- To evaluate the causes of conflict in the Middle East

Vocabulary

superpower
occupation
demilitarized zone

The United States had managed to contain communism in Europe through a combination of bold action and economic aid. In Asia and the Middle East, several efforts to stem the spread of communism were also successful. However, in the small Asian nation of Korea, the Cold War suddenly turned "hot."

◆ EAST ASIA AFTER THE WAR

When Japan was defeated in World War II, it lost its empire and occupied territories, which included a large part of China, Korea, the Philippines, and Southeast Asia. The United States and the Soviet Union were now **superpowers,** the strongest nations in the world. As rivals for world power, they competed for influence in Asia—along with Communist China, a new Asian giant.

The Occupation of Japan

Having been largely responsible for Japan's defeat, the United States established the policies of its **occupation,** the control over a conquered nation by a foreign power. General Douglas MacArthur, the American commander of the occupation forces, oversaw the disbanding of Japan's army and the removal of its military leaders from power. Japan adopted a new democratic constitution that provided for free elections, political parties, labor unions, and land reform. For the first time, Japanese women were granted legal rights, including suffrage.

With nearly $2 billion in American aid, the Japanese rebuilt their ruined country. By the time the United States ended its occupation in 1952, Japan had regained its industrial strength. Like West Germany, Japan was no longer an enemy; it was a strong ally of the United States.

The Rise of Communism in China

Since the 1920s, Chinese Nationalists (led by Chiang Kai-shek) and Communists (led since 1935 by Mao Zedong) had battled for control of China. Although Chiang was the official head of the government, his failure to make much-needed reforms, such as redistributing land to the poor and fighting corruption in government, lost him popular support. In contrast, Mao won a large following among the Chinese peasants with promises of economic progress. The Japanese invasion of China in 1937 had forced the Nationalists and the Communists into an uneasy truce. But after the

In 1949, Mao Zedong became the leader of the People's Republic of China. He is shown here at a Communist rally. ▼

◄ U.S. soldiers marched into the Naktong River valley of South Korea to battle the Communists. Along the same dirt road, South Korean women and children fled the Communists.

defeat of Japan in 1945, civil war again erupted. The United States, which supported the Nationalists, tried to get the two sides to share power. They refused, and the fighting continued.

Soon it was clear that only large amounts of U.S. military and economic aid could possibly save the Nationalists. President Truman was unwilling to make such an all-out effort because he did not believe Chiang would be successful.

China fell to the Communists, and in October 1949, Mao established the People's Republic of China. Chiang and the Nationalists fled to the island of Formosa, later known as Taiwan. The United States insisted that the Taiwan government was the legal government of China. It refused to recognize the People's Republic and kept the UN from admitting Communist China to China's seat on the Security Council. Mao, for his part, entered into an alliance with the Soviet Union.

How did the Communists come to power in China?

◆ **THE KOREAN WAR**

Unrest also rocked China's neighbor Korea. From 1910 to 1945, Korea had been a Japanese colony. After World War II, Korea was divided along the 38th parallel of latitude. The United States and the Soviet Union were unable to agree on a plan to unify the country. U.S. troops occupied South Korea, and Soviet troops occupied North Korea.

On June 25, 1950, North Korean troops, armed with Soviet artillery and tanks, swept across the 38th parallel into South Korea. North Korea's goal was to reunify North and South Korea under a Communist government. President Truman and the American people were outraged at North Korea's invasion. The President quickly committed troops, under General Douglas MacArthur, to a UN force that was sent to help the South Koreans fight. Truman explained his decisive action, saying,

❝ I recalled some earlier instances: Manchuria, Ethiopia, Austria. I remembered how each time that the democracies failed to act it had encouraged the aggressors to go ahead. ❞

Although other countries also supplied soldiers, Americans accounted for about 90 percent of the UN force, making the Korean War very much an American war. Because Truman never went before

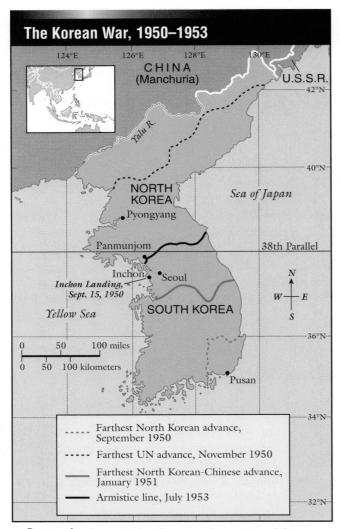

The Korean War, 1950–1953

CHINA (Manchuria)

U.S.S.R.

Yalu R.

NORTH KOREA

Sea of Japan

Pyongyang

Panmunjom

38th Parallel

Inchon
Seoul
*Inchon Landing,
Sept. 15, 1950*

Yellow Sea

SOUTH KOREA

0   50   100 miles
0   50   100 kilometers

Pusan

N
W — E
S

42°N
40°N
36°N
34°N
32°N

124°E   126°E   128°E   130°E

- - - - - Farthest North Korean advance, September 1950
- - - - - Farthest UN advance, November 1950
———— Farthest North Korean–Chinese advance, January 1951
———— Armistice line, July 1953

▲ **Geography** *An armistice line was drawn to end the war in 1953.* **Interpreting the Map** *To what line of latitude, farthest north, did the UN forces advance?*

Congress to ask for a formal declaration of war, the government officially referred to the U.S. intervention in Korea as a police action, not a war.

Early Days of the Conflict

At first, the ill-equipped UN soldiers were no match for the North Korean army with its Soviet tanks. During the first six weeks of fighting, the North Koreans advanced, driving back the UN troops to the southeastern tip of Korea. In September 1950, however, General MacArthur launched a brilliant amphibious attack at Inchon. In about two weeks, UN forces drove the North Koreans back across the 38th parallel, shown on the map on this page.

Chinese Involvement in Korea

With President Truman's approval, MacArthur advanced into North Korea, hoping to conquer it and set up an American-backed government. MacArthur chased the North Koreans all the way to the Chinese border.

Suddenly, an army of 300,000 Chinese launched an assault on MacArthur's troops. The Americans suffered heavy losses and were pushed back to the 38th parallel boundary. There, with both armies poised along the boundary, the war reached a stalemate.

Truman Versus MacArthur

General MacArthur believed he could win the war if UN forces blockaded and bombed China and if Chiang Kai-shek's Nationalist troops returned to invade China. But President Truman feared that an attack on China would draw the Soviet Union in, leading to World War III. He ordered MacArthur to limit his war plans.

Defiant, MacArthur publicly challenged Truman's order. "In war," he declared, "there can be no substitute for victory." Many Americans agreed with him. They wanted the Communists out of both China and Korea. Under the Constitution, the President, not a general, commands the armed forces and directs foreign policy. President Truman fired General MacArthur for insubordination.

The Korean War did not end until 1953, when the two sides signed an armistice agreement. The agreement established a **demilitarized zone,** or DMZ, between North and South Korea. A demilitarized zone is an area in which military forces are prohibited. In addition, an armistice line was set between the two countries approximately where it had been before the war. In the end, more than 54,000 Americans and nearly two million Koreans and Chinese had lost their lives in the fighting.

Why did President Truman think it was necessary to go to war in Korea?

◆ THE COLD WAR AND THE MIDDLE EAST

The United States and the Soviet Union also competed fiercely in the Middle East. A major source of conflict was between Arabs and Jews, who both claim homelands in the region.

Trouble in Israel

After World War II, Jewish survivors of the Holocaust and other Jews from around the world flocked to Palestine. The Jews were overjoyed to finally get the national homeland that the British had promised them at the end of World War I. But Arabs and Jews clashed in the British-controlled territory.

The Arabs, like the Jews, claimed that the land had been promised to them by God. Hoping to satisfy both sides, the UN approved a plan to divide Palestine into two states—one Arab, the other Jewish. But the Arabs wanted Palestine to be an all-Arab state.

On May 14, 1948, the Jews announced the creation of the new, independent state of Israel in their section of Palestine. The United States immediately recognized Israel as a legitimate state. In response to the establishment of Israel, Israel's Arab neighbors sent in armies. The Israeli army pushed the Arabs back and captured about half the land pledged to the new Arab state. Hundreds of thousands of Palestinian Arabs fled to neighboring countries. Many gathered in refugee camps in Jordan, Lebanon, and Syria.

In 1949, a UN team arranged for an end to the war, but the Arab nations refused to recognize the state of Israel. Palestinian Arabs were determined to regain their land. This would mark the beginning of a series of Middle East conflicts between Palestinian Arabs and Israelis.

The Suez Crisis

Egypt's leader, Gamal Abdel Nasser, tried to benefit from Cold War rivalries. Though he pursued anti-Communist policies at home, he asked for and received economic aid from both the Soviet Union and the United States. In 1955 the United States offered to lend Egypt $56 million to build the giant Aswan High Dam on the Nile River. However, when Nasser accepted arms from the Soviet Union, the United States changed its mind about the loan. An angry Nasser then seized the Suez Canal and barred Israeli ships from passing through it.

Nasser's action alarmed Britain and France, who needed to transport their oil imports through the Suez Canal. Along with Israeli forces, they attacked Egypt. Supported by the United States and the Soviet Union, the UN called on Britain, France, and Israel to withdraw their troops from Egypt. They complied, and the Suez Canal remained under Egyptian control. The Soviets used the crisis to establish closer ties with Egypt and to increase Soviet influence in the Middle East.

The Eisenhower Doctrine

In 1957, the United States announced a new policy, aimed at checking Soviet influence in the Middle East. The Eisenhower Doctrine, named for Dwight D. Eisenhower, promised U.S. economic and military aid to any Middle Eastern nation threatened by a Communist-controlled country.

The Eisenhower Doctrine was first applied in 1958 when rebels, believed to be influenced by Nasser and the Soviet Union, overthrew the government of Iraq. Fearing a similar revolt in his own country, the ruler of Lebanon requested U.S. assistance. Eisenhower sent in 6,000 marines, and order was soon restored.

 How did the United States try to counteract Soviet influence in the Middle East?

Section 2 Review

Check Understanding

1. **Define** (a) superpower (b) occupation (c) demilitarized zone

2. **Explain** how the American occupation affected Japan.

3. **Identify** Chiang Kai-shek and Mao Zedong.

4. **Describe** the disagreement between Truman and MacArthur.

5. **Explain** how Nasser tried to benefit from the Cold War.

Critical Thinking

Synthesizing Why might many Americans have sided with MacArthur against Truman over policy in China and Korea?

Write About Culture

Connecting Past and Present Write a news article explaining why conflict exists today between the Jews and the Arabs over territory in Israel.

Section 3

The Cold War at Home

PREVIEW

Objectives

- To describe the Cold War policies of the Eisenhower administration

- To analyze the U.S. government's response to fear of the spread of communism

- To explain how rivalry between the United States and the Soviet Union resulted in an arms race and a space race

Vocabulary

massive retaliation	McCarthyism
brinkmanship	fallout
summit conference	space race
perjury	

During the 1950s, U.S. leaders sought new strategies for dealing with the Cold War. Many Americans came to believe that there were enemies inside the United States as well as behind the iron curtain. This climate of fear and suspicion produced another Red Scare.

◆ EISENHOWER BECOMES PRESIDENT

By the election of 1952, Americans were ready for a change. The Korean War still raged, and many people felt that President Truman had not done enough to stop the advance of communism. Dwight Eisenhower, the Republican candidate and a World War II hero, won a huge victory, in part by promising to go to Korea and end the war.

A New Foreign Policy

Eisenhower's secretary of state, John Foster Dulles, took a tough stand against communism. To Dulles, communism was an evil that needed to be wiped out. He attacked Truman's policy of containment, arguing that it was not enough just to control the spread of communism. Rather, he wanted to free the nations of Eastern Europe from Soviet rule. Dulles urged the people of Eastern Europe to rise up against Soviet domination.

Dulles also rejected fighting limited wars such as the Korean War. Instead he announced that if necessary, the United States would use nuclear weapons against the Soviets. The policy of all-out nuclear warfare was called **massive retaliation.** Dulles realized that using threats of nuclear attack was a dangerous tactic. The United States must be willing and able to go to the brink of war without going over the edge, said Dulles. Critics nicknamed this policy **brinkmanship.** Dulles defended the policy, saying,

> The ability to get to the verge of war is a necessary art. If you cannot muster it, you inevitably get into wars. If you try to run away from it, if you are scared to go to the brink, you are lost.

The Geneva Summit

Despite Dulles' tough words, Eisenhower hoped to ease Cold War tensions. Stalin's death in 1953 and the rise to power of new leaders in the Soviet Union gave the President this opportunity.

In July 1955, Eisenhower met with leaders from Britain, France, and the Soviet Union in Geneva, Switzerland, to discuss how relations could be improved. The press called the meeting a **summit conference** because it involved the highest officials of each country. At the Geneva summit, Eisenhower put forward an "open skies" proposal. Each side would allow the other to take aerial photographs of its military preparations. The Soviets and the Communist party leader, Nikita Khrushchev (kroo-shof´), rejected the plan, but the summit produced a new feeling of goodwill between the two nations.

Khrushchev became Soviet premier in 1958. He and Eisenhower made plans to meet at another summit conference in Paris in May 1960.

The U-2 Incident

The goodwill did not last long. On May 1, 1960, the Soviets shot down a U.S. plane, called a U-2, deep within their territory. At first, the United States claimed that the plane was on a weather mission. But the captured pilot, Gary Francis Powers, confessed to

◀ Members of the press recorded the proceedings as the House Un-American Activities Committee investigated accusations that there were Communists in the movie industry.

being a spy. Unknown to most Americans, U.S. spy planes had been photographing Soviet military sites since 1956.

At the Paris summit, held later in May as scheduled, a furious Khrushchev demanded that the spy flights cease immediately. He also wanted the United States to apologize for "past acts of aggression." When Eisenhower refused to apologize, Khrushchev stormed out, and the conference broke up. Eisenhower later regretted that the U-2 incident had cost him Khrushchev's goodwill.

How were Soviet-U.S. relations strained during the Eisenhower administration?

◆ McCARTHYISM AND THE RED SCARE

During the 1950s, fear of spies grew. Many Americans were alarmed because they believed that agents of communism were secretly gaining strength in the United States.

The Hunt for Spies Begins

After World War II, the House Un-American Activities Committee (HUAC) launched a search for Communists within the nation. One of its first targets was the entertainment industry. During the late 1940s, HUAC hunted for actors, writers, and directors who had joined Communist organizations or had sympathized with Communist issues. Those who refused to testify at HUAC's public hearings were regarded as guilty and were blacklisted, or put on a list of people not to employ. Many in the movies, TV, and radio lost their jobs, and their reputations were ruined. Some continued to work by hiding their identities.

HUAC's most famous case involved Alger Hiss, a former State Department official charged with passing top-secret documents to the Soviets. Whittaker Chambers, a former Communist agent, claimed that Hiss had provided him with the State Department documents. Hiss could not be tried for treason because too much time had passed. However, when Hiss denied the charges, he was tried, convicted, and sent to prison for **perjury,** or lying under oath.

Two other suspected spies, Ethel and Julius Rosenberg, received harsher punishment. The Rosenbergs were charged with passing atomic secrets to the Soviets during World War II, making it possible for the Soviets to make their own atomic bomb. Although they continued to maintain their innocence, a jury convicted the Rosenbergs of treason, and they were executed in 1953.

The Rise and Fall of McCarthy

One man, Senator Joseph R. McCarthy of Wisconsin, built his career by threatening to expose Communists. In a speech in Wheeling, West Virginia, in 1950, McCarthy claimed to have in his hands a list of 205 known Communists currently working in the State Department. McCarthy refused to show the list to anyone. As it turned out, he did not need to. Many Americans were eager to believe him.

Soon the nation was in the grip of another Red Scare that became known as **McCarthyism.** McCarthyism meant that anyone could be perceived as disloyal or treasonous by supporting communism or even questioning capitalism. The slightest unconfirmed hint of communism ruined many careers.

When McCarthy falsely charged that the U.S. Army was filled with Communists, the army fought back. The Senate voted to censure McCarthy. Condemned by the Senate, McCarthy soon dropped out of public view. But the fears he had fueled remained.

 What caused the rise of McCarthyism?

◆ THE ARMS AND SPACE RACES

In 1946 the United States proposed a plan to ban further use of the atomic bomb. In addition, it recommended that atomic energy be put under the control of an international agency. The Soviets, who were rapidly developing their own atomic bomb, came back with an alternate plan. Their proposal would result in the destruction of all existing nuclear weapons. Neither side would accept the other's proposal.

A nuclear arms race was on. In 1949, the Soviets exploded their first atomic bomb. Americans were stunned. They had not expected the Soviets to have and test atomic weapons so soon. The terrified nation pressured American scientists to create an even more powerful bomb.

In 1952, Americans exploded the first hydrogen bomb, or H-bomb. Soon, though, the Soviets had their own hydrogen bomb. These weapons were vastly more destructive than the atomic bomb. Communist China joined the race by testing its first atomic bomb in 1964, and a hydrogen bomb three years later. Great Britain and France also developed nuclear weapons.

The United States continued to test atomic bombs after World War II. The test in the photograph below was made over Bikini Atoll in the Pacific Ocean in 1946. ▼

▲ *The Soviet Union sent a dog, Laika, into space aboard the satellite* Sputnik 2. *That satellite launch was commemorated on this Soviet stamp.*

Toward a Test Ban

Nuclear weapons did not have to be used in a war to be dangerous. The process of testing them resulted in fatalities and contamination from **fallout.** Fallout is the settling of radioactive particles that result from a nuclear blast. After the United States exploded its second H-bomb at Bikini Atoll in the Pacific Ocean, fish that were caught more than 1,000 miles away were found to be radioactive. Scientists feared that continued testing would contaminate the earth's atmosphere.

A halt to nuclear testing was both the way to avoid this danger and the first step toward ending the deadly nuclear arms race. Many people feared that nuclear bombs presented a threat to health and to the very existence of the human race. In 1958, the United States, the Soviet Union, and Great Britain began test-ban talks in Geneva but were unable to reach an agreement.

The Launch of *Sputnik*

In the fall of 1957, the news that the Soviets had sent the first and second satellites, *Sputnik 1* and *Sputnik 2*, into space shocked many Americans. Not only were they astonished that the Soviets had beaten them into space, but they were alarmed to learn that the rockets used to launch the satellites could also carry nuclear warheads.

The United States and the Soviets were now also in a **space race**—a competition in technology to gain prominence in space. In January 1958, the Americans launched their own satellite, *Explorer 1.* That same year, Congress established the National Aeronautics and Space Administration (NASA) to coordinate the country's space program.

Many Americans believed the Soviets were ahead in the space race. In 1958, Congress passed the National Defense Education Act, with the goal of producing more scientists and teachers. The money also helped to fund more laboratories and scientific equipment for high schools and colleges.

How did the arms race and the space race demonstrate U.S.-Soviet competition?

Section 3 Review

Check Understanding

1. **Define** (a) massive retaliation (b) brinkmanship (c) summit conference (d) perjury (e) McCarthyism (f) fallout (g) space race

2. **Explain** the Eisenhower administration's approach to the Cold War.

3. **Discuss** how the U-2 incident affected U.S. and Soviet relations.

4. **Describe** the way many people responded to the fear of the spread of communism.

5. **Explain** why the United States proposed a plan that would put atomic energy under the control of an international agency.

Critical Thinking

Analyzing Why were some Americans willing to believe Senator Joseph McCarthy's charges against people?

Write About History

◆**Connecting Past and Present** John Foster Dulles made his comment about brinkmanship more than 35 years ago. Write a newspaper editorial, supporting or opposing the truth of his ideas today.

Emerging Nations and the Cold War

PREVIEW

Objectives

- To describe the results of independence movements in Africa and Asia

- To explain what problems the new African and Asian nations faced

- To analyze why the United States began sending military advisors to Vietnam during the 1950s

Vocabulary

nonviolent resistance   domino theory
Vietminh   Viet Cong

During the 1950s, former colonies in Asia and Africa gained their independence. In the 1950s and 1960s, new faces joined familiar ones in the UN General Assembly. On one day alone, September 20, 1960, a total of 16 new African nations were admitted to the UN. The United States and the Soviet Union soon competed to win allies among these new nations.

◆ AFRICANS PUSH FOR INDEPENDENCE

In 1957, *Life* magazine featured Kwame Nkrumah (kwä´-mē en-´krü-mə), the prime minister of the new nation of Ghana, on its cover. The former British colony was the first African nation to gain independence after World War II. By 1970, there would be 50 new African nations.

During World War II, hundreds of thousands of Africans had fought alongside European and American soldiers to free the world from Nazi rule. After the war, they were ready to win freedom for themselves.

Some former colonies, like Ghana, achieved independence through peaceful means. Others, such as the British colony of Kenya, where the white ruling minority refused to give up power, had to fight for it.

Some of the new African countries were ill-prepared for nationhood. They had little experience in self-government, except on the local level. Boundaries between countries had been created for the convenience of Europeans, with no regard for the different ethnic groups lumped together under one government. Often, tribal loyalties remained stronger than national loyalty. Tension between groups led to feuds and even civil war.

Underdeveloped economies also caused problems. Most Africans still lived by subsistence farming, providing for their own needs. The colonial powers had used Africa's rich natural resources for their own industries rather than for the development of local industries. Africans desperately needed funds to develop their countries. But if they turned to outside nations for help, they ran the risk of foreign control.

The United States and the Soviet Union both welcomed the end of colonial rule in Africa. Each hoped to have the newly emerging nations as allies. In the early Cold War years, however, the superpowers were too caught up in rivalries in Europe and Asia to pay much attention to Africa.

 What problems did the nations of Africa face after gaining independence?

Prime Minister Kwame Nkrumah celebrated the independence of Ghana, the first African nation to gain independence after World War II. ▼

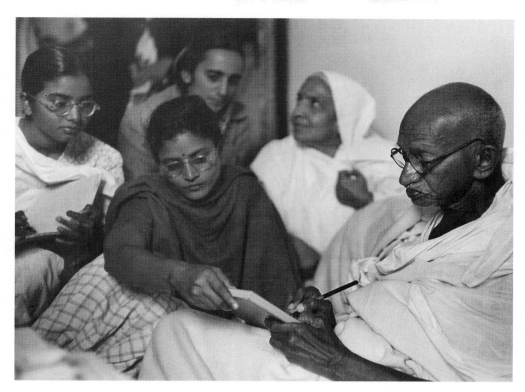

◀ *Mohandas K. Gandhi, shown here with a crowd of followers, led the independence movement in India.*

◆ ASIANS GAIN INDEPENDENCE

Many Asians had hungered for independence well before World War II ended. In Asia, which had a long history of colonial rule, nationalism arose sooner than it did in Africa. While most of Africa did not come under foreign control until the late 1800s, parts of Asia were colonized during the 1700s and 1800s.

In 1946, the Philippines gained independence, which the United States had promised 12 years before. The change occurred peacefully.

The following year, the British finally returned full independence to India. Mohandas K. Gandhi (mō´-hən-däs gän´-dē) headed the independence movement. Gandhi believed in using **nonviolent resistance** to achieve his goals. Through strikes, fasts, and protest marches, Gandhi and his followers forced the British to take the first steps toward allowing self-rule for India in the 1930s. But bitter fighting at the time of independence between India's two main religious groups, the Hindus and the Muslims, made it necessary to establish two separate countries. One was India, which was mostly Hindu; the other was Pakistan, which was mostly Muslim.

Elsewhere in Southeast Asia, independence was achieved only after a long and violent struggle.

This was true of both Indonesia (the former Dutch East Indies) and the French colony of Indochina. Like the new African nations, the new countries of Asia faced serious economic and political problems. These problems frequently had come about as a result of colonial rule. But most of the countries were determined to develop in their own way, without direction from either the United States or the Soviet Union.

The United States did, however, persuade a few Asian nations to join in a military alliance. In September 1954, Australia, New Zealand, Pakistan, the Philippines, and Thailand joined Britain, France, and the United States to form the Southeast Asia Treaty Organization (SEATO). Like NATO, SEATO was organized to provide security against Communist aggression. All member nations pledged to aid each other militarily in the event of an attack. SEATO would also protect the new nations of Cambodia, Laos, and South Vietnam. SEATO was especially important to the United States in view of the growing conflict in Vietnam.

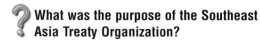

What was the purpose of the Southeast Asia Treaty Organization?

◆ TENSION IN SOUTHEAST ASIA

Before World War II, Vietnam, along with Laos and Cambodia, was part of the French colony of Indochina. Vietnamese nationalists, led by Ho Chi Minh, a Communist, hoped to win independence. Japan conquered Indochina during World War II, but Ho and his followers, the **Vietminh,** continued to work for freedom. After the defeat of Japan, Ho declared Vietnam independent.

France Fights to Regain Vietnam

In 1945, the French sent troops to reconquer Vietnam. They soon won control of cities in the south. The Vietminh fled into the mountains, where they launched guerrilla attacks against the French. This guerrilla warfare took a heavy toll.

The French asked the United States for help. At first, the Americans had opposed France's effort to regain Vietnam. But fearing that communism would spread throughout Vietnam, the United States agreed to provide aid. Both Truman and Eisenhower sent military supplies and military advisors to help the French troops. After 1949, the People's Republic of China aided the Vietminh.

Despite American help, French troops were trapped at the fortress of Dien Bien Phu. France appealed to the United States to launch an air strike against the Vietminh. Eisenhower refused. He feared the United States would become involved in another treacherous ground war like the Korean War. Dien Bien Phu fell to the Vietminh on May 7, 1954.

A Divided Vietnam

In 1954, an international conference was held in Geneva, Switzerland, to decide the fate of Vietnam. The Geneva Agreements called for an end to the fighting between the French and the Vietminh. They divided Vietnam into two regions, with the Vietminh in control of the north and the French in control of the south, as shown on the map on page 499. The Vietnamese were to hold free elections in 1956, with the goal of uniting the country under one government.

The French soon withdrew from South Vietnam. They left in power an anti-communism government, headed by Ngo Dinh Diem. Diem's government was weak and corrupt. Without outside help, it would topple. The United States feared that South Vietnam would then fall to the Communists, starting a chain reaction that would end with all of Asia under the rule of communism. This became known as the **domino theory.** As Eisenhower explained,

In April 1954, the Vietnamese army took back the city of Hongay from the French. The people of the city joyously greeted the soldiers as they rode through the streets in triumph. ▶

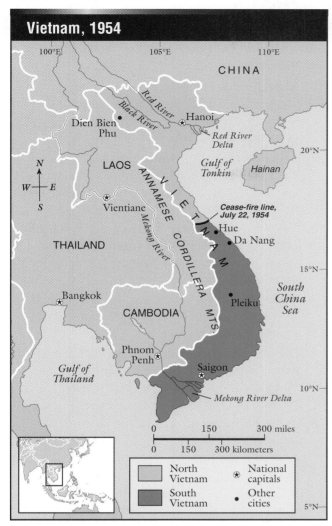

Vietnam, 1954

CHINA

Red River
Black River
Dien Bien Phu
Hanoi
Red River Delta
20°N
LAOS
Gulf of Tonkin
Hainan
Vientiane
Hue
Cease-fire line, July 22, 1954
Da Nang
15°N
THAILAND
Pleiku
South China Sea
Bangkok
CAMBODIA
Phnom Penh
10°N
Saigon
Gulf of Thailand
Mekong River Delta
5°N

0   150   300 miles
0   150   300 kilometers

| North Vietnam | ⊛ National capitals |
| South Vietnam | • Other cities |

▲ **Geography** *This map shows how Vietnam was partitioned according to the Geneva Agreements.* **Interpreting the Map** *At about what point of latitude was the cease-fire line of 1954?*

> You have a row of dominoes set up, you knock over the first one, and what will happen to the last one is the certainty that it will go over very quickly. **,,**

U.S. Involvement Grows

Eisenhower feared that the dominoes might include the Southeast Asian nations of Thailand, Malaysia, Indonesia, Burma, and the Philippines. All were facing Communist-led rebel movements.

Eisenhower pledged economic and military support to Diem's government. He had already made sure that SEATO's protection extended to South Vietnam.

During the mid-1950s, he used SEATO to send the first American military advisors to South Vietnam.

In spite of huge amounts of American aid, Diem's government remained corrupt and shaky. South Vietnamese Communists, called the **Viet Cong**, attacked Diem's strong-man rule. The United States responded by sending in more military advisors. During Eisenhower's administration, 800 military advisors were sent to South Vietnam. Many more would follow.

 How did the United States first become involved in Vietnam?

Section 4 Review

Check Understanding

1. **Define** (a) nonviolent resistance (b) Vietminh (c) domino theory (d) Viet Cong

2. **Identify** Kwame Nkrumah and Mohandas K. Gandhi.

3. **Explain** why the United States decided to help the French regain Vietnam.

4. **Discuss** why Eisenhower believed the United States had to support Diem's government.

Critical Thinking

Analyzing In what way was increasing the number of military advisors in Vietnam a dangerous course for the United States?

Write About History

◆**Connecting Past and Present** Nations that gained independence in recent times faced several problems that confronted the United States when it struggled for independence in the 1700s. In what ways were their struggles similiar? How were they different? Write a brief essay.

Chapter 24
Review

CHAPTER SUMMARY

Section 1

After World War II, the Soviets were in control of several countries in Eastern Europe. That led to a Cold War between the Soviet Union and the United States. The United States moved to contain communism through economic aid and the formation of NATO.

Section 2

In Asia, the United States helped Japan rebuild, while China embraced communism. North Korea invaded South Korea, and UN forces led by the United States intervened to save South Korea from the Communists. The war ended in 1953, but Korea remained a divided country. In the Middle East, the creation of Israel sparked conflict with Arab countries. Both the United States and the Soviet Union sought influence and power in the region.

Section 3

The Cold War continued during the Eisenhower years. There was some attempt to repair the relationship between the United States and the Soviet Union, but the U-2 incident cooled relations again. Communists were seen as threats by some people in the United States. Meanwhile, the Americans and the Soviets competed with one another in the space and arms races.

Section 4

New nations formed in Africa but faced many problems. In Asia, India fought for and gained independence. Eisenhower—afraid that if Vietnam fell to communism, all of Asia would follow—sent military advisors to South Vietnam.

Connecting ◆ Past and Present

The arms race and the space race characterized the competitive relationship between the Soviet Union and the United States during the Cold War. In what ways do Russia and the United States cooperate today?

Using Vocabulary

Select the letter of the phrase that best completes each sentence.

1. A **satellite** is (a) a policy of containing communism; (b) a nation economically or politically dependent on another nation; (c) a continuation of a previous policy.

2. Under the policy of **containment,** the United States (a) provided aid to European countries; (b) tried to win the space race; (c) tried to halt the spread of communism.

3. The term **superpower** referred to which of the following two nations? (a) China and North Korea; (b) Vietnam and France; (c) the United States and the Soviet Union.

4. **McCarthyism** (a) was named for a U.S. ship; (b) was the idea of a Soviet spy; (c) included unproved charges of treason.

5. The **domino theory** was the reason the United States (a) became involved in Vietnam; (b) airlifted food to Berlin; (c) promised freedom to the Philippines.

6. Under **occupation,** (a) a nation is controlled by the military of the victors; (b) economic progress is made; (c) information is distributed.

7. The **Vietminh** were (a) a pro-Communist group in Vietnam; (b) pro-French soldiers in Vietnam; (c) trained by the United States to help the French fight.

8. The **iron curtain** was (a) a protective cloth for soldiers; (b) a resource found in England; (c) the border between the Communist and democratic nations of Europe.

Check Understanding

1. **Discuss** the aims of the United Nations.

2. **Explain** the steps the Soviet Union took after the war to expand its influence in Eastern Europe.

3. **Describe** how the Marshall Plan was part of an effort to stop the spread of communism.

4. **Relate** how the United States dealt with Japan after the war.

5. **Explain** how the Korean War began.

6. **Describe** how the creation of Israel caused conflict in the Middle East.

7. **Identify** Joseph McCarthy and explain what he did.

8. **Describe** the development of the space race.

9. **Describe** two of the problems that the new African and Asian nations faced.

10. **Explain** why the United States got involved in Vietnam in the late 1950s.

Critical Thinking

1. **Analyzing Information** What was the U.S. attitude toward the Soviets after World War II?

2. **Comparing** Compare and contrast the Truman Doctrine and the Eisenhower Doctrine.

3. **Making Inferences** How might the Soviets have reacted to the views of John Foster Dulles?

4. **Analyzing Information** What motivated Congress to pass the National Defense Education Act in 1958?

◆ **Connecting Past and Present** How do you think the tensions with the Soviet Union in the Cold War affect our relations today with Russia?

Interpreting the Timeline

Use the timeline on pages 480–481 to answer these questions.

1. What happened in Asia the year that Senator McCarthy made charges against U.S. officials?

2. In what year did Churchill describe the Communist takeover in Eastern Europe as the falling of an iron curtain?

3. What was one U.S. response to the Soviet launch of *Sputnik 1*?

Writing to Show Cause and Effect

The Cold War affected the lives of most Americans in the 1950s. **Write** a short essay, explaining the causes of the Cold War and the effects that it had on American society.

Putting Skills to Work

INTERPRETING SPECIAL-PURPOSE MAPS

In the Building Skills lesson on page 487, you learned that special-purpose maps focus on a specific topic rather than give a general idea of an area. Look at the map below, which shows sources for coal and iron ore in Western Europe. Answer the questions that follow.

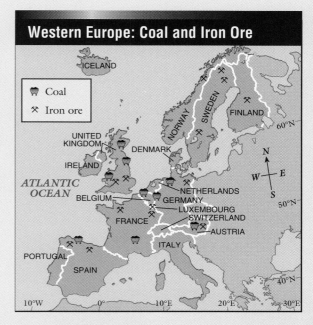

Western Europe: Coal and Iron Ore

1. In what areas of France is iron ore found?

2. What resource is found in Sweden?

3. Which countries have coal and iron ore?

Portfolio Project

A COLD WAR DOCUMENTARY

Work with several classmates to prepare a storyboard for a documentary about one of the following events in the Cold War: the Berlin Blockade, the Korean War, or the U-2 incident. Use library resources as well as this textbook to help you find information on your subject.

U.S. AND SOVIET RELATIONS

In the 1950s and 1960s, the United States and the Soviet Union were firmly locked in the Cold War. The nuclear arms race threatened their futures, redirected their economies, and promoted fears of coming doom.

Then In American popular culture, Soviets were once the symbol of evil. In the TV cartoon show *Rocky and Bullwinkle*, the bumbling spies Boris Badenov and Natasha Fatale plotted the downfall of American heroes in thick Russian accents. British writer Ian Fleming used the Soviets as villains in his James Bond novels, and John Le Carré explored the dark side of the Cold War.

Since there were no real battles to fight in the Cold War, Americans celebrated other victories. They rejoiced when a young pianist from Texas named Van Cliburn won the 1958 Tchaikovsky piano competition in Moscow. They were pleased when Russian ballet dancer Rudolf Nureyev defected to France. They were thrilled when the U.S. hockey team defeated the Soviets in the 1980 Winter Olympics.

Now When the Soviet Union collapsed in 1991, the tensions of the Cold War eased. The changed relationship between Russia (the leading nation of the former Soviet Union) and the United States is startling. McDonald's, a symbol of American capitalism, has two restaurants in Moscow. Just as surprising is the sight of Americans and Russians cooperating in space. The United States, in response to the Soviet launch of *Sputnik*, had stepped up its own space program. Today, Russian and American astronauts are planning to work together on ambitious projects in space.

You Decide

Since the fall of the Soviet Union, the United States has provided Russia with financial assistance. Do you think the United States should continue to provide financial assistance to Russia? Why or why not?

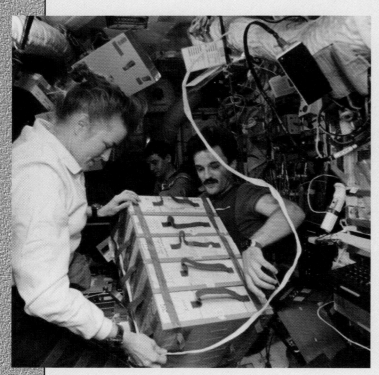

▲ In this photograph, American astronaut Shannon W. Lucid works with Russian cosmonaut Aleksandr Kaleri on the Mir Space Station.

Unit 8

Opportunities in a Changing Society 1945–1969

> " I have a dream that one day this nation will rise up and live out the true meaning of its creed: We hold these truths to be self-evident, that all men are created equal.... I have a dream that my four little children will one day live in a nation where they will not be judged by the color of their skin, but by the content of their character. "
>
> *Rev. Dr. Martin Luther King, Jr., in a speech at the March on Washington, August 28, 1963*

Chapter 25   Americans Find Prosperity (1945–1960)

Chapter 26   The Civil Rights Movement (1947–1965)

Chapter 27   A New Frontier and a Great Society (1960–1969)

▲ The nation watched much of the 1965 civil rights march from Selma to Montgomery, Alabama, unfold on television. ◆ **Connecting Past and Present** *What do the American flags say about this march? What symbols do people use to express their pride in their nation or support for a cause today?*

Chapter 25
Americans Find Prosperity 1945–1960

CHAPTER PREVIEW

Section 1 Adjusting to Peacetime

The American economy underwent a major shift as the nation moved from war to peace. Two Presidents, Truman and Eisenhower, blazed different trails in the prosperous postwar years.

Section 2 The Good Years

In the years after World War II, Americans produced more goods than ever before, and many people enjoyed a higher standard of living.

Section 3 Popular Culture of the '50s

Television, rock 'n' roll, and the Beats were part of a new culture that arose in the years after World War II.

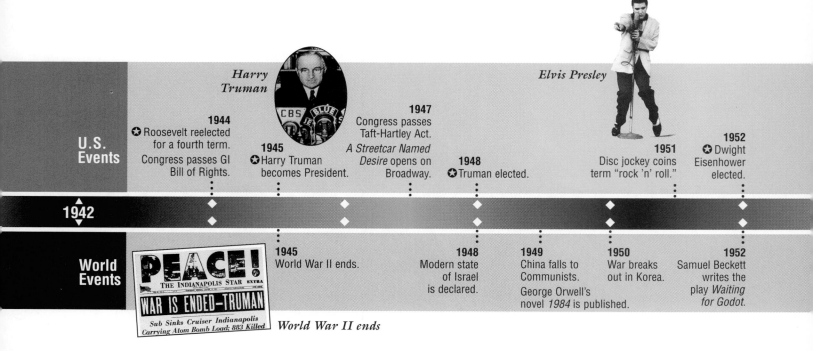

Harry Truman

Elvis Presley

U.S. Events

1944
✪ Roosevelt reelected for a fourth term.
Congress passes GI Bill of Rights.

1945
✪ Harry Truman becomes President.

1947
Congress passes Taft-Hartley Act.
A Streetcar Named Desire opens on Broadway.

1948
✪ Truman elected.

1951
Disc jockey coins term "rock 'n' roll."

1952
✪ Dwight Eisenhower elected.

1942

World Events

PEACE!
THE INDIANAPOLIS STAR EXTRA
WAR IS ENDED—TRUMAN
Sub Sinks Cruiser Indianapolis Carrying Atom Bomb Load; 883 Killed

World War II ends

1945
World War II ends.

1948
Modern state of Israel is declared.

1949
China falls to Communists.
George Orwell's novel *1984* is published.

1950
War breaks out in Korea.

1952
Samuel Beckett writes the play *Waiting for Godot.*

▲ Rock 'n' roll was seen and heard in millions of homes in the 1950s, when the television show "American Bandstand" was first broadcast.
◆◆ **Connecting Past and Present** *What age are most of the people in the photo? How is television used to promote popular music today?*

Portfolio Project

AN ORAL HISTORY

Oral histories are people's spoken accounts of the past. When historians study events in the recent past, they often interview people who experienced those events. These interviews, based on firsthand recollections, can show how important events affected individuals. As you read this chapter, watch for key events, and note questions that you would like to ask of people who lived in the 1950s. At the end of the chapter, you will compile an oral history of the decade.

Jonas Salk

Lorraine Hansberry, playwright

1954
Jonas Salk successfully tests polio vaccine.

Phrase "under God" added to the Pledge of Allegiance.

1956
✪ Eisenhower reelected.

Congress passes funding for Federal Aid Highway Act of 1956.

1959
A Raisin in the Sun opens on Broadway.

1960
✪ John F. Kennedy elected.

1963
✪ Lyndon B. Johnson becomes President.

1964

1955
Soviets create Warsaw Pact to challenge NATO.

1956
Revolution breaks out in Communist Hungary.

1957
Ghana becomes first West African colony to win its independence.

1959
Fidel Castro comes to power in Cuba.

1963
Military coup overthrows the government of Ngo Dinh Diem of South Vietnam.

Fidel Castro, Cuban leader

Section 1

Adjusting to Peacetime

PREVIEW

Objectives

- To describe the postwar economy and the importance of GIs to it

- To explain how the Truman administration guided the U.S. economy in its transition from wartime to peacetime

- To analyze why Eisenhower's administration was well suited to the needs of the time

Vocabulary

Dixiecrat   Fair Deal
special session   recession
whistle-stop tour   military-industrial complex

Franklin Roosevelt died suddenly on April 12, 1945. His Vice President, Harry Truman, succeeded him. Truman's aggressive personality suited the confrontational mood of the Cold War. He linked the Soviet threat in Europe to the need for a strong President.

◆ TRUMAN AND THE ECONOMY

Even though World War II ended soon after Truman became President, it did not signify an end to the challenges facing the United States. In fact, the postwar years brought about many new problems. Soldiers and sailors returned to the United States and had to look for work. At the same time, millions of civilians lost their jobs. Wartime industries had to be converted to meet peacetime needs, producing such items as cars and refrigerators instead of ships and tanks. This change had to take place quickly and smoothly.

The GI Bill of Rights

One of the most pressing responsibilities was the need to help veterans of World War II. The government aided returning soldiers by passing the Serviceman's Readjustment Act of 1944, popularly known as the GI Bill of Rights. It allowed veterans to apply for low-cost loans to buy houses or farms, or to start businesses. The bill also provided a full year of unemployment pay for any veteran who could not find work.

Probably the most important part of the law was the aid it gave to veterans who wanted an education. Each American soldier, or GI, was eligible to receive $500 a year to pay for the cost of attending college. The law also gave GIs up to $75 a month for living expenses. This was a great deal of money at a time when rent for an apartment might be $40 a month.

Of the ten million veterans who returned, about eight million used the GI Bill to further their education, helping the United States take a giant step toward the goal of full education for all. One veteran later remembered,

> The GI Bill of Rights . . . had more to do with thrusting us into a new era than anything else. Millions of people whose parents or grandparents had never dreamed of going to college saw that they could go. . . . I think it made us a far more democratic people.

Inflation and Labor Unrest

After a decade of economic depression and years of war, many Americans were eager to begin living the good life. One obstacle to prosperity appeared shortly after the war—higher prices. During World War II, the government had controlled both prices and wages in order to save money needed for the war effort. In 1946, when the government ended these controls, businesses were free to raise prices on the goods they made or sold. The result was rapid inflation. By 1948, prices were on average almost 32 percent higher than in 1945. Practically every kind of consumer product— from automobiles to pots and pans—rose in price. A headline in the New York *Daily News* referred to the higher price of meat, "Prices Soar, Buyers Sore, Steers Jump Over the Moon."

The situation grew worse as American consumers bought goods as fast as factories could make them. Because the demand for products was greater than the supply, manufacturers had no reason to keep their prices down. Prices continued to rise through 1948 until factory production at last caught up with demand.

◄ Workers across the nation felt the impact of the dramatic increase in inflation. These steel workers in Buffalo, New York, went on strike in early 1946.

Though prices for consumer goods were rising rapidly during this time, wages were not. Demanding more pay to cover the higher cost of living, many workers went out on strike. During 1946 alone, for example, more than five million people went out on strike in hopes of winning higher pay. At one point that year, meat packers and auto, steel, electrical, and communications workers were all out on strike. The economic impact on the country was serious.

The coal miners' strike in April 1946 dealt an especially severe blow to the economy. At that time, coal provided more than half of all industrial energy. Without coal, much of the nation's economy was crippled. Electric power production had to be cut back. Steel companies were unable to operate their mills, and car companies had to shut down their assembly lines. Truman let the strike continue for a few weeks. Then, like Franklin Delano Roosevelt before him, Truman took strong action. He seized control of the mines and ordered the miners back to work.

The Taft-Hartley Act

Truman's actions pleased few people. His tough stand on strikes made labor unions angry. His continuation of Roosevelt's policies made critics of the New Deal suspicious. The high rate of inflation upset just about everyone. By the fall of 1946, many people were fed up with the President. Truman rated lower in public approval than any twentieth-century President except Herbert Hoover.

Americans showed their dislike of Truman in the congressional election of 1946. Campaigning on the slogan "Had Enough?" the Republicans took control of both houses of Congress. With this new majority, in 1947 the Republicans passed the Taft-Hartley Act, which greatly limited the power that unions had gained during the New Deal. Among the many new rules was one that gave government the power, if a strike might cause a national emergency, to declare an 80-day "cooling off" period prior to the strike. Another rule banned unions from using dues collected from members for political contributions. Still another outlawed closed shop agreements, in which an employer hires only union members. The Republicans hoped that without closed shops, union power would fade. Horrified, labor leaders denounced the Taft-Hartley Act as a "slave labor bill." Truman vetoed the bill, but the Republican-controlled Congress passed it again and overrode his veto.

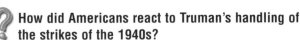

How did Americans react to Truman's handling of the strikes of the 1940s?

◆ THE ELECTION OF 1948

By the summer of 1948, few political observers gave Truman much hope of winning the presidential election. Even within his own Democratic party, people were angry with him. Truman had issued executive orders in July 1948 desegregating the armed forces and banning discrimination in the federal civil service. During the Democratic Convention, the entire Mississippi delegation and half of the Alabama delegation walked out, protesting Truman's pro-civil rights position. Not long after, white southern Democrats, called **Dixiecrats,** organized a political party called the States' Rights party. They nominated, as their candidate for President, the governor of South Carolina, Strom Thurmond. Meanwhile, liberal Democrats thought Truman was not doing a good job defending many New Deal programs. They, too, broke from the regular Democratic party and formed the Progressive party, under the leadership of Henry A. Wallace. He had been Franklin Roosevelt's Vice President during Roosevelt's third term.

The Great Upset

The Republicans, confident of victory, chose a moderate candidate they hoped would appeal even to Democrats. This candidate was Thomas Dewey, the governor of New York. Dewey had built a reputation as a battler against organized crime. Convinced that Truman could not win, Dewey did not campaign

▲ Harry Truman was photographed after he had defeated Dewey in the 1948 presidential election. The famous headline error indicates how close the race was.

aggressively or make many speeches. When he did make speeches, his somewhat cold and stiff manner did not project a compelling image.

Truman knew how to use the office of the President to his advantage. In July 1948, he struck a major blow at the Republicans by calling the Republican-controlled Congress into **special session.** A special session is an extra meeting of Congress outside the months in which it usually meets. It was the first special session in an election year in almost 100 years. Truman challenged Congress to pass laws to stop inflation, end the housing shortage that had resulted from soldiers returning home, fund medical insurance, aid education, and protect civil rights. Early in the campaign, the Republicans had claimed to be in favor of all of these policies. In the special session, however, the Republicans did not strongly support them. Truman persuaded many Americans to vote for him when he showed that the Republicans had not made good on their promises.

In September, Truman took his case to the people. He set out on a long **whistle-stop tour** of the country. On a whistle-stop tour, political candidates make brief appearances in many small towns. Truman delivered as many as a dozen speeches a day, lashing out at the Republicans and calling them "tools of big business." Fear of the Republicans won the bulk of organized labor back from the Progressive party. In addition, Truman's recognition of the new state of Israel in May 1948 encouraged many Jewish voters to support the Democratic party.

Study Hint

A Venn diagram, such as the one on page 363, is useful to note similarities and differences between people, places, or events. Use one to compare the presidencies of Truman and Eisenhower. Draw two large overlapping circles. Where the circles overlap, list ways the presidencies are alike. Where the circles do not overlap, list differences between the presidencies.

Neither the Republicans nor the press realized that Truman was making progress toward election. In October, *Newsweek* magazine polled 50 leading political writers. All 50 predicted a Dewey victory. Even on election day the *Chicago Tribune*, a morning newspaper, printed a headline, "Dewey Defeats Truman." But the *Tribune* was printed far too early, before all the votes were counted. Truman won the election with 304 electoral votes to 189 for Dewey. The States' Rights party won 39 electoral votes, all in the South. The Progressive party did not win any electoral votes.

The Fair Deal

Armed with his victory, Truman introduced a program he called the **Fair Deal.** Based on Franklin Roosevelt's New Deal, the Fair Deal called for the repeal of the Taft-Hartley Act, a higher minimum wage, government-backed health insurance, and federal funding for public schools and urban housing.

Many Democrats had been swept into Congress by the election, so Truman was able to get some of the laws he wanted passed. Congress raised the minimum wage from 40 to 75 cents an hour and passed a law promoting the clearing of slums and the building of low-income housing. The Social Security Act of 1950 increased the number of people covered under the Social Security Act of 1935. However, Republicans and southern Democrats joined to block many of Truman's Fair Deal proposals, including national health insurance, aid for farmers, and a law to banish discrimination in hiring. Bills to weaken southern segregation, such as making lynching a federal crime and outlawing the poll tax, were also defeated. Truman's domestic policies were deadlocked by the end of his term. By then, his Cold War foreign policy was drawing the nation's attention.

Why were Republicans so confident of victory in 1948?

◆ THE EISENHOWER YEARS

By the 1952 presidential election, Democrats had been in the White House for almost 20 years. The Republicans had a new slogan: "It's time for a change." The candidate chosen by Republicans to effect this change was the well-known World War II general, Dwight D. Eisenhower.

Eisenhower, who had led the Allied forces in Western Europe and had planned the D-day invasion of Normandy in 1944, was one of the most popular American heroes of World War II. After the war, Eisenhower had retired from the army and become president of Columbia University in New York City for a short time. Then he returned to Europe to serve as commander of the forces of the North Atlantic Treaty Organization (NATO).

Eisenhower, whose nickname was "Ike," represented firmness, friendliness, and honesty to millions of Americans. In 1952, he won the Republican nomination for President and chose as his running mate California senator Richard M. Nixon. While Eisenhower was known as a moderate Republican, Nixon was known for his strong anti-Communist views.

Truman, whose popularity had sunk to an all-time low after he dismissed MacArthur as commander of the UN troops in Korea, decided not to seek reelection. The Democrats chose Governor Adlai Stevenson of Illinois as their presidential candidate. Though Stevenson showed a command of major issues, he could not overcome Eisenhower's popularity. The Republican campaign slogan, "I Like Ike," captured the national mood. Eisenhower won a smashing victory, receiving 6.6 million more popular votes than Stevenson. In the electoral college, Eisenhower won 442 votes as opposed to 89 for Stevenson. The Republicans also won a slim majority in both houses of Congress.

Eisenhower's easygoing ways were compatible with the nation's desire to enjoy peacetime prosperity.

Eisenhower's campaign slogan, "I Like Ike," appeared across the nation, stirring wide public support. ▼

Americans wanted a period of calm and steady government, not continued reminders of the postwar challenges they faced. Eisenhower promised to "steer a course right down the middle." This meant continuing some of the programs of the New Deal while, at the same time, trying to halt the growth of the federal government. It also meant keeping government from tampering with the economy.

Eisenhower did propose new programs for clearance of urban slums and for the construction of public housing. Also, in April 1953, he signed a bill creating the Department of Health, Education, and Welfare as a major department in government. Its function was to manage federal food, drug, health, and educational programs and oversee Social Security.

An Interstate Highway System

Improvements to the U.S. highway system were a highlight of Eisenhower's presidency. Dreaming of a highway network that would speed travel between the states, he proposed a national interstate highway system to be funded by government bonds and special taxes. Congress authorized funding for this system of highways by passing the Federal Aid Highway Act of 1956. It proposed building 40,000 miles of new highways at a total cost of $41 billion. In signing the bill, Eisenhower noted proudly,

> **The amount of concrete poured to form these roadways would build six sidewalks to the moon.**

The new highway system boosted the U.S. economy, especially the automobile and trucking industries. Highways eventually linked every state in the contiguous United States, as shown on the map below. Highways near major cities proved an ideal way to transport goods from manufacturing centers to markets. By 1960, truckers were carrying about half the country's freight and using parts of the new highway system to do so. The interstate system also made it possible for Americans to travel more easily for business or pleasure. As a result, businesses sprang up in suburban areas, and the travel and tourism industry grew.

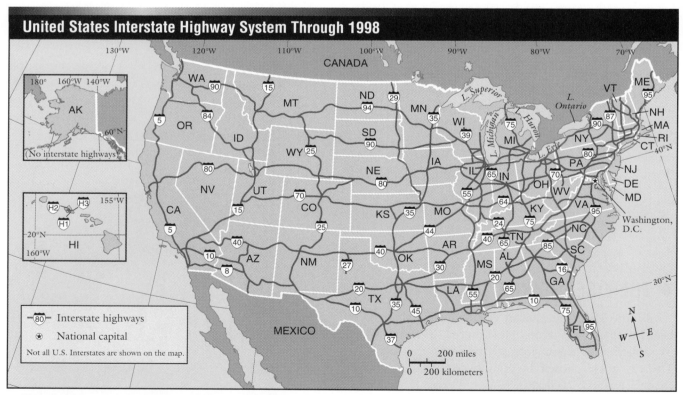

United States Interstate Highway System Through 1998

▲ **Geography** *The interstate highway system was begun during the Eisenhower administration. Today, it is considered nearly complete.* **Interpreting the Map** *How are major highways that run north-south numbered? How are those that run east-west numbered?*

However, the growth of the interstate highway system also had other kinds of results. The efficiency of the new highways caused railroads to lose a good deal of their business. Many lines folded, and others cut back on service. The railroads suffered even more as people began using their cars instead of trains to travel long distances. Also, towns that were not located near interstates noticed that their economies declined due to a decrease in business. Increasing traffic on highways also brought more pollution, traffic jams, and accidental deaths. In addition, the roads made it easier for more people to leave the cities and move to the suburbs.

A Second Term

In September 1955, Eisenhower suffered a heart attack, but his health improved, and early in 1956, he announced he would seek another term. Eisenhower's Democratic opponent was Adlai Stevenson, the same candidate who had opposed him in 1952. This time, Stevenson warned against Republican broken promises while Eisenhower ran on a record of "peace, progress, and prosperity." Eisenhower's popularity led to a one-sided campaign. He won by an even larger margin than in 1952.

A highlight of Eisenhower's second term was the admission of Alaska and Hawaii as the 49th and 50th states in 1959. Another highlight was the American economy, which, in general, continued to prosper during this time. However, several **recessions,** or slowdowns, did mark the economy. During this period, Eisenhower used government spending to get the economy going again, just as the Democrats had during the New Deal. The amounts were small because Eisenhower was uncomfortable with massive government spending. Government debt remained high, bolstered by military spending, foreign aid, and expenses relating to World War II veterans who had returned home.

Much of Eisenhower's second term was marked by foreign policy crises in several developing nations around the world. In 1956, a short but bitter war flared in the Middle East as Great Britain, France, and Israel invaded Egypt. Also in 1956, a revolution against Communist rule in Hungary was brutally put down by Soviet armed forces. In 1959, Communist revolutionaries took over Cuba, barely 90 miles from the United States coast. When confronted with the presence of a Communist government so near the United States, Eisenhower used every means available

to him to stop it, including trade embargoes and economic and military aid.

By the end of Eisenhower's second term, he had become concerned that the alliance between the United States military and the huge defense industry was growing too close. He called this alliance the **military-industrial complex.** Eisenhower acknowledged that in the future the nation would need a strong military and large defense industries, but he warned that such an alliance could result in "misplaced power."

 According to Eisenhower, what role should government play in the economy?

Section 1 Review

Check Understanding

1. **Define** (a) Dixiecrat (b) special session (c) whistle-stop tour (d) Fair Deal (e) recession (f) military-industrial complex

2. **Explain** how the Taft-Hartley Act affected labor and strikes.

3. **Describe** how Truman used the power of the presidency to upset Dewey in the 1948 election.

4. **Discuss** why Eisenhower's personality and his "middle of the road" approach were well suited for the time period.

Critical Thinking

Synthesizing How did the problems the United States faced after World War II compare with the problems it faced after World War I?

Write About Culture

Connecting Past and Present Write an essay explaining why the interstate highway system is more important or less important today than it was in the 1950s.

BUILDING SKILLS

....

Evaluating Media: Truman's Election of 1948

Evaluating media involves examining the kind and quality of information offered by television, radio, newspapers, magazines, and even the Internet. These broadcast and print sources offer facts about current events, as well as interpretations and in-depth analyses of people, situations, and issues that make up history.

Here's How

Follow these steps to evaluate media:

1. Study the coverage. Is the treatment of the subject hasty and shallow, or is it detailed and complete? What kind of background information is provided? Are cause-and-effect relationships explained? Can all the facts be verified?

2. Check for fairness and accuracy. Is the coverage balanced, or can you detect a bias? What kinds of adjectives are used to chronicle the event?

3. Determine the degree of immediacy and interest. Is the event or issue reported on the scene, or is it secondhand? Is the person, event, or issue presented in an interesting way?

Here's Why

Historians use and evaluate many kinds of sources to enrich their understanding of a period, person, issue, or event. Whether listening to a news conference on the radio, watching a documentary on television, or doing research on the Internet, like a historian you need to evaluate the accuracy and quality of what you see, hear, and read.

Practice the Skill

The newspaper article below appeared in *The New York Times* on November 4, 1948. Read what the reporter, Arthur Krock, has to say about President Truman's presidential victory. Use the steps in *Here's How* to evaluate the article, then answer the three questions below.

In the political history of the United States, this achievement by Mr. Truman will be set down as a miracle of electioneering for which there are few if any parallels. His victory made him the undisputed national leader of the Democratic party, [which has been] bitterly divided for the past few years . . . since the death of Franklin D. Roosevelt, whom Mr. Truman succeeded from the office of Vice President.

1. What point of view does the writer communicate about President Truman's victory?

2. How does this coverage of the topic differ from that provided in this textbook on pages 508–509?

3. How does this article contribute to your understanding of Truman's election campaign?

Apply the Skill

Choose a current event that interests you and examine its treatment in at least three of the following media: a radio talk show; a television documentary or news magazine; a daily newspaper; an Internet news group. Use the *Here's How* steps to evaluate each medium. Then write an essay in which you compare and contrast the way the media present the subject.

The Good Years

PREVIEW

Objectives

- To analyze how and why the American economy expanded during the 1950s

- To evaluate the dramatic changes that the growing economy brought to American life

- To describe how the gap between middle-class Americans and poor Americans grew in the 1950s

Vocabulary

affluence	service industry
productivity	white-collar job
automation	baby boom
blue-collar job	urban renewal

The 1950s have often been called the "age of affluence" because of the financial comfort and security that characterized the decade. Unemployment was low and wages were high. People had money to spend and to save, and most of the nation prospered.

◆ AN EXPANDING ECONOMY

In the postwar years, the United States enjoyed a time of rapid economic growth. The economy expanded rapidly. When an economy expands, more goods are produced and sold, and new jobs are created. The boom reached its peak in the 1950s, when the average American's annual income nearly doubled from $1,526 to $2,788 per person.

The expansion was created by a nationwide increase in spending. During World War II, Americans had saved $150 billion. Now, they rushed to buy cars, televisions, refrigerators, and even houses—all the things they had not been able to get during the war. As their wages rose, they had even more money to spend.

Productivity and Prosperity

During the 1950s, there were plenty of goods for Americans to buy. **Productivity,** or the rate at which goods are produced or services are performed, increased at a rapid rate during the decade. Behind this increased productivity was **automation,** or the use of machines to do work formerly done by people. Between 1947 and 1957, Americans spent nearly $300 billion on new factories and industrial machines. Automation cut the time required to make countless products. For example, between 1945 and 1960, the length of time it took to produce an automobile was cut in half, from 310 hours to 155 hours.

High productivity allowed the United States to manufacture and consume more goods than any other country. In 1950, the United States built over eight million cars, which was more than 75 percent of all the autos produced worldwide in that year. New homes were built at the rate of about 1.4 million per year. More than one half of all the factory goods produced in the world during the 1950s were made in the United States.

Farmers, too, found ways to increase productivity. Between 1947 and 1957, U.S. farms produced more meat, wheat, and corn than in any other decade.

American magazines celebrated this time of general prosperity. One 1950s news magazine boasted,

> **There has been an explosive increase in production of all kinds, along with a record increase in . . . earnings, so that people have been able to buy and build more than ever before. . . . All told, [this] has been a real age of miracles.**

Increased productivity led to a work week that averaged 40 hours, and this shorter work week led to more leisure time. Instead of struggling to make a living, Americans now spent about $1 on leisure out of every $6 they earned. They golfed, gardened, traveled, watched television, and enjoyed countless other activities in larger numbers than ever before.

The Growth of a Service Economy

The huge boom in output took place while the U.S. economy was becoming less industrial and agricultural. Before the 1950s, the economy had largely been based on industries like manufacturing and mining. Jobs in these fields are called **blue-collar jobs,** after the work shirts worn by manual laborers. In the 1950s, more Americans moved into jobs in **service industries.** These are businesses such as medicine, law, insurance, banking, sales, and entertainment—anything that includes work done for others. Many such jobs are referred to as **white-collar jobs,** after the white shirts that most male office workers wore during the early part of this century. In 1940, only about one third of American workers held white-collar jobs. By 1960 more than half of all American workers had jobs in service fields. A majority of those service jobs were considered white-collar.

Left Out of the Prosperity

Despite the general prosperity of the 1950s, not all Americans benefited. The gap between the rich and the poor grew wider during the 1950s. By 1957, one quarter of the population still lived in poverty. In 1960, one out of five Americans lived below the poverty level, then defined as a 4-person family with an annual income below $3,000. Forty percent of American homes did not have a private bathroom with hot running water and a flush toilet.

Although many poor people were elderly and white, the burden of poverty fell heavily on African Americans and Latinos, who earned only about 60 percent of the income of white workers. Many Latinos had to move from place to place to find jobs, earning low wages harvesting crops that could not be handled by machines. Native Americans who had lost their land often moved to the cities, where lack of job training kept them in low-paying jobs. It became increasingly difficult for those with little formal education to find steady work that paid well. The unemployment rate for African Americans, Latinos, and Native Americans was often nearly double the rate for whites.

Many Americans were not aware of the widespread poverty in which African Americans, Latinos, Native Americans, and many rural whites were forced to live. As the middle class moved to the suburbs, they left the poor behind in the cities. Writer Ralph Ellison summed up the experience of many African Americans in his 1952 novel, *Invisible Man:*

> **I am an invisible man. I am invisible, understand, simply because people refuse to see me.**

While millions of Americans enjoyed the affluent life, a sense of resentment grew among poor Americans.

They could see the wealth around them, but they could not get it for themselves. No massive social welfare programs like those of the New Deal were introduced to help them break out of poverty.

? Why were many Americans unaware of widespread poverty during the 1950s?

◆ NEW LIVING PATTERNS

The years after World War II saw huge changes in the way people lived in the United States. The American population grew, and many people moved. The places in which people lived, both cities and towns, were changing, too. Finally, the roles of women and men changed in surprising ways.

Baby Boomers

After World War II, the population of the United States increased dramatically. Marriage rates surged as soldiers returned home. Confident that the bad times were behind them, many married couples started families. Births per year increased from about 2.5 million in 1940 to more than 4 million in 1955. This increase in the birth rate began in 1946 and was called the **baby boom.** Before it slowed in 1964, it created the largest population increase the United States had ever known.

Just as the prosperity of the 1950s encouraged people to have children, the large number of new

Social Issues *As suburbs developed, Americans moved out of the cities.* **Interpreting the Graph** *Where were most Americans living by 1960?* ▼

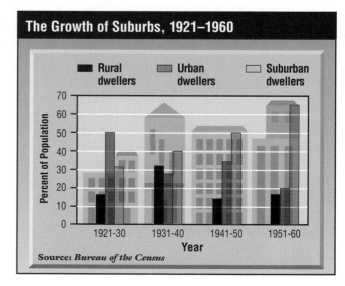

The Growth of Suburbs, 1921–1960

Source: *Bureau of the Census*

children fueled economic growth. Businesses rushed to provide services for this huge new market created by "baby boomers," as these children were called. Builders constructed thousands of schools, books on child care were written by experts like pediatrician Dr. Spock, and teachers were in great demand.

Growth of the Suburbs

As their families grew, Americans of the 1950s wanted their own homes. Using the GI Bill, many families of veterans were able to get loans to buy houses. They soon created a huge demand for housing, which builders struggled to meet. One way to do so was to build in the suburbs, the communities around urban areas. Thus, after World War II, the suburbs became the fastest-growing part of the American landscape. On average, some 3,000 acres of land were bulldozed for new suburbs every single day during the 1950s. By 1960, one out of four Americans lived in these communities, as shown on the graph on page 514.

One development that set the pattern for suburban growth was Levittown. In 1946, builder William Levitt bought a large piece of farmland on Long Island, near New York City. He divided it up and built 17,450 homes—a completely new community—which he named "Island Trees." The name was later changed to Levittown.

Levitt made his houses affordable by borrowing Henry Ford's principles of mass production and applying them to home building. Entire rows of houses were built using the same plan. Kitchens, bathrooms, and bedrooms in each house were nearly identical. Workers put the same type of oven in every kitchen and put up wall coverings that came in ready-made sheets. With these shortcuts, houses could be built in weeks, not months. Most of the houses looked alike, but buyers did not mind. They were happy to have a home of their own. A 1947 Levitt home cost $7,990, and the demand far exceeded the supply.

The surge to the suburbs created great opportunities for businesses. Before the 1950s, suburbanites had to travel to the city for shopping, medical care, and entertainment. Now, they could find all the goods and services they needed close at hand as stores, offices, and hospitals sprang up nearby.

A few of the new suburbs were open to people of all backgrounds, but most were not. Secret rules often barred house sales to African Americans, Italian Americans, Latinos, and Jews. The Levitt organization

▲ Houses built in Levittown had two bedrooms, a fireplace, and a built-in TV. One tree was planted every 28 feet along each street.

publicly refused to sell houses to African Americans until forced to do so by the U.S. courts in the mid-1960s. The 1959 play *A Raisin in the Sun,* by the African American playwright Lorraine Hansberry, deals in part with the problems an African American family faces in trying to move from Chicago to a mostly white suburb.

Changing Cities

As middle-class city dwellers moved out, the cities began to lose income from the loss of tax revenue. City governments could no longer afford to provide many public services. Some large cities suffered a decline in total population during the 1950s, something that had never happened before in the United States. Among them were Detroit, St. Louis, San Francisco, and Washington, D.C.

Meanwhile, the trends that had led poor people to leave farms and come to the cities were continuing. For example, about 1.85 million African Americans moved from the rural South to the cities of the North during the 1950s. With the flight of the middle class to the suburbs, the central cities more and more became home to the very rich and the very poor. Slum neighborhoods grew.

As the slums spread, federal, state, and local governments responded by completing hundreds of urban renewal projects. These projects aimed at replacing slum areas with improved residential, commercial, or industial areas. However, these urban renewal projects often succeeded only in bulldozing vital neighborhoods and relocating their residents to huge apartment buildings. Eventually, these buildings became associated with poverty and crime.

? What caused the growth of suburbs in the 1950s?

◆ NEW FORCES AFFECT SOCIETY

The nation was changing economically and geographically. Other changes were occurring as well.

Women and the Work Force

In 1943, women made up 25 percent of all workers in the wartime auto industry. By 1950, however, they made up only 10 percent. Managing a home and raising a family became the goals of many women. Others who wanted a career in business faced social pressures to limit that career.

Newspapers, magazines, and television helped shape the view of women. Most commercials showed women happily doing housework. Popular television programs, such as *Father Knows Best,* seldom suggested that women might have careers other than in the home.

As the 1950s progressed, more women were willing to challenge society's limited view. By the end of the 1950s, more American women were working outside the home than at any other time in history. By 1960, women held one third of the nation's jobs. About half of those women workers were married.

Many women, working in a culture that assumed women should be at home, faced job discrimination. Promotions were limited: only about 6 percent of all women workers held executive positions. Pay, too, was lower. On average, women with college degrees earned only $3,758, while men with high-school diplomas brought in average annual salaries of about $4,400.

Advances in Health

Dramatic improvements in medical care and medical research—in part funded by the government—allowed many Americans to enjoy longer and healthier lives. Many dreaded epidemic diseases disappeared due to vaccines and "wonder drugs" that were developed to eradicate such diseases.

Perhaps the most important medical advance was the conquest of polio. This paralyzing disease often

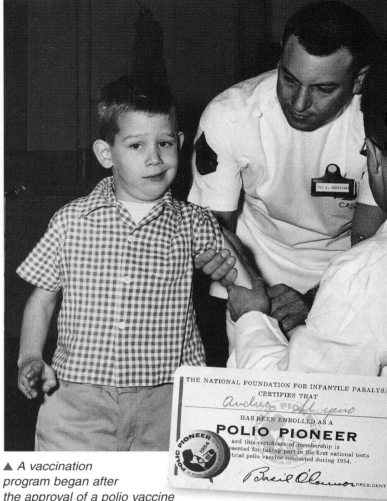

▲ A vaccination program began after the approval of a polio vaccine in 1955. Certificates were issued to the first children who got the vaccine.

struck children. Many Americans knew that it had attacked Franklin Roosevelt and could have ended his career in politics. In 1950 alone, nearly 33,000 people were stricken with polio.

In 1954 a researcher named Jonas Salk successfully tested a vaccine against the disease. Another researcher, Albert Sabin, developed another vaccine against the disease in 1959. Effective use of these vaccines meant that by the end of the decade, the number of reported cases dropped to only 2,200. By the 1960s, polio was practically wiped out in the United States.

Several other common diseases, such as pneumonia, rheumatic fever, and tuberculosis, became less of a threat during the 1950s. The discovery of antibiotics brought many diseases caused by bacteria under control. The flu and measles, while not treatable with antibiotics, began to yield to new vaccines.

Additionally, surgeons invented techniques to repair damaged blood vessels with artificial fibers. For the first time they transplanted corneas, the clear covering of the eyes. They began to move bone and tissue from one place in the body to another. This helped give renewed health to the sick.

A Bill for Education

Although American science made great progress in the 1950s, the Soviet launch of *Sputnik 1* in 1957 led many people to question the quality of American education. A debate over how children should be educated had raged for most of the decade. Concerned experts charged that education in the United States was weak. Said *Life* magazine,

> "The schools are in terrible shape. What has long been an ignored national problem, *Sputnik* has made a recognized crisis."

Many parents agreed that schools had failed to challenge young people. Critics demanded tougher courses, especially in science and math. These subjects, according to educators, held the key to victory in the space race. In response, Congress passed the National Defense Education Act. This bill provided nearly $900 million for college and graduate school loans, science laboratories in state universities, and instruction in science and math.

A Growing Interest in Religion

During the 1950s, organized religious groups grew more powerful, perhaps because people sought a firm foundation in a changing world. Church membership grew twice as fast as the population. The number of new church buildings doubled between 1950 and 1957. Christian Bibles sold at the rate of ten million a year. Religious songs hit the bestseller charts, and religious films such as *Ben Hur, The Ten Commandments,* and *The Robe* were popular at the box office.

Several religious leaders from different backgrounds had national programs on radio and network television. Baptist preacher Billy Graham began his career with a radio show first broadcast in 1950. Archbishop Fulton J. Sheen gave Roman Catholics a voice in a country that had often shown intolerance toward their religion. Norman Vincent Peale, a popular minister in the Reformed Church of America,

advanced ideas that Americans received with enthusiasm. In his book *The Power of Positive Thinking*, Peale said that by adopting a positive attitude, one could achieve success. These religious leaders all stressed individual solutions to problems and did not advocate social or political activism. Their emphasis on the importance of belonging and conforming meshed well with suburban, family-centered life.

Political leaders, too, encouraged the trend toward religion. In an effort to combat communism, Congress itself added the phrase "under God" to the Pledge of Allegiance in 1954. In 1956 it adopted "In God We Trust" as the national motto.

 How did American society change during the 1950s?

Section 2 Review

Check Understanding

1. **Define** (a) affluence (b) productivity (c) automation (d) blue-collar job (e) service industry (f) white-collar job (g) baby boom (h) urban renewal

2. **Explain** why the middle class prospered and grew during the 1950s.

3. **Describe** at least two dramatic economic changes that took place in the 1950s.

4. **Explain** why the gap between the middle class and the poor became greater in the 1950s.

Critical Thinking

Connecting Past and Present Compare the mood of the middle class in the 1950s to the mood of the middle class today. Consider feelings about the economy and about religion, education, and living patterns.

Write About Economics

Write an essay in which you discuss the effects that automation had on the U.S. economy in the 1950s.

Popular Culture of the '50s

PREVIEW

Objectives

- To analyze how television changed American life and the way Americans viewed their society and the world

- To examine why rock 'n' roll gained popularity and how it became a symbol of the younger generation

- To evaluate the reasons why some Americans rejected the standards of society

Vocabulary

rhythm and blues
generation gap
alienation

The booming economy, the huge shifts in population, and the scientific advances of the 1950s led to major changes in American life. In the years following World War II, the culture of the United States reflected a desire for the good life. People were deeply influenced by television, music, and the rise of a new group of consumers—teenagers.

◆ THE POWER OF TELEVISION

Today, people take television for granted. However, to Americans of the 1950s, television was a marvel. Everyone wanted to watch it. Lucky people who owned sets invited neighbors and friends over for long hours of evening television viewing.

As more people witnessed this new technology, they wanted sets of their own. By 1950, about 4 million American households owned television sets, as shown in the graph on this page. In 1956, Americans were buying about 20,000 television sets a day. By 1960, nearly nine in every ten American families owned at least one television set, which was turned on an average of five hours per day.

Television in the 1950s was an exciting medium in many ways. Videotape had not yet been invented, so most shows were broadcast live. Early programs included original dramas by top writers, sporting events, comedy-variety shows, and situation comedies about urban families. One series offered opera, symphony, and ballet, while another provided coverage of controversial public issues. This bold television programming is one reason the early 1950s is sometimes called the Golden Age of Television.

Television changed family life. Before television, families tended to share a variety of activities in the evenings, including reading together, singing and playing musical instruments, listening to the radio, or simply talking about the day's events. During the 1950s, in many families, watching television became the most important common activity of family life. In fact, by 1956, Americans were spending almost as much time watching television every week as they spent working for pay. The first frozen dinners, marketed as "TV dinners," appeared in 1954, designed for families who wanted to combine mealtime and television viewing.

Television changed political campaigns. During the 1952 presidential campaign, television brought visual images of politicians into American living rooms. Local politics changed too, as local politicians became national political figures overnight. Those who made a better impression on television could sway voters more easily. Candidates who had money

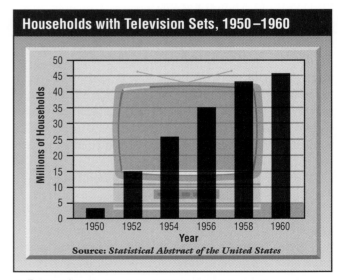

Households with Television Sets, 1950–1960

Millions of Households (y-axis: 0, 5, 10, 15, 20, 25, 30, 35, 40, 45, 50)

Year (x-axis: 1950, 1952, 1954, 1956, 1958, 1960)

Source: *Statistical Abstract of the United States*

▲ **Economics** *By the late 1950s, television sets were common in American homes.* **Interpreting the Graph** *When was the greatest increase in the number of households with television sets?*

▲ *In many families, watching television replaced other more active and interactive pastimes.*

could buy more advertising and television time. Ever since then, television image-making has been one of the most crucial factors in many elections.

Finally, television demonstrated a unique ability to create and support fads and trends across the country. In 1953 a magazine, *TV Guide,* was introduced. It soon became the best-selling magazine in the country. Successful television advertising campaigns made household names out of previously unknown products. A classic example occurred when Walt Disney produced a series of four one-hour shows on the life of frontier legend Davy Crockett. The tremendous popularity of the series instantly created a $300 million industry of Davy Crockett shirts, coonskin caps, and toys. Major automobile companies such as Pontiac, gasoline companies such as Texaco, and appliance companies such as Westinghouse and Gillette sponsored entire programs. Through television, such companies found a whole new way to introduce consumers to their products.

How did television change politics and advertising during the 1950s?

◆ ROCK 'N' ROLL

Perhaps television's greatest effect was on young people. Teenagers of the 1950s were the first "TV generation." In fact, the term *teenager,* describing someone from 13 to 19 years of age, entered standard usage at this time. According to the *Dictionary of American Slang,* edited by Harold Wentworth, the United States is the only country to coin a word for this age group. Among the programs teenagers loved to watch were afternoon shows in which teens danced to the latest music. Many teenagers were attracted to the television show *American Bandstand,* which featured popular, trendy songs and music.

A new sound called **rhythm and blues** combined blues and jazz forms. The deepest roots of this sound go back to the music that enslaved Africans brought with them to the Americas. Until the 1950s, most African American musicians performed only before African American audiences. With a few exceptions, recordings by African American artists were not played on major radio stations.

With the mass migration of African Americans to northern cities in the 1950s, however, urban radio stations started playing rhythm and blues. When young white listeners discovered this new music on the radio, they liked it. They began buying rhythm and blues on records. Alan Freed, a white disc jockey, began playing the music on his radio program, calling it "rock 'n' roll."

From that beginning, rock 'n' roll caught on across the nation. Soon African American musicians were scoring big hits, and teens became familiar with instrumentalists and singers such as Chuck Berry, Little Richard, Ray Charles, B.B. King, and Fats Domino. Familiarity with the music set the stage for a white rock 'n' roll singer. With hips gyrating, knees bending, and voice pleading, Elvis Presley soon became a teen idol and national star. He appeared on network television shows and starred in movies. Many of his songs, such as "Heartbreak Hotel," "Hound Dog," "Don't Be Cruel," and "All Shook Up," were written by African American musicians. Many of the songs sung by Presley shot to the top of the music charts.

Elvis opened the doors to a whole new generation of rock 'n' rollers: Jerry Lee Lewis, Buddy Holly, the Everly Brothers, and Roy Orbison. Ritchie Valens recorded "La Bamba," which became a hit even with people who could not understand its Spanish words. Teenagers across the country—African American, white, and Latino—were united by a feeling that rock 'n' roll was their music. It was an attitude, a celebration of being young, and a sense of having something that parents could not understand or appreciate.

Chuck Berry, a songwriter and guitarist, was especially good at capturing the teen spirit with humor and understanding. He composed hits about the joys and frustrations of school ("School Days"), cars ("Maybelline"), and becoming a rock 'n' roller ("Johnny B. Goode").

Adults had a hard time understanding rock 'n' roll in general and Elvis Presley in particular. To many adults, it seemed rock 'n' roll attacked authority and as a result could be connected with everything that people should avoid, from drug use to organized crime. During the 1950s and even during the 1960s, rock 'n' roll music was a symbol of all that was different about the generation that grew up after World War II. A **generation gap** was growing in the United States—a vast difference in tastes and values between young people and their parents.

What are the roots of rock 'n' roll music?

◆ REJECTING SOCIETY

Further evidence of the generation gap surfaced in the movies many Americans viewed. While many older Americans continued to flock to westerns and war movies that presented a clear line between good and evil, teens idolized a new breed of movie heroes—people who were in rebellion against society. Movies of the 1950s such as *Rebel Without a Cause* and *The Wild One* featured young people who rejected the values of their elders.

Though teenagers may have rebelled in their choices of music and heroes, most eventually blended into the mainstream of American society. There were some young people and adults, however, who rejected society's values. They were called Beats. Coined by writer Jack Kerouac, the term referred to those who expressed "a weariness with all forms of the modern industrial state"—conformity, militarism, and blind faith in technological progress. The Beats became known for expressing their **alienation** from those around them. Alienation is the feeling that one is different from everyone else and does not fit in.

Beat poets, such as Allen Ginsberg and Lawrence Ferlinghetti, wrote about what they viewed as the materialism and sameness of 1950s middle-class life. Writer Kerouac's novel *On the Road* became a Beat classic. It tells the story of a group of friends who crisscross the country by car in search of adventure and inner peace.

Stars like Chuck Berry, Little Richard, and Elvis Presley skyrocketed to the top of the music charts with the rock 'n' roll sounds of the mid-'50s. ▼

◀ James Dean starred in Rebel Without a Cause. *In a still photograph from the movie, he is shown arguing with his parents, symbolizing the alienation many young people of the '50s felt.*

In his poem "Howl," Ginsberg described the mood of his alienated peers.

"I saw the best minds of my generation destroyed by madness . . .
who wandered around and around
at midnight in the railroad yard
wondering where to go."

Although they were not considered Beats, writers of the generation such as J.D. Salinger and Saul Bellow also wrote about characters who rebelled against conformity and society. In *The Catcher in the Rye,* Salinger's hero, Holden Caulfield, is a teenager who fights values he considers to be false. In *The Adventures of Augie March,* Bellow's main character revolts against purposelessness and tries to remain true to himself.

By the late 1950s, the writings and insights of many of the Beats were accepted into mainstream American society. Other Beats laid the groundwork for the next generation of young people, who would express the alienation they felt from society in the 1960s.

In what way did the Beats rebel against society?

Section 3 Review

Check Understanding

1. **Define** (a) rhythm and blues (b) generation gap (c) alienation

2. **Explain** why rock 'n' roll became an important symbol of young people.

3. **Evaluate** the reasons why some Americans rejected the standards of society.

Critical Thinking

Identifying Central Issues Why do you suppose many adults worried so much about the impact of rock 'n' roll in the 1950s?

Write About Culture

◆ **Connecting Past and Present** Write an essay explaining how television has affected American life both today and during the 1950s.

Chapter 25
Review

CHAPTER SUMMARY

Section 1
The United States faced a difficult transition from a wartime to a peacetime economy, with unemployment, inflation, and labor troubles. Discontent led many Americans to expect President Harry Truman's defeat in the election of 1948. However, Truman pulled off one of the greatest election upsets in U.S. history. Truman's Fair Deal program attempted to continue Roosevelt's New Deal. Dwight D. Eisenhower, who served for two terms during the 1950s, pursued a moderate course, continuing some New Deal programs without expanding the role of government.

Section 2
In general, the 1950s were a time of economic boom. A surge in buying power created widespread affluence among the American middle class. This affluence brought dramatic changes in styles of living. Postwar families had children in record numbers, creating the baby boom and leading to suburban growth. At the same time, religion gained increased popularity, and medicine made significant advances. The general prosperity helped conceal the widening gap between the middle class and the poor in the United States.

Section 3
In the 1950s, television became an important part of American culture. Rock 'n' roll music also emerged, capturing the imagination of the young and becoming a key element in youthful rebellion against parental authority. The Beat movement rejected pressure to conform to commonly accepted standards of American society.

Connecting ◆◆ Past and Present

In the 1950s, rock 'n' roll music was viewed as a way of expressing teenage rebellion against society. Is some popular music today viewed in the same way? Explain your answer.

Using Vocabulary

From the list below, select the term that best completes each sentence.

productivity	automation
affluence	urban renewal
Fair Deal	recession
alienation	blue-collar job

1. The _____ was Truman's attempt to continue the policies of Franklin Roosevelt.

2. The rate at which goods are produced or services are performed is called _____ .

3. Clearing out a slum and replacing it with an industrial park is an example of an _____ project.

4. During a _____ , or slowdown in the economy, a government may spend to get the economy moving.

5. _____ is the use of machines to do work formerly done by people.

6. Someone who works in a factory might be said to have a _____ .

7. _____ is financial comfort and security.

8. Those who feel they do not belong may feel a sense of _____ from society.

Check Understanding

1. **Explain** how and why the U.S. economy changed during the 1950s.

2. **Analyze** why Harry Truman's election in 1948 was such a surprise to Americans.

3. **Discuss** how the GI Bill helped veterans.

4. **Describe** the impact of the interstate highway system on the United States.

5. **Evaluate** why inflation was a problem after World War II.

6. **Describe** why middle-class Americans overlooked the growing gap between themselves and the poor during the 1950s.

7. **Explain** how television affected the young.

8. **Discuss** why Eisenhower's campaign slogan was so appropriate for him and the public.

9. **Explain** the reasons for the rise of the Beats in the 1950s.

10. **Describe** the importance of William Levitt, Jonas Salk, and Chuck Berry.

Critical Thinking

1. **Applying Information** Television impacted society in the 1950s. In what ways was this impact positive? Explain your answer.

2. **Comparing** Compare the challenges Truman faced during his presidency with the challenges Eisenhower faced.

3. **Understanding Causes and Effects** What were the causes and effects of the growth of the suburbs in the 1950s?

4. **Making Inferences** Why were women's roles limited in the 1950s?

◆ **Connecting Past and Present** During the 1950s, poor people were often "invisible" to those who benefited from the prosperous times. Can middle-class Americans ignore the poverty of others today? Why or why not?

Interpreting the Timeline

Use the timeline on pages 504–505 to answer these questions.

1. How many years did Harry Truman serve as President of the United States without being elected to that office?

2. Which event shows that Congress recognized that there was an increased interest in religion in the United States?

3. Which events on the timeline illustrate the spread of communism?

Putting Skills to Work

EVALUATING MEDIA

In the Building Skills lesson on page 512, you learned that evaluating media involves examining the kind and quality of information offered by print and broadcast resources. Read the following comments offered by Frank Sinatra, a popular singer whose career began in the 1930s, in a *New York Times* interview from January 12, 1958. Then answer the questions below.

Rock 'n' roll ... is sung, played and written for the most part by [mentally deficient] goons and by means of its almost imbecilic repetition and sly, lewd, in plain fact, dirty lyrics ... it manages to be the [warlike] music of every sideburned delinquent on the face of the earth.

1. Is Frank Sinatra's assessment of rock 'n' roll based on fact or opinion? How can you tell? What bias can you detect?

2. Sinatra was particularly well known for his ballads and other romantic songs. How do you think that his experience in the music world influenced his opinions about rock 'n' roll?

3. How might parents and teenagers in the 1950s have reacted to Sinatra's comments? How do you feel about them today?

Writing to Express a Point of View

Suppose you are a teenager in the 1950s. Your parents want to ban rock 'n' roll from your home. **Write** a short argument in which you explain why you like the music and why your parents should allow you to listen to it. Make a respectful, not confrontational, argument. In it, offer evidence that reassures your parents that rock 'n' roll is not connected with crime or other social problems.

 *Portfolio Project*

AN ORAL HISTORY

Choose one of the topics from this chapter, such as Eisenhower's presidency, the development of the U.S. highway system, the growth of the suburbs, or the power of television. Brainstorm a short list of questions about the topic, and interview three to five adults who grew up during the 1950s to get their firsthand recollections of the time period. With your classmates, organize the responses according to topics and compile them in a binder, forming an oral history of the time period.

Chapter 26
The Civil Rights Movement 1947–1965

CHAPTER PREVIEW

Section 1 The Roots of the Movement

Steps taken during and after World War II set the stage for important advances against segregation beginning in the 1950s.

Section 2 Combating Segregation in Education

The rule of "separate but equal," which was the basis of school segregation for more than half a century, was overturned.

Section 3 The Tactics of Nonviolence

Protests such as boycotts, sit-ins, and marches took place throughout the South during the civil rights movement.

Section 4 Political Action for Civil Rights

The Freedom Summer project launched a massive drive to register voters in the South and to challenge segregation.

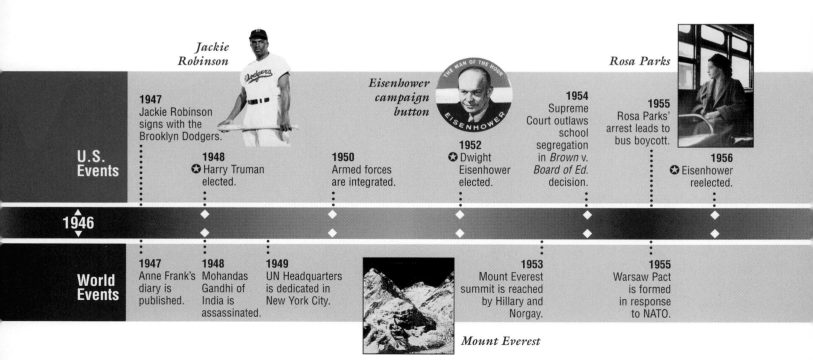

Jackie Robinson

Eisenhower campaign button

Rosa Parks

U.S. Events

1947 Jackie Robinson signs with the Brooklyn Dodgers.

1948 ✪ Harry Truman elected.

1950 Armed forces are integrated.

1952 ✪ Dwight Eisenhower elected.

1954 Supreme Court outlaws school segregation in *Brown* v. *Board of Ed.* decision.

1955 Rosa Parks' arrest leads to bus boycott.

1956 ✪ Eisenhower reelected.

◀ 1946 ▶

World Events

1947 Anne Frank's diary is published.

1948 Mohandas Gandhi of India is assassinated.

1949 UN Headquarters is dedicated in New York City.

1953 Mount Everest summit is reached by Hillary and Norgay.

1955 Warsaw Pact is formed in response to NATO.

Mount Everest

Portfolio Project

AN INTERNET WEBSITE

The Internet is an exciting means of communication, entertainment, and education. One way to actively use the Internet is to create a Website—with text and graphics, sounds and videos—on a subject of interest. As you read this chapter, keep in mind the elements that would make an interesting Website dealing with the civil rights movement. At the end of the chapter, you will construct a Website on a topic of your choice.

▲ On August 28, 1963, more than 200,000 people gathered in Washington, D.C., to show their support for the civil rights bill proposed by President Kennedy. ◆ **Connecting Past and Present** Why was the rally held in Washington, D.C.? What issues could capture nationwide support today?

Martin Luther King, Jr.

1960
✪ John F. Kennedy elected.
Sit-ins begin in southern states.
John Updike's novel *Rabbit, Run* is published.

1961
Freedom Riders travel through the South.

1963
✪ Lyndon B. Johnson becomes President.
Martin Luther King, Jr., speaks at the March on Washington.

1964
✪ Johnson elected.
Civil Rights Act is passed.

1965
Malcolm X is assassinated.
Voting Rights Act expands African American voter registration.

1968

1958
Apartheid policies strengthened in South Africa.

1959
Fidel Castro takes over Cuban government.

1962
World population is estimated at 3.1 billion.

sharing is caring
THE SALVATION ARMY
God bless you

1965
Salvation Army is 100 years old.

Salvation Army

The Roots of the Movement

PREVIEW

Objectives

- To examine the patterns of segregation and discrimination that African Americans faced in the North and in the South

- To explain how small advances after World War II raised hopes that African Americans might soon win full civil rights

Vocabulary

unethical
integrate

The civil rights movement of the 1950s and 1960s was driven by ordinary citizens all over the United States. These black and white Americans were determined to end the racial inequality and segregation that had become common in the North and the South. African Americans and their white supporters began to demand that their civil rights be recognized and respected. It would take a while longer before others—including Latinos, Native Americans, and Asian Americans—would demand that their rights be recognized.

◆ AFRICAN AMERICANS IN THE POSTWAR YEARS

More than a million African American soldiers served in World War II. For most of the war, they served in segregated, entirely African American military units that were often commanded by white officers. Life for African Americans in the armed forces was as segregated as life at home.

When African American soldiers returned from war, they found that they still lagged behind the rest of the nation in their political and economic rights. In both the North and the South, African Americans faced a deeply ingrained system that kept them segregated in jobs, housing, and education.

Legal Segregation in the South

In the years since Reconstruction, southern legislatures had transformed segregation from custom into law. Jim Crow laws created two worlds, one for whites and one for African Americans and others whose skin color was not white. Each world had its own neighborhoods, shops, drinking fountains, restaurants, schools, and even funeral homes and cemeteries. These Jim Crow laws were "justified" by the 1896 *Plessy* v. *Ferguson* Supreme Court decision, which determined that public facilities could be separate for whites and African Americans as long as they were of equal quality. Over the years, the Supreme Court continued to uphold the "separate but equal" ruling in the *Plessy* case.

Southern states restricted the political power of African Americans by preventing them from voting. Some white Southerners used threats and violence to scare African Americans away from the polls. In some states, poll taxes required voters to pay a fee each time they voted. Few African Americans in the South could afford the tax and therefore were prevented from voting. In some places, African American voters who could afford to pay the poll tax later discovered that their receipts, written on blue instead of pink paper, disqualified them from voting.

A number of states included grandfather clauses in their voting laws, which said that any person, white or black, whose father or grandfather had voted in 1867 could now vote. Since African Americans in southern states had not been allowed to vote until 1868, it was unlikely they could vote now. Such tactics left African Americans with no voice in the government and no political power to change their status.

De Facto Segregation in the North

There were no Jim Crow laws in the North, but segregation there was just as real. De facto segregation, or separation by race in practice, if not in law, created a society in which African Americans who lived in the North faced nearly as segregated a life as many African Americans in the South. Although not segregated by law, many African Americans lived in separate neighborhoods, usually with poor, run-down housing. Especially after World War II, many middle-class whites moved to suburban communities where African Americans were not welcome. Many African American families stayed in the urban neighborhoods that whites had left.

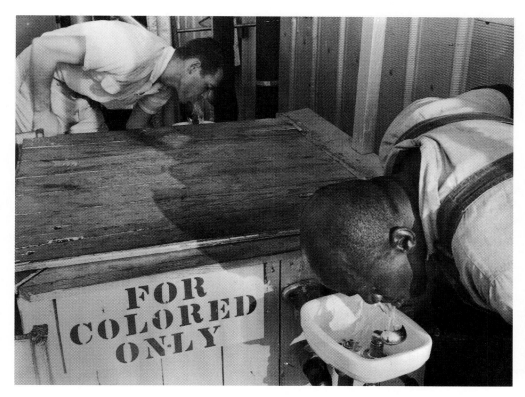

▲ *Legalized segregation according to race was part of daily life in the South. Signs like the one shown here were placed at drinking fountains.*

Northern schools were often segregated as well. Because many students attended neighborhood schools, children from African American neighborhoods attended schools in which most students were African American. These schools often received fewer funds than white schools and thus were poorly equipped.

African Americans in the North also faced widespread discrimination in the workplace. White employers usually reserved the best jobs for other whites. As a result, qualified African Americans had a hard time finding good jobs, and the average income of African Americans remained lower than that of whites.

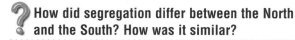 **How did segregation differ between the North and the South? How was it similar?**

◆ A CHANGING SOCIETY

After World War II, more white Americans were willing to fight racial discrimination. The battle against the Nazis, whose racist policies had ordered the murder of nearly 12 million Jews, Gypsies, and others, caused many white Americans to question the racial policies of the United States. They began to realize that judging another human according to skin color was both dangerous and **unethical,** or not according to the principles of proper conduct.

In this new political climate, African Americans began to look to the future with hope. They worked together and with their white supporters to promote their cause and demand results.

Integrating the Armed Forces

One of the first breakthroughs against segregation came in 1948. African American soldiers returning home from World War II brought back bitter tales of their shabby treatment in segregated units. African American civil rights leaders threatened to mount a massive protest unless the government **integrated** the military, or opened it to all people without restriction. Many white Northerners backed their demand.

President Truman supported their demand as well and issued an executive order requiring "equality of treatment and opportunity" in the armed forces. When asked whether "equality of treatment" meant integration, Truman replied, "Yes." His firm stand on the issue was one of the first examples of the federal government's support for integration. Despite some resistance, by 1950 all the armed services had begun to place African Americans in integrated units and employed them in jobs previously available only to white soldiers. In 1954, Benjamin Oliver Davis, Jr., became the first African American general in the United States Air Force.

▲ *Jackie Robinson—shown sliding into home plate— was the first African American elected to the National Baseball Hall of Fame.*

African American novelists and poets not only gained widespread popularity, but they also helped portray the misery and inequalities of African American life. Both Richard Wright, the "father of the American black novel," and James Baldwin wrote about the patterns of discrimination that African Americans faced in white society. Gwendolyn Brooks turned the lives of women living in urban ghettos into rhythmic poetry. Such works became popular among people of all races in the postwar period. Still, there were limited opportunities during the 1950s and 1960s for the majority of African Americans who were interested in pursuing careers as writers, actors, and artists.

Why were white Americans more receptive to civil rights causes in the years following World War II?

Breaking the Color Barrier in Baseball

One of the best-known victories for African Americans in the postwar years came in sports. African Americans had been excluded from major league baseball since its beginnings. In 1945, the Brooklyn Dodgers broke this racial barrier by signing a player named Jackie Robinson to a contract. Robinson had been a star athlete at the University of California at Los Angeles before playing in the Negro Baseball League.

Robinson's first months in the major leagues were a test of endurance. He was ignored by many other players and jeered by fans. Soon, however, his competitiveness and daring play won him huge numbers of white and African American fans. In 1962, he became the first African American elected to the National Baseball Hall of Fame. More important, Robinson paved the way for other African American athletes to compete in baseball and other professional sports.

African Americans in the Arts

After World War II, the works of African American actors, artists, writers, and musicians gained national recognition. Jazz and pop music by Harry Belafonte and other performers emerged from African American communities. Mahalia Jackson sang gospel music to enthusiastic white and African American audiences. Sidney Poitier was named best actor in a dramatic role in 1963.

Section 1 Review

Check Understanding

1. **Define** (a) unethical (b) integrate

2. **Analyze** how *Plessy* v. *Ferguson* was used to support southern segregation.

3. **Describe** how white Southerners prevented African Americans from voting.

4. **Identify** how small advances after World War II raised hopes that African Americans might soon win full civil rights.

Critical Thinking

Evaluating Information From your perspective, why might it be more difficult to battle against de facto segregation than segregation imposed by law? Explain.

Write About Citizenship

◆ **Connecting Past and Present** Write a paragraph telling how sports and the arts today are the same as or different from the way they were in the 1940s.

BUILDING SKILLS

Choosing a Topic and Purpose for Research: Civil Rights

Choosing a topic and purpose are the first two steps to writing an interesting, high-quality research report. A good research report is built gradually in a sequence of logical steps.

The first step is to choose a topic that will be interesting and meaningful both to you and to your readers—your audience.

Here's How

Follow these steps to select a topic and purpose for your audience:

1. Choose a topic that interests you and that can be easily researched. Select several possible topics. Then, check what resources are available in the library. If there is only a little information on a topic, eliminate it.

2. Before deciding on the exact topic of your research paper, consider your purpose for writing, or what you want to accomplish. Do you want to explain, summarize, persuade, recommend, or entertain?

3. Narrow your topic. You cannot write effectively about a general topic, such as civil rights, because there is too much information about it. You can, however, write effectively about a famous civil rights leader, a specific time period, or a particular location or event.

4. Consider the audience for your research paper. Will the people who read your paper have a great deal of knowledge about the subject? What will you need to tell them to help them understand? How will you organize your material? What vocabulary will you use?

Here's Why

As a writer you must coordinate all of the elements of your writing effectively. By carefully attending to topic, purpose, and audience, you will lay the groundwork for a research paper that communicates logically and effectively.

Practice the Skill

1. Each of the following topics is too broad. Narrow the topics by selecting one example or person that represents the topic, by substituting a brief time period for a long one, or by limiting the topic to a specific condition, place, or purpose. Write a narrower topic for each one.
   a. Segregation
   b. Important Civil Rights Court Cases
   c. African Americans in the Army

2. List two different purposes and audiences for each of the following topics.
   a. Civil Rights in the Early 1960s
   b. Discrimination in the Workplace
   c. The Brooklyn Dodgers and the Color Barrier

Apply the Skill

Choose an interesting topic for a research paper. Do some research to make sure that there are enough resources. Then decide on a purpose for your research paper, and think about the people who will read it. Write a paragraph that summarizes your topic and the goals for your paper.

Section 2

Combating Segregation in Education

PREVIEW

Objectives

- To analyze why segregated schools were separate but not equal

- To explain how the Supreme Court decision in *Brown* v. *Board of Education of Topeka* shattered the doctrine of "separate but equal"

- To describe the steps taken by white Southerners to resist school integration

- To analyze why President Eisenhower sent federal troops into the South to enforce school integration

Vocabulary

desegregate
federalize

During the 1940s, the National Association for the Advancement of Colored People, or NAACP, challenged the idea of separate but equal facilities at training schools and in graduate programs with some success. In the 1950s, leaders of the NAACP and other civil rights leaders decided it was time to focus their attention on integrating public elementary, junior, and high schools.

◆ UNEQUAL SCHOOLS

In the South, African American children attended segregated schools. Many traveled miles to poorly equipped, understaffed, and overcrowded buildings. Many segregated schools did not even have indoor plumbing. Students sat at battered desks and shared books because there were not enough to go around. White children, on the other hand, often walked to nearby schools that had better equipment, well-trained teachers, and books that were more up to date. Clearly, African American and white schools were "separate"—in the language of *Plessy* v. *Ferguson*. Just as clearly, however, they were not "equal."

Brown v. Board of Education of Topeka

In Topeka, Kansas, an African American third-grader named Linda Brown had to walk nearly a mile and pass through a dangerous railroad switchyard in order to reach her segregated school. Yet the all-white Sumner School was only seven blocks from her house. In 1950, Linda's father, Oliver Brown, decided to enroll her in the Sumner School. The principal refused the application, saying that the school was for whites only.

Brown decided to take legal action. With the help of the local chapter of the NAACP, he and seven other African American parents sued the Topeka Board of Education to gain the right for their children to attend the neighborhood school.

Brown and the NAACP lost the case in Kansas. The judges argued that the 1896 *Plessy* v. *Ferguson* decision allowed Topeka to provide "separate but equal" schools for students of different races. Since there was another school for Linda Brown to attend, the local all-white school did not have to accept her. Brown did not give up, however. He appealed the case all the way to the United States Supreme Court.

Thurgood Marshall and Victory in the Supreme Court

To present the case in the Supreme Court, Brown hired Thurgood Marshall, a lawyer who specialized in civil rights cases. For more than ten years, Marshall had served as legal director of the NAACP. Later, he would become the first African American Supreme Court justice.

During his years with the NAACP, Marshall fought legal segregation in educational institutions. He began by concentrating on segregation in graduate, law, and professional training schools, hoping that judges would be more sympathetic to well-educated African Americans.

In presenting *Brown* v. *Board of Education of Topeka*, Marshall argued that the very fact that a school was segregated meant it was unequal. Separate schools received separate money from the state, separate teachers, and separate building facilities. With these differences, separate schools could never be truly equal. In addition to his legal arguments, Marshall produced testimony from psychologists demonstrating that segregation lowered the self-esteem of African American children. Segregated schools, Marshall concluded, violated the Fourteenth Amendment to the Constitution, which promises all Americans "equal protection of the laws." That means that all people, no matter what their background, should be able to attend the same neighborhood public schools.

On May 17, 1954, the Supreme Court handed down its unanimous decision. Ruling in favor of Brown, the Court declared segregation unconstitutional. Chief Justice Earl Warren read the unanimous decision:

" We conclude that in the field of public education, the doctrine of 'separate but equal' has no place. Separate educational facilities are [always] unequal. "

The *Brown* decision was a historic Supreme Court case that changed American history. More than 50 years of legal segregation beginning with *Plessy* v. *Ferguson* was over. The concept of "separate but equal" was legally dead.

What reason did the Supreme Court give for overturning *Plessy* v. *Ferguson*?

◆ INTEGRATING SCHOOLS

At first, many southern schools refused to **desegregate,** or end segregation. In 1955, the Supreme Court ordered American schools to begin desegregation "with all deliberate speed." In some areas, however, white politicians and school boards decided they could interpret the phrase "all deliberate speed" to mean 25 years—or perhaps never. In Virginia, the governor defied the ruling by proposing that state aid be denied to any Virginia school system that integrated its classes. More than a decade after the *Brown* ruling, thousands of public schools still had 100 percent white or African American enrollments.

Resistance in Little Rock

A key test of the Supreme Court ruling came in 1957 in Little Rock, Arkansas. A federal court had ordered Little Rock's Central High School to enroll nine African American students. Arkansas' governor, Orval Faubus, was determined to resist. The preceding year, Faubus had told a crowd of supporters, "No school district will be forced to mix the races as long as I am governor of Arkansas." He called out the

President Eisenhower ordered that African American students be protected by national guardsmen under federal command and by army paratroopers as they walked to Central High School in Little Rock, Arkansas, in 1957. ▼

Arkansas National Guard to prevent the African American students from attending the school.

On the morning of September 4, the African American students—the "Little Rock nine"—arrived at the school. There, a mob of white people taunted and insulted them. When they tried to enter the building, national guardsmen turned them away. Years later, Elizabeth Eckford, one of the African American students, described that attempt to enter Central High:

> The crowd moved in closer, and began to follow me, called me names. Then my knees started to shake and all of a sudden I wondered whether I could make it to the center entrance a block away. It was the longest block I ever walked in my whole life.

The incident at Little Rock became the focus of the national media. A photograph of Elizabeth Eckford walking past a jeering white mob appeared in almost every newspaper in the country.

Like many other people, President Eisenhower was troubled by these images. Eisenhower did not believe that the federal government should interfere in local affairs. But by using the National Guard to defy a Supreme Court order, Governor Faubus had challenged the authority of the federal government. Eisenhower decided it was time to act.

Eisenhower **federalized** Arkansas' National Guard, putting it under the control of the federal government. Then he sent 1,000 paratroopers to Little Rock to enforce integration. Under the protection of these armed forces, the nine African American students at last entered Central High School on September 23. Said one student, Minnijean Brown, "For the first time in my life, I feel like an American citizen."

A Year of Turmoil

Central High was integrated, but the struggle was not over. For several more weeks, armed soldiers had to escort the nine African American students into the school for their protection. Once inside, they still faced problems. Some white students greeted them with kicks, shoves, and obscenities. The torment continued for a school year.

The following August, Governor Faubus announced that he was closing Little Rock's high schools in order

to prevent "violence and disorder." The schools remained closed during the 1958–1959 school year. In place of public schools, the state set up "private" academies, which African Americans could not attend.

In time, the courts forced Little Rock's schools to reopen, and some African American students were enrolled. Slowly, other schools throughout the South desegregated. A new civil rights act increased federal power to protect the civil rights of African Americans. Still, after Little Rock, it was clear that more than a court order was needed to end segregation.

 How did the U.S. government act to desegregate schools in the South?

Section 2 Review

Check Understanding

1. **Define** (a) desegregate (b) federalize

2. **Identify** Thurgood Marshall and his role in *Brown* v. *Board of Education of Topeka*.

3. **Explain** how the Supreme Court decision in *Brown* v. *Board of Education of Topeka* shattered the doctrine of "separate but equal."

4. **Describe** the steps taken by some people to resist school integration.

5. **Explain** why President Eisenhower sent federal troops to Little Rock in September 1957.

Critical Thinking

Supporting a Generalization Find at least two facts in this section to support the following generalization: The federal government supported the Supreme Court's decision in *Brown* v. *Board of Education of Topeka*.

Write About Citizenship

Connecting Past and Present Write a letter to the editor of the school newspaper that compliments or criticizes the way the student body of your school treats newcomers.

Section 3

The Tactics of Nonviolence

PREVIEW

Objectives

- To explain why African Americans organized a bus boycott in Montgomery, Alabama

- To recognize the role of Dr. Martin Luther King, Jr., in the civil rights movement

- To examine the importance of the 1963 March on Washington

Vocabulary

theology	Freedom Ride
sit-in	civil disobedience

While the courts struggled with legal issues of school segregation, African Americans were acting to secure other civil rights. In the South, they developed methods of mass protest to bring their case to the public.

◆ THE MONTGOMERY BUS BOYCOTT

On December 1, 1955, an African American woman named Rosa Parks climbed aboard a bus in Montgomery, Alabama. After a long day's work as a seamstress in a department store, she took a seat toward the middle of the bus, where African Americans were permitted to sit.

As the bus filled, several white passengers were left standing. The driver ordered Parks and three other African Americans to give up their seats so that the whites could sit. The three other African Americans obeyed. Parks, however, politely but firmly refused to move. Furious, the driver called the police. Parks was arrested and sent to jail for violating Montgomery's segregation laws.

News of Parks' arrest spread quickly through Montgomery's African American community. To express their outrage at the city's segregation laws, the local NAACP and other organizations decided to organize a one-day boycott of the city's buses. They

asked African Americans, who accounted for nearly 75 percent of Montgomery's riders, to stop riding the buses for a day. Organizers knew that a boycott would cost the bus company a lot of money.

Dr. King and the Bus Boycott

The NAACP contacted African American ministers all over Montgomery to help with the boycott. Among them was a 26-year-old minister who had recently been appointed to serve at a Montgomery church, Dr. Martin Luther King, Jr.

King was the son and grandson of Baptist ministers. He graduated from Morehouse College and later earned a degree in **theology,** the study of religious faith and practice, at Boston University. He was an outspoken supporter of the movement to win civil rights for African Americans. He believed that African Americans should gain their rights without the use of violence even when violence was used against them. He developed his philosophy of nonviolent resistance from the ideas of Mohandas Gandhi, a religious and political leader from India who had used nonviolent protests to free his people from British colonial rule.

King's philosophy of nonviolent protest won the support of local civil rights leaders across the nation—beginning in Montgomery. All day long, on Monday, December 5, 1955, Montgomery's buses traveled the streets almost empty. African Americans filled the city's sidewalks, walking or waiting for taxis or for rides in friends' cars, many of which belonged to whites who supported the boycott.

The Boycott Becomes a Movement

Strengthened by success, the people of Montgomery's African American community decided to continue the boycott. They created the Montgomery Improvement Association (MIA) to direct the protest and elected Martin Luther King as its president. The MIA drew up a list of formal demands, including courteous treatment for African Americans on buses and a "first-come, first-served" policy. African Americans would sit in the back of the bus, but they would not have to give up their seats to anyone. The MIA also demanded that the bus company hire African American drivers on routes that had a large proportion of African American passengers. Until the company met these demands, African Americans in Montgomery would refuse to ride the city's buses.

The boycott lasted 381 days. At first, city officials ignored the protest. But by the end of the first month,

Chapter 26 ◆ 533

white businesses in the downtown area were beginning to suffer from the loss of trade. The loss of passengers was also crippling the city's bus company. As the boycott continued, African Americans continued to walk, form car pools, or stay home.

Frustrated and angry, Montgomery's white citizens fought back. Employers threatened to fire African Americans if they did not abandon the boycott. Police repeatedly stopped African American drivers and demanded to see their licenses and insurance papers. They falsely arrested many for speeding. King himself was arrested for speeding and jailed for several days.

When threats failed to work, some white people turned to violence. They threw bricks through the windows of African American homes and bombed two African American churches. In January 1956, white citizens threw a bomb at King's house. It exploded on his porch, shattering the front windows and sending shards of glass into the house. An angry crowd of African Americans gathered to demand revenge, but King defused their fury with a call for nonviolence:

> "We must love our white brothers no matter what they do to us. If I am stopped, this movement will not stop, for what we are doing is right. What we are doing is just—and God is with us."

As news of the boycott spread, support poured in from around the world. African Americans and whites alike responded warmly to King's nonviolent protest. Donations helped the boycott continue and grow stronger. Dr. King and the other leaders increased their demands. At first, African Americans had been willing to accept segregated seats in the back of the bus. Now, wanting full equality, they filed a lawsuit in federal court charging that Alabama's system of bus segregation was illegal.

In December 1956, the United States Supreme Court agreed, ruling unanimously that segregation on Alabama buses was unconstitutional. On December 21, King and several other African Americans climbed into Montgomery's first integrated bus. The bus driver greeted them with a smile, saying, "We are glad to have you with us this morning."

How did Dr. Martin Luther King, Jr., help end segregation on Montgomery's buses?

◆ MORE NONVIOLENT PROTESTS

The success of the Montgomery bus boycott stirred people across the nation. The peaceful protesters who had used alternate means to get to work for more than a year in Montgomery gave courage to African Americans throughout the South. Soon, many more groups of people began to stage nonviolent protests against other segregation laws, such as laws affecting seating at theaters and restaurants and laws about using department store dressing rooms.

Sit-ins Across the South

In February 1960, four African American college students in Greensboro, North Carolina, decided to demonstrate against segregation of restaurant lunch counters. Entering a downtown five-and-dime store called F. W. Woolworth, they sat at its "whites-only" lunch counter. When the waitress would not serve them, they refused to leave. They stayed at the counter until the store closed. The next day, 20 students returned to continue the protest through July, when the lunch counter was desegregated at last.

These protests came to be called **sit-ins**. When television cameras captured the protesters on film, sit-ins began to spread throughout the South. Soon, thousands of young African Americans and white supporters were "sitting-in," not only at lunch counters but also at segregated movie theaters, department stores, drugstores, and libraries. After a while, hundreds of sit-ins were taking place at the same time.

The authorities had a hard time dealing with the sit-ins. As soon as the police arrested one group of protesters, another group took its place. Although angry whites hurled insults or dumped food on them, the protesters never fought back. If they were knocked down, they brushed themselves off and took their seats again.

The support of Martin Luther King and other African American leaders gave the nonviolent sit-ins a burst of energy. King praised those who took part in sit-ins. Over the next year, an estimated 70,000 black and white students took part in sit-ins. Some 3,600 served time in jail. White merchants, whose businesses were suffering, grew eager to settle. By 1961, segregated lunch counters had nearly disappeared from the South.

Marching in Birmingham

In 1963, King turned his attention to Birmingham, Alabama. Despite eight years of civil rights protests, Birmingham remained a symbol of white

◄ The image of these protesters being splattered with food appeared in magazines and newspapers across the country. Their nonviolent reaction to the jeering crowds sent a powerful message about the injustice of segregated lunch counters.

racism at its most extreme. King called it the most segregated city in America. He believed that a victory over Jim Crow laws in Birmingham would inspire African Americans throughout the South to challenge the system. King arrived in Birmingham on April 3, 1963. He planned to organize a boycott of segregated stores and to stage nonviolent sit-ins and marches throughout the city.

Leading segregationists vowed to oppose the protests with force. Eugene "Bull" Connor, the Birmingham police chief, promised that "blood would run in the streets of Birmingham" before he would allow the city to be integrated.

To block the protesters, Connor had obtained a court order banning all demonstrations. When King and the other leaders of the march defied the order, the police arrested and jailed them. King was put in solitary confinement in a nearly dark cell. There, he wrote the famous "Letter from a Birmingham Jail," which said that it was time for African Americans to gain their civil rights.

After a week, King and the other leaders posted bail and were released from jail. Their protests continued. On May 2, high school and college students joined the adults on the march in Birmingham. Bull Connor decided to arrest them all. Nine hundred youths filled the Birmingham jails that night.

Still, the marches continued. The next day, 25,000 people turned out to march in Birmingham. When they refused to stop, the police set dogs on them and beat them with clubs. Bull Connor ordered his men to spray high-pressure fire hoses into the crowd. The force of the water hurled the men, women, and children to the ground and slammed them against buildings and cars.

As the marches continued, television cameras captured images of clashing protesters and police that were watched by alarmed Americans across the nation. Even Birmingham's white population was becoming alarmed. Finally, in mid-May, a compromise was reached, and protesters agreed to end the massive demonstrations. In return, city officials agreed to desegregate restrooms, lunch counters, department store fitting rooms, and drinking fountains within 90 days. They also agreed to open employment opportunities to African Americans. The demonstrators had won a significant victory in Birmingham.

The Freedom Riders

While sit-ins shook the South, James Farmer, a leader of the Congress of Racial Equality (CORE), organized a protest that challenged the effectiveness of the court order outlawing segregation on interstate buses and in bus terminals. In May 1961,

13 white and black protesters climbed aboard two buses and set out from Washington, D.C., on what they called the **Freedom Ride.** They planned to travel throughout the South and deliberately break segregation rules in bus terminals, restaurants, restrooms, and waiting rooms. This kind of protest is known as **civil disobedience**—refusing to obey governmental demands or laws in order to bring about change.

At first, the riders had few problems. However, as they traveled farther south, angry mobs of whites awaited them. In Anniston, Alabama, 40 white youths burned the bus and severely beat both black and white riders. Similar scenes were repeated in Birmingham and again in Montgomery. Dr. King appealed to the riders to turn back, but they refused.

The violence against the Freedom Riders shocked the nation. At every stop there was more violence, and the injured riders were replaced by new volunteers. In response to public pressure, the federal government assigned federal marshals to protect the Freedom Riders. The route of the Freedom Ride is shown on the map below.

The Freedom Riders' protest was a success even though the buses did not reach their original destination of New Orleans, Louisiana. When they reached Jackson, Mississippi, the protesters were arrested. However, the violence directed toward them and the injuries they had suffered focused attention on the unfair conditions in bus stations in the South. As a result, the federal government issued tougher regulations that barred segregation in interstate travel. The government also put pressure on local communities to obey these rules. In the next few years, WHITE and COLORED signs were pulled down from waiting rooms in hundreds of southern bus, train, and airport terminals.

The March on Washington

By 1963, the civil rights movement had gained great momentum. To demonstrate their strength, leaders planned a march that would send a message to the whole nation. They decided to gather in Washington, D.C., to mark the one-hundredth anniversary of the Emancipation Proclamation.

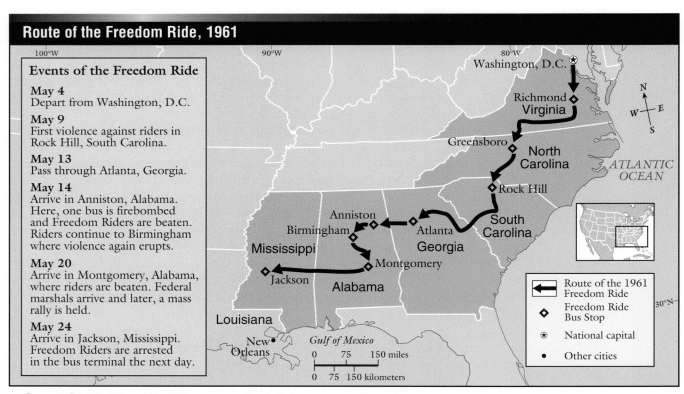

Route of the Freedom Ride, 1961

Events of the Freedom Ride

May 4
Depart from Washington, D.C.

May 9
First violence against riders in Rock Hill, South Carolina.

May 13
Pass through Atlanta, Georgia.

May 14
Arrive in Anniston, Alabama. Here, one bus is firebombed and Freedom Riders are beaten. Riders continue to Birmingham where violence again erupts.

May 20
Arrive in Montgomery, Alabama, where riders are beaten. Federal marshals arrive and later, a mass rally is held.

May 24
Arrive in Jackson, Mississippi. Freedom Riders are arrested in the bus terminal the next day.

▲ **Geography** The Freedom Ride protest showed that in spite of legislation, interstate travel was not safe or integrated. **Interpreting the Map** What was the significance of the direction of the protest route?

◀ Dr. Martin Luther King, Jr., delivered his famous "I Have a Dream" speech at the March on Washington on August 28, 1963.

On August 28, 1963, about 200,000 marchers arrived in Washington to pressure Congress to pass important civil rights legislation. Many speakers addressed the crowd that day, but none moved the crowd like Dr. King, whose "I Have a Dream" speech is a landmark of American history. After describing his dream of racial harmony, he ended with these words:

" When we let freedom ring . . . from every state and every city, we will be able to speed up that day when all of God's children, black men and white men, Jews and Gentiles, Protestants and Catholics, will be able to join hands and sing in the words of the old Negro spiritual, 'Free at last! Free at last! Thank God almighty, we are free at last!' "

The following year, Congress passed and President Lyndon Johnson signed the most sweeping civil rights legislation in the country since Reconstruction. The Civil Rights Act of 1964, which had been proposed by President Kennedy, protected the right of all citizens to vote, banned discrimination in hiring, and outlawed segregation in public places.

? What methods did African Americans and their white supporters use in the struggle for civil rights in the 1960s?

Section 3 Review

Check Understanding

1. **Define** (a) theology (b) sit-in (c) Freedom Ride (d) civil disobedience

2. **Explain** the events that caused African Americans to organize a bus boycott in Montgomery, Alabama.

3. **Describe** the accomplishments of Dr. Martin Luther King, Jr., in the civil rights movement.

4. **Explain** the impact of the March on Washington in August 1963.

Critical Thinking

◆ **Connecting Past and Present** When are the methods of civil disobedience and nonviolence used in protest today? Give at least one example.

Write About History

Write a speech that might have inspired people in your community to participate in a boycott, a sit-in, a freedom ride, or a protest march to end segregation during the 1960s.

POINT *of* VIEW

LETTER FROM A BIRMINGHAM JAIL

While Dr. Martin Luther King, Jr., was in jail in Birmingham, he was troubled by a letter that appeared in a local newspaper. The writers of the letters were clergymen from Alabama. All were white; some were Catholic, some were Protestant, and one was Jewish.

These clergymen supported King's goals, but they criticized his tactics as "unwise and untimely." They criticized his protests for "spreading hatred between the races." They also called King an outsider to Birmingham.

King decided to respond to the clergymen. Although he was not allowed to have any writing materials, his lawyers smuggled a pen into the jail. Using toilet paper and the edges of newspapers, King wrote one of the most important documents of the civil rights movement, "Letter from a Birmingham Jail." In eloquent language, King explained the reasons for his protest. He argued that people have a "moral responsibility to disobey unjust laws." King noted that there is no good time for protests and that African Americans had waited too long to gain their rights. King's letter was printed. More than one million copies were sent to newspapers, civil rights activists, and church leaders.

We have waited for more than 340 years for our constitutional and God-given rights.... Perhaps it is easy for those who have never felt the stinging darts of segregation to say, "Wait." This wait has almost always meant "Never."

But when you have seen vicious mobs lynch your mothers and fathers at will; ... when you have seen hate-filled policemen curse, kick, and even kill your black brothers and sisters; ... when you have to concoct [make up] an answer for a five-year-old son who is asking: "Daddy, why do white people treat colored people so mean?"... when you are harried by day and haunted by night by the fact that you are a Negro, living constantly at tip-toe stance never quite knowing what to expect next, then you will understand why we find it difficult to wait.

Dr. Martin Luther King, Jr., "Letter from a Birmingham Jail," April 1963

Examining Point of View

1. Why does King believe African Americans cannot wait to take action for their rights?

2. How does King's role as a parent affect his point of view?

3. Why might the other clergymen have seen King as spreading hatred between the races?

4. What might be the consequences of civil disobedience?

What's Your Point of View?

Identify a social problem in your community and decide what you and others could do to correct the problem. How urgent is the problem? What are the possible consequences if it is not corrected soon?

Write a letter to the editor of a newspaper in which you describe the social problem you have identified. Suggest solutions and tell why you are convinced that people should not wait to correct the problem.

Section 4

Political Action for Civil Rights

PREVIEW

Objectives

- To explain why volunteers launched a massive drive to register voters in the South

- To describe how the Democratic party was challenged at the 1964 presidential convention

- To analyze the effects of the Voting Rights Act of 1965

Vocabulary

voter registration
Freedom Summer
coalition

On July 2, 1964, Dr. Martin Luther King, Jr., and other civil rights leaders joined President Johnson as he signed the new Civil Rights Act into law. The success of the legislation was a triumph for African Americans and civil rights workers all over the country. It was only the beginning, however, of equal political representation for African Americans in federal and state governments.

During the summer of 1964, an organization called the Student Nonviolent Coordinating Committee, or SNCC, planned a massive **voter registration** drive in southern states. The goal of voter registration programs was to get people's names on the official list of voters so that they could participate in elections. SNCC (pronounced SNIK) also planned to open African American schools and to challenge the all-white Democratic political parties of the South. Over the next few years, SNCC fought segregation through nonviolent confrontation and mass action in most civil rights battles.

◆ FREEDOM SUMMER

The SNCC campaign became known as **Freedom Summer** and attracted over 1,000 young volunteers to the South to take part. Many of the volunteers were white college students from the North, who joined the summer project to help the cause. Some of the volunteers would witness segregation for the first time. One volunteer wrote on his application, "I want to work in Mississippi because I feel it is my duty as an American to end segregation in this country." Another wrote,

> **I'm going because the worst thing after burning churches and murdering children is keeping silent.**

Tough Battle in Mississippi

Of all the southern states, Mississippi, the poorest state in the nation, presented the greatest challenge to civil rights workers. Mississippi's white population had some of the nation's most militant segregationists. Between 1882 and 1952, Mississippi had 534 reported lynchings, more than any other state in the nation. When Freedom Summer began in 1964, less than 7 percent of Mississippi's 400,000 voting-age African Americans were registered voters. In the five Mississippi counties that had the largest African American populations, not a single African American was registered to vote.

Various tactics were used to prevent African Americans from voting. Those who tried to register were often fired by their white employers or refused loans to buy farm equipment and seed. African American sharecroppers were forced from their homes and thrown off the land. When these kinds of tactics failed, the Ku Klux Klan was called in to terrorize African Americans who wanted to exercise their right to vote.

The literacy test was another way to deny African Americans suffrage. Only those who passed the test were allowed to vote, but white officials rigged the results by giving easy tests to whites and more difficult ones to African Americans. The tests for African Americans sometimes included such nonsensical questions as "How many bubbles are in a bar of soap?" Other literacy test questions asked the prospective African American voter to recite, word by word, the Constitution of the United States, or to interpret complicated portions of the state constitution. Tests like these kept most African Americans from being allowed to vote.

Violence Against the Volunteers

Civil rights workers during Freedom Summer faced many obstacles in their drive to register African American voters. Some Mississippi communities passed laws that banned certain civil rights activities. For example, one community made it illegal to pass out leaflets calling for boycotts. The penalty for breaking the law was prison. People in some communities used intimidation and violence to stop the volunteers.

Early in the summer of 1964, three young civil rights workers—Andrew Goodman, James Chaney, and Mickey Schwerner—were reported missing. The three had been stopped for speeding in a Mississippi town, held in jail for a few hours, and then released. No one ever saw them alive again.

Pressured by the young men's parents, the Federal government sent FBI agents to investigate their disappearance. Local authorities did not cooperate with the investigation, and it was over a month before their bodies were found buried under a dam wall. They had been beaten and then shot to death.

People throughout the United States were shocked by the murders, but African Americans in Mississippi were especially angry. The three civil rights workers had been murdered because they tried to register African Americans to vote. Their murders illustrated the ugliness of southern racism.

Throughout Freedom Summer, segregationist groups attacked and intimidated the civil rights volunteers. The Ku Klux Klan held rallies at which speakers made violent threats against the civil rights workers. Some especially targeted the white students who worked alongside African American volunteers. By the end of the summer, angry white segregationists had burned 35 African American churches and bombed 30 houses and other buildings. In addition to the three young volunteers who were murdered, there were 1,000 arrests, 80 beatings, and 35 shooting incidents. In spite of the threats and violence, however, Freedom Summer was a success. Student volunteers helped register 17,000 African Americans to vote in Mississippi.

Freedom Schools

In addition to the voter registration drive, the SNCC volunteers also set up more than 40 Freedom Schools. These schools helped to provide Mississippi's African Americans with the education that the state's Jim Crow system had denied them. The Freedom

▲ Civil rights volunteers encouraged African Americans to exercise their right to vote. This volunteer's bag says, "Be a first-class citizen. Register to vote!"

Schools taught such subjects as reading and math. However, volunteers also taught African American history, including information about the lives of African American heroes, such as Frederick Douglass and Sojourner Truth. Mississippi's African American students also learned—many for the first time—that the Supreme Court had outlawed school segregation ten years earlier.

Students who attended the Freedom Schools were dedicated, often attending school in the face of danger. For example, after whites firebombed the McComb Freedom School, 75 students appeared for class the next morning. Throughout the summer more than 3,000 students attended Freedom Schools.

? What was the goal of Freedom Summer?

◆ FREEDOM DEMOCRATIC PARTY

In April 1964, a **coalition**, or temporary alliance for joint action, of SNCC and other major civil rights groups formed the Mississippi Freedom Democratic party (MFDP). Their goal was to unseat, or replace, the whites-only state Democratic party. They wanted to be recognized as the official Mississippi delegation to the Democratic National Convention, which would select the Democratic candidate for President in 1964. Throughout the summer, volunteers like Fannie Lou Hamer worked to register members for the MFDP. By August, they had recruited over 80,000 members.

The Democratic Convention took place at the end of August. The MFDP chose to send 68 delegates to the convention. All but four of them were African American. The MFDP leaders publicized the experiences of Fannie Lou Hamer and other members to demonstrate that Mississippi continued to exclude African Americans from the political process. In this way, they hoped to discredit the white Democrats and persuade convention officials to recognize the MFDP as the legitimate Democratic party of Mississippi.

The leader of the national Democratic party, President Lyndon Baines Johnson, could not recognize the MFDP without excluding the white Democratic delegates. He heard speeches by MFDP leaders and offered a compromise. The convention would seat two MFDP delegates and allow them to vote as "delegates at large." Their votes would be counted in addition to the votes of the white delegates from Mississippi. The remaining MFDP delegates could remain at the convention as "honored

Person to Person

Fannie Lou Hamer

At the Democratic National Convention in 1964, an African American woman named Fannie Lou Hamer played a powerful role in exposing the inequalities of Jim Crow laws that restricted voter rights in the South.

When Fannie Lou Hamer registered to vote in her home state of Mississippi, she was fired from her job and evicted from her home. The next time Hamer registered to vote, she told the town clerk, "Now you can't have me fired 'cause I'm already fired, and I won't have to move now, because I'm not livin' in no white man's house. I'll be back here every 30 days until I become a registered voter."

Hamer's commitment to the political struggle of the state's African Americans led her to become a delegate

▲ Fannie Lou Hamer (1917–1977)

from the Mississippi Freedom Democratic Party to the Democratic National Convention. As a delegate, she led a protest after the party was barred from the convention floor. She also aired her story on national television. "Is this America," she asked, "the land of the free and the home of the brave, where we are threatened daily because we want to live as decent human beings?"

Fannie Lou Hamer, known as the "Spirit of Civil Rights," helped convince Americans that Mississippi was not democratically represented. Partly because of her efforts, an integrated delegation was seated at the 1968 Democratic Convention.

Looking Back: What challenges did Hamer face in an effort to vote?

guests" but would not be permitted to vote as delegates. In addition, all Mississippi Democrats would have to take a loyalty oath, swearing to support the Democratic presidential candidate nominated by the convention.

The Freedom Democrats debated the proposed compromise carefully. At last, they decided to reject it and left the convention. They would not settle for less than full representation. "We did not come all this way for just two seats," Hamer declared.

The discriminatory practices of Mississippi's state Democratic party were exposed to all the delegates at the convention. Four years later, at the 1968 Democratic Convention, the MFDP once again challenged the state Democratic party. This time, the MFDP won. Their party was recognized as the official delegation from Mississippi. Since then, all state delegations to Democratic national conventions have been integrated.

 What was the goal of the Mississippi Freedom Democratic Party?

◆ VOTING RIGHTS ACT OF 1965

After President Lyndon Johnson won the 1964 election in a landslide, capturing an overwhelming 94 percent of the African American vote, civil rights leaders believed that the time was right for further legislation to ensure that African Americans could exercise their right to vote. Martin Luther King, Jr., chose the city of Selma, Alabama, for the start of a nonviolent march to Montgomery, the state capital. The march was intended to draw attention to the issue of voting rights. As the march began on March 7, 1965, state troopers ordered the marchers to retreat. When they refused, the troopers attacked them. Television sets aired the entire spectacle on the nightly news.

The shocking events in Selma forced President Johnson to demand new voting laws that addressed African American rights. On March 15, he addressed a joint session of Congress and a national television audience. In a stirring speech, the President fused the political power of his office with the moral power of

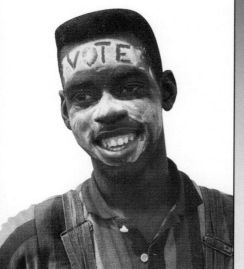

Citizenship *After voter registration campaigns, such as Freedom Summer, thousands of African Americans voted for the first time.* **Interpreting the Chart** *Which state had the most registered voters in 1966? Which state had the greatest percentage increase in registered voters from 1960 to 1966?* ▶

African American Voter Registration in the South, 1960–1966		PERCENT INCREASE
STATE	▓ Voter registration in 1960 ▓ Voter registration in 1966	
	0 100,000 200,000 300,000 400,000	
Alabama		279
Arkansas		58
Florida		66
Georgia		67
Louisiana		53
Mississippi		695
North Carolina		34
South Carolina		229
Tennessee		22
Texas		76
Virginia		105

Sources: U.S. Department of Commerce, Bureau of the Census, *Statistical Abstract of the United States*

the civil rights movement. His words would ring true to the hundreds of thousands of civil rights workers and protesters.

> [It] is . . . really all of us who must overcome the crippling legacy of bigotry and injustice. And we shall overcome.

Soon after, the Voting Rights Act of 1965 was passed by Congress. The act was aimed directly at six states and part of a seventh that had regularly used literacy tests to keep African Americans from voting. It provided that if less than 50 percent of the voting-age citizens were registered, then racial discrimination could be presumed. In such cases, federal supervision of registration would take place, automatically suspending literacy tests. Eligible African American citizens would be allowed to enroll even if they could not read or write. If local governments refused to eliminate literacy tests, the President could send federal examiners to register voters in the state.

In 1960, before the passage of the Voting Rights Act, about 1.5 million African Americans had registered to vote in the South. By 1966, however, one year after the act was passed, over 2.5 million African Americans in the South were registered voters. The numbers of registered voters in each southern state in 1960 and 1966 are shown on the chart on page 542. The numbers of registered African American voters continued to climb to over 3.5 million by 1970.

The act ushered in a new era in American politics. As African Americans began to be represented in local, state, and federal levels of government, they began to change the political culture of the United States. Ten years after the Montgomery bus boycott, the civil rights movement had reached a peak of national influence.

For some African Americans, however, the legislative accomplishments were too little, too late. Impatient with the slow pace of the civil rights movement, many turned to more radical leaders. Some of them, such as Malcolm X and Stokely Carmichael, advocated pride and "black power," rather than peaceful resistance, to obtain rights.

 How did the Selma march influence passage of the Voting Rights Act of 1965?

Section 4 Review

Check Understanding

1. **Define** (a) voter registration (b) Freedom Summer (c) coalition

2. **Explain** why civil rights volunteers went to Mississippi in the summer of 1964.

3. **Describe** some tactics that were used to prevent African Americans from voting in Mississippi.

4. **Evaluate** the effects of the Voting Rights Act.

Critical Thinking

◆ **Connecting Past and Present** Why are national and local voting drives just as important today as they were in the early 1960s?

Write About Citizenship

Write an essay in which you evaluate the effectiveness of the MFDP.

Chapter 26
Review

CHAPTER SUMMARY

Section 1

African American soldiers returned home after World War II to find discrimination was still part of everyday life. In the South, African Americans faced Jim Crow laws; in the North, they faced de facto segregation.

Section 2

After the 1954 Supreme Court ruling declaring school segregation unconstitutional, a few southern schools integrated, but many whites in the South resisted. It took the intervention of federal troops to force integration at Central High School in Little Rock, Arkansas, in 1957.

Section 3

In 1955, African Americans protesting discrimination staged a year-long bus boycott in Montgomery, Alabama. The boycott sparked other protests, including the Freedom Ride, and brought the young minister Dr. Martin Luther King, Jr., to national prominence.

Section 4

The civil rights movement focused on massive voter registration drives in 1964. Violence against volunteers and protesters caught the attention of a national television audience and convinced the nation that voting rights for African Americans must be assured. The passage of the Voting Rights Act of 1965 helped increase the influence of African Americans in the South.

Connecting ◆◆ Past and Present

Identify the social issues that provoke protests today. Compare them to the social issues in this chapter.

Using Vocabulary

Select the letter of the phrase that best completes each sentence.

1. When the government **integrated** the military, it (a) required equal treatment and opportunity for all soldiers; (b) made sure all soldiers could vote; (c) prevented African Americans from becoming officers; (d) ensured that African Americans were not the only ones sent to war.

2. A **sit-in** was (a) a violent reaction to segregated buses; (b) a type of labor strike; (c) a nonviolent protest at white lunch counters; (d) an unsuccessful attempt to register voters.

3. When President Eisenhower **federalized** Arkansas' National Guard, he (a) made them employees of the state; (b) paid them federal instead of state wages; (c) forced them to integrate; (d) put them under the control of the federal government.

4. **Theology** is (a) the study of religious faith and practice; (b) the study of nonviolence; (c) the study of African American history; (d) a nonviolent protest technique.

5. When African Americans used **civil disobedience** to change laws, they (a) used force against police officers; (b) broke what they considered unjust laws; (c) asked lawyers to get temporary relief from unjust laws; (d) rewrote unjust laws.

6. **Freedom Summer** was a campaign to (a) register African American voters; (b) gain access to segregated schools; (c) integrate all interstate buses and trains; (d) enroll African American students in college.

7. In battling the Nazis during World War II, many Americans discovered that judging people by their skin color was **unethical,** or (a) a waste of time; (b) not according to the principles of proper conduct; (c) an economic system; (d) unconstitutional.

8. The Mississippi Freedom Democratic party was formed by a **coalition,** or a (a) political convention; (b) sit-in; (c) voter registration drive; (d) temporary alliance of several groups.

Check Understanding

1. **Describe** the difference in the patterns of segregation and discrimination between the North and the South.

2. **List** the ways states in the South kept African Americans from voting.

3. **Discuss** two victories that African Americans gained soon after World War II.

4. **Explain** Thurgood Marshall's argument in *Brown* v. *Board of Education of Topeka*.

5. **Explain** why President Eisenhower sent federal troops into the South to enforce school segregation.

6. **Explain** why African Americans organized a bus boycott in Montgomery, Alabama.

7. **Identify** Dr. Martin Luther King, Jr., and tell why he was important to the civil rights movement.

8. **Discuss** the importance of the March on Washington in 1963.

9. **Describe** how the Mississippi Freedom Democratic party challenged the national Democratic party in 1964.

10. **Explain** the provisions and the impact of the Voting Rights Act of 1965.

Critical Thinking

1. **Interpreting** Why do you think different patterns of segregation developed in the North and the South?

2. **Analyzing** Why did the Supreme Court change its earlier opinion and rule that it was not constitutional to allow "separate but equal" educational facilities?

3. **Making Inferences** Why did civil rights workers meet with violence in the South?

4. **Understanding Points of View** Many African Americans have supported the practice of busing across school district boundaries to achieve integration. Others have opposed it. Why have parents disagreed with each other over busing?

◆ **Connecting Past and Present** People still debate the merits of busing students to achieve integration. Explain why this issue remains controversial today.

Putting Skills to Work

CHOOSING A TOPIC AND PURPOSE FOR RESEARCH

In the Building Skills lesson on page 529, you learned that the first steps to writing an effective research paper are choosing a topic, a purpose, and an audience. Practice these steps by completing the following tasks.

1. Limit these topics in two different ways.
   a. African American organizations
   b. Famous African Americans

2. Identify two different purposes and audiences for these topics.
   a. Ending Segregation in Schools
   b. The Montgomery Bus Boycott

Interpreting the Timeline

Use the timeline on pages 524–525 to answer these questions.

1. List the events that involve federal actions to fight segregation.

2. How long after the Supreme Court ruling on school segregation was the Civil Rights Act passed?

3. Which events shown on the timeline may have inspired civil rights activists? Explain your choices.

Writing to Create

It is the end of the 1957–1958 school year at Little Rock's Central High School. You are a graduating senior. **Write** a letter to a friend describing what has happened in the school regarding integration.

Portfolio Project

AN INTERNET WEBSITE

Choose some aspect of the civil rights movement that interests you and that you think would make a good Website. Write the text that describes the person, issue, or event you have chosen. Then use information from your text to construct a Website that includes visuals and sounds. Remember that your goal is to bring this time in history to life for Web browsers.

Chapter 27
A New Frontier and a Great Society 1960–1969

CHAPTER PREVIEW

Section 1 The New Frontier

The first President born in the twentieth century, John F. Kennedy, asked Americans to meet the challenges and opportunities of a New Frontier.

Section 2 Foreign Policy in the Early 1960s

Kennedy was challenged many times by the Soviet Union during his brief administration, but his resolve during crises involving Berlin and Cuba forced the Soviets to back down.

Section 3 The Great Society

Lyndon Johnson won passage of far-reaching legislation, including a civil rights act, Medicare and Medicaid programs, and immigration reform.

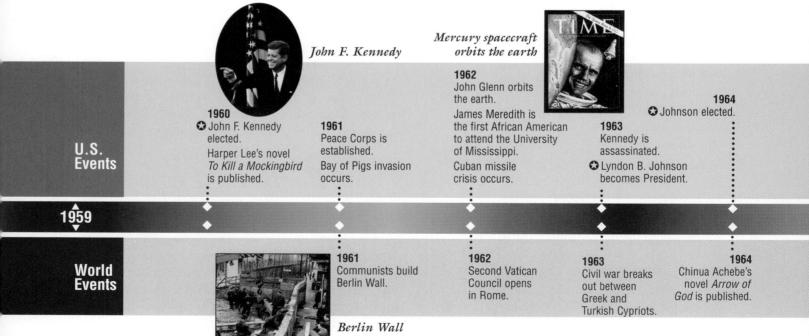

John F. Kennedy

Mercury spacecraft orbits the earth

U.S. Events

1960
✪ John F. Kennedy elected.
Harper Lee's novel *To Kill a Mockingbird* is published.

1961
Peace Corps is established.
Bay of Pigs invasion occurs.

1962
John Glenn orbits the earth.
James Meredith is the first African American to attend the University of Mississippi.
Cuban missile crisis occurs.

1963
Kennedy is assassinated.
✪ Lyndon B. Johnson becomes President.

1964
✪ Johnson elected.

▲ **1959** ▼

World Events

1961
Communists build Berlin Wall.

Berlin Wall

1962
Second Vatican Council opens in Rome.

1963
Civil war breaks out between Greek and Turkish Cypriots.

1964
Chinua Achebe's novel *Arrow of God* is published.

▲ *President John F. Kennedy's children sometimes visited their father in the Oval Office.* ◈ **Connecting Past and Present** *What qualities of President Kennedy are conveyed in this photograph? What characteristics contribute to a President's popularity today?*

Portfolio Project

A WRITTEN DIALOGUE

In this chapter, you will read about a number of key events that occurred during the presidencies of John Kennedy and Lyndon Johnson. As you read the chapter, think about the way people might have talked about these events at the time they happened. At the end of the chapter, you will write a dialogue, or conversation between two or more people, that might have occurred. The dialogue will be the basis for a dramatic oral reading that will bring the people, the time period, and the event to life for your classmates.

1965
Immigration and Nationality Act alters quotas. Voting Rights Act is passed.

1966
Supreme Court rules people accused of crimes must be informed of rights.

Coretta Scott King and sons at King's funeral

1968
✪ Richard Nixon elected. Martin Luther King, Jr., is assassinated.

1969
Chief Justice Earl Warren retires from U.S. Supreme Court.

1970

1965
India and Pakistan fight over control of Kashmir.

1967
Israeli-Arab Six-Day War is fought. The Beatles release *Sgt. Pepper's Lonely Hearts Club Band.*

The Beatles

1968
Violence erupts between Catholics and Protestants in Northern Ireland.

Section 1

The New Frontier

PREVIEW

Objectives

- To identify the factors that determined the results of the election of 1960

- To describe the reasons John Kennedy's ideals appealed to people eager for change

- To explain Kennedy's New Frontier programs

Vocabulary

New Frontier   mandate
missile gap   Peace Corps

Dwight Eisenhower had steered the nation through a period of relative prosperity in the latter half of the 1950s. However, as the nation approached a new decade and the next presidential election, Americans seemed eager for change. Increasingly, they called for greater attention to the nation's domestic problems, such as poverty, the quality of health care, and struggles over civil rights. The President elected in 1960 would have to deal with these issues.

◆ THE 1960 ELECTION

In July 1960, the Democratic National Convention met in Los Angeles to choose a presidential candidate. One possible candidate was John Fitzgerald Kennedy, a Massachusetts Democrat who had served in the House of Representatives and was serving as a senator from Massachusetts. Kennedy was a member of a powerful Boston family with Irish roots that had made a fortune in business, real estate, and the stock market. As a potential candidate, Kennedy had waged a vigorous campaign, giving more than 300 speeches in a few short months and winning the loyalty of many supporters.

The Democratic Candidate

Many Democratic leaders doubted Kennedy's ability to win the election. One major concern was his youth. Kennedy was only 43 years old, and some leaders

and voters wondered whether he had the experience needed to run the country. Another concern was Kennedy's religion. If elected, he would be the first Roman Catholic President, and some voters feared that as President his decision making might be influenced by the Pope and the Roman Catholic Church.

Kennedy defused the issue of his religion during his campaign. He said that any President who did not hold the Constitution as the highest authority of the land would be violating a trust. During one of his campaign speeches, he emphasized this point by saying,

> **If this election is decided on the basis that forty million Americans lost their chance of being President on the day they were baptized, then it is the whole nation that will be the loser in the eyes of history.**

Kennedy, often known by his initials, JFK, won the Democratic nomination and chose Lyndon Baines Johnson, the Senate majority leader, as his running mate for Vice President. Democrats hoped that Johnson, a Texan, would help the Democratic ticket win several crucial southern states.

In accepting the nomination, Kennedy stirred many Americans with his vision of a **New Frontier,** a set of challenges and opportunities for Americans. In one of Kennedy's memorable speeches, he introduced his idea for a New Frontier:

> **We stand today on the edge of a New Frontier—the frontier of the 1960s. A frontier of unknown opportunities and perils. A frontier of unfulfilled hopes and threats. . . . The New Frontier of which I speak is not a set of promises. It is a set of challenges. It sums up not what I intend to offer the American people, but what I intend to ask of them.**

The New Frontier became the label for Kennedy's vision of progress at home. It was not an organized set of laws for economic change like Roosevelt's New Deal. Instead, it was a guiding ideal that he acted upon.

The Campaign

Kennedy's Republican opponent was Richard M. Nixon, who had served as Vice President under Eisenhower. Nixon was known for his strong anti-Communist views. He had many years of experience in government, and also was known for his expertise in foreign policy.

During the campaign, Kennedy claimed that the Republicans had allowed the United States to fall behind the Soviet Union in military strength. Spending less money than the Soviets on basic as well as state-of-the-art weaponry had created what was called the **missile gap.** Kennedy promised to close the gap by spending more on defense and by improving science education in the United States. Kennedy also charged that Eisenhower and Nixon had ignored social issues such as poverty, health care, and care of the elderly. He promised that as President he would deal actively with these problems.

The polls swung in Kennedy's favor after four televised debates between the candidates in September and October of 1960. Many people who watched the debates thought that Kennedy looked calm and confident. In contrast, Nixon appeared tired and strained. After the debates, polls showed that people listening to the debates on the radio thought that Nixon had "won" them. However, television viewers thought that Kennedy had won. Political analysts agreed that the 1960 election moved television to the center of presidential politics, making image and physical appearance more important than ever.

When the votes were tallied, Kennedy had won one of the closest presidential elections in United States history. Out of the 68.8 million votes cast, Kennedy received only 118,574 more votes than Nixon. Kennedy, however, did fairly well in the South, but he carried most of the Northeast and Midwest.

What factors led to Kennedy's victory in the 1960 election?

◆ THE KENNEDY PRESIDENCY

Kennedy assumed the presidency on January 20, 1961. His inaugural address, now considered one of the most memorable speeches in modern American history, was brief but stirring. In his speech, Kennedy portrayed the United States as both a seeker of peace and a firm defender of the weak against aggression. Challenging Americans to action, he said,

> In the long history of the world, only a few generations have been granted the role of defending freedom in its hour of maximum danger. I do not shrink from this responsibility. I welcome it. And so, my fellow Americans, ask not what your country can do for you. Ask what you can do for your country.

Surrounded by supporters who included college professors, Hollywood movie stars, and talented writers and artists, Kennedy gave the presidency an atmosphere of celebrity and glamour. Much later, his widow, Jacqueline Bouvier Kennedy, compared the Kennedy White House to Camelot, the legendary site of King Arthur's court. Like King Arthur, John Fitzgerald Kennedy dreamed of transforming his country into one that would use power to achieve positive ends. Immortalized in a 1960 Broadway musical, Camelot conveyed the same sense of youthfulness, excellence, hope, and idealism as the Kennedy White House did to many Americans.

Insisting on direct control of details that other Presidents had left to advisors and appointees, Kennedy

Kennedy's inaugural address was delivered on a cold January day in 1961. Former President Eisenhower and Jacqueline Kennedy look on from behind the podium. ▼

did much to change and strengthen the executive branch. People who were members of the White House staff took on many of the decision-making and advisory roles previously held by Cabinet members. This increased Kennedy's authority, since these appointees, unlike Cabinet members, did not have to go through congressional confirmation proceedings. Kennedy's aides, "the best and the brightest" as he called them, dominated policy making. With people such as McGeorge Bundy directing foreign affairs and Theodore Sorensen as a special counsel, speechwriter, and chief of staff, Kennedy began a pattern still in place today—whereby American Presidents increasingly govern through small groups of fiercely loyal aides.

How did Kennedy's personal style differ from that of previous Presidents?

◆ NEW FRONTIER PROGRAMS

Attempting to rival Franklin Roosevelt's first 100 days in office, Kennedy presented an ambitious New Frontier program to Congress. He proposed that Congress raise the minimum wage, approve federal assistance to public schools, and provide medical insurance to supplement private insurance for people over 65. He also wanted Congress to provide aid to poor areas of the country and guarantee federal aid for housing.

Kennedy had difficulty getting his major bills passed. Having won the election by a small margin, he was unable to claim a national **mandate,** or complete support, for his programs. Although Democrats controlled both houses of Congress, the party was divided between northern and southern Democrats. Southern Democrats, for the most part conservatives, did not want the federal government to become further involved in issues such as housing, education, and wages. Believing that these issues should be left to the states, they joined with Republicans to block many of Kennedy's proposals.

Despite some legislative defeats, Kennedy won important victories. In April 1961, Congress voted to provide millions of dollars in aid to areas of the country suffering from severe unemployment. In June 1961, Congress provided money for housing for the elderly and the poor, and for college students. Minimum wage legislation helped increase the average annual income of families, as shown on the graph on this page. In addition, social security benefits were extended to more Americans. Antipollution laws were passed.

Civil Rights

During the 1960 campaign, Kennedy took a strong stand in support of civil rights. In a later speech, he pointed to inequalities faced by African Americans in the early 1960s:

> The Negro baby born in America today has about one-half as much chance of completing a high school as a white baby born in the same place on the same day, one-third as much chance of completing college . . . a life expectancy which is seven years shorter, and the prospects of earning only half as much.

Despite supporting civil rights, however, the President was reluctant to anger white southern congressional leaders whose support he needed to pass other parts of his New Frontier program. At first, Kennedy took mild measures to ensure civil rights. In 1961, he supported passage of the Twenty-third Amendment, which allowed residents of the District of Columbia, largely African Americans, to vote in presidential elections. He called for outlawing the poll tax in federal elections. Kennedy also appointed a number of African Americans to important government

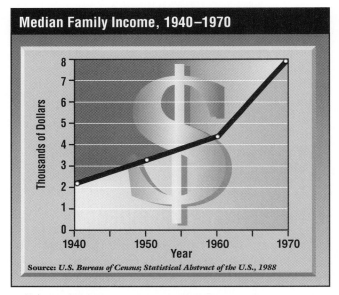

▲ **Economics** *The median annual income of families in the United States rose greatly during the period 1940–1970.* **Interpreting the Graph** *How much did median annual income increase between 1955 and 1965?*

◀ *This Peace Corps volunteer is working on an irrigation project in the Asian nation of Nepal.*

positions, including Thurgood Marshall, who became a judge of the U.S. Court of Appeals.

Many African American leaders believed that Kennedy was not moving fast enough to ensure civil rights. Kennedy considered proposing legislation banning discrimination in voting and employment, but he hesitated. He believed that such a proposal would result in too much opposition from white Southerners.

Then, in September 1962, an African American Air Force veteran named James Meredith attempted to enroll at the University of Mississippi. Violence broke out, and Kennedy sent federal troops to make sure Meredith would be allowed to attend classes.

From this point on, Kennedy became actively involved in the cause of civil rights. However, more violence would occur before he actually proposed a civil rights bill to Congress. In September 1963, members of the Ku Klux Klan bombed a church in Birmingham, Alabama, killing four African American children. This violence led Kennedy to propose a civil rights bill guaranteeing equal access to all public accommodations and outlawing discrimination in voting and employment. It would fall to Kennedy's successor, Lyndon Johnson, to win approval of the Civil Rights Act.

Kennedy made a significant contribution to women's rights with his Presidential Commission on the Status of Women, led by Eleanor Roosevelt. The commission's 1963 report was the most comprehensive study of women's lives ever produced by the federal government, documenting the discrimination women faced in the workplace and in the legal system. It called for federally supported day-care programs, continuing-education programs for women, and an end to sex bias in social security and unemployment benefits.

The Peace Corps

Another important part of Kennedy's New Frontier agenda was a proposal to institute the **Peace Corps.** The group represented the President's promise to direct the idealism of a new generation. The Peace Corps is a federal agency that sends trained volunteers to developing countries overseas. Besides teaching modern methods of farming and manufacturing, volunteers help establish schools and health centers.

The Peace Corps was aimed at improving living conditions throughout the world while reducing Communist influence. The hard work of Peace Corps volunteers eventually won the United States many friends around the world.

The Space Race Begins

A keystone of Kennedy's program was exploration of the new frontier of space. After *Sputnik 1*

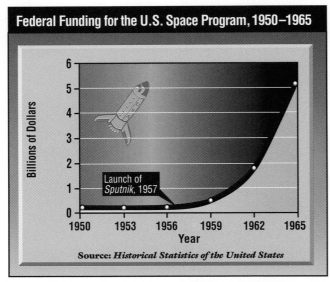

Federal Funding for the U.S. Space Program, 1950–1965

Billions of Dollars

Launch of *Sputnik*, 1957

Year

Source: *Historical Statistics of the United States*

▲ **Economics** *The race to put a man on the moon consumed U.S. engineers for 15 years.* **Interpreting the Graph** *What event marked the beginning of the massive increase in government spending on the space program?*

and *2* were launched in 1957, the Soviet Union sent other satellites into orbit. In April 1961, Soviet cosmonaut Yuri Gagarin became the first human to orbit the earth. Vice President Lyndon Johnson voiced the concerns of many Americans about the Soviet Union's technological advances when he said,

> Control of space means control of the world. From space, the masters . . . would have the power to control the earth's weather, to cause drought and flood, to change the tides and raise the levels of the sea, to divert the Gulf Stream and change temperate climates to frigid.

In May 1961, Kennedy announced the creation of the Apollo program, promising that the United States would put an American on the moon before 1970. In spite of the estimated costs—a staggering $30 to $40 billion over a ten-year period—President Kennedy believed that it was vital for the United States to show its technological abilities and beat the Soviets to the moon. He declared it was "time for this nation to take a clearly leading role in space achievement, which in many ways may hold the key to our future on earth." Many scientists debated the scientific value of putting a person on the moon, and many citizens pointed to

the need for greater spending on public education and social welfare programs. However, government funding began for a U.S. space program, as shown on the graph on this page. Nine months later, in February 1962, John Glenn became the first American to orbit the earth. His flight lasted 4 hours and 55 minutes and covered 81,000 miles.

 What events forced Kennedy to show greater support for civil rights legislation?

Section 1 Review

Check Understanding

1. **Define** (a) New Frontier (b) missile gap (c) mandate (d) Peace Corps

2. **Identify** the issues that threatened Kennedy's candidacy for President in 1960.

3. **Describe** how President Kennedy's style appealed to people eager for change.

4. **Explain** why Kennedy had difficulties getting some of his New Frontier legislation passed by Congress.

5. **Describe** the factors that led Kennedy to propose putting an American on the moon by 1970.

6. **Explain** Kennedy's position on civil rights.

Critical Thinking

Analyzing a Quotation Reread Lyndon Johnson's comment about the space race on this page. Did his prediction turn out to be true? Explain your response.

Write About Government

◆**Connecting Past and Present** The presidential debates of 1960 highlighted the impact that television could have on the outcome of a political campaign. How important a role does television play in campaigns today? Explain in writing.

CONNECTING HISTORY & Science

RACE TO THE MOON

On July 20, 1969, almost six months before the deadline set by President Kennedy, close to a billion people gazed in awe at television screens as American astronauts Neil Armstrong and Edwin "Buzz" Aldrin landed on the moon. All over the world, people watched as Armstrong left footprints in moon dust. Not everyone understood his declaration, "That's one small step for a man, one giant leap for mankind," but there was no mistaking his action of planting the American flag on the surface of the moon.

The landing of the lunar module of *Apollo 11* was the culmination of nine and a half years of intensive work that began during the Kennedy administration. Starting from small satellites that explored space and progressing to crewed flights that orbited the earth and the moon, the National Aeronautics and Space Administration (NASA) worked tirelessly to meet President Kennedy's challenge to land a man on the moon before the end of the 1960s.

The space program was both a controversial and a political issue during the 1960s. Some scientists believed that robots and instruments could collect information in space more safely than humans could, while others appreciated that science, industry, and education might benefit from the technological advances made in the effort to put men on the moon. Some politicians questioned the wisdom of spending so much money and energy on a project of questionable scientific value, while others saw the moon landing, whether scientifically valuable or not, as a victory of capitalism over communism. Regardless of the disagreement, however, the New Frontier was actually reached in space, if not on the earth, on July 20, 1969.

Making the Scientific Connection

1. What did Neil Armstrong mean when he said, "That's one small step for a man, one giant leap for mankind"?

2. Why was the space program a controversial issue?

3. Are American attitudes toward the space program the same today as they were during the 1960s? Explain your answer.

Connecting Past and Present

Some Americans feel that money spent on space travel and research would be better spent on the earth. Others believe that discoveries made in space could benefit life on the earth. Do you think Congress should fund space exploration today? Write a short speech in which you make a case either for abandoning space exploration or for continuing to support it.

Astronauts Neil Armstrong (left) and Buzz Aldrin (right) explored the moon's surface while Michael Collins (center) manned Apollo 11 *as it circled the moon.* ▼

BUILDING *SKILLS*

Conducting Research: The Postwar Era

Conducting research is the process of examining various kinds of resources for information. It also means assessing the data you collect, synthesizing your findings, and drawing your own conclusions.

Here's How

Follow these steps to conduct research:

1. Use both primary and secondary sources.
2. Select the kinds of references you need. General background materials will give you an overview of your topic, while specialized materials offer more detailed information. Encyclopedias are good for a general summary and a list of cross-references that can give you ideas for other references to consult.
3. Use the library catalog system to find the materials you need. You can search this system according to author, book title, or subject.
4. Search computer databases to find specific books and articles about your topic. When you conduct a search by entering key words, you get back a list of every source that contains those words.
5. If possible, use the Internet to gather information. It can connect you to universities, libraries, news organizations, government agencies, businesses, and individuals worldwide.
6. Assess the usefulness of your sources by evaluating each one for its relevance, timeliness, level of specialization, expertise, and purpose.
7. Keep an accurate list of your resources. Include title, author, publisher, publication date, and any other information that will help you or someone else locate the same information again.

Here's Why

Doing a research paper gives you a chance to learn about a topic and to pass some of your knowledge on to others. The better your research is, the more you will learn. Good information from reliable sources, especially information that can be found in two or more sources, will give you the materials and the confidence to write an interesting paper that is logical and meaningful.

Practice the Skill

Use a library to complete these tasks.

1. Using the Peace Corps as a starting point, find two different articles in an encyclopedia that cover this topic. Write the names of the two articles and at least three related articles that are cross-referenced.
2. Use the *Readers' Guide to Periodical Literature*, which is a list of articles that appear in national magazines, or the Internet. Find the name of one article from the last ten years about each of the following topics: John Fitzgerald Kennedy, Jacqueline Kennedy, the missile gap, the space race, and the Twenty-third Amendment.

Apply the Skill

For the topic you chose in Chapter 26 for your research paper, make a list of the resources you plan to use. Include at least one encyclopedia article, two books, and three magazine or newspaper articles. If possible, include one Internet site. For each source that you list, write a brief evaluation of its relevance, timeliness, level of specialization, expertise, and purpose.

Foreign Policy in the Early 1960s

PREVIEW

Objectives

- To explain how the Bay of Pigs invasion affected U.S. relations with countries in Latin America

- To discuss the impact of Soviet threats to West Berlin

- To describe how Kennedy handled the Cuban missile crisis

Vocabulary

Third World
exile
quarantine

The Kennedy years, like the years of the Eisenhower administration, were dominated by the Cold War. During the 1960s, leaders of the Soviet Union were ready to challenge the United States, sensing they had an advantage in such weapons as missiles. Communism, supported by the Soviet Union, seemed to be spreading in areas known as the **Third World,** the developing nations of the Middle East, Africa, and Latin America that were not aligned with either the United States or the Soviet Union. The *First World* referred to the Western democracies and the *Second World* referred to the Communist bloc.

Kennedy believed there were two ways of fighting communism. The first was to increase U.S. military might and convince the Soviets that the United States was prepared to use that might if necessary. The second was to build support in the Third World by offering economic aid, technology, and advice.

◆ TROUBLE IN LATIN AMERICA

Cuba, located only 90 miles from the southern tip of Florida, was a place where the tensions of the Cold War became serious. In 1959, rebel forces under the command of Fidel Castro had overthrown Cuban dictator Fulgencio Batista. At first, Castro promised to bring democracy to Cuba. This promise won him substantial support from the Cuban people and from other countries as well. The United States recognized the new regime and tried to establish friendly relations with Castro.

As the months passed, however, it became clear that Castro had no faith in democracy. Rather, as he announced in 1961, he was a Communist, determined to transform the Cuban economy and ally the country with the Soviet Union. Castro's government became more repressive, and middle-class and wealthy Cubans began to flee to the United States.

Tensions grew between Cuba and the United States when Castro seized Cuba's private businesses and placed them under the government's control. A number of U.S. companies had important interests in many Cuban industries, especially the sugar industry. U.S. businesses owned about 40 percent of sugar-producing businesses in Cuba. When Castro took over these industries and replaced their American owners, the friendly relationship between the United States and Cuba ended abruptly. Believing that the United States was trying to overthrow him, Castro asked the Soviets for massive shipments of military weapons to build up his defenses.

The Bay of Pigs Invasion

In his last year as President, Eisenhower had approved a secret plan to replace Castro. According to the plan, the Central Intelligence Agency (CIA) would give military training and arms to 1,500 Cuban **exiles,** who had left their country either by force or voluntarily to live in the United States. These exiles, who became known as the Cuban Brigade, planned to return to Cuba and overthrow the Castro regime. When Kennedy took office, he continued the training of the Brigade. Allen Dulles, head of the CIA, assured the President that Cubans would rise up to support the invasion as soon as the exiles landed in Cuba.

Kennedy's administration tried to keep the invasion plan a tightly held secret. However, several reporters found out about the upcoming invasion. At the President's request, they did not publish the news.

On April 17, 1961, the land invasion began. About 1,500 Cuban exiles and a few Americans landed at the Bay of Pigs in Cuba, about 90 miles from Havana, as shown on the map on page 556. The Cuban people did not rise up against Castro. Instead, when they heard that the United States had backed the invasion, Cubans rallied in support of Castro. Castro's forces moved swiftly to trap the invaders. In three days, they killed more than 100 of the invaders and took the rest as prisoners.

Americans were shocked to learn how deeply involved the U.S. government had been. Kennedy himself was in an embarrassing position. Conservatives attacked him for not providing enough arms for the invasion to succeed. Liberals attacked him for supporting the invasion of an independent nation. Latin Americans considered it another example of the United States resorting to big-stick diplomacy. Throughout the Third World, the United States was criticized for attacking a smaller country.

Kennedy took the full blame for the invasion and its failure. He acknowledged that he had used poor judgment but criticized the CIA for overestimating the strength of the anti-Castro opposition in Cuba. In December 1962, Castro released the prisoners after the United States provided medicine and food to Cuba worth $42 million.

The Alliance for Progress

During the 1950s, the image of the United States in Latin America had suffered. Many Latin Americans believed that the United States had too much influence in their region. In 1961, Kennedy attempted to change that perception by creating a program known as the Alliance for Progress. The Alliance was a joint effort to provide economic assistance to Latin America over a period of ten years. Kennedy called the Alliance

> **❝ . . . a vast cooperative effort . . . to satisfy the basic needs of the American people for homes, work and land, health and schools. ❞**

The Alliance for Progress pledged United States participation in four ways—economic assistance, support for more equal distribution of land and taxes, efforts to ensure democracy, and assistance in countering communism. The Alliance also promised to improve education, nutrition, and medical services in Latin American countries. To attain these goals, the United States committed $20 billion to the project, with the Latin American nations responsible for the rest.

The results of the Alliance proved disappointing. Economic growth increased in Latin America but not as much as Kennedy had hoped. Furthermore, Latin

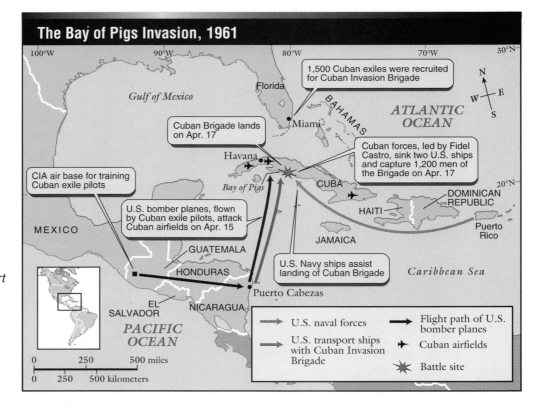

Geography *Kennedy's effort to overthrow the government of Cuba in 1961 ended disastrously.* **Interpreting the Map** *How were Nicaragua and Guatemala involved in the plan?* ▶

The Bay of Pigs Invasion, 1961

- 1,500 Cuban exiles were recruited for Cuban Invasion Brigade
- Cuban Brigade lands on Apr. 17
- Cuban forces, led by Fidel Castro, sink two U.S. ships and capture 1,200 men of the Brigade on Apr. 17
- CIA air base for training Cuban exile pilots
- U.S. bomber planes, flown by Cuban exile pilots, attack Cuban airfields on Apr. 15
- U.S. Navy ships assist landing of Cuban Brigade

Gulf of Mexico • Florida • Miami • BAHAMAS • ATLANTIC OCEAN • Havana • Bay of Pigs • CUBA • DOMINICAN REPUBLIC • HAITI • Puerto Rico • MEXICO • GUATEMALA • HONDURAS • JAMAICA • Caribbean Sea • Puerto Cabezas • EL SALVADOR • NICARAGUA • PACIFIC OCEAN

- → U.S. naval forces
- → U.S. transport ships with Cuban Invasion Brigade
- → Flight path of U.S. bomber planes
- ✈ Cuban airfields
- ✳ Battle site

0 250 500 miles
0 250 500 kilometers

◀ The Berlin wall became a symbol of the differences between the Communist world and the free world. Kennedy's visit in June 1963 bolstered the spirits of West Berliners.

American countries made few of the reforms in land distribution and taxes proposed by the Alliance, and few countries adopted democratic governments. In fact, during a ten-year period after 1961, military leaders took over the governments of Honduras, Ecuador, and Peru. By the 1970s, the Alliance had lost most of its support both in the United States and Latin America.

How did Kennedy attempt to deal with problems in Latin America?

◆ RELATIONS WITH THE SOVIET UNION

The failure of the Bay of Pigs invasion had a major impact on relations with the Soviet Union. After the invasion, Kennedy made plans for a summit conference in Vienna, Austria, with Soviet leader Nikita Khrushchev. A summit conference is a meeting of the leaders of two or more countries. Kennedy believed that the two leaders had to work out better channels of communication if the threat of nuclear war was to be avoided.

If anything, the Vienna summit conference worsened, rather than improved, superpower relations. There were only brief moments of agreement between the two leaders. Khrushchev criticized Kennedy for U.S. involvement in the Bay of Pigs. Kennedy faulted Khrushchev for supporting Communist revolutions in other countries. Khrushchev boasted about Soviet superiority in space exploration. Both leaders admitted the need for a ban on nuclear arms, but they could not come to any agreement about how to achieve it.

The Berlin Wall

One of the toughest issues the two leaders discussed concerned the city of Berlin. The former capital of Germany was located deep within Communist-controlled East Germany. At the end of World War II, the city had been split into sectors. West Berlin was democratic and allied with the Western nations while East Berlin was controlled by Communists and allied with the Soviet Union.

At the Vienna conference, Khrushchev challenged the West over Berlin. He told a stunned Kennedy that Berlin should be united as one city within East Germany. Kennedy responded that the United States would never allow this. He saw West Berlin as a center of democracy in the midst of hostile Communist territory. He pointed out to Khrushchev that nearly three million East Germans had already escaped to West Berlin in search of a better life.

Their differences over Berlin created an ominous atmosphere during the closing minutes of the meeting. As the two leaders separated, Kennedy, thinking of a possible challenge over Berlin, remarked, "It will be a cold winter." Both men returned home ready to build up their countries' military strength.

Late that summer, the East German government began building a wall between East Berlin and West Berlin. The 12-foot high, 103-mile long wall, made of concrete and topped with barbed wire, was referred to as "the wall of shame" by people in both East Berlin and West Berlin. It was meant to prevent more East Germans from fleeing to West Berlin.

The construction of the Berlin Wall greatly changed the lives of the people of East Berlin and West Berlin, as well as East Germany and West Germany. The Wall now officially separated East Berlin from West Berlin, making casual contact between friends and families on both sides, as well as trade in goods and services, extremely difficult. The Wall did succeed at stemming the flow of people to West Berlin, but it would remain a symbol of East German communism for nearly 30 years. In the years that followed its construction, hundreds of people from East Berlin made desperate attempts to escape over the Wall to West Berlin. Some people succeeded. Others were shot or captured by the East Germans as they tried to escape.

In June 1963, Kennedy traveled to West Germany to show American support for democracy. Kennedy portrayed divided Berlin as a symbol of the vast differences between the Communist world and Western democracy. Kennedy said,

> **There are many people in the world who really don't understand what is the great issue between the free world and the Communist world. Let them come to Berlin! There are some who say that communism is the wave of the future. Let them come to Berlin!**

As the crowd of West Berliners applauded, he said that all people who were free should support Berliners by considering them fellow citizens. Then to ringing cheers, he said, "*Ich bin ein Berliner*," by which he meant, "I am a Berliner." That commitment assured the people of Berlin that the United States would continue to support the city.

The Cuban Missile Crisis

A year after the Berlin crisis, the world was plunged into an even more dangerous situation. Once again, Cuba was at the center of the conflict. In the summer of 1962, the Soviet Union began offering increased military and economic aid to Cuba. Castro had asked for Soviet military hardware because he said he feared an invasion by the United States. In April 1962, Soviet leader Nikita Khrushchev decided to place missiles in Cuba. Castro agreed in July, and 60 missiles and their nuclear warheads were sent to Cuba hidden on board civilian ships.

To find out what was going on in Cuba, Kennedy sent American spy planes to fly over the country. The planes brought back alarming information. The Soviet Union had installed nuclear missiles that could easily destroy cities in the eastern part of the United States.

The President immediately called in his closest advisors. Over a tense six-day period, the group debated several options. One option was to launch an immediate air attack on Cuba. Another option was to **quarantine** Cuba. This would isolate the island by forming a naval blockade around it.

On October 22, Kennedy appeared on television to announce the presence of nuclear missiles on Cuba. He also announced that a quarantine would prevent further Soviet weapons from reaching the island. Kennedy insisted that the Soviets withdraw

Study Hint

As you read this chapter, you will learn how to organize important ideas to help you remember them. Make a list or chart of ideas and details that you think are related. Then find out how these ideas are related, and make a name or title for the category that identifies, or classifies, them.

◀ *Cuban immigrants in the United States watched with fear as Kennedy announced the presence of nuclear warheads in their homeland.*

the missiles immediately. He warned that if any of the missiles were launched from Cuba, it would be regarded as a Soviet attack on the United States. He then placed the United States military on full alert and ordered a fleet of American ships to blockade Cuba.

Tension mounted as Soviet ships steamed toward the blockade. The superpowers seemed on the brink of a nuclear war. Then, on October 24, 1962, Khrushchev ordered the ships to turn back. Four days later, he ordered the bases on Cuba to be dismantled, provided the United States agreed to stay out of Cuban affairs and removed missiles in Turkey aimed at the Soviet Union. Said United States secretary of state Dean Rusk,

❝We were eyeball to eyeball, and the other guy just blinked.❞

A UN inspection team monitored the removal of the missiles. Kennedy ended the quarantine on November 20. He and Khrushchev agreed nine months later to ban above-ground nuclear testing.

In what ways did the Berlin Wall and the Cuban missile crisis intensify the Cold War with the Soviet Union?

◆ THE ASSASSINATION OF THE PRESIDENT

Two years and ten months after he became President, Kennedy made a political tour of Texas. He believed that appearing in the state in person might increase his popularity there. In addition, he believed that his presence in Texas could heal a split in the state Democratic party. Kennedy was greeted warmly as he traveled around the state. On November 22, 1963, John and Jacqueline Kennedy arrived in Dallas. Thousands of enthusiastic people were waiting to greet them at the airport. Kennedy was in high spirits as he waved to the crowd from his motorcade.

Suddenly, shots rang out, and Kennedy slumped in his seat. The motorcade rushed to the nearest hospital where, after attempts to revive him failed, he was pronounced dead. Later, aboard a plane carrying the President's body back to Washington, Vice President Lyndon Baines Johnson took the presidential oath of office.

Lee Harvey Oswald was arrested and charged with the President's assassination. Oswald had fired on the motorcade with a high-powered rifle from a building overlooking the route. Two days later, as millions of Americans watched on television, a nightclub operator

Vice President Lyndon Johnson is sworn in as President in the cabin of the presidential plane after Kennedy's assassination. Kennedy's widow, Jacqueline, stands to the right. Johnson's wife, Lady Bird, stands to the left. ▶

named Jack Ruby shot and killed Oswald as the police were escorting him from the police station to the county jail. Ruby was captured, tried, and convicted of Oswald's murder.

To investigate Kennedy's assassination, President Johnson set up the Warren Commission, headed by Supreme Court Chief Justice Earl Warren. The commission studied the evidence to determine whether Oswald had acted alone or whether others had been involved in the assassination. Although the commission decided that Oswald had acted alone, many Americans thought that the evidence pointed to additional participants. In the late 1970s, the House Select Committee on Assassinations disputed the findings of the Warren Commission. The assassination of President Kennedy has remained one of the most argued issues in U.S. history.

Kennedy's assassination threw the country into mourning. Schools and businesses closed. Even those who had criticized Kennedy were shocked and saddened by his death. From around the world, expressions of grief poured in to the Kennedy family and to the nation. Though Kennedy's administration had been brief, he had inspired many people with his efforts to spread democracy and with his hope for a better tomorrow.

 How did the assassination of John F. Kennedy affect the nation?

Section 2 Review

Check Understanding

1. **Define** (a) Third World (b) exile (c) quarantine

2. **Explain** why the Bay of Pigs invasion failed.

3. **Identify** the reasons why the Communists built a wall between East Berlin and West Berlin.

4. **Describe** the outcome of the U.S. quarantine of Cuba.

Critical Thinking

◆**Connecting Past and Present** How have U.S. relations with Cuba improved today? In what ways is that relationship still unfriendly?

Write About Government

Write a paragraph explaining how the photograph on this page shows the orderly succession of power in the U.S. government as provided in the U.S. Constitution.

The Great Society

PREVIEW

Objectives

- To identify measures that were part of Johnson's war on poverty

- To summarize how the voting rights and immigration reform laws changed the political landscape of the United States

- To explain how Supreme Court decisions of the 1960s had a lasting impact on American society

Vocabulary

filibuster	political asylum
Great Society	Miranda warning
Medicare	gerrymander
Medicaid	

Within hours of being sworn in as President of the United States, Lyndon Baines Johnson set to work preparing a speech to Congress. The speech proved to be one of the most important of his career. People throughout the world were eager to know if Johnson could inspire the same confidence that Kennedy had.

◆ JOHNSON'S FIRST REFORMS

Johnson's first speech as President calmed many fears. He expressed his regret at the death of President Kennedy. Then, he began speaking about the policies he supported. To the discomfort of opponents of civil rights, Johnson, a Southerner, urged Congress to honor Kennedy's memory by quickly passing his civil rights bill. He also asked Congress to pass a bill cutting taxes.

Action on Civil Rights

Winning passage of the civil rights bill was a difficult task. Johnson had been actively supporting civil rights since the late 1950s. His leadership in this area led some of his fellow white southern lawmakers to feel that they had been betrayed. On the other hand, many

civil rights leaders distrusted Johnson because he had southern roots. Johnson intended to win their confidence. He used all his powers of persuasion to sway the representatives to endorse the bill. On January 31, 1964, he presented his new version of a civil rights bill and urged Congress to pass it without delay.

Although the bill passed the House of Representatives, serious problems arose when it got to the Senate. Johnson suspected that some senators intended to **filibuster,** delaying a vote on a bill by giving long speeches.

This tactic had been used before. For example, in 1957, Senator Strom Thurmond of South Carolina had spoken for 24 hours and 18 minutes against what became the Civil Rights Act of 1957. Johnson, the Senate majority leader, used his skills at negotiating and compromise to get this bill, which attempted to remove restrictions on African American voters, passed. This law was strengthened by the Civil Rights Act of 1960, which Johnson also championed and got passed, in spite of another lengthy filibuster by some white southern legislators.

The Civil Rights Act that was finally passed in July 1964 was the most sweeping piece of civil rights legislation in U.S. history. It prohibited discrimination in public places on the basis of race, ending segregation

President Lyndon Johnson shakes hands and offers a pen to Rev. Dr. Martin Luther King, Jr., after signing the Civil Rights Act of 1964. ▼

in most hotels, restaurants, department stores, and other facilities open to the general public. The act also prohibited racial discrimination by employers, unions, and employment agencies. It set up the Equal Employment Opportunity Commission to ensure that all people would receive fair treatment. In addition, the act outlawed discrimination in schools, giving the attorney general the power to file suit in court to speed up desegregation. Finally, it extended the power of the federal government to protect the voting rights of African Americans. At the signing of the act, Johnson summed up why the bill was just and in keeping with the principles of the nation. Listeners were reminded of the Declaration of Independence when he said,

> We believe that all men are created equal, yet many are denied equal treatment. We believe that all men have certain unalienable rights, yet many Americans do not enjoy those rights. We believe that all men are entitled to the blessings of liberty, yet millions are being deprived of those blessings, not because of their own failures but because of the color of their skin.

War on Poverty

Since the end of World War II, advances in technology had changed the causes of poverty in the United States. Many jobs were eliminated because of automation. In other cases, job requirements were raised, creating less demand for unskilled labor. Although skilled workers were generally well paid, those without skills found fewer jobs available and received lower pay for the jobs they did find.

Poverty was most prevalent among the very young, the elderly, and immigrant groups. Unemployment was double the rate among teenagers and young adults as it was in the nation as a whole. Many retired people were unable to live in comfort on the small payments provided by Social Security. Discrimination often barred African Americans and other groups from steady, well-paid jobs.

In an attempt to eliminate poverty in the United States, Johnson attacked it in two ways. One method was to offer direct financial assistance to poor people. The other was to offer them programs that would give them a chance to improve their employment skills. Johnson used the Democratic majorities in the House and Senate to push through the most ambitious reform program since the New Deal.

Lady Bird Johnson and the President were active proponents of Head Start. In this photograph, the First Lady works with students in a preschool program. ▶

In August 1964, Johnson won passage of the Economic Opportunity Act, which established the Office of Economic Opportunity to run antipoverty programs. Its purpose was to help young people and adults find a way out of poverty. To do this, it funded community action programs, youth centers, and work-experience programs. It offered services to needy children, migrant workers, and other people from disadvantaged backgrounds.

Some of the programs started by the Economic Opportunity Act are still in existence today. One of them is the Job Corps, an organization that resembles FDR's Civilian Conservation Corps of the 1930s. Instead of paying unemployed young people to work on the land, however, the Job Corps pays them while they train for industrial jobs. Another program, Project Head Start, was designed to help preschool children from low-income families. Head Start funds play groups, day care, and activities designed to help children get ready for elementary school. It also offers educational services to parents, medical and dental care, and nutritious meals. Yet another program created was VISTA, which stands for Volunteers in Service to America. VISTA volunteers work in urban areas and on Indian reservations, providing drug counseling, homeless shelters for runaways, and educational programs for adults and children.

As ambitious as it was, the war on poverty suffered from limited funding, and many elements of it did not last past Johnson's term in office. A 1970 study concluded,

"More than five years after the passage of the Economic Opportunity Act, the war on poverty has barely scratched the surface. Most poor people have never had contact with it, except perhaps to hear the promises of a better life to come."

In what ways did Johnson hope to eliminate poverty in the United States?

◆ JOHNSON'S GREAT SOCIETY

Johnson decided to seek reelection in 1964. His chances for another term looked good. LBJ, as Johnson was called, had not only led the nation though the grim

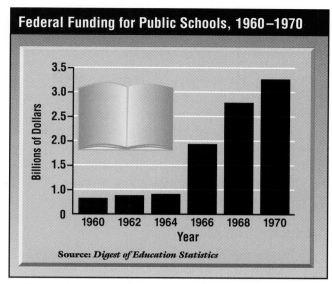

Federal Funding for Public Schools, 1960–1970

Source: *Digest of Education Statistics*

▲ **Economics** *Johnson's Great Society program included plans to increase funding for public schools.* **Interpreting the Graph** *How much federal money went to public education in 1966, 1968, and 1970?*

days after Kennedy's assassination, but he had also been able to get Congress to pass a number of important laws. His push for civil rights had won the strong support of many African Americans, and his war on poverty met the approval of unions, low-income workers, and others.

The Democratic party nominated Johnson for the presidency, and the Republican party nominated Senator Barry Goldwater of Arizona. Goldwater, a conservative, opposed many of Johnson's policies. As the campaign progressed, the differences between the two candidates became increasingly apparent. Goldwater had voted against the Civil Rights Act of 1964, whereas Johnson was intensely proud of the act. While Goldwater stressed "doing it on one's own" without financial aid from the federal government, Johnson maintained that government assistance was necessary to end poverty. Goldwater stressed the need for a strong anti-Communist policy and even suggested that he might use nuclear weapons in Vietnam. In contrast, Johnson seemed more likely to bring peace to the nation.

LBJ won 61 percent of the 70 million votes cast, an even higher percentage than Roosevelt had won in 1936. By capturing 44 states, Johnson won 486 electoral votes, compared with Goldwater's 52. With this victory, LBJ was ready to launch a new program.

The Launch of a New Plan

With the election behind him, Johnson presented a new legislative program for the country that he called the **Great Society.** He had several goals for his first full term, including more federal aid for housing, no-cost medical insurance for the elderly, and federal aid to make a college education more available to poor people. He also wanted to change the immigration laws to allow more people from Asia, eastern Europe, and Latin America into the country.

Johnson accomplished most of these goals. By 1966, he won approval for urban redevelopment and aid to education, as shown on the graph on page 563. By 1968, he had sponsored bills providing housing assistance, further aid to education, and conservation.

Medicare and Medicaid

One of the most important of Johnson's Great Society programs was **Medicare,** low-cost health insurance for people over 65 years old that helps pay for such health care costs as hospital bills and doctors' care. The Medicare bill, passed in 1965, was the first major change in the Social Security system since 1935.

Medicaid was another Great Society health program. While Medicare supports the elderly, Medicaid provides assistance to low-income and disabled Americans. Under it, the federal and state government pays for doctors, treatment in clinics, prescriptions, and some nursing-home care, dental care, and eyeglasses.

Reform in Immigration and Voting Rights

The Immigration and Nationality Act of 1965 was an attempt to change an immigration policy that had been in effect since 1924. That older policy had established a quota system that favored immigrants from countries in northern and western Europe over those from other countries. Many immigrants from Asia were prohibited from entering the country.

The Immigration and Nationality Act of 1965 altered the quota system. Effective July 1, 1968, 170,000 immigrants from the Eastern Hemisphere and 120,000 from the Western Hemisphere were allowed to enter the United States each year. It established guidelines for entry based on skills the immigrants possessed or need for **political asylum,** protection from oppression by rulers in one's homeland. The act allowed many more immigrants to come to the United States from Latin America, Asia, and eastern Europe. The old system of controlling immigration based on trying to keep the United States primarily a European American nation came to an end.

In 1965, Congress also passed the Voting Rights Act. The act was largely a reaction to the violence faced by African Americans who attempted to register to vote in some places in the South. This law created widespread reforms in the nation's voting laws. Literacy tests could no longer be used to keep people from voting. The Voting Rights Act led to increased voter registration in the South. This resulted in the election of many more African American candidates to local and state offices.

What different groups of people benefited from Johnson's Great Society program?

◆ LANDMARK SUPREME COURT DECISIONS

Along with the reforms of the Johnson administration came a series of Supreme Court decisions that supported the Great Society. They ushered in a new era of active Supreme Court involvement in the social changes of the 1960s. Additionally, the racial makeup of the Court was diversified when, in 1967, Johnson appointed Thurgood Marshall as the first African American Supreme Court Justice.

Leading the Supreme Court in these landmark decisions was Chief Justice Earl Warren. Warren was appointed to the Supreme Court in 1953 and remained there until 1969. He was such an important force in the Supreme Court rulings of the 1960s that the Court came to be known as the Warren Court.

The Warren Court made sweeping Supreme Court decisions. Earl Warren is seated in the middle of the front row, and Thurgood Marshall is at top right. ▼

The Rights of the Accused

Three Supreme Court decisions in the 1960s changed the way the police treated people suspected of crimes. In *Gideon* v. *Wainwright* (1963), the Court ruled that those who could not afford to hire a lawyer to argue a criminal case must be assigned one free of charge by the state.

In *Escobedo* v. *Illinois* (1964), Danny Escobedo, who had been arrested on suspicion of murder, was not allowed to see his lawyer. After hours of questioning by the police, Escobedo confessed to firing the shot that killed the victim. Afterwards he was convicted. In 1964, Escobedo appealed his conviction to the Supreme Court, which reversed the decision. The Court ruled that Escobedo's confession could not be used as evidence because he had been denied a lawyer. According to the Court, anyone who is taken into custody has the right to have a lawyer.

The 1966 case known as *Miranda* v. *Arizona* strengthened the rights of the accused even further. Ernesto Miranda was arrested in Phoenix in connection with a rape and kidnapping. After the victim identified him, Miranda confessed to the crime without being informed of his rights. It is the duty of the police to remind suspects of their right to remain silent, and that anything they say can be used against them in court. For those reasons, the Supreme Court ruled that Miranda's signed confession could not be admitted as evidence to convict him.

All three of these cases had far-reaching effects on the criminal justice system. After these rulings, the police had to make certain that they informed people of their rights. The statement of these rights is known as the **Miranda warnings:**

> You have the right to remain silent. Anything you say may be held against you in a court of law. You have the right to an attorney.

The statement of these rights continues to be read today. Since 1966 the ruling on the *Miranda* case has become highly controversial. Many Americans believe that the Supreme Court was too soft on crime, making it difficult for the police to do their job effectively. Other people, defending the Court's decisions, say that the *Miranda* ruling protects citizens from being abused by overly eager police.

One Person, One Vote

In the past, state legislatures had sometimes drawn up election districts on the basis of land area. Therefore, rural districts with few people could have greater representation than urban districts with many people. Politicians also frequently resorted to **gerrymandering,** or creating election districts that were shaped in order to ensure reelection.

In 1962, in a case referred to as *Baker* v. *Carr*, the Supreme Court ruled that election districts had to be roughly equal in population. The decision gave every American roughly the same power when casting his or her vote.

 What was one of the major rulings of the Warren Court? Why was it important?

Section 3 Review

Check Understanding

1. **Define** (a) filibuster (b) Great Society (c) Medicare (d) Medicaid (e) political asylum (f) Miranda warning (g) gerrymander

2. **Identify** the main provisions of the Civil Rights Act of 1964.

3. **Describe** the central aim of the Economic Opportunity Act.

4. **Describe** how the Voting Rights Act changed political activity in the United States.

5. **Analyze** the significance of the Supreme Court's *Gideon* and *Escobedo* rulings.

Critical Thinking

Identifying Cause and Effect What was the cause and effect of *Miranda* v. *Arizona*?

Write About Government

◆ **Connecting Past and Present** Write a paragraph about how certain laws passed during Johnson's administration affect life today.

Chapter 27
Review

CHAPTER SUMMARY

Section 1

John F. Kennedy, a Catholic and the youngest person to become President, won one of the closest presidential elections in U.S. history. During his term he was able to get few of his New Frontier initiatives passed, although he did establish the Peace Corps and made some first steps on civil rights issues.

Section 2

The Cold War dominated Kennedy's administration. Relations between the United States and the Soviet Union worsened after the United States backed an invasion of Castro's Cuba, which failed. The Soviets built the Berlin Wall to keep East Germans from escaping to West Berlin, further straining U.S.-Soviet relations. Cuba was the center of yet another crisis in 1962, when the United States quarantined Cuba to force the Soviets to remove nuclear missiles.

Section 3

Lyndon Johnson, who became President after Kennedy's assassination, engineered important civil rights legislation and a war on poverty. In 1964, Johnson was elected President and set forth the Great Society program, which included Medicare and Medicaid programs. The Immigration and Nationality Act of 1965 changed United States immigration policy for the first time since the 1920s. Important Supreme Court decisions signaled the Court's involvement in the social issues of the 1960s.

Connecting ◆◇◆ Past and Present

Would Americans today support a call for action such as Kennedy made in his inaugural address? Explain your answer.

Using Vocabulary

From the list below, select the term that best completes each sentence.

New Frontier	Peace Corps
Third World	quarantine
mandate	Great Society
Miranda warning	Medicare

1. Johnson's program to insure elderly Americans against the cost of health care was called _____.

2. Kennedy's ambitious program for social change was called the _____.

3. Johnson's legislative program for the country after his election in 1964 was called the _____ program.

4. The _____ is the part of the world containing developing countries.

5. The _____ sends volunteers to developing countries to help teach modern methods of farming and establish schools.

6. Suspects arrested for a crime must be given the _____ by the police.

7. A _____ isolates a location by forming a naval blockade around it.

8. If a leader has a _____ for a program, he or she might be able to say that there is complete support for it.

Check Understanding

1. **Discuss** the factors that most influenced the 1960 presidential election.

2. **Describe** Kennedy's leadership style.

3. **List** three of the measures that Kennedy proposed as part of his New Frontier initiative.

4. **Explain** why the Bay of Pigs invasion was a major setback to the Kennedy Administration.

5. **Identify** the two ways Kennedy wanted to fight communism.

6. **Summarize** what happened during the Cuban missile crisis.

7. **List** four major pieces of legislation Johnson was able to get Congress to pass.

8. **Explain** how the Voting Rights Act of 1965 and the Immigration and Nationality Act of 1965 changed the political landscape in the United States.

9. **Discuss** how Supreme Court decisions in the 1960s affected society.

10. **Discuss** the goals of Johnson's Great Society program.

Critical Thinking

1. **Applying Information** Why are Kennedy and his administration often compared with a legendary king and his mythical kingdom?

2. **Comparing** Compare the administrations of Kennedy and Johnson.

3. **Evaluating Information** After the Cuban missile crisis, secretary of state Dean Rusk said, "We were eyeball to eyeball, and the other guy just blinked." What did Rusk mean?

4. **Inferring** What arguments do you think opponents used to try to block Johnson's Great Society program?

5. **Connecting Past and Present** Which pieces of legislation enacted during Johnson's or Kennedy's presidency do you believe have had the most lasting effect on American society?

Interpreting the Timeline

Use the timeline on pages 546–547 to answer these questions.

1. In which years were people's rights affected by events in the United States?

2. Which events in 1961 and 1962 were related?

3. Which events reflect the conflicts taking place in foreign countries?

Putting Skills to Work

CONDUCTING RESEARCH

In the Building Skills lesson on page 554, you learned about the different kinds of resources that you can use to write an effective research paper. Practice these skills by completing three of the following four tasks.

1. List three specific resources you would check to find out more about the Bay of Pigs invasion.

2. List one book or magazine article written in the last five years that evaluates Kennedy's presidency.

3. Use the card catalog system to find the titles and authors of three books about Kennedy and the Soviet Union.

4. Use a computer database to find information about Kennedy's assassination. Remember to make your key words as specific as possible.

Writing to Express an Opinion

Some historians say that the Kennedy administration brought a mood of vitality and excitement to the nation. **Write** an essay in which you explain what kind of national mood you would try to create if you were President and how you would go about doing it. Back up your statements with examples from the administrations of Kennedy and Johnson.

 *Portfolio Project*

A WRITTEN DIALOGUE

Select one event that occurred during the presidency of either Kennedy or Johnson. Write a dialogue that might have occurred between two people who witnessed or took part in the event. Consider what these people would have thought and felt as well as how they would have acted. When you have completed the dialogue, choose a partner and perform it for the class.

THE AMERICAN CAR

Americans' passion for their cars dates back to at least the years between 1910 and 1920, when Henry Ford's mass production methods made the automobile affordable. Just about every driver remembers the first car he or she owned, no matter how unimpressive or beat up it might have been. Although tastes have changed and driving habits have been modified by the times, for most Americans the car remains a practical necessity as well as a symbol of freedom.

Then The automobiles of the 1950s and early 1960s were cars for people who had something to celebrate. World War II was over, and huge, gas-guzzling, gleaming wonders were the reward. According to one auto dealer, "A guy comes in, and he looks at the shape, and that's all. Nobody wants to know how it's made or how it runs, or even if it runs." The new car buyer was concerned mainly with style, size, and power. At 30 cents a gallon for gas, most Americans cared little about fuel economy or efficiency.

The formerly basic automobile turned into a work of art. With huge metallic bodies, bright colors, sweeping tail fins, and fake air vents, some vehicles looked more like rockets or battleships than cars. Manufacturers competed to design models with bigger engines, wider bodies, and fancier grill work.

The automobiles of the '50s and early '60s occasionally cruise by on the roads even now. Next to the smaller and sleeker cars—as well as the bulky sports utility vehicles—of today, these classics are colorful reminders of a time when style was king.

Now Much has happened to change the way automobiles are built, how they run, and how they look. Finless and chromeless cars are dull in comparison with their ancestors. However, many car owners are much more concerned about safety, reliability, and efficiency than were drivers of the 1950s. Consumers today look for features such as air bags, anti-lock brakes, and daytime running lights that were not available even ten years ago.

The car of today may remain an expression of an individual's personality, but it is also a matter of practicality. Whether people regard driving as a source of recreation or a means of transportation, their cars continue to be vehicles of personal freedom.

You Decide

What are some of the reasons that have caused a change in people's ideas about styling, gas mileage, and safety of cars? Is a car still considered a status symbol? Why or why not?

▲ A 1950s Cadillac

Unit 9

Foreign and Domestic Challenges 1960–1981

> " The world will not be the same for our children, or even for ourselves... because ours is a time of change; rapid and fantastic change...shaking old values, and uprooting old ways. Our destiny...will rest on the unchanged character of our people, and on their faith. "
>
> *Lyndon B. Johnson, Inaugural Address, January 20, 1965*

▲ During the Vietnam War, protests against U.S. involvement were often dramatic.
◈ **Connecting Past and Present** *What is the protester trying to show by putting the flower into the rifle? How do people peacefully protest today?*

Chapter 28
The Fight for Social Change 1960–1980

CHAPTER PREVIEW

Section 1 African American Protests

Frustration over the slow pace of acheiving equal rights contributed to a split in the civil rights movement and to the rise of new leaders.

Section 2 Women's Rights

Feminism took on a new energy as women sought equal treatment in employment, education, and politics.

Section 3 Latino Civil Rights

Prejudice and poverty stimulated an active Latino civil rights movement.

Section 4 Native American and Asian American Rights

Native Americans and Asian Americans, motivated by the successes of African Americans and Latinos, organized for their rights.

Malcolm X

César Chávez

U.S. Events

1960
✪ John F. Kennedy elected.

1962
National Farm Workers Association is organized by César Chávez.

1963
Kennedy is assassinated.
✪ Lyndon B. Johnson becomes President.

1964
✪ Johnson elected.
Martin Luther King, Jr., wins the Nobel Peace Prize.

1965
Malcolm X is assassinated.
Freedom Flights bring refugees from Cuba.
Immigration Act opens Asian immigration.

1966
Black Panther party is formed.
National Organization for Women is founded.

1968
✪ Richard Nixon elected.
Kerner Commission issues report on urban riots.
Martin Luther King, Jr., is assassinated.

1959

World Events

1961
V.S. Naipaul's novel *A House for Mr. Biswas* is published.

1963
France vetoes British membership in the Common Market.

1966
Red Guards are formed in Communist China to promote extremist socialism.

1969
Soviet and Chinese forces clash in Manchuria.

Red Guards

Portfolio Project

A VOICE FOR CHANGE

In the 15 years between 1964 and 1979, Americans were more divided than they had been at any time since the Civil War. Individuals and groups expressed their points of view in a variety of ways—through art, literature, music, and politics. As you read this chapter, think about the strategies that people used in their struggles for change. At the end of the chapter, you will express your point of view on an issue, using an effective and appropriate strategy.

▲ Shirley Chisholm, the first African American woman elected to Congress, crusaded for equal rights for women in the 1970s.
◆◆ **Connecting Past and Present** *How is the crowd reacting to Chisholm's call for equality? What rights do people work for today?*

Wounded Knee standoff

Female cadet

1972
✪ Richard Nixon reelected.
Ms. magazine begins publication.

1973
Armed standoff by Native Americans occurs at Wounded Knee.

1974
Richard Nixon resigns.
✪ Gerald Ford becomes President.

1975
Military academies open to women.
E.L. Doctorow's novel *Ragtime* is published.

1976
✪ Jimmy Carter elected.

1978
Over 50,000 refugees from Laos, Cambodia, and Vietnam enter U.S.

1980
✪ Ronald Reagan elected.

1981

1971
UN votes to admit Communist China.

1975
World population is estimated at 4 billion.

1977
Egyptian president Anwar el-Sadat visits Israel.

1980
Polish workers start Solidarity union under Lech Walesa.

United Nations

African American Protests

PREVIEW

Objectives

- To describe the views of black nationalists

- To explain the causes and effects of riots in cities during the summers of 1964 through 1968

- To discuss the impact of the Black Power movement on the struggle to end discrimination against African Americans

Vocabulary

Black Power
Black Panther

By 1964, the civil rights movement was a major factor in American politics. Led by Martin Luther King, Jr., the movement had made some progress using nonviolent methods to gain civil rights, as shown on the chart on page 575. For example, thousands of African Americans in the South were now able to vote. However, change came slowly, and frustration and anger grew in the African American community, especially as militant white segregationists confronted peaceful protesters with violence.

Many civil rights leaders disagreed about what direction they should take. Some preferred to continue with peaceful protest and integration. Others supported a militant response to the violence they encountered.

◆ NEW VOICES FOR CIVIL RIGHTS

In 1964, Martin Luther King, Jr., won the Nobel Peace Prize for bringing about change without violence. Though this prize reflected the world's admiration, in the United States Dr. King had many critics.

Black Nationalism

The new voices in the civil rights movement were younger, louder, and angrier. Many were bitter about how long it was taking to achieve equal rights. Some African Americans turned to black nationalism, a belief in the separate identity and racial unity of the African American community. Black nationalists did not believe integration into white society would benefit African Americans. Instead, they believed in establishing a separate African American society or nation.

Black nationalism was an idea that appealed to many urban African Americans in the North. Previously, the civil rights movement had worked mainly to change unfair laws that enforced segregation in the South. Though racial discrimination in the North was not as obvious, it seriously limited African Americans' chances for advancement in jobs, housing, and education. Many young urban African Americans felt both hopeless and angry. They were angry at white society—at slum landlords, at store owners who charged high prices, at city officials, at the justice system, and at the unjust treatment they sometimes received from white police officers who patrolled African American neighborhoods.

Malcolm X

The best-known black nationalist of this period was Malcolm X. He joined the Nation of Islam, a group often called the Black Muslims, when he was 27 years old. The message of the Nation of Islam was one of self-help and separation from white society.

Born Malcolm Little, he rejected his last name as a slave name when he joined the Black Muslims. He took the letter *X* as a symbol of his missing African name and became a minister of the Nation of Islam. His fiery speeches thrilled audiences and won many followers.

Malcolm X offered a dramatic contrast to Martin Luther King, Jr. Instead of preaching integration, Malcolm X asked why any African American would want to join white society. He spoke directly to white people, saying,

> **What you don't realize is that black people today don't think it is any victory to live next to you or enter your society. This is what you have to learn—that the black man has finally reached the point where he doesn't see what you have to offer.**

Malcolm X urged African Americans to use "any means necessary" to achieve equal rights. This position upset moderate civil rights leaders, both

African American and white, who were committed to using only nonviolent methods.

After a trip in 1964 to Mecca, in Saudi Arabia—the city that Muslims consider holy—Malcolm X underwent a turning point in his thinking. He changed his name to Al Hajj Malik al-Shabazz and adopted the view that not all white people were evil. It was possible, he thought, to work with all people around the world to create freedom and equality for everyone. He continued to stress self-determination and self-defense for African Americans. "We won't get our problems solved depending on the white man," he declared.

Malcolm X's changed opinions earned him a number of enemies, including members of the Nation of Islam who considered him a traitor for rejecting their message of separatism. In February 1965, he was assassinated while giving a speech at a rally in Harlem in New York City. Three members of the Nation of Islam were arrested, convicted of his murder, and sentenced to long terms in prison.

Black Power

A dramatic event in the fight for equal rights occurred early in 1966. James Meredith, the first African American to attend the University of Mississippi, announced that he would walk to Jackson, the state capital, as a way to encourage more African Americans in Mississippi to register to vote. As Meredith walked along the highway, a sniper with a shotgun wounded him.

Dr. Martin Luther King, Jr.; Stokely Carmichael, the newly elected leader of the Student Nonviolent Coordinating Committee (SNCC); and Floyd McKissick of the Congress of Racial Equality (CORE) decided to finish Meredith's march. As the march began on June 7, King tried to rally the crowd with the traditional cry of "Freedom Now!" Carmichael, however, used a new phrase to express protest: **Black Power.** Its symbol was a raised, clenched fist.

Meredith's shooting had convinced groups such as SNCC that peaceful marches were not effective. The split between militant and moderate views began to grow wider. Stokely Carmichael challenged moderate leaders with these words:

> We've been saying freedom for six years—and we haven't got anything.
> What we're going to start saying now is 'Black Power'!

▲ Malcolm X, who rejected his last name when he joined the Black Muslims, urged African Americans to pursue a path of self-determination.

Black Power meant different things to different people. To some, it meant creating African American political parties. To others, it meant that African Americans should establish their own businesses. Using the idea of Black Power, some self-help groups promoted ideas of racial unity for African Americans and instilled a sense of pride with the phrase "Black is beautiful." Other Black Power leaders supported urban disturbances as expressions of rebellion against poverty and lack of power.

The best-known revolutionary militant group was the **Black Panther** party. Formed by Bobby Seale and Huey Newton in Oakland, California, in 1966, the Black Panthers wanted African Americans to control their own communities and to fight police abuse. They demanded that the federal government rebuild decaying city ghettos. They also demanded that African Americans be released from jail and tried again by African American juries. They called for armed rebellion, if necessary, to win their goals. Although the Panthers had frequent violent encounters with police, they had another side as well. They developed day-care programs and sponsored free breakfasts for African American children. Some African American leaders urged Huey Newton, Bobby Seale, and other Black

Panthers to abandon their militant views. They feared militancy would frighten white people whose support they needed to get civil rights measures through Congress. The new young leaders refused, and a split widened—with SNCC and the Black Panthers on one side and more conservative groups, such as the NAACP, on the other.

Throughout the late 1960s, Black Power continued to grow. College students demonstrated for black studies programs. Parents gave their children African names, and well-known people, such as the playwright and poet Imamu Amiri Baraka (formerly LeRoi Jones), the boxer Muhammad Ali (formerly Cassius Clay), and the civil rights leader Kwame Toure (formerly Stokely Carmichael), rejected what they called their "slave names."

How did the ideas of the Black Power movement differ from those of Martin Luther King, Jr.?

◆ CONFLICT IN THE CITIES

While some activists were advocating Black Power, Martin Luther King, Jr., continued to preach nonviolence and racial harmony. King worried, however, about the divisions between militants and moderates in the African American community. African Americans' frustration with poverty, particularly in urban areas, led to riots.

The Assassination of Dr. King

In 1966, Dr. King led a rally in Chicago against poverty, unemployment, poor schools, and housing discrimination. As King and his supporters marched through white neighborhoods, angry people threw rocks and bottles at them. Soon after the march, white leaders in Chicago agreed to stop unfair housing practices but did little to carry out the plan.

In 1968, King organized the Poor People's Campaign in an effort to improve economic opportunities for people of all races. In April 1968, he traveled to Memphis, Tennessee, in support of a strike by African American sanitation workers. There Dr. King spoke about the future in words that suggested he knew his life was in danger:

> " I may not get there with you, but I want you to know tonight that we as a people will get to the promised land. "

The Black Panthers' goals included fighting police abuse and rebuilding decaying ghettos. These Black Panthers, demonstrating outside a courthouse, are wearing the Panthers' characteristic clothing—black leather jackets and black berets. ▶

Major Civil Rights Actions, 1865–1970

CIVIL RIGHTS LEGISLATION, 1865–1957

1865—13th Amendment	Abolishes slavery throughout the United States
1868—14th Amendment	Extends citizenship to formerly enslaved persons
1870—15th Amendment	Prohibits states from denying the right to vote because of race
1883—Supreme Court ruling	Federal laws preventing racial discrimination by private individuals deemed unconstitutional
1896—Supreme Court ruling	*Plessy* v. *Ferguson* establishes separate but equal public facilities for whites and African Americans.
1946—Supreme Court ruling	Segregation on interstate buses is ruled illegal.
1954—Supreme Court ruling	*Brown* v. *Board of Education of Topeka* rules that segregation in public schools is unconstitutional.
1955—Supreme Court ruling	Authorizes desegregation in public schools
1957—Civil Rights Act	Establishes Commission on Civil Rights to ensure enforcement of federal civil rights laws

MAJOR EVENTS OF THE CIVIL RIGHTS MOVEMENT, 1955–1968

1955—Montgomery bus boycott	Dr. Martin Luther King, Jr., leads boycott against an Alabama bus company's segregation policies.
1960—Greensboro Sit-in	Students protest against segregated lunch counters at an F. W. Woolworth store in Greensboro, North Carolina.
1961—Freedom Ride	Protests against segregation in interstate transportation facilities
1962—University integration	James Meredith becomes first African American to enroll at the University of Mississippi.
1963—March on Washington	200,000 people, led by Dr. King, march to Washington, D.C., to show support for civil rights bill.
1965—Selma March	State troopers, defying a federal court order, attack peaceful demonstrators in Selma, Alabama.
1965—Watts (Los Angeles) Riot	Five days of rioting, after police arrest an African American, result in 34 deaths and $200 million in property damage.
1967—Summer of riots	Riots break out in 75 U.S. cities.
1968—Kerner Commission	Reports that the nation is moving toward two societies, "one black, one white—separate and unequal"
1968—Dr. King assassinated	Dr. King is shot dead while supporting striking sanitation workers in Memphis, Tennessee.

CIVIL RIGHTS LEGISLATION, 1960–1970

1960—Civil Rights Act	Authorizes referees to help African Americans register to vote
1964—24th Amendment	Prohibits poll taxes in federal elections
1964—Civil Rights Act	Directs businesses to serve all people without regard to race, color, religion, or national origin; establishes Equal Opportunity Employment Commission to handle complaints of unfair employment practices; authorizes federal government to cut funds to segregated schools
1965—Voting Rights Act	Eliminates voter literacy tests as a means of discrimination
1966—Supreme Court ruling	Prohibits poll taxes in state and local elections
1968—Civil Rights Act	Ends discrimination in sale or rental of housing; establishes strict measures to control rioting
1968—Supreme Court ruling	Bans all housing discrimination
1970—Congressional Law	Safeguards voting rights of illiterate voters by banning literacy tests in all states

▲ **Government** *This chart shows events and legislation related to the civil rights movement.* **Interpreting the Chart** *How do the major events reflect the variety of approaches and reactions people had to the civil rights movement?*

That was King's last speech. The next evening, he was shot as he stood on a motel balcony. The death of the man who had continuously preached nonviolence sparked urban riots in more than 100 cities. For many people, the death of King marked the beginning of the end of the civil rights movement.

Urban Riots

By the mid-1960s, African Americans had become near majorities in the nation's cities. The exodus of whites to the suburbs had reduced the tax base for public services so that schools, hospitals, and recreational facilities were often poorly funded and unable to provide adequate services.

Urban pressures frequently reached a boiling point during the summers of 1964 through 1968. African Americans lashed out against the political and economic domination of their communities by whites and against police abuse, by destroying white-owned property. In the Watts section of Los Angeles, for example, a 1965 riot grew out of the arrest of an African American for a traffic violation. It resulted in $200 million in property damage, 34 deaths, and nearly 4,000 arrests. In Detroit, in 1967, the nation's most violent race riot occurred. Army tanks and national guardsmen had to be called in after 43 people were killed. In Newark, New Jersey, that same summer and in Washington, D.C., and Cleveland in 1968, there were also destructive riots.

The Kerner Commission

Initially, these disturbances led to badly needed reforms. After the riot in Watts, President Johnson set up a task force, a temporary group created to accomplish a goal, headed by Deputy Attorney General Ramsey Clark. Funds were allocated for antipoverty programs, but they did not fully address the problem.

In 1967, President Johnson set up the National Advisory Commission on Civil Disorders, chaired by Illinois governor Otto Kerner. Thereafter known as the Kerner Commission, its job was to investigate the causes of the urban riots. The group blamed the riots on white racial prejudice and discrimination, pointing to poverty, segregated schools, and poor housing as the causes for African Americans' anger. In its 1968 report, the commission warned,

"Our nation is moving toward two societies, one black, one white—separate and unequal."

The Kerner Commission recommended a more extensive public housing program, integrated schools, and funding for income supplements. Congress ignored the warning and the recommendations. About the only change to come out of the Kerner Commission was the Open Housing Law, which extended the protections against discrimination in the sale or rental of housing provided in the 1964 Civil Rights Act. The new law also included strict measures to control rioting by requiring up to five years in prison for anyone traveling across state lines to "organize, promote, encourage, participate in, or carry on a riot."

 What was the government's response to the urban riots?

Section 1 Review

Check Understanding

1. **Define** (a) Black Power (b) Black Panther

2. **Identify** the injustices against African Americans that led to disturbances in cities.

3. **Describe** one issue over which militant civil rights leaders differed with moderate leaders.

4. **Discuss** how the Black Power movement tried to end discrimination.

Critical Thinking

Connecting Past and Present In your opinion, which ideas of the civil rights leaders from the 1960s have the most influence today?

Write About Citizenship

You are present at a meeting between Dr. Martin Luther King, Jr., and Malcolm X before Malcolm's visit to Mecca. Write a dialogue that might have taken place between the two leaders over the way to end discrimination against African Americans.

BUILDING SKILLS

Taking Notes and Outlining: Americans Fight for Social Change

Taking notes and outlining are important steps in writing a research paper. These steps will help you collect and organize your research. There are a number of different methods for notetaking and outlining. Any of them will help you to record facts and supporting details so that you can put them together logically and effectively.

Here's How

Follow these steps to take notes and outline:

1. Skim or quickly read the information you have found, and decide what main ideas you will use in your research paper.

2. Record each main idea on an index card or on a separate sheet of paper. In your own words, add notes about each main idea.

3. If you are using quotations, copy them carefully, with punctuation, capitalization, and spelling exactly as in the original. Be sure to write the source of the information.

4. Arrange the notecards or pieces of paper so that facts about each main idea are grouped together.

5. Create an outline by identifying the main ideas with Roman numerals. Subtopics are labeled with capital letters, and supporting details are labeled with Arabic numerals.

Here's Why

Recording main ideas, subtopics, and supporting details so that you can put them in a logical order before you begin to write will make drafting your research paper easier and faster.

Practice the Skill

Copy the outline below into your notebook. Complete the outline using the information on pages 573–574 from Section 1.

Topic: The Rise of the Black Panthers

I. The Black Panther movement
  A. Origins of the Black Panthers
    1. The group was formed in 1966.
    2. They were formed in Oakland, CA.
  B. Initial founders of the Black Panthers
    1.
    2.
  C. Reasons for founding
    1.
    2.
II. Actions taken by the Black Panthers
  A.
    1.
    2.
  B.
    1.
    2.

Apply the Skill

Based on the topic and purpose you chose in the Building Skills lesson in Chapter 26 and the sources you chose in the Building Skills lesson in Chapter 27, take notes on main ideas and details. Organize your notes so that all the related ideas are grouped together. Finally, turn your notes into an outline.

Women's Rights

Objectives

- To discuss why the women's movement took on a new energy in the 1960s

- To explain the steps women took to gain equal treatment in employment, education, and politics

- To describe the laws that were passed in the 1960s and 1970s to protect women from discrimination

Vocabulary

feminism
lobby
gender

The effects of the civil rights movement rippled through American society. Beginning in the 1960s, other groups sought equal rights. Though women were not a minority, they still faced economic and social disadvantages. Many women desired more active and inclusive roles. They wanted more choices in education, jobs, political activity, and their personal lives.

◆ EQUALITY FOR WOMEN

Many women wanted a broader choice of jobs. Some jobs, such as those of nurse, secretary, teacher, and sales clerk, were traditionally considered "women's work." Though the atmosphere of the 1950s put pressure on women to remain homemakers, large numbers of women continued to work outside the home. By 1960, over one third of all women were working in jobs outside the home.

Women had little equality at work, however. Most jobs that women held outside the home were low-paying. Few women were managers or executives. Even a woman doing the same job (or a similar job) as a man earned less than he did—only 63 cents for each dollar that a man earned in 1960. More women were going to college in the 1960s, but many felt frustrated when they were discouraged from going into medicine, law, or science. Women had little presence in politics or government.

In 1963, a new book, *The Feminine Mystique,* expressed the feelings of many women. Writer Betty Friedan described how many of the women who had graduated with her in 1942 from Smith College were unfulfilled and dissatisfied with their home-centered lives. They wanted more outlets for their talents and ambitions. Friedan identified "the feminine mystique"—the idea that women wanted to remain at home—as the main source of the problem.

> **We can no longer ignore that voice within women that says: 'I want something more than my husband and my children and my home.'**

NOW Sets Goals

It was these desires that led to the movement for women's equality, sometimes called **feminism.** This was neither a new term nor a new idea. In the 1800s women had worked for the right to vote and for equality in education and in jobs. The term *feminism* was first used in 1895 to describe the advocacy of political, economic, and social equality of men and women. Feminists were those who believed in the theory or who worked to put it into practice.

In 1966, Betty Friedan and other feminists created the National Organization for Women, or NOW. The organization grew quickly. In its first year, membership went from 300 charter members to 1,200.

NOW's basic goals were "true equality for all women" and "a fully equal partnership of the sexes." At first, its focus was primarily on economics and jobs. NOW criticized the fact that few women earned graduate and professional degrees and that almost none held high-level jobs in government, industry, or business.

Later, NOW broadened its concern to include other matters, among them the division of responsibilities among family members. NOW supported an equal partnership between women and men in marriage and home life. It objected to advertisers and the media who presented women only as homemakers. Finally, NOW tried to ensure that it did not become part of any political party. Rather, its members would work for the election of candidates who supported the group's aims.

▲ *In the late 1960s and early 1970s, demonstrations such as this one demanding equal rights for women were common.*

NOW also worked to change the laws governing a woman's right to choose an abortion. In *Roe* v. *Wade* (1973), the Supreme Court ruled that a state could not prevent a woman from having an abortion during the first three months of pregnancy. The Court made this decision in order to maintain the privacy of the doctor-patient relationship, not to affirm a woman's right to control her own body, as feminists had wanted. However, this decision changed abortion laws in 46 states.

New Laws Promise Equality

Even before NOW began to **lobby,** or try to persuade legislators, women had gained some rights. Many provisions of civil rights laws protected women and other groups, as well as African Americans. For example, the Equal Pay Act of 1963 prohibited discrimination in compensation for "equal work" on the basis of sex.

Though the Civil Rights Act of 1964 was drafted primarily to benefit African Americans, a section of the law became important to the women's movement. That section, Title VII, stopped private employers from discriminating against workers on the basis of race, color, religion, national origin, or **gender** (classification by sex). It set up the Equal Employment Opportunity Commission (EEOC) to deal with job discrimination. Title IX of the Education Amendments Act of 1972 prohibited sex discrimination in educational programs that received government money, which was especially good news for women athletes. The act required schools to financially support sports programs for women and girls as much as programs for men and boys. The Equal Credit Opportunity Act (1975) made it easier for women to borrow money, obtain credit cards, and take out home mortgages in their own names. Previously, a married woman often had to get her husband's signature on financial contracts.

? **What were the goals of the founders of NOW?**

◆ PROGRESS AND SETBACKS

By the 1970s, the efforts of the women's movement were paying off. New opportunities opened up in hundreds of fields. For the first time, women were obtaining jobs as FBI agents, commercial airline pilots, astronauts, rabbis, and Episcopal priests. Each of the U.S. military academies began to admit women and train them as officers. A television network hired the first woman to co-host the network news, Barbara Walters.

For the most part, the media did not take the women's movement seriously. Television, newspaper, and magazine advertisements still showed women as dependent on men. For this reason, in 1972 journalist Gloria Steinem began a new magazine called *Ms.,* which aimed to take women's issues seriously. When it was first launched, *Ms.* called itself "the new magazine for women" and covered ideas that were not usually discussed in other women's magazines. Over the years, *Ms.* has tackled many important issues, from sexual harassment in the workplace to women in the military. The magazine also gave many women a new title. Being called "Miss" or "Mrs." automatically defined a woman as single or married, but "Ms." was neutral. It soon became the title that many women chose to use.

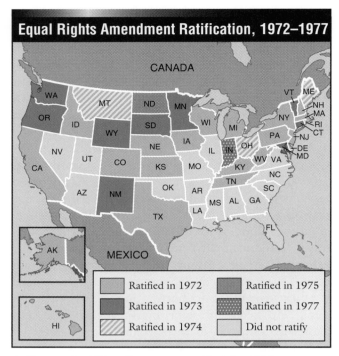

Equal Rights Amendment Ratification, 1972–1977

CANADA

MEXICO

	Ratified in 1972		Ratified in 1975
	Ratified in 1973		Ratified in 1977
	Ratified in 1974		Did not ratify

▲ **Geography** *Thirty-five states ratified the ERA.*
Interpreting the Map *Which two states were the last to ratify?*

Women's Liberation

Just as the civil rights movement had its conservative and militant branches, so too did the women's movement. The more radical women were often younger, less formal, and more dramatic than the members of NOW. Many members in the more militant branches of the women's liberation movement had participated in the civil rights struggle. Adopting the slogan *Sisterhood is powerful,* they organized groups and staged sit-ins at the offices of national magazines to protest media depictions of women that they considered demeaning. They lobbied for the admission of women to all-male colleges, such as Yale and Princeton, and were instrumental in setting up women's studies programs at many universities. Others established health clinics, day-care centers, rape-crisis centers, and shelters for women fleeing abusive relationships.

By the early 1970s, the women's movement had fostered a sense of community that provided support to many women. Sisterhood did not always unite women across race or class lines, however. Much of the women's liberation movement remained white and middle-class. African American women formed their own groups to address their distinct cultural and political concerns, as did Latina women.

The Equal Rights Amendment

The women's movement experienced many setbacks. For example, activists had tried since the 1920s to pass an amendment to the Constitution that would guarantee women's rights. In 1972, Congress passed the Equal Rights Amendment, known as the ERA. The ERA stated that men and women must be treated equally by law. Opinions were divided over whether the ERA was needed. Opponents argued that it would hurt family life and force women to serve in the military. Before the ERA could become law, 38 state legislatures had to ratify it within 10 years. But only 35 state legislatures approved the ERA, so the amendment died in 1982. The states that ratified the ERA are shown on the map on this page.

 What were the arguments for and against the ERA?

Section 2 Review

Check Understanding

1. **Define** (a) feminism (b) lobby (c) gender

2. **Explain** why the feminist movement gained strength and energy during the 1960s.

3. **Discuss** what women did to seek equal treatment in employment, education, and politics in the 1960s.

4. **Describe** the division of opinion about the need for the Equal Rights Amendment.

5. **Explain** the new laws that helped women gain equality in the 1970s.

Critical Thinking

◆**Connecting Past and Present** How have women's lives changed since the 1970s? In what professions have women gained prominence since the 1970s?

Write About History

Write a list of questions you would ask a woman who lived through the 1960s and 1970s.

Section 3

Latino Civil Rights

PREVIEW

Objectives

- To explain how the struggles of Mexican American farm workers led to an active Latino civil rights movement

- To discuss why Puerto Ricans migrated to the mainland United States

- To describe how Cubans who fled Castro's government established a presence in the United States

Vocabulary

bilingual
commonwealth
political exile

Latinos come from many cultures in Latin America, including the Caribbean. The largest Latino groups are Mexican Americans, Puerto Ricans, and Cuban Americans. There are also sizable communities from Colombia, the Dominican Republic, El Salvador, Guatemala, and other countries of Central America. Latinos came by themselves or with their families to live in the United States. About 90 percent of them live in large cities.

In the 1960s and 1970s, the Latino population in the United States increased faster than that of any other group, but its development as a political force grew more slowly. Like other ethnic groups, Latinos faced widespread discrimination in jobs, education, and housing.

◆ MEXICAN AMERICANS

Mexican Americans are the largest group of Latinos in the United States, making up about 63 percent of the Latino population. Mexicans have a long history in the United States. Many lived in California and the Southwest even before those lands became part of the United States, but the annexation of Texas and the U.S. victory in the war with Mexico made them a minority in a dominant Anglo, or English-speaking, society. While Mexican heritage is still strongest in the Southwest and California, there are large Mexican American communities in Chicago, New York, Milwaukee, and other U.S. cities.

The civil rights movement of the 1960s and 1970s encouraged voters to exercise their rights. In the early 1960s, voters in Texas, California, and New Mexico elected the first Mexican Americans to the House of Representatives and the Senate, including Joseph Montoya and Henry B. Gonzalez. President Lyndon Johnson also named several Latinos to important government positions, and in 1974, voters in two states elected Mexican Americans as governors—Jerry Apodaca in New Mexico and Raúl Castro in Arizona. During Nixon's administration, which began in 1969, Romana A. Banuolos was appointed treasurer of the United States.

Latino political gains were not always accompanied by economic gains. Limited job opportunities forced some Latinos to work as migrant farm laborers, traveling from farm to farm and living in temporary shacks. They spent days in the hot sun, picking fruit or vegetables for very low pay. Children, who worked long hours in the fields, did not go to school. César Chávez, a leader in the struggle for Latino civil rights, helped migrants improve their working conditions.

César Chávez Leads the Farm Workers

Like Martin Luther King, Jr., César Chávez was committed to using nonviolent methods in order to achieve better conditions. He believed that actions such as strikes and boycotts could effectively bring about change. He also admired the Indian leader Mohandas Gandhi, who had preached nonviolence. Like Gandhi, Chávez used hunger strikes to gain attention and win support.

In 1962, Chávez began to fight for better labor conditions and higher wages for grape pickers in California. He organized a union that eventually became the United Farm Workers of America (UFW).

In 1965, Chávez's group joined other workers in a strike against powerful California grape growers. Chávez and Dolores Huerta, another activist, led a peaceful march of workers from Delano, California, to the state capitol in Sacramento. As a result of the publicity, wine grape growers agreed to bargain with the union. However, the growers of table grapes refused.

Chávez and Huerta then called for a boycott in 1968 of California-grown grapes. Soon, people across the country knew about the farm workers' cause. An estimated 17 million Americans showed their support by refusing to buy the grapes. The boycott hurt business so much that table grape growers eventually gave in to workers' demands, ending the boycott in 1978. Future boycotts won better conditions for workers who picked lettuce and other crops in California. Chávez broadened the struggle for better wages and union recognition into a campaign for workers' dignity.

The Chicano Movement

Like the black nationalists who were proud of their African heritage, Mexican American high school and college students took pride in their roots. They identified *la raza* ("the race" or "people") as the source of their common language, religion, and heritage. Calling themselves Chicano and Chicana instead of Mexican American to express their cultural nationalism, they demanded equality with Anglos. The Chicano rights movement was called *el Movimiento,* or "the movement."

Between 1965 and 1969, the Chicano movement reached its peak of activism. Students staged strikes in East Los Angeles high schools to demand Mexican American literature and history courses. They wanted to study writers such as Gary Soto, Denise Chávez, and Rolando Hinojosa. In 1967 a group of students formed the Brown Berets, modeled on the Black Panthers, to address housing, employment, and other community issues. A cultural movement spread from college campuses into the Latino community. This movement included literary journals that were published and theatrical companies and music groups that toured across the country. Murals illustrating ethnic themes were painted on buildings in Los Angeles.

Chicano nationalism inspired a variety of regional political movements in the late 1960s. Rodolfo "Corky" Gonzales's Crusade for Justice was formed in 1965 to build Chicanos' political power and influence, and to foster cultural pride. The Crusade, which started in Denver, established a day-care center, a legal defense fund, a ballet company, a weekly newspaper, and a **bilingual** school. *Bilingual* means "using two languages." In Crystal City, Texas, Jose Angel Gutierrez formed the political party La Raza Unida, or "the United People." It increased Mexican American representation in local government and established social and cultural programs.

Efforts to provide self-help for Mexican Americans led to the founding of the Mexican American Legal

▲ *Dolores Huerta (pictured above) and César Chávez mobilized consumers to support better working conditions for farm workers by boycotting grapes.*

Defense and Education Fund (MALDEF) in 1968. MALDEF provided educational services and legal help in civil rights cases. It also encouraged Chicanos and Chicanas to become lawyers and community leaders.

What were the goals of the Chicano movement?

◆ PUERTO RICANS ON THE MAINLAND

The United States and Puerto Rico have had a unique relationship since the island became an American territory at the end of the Spanish-American War. In 1952, Puerto Rico became a **commonwealth,** a self-governing area, although it still maintained an association with the United States. Puerto Ricans elect their own officials, and they have a delegate in the U.S. House of Representatives who takes part in debates but does not have a vote. Puerto Ricans are U.S. citizens and have many of the same rights and obligations, although they do not vote in national general elections or pay federal income tax.

During the 1940s and 1950s, as air travel became more affordable, more than 545,000 Puerto Ricans flocked to the mainland United States. Today about a third of the Puerto Ricans on the mainland live in New York City. Newark, Philadelphia, and Chicago are other cities with large Puerto Rican communities.

Activist Groups

Since about 1964, the Puerto Rican Community Development Project has worked to improve education, family life, and health care in New York's Puerto Rican community. It has helped develop other educational programs, such as ASPIRA (from the Spanish word for *aspire,* "to have a strong goal"). ASPIRA works to develop community leadership in cities with large Puerto Rican communities.

Like MALDEF, the Puerto Rican Legal Defense and Education Fund works for Latinos' legal rights. In the 1970s, it sued successfully to get bilingual education in New York City schools. The fund also helped increase the number of Latinos who worked in city government.

The Nuyorican Cultural Movement

Like other Latinos, Puerto Ricans cherish their culture and traditions of music, art, and dance. The Puerto Rican Dance Theatre began in 1970. At about the same time, the Nuyorican cultural movement emerged in New York's large Puerto Rican community. The term *Nuyorican* comes from the time when most Puerto Ricans on the mainland lived in New York City. The term refers to a second-generation Puerto Rican who is born and raised on the mainland of the United States. Nuyorican culture is a blend of cultures from Puerto Rico and the mainland United States.

 What were some organizations and programs that helped the Puerto Rican community living on the United States mainland?

◆ CUBAN AMERICANS

Most Latinos came to the United States to look for jobs and a better way of life. However, many Cubans came for a different reason. Until the 1950s, the Cuban American community was quite small. It was centered in Tampa and Miami, in Florida. A smaller group lived in the New York and New Jersey area. Cubans could travel freely between Cuba and the United States.

Everything changed in 1959, when Fidel Castro took control of the Cuban government. When Castro's Communist government took over businesses and private property, thousands saw their way of life shattered. Many Cubans fled to the United States, becoming **political exiles,** people who leave their country for reasons relating to persecution or abuse by their government. Between 1959 and 1962, more than 250,000 Cubans fled to the United States.

◀ *The Latino bandleader and composer Tito Puente (bottom left) was responsible for popularizing Latin musical styles such as the cha-cha, mambo, and salsa. Puente's ability to play the clarinet, saxophone, piano, and many types of drums earned him the nickname* El Rey (the King) *of big-band mambo.*

During the Cuban Missile Crisis in 1962, Castro stopped allowing Cubans to leave legally. However, Cubans continued to come to the United States in small boats or on flimsy rafts through the choppy waters of the Florida Strait.

In 1965, the Cuban and U.S. governments co-operated to set up "Freedom Flights." These airlifts brought about 250,000 people to the United States. Cuba was losing so many skilled and educated people, however, that in April 1973, Castro stopped the flights from leaving the country.

The Mariel Boatlift

In 1980, Castro's government lifted the travel ban. Anyone who wanted to leave could exit at the port of Mariel. Cuban Americans in a convoy of small boats quickly left Florida to pick up relatives in Cuba. An unwelcome surprise awaited them when they reached Mariel, however. Castro announced that they could not pick up their friends and relatives unless they also agreed to take along other Cubans, including people from the island's prisons and mental hospitals.

Between April and September 1980, the Mariel boatlift brought some 125,000 people, known as Marielitos, to U.S. shores. Most of the 26,000 ex-prisoners had been jailed for political reasons or for minor crimes. Eventually, the United States accepted all but 2,746 of the refugees.

Success for Cuban Americans

Most of the early Cuban exiles were well-educated people from professional families. The exiles who came later were often small business owners and service workers who were at ease with city life and American culture. They were literate in Spanish and learned English easily. As a result, the Cuban American community generally had fewer social and economic problems than other Latino communities, which were frequently plagued by poverty. Other Americans looked at the Cuban newcomers as stable and hard-working.

Most Cubans settled in a section of Miami called Little Havana. As others came, they moved in with family members. Soon, entrepreneurs started Cuban-owned businesses. Those who came later often had both family ties and a place to work. Cuban culture and the Spanish language added flavor to life in south Florida.

Political exiles influenced Cuban American political movements. Many Cuban exiles hated Castro because he had taken away much of what had belonged to

them. They organized anti-Castro resistance groups with the aim of overthrowing the Castro government. As time passed, though, some Cuban Americans began to discuss having closer ties with Cuba.

Political changes in Cuba have been a major issue for Cuban Americans. They have lobbied and elected Latinos to political office in order to support their efforts to influence U.S. policies toward Cuba and toward immigration. Some Cuban Americans' activities have helped ensure the continuing opposition of the United States government to the Castro government.

 What advantages did Cuban Americans in the United States have in the 1960s?

Section 3 Review

Check Understanding

1. **Define** (a) bilingual (b) commonwealth (c) political exile

2. **Analyze** the methods César Chávez used to help migrant farm workers gain their rights.

3. **Describe** some of the goals of the Chicano movement.

4. **Explain** why large numbers of Puerto Ricans migrated to the United States mainland.

5. **Explain** how Castro affected Cuban immigration to the United States.

Critical Thinking

Connecting Past and Present How would you compare the struggle of Mexican Americans in the 1960s and 1970s with the difficulties they encountered in the 1930s? In what ways has life improved for them? In what ways has it stayed the same?

Write About Culture

Write a paragraph explaining why you think Chicanos wanted to have their literature and history taught in U.S. schools.

POINT *of* VIEW

CÉSAR CHÁVEZ

César Chávez led migrant farm workers in the struggle for better working conditions and higher wages. He refused all outside support, including money from the American Federation of Labor, because he believed that farm workers need to exercise their own power. Chávez was a passionate speaker who believed in the justness of the farm workers' cause. Through the years, Chávez worked tirelessly to build a union that would protect and fight for the rights of migrant farm workers. The movement was about more than just wages, however. César Chávez also encouraged the dignity and pride of the Latino population. In these comments, he discusses what moved him to devote his life to the struggle.

I remember with strong feelings the families who joined our movement and paid dues long before there was any hope of winning contracts. Sometimes, fathers and mothers would take money out of their meager food budgets just because they believed that farm workers could and must build their own union. I remember thinking then that with spirit like that we had to win. No force on earth could stop us.

• • • •

[Farm workers] are involved in the planting and the cultivation and the harvesting of the greatest abundance of food known in this society. They bring in so much food to feed you and me and the whole country and enough food to export to other places. The ironic thing is that after they have made this tremendous contribution, they don't have any money or any food left for themselves.

• • • •

It is not enough to teach our young people to be successful . . . so they can realize their ambitions, so they can earn good livings, so they can accumulate the material things that this society bestows. Those are worthwhile goals. But it is not enough to progress as individuals while our friends and neighbors are left behind.

Examining Point of View

1. Why did César Chávez became a labor organizer?
2. Based on these passages, what qualities do you think César Chávez had?
3. What do you think Chávez meant when he said, "it is not enough to progress as individuals while our friends and neighbors are left behind"?
4. What goals does César Chávez identify as important ones to fight for?

What's Your Point of View?

Chávez explained the reason he devoted his life to work for the rights of migrant workers in this way: "If you're outraged at conditions, then you can't possibly be free or happy until you devote all your time to changing them. . . . We can't change anything if we want to hold on to a good job, a good way of life, and avoid sacrifice."

Write an essay in which you agree or disagree with Chávez's point of view. For what cause would you be willing to make a sacrifice?

Native American and Asian American Rights

PREVIEW

Objectives

- To explain what rights Native Americans sought in the 1960s and 1970s

- To describe the reasons why hundreds of thousands of Asians came to the United States after 1965

Vocabulary

life expectancy
termination
nisei

The experiences of Native Americans and Asian Americans have been very different. However, movements they formed in the 1960s paralleled efforts of other groups who tried to gain equality and respect in American society.

◆ NATIVE AMERICANS CLAIM THEIR RIGHTS

Every new immigrant group coming to the United States has had to overcome prejudice and discrimination. However, even the people who lived here first, the Native Americans, have had to fight for acceptance.

By the 1960s, many Native Americans had lost hope in their ability to break out of the cycle of poverty. Poverty was a way of life on most reservations, where living conditions were bleak because of a lack of good food, fresh water, health care, and job opportunities. The Native American's **life expectancy,** the number of years an individual is expected to live based on statistics, was short compared with other ethnic groups. Rates of suicide and alcohol abuse were high.

Changing Government Policies

Many people blamed the federal government for the plight of Native Americans. Over the years,

government policies changed frequently, and few showed any understanding of Native American ways of life. For example, at one time, the government broke up tribal lands, gave some of the land to individuals, and then sold the rest. Then the federal government changed its policy in 1934 with the Indian Reorganization Act. This act recognized Native American nations as sovereign, or independent, political units with a right to their land. The act also allowed many Native American nations to set up their own governments.

Policies changed again in the 1950s. Responding to pressure groups, including mining and other economic interests wishing to exploit the resources on Native American reservations, Congress adopted a policy known as **termination.** It meant that the federal government would no longer provide federal programs and economic support to reservations. Native American schools were closed, aid programs ended, and Native Americans were encouraged to leave reservations. This policy also meant that some nations would no longer be recognized as political organizations. Some large Native American nations, including the Klamath of Oregon and the Menomonee in Wisconsin, and more than 100 smaller nations were forced to disband.

Programs to help Native Americans became the responsibilities of individual states, which now controlled Native American lands within their borders. Native Americans lost control of large areas of their

Study Hint

By forming a study group, you can improve your performance on tests. Members of a study group can help explain parts of the material that they understand well. Form a study group and have each member focus on one section of this chapter. When you meet, each member will provide the group with a summary of the section studied.

◄ These Native Americans lead a federal government negotiator (in the car) out of Wounded Knee. During the standoff, two Native Americans were killed and many buildings were destroyed.

lands as the states sold rights to reservation land to oil, mining, and lumber companies.

The Bureau of Indian Affairs offered money to Native Americans to move to cities. However, once the money was spent, Native Americans had to take poorly paid jobs. Many became dependent on government social services.

Building an Identity

The scars left by the termination policies helped mobilize a new movement to defend Native American rights. The movement also helped build a strong sense of identity among Native Americans.

The main militant activity began in Minneapolis in 1968, when a group of activists from the Ojibwa nation started the American Indian Movement (AIM). At first, AIM focused on the problems of urban Native Americans, such as jobs and health care.

AIM also set up what it called survival schools to give young people a sense of their history and traditions. One AIM leader, Clyde Bellecourt explained to white people,

" This is all we have left here. Our way of life. And it was told to us that if our drum was ever stilled, you too would be through as a nation. "

Protests led by Native Americans focused mainly on changing federal government policies. In November 1969, for example, about 80 protesters took over Alcatraz Island in San Francisco Bay, the site of an abandoned federal prison. The protesters demanded control of the island, basing their claim on an 1878 treaty that allowed Native American men to control unused federal lands. The militants demanded government funds for an Indian cultural center and university. The occupation of Alcatraz lasted more than a year until federal marshals removed the last few protesters.

AIM activist Russell Means led a number of protests to publicize Native American grievances. For example, Means and nearly 200 Sioux seized the village of Wounded Knee, South Dakota, in 1973, where 83 years earlier, U.S. cavalry troops had massacred about 350 Sioux men, women, and children. The 1973 conflict at Wounded Knee was designed to protest living conditions at the neighboring Pine Ridge reservation. Armed AIM activists asked only that the federal government uphold treaty rights, but FBI agents and federal marshals surrounded the reservation. The standoff continued for 71 days. Eventually, federal officials met with tribal leaders and a compromise was reached.

Termination Ends

Several Native American groups won small parts of what had earlier been taken from them. For example,

President Nixon returned Blue Lake to the Pueblo Indians in Taos, New Mexico, and backed Congress in granting Alaskan Native Americans legal title to 40 million acres and compensation of nearly $1 billion. Despite these victories, tribal lands continued to suffer from industrial and government dumping and other commercial uses.

The 1960s marked the beginning of a Native American renaissance. Books like Vine Deloria, Jr.'s *Custer Died for Your Sins* (1969) and Dee Brown's *Bury My Heart at Wounded Knee* (1971) joined John Neihardt's *Black Elk Speaks* (1932) to reach millions of readers inside and outside Native American communities. These successes inspired other works about Native American life that also attracted large audiences.

? What actions did Native Americans take to create a change in government policies?

◆ ASIAN AMERICAN COMMUNITIES

Americans of Asian descent are even more diverse than those of Latin American descent. They speak many different languages, follow different religions, and have different traditions. Discriminated against by policy and law, they joined the civil rights movements of the 1960s in an attempt to end the prejudice they faced.

Asian Immigration

The Immigration Act of 1965 enabled increased immigration from Asia. In the 1970s alone, more than 1.5 million Asians arrived in the United States. This new wave also brought a strikingly different group of Asian immigrants. In 1960, the Asian American community was primarily composed of Chinese, Japanese, and Filipinos. However, by 1990, the Asian American population also included a significant percentage of Koreans, Asian Indians, Vietnamese, Laotians, and Cambodians. Many of these Asians had been able to come to the United States during the 1970s as a result of polices in the Immigration Act of 1965.

Getting used to life in the United States was often difficult. Like earlier immigrants, some newcomers met with hostility and prejudice. Some local workers and business owners resented competition from these Asian immigrants. To feel more at home, new immigrants settled near friends and relatives. Large cities—such as New York, Seattle, Minneapolis, and Los Angeles—soon included Asian neighborhoods.

A Wartime Legacy

The discrimination that Americans of Japanese descent faced during World War II continued into the 1960s. It was one of the first issues taken up by

In the late 1970s, many Vietnamese immigrants, such as the ones shown here, made part of the journey to the United States on flimsy, overcrowded boats. ▶

▲ In 1964, Patsy Takemoto Mink became the first Asian American woman in Congress.

in the garment industry. Others led campaigns that reflected the diversity of the Asian American population. Filipino Americans, for example, organized to educate themselves and other Americans about the destructive role of U.S.-backed Philippine dictator Ferdinand Marcos. Artists, writers, filmmakers, and historians sought to honor the Asian American past as well as to advance their cultural identity. Fiction writers, such as Frank Chin, Maxine Hong Kingston, and Amy Tan, found large audiences both inside and outside their communities. After generations of discrimination, these writers began to forge an identity and pride that was characteristically Asian American.

 How did Asian Americans advance their fight for civil rights?

the Japanese American Citizens League (JACL), a civic group formed by **nisei** (nē´-sā´), or second-generation Japanese Americans. The JACL became a leading organization working for Asian American civil rights in the 1960s and 1970s. It lobbied Congress to pay Japanese Americans for the financial losses they had suffered during World War II. The Civil Liberties Act of 1988 included an apology and some payments to victims of internment.

Joining the Civil Rights Movement

When Hawaii became a state in 1959, it elected the first Asian American to the Senate, Hiram Fong. Senator Fong's parents had come to Hawaii from China. Representative Daniel K. Inouye was born in Honolulu, Hawaii, to Japanese American parents. In 1962, Inouye was elected to the Senate. In 1964, Patsy Takemoto Mink, a Japanese American, became the first Asian American woman elected to Congress.

As civil rights movements gained steam in the 1960s, Asian students joined in the struggles. Students at San Francisco State College, for example, organized the Third World Liberation Front (TWLF), which included Asian Americans, Latinos, and African Americans. In November 1968, the TWLF asked for and won a school of ethnic studies at the college. In many Asian American communities, students helped set up community centers and self-help groups.

Some young Asian activists in San Francisco and New York, modeling themselves after the Black Panthers, became trade union organizers who attempted to raise the low wages of Asian immigrants

Section 4 Review

Check Understanding

1. **Define** (a) life expectancy (b) termination (c) nisei

2. **Explain** some of the problems that Native Americans faced in the 1950s and 1960s.

3. **List** the different ways Native Americans tried to improve political and social conditions.

4. **Describe** some of the reasons why getting used to life in the United States was often difficult for Asian Americans.

Critical Thinking

◆ **Connecting Past and Present** In what ways are Native Americans and Asian Americans better off today than they were in the 1960s and 1970s? In what ways do they continue to face discrimination?

Write About Culture

Have a discussion about the countries and cultures represented in your classroom. Then write a brief essay describing the ethnic diversity of your class.

Chapter 28
Review

CHAPTER SUMMARY

Section 1
Throughout the 1960s, the majority of African Americans continued to support civil rights leader Martin Luther King, Jr., and his goal of integration. However, Malcolm X and other leaders sought a more aggressive approach to bring about change and equality.

Section 2
In the 1960s and 1970s, women achieved some notable victories in education, employment, and politics. The National Organization for Women worked for equal pay and access to better jobs. Intensive lobbying led to a number of laws that protected against discrimination on the basis of gender, although the Equal Rights Amendment was not ratified.

Section 3
The Latino rights movement gathered strength during the 1960s. The struggle of migrant farm workers in the California grape industry inspired the Chicano Movement, or *el Movimiento*. Puerto Ricans also organized to gain rights, improve their lives, and preserve their culture. Cubans made rapid progress in establishing their presence in the United States.

Section 4
Native Americans' efforts to improve their lives helped to change discriminatory federal policies and reestablish tribal lands. Large numbers of Asians immigrated to the United States with the changing of immigration laws in 1965. Attempting to overcome prejudice, many joined the civil rights movement.

Connecting ◆◆ Past and Present

How do you think the activities of ethnic groups in the 1960s and 1970s changed American ways of life? How might life have been different today without the activities of these groups?

Using Vocabulary

From the list below, select the term that best completes each sentence.

Black Power	feminism
commonwealth	gender
lobby	political exile
termination	nisei

1. Second-generation Japanese Americans are known as _____ .

2. The women's movement for equality is also called _____ .

3. The policy of _____ meant that the federal government would no longer provide economic support to Native American reservations.

4. _____ could mean creating African American political parties or establishing African American businesses.

5. To _____ means to influence legislators to pass certain laws.

6. A _____ is one who leaves his or her country for reasons relating to the government.

7. The Civil Rights Act of 1964 forbade discrimination against workers because of race, religion, national origin, or _____ .

8. A _____ is a self-governing area.

Check Understanding

1. **Describe** how anger and frustration about discrimination against African Americans led to disturbances in cities.

2. **Explain** the split in approaches taken by African American leaders in the 1960s.

3. **Discuss** the impact of the Black Power movement on the struggle to end discrimination.

4. **Explain** the steps women took to gain equal treatment in employment, education, and politics.

5. **Identify** the Equal Rights Amendment and explain what happened to it.

6. **Summarize** how the struggles of Mexican American farm workers led to an active Latino civil rights movement.

7. **Discuss** why Puerto Ricans migrated to the mainland United States during the 1960s and 1970s.

8. **Explain** why Cubans migrated to the United States after 1959.

9. **Explain** the rights that Native Americans sought to gain in the 1960s and 1970s.

10. **Describe** the reasons why over one million Asians came to the United States after 1965.

Critical Thinking

1. **Comparing and Contrasting** Compare and contrast the ideas of Martin Luther King, Jr., and Malcolm X.

2. **Drawing Conclusions** How and why did the political goals of the Mexican American community differ from those of the Cuban American community?

3. **Making Inferences** Why do you think the government changed its policies toward Native Americans during the 1960s?

4. **Formulating Questions** Choose one person who appears in this chapter and write three questions that you would ask that person if you had the chance to interview him or her.

Connecting Past and Present In the 1960s and 1970s, women made great strides through the women's movement. What are some issues that women face today that are different from their earlier concerns?

Interpreting the Timeline

Use the timeline on pages 570–571 to answer these questions.

1. How many years separated the founding of the National Organization for Women (NOW) from the publication of *Ms.* magazine?

2. Which events affected immigration to the United States?

3. Which events support the statement that the 1960s were marked by violence?

Putting Skills to Work

TAKING NOTES AND OUTLINING

In the Building Skills lesson on page 577, you learned how to record main ideas, subtopics, and supporting details, and how to turn your notes into an outline. Organize the following notes into a formal outline.

- Summers of mid-1960s filled with angry demonstrations and riots in the cities
- Many urban problems—poor transportation, little crime control, undependable garbage collection, lack of money for good schools
- Riots happened in Watts (Los Angeles), California; Detroit, Michigan; Newark, New Jersey; Washington, D.C.; Cleveland, Ohio.
- Riots resulted in property damage, many deaths and arrests.
- Incidents grew out of feelings of political domination and frustration at police abuse.
- Commission appointed by Johnson recommended that government should rebuild ghettos, provide more public housing, integrate schools, create new jobs, and treat all citizens as equals.

Writing to Persuade

Choose an issue from this chapter, such as integration, eliminating prejudice, or obtaining equal rights. Take a stand on the issue from the perspective of an ethnic group. **Write** a letter to the editor of your local newspaper about the best ways to deal with the issue.

 *Portfolio Project*

A VOICE FOR CHANGE

Select an issue from among the following: the need for minorities to unite to fight discrimination; discrimination in the workplace; the farm workers' struggle in California; or support for Native Americans. Select a strategy to express your point of view on the issue. For example, you might write a protest song, draw a political cartoon or a poster, or write a persuasive speech. Express your point of view using your selected strategy, and share your finished project with your class. Explain why you chose the particular strategy to express your point of view.

Chapter 29
The Vietnam War
1960–1973

CHAPTER PREVIEW

Section 1 Cold War Politics and the Vietnam War

U.S. involvement in Vietnam began as part of the Cold War policy to contain communism, but escalated to the point that U.S. troops were fighting a full-scale war.

Section 2 A War Fought in Public

In the United States, public opinion about the Vietnam War changed as casualties mounted. The influence of the media's coverage played an important role in how people reacted to the war.

Section 3 The War Ends

In 1973, the last U.S. combat troops left Vietnam, giving people the opportunity to assess the long-term effects of the war on U.S. society and politics.

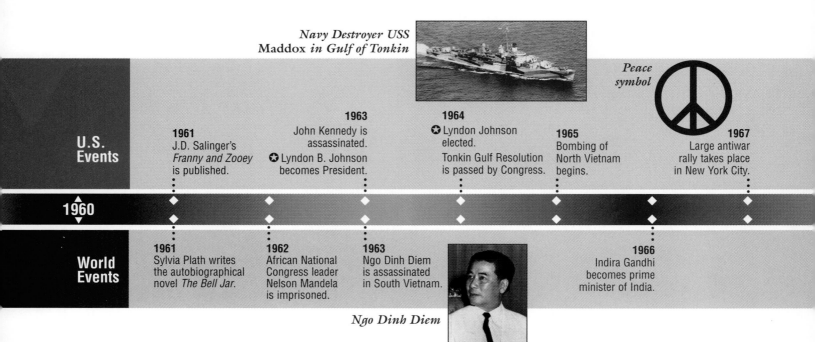

Navy Destroyer USS Maddox in Gulf of Tonkin

Peace symbol

U.S. Events

1961
J.D. Salinger's *Franny and Zooey* is published.

1963
John Kennedy is assassinated.
✪ Lyndon B. Johnson becomes President.

1964
✪ Lyndon Johnson elected.
Tonkin Gulf Resolution is passed by Congress.

1965
Bombing of North Vietnam begins.

1967
Large antiwar rally takes place in New York City.

1960

World Events

1961
Sylvia Plath writes the autobiographical novel *The Bell Jar.*

1962
African National Congress leader Nelson Mandela is imprisoned.

1963
Ngo Dinh Diem is assassinated in South Vietnam.

1966
Indira Gandhi becomes prime minister of India.

Ngo Dinh Diem

Portfolio Project

PROTEST SONGS

The Vietnam War era was a time of great social and political change in the United States. As the war escalated, protest against it increased. Popular songs of the era commented on the war and other social and political issues. As you read the chapter, note the reasons that some people supported the war while others protested against it. At the end of the chapter, you will summarize and evaluate a protest song.

▲ *A squadron of U.S. transport helicopters lands in Vietnam.*
◆**Connecting Past and Present** *Why are the helicopters flying behind each other, rather than side by side? What strategies do armies use to protect themselves in foreign countries today?*

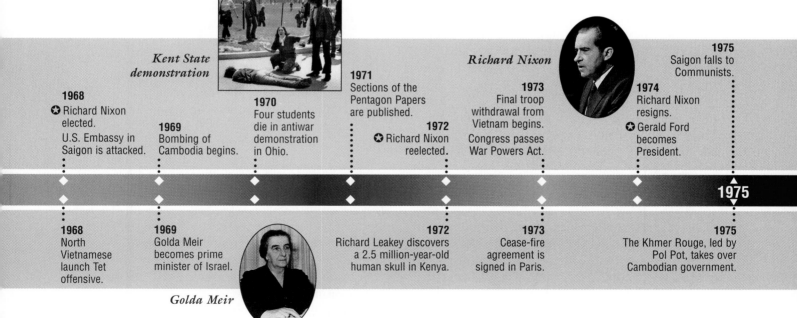

Kent State demonstration

1968
✪ Richard Nixon elected.
U.S. Embassy in Saigon is attacked.

1969
Bombing of Cambodia begins.

1970
Four students die in antiwar demonstration in Ohio.

1971
Sections of the Pentagon Papers are published.

1972
✪ Richard Nixon reelected.

Richard Nixon

1973
Final troop withdrawal from Vietnam begins.
Congress passes War Powers Act.

1974
Richard Nixon resigns.
✪ Gerald Ford becomes President.

1975
Saigon falls to Communists.

1975

1968
North Vietnamese launch Tet offensive.

1969
Golda Meir becomes prime minister of Israel.

Golda Meir

1972
Richard Leakey discovers a 2.5 million-year-old human skull in Kenya.

1973
Cease-fire agreement is signed in Paris.

1975
The Khmer Rouge, led by Pol Pot, takes over Cambodian government.

Section 1

Cold War Politics and the Vietnam War

PREVIEW

Objectives

- To describe the political situation in Vietnam during the 1960s

- To explain why U.S. involvement in Vietnam escalated during the 1960s

- To analyze the effects of the Gulf of Tonkin Resolution

Vocabulary

depose
coup d'etat
escalation

In 1946, the people of Vietnam began fighting a war for independence from French domination. The independence movement against French rule was led by Ho Chi Minh (hō´ chē´ mǐn´). In 1954, after years of fighting a difficult and costly war, the French finally agreed to leave Vietnam. Nineteen nations—including France, the United States, Vietnam, Communist China, and the Soviet Union—met in Geneva, Switzerland, in 1954 to create a treaty called the Geneva Accords. Under the terms of the treaty, Vietnam was to be temporarily split at the 17th parallel, as shown on the map on page 595. North of the parallel, North Vietnam would be controlled by Ho Chi Minh. South Vietnam would be ruled by Ngo Dinh Diem (nō´ din´ dē´-ĕm), an anti-Communist.

◆ THE VIETNAM WAR BEGINS

The division between North and South Vietnam was to end with elections in 1956. In these elections, the Vietnamese would vote for one leader to unite both countries and determine the type of government the new country was to have. At the time of the Geneva Convention, however, South Vietnam and the United States were afraid that Ho Chi Minh's Communist government would win such elections, so South Vietnam and the United States did not sign the Geneva Accords. President Eisenhower did not want to abandon Vietnam to the Communists. Ngo Dinh Diem canceled the elections in 1956, seeking to create an independent, non-Communist South Vietnam based on U.S. support. Ho Chi Minh saw war as the only way to unite North and South Vietnam.

The United States Gets Involved

America's Cold War against communism in the 1950s and 1960s played a big part in U.S. involvement in Vietnam. Ho Chi Minh's government in North Vietnam was Communist, and it was supported by the Soviet Union and Communist China. The United States supported the anti-communism ruler, Ngo Dinh Diem, in the South. With the threat of civil war in Vietnam, Americans began to fear the spread of communism that would take place if Ho Chi Minh won an election. Many people in the United States believed in the domino theory, which said that if Vietnam fell to communism, the remainder of Southeast Asia would follow and communism would soon threaten the rest of the world.

Diem's Government

In spite of support for Diem from the United States, many South Vietnamese opposed him, pointing out corruption and problems in the government. Diem had promised democracy and freedom, but ruled as a dictator. The South Vietnamese people who opposed Diem formed an organization in 1957, called the Viet Cong, to fight against Diem's government. Later, the Viet Cong would be known as the National Liberation Front (NLF). In 1959, the Viet Cong joined the North Vietnamese in their fight to topple the government of South Vietnam and to unite the country. This marked the beginning of the Vietnam War.

As Ho Chi Minh's North Vietnamese soldiers and the Viet Cong became more aggressive in their efforts to overthrow Diem's government, the United States began to supply weapons and military advisors to the government of South Vietnam. With U.S. support, Diem's army became large and powerful. To fight against this large army, the Viet Cong used guerrilla warfare, a method of fighting that consisted of surprise attacks and sabotage. Guerrillas hid among the general population, then struck and disappeared into the countryside or into nearby villages. Because Diem's soldiers could not always identify their enemies, fighting the Viet Cong proved to be extremely difficult.

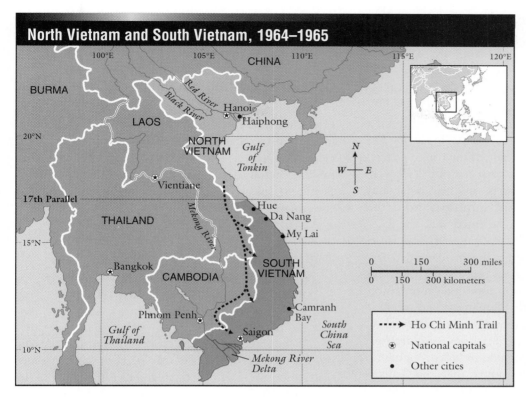

North Vietnam and South Vietnam, 1964–1965

◀ **Geography** *The Geneva Accords divided Vietnam at the 17th parallel.* **Interpreting the Map** *What countries border Vietnam? Through what countries did the Ho Chi Minh Trail pass?*

United States Increases Involvement

During the early 1960s, Kennedy sent economic aid to South Vietnam and increased the number of U.S. military advisors to train South Vietnamese troops from about 900 to about 16,000. Under the Geneva Accords, foreign countries were permitted to offer military training to South Vietnam. The treaty did not permit foreign advisors in direct combat. Increasingly, however, U.S. advisors began to play more direct roles in combat.

Diem's government continued to lose popular support because of charges of corruption and dictatorial tactics. Various South Vietnamese military leaders conspired to **depose** him, or remove him from power. On November 2, 1963, these leaders, who were supported by the United States, assassinated Diem after a **coup d'etat** (kōō´ dā-tä´), or violent overthrow of a government. General Duong Van Minh seized power in Saigon, the capital of South Vietnam. He was the first of many military officers to rule the country.

Three weeks later, on November 22, 1963, President Kennedy was assassinated in Dallas, and Lyndon Johnson, the Vice President, became President. Johnson was now in charge of U.S. policy in Vietnam.

How did Cold War politics affect the United States' decision to get involved in Vietnam?

◆ THE CONFLICT WIDENS

President Johnson believed that with help from the United States, South Vietnam would quickly overcome Ho Chi Minh's forces. He believed that the North Vietnamese forces were weak and that U.S. military power was much stronger. Beyond that, he believed that the fight against communism was morally right.

Yet, even as Johnson took office, the situation in Vietnam was rapidly changing. This was particularly true in South Vietnam's Mekong Delta region, where 40 percent of the population lived. The Mekong region was becoming a stronghold of the Viet Cong. In addition, North Vietnam was sending arms and soldiers down the Ho Chi Minh Trail, a network of roads and paths that cut through the thick rain forests of neighboring Laos and Cambodia, into South Vietnam.

In 1964, Secretary of Defense Robert McNamara realized that South Vietnam's hold over the Mekong Delta was not as strong as U.S. leaders had thought. The Viet Cong had been winning support from the people and gaining control over the South. McNamara told only President Johnson of his concern. To the public, McNamara stated that the war was going well. Based on information from such leaders as McNamara, most Americans supported an increase of U.S. military advisors and military aid in Vietnam.

The Gulf of Tonkin Incident

A turning point in U.S. involvement in the war in Vietnam occurred in early August 1964. On August 2, the U.S. Navy reported that enemy patrol boats had attacked the U.S. destroyer *Maddox* in the Gulf of Tonkin, off the North Vietnamese coast.

The *Maddox* left the Gulf of Tonkin but returned a day later with another destroyer, the *C. Turner Joy.* On August 4, 1964, the two ships cruised the rough waters. Mist and fog made it difficult to see. Both destroyers reportedly detected enemy boats on their radar and opened fire in order to avoid torpedoes from the attackers. It has never been confirmed that the U.S. ships were actually attacked. Pilots flying overhead failed to spot enemy boats. However, the incident had far-reaching effects. Upon hearing reports of a second enemy attack, President Johnson appeared on television and explained that the North Vietnamese had fired on U.S. ships and that the United States was retaliating. As Johnson spoke to the nation, U.S. planes were destroying gunboats and fuel storage tanks in North Vietnam.

Taking advantage of the anger that the Tonkin attack stirred, Johnson sent a resolution to Congress that would give him broad powers to take all measures to prevent further aggression by the North. Johnson asked Congress to give him the powers to take "all necessary measures to repel any armed attack against the forces of the United States." Congress passed the Tonkin Gulf Resolution overwhelmingly on August 7.

Study Hint

When you answer a multiple-choice question on a test, first eliminate the answers that you know are incorrect. Then choose the best or closest alternative from among the remaining choices. Try this technique when you reach the vocabulary section of the Chapter Review on page 608.

The resolution gave the President unlimited power and the freedom to conduct operations in Vietnam without actually having Congress declare war.

Operation Rolling Thunder

President Johnson's stand against the Vietnamese Communists gained him a great deal of popularity in the United States. One reason he won a landslide victory in the 1964 presidential election was that he had acted decisively in Vietnam. In addition, President Johnson had made a campaign promise to the American people:

> **I am not about to send American boys away from home to do what Asian boys ought to be doing for themselves.**

At the same time that President Johnson made this promise, however, he and his advisors were making plans to bomb North Vietnam and its capital, Hanoi. In February 1965, a military base in South Vietnam was attacked by Viet Cong forces, killing eight Americans. In response, Johnson ordered the first bombing of North Vietnam. This attack by the United States began Operation Rolling Thunder—a series of air strikes against Hanoi and other parts of North Vietnam. For three and a half years, the United States dropped about 800 tons of bombs each day on the North in order to discourage the enemy and destroy its ability to fight. Although these bombing raids caused immense damage and many deaths, they only stiffened the resolve of the North Vietnamese and the Viet Cong to drive the United States-backed forces out. According to one North Vietnamese doctor,

> **There was extraordinary fervor then. The Americans thought that the more bombs they dropped, the quicker we would fall on our knees and surrender. But the bombs heightened rather than dampened our spirits.**

Once Operation Rolling Thunder began, many people realized that the administration's actions contradicted messages the President gave in his speeches. For example, the President had promised in his

◄ Armed U.S. helicopters fired on North Vietnam shortly after Congress passed the Tonkin Gulf Resolution.

campaign that U.S. soldiers would not fight in Vietnam. However, in March 1965, he sent thousands of men to fight in the rain forests of Vietnam. Indeed, Johnson found it difficult to hold the line against future **escalation,** or increasing involvement, in the war. Time and again, he publicly promised that no new troops would be sent to Vietnam. However, President Johnson continually gave in to requests for more soldiers by General William Westmoreland, the U.S. commander in South Vietnam. By June 1965, more than 50,000 U.S. soldiers were fighting the Viet Cong.

At the beginning of U.S. involvement in the Vietnam conflict, most people in the country supported the President. They regarded his actions as an attempt to stop communism. A poll that was conducted in 1965 demonstrated this support—61 percent of Americans thought U.S. policy in Vietnam was well-founded.

However, as the war continued, many Americans began to distrust U.S. policies. For the first time, combat footage appeared nightly on the television news. Night after night, people sat in their homes and saw images of soldiers being killed while the President and others spoke positively of the United States' efforts to win the war. The violence on television seemed to contradict the government's optimistic portrayal of the events in Vietnam. Over time, this contradiction would lead many to question their faith in the government.

How did the North Vietnamese and the Viet Cong react to Operation Rolling Thunder?

Section 1 Review

Check Understanding

1. **Define** (a) depose (b) coup d'etat (c) escalation

2. **Describe** the political differences between the governments of South Vietnam and North Vietnam.

3. **Identify** the Viet Cong and their goals and strategies during the war.

4. **Explain** two events that led to increased U.S. involvement in Vietnam.

Critical Thinking

Expressing a Point of View Explain why you think President Johnson asked Congress to pass the Tonkin Gulf Resolution.

Write About Government

Connecting Past and Present Write about the foreign countries and world events in which the United States is involved today.

BUILDING SKILLS

....

Writing a Research Report: Cold War Politics and Vietnam

Writing a research report involves synthesizing the information you collected from primary and secondary sources about the topic you have chosen. Your goal is to give your audience a new understanding of the person, event, or issue.

Here's How

Follow these steps to write a research report:

1. Begin by writing a thesis statement—a declarative sentence that summarizes the main idea of your report.

2. Using your notes and your outline, draft the introductory paragraph of your report.

3. Next, draft the body of your report. Usually, a paragraph will begin with a topic sentence that states a main idea from your outline. The rest of the sentences in the paragraph should be details and examples from your notecards.

4. Decide when your sources of information should be documented. Always provide footnotes for direct quotations, summaries of an author's ideas, statistics, facts that are not common knowledge, and disputable facts.

5. Draft a brief concluding paragraph that summarizes your ideas.

6. Revise and edit your research report. Reorganize it as needed to make your points clear. Improve sentences by adding effective modifiers or by changing sentence length and structure. Then write the final copy of your research report.

Here's Why

Writing a research report adds dimension to your understanding of history. By investigating a subject you are interested in, you become an expert who can increase the knowledge of your audience.

Practice the Skill

Read the following outline about the events that led to U.S. involvement in the Vietnam War. Then write a thesis statement and an introductory paragraph for a research report based on these notes.

I. Effects of Geneva Accords (signed in 1954)
  A. Vietnam is divided at the 17th parallel.
    1. Communist leader Ho Chi Minh rules North Vietnam.
    2. Anti-Communist leader Ngo Dinh Diem rules South Vietnam.
  B. Diem cancels elections in 1956.
    1. Ho Chi Minh, supported by the Soviet Union and Communist China, attacks South Vietnam.
    2. United States fears spread of communism and sends military advisors to South Vietnam.

II. United States involvement increases.
  A. Congress passes Tonkin Gulf Resolution (1964).
    1. President's powers to prevent aggression in Vietnam are increased.
    2. President can take action without Congress declaring war.
  B. Operation Rolling Thunder takes place (1965).
    1. South Vietnam military base is attacked by the Viet Cong.
    2. U.S. begins bombing of North Vietnam.

Apply the Skill

Using the topic you chose in Chapter 26, the research you did in Chapter 27, and the notes and outline you made in Chapter 28, write a first draft of your research report.

Section 2

A War Fought in Public

PREVIEW

Objectives

- To explain the difficulties U.S. forces faced in fighting the Viet Cong

- To analyze events in the Vietnam War that affected how Americans viewed the war

- To describe the reasons why antiwar protests in the United States increased during the middle and late 1960s

Vocabulary

napalm

conscientious objector

teach-in

moratorium

deferment

During the 1960s, as U.S. involvement in Vietnam increased, the nation was becoming profoundly divided over the United States' role in the war and its overall responsibility in world affairs. While many people continued to support the U.S. role in the war as a fight against communism, others began to question the purpose of the war.

◆ FIGHTING THE WAR IN VIETNAM

By 1966, U.S. troops were fully engaged in the war and were suffering heavy casualties. They had abandoned hopes of fighting a short war. This was due, in part, to the enemy's refusal to fight large-scale battles. Instead, a series of small, quick clashes kept U.S. soldiers on the defensive and wore them down. Though armed with powerful B-52 bomber planes, helicopters, and advanced infantry rifles, U.S. soldiers still found that it was not easy fighting the almost-invisible Viet Cong. In order to flush enemies out of their hiding places, U.S. forces routinely dropped **napalm** bombs to burn jungles. Napalm is a jellied gasoline compound that not only destroys plants but also burns flesh on contact. An eyewitness from North Vietnam described what happened in July 1967 when his village, Vinh Quang, was bombed with napalm:

"Then the bombing began again, this time with napalm, and the village went up in flames. The napalm hit me, and I must have gone crazy. I felt as if I were burning all over, like charcoal, and I lost consciousness. Comrades took me to the hospital, and my wounds didn't begin to heal until six months later."

Whatever advantages the United States seemed to have in terms of superior equipment did not have the desired effect. The Viet Cong were able to use guerrilla warfare techniques to their advantage. They became experts in laying mines and booby traps along

▲ This Viet Cong booby trap could be rigged to fall from a tree on a soldier below. Its metal had been shredded so that its jagged edges pointed in all directions.

jungle paths. The Viet Cong were able to disappear into the rain forest without a trace. Sometimes they hid in underground tunnels, waiting to ambush unsuspecting troops. Frustrated U.S. soldiers on the ground often could not even find the enemy to fight. Tim O'Brien, a veteran and an author, wrote about his experiences on patrol:

> Should you put your foot to that flat rock or the clump of weeds to its rear? Paddy dike or water? You wish you were Tarzan, able to swing with the vines. You try to trace the footprints of the man to your front. You give it up when he curses you for following too closely; better one man dead than two. The moment-to-moment, step-by-step decision-making preys on your mind.

The Vietnamese knew the terrain, the rain forest, and the waterways; the Americans did not. The United States was fighting on foreign soil, defending a government in the South whose own soldiers could not defend it effectively. As Secretary of Defense McNamara told journalists in 1965, "It will be a long war."

The Tet Offensive

On January 30, 1968, many people in South Vietnam were celebrating Vietnam's most important holiday, the lunar New Year called Tet. However, it was on this day that the war in Vietnam changed drastically. While people in the South Vietnamese city of Saigon celebrated the holiday by setting off firecrackers and fireworks, nearly 85,000 Viet Cong and North Vietnamese soldiers launched a surprise attack. The North Vietnamese and Viet Cong attacked 12 U.S. air bases and more than 100 cities and towns in South Vietnam, including Saigon. In the early morning hours, the Viet Cong attacked the U.S. embassy in Saigon and bombed the U.S. military complex at Camranh Bay, causing enormous damage. The Tet offensive showed that no place in South Vietnam—not even the American embassy—was safe from attack.

The Tet offensive stunned the United States and the world. Previously, the Viet Cong had only controlled the countryside; the cities had been considered safe from attack. Now it was clear that the Viet Cong could strike anywhere. Particularly troubling was the

Rather than fight large-scale battles, the Viet Cong often made small attacks on unsuspecting U.S. troops and then disappeared into the forests before U.S. forces could find them. Here, a wounded U.S. soldier is helped to safety. ▶

fact that U.S. intelligence had failed to pick up any signs that a massive attack was coming.

From the North Vietnamese point of view, the Tet offensive failed because it did not trigger a massive uprising as the North Vietnamese and the Viet Cong had wanted. They had hoped that many of the Vietnamese in the South would join them in the fight against the United States. However, the Tet offensive did have a great impact on Americans. Far from inspiring them to support the war, the images of destruction shown on TV caused many Americans to question whether the United States should continue to be involved in Vietnam. Before the Tet offensive, most news broadcasts had been supportive or objective in presenting information about the war. Afterward, many broadcasts became openly critical of U.S. involvement. After the Tet offensive, a poll showed that only 26 percent of Americans approved of how the President was handling the war. Many Americans began to call for removal of U.S. troops from Vietnam.

The My Lai Massacre

Another event that caused the U.S. public to question American involvement in Vietnam happened at My Lai (mē´ lī´). In November 1969, newspapers reported an incident that had occurred in South Vietnam on March 16, 1968. On that day, helicopters dropped a company of U.S. soldiers into the small village of My Lai. The soldiers expected to find a Viet Cong battalion there. Instead, they found old women, children, and men. Believing that the villagers were helping the Viet Cong and hiding weapons, the soldiers shot the innocent villagers, as many as 450 people. The incident was kept secret for over a year, but once it became known, 25 officers were charged in the massacre and the cover-up. The details of the My Lai Massacre and the trial of the company's commander, Lt. William L. Calley, Jr., caused even more people to question U.S. involvement in the war.

What factors caused Americans to question the war effort?

◆ DIVIDED OPINIONS ABOUT U.S. INVOLVEMENT

The U.S. government was well aware that it needed public support to continue the war. The war was unpopular with many Americans who came to learn that many South Vietnamese people did not

▲ *College students, like those in this photograph, were among the most vocal opponents of the Vietnam War.*

support their own government. As early as 1965, President Johnson told his staff his concerns about maintaining the American public's support.

> **Our people won't stand firm in the face of heavy losses, and they can bring the government down.**

In order to win over the American people, the government allowed print and television journalists to cover the fighting. U.S. generals spoke positively on camera about search-and-destroy missions and favorable "kill ratios"—the number of enemy soldiers killed compared to U.S. soldiers killed. But viewers saw the war's violence and destruction on television as well.

In addition to the death and violence reported in the news, there were other issues that concerned Americans about U.S. involvement in the war. Between 1964 and 1967, the war's cost rose to $20 billion per year. To some Americans, this seemed a lot of money to spend on a war in a small faraway country.

Above all, there was no clear answer as to how many U.S. troops would be needed to win the war, or if it was even possible to win. In December 1965, there were about 185,000 troops in Vietnam; by December 1966, the number had reached over 385,000. In March 1969—the peak of U.S. involvement—541,500 U.S. soldiers were in Vietnam. Many Americans wanted to know how many more soldiers were going to be sent to

Four students from Kent State University, in Ohio, were killed by national guardsmen during an antiwar demonstration. ▶

Vietnam. Others wanted to set a time limit on how long U.S. troops would remain there.

On the other hand, a sizable number of Americans believed strongly that communism had to be stopped in Vietnam and that Ho Chi Minh and the Viet Cong were directly controlled by China and the Soviet Union. If the Communists won in Vietnam, they feared, eventually the United States and other democracies would be surrounded by enemy governments.

Antiwar Protests

Between 1965 and 1971, the peace movement in the United States attracted many people, especially those between the ages of 17 and 25. College students as well as high school students took a stand against the war, demanding the immediate withdrawal of U.S. troops from Vietnam. Some of these people were **conscientious objectors,** people who oppose war for moral or religious reasons. Many colleges around the country organized **teach-ins,** or meetings to raise awareness about events in Southeast Asia. Students also protested military recruitment and war-related research conducted on campus. While some protesters marched, others held vigils or distributed leaflets door-to-door. **Moratoriums,** or the suspension of work and classes as a sign of protest, also became prevalent.

Antiwar demonstrations often attracted large crowds. In April 1967, almost 400,000 people attended a rally in New York City's Central Park. In October 1967, over 100,000 people protested for peace at the Lincoln Memorial in Washington, D.C. About half of these protesters marched to the Pentagon, where they were turned back by soldiers and tear gas. During the first six months of 1968, more than 220 demonstrations against the war occurred. In May 1970, an antiwar protest at Kent State University, in Ohio, ended with the deaths of four students and the wounding of nine others when National Guard troops fired into a crowd of protesters who were throwing rocks at them.

Opponents of the war also protested the 1965 Selective Service Act, which required men to register for the draft when they became 18. In theory, all who registered were eligible to be drafted. However, male undergraduates could receive an educational **deferment,** or postponement, which enabled them to delay army service until they graduated. Opponents of the draft pointed out that the majority of college students were white and from middle-class or upper middle-class families. As a result, the burden of serving in Vietnam unfairly fell upon African Americans, Latinos, and other minorities, as well as poor whites—those who could not afford to attend college and were thus not eligible for deferment. Even when a lottery system was instituted to make the draft system more random, some people publicly burned their draft cards as a sign of protest, facing a five-year jail term and a $10,000 fine. Some men went to jail rather than be drafted; others fled to Canada or Europe.

The Election of 1968

The election of 1968 took on added importance because of the tension in the United States related to the Vietnam War. Several Democratic candidates, notably Eugene McCarthy and Robert Kennedy, openly challenged President Johnson on the war and his failure to pursue Great Society programs. By 1968, even Johnson himself had come to believe that the war could not be won in the traditional sense and that, at best, a stalemate might be achieved. He also realized that public opinion was too divided to enable the federal government to continue funding the war, and that continuing to do so might wreck the Democratic party. As a result, Johnson decided to negotiate with the North Vietnamese and halt further bombing raids. Then, in a speech on March 31, 1968, the President surprised the American public by announcing that he would not seek reelection.

With Johnson's withdrawal from the presidential race, Robert Kennedy, Eugene McCarthy, and Hubert Humphrey (Johnson's Vice President) were left to seek the Democratic party's nomination. However, just after midnight on June 5, Robert Kennedy was assassinated as he was leaving his California primary victory party. Only McCarthy and Humphrey were now in the race.

The week-long Democratic National Convention took place in Chicago in August. Thousands of antiwar demonstrators converged on the city, and emotions ran high. Clashes between demonstrators and the Chicago police led to many injuries as police clubbed the demonstrators.

Inside the convention hall, the candidates were fighting their own battles. Although Humphrey, who supported Johnson's policies, won the Democratic nomination, his candidacy was damaged by the violence and political differences expressed at the convention. Democrats could not agree about their position on the war. Convention organizers tried to declare Humphrey's nomination unanimous, but many delegates refused to endorse him.

The Republican National Convention, held in Miami Beach, was very different. Richard Nixon won the nomination on the first ballot, and the proceedings were orderly. In his acceptance speech, Nixon said,

> **I pledge to you tonight that the first priority foreign policy objective of our next administration will be to bring an honorable end to the Vietnam War.**

Alabama governor George Wallace was a third party candidate for President. As governor, he had pledged to enforce segregation. Wallace criticized antiwar protesters during his presidential campaign. He believed that Americans should continue to fight until they achieved victory in Vietnam. Referring to the antiwar movement and the urban disturbances, he promised to restore "law and order" in the country.

In the 1968 presidential election, Richard Nixon defeated Hubert Humphrey by only 500,000 votes out of more than 70 million cast. Wallace earned 13.5 percent of the vote.

 What was the major issue in the election of 1968?

Section 2 Review

Check Understanding

1. **Define** (a) napalm (b) conscientious objector (c) teach-in (d) moratorium (e) deferment

2. **Explain** the media's role in influencing U.S. opinion of the war in the middle to late 1960s.

3. **Describe** the methods antiwar protesters used to express their opinions.

4. **Describe** the events of the war that had the greatest impact on public opinion.

Critical Thinking

Analyzing What were some of the reasons that many Americans opposed the Vietnam War?

Write About Citizenship

Connecting Past and Present Write an essay comparing the influence of the media on public opinion during the Vietnam War with its influence on public opinion today.

Section 3

The War Ends

PREVIEW

Objectives

• To describe how President Nixon's policies affected American public opinion about the Vietnam War

• To analyze why Nixon's actions regarding Vietnam heightened antiwar feelings in the United States

• To explain how a cease-fire was negotiated to end U.S. involvement in the Vietnam War

• To analyze why the end of the war in Vietnam did not immediately resolve Americans' sentiments toward the war

Vocabulary

Vietnamization
incursion
envoy

President Nixon's election gave the American people hope that an end to the war in Vietnam would come soon. However, despite the President's earlier pledge, the war continued for another four years.

◆ THE FINAL YEARS

In February 1969, President Nixon ordered U.S. planes to start bombing the Ho Chi Minh Trail in Cambodia to stop the North Vietnamese from sending troops and supplies to the Viet Cong in the South. The bombing of Cambodia was a bold and controversial move because Cambodia was a neutral country. Vietnamese Communists had been storing weapons and supplies in Cambodia throughout much of the war, however, so Nixon felt the bombing was justified.

Although planned as a short-term strategy, the Cambodia bombing campaign continued for 14 months. The facts of the bombing missions were kept secret, even from Congress and the media. Official government documents were altered to state that bombings had taken place in Vietnam, not Cambodia.

Vietnamization

In the middle of 1969, Nixon began a policy he termed **Vietnamization,** an attempt to transfer the burden of the war to the South Vietnamese army. The United States would provide military and economic aid, but not troops, to South Vietnam. Troop withdrawal began, and by August about 25,000 soldiers had returned home. On April 20, 1970, Nixon withdrew another 150,000 troops from Vietnam.

However, ten days later, the President announced that he had ordered United States and South Vietnamese forces into Cambodia. He said the invasion would help ease troop withdrawal. Calling the movement of troops into Cambodia an **incursion,** or raid, Nixon acted without notifying Congress. On television, he defended his actions by stating,

> "If, when the chips are down, the world's most powerful nation, the United States of America, acts like a pitiful helpless giant, the forces of totalitarianism and anarchy will threaten free nations and free institutions throughout the world."

Nixon's announcement set off another round of antiwar demonstrations, including the one that took place at Kent State University, in Ohio. In late 1970, a

Nixon announced in April 1970 that U.S. troops would attack North Vietnamese bases in Cambodia. He is shown here pointing to a map of Southeast Asia. ▼

▲ This air force photo of the Ho Chi Minh trail in 1971 shows the results of bombings by U.S. planes. In the photo, DMGD *means "damaged,"* DEST *means "destroyed,"* TRK *means "truck,"* and PROB *means "probably."*

poll showed that 65 percent of Americans wanted the United States to withdraw from Southeast Asia. In December 1970, Congress reacted to Nixon's invasion of Cambodia by repealing the Tonkin Gulf Resolution, which had given the President the authority to order the invasion without a declaration of war on Vietnam. However, in 1971, without using U.S. troops, the United States provided military aid as South Vietnamese troops invaded Laos, a neighboring country. In 1971, the United States dropped more than 800,000 tons of bombs on Laos, Cambodia, and Vietnam.

Even more Americans turned against the war after June 13, 1971, when *The New York Times* published sections from the Pentagon Papers, a study of U.S. policies in Vietnam authorized by Secretary of Defense Robert McNamara. This 7,000-page document was the secret history of the United States' involvement in the Vietnam War. The Pentagon Papers showed that plans for entering the war were being developed even as President Johnson was promising that the United States would not send troops there. In addition, the story in *The New York Times* reported that Nixon was ordering the bombings while conducting peace negotiations with the North Vietnamese.

One of the authors of the Pentagon Papers was Daniel Ellsberg, a former Department of Defense official. Believing that the public should be allowed to

read the report, he gave it to the press. The U.S. Justice Department brought charges of theft, conspiracy, and espionage against Ellsberg. Some of Nixon's close advisors had thieves wiretap Ellsberg's phone and break into the office of Ellsberg's former psychiatrist to steal information about him. Because of this illegal conduct by the government, the judge in the case dismissed all charges against Ellsberg in 1973.

The Justice Department used a Supreme Court order of June 30, 1971, to prevent *The New York Times* from publishing the entire report because the information would put the national security of the United States in danger. *The New York Times* resisted the order on the grounds that the government was trying to censor the free press, which is a violation of rights guaranteed in the First Amendment. In the case of *The New York Times Company* v. *United States,* the Supreme Court threw out the government's request, stating that if the government was allowed to halt publication of the news through use of the courts, it would "destroy the fundamental liberty and security" of the citizens it is supposed to protect.

U.S. Withdrawal from Vietnam

Secret negotiations to end the war had begun in Paris in August 1969, when Henry Kissinger, Nixon's

envoy, or diplomatic representative, met with Le Duc Tho, the North Vietnamese representative. It took more than three years for the two sides to reach an agreement. During that time, Nixon continued the process of Vietnamization and gradually withdrew U.S. troops from Vietnam. By the end of 1972, more than 400,000 troops had been withdrawn.

On January 27, 1973, a cease-fire agreement was signed in Paris. According to the treaty, the Northern and Southern forces were to stay in the territory they controlled at the time, and all U.S. troops were to leave within 60 days. As part of the treaty, North Vietnamese officials were to release U.S. prisoners of war.

 What was the importance of *The New York Times Company* v. *United States* case?

◆ THE AFTERMATH OF WAR

After the last United States troops left Vietnam on March 29, 1973, fighting continued despite the cease-fire agreement. Without direct U.S. military support, the South Vietnamese army disintegrated as North Vietnamese troops poured into the South. Two years later, on April 30, 1975, Communist forces captured Saigon and reunited the North and the South. The war was over. All of Vietnam had a Communist government led by a group of Communist party leaders. Laos and Cambodia eventually also became Communist, but the rest of Southeast Asia did not. It seemed as if the domino theory was only partially proven correct.

Vietnam Veterans

For many soldiers, the return to the United States was a difficult adjustment. Many Americans at home did not honor the soldiers' great sacrifices. Veterans re-entered a society strongly divided over the cause for which they had risked their lives. Many veterans felt the government had betrayed them.

Although most veterans succeeded in civilian society, some suffered from posttraumatic stress disorder, characterized by flashbacks of war scenes, an inability to function in society, and severe emotional depression. Other veterans returned with drug addiction problems.

Slowly these scars have begun to heal. Americans have tried to publicly acknowledge the contributions of the Vietnam veterans. The building of the Vietnam Veterans Memorial in Washington, D.C., in 1982, helped in this effort. The memorial has become a place for Americans to ponder the war and honor the dead.

Maya Ying Lin

Fingers slowly trace the names on the black wall. Family and friends of dead soldiers leave flowers, pictures, and notes. A visit to the Vietnam Veterans Memorial in Washington, D.C., is an emotional one. What is surprising to many is that the designer was a student who won a design contest sponsored by the Vietnam Veterans' Memorial Fund.

The announcement that Maya Lin, an architecture student at Yale University, had won the national competition in 1981 made headlines. No one had expected the winner to be a woman who was four years old when U.S. soldiers began fighting in Vietnam.

To some, Lin's design was breathtaking in its simplicity. Two angled black granite walls were etched with the names of more than 58,000 Americans

▲ Maya Ying Lin (1959–   )

killed in Vietnam. To others, the design was a disgrace. They thought the monument did nothing to honor the soldiers' sacrifices.

Controversy raged over the design, but Maya Lin resisted suggestions that there be a golden inscription or a flag. She felt the focus should be on the names. As Lin said of her design, "It does not glorify the war or make an antiwar statement. It is a place for private reckoning."

Today, the Vietnam Veterans Memorial (often called the Wall) is a popular attraction in Washington. Thanks to Maya Lin's determination and creativity, the memorial continues to have the power to move people.

Looking Back: Why do you think Lin's design for the Vietnam Veterans Memorial was controversial?

▲ *The names of more than 58,000 Americans killed in Vietnam are engraved on the Vietnam Veterans Memorial, erected in 1982.*

Not far from the Vietnam Veterans Memorial is the Vietnam Women's Memorial, dedicated in 1993 to honor American women who served in Vietnam. This bronze statue, designed by Glenna Goodacre, is a tribute to over 10,000 women who volunteered for duty in Vietnam. About 90 percent were nurses, while others performed duties as doctors, air-traffic controllers, communication specialists, and clerks.

Effects of the War

The United States paid a high price to fight the war in Vietnam. About 58,000 Americans died, and 300,000 were wounded. More than $150 billion was spent on the war.

The war also resulted in new legislation. First, Congress passed the War Powers Act of 1973. The act restricted the President's ability to send troops into combat to situations in which the United States, its territories or possessions, or its armed forces are attacked. In addition, the act stated that the President could not send troops into action for longer than 90 days without the authorization of Congress. President Nixon vetoed the War Powers Act, but Congress overrode his veto.

Another major effect was the passage in 1971 of the Twenty-sixth Amendment, which lowered the voting age from 21 to 18. Supporters of the amendment pointed out that if 18-year-olds were old enough to be drafted, they should also be allowed to vote.

The Vietnam War was a turning point in the Cold War. It caused U.S. officials to realize that even a superpower like the United States had to choose when and where to exercise its power.

The Vietnam War had other profound effects on U.S. society. On a number of occasions during the Vietnam War, the government and military establishment created feelings of mistrust between U.S. citizens and their elected leaders. In addition, after the war more than two million people left their homes in Vietnam, Laos, and Cambodia in order to find a more stable and safe life. Many of these immigrants who entered the United States in the 1970s and 1980s have had a strong impact on the country.

? **How did the Vietnam War affect American society?**

Section 3 Review

Check Understanding

1. **Define** (a) Vietnamization (b) incursion (c) envoy

2. **Describe** the reasons why the United States forces fought part of the Vietnam War in Cambodia.

3. **Explain** why the contents of the Pentagon Papers created a controversy in America.

4. **Explain** how the cease-fire agreement led to a Communist victory in Vietnam.

5. **Analyze** how Vietnam veterans were affected by the way Americans at home felt about the war.

Critical Thinking

Drawing Conclusions Did Nixon achieve a "peace with honor"? Explain.

Write About History

◆**Connecting Past and Present** Write some interview questions that you would want to ask someone who participated in the Vietnam War.

Chapter 29
Review

CHAPTER SUMMARY

Section 1

The United States was afraid that South Vietnam would unite with Communist-controlled North Vietnam, and that the entire country, as well as all of Southeast Asia, would eventually become Communist. To halt the spread of communism, the United States at first sent weapons and military advisors to support South Vietnam. When U.S. battleship destroyers patrolling in the Gulf of Tonkin were reportedly attacked, Congress passed the Tonkin Gulf Resolution, giving President Johnson power to increase involvement in Vietnam without a declaration of war.

Section 2

As U.S. involvement in Vietnam increased and casualty rates rose, some Americans began to question the United States' role in the war. The vivid images and reporting from newspapers and television convinced some that the war could not be won. As antiwar sentiment mounted, Johnson decided not to run again for President. Violence and party disunity at the Democratic Convention contributed to a Republican victory in the election of 1968.

Section 3

President Nixon's actions in Cambodia resulted in an escalation of the war, but finally, in 1973 the United States negotiated a cease-fire to withdraw from Vietnam. With the United States out of Vietnam, the Vietnamese Communists took control of South Vietnam in 1975. The aftermath of the war resulted in the War Powers Act, which limited the ability of a President to wage war without support of Congress. The U.S. voting age was reduced to 18, the same age at which men could be drafted.

Connecting ◆◆ Past and Present

If a war were declared today, should the U.S. government make all information about that war available to its citizens? Explain.

Using Vocabulary

Select the letter of the phrase that best completes each sentence.

1. A **moratorium** is (a) a person opposed to war; (b) a surprise attack; (c) a suspension of activity; (d) a war with no clear winner.

2. A **coup d'etat** is (a) a war fought by paid soldiers; (b) a violent overthrow of a government; (c) a puppet government; (d) the general in a guerrilla war.

3. One of the characteristics of **napalm** is that it (a) burns flesh on contact; (b) inflicts wounds that heal quickly; (c) blows up when it is stepped on; (d) is only effective during surprise attacks.

4. **Vietnamization** was (a) a proposal sponsored by the United Nations; (b) a policy promoted by Communist Russia; (c) the attempt by the United States to turn Cambodia into part of South Vietnam; (d) an attempt to transfer the responsibility of the war to the South Vietnamese.

5. An **envoy** is (a) a group of ships that travel together to protect each other; (b) a guerrilla fighter; (c) a member of the navy; (d) a diplomatic representative.

Check Understanding

1. **Describe** the differences in the governments of North and South Vietnam when the war began.

2. **Explain** how the domino theory led to U.S. involvement in the Vietnam War.

3. **Identify** the Tonkin Gulf Resolution and explain how it led to the escalation of U.S. involvement in the Vietnam War.

4. **Summarize** U.S. involvement in the Vietnam War from 1965 to 1968.

5. **Explain** how U.S. opinion toward involvement in Vietnam changed after 1965.

6. **List** three ways people in the United States protested the war in Vietnam.

7. **Describe** the scenes at the Republican and Democratic party conventions in 1968.

8. **Describe** how Nixon's actions in Cambodia heightened antiwar feeling in the United States.

9. **Explain** the goals of the policy of Vietnamization.

10. **Summarize** how the Vietnam War ended for the United States and for Vietnam.

Critical Thinking

1. **Applying Information** Explain the link between U.S. involvement in Vietnam and the Cold War.

2. **Drawing Inferences** Why do you think Johnson decided not to seek the presidency in 1968?

3. **Examining Evidence** What were the reasons for the distrust of the federal government that some Americans felt after the war?

4. **Defending a Position** Why do you think Nixon broke his campaign promise and escalated U.S. involvement in the Vietnam War?

◆ **Connecting Past and Present** If a U.S. ship reported being attacked today, what reasons might the President need in order to justify an attack on a foreign country?

Interpreting the Timeline

Use the timeline on pages 592–593 to answer these questions.

1. How much time passed between Nixon's first election as President and the final withdrawal of U.S. troops from Vietnam?

2. In which year did the bombing of North Vietnam begin?

3. Which American events reflect public reaction to involvement in Vietnam during the 1960s and 1970s?

Writing to Express a Point of View

Take the point of view of one of two brothers: an antiwar protester who avoided the draft, or a soldier who went to fight in the Vietnam War. **Write** a letter to the other brother explaining the motives behind your actions. Give reasons, facts, and examples to back up your position.

Putting Skills to Work

WRITING A RESEARCH REPORT

In the Building Skills lesson on page 598, you learned how to write a research report. Use the guidelines in step 4 of *Here's How* on page 598 to determine which of the following notes would require documentation if they were to be used in a report. Be prepared to explain why you would or would not document each of the notes.

1. A majority of Americans believed in the domino theory, which said that if Vietnam fell to communism, then the rest of Southeast Asia and the world would become Communist as well.

2. The Viet Cong was later called the National Liberation Front.

3. During the early 1960s, President Kennedy sent economic aid to South Vietnam and increased military advisors from 3,000 to 16,000.

4. According to General Maxwell Taylor, "a sequence of crises, political and military," forced Johnson "to choose between accepting defeat or introducing American combat forces."

5. Ngo Dinh Diem was assassinated on November 2, 1963.

 *Portfolio Project*

PROTEST SONGS

Songs like "Blowing in the Wind," "We Shall Overcome," and "The Times They Are A-Changin'" were well-known protest songs of the 1960s and 1970s. Folk music by such writers as Pete Seeger, Bob Dylan, and Joan Baez not only reflected the values of many young people but also helped to influence them. Find examples of some protest songs and analyze their opinions of the Vietnam War. Write a summary and evaluation of one protest song, and include your analysis in your portfolio.

Chapter 30
Searching for Stability
1969–1981

CHAPTER PREVIEW

Section 1 Foreign Policy in the 1970s

After the end of the Vietnam War, the United States enjoyed friendlier relations with the Soviet Union and China.

Section 2 Economic and Political Difficulties at Home

The United States suffered from both inflation and economic stagnation in the 1970s. It also faced its greatest constitutional crisis since the Civil War.

Section 3 A New Approach to Foreign Policy

The United States went from the triumph of the Camp David Accords to the Iran hostage crisis during the presidency of Jimmy Carter.

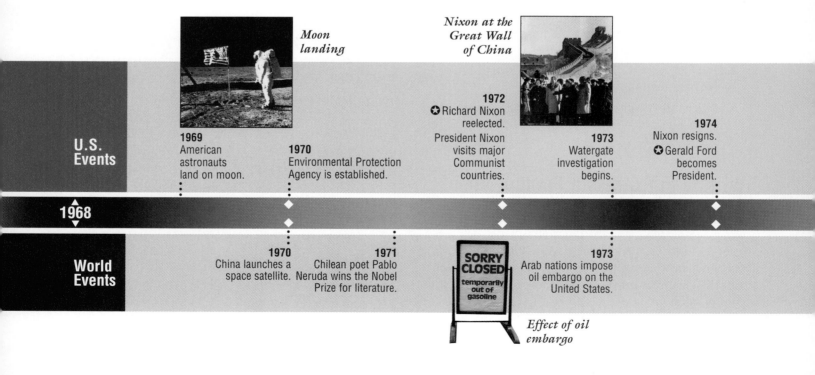

Moon landing

Nixon at the Great Wall of China

U.S. Events

1969
American astronauts land on moon.

1970
Environmental Protection Agency is established.

1972
✪ Richard Nixon reelected.
President Nixon visits major Communist countries.

1973
Watergate investigation begins.

1974
Nixon resigns.
✪ Gerald Ford becomes President.

▲ 1968 ▼

World Events

1970
China launches a space satellite.

1971
Chilean poet Pablo Neruda wins the Nobel Prize for literature.

SORRY CLOSED
temporarily out of gasoline

1973
Arab nations impose oil embargo on the United States.

Effect of oil embargo

Portfolio Project

A POSITION PAPER

Every President depends on advisors to provide educated recommendations in the form of position papers. A position paper is a policy report that usually explains and recommends a particular course of action. As you read the chapter, look for problems that absorbed the energies of a President in the 1970s. At the end of the chapter, you will write a position paper recommending a way to solve a problem.

▲ *The Great Seal of the United States is displayed in the center of the Oval Office.* ◈ **Connecting Past and Present** *Why do you think the eagle holds 13 arrows—representing war—on one side and an olive branch—representing peace—on the other? What symbols would you choose to represent the United States today?*

Anwar el-Sadat, Jimmy Carter, and Menachem Begin

American hostages

1976
✪ Jimmy Carter elected.
Alex Haley's novel *Roots* is published.

1979
Israeli-Egyptian peace treaty is signed.
Militant Iranians seize American hostages.

1980
U.S. boycotts summer Olympics.
✪ Ronald Reagan elected.

1981
Iran releases American hostages.

1982

1977
Panama Canal treaty is signed to return canal ownership to Panama by the end of 1999.

1979
Margaret Thatcher becomes British prime minister.
Shah of Iran is overthrown.

Margaret Thatcher

Foreign Policy in the 1970s

PREVIEW

Objectives

- To explain how President Nixon established diplomatic ties with China

- To analyze the goals of détente and how détente changed relations between the United States and the Soviet Union

- To describe how Gerald Ford continued Nixon's policy of détente

Vocabulary

normalize   subversion

bloc   Marxist

détente

Richard Nixon put a high priority on leaving the Vietnam conflict behind and moving ahead in other areas of diplomacy. Together with his main foreign policy advisor, Henry Kissinger, he crafted a foreign policy that began to wind down the Vietnam War and relax the tensions of the Cold War.

This policy emphasized a practical approach toward international politics. It moved U.S. relations with the world's largest Communist nations—China and the Soviet Union—toward a safer, more positive position.

◆ NIXON IN CHINA

Since the Communist victory in China in 1949, relations between the United States and the People's Republic of China had been hostile. The United States had fought bitter battles with Chinese troops during the Korean War. Furthermore, the United States did not even recognize the Communist government as the legitimate government of China. Instead, the United States continued to recognize the Republic of China, the Nationalist government in Taiwan, as the "real" China, supporting it with large amounts of military and economic aid.

During his political career, Richard Nixon had favored strong anti-Communist policies. He had attacked some liberals at home as Communist sympathizers, and he had criticized the brutality of China's leaders. Americans were thus surprised when, in July 1971, President Nixon announced on television that relations between the United States and the People's Republic of China would start to **normalize,** or be renewed by the establishment of diplomatic contacts.

Nixon and Kissinger realized that China was the world's most populous nation. They also knew that its Communist government was not going to be replaced, no matter what the United States did. Furthermore, the People's Republic had diplomatic relations with most of the world's nations. Many members of the United Nations (UN) pressured the United States to give Taiwan's seat in the UN to the huge People's Republic of China.

Chinese and Soviet Relations

During the 1960s, China had grown increasingly more hostile to its Communist neighbor, the Soviet Union. This forced a change in the U.S. government's thinking toward communism in general. In the 1950s and early 1960s, the United States had seen all Communist countries as part of a solid, threatening **bloc,** or a group of nations united for a common action. Now it was clear that there were serious differences between Communist nations. Chairman Mao Zedong, head of the Chinese Communists, thought that Soviet leaders were not aggressive enough in

Study Hint

To help you remember important ideas, try to predict the outcome of the historical events that you are reading about. Verify your prediction as you continue to read and learn more information about the topic. If your prediction was not correct, revise it in light of the new information that you have learned.

▲ *Richard and Pat Nixon toured the Great Wall on their visit to China in 1972.*

their relations with the West. Furthermore, a series of battles along the boundary between China and Siberia, a part of the Soviet Union, increased tensions between China and the Soviet Union.

Nixon and Kissinger believed that the United States should work toward peaceful relations with both countries. They also believed that Nixon was the ideal President to lead this change. Because Nixon had long held strong anti-Communist views, he was in a solid position to tell the American people that times had changed. A more liberal leader than Nixon would have risked being labeled as "soft on communism."

A Successful Trip to China

The first official interaction between China and the United States in over two decades occurred in April 1971, when the Chinese hosted a table tennis team from the United States. Then, in 1972, a year after announcing U.S. intentions to establish contact with China, Nixon decided to make an official visit to the People's Republic of China. Though the announcement came as a surprise, Kissinger had been secretly negotiating the trip with the Chinese for more than a year.

In February 1972, Nixon and his wife, Pat, flew to the capital city of Beijing. They toured the Great Wall and other historic spots before Nixon met with Chairman Mao and Premier Zhou Enlai (jõ´ en´-lĭ´). TV cameras and newspaper photographers captured the historic moment for the world to witness as the leaders celebrated the start of a new era in East-West diplomacy.

There were still many steps to take, but the hostility of the Cold War was easing. Now, it was hoped, the two countries might begin to open their economic, cultural, and scientific markets to each other, advancing trade and communication on both sides.

Why was Nixon in a good position to improve relationships with Communist China?

◆ OTHER FOREIGN POLICY DECISIONS

The establishment of U.S. relations with China led to other changes in American foreign policy as well— including improved relations with the Soviet Union. Soviet leaders became concerned over the new friendship between China and the United States. They could easily imagine an alliance between the United States and China directed against the Soviet Union. As a result of this underlying concern, the Soviet Union decided to ease tensions with the United States by establishing friendly diplomatic relations.

The SALT treaty between the United States and the Soviet Union attempted to limit each country's buildup of nuclear missiles, such as the ones featured in this Soviet parade. ▶

In May 1972, only a few months after visiting Beijing, President Nixon flew to Moscow. This was yet another history-making event, since no American President had ever before visited the Soviet Union. The aim of the visit was to establish **détente** (dā-tänt´), a relaxation of tensions, between East and West. As Nixon declared,

❝There must be room in this world for two great nations with different systems to live together and work together.❞

Nixon and Kissinger intended to show that China, the Soviet Union, and the United States could benefit from cooperating on several key issues. They also hoped to weaken the support that China and the Soviet Union were extending to other Communist nations.

Limiting Nuclear Weapons

In Moscow, President Nixon had cordial meetings with the Communist party leader Leonid Brezhnev (lā-ō-nēd´ brezh´-nef). Most importantly, the two leaders continued the Strategic Arms Limitation Talks, known as SALT, which had been ongoing for several years.

The goal of the SALT talks was to ease what was perhaps the greatest concern of people throughout the industrialized world—the buildup of nuclear weapons. For decades, American leaders had maintained that the United States' insurance against a Communist attack, and its continuing role as a world leader, rested in its storehouse of weaponry. In fact, both the United States and the Soviet Union had enough weapons to destroy each other several times. In addition to causing worldwide concern, the buildup of nuclear weapons by both the Soviets and the Americans caused the most severe tensions of the Cold War.

Now, the SALT talks had progressed past the negotiation stage to the point where the leaders could actually sign a treaty limiting the increase of nuclear weapons. Under the SALT treaty, the two nations would for five years limit the number of certain offensive nuclear missiles they had. In addition each nation was limited to two defensive missile sites. Later this number was reduced to one. Although the SALT agreement did not limit weapons other than missiles, it was a start toward ending the nuclear arms race.

Détente also encouraged the superpowers to communicate about other issues. In addition to discussing trade agreements and shared technology, the United States agreed to sell grain to the Soviet Union, which had suffered several crop failures.

Intervention in Chile

Even with détente, American foreign policy remained strongly anti-Communist. Nixon and Kissinger believed in helping American allies resist Communist **subversion,** the undermining of a government. The United States supported pro-American, anti-Communist governments, whether they were democracies or dictatorships.

This policy became controversial when, in 1970, the people of Chile elected a Socialist leader, Salvador Allende Gossens (ä-yĕn-dā´ gô-sens), as their president. Allende was the first **Marxist** to win a democratic election in the Americas. A Marxist is one who follows the ideas of the nineteenth-century Communist writer Karl Marx.

Allende's Socialist government nationalized a number of major industries, such as copper mining and banking, and supported land reform. The government planned to divide large land holdings for distribution to landless farmers. Each of these actions threatened American business interests in Chile.

Nixon and Kissinger feared that Socialist Chile would ally with Cuba and the Soviet Union. They thought this alliance might start a Communist domino effect in Latin America. As a result, the United States cut off all aid to Chile. At the same time, the Central Intelligence Agency (CIA) spent millions of dollars financing anti-government opposition in Chile. When a group of military officers plotted to overthrow Allende, the CIA supported them. Allende was overthrown and assassinated in 1973. A military group took control of the government and banned political activity by the opposition. Even though the new Chilean leaders abolished civil liberties, executed thousands of people, and ended economic reform, the United States resumed trade and economic relations with Chile because its government was no longer under Communist influence.

? How did the United States' actions in Chile reflect the U.S. government's anti-Communist policies?

◆ DÉTENTE CONTINUES

Gerald Ford, who became President in August 1974, retained Henry Kissinger as secretary of state and tried to continue Richard Nixon's foreign policies. Ford worked for détente by traveling to China and the Soviet Union. Although he had served in the House of Representatives for 25 years, he had little firsthand knowledge of foreign affairs.

◄ President Ford tried to continue Nixon's policy of détente. During Ford's first overseas trip as President, in 1974, he met with Soviet leader Leonid Brezhnev (right) in Vladivostok, an important port city in the eastern Soviet Union.

▲ *Representatives from over 30 countries met in Helsinki, Finland, in 1975, to sign the Helsinki Accords. The accords reflected the ongoing attempt to achieve détente among many of the world's leading powers.*

Crises Continue in Southeast Asia

During this period of eased relations between the United States and Communist countries, conflicts still arose. In May 1975, a few weeks after the fall of Saigon to the Vietnamese Communists, a U.S. merchant ship bound for Thailand, the *Mayaguez,* had mistakenly entered Cambodian waters. Soon after, Cambodian soldiers boarded and captured the ship.

President Ford sent U.S. Marines to retake the *Mayaguez,* unaware that the Cambodians had already released the ship's crew. Some Americans criticized the operation because 40 United States soldiers died in the clash with Cambodian soldiers. In addition, President Ford had acted without consulting Congress. Most Americans, however, strongly supported the President's actions because they believed it demonstrated America's strength.

Agreements at Helsinki

In Europe, the Cold War thawed slightly with the signing of an arms control agreement in 1975, called the Helsinki Accords. The idea for a meeting on European security was generated by the Soviet Union.

Delegates from the United States, the Soviet Union, Canada, and about 30 European nations met in Helsinki, Finland. They discussed arms control and cooperation between nations, and they agreed that national boundaries would only be changed peacefully. Another goal of the meeting was to create a balance of

power between NATO and Warsaw Pact forces in Europe. Finally, the Helsinki Accords spelled out standards of human rights that all attending nations pledged to observe. The meeting also gave President Ford another opportunity to meet with Leonid Brezhnev and begin discussions about a new SALT treaty. Speaking at the Helsinki meeting, Ford said,

> **Peace is not a piece of paper. History will judge this conference not by what we say here today but by what we do tomorrow—not by the promises we make but by the promises we keep.**

 How did the Helsinki Accords pursue the goals of détente?

Section 1 Review

Check Understanding

1. **Define** (a) normalize (b) bloc (c) détente (d) subversion (e) Marxist

2. **Explain** President Nixon's reasons for changing United States policy toward the People's Republic of China.

3. **Describe** the goals of détente and explain how this policy changed relations between the United States and the Soviet Union.

4. **Explain** how Gerald Ford attempted to continue Nixon's policy of détente.

Critical Thinking

Connecting Past and Present What foreign policy negotiations are currently in process?

Write About History

Write a headline and a news story that might have appeared in a Chinese or Soviet newspaper following President Nixon's visit to either country.

BUILDING *SKILLS*

Presenting an Oral Report: Nixon's Foreign Policy

Presenting an oral report is like a written report in that it is a way to communicate information about a subject. Whether you are writing or speaking about a subject, you should select a topic and a purpose that are appropriate for your audience, do research, and organize your material so that it makes a point clearly and directly. An oral report is different from a written report in its delivery. When you present a report orally, you can use your voice and gestures to emphasize ideas.

Here's How

Follow these steps to present an oral report:

1. Choose a topic and a purpose that are appropriate for the audience.

2. Research information about your topic. Depending on whether you want to describe an event, explain a process, or persuade your audience, organize your material so it fits your purpose.

3. As you plan and organize your report, use notecards. Write short notes or cues that will help you remember the order in which you want to present information. Avoid long, complicated sentences.

4. Be sure to create a strong introduction and conclusion for your oral report. Your speech should arouse curiosity and attention at the beginning and leave a lasting impression at the end.

5. Identify places in your text where you want to pause, and highlight the words you want to emphasize.

6. Prepare visuals—such as charts, graphs, pictures, photographs, summary statements, or lists—to supplement your report. Make them large enough to be easily seen and read by your audience.

7. Rehearse your presentation. Try to refer to your notes only briefly. Practice so you can speak directly to your audience.

8. When the time comes to deliver your speech, pause before you begin, and concentrate on your opening lines. Make eye contact. Speak slowly and clearly. Allow time for the audience to respond and ask questions. At the conclusion, thank your audience for their attention.

Here's Why

Giving an oral report is more than just reading what you have written. An inviting introduction, your tone of voice and gestures, the visuals you share, and your summary can add the special touches that increase interest in members of your audience.

Practice the Skill

Choose one of the following subjects, narrow it to a topic, and cover it in a five-minute oral report. Write an introduction for your report that will grab your listeners' attention, summarize your topic and purpose, and give listeners an idea of what they can expect from the rest of the report.

- Nixon's foreign policy toward China and the Soviet Union
- Strategic Arms Limitation Talks (SALT)
- U.S. intervention in Chile

Apply the Skill

Choose a subject that interests you. Follow the eight steps in *Here's How* to develop and present an oral report.

Section 2

Economic and Political Difficulties at Home

PREVIEW

Objectives

- To identify the domestic problems facing the United States during the 1970s

- To describe the events and effects of Watergate

- To explain how Gerald Ford led the nation in the post-Watergate years

- To examine Jimmy Carter's domestic record as President

Vocabulary

revenue sharing	stagflation
affirmative action	executive privilege
impound	

During Nixon's first presidential term, he and his foreign policy team had taken some bold and successful steps in expanding America's role in foreign policy. For many Americans, however, Richard Nixon would forever be associated with the political scandal at the Watergate complex. That scandal would eventually force Nixon to resign in 1974.

◆ DOMESTIC PROBLEMS CHALLENGE THE NATION

Though Richard Nixon's main interest was in foreign policy, he also hoped to change the direction of domestic policy. His administration pursued goals that were very different from those of Presidents Kennedy and Johnson.

Nixon believed that the federal government had grown too large and too distant from the American people. In August 1969, he announced a program that he called a New Federalism. It was a plan for turning over responsibility for social programs to the states. Nixon believed that smaller units of government were more responsive to people's needs. Nixon stated,

> "After a third of a century of power flowing from the people and the states to Washington, it is time for a new federalism in which power, funds, and responsibility will flow from Washington to the states and to the people."

To demonstrate this new flow of power, Nixon proposed what he called **revenue sharing.** In the revenue sharing program of 1972, Nixon distributed more than $30 billion of federal money to the states. The states were free to spend this money as they thought necessary. This reflected Nixon's view that individual states were more capable of handling their government and economic affairs than was the federal government. Nixon therefore reduced funding for many federal programs, including urban renewal, job training, education, and social welfare. Congress, controlled by Democrats, blocked Nixon's efforts to cut dozens of other federal programs. With less money for programs, state and local governments feared they would have fewer funds than they had before revenue sharing.

A New Direction in Civil Rights

In the area of civil rights, which continued to be a major issue for the nation, President Nixon took a very different approach than Kennedy or Johnson had. Nixon knew that he had little support from African American voters, so he hoped to win the votes of white Southerners instead. For this reason, civil rights laws were not always enforced during his administration.

In addition, Nixon took a strong stand on the controversial issue of school busing. In order to avoid schools composed solely of African American students or white students, federal courts had ordered the busing of students from one school district to another as a way of creating racially mixed schools. Nixon, however, opposed busing and ordered federal aid, which had been cut off for segregated schools, to resume to schools that remained segregated. Yet his administration did support **affirmative action,** a program to help minorities find jobs in fields that had been previously closed to them.

Nixon and the Environment

Sparked by Rachel Carson's *Silent Spring*, a book that warned of wildlife devastation caused by pesticides, concern for the environment had steadily risen during

618 ◆ Unit 9

the 1960s and 1970s. In response, Congress passed a number of laws to clean up water and air. The Environmental Protection Agency (EPA) was established in 1970 to monitor and enforce those laws. The EPA is an independent government agency that controls all government programs that fight pollution. The EPA's first target was use of the pesticide DDT, which was responsible for the death of much wildlife. Congress also established the Office of Environmental Quality, which enforced fines levied on oil companies to pay for the costs of cleaning up oil spills.

Nixon was not much of a supporter of environmental concerns. In 1973, he **impounded,** or refused to release, $6 million that Congress had allocated for water pollution control. Congress sued the President to force him to release the impounded funds.

The Occupational Safety and Health Agency (OSHA) was also created by Congress during the Nixon administration. This agency tries to ensure worker safety from dangerous machines and from toxic, or poisonous, chemical pollutants.

The Supreme Court

One way that Presidents can have a lasting influence is by appointing judges to the Supreme Court. Because justices may stay in office as long as they live, they are likely to serve long after the administration of the President who names them. Nixon believed that the Supreme Court under Chief Justice Earl Warren was too liberal and too concerned with the

In 1962, Rachel Carson wrote Silent Spring, *a book about the dangers posed by chemicals in the environment.* ▼

rights of criminal defendants. One of Nixon's campaign issues had been stricter "law and order" policies. When he had the unusual chance to name four new members to the Supreme Court, he chose justices with conservative views.

The first was a new chief justice, Warren Burger, who replaced Earl Warren upon his retirement in 1969. Nixon also nominated justices Harry Blackmun, Lewis Powell, Jr., and William Rehnquist, all of whom were seen as politically moderate or conservative. The Burger Court was more conservative than the Warren Court, but many of its rulings displeased Nixon and other conservatives. For example, Nixon opposed busing of students to achieve racial integration. However, in the case *Swann* v. *Charlotte-Mecklenburg Board of Education,* the Supreme Court ruled that busing may be used to end segregation in schools.

Economics and Energy

Perhaps Nixon's major domestic challenge was the relatively unstable economy. The billions of dollars that had been spent on the Vietnam War had increased deficit spending, or spending more money than is collected in taxes. Unemployment was rising. At the same time, the economy was suffering from inflationary pressures. Economists had expected that a rise in unemployment would slow inflation. When large numbers of people are unemployed, they do not have enough money to make major purchases, so prices usually come down. In the 1970s, however, a variety of factors caused inflation to continue, even as the economy remained stagnant, or not growing. Economists named this difficult situation **stagflation,** a term that combined the words *inflation* and *stagnation*.

International pressures also hurt the U.S. economy. The Organization of Petroleum Exporting Countries (OPEC) sets world oil prices and output rate. In the 1970s, Egypt and Syria, both Arab nations, were at war with Israel. In support of Egypt and Syria, the Arab members of OPEC placed an embargo on oil shipments to the United States, an ally of Israel.

The Arab oil embargo of 1973 led to an energy crisis for Americans. Shortages of gasoline caused long lines, high prices, and frustrated drivers at the gas pumps. The price of a barrel of crude oil rose from $1.80 in 1971 to $11.65 in 1974. Higher oil prices pushed the U.S. inflation rate even higher.

Astronaut Neil Armstrong photographed fellow Apollo 11 astronaut Edwin E. Aldrin, Jr., as he walked on the surface of the moon on July 20, 1969. ▶

Triumph in the Space Race

While the nation faced economic and environmental problems, it achieved a historic success in its space program. Since President Kennedy's 1961 pledge to support a space research program, a chief goal of the U.S. government had been to be the first country to place a person on the moon. Rapid progress had been made toward that goal during the 1960s. By 1968, an Apollo spacecraft with astronauts aboard circled the moon, taking detailed pictures before returning to Earth.

In July 1969, billions of people around the world watched as astronaut Neil Armstrong became the first person to set foot on the moon. Cameras recorded the first steps on the moon's surface. Pictures showed the American flag planted on the moon's surface, and Apollo's astronauts playfully jumping vast distances in the moon's weak gravity field. The astronauts collected moon rocks and returned safely to Earth.

The United States initiated other moon landings over the following years, and launched a number of robotic space probes. One such probe, sent to Mars during the Viking mission, radioed pictures of Mars to fascinated viewers on Earth in 1976.

 What two economic trends caused the situation known as stagflation?

◆ THE WATERGATE SCANDAL

Richard Nixon was concerned that he might become a one-term President. Along with his close inner circle of advisors—Henry Kissinger, H.R. Haldeman, and John Ehrlichman—Nixon used a variety of questionable political methods to undermine the presidential campaigns of Democrats Edmund Muskie and George McGovern. Although McGovern warned Americans that Nixon's administration was corrupt, his message was ignored, and President Nixon was reelected by a landslide in 1972.

A Scandal Unfolds

Just after Nixon's reelection, a startling scandal began to surface. In June 1972, police had arrested five men for breaking into the headquarters of the Democratic party. These headquarters were in the Watergate complex of buildings in Washington, D.C.

It was soon revealed that some of the Watergate burglars had ties to Nixon's reelection organization, the Committee for the Reelection of the President. Journalists found evidence that the "burglars" were trying to wiretap the phones in the Democratic party headquarters. They also uncovered plans to sabotage Democratic presidential candidates in various ways, such as stealing documents and spreading rumors.

Early in 1973, evidence revealed that the Watergate break-in was part of a larger plan of spying. The burglars had been paid out of a secret fund taken from Republican party campaign money. High-level White House staff members knew about the plan and had worked to cover it up.

In April 1973, Nixon went on television to deny any personal knowledge of the crimes or the cover-up. He announced that his closest aides, Haldeman and Ehrlichman, had resigned. His legal advisor, John Dean, was fired. Archibald Cox, a law professor, was named special prosecutor to carry out an investigation.

In May 1973, a Senate committee began official hearings on the Watergate incident. A parade of witnesses told their stories to senators who questioned them. John Dean now admitted to the committee that Nixon had known about the cover-up. Dean also revealed how the White House planned to harass people on its "enemies list" with tax audits and other threatening tactics. As committee hearings continued, Senator Howard Baker of Tennessee asked a question that summed up what the committee members wanted to know most:

> **What did the President know, and when did he know it?**

Oval Office Tapes

When a White House aide testified that Nixon had tape-recorded conversations in the Oval Office since 1971, a battle for those audiotapes began. Both the Senate committee and the court where various Watergate figures were on trial vied for the tapes.

At first the President claimed **executive privilege,** the principle that members of the executive branch of government cannot legally be forced to disclose their confidential communications if these disclosures would harm the operations of the executive branch. Under executive privilege, President Nixon refused to release the tapes.

In October 1973, Special Prosecutor Archibald Cox sued the White House for release of the tapes. Nixon ordered Attorney General Elliot Richardson to fire Cox. Richardson resigned instead. Deputy Attorney General William Ruckelshaus also resigned after being ordered to fire Cox. Nixon then named Robert Bork as the Attorney General. Bork finally dismissed Cox. Soon after, impeachment charges against the President were introduced in the House of Representatives.

History provided little guidance for members of Congress as they moved through the impeachment process. However, the evidence against President Nixon

◀ **Government** *President Nixon's tape-recorded conversations in the Oval Office revealed that Nixon not only knew about the Watergate cover-up, but that he had authorized it.* **Interpreting the Cartoon** *What does this cartoon imply about privacy in the Nixon White House?*

seemed overwhelming to representatives such as Barbara Jordan from Texas, who said,

> The framers confided in the Constitution the power if need be to remove . . . a President swollen with power and grown tyrannical.

The Watergate scandal took several months to unravel, from the fall of 1973 into the summer of 1974. A number of officials went on trial for conspiracy and perjury, or lying under oath, in the cover-up. In all, 40 officials of Nixon's administration were indicted for crimes including burglary, perjury, and obstruction of justice.

In the summer of 1974, investigators appealed to the Supreme Court for release of the Oval Office tapes. The Court unanimously ordered Nixon to release transcripts, or written accounts, of some tapes. The transcripts showed beyond all doubt that the President not only knew about the Watergate cover-up, but that he had also authorized it. It appeared that Nixon had obstructed justice by urging aides to lie to the FBI and had abused presidential power by using the FBI and Internal Revenue Service (IRS) to investigate and punish his so-called political enemies.

Pictured (from left) are Richard Nixon and his inner circle of advisors: H.R. Haldeman, chief of staff; Henry Kissinger, national security advisor; and John Ehrlichman, chief advisor for domestic affairs. ▼

Nixon Resigns

Nixon was a President in very serious trouble. The public no longer believed him, and even his strongest supporters in Congress could no longer defend him. It appeared that impeachment by the House of Representatives could not be avoided. Finally, on August 9, 1974, Nixon became the first President in the history of the United States to resign from office.

The Watergate scandal was a difficult experience for the United States. Although there had been other scandals, a President had never resigned from office. Watergate shook the confidence many Americans had in their government. However, the scandal also confirmed to many Americans that the system of checks and balances still worked. Congress had investigated the scandal, brought it to public notice, and threatened to impeach the President. The Supreme Court had reviewed the actions of the President and of Congress. As a result, the Supreme Court had forced the President to turn over the Oval Office tapes that finally led to his resignation. Watergate also showed that the American system was strong enough to guarantee a peaceful transition of power under difficult conditions.

What evidence led Richard Nixon to resign from office in 1974?

◆ GERALD FORD STEPS IN

The man who replaced Nixon as President came to hold the office in a unique way. One year earlier, Gerald Ford had been the House minority leader. He was a well-liked politician, but he did not have a reputation for bold leadership. In October 1973, Nixon had appointed Ford as Vice President. Ford replaced Spiro Agnew, who had resigned when it was revealed that he had been taking bribes. The Twenty-fifth Amendment to the Constitution gives the President the power to appoint a Vice President with the consent of the Senate if the office becomes vacant. When Gerald Ford took office as President, he became the only President who was not elected to either the presidency or the vice presidency.

On becoming President, Gerald Ford chose former New York Governor Nelson Rockefeller to fill his old office. For the first time in history, both the President and Vice President had been appointed, not elected, to office.

The Nixon Pardon

Unfortunately for Ford, one of his first decisions was his most unpopular. After reassuring the public that "our long national nightmare is over," he pardoned former President Nixon for "all offenses." That blanket pardon protected Nixon from being prosecuted for anything he had done during his presidency. The pardon shocked and outraged much of the American public, who believed that Nixon should have been openly investigated.

President Ford contended that he meant the pardon as a way "to firmly shut and seal this book on Watergate." However, many Americans thought that the pardon was aimed at ending what was a political embarrassment to Republicans. Aides who had been loyal to Nixon were already in prison, and many people thought it was unfair that the national leader did not receive any punishment. The pardon particularly angered many Americans because Nixon continued to deny that he had done anything wrong. Americans showed their anger in the congressional elections in the fall of 1974, voting a large number of Republicans out of office.

Economic Problems

Ford inherited the nation's economic problems that Nixon had been unable to solve. Stagflation was causing hardship among many Americans as oil prices soared and prices for other consumer goods continued to rise. In addition, and perhaps worst of all, unemployment continued to climb, reaching double-digit figures by 1974. Any action taken to fix one problem seemed to make another worse.

As President, Gerald Ford lacked a clear program and offered few initiatives to put the economy on the road to recovery. His first economic program depended on rebuilding people's confidence. Ford instituted a program called "Whip Inflation Now," or WIN. It asked the American people to voluntarily fight high prices and save energy in simple, everyday ways— by planting gardens, by turning down the heat, and by spending less money. Few people changed their habits or took the program seriously.

Ford maintained that if he increased government spending to bring down unemployment, inflation would rise. Consequently, he did little to increase spending, and the recession continued to worsen.

 **Why did President Ford pardon former President Nixon?**

▲ Campaign buttons supporting Carter for President in 1976 played on his trademark toothy grin and his career as a peanut farmer before he became governor of Georgia.

◆ JIMMY CARTER'S PRESIDENCY

The economy was one major issue in the election of 1976. Another issue was the American public's distrust of politicians and government in general. Ford won the Republican nomination in a tough primary fight against Ronald Reagan, former governor of California.

The Democrats nominated Jimmy Carter, who had been governor of Georgia. With no experience in national politics, Carter used this as an advantage in his campaign. Carter emphasized the issue of trust. He and his running mate, Senator Walter Mondale, of Minnesota, won the election by a narrow margin.

From the beginning, the Carter administration was clearly different. As a mark of his concern with education and energy conservation, the President won congressional approval for two new Cabinet-level departments, the Department of Education and the Department of Energy. The Department of Energy brought together the many federal programs that promoted energy conservation.

Carter won approval for more of his presidential appointments than had previous Presidents. He named many more women, Hispanics, and African Americans to his Cabinet and staff. He also named many women as federal judges. Two women were appointed to Cabinet posts. Patricia Roberts Harris became secretary of the Department of Housing and Urban Development, and Juanita Kreps became secretary of the Department of Commerce.

Economic Problems Continue

At first, Carter tried to boost government spending, which would create new jobs and thus fight unemployment. Increased spending stimulated the economy

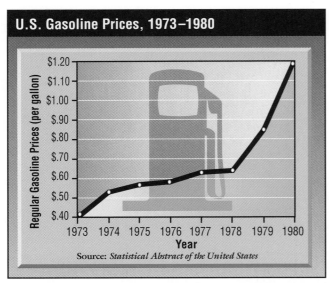

U.S. Gasoline Prices, 1973–1980

Source: *Statistical Abstract of the United States*

▲ **Economics** *Gasoline prices nearly doubled between 1978 and 1980.* **Interpreting the Graph** *In which earlier one-year period was there a dramatic increase in price?*

somewhat, but it also caused inflation rates to soar to an unhealthy 10 percent. Carter then took the opposite approach and asked for spending cuts to control inflation.

The economy continued to weaken, and unemployment rates continued to rise. Interest rates soared, hurting people who wanted to borrow money to buy houses or cars. Unemployment jumped from 5.8 percent in 1979 to 7.1 percent in 1980. Americans began to doubt that the Carter administration had a real plan to improve the economy. The constant changes in Carter's approach led them to believe that the government did not have a consistent policy.

A New Energy Crisis

One of the driving forces of inflation was the high price of oil. Despite the energy crisis of 1973, Americans continued to use huge quantities of imported oil, especially as fuel. OPEC continued to raise the price of oil. The price for oil products, especially gasoline, rose dramatically in the United States during the late 1970s, as the graph above shows. Carter made energy conservation a major goal. He wanted the country to be less dependent on imports and more immune to OPEC's sudden demands for price increases.

One responsibility of President Carter's Department of Energy was to look for new energy sources. Carter believed that finding alternative fuels would be a solution to the oil problem. The National Energy Act of 1978

loosened price controls on natural gas and domestic oil, with the assumption that higher prices would cut usage. The act discouraged "gas-guzzling" cars and gave tax credits to people who conserved energy by insulating their homes or using solar power.

Again, people faced long lines at the gas station. High prices for oil brought higher prices for many other consumer goods. By 1980, Americans were paying $62 billion a year for imported oil. This was almost double the amount they had paid in 1976. As Americans approached the election year of 1980, they had serious doubts about Carter's ability to improve the economy.

 What were the most serious domestic problems of Jimmy Carter's presidency?

Section 2 Review

Check Understanding

1. **Define** (a) revenue sharing (b) affirmative action (c) impound (d) stagflation (e) executive privilege

2. **Describe** the economic problems facing the United States during the 1970s.

3. **Identify** the events that led to Richard Nixon's resignation as President.

4. **Analyze** the reasons why Ford's pardon of Nixon was unpopular with the public.

5. **Evaluate** Jimmy Carter's domestic record as President.

Critical Thinking

Connecting Past and Present What effects of Watergate are apparent today? Has Americans' trust in government been restored?

Write About Government

Do you agree with President Ford's decision to pardon Richard Nixon? Write a brief essay describing what punishment, if any, you think President Nixon should have received.

Section 3

A New Approach to Foreign Policy

PREVIEW

Objectives

- To explain President Carter's approach to foreign policy
- To discuss Carter's success in bringing about a peace agreement between Israel and Egypt
- To trace the events leading to the Iran hostage crisis and its resolution

Vocabulary

shuttle diplomacy
dissident
ayatollah

Jimmy Carter's firm religious faith and strong sense of morality brought a new tone to United States foreign policy, and Carter achieved some important successes. However, a favor to an old ally—the shah, or emperor of Iran—brought on a crisis that deeply upset Americans. Along with economic problems, the situation led to President Carter's political downfall. After just one term, he lost the presidency in the election of 1980.

◆ CARTER'S FOREIGN POLICY

In foreign policy, Jimmy Carter tried to promote human rights around the globe. Relying on the United States' role as a world superpower, he tried to influence other nations to follow a foreign policy that supported democracy and freedom. Many of his speeches carried this message:

"As long as I am president, the government of the United States will continue, throughout the world, to enhance human rights. No force on earth can separate us from the commitment."

Early Successes

Though Carter had little experience with diplomacy when he became President, he soon proved to be a skillful peacemaker. During his presidency, the United States took some historic steps in foreign relations.

One step was an agreement to return the Panama Canal to Panama. To most people in Latin America, United States' control of the Canal Zone was old-fashioned "big-stick" imperialism. To many Americans, however, the canal was a symbol of U.S. power and prestige. Many Americans insisted that control of the canal was necessary to protect American security.

President Carter signed the Panama Canal treaties in 1977. After heated debate, the Senate narrowly approved them. According to the treaties' terms, the United States would return the canal to Panama by December 31, 1999. The treaties ensured that the canal would continue to remain open to all nations after its return to Panama. The United States reserved the right to step in with military force if necessary to keep it open.

Another major advance in foreign policy was a follow-up to President Nixon's historic visit to China. In January 1979, the United States and the People's Republic of China established diplomatic relations. Both countries hoped to open up their markets to trade. The United States also hoped recognition of China would lead to a better bargaining position with the Soviet Union. Still in conflict with China, the Soviet Union feared an alliance between China and the United States.

Carter applied his policies toward Africa, too. He named Andrew Young, a civil rights leader, to be ambassador to the United Nations. Young also oversaw a new policy toward African nations that were becoming independent from colonial rule. This policy called for support of rule by the black majority in countries such as South Africa and Rhodesia. For the first time, U.S. diplomats spoke out against the rule of South Africa by its white minority and the country's policy of racial separation.

An Agreement at Camp David

Carter's biggest diplomatic risk also brought his greatest success. The Middle East was a constant source of tension, with conflicts between Israel and its neighboring Arab nations exploding into open warfare several times. In 1977, Egypt's president, Anwar el-Sadat, made a dramatic gesture toward peace by making a visit to Israel. Before then, no Arab nation had ever officially recognized Israel's right to exist as a nation.

President Anwar el-Sadat of Egypt (left) and Prime Minister Menachem Begin of Israel (right) were awarded the 1978 Nobel Peace Prize. They are shown here at Camp David with Jimmy Carter. ▶

American diplomats began to adopt the **shuttle diplomacy** begun by Henry Kissinger, moving back and forth between Israel and Egypt in an effort to reach agreements. Carter then invited Sadat and Menachem Begin (ma-näkh´-am bā´-gin), Israel's prime minister, to meet at Camp David, the presidential retreat in Maryland. In September 1978, the three leaders began intense discussions. After two weeks, Sadat and Begin shook hands and signed what were known as the Camp David Accords. In 1979, the leaders formalized the Accords in the Camp David Treaty. According to the terms of the agreement, Egypt became the first Arab nation to extend diplomatic recognition to Israel, and Israel agreed to withdraw its troops from the occupied Sinai peninsula. The Camp David Accords and Treaty could not guarantee peace in the complicated politics of the Middle East, but they were a historic first step.

The End of Détente

Relations between the United States and the Soviet Union were sometimes strained. U.S. recognition of China and their exchange of ambassadors increased tensions between the Soviet Union and the United States. In addition, President Carter openly supported Soviet

dissidents, people who disagree with a government policy or rule. Soviet dissidents were actively campaigning for greater freedom in the Soviet Union.

The signing of an arms agreement, known as SALT II, in June 1979, did not help U.S.-Soviet relations. This agreement was meant to reduce even further the number of nuclear warheads and missiles held by each superpower, but the Senate opposed the treaty because it feared the agreement threatened U.S. military strength.

The future of the proposed treaty was put in further jeopardy when Soviet troops invaded neighboring Afghanistan in order to support a Soviet-backed government there. In response, Carter withdrew the treaty from Senate consideration. The President also put an embargo on sales of grain and electronics to the Soviet Union. He then cancelled the participation of U.S. teams at the 1980 summer Olympic Games, which were to be held in Moscow. Finally, he issued the Carter Doctrine, which warned the Soviets that the United States would fight to protect its interests in the Persian Gulf.

President Carter had a mixed record in foreign policy. Although he had made a strong commitment to human rights, his policy was ignored by some American allies and opposed by others. Soviet leaders viewed Carter's emphasis on human rights as interference. By the end of his term in office, relations between the United States and many of its allies were poorer than they had been in years.

? **What were the Camp David Accords, and why were they important?**

◆ THE IRAN HOSTAGE CRISIS

One other foreign policy crisis critically damaged American prestige and Jimmy Carter's public support. Since the 1950s, the United States had supported the shah of Iran. The shah was on good terms with the United States, and, under his rule, Iran became a major supplier of oil to the United States.

Over the years, the shah had become unpopular in his country. Both traditional Muslims and liberal reformers disliked his policies, which included torturing and executing prisoners without a trial. The most vocal opponents were led by **ayatollahs** (ī´-ya-tō´-las)—high-ranking religious leaders in the branch of Islam that most Iranians practice. The ayatollahs opposed efforts to modernize Iran, and they held the United States responsible for many of the shah's unpopular actions.

Early in 1979, a revolution overthrew the shah, who fled the country. In October 1979, President Carter permitted the critically ill shah to enter the United States for medical treatment. The Ayatollah Khomeini (ī´-ya-tō´-la kō-mān´-ē), an elderly Muslim religious leader, replaced the shah as the leader of Iran. His revolutionary government set up a strict Islamic state, which promoted hatred of American ways and Western influence.

Many of the Ayatollah's devoted followers reacted with fury when they learned that the exiled shah had been admitted to the United States. They demanded that he be returned to Iran to face trial. For days, militants protested outside the United States Embassy in Tehran, shouting "Death to Carter! Death to America!"

Iranians Seize the U.S. Embassy

On November 4, the militants seized the U.S. embassy and took as hostages 66 Americans, mainly diplomats and embassy staff. The seizure was a violation of international law, since countries are required to protect all foreign embassies. The Iranian government claimed it was unable to control the militants.

A few hostages were quickly released, but more than 50 remained. Iran refused to release them unless Carter sent the shah back to Iran for trial. The hostages were questioned, accused of spying, and threatened. Some were blindfolded and beaten. Loudspeakers broadcast anti-American slogans outside their prison. One hostage described the experience this way:

> **❝The biggest fear was not knowing what the future held and not knowing what was happening to my colleagues. And then there was the undercurrent; the threats of trials and executions.❞**

President Carter tried to apply pressure on Iran, but nothing he did ended the crisis. He broke diplomatic relations with Iran and made Iranians' assets in the United States unavailable to them. Finally, in desperation, he sent American commandos on a rescue mission. However, the raid failed when dust storms disabled several helicopters. Eight American soldiers died in the raid.

The hostage crisis continued for more than a year. The shah died in July 1980, but the Iranians still would not release the hostages. Diplomats continued to negotiate in secret with intermediary countries as the presidential election of 1980 approached.

Shortly after Americans were taken hostage from their embassy in Tehran, they were forced to pose, blindfolded, with a few of their Iranian captors. ▼

The 1980 Election

The hostage crisis was devastating to Jimmy Carter's presidency. In addition, severe inflation and the collapse of détente with the Soviet Union reduced Carter's chances for reelection.

To oppose President Carter, the Republicans nominated former California governor Ronald Reagan. Four years earlier, Reagan had narrowly lost the Republican nomination to Gerald Ford. As Reagan campaigned around the country, he announced an economic plan that appealed to many voters. He promised to fight for an across-the-board tax cut for everyone. Americans knew how to spend their money better than the government did, he declared. He asked voters if they were better off in 1980 than they had been in 1977, when Carter took office.

Reagan also criticized Carter as weak and indecisive. He promised to restore American prestige in the world and to revitalize the U.S. economy. Reagan declared,

> **We have every right to dream heroic dreams. . . . It is time for us to realize that we are too great a nation to limit ourselves to small dreams. We're not, as some would have us believe, doomed to an inevitable decline.**

In the summer of 1980, polls showed that only 21 percent of Americans approved of Carter's performance as President. This was the lowest rating given to a President since the 1930s.

Ronald Reagan won the election of 1980 by a wide margin—51 percent of the vote to Carter's 41 percent. A third-party candidate, John Anderson, won 7 percent of the vote. The electoral vote was even more clear-cut. Reagan won 489 electoral votes to Carter's 49. Moreover, the Republicans gained a majority in the Senate for the first time since the election of Eisenhower in 1952. Voter turnout, however, showed a lack of interest in the political process. Only slightly more than half of the eligible voters cast their votes.

Reagan's election broke the stalemate over the hostages in Iran. After 444 days, Iran finally released the hostages. Their plane left Tehran on January 20, 1981, which was Reagan's inauguration day.

? What factors made it possible for Ronald Reagan to win the 1980 election?

▲ Reagan's promise to lower taxes, promote conservative values, and strengthen the national defense appealed to Americans who were weary of the political and social turmoil of the 1960s and 1970s.

Section 3 Review

Check Understanding

1. **Define** (a) shuttle diplomacy (b) dissident (c) ayatollah

2. **Explain** Carter's goals for American foreign policy.

3. **Summarize** the argument for and against returning the Panama Canal to Panama.

4. **Discuss** why the Camp David Accords marked an important change in policy between Israel and its Arab neighbors.

5. **Describe** how the Iran hostage crisis was resolved.

Critical Thinking

◆ **Connecting Past and Present** How have relations in the Middle East changed since the Camp David Accords? Support your ideas with facts.

Write About History

Write a brief article about how Carter's approach to foreign policy was different from Nixon's.

CONNECTING HISTORY & Citizenship

CLEMENCY AND PARDONS FOR DRAFT RESISTERS

The war in Vietnam tested the ideals of citizenship as much as any event in American history. There had always been people who objected to wars the United States fought. However, never before in American history—even during the Civil War—had so many Americans opposed a war.

Americans had a strong tradition of patriotism. For 200 years, most Americans had believed in the necessity of the wars their government had asked them to fight. During the 1960s, however, many Americans came to believe U. S. involvement in Vietnam was unjust. Some American men fled to Canada or Europe to resist the draft, while others went to jail rather than be drafted.

Some Americans feared that the war resisters symbolized the breakdown of American society. How could democracy survive, they asked, if each person could choose which wars to fight? The debate tore American society apart.

With the end of the war, there were calls for a pardon for draft resisters. Yet bitter feelings remained. Returning soldiers deeply resented those who had refused to fight. Many others who had left the country feared legal action if they returned.

Both Presidents Ford and Carter moved to heal the country with amnesty programs. Amnesty is protection from legal action. Soon after President Ford pardoned Nixon, Ford set up a program of clemency. Clemency is mercy or leniency. To earn clemency, those who had evaded the draft were required to give two years of public service and take an oath of allegiance to the United States. This offer pleased few Americans. Those who had opposed the war thought it was too harsh. Others, especially veterans' organizations, thought it was unfair to those who had fought in Vietnam. Only about 8,000 of the more than 150,000 eligible draft resisters took advantage of the program. Many draft resisters refused the offer because acceptance would have been admission that they had done something wrong.

On his first day as President, Carter issued a full pardon to draft resisters. A quarter of a million men who had never registered were also pardoned. "I think it is time to get the Vietnam War over," Carter said.

Making the Citizenship Connection

1. Why do you think Presidents Ford and Carter offered amnesty programs to draft resisters?

2. Do you think a person can be a good citizen and resist his or her government? Explain your answer.

3. What do you think should have been done with those who had resisted the draft during the Vietnam War?

Connecting Past and Present

If a situation similar to the Vietnam War occurred today, how do you think you and your friends might react? Would you go to war or express your opposition to the government?

▲ *Some war resisters who had burned draft registration cards were granted full pardons by President Carter.*

Chapter 30
Review

CHAPTER SUMMARY

Section 1
At the end of the Vietnam War, President Nixon attempted to relax Cold War tensions. In 1972, he made a historic visit to China. At the same time, Nixon established warmer relations with the Soviet Union. The United States continued to oppose Marxist governments in Latin America, which led to intervention in Chile. Gerald Ford continued Nixon's détente policies. When Cambodian soldiers seized the American ship *Mayaguez*, Ford sent the U.S. Marines to retake the ship.

Section 2
Nixon reduced federal funds for social programs, claiming that they should be run by the states. Stagnation and inflation hurt the U.S. economy. The key event of Nixon's second term was the Watergate scandal, which led to his resignation in 1974. Gerald Ford served the remainder of Nixon's term. Ford's pardon of Nixon shocked and outraged many Americans. Jimmy Carter, elected in 1976, was unable to boost the economy out of its persistent stagflation. Unemployment increased and interest rates soared, diminishing President Carter's popularity with the American people.

Section 3
Carter attempted to base his foreign policy on human rights considerations. His greatest success was bringing together Israel and Egypt to sign the Camp David Accords. The seizing of more than 50 American hostages by Iranian militants dominated the last year of Carter's presidency. As the crisis dragged on, Carter's popularity decreased. Ronald Reagan easily defeated Carter in the 1980 election.

Connecting ◆ Past and Present

What problems in international relations that existed in the 1970s are still problems today?

Using Vocabulary

Select the letter of the phrase that best completes each sentence.

1. President Nixon claimed **executive privilege** when asked to turn over tapes of White House conversations, which means (a) governing in an office; (b) not having to disclose communications because they might harm the presidential branch; (c) destroying evidence; (d) lying under oath.

2. Trying to **normalize** relations involves (a) breaking contacts; (b) establishing diplomatic connections; (c) initiating an embargo; (d) signing a peace treaty.

3. A **bloc** is (a) a place where hostages are kept; (b) an object in the path of a person; (c) the Watergate burglars; (d) a group of countries united for common action.

4. **Shuttle diplomacy** is (a) taking short trips on the space shuttle; (b) trading food for space technology; (c) foreign policy efforts that require traveling back and forth; (d) withdrawal of troops from neutral countries.

5. Jimmy Carter openly supported Soviet **dissidents,** people who (a) shun all violence; (b) favor arms buildups; (c) fight high prices; (d) disagree with a government policy or rule.

Check Understanding

1. **Explain** why President Nixon's 1972 visit to the People's Republic of China was historic.

2. **Describe** how détente affected relations between the United States and the Soviet Union.

3. **List** two economic problems the United States faced in the 1970s.

4. **Summarize** the events of the Watergate scandal.

5. **Discuss** how Gerald Ford continued President Nixon's policy of détente.

6. **Explain** the issues in the election of 1976.

7. **Describe** how Jimmy Carter attempted to solve the nation's economic problems.

8. **Discuss** how President Carter's approach to foreign policy differed from the foreign policy of the Presidents immediately before him.

9. **Describe** how Carter helped engineer the Camp David Accords.

10. **Explain** what led to the Iran hostage crisis and how it was resolved.

Critical Thinking

1. **Drawing Conclusions** Why did United States foreign policy toward major Communist nations begin to change in the 1970s?

2. **Understanding Causes and Effects** What were the effects of Watergate on the nation?

3. **Comparing and Contrasting** Based on their strengths and weaknesses, were Nixon and Carter alike or different as Presidents? Explain your answer.

4. **Identifying Alternatives** President Carter lost much of his popularity during the hostage crisis. How might he have handled the crisis differently?

◆ **Connecting Past and Present** How did the period of détente affect the way Americans live today?

Interpreting the Timeline

Use the timeline on pages 610–611 to answer these questions.

1. Name two events related to space exploration.

2. Who was President of the United States when the Iranians released the American hostages?

3. Name one event that positively affected Carter's presidency and one event that negatively affected his presidency.

Writing to Persuade

President Jimmy Carter wanted American foreign policy to set a moral standard for the world. He tried to encourage other nations to support democracy and freedom. **Write** a speech evaluating the role human rights played in Carter's foreign policy. Consider whether the United States should have a right to set a moral standard and interfere in the affairs of another country. Make your argument a strong one by citing examples from American history.

Putting Skills to Work

PRESENTING AN ORAL REPORT

As you learned in the Building Skills lesson on page 617, oral reports require a different kind of preparation than written reports. The following paragraphs are part of an oral report. Practice delivering this material so that you can present it well to your class. Listen to your classmates' presentation of the material, and compare the results. What kinds of delivery made certain presentations more successful than others?

Nixon's two major trips abroad turned out to be great successes at home as well. By the fall of 1972, Nixon's popularity at home was quite high. Many people forgot the lingering problem of Vietnam and Nixon's expansion of the war into Cambodia in 1970. Now he seemed to have a new image—that of peacemaker.

In November, Nixon defeated his Democratic rival George McGovern in a landslide. McGovern had campaigned on a strong antiwar platform. He had also called Nixon's administration the most "corrupt in U.S. history." But McGovern's charge had little effect on the voters in November.

 *Portfolio Project*

A POSITION PAPER

Choose a problem that occupied a President during the 1970s. It could be a domestic problem, such as stagflation or Watergate. It could also be a foreign policy problem, such as arms limitation, the Iran hostage crisis, or the Arab-Israeli dispute. Write a position paper to the President who was in office at the time, recommending a course of action. Use the material in this chapter as well as library resources to provide the specific facts you will need to support your recommendations. Compare your solutions with those of your classmates.

NEWS MEDIA AND THE GOVERNMENT

The First Amendment to the Constitution guarantees freedom of the press, which includes the right of the news media to question and criticize the government and its leaders. Not only is a free press vital in keeping government responsible to its citizens, but it is also the most powerful means for creating and shaping public opinion. For over two centuries, the news media has served as an important channel between government and the governed.

Then In June 1972, two young reporters from the *Washington Post*, Bob Woodward and Carl Bernstein, began to report an astonishing story. They had uncovered evidence that what the White House had called a "third-rate burglary" was actually part of a bigger story about abuse of presidential power. In an attempt to divert attention from the conduct of the President, the Nixon administration continuously questioned the conduct and the motives of the press. If it had not been for the two reporters from the *Washington Post,* the American public might never have known about Watergate. Other newspapers, news magazines, and TV networks did not pursue the story. Some even accused the *Post* of overplaying the facts. As a result of poor coverage, Watergate was not an issue in the 1972 presidential election.

Now When Woodward and Bernstein broke the Watergate story, they followed rules of journalism that were standard for the time. Before they printed any details obtained in an interview, they confirmed the facts with at least one other source. Today, technology—such as communications satellites and lightweight minicams, or videotape cameras—makes it possible for people to receive news as it happens. Cable television broadcasts news around the clock, and news on the Internet is often reported moments after it happens, although it has not always been checked for accuracy.

Woodward and Bernstein felt responsible for giving readers the truth about the public figures who were elected to serve them. Today, the news media is frequently driven by commercial interests. News is sometimes reduced to gossip as sensational aspects of a story are featured. A blizzard of information may be presented, but often speed and ratings take priority over thoroughness, quality, and accuracy.

▲ Washington Post *reporters Carl Bernstein (left) and Robert Woodward (right) followed a trail of leads to uncover the Watergate scandal. The* Washington Post *won the Pulitzer Prize in journalism for its reporting of the scandal.*

You Decide

1. Woodward and Bernstein believed that an informed public provides the best government. Do you agree or disagree? Explain your views.

2. Should limits be placed on the American press in how it presents news? If so, what limits?

Entering a New Century 1980–the future

> **The personal-computer revolution happened and it has affected millions of lives. It has led us to places we had barely imagined. We are all beginning another great journey.... I think this is a wonderful time to be alive. There have never been so many opportunities to do things that were impossible before.**
>
> *Bill Gates,*
> *in his autobiography*
> The Road Ahead, *1995*

▲ *Several young people in New York City register to vote in an upcoming election.*
 Connecting Past and Present *How do you think these first-time voters feel about participating in their government? How might a picture of voter registration in the early 1900s differ from this one?*

Chapter 31
Challenges at Home and Abroad 1980–1998

CHAPTER PREVIEW

Section 1 Politics and Presidents

Ronald Reagan launched an era of economic and social conservatism that was continued by his successor, George Bush. Concerns about the economy during Bush's term led to his defeat and to the victory of Bill Clinton in 1992.

Section 2 A Time of Mixed Gains

During the 1980s and early 1990s, progress toward equality was made by African Americans, women, Latinos, and Native Americans. Yet, despite gains made in politics and education, minorities continued to struggle against inequality and discrimination.

Section 3 A Changing World

Americans celebrated the end of the Cold War, but soon found themselves concerned with crises in the Middle East, Africa, Eastern Europe, and Latin America.

Jesse Jackson campaign button

U.S. Events

1980
✪ Ronald Reagan elected.

Sandra Day O'Connor

1981
Sandra Day O'Connor becomes first woman appointed to the Supreme Court.

1983
Reagan proposes Star Wars program.

Martin Luther King, Jr.'s birthday becomes a federal holiday.

1984
✪ Ronald Reagan reelected.

Jesse Jackson forms the Rainbow Coalition.

1986
Iran-Contra affair is exposed.

1988
✪ George Bush elected.

Toni Morrison wins the Pulitzer Prize for the novel *Beloved*.

1978

World Events

1979
Islamic republic is formed in Iran.

1983
Lech Walesa of Poland is awarded Nobel Peace Prize.

Lech Walesa

1985
Mikhail Gorbachev proposes *glasnost* policy in U.S.S.R.

Gabriel García Márquez's novel *Love in the Time of Cholera* is published.

Portfolio Project

A TIME CAPSULE

A time capsule is a sealed container that holds artifacts, which are objects produced and used by people. The capsule is meant to give people in the future an idea of what life was like during a particular era. At the end of this chapter, you will prepare a list of items to place in a time capsule that will give people in the future a picture of the United States in the 1980s and 1990s. As you read the chapter, look for ideas for items to include in the capsule.

▲ Bill Clinton, George Bush, and Ronald Reagan were among the five Presidents who attended the funeral of Richard Nixon in 1994.
◆◇ Connecting Past and Present *How does the photograph convey the mood of the occasion? In what ways do we commemorate past Presidents?*

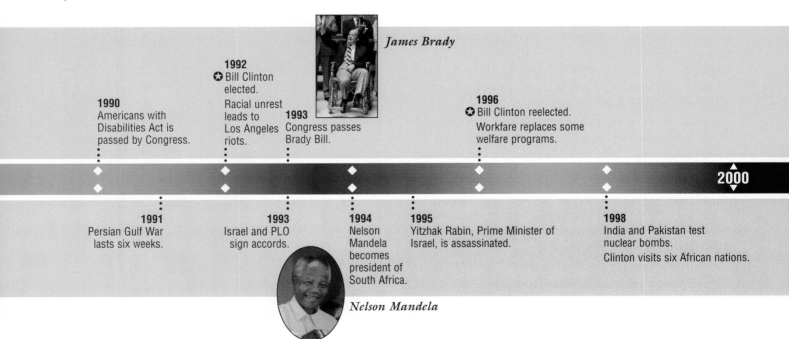

James Brady

1990
Americans with Disabilities Act is passed by Congress.

1992
✪ Bill Clinton elected.
Racial unrest leads to Los Angeles riots.

1993
Congress passes Brady Bill.

1996
✪ Bill Clinton reelected.
Workfare replaces some welfare programs.

1991
Persian Gulf War lasts six weeks.

1993
Israel and PLO sign accords.

1994
Nelson Mandela becomes president of South Africa.

1995
Yitzhak Rabin, Prime Minister of Israel, is assassinated.

1998
India and Pakistan test nuclear bombs.
Clinton visits six African nations.

2000

Nelson Mandela

Section 1

Politics and Presidents

PREVIEW

Objectives

- To analyze how Ronald Reagan launched a new era of conservatism in the 1980s

- To describe how George Bush dealt with an economic slowdown in the United States

- To describe Bill Clinton's program to lead the United States into the twenty-first century

Vocabulary

supply-side economics
federal deficit
downsize

The 1960s and 1970s proved to be decades of turbulence and change in the United States. By 1980, however, the mood of the country had shifted. That year the American people elected as President the former governor of California, Ronald Reagan.

◆ THE REAGAN YEARS

President Reagan reduced funding for many social programs that had been part of the Great Society. He also openly criticized Soviet policies, more than previous Presidents had. He called the Soviet Union an "evil empire" and took firm action to stop Communist-led uprisings in Latin America and Africa.

Because of Reagan's popularity, the 1980s are often called the Reagan Era. He won reelection in 1984 easily. In 1988, the American people voted Reagan's Vice President, George Bush, into the White House. Bush continued many of the conservative policies Reagan had introduced in the early 1980s.

The Great Communicator

At their presidential convention in 1980, the Republicans nominated Ronald Reagan to run against Jimmy Carter. Reagan was a former actor who had entered politics and served two terms as governor of California. His friendly and assured style earned him the nickname "the Great Communicator."

Reagan deeply believed in free enterprise and the ability of individual Americans to solve their own problems. These were the kinds of optimistic ideas that many Americans wanted to hear. Reagan defeated Carter with a large majority of the vote. Worried about domestic economic problems as well as international terrorism, Americans wanted upbeat and confident leaders. Reagan projected a tough, "can-do" message that many Americans admired. As he said in 1981,

> The free enterprise system has given us the greatest standard of living in the world. . . . It has enabled industrious Americans from the most humble of backgrounds to climb to the top. . . .

When Iran released the American hostages on the same day that Reagan took office, many Americans felt that Reagan's tough new style in dealing with domestic and foreign problems was already producing results.

Ronald and Nancy Reagan celebrated Reagan's landslide reelection in 1984, in which he carried 49 of the 50 states. ▼

The New Right

Reagan's 1980 victory was due in part to strong support from several well-organized conservative groups. Together these groups made up the New Right, a movement that supported a conservative agenda. Some members of the New Right were business owners and executives concerned about the economy. These conservatives wanted lower taxes and less government regulation of business.

Others in the New Right cared more about social issues. In their view, the United States in the 1960s and 1970s was becoming too passive toward issues like drug use and sexuality. Many of them questioned the value of special programs that were created for women and minorities. A large number wanted to allow students to pray in public schools. Many conservatives wanted to restore what they saw as traditional, or family, values. A group called the Moral Majority, led by Jerry Falwell, spearheaded this part of the New Right coalition.

The New Right had many followers, especially in the South and West. It was well organized and well funded. New Right groups were expert at using mail and telephone campaigns to gain supporters and to circulate information. They raised millions of dollars to support conservative candidates for Congress, for state legislatures, and for local governments.

A Dramatic Beginning

President Reagan's first year in office was marked by near tragedy. Just two months after his inauguration, as Reagan walked to a limousine in Washington, D.C., a young man named John Hinckley, Jr., fired six bullets at him. One bullet entered Reagan's chest and lodged only a few centimeters from his heart. The 70-year-old President walked from the ambulance into the hospital himself and recovered quickly. His good humor in the face of adversity astonished Americans. "I hope you're all Republicans," he quipped to the surgeons who removed the bullet from his chest. His courage won the admiration of many Americans.

Press secretary James Brady, who was accompanying the President, was not as lucky as Reagan. During the shooting, one of the bullets from Hinckley's handgun hit Brady, causing considerable paralysis. The incident inspired James Brady and his wife, Sarah, to launch a battle to restrict the purchase of handguns. In 1993, Congress passed the Brady Bill, which established a waiting period and required a background check of people who wanted to buy handguns.

▲ Jerry Falwell, a leader of the Moral Majority, advocated traditional family values and political conservatism in the 1980s.

A few months into Reagan's administration, air traffic controllers across the country went on strike. Reagan threatened to fire the strikers—who were federal employees—if they did not go back to work. Strikes by workers whose service was critical to the country were considered illegal. Few believed that the President would fire workers who were vital to the nation's transportation system. In August 1981, however, Reagan dismissed nearly all the 10,000 air traffic controllers. As airports scrambled to hire and train new air traffic controllers, organized labor got the message: Reagan would be tough on unions that promoted illegal strikes.

Shrinking the Government

Reagan moved quickly to make good on some of his campaign promises. As governor of California, he had cut spending and balanced the budget. Reagan pledged to do the same thing for the nation. Cutting federal taxes, he said, would give individuals and businesses more money, causing the economy to grow. Reagan believed in an economic theory known as **supply-side economics.** This theory held that cutting taxes on businesses and individuals would result in more money being available for people to invest in new goods and services. Businesses would need to employ more people and produce more goods to meet the increased demand. This would cause the economy to expand quickly, putting back into circulation the money the government had lost by cutting taxes.

The theory of supply-side economics was untested. But the prospect of tax cuts was so popular that both Republicans and Democrats in Congress supported Reagan's plan. In July 1981, Congress voted to reduce federal income taxes about 25 percent over the next three years. Taxes went down for all Americans, but the percent of reduction for high-income people was larger than for anyone else. It was the biggest tax cut in the nation's history, and it reduced government revenue nearly $750 billion over the following five years.

Reagan also urged Congress to cut spending on more than 80 federal programs, including education, medical research, housing, and social services. While Reagan reduced spending in these areas, he nearly doubled military spending.

In March 1983, Reagan announced an ambitious new program to protect the United States from nuclear missile attack. The program, officially called the Strategic Defense Initiative, quickly became known as Star Wars, after the popular film. The Star Wars program involved placing satellites armed with missiles or lasers in outer space. From space, enemy missiles would be intercepted and shot down before they reached their targets.

Many scientists, claiming that no antimissile system could really protect the nation from an enemy attack, criticized the Star Wars program. Others complained that the budget for it—$26 billion to start—was too high. They opposed cutting social programs while increasing money for military projects. By the mid-1990s, the government had spent more than $40 billion on Star Wars.

Reagan's Economic Policies

Reagan's economic policies had several positive effects. Under President Carter, inflation had soared to 17 percent. Under Reagan, it dropped back to 5 percent. The economy created jobs at a rapid pace, adding 20 million people to the employment rolls during Reagan's two terms in office.

However, the combination of tax cuts and higher military spending also had negative results. Though the economy grew rapidly, **federal deficits** increased. The federal deficit is the amount of money the government spends in a year that is not covered by the taxes and other monies it collects in that year.

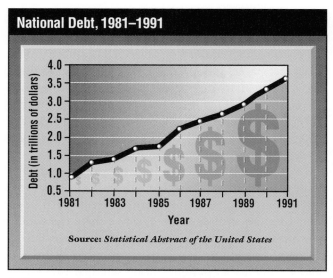

▲ **Economics** *The national debt increased in the 1980s.* **Interpreting the Graph** *If you compare yearly changes in the national debt, what pattern do you see?*

The federal government had been running deficits for years. But under Reagan, deficits soared, jumping from $79 billion in 1981 to $221 billion in 1986. The increase in deficits during the Reagan years was larger than that of all previous Presidents combined. It was so large that by 1988, the national debt—all the annual deficits added up—was more than $2.6 trillion, as shown in the chart above. Large annual deficits and a growing national debt began to undermine confidence in the economy. Experts both in the United States and abroad worried that the economy could not support these huge imbalances of revenue and expenditure.

Republicans and Democrats accused each other of causing the federal deficits. Reagan said that the problem lay with Congress, which had passed the tax cuts but had not cut government spending. Democrats charged that supply-side economics simply did not work. They said the idea that the government could cut taxes and increase military spending without running a deficit was absurd.

Congress passed the Gramm-Rudman-Hollings Act in 1985, putting pressure on the President and Congress to balance the federal budget each year. If they were unable to reduce the deficit to within certain limits, the act required automatic cuts in federal spending. Although a 1986 Supreme Court ruling invalidated a portion of the law, its main part remained. The intent of the law was to balance the federal budget by 1991. It did not succeed.

Reagan's Second Term

In 1984, Democrats tried to turn back Reagan's conservative revolution. To run against Reagan, the Democrats nominated Walter Mondale, who had served as Jimmy Carter's Vice President. They chose Geraldine Ferraro, a New Yorker, as the candidate for Vice President. Ferraro was the first woman to run for Vice President with the support of a major political party. When she spoke before the Democratic Convention in San Francisco, she knew she was making history:

“By choosing an American woman to run for our nation's second-highest office, you send a powerful message to all Americans. There are no doors we cannot unlock. We will place no limits on achievement.”

Although Ferraro attracted strong support from women, Reagan and Vice President George Bush easily defeated their Democratic rivals. In the election, Reagan won 59 percent of the popular vote, sweeping every state except Mondale's home state of Minnesota and the District of Columbia.

Reagan made use of the President's power to appoint conservative federal court judges. He also filled three vacancies on the Supreme Court. During his first term, he had appointed Sandra Day O'Connor associate justice of the Supreme Court, the first woman to serve on the Court. His later appointments, Anthony Kennedy and Antonin Scalia, gave the Court a stronger conservative voice than it had had for decades.

The Supreme Court began to chisel away at some of the liberal rulings of the 1960s and 1970s. Several Court decisions limited programs that promoted affirmative action. Affirmative action refers to programs that encourage the hiring of groups that have been discriminated against in the past, especially women and minorities. In several cases the Court now found that affirmative action was unfair to white male job applicants. As the Court's decisions on these cases agreed with the views of some opponents of affirmative action, supporters of affirmative action were alarmed. In addition, the Court allowed the execution of criminals who were under 18 years old when they committed murder.

Why did federal deficits grow during Reagan's administration?

◆ GEORGE BUSH AS PRESIDENT

George Bush, who served as Vice President under Reagan, won the Republican nomination for President in 1988. Bush, originally from New England, had moved to Texas and made a career in the oil business. He also served in the Congress as representative from Texas, at the United Nations, and as director of the Central Intelligence Agency before becoming Vice President. Bush chose Dan Quayle, a senator from Indiana, to be his running mate.

For the Democratic nomination, a tight race developed between Michael Dukakis, the governor of Massachusetts, and Jesse Jackson. Jackson, a civil rights activist from Chicago, crisscrossed the nation, electrifying audiences with his speeches. Jackson surprised the experts by winning primaries in Mississippi, Alabama, and Louisiana. Dukakis, Massachusetts governor during a period of economic growth in the state, emerged from the primaries with enough votes to secure the Democratic nomination.

The Election of 1988

At the start of the campaign, polls showed Dukakis well ahead of Bush. Many voters saw Bush as a wealthy person who was not able to identify with their problems.

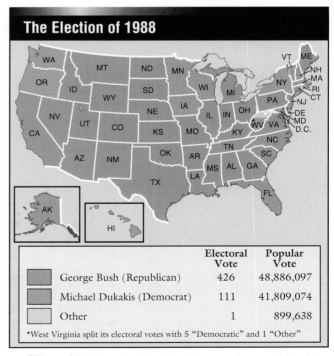

The Election of 1988

		Electoral Vote	Popular Vote
	George Bush (Republican)	426	48,886,097
	Michael Dukakis (Democrat)	111	41,809,074
	Other	1	899,638

*West Virginia split its electoral votes with 5 "Democratic" and 1 "Other"

▲ **Citizenship** *George Bush easily won the presidential election of 1988.* **Interpreting the Map** *By approximately how many popular votes did Bush defeat Dukakis?*

Bush gained the support of some voters when he tried to portray Dukakis as soft on crime. One Bush campaign commercial featured Willie Horton, a convicted murderer. While out of a Massachusetts prison on a furlough, Horton committed another crime. Bush's ad implied that Dukakis had supported Horton's release. Both Bush and Dukakis soon were creating a series of campaign commercials that pointed out each other's negative aspects.

Bush also scored points with voters when he promised not to raise taxes. "Read my lips," Bush said again and again at campaign stops. *"No new taxes!"* Bush won the election by a comfortable margin. However, only about 57 percent of the voting-age population turned out on election day.

Bush's Domestic Policies

As President, Bush continued many of Ronald Reagan's policies. However, he softened the more militant tone of the Reagan years, calling for "a kinder, gentler nation." In addition, Bush took some initiatives of his own. He wanted to improve public education and said he hoped that Americans would remember him as "the education President." However, his plans to increase spending on education were overshadowed by concern with the impact of new spending on the federal deficit.

Bush also called for an all-out war on drugs. In his inaugural address, Bush declared,

“ When that first cocaine was smuggled in on a ship it may as well have been a deadly bacteria, so much has it hurt the body, the soul, of our country. . . . ”

Bush asked Congress for more than $7 billion to fund an antidrug program. The program called for more police and more customs agents to keep drugs from getting into the country. It also established an office of National Drug Control Policy, which would have a powerful leader. Bush also called for stiff prison sentences for drug dealers.

The main domestic issue of the Bush years was the huge national debt. During Bush's term of office, the national debt continued to increase, reaching $4 trillion. Bush came to the conclusion that the only way to cut federal deficits was to both reduce spending and raise taxes. Despite his campaign promise of

"no new taxes," Bush decided in 1990 to support a plan that would still aim to balance the federal budget, though 1991 was an unrealistic goal. However, Bush's plan included new taxes. Bush's call for a tax increase outraged many of his supporters.

In 1991, the U.S. economy fell into a steep slump. Many people believed that the tax hike had led to a recession. The economic slowdown had a deep impact on banks, which had lent money to risky business projects that had gone bankrupt. Several banks, as well as savings and loans institutions, began to fail. Savings and loans, or S&Ls, are small banks that usually concentrate on savings accounts and loans for home mortgages. Many depositors lost their money. The federal government spent billions of dollars to take over the failed S&Ls and dispose of their assets.

As unemployment soared, businesses went bankrupt, and the budget remained unbalanced, Bush's popularity declined. Changes in Eastern Europe and a threat to the nation's oil supply had forced Bush to make foreign policy a priority. Many Americans started to feel that the President cared more about foreign policy than about problems at home.

What domestic issues became the main concerns of George Bush's presidency?

Reluctant to tamper with the economy, President Bush said, "I'm just going to stay the course." Eventually, he raised taxes, which upset many people.▼

◆ NEW DIRECTIONS IN POLITICS

As the 1992 elections approached, the American public seemed more dissatisfied with government. The economy remained mired in recession. Every week it seemed that a major company announced massive **downsizing,** or laying off workers in order to cut costs.

Women's views gained more prominence. Many more women announced they would run for public office in 1992. Some of them ran in reaction to the controversy surrounding President Bush's 1991 nominee to the Supreme Court, Clarence Thomas. During Thomas's nomination hearings, a professor of law, Anita Hill, came forward to accuse Thomas of sexual harassment. Thomas strongly denied the charges. Saying there was not enough evidence to support the charges, the Senate confirmed Thomas, and he took his seat on the Supreme Court. But many women identified with Hill, and the public airing of the harassment charge made many people more aware of the problem.

The 1992 Election

The 1992 campaign reflected the worries of many Americans. On radio call-in shows, in gatherings with the candidates, in letters to the editor, and in social conversations, people voiced their fears about the future. Many said they disliked both major parties. That mood opened the way for the third-party candidacy of Texas billionaire Ross Perot. Perot drew people's attention by claiming that the government was wasteful and inefficient.

Discontent also ran deep in the two major parties. President Bush faced a challenge for the Republican nomination from Pat Buchanan, a conservative journalist. Buchanan kept up his attacks on Bush for being out of touch with the average American. Though Bush won the nomination of his party, Buchanan's fierce attacks had weakened him, and some people began to question Bush's ability to lead.

The Democrats saw the rise of Governor Bill Clinton of Arkansas, a newcomer to national politics. Nominated by the Democrats, Clinton stressed the country's economic problems throughout the campaign. With a popular slogan, "It's the economy, stupid," Clinton convinced the American people that he was better able to deal with their concerns. In November 1992, Americans elected Bill Clinton to be their President.

▲ During the 1992 campaign, Bill Clinton conducted town meetings across the country. At each meeting, voters spoke out on issues that concerned them.

Clinton's Early Programs

One of President Clinton's first concerns was to address the problems of health care. The cost of medical care and health insurance was skyrocketing, and almost 25 million Americans had no medical coverage at all. To begin to solve the problem, Clinton named his wife, Hillary Rodham Clinton, to lead a study of health care reforms. After the study was completed, he proposed a national health insurance program that would provide coverage to all Americans.

Though the proposals for a national health care system failed to gain support, other Clinton programs had more success. Clinton won approval of a budget that included a significant cut in spending and a tax increase on the wealthiest Americans. Clinton also

▲ First Lady Hillary Rodham Clinton was in charge of the President's health care plan. She is shown here in 1994 at a rally with other supporters of health care reform.

won passage of a law that required many employers to give workers, both men and women, unpaid leave to attend to urgent family responsibilities. Workers would not be penalized for taking time off for illness in the family or for the birth of a child.

Tackling a Second Term

In the congressional elections held in 1994, the Republicans won control of both houses of Congress for the first time since 1954. Led by House Speaker Newt Gingrich, of Georgia, the Republicans set out to promote a conservative agenda called the "Contract with America." It pledged to reduce the size of government and promised a number of reforms.

With Congress controlled by Republicans, Clinton had little hope of passing his own program. As elections approached in 1996, some experts predicted that Clinton would lose. However, many Americans favored Clinton's actions. When Republicans discussed cutting Medicare and Social Security benefits, Clinton led the effort to preserve those programs. Many voters, thinking that the Republicans had cut too many social programs, credited Clinton with saving them.

To oppose Clinton, the Republicans nominated Bob Dole, a senator from Kansas. During the campaign,

Dole spoke of building a bridge to the past, while Clinton declared that he would build a bridge to the future. Ross Perot once again ran as a third-party candidate. Clinton won the election with 49 percent of the popular vote. Republicans retained control of both houses of Congress.

Toward the Year 2000

In Clinton's second term, a great deal of attention focused on the accusations of special prosecutor Kenneth Starr. Clinton and others in his administration had been the subjects of a number of ongoing investigations into possible wrongdoing. On December 19, 1998, Bill Clinton was impeached by the House of Representatives on two charges—perjury and obstruction of justice. On February 12, 1999, President Clinton was acquitted of both charges by the U.S. Senate.

 What issues were important to Bill Clinton during his presidency?

Section 1 Review

Check Understanding

1. **Define** (a) supply-side economics (b) federal deficit (c) downsize

2. **Describe** how Ronald Reagan changed the nation's political course in the 1980s.

3. **Identify** Bill Clinton's focus in the 1992 election.

Critical Thinking

◆ **Connecting Past and Present** In the 1980s, Ronald Reagan said that Americans have the "right to dream heroic dreams." Why would this pledge still have appeal today?

Write About Economics

Write a brief article explaining why you think it is important or unimportant for the federal government to balance the budget each year.

BUILDING *SKILLS*

Making a Study Plan: Understanding and Reviewing

Making a study plan is the first step to improving your grades and doing well on tests. In addition to recording your assignments accurately and having whatever materials you need, you can use certain techniques to help you remember what you learn. SQ3R, which stands for *Survey, Question, Read, Recite,* and *Review,* is a study plan that can make you a more efficient student.

Here's How

Follow these steps to use the SQ3R study plan:

1. Survey the material. Get a general idea of what the chapter or section is about by scanning titles and headings. Also look at maps, charts, tables, and photographs. Then read the introduction and the conclusion or summary.

2. Make up questions. Decide what questions you should be able to answer after reading the material. Turn chapter objectives and headings and subheadings into questions. Ask *who, what, where, when, why,* and *how* questions. Write your questions in a notebook.

3. Read the material. As you read, try to answer the questions. Write down answers as you find them. Look specifically for facts, names, definitions, and dates that will be on a test. Also, find the main ideas in each section that will be the focus of an essay test.

4. Recite. Answer each of the questions you have asked in your own words. Either recite the answers to a study partner or write them down. Do not refer to your notes.

5. Review the material. Verify your answers by rereading portions of the material.

Here's Why

SQ3R is a study plan that will help you understand what you read. By using it each time you have an assignment, you will be prepared for the next test.

Practice the Skill

Try out the five steps of SQ3R on Section 1 of this chapter, pages 636–642. Think of how you might modify the plan to meet your individual needs.

Apply the Skill

Use SQ3R on a reading assignment. The chart below will help you.

Making a Study Plan

Survey	Skim over the material to get an idea of what it is about.
Question	Prepare a list of questions.
Read	Read the material in order to answer the questions you formulated, taking notes if you want to.
Recite	Answer the questions without referring to your notes.
Review	Reread the material to check your answers.

Section 2

A Time of Mixed Gains

PREVIEW

Objectives

- To evaluate the impact of Latino communities in the United States

- To examine the progress of African Americans and other groups

- To explain why racial disturbances continued to plague the nation

Vocabulary

Rainbow Coalition
underclass
workfare

The struggle for equality of political and economic opportunity occupied Americans in the 1980s and 1990s. These struggles took different forms. During the Reagan era, the federal government backed away from actively supporting affirmative action for women and minorities. Instead, as women, African Americans, and Latinos won new positions in government and business, they defended their own interests in many ways.

◆ MAKING PROGRESS

In the 1980s and 1990s, members of minority groups and poor people of all races became more active in politics. For the first time, African Americans became mayors of the nation's largest cities—New York, Los Angeles, and Chicago. When elected by Virginians to be their governor, Douglas Wilder became the first African American to serve as governor. Federico Peña and Henry Cisneros, both Mexican Americans, became the mayors of Denver and San Antonio, respectively. Both later served in Bill Clinton's Cabinet. Ben Nighthorse Campbell, a Native American, was elected senator from Colorado in 1992. In 1992, Nydia Velázquez became the first Puerto Rican woman to be elected to Congress. The number of women who entered politics continues to grow.

Latino Communities

Hispanic Americans are a diverse group, coming from many countries and cultures. Latino roots connect to Spain, Mexico, the Caribbean islands, and the Spanish-speaking countries of Central and South America. By 2010, Hispanics will be the largest minority group in the United States, making up more than 20 percent of the population.

The political clout of Latinos increases as Latino participation in the democratic process grows. By the year 2001, Latino voter registration is expected to be 8.5 million—up from 6.6 million in 1997. Since 1976, the percentage of Latinos voting in presidential elections has grown at an average rate of 15 percent. In contrast, the voter turnout in 1996 for the general population declined 10 percent.

Latinos are also making progress in the economic arena. In 1997, the U.S. Hispanic Chamber of Commerce reported that the number of Hispanic-owned businesses—barely 100,000 in 1979—had grown to more than 1,000,000. The impact of Latinos in the U.S. marketplace and at the polling booth increases every year.

Jesse Jackson's supporters in the elections of the 1980s included members of labor unions. This photograph shows him speaking to members of the Communications Workers of America. ▼

African American Gains

African Americans played an increasingly important role in the political mainstream of the 1980s. One sign of their new power was the debate over making the birthday of Martin Luther King, Jr., a national holiday. African Americans and other leaders appealed to Congress to honor King. In 1983, Congress passed a bill, which President Reagan signed, declaring King's birthday the nation's tenth federal holiday.

Another sign of the growing political strength of African Americans was Jesse Jackson's success in the 1984 and 1988 presidential campaigns. Jackson was a prominent leader of the civil rights movement in the 1960s. He had worked closely with Martin Luther King, Jr., and was with King when King was assassinated in Memphis in 1968. In 1984, Jackson formed the **Rainbow Coalition,** which brought together many different groups of people to promote opportunities for minorities.

In the fields of education and employment, African Americans made significant progress after the 1970s. In 1960, 3 percent of African American adults had graduated college. By 1996, the number of college graduates was 15 percent. The education gap between African Americans and whites was narrowing. In 1997, 86 percent of African Americans, ages 25–29, had graduated high school. The figure for whites was 87 percent. Increased education has led to higher-paying jobs. By the mid 1990s, 28 percent of African American families earned between $25,000 and $50,000 a year; 10 percent earned between $50,000 and $75,000; 6 percent earned more than $75,000.

Inequality Continues

Despite this progress, inequality remained a serious problem. While more than 20 percent of African Americans had professional, technical, or managerial positions, more than 50 percent of whites were employed in such jobs. African American unemployment was nearly double that of whites, and nearly a third of African Americans lived in poverty.

Inequality and discrimination against African Americans kept racial tensions high in the country. In 1991, these tensions exploded in Los Angeles, California. Four white Los Angeles police officers were caught on videotape beating Rodney King, an African American motorist they had pulled over for speeding. News programs broadcast the tape over and over. The beating shocked many people who thought that the officers' guilt seemed obvious.

Person ◆ *to* ◆ *Person*

Ben Nighthorse Campbell

In 1992, when Ben Nighthorse Campbell won the Colorado senatorial election, he became the first Native American in over 60 years to serve in the Senate.

Campbell was born in California in 1933. His father was a member of the Northern Cheyenne nation and his mother was of Portuguese descent. In 1876, his great-grandfather fought at Little Bighorn, where Colonel Custer's troops were defeated by the Cheyenne and the Sioux.

After graduating from San Jose State University, Campbell attended Meiji University in Tokyo. He served in the Colorado state legislature from 1983 to 1986.

Elected to the U.S. Congress in 1986, Campbell became a leader in public lands and natural resources policies. He sponsored and fought for legislation to protect the Colorado wilderness and legislation to settle the water rights of Native Americans. When the Smithsonian Institution established the National Museum of the American Indian, it was largely as a result of Campbell's efforts.

In 1992, Campbell was elected to the Senate. Though Campbell is aware of his commitment to address the problems of the entire United States, he is especially concerned with Native American issues. He says, "You are measured by how much you've given to people, how much you help people."

▲ Ben Nighthorse Campbell (1933–)

Looking Back: As a U.S. senator, what problems are particularly important to Ben Nighthorse Campbell?

On April 29, 1992, a jury found the officers not guilty. Los Angeles exploded in the worst urban violence since the 1960s. Looting spread in the central city, and rioters burned more than 1,000 stores. More than 50 people died, and the city suffered more than $1 billion in damage. The riots in Los Angeles reflected an anger and despair that lay just below the surface in several American cities.

Later, the four police officers were tried in another location, charged with a federal offense—violating Rodney King's civil rights. Two of the four officers were found guilty by a jury and sent to prison.

What political and economic progress was made by African Americans and Latinos in the 1990s?

◆ NEW POLICIES

Many men and women formerly excluded from the U.S. work force became salaried employees in the 1990s. New policies made jobs available to more people.

From Welfare to Workfare

Since the 1980s, criticism of the welfare system had continued to grow. Welfare, many claimed, locked families into a cycle of poverty from which children rarely escaped. Some critics spoke of an **underclass** of poor Americans, people who were prevented by poverty from gaining the education or skills they needed to improve their lives.

Welfare policies also came under assault because of their cost. Both federal and state governments were looking for ways to reduce government spending. In August 1996, the President and the Congress agreed on a welfare reform plan. Since the Great Depression of the 1930s, the federal government had guaranteed welfare benefits to the needy. The new law ended that guarantee. Instead, it encouraged states to set up **workfare** programs. Under workfare, people who are receiving welfare have to work in jobs that are created or found for them by local agencies. To refuse to participate in the workfare program means risking the loss of benefits. The law also prohibited welfare benefits for more than five years. A year after the reform passed, welfare rolls sharply declined. President Clinton celebrated welfare reform's success, saying,

> A lot of people said that welfare reform would never work. . . . But a year later, I think it's fair to say the debate is over. We now know that welfare reform works.

After the L.A. riots, some high school students, along with their biology teacher, started a community garden. Their efforts grew into a business, called Food from the Hood. The company produces salad dressing that is sold in about 2,000 stores across the country. The profits are used to fund college scholarships. ▶

In 1990, there were many demonstrations in support of the passage of the Americans with Disabilities Act.

However, data collected by the U.S. Census Bureau showed that employers were changing their attitudes about hiring people with disabilities. More than 22 million Americans have some kind of physical or mental disability. In the years from 1991 to 1994, the percentage of employed people with severe disabilities increased from 23 to 26 percent. This meant that about 800,000 more severely disabled individuals were working in 1994 than in 1991. A 1997 survey found that three quarters of the largest U.S. companies were hiring people with disabilities.

 What are two policies of the 1990s that affected the U.S. work force?

Yet, many Americans questioned the success of welfare reform. Critics pointed out that welfare rolls were decreasing even before the reform went into effect. They said that a strong job market allowed people to find jobs and get off welfare. Critics also worried about the effects the new welfare law would have on families. They feared there would be no one to care for children when single mothers went to their jobs. They were concerned that the reform's long-term negative effects on society would outweigh the short-term benefits.

Americans with Disabilities

The Americans with Disabilities Act (ADA), which Congress passed in 1990, has been called the most sweeping civil rights bill ever passed. The ADA's goal was to help disabled people find work and become more independent. The law required employers to create a workplace that accommodates disabled workers. The ADA also said that public buildings and public transportation had to be made accessible.

Many companies balked at the cost of accommodating the disabled. New construction, they claimed, would be too expensive. As a result, the act led to thousands of lawsuits that tried to force communities to live up to the law. The Empire State Building, in New York City, had to spend more than $2 million removing barriers so that disabled people could use its observation deck.

Section 2 Review

Check Understanding

1. **Define** (a) Rainbow Coalition (b) underclass (c) workfare

2. **Discuss** two examples of the progress made by minorities during the 1980s and 1990s.

3. **Explain** why riots broke out in Los Angeles in 1992.

4. **Evaluate** the pros and cons of the welfare reform plan.

5. **Explain** how society benefits from the Americans with Disabilities Act.

Critical Thinking

Making Inferences Why did many Americans support welfare reform?

Write About Citizenship

Connecting Past and Present Write a paragraph summarizing the accomplishments of women, African Americans, and Latinos in politics in the 1980s and early 1990s. How have their accomplishments made an impact on American society today?

Section 3

A Changing World

PREVIEW

Objectives

- To explain how and why the Cold War ended after half a century

- To describe the factors that led to the end of apartheid in South Africa

- To discuss U.S. policies toward the Marxist movements in Nicaragua

- To explore U.S. involvement in Middle Eastern affairs

Vocabulary

glasnost
apartheid
sanction

Sandinista
contra

In 1992, Mikhail Gorbachev, former leader of the Soviet Union, made a historic visit to Fulton, Missouri. In that small town, 46 years earlier, British prime minister Winston Churchill had warned that an "iron curtain" divided Europe. When Churchill spoke in the mid-1940s, the Communist regimes of Eastern Europe were just gaining power. Churchill's speech announced the beginning of the Cold War.

Gorbachev came to Fulton in 1992 to declare the Cold War was over. The speech marked an astonishing shift in world history. At the beginning of the 1980s, few people predicted the collapse of communism in Eastern Europe and the Soviet Union, but a series of events paved the way for its sudden end.

◆ THE COLD WAR ENDS

At the start of the 1980s, the Cold War seemed to be heating up, not winding down. A few weeks after taking office, Ronald Reagan expressed his belief that the Soviet Union wanted "world domination through world rule of Communist states."

Believing that the United States lagged behind the Soviet Union in military might, Reagan launched a

massive military buildup. Congress approved large spending increases for the armed forces. By 1989, the military budget was approximately double its 1980 level, as shown on the graph below.

While U.S. military strength was increasing, the Soviet Union was also building up its military strength. Since the Soviets had far less money than the Americans, new military spending put a huge strain on their economy. This crisis became the responsibility of the new Soviet leader, Mikhail Gorbachev.

Gorbachev believed the Soviet Union had to change. In 1985, he called for a policy of **glasnost**, or openness, to make the Soviet system more democratic. He also called for reforms to make the economy respond to people's needs. However, the Soviet economy continued to weaken. As it did, Gorbachev felt pressured to reduce the burden of military spending. As a result, the Soviet leader was eager to sign arms-control treaties with the United States. In 1987, Gorbachev and Ronald Reagan agreed to eliminate a large part of their nations' nuclear missile weaponry.

The Fall of Communism

Although Gorbachev was interested in reform, his primary goal was to preserve the Communist system in his country. In the end, however, his reforms could not prevent the fall of communism and the breakup of the Soviet Union.

The collapse of communism began in Eastern Europe, not in the Soviet Union. Previously, only the

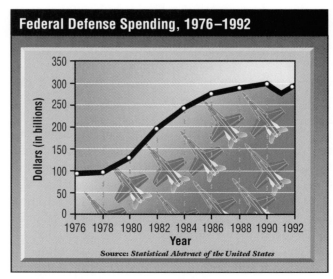

Federal Defense Spending, 1976–1992

Dollars (in billions) — Year axis: 1976 1978 1980 1982 1984 1986 1988 1990 1992

Source: *Statistical Abstract of the United States*

▲ **Economics** *Federal defense spending soared during the 1980s.* **Interpreting the Graph** *How much did federal defense spending increase between 1982 and 1984?*

threat of a Soviet military invasion had kept Communist regimes in power in Eastern Europe. By 1989, reformers realized that Gorbachev would not order military force against them. They saw that the strain on the Soviet economy prevented long and costly Soviet military operations in Eastern Europe.

Once it began, the democracy movement spread through such Eastern European nations as Poland, Czechoslovakia, Yugoslavia, and Hungary. In one country after another, small protests one week turned into mass demonstrations the next. Faced with overwhelming opposition from their own people, Communist leaders fled their countries. In East Germany in 1989, huge crowds broke through the wall that had divided Berlin. The Berlin Wall became the scene of a week-long party celebrating the peaceful overthrow of Communist rule in East Germany.

The Breakup of the Soviet Union

In 1991, the pro-democracy movement in Eastern Europe spilled over into the Soviet Union. Republic after republic declared its independence from the Soviet Union. A new federation, the Commonwealth of Independent States, replaced the old Soviet Union. The Commonwealth was made up of 11 of the 15 former Soviet republics. Russia was the largest of the old Soviet republics.

George Bush, who was President when the movement for democracy swept across much of Eastern Europe, declared,

> Communism died this year. . . . The biggest thing that has happened in the world in my life, in our lives, is this: by the grace of God, America won the Cold War.

At first, the countries of Eastern Europe and the former Soviet Union celebrated their new freedom. Reality set in quickly, however. The Communists had left economic chaos behind. Huge, state-owned companies were a burden on the economy. But the new governments were reluctant to close inefficient companies because there were no other jobs available.

In Russia the economy went into a drastic slump. Production dropped, inflation soared, and imported goods flooded the country. Ordinary Russians began to ask if *democracy* was just another word for *poverty*.

Angry and confused, Russians turned against Gorbachev. In December 1991 Gorbachev resigned,

▲ Hardline Communists attempted to overthrow Gorbachev in 1991. In this photograph, his supporters carry a giant Russian flag in Red Square to celebrate his triumph. He resigned, however, a few days later.

and Boris Yeltsin replaced him as the leader of Russia. Yeltsin favored a free-market economy. As Yeltsin dismantled the old state-owned economy, Russians began to build a free-enterprise system. However, conditions for many Russians worsened. Some Russians even called for the return of Communist rule.

Cooperation Between Russia and the U.S.

The fall of communism radically changed the relationship between the United States and Russia. No longer rivals and potential enemies, the two nations moved to cooperate in a variety of areas. For the United States, it was vital that Russia develop into a democracy. Therefore, U.S. economic advisors helped Russia complete the change to a free-market economy.

George Bush pledged $1.5 billion in aid to help Russia get through the worst of the economic crisis.

Another key area of cooperation was space exploration. In 1997, Russian cosmonauts and American astronauts lived together for months on *Mir,* a space station orbiting many miles above the earth. Looking to the future, the two countries are planning more projects, including a new international space station.

 What caused communism to collapse in Eastern Europe and the Soviet Union?

◆ AN END TO APARTHEID

Democracy arrived in another part of the world—South Africa—in the 1990s. Political change in South Africa was the result of a popular movement inside the country as well as pressures exerted from the world community. The country was urged to change the political and social structures that had been in place there for many years.

For hundreds of years, South Africa was a country of several cultures, as Dutch and British settlers were drawn to the land by its wealth of natural resources. By the late 1940s, white settlers had created a system of complete separation of the races, known by the Dutch word **apartheid** (ə-pär´-tāt), meaning separation. Apartheid denied black Africans any political voice, forced them to live in separate areas, and restricted them to low-paying jobs.

Black South Africans struggled for many years to end apartheid. The African National Congress (ANC) was a coalition of groups whose goal was to build a democratic South Africa. In 1962, police arrested a young ANC leader named Nelson Mandela for anti-government activities. Mandela spent the next 28 years in prison. Even from his cell, Mandela stayed in touch with events beyond the prison walls and continued to lead the anti-apartheid movement.

The anti-apartheid struggle took a new turn in the 1980s. A wave of demonstrations in the United States and Europe demanded that companies stop doing business with the apartheid regime. The tactics were effective. By the late 1980s, many U.S. and European companies had closed their branches in South Africa. In 1986, Congress imposed strict **sanctions** on U.S. companies doing business with South Africa. A sanction is a measure, such as a trade boycott, taken against a nation that defies international law.

In the meantime, black South Africans stepped up their protests. The apartheid government was feeling pressure from both inside and outside the country. In February 1990, the government released Nelson Mandela from prison and began to end racial segregation. In 1994, South Africa held its first truly democratic election. The ANC won a landslide victory, and Nelson Mandela became president of the new South Africa. Mandela noted that black South Africans had been inspired by several Americans, including Martin Luther King, Jr., and Abraham Lincoln. Mandela also spoke of the impact of the Declaration of Independence on the anti-apartheid movement. Mandela noted that the Declaration of Independence served as an inspiration, saying:

In Johannesburg, voters celebrated the victory of Nelson Mandela and the African National Congress in South Africa's first democratic election, held in May 1994. ▼

> " [South Africans] could not have known of your Declaration of Independence and not elected to join in the struggle to guarantee the South African people's life, liberty, and the pursuit of happiness. "

Today, South Africa has a democratic government and a slowly improving economy. In addition, the United States has a much closer relationship with a multiracial South Africa, as Americans of all ethnic backgrounds can now travel freely to the country. Furthermore, a resumed relationship between American companies and the South African government has benefited both economies.

 What internal and external pressures led to the end of apartheid in South Africa?

Study Hint

When you read about a topic, think back to what you already know. Use this known information to help you understand new aspects of the topic. When you read about relations in Latin America today, recall what you learned about U.S. relations with Latin America in the past.

◆ RELATIONS WITH LATIN AMERICA

Since the nations of Latin America won their independence from European countries, the region has been of special interest to the United States. U.S. policy has attempted to protect American investments in the region. In the 1980s, political turmoil again led to direct U.S. intervention.

Sandinistas in Nicaragua

For decades, dictators ruled the small Central American nation of Nicaragua. Because the dictators were anti-Communist, the United States supported them with military aid and other forms of assistance. In 1979, a popular movement overthrew the dictatorship and took power. The rebels called themselves **Sandinistas,** after Augusto Sandino, a patriotic hero from the 1920s.

At first, the Sandinista leadership included moderates. However, Communist leaders soon took control of the organization. When Ronald Reagan became President in 1981, he warned that the Sandinistas were creating another Communist Cuba in Central America.

Reagan ordered the Central Intelligence Agency to organize a rebel army to fight the Sandinistas. The CIA recruited Nicaraguans opposed to the new government and provided them with money, guns, and training. Because they opposed the Sandinistas, the guerrillas were called **contras,** a Spanish word

meaning "against." Soon the Sandinistas were fighting a civil war against a U.S.-backed army.

The contra war divided Americans. Many criticized the contras for violating human rights by attacking civilians. Other Americans supported the contras because they feared that the Sandinistas would spread communism in Central America. Congress approved military aid to the contras at first. Then it passed a law forbidding all aid to either side.

In 1986, newspapers revealed that members of the Reagan administration had violated this law by secretly giving money to the contras. The money, it was claimed, had come from the secret sale of weapons to Iran.

President Reagan, who claimed to know nothing about the illegal arms deal, appointed a special committee to investigate. As investigators probed what became known as the Iran-Contra affair, officials admitted that they had planned to use the money from the weapons sale to create a secret military unit in Nicaragua. The unit would carry out missions without the knowledge of the American people. A congressional hearing led to the indictment and conviction of several government officials.

The Nicaraguan conflict finally ended in 1989. The United States pressured the Sandinistas to hold free and open elections. They did, and Nicaraguan voters turned them out of office. The new government of Violeta Barrios de Chamorro launched programs to reduce the size of the national army. The United States stopped funding the contras

▲ President Violetta Barrios de Chamorro led 21 heads of state during a Latin American summit meeting in Nicaragua in 1991.

and instead gave aid to the new government. With this aid, the Nicaraguans worked to improve the economy, which remains one of the poorest in Latin America.

Intervening in Panama and Haiti

Like Ronald Reagan, George Bush also faced difficult decisions in Central America. This time the trouble spot was Panama, where in 1983, General Manuel Noriega had seized power. At first, Noriega's relations with the United States were good. They went bad when it was suspected that Noriega was trafficking in drugs.

In 1989, when Panamanian soldiers killed a U.S. soldier, President Bush ordered 14,000 American troops into Panama. After brief but bloody fighting, Noriega surrendered. He was brought to the United States to stand trial on drug-smuggling charges. Noriega was convicted and sentenced to 40 years in prison.

A very different situation led to U.S. intervention in Haiti. After many years of dictatorship, Haitians freely elected Jean-Bertrand Aristide to be president in 1990. Less than a year later, the Haitian military overthrew Aristide and imposed a dictatorship. Thousands of Haitians took to the sea in flimsy boats to reach the safety of the United States.

The United States and other nations pressured Haiti's military dictators to restore democracy. The military at first agreed to the plan, but then went back on their agreement. With a U.S. force on its way toward Haiti, the military rulers finally agreed to accept Aristide as the leader of Haiti. Thousands of American troops landed with Aristide to maintain order. Most of the soldiers left in six months. They restored water and electricity and trained a new police force. In 1996, when Aristide's term of office ended, he turned over power to his long-time ally, Rene Preval.

? How has the United States dealt with internal conflicts in Latin America?

◆ PROGRESS AND SETBACKS IN THE MIDDLE EAST

Because the Middle East is the source of much of the oil that is consumed by Americans, the region is of great interest to the United States. Concern grows as conflict continues among several of the Middle East nations. American diplomats travel back and forth attempting to help settle the disputes that threaten the region.

The Gulf War

In 1990, Saddam Hussein, dictator of Iraq, invaded oil-rich Kuwait and seized control of the country. There were two important reasons for the United States to oppose Hussein. The first was the threat to the oil supply. The second was the fear that this aggression would lead to a larger war. However, President Bush did not want to act alone. He formed a United Nations alliance with other nations that were also upset by Hussein's actions. The alliance included Egypt, Saudi Arabia, Syria, Pakistan, France, Italy, and Great Britain.

Despite the powerful coalition, Iraq refused to withdraw from Kuwait. On January 17, 1991, the allies launched an attack they called Operation Desert Storm. The attack began with a massive bombing campaign that destroyed Iraq's air defense centers, leaving the coalition in command of the skies over Iraq. By February 28, the Persian Gulf War was over and Kuwait was free. Two heroes of the war were Norman Schwarzkopf, the commanding general, and Colin Powell, the chairman of the Joint Chiefs of Staff.

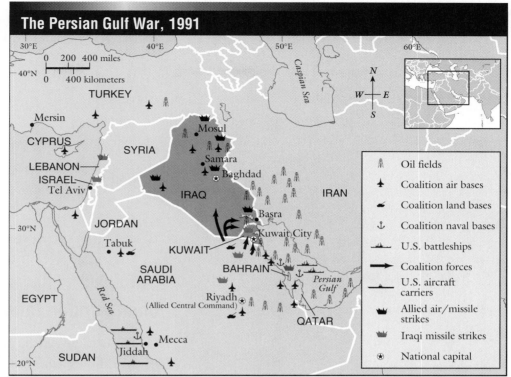

The Persian Gulf War, 1991

Geography *The locations of oil fields and pipelines were important in the Persian Gulf War.* **Interpreting the Map** *Which country had the greatest number of oil fields? What was the relationship of these oil fields to the Persian Gulf?* ▶

In the Persian Gulf War, depicted in the map above, about 150 Americans died in battle and about 100,000 Iraqis were killed. The coalition set conditions to ensure that Iraq would not rebuild its military. For years after the defeat, Hussein would violate the terms of the agreement. Throughout the late 1990s, Hussein tried to block UN teams from inspecting Iraqi facilities to see if weapons for chemical warfare were manufactured there.

Israel and Palestine

The United States has also played a crucial role in trying to resolve the conflict between Israel and its Arab neighbors. Under pressure from the United States, the Palestine Liberation Organization (PLO) promised to stop terrorist activities. In 1993 and 1995, the PLO and Israel reached an agreement that gave the Palestinians control of the Gaza Strip and parts of the West Bank.

The peace process still has a long way to go. Frequent outbreaks of violence continue to occur on both sides. However, many Arabs and Israelis agree that diplomatic negotiations are the only way to resolve their conflicts. The United States continues to work to help bring about a fair and lasting peace in the region.

 What are the causes of continuing conflict in the Middle East?

Section 3 Review

Check Understanding

1. **Define** (a) glasnost (b) apartheid (c) sanction (d) Sandinista (e) contra

2. **Analyze** the role of Gorbachev in bringing about an end to the Cold War.

3. **Identify** Nelson Mandela and describe his role in ending apartheid in South Africa.

Critical Thinking

Making Inferences Why did the United States act with other nations in the Persian Gulf War?

Write About Economics

◆**Connecting Past and Present** Write the headline and the first paragraph of an editorial about how the end of the Cold War has affected U.S. politics and economics in the past decade.

Chapter 31
Review

CHAPTER SUMMARY

Section 1
Ronald Reagan's election in 1980 reflected a conservative mood in the nation. Reagan cut taxes and slashed federal social spending programs. He pushed ahead with his conservative agenda in his second term. George Bush won the election in 1988. A poor economy and unfulfilled campaign promises led to Bush's defeat and the victory of Democrat Bill Clinton in 1992. In 1994, disappointment with Clinton led to a Republican victory in both houses of Congress. However, Clinton won reelection in 1996.

Section 2
Members of minority groups made some significant political, educational, and economic gains in the 1980s and 1990s, but inequality remained an issue. Racial tensions led to riots in Los Angeles in 1992.

Section 3
The 1980s and 1990s were years of remarkable change. Communism in Eastern Europe and the Soviet Union collapsed. While the Cold War was over, the United States faced new complexities in its foreign affairs. The United States became involved in Nicaragua, Haiti, and Panama. When Iraq invaded Kuwait, the United States led UN forces in the Persian Gulf War.

Connecting ◆ Past and Present

In past decades, the United States increasingly focused on foreign affairs. Yet when polled, the American people consistently said that they were most concerned with events in the United States. Where should the focus of the United States be today, at home or abroad? Explain your answer.

Using Vocabulary

For each term below, write a sentence that shows its meaning.

1. federal deficit
2. sanction
3. contra
4. Rainbow Coalition
5. underclass
6. workfare
7. glasnost
8. apartheid
9. Sandinista
10. downsize

Check Understanding

1. **Explain** the agenda of the New Right.
2. **List** three elements of the conservative agenda of President Reagan.
3. **Explain** the campaign promise that George Bush did not fulfill and list the results of this failure.
4. **Describe** the role the economy played in the 1992 presidential election.
5. **Identify** the Americans with Disabilities Act and describe its significance.
6. **Identify** the causes of conflict in the Middle East.
7. **Explain** how the welfare system changed in 1996.
8. **Summarize** the events that led to the end of the Cold War.
9. **Describe** how U.S. policy toward South Africa changed with the end of apartheid.
10. **Explain** why the United States fought in the Persian Gulf War.

Critical Thinking

1. **Drawing Conclusions** Why do you think Americans rejected Carter and elected Reagan so decisively?

2. **Comparing** Compare the attitudes of Reagan, Bush, and Clinton toward federal budget deficits.

3. **Analyzing** How did President Reagan think supply-side economics would benefit the country?

4. **Comparing** Compare the reasons the United States intervened in Nicaragua with the reasons the United States intervened in Panama.

◆ **Connecting Past and Present** What in the Declaration of Independence inspired the anti-apartheid movement in South Africa?

Writing to Show Cause and Effect

Write an essay describing how the economy affected presidential politics in the 1980s and 1990s. Use specific examples to show cause and effect. Describe issues such as the balanced budget, recession, health care, welfare reform, and aid to education.

Interpreting the Timeline

Use the timeline on pages 634–635 to answer these questions.

1. Who was the first woman appointed to the Supreme Court?

2. In what year was the Iran-Contra affair exposed?

3. Which events reflect peaceful progress being made in foreign countries?

Putting Skills to Work

MAKING A STUDY PLAN

In the Building Skills lesson on page 643, you learned to use SQ3R as a study plan. Now try it out on the next chapter. Follow these steps:

- Survey the material carefully.
- Then create questions based on the objectives, main headings, and subheadings.
- After you have read the chapter, reread it to find answers to your questions, taking notes if necessary.
- Answer the questions by reciting them aloud or by writing them down. Make sure you use your own words and do not refer to your notes.
- Finally, review the material to see if your answers are correct.

Portfolio Project

A TIME CAPSULE

Time capsules are often prepared to commemorate a notable event. If you were preparing a time capsule to depict the last 25 years of the twentieth century, what items would you include in it? Remember that the capsule is intended to show people in the distant future what life was like during this period.

Go back over the chapter and review its main ideas and notable events. Of these ideas and events, which would most educate people in the future about the last quarter of the twentieth century? What artifacts would be most representative of these ideas and events? Think of music CDs, newspaper articles, videos, books, clothing, photographs, and any other items that would fit into a capsule measuring five feet by ten feet.

Chapter 32
Americans Face the Future 1985–the future

CHAPTER PREVIEW

Section 1 The United States and the World

With the collapse of communism in the Soviet Union and Eastern Europe, the United States is the only remaining superpower.

Section 2 Conserving the Environment

Americans are working to clean up their environment and limit their consumption of nonrenewable energy sources.

Section 3 Science Changes the Way We Live

Technological innovations have led to changes in communication, medicine, entertainment, and in the workplace.

Section 4 A Nation of Diversity

As the United States enters a new century, complexities and challenges accompany growth and prosperity.

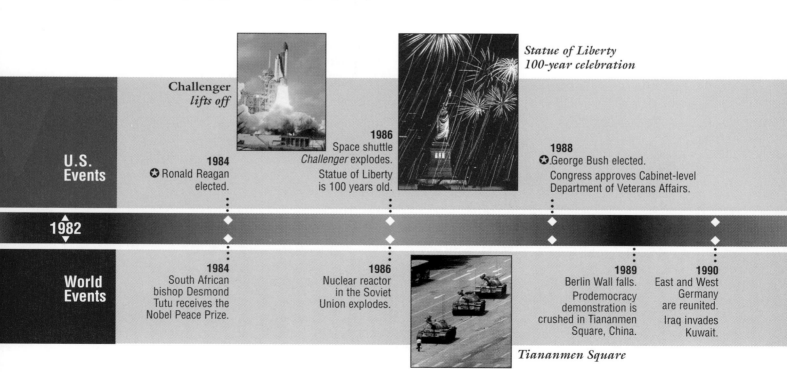

Statue of Liberty 100-year celebration

Challenger *lifts off*

U.S. Events

1984
✪ Ronald Reagan elected.

1986
Space shuttle *Challenger* explodes.
Statue of Liberty is 100 years old.

1988
✪ George Bush elected.
Congress approves Cabinet-level Department of Veterans Affairs.

▲ **1982** ▼

World Events

1984
South African bishop Desmond Tutu receives the Nobel Peace Prize.

1986
Nuclear reactor in the Soviet Union explodes.

1989
Berlin Wall falls.
Prodemocracy demonstration is crushed in Tiananmen Square, China.

1990
East and West Germany are reunited.
Iraq invades Kuwait.

Tiananmen Square

Portfolio Project

A BRIEFING PAPER

Government officials and company executives have little time to read long, complicated documents. To keep them informed, summaries of the most important issues—called briefing papers—are often written for them. As you read this chapter, look for information that would help a newcomer to the United States understand the future challenges that face the country. At the end of this chapter, you will write a briefing paper directed at people who are making new homes in this country.

▲ *The solar panels on this satellite collect energy that enables the satellite to receive and transmit signals to Earth.* ◆◆ **Connecting Past and Present** *Why is solar energy a good source of power for a satellite? How is solar energy used on Earth today?*

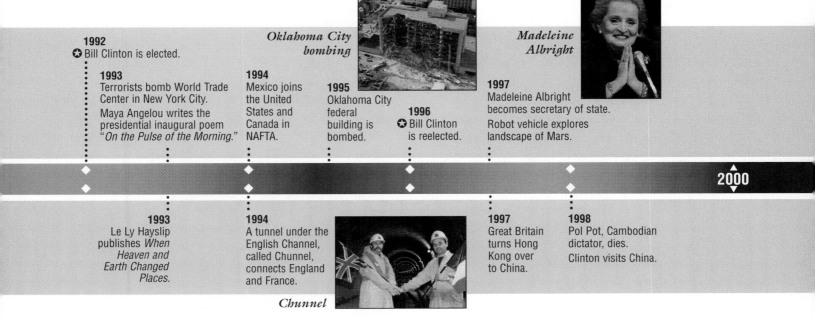

1992
✪ Bill Clinton is elected.

1993
Terrorists bomb World Trade Center in New York City.

Maya Angelou writes the presidential inaugural poem "*On the Pulse of the Morning.*"

Oklahoma City bombing

1994
Mexico joins the United States and Canada in NAFTA.

1995
Oklahoma City federal building is bombed.

1996
✪ Bill Clinton is reelected.

Madeleine Albright

1997
Madeleine Albright becomes secretary of state.

Robot vehicle explores landscape of Mars.

2000

1993
Le Ly Hayslip publishes *When Heaven and Earth Changed Places.*

1994
A tunnel under the English Channel, called Chunnel, connects England and France.

Chunnel

1997
Great Britain turns Hong Kong over to China.

1998
Pol Pot, Cambodian dictator, dies.

Clinton visits China.

Section 1

The United States and the World

PREVIEW

Objectives

- To explain how the end of the Cold War created new power relationships among the nations of the world

- To describe the characteristics of the new global economy

- To analyze the new economic challenges that the United States faces

Vocabulary

ethnic cleansing	quality control
human rights	Pacific Rim
interdependent	multinational
trade deficit	

The Cold War shaped American life from the 1940s to the late 1980s. With the collapse of communism, the Cold War came to an end. In the post-Cold War world, the United States would face new challenges and forge new relationships.

◆ CONFLICTS AROUND THE WORLD

When the Cold War ended in the late 1980s, the United States emerged as the world's only military superpower. No longer was there an arms race with a powerful Soviet Union. Americans became increasingly aware that in the new emerging world, economic power would be as important as military strength.

During the Cold War, the Soviet Union and its allies were seen as military threats to the United States. Today, the United States faces foreign policy challenges that are more complicated than those of the Cold War. These challenges include regional conflicts and civil wars in Asia, the Middle East, Africa, and Europe. In the spring of 1998, a major concern arose over the testing of nuclear bombs by India and Pakistan.

Uprising in China

The end of the Cold War did not mean the triumph of democracy throughout the world. In the late 1990s, democracy was still struggling in much of Africa, the Middle East, and East Asia. In China, a movement to embrace democracy challenged the Communist government, but after a dramatic confrontation, communism remained in place.

Young university students spearheaded China's prodemocracy uprising. In 1989, thousands of students and workers gathered in Tiananmen Square in downtown Beijing. The protesters demanded free speech, democracy, and an end to corruption.

Throughout the world, people wondered if the world's largest dictatorship would become more democratic. The answer came quickly. Instead of agreeing to the reforms, China's leaders crushed the uprising. Chinese troops killed hundreds of workers and students and jailed many more.

Today China is still firmly in the grip of its Communist leaders. They have brought many reforms to China's economy, but they maintain a strict political dictatorship. Action against political dissenters is quick and harsh. Americans debate whether the United States should be friendly toward a nation that has mistreated dissenters. Many Americans strongly opposed a 1997 visit to the United States by China's leader, Jiang Zemin (jē´-äng zemin´).

Chinese university students came face-to-face with the government's military forces on Tiananmen Square in 1989. ▼

Violence in Somalia and Bosnia

American policymakers feel a great responsibility to help other countries who turn to them for help. But they are reluctant to send U.S. troops into conflicts that may drag on with no clear goal. Events in Eastern Europe and Africa in the 1990s demonstrated the risk of intervening in civil wars. Although people everywhere hoped that a new era of peace would follow the Cold War, problems in the world persisted.

In Africa, the end of the Cold War was the beginning of new struggles. In 1991, fierce fighting broke out in Somalia as rival armies fought to control the nation. The violence kept farmers from planting their fields. This led to widespread starvation.

To deal with the famine, Americans joined a UN peacekeeping force that entered the country in October 1992. The troops handed out food to the starving civilians, but they had little success in keeping the peace.

Though the peacekeepers were in Somalia to help its people, they soon came under attack from rival Somali factions. In the summer of 1993, Somali fighters killed several American soldiers and dragged their bodies through the streets. President Clinton recalled American troops from Somalia in early 1994. With the U.S. troops gone, the conflict between Somali factions resumed.

In Eastern Europe, the rise of independent governments led to unexpected violence. There, the old Communist regimes had dominated and suppressed rivalries between different ethnic groups. The fall of communism unleashed conflicts between these groups.

In the former Yugoslavia, Europe experienced the worst violence since World War II. Yugoslavia split into three countries—Croatia, Serbia, and Bosnia and Herzegovina. Croats, Muslims, and Serbs fought for control in Bosnia. In areas under dispute, soldiers drove innocent people from their homes. American negotiators tried to end the fighting, but the killing went on. Serbian troops followed a policy of **ethnic cleansing**—emptying villages of their Muslim and Croat inhabitants and killing many of the men.

In April 1994, NATO forces at last intervened forcefully. American and European bombers attacked Serbian artillery positions. Fearing they were losing ground, the Serbs signed a peace treaty in Dayton, Ohio, in November 1995. The fighting stopped at last, and Bosnians began to recover from the war. The United States and other NATO nations pushed to put mass murderers on trial for war crimes—as the Allies had done after World War II.

▲ Two New York City police officers comforted an injured woman immediately after the bombing of the World Trade Center in 1993.

Terrorism

Since 1988, fighting terrorism has been a major concern of the United States. In that year, terrorists blew up an American jet over Lockerbie, Scotland, killing all 259 people on board. In 1993, six people were killed when terrorists set off a bomb at the World Trade Center in New York City.

It is difficult for the United States or the UN to stop terrorism. Terrorist groups are usually small and undercover. Although a few countries secretly finance terrorist activities, terrorists do not openly represent a government. As a result, pressure cannot be applied to terrorists as it can to a nation.

Many terrorist attacks have been directed against American policies in the Middle East. Americans hope that a lasting peace in the Middle East will bring an end to the terrorist activities of militant groups.

However, not all terrorist activities stem from outside the United States. In 1995, American terrorists bombed the federal building in Oklahoma City, killing 168 people. The people responsible for the bombing were Americans protesting policies of the U.S. government. Two men were arrested, tried in court, and convicted of the crime.

The FBI and CIA are increasingly focused on collecting information about terrorist groups and preventing attacks. In recent years, American and foreign agents have made a number of arrests and have foiled several planned attacks.

Human Rights

The basic freedoms that everyone deserves to have are called **human rights.** After World War II, the United Nations unanimously approved a Declaration of Human Rights. It echoed the words of the Declaration of Independence in proclaiming,

> **All human beings are born free and equal in dignity and rights. They are endowed with reason and conscience and should act towards one another in a spirit of brotherhood.**

It is not easy to achieve such high ideals. During the Cold War, both the Soviet Union and the United States supported governments that violated human rights. After the Cold War, the United States found it difficult to persuade some governments to respect the basic rights of their citizens.

Yet there are definite signs of progress. Since the Cold War ended, concern about human rights has grown. Groups such as Amnesty International have focused world attention on regimes that abuse human rights. World pressure has resulted in some notable successes. For example, a widespread economic embargo forced South Africa to end the policy of apartheid.

At other times, more active measures have been taken. In Haiti, Somalia, and Bosnia, the United States intervened to stop violence and defend human rights. But many people believe that U.S. intervention has to be limited. In the mid-1990s, the United States cut its defense budget. As a result, several military bases were closed, and fewer weapons were purchased.

Also, many Americans question the wisdom of sending troops into dangerous situations that present no direct threat to U.S. security. For that reason, a large number of Americans opposed U.S. intervention in Somalia and Bosnia. American Presidents have argued that small conflicts, if unresolved, can develop into larger ones.

? **What are the arguments for and against U.S. intervention in foreign conflicts?**

◆ LIVING IN A GLOBAL ECONOMY

Today, the economy of the United States and the economies of other countries are **interdependent.** This means that the economies of nations around the world depend on each other. For example, the United States sells beef, wheat, airplanes, cars, and computers in markets all over the globe. In turn, it imports oil from Mexico, televisions from Japan, and toys from China. Nations invest in one another's stock markets. Service industries in many countries expand as the rate of tourism continues to grow. Economic interdependence means that decisions and events beyond the borders of the United States affect its economy in important ways.

Growing Competition

For 30 years after World War II, the United States was unchallenged as the world's economic leader. However, by the 1970s, the American economy faced new competition. Low-cost, high-quality cars, televisions, and other goods from Japan found enthusiastic buyers in the United States. As a result, a **trade deficit** developed—that is, the value of the goods that the United States imported was more than the value of the goods it exported. Americans bought more products than they sold. As consumers bought fewer U.S.

▲ *The toys being made in this factory in China will be sold in stores throughout the world.*

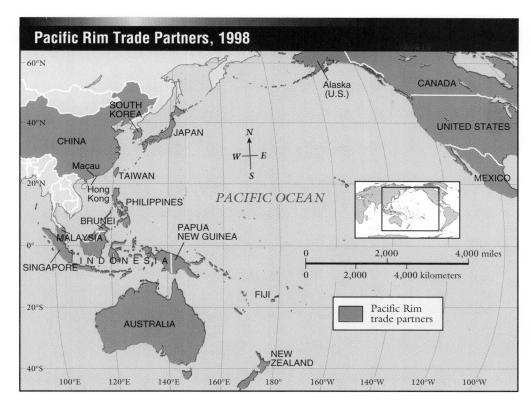

Pacific Rim Trade Partners, 1998

Pacific Rim trade partners

◀ **Economics** *Many countries that border on the Pacific Ocean are trade partners.* **Interpreting the Map** *What trade partner is directly south of Papua New Guinea?*

cars and appliances, American auto and steel companies laid off hundreds of thousands of their workers.

In recent years, American industry has rebounded. Many companies have modernized their plants, adding new machinery controlled by sophisticated computers. American manufacturers also pay more attention to **quality control,** making sure that the goods produced are consistently well made. New U.S. factories are more efficient and more profitable.

Despite this progress, many American industries may never again offer the number of high-paying jobs that they did before the 1980s. The price of American goods competes with lower-priced products made in countries where wages are lower. Competitive pressure has led some U.S. industries to continue to downsize and to modernize. Automation requires fewer employees to run a company.

While the U.S. economy is still the largest in the world, it faces competition from other countries. Japan and Germany are economically strong. In the 1980s and much of the 1990s, many of the countries of the **Pacific Rim,** nations with a boundary that touches the Pacific Ocean, had high growth rates. Pacific Rim countries include South Korea, Taiwan, Singapore, Indonesia, and Malaysia. The map above shows the Pacific Rim countries that are major trade partners. In the late 1990s, there was an economic decline in a few

Pacific Rim countries. A gradual recovery was expected. The economy of the People's Republic of China is the fastest growing in the region. In the 1990s, China's economy increased at an average rate of about 11 percent a year. Its growth rate will soon place it among the world's leading economic powers.

The United States also faces increasing competition from Europe. The nations of Western Europe have taken steps to unify their economies by forming a European Union. In 1999, 11 European nations started to use a common currency called the euro. By 2002, the euro will have replaced the French franc, Italian lira, British pound, German mark, and other currencies of the nations of Europe. The European Union will be a powerful trading group.

The NAFTA Treaty

Faced with competition from Europe and Asia, the United States joined with other nations of North America to create its own trade organization. In 1992, the United States, Canada, and Mexico signed the North American Free Trade Agreement, or NAFTA. NAFTA, which went into effect in 1994, seeks to promote trade between the nations of North America. This means that most goods produced in the three nations can move from nation to nation without tariffs. The

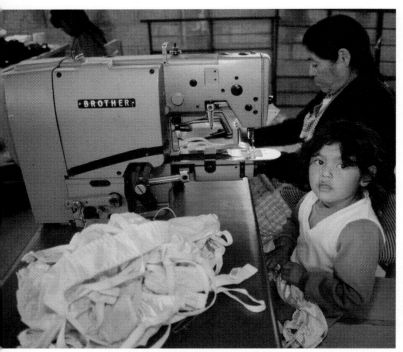

▲ *A shortage of day care in Mexico makes it necessary for a woman employed in an American factory to bring her child to work.*

trade agreement encourages the formation of foreign-owned factories in Mexico that produce goods that are exported to the United States and other countries.

Before Congress approved the treaty, Americans fiercely debated NAFTA. Supporters claimed that reducing tariffs on imports would benefit the U.S. economy. Canadians and Mexicans, they said, would buy more U.S. goods, creating new jobs for Americans. Opponents of NAFTA warned that U.S. companies would move to Mexico, where wages are much lower. They also charged that Mexican workers are exploited by low wages and poor working conditions. Since NAFTA took effect, some American factories have moved south of the border. But the loss of jobs has been smaller than critics of NAFTA had predicted. In the meantime, trade between Canada, Mexico, and the United States has surged. NAFTA has re-established a free trade area with a population of 360 million and a total economic output of $6 trillion annually. It is the second largest free trade area in the world after the European Union, which has a population of 375 million and a total economic output of $7 trillion annually.

A large corporation that has operations in several countries is called a **multinational.** Multinationals, such as General Electric in the United States and Mitsubishi in Japan, have spurred economic interdependence. Because multinationals do business in so many countries, they are beyond the control of any one government. If taxes or wages rise too high in one country, multinationals simply move production to another one. Critics say that multinationals exploit workers by building factories where they can pay employees the lowest wages. The companies reply that they provide employment that would not otherwise be available.

 What are the characteristics of the world's economy in the post-Cold War era?

Section 1 Review

Check Understanding

1. **Define** (a) ethnic cleansing (b) human rights (c) interdependent (d) trade deficit (e) quality control (f) Pacific Rim (g) multinational

2. **Describe** the changes that the collapse of communism brought to international relations.

3. **Explain** how the United States cooperated with the United Nations in Somalia.

4. **Identify** the economic challenges the United States faces in the future.

5. **Identify** the European Union.

6. **Give** the arguments made for and against NAFTA.

Critical Thinking

◆**Connecting Past and Present** How do you think economic interdependence has changed relationships between nations today?

Write About Government

It is a presidential election year. The candidate of your choice has asked you to produce a TV commercial about whether the United States should protect human rights around the world. Write a storyboard for a commercial, describing the candidate's point of view.

BUILDING SKILLS

....

Taking a Test: Preparing for Your History Exam

Taking a test involves using your knowledge of a given topic to answer different types of questions, often in a limited amount of time. There are some basic test-taking skills that you can master in order to improve your test scores.

Here's How

Follow these steps to take a test:

1. Skim the whole test quickly. Get a sense of how much time you will need to complete each part of the test.

2. Read each question carefully before you answer. You must understand the question to answer it correctly.

3. Look for key words in the questions. The following direction words tell you how to organize your answer.

Key Direction Words	
compare	show similarities
contrast	show differences
explain	inform about facts or give directions
tell why	give reasons
list	give examples
review	summarize
describe	create a vivid picture
show	demonstrate logically
trace	discuss origin and development
identify	place the person or event in time, relate to other people or events
discuss	present ideas
define	give the meaning
illustrate	give examples
evaluate	give good and bad points and come to a conclusion

4. Answer the easiest questions first. This assures that you will answer everything you know best before the time runs out.

5. In multiple-choice tests, read all choices before you choose an answer so that you are sure you are choosing the best one. If you are unsure of an answer, try to eliminate the choices that are obviously wrong. Then you can make an educated guess regarding the remaining possibilities.

6. Try to leave a few minutes to look over your work.

Here's Why

Becoming "test wise" is a practical way of improving your grades.

Practice the Skill

With a partner, analyze each of the five items in the Check Understanding part of the Section 1 Review on page 662. For example, the first item requires you to give the meaning of seven vocabulary terms from the section.

Apply the Skill

Using the material in Section 1, write five questions. Use key direction words from the chart when formulating your questions. Try to make them as challenging as possible. Exchange questions with a partner. Answer each other's questions; then together check the answers. Make sure all answers are appropriate to the key direction words. Explore how the questions and the answer choices might have been more effectively expressed.

Section 2

Conserving the Environment

PREVIEW

Objectives

- To identify environmental problems facing the United States and the world

- To examine how concerns about nuclear power have spurred the search for alternative energy sources

- To describe concerns over the possibility of global warming

Vocabulary

acid rain	global warming
renewable	greenhouse effect
deforestation	

Most Americans are aware that economic progress has taken its toll on the environment. Before the Industrial Revolution, the use of fuels was limited. Today, nearly all air and water pollution is the result of modern cars, power plants, and factories.

◆ ENVIRONMENTAL PROBLEMS

One problem directly related to industrialization is **acid rain,** rain polluted with sulfuric acid. Acid rain has become a worldwide problem, contaminating air and water—even killing fish. In the Ohio Valley, electric plants produce energy by burning coal. Power plant chimneys shoot tons of sulfur dioxide into the air. Winds then carry the gas east, where it mixes with rain and falls to Earth. Similarly, factories in central and eastern Europe send acid rain into Scandinavia and Siberia, where it is destroying forests. In parts of China, pollution is already so bad that brown snow sometimes falls.

The United States, one of the world's largest producers of acid rain, has begun to address the problem by trying to limit the output of chemicals that cause acid rain. The Environmental Protection Agency

(EPA) has put a limit on the amount of sulfur dioxide that power plants may produce. To meet this requirement, coal-burning plants in the Midwest are switching to cleaner fuel. In recent years, the output of sulfur dioxide has slowly dropped.

Lakes and rivers in the United States are cleaner today than they were 25 years ago. The Clean Water Act of 1972, which set new standards for controlling pollution, helped bring back life to many bodies of water. For example, for many years New Yorkers were unable to swim or fish in the Hudson River. Chemical plants and other factories had dumped toxic waste into the river for many decades. Today the cleanup of the Hudson has been so effective that upstate New Yorkers have begun to swim in the river and even eat fish caught in its waters.

Communities are also taking steps to reduce waste materials by recycling cans, bottles, and newspapers. Recycling means reusing the metal, glass, plastic, and paper that was once treated as waste. Many cities now sell their trash to recycling companies instead of burying it in landfills or dumping it in the ocean. Appliances such as refrigerators and washers are recycled and their metal is reused. In 1996, about 45 million large appliances were recycled. They produced 2.8 million tons of recycled steel—equal to the steel in 48 aircraft carriers.

 What problems have been identified as threats to the environment?

◆ MAINTAINING ENERGY SUPPLIES

Americans use more energy than people in any other nation. Although they make up only 4 percent of the world's population, Americans own 25 percent of the world's cars and trucks. They consume 25 percent of the world's total energy supplies. With about 260 million people, the United States uses as much energy as the combined 2.2 billion people of China and India.

The Oil Crisis

Most Americans did not worry about energy supplies until the 1970s, when oil-producing nations in the Middle East stopped selling oil to the United States. At that time, the federal government ordered U.S. automakers to build cars that used fuel more efficiently. By the mid-1980s, the average American automobile got twice the gas mileage that was common in the early 1970s.

664 ◆ Unit 10

Despite these advances, the United States did not lose its dependence on foreign oil. Today, Americans import even more oil than they did in 1973.

Nuclear Energy

The energy crisis led to the exploration of new sources of energy. Nuclear power seemed like the best alternative. The issue of nuclear safety, however, became a public issue with an accident at Three Mile Island, a nuclear power plant in Pennsylvania. It was feared, mistakenly, that dangerously toxic fumes had escaped into the atmosphere. Then, in 1986, an explosion at the Chernobyl nuclear plant in the Soviet Union killed 31 people and sent a huge radioactive cloud across Europe.

Today many Americans feel that the risks of nuclear power are greater than its benefits. Plans to build a number of new nuclear power plants have been scrapped, and several plants have been shut down. Less than 10 percent of our total energy demand is currently supplied by nuclear power.

Solar and wind energy are alternative sources of power. In the Southwest, solar panels are being used to convert the sun's rays into electric current. On California hills, giant windmills harness the breeze to produce electricity. Because these sources of energy will never run out, they are called **renewable.**

Sources of energy that are not renewable—oil, coal, and wood—are the most commonly used sources of energy today. But scientists believe that renewable energy could ease U.S. energy problems. They are working to invent practical ways to use renewable energy, such as interlocking solar shingles that would turn a roof into a giant solar panel.

Protecting Forests

When European settlers first came to North America, a dense forest stretched from Maine to Florida. Since then, all but 5 percent of the nation's original forest has been cut. Today, scientists believe that this process, called **deforestation,** is a serious threat to the environment throughout the world, especially in Brazil and Indonesia. In heavily logged areas, topsoil has been washed away. Trees produce oxygen, and cutting them down reduces the natural supply of oxygen. It also destroys the habitat of many animals. Some species of animals, such as the Indian tiger and the European bison, are approaching extinction, or dying out, because of deforestation.

Global Warming

Another environmental issue is **global warming,** which is the theory that the earth's average temperature

◀ The Three Mile Island nuclear power plant still operates on the Susquehanna River in central Pennsylvania. The plant itself is the square building in the center of the photograph; its four cooling towers surround it.

◀ Deforestation is a major problem in the Amazon rain forest of Brazil. It can result from large logging projects, or from farming methods of cutting and burning patches of forest for farmland.

is slowly rising. A major cause of global warming appears to be increased energy consumption. As nations become more industrialized, gases such as carbon dioxide and methane build up. The sun heats the earth, and the gases—forming a barrier—trap the heat. The process by which the planet is kept from cooling off is called the **greenhouse effect.**

Global warming may have serious consequences. Rising temperatures may melt ice fields and raise the level of the world's oceans. Looking for ways to slow down global warming, scientists and world leaders met in Rio de Janeiro in 1992. Many scientists are hopeful that dependence on nonrenewable energy sources will be reduced by the year 2010.

Referring to the earth's environmental problems, Vice President Al Gore has written,

> ". . . this crisis will be resolved only if individuals take some responsibility for it. By educating ourselves and others . . . each one of us can make a difference."

? What major problems have to be addressed to conserve the environment?

Section 2 Review

Check Understanding

1. **Define** (a) acid rain (b) renewable (c) deforestation (d) global warming (e) greenhouse effect

2. **Describe** a result of the 1970s energy crisis.

3. **Identify** the reasons for concern over global warming.

Critical Thinking

◆ **Connecting Past and Present** Why is global warming a greater concern today than in the past?

Write About Citizenship

For a debate on energy conservation, prepare a list of points that supports your position: <u>Resolved:</u> Government regulations on fuel conservation are a threat to freedom.

Section 3

Science Changes the Way We Live

PREVIEW

Objectives

- To describe how technological advances have changed American lives at home, at work, and at play

- To explain how space exploration has spurred technological advances

- To describe scientific advances in health care

Vocabulary

computer literate	genetic engineering
telecommunications	clone

Technology, though contributing to many of today's environmental problems, has improved modern life in many ways. Technology has significantly changed the way Americans work, study, and play.

◆ THE REVOLUTION IN TECHNOLOGY

The first computers were clumsy giants. The Electronic Numerical Integrator and Calculator (ENIAC), built at the University of Pennsylvania in 1946, weighed 30 tons and was as big as a railroad freight car. Today's laptop computers are far more powerful, yet they weigh only a few pounds. In development are computers, storing vast amounts of information, that will be the size and shape of wallets. Technology is changing so rapidly that state-of-the-art computers sold one year become outdated by the next.

Computers in Daily Life

At first, only scientists and military personnel had access to computers. ENIAC, for example, was used to speed up calculations for military engineers. Today, computers are used by workers in gas stations, video stores, restaurants, offices, and in almost every other workplace. Many families do their taxes and keep track of their expenses with personal computers. Students use word processing to write school reports.

Computers have made revolutionary changes in the way people get and use information. Individuals, organizations, and businesses—with modems—can connect to Internet sites all over the world. The Internet refers to a network of computers connected together. Workers use e-mail to communicate over distances almost instantly. Knowledge formerly obtained through research in a library now can be accessed at home through the Internet. Over the Internet, people can read international newspapers and magazines, shop for goods, and exchange information with others who have similar interests.

Many of today's jobs require workers to be **computer literate**, that is, to have the basic skills needed to use a computer. A computer-literate person has an advantage over those who do not possess the skills to use computers. More and more, businesses and industries are relying on computers to organize, store, create, and transmit information.

The computer has changed the nature of the workplace. Each year, there are advances made in **telecommunications**—communication at a distance, often by cable, telephone, and television. Many people can now work at home, exchanging information with employers, clients, or customers using modems, telephones, and fax machines.

As more computers are connected to the Internet, more and more people will have access to information—and to each other. People in remote areas will become actively involved with the rest of the world. Businessman Lawrence Ellison said in an interview in 1997,

> The Information Age! And there's a chance that what we do will change everything: It will change the way we communicate amongst ourselves, the way we entertain, the way we work.

Technology and Entertainment

New technology has also made startling changes in the media. Twenty-five years ago, choices for television viewers were limited. In most areas of the United States, people could watch a few major networks, one or two local stations, and a publicly supported station. Today, with satellite dishes and cable, some viewers

▲ *The Women's National Basketball Association has many star players and a growing number of loyal fans who come to cheer on their teams.*

have hundreds of choices. The great number of choices has led to tremendous growth in the entertainment and communications industries. Several businesses have merged to form large international companies.

The media has had a dramatic effect on sports. Cable channels and the networks bid against each other for rights to broadcast sports events. As the audience for sports has expanded, an interest in women's sports has grown. This has resulted in new professional women's leagues. In 1996 the Women's National Basketball Association (WNBA) was formed.

Technology will soon make all kinds of entertainment choices conveniently accessible. Computers with enormous capacities—called servers—will make it possible to store movies, television programs, and all sorts of other digital information. This will enable people to request whatever they want from a long list of available programs.

Technology and the Space Age

Many technological changes have originated with the U.S. space program. A number of innovations designed for outer space have turned out to be useful on Earth. Food dehydration, nonstick pots and pans, and advances in laser surgery have, for instance, been developed by NASA engineers.

In the 1990s, NASA launched half a dozen missions into orbit around Earth. Shuttle astronauts sent satellites into space in order to test the reaction of chemicals and other materials in a zero-gravity environment. NASA's future projects include the International Space Station (ISS). Scientists from the United States, Russia, the European Space Agency, Canada, and Japan will work on the project. Construction of the 470-ton outpost is expected to be completed in 2004.

In recent years, NASA has focused on sending unmanned mechanical probes into space to explore the solar system. In 1997, people marveled at pictures taken by a robot vehicle that analyzed Martian rocks and radioed its findings to Earth. NASA's long-range hope is to send a human crew to Mars. At NASA and at other research centers, studies are under way to develop the technology that eventually will make such a mission possible. A trip to Mars requires the development of lighter, partly inflatable space ships, systems to recycle wastes and produce food, and ways to make rocket fuel on Mars so that it does not have to be transported from Earth.

How has technology changed the way people live in the twentieth century?

◆ ADVANCES IN HEALTH

New technology has brought about revolutionary changes in the practice of medicine. Doctors now use techniques such as sonograms, CAT scans, and MRIs to see parts of the body that ordinary X-rays cannot. Sonograms are computer-analyzed pictures of the body based on the reflection of sound waves. A CAT scanner rotates 180 degrees around a patient's body, emitting a pencil-thin X-ray beam. A computer analyzes the data. An MRI allows physicians to see through bones and organs, eliminating the need for some exploratory surgery. The MRI uses a powerful magnet and radio waves to produce signals that are translated by a computer.

Genetic Engineering

Scientists have also made advances in the study of genes, which contain the code that gives each living thing its distinct characteristics. Scientists can now manipulate genes to change certain characteristics of plants and animals. This is called **genetic engineering.** Genetic engineering projects include plans to create trees that grow faster, beef that contains less fat, and plants that have more nutritional value. Researchers hope to be able to prevent some diseases by altering the particular genes that cause them.

Some of the most startling research has come in the field of **cloning,** or using the genetic material in the cells of a plant or animal to create an identical copy of the original. In 1997, Scottish researchers made a breakthrough when they reported that genes of a sheep were used to create an identical lamb. Despite several successes, genetic engineering has raised concern. Some people question the wisdom of changing genetic material. Some worry about harmful bacteria that may result from experimentation. To offset these concerns, the National Institutes of Health have set guidelines for scientists working with genes.

Fighting Disease

In recent years, hope has surged over advances made in the decades-old fight against cancer. In 1998, a conference of cancer specialists issued reports that told about new approaches in controlling the disease. Scientists are making strides in developing drugs that will prevent or reduce the risk of certain cancers or that will keep cancerous tumors in check for long periods of time. In addition, laboratory advances in biology and genetics are offering new improvements in treatments.

Scientists continue to look for a cure for Acquired Immune Deficiency Syndrome, the medical condition known as AIDS. AIDS destroys the body's immune

In this photograph, a physician analyzes the images of a patient's brain created by magnetic resonance imaging—MRI. ▼

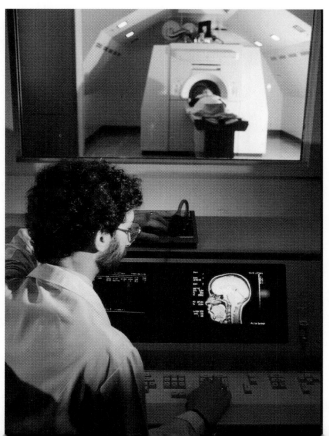

system, leaving it defenseless against other diseases that invade the body.

Prevention remains the only reliable defense against AIDS. HIV, the virus that may lead to AIDS, enters the body by contact with the body fluids of an infected person. In recent years, the increase of new infections in the United States has slowed, and the number of deaths has actually declined. By the late 1990s, AIDS remained the number-one cause of death for all Americans between 25 and 44 years old.

Today, doctors have made progress using a combination of strong drugs in the treatment of AIDS. These drugs have reduced the level of the virus in some patients who, though not cured, survive far longer than AIDS patients did a few years before. A cure for AIDS still seems far off, but the current treatments and the continuing research are encouraging signs.

How have scientific advances affected health care?

Section 3 Review

Check Understanding

1. **Define** (a) computer literate (b) telecommunications (c) genetic engineering (d) clone

2. **Describe** how technological advances have changed the way Americans work, study, and play.

3. **Explain** how people have benefited from advances in medicine.

Critical Thinking

Connecting Past and Present What job skills needed today were also useful in the past? What skills—not needed in the past—are important today?

Write About Culture

Write an outline for a magazine article about cloning. Include arguments for and against further experimentation with this technique.

CONNECTING HISTORY
& Science

SURGICAL TECHNIQUES

In the past a medical operation often meant pain and long recovery periods. Modern technology, however, has made possible new procedures that are efficient, accurate, and less stressful to patients. The use of the laser beam is one such development.

Today laser surgery is commonplace. In laser surgery, surgeons use an intense beam of light to operate without breaking the skin. For instance, a surgeon can skillfully direct a laser beam into a patient's eye, changing the shape of the lens. When the operation is over, the patient no longer needs glasses.

Another technical marvel is microsurgery. Using a microscope and tiny needles, surgeons can direct laser beams on blood vessels and cells. With microsurgery, they can remove brain tumors, leaving no visible trace of the invasive procedure.

Today's surgeons also use ultrasonic waves to avoid surgery. These high-frequency sound waves can break up gall bladder stones and kidney stones, making surgery to remove them unnecessary.

With cryosurgery, another new technique, doctors use extremely low temperatures to destroy diseased tissue. Cryosurgery may be used in combination with microsurgery for very delicate operations on the brain.

Many of the new surgeries are much less painful than older treatments. With the new techniques, surgeons need to touch very little of the tissue that surrounds the affected area when they operate. When less of the body is affected, healing is faster and the risk of infection is reduced.

Another technique that was unthinkable years ago is transplant surgery. Surgeons today can replace damaged hearts, livers, lungs, and kidneys with healthy organs from donors. A successful transplant can mean a longer life for a seriously ill person.

Making the Scientific Connection

1. What is laser surgery?
2. What is cryosurgery?
3. Why are some new techniques less difficult for the patient?
4. Why do you think so many new techniques are used for surgery on the brain?

Connecting Past and Present

Write a dialogue between a current student of surgery and a doctor who performed operations 50 years ago. Have them tell each other about treating patients in their time.

A surgeon shines a yellow laser beam into the eye of a patient during laser eye surgery. ▼

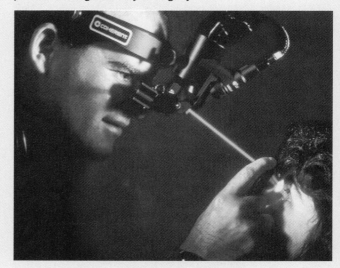

Section 4

A Nation of Diversity

PREVIEW

Objectives

- To explore the effects of immigration on American cities

- To describe the cultural diversity of the United States since the 1980s

- To discuss the impact of social and economic changes in the U.S. population

Vocabulary

multicultural
Sun Belt
reapportion

The face of the United States has changed in many ways since the nation's birth in 1776. In the 1800s, waves of Irish, German, Italian, Chinese, and eastern European immigrants reached American shores. In recent years, increasing numbers of newcomers from the Middle East, East Asia, Latin America, and the Caribbean have contributed to the American scene.

◆ RECENT IMMIGRANTS

More immigrants arrived in the United States in the 1980s than in any previous decade. According to the Census Bureau, even more immigrants have come to the United States in the 1990s. Yet, while the number of newcomers is large, they make up a smaller percentage of the population than they did in the early 1900s. In 1910, immigrants were 15 percent of the total population. In 1995, immigrants in the United States were about 10 percent of the total population.

Today nearly 90 percent of immigrants come to the United States from Asia, Latin America, and the Caribbean. The largest percentage come from Mexico, the Philippines, and Vietnam. Many people also come to the United States from China, Cuba, Korea, India, Russia, and the Dominican Republic.

The 1990 census shows that 70 percent of recent newcomers move to six states: California, New York, Texas, Florida, New Jersey, and Illinois. In fact, over 40 percent of new immigrants live in California and New York. Many of them settle, as immigrants did in the past, in metropolitan areas.

Immigrant Communities

In Los Angeles, New York, Chicago, San Antonio, Miami, and other cities, the newcomers have built vibrant communities. Since many immigrants come to the United States to be with relatives, they often live in tight-knit family groups. Many work long hours in low-paying jobs and learn English in night classes. At first, they may settle in places like Chinatown, Little Havana, or Little Kiev with others from their former country. There they can enjoy familiar foods, speak their native language, and celebrate national holidays.

Many American cities have large ethnic neighborhoods. For example, most of the residents in New York City's Brighton Beach are Russian immigrants. There, people can eat eight-course Russian meals and hear the latest gossip from Moscow. In Miami, *Calle Ocho*, or Eighth Street, is the center of the city's prosperous Cuban American community.

In America, some people celebrate traditions from both their old and new homelands. These people from an Indian community in Chicago enjoy a street festival. ▼

◀ *American colleges and universities today attract immigrants, children of immigrants, and students whose families have lived in the United States for generations.*

Mexican American communities in the Southwest include recent arrivals and families who have lived in the region for generations.

Debating Immigration

The large number of immigrants has reopened debate about the effect of the newcomers on the American economy. Some people argue that immigrants take jobs away from American citizens. They believe that the surge in immigration has strained the facilities that provide education, medical care, and welfare to U.S. citizens.

Other Americans defend the role immigrants play in the economy. They point out that the newcomers often open new businesses. Some immigrants are highly trained doctors, engineers, and scientists. Nearly 30 percent of the Americans who have won Nobel prizes in chemistry, physics, and medicine were born in other countries. In addition, American culture has been enlivened by the foods, music, dances, art, fashions, and customs that people have brought from around the world.

Immigration has changed our sense of who we are as a nation. In earlier times, immigrants were encouraged—sometimes forced—to give up the language and customs of their native land. Today, many Americans accept the idea that theirs is a **multicultural** land, one that is marked by cultural diversity.

Others have questioned the notion of ethnic identity. They argue that people should not think of themselves as Chinese Americans, African Americans, German Americans, or Cuban Americans. They say that ethnic traditions should be discarded and that the people of this country should think of themselves as Americans. They believe the nation should emphasize the rights of individuals rather than the rights of groups. Some say that people in a culturally diverse society can observe their individual traditions and still accept the principles of democracy upon which the United States was founded. One's cultural heritage can be respected, while the continually evolving American traditions and customs can be shared.

What differing positions have Americans taken toward multiculturalism?

◆ A CHANGING POPULATION

As Americans enter the twenty-first century, they can take pride in their accomplishments. Their nation is strong. Many problems have been tackled; some have been solved. Yet there is much to do. Women still lag behind men in earning power and opportunities. Many families live in poverty. The strength of American society is recognizing problems that exist and continuing to make efforts to solve them.

The Wage Gap

The U.S. economy performed well through much of the 1980s and 1990s. The overall prosperity, however, hid the underlying difficulties experienced by many Americans. Because of the decline of U.S. manufacturing, decent-paying jobs that required little schooling were becoming rare. Millions of jobs in auto plants, steel mills, and other factories had been disappearing since the 1960s. Workers were being replaced by computers, and many owners were moving their businesses to other countries.

Today, many high-wage jobs demand a college degree or technical training. It is hard for high-school graduates without needed skills to find jobs with good pay. As a result, there is a growing wage gap between skilled and unskilled workers.

Americans Moving and Aging

From 1980 to 1990, the U.S. population increased by about 25 million people, as shown on the chart of population growth on this page. The fastest growing American states were in the South and Southwest, a region known as the **Sun Belt.** California, Texas, and Florida had the biggest population increases.

Americans continue to move to the Sun Belt for many reasons. Many retired people are attracted to the warmer climate. Mild winters in the Sun Belt mean lower heating bills. Job opportunities open up to serve the growing population. Many immigrants also move to the Sun Belt because of the economic opportunities.

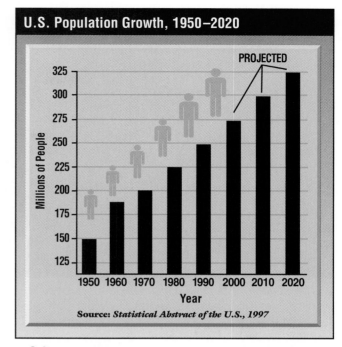

U.S. Population Growth, 1950–2020

Source: *Statistical Abstract of the U.S., 1997*

▲ **Culture** *By 2020, it is projected that the population of the United States will have more than doubled since 1950.* **Interpreting the Graph** *In which decade was population growth most dramatic?*

The makeup of Congress today reflects the shift in population. After each census, seats in the House of Representatives are **reapportioned,** or redistributed, based on population. Northern states have steadily lost House seats to the South and West. After the 1990 census, New York lost three representatives in the House, while California gained seven.

Americans over 65 are a growing segment of the population. Senior citizens are healthier and more active than ever before. They take college courses, dance, jog, and exercise to stay fit. In 1930, the average life expectancy was 63 years, while now it is 77. By the year 2010, nearly 40 million Americans will be over 65 years old. More than 6 million will be 85 years old or older.

This aging, or "graying," of America poses several problems, according to Deborah Sullivan, a sociologist at Arizona State University. She has said,

> "The graying of America will impact social security and retirement funds. There is no doubt about that. Health care, family structure, and social services also will be seriously affected."

Study Hint

As you study, read and review material carefully. Ask yourself questions to explore main ideas and important details. Then formulate answers, rereading information if necessary.

▲ *The Statue of Liberty continues to be a source of inspiration to Americans, as well as to visitors from around the world.*

the Great Depression and expanded the goal of equality for all Americans. Today, Americans are using hard work and ingenuity to keep ahead in a changing world. With its technological leadership and democratic traditions, the United States faces the future with confidence.

That future will bring its own challenges. The information revolution of the 1990s has brought sweeping changes to American society. Preparing people to use the new information presents a challenge to the education system. Another challenge will be to ensure that all people have access to that information.

Again and again, Americans have proven that they can overcome obstacles and adapt to new conditions. In the future, as in the past, Americans will draw strength from their diversity and their commitment to freedom and equality.

 What are some characteristics of the changing American society?

New Strides for Women

In 1970, only 18 percent of American women had graduated from college. Today, more women than men attend college. In the past many professional schools had quotas, or certain numbers of particular groups of students that could be accepted. The purpose of some quotas was to limit the number of women students. Laws and societal attitudes have changed. In the 1980s, almost 40 percent of the U.S. engineers and scientists were women. By 1997, women made up 40 percent of law-school graduates. The gap continues to close.

Women have become more prominent on the national level. In 1993, President Clinton appointed Ruth Bader Ginsburg to the Supreme Court. That same year, Janet Reno became the first woman U.S. attorney general. In 1997, Madeleine Albright became the first woman secretary of state. The accomplishments of such leaders have encouraged women in politics and other fields. Much remains to be done, however, before women reach full equality. Women are still paid less than men for the same work. On average, many professional women—doctors, lawyers, accountants—earn only 60 percent as much as men in the same fields.

Confidence in the Future

In this century, Americans fought in two world wars and survived a long Cold War. The country overcame

Section 4 Review

Check Understanding

1. **Define** (a) multicultural (b) Sun Belt (c) reapportion

2. **Discuss** how immigration has affected American life.

3. **Explain** the causes of the rising population in the Sun Belt.

4. **Describe** some of the challenges that the United States faces as it enters the twenty-first century.

Critical Thinking

Analyzing Why do anti-immigrant feelings often increase when unemployment rises?

Write About Government

◆ **Connecting Past and Present** Choose a person from early U.S. history. What would be his or her impression of the country today? Write a report of the person's observations.

POINT of VIEW

SHOULD WE REFORM IMMIGRATION LAWS?

Immigration has long stirred debate in America. Most Americans are descendants of people who came from other countries. While many American citizens believe that we should continue to welcome immigrants to the United States, others want to limit the number of newcomers who are permitted to enter. In the first passage below, Spencer Abraham, U.S. senator from Michigan, supports immigration. In the second excerpt, Yeh Ling-Ling, himself an immigrant, calls for curbs. Both writers focus on how immigration affects the economy of the country.

Immigrants are the ultimate entrepreneurs. They are people willing to risk it all in a new and different land. Immigrants also create a "brain gain" for the United States. Highly-educated, highly-skilled immigrants are essential to the competitiveness of America's high-tech industries. After recruiting on American campuses, these companies still do not have enough highly-skilled engineers, scientists, and computer specialists. Only because their need is real do companies go through the trouble, expense, and government paperwork necessary to hire foreign workers.

Sen. Spencer Abraham, Michigan Republican,
from a letter published in the
Washington Times, *Jan. 11, 1996*

Almost every week, we hear about thousands of our workers losing their jobs. Yet in 1992, more than 750,000 legal immigrants of working age were admitted to this country. In addition, we admit annually more than 60,000 foreign professionals on extended work visas. Many of these "temporary workers" enter skilled occupations, such as computer programming and engineering, where there have been massive layoffs. If the United States continues with an immigration policy that operates as if we had a labor shortage, how can we expect unemployed Americans and welfare recipients to find jobs?

Yeh Ling-Ling,
from a letter published in the
Los Angeles Times, *in 1994*

Examining Point of View

1. Why does Senator Abraham believe immigration is a "brain gain"?

2. What additional facts would you need to know to choose which argument is more persuasive?

3. What difficulties does Yeh see as a result of immigration?

4. Compare the two views on how immigration affects the U.S. economy.

What's Your Point of View?

Does the United States have a responsibility to those who, like many of our ancestors, are looking for a better life? Or should we limit the number of immigrants allowed into the country?

Write an essay, taking one side of the issue. Be sure to support your position.

Chapter 32
Review

CHAPTER SUMMARY

Section 1
When the Cold War ended, the United States became the world's only superpower. The risk of nuclear war between superpowers lessened, but regional conflicts broke out around the world. The United States faced difficult decisions about becoming involved in foreign crises. With the world's economies becoming increasingly interdependent, economic power became as important as military strength. Confronting terrorism and human rights violations became major goals of the United States.

Section 2
Increasingly, many Americans have become concerned with their environment. People throughout the world are taking steps to deal with acid rain, toxic waste dumping, and the maintenance of adequate supplies of energy. Deforestation and global warming have highlighted the need for international cooperation.

Section 3
Technology has revolutionized American life. It has led to advances in telecommunications, medicine, space exploration, and entertainment.

Section 4
Immigrants from Asia, Latin America, the Middle East, and the Caribbean have changed American cities. Changes in American society include increased life expectancy, increased mobility, and the aging of the population. Acknowledging that some problems still exist, the United States looks to the future with confidence.

Connecting ◆▶ Past and Present

In what ways does the United States today reflect the ideals of the early founders of the nation?

Using Vocabulary

Select the letter of the phrase that best completes each sentence.

1. A **multinational** (a) is always profitable; (b) is a large company with operations all over the world; (c) cannot be taxed; (d) is run by governments.

2. **Human rights** are (a) basic freedoms that every human being should have; (b) decided by state governments; (c) ratified by Congress; (d) available only to Americans.

3. **Acid rain** is rain polluted by (a) carbon monoxide; (b) sulfur dioxide; (c) hydrochloric acid; (d) citrus acid.

4. **Telecommunications** is (a) to take the bus to work; (b) to work in an office with child care on site; (c) using a bicycle to get where you need to go; (d) communication at a distance.

5. **Genetic engineering** is (a) outlawed by the Geneva Convention; (b) manipulating genes to change certain characteristics; (c) the same as cloning; (d) outlawed by Congress.

6. **Multicultural** is (a) a maximum number; (b) a minimum number; (c) cultural diversity; (d) a book in several languages.

7. When seats in the House of Representatives are **reapportioned**, (a) the seats must be based on the number of immigrants in a district; (b) the seats are given to appointed members; (c) the voters decide where the districts should be; (d) the seats are distributed based on population.

8. The **Sun Belt** is (a) a region in the South and Southwest United States; (b) an area around the Equator; (c) the hottest part of the globe; (d) a region in South America.

9. A **trade deficit** develops when a country (a) imports and exports the same amount of goods; (b) manufactures more equipment than it needs; (c) cuts off diplomatic relations with another country; (d) imports more goods than it exports.

10. **Deforestation** is (a) planting many trees; (b) flooding the land; (c) cutting down many trees; (d) building homes in the forest.

Check Understanding

1. **Explain** how the end of the Cold War changed the balance of power in the world.

2. **Describe** the global economy and how it affects the United States.

3. **List** three environmental problems the United States faces, and describe some of the solutions Americans have found for them.

4. **Explain** how concerns about nuclear power have spurred the search for alternative energy sources.

5. **Summarize** the factors that many scientists believe are leading to global warming.

6. **Describe** the way rapid technological advances have changed the nature of the American workplace.

7. **Identify** advances in medical science made possible by new technology.

8. **Explain** how recent immigration has changed the nature of American cities.

9. **Describe** the advances made by women in the workplace.

10. **Describe** the global economic and environmental concerns the United States has faced since the end of the Cold War.

Critical Thinking

1. **Evaluating Information** What do you think is the most important environmental threat the United States faces?

2. **Analyzing** What are the major benefits of recent technological changes? What are the major problems?

3. **Defending a Position** As the world's only superpower, should the United States take an active role in solving conflicts throughout the world? Support your position with reasons.

4. **Applying Information** Which of the technological changes of the past few years do you think has had the greatest effect on your life? Explain your answer.

5. **Connecting Past and Present** What accounts for the differences in the way Americans spend their leisure time now from the ways they did in the past?

Putting Skills to Work

TAKING A TEST

The Building Skills lesson on page 663 provided some practical strategies for taking a test. Choose two sections of the Chapter Review and treat them as if they were a test. Check your answers against the material in the textbook or ask a classmate to evaluate what you know. Use the test-taking suggestions on your next history exam.

Interpreting the Timeline

Use the timeline on pages 656–657 to answer these questions.

1. In what year and country did the Tiananmen Square demonstration occur?

2. In what year did a third partner join the North American Free Trade Association?

3. In what years did terrorist events occur in the United States?

Writing to Predict

What does the future hold for this country? Choose a specific subject, such as work, play, world affairs, scientific advances, or space exploration. Think about the trends you read about in this chapter that will affect that subject. **Write** your predictions supposing that today's trends continue. Be sure to support your predictions with specific facts.

 *Portfolio Project*

A BRIEFING PAPER

Choose one of the challenges facing the United States as it enters a new century. Possible topics include changes in economics, population, the environment, technology, medicine, or recreation. Write a briefing paper for newcomers to this country, preparing them for how future developments in one of these areas may affect their lives.

Connecting Past and Present

THE INFORMATION SUPERHIGHWAY

Acquiring information has commonly meant using a telephone, a library, a catalogue, or some other kind of resource or informational tool. The computer has revolutionized the ways we can now access information.

When the computer was introduced, few people guessed how fast, or how far, it would develop. As more and more people purchase computers—and as these computers are interconnected globally—the Internet is expanding. In the 1950s, a massive construction project crisscrossed the United States with a vast grid of interstate highways. The technological network that connects computers from around the world is called the "information superhighway."

Then The first computers took up the space of a large room. When the first personal computers were introduced in the 1970s, they were bulky and expensive. Even so, in 1982, 2.8 million computers were purchased. In those days computers were used mostly for typing and record keeping. In the 1990s, the use of e-mail (electronic mail) started to become widespread.

Now Today, people everywhere can be connected to each other with their computers. The computer has gone from being a versatile typewriter to a means—through the Internet—of worldwide communication. For the first time in history, knowledge stored all over the world is available to anyone who is linked to the global network. In addition, experts in various fields have established special-interest Internet sites. People on the "superhighway" can ask questions about a subject and have it answered by these experts right away—or later, by e-mail. It is projected that by the year 2001, there will be 500 million people connected to the Internet. Some people say that the Internet has become the instrument for the greatest change in communication since the invention of writing.

You Decide

1. How do modern computers affect the way information can be accessed and transmitted?

2. Do you think the constitutional amendment that guarantees freedom of the press should apply to the Internet? Explain.

On the left is ENIAC, the world's first electronic digital computer, developed in the 1940s. On the right is a modern laptop computer. ▼

Reference Center

160°W 140°W 120°W 100°W 80°W 60°W 40°W 20°W

80°N

ARCTIC OCEAN

Greenland (Den.)

Arctic Circle

Alaska (U.S.)

60°N

ICELAND

ALEUTIAN IS. (U.S.)

CANADA

NORTH AMERICA

UNITED KINGDOM

40°N

UNITED STATES

AZORES" (Port.)

BERMUDA (U.K.)

ATLANTIC OCEAN

SPAI

MIDWAY I. (U.S.)

MOROCC

MEXICO

Western Sahara (Mor.)

Tropic of Cancer

20°N

HAWAII (U.S.)

CUBA

DOM. REP.

MAURITANIA

GUATEMALA

Caribbean Sea

CAPE VERDE

SENEGAL

GUYANA

VENEZUELA

SURINAME

GAMBIA

GUINEA-BISSAU

MAL

GUINEA

0° Equator

GALÁPAGOS IS. (Ecuador)

COLOMBIA

French Guiana (Fr.)

SIERRA LEONE

LIBERIA

COTE DIVOIRE

TOG

EQUATORIAL GUINEA

ECUADOR

SOUTH AMERICA

SÃO TOMÉ AND PRÍNCIPE

PACIFIC OCEAN

SAMOA

PERU

BRAZIL

AMERICAN SAMOA (U.S.)

FRENCH POLYNESIA (Fr.)

BOLIVIA

TONGA

20°S

PITCAIRN I. (U.K.)

Tropic of Capricorn

PARAGUAY

EASTER I. (Chile)

CHILE

URUGUAY

ARGENTINA

40°S

FALKLAND IS. (U.K.)

ATLANTIC OCEAN

60°S

Antarctic Circle

80°S

Central America and the Caribbean

UNITED STATES

30°N

0   150   300 miles
0   150   300 kilometers

Gulf of Mexico

25°N

Tropic of Cancer

B A H A M A S

20°N

CUBA

ATLANTIC OCEAN

MEXICO

CAYMAN ISLANDS (U.K.)

GREATER ANTILLES

TURKS AND CAICOS IS. (U.K.)

BR. VIRGIN IS. (U.K.)

BELIZE

JAMAICA

HAITI

DOMINICAN REPUBLIC

Puerto Rico (U.S.)

VIRGIN ISLANDS (U.S.)

ANTIGUA AND BARBUDA

GUATEMALA

15°N

N
W   E
S

Hispaniola

W E S T   I N D I E S

ST. KITTS AND NEVIS

GUADELOUPE (Fr.)

HONDURAS

DOMINICA

MARTINIQUE (Fr.)

EL SALVADOR

NICARAGUA

C E N T R A L   A M E R I C A

Caribbean Sea

NETH. ANTILLES (Neth.)

ARUBA

ST. LUCIA

ST. VINCENT AND THE GRENADINES

BARBADOS

GRENADA

LESSER ANTILLES

TRINIDAD AND TOBAGO

10°N

COSTA RICA

PANAMA

COLOMBIA

VENEZUELA

90°W   85°W   80°W   75°W   70°W   65°W   60°W

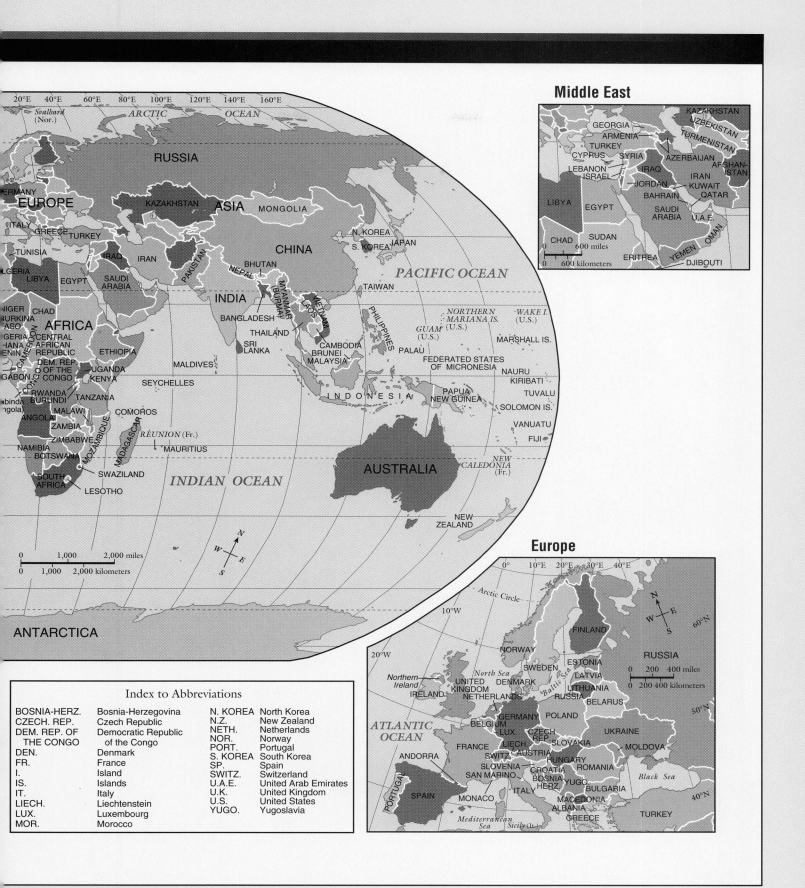

Middle East

ARCTIC OCEAN

20°E 40°E 60°E 80°E 100°E 120°E 140°E 160°E

Svalbard (Nor.)

RUSSIA

EUROPE

GERMANY

ITALY
GREECE
TURKEY

TUNISIA

ALGERIA
LIBYA
EGYPT

NIGER
CHAD
BURKINA
FASO

AFRICA

NIGERIA
CENTRAL
GHANA
AFRICAN
BENIN
REPUBLIC

CAMEROON

DEM. REP. OF THE CONGO

GABON
CONGO
KENYA
UGANDA

RWANDA
BURUNDI
TANZANIA

(Cabinda)
Angola

ANGOLA
MALAWI
ZAMBIA
ZIMBABWE

NAMIBIA
BOTSWANA

SOUTH
AFRICA
LESOTHO
SWAZILAND

ASIA

KAZAKHSTAN

MONGOLIA

IRAQ
IRAN
PAKISTAN

SAUDI
ARABIA

NEPAL
BHUTAN

INDIA

BANGLADESH

MYANMAR
(BURMA)

THAILAND

SRI
LANKA

MALDIVES

ETHIOPIA

SEYCHELLES

COMOROS

MOZAMBIQUE

MADAGASCAR

RÉUNION (Fr.)

MAURITIUS

CHINA

N. KOREA
S. KOREA
JAPAN

TAIWAN

VIETNAM
LAOS

CAMBODIA
BRUNEI
MALAYSIA

PHILIPPINES

PALAU

INDONESIA

PAPUA
NEW GUINEA

PACIFIC OCEAN

*NORTHERN
MARIANA IS.
(U.S.)*

*GUAM
(U.S.)*

*WAKE I.
(U.S.)*

MARSHALL IS.

FEDERATED STATES
OF MICRONESIA

NAURU
KIRIBATI
TUVALU
SOLOMON IS.

VANUATU

FIJI

*NEW
CALEDONIA
(Fr.)*

INDIAN OCEAN

AUSTRALIA

NEW
ZEALAND

0   1,000   2,000 miles
0   1,000   2,000 kilometers

N
W   E
S

ANTARCTICA

Middle East

KAZAKHSTAN
UZBEKISTAN
TURKMENISTAN

GEORGIA
ARMENIA
TURKEY
CYPRUS
SYRIA
AZERBAIJAN
AFGHANISTAN

LEBANON
ISRAEL
IRAQ
IRAN
JORDAN
KUWAIT
BAHRAIN
QATAR

LIBYA
EGYPT
SAUDI
ARABIA
U.A.E.

CHAD   600 miles
SUDAN
600 kilometers
ERITREA
YEMEN
OMAN
DJIBOUTI

Europe

0°   10°E   20°E   30°E   40°E

Arctic Circle

10°W

20°W

FINLAND

NORWAY

RUSSIA

0   200   400 miles
0   200 400 kilometers

60°N

*Northern
Ireland*

UNITED
KINGDOM

IRELAND

North Sea

SWEDEN

DENMARK

NETHERLANDS

ESTONIA
LATVIA
LITHUANIA
RUSSIA
BELARUS

Baltic Sea

50°N

**ATLANTIC
OCEAN**

GERMANY
POLAND

BELGIUM
LUX.
CZECH
REP.
SLOVAKIA

ANDORRA

FRANCE

SWITZ.
LIECH.
AUSTRIA
HUNGARY
SLOVENIA
CROATIA
SAN MARINO
BOSNIA-
HERZ.
YUGO.
ITALY

PORTUGAL

SPAIN

MONACO

UKRAINE

MOLDOVA

ROMANIA

Black Sea

BULGARIA
MACEDONIA
ALBANIA
GREECE

TURKEY

40°N

*Mediterranean
Sea*
Sicily (It.)

Index to Abbreviations

BOSNIA-HERZ.	Bosnia-Herzegovina	N. KOREA	North Korea
CZECH. REP.	Czech Republic	N.Z.	New Zealand
DEM. REP. OF THE CONGO	Democratic Republic of the Congo	NETH.	Netherlands
		NOR.	Norway
DEN.	Denmark	PORT.	Portugal
FR.	France	S. KOREA	South Korea
I.	Island	SP.	Spain
IS.	Islands	SWITZ.	Switzerland
IT.	Italy	U.A.E.	United Arab Emirates
LIECH.	Liechtenstein	U.K.	United Kingdom
LUX.	Luxembourg	U.S.	United States
MOR.	Morocco	YUGO.	Yugoslavia

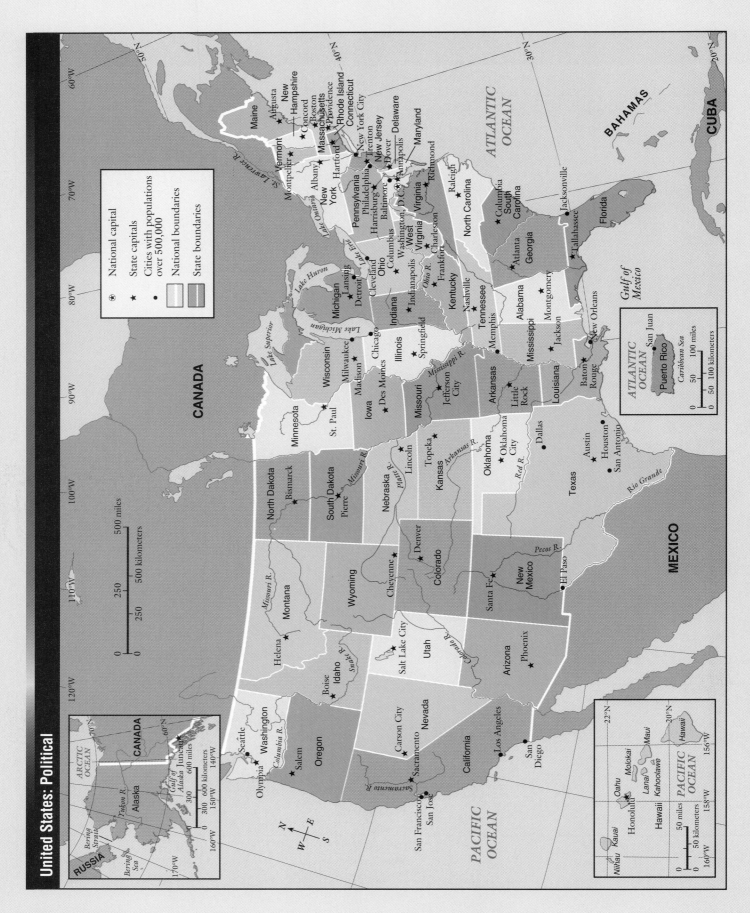

National capital ✪

State capitals ★

Cities with populations over 500,000 •

National boundaries

State boundaries

CANADA

RUSSIA

ARCTIC OCEAN

Bering Strait

Bering Sea

Alaska

Yukon R.

Gulf of Alaska

Juneau ★

70°N

60°N

170°W   160°W   150°W   140°W

300   600 miles

300   600 kilometers

MEXICO

PACIFIC OCEAN

ATLANTIC OCEAN

BAHAMAS

CUBA

Gulf of Mexico

ATLANTIC OCEAN

Caribbean Sea

Puerto Rico

San Juan

50   100 miles

50   100 kilometers

PACIFIC OCEAN

22°N

20°N

Niihau   Kauai   Oahu   Honolulu   Molokai   Lanai   Maui   Kahoolawe   Hawaii   Hawaii

50 miles

50 kilometers

160°W   158°W   156°W

500 miles

500 kilometers

250

250

0

Washington
Seattle
Olympia ★
Oregon
Salem ★
Columbia R.
Snake R.
Idaho
Boise ★
Nevada
Carson City ★
California
Sacramento ★
San Francisco
San Jose
Los Angeles
San Diego
Sacramento R.

Montana
Helena ★
Wyoming
Cheyenne ★
Utah
Salt Lake City ★
Arizona
Phoenix ★
Colorado
Denver ★
New Mexico
Santa Fe ★
El Paso
Colorado R.
Pecos R.
Rio Grande

Missouri R.

North Dakota
Bismarck ★
South Dakota
Pierre ★
Nebraska
Lincoln ★
Kansas
Topeka ★
Oklahoma
Oklahoma City ★
Texas
Austin ★
Houston
San Antonio
Dallas
Platte R.
Arkansas R.
Red R.

Minnesota
St. Paul ★
Iowa
Des Moines ★
Missouri
Jefferson City ★
Arkansas
Little Rock ★
Louisiana
Baton Rouge ★
New Orleans
Mississippi R.
Missouri R.

Wisconsin
Madison ★
Milwaukee
Illinois
Springfield ★
Chicago
Michigan
Lansing ★
Detroit
Indiana
Indianapolis ★
Mississippi
Jackson ★
Memphis

Lake Superior
Lake Michigan
Lake Huron
Lake Erie
Lake Ontario
St. Lawrence R.

CANADA

Ohio
Columbus ★
Cleveland
Kentucky
Frankfort ★
Tennessee
Nashville ★
Alabama
Montgomery ★
Georgia
Atlanta ★
Ohio R.

Maine
Augusta ★
New Hampshire
Concord ★
Vermont
Montpelier ★
Massachusetts
Boston ★
Rhode Island
Providence ★
Connecticut
Hartford ★
New York
Albany ★
New York City
Pennsylvania
Harrisburg ★
Philadelphia
New Jersey
Trenton ★
Delaware
Dover ★
Maryland
Annapolis ★
Washington, D.C. ✪
West Virginia
Charleston ★
Virginia
Richmond ★
Baltimore

North Carolina
Raleigh ★
South Carolina
Columbia ★
Georgia
Florida
Tallahassee ★
Jacksonville

N
W   E
S

30°N
40°N
50°N

60°W   70°W   80°W   90°W   100°W   110°W   120°W

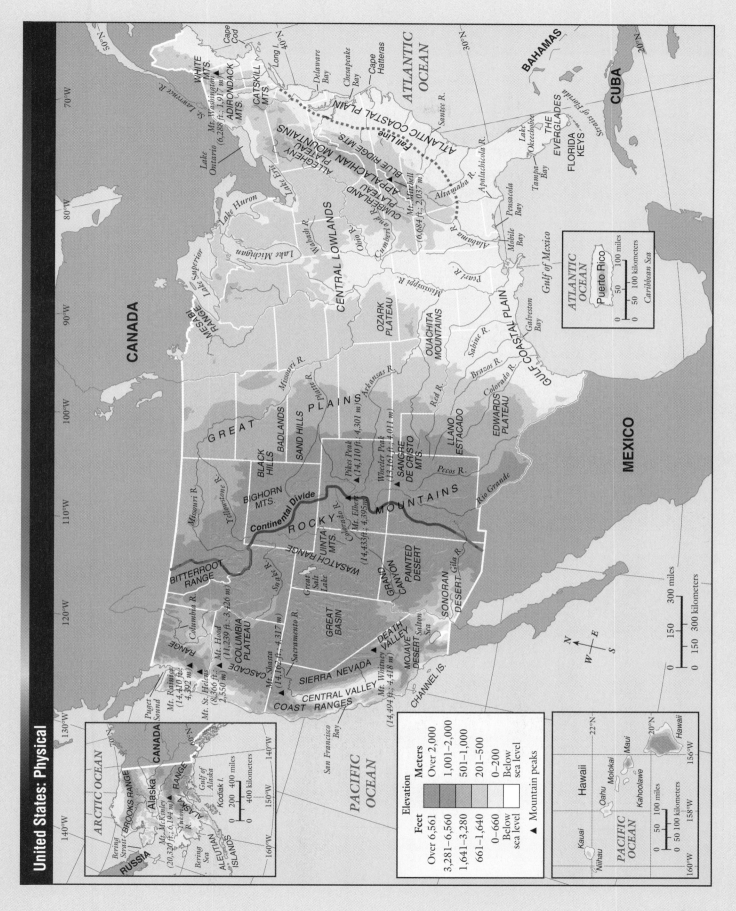

United States: Physical

Atlas ◆ 683

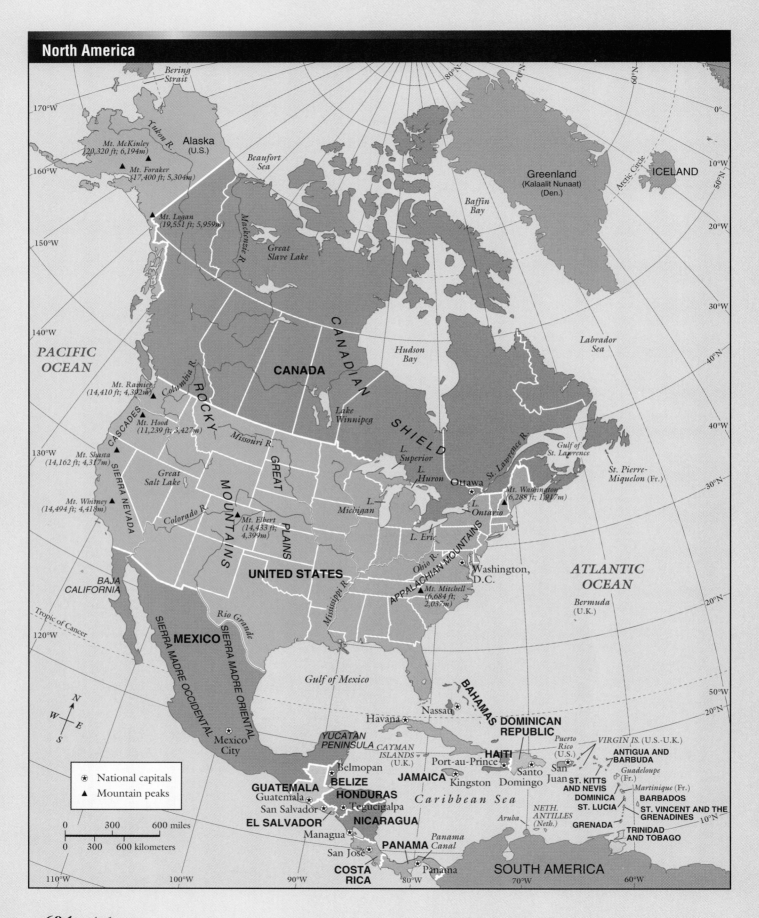

North America

Bering Strait

Mt. McKinley (20,320 ft; 6,194m) ▲
Mt. Foraker (17,400 ft; 5,304m) ▲

Alaska (U.S.)

Yukon R.

Beaufort Sea

▲ *Mt. Logan (19,551 ft; 5,959m)*

Mackenzie R.

Great Slave Lake

ICELAND

Greenland
(Kalaalit Nunaat)
(Den.)

Arctic Circle

Baffin Bay

PACIFIC OCEAN

CANADIAN SHIELD

Labrador Sea

CANADA

Hudson Bay

Mt. Rainier (14,410 ft; 4,392m) ▲

Columbia R.

ROCKY

CASCADES

Mt. Hood (11,239 ft; 3,427m) ▲

Missouri R.

Lake Winnipeg

L. Superior

St. Lawrence R.

Gulf of St. Lawrence

St. Pierre-Miquelon (Fr.)

Mt. Shasta (14,162 ft; 4,317m) ▲

SIERRA NEVADA

Great Salt Lake

MOUNTAINS

GREAT

L. Huron

Ottawa ✪

▲ *Mt. Washington (6,288 ft; 1,917m)*

Mt. Whitney (14,494 ft; 4,418m) ▲

Colorado R.

Mt. Elbert (14,433 ft; 4,399m) ▲

PLAINS

L. Michigan

L. Ontario

L. Erie

UNITED STATES

Ohio R.

APPALACHIAN MOUNTAINS

✪ Washington, D.C.

ATLANTIC OCEAN

BAJA CALIFORNIA

Mississippi R.

▲ *Mt. Mitchell (6,684 ft; 2,037m)*

Bermuda (U.K.)

Tropic of Cancer

MEXICO

Rio Grande

SIERRA MADRE ORIENTAL

SIERRA MADRE OCCIDENTAL

Gulf of Mexico

BAHAMAS

Nassau ✪

Havana ✪

DOMINICAN REPUBLIC

✪ Mexico City

YUCATAN PENINSULA

CAYMAN ISLANDS (U.K.)

Puerto Rico (U.S.)

VIRGIN IS. (U.S.-U.K.)

ANTIGUA AND BARBUDA

Belmopan ✪

HAITI

Port-au-Prince ✪

Santo Domingo

San Juan

Guadeloupe (Fr.)

ST. KITTS AND NEVIS

JAMAICA

Kingston ✪

Martinique (Fr.)

DOMINICA

BARBADOS

GUATEMALA

BELIZE

HONDURAS

Tegucigalpa ✪

Caribbean Sea

ST. LUCIA

ST. VINCENT AND THE GRENADINES

Guatemala ✪

San Salvador ✪

NICARAGUA

NETH. ANTILLES (Neth.)

Aruba

GRENADA

EL SALVADOR

Managua ✪

Panama Canal

TRINIDAD AND TOBAGO

PANAMA

San José ✪

Panama ✪

COSTA RICA

SOUTH AMERICA

| ✪ | National capitals |
| ▲ | Mountain peaks |

0   300   600 miles

0   300   600 kilometers

N
W   E
S

South America

CENTRAL
AMERICA

Caribbean Sea

Caracas

VENEZUELA

GUYANA

SURINAME

French Guiana
(Fr.)

Orinoco R.

Georgetown

Paramaribo

Cayenne

10°N

N

W   E

S

Bogotá

L L A N O S

GUIANA HIGHLANDS

COLOMBIA

*Mapelo I.
(Colombia)*

Quito

Amazon R.

Equator

0°

ECUADOR

▲ *Mt. Chimborazo
(20,561 ft; 6,268m)*

PERU

A N D E S

AMAZON BASIN

B R A Z I L

Brasília

São Francisco R.

*BRAZILIAN
HIGHLANDS*

10°S

▲ *Mt. Huascarán
(22,205 ft; 6,960m)*

Lima

M O U N T A I N S

La Paz

BOLIVIA

Sucre

Paraguay R.

Tropic of Capricorn

PARAGUAY

20°S

*San Felix I.
(Chile)*   *San Ambrosio I.
(Chile)*

Asunción

CHILE

ARGENTINA

PAMPAS

Uruguay R.

URUGUAY

*Juan Fernández Is.
(Chile)*

▲ *Mt. Aconcagua
(22,834 ft; 6,959m)*

Santiago

Buenos Aires

Montevideo

ATLANTIC OCEAN

30°S

PACIFIC OCEAN

PATAGONIA

⊛ National capitals

▲ Mountain peaks

40°S

*Strait of
Magellan*

*FALKLAND IS. (U.K.)
(MALVINAS IS.)*

0   400   800 miles

0   400   800 kilometers

*TIERRA
DEL FUEGO*

*Cape
Horn*

50°S

100°W   90°W   80°W   70°W   60°W   50°W   40°W   30°W   20°W   10°W

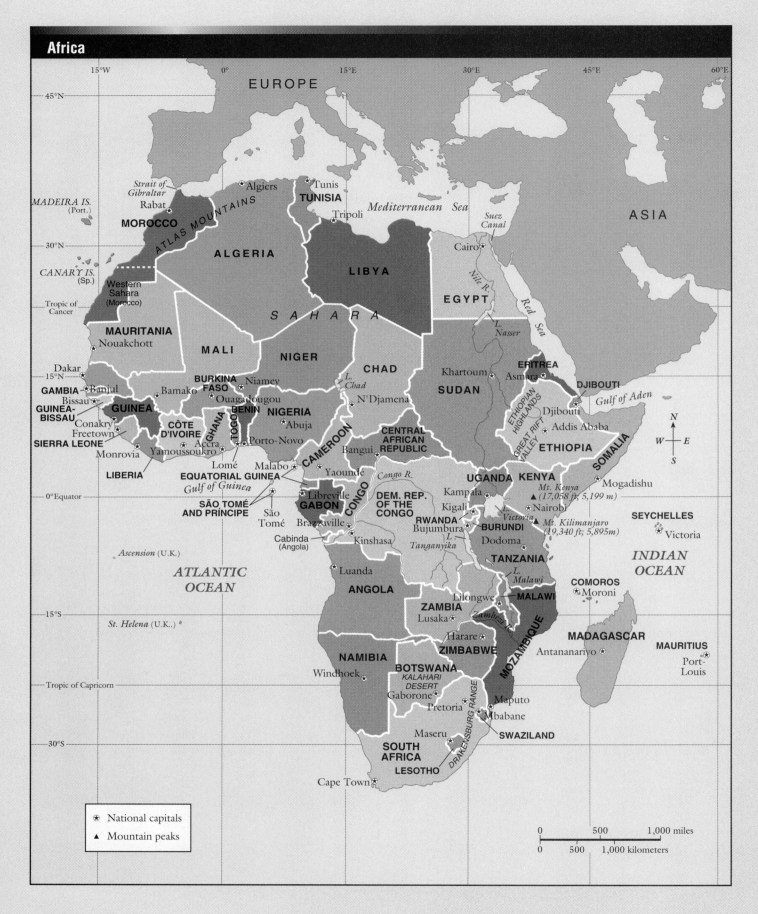

Africa

EUROPE

ASIA

MADEIRA IS.
(Port.)

Strait of Gibraltar

Algiers ✳

Tunis ✳
TUNISIA

Mediterranean Sea

Rabat ✳
MOROCCO

Tripoli ✳

Suez Canal

ALGERIA

LIBYA

Cairo ✳

CANARY IS.
(Sp.)

Western
Sahara
(Morocco)

Tropic of
Cancer

S A H A R A

EGYPT

Nile R.

Red Sea

L. Nasser

MAURITANIA

Nouakchott ✳

MALI

NIGER

CHAD

Khartoum ✳

ERITREA

Asmara ✳

DJIBOUTI

Dakar ✳

L. Chad

SUDAN

ETHIOPIAN HIGHLANDS

Djibouti ✳

Gulf of Aden

BURKINA FASO

Niamey ✳

Addis Ababa ✳

GAMBIA ✳ Banjul

Bamako ✳

Ouagadougou ✳

N'Djamena ✳

Bissau ✳
GUINEA-BISSAU

GUINEA

BENIN

NIGERIA

Abuja ✳

CENTRAL AFRICAN REPUBLIC

GREAT RIFT VALLEY

ETHIOPIA

Conakry ✳

CÔTE D'IVOIRE

GHANA

TOGO

Freetown ✳

SIERRA LEONE

Accra ✳

Porto-Novo ✳

CAMEROON

Bangui ✳

SOMALIA

Monrovia ✳

Yamoussoukro ✳

Lomé ✳

Malabo ✳

UGANDA

KENYA

Mogadishu ✳

LIBERIA

EQUATORIAL GUINEA

Yaoundé ✳

Congo R.

Kampala ✳

*▲ Mt. Kenya
(17,058 ft; 5,199 m)*

SÃO TOMÉ AND PRÍNCIPE

Gulf of Guinea

São Tomé ✳

GABON

Libreville ✳

CONGO

DEM. REP. OF THE CONGO

Kigali ✳

RWANDA

Bujumbura ✳

L. Victoria

✳ Nairobi

SEYCHELLES

✳ Victoria

Ascension (U.K.)

Brazzaville ✳

BURUNDI

*▲ Mt. Kilimanjaro
(19,340 ft; 5,895m)*

Cabinda
(Angola)

Kinshasa ✳

L. Tanganyika

Dodoma ✳

*INDIAN
OCEAN*

0° Equator

*ATLANTIC
OCEAN*

Luanda ✳

TANZANIA

L. Malawi

COMOROS

Moroni ✳

ANGOLA

Lilongwe ✳

MALAWI

ZAMBIA

MADAGASCAR

St. Helena (U.K.)

Lusaka ✳

Zambezi R.

Harare ✳

MAURITIUS

Antananarivo ✳

Port-
Louis ✳

NAMIBIA

ZIMBABWE

MOZAMBIQUE

Tropic of Capricorn

Windhoek ✳

BOTSWANA

*KALAHARI
DESERT*

Gaborone ✳

Pretoria ✳

DRAKENSBURG RANGE

Maputo ✳
Mbabane ✳

Maseru ✳

SWAZILAND

**SOUTH
AFRICA**

LESOTHO

Cape Town ✳

N

W   E

S

| ✳ National capitals |
| ▲ Mountain peaks |

| 0 | 500 | 1,000 miles |
| 0 | 500 | 1,000 kilometers |

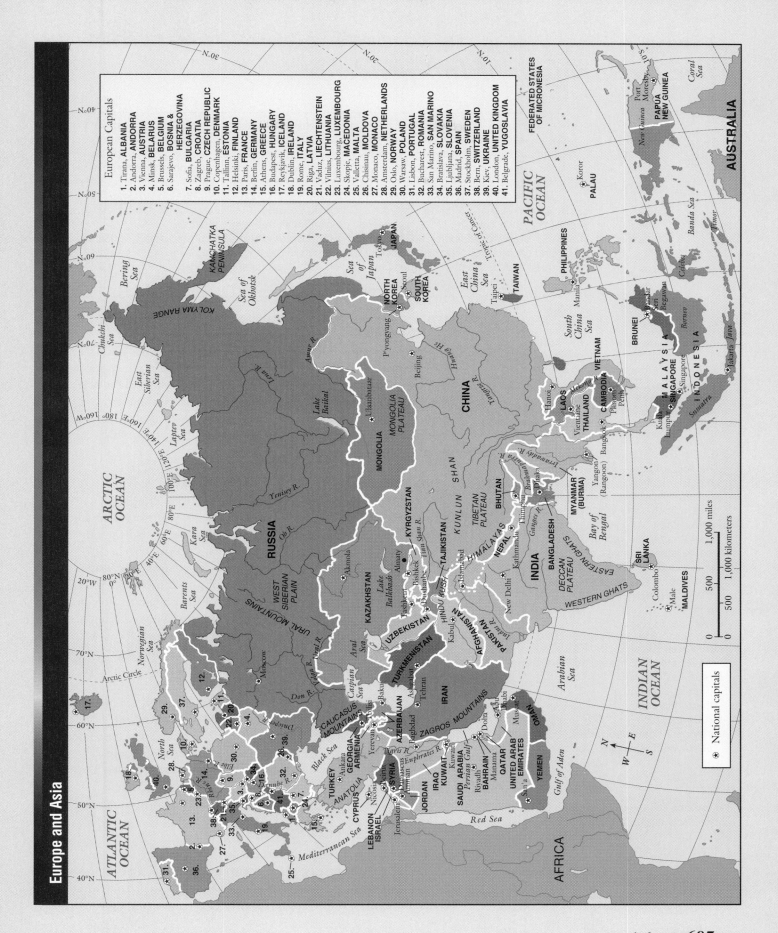

Europe and Asia

European Capitals

1. Tirana, ALBANIA
2. Andorra, ANDORRA
3. Vienna, AUSTRIA
4. Minsk, BELARUS
5. Brussels, BELGIUM
6. Sarajevo, BOSNIA & HERZEGOVINA
7. Sofia, BULGARIA
8. Zagreb, CROATIA
9. Prague, CZECH REPUBLIC
10. Copenhagen, DENMARK
11. Tallinn, ESTONIA
12. Helsinki, FINLAND
13. Paris, FRANCE
14. Berlin, GERMANY
15. Athens, GREECE
16. Budapest, HUNGARY
17. Reykjavik, ICELAND
18. Dublin, IRELAND
19. Rome, ITALY
20. Riga, LATVIA
21. Vaduz, LIECHTENSTEIN
22. Vilnius, LITHUANIA
23. Luxembourg, LUXEMBOURG
24. Skopje, MACEDONIA
25. Valletta, MALTA
26. Chisinau, MOLDOVA
27. Monaco, MONACO
28. Amsterdam, NETHERLANDS
29. Oslo, NORWAY
30. Warsaw, POLAND
31. Lisbon, PORTUGAL
32. Bucharest, ROMANIA
33. San Marino, SAN MARINO
34. Bratislava, SLOVAKIA
35. Ljubljana, SLOVENIA
36. Madrid, SPAIN
37. Stockholm, SWEDEN
38. Bern, SWITZERLAND
39. Kiev, UKRAINE
40. London, UNITED KINGDOM
41. Belgrade, YUGOSLAVIA

✯ National capitals

The Declaration of Independence

By June 1776, the American colonists realized that they must break free of Great Britain. Their efforts to make peace with King George III had failed. Thomas Jefferson was chosen to write a document telling the world why the colonies wanted to become independent. One of the most important goals of this document was to describe the basic rights on which the nation was founded, and the ways the government must protect them. These rights are the same today as they were in 1776.

On July 4, 1776, the Continental Congress accepted the Declaration of Independence. Ever since then, the United States has celebrated its freedom on that day.

Below is the text of the Declaration of Independence using modern spelling, punctuation, and capitilization. The titles in bold are not a part of the original document. They have been added to help you understand the text. Explanations and definitions accompany the text in the margin.

PREAMBLE

Preamble
In the opening paragraph the colonists explain that they will state the reasons why they are breaking away from Britain.

political bands alliances
powers of the earth other countries

When in the Course of human events, it becomes necessary for one people to dissolve the **political bands** which have connected them with another and to assume, among the **powers of the earth**, the separate and equal station to which the laws of nature and of nature's God entitle them, a decent respect to the opinions of mankind requires that they should declare the causes which impel them to the separation.

A NEW THEORY OF GOVERNMENT

A New Theory of Government
The colonists believed that humans are created equal and have equal rights to life, liberty, and the pursuit of happiness. Governments are formed to protect these rights. When a government threatens or takes away these rights, then the people have the right to change or do away with that government. The long history of abuses committed against the colonies by King George III of England shows the colonists that they should revolt against his rule.

endowed given
unalienable not able to be taken away
instituted created
consent agreement
effect bring about
prudence care
evinces a design to reduce them under absolute despotism makes a plan to put them under the absolute control of King George III

We hold these truths to be self-evident, that all men are created equal; that they are **endowed** by their Creator with certain **unalienable** rights; that among these are life, liberty, and the pursuit of happiness. That to secure these rights, governments are **instituted** among men, deriving their just powers from the **consent** of the governed; that whenever any form of government becomes destructive of these ends, it is the right of the people to alter or to abolish it, and to institute a new government, laying its foundation on such principles, and organizing its powers in such form, as to them shall seem most likely to **effect** their safety and happiness. **Prudence**, indeed, will dictate that governments long established should not be changed for light and transient causes; and, accordingly, all experience hath shown that mankind are more disposed to suffer, while evils are sufferable, than to right themselves by abolishing the forms to which they are accustomed. But when a long train of abuses and usurpations, pursuing invariably the same object, **evinces a design to reduce them under absolute despotism**, it is their right, it is their duty, to throw off such government and to provide new guards for their future security.

REASONS FOR INDEPENDENCE

Reasons for Independence
This section lists 27 reasons for separation from Britain. They can be divided into three parts:

1. Abuses by King George III
2. Abuses by Parliament
3. Acts of war against the colonies

Such has been the patient sufferance of these colonies, and such is now the necessity which constrains them to alter their former systems of government. The history of the present King of Great Britain is a history of repeated injuries and usurpations, all having, in direct object, the establishment of an absolute tyranny over these States. To prove this, let facts be submitted to a candid world.

ABUSES BY KING GEORGE III

He has refused his **assent** to laws the most wholesome and necessary for the public good.

He has forbidden his governors to pass laws of immediate and pressing importance, unless suspended in their operation till his assent should be obtained; and, when so suspended, he has utterly neglected to attend to them.

He has refused to pass other laws for the accommodation of large districts of people, unless those people would **relinquish** the right of representation in the legislature, a right inestimable to them and formidable to tyrants only.

He has called together legislative bodies at places unusual, uncomfortable, and distant from the depository of their public records, for the sole purpose of **fatiguing** them into **compliance** with his measures.

He has **dissolved** representative houses repeatedly, for opposing with manly firmness his invasion on the rights of the people.

He has refused, for a long time after such dissolutions, to cause others to be elected, whereby the legislative powers, incapable of **annihilation**, have returned to the people at large for their exercise; the state remaining, in the meantime, exposed to all the dangers of invasion from without, and **convulsions** within.

He has **endeavored** to prevent the population of these States; for that purpose, obstructing the laws of naturalization of foreigners, refusing to pass others to encourage their migration **hither**, and raising the conditions of new **appropriations** of lands.

He has obstructed the administration of justice by refusing his assent to laws for establishing judiciary powers.

He has made judges dependent on his will alone for the **tenure** of their offices and the amount and payment of their salaries.

He has **erected** a multitude of new offices and sent hither swarms of officers to harass our people and eat out their substance.

He has kept among us, in times of peace, standing armies without the consent of our legislatures.

He has affected to **render** the military independent of, and superior to, the civil power.

ABUSES BY PARLIAMENT

He has combined with others to subject us to a **jurisdiction** foreign to our Constitution and unacknowledged by our laws, giving his assent to their acts of pretended legislation:

For **quartering** large bodies of armed troops among us;

For protecting them by a **mock** trial from punishment for any murders which they should commit on the inhabitants of these States;

Abuses by King George III
- Ignoring laws that the colonies needed him to pass
- Demanding, as a requirement for his approval of certain laws, that the colonies stop requesting representation in Parliament
- Interfering with the operations of colonial legislatures
- Refusing to set up courts in the colonies
- Sending officers, such as tax collectors and customs officials, who are taking needed supplies from the colonists

---

assent agreement
relinquish give up
fatiguing exhausting
compliance agreeing
dissolved broken up
annihilation destruction
convulsions disturbances and riots
endeavored tried
hither here
appropriations grants
tenure term of office
erected set up
render make

 How were the colonists' inalienable rights—life, liberty, and the pursuit of happiness—taken away by King George III?

Abuses by Parliament
- Housing troops in colonists' homes
- Blocking trade with other countries
- Taxing the colonies without allowing them to be represented in Parliament
- Not allowing jury trials

---

jurisdiction authority
quartering housing
mock false

For cutting off our trade with all parts of the world;

For imposing taxes on us without our consent;

For depriving us, in many cases, of the benefits of trial by jury;

For **transporting us beyond seas** to be tried for pretended offenses;

For abolishing the free system of English laws in a neighboring province, establishing therein an **arbitrary government**, and enlarging its boundaries, so as to render it at once an example and fit instrument for introducing the same **absolute rule** into these Colonies;

For taking away our charters, abolishing our most valuable laws, and altering, fundamentally, the powers of our governments;

For suspending our own legislatures and declaring themselves **invested with power** to legislate for us in all cases whatsoever.

ACTS OF WAR AGAINST THE COLONIES

He has **abdicated** government here by declaring us out of his protection and waging war against us.

He has plundered our seas, ravaged our coasts, burnt our towns, and destroyed the lives of our people.

He is, at this time, transporting large armies of foreign mercenaries to complete the works of death, desolation, and tyranny already begun with circumstances of cruelty and **perfidy** scarcely paralleled in the most **barbarous** ages, and totally unworthy, the head of a civilized nation.

He has **constrained** our fellow citizens, taken captive on the high seas, to bear arms against their country, to become the executioners of their friends and brethren, or to fall themselves by their hands.

He has excited domestic **insurrections** amongst us and has endeavored to bring on the inhabitants of our frontiers, the merciless Indian savages, whose known rule of warfare is an undistinguished destruction of all ages, sexes, and conditions.

TAKING ACTION

In every stage of these oppressions, we have **petitioned** for **redress** in the most humble terms; our repeated petitions have been answered only by repeated injury. A prince whose character is thus marked by every act which may define a tyrant is unfit to be the ruler of a free people.

Nor have we been **wanting in attentions to our British brethren.** We have warned them, from time to time, of attempts by their legislature to extend an **unwarrantable** jurisdiction over us. We have reminded them of the circumstances of our emigration and settlement here. We have appealed to their native justice and **magnanimity**, and we have **conjured** them, by the ties of our **common kindred**, to disavow these **usurpations**, which would inevitably interrupt our connections and correspondence. They too have

---

transporting us beyond seas sending colonists to England for trial
arbitrary government unjust rule
absolute rule dictatorship
invested with power having the power

Acts of War Against the Colonies
The third and final set of complaints provides examples in which the British committed acts of war against the colonies.

The colonists were angry at the British for kidnapping American sailors and other citizens, and then trying to force these kidnapped Americans to fight against the colonies. Colonists in the West feared that the British had tried to rally Native Americans to attack them.

abdicated given up
perfidy dishonesty
barbarous savage, uncivilized
constrained forced
insurrections revolts

Taking Action
The colonists asked the British government and citizens for justice but they received only bad treatment. The Declaration states boldly that a king who allows this abuse is not fit to rule a free country.

petitioned asked
redress relief
wanting in attentions to our British brethren ignoring the British people
unwarrantable unforgivable
magnanimity kindness
conjured called upon
common kindred relatives
usurpations seizing people's rights by force

been deaf to the voice of justice and of **consanguinity**. We must, therefore, acquiesce in the necessity which denounces our separation, and hold them, as we hold the rest of mankind, enemies in war, in peace, friends.

INDEPENDENCE

We, therefore, the representatives of the United States of America, in general Congress assembled, appealing to the Supreme Judge of the world for the **rectitude of our intentions**, do, in the name, and by the authority of the good people of these colonies, solemnly publish and declare, that these united colonies are, and of right ought to be free and independent states; that they are **absolved from all allegiance** to the British Crown, and that all political connection between them and the State of Great Britain, is and ought to be, totally dissolved; and that, as free and independent states, they have full power to **levy** war, conclude peace, contract alliances, establish commerce, and to do all other acts and things which independent states may of right do. And for the support of this declaration, with a firm reliance on the protection of Divine Providence, we mutually pledge to each other our lives, our fortunes, and our sacred honor.

· ·

John Hancock, *President of the Continental Congress (Massachusetts)*

NEW HAMPSHIRE	PENNSYLVANIA	VIRGINIA
Josiah Bartlett	Robert Morris	George Wythe
William Whipple	Benjamin Rush	Richard Henry Lee
Matthew Thornton	Benjamin Franklin	Thomas Jefferson
	John Morton	Benjamin Harrison
MASSACHUSSETTS	George Clymer	Thomas Nelson, Jr.
Samuel Adams	James Smith	Francis Lightfoot Lee
John Adams	George Taylor	Carter Braxton
Robert Treat Paine	James Wilson	
Elbridge Gerry	George Ross	SOUTH CAROLINA
		Edward Rutledge
NEW YORK	DELAWARE	Thomas Heyward, Jr.
William Floyd	Caesar Rodney	Thomas Lynch, Jr.
Philip Livingston	George Read	Arthur Middleton
Francis Lewis	Thomas McKean	
Lewis Morris		CONNECTICUT
	MARYLAND	Roger Sherman
RHODE ISLAND	Samuel Chase	Samuel Huntington
Stephen Hopkins	William Paca	William Williams
William Ellery	Thomas Stone	Oliver Wolcott
	Charles Carroll of Carrollton	
NEW JERSEY		GEORGIA
Richard Stockton		Button Gwinnett
John Witherspoon	NORTH CAROLINA	Lyman Hall
Francis Hopkinson	William Hooper	George Walton
John Hart	Joseph Hewes	
Abraham Clark	John Penn	

Independence
The final paragraph was a formal declaration of independence. It stated that the colonies are, and should be, free from the control of Britain. They should have all of the rights of an independent nation, including the rights to make war and peace, to create treaties with other nations, and to regulate trade. With the protection of God, the signers pledged to fight for the independence of the colonies.

consanguinity family
rectitude of our intentions morality and rightness of their plan to declare independence
absolved from all allegiance no longer loyal to
levy make

Connecting ◆◆ Past and Present

How have the Declaration's ideas about equality, justice, and liberty served as an inspiration for people today who feel they are being treated unfairly?

The Constitution of the United States

The writers of the Constitution constructed a document flexible enough to be used in today's world. Almost every part of your life is touched by this document. The newspapers and magazines that you read are free to print the news because of freedom of speech and the press protected in the Constitution. Schools were desegregated based on the promises of equal rights in the Constitution. Even your right to have clubs and sports teams at school is guaranteed in the Constitution by the right to meet freely with other people.

Below is the full text of the Constitution using modern spelling, punctuation, and capitalization. Portions which no longer apply or have been changed are crossed out. The titles in bold were not a part of the original document. They have been added to help you understand the text. Explanations and definitions accompany the text in the margin.

Preamble
The purpose of government is to protect freedom, equality, justice, and safety.

tranquility peace
posterity future generations

The Legislative Branch
Outlines the structure and rules for the lawmaking branch of the government.

Section 1: A Two-House Congress
The legislative branch has two houses: the House of Representatives and the Senate.

Elections
States must hold elections for the House of Representatives every two years.

requisite required

Qualifications:
A representative must:
• be at least 25 years old
• have been a citizen of the United States for seven years
• be a resident of the state which elected the representative

Number of Representatives
The number of representatives from a state is based on its population. The total number of representatives in the House is limited to 435.

enumeration census, or count of the population

PREAMBLE

We the people of the United States, in order to form a more perfect Union, establish justice, insure domestic **tranquility**, provide for the common defense, promote the general welfare, and secure the blessings of liberty to ourselves and our **posterity**, do ordain and establish this Constitution for the United States of America.

ARTICLE I: THE LEGISLATIVE BRANCH

Section 1: A Two-House Congress

All legislative powers herein granted shall be vested in a Congress of the United States, which shall consist of a Senate and House of Representatives.

Section 2: The House of Representatives

1. Elections The House of Representatives shall be composed of members chosen every second year by the people of the several states, and the electors in each state shall have the qualifications **requisite** for electors of the most numerous branch of the state legislature.

2. Qualifications No person shall be a representative who shall not have attained to the age of twenty-five years, and been seven years a citizen of the United States, and who shall not, when elected, be an inhabitant of that state in which he shall be chosen.

3. Number of Representatives Representatives and direct taxes shall be apportioned among the several states which may be included within this Union, according to their respective numbers, which shall be determined by adding to the whole number of free persons, including those bound to service for a term of years, and excluding Indians not taxed, three fifths of all other persons. The actual **enumeration** shall be made within three years after the first meeting of the Congress of the United States, and within every subsequent term of ten years, in such manner as they shall by law direct. The number of representatives shall not exceed one for every thirty thousand, but each state shall have at least one representative;

and until such enumeration shall be made, the state of New Hampshire shall be entitled to choose three, Massachusetts eight, Rhode-Island and Providence Plantations one, Connecticut five, New-York six, New Jersey four, Pennsylvania eight, Delaware one, Maryland six, Virginia ten, North Carolina five, South Carolina five, and Georgia three.

4. Vacancies When vacancies happen in the representation from any state, the executive authority thereof shall issue writs of election to fill such vacancies.

5. Officers and Impeachment The House of Representatives shall choose their Speaker and other officers; and shall have the sole power of impeachment.

Section 3: The Senate

1. Number of Senators The Senate of the United States shall be composed of two senators from each state, chosen by the Legislature thereof, for six years; and each senator shall have one vote.

2. Three Classes Immediately after they shall be assembled in consequence of the first election, they shall be divided as equally as may be into three classes. The seats of the senators of the first class shall be vacated at the expiration of the second year, of the second class at the expiration of the fourth year, and of the third class at the expiration of the sixth year, so that one third may be chosen every second year; and if vacancies happen by resignation, or otherwise, during the recess of the legislature of any state, the executive thereof may make temporary appointments until the next meeting of the legislature, which shall then fill such vacancies.

3. Qualifications No person shall be a senator who shall not have attained to the age of thirty years, and been nine years a citizen of the United States, and who shall not, when elected, be an inhabitant of that state for which he shall be chosen.

4. Senate President The Vice President of the United States shall be president of the Senate, but shall have no vote, unless they be equally divided.

5. Officers The Senate shall choose their other officers, and also a president **pro tempore**, in the absence of the Vice President, or when he shall exercise the office of President of the United States.

6. Impeachment Trials The Senate shall have the sole power to try all impeachments. When sitting for that purpose, they shall be on oath or **affirmation**. When the President of the United States is tried, the Chief Justice shall preside: And no person shall be convicted without the concurrence of two-thirds of the members present.

7. Punishment for Impeachment Judgment in cases of impeachment shall not extend further than to removal from office, and disqualification to hold and enjoy any office of honor, trust or profit under the United States; but the party convicted shall nevertheless be liable and subject to **indictment**, trial, judgment and punishment, according to law.

 Name three differences between the House of Representatives and the Senate.

Section 3: The Senate
Senators are elected every six years. The framers made Senate seats longer than House seats to make the Senate more stable. The Vice President of the United States is the president of the Senate.

Qualifications
A senator must:
• be at least 30 years old
• have been a citizen for nine years
• live in the state that he or she will represent

Senate President
The Vice President of the United States has the title of president of the Senate but can vote only when there is a tie.

Impeachment Trials
The House of Representatives has the power to impeach, or accuse, government officials of wrongdoing by voting a "bill of impeachment." The Senate then decides whether the official is guilty. If two thirds of the senators agree, the official is removed from office.

---

pro tempore for the time being
affirmation formal declaration
indictment accusation

Section 5: Rules and Records

Each house is responsible for overseeing its elections, determining the rules, and punishing members for violation of such rules. Each house must keep a record of its proceedings and votes so that people know how their representatives voted on bills.

---

quorum the smallest number of members that must be present in order to conduct business
concurrence agreement
adjourn stop meeting

Section 6: Payment and Immunity

Members of Congress are paid from the national treasury. Congressional immunity protects members of Congress from punishment for anything said in Congress and allows members of Congress to speak freely. It does not protect members of Congress from arrest for criminal offenses.

---

compensation salary
ascertain to make certain
felony a serious crime
breach break
emoluments payments

Section 4: Congressional Elections

1. Regulations The times, places, and manner of holding elections for senators and representatives, shall be prescribed in each state by the legislature thereof; but the Congress may at any time by law make or alter such regulations, except as to the places of choosing senators.

2. Sessions The Congress shall assemble at least once in every year, ~~and such meeting shall be on the first Monday in December, unless they shall by law appoint a different day.~~

Section 5: Rules and Records

1. Quorum Each house shall be the judge of the elections, returns and qualifications of its own members, and a majority of each shall constitute a **quorum** to do business; but a smaller number may adjourn from day to day, and may be authorized to compel the attendance of absent members, in such manner, and under such penalties as each house may provide.

2. Rules and Conduct Each house may determine the rules of its proceedings, punish its members for disorderly behavior, and, with the **concurrence** of two-thirds, expel a member.

3. Record Keeping Each House shall keep a journal of its proceedings, and from time to time publish the same, excepting such parts as may in their judgment require secrecy; and the yeas and nays of the members of either house on any question shall, at the desire of one-fifth of those present, be entered on the journal.

4. Adjournment Neither house, during the session of Congress, shall, without the consent of the other, **adjourn** for more than three days, nor to any other place than that in which the two houses shall be sitting.

Section 6: Payment and Immunity

1. Salary The senators and representatives shall receive a **compensation** for their services, to be **ascertained** by law, and paid out of the treasury of the United States. They shall in all cases, except treason, **felony**, and **breach** of the peace, be privileged from arrest during their attendance at the session of their respective houses, and in going to and returning from the same; and for any speech or debate in either house, they shall not be questioned in any other place.

2. Restrictions No senator or representative shall, during the time for which he was elected, be appointed to any civil office under the authority of the United States, which shall have been created, or the **emoluments** whereof shall have been increased during such time; and no person holding any office under the United States, shall be a member of either house during his continuance in office.

Section 7: How a Bill Becomes a Law

1. Tax Bills All bills for raising revenue shall originate in the House of Representatives; but the Senate may propose or concur with amendments as on other bills.

2. Approving a Bill Every bill which shall have passed the House of Representatives and the Senate, shall, before it become a law, be presented to the President of the United States; if he approves he shall sign it, but if not he shall return it, with his objections to that house in which it shall have originated, who shall enter the objections at large on their journal, and proceed to reconsider it. If after such reconsideration two-thirds of that house shall agree to pass the bill, it shall be sent, together with the objections, to the other house, by which it shall likewise be reconsidered, and if approved by two-thirds of that house, it shall become a law. But in all such cases the votes of both houses shall be determined by yeas and nays, and the names of the persons voting for and against the bill shall be entered on the journal of each house respectively. If any bill shall not be returned by the President within ten days (Sundays excepted) after it shall have been presented to him, the same shall be a law, in like manner as if he had signed it, unless the Congress by their adjournment prevent its return, in which case it shall not be a law.

3. President's Role Every order, resolution, or vote to which the concurrence of the Senate and House of Representatives may be necessary (except on a question of adjournment) shall be presented to the President of the United States; and before the same shall take effect, shall be approved by him, or being disapproved by him, shall be repassed by two-thirds of the Senate and House of Representatives, according to the rules and limitations prescribed in the case of a bill.

Section 8: Congress' Powers

1. Taxation The Congress shall have power to lay and collect taxes, duties, imposts and excises, to pay the debts and provide for the common defense and general welfare of the United States; but all duties, imposts and excises shall be uniform throughout the United States;

2. Borrow Money To borrow money on the credit of the United States;

3. Trade To regulate commerce with foreign nations, and among the several states, and with the Indian tribes;

4. Naturalization, Bankruptcy To establish a uniform rule of naturalization, and uniform laws on the subject of bankruptcies throughout the United States;

5. Money To coin money, regulate the value thereof, and of foreign coin, and fix the standard of weights and measures;

6. Counterfeiting To provide for the punishment of counterfeiting the securities and current coin of the United States;

Section 7: How a Bill Becomes a Law
All taxation bills for raising revenues, or income, must start in the House of Representatives.

Approving a Bill
After both the House and Senate pass a bill, it goes to the President. The President may sign the bill, in which case the bill becomes a law. The President may also veto, or reject, the bill. A veto sends it back to Congress. Congress then may override the veto with a two-thirds majority in both houses of Congress.

 Why is it important that the name of each congress person, and how he or she voted, is recorded in an official journal?

President's Role
When both the Senate and the House vote to pass a bill, they must present it to the President. He may either pass or veto it. If he vetoes it, it can still be passed by a two-thirds majority vote in the House and Senate.

Section 8: Congress' Powers
The first 17 clauses are "enumerated powers." They are specific powers which include the right to:

- tax
- borrow money
- regulate trade
- provide a post office
- raise an army and navy
- declare war

7. **Post Offices** To establish post offices and post roads;

8. **Copyrights and Patents** To promote the progress of "science and useful arts," by securing for limited times to authors and inventors the exclusive right to their respective writings and discoveries;

9. **Federal Court** To constitute **tribunals** inferior to the Supreme Court;

10. **International Law** To define and punish piracies and felonies committed on the high seas, and offenses against the law of nations;

11. **War** To declare war, ~~grant letters of **marque** and **reprisal**~~, make rules concerning captures on land and water;

12. **Army** To raise and support armies, but no appropriation of money to that use shall be for a longer term than two years;

13. **Navy** To provide and maintain a navy;

14. **Rules for Armed Forces** To make rules for the government and regulation of the land and naval forces;

15. **Militia** To provide for calling forth the militia to execute the laws of the Union, suppress insurrections, and repel invasions;

16. **Rules for Militia** To provide for organizing, arming, and disciplining the militia, and for governing such part of them as may be employed in the service of the United States, reserving to the states respectively, the appointment of the officers, and the authority of training the militia according to the discipline prescribed by Congress;

17. **District of Columbia** To exercise exclusive legislation in all cases whatsoever, over such district (not exceeding ten miles square) as may, by cession of particular states, and the acceptance of Congress, become the seat of the government of the United States, and to exercise like authority over all places purchased by the consent of the legislature of the state in which the same shall be, for the erection of forts, magazines, arsenals, dockyards, and other needful buildings; and

18. **Elastic Clause** To make all laws which shall be necessary and proper for carrying into execution the foregoing powers, and all other powers vested by this Constitution in the government of the United States, or in any department or officer thereof.

Section 9: Powers Denied Congress

1. **Slavery** ~~The migration or importation of such persons as any of the states now existing shall think proper to admit, shall not be prohibited by the Congress prior to the year one thousand eight hundred and eight, but a tax or duty may be imposed on such importation, not exceeding ten dollars for each person.~~

2. **Habeas Corpus** The privilege of the **writ of habeas corpus** shall not be suspended, unless when in cases of rebellion or invasion the public safety may require it.

Connecting ◆ Past and Present

Which three of Congress' 17 "enumerated powers" do you think are most important in today's world? Explain your answer.

The "Elastic Clause"
The 18th clause is known as the "necessary and proper," or "elastic clause." This clause gives Congress the power to make laws that are necessary to carry out the 17 "enumerated powers."

Section 9: Powers Denied Congress
These are the powers that Congress does not have. This clause reflects the framers' fear of creating a government that was too powerful.

3. Illegal Punishment No bill of **attainder** or **ex post facto law** shall be passed.

4. Direct Tax No capitation, ~~or other direct~~, tax shall be laid, unless in proportion to the census or enumeration herein before directed to be taken.

5. Export Taxes No tax or duty shall be laid on articles exported from any state.

6. Trade Preferences No preference shall be given by any regulation of commerce or revenue to the ports of one state over those of another: nor shall vessels bound to, or from, one state, be obliged to enter, clear, or pay duties in another.

7. Spending Public Money No money shall be drawn from the treasury, but in consequence of appropriations made by law; and a regular statement and account of the receipts and expenditures of all public money shall be published from time to time.

8. Titles of Nobility No title of nobility shall be granted by the United States: and no person holding any office of profit or trust under them, shall, without the consent of the Congress, accept of any present, emolument, office, or title, of any kind whatever, from any king, prince, or foreign state.

Section 10: Powers Denied the States

1. Restrictions No state shall enter into any treaty, alliance, or confederation; grant letters of marque and reprisal; coin money; emit bills of credit; make any thing but gold and silver coin a tender in payment of debts; pass any bill of attainder, ex post facto law, or law impairing the obligation of contracts, or grant any title of nobility.

2. Import and Export Taxes No state shall, without the consent of the Congress, lay any imposts or duties on imports or exports, except what may be absolutely necessary for executing its inspection laws; and the net produce of all duties and imposts, laid by any state on imports or exports, shall be for the use of the treasury of the United States; and all such laws shall be subject to the revision and control of the Congress.

3. Wartime and Peacetime Restraints No state shall, without the consent of Congress, lay any **duty of tonnage**, keep troops, or ships of war in time of peace, enter into any agreement or compact with another state, or with a foreign power, or engage in war, unless actually invaded, or in such imminent danger as will not admit of delay.

ARTICLE II: THE EXECUTIVE BRANCH

Section 1: The Presidency

1. Terms of Office The executive power shall be vested in a President of the United States of America. He shall hold his office during the term of four years, and, together with the Vice President, chosen for the same term, be elected, as follows.

---

attainder punish a person without a trial
ex post facto law a law which punishes someone for an action that was legal when the action was performed

Trade Preferences
No state's ports will be favored over those of another.

Spending Public Money
Money from the treasury may only be used when the law allows. The use of this money must be accounted for and made public knowledge.

Titles of Nobility
A U.S. official may not hold a title of nobility. A federal officer may not accept a gift from a foreign government without the consent of Congress.

Section 10: Powers Denied the States
The framers of the Constitution understood the dangers of a powerful federal government, but they also wanted to prevent the 13 states from acting like independent nations. Some powers are denied to the states because they are given to Congress. These include the powers to:
• make treaties with other nations
• print money
• declare war
• tax trade

Powers that are denied to both Congress and to the states include the powers to:
• pass bills of attainder
• pass ex post facto laws
• grant titles of nobility
• tax exports

---

duty of tonnage charge per ton

The Executive Branch
Article II of the Constitution gives the President "executive power." This is the power to enforce laws of the U.S. government. The first clause sets the term of office at four years.

The Electoral System
The second clause establishes the electoral college, though the term is not used in the Constitution. The electoral college is a body of presidential "electors" chosen in each state.

2. The Electoral System Each state shall appoint, in such manner as the legislature thereof may direct, a number of electors, equal to the whole number of senators and representatives to which the state may be entitled in the Congress; but no senator or representative, or person holding an office of trust or profit under the United States, shall be appointed an elector.

3. Original Method for Electing the President ~~The electors shall meet in their respective states, and vote by ballot for two persons, of whom one at least shall not be an inhabitant of the same state with themselves. And they shall make a list of all the persons voted for, and of the number of votes for each; which list they shall sign and certify, and transmit sealed to the seat of the government of the United States, directed to the president of the Senate. The president of the Senate shall, in the presence of the Senate and House of Representatives, open all the certificates, and the votes shall then be counted. The person having the greatest number of votes shall be the President, if such number be a majority of the whole number of electors appointed; and if there be more than one who have such majority, and have an equal number of votes, then the House of Representatives shall immediately choose by ballot one of them for President; and if no person have a majority, then from the five highest on the list the said House shall in like manner choose the President. But in choosing the President, the votes shall be taken by states, the representation from each state having one vote; A quorum for this purpose shall consist of a member or members from two thirds of the states, and a majority of all the states shall be necessary to a choice. In every case, after the choice of the President, the person having the greatest number of votes of the electors shall be the Vice President. But if there should remain two or more who have equal votes, the Senate shall choose from them by ballot the Vice President.~~

4. Time of Elections The Congress may determine the time of choosing the electors, and the day on which they shall give their votes; which day shall be the same throughout the United States.

Requirements for President
To be President, a person must:
- have been born a citizen of the United States
- be 35 years old
- have been a resident of the United States for at least 14 years

5. Requirements for President No person except a natural-born citizen, or a citizen of the United States, at the time of the adoption of this Constitution, shall be eligible to the office of President; neither shall any person be eligible to that office who shall not have attained to the age of thirty-five years, and been fourteen years a resident within the United States.

Why do you think a person must have been born in the United States in order to be eligible to be President?

6. President's Successor In case of the removal of the President from office, or of his death, resignation, or inability to discharge the powers and duties of the said office, the same shall devolve on the Vice President, and the Congress may by law provide for the case of removal, death, resignation or inability, both of the President and Vice President, declaring what officer shall then act as President, and such officer shall act accordingly, until the disability be removed, or a President shall be elected.

7. Salary The President shall, at stated times, receive for his services, a compensation, which shall neither be increased nor diminished during the period for which he shall have been elected, and he shall not receive within that period any other emolument from the United States, or any of them.

8. Oath Before he enters on the execution of his office, he shall take the following oath or affirmation: "I do solemnly swear (or affirm) that I will faithfully execute the office of President of the United States, and will to the best of my ability, preserve, protect and defend the Constitution of the United States."

Section 2: Presidential Powers

1. Military The President shall be Commander-in-Chief of the Army and Navy of the United States, and of the militia of the several states, when called into the actual service of the United States; he may require the opinion, in writing, of the principal officer in each of the executive departments, upon any subject relating to the duties of their respective offices, and he shall have power to grant reprieves and pardons for offenses against the United States, except in cases of impeachment.

2. Checks and Balances He shall have power, by and with the advice and consent of the Senate, to make treaties, provided two-thirds of the Senators present concur; and he shall nominate, and by and with the advice and consent of the Senate, shall appoint ambassadors, other public ministers and consuls, judges of the Supreme Court, and all other officers of the United States, whose appointments are not herein otherwise provided for, and which shall be established by law; but the Congress may by law vest the appointment of such inferior officers, as they think proper, in the President alone, in the courts of law, or in the heads of departments.

3. Filling Vacancies The President shall have power to fill up all vacancies that may happen during the recess of the Senate, by granting commissions which shall expire at the end of their next session.

Section 3: State of the Union

He shall from time to time give to the Congress information of the state of the Union, and recommend to their consideration such measures as he shall judge necessary and **expedient**; he may, on extraordinary occasions, convene both houses, or either of them, and in case of disagreement between them, with respect to the time of adjournment, he may adjourn them to such time as he shall think proper; he shall receive ambassadors and other public ministers; he shall take care that the laws be faithfully executed, and shall commission all the officers of the United States.

Section 4: Impeachment

The President, Vice President, and all civil officers of the United States, shall be removed from office on impeachment for, and conviction of treason, bribery, or other high crimes and **misdemeanors**.

Section 2: Presidential Powers
This section gives the President the powers to:
- head the nation's armed forces
- get information from the head of each executive
- grant pardons in federal cases

Checks and Balances
The framers feared the possibility of one branch becoming too powerful. One result was the creation of checks and balances, which allows one branch to check the actions and to balance the powers of the other branches. The President has the power to make treaties with other governments, but the Senate must approve the treaties for them to be valid. The Senate must also confirm all Presidential appointments of judges, Cabinet members, and ambassadors.

Section 3: State of the Union
The President delivers a State of the Union message to Congress shortly after the beginning of each congressional session. In this message the President can suggest laws that should be made.

expedient proper

misdemeanors misbehaviors, less serious crimes

Section 1: The Court System

The Supreme Court is our nation's highest court. Its judges are appointed by the President, with the approval of the Senate, and may hold office for life. Congress has the power to establish other federal courts.

vested held completely
ordain to establish by law

Judicial Review

Nowhere in the Constitution does the term "judicial review" appear. Yet, judicial review is one of the most important activities of the Supreme Court—the power to decide whether or not a law is constitutional, or in accord with the rules of the Constitution. Judicial review is an important element of the system of checks and balances. Over the years, the Supreme Court has declared many laws unconstitutional.

equity fairness
consul government official who looks after our government's interests in another country
admiralty officials in charge of the navy

Trial by Jury

The right to be judged by a group of citizens and not only by a judge is granted to anyone accused of a federal crime.

Section 3: Treason

Treason is the act of being disloyal to one's own country. It is the only crime defined in the Constitution.

levying to start or wage (war)

Punishment

Congress has the power to decide the punishment for someone convicted of treason, but the punishment cannot extend to the convicted person's family.

Section 1: State Acts and Records

Each state must respect the laws, official records, and court decisions of another state. Birth certificates, marriage certificates, and wills that are valid in one state must be recognized as valid in all states.

ARTICLE III: THE JUDICIAL BRANCH

Section 1: The Court System

The judicial power of the United States, shall be **vested** in one Supreme Court, and in such inferior courts as the Congress may from time to time **ordain** and establish. The judges, both of the Supreme and inferior courts, shall hold their offices during good behavior, and shall, at stated times, receive for their services, a compensation, which shall not be diminished during their continuance in office.

Section 2: Authority of the Courts

1. Federal Courts and Judges The judicial power shall extend to all cases, in law and **equity**, arising under this Constitution, the laws of the United States, and treaties made, or which shall be made, under their authority; to all cases affecting ambassadors, other public ministers and **consuls**; to all cases of **admiralty** and maritime jurisdiction; to controversies to which the United States shall be a party; to controversies between two or more states; ~~between a state and citizens of another State~~; between citizens of different states; between citizens of the same state claiming lands under grants of different states, and between a state, or the citizens thereof, and foreign states, ~~citizens or subjects~~.

2. The Supreme Court In all cases affecting ambassadors, other public ministers and consuls, and those in which a state shall be party, the Supreme Court shall have original jurisdiction. In all the other cases before mentioned, the Supreme Court shall have appellate jurisdiction, both as to law and fact, with such exceptions, and under such regulations as the congress shall make.

3. Trial by Jury The trial of all crimes, except in cases of impeachment, shall be by jury; and such trial shall be held in the state where the said crimes shall have been committed; but when not committed within any state, the trial shall be at such place or places as the Congress may by law have directed.

Section 3: Treason

1. Explanation Treason against the United States, shall consist only in **levying** war against them, or in adhering to their enemies, giving them aid and comfort. No person shall be convicted of treason unless on the testimony of two witnesses to the same overt act, or on confession in open court.

2. Punishment The Congress shall have power to declare the punishment of treason, but no attainder of treason shall work corruption of blood, or forfeiture except during the life of the person attainted.

ARTICLE IV: RELATIONS AMONG THE STATES

Section 1: State Acts and Records

Full faith and credit shall be given in each state to the public acts, records, and judicial proceedings of every other state. And the

Congress may by general laws prescribe the manner in which such acts, records, and proceedings shall be proved, and the effect thereof.

Section 2: Citizens' Rights

1. Citizenship The citizens of each state shall be entitled to all privileges and immunities of citizens in the several states.

2. Criminal Jurisdicton A person charged in any state with treason, felony, or other crime, who shall flee from justice, and be found in another state, shall on demand of the executive authority of the state from which he fled, be delivered up, to be removed to the state having jurisdiction of the crime.

3. Escaped Slaves ~~No Person held to service or labor in one state, under the laws thereof, escaping into another, shall, in consequence of any law or regulation therein, be discharged from such service or labor, but shall be delivered up on claim of the party to whom such service or labor may be due.~~

Section 3: New States

1. Admission New states may be admitted by the Congress into this Union; but no new state shall be formed or erected within the jurisdiction of any other state; nor any state be formed by the junction of two or more states, or parts of states, without the consent of the legislatures of the states concerned as well as of the Congress.

2. Congressional Power The Congress shall have power to dispose of and make all needful rules and regulations respecting the territory or other property belonging to the United States; and nothing in this Constitution shall be so **construed** as to prejudice any claims of the United States, or of any particular state.

Section 4: United States' Guarantee

The United States shall guarantee to every state in this Union a republican form of government, and shall protect each of them against invasion; and on application of the legislature, or of the executive (when the legislature cannot be convened) against domestic violence.

ARTICLE V: AMENDING THE CONSTITUTION

The Congress, whenever two-thirds of both houses shall deem it necessary, shall propose amendments to this Constitution, or, on the application of the legislatures of two-thirds of the several states, shall call a convention for proposing amendments, which, in either case, shall be valid to all intents and purposes, as part of this Constitution, when ratified by the legislatures of three-fourths of the several states, or by conventions in three-fourths thereof, as the one or the other mode of ratification may be proposed by the Congress; provided that ~~no amendment which may be made prior to the year one thousand eight hundred and eight shall in any manner affect the first and fourth clauses in the ninth section of the first article; and that~~ no state, without its consent, shall be deprived of its equal suffrage in the Senate.

If a person charged with a crime flees to another state, what action is that state required to take? Why do you think this is so?

Escaped Slaves
This clause was nullified by the Thirteenth Amendment (1865) which abolished slavery.

person held to service or labor an enslaved person

Section 3: New States
Only Congress can admit new states to the Union.

construed interpreted

Section 4: United States' Guarantee
A republican form of government is one in which the citizens choose, through voting, who will represent them in government. The government exists only by the consent, or will, of the citizens.

Amending the Constitution
These procedures are necessary to amend, or change, the Constitution. The process is very difficult. Since 1789, only 33 amendments have been proposed and 27 have been ratified.

There are two ways of proposing an amendment:
• by a two-thirds vote in Congress
• by a national convention called by Congress at the request of two-thirds of the state legislatures

debts money, goods, or services owed to another person or group

Supreme Law
Federal laws are superior to state laws. No state may make a law that conflicts with the Constitution, a law of Congress, or a treaty.

Supporting the Constitution
All government officials must support the Constitution. However, no religious test will ever be necessary for anyone to hold office.

How many states are needed to ratify the Constitution in order for it to take effect?

ARTICLE VI: NATIONAL DEBTS AND RATIFICATION

1. Debts All **debts** contracted and engagements entered into, before the adoption of this Constitution, shall be as valid against the United States under this Constitution, as under the Confederation.

2. Supreme Law This Constitution, and the laws of the United States which shall be made in pursuance thereof; and all treaties made, or which shall be made, under the authority of the United States, shall be the supreme law of the land; and the judges in every state shall be bound thereby, anything in the Constitution or laws of any state to the contrary notwithstanding.

3. Supporting the Constitution The senators and representatives before mentioned, and the members of the several state legislatures, and all executive and judicial officers, both of the United States and of the several states, shall be bound by oath or affirmation, to support this Constitution; but no religious test shall ever be required as a qualification to any office or public trust under the United States.

ARTICLE VII: RATIFICATION

The ratification of the conventions of nine states, shall be sufficient for the establishment of this Constitution between the states so ratifying the same.

Done in convention by the unanimous consent of the states present the seventeenth day of September in the year of our Lord one thousand seven hundred and eighty seven and of the independence of the United States of America the twelfth. In witness whereof we have hereunto subscribed our names

George Washington, *President and deputy from (Virginia)*

NEW HAMSPHIRE
John Langdon
Nicholas Gilman

MASSACHUSETTS
Nathaniel Gorham
Rufus King

CONNECTICUT
William Samuel
  Johnson
Roger Sherman

NEW YORK
Alexander Hamilton

NEW JERSEY
William Livingston
David Brearley
William Paterson
Jonathan Dayton

PENNSYLVANIA
Benjamin Franklin
Thomas Mifflin
Robert Morris
George Clymer
Thomas FitzSimons
Jared Ingersoll
James Wilson
Gouverneur Morris

DELAWARE
George Read
Gunning Bedford
John Dickinson
Richard Bassett
Jacob Brown

MARYLAND
James McHenry
Daniel of St.
  Thomas Jenifer
Daniel Carroll

VIRGINIA
John Blair
James Madison

NORTH CAROLINA
William Blount
Richard Dobbs
  Spaight
Hugh Williamson

SOUTH CAROLINA
John Rutledge
Charles Cotesworth
  Pinckney
Charles Pinckney
Pierce Butler

GEORGIA
William Few
Abraham Baldwin

AMENDMENTS TO THE CONSTITUTION
First Amendment: Religious and Personal Freedom
(Ratified December 15, 1791)

Congress shall make no law respecting an establishment of religion, or prohibiting the free exercise thereof; or **abridging** the freedom of speech, or of the press; or the right of the people peaceably to assemble, and to petition the government for a **redress** of grievances.

Second Amendment: Right to Keep Arms
(Ratified December 15, 1791)

A well-regulated militia, being necessary to the security of a free state, the right of the people to keep and bear arms, shall not be infringed.

Third Amendment: Housing of Troops
(Ratified December 15, 1791)

No soldier shall, in time of peace be **quartered** in any house, without the consent of the owner, nor in time of war, but in a manner to be prescribed by law.

Fourth Amendment: Search and Seizure
(Ratified December 15, 1791)

The right of the people to be secure in their persons, houses, papers, and effects, against unreasonable searches and seizures, shall not be violated, and no **warrants** shall issue, but upon probable cause, supported by oath or affirmation, and particularly describing the place to be searched, and the persons or things to be seized.

Fifth Amendment: Rights of Accused Persons
(Ratified December 15, 1791)

No person shall be held to answer for a capital, or otherwise infamous crime, unless on a presentment or indictment of a grand jury, except in cases arising in the land or naval forces, or in the militia, when in actual service in time of war or public danger; nor shall any person be subject for the same offense to be twice put in jeopardy of life or limb; nor shall be compelled in any criminal case to be a witness against himself, or be deprived of life, liberty, or property, without due process of law; nor shall private property be taken for public use, without just compensation.

Sixth Amendment: Criminal Court Procedures
(Ratified December 15, 1791)

In all criminal prosecutions, the accused shall enjoy the right to a speedy and public trial, by an impartial jury of the state and district wherein the crime shall have been committed, which district shall have been previously ascertained by law, and to be informed of the nature and cause of the accusation; to be confronted with the witnesses against him; to have compulsory process for obtaining witnesses in his favor, and to have the assistance of counsel for his defense.

Amendments to the Constitution
The first 10 amendments, which became part of the Constitution in 1791, are known as the Bill of Rights. These amendments were intended to restrict the federal government.

First Amendment
Protects certain personal freedoms, such as freedom of religion, freedom of the press, and the freedom of political rights.

abridging limiting or restricting
redress correction

Second Amendment
Guarantees the right of state militias to keep arms.

Third Amendment
Prohibits the government from using private homes to house soldiers.

quartered lodged or housed

Fourth Amendment
Protects citizens from government searches or seizures of their property without a valid reason.

warrant a legal document explaining why a search is needed and where the search will be carried out

Fifth Amendment
Rights protected here include:

- A person cannot be tried in a federal court for a serious crime without a formal accusation from a grand jury.

- A person found guilty of a crime in federal court cannot be tried again for the same offense in a federal court.

- People accused of a crime cannot be forced to say anything that might help the government convict them.

Sixth Amendment

- Accused people are entitled to a public trial by a jury, held soon after the person has been accused of the crime.

- Accused people must be told the nature of the charges against them.

- Accused people have the right to a lawyer whether or not they can afford one.

Seventh Amendment
No judge can overturn the decision of a jury because the judge disagrees with the jury's findings. Judges can set aside a verdict, however, if they find that the trial court made legal errors.

common law refers to laws established by judges in past cases

Eighth Amendment
The government may not set bail or impose punishments that are not in proportion to the crime.

Ninth Amendment
People have rights not listed in the Constitution. This was included to meet criticisms that a government might justify oppression by saying that it is not prohibited by the Bill of Rights.

Tenth Amendment
This amendment limits federal power. It states that powers not given to the federal government and not denied to the states belong to the states or to the people.

Eleventh Amendment
The juducial branch's power is limited to specific kinds of cases.

Twelfth Amendment
Originally, the Constitution established that presidential electors voted for two persons. The person who got the most votes was elected President. The person who got the second most electoral votes was elected Vice President. In the 1800 Presidential election Thomas Jefferson and Aaron Burr, running on the same ticket, received an equal number of electoral votes. This electoral tie resulted in a bitter deadlock. The Twelfth Amendment sought to prevent this problem from happening again by instructing electors to cast separate ballots for President and Vice President.

Seventh Amendment: Trial by Jury in Civil Cases
(Ratified December 15, 1791)

In suits at **common law**, where the value in controversy shall exceed twenty dollars, the right of trial by jury shall be preserved, and no fact tried by a jury, shall be otherwise reexamined in any court of the United States, than according to the rules of the common law.

Eighth Amendment: Limits on Bail, Fines, and Punishments
(Ratified December 15, 1791)

Excessive bail shall not be required, nor excessive fines imposed, nor cruel and unusual punishments inflicted.

Ninth Amendment: Rights Retained by the People
(Ratified December 15, 1791)

The enumeration in the Constitution, of certain rights, shall not be construed to deny or disparage others retained by the people.

Tenth Amendment: Powers Reserved to the States
(Ratified December 15, 1791)

The powers not delegated to the United States by the Constitution, nor prohibited by it to the states, are reserved to the states respectively, or to the people.

Eleventh Amendment: Suits Against States
(Ratified February 7, 1795)

The judicial power of the United States shall not be construed to extend to any suit in law or equity, commenced or prosecuted against one of the United States by citizens of another state, or by citizens or subjects of any foreign state.

Twelfth Amendment: Election of President and Vice President
(Ratified June 15, 1804)

The electors shall meet in their respective states, and vote by ballot for President and Vice President, one of whom, at least, shall not be an inhabitant of the same state with themselves; they shall name in their ballots the person voted for as President, and in distinct ballots the person voted for as Vice President, and they shall make distinct lists of all persons voted for as President, and of all persons voted for as Vice President, and of the number of votes for each, which lists they shall sign and certify, and transmit sealed to the seat of the government of the United States, directed to the president of the Senate; the president of the Senate shall, in the presence of the Senate and House of Representatives, open all the certificates and the votes shall then be counted; the person having the greatest number of votes for President, shall be the President, if such number be a majority of the whole number of electors appointed; and if no person have such majority, then from the persons having the highest number not exceeding three on the list of those voted for as President, the House of Representatives shall choose immediately, by ballot, the President. But in choosing the President, the votes shall be taken by states, the representation from each state having one vote; a **quorum** for this purpose shall consist of a member or members from two-thirds of the states, and a majority of all the states shall be necessary to a choice. And if the House of Representatives shall not choose a President whenever the right of choice shall **devolve** upon them, ~~before the fourth day of March next following,~~ then the Vice President shall act as President, as in the case of the death or other Constitutional disability of the President. The person having the greatest number of votes as Vice President, shall be the Vice President, if such number be a majority of the whole number of electors appointed, and if no person have a majority, then from the two highest numbers on the list, the Senate shall choose the Vice President; a quorum for the purpose shall consist of two-thirds of the whole number of senators, and a majority of the whole number shall be necessary to a choice. But no person Constitutionally ineligible to the office of President shall be eligible to that of Vice President of the United States.

Thirteenth Amendment: Abolition of Slavery
(Ratified December 6, 1865)

Section 1
Neither slavery nor involuntary servitude, except as a punishment for crime whereof the party shall have been duly convicted, shall exist within the United States, or any place subject to their jurisdiction.

Section 2
Congress shall have the power to enforce this article by appropriate legislation.

Fourteenth Amendment: Rights of Citizens
(Ratified July 9, 1868)

Section 1
All persons born or naturalized in the United States, and subject to the jurisdiction thereof, are citizens of the United States and of the state wherein they reside. No state shall make or enforce any law which shall abridge the **privileges or immunities** of citizens of the United States; nor shall any state deprive any person of life, liberty, or property, without due process of law; nor deny to any person within its jurisdiction the equal protection of the laws.

Section 2
Representatives shall be apportioned among the several states according to their respective numbers, counting the whole number of persons in each state, ~~excluding Indians not taxed~~. But when the right to vote at any election for the choice of electors for President and Vice President of the United States, representatives in Congress, the executive and judicial officers of a state, or the members of the legislature thereof, is denied to any of the ~~male~~ inhabitants of such state, ~~being twenty-one years of age,~~ and

 How did the Thirteenth and Fourteenth Amendments increase Americans' freedoms and rights?

citizens of the United States, or in any way abridged, except for participation in rebellion, or other crime, the basis of representation therein shall be reduced in proportion which the number of such male citizens shall bear to the whole number of ~~male~~ citizens ~~twenty-one years of age~~ in such state.

Section 3

No person shall be a senator or representative in Congress, or elector of President and Vice President, or hold any office, civil or military, under the United States, or under any state, who, having previously taken an oath, as a member of Congress, or as an officer of the United States, or as a member of any state legislature, or as an executive or judicial officer of any state, to support the Constitution of the United States, shall have engaged in insurrection against the same, or given aid or comfort to the enemies thereof. But Congress may, by a vote of two-thirds of each house, remove such disability.

Section 4

The validity of the public debt of the United States, authorized by law, including debts incurred for payment of pensions and bounties for services in suppressing insurrection or rebellion, shall not be questioned. But neither the United States nor any state shall assume or pay any debt or obligation incurred in aid of insurrection or rebellion against the United States, or any claim for the loss or emancipation of any slave; but all such debts, obligations, and claims shall be held illegal and void.

Section 5

The Congress shall have power to enforce, by appropriate legislation, the provisions of this article.

Fifteenth Amendment: Right to Vote
(Ratified February 3, 1870)

Section 1

The right of citizens of the United States to vote shall not be denied or abridged by the United States or by any state on account of race, color, or **previous condition of servitude**.

Section 2

The Congress shall have the power to enforce this article by appropriate legislation.

Sixteenth Amendment: Income Tax
(Ratified February 3, 1913)

The Congress shall have power to lay and collect taxes on incomes, from whatever source derived, without apportionment among the several states, and without regard to any census or enumeration.

Section 3
Prohibits former Confederate leaders from voting or holding office. This provision was partly revoked in 1872. It was eliminated completely in 1898 so that former Confederate officers could fight in the Spanish-American War.

Fifteenth Amendment
Neither the United States nor any state can deny the right to vote to any persons because of race or because they were once slaves.

previous condition of servitude refers to people who were formerly enslaved

Sixteenth Amendment
Congress is allowed to collect taxes on people's income.

Seventeenth Amendment: Direct Election of Senators

(Ratified April 8, 1913)

Section 1

The Senate of the United States shall be composed of two senators from each state, elected by the people thereof, for six years; and each senator shall have one vote. The electors in each state shall have the qualifications **requisite** for electors of the most numerous branch of the state legislatures.

Section 2

When vacancies happen in the representation of any state in the Senate, the executive authority of such state shall issue writs of election to fill such vacancies: Provided, that the legislature of any state may empower the executive thereof to make temporary appointments until the people fill the vacancies by election as the legislature may direct.

Section 3

~~This amendment shall not be so construed as to affect the election or term of any senator chosen before it becomes valid as part of the Constitution.~~

Eighteenth Amendment: Prohibition

(Ratified January 16, 1919)

Section 1

~~After one year from the ratification of this article the manufacture, sale, or transportation of intoxicating liquors within, the importation thereof into, or the exportation thereof from the United States and all territory subject to the jurisdiction thereof for beverage purposes is hereby prohibited.~~

Section 2

~~The Congress and the several states shall have concurrent power to enforce this article by appropriate legislation.~~

Section 3

~~This article shall be inoperative unless it shall have been ratified as an amendment to the Constitution by the legislatures of the several states, as provided in the Constitution, within seven years from the date of the submission hereof to the states by the Congress.~~

Nineteenth Amendment: Women's Right to Vote

(Ratified August 18, 1920)

Section 1

The right of the citizens of the United States to vote shall not be denied or abridged by the United States or by any state on account of sex.

Section 2

Congress shall have power to enforce this article by appropriate legislation.

Seventeenth Amendment
Senators are elected directly by the voters every six years, instead of by the state legislatures.

---

requisite required, necessary

Eighteenth Amendment
This is the only amendment to be completely repealed. It prohibited the making, selling, and transporting of alcohol. It was part of a national effort to reduce the problems associated with the abuse of alcohol. It was repealed by the Twenty-first Amendment in 1933.

 How did the Fifteenth and Nineteenth Amendments expand voting rights to Americans?

Nineteenth Amendment
In 1920, women finally won the right to vote—suffrage—in both national and state elections. The struggle for woman suffrage had gone on for almost 75 years before passage of the Nineteenth Amendment.

Twentieth Amendment: Presidential Terms
(Ratified January 23, 1933)

Section 1

The terms of President and Vice President shall end at noon on the 20th day of January, and the terms of senators and representatives at noon on the 3rd day of January, of the years in which such terms would have ended if this article had not been ratified; and the terms of their successors shall then begin.

Section 2

The Congress shall assemble at least once in every year, and such meeting shall begin at noon on the 3d day of January, unless they shall by law appoint a different day.

Section 3

If, at the time fixed for the beginning of the term of President, the President-elect shall have died, the Vice President-elect shall become President. If a President shall not have been chosen before the time fixed for the beginning of his term, or if the President-elect shall have failed to qualify, then the Vice President-elect shall act as President until a President shall have qualified; and the Congress may by law provide for the case wherein neither a President-elect nor a Vice President-elect shall have qualified, declaring who shall then act as President, or the manner in which one who is to act shall be selected, and such person shall act accordingly until a President or Vice President shall have qualified.

Section 4

The Congress may by law provide for the case of the death of any of the persons from whom the House of Representatives may choose a President whenever the right of choice shall have devolved upon them, and for the case of the death of any of the persons from whom the Senate may choose a Vice President whenever the right of choice shall have devolved upon them.

Section 5

Sections 1 and 2 shall take effect on the 15th day of October following the ratification of this article.

Section 6

This article shall be inoperative unless it shall have been ratified as an amendment to the Constitution by the legislatures of three-fourths of the several states within seven years from the date of its submission.

Twenty-first Amendment: Repeal of Prohibition
(Ratified December 5, 1933)

Section 1

The eighteenth article of amendment to the Constitution of the United States is hereby repealed.

Section 2

The transportation or importation into any state, territory, or possession of the United States for delivery or use therein of intoxicating liquors, in violation of the laws thereof, is hereby prohibited.

Section 3

This article shall be inoperative unless it shall have been ratified as an amendment to the Constitution by conventions in the several states, as provided in the Constitution, within seven years from the date of the submission hereof to the states by the Congress.

Twenty-second Amendment: Limitation of Presidential Terms
(Ratified February 27, 1951)

Section 1

No person shall be elected to the office of President more than twice, and no person who has held the office of President, or acted as President, for more than two years of a term to which some other person was elected President shall be elected to the office of the President more than once. ~~But this article shall not apply to any person holding the office of President when this article was proposed by the Congress, and shall not prevent any person who may be holding the office of President, or acting as President, during the term within which this article becomes operative from holding the office of President or acting as President during the remainder of such term.~~

Section 2

~~This article shall be inoperative unless it shall have been ratified as an amendment to the Constitution by the legislatures of three-fourths of the several states within seven years from the date of its submission to the states by the Congress.~~

Twenty-third Amendment: Presidential Electors for the District of Columbia
(Ratified March 29, 1961)

Section 1

The district constituting the seat of government of the United States shall appoint in such manner as the Congress may direct: A number of electors of President and Vice President equal to the whole number of senators and representatives in Congress to which the district would be entitled if it were a state, but in no event more than the least populous state; they shall be in addition to those appointed by the states, but they shall be considered, for the purposes of the election of President and Vice President, to be electors appointed by a state; and they shall meet in the district and perform such duties as provided by the twelfth article of amendment.

Section 2

The Congress shall have power to enforce this article by appropriate legislation.

Twenty-second Amendment
Before Franklin D. Roosevelt's four terms, no President served more than two terms. This tradition had started with George Washington. This amendment made the two-term tradition into a law.

Why do you think the President is prevented from serving more than two terms?

Twenty-third Amendment
By the time this amendment was ratified in 1960, more than 781,000 people lived in Washington, D.C. However, the Constitution had no provisions for allowing residents of the District of Columbia to vote in presidential elections. Now the District of Columbia has three electoral college votes.

Twenty-fourth Amendment

Poll taxes require people to pay taxes before they are able to vote. The poll tax was often used to prevent African Americans from voting.

Twenty-fifth Amendment

This amendment establishes procedures if the President dies, resigns, or is temporarily disabled. It creates two ways of dealing with the transition of power. If the President notifies Congress, in writing, that he or she is too sick to perform the duties of the presidency, then the Vice President assumes the Presidency until the President recovers. If the President is unable or unwilling to notify Congress, then the Vice President and a majority of the Cabinet can declare the President disabled and allow the Vice President to assume the duties of the presidency. This amendment also states that if a vacancy exists in the office of the Vice President, the President nominates a Vice President and a majority of both houses of Congress must approve.

Twenty-fourth Amendment: Abolition of Poll Taxes in National Elections

(Ratified January 23, 1964)

Section 1

The right of citizens of the United States to vote in any primary or other election for President or Vice President, for electors for President or Vice President, or for senator or representative in Congress, shall not be denied or abridged by the United States or any state by reason of failure to pay any poll tax or other tax.

Section 2

The Congress shall have power to enforce this article by appropriate legislation.

Twenty-fifth Amendment: Presidential Disability and Vice-Presidential Vacancies

(Ratified February 10, 1967)

Section 1

In case of the removal of the President from office or of his death or resignation, the Vice President shall become President.

Section 2

Whenever there is a vacancy in the office of the Vice President, the President shall nominate a Vice President who shall take office upon confirmation by a majority vote of both houses of Congress.

Section 3

Whenever the President transmits to the president pro tempore of the Senate and the speaker of the House of Representatives his written declaration that he is unable to discharge the powers and duties of his office, and until he transmits to them a written declaration to the contrary, such powers and duties shall be discharged by the Vice President as acting President.

Section 4

Whenever the Vice President and a majority of either the principle officers of the executive departments or of such other body as Congress may by law provide, transmit to the president pro tempore of the Senate and the speaker of the House of Representatives their written declaration that the President is unable to discharge the powers and duties of his office, the Vice President shall immediately assume the powers and duties of the office as acting President.

Thereafter, when the President transmits to the president pro tempore of the Senate and the speaker of the House of Representatives his written declaration that no inability exists, he shall resume the powers and duties of his office unless the Vice President and a majority of either the principal officers of the executive department or of such other body as Congress may by law provide, transmit within four days to the president pro tempore of the Senate and the speaker of the House of Representatives their written declaration that the President is unable to discharge the powers and duties of his office. Thereupon Congress shall decide the issue, assembling within forty-eight hours for that purpose if not in session. If the Congress, within twenty-one days after receipt of the latter written declaration, or, if Congress is not in session, within twenty-one days after Congress is required to assemble, determines by two-thirds vote of both houses that the President is unable to discharge the powers and duties of his office, the Vice President shall continue to discharge the same as acting President; otherwise, the President shall resume the powers and duties of his office.

Twenty-sixth Amendment: Eighteen-Year-Old Vote
(Ratified July 1, 1971)

Section 1
The right of the citizens of the United States who are 18 years of age or older, to vote shall not be denied or abridged by the United States or by any state on account of age.

Section 2
The Congress shall have power to enforce this article by appropriate legislation.

Twenty-seventh Amendment: Congressional Compensation
(Ratified May 7, 1992)

No law, varying the compensation for the services of the senators and representatives, shall take effect until an election of representatives shall have intervened.

Twenty-sixth Amendment
The right to vote is extended to 18-year-olds in all elections. Granting the right to vote had become an issue during the 1960s when 18-year-old men were forced to register for the draft but were prohibited from voting.

Twenty-seventh Amendment
Congress may raise members' salaries, but the raise only takes effect after the next congressional elections. This allows voters to speak out on proposed raises. The Twenty-seventh Amendment was proposed in 1789, but was not ratified until 1992.

Connecting ◆ Past and Present

Which three amendments passed since 1800 do you think have had the most significant impact on American society today? Explain your answer.

The Emancipation Proclamation

On September 22, 1862, President Abraham Lincoln issued a statement (a preliminary proclamation) on the abolition of slavery in the Confederacy. Lincoln declared that on January 1, 1863, all enslaved people living in areas which were in rebellion against the United States would be freed.

On January 1, 1863, Abraham Lincoln formally issued the Emancipation Proclamation. All slaves in areas controlled by the Confederacy were now declared to be free.

"I never, in my life, felt more certain that I was doing right than I do in signing this paper." These were the words that President Abraham Lincoln spoke just before he signed the Emancipation Proclamation.

---

emancipation freedom from bondage
proclamation an announcement

---

repress to dominate or control; to hold back

---

aforesaid already mentioned

 Which Constitutional amendments are related to the ideas in the Emancipation Proclamation?

---

countervailing evidence that shows something is not true

By the President of the United States of America

A Proclamation

Whereas on the 22nd day of September, A.D. 1862, a proclamation was issued by the President of the United States, containing, among other things, the following, to wit:

"That on the 1st day of January, A.D. 1863, all persons held as slaves within any State or designated part of a State the people whereof shall then be in rebellion against the United States shall be then, thenceforward, and forever free; and the executive government of the United States, including the military and naval authority thereof, will recognize and maintain the freedom of such persons and will do no act or acts to **repress** such persons, or any of them, in any efforts they may make for their actual freedom.

"That the executive will on the 1st day of January **aforesaid**, by proclamation, designate the States and parts of States, if any, in which the people thereof, respectively, shall then be in rebellion against the United States; and the fact that any State or the people thereof shall on that day be in good faith represented in the Congress of the United States by members chosen thereto at elections wherein a majority of the qualified voters of such States shall have participated shall, in the absence of strong **countervailing** testimony, be deemed conclusive evidence that such State and the people thereof are not then in rebellion against the United States."

Now, therefore, I, Abraham Lincoln, President of the United States, by virtue of the power in me vested as Commander-In-Chief of the Army and Navy of the United States in time of actual armed rebellion against the authority and government of the United States, and as a fit and necessary war measure for **suppressing** said rebellion, do, on this 1st day of January, A.D. 1863, and in accordance with my purpose so to do, publicly proclaimed for the full period of one hundred days from the first day above mentioned, order and designate as the States and parts of States wherein the people thereof, respectively, are this day in rebellion against the United States the following, to wit:

Arkansas, Texas, Louisiana (except the parishes of St. Bernard, Palquemines, Jefferson, St. John, St. Charles, St. James, Ascension, Assumption, Terrebone, Lafourche, St. Mary, St. Martin, and Orleans, including the city of New Orleans), Mississippi, Alabama, Florida, Georgia, South Carolina, North Carolina, and Virginia (except the forty-eight counties designated as West Virginia, and also the counties of Berkeley, Accomac, Northhampton, Elizabeth City, York, Princess Anne, and Norfolk, including the cities of Norfolk and Portsmouth), and which **excepted parts** are for the present left precisely as if this proclamation were not issued.

And by virtue of the power and for the purpose aforesaid, I do order and declare that all persons held as slaves within said designated States and parts of States are, and **henceforward** shall be, free; and that the Executive Government of the United States, including the military and naval authorities thereof, will recognize and maintain the freedom of said persons.

And I hereby enjoin upon the **people so declared to be free** to **abstain** from all violence, unless in necessary self-defense; and I recommend to them that, in all cases when allowed, they labor faithfully for reasonable wages.

And I further declare and make known that such persons of suitable condition will be received into the armed service of the United States to garrison forts, positions, stations, and other places, and to man vessels of all sorts in said service.

And upon this act, sincerely believed to be an act of justice, warranted by the Constitution upon military necessity, I invoke the considerate judgment of mankind and the gracious favor of Almighty God.

suppressing ending or holding back

Areas that are considered a part of the Confederacy will be affected by the Proclamation.

These are the areas still rebelling against the United States. Slaves living in areas that are not listed are not freed.

excepted parts states and parts of states that are not affected by the Emancipation Proclamation

Enslaved people living in the areas mentioned above are now free and the United States will fight for their freedom.

henceforward from now on
people so declared to be free freed slaves
abstain do without

President Lincoln encourages the newly freed slaves to join the Union's armed forces. (Nearly 180,000 former slaves joined the Union Army to fight against the Confederacy.)

Connecting ◆ Past and Present

In what ways did the Emancipation Proclamation pave the way for future civil rights laws?

The Seneca Falls Declaration of Sentiments

In 1848, Elizabeth Cady Stanton and Lucretia Mott held a women's rights convention in Seneca Falls, New York. The women and men at the meeting demanded more rights for women, including better education and job opportunities and the right to vote.

The words of the Seneca Falls Declaration of Sentiments of 1848 look both to the past and to the future. By paralleling the words of the Declaration of Independence (see page 688), the writers showed how many parts of the 1776 Declaration did not apply to women. The Declaration of Sentiments looked to the future, however, as its ideas inspired fighters for women's rights throughout the 1800s and into the 1900s.

The Seneca Falls Declaration of Sentiments (Excerpts)

The opening words parallel the preamble to the Declaration of Independence.

one portion of the family of man women
impel encourage or demand

When, in the course of human events, it becomes necessary for **one portion of the family of man** to assume among the people of the earth a position different from that which they have hitherto occupied, but one to which the laws of nature and nature's God entitle them, a decent respect to the opinions of mankind requires that they should declare the causes that **impel** them to such a course.

These words also parallel the Declaration of Independence, with the addition of the crucial word "women" to the phrase "all men and women are created equal."

self-evident obvious
consent agreement

We hold these truths to be **self-evident**: that all men and women are created equal; that they are endowed by their Creator with certain inalienable rights; that among these are life, liberty, and the pursuit of happiness; that to secure these rights governments are instituted, deriving their just powers from the **consent** of the governed. . . .

The history of mankind is a history of repeated injuries and usurpations on the part of man toward woman, having in direct object the establishment of an absolute tyranny over her. . . .

Women demand all the rights and privileges that they should have as citizens of the United States, especially the right to vote.

degradation lowering in value
aggrieved hurt or injured
fraudulently dishonestly

Now, in view of not allowing one half the people of this country to vote, of their social and religious **degradation** . . . and because women do feel themselves **aggrieved**, oppressed, and **fraudulently** deprived of their most sacred rights, we insist that they have immediate admission to all the rights and privileges which belong to them as citizens of the United States.

The authors understand that they may be misunderstood. However, gaining equal rights is so important that they will do whatever is necessary.

In entering upon the great work before us, we anticipate mistaken ideas, misrepresentations, and ridicule; but we shall make every effort within our power to secure our object.

Connecting ◆ Past and Present

In what year was an amendment to the Constitution passed that guaranteed a right the authors of the Declaration of Sentiments were fighting for? What was the right?

Chief Joseph's Speech

Chief Joseph led a group of Native Americans called the Nez Percé. Chief Joseph was known to the Nez Percé as Hin-mah-too-yah-lat-kekt, or Thunder Rolling Down the Mountain. The Nez Percé were a peaceful nation who lived in the valley of the Walla Walla in Oregon.

The U.S. government promised Chief Joseph that his people would live on their ancestral land forever. The government broke that promise. In 1877 the Nez Percé were forced to live on an Oklahoma reservation, where many died from disease and starvation. Chief Joseph wrote the following speech to describe the hardships the Nez Percé faced.

"I have heard talk and talk, but nothing is done. Good words do not last long unless they amount to something. Words do not pay for my dead people. They do not pay for my country, now overrun by **white men**. Good words will not give my people good health and stop them from dying. Good words will not get my people a home where they can live in peace and take care of themselves. I am tired of talk that comes to nothing. It makes my heart sick when I remember all the good words and broken promises.

"The earth is our mother. She should not be disturbed by hoe or plough. We want only to **subsist** on what she freely gives us.

"I believe much trouble and blood would be saved if we opened our hearts more. I will tell you in my way how the Indian sees things. The white man has more words to tell you how they look to him, but it does not require many words to speak the truth.

"If the white man wants to live in peace with the Indian, . . . we can live in peace. There need be no trouble. Treat all men alike . . . give them all the same law. Give them all an even chance to live and grow. You might as well expect the rivers to run backward as that any man who is born a free man should be contented when penned up and denied liberty to go where he pleases. We only ask an even chance to live as other men live. We ask to be recognized as men. Let me be a free man . . . free to travel . . . free to stop . . . free to work . . . free to choose my own teachers . . . free to follow the religion of my Fathers . . . free to think and talk and act for myself."

white men American settlers

subsist live or survive

To live in peace with the Native Americans, the settlers need to respect them and treat them with equality. Chief Joseph asks how a Native American, who has been born free, can be happy caged up in a reservation.

Connecting Past and Present

Chief Joseph discussed issues such as equality, freedom, and respect for the environment. Do these issues have the same importance for Americans today? Explain your answer.

	Years in Office	Vice President	Political Party	State[+]	
1 George Washington Born: 1732 Died: 1799	1789–1797	John Adams	Federalist	Virginia	
2 John Adams Born: 1735 Died: 1826	1797–1801	Thomas Jefferson	Federalist	Massachusetts	
3 Thomas Jefferson Born: 1743 Died: 1826	1801–1809	Aaron Burr, George Clinton	Democratic-Republican	Virginia	
4 James Madison Born: 1751 Died: 1836	1809–1817	George Clinton, Elbridge Gerry	Democratic-Republican	Virginia	
5 James Monroe Born: 1758 Died: 1831	1817–1825	Daniel D. Tompkins	Democratic-Republican	Virginia	
6 John Quincy Adams Born: 1767 Died: 1848	1825–1829	John C. Calhoun	Democratic-Republican	Massachusetts	
7 Andrew Jackson Born: 1767 Died: 1845	1829–1837	John C. Calhoun, Martin Van Buren	Democratic	Tennessee (SC)	
8 Martin Van Buren Born: 1782 Died: 1862	1837–1841	Richard M. Johnson	Democratic	New York	
9 William Henry Harrison* Born: 1773 Died: 1841	1841	John Tyler	Whig	Ohio (VA)	
10 John Tyler Born: 1790 Died: 1862	1841–1845	None	Whig	Virginia	
11 James K. Polk Born: 1795 Died: 1849	1845–1849	George M. Dallas	Democratic	Tennessee (NC)	
12 Zachary Taylor* Born: 1784 Died: 1850	1849–1850	Millard Fillmore	Whig	Louisiana (VA)	
13 Millard Fillmore Born: 1800 Died: 1874	1850–1853	None	Whig	New York	
14 Franklin Pierce Born: 1804 Died: 1869	1853–1857	William R. King	Democratic	New Hampshire	
15 James Buchanan Born: 1791 Died: 1868	1857–1861	John G. Breckinridge	Democratic	Pennsylvania	
16 Abraham Lincoln** Born: 1809 Died: 1865	1861–1865	Hannibal Hamlin, Andrew Johnson	Republican	Illinois (KY)	
17 Andrew Johnson Born: 1808 Died: 1875	1865–1869	None	Union	Tennessee (NC)	
18 Ulysses S. Grant Born: 1822 Died: 1885	1869–1877	Schuyler Colfax, Henry Wilson	Republican	Illinois (OH)	
19 Rutherford B. Hayes Born: 1822 Died: 1893	1877–1881	William A. Wheeler	Republican	Ohio	
20 James A. Garfield** Born: 1831 Died: 1881	1881	Chester A. Arthur	Republican	Ohio	

[+] State of residence at time of election. If state of birth is different, it is shown in parentheses.
* died in office   ** assassinated while in office   ***resigned while in office

		Years in Office	Vice President	Political Party	State*	
21	**Chester A. Arthur** Born: 1830 Died: 1886	1881–1885	None	Republican	New York (VT)	
22	**Grover Cleveland** Born: 1837 Died: 1908	1885–1889	Thomas A. Hendricks	Democratic	New York (NJ)	
23	**Benjamin Harrison** Born: 1833 Died: 1901	1889–1893	Levi P. Morton	Republican	Indiana (OH)	
24	**Grover Cleveland** Born: 1837 Died: 1908	1893–1897	Adlai E. Stevenson	Democratic	New York (NJ)	
25	**William McKinley**** Born: 1843 Died: 1901	1897–1901	Garrett Hobart, Theodore Roosevelt	Republican	Ohio	
26	**Theodore Roosevelt** Born: 1858 Died: 1919	1901–1909	Charles W. Fairbanks	Republican	New York	
27	**William Howard Taft** Born: 1857 Died: 1930	1909–1913	James S. Sherman	Republican	Ohio	
28	**Woodrow Wilson** Born: 1856 Died: 1924	1913–1921	Thomas R. Marshall	Democratic	New Jersey (VA)	
29	**Warren G. Harding*** Born: 1865 Died: 1923	1921–1923	Calvin Coolidge	Republican	Ohio	
30	**Calvin Coolidge** Born: 1872 Died: 1933	1923–1929	Charles G. Dawes	Republican	Massachusetts (VT)	
31	**Herbert C. Hoover** Born: 1874 Died: 1964	1929–1933	Charles Curtis	Republican	California (IA)	
32	**Franklin D. Roosevelt*** Born: 1882 Died: 1945	1933–1945	John N. Garner, Henry A. Wallace, Harry S Truman	Democratic	New York	
33	**Harry S Truman** Born: 1884 Died: 1972	1945–1953	Alben W. Barkley	Democratic	Missouri	
34	**Dwight D. Eisenhower** Born: 1890 Died: 1969	1953–1961	Richard M. Nixon	Republican	New York (TX)	
35	**John F. Kennedy**** Born: 1917 Died: 1963	1961–1963	Lyndon B. Johnson	Democratic	Massachusetts	
36	**Lyndon B. Johnson** Born: 1908 Died: 1973	1963–1969	Hubert H. Humphrey	Democratic	Texas	
37	**Richard M. Nixon***** Born: 1913 Died: 1994	1969–1974	Spiro T. Agnew, Gerald R. Ford	Republican	New York (CA)	
38	**Gerald R. Ford** Born: 1913	1974–1977	Nelson A. Rockefeller	Republican	Michigan (NE)	
39	**James E. Carter, Jr.** Born: 1924	1977–1981	Walter F. Mondale	Democratic	Georgia	
40	**Ronald Reagan** Born: 1911	1981–1989	George H.W. Bush	Republican	California (IL)	
41	**George H.W. Bush** Born: 1924	1989–1993	J. Danforth Quayle	Republican	Texas (MA)	
42	**William J. Clinton** Born: 1946	1993–	Albert Gore, Jr.	Democratic	Arkansas	

THE FIFTY STATES

State (U.S. government abbreviation)	Date of Entry into Union (Order of entry)	Total Area in Square Miles (Rank)	Population (in thousands), estimated 2000	Capital	State Nickname	Number of Representatives in House
Alabama (AL)	1819 (22)	52,423 (30)	4,451	Montgomery	Heart of Dixie	7
Alaska (AK)	1959 (49)	656,424 (1)	653	Juneau	The Last Frontier	1
Arizona (AZ)	1912 (48)	114,006 (6)	4,798	Phoenix	Grand Canyon State	6
Arkansas (AR)	1836 (25)	53,182 (29)	2,631	Little Rock	Land of Opportunity	4
California (CA)	1850 (31)	163,707 (3)	32,521	Sacramento	Golden State	52
Colorado (CO)	1876 (38)	104,100 (8)	4,168	Denver	Centennial State	6
Connecticut (CT)	1788 (5)	5,544 (48)	3,284	Hartford	Constitution State	6
Delaware (DE)	1787 (1)	2,489 (49)	768	Dover	First State	1
Florida (FL)	1845 (27)	65,756 (22)	15,233	Tallahassee	Sunshine State	23
Georgia (GA)	1788 (4)	59,441 (24)	7,875	Atlanta	Empire State of the South	11
Hawaii (HI)	1959 (50)	10,932 (43)	1,257	Honolulu	Aloha State	2
Idaho (ID)	1890 (43)	83,574 (14)	1,347	Boise	Gem State	2
Illinois (IL)	1818 (21)	57,918 (25)	12,051	Springfield	Land of Lincoln	20
Indiana (IN)	1816 (19)	36,420 (38)	6,045	Indianapolis	Hoosier State	10
Iowa (IA)	1846 (29)	56,276 (26)	2,900	Des Moines	Hawkeye State	5
Kansas (KS)	1861 (34)	82,282 (15)	2,668	Topeka	Sunflower State	4
Kentucky (KY)	1792 (15)	40,411 (37)	3,995	Frankfort	Bluegrass State	6
Louisiana (LA)	1812 (18)	51,843 (31)	4,425	Baton Rouge	Pelican State	7
Maine (ME)	1820 (23)	35,387 (39)	1,259	Augusta	Pine Tree State	2
Maryland (MD)	1788 (7)	12,407 (42)	5,275	Annapolis	Old Line State	8
Massachusetts (MA)	1788 (6)	10,555 (44)	6,199	Boston	Bay State	10
Michigan (MI)	1837 (26)	96,705 (11)	9,679	Lansing	Wolverine State	16
Minnesota (MN)	1858 (32)	86,943 (12)	4,830	St. Paul	Gopher State	8
Mississippi (MS)	1817 (20)	48,434 (32)	2,816	Jackson	Magnolia State	5
Missouri (MO)	1821 (24)	69,709 (21)	5,540	Jefferson City	Show Me State	9
Montana (MT)	1889 (41)	147,046 (4)	950	Helena	Treasure State	1
Nebraska (NE)	1867 (37)	77,358 (16)	1,705	Lincoln	Cornhusker State	3
Nevada (NV)	1864 (36)	110,567 (7)	1,871	Carson City	Silver State	2
New Hampshire (NH)	1788 (9)	9,351 (46)	1,224	Concord	Granite State	2
New Jersey (NJ)	1787 (3)	8,722 (47)	8,178	Trenton	Garden State	13
New Mexico (NM)	1912 (47)	121,598 (5)	1,860	Santa Fe	Land of Enchantment	3
New York (NY)	1788 (11)	54,471 (27)	18,146	Albany	Empire State	31
North Carolina (NC)	1789 (12)	53,821 (28)	7,777	Raleigh	Tar Heel State	12
North Dakota (ND)	1889 (39)	70,704 (19)	662	Bismarck	Flickertail State	1
Ohio (OH)	1803 (17)	44,828 (34)	11,319	Columbus	Buckeye State	19
Oklahoma (OK)	1907 (46)	69,903 (20)	3,373	Oklahoma City	Sooner State	6
Oregon (OR)	1859 (33)	98,386 (9)	3,397	Salem	Beaver State	5
Pennsylvania (PA)	1787 (2)	46,058 (33)	12,202	Harrisburg	Keystone State	21
Rhode Island (RI)	1790 (13)	1,545 (50)	998	Providence	Ocean State	2
South Carolina (SC)	1788 (8)	32,008 (40)	3,858	Columbia	Palmetto State	6
South Dakota (SD)	1889 (40)	77,121 (17)	777	Pierre	Mount Rushmore State	1
Tennessee (TN)	1796 (16)	42,146 (36)	5,657	Nashville	Volunteer State	9
Texas (TX)	1845 (28)	268,601 (2)	20,119	Austin	Lone Star State	30
Utah (UT)	1896 (45)	84,904 (13)	2,207	Salt Lake City	Beehive State	3
Vermont (VT)	1791 (14)	9,615 (45)	617	Montpelier	Green Mountain State	1
Virginia (VI)	1788 (10)	42,777 (35)	6,997	Richmond	Old Dominion	11
Washington (WA)	1889 (42)	71,302 (18)	5,858	Olympia	Evergreen State	9
West Virginia (WV)	1863 (35)	24,231 (41)	1,841	Charleston	Mountain State	3
Wisconsin (WI)	1848 (30)	65,499 (23)	5,326	Madison	Badger State	9
Wyoming (WY)	1890 (44)	97,818 (10)	525	Cheyenne	Equality State	1
District of Columbia (DC)		68 (51)	523			1 (non-voting)

Commonwealths and Territories	Total Area in Square Miles	Population (in thousands), estimated 2000				Capital
Puerto Rico (PR)	3,508	3,908				San Juan
Guam (GU)	217	171				Agana
U.S. Virgin Islands (VI)	171	99				Charlotte Amalie
American Samoa (AS)	90	69				Pago Pago
N. Mariana Islands (MP)	189	44				Saipan

Glossary

A

abdicate to formally give up one's power or office (p. 346)

abolition the act of doing away with slavery (p. 155)

acid rain a rain polluted with sulfuric acid (p. 664)

affirmative action a program to help minorities find jobs in fields that had been previously closed to them (p. 618)

affluence financial security and wealth (p. 513)

alienation the feeling that one is different from everyone else and does not fit in (p. 520)

ally a nation or person that is associated with another for a common cause or purpose (p. 329)

amend to change (p. 97)

amnesty a government pardon for political offenses (p. 210)

amphibious landing a military maneuver in which soldiers are brought close to shore by boat and swim or wade to land (p. 448)

anarchist a person who wants to do away with all forms of government (p. 265)

annex to take possession of (p. 118)

Antifederalist an opponent to the Constitution (p. 95)

anti-Semitic prejudiced against Jewish people (p. 405)

apartheid a policy that promoted complete separation of the races in Africa (p. 650)

appeasement a policy of giving in to avoid more trouble (p. 427)

aristocrat a person of the ruling class (p. 28)

armistice a cease-fire (p. 350)

arms race a competition to build weapons (p. 329)

arsenal a warehouse where weapons and ammunition are stored (p. 178)

artisan a craftsperson (p. 108)

assassinate to murder (p. 203)

assembly a lawmaking body (p. 56)

assembly line a row of factory workers who put together a product part by part as it passes by on a conveyor belt (p. 361)

assimilate to be absorbed into the culture of a population or group (p. 233)

astrolabe an instrument that shows distance north and south of the equator (p. 15)

automation the use of machines to do work formerly done by people (p. 513)

autonomy independence (p. 322)

ayatollah a high-ranking religious leader in a branch of Islam (p. 627)

B

baby boom the name given to the increase in births between 1945 and 1964—the largest population increase in the United States to date (p. 514)

backcountry the remote, less developed part of a region (p. 46)

bank holiday the closing of all the nation's banks for four days by President Roosevelt (p. 400)

barrio a Latino neighborhood (p. 348)

Bessemer process a process that blasts air at molten iron to turn it into high quality steel (p. 252)

bicameral having two legislative houses (p. 91)

Big Three the three leaders of the strongest Allied powers; Winston Churchill, Joseph Stalin, and Franklin Roosevelt (p. 445)

bilingual using two languages (p. 582)

bill of rights a list of basic freedoms as in the first ten amendments to the Constitution (p. 96)

Black Cabinet a group of African Americans brought together by President Roosevelt to advise him (p. 413)

black codes a series of laws aimed to limit the freedom African Americans gained with the passage of the Thirteenth Amendment and the Civil Rights Bill (p. 212)

blacklist a list of persons who are disapproved of or are to be punished or boycotted (p. 265)

black nationalism a political movement begun in the 1920s seeking to establish a separate homeland for African Americans; also refers to a belief in the separate identity and racial unity of the African American community (p. 374)

Black Panther a militant political party formed in Oakland, California, in 1966 that wanted African Americans to control their own communities (p. 573)

Black Power a political movement emphasizing racial separation and stressing unity and racial pride (p. 573)

blitzkrieg "lightning war" (p. 428)

bloc a group of nations united for a common action (p. 612)

blue-collar job employment in an industry like manufacturing and mining, so termed because of the work shirts worn by manual laborers (p. 513)

bonanza a source of sudden wealth (p. 237)

bond a certificate of debt that a government or business may issue to raise money (p. 98)

Bonus Army the group of jobless World War I veterans who marched on Washington, D.C., demanding their monetary bonuses (p. 384)

boom town a mining camp that seemed to spring up overnight (p. 138)

bootlegger a person who made liquor or smuggled it into the country (p. 368)

border ruffian an armed proslavery person (p. 176)

border state one of the four slave states located between the North and the South that stayed in the Union during the Civil War (p. 185)

bounty a reward (p. 196)

boycott an economic protest in which people refuse to buy certain goods (p. 68)

Brain Trust President Roosevelt's group of advisors, so named because many of its members were college professors, lawyers, and economists (p. 399)

branch line a smaller railroad line that reaches out to major cities (p. 254)

brinkmanship the policy in which the United States must be able to go to the brink of war without going over the edge (p. 492)

buffalo soldier a term given to an African American who guarded Native American reservations (p. 233)

C

Cabinet the group of department heads who serve as the President's chief advisors (p. 98)

Californio a citizen of California (p. 27)

canal a channel dug out of the ground and filled with water (p. 111)

capitalism the system in which privately owned businesses, farms, and factories compete with one another for profits (p. 260)

capitalist a person with money to invest in business to make a profit (p. 108)

carpetbagger a Northerner who moved to the South after the Civil War for political or economic gain (p. 216)

cash-and-carry policy a government procedure in which nations at war could buy nonmilitary goods from the United States as long as they paid cash and carried the goods home on their own ships (p. 434)

cash crop a crop that is grown for sale rather than for use by a farmer (p. 30)

casualty anyone hurt or killed, as in an accident or in battle (p. 190)

cede to surrender possession of (p. 65)

censorship the silencing of free speech (p. 195)

censure to officially reprimand (p. 297)

charter a written document from the government (p. 30)

checks and balances a system in which each branch of the government has powers that limit and control those of the other branches (p. 94)

circulation the average number of readers of a publication (p. 283)

city manager a professional manager who runs the government of a city (p. 301)

civil disobedience refusing to obey governmental demands or laws in order to bring about change (p. 536)

civilian a person who is not in the military (p. 337)

civilization the society and culture of a particular people, place, or period (p. 8)

civil liberty the right to a freedom, such as speech, thought, and action (p. 349)

civil rights political, economic, and social rights (p. 36)

clone to use genetic material in the cells of a plant or animal to create an identical copy of the original (p. 669)

closed shop a business that only hires union members (p. 266)

coalition a temporary alliance for joint action (p. 541)

Cold War a state of tension and hostility that stopped short of actual fighting between the United States and the Soviet Union (p. 483)

collective bargaining negotiations between a union and their employer about hours, wages, and other working conditions (p. 407)

colony a settlement made up of people who retain ties to their homeland (p. 10)

commerce the large-scale buying and selling of goods that goes on between cities or countries (p. 11)

common a land shared by all inhabitants of a place (p. 44)

commonwealth a self-governing area (p. 582)

communal shared by members of a community (p. 135)

Communist someone who believes that the government, not individuals, should own property and businesses (p. 343)

company town a community in which workers live in company-owned housing and shop from company-owned stores (p. 263)

compass an instrument that shows direction (p. 15)

compromise a settlement of differences in which both sides give up something they want (p. 91)

computer literate to have the basic skills needed to use a computer's basic functions (p. 667)

concentration camp a large prison camp (p. 426)

confederation a union of independent states or nations that decide to work or act together (p. 86)

conquistador the Spanish term for conqueror, or one who gains control by winning a war (p. 17)

conscientious objector a person who opposes war for moral reasons (p. 602)

conscription the drafting of people into the armed forces (p. 196)

conservative a person who wants to preserve the current system or power structure (p. 404)

constitution a document that states the principles according to which a nation is governed (p. 86)

constitutional monarchy a system of government in which democratically elected officials governed in the name of a ruler (p. 430)

containment the restriction of the strategic power of a nation by another nation (p. 485)

contra a Nicaraguan guerrilla who opposed the Sandinistas (p. 651)

convoy system the accompaniment of supply and troop transports by warships to provide safe passage (p. 343)

cooperative an organization jointly owned by those who use its services (p. 246)

corporation a business authorized by law to act as one person, though often made up of several people (p. 258)

corps a specialized branch of the armed forces (p. 471)

cotton gin a machine that removes seeds from cotton (p. 114)

coup d'etat a sudden and violent overthrow of a government (p. 595)

coureur de bois a fur trader, in French (p. 62)

credit a form of borrowing where a buyer pays later for a purchase (p. 222)

Crusades religious wars (p. 10)

cryptologist an expert who makes and deciphers codes (p. 451)

D
....

declaration a formal statement (p. 73)

de facto discrimination in practice instead of by law (p. 284)

default to fail to pay money on a loan (p. 381)

deferment a postponement (p. 602)

deficit spending paying out more than is collected in taxes (p. 410)

deforestation the cutting down of forests and trees (p. 665)

demilitarized zone an area from which military forces are prohibited (p. 490)

denounce to sharply condemn (p. 68)

deployment the sending out of armed forces ready for battle (p. 486)

deport to be sent out of a country (p. 371)

depose to remove from power (p. 595)

depth charge a special bomb designed to explode underwater (p. 343)

desegregate to end segregation or separation (p. 531)

détente a relaxation of tensions (p.614)

detention center a place in which people are temporarily held in custody (p. 279)

dictator a ruler with absolute power (p. 424)

diplomatic relations official ties (p. 338)

direct primary an election in which the members of a political party choose the party's candidates for office (p. 302)

disarmament the reduction of weapons (p. 433)

discrimination the unjust treatment of one individual by another based on prejudice (p. 284)

disenfranchise to be denied rights of citizenship, especially the right to vote (p. 215)

dissenter a person who refuses to conform to the authority of an established institution, such as a church (p. 34)

dissident a person who disagrees with a government policy or rule (p. 626)

Dixiecrat a white southern member of the States' Rights party (p. 508)

dollar diplomacy the use of the United States' economic power to win its foreign policy goals (p. 325)

domino theory the fear that a country would fall to the Communists, starting a chain reaction (p. 498)

downsize to lay off workers in order to cut costs (p. 641)

draft a process for selecting people for military service (p. 342)

drought a long period without any rainfall (p. 126)

due process the required procedures of the law (p. 195)

duty a tax (p. 47)

E
....

electoral college a group of electors from each state chosen by the voters to perform the offical duty of electing the President and Vice President of the United States (p. 93)

emancipation freeing (p. 197)

embargo a ban (p. 102)

empire a land and people controlled by one ruler (p. 8)

encomienda system a practice in which Native Americans were forced to work for Spanish lords (p. 17)

Enlightenment the belief that the spread of new ideas and reason would improve the world (p. 55)

entrepreneur a business person who takes a risk in hope of earning a profit (p. 282)

envoy a diplomatic representative (p. 606)

escalation an increasing involvement (p. 597)

ethnic sharing a common racial, national, religious, or cultural tradition (p. 278)

ethnic cleansing a policy of violently ejecting villages of a particular ethnic group or groups (p. 659)

executive order an order issued by the President (p. 474)

executive privilege the principle that members of the executive branch of government cannot legally be forced to disclose their confidential communications if they would harm operations of the executive branch (p. 621)

exile a person who leaves their own country, either by force or voluntarily (p. 555)

Exoduster an African American who settled on the Great Plains in the 1870s and 1880s (p. 244)

expatriate a person who leaves their homeland to live in another country (p. 365)

export to send a product abroad (p. 47)

extremist a person who deviates from the political opinions held by most people (p. 179)

F

factory system a system that brought workers and machines together in one place to produce goods (p. 108)

Fair Deal President Truman's program which called for a higher minimum wage, repeal of the Taft-Hartley Act, government-backed medical insurance, and federal funding for public schools and urban housing (p. 509)

fallout the minute poisonous atoms that fall to Earth after a nuclear blast (p. 495)

famine a long period in which there is not enough food (p. 25)

federal deficit the amount of money the government spends that is not covered by the taxes it collects (p. 638)

Fascist a person who believes in fascism, a political system in which a dictator rules over a state (p. 425)

federalism a form of government that divides power between the national government and the state governments (p. 93)

Federalist a supporter of the Constitution and a strong central government (p. 95)

federalize to put under the control of the federal government (p. 532)

feminism a movement for women's equality (p. 578)

filibuster delaying a vote on a bill by giving long speeches (p. 561)

fireside chat an informal radio speech to the American people by President Roosevelt (p. 399)

foreclose to seize possession of a borrower's property when the borrower has not made payments to the lender (p. 382)

forty-niner a gold seeker who rushed to California in 1849 (p. 138)

foxhole a shallow pit that provides safety from enemy gunfire (p. 471)

Free-Soiler a person who opposed slavery and popular sovereignty (p. 170)

free state a state that banned slavery (p. 168)

Freedmen's Bureau an agency established at the end of the Civil War to help newly emancipated African Americans adjust to freedom (p. 220)

Freedom Ride an organized trip by the Congress of Racial Equality from Washington, D.C., through southern cities to protest discrimination (p. 536)

Freedom Summer a name given to the 1964 SNCC campaign to provide support for voter registration in the Deep South (p. 539)

frontier a region that marks the point of farthest settlement in a territory (p. 45)

fugitive one who is running away or escaping from the law (p. 170)

G

gender classification by sex (p. 579)

generation gap a vast difference in tastes and values between young people and their parents (p. 520)

genetic engineering the changing of genes to improve the usefulness of plants and animals (p. 668)

genocide the deliberate murder of an entire people (p. 456)

gerrymander to create an election district that is strangely shaped in order to ensure reelection (p. 565)

Ghost Dance a Native American religious movement formed around a ritual dance that would restore their lands and their traditional ways of life (p. 233)

Gilded Age a period in which business leaders possessed unequaled wealth that often concealed widespread corruption (p. 296)

glacier a giant sheet of ice (p. 4)

glasnost openness, in Russian (p. 648)

global warming a scientific theory that the earth's average temperature is slowly rising (p. 665)

graduated income tax a tax that assesses money owed to the government based on income (p. 306)

Great Migration the movement of more than 1.4 African Americans from the South to the North between 1890 and 1920 (p. 284)

Great Society the name of President Johnson's legislative program which included a civil rights act, Medicare, Medicaid, and immigration reform (p. 564)

greenhouse effect the process by which the planet is kept from cooling off (p. 666)

griot a storyteller (p. 13)

guerrilla a fighter, not part of a regular army, who makes surprise attacks on an enemy (p. 322)

H

hacienda a huge estate (p. 27)

Harlem Renaissance the artistic output of African American writers, painters, and musicians who lived in Harlem during the 1920s (p. 365)

heir a person next in line to inherit (p. 331)

Hessian a hired soldier, or mercenary, from the state of Hesse, Germany (p. 75)

Holocaust Hitler's policy of killing Jews (p. 456)

homesteader a settler on free land made available by the Homestead Act (p. 242)

Hooverville a shantytown (p. 383)

horizontal integration a merger of competing businesses or individual claims in the same business (p. 260)

human rights the set of basic freedoms that every human being deserves to have (p. 660)

Hundred Days the period of presidential activity during FDR's first term (p. 400)

hydroelectric power electricity produced by water power (p. 401)

I

ideal a perfect model (p. 73)

impeachment a charge and trial of a public official, such as the President, on charges of a serious crime (p. 215)

imperialism the policy of one nation gaining control of other territories and using them to build a foreign empire (p. 314)

import to buy from another nation (p. 47)

impound to refuse to release (p. 619)

impressment the act of seizing someone and forcing them into service (p. 102)

inauguration a formal ceremony to officially induct a President into office (p. 98)

incursion a raid (p. 604)

indentured servant a worker bound to a contract in which a master paid their fare in return for freedom once their debt was repaid (p. 31)

inflation a steep rise in the price of goods (p. 370)

installment plan the payment of a small amount toward the total price of an item with an additional fixed amount plus interest that is paid each month until the full price is paid (p. 362)

insurrection a rebellion against established authority (p. 178)

integrate to open to people of all races without restriction (p. 527)

interdependent the link among countries that make up the world economy (p. 660)

interest rate the rate that Federal Reserve banks charge other banks for borrowing money (p. 306)

internment camp a prison camp (p. 477)

ironclad warship a vessel covered for battle with protective iron plates (p. 192)

iron curtain the border between the Communist nations and the democratic nations of Europe (p. 483)

isolationism the policy of staying out of the political affairs of other countries (p. 314)

isthmus a narrow strip of land (p. 323)

J

Jazz Age the name given to the 1920s because of the tremendous popularity of jazz in America during that decade (p. 364)

Jim Crow laws laws that separated races in all aspects of southern life (p. 223)

jingoism aggressive patriotism (p. 316)

joint-stock company an organization in which people invest money and share both the risks and the profits (p. 30)

judicial review the Supreme Court's power to declare a law unconstitutional (p. 101)

K

kamikaze pilots who deliberately committed suicide by crashing their airplanes, loaded with bombs, into enemy ships (p. 457)

kerosene an oil-based liquid produced from crude oil (p. 252)

kickback an illegal payment made in return for a favor or service (p. 297)

kinship a relationship based on common ancestors (p. 13)

kitchen cabinet a group of President Andrew Jackson's friends and supporters who met informally at the White House (p. 119)

L

labor union a group of workers who organize to protect their rights and working conditions (p. 146)

lend-lease plan the Presidential power to lend or lease arms and other supplies to any country whose defense is vital to the United States (p. 435)

libel a false statement in writing to injure a person's reputation (p. 57)

liberal a person who believes in using government resources to bring about social and economic change (p. 404)

life expectancy the number of years individuals are expected to live based on statistics (p. 586)

literacy rate the proportion of people who can read (p. 173)

lobby to try to persuade legislators (p. 579)

lockout the shutdown of a plant to bring striking workers to terms (p. 265)

Loyalist a person who remained faithful to the British king (p. 74)

lynch to hang (p. 222)

M

mandate complete support (p. 550)

Manhattan Project a research effort by a team of Allied scientists to build an atomic bomb (p. 457)

Manifest Destiny the belief that the United States had the right to extend its boundaries to the Pacific Ocean (p. 136)

martial law temporary rule by the army instead of elected officials (p. 185)

Marxist a person who follows the ideas of the nineteenth century writer Karl Marx (p. 615)

massacre the merciless killing of many people (p. 69)

mass media a mode of communication that reaches large numbers of people (p. 362)

mass production the making of many items in a short period of time (p. 110)

massive retaliation the use of nuclear weapons by one nation against another (p. 492)

McCarthyism named for Sen. Joseph McCarthy, a political tactic by which anyone could be perceived as disloyal or treasonous by appearing to support communism (p. 494)

mechanical reaper a machine for harvesting grain (p. 146)

Medicaid a government-funded medical insurance program for low-income and disabled Americans of any age (p. 564)

Medicare a government-funded medical insurance program for people over 65 (p. 564)

mercenary a hired soldier (p. 75)

mercantile system an economic system based on the theory that a nation grew in strength by building up its gold supply and expanding its trade (p. 47)

merit system a system in which jobs are granted on the basis of ability (p. 298)

mestizo a person of mixed Spanish and Native American ancestry (p. 27)

Middle Passage the part of a triangular trade route that took enslaved Africans to the West Indies (p. 50)

migrant a worker who travels from job to job (p. 277)

migrate to move (p. 4)

militant ready to fight; aggressive (p. 155)

militarism an aggressive policy put forth by the military or by people who follow the ideals of the military (p. 430)

military-industrial complex President Eisenhower's term for the close alliance between the U.S. military and the huge defense industry (p. 511)

militia an army of citizens who serve in times of emergency (p. 56)

minuteman an armed colonial militiaman who believed he could be ready for action at a minute's notice (p. 71)

Miranda warnings the statement an arrested person must legally hear that he or she has the right to have an attorney and the right to remain silent (p. 565)

missile gap the term for the lack of military strength of the United States as compared to the Soviet Union (p. 549)

mission a religious organization that spreads its faith or provides educational and other assistance (p. 25)

mobilize to call to duty, as in troops (p. 331)

moderate avoiding extremes (p. 210)

monarch a ruler (p. 11)

monopoly exclusive control (p. 11)

moratorium a period when all work and school activity is stopped as a sign of protest in order to bring about change (p. 602)

mountain man a fur trapper or trader who went west (p. 134)

muckraker a journalist who investigated and exposed corrupt practices in government and unions (p. 301)

multicultural a society that is marked by cultural diversity (p. 672)

multinational a large corporation that has operations in several countries (p. 662)

muster to call together (p. 65)

N

napalm a petroleum jelly compound that can burn flesh on contact (p. 599)

nationalism pride in one's country (p. 103)

nationalize to take government control of (p. 434)

nativism feelings of resentment toward immigrants (p. 150)

navigator a person who plans and directs the course of a ship (p. 15)

Nazi Hitler's National Socialist party (p. 426)

neutral supporting neither side in a dispute (p. 78)

New Deal the promises and programs initiated by President Roosevelt in response to the Great Depression in order to advance economic recovery and social welfare (p. 398)

New Frontier the set of challenges and opportunities for Americans named by President John F. Kennedy (p. 548)

nisei second-generation Japanese Americans (p. 589)

nomad any of a people constantly on the move in search of food (p. 4)

nonviolent resistance the use of strikes, fasts, and protest marches to achieve one's goals (p. 497)

normalize to establish diplomatic contacts (p. 612)

nullify to cancel (p. 100)

O

occupation the control over a conquered nation by a foreign power (p. 488)

oral history a recorded story of a particular group of people (p. 417)

P

Pacific Rim nations with a boundary of the Pacific Ocean (p. 661)

pacifist a person opposed to any war (p. 349)

pardon to release from punishment (p. 215)

partisan a person who strongly supports a cause (p. 448)

patent a grant that gives an inventor the sole right to make, use, and sell an invention for a set period of time (p. 252)

Patriot a person who favored independence (p. 74)

patroon the owner of a manorial estate given by the Dutch government (p. 35)

Peace Corps a federal agency that sends trained volunteers to help developing countries overseas (p. 551)

peninsula a narrow finger of land surrounded on three sides by water (p. 77)

perjury to lie under oath (p. 493)

philanthropist a person who donates to museums, libraries, and other public works (p. 259)

Pilgrim a religious traveler to a new land (p. 32)

pilgrimage a religious journey (p. 12)

plantation a large farm that grows one major crop (p. 15)

platform a statement of political beliefs and policies (p. 247)

pogrom an organized attack on unarmed people (p. 273)

political asylum the protection of immigrants from oppression by rulers in their homeland (p. 564)

political exile a person who leaves a country for reasons relating to government (p. 583)

political left a liberal position (p. 404)

political right a conservative position (p. 404)

poll tax a sum of money that was paid before someone could vote (p. 223)

popular sovereignty a practice in which the people who settled in the new territories would vote to decide their own policies, such as whether to allow slavery (p. 169)

Populist a political party which supported political issues important to farmers in the late 1800s (p. 247)

preamble the first section of the Declaration of Independence, which states basic principles of democracy (p. 73)

precedent an example (p. 99)

presidio a fort (p. 27)

price-fixing the practice of several companies raising or lowering their prices in order to drive competitors out of business (p. 307)

productivity the rate at which goods are produced or services are performed (p. 513)

prohibition the period (1919-1933) during which the Eighteenth Amendment to the Constitution banned the making, selling, or transporting of alcohol (p. 367)

propaganda the promotion of certain ideas to advance, damage, or destroy a cause (p. 69)

protectorate an independent country that is actually controlled by more powerful country (p. 316)

proviso a part of a document that makes restrictions (p. 169)

public works construction projects financed with public funds (p. 392)

Pullman car a first class train car that provided passengers with reclining seats and sleeping spaces (p. 255)

Puritan an English person who wanted to simplify the traditions of the Church of England (p. 33)

Q

quality control a manufacturer's check of whether or not a product is consistently well made (p. 661)

quarantine to isolate (p. 558)

quota a proportional share or allotment (p. 371)

R

radical drastic or extreme (p. 210)

railhead the end of a track (p. 238)

railroad time a standard time system for accurate train scheduling (p. 254)

Rainbow Coalition an organization formed by Jesse Jackson in 1984 which brought many groups together to promote opportunities for minorities (p. 645)

rancho a large cattle farm (p. 130)

ratify to approve (p. 86)

rationing a government control of food, gasoline, and other vital goods (p. 465)

reapportion to redistribute (p. 673)

rebate a discount or partial refund (p. 259)

recall a reform that allows voters to remove an elected official from office (p. 302)

recession a slowdown in the economy (p. 511)

reconnaissance an exploratory examination (p. 200)

Reconstruction the era of rebuilding the South after the Civil War by reuniting the South into the Union and redefining the status of African Americans (p. 210)

Red Scare the period during the 1920s when there were worries about a Communist takeover (p. 371)

reenlistment signing up again for service in an army (p. 233)

refugee a person who flees difficult political, social, or economic conditions in search of a better place to live (p. 386)

relief a direct money payment for the unemployed (p. 392)

renewable a source of energy that will never run out (p. 665)

reparation the payment of damages (p. 352)

repatriation to return to the country of one's birth (p. 415)

repeal to cancel (p. 175)

representative a person selected to act for others (p. 63)

republic a government in which the citizens rule through elected representatives (p. 350)

reservation a tract of public land set aside for special use, as for Native Americans (p. 230)

resolution a formal expression of intention (p. 160)

restriction a limitation (p. 51)

revenue sharing a Nixon program in which more than $30 billion of federal money could be spent by the states (p. 618)

revival a reawakening (p. 152)

rhythm and blues a type of music that combines blues and jazz forms (p. 519)

right-of-way a strip of land on which a railroad, highway, or power line is built (p. 243)

royal colony a group of settlers still living under a king's control (p. 37)

rural pertaining to the country or country life (p. 146)

S
....

sabotage secret acts against the government (p. 477)

sanction a measure, such as a trade boycott, taken against a nation that defies international law (p. 650)

Sandinista a rebel who helped to overthrow the Nicaraguan dictatorship in 1979 (p. 651)

sanitation disposal of waste (p. 50)

satellite a nation that is economically or politically under the control of another country (p. 482)

scab a negative term for a person hired to replace a striking worker (p. 265)

scalawag a southern white person who sided with the Republicans (p. 216)

scapegoat a person or people unfairly blamed for a situation or a problem (p. 273)

scorched-earth policy a plan in which a retreating army burns or destroys its own crops and other valuable materials, leaving behind only burnt ground (p. 443)

scrip a certificate of a right to receive something, for use in, for example, the company store (p. 263)

secede to withdraw (p. 179)

sectionalism loyalty to a region, rather than a whole country (p. 169)

segregation the separation of races (p. 223)

self-determination the right of a nation to decide its own political status (p. 351)

self-sufficient the ability to provide without the aid of others (p. 154)

semi-sedentary a way of life for people who settled on fertile lands but followed game during hunting seasons (p. 126)

separation of powers the system of dividing the powers of government among different branches (p. 93)

Separatist an English person who broke away from the Church of England (p. 32)

service industry a field such as medicine, law, education, or sales, in which work is provided for others (p. 513)

settlement house a community center that provides for the poor (p. 288)

sharecropping a system where a farm worker is given land, seed, and tools in return for a part of the crops that are harvested (p. 222)

shuttle diplomacy the moving back and forth between countries in an effort to reach agreement (p. 626)

siege a blockade of a city so that food, fuel, and other supplies cannot enter (p. 443)

sit-down strike a tactic to prevent employers from hiring other workers during a strike (p. 409)

sit-in an act of occupying seats in a racially segregated establishment in organized protest against discrimination (p. 534)

slave state a state that permitted slavery (p. 168)

soap opera a daytime drama originally broadcast on the radio, whose advertisers were often soap companies (p. 416)

Social Darwinism an extension of a scientific theory into business that argued that if government would stay out of the affairs of business, the strong would survive and the weak would fail (p. 260)

social gospel movement the drive to introduce youths to habits and skills based on Christian teachings to escape poor living conditions (p. 288)

socialism an economic and political system in which society as a whole, rather than private individuals, owns property, operates businesses, and provides for its members (p. 153)

space race a competition in technology to gain prominence in space (p. 495)

speakeasy an illegal saloon or bar (p. 368)

special session an extra meeting of Congress outside the months in which it usually meets (p. 508)

sphere of influence a territorial area over which one nation has political and economic influence (p. 319)

spiritual an expressive religious song (p. 115)

spoils system the giving of federal jobs to supporters (p. 119)

sponsor to pay for (p. 416)

squatter a person who settles land without having a legal claim (p. 245)

stagflation the economic situation when prices come down as a result of unemployment (p. 619)

stalemate a deadlock or a standstill (p. 191)

steerage a large open area beneath a ship's deck (p. 273)

stock a share of ownership in a business (p. 258)

strike a work stoppage to protest an act or condition (p. 148)

subsistence providing just enough food to live on (p. 44)

suburb a community at the edge of a city (p. 282)

subversion the undermining of government (p. 615)

suffrage the right to vote (p. 160)

summit conference a meeting of the highest officials of various countries to discuss how relations could be improved (p. 492)

Sun Belt the region of states in the South and Southwest (p. 673)

superpower the strongest nations in the world (p. 488)

supply-side economics an economic theory which holds that cutting taxes of businesses and individuals would result in more money being available for people to invest in new goods and services (p. 637)

surplus more of a quantity than what is needed (p. 5)

survey an examination and measurement of a region to determine its boundaries (p. 86)

sweatshop a factory where workers labor under unhealthy conditions for long hours and little pay (p. 286)

T

tabloid a newspaper that focuses primarily on sensational events (p. 365)

tariff a system of duties placed on imports or exports (p. 93)

task force a group of experts organized to solve a specific problem (p. 287)

tax money paid to a government in return for services (p. 33)

teach-in a meeting to raise awareness about an event (p. 602)

Tejano a Mexican who lived in Texas (p. 131)

telecommunications communication at a distance, as by cable, telephone, and television (p. 667)

temperance a movement that supports limited drinking or total rejection of alcoholic beverages (p. 158)

tenant farmer a farmer who paid for the right to work someone else's land (p. 387)

tenement an apartment building that often did not meet the standards for sanitation and safety (p. 147)

termination a Congressional policy ending federal programs to reservations (p. 586)

terrorist a person who is willing to use violence to promote a cause (p. 331)

textile cloth (p. 108)

theology the study of religious faith and practice (p. 533)

Third World a term for the developing nations of the Middle East, Africa, and Latin America that were not aligned with either the United States or the Soviet Union (p. 555)

Three R's President Roosevelt's three goals for fighting the Great Depression: relief, recovery, and reform (p. 399)

thresher a machine that separates kernels of the wheat plant from the husks (p. 146)

tipi a shelter built with buffalo hides (p. 127)

total war war against civilians and resources as well as against armies (p. 201)

totalitarian state a place where an individual, group, or government has total control over citizens' lives (p. 426)

trade deficit the importation of more goods than a country has exported (p. 661)

transcontinental spanning the continent (p. 230)

treasury a reserve of money (p. 87)

tribute a forced payment from a conquered people (p. 8)

trust a legal agreement under which stockholders of different companies in one industry turn over their stock to one group of directors (p. 260)

tsar a powerful emperor (p. 339)

turnpike a road that charges tolls (p. 110)

U

unconstitutional a law that violates the Constitution (p. 94)

underclass poor Americans who are prevented by poverty from gaining the education or skills they need (p. 646)

Underground Railroad escape routes enslaved African Americans followed to reach freedom in the North (p. 173)

unethical not according to the principles of proper conduct (p. 527)

urban pertaining to the city or city life (p. 146)

urban renewal a government project aimed at clearing out slum areas and replacing them with residential, commercial, or industrial development (p. 516)

utopia a perfect society on Earth (p. 152)

V

vaquero a cowhand (p. 27)

vaudeville a variety show that features singing, dancing, and comedy skits (p. 283)

vertical integration controlling all aspects of an industry, including raw materials, transportation systems, and all stages of the manufacturing process (p. 259)

veto to reject (p. 94)

Viet Cong a South Vietnamese Communist (p. 499)

Vietminh a Vietnamese nationalist group led by Ho Chi Minh (p. 498)

Vietnamization an attempt by Nixon to transfer the burden of the Vietnam War to the South Vietnamese army (p. 604)

vigilante committees a group of people who make and enforce its own laws (p. 240)

voter registration a drive to get people on official lists of voters so that they can participate in elections (p. 539)

W

wagon train many wagons traveling together (p. 134)

war of attrition a war in which the weaker army inflicts continuous losses of soldiers and supplies that gradually add up to an unbearable burden for the other side (p. 190)

water rights the determination of who had the right to use water that flowed from one person's land to another (p. 140)

whistle-stop tour a term for a trip in which a political candidate makes brief appearances in many small towns (p. 508)

white-collar job a job so named because of the white shirts worn at one time by most male office workers; often a job in a service industry (p. 514)

wildcat strike a protest in which workers walk off the job without union approval (p. 467)

workfare a law in which recipients of welfare may risk receiving benefits if they do not work for the local government (p. 646)

Y

yellow-dog contract an agreement that requires newly hired employees to promise to never join a labor union (p. 266)

yellow journalism the publishing of wildly sensational news stories (p. 317)

Index

Camranh Bay, 600
Canals, 111, 112*m*
Cane Ridge, Kentucky, religious revival in, 152
Capone, Al, 368
Carmichael, Stokely, 543, 573, 574
Carnegie, Andrew, 252, 259, 260, 266, 283
Carnegie Steel, 266
Carolinas, settlement of, 39
   See also North Carolina, South Carolina
Carpetbaggers, 216, 216*p*
Carranza, Venustiano, 326–327
Carson, Rachel, 618–619, 619*p*
Carter, Jimmy, 626*p*, 639
   administration of, 623–624
   and draft resisters, 629
   in election of 1980, 628, 628*p*, 636
   foreign policy of, 625–628
Carter Doctrine, 626
Carver, George Washington, 285
Carvey, William Harvey, 199
Cass, Lewis, 170
Castro, Fidel, 555, 583–584
Castro, Raúl, 581
Catcher in the Rye (Salinger), 521
Catlin, George, 126
Catt, Carrie Chapman, 307, 308
Cattle boom, end of, 238–239
Cavada, Federico Fernández, 200
Cayuga, 7
Censorship, 195, 356
Centennial Exhibition, 255
Central America
   Aztec civilization in, 8, 24
   Mayan civilization in, 8
Central Intelligence Agency (CIA), 556, 615, 651
Central Pacific Railroad, 243, 253
Central Powers, 337
   in World War I, 336
   in World War II, 331
Century of Dishonor, A (Jackson), 233
Chamberlain, Neville, 427
Chambers, Whittaker, 493
Chamorro, Violeta Barrios de, 651, 652*p*
Champlain, Samuel de, 27
Chaney, James, 540
Chaplin, Charlie, 366
Charles, Ray, 519
Charles I (King of England), 37
Charles II (King of England), 36
Charleston, South Carolina
   capture of, in Revolutionary War, 77
   racial riots in, 374
Chaves, Manuel, 200
Chávez, César, 581–582, 585, 585*p*
Chávez, Denise, 582
Checks and balances, 94
Cherokee people, 79, 127
   and New Deal, 414
   removal of, 120–121, 121*p*
Cheyenne people, 126, 230–231, 231*p*
Chiang Kai-shek, 431, 431*p*, 454, 488, 490
Chicago
   African Americans in, 373–374
   great fire in, 281–282
   growth of, 146, 274
   immigrants in, 149, 286
   jazz in, 364

   racial riots in, 284, 374
   settlement houses in, 288
   skyscrapers in, 281–282, 281*p*
   suburbs of, 282
Chicano movement, 582
Chickasaw people, 120–121
Children in work force, 264, 264*p*
Chile, U.S. intervention in, 615
Chin, Frank, 589
China
   Boxer Rebellion in, 320, 320*p*
   Civil War in, 431
   communism in, 488–489, 488*p*
   economic growth of, 661
   establishment of People's Republic of, 489
   immigrants from, 277, 278*p*
   Japanese aggression toward, 431–432, 432*p*
   Nixon's visit to, 612–613, 613*p*, 625
   open door policy in, 319–320
   Opium War in, 315
   relations with Soviet Union, 612–613
   Tiananmen Square in, 658, 658*p*
   and World War II, 454
Chinatowns, 277
Chinese Exclusion Act (1882), 279
Chinese workers
   immigration of, 139
   and transcontinental railroad, 253
Chippewa people, 67
Chisholm, Shirley, 571*p*
Chivington, John M., 231
Choctaw people, 120–121
Christians and Christianity, 10, 15, 17, 152–153
   in Spanish settlements (Catholicism), 25–26
   in colonial America, 32–33, 34, 35, 36–37
   social gospel movement and, 287–288
Churchill, Winston, 336, 435, 445, 454, 454*p*, 482–483, 485, 648
Church of England, 32, 33
Cigarmakers' Union, 266
Cincinnati, immigrants in, 149
Cinqué, Joseph, 116
Cisneros, Henry, 644
Cities
   corruption in, 297
   crime in, 287
   decline of, 515
   growth of American, 146
   life and work in, 147, 286–287
   lure of, 281–283
   urban renewal projects in, 515–516
Civilian Conservation Corps (CCC), 402, 563
Civil Rights Act (1866), 214
Civil Rights Act (1957), 561
Civil Rights Act (1960), 561
Civil Rights Act (1964), 537, 551, 561, 561*p*, 563, 576, 579
Civil rights movement
   Asian Americans in, 588–589
   Birmingham marches in, 534–535
   and Dwight D. Eisenhower, 531–532, 531*p*
   effects of, 578
   freedom rides in, 535–536, 536*m*
   Freedom Summer in, 539–541
   and John F. Kennedy, 550–551
   Latinos in, 581–584, 582*p*, 583*p*
   legislation in, 575*c*
   and Lyndon Johnson, 551, 561–562, 561*p*
   major events in, 575*c*

   March on Washington in, 536–537, 537*p*
   Montgomery bus boycott in, 533–534
   Native Americans in, 586–588
   under Nixon, 618
   school integration in, 531–532, 531*p*
   Selma to Montgomery march in, 503*p*
   sit-ins in, 534, 535*p*
   under Wilson, 307
   See also African Americans
Civil War
   in China, 431
   in Greece, 484
Civil War (1861–1965)
   African Americans in, 198–199, 198*p*
   battles and strategies in, 187–188, 188*p*, 190–194, 191*m*, 192*p*, 201–202, 202*m*
   beginning of, 179
   casualties in, 190
   costs and effects of, 203–204
   effect of, on cattle drives, 237
   end of, 201–203
   Hispanics in, 200
   North's blockade against South, 191–192
   opposition to, 195
   preparing for, 186–187
   raising armies for, 196
   soldiers in, 182*p*, 183*p*, 196
   strengths of North and South, 186–187, 187*c*
   technology in, 205, 205*p*
   women in, 199–200, 199*p*
Clalin, Francis, 199*p*
Clark, Ramsey, 576
Clark, William, 102, 102*p*, 134
Clay, Henry, 119, 120, 168, 170
Clayton, Horace, 413
Clayton Antitrust Act (1914), 306–307
Clean Water Act (1972), 664
Clemenceau, Georges, 351*p*, 352
Clermont (steamboat), 111, 111*p*
Cleveland, Grover, 298, 298*p*
   in election of 1892, 247
   foreign policy under, 316
   and immigration policy, 279
   and labor relations, 267
Cleveland, Ohio, growth of, 274
Clinton, George, 95
Clinton, William Jefferson, 420, 634–635*p*
   in election of 1992, 641, 641*p*
   in election of 1996, 642
   impeachment of, 642
Cody, William F., 230
Cohan, George M., 343, 343*p*
Cold War
   in Asia, 488–490
   beginning of, 482–486
   brinkmanship in, 492
   containment in, 492
   and détente, 614, 615–616
   under Eisenhower, 492–495
   and emerging nations, 496–499, 496*p*, 497*p*, 498*p*, 499*m*
   end of, 648–650, 658
   foreign policy challenges in, 658
   and Middle East, 490–491
   and signing of Helsinki Accords, 616
Collective bargaining, 407
College of William and Mary, 56, 56*p*
Colleges and universities
   for African Americans, 220
   early, 56, 56*p*
Collier, John, 413

Jackson, Jesse, 644*p*, 645
Jackson, Mahalia, 528
Jamaica, early explorations of, 17
James I (King of England), 30
James II (King of England), 37
Jamestown, 22*p*, 30–31, 31*p*, 32
Japan
    constitutional monarchy in, 430
    Gentleman's Agreement with, 279
    immigrants from, 277–278
    invasion of Pearl Harbor by, 435–436, 436*p*
    militarism in, 430
    occupation of, 488
    Perry's visit to, 315
    U.S. relations with, 319
    in World War I, 336
    in World War II, 331, 430–432, 443–445,
        451–452, 451*p*, 452*p*, 458*m*
Japanese Americans in World War II,
    476–477, 476*m*, 477*p*
Jay, John, as author of *Federalist Papers*, 95
Jazz Age, 359*p*, 364–365, 364*p*, 380
Jefferson, Thomas, 72
    as author of Declaration of Independence, 74
    and Bank of the United States, 98–99
    in election of 1796, 100
    in election of 1804, 102
    and Louisiana Territory, 101–102
Jews
    and creation of Israel, 491
    discrimination against, 515
    immigration of, 273
    in World War II, 426
Jiang Zemin, 658
Jim Crow laws, 223, 284, 373, 406, 526, 535
Job Corps, 563
Johnson, Albert, 371
Johnson, Andrew, 211*p*
    impeachment charges against, 215–216,
    and Radical Reconstruction, 214–215
    Reconstruction plan of, 211
Johnson, Cornelius, 416
Johnson, Lady Bird, 562*p*
Johnson, Lyndon Baines, 537, 601
    and civil rights movement, 539, 541, 551,
        561–562, 561*p*, 576
    in election of 1964, 542, 563
    in election of 1968, 603
    and Great Society, 563–564, 563*c*
    and Latino appointments, 581
    taking oath of office by, 559, 560*p*
    as Vice President, 548, 552
    and Vietnam War, 595, 596–597
    and War on Poverty, 562–563
Johnston, Joseph E., 190
Jones, Absalom, 152
Jones, Mary Harris, 264
Jones Act (1917), 280, 322
Jordan, Barbara, 622
Joseph, Chief, 232
Journalism
    and anti-Japanese sentiment, 278
    and newspaper circulation, 283
    Riis contribution to, 287
    role of Tarbell, 262
    yellow, 317
Judicial branch, 94
Judiciary Act (1789), 100
The Jungle (Sinclair), 303

K

Kansas, battle over slavery in, 176–177
Kansas-Nebraska Act (1854), 175
Kelley, Oliver, 246
Kellogg-Briand Pact (1928), 433
Kelly, William, 252
Kennedy, Anthony, 639
Kennedy, Jacqueline Bouvier, 549, 549*p*,
    559, 560*p*
Kennedy, John F., 546*p*, 547*p*
    administration of, 549–550
    assassination of, 559–560, 595
    and civil rights movement, 537, 550–551
    in election of 1960, 548–549
    and foreign policy, 555–559, 556*m*, 557*p*
    inauguration of, 549*p*
    and New Frontier, 548, 550–552
    and space research, 620
    and Vietnam War, 595
Kennedy, Robert
    assassination of, 603
    and election of 1968, 603
Kent State University, antiwar protest at, 602,
    602*p*, 604
Kentucky
    as border state, 185
    Revolutionary War in, 77
Kentucky Resolutions, 100
Kenya, independence of, 496
Kerner Commission, 576
Kerouac, Jack, 520
Key, Francis Scott, 103
Khomeini, Ayatollah, 627
Khrushchev, Nikita, 492, 557, 558
Kier, Samuel, 252
King, Martin Luther, Jr., 533, 534, 539,
    561*p*, 645, 650
    assassination of, 574, 576
    and "I Have a Dream" speech, 503, 537
    as leader of civil rights movement, 572
    letter from a Birmingham jail, 538
    teachings of, 574
    and voting rights, 542
    as winner of Nobel Peace Prize, 572
King, Rodney, 645, 646
Kingston, Maxine Hong, 589
Kissinger, Henry, 605–606, 612–615, 620,
    622*p*, 626
Knights of Labor, 265–266, 265*p*, 266*p*
Know-Nothings, 150
Korean immigrants, 278
Korean War, 488–490, 489*p*, 490*m*
Kreps, Juanita, 623
Ku Klux Klan (KKK), 224–225, 225*p*, 284,
    374, 374*p*
    and civil rights movement, 539, 540, 551
Kuwait, 356
    and Gulf War, 652–653, 653*m*

L

Labor
    organization of, 147–148
    sweatshop, 286–287
    in World War I, 347–348
    See also Work force

Labor movement
    under Franklin Roosevelt, 407, 409
    in 1920s, 370
    strikes in, 266–267, 267*p*, 506–507, 507*p*
    and World War II, 466–467, 467*p*
Lake Erie, 111
Lakota people, 231
Land bridge and migration routes, 4*m*
Landon, Alfred, 407
Land Ordinance (1785), 87, 87*m*
Land rushes, Oklahoma, 245
Lange, Dorothea, 417
Laos, 497
    Communist takeover of, 606
    in World War II, 435
La Raza Unida, 582
La Salle, Robert de, 27–28
Las Casas, Bartolomé de, 17, 24–25
Laser surgery, 670, 670*p*
Latin America
    and dollar diplomacy, 325–326
    foreign policy in, under Kennedy,
        555–557
    Good Neighbor policy in, 434
    immigration from, 279–280
    and Monroe Doctrine, 118
    and Roosevelt Corollary to Monroe
        Doctrine, 324–325
    Big Stick policy in, 323
    U.S. relations with, 651–652
Latinos. *See* Hispanics
Latvia, post World War I, 353
League of Nations, 353
    and Japanese aggression, 430
League of the Iroquois, 7, 93
Le Duc Tho, 606
Lee, Richard Henry, 72, 73, 95–96
Lee, Robert E., 190
    as Confederate General, 187, 190–191,
        193–194, 201
    and John Brown's raid, 178
    surrender of, 201–203
Lend-Lease Act (1941), 435
Lenin, Vladimir, 343, 425
Leningrad in World War II, 443
"Letter from a Birmingham Jail," 535
Letters from a Federal Farmer (Lee), 95–96
Levittown, 515, 515*p*
Lewis, John L., 409
Lewis, Meriwether, 102, 102*p*, 134
Lewis, Sinclair, 365
Leyte Island in World War II, 457
The *Liberator*, 155
Liberty bonds, 347, 349
Liberty League, 406
Libraries, 283
Libya and World War II, 442
Life expectancy
    changes in, 673
    for Native Americans, 586
Liliuokalani, 315–316, 316*p*
Lincoln, Abraham, 184*p*, 650
    and transcontinental railroad, 230
    assassination of, 203
    debate with Douglas, 178
    and declaration of martial law, 185

resignation of, 622
and veto of War Powers Act, 607
as Vice President, 509
and Vietnam War, 604–606, 604*p*
and Watergate scandal, 620–622, 621*p*
Nkrumah, Kwame, 496, 496*p*
Noriega, Manuel, 652
Normandy, 449–450, 449*p*
North
strengths of, pre-Civil War, 186, 187*c*
widening gap from South, 173–175
North America, 1*p*, 4*m*
first settlers of, 4–5
Native American cultures in, 5, 6*m*, 7
Spanish in, 130–132
North American Free Trade Agreement
(NAFTA), 661–662
North Atlantic Treaty Organization
(NATO), 485–486, 509
North Carolina, 38*c*
and ratification of Constitution, 96, 97
Revolutionary War in, 77
secession of, 184
slaves in, 51
Northup, Solomon, 174
Northwest Ordinance (1787), 87
Northwest Territory, 102
Nuclear energy, 665, 665*p*
Nuclear weapons, test ban for, 494*p*, 494–495
Nuremberg Trials, 457
Nuyorican cultural movement, 583
Nye, Gerald P., 433

O

Oahu Island, 315
O'Brien, Tim, 600
Occupational Safety and Health Agency
(OSHA), 619
O'Connor, James F., 437
O'Connor, Sandra Day, 639
Oglethorpe, James, 39
Ohio River valley, settlement of, 62–63
Oil crisis, 664–665
Oil industry, 252
role of Rockefeller in, 260
Ojibwas, 5, 587
Okinawa in World War II, 458
Oklahoma City bombing, 659
Oklahoma land rushes, 245
Olympics
in 1936, 416
in 1980, 626
Omaha, Nebraska, growth of, 253
Oneida people, 7, 154
O'Neill, Eugene, 365
Onondaga people, 7
On the Road (Kerouac), 520
Open Door Notes, 320
Open door policy in China, 319–320
Open Housing law, 576
Operation Desert Storm, 652
Operation Overlord, 449
Operation Rolling Thunder, 596–597
Operation Torch, 447
Opium War, 315

Oregon
settlement of, 136, 242
statehood for, 137
Oregon Trail, 135, 138
Organization of Petroleum Exporting
Countries (OPEC), 619, 624
Orlando, Vittorio, 351*p*, 352
O'Ryan, John F., 437
Oswald, Lee Harvey, 559–560
Otis, James, 68, 79
Ottawa people, 67
Ottoman Empire, 331
pre-World War I, 329, 330–331
in World War I, 336
"Over There" (Cohan), 343, 343*p*
Owens, Jesse, 416
Owens, Robert, 154

P

Pacific Rim, 661, 661*m*
Paine, Thomas, 72–73, 72*p*
Pakistan
creation of, 497
as member of SEATO, 497
Pale of Settlement, 273
Palestine, 491
conflict between Israel and, 653
Palestine Liberation Organization
(PLO), 653
Palmer, A. Mitchell, 371
Panama
U.S. intervention in, 652
U.S. relations with, 323–324
Panama Canal, 328
building, 324, 328*m*
treaties involving, 625
Paris in World War I, 344
Paris Peace Conference, 351–353
Paris summit (1960), 493
Parker, John, 71
Parks, Rosa, 533
Passos, John Dos, 365
Patriots, 74
Patton, George S., 448, 450, 456
Paul, Alice, 308
Pawnee people, 126, 134
Pawtucket, Rhode Island, textile mill in, 108
Payne-Aldrich Tariff Act (1909), 304
Peace Corps, 551, 551*p*
Peace Democrats, 195, 195*p*
Peale, Norman Vincent, 517
Pearl Harbor, 315, 435–436, 436*p*, 451,
466, 473, 476
Peña, Federico, 644
Pendleton Civil Service Act (1883), 298
Penn, William, 23*p*, 36, 45
Pennsylvania, 38*c*
and ratification of Constitution, 96
religious toleration in, 45
settlement of, 23*p*, 36
Pennsylvania, University of, 48
Pennsylvania Railroad, 259
Pennsylvania Rock Oil Company, 252
Pentagon Papers, 605
People for the Ethical Treatment of Animals
(PETA), 82

Perkins, Frances, 399, 399*p*, 411
Perot, Ross, 641
Perry, Matthew, 315, 315*p*
Pershing, John J., 342–343, 346
Philadelphia, 91*p*
African Americans in, 52, 373–374
Constitutional Convention at, 90
growth of, 48, 146
public safety in, 147
in Revolutionary War, 77
unions in, 148
Philippines
independence for, 497
as member of SEATO, 497
in Spanish-American War, 317–318, 319
U.S. control of, 322
in World War II, 430–431, 435, 443–444,
444*p*, 457
Pickett, George, 193–194
Pierce, Franklin, 171
Pilgrims, 32–33, 32*p*
Pinchback, P. B. S., 217
Pine Ridge reservation, 587
Pitcher, Molly, 78
Pitt, William, 65
Platt Amendment, 322
Pledge of Allegiance, 517
Plessy v. *Ferguson*, 526, 530, 531
Plymouth, 32–33, 38*c*
Pocahontas, 30
Pogroms, 273
Poison gas in World War I, 336
Poitier, Sidney, 528
Poland
communism in, 482
democracy movement in, 649
fall of, 434
Germany takeover of, 427–428, 428*p*, 456
invasion of, 434
as member of Warsaw Pact, 486
post-World War I, 352
Polio, 516, 516*p*
Political campaigns, impact of television on,
518–519
Political parties, development of first, 100
Polk, James
in election of 1844, 136
and war with Mexico, 137
Poll taxes, 223
Ponce de León, Juan, 17*c*, 25
Pontiac, 67
Poor People's Campaign, 574
Poor Richard's Almanac, 48
Popé, 26
Population,
changing, 672–674, 673*c*
Populists, 247
Port Arthur, 319
Portsmouth, growth of, 44
Portsmouth Conference, 319
Portugal
emergence of, as nation, 11
exploration and settlement by, 15–16, 17*c*
Pound, Ezra, 365
Powell, Colin, 652
Powell, Lewis, Jr., 619
The Power of Positive Thinking (Peale), 517
Powers, Gary Francis, 492
Powhatan, 30

Tikal, 8
Tilden, Samuel J., 218
Timber Culture Act (1873), 243
Time zones, 254
Tippecanoe, Battle of, 103
Tobacco, 30, 37, 39
Tocqueville, Alexis de, 109
Toleration Act (1649), 37
Tombouctou, 12
Tompkins, Sally Louisa, 200
Tonkin Gulf Resolution, 596
    repeal of, 605
Toure, Kwame, 574
Townshend Acts (1767), 68
Trade
    deficit in, 660
    fur, 62, 82
    interstate, 93
    with Native Americans, 62, 62p
    and North American Free Trade Agreement
      (NAFTA), 661–662
    slave, 25, 51, 51p
    triangular, 50–51, 50m
    with West African kingdoms, 12, 14m
Trail of Tears, 121, 121p
Transcontinental railroad, 230, 253–254, 254p
Transcontinental Railroad Act (1862), 243
Transplant surgery, 670
Transportation and western settlement,
    110–111
Travis, William B., 132
Trench warfare in World War I, 336, 337,
    337p
Trenton, capture of, in Revolutionary War, 76
Triangle Shirtwaist factory, fire in, 286–287
Triangular trade, 50–51, 50m
Triple Alliance, 329
Triple Entente, 330
Truman, Harry S, 490
    and atomic bomb, 458
    and Berlin blockade, 484
    and economy, 506–507, 507p
    in election of 1948, 508–509, 508p
    and Fair Deal, 509
    and integration of armed forces, 527–528
    and Korean War, 489–490
    and labor movement, 507
    and Marshall Plan, 484–485
    and United Nations, 482
    and World War II, 457–458
Truman Doctrine, 485
Truth, Sojourner, 160, 200
Tubman, Harriet, 174, 174p, 200
Turner, Nat, 116
Turnpikes, 110–111
Tuskegee Institute, 285, 285p
Twain, Mark, 241, 283, 296
Tweed, William Marcy, 297, 297p
Twelfth Amendment, 100
Twelve Years a Slave (Northup), 174
Twenty-fifth Amendment, 622
Twenty-first Amendment, 368
Twenty-sixth Amendment, 607
Twenty-third Amendment, 550
Tydings-McDuffie Act, 430
Typewriter, 255–256

U

U-2 incident, 492–493
Uncle Tom's Cabin (Stowe), 174-175
Underground Railroad, 166p, 167p,
    173–174, 173m, 244, 284
Underwood-Simmons Tariff Act (1913), 306
Unemployment
    among Mexican Americans, 415
    in Great Depression, 382–383, 382p
    in 1920s, 370
Union League, 217
Union Pacific Railroad, 243, 253, 297
United Farm Workers of America (UFW),
    581–582, 582p
United Mine Workers, 409, 467
United Nations (UN), 482, 483c, 612
    peacekeeping force in Somalia and
      Bosnia, 659
United States Steel Corporation, 259
United States v. Reese, 223
Universal Negro Improvement Association
    (UNIA), 375
Urban League, 348
Urban renewal projects, 515–516
Urban riots, 576
Utopian communities, 153–154

V

Valens, Ritchie, 519
Valley Forge, 77, 77p
Van Buren, Martin, 170
Vanderbilt, Cornelius, 296–297
Vanzetti, Bartolomeo, 372, 372p
Velaquez, Loreta Janeta, 200
Venezuela, crisis between Britain and, 324
Veracruz, U.S. seizure of, 326
Versailles, Treaty of, 352–353, 424, 426
Vesey, Denmark, 115–116
Vicksburg, Mississippi, in Civil War, 193
Victor Emmanuel III, 448
Victory bonds, 347
Vienna summit conference, 557
Viet Cong, 499, 594, 599, 600
Vietminh, 498
Vietnam
    division of, 498–499, 499m
    French policies in, 498, 498p
    immigrants from, 588p
    U.S. involvement in, 499
    in World War II, 435
Vietnamization, 604–605
Vietnam veterans, treatment of, 606–607
Vietnam Veterans Memorial, 606–607, 607p
Vietnam War, 569p
    aftermath of, 604–605, 605–606, 605p
    beginning of, 594–595, 595m
    divided opinions about U.S. involvement
      in, 601–605, 602p
    effects of, 606
    escalation of, 596–597
    fighting, 599–601, 599p, 600p
    final years, 604–605, 605p
    U.S. involvement in, 601–602
    U.S. withdrawal from, 605–606
Vietnam Women's Memorial, 607

Vigilante committees, 240
Viking mission, 620
Vikings, 10
Villa, Francisco "Pancho," 327, 327p, 343
Violence
    and Ku Klux Klan (KKK), 284
    and labor unions, 265
Virginia, 38c
    House of Burgesses in, 31, 37, 70
    and ratification of Constitution, 96, 97
    secession of, 184
    settlement of, 30–31, 37
    slaves in, 51, 52
Virginia City, Nevada, 241
Virginia Company, 31
Virginia Plan, 91
Virginia Resolutions, 100
VISTA, 563
Voting rights
    of African Americans, 225, 539, 540p,
      542–543, 542p, 564
    reform in, 564
    for women, 307–308, 309, 347, 367
Voting Rights Act (1965), 564

W

*Wabash, St. Louis and Pacific Railroad
    Company v. Illinois*, 299
Wade-Davis Bill, 210–211
Wagner, Robert, 406
Wagon trains, 134–135, 134p
Wake Island, in World War II, 443–444
Wald, Lillian D., 288
Wallace, Henry A., 508
War bonds, 466, 466p
War Democrats, 195
War for Independence. *See* Revolutionary War
War Hawks, 102
War Industries Board (WIB), 347
War Mobilization, Office of, 465
Warner, Charles, 296
War of 1812, 102–103
    and growth of American industry, 109
War on Poverty, 562–563
War Powers Act (1973), 607
War Production Board (WPB), 464–465
Warren, Earl, 531, 560, 564, 619
Warren Commission, 560
Warsaw Pact, 486, 486m
Washington, D.C.
    African American ghettos in, 374
    changes in, 515
    destruction of, in War of 1812, 103
    march on, 384, 536–537, 537p
Washington, George, 61p
    administration of, 98–99
    Cabinet of, 98
    at Constitutional Convention, 84p, 85p, 90
    farewell address of, 99
    as Federalist, 95
    and French and Indian War, 64
    inauguration of, 98
    and Whiskey Rebellion, 99
Washington Naval Conference (1921), 433
Washington-on-the-Brazos, 132
Watergate scandal, 620–622
Watson, Thomas A., 255

Watt, James, 108
Weaver, James, 247
Weaver, Robert C., 413
Webster, Daniel, 120, 170–171
Weld, Theodore, 155
Welfare reform, 646
Wells, Ida B., 285
Wentworth, Harold, 519
West African kingdoms, 14m
   agriculture in, 13, 14
   culture of, 13–14
   Ghana, 12
   Mali, 12
   Songhai, 12–13
   trade with, 12
Western settlement, 110–111, 130–132,
   228p, 229p, 239m
   Exodusters in, 244–245
   farming in, 242–247, 243p, 244p, 246p
   Grange in, 246–247, 246p
   homesteaders in, 242–243, 244p
   land rushes in, 245
   and Manifest Destiny, 136–137
   mining in, 138–139, 239–241, 240p
   Mormons in, 135–136
   and Native Americans, 126–128, 134,
      230–234, 231p, 232m, 233p, 234p
   overland trails in, 134–135, 134p, 135
   and Populists, 247
   railroads in, 243
   ranchers in, 237–239, 237p, 238p, 239m
   and war with Mexico, 137
   women in, 243–244, 243p
Western Union Telegraph Company, 255
Westinghouse, George, 254
Westmoreland, William, 597
Weyler, Valeriano, 316
Whig party, on Compromise of 1850, 171
   formation of, 169
Whiskey Rebellion, 99, 99p
White, Walter, 412
Whitefield, George, 55p
Whitney, Eli, 110, 114, 115p, 117, 117p
Wilhelm, Kaiser, abdication of, 346
Willard, Emma, 161
Williams, Roger, 34
Willkie, Wendell, 410
Wilmot Proviso, 169
Wilson, James, and signing of Constitution,
   92–93
Wilson, Woodrow, 360
   election of, 305–306, 305p
   foreign policy under, 329
   and moral diplomacy, 325–326
   and peace negotiations, 351–353, 351p
   as President, 306–307
   and United Nations, 482
   and women's rights, 347
   and World War I, 337, 338–340
Wolfe, James, 65
The Woman in Battle (Velaquez), 200
Women
   in arts, 416
   in Civil War, 199–200, 199p
   colonial, 48, 48p
   and Declaration of Independence, 74
   education of, 161
   equal rights for, 367
   in factory system, 109–110
   and gold mining, 139

   in government, 674
   and New Deal, 411, 412, 411p
   in politics, 641, 642p, 644
   and reform movements, 159
   in Revolutionary War, 78, 78p
   rights of, 641, 674
   in sports, 366
   and spread of public education, 157
   and suffrage movement, 307–308, 307m
   and the temperance movement, 158, 158p
   and Western settlement, 243–244, 243p
   in work force, 250–251, 251p, 256, 264,
      367, 367c, 369, 369p, 373, 516
   in World War I, 347, 348p, 367
   in World War II, 469–471, 469p, 470p,
      471p
Women Accepted for Volunteer Emergency
   Service (WAVES), 471, 471p
Women's Auxiliary Army Corps
   (WAAC), 471
Women's National Basketball Association
   (WNBA), 668, 668p
Women's rights movement, 159–161, 160p,
   347, 551, 578–580, 579p
Woodruff, Hale, 365
Woods, Granville, 254
Woodson, Carter, 285
Work force
   African Americans in, 265, 265p, 373,
      474–475
   on assembly line, 380
   children in, 264, 264p
   in Great Depression, 383–384, 384p
   immigrants in, 264
   Latinos in, 475
   life of, 263–265
   in 1920s, 361–362, 361p
   women in, 250–251, 256, 264, 367,
      367c, 369, 369p, 373, 469–470, 469p,
      470p, 516
   See also Labor unions
Works Progress Administration (WPA), 417
World Antislavery Convention, 159
World Trade Center, bombing of, 659, 659p
World War I, 293p, 345m
   African Americans in, 342, 342p, 348
   armistice following, 350
   battles in, 344–346
   causes of, 329–331
   costs of, 347, 350–351
   debts from, 424
   destruction from, 335p
   end of, 350–351
   Europe after, 352m
   German retreat in, 346
   home front in, 347–349
   Mexican Americans in, 348
   peace negotiations following, 350p,
      351–353
   propaganda in, 348–349, 349p
   Russia in, 343–344
   technology in, 336–337
   trench warfare in, 336, 337
   U.S. entrance into, 339–340
   U.S. neutrality in, 337, 338–340
   U.S. preparation for, 342–343
   women in, 347, 348p, 367
World War II, 450m
   in Africa, 442, 442p, 445, 447
   African Americans in, 472–475, 473p
   Allies' strategy in, 445, 445p

   atomic bomb in, 457–458
   battle conditions in, 440–441p
   Battle of the Bulge in, 455
   Berlin in, 455–456
   blitzkrieg in, 443, 443p
   and bombing of Pearl Harbor, 315,
      435–436, 436p, 451, 466, 473, 476
   Cairo in, 454, 454p
   China in, 454
   costs of, 458–459
   D-day invasion of, 449–451, 449p
   destruction of Germany in, 458
   draft in, 434, 434p, 442
   and Dwight Eisenhower, 449
   economy following, 513–514
   end of, 454–456, 459p
   events leading to, 435c
   France in, 450–451
   and Franklin Roosevelt, 464
   and Harry Truman, 457–458
   Hitler in, 445, 447, 454, 455, 456
   homefront in, 462p, 463p, 464–467,
      464c, 465p, 466p, 467p
   internal migration in, 472
   invasion of Pearl Harbor in, 435–436, 436p
   Italy in, 448
   Japanese Americans in, 476–477, 476m,
      477p
   Japan in, 451–452, 451p, 452p, 458m
   Jews in, 456–457, 456p
   and labor movement, 466–467, 467p
   Latinos in, 475–476, 475p
   and Libya, 442
   Midway Islands in, 451–452
   Normandy invasion in, 421p
   Sicily in, 447–448
   in Soviet Union, 442–443, 443p, 448–449,
      454–455, 455p
   submarines in, 435
   and Tobruk, 442
   U.S. defense spending in, 464, 464c
   and U.S. neutrality, 433–435
   women in, 469–471, 469p, 470p, 471p
Wounded Knee, South Dakota, 233, 587
Wovoka, 233
Wright, Richard, 417, 528

Y

Yalta Conference, 454–455, 454p
Yamamoto Isaroku, 451, 452
Yellow-dog contracts, 266
Yellow journalism, 317
Yeltsin, Boris, 649
Yorktown, Battle of, 77–78
Young, Andrew, 625
Young, Brigham, 135–136
Yugoslavia
   communism in, 482, 484
   democracy movement in, 649
   post-World War I, 353

Z

Zapata, Emiliano, 326, 326p
Zavala, Lorenzo de, 132
Zenger, John Peter, 57, 57p
Zhou Enlai, 613
Zimmermann telegram, 339
Zoot suit riots, 475–476

Photo Credits

p. iii (t) The Granger Collection; p. iii (b) North Wind Picture Archives; p. iv (t) Corbis-Bettmann; p. iv (b) Smithsonian Institute; p. v (t) Library of Congress; p. v (m) Stephen G. St. John, (c) National Geographic; p. v (b) Courtesy of The Oakland Museum of California; p. vi (t) AP/Wide World Photos; p. vi (b) AP/Wide World Photos; p. vii (t) The Granger Collection; p. vii (b) Stock Montage; p. viii (t) Classic PIO Library; p. viii (b) The Granger Collection; p. ix (t) Archive Photo; p. ix (m) Corbis-Bettmann; p. ix (b) Courtesy of General Motors; p. x (t) UPI/Corbis-Bettmann; p. x (m) Corbis-Bettmann; p. x (b) Prentice Hall, Inc.; p. xi (t) Johnson, Gamma Liaison, Inc.; p. xi (b) Reuters/Corbis-Bettmann; p. xvii (b) Prentice Hall, Inc.; p. xviii (b) Photo Disc., Inc.; p. xviii (m) Silver Burdett Ginn; p. xviii (t) The Granger Collection; p. xix (tl) UPI/Corbis-Bettmann; p. xix (br) Archive Photo; p. xix (bl) Superstock; p. xxii (mr) UPI/Corbis-Bettmann; p. xxii (ml) UPI/Corbis-Bettmann; p. xxii (tl) Photo Researchers, Inc.; p. xxii (bl) Corbis-Bettmann; p. xxii (tr) The Granger Collection; p. xxii (mr) Culver Pictures; p. xxii (br) Library of Congress; p. xxix (tr) Library of Congress.

Unit 1: p. 1 Christie's Images; p. 2 (t) Kathy Schneider/The Image Bank; p. 2 (b) Corbis-Bettmann; p. 3 (main) The Granger Collection; p. 3 (t) Commune De Genova; p. 3 (b) Simon and Schuster; p. 7 Courtesy of Trans World Airlines; p. 8 The Granger Collection; p. 11 Corbis-Bettmann; p. 13 The Granger Collection; p. 15 The Granger Collection; p. 16 Corbis-Bettmann; p. 18 The Granger Collection; p. 22 (t) A. H. Robbins Company; p. 22 (bl) Brown Brothers; p. 22 (br) Library of Congress; p. 23 (main) The Granger Collection; p. 23 (tr) Corbis-Bettmann; p. 23 (tl) Corbis-Bettmann; p. 23 (b) Culver Pictures, Superstock; p. 25 The Granger Collection; p. 27 Harold Sund, Image Bank; p. 31 National Park Service; p. 32 Library of Congress; p. 35 Corbis-Bettmann; p. 42 (t) Culver Pictures; p. 42 (bl) Air India Library; p. 42 (br) Art Resource, NY; p. 43 (main) The Granger Collection; p. 43 (tl) Photo Researchers, Inc.; p. 43 (tr) The Granger Collection; p. 43 (b) Corbis-Bettmann; p. 45 Culver Pictures; p. 46 Culver Pictures; p. 48 The Granger Collection; p. 51 Library of Congress; p. 53 The Granger Collection; p. 54 The Granger Collection; p. 55 The Granger Collection; p. 56 Bill Geiger; p. 57 Corbis-Bettmann; p. 60 (t) Corbis-Bettmann; p. 60 (b) National Portrait Gallery, Edinburgh; p. 61 (main) Corbis-Bettmann; p. 61 (t) Corbis-Bettmann; p. 61 (b) The Peabody Museum; p. 62 Culver Pictures; p. 64 Library of Congress; p. 68 Colonial Williamsburg Foundation; p. 69 Corbis-Bettmann; p. 70 Library of Congress; p. 72 (t) The Granger Collection; p. 72 (b) Library of Congress; p. 73 North Wind Picture Archives; p. 77 Library of Congress; p. 78 Corbis-Bettmann; p. 82 Barbara Rios, Photo Researchers.

Unit 2: p. 83 The Granger Collection; p. 84 (t) Library of Congress; p. 84 (b) Giraudon, Art Resource; p. 85 (main) Library of Congress; p. 85 (t) Montana State Capitol Building; p. 85 (bl) Beethoven-Archive; p. 85 (br) Columbus Memorial Library; p. 91 Independence National Historic Park Collection; p. 92 Museum of Art, Rhode Island School of Design; p. 96 Corbis-Bettmann; p. 99 Corbis-Bettmann; p. 100 Corbis-Bettmann; p. 102 (t) The Granger Collection; p. 102 (b) The Granger Collection; p. 103 Field Museum of Natural History; p. 106 (main) Munson-Williams-Proctor Institute; p. 106 (t) Library of Congress; p. 106 (b) Library of Congress; p. 107 (t) The Granger Collection; p. 107 (b) Corbis-Bettmann; p. 109 Smithsonian Institute; p. 111 Culver Pictures; p. 114 Corbis-Bettmann; p. 115 The Granger Collection; p. 117 Smithsonian Institute; p. 120 Corbis-Bettmann; p. 121 Corbis-Bettmann; p. 124 (tl) The Granger Collection; p. 124 (r) The Granger Collection; p. 125 (tr) Courtesy of the State of California; p. 125 (b) The Granger Collection; p. 126 (main) Library of Congress; p. 127 The Granger Collection; p. 128 E.R. Degginger, Bruce Coleman; p. 131 Culver Pictures; p. 133 Bill Pogue, Stockhouse Inc.; p. 134 Culver Pictures; p. 139 California State Library; p. 140 National Archives; p. 141 The Granger Collection; p. 144 (t) Library of Congress; p. 144 (b) The Granger Collection; p. 145 (main) Culver Pictures; p. 145 (t) Lynn Historical Society; p. 145 (b) Library of Congress; p. 147 Culver Pictures; p. 148 The Granger Collection; p. 149 The Granger Collection; p. 152 The Granger Collection; p. 153 The Philadelphia Free Public Library; p. 154 Christie's Images; p. 156 (t) Sophia Smith Collection; p. 156 (b) Culver Pictures; p. 157 The Granger Collection; p. 158 Stock Montage; p. 160 Lynn Historical Society; p. 161 Corbis-Bettmann; p. 164 CDA Culver Pictures.

Unit 3: p. 165 The Granger Collection; p. 165 The Granger Collection; p. 166 (tl) Library of Congress; p. 166 (tr) Library of Congress; p. 166 (b) Corbis-Bettmann; p. 167 (main) The Granger Collection; p. 167 (tl) Library of Congress; p. 167 (tr) Library of Congress; p. 167 (b) Corbis-Bettmann; p. 170 American Antiquarian Society; p. 172 New-York Historical Society; p. 174 Library of Congress; p. 177 (b) Corbis-Bettmann; p. 177 (t) The Granger Collection; p. 181 The Granger Collection; p. 182 (t) Library of Congress; p. 182 (m) Corbis-Bettmann; p. 182 (b) C. Marvin Lang; p. 183 (main) Library of Congress; p. 183 (t) Library of Congress; p. 184 Library of Congress; p. 186 The Granger Collection; p. 188 The Granger Collection; p. 190 The Granger Collection; p. 192 The Granger Collection; p. 193 The Granger Collection; p. 194 Library of Congress; p. 195 The Granger Collection; p. 196 Courtesy of the Historical Society of Delaware; p. 197 The Granger Collection; p. 198 Library of Congress; p. 199 Boston Public Library; p. 199 Boston Public Library; p. 205 Stephen G. St. John, (c) National Geographic; p. 208(t) Library of Congress; p. 208(b) Library of Congress; p. 209 (main) Library of Congress; p. 209 (tr) Library of Congress; p. 209 (tl) Library of Congress; p. 209 (b) Photograph © Board of Trustees, Widener Collection, National Gallery of Art, Washington; p. 211 Library of Congress; p. 213 Library of Congress; p. 215 Library of Congress; p. 216 (t) The Granger Collection; p. 216 (b) National Geographic Society; p. 217 Library of Congress; p. 221 Culver Pictures; p. 222 Schomberg Collection, New York Public Library; p. 225 Harper's Weekly; p. 226 Courtesy of Teach For America.

Unit 4: p. 227 Library of Congress; p. 228 (tl) Corbis-Bettmann; p. 228 (tr) Library of Congress; p. 229 (main) Nebraska State Historical Society; p. 229 (tl) The Granger Collection; p. 231 The Granger Collection; p. 233 The Granger Collection; p. 234 New York Public Library; p. 234 New York Public Library; p. 235 (l) Corbis-Bettmann; p. 235 (r) The Granger Collection; p. 237 Courtesy of The Oakland Museum of California; p. 238 Schomberg Center for Research in Black Culture; p. 240 The Granger Collection; p. 243 Kansas State Historical Society; p. 244 Solomon D. Butcher Collection, Nebraska State Historical Society; p. 246 The Granger Collection; p. 250 (t)The Granger Collection; p. 251 (main) Corbis-Bettmann; p. 251 (tl) Library of Congress; p. 251 (tr) The Granger Collection; p. 253 The Granger Collection; p. 254 AP/Wide World Photos; p. 255 The Granger Collection; p. 260 Bettmann; p. 262 (l) Library of Congress; p. 262 (r) UPI/Corbis-Bettmann; p. 264 Corbis-Bettmann; p. 265 The Granger Collection; p. 266 Library of Congress; p. 267 The Granger Collection; p. 270 (t) The Granger Collection; p. 270 (b) PhotoDisc, Inc.; p. 271 (main) The Granger Collection; p. 271 (t) New-York Historical Society; p. 271 (bl) Corbis-Bettmann; p. 271 (br) Corbis-Bettmann; p. 275 Museum of the City of New York; p. 278 The Granger Collection; p. 280 Florida State Archives; p. 281 Brown Brothers; p. 282 The Granger Collection; p. 283 UPI/Corbis-Bettmann; p. 285 The Granger Collection; p. 287 New-York Historical Society; p. 288 The Granger Collection; p. 289 George Eastman House; p. 292 Museum of the City of New York.

Unit 5: p. 293 Library of Congress; p. 294 (t) Culver Pictures; p. 294 (bl) Corbis-Bettmann; p. 294 (br) Air France; p. 295 FPG; p. 295 (tl) Corbis-Bettmann; p. 295 (b) Corbis-Bettmann; p. 297 The Granger Collection; p. 298 Library of Congress; p. 299 Culver Pictures; p. 301 UPI/Corbis-Bettmann; p. 302 (t) Brown Brothers; p. 302 (b) UPI/Corbis-Bettmann; p. 303 Corbis-Bettmann; p. 304 The Granger Collection; p. 305 Library of Congress; p. 308 AP/Wide World Photos; p. 312 (tl) The Granger Collection; p. 312 (tr) National Archives; p. 312 (b) Library of Congress; p. 313 (main) Corbis-Bettmann; p. 313 (tr) UPI/Corbis-Bettmann; p. 313 (t) National Archives; p. 313 (bl) AP/Wide World Photos; p. 315 Library of Congress; p. 316 Library of Congress; p. 317 The Granger Collection; p. 319 Library of Congress; p. 320 Corbis-Bettmann; p. 321 Corbis-Bettmann; p. 323 Corbis-Bettmann; p. 325 The Granger Collection; p. 326 Library of Congress; p. 327 Culver Pictures; p. 331 Culver Pictures; p. 334 (tl) AP/Wide World Photos; p. 334 (tr) Corbis-Bettmann; p. 334 (b) UPI/Corbis-Bettmann; p. 335 (main) Corbis-Bettmann; p. 335 (t) UPI/Bettmann; p. 335 (b) UPI/Bettmann; p. 337 National Archives; p. 339 The Granger Collection; p. 340 Centro de Estudios Puertorriquenos, Hunter College; p. 342 The Granger Collection; p. 343 (t) The Granger Collection; p. 343 (b) The Granger Collection; p. 344 Library of Congress; p. 346 National Archives;